Simply Visual Basic® 2010
Fourth Edition

Deitel® Series Page

How To Program Series

Android How to Program
C++ How to Program, 8/E
C How to Program, 7/E
Java™ How to Program, 9/E
Java™ How to Program, Late Objects Version, 8/E

Internet & World Wide Web How to Program, 5/E
Visual C++® 2008 How to Program, 2/E
Visual Basic® 2010 How to Program
Visual C#® 2010 How to Program, 4/E

Simply Series

Simply C++: An App-Driven Tutorial Approach
Simply Java™ Programming: An App-Driven Tutorial
  Approach

Simply C#: An App-Driven Tutorial Approach
Simply Visual Basic® 2010: An App-Driven Approach,
  4/E

CourseSmart Web Books

www.deitel.com/books/CourseSmart/
C++ How to Program, 5/E, 6/E, 7/E & 8/E
Simply C++: An App-Driven Tutorial Approach
Java™ How to Program, 6/E, 7/E, 8/E & 9/E
Simply Visual Basic 2010: An App-Driven Approach, 4/E

Visual Basic® 2008 How to Program
Visual Basic® 2010 How to Program
Visual C#® 2008 How to Program, 3/E
Visual C#® 2010 How to Program, 4/E

Deitel® Developer Series

AJAX, Rich Internet Applications and Web Development for Programmers
Android for Programmers: An App-Driven Approach
C++ for Programmers

C# 2010 for Programmers
iPhone® for Programmers: An App-Driven Approach
Java™ for Programmers, 2/E
JavaScript for Programmers

LiveLessons Video Learning Products

www.deitel.com/books/LiveLessons/
Android App Development Fundamentals
C++ Fundamentals
Java™ Fundamentals
C# 2010 Fundamentals

iPhone® App Development Fundamentals
JavaScript Fundamentals
Visual Basic Fundamentals

To receive updates on Deitel publications, Resource Centers, training courses, partner offers and more, please register for the free *Deitel® Buzz Online* e-mail newsletter at:

    www.deitel.com/newsletter/subscribe.html

and join the Deitel communities on Twitter®

    @deitel

Facebook®

    facebook.com/DeitelFan

and Google+

    gplus.to/deitel

To communicate with the authors, send e-mail to:

    deitel@deitel.com

For information on government and corporate *Dive-Into® Series* on-site seminars offered by Deitel & Associates, Inc. worldwide, visit:

    www.deitel.com/training/

or write to

    deitel@deitel.com

For continuing updates on Prentice Hall/Deitel publications visit:

    www.deitel.com
    www.pearsonhighered.com/deitel/

Visit the Deitel Resource Centers for additional information that will help you master programming languages, software development, Android and iPhone/iPad app development, and Internet- and web-related topics:

    www.deitel.com/ResourceCenters.html

Simply Visual Basic® 2010
Fourth Edition

Paul Deitel
Deitel & Associates, Inc.

Harvey Deitel
Deitel & Associates, Inc.

Abbey Deitel
Deitel & Associates, Inc.

PEARSON

Boston Columbus Indianapolis New York San Francisco Upper Saddle River
Amsterdam Cape Town Dubai London Madrid Milan Munich Paris Montreal Toronto
Delhi Mexico City Sao Paulo Sydney Hong Kong Seoul Singapore Taipei Tokyo

Editorial Director: *Marcia J. Horton*
Editor-in-Chief: *Michael Hirsch*
Executive Editor: *Tracy Johnson (Dunkelberger)*
Associate Editor: *Carole Snyder*
Vice President, Marketing: *Patrice Jones*
Marketing Manager: *Yezan Alayan*
Marketing Coordinator: *Kathryn Ferranti*
Vice President, Production: *Vince O'Brien*
Managing Editor: *Jeff Holcomb*
Associate Managing Editor: *Robert Engelhardt*
Operations Specialist: *Lisa McDowell*
Art Director: *Anthony Gemmellaro*
Cover Design: *Paul Deitel, Harvey Deitel, Abbey Deitel, Anthony Gemmellaro*
Cover Photo Credit: © *sssteps / iStockphoto.com*
Media Editor: *Daniel Sandin*

Credits and acknowledgments borrowed from other sources and reproduced, with permission, in this textbook appear on page vi.

Library of Congress Cataloging-in-Publication Data

```
Deitel, Paul J.
  Simply Visual Basic 2010 / Paul Deitel, Harvey Deitel, Abbey Deitel. --
4th ed.
      p. cm. -- (Simply series)
  Rev. ed. of: Simply visual Basic 2008. c2009.
  Includes index.
  ISBN-13: 978-0-13-299060-8
  ISBN-10: 0-13-299060-1
1.  Microsoft Visual BASIC. 2.  BASIC (Computer program language)  I.
Deitel, Harvey M., II. Deitel, Abbey. III. Deitel, Paul J. Simply Visual
Basic 2008. IV. Title.
  QA76.73.B3D455 2013
  005.2'762--dc23
                                            2011053218
```

10 9 8 7 6 5 4 3 2 1

ISBN-10:   0-13-299060-1
ISBN-13: 978-0-13-299060-8

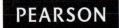

Trademarks:

Brief Table of Contents

PREFACE

Welcome to the Visual Basic® 2010 programming language and the world of Microsoft® Windows®, and Internet and web programming with Microsoft's .NET 4.0 platform! At Deitel & Associates, we write programming language textbooks, professional books and LiveLessons video products for Pearson and deliver programming courses at corporate, government, military and academic organizations worldwide. This book, which is part of our *Simply* series, has been updated based on Visual Studio 2010 and .NET 4.0. Our goal was to write a book that focuses on core concepts and features while keeping the discussion as simple as possible. The book is intended for readers using recent versions of Windows®.

To achieve this goal, we implemented an innovative teaching methodology. We present the core concepts of leading-edge computing technologies using the APP-DRIVEN approach, combined with the DEITEL® signature LIVE-CODE approach of teaching programming using complete, working, real-world apps. We merged the notion of a lab manual with that of a conventional textbook, creating a book that works well in a traditional classroom setting or with students sitting at computers and building each example app as they read the chapters. The book is also appropriate for online distance learning courses.

As students work through the chapters, they learn conventional and visual programming fundamentals, graphical-user-interface (GUI) components, file processing, database processing and web-based apps development. Most sections are followed by self-review questions with answers, so that students receive immediate feedback.

We believe that this book and its support materials provide students and professionals with an informative, interesting, challenging and entertaining Visual Basic educational experience. We provide a suite of supplementary materials that help instructors maximize their students' learning experience.

As you read the book, if you have questions, e-mail us at deitel@deitel.com; we'll respond promptly. For updates on this book and its supporting Visual Basic software, visit www.deitel.com/books/SimplyVB2010/, join our social networking communities on Facebook (www.deitel.com/deitelfan), Twitter (@deitel) and Google+ (gplus.to/deitel), and subscribe to the *Deitel® Buzz Online* newsletter (www.deitel.com/newsletter/subscribe.html).

Here are some of the key features of the fourth edition of *Simply Visual Basic 2010*:

■ *New Chapter 1.* The new Chapter 1 engages students with intriguing facts and figures to get them excited about learning to program. The chapter includes a table of some of the research made possible by computers and the Internet, current technology trends and hardware discussion, the data hierarchy, a new section on social networking, a table of popular web services, a table of business and technology publications and websites that will help you keep up with the latest technology news and trends, and updated exercises. Students also get hands-on experience by test-driving a fun painter app.

■ *Making a Difference Exercises Set.* We encourage you to use computers and the Internet to research and solve problems that really matter. These new exercises are meant to increase awareness of important issues the world is facing. We hope you'll approach them with your own values, politics and beliefs.

■ *Up-to-date with Visual Basic 2010, the Visual Studio 2010 IDE and .NET 4.*

■ *LINQ.* LINQ (Language-Integrated Query) is one of the most important newer features in Visual Basic. LINQ provides a uniform syntax for querying data, and it enables insert, update and delete operations. Strong typing enables Visual Studio to provide *IntelliSense* support for LINQ operations and results. LINQ can be used on different types of data sources, including collections (LINQ to Objects, Chapters 20, 21 and 23) and databases (LINQ to SQL, Chapters 27 through 29). Many of the new Visual Basic language features we cover were introduced to support LINQ.

■ *Databases.* We use real-world apps to teach the fundamentals of database programming using the free Microsoft SQL Server Express Edition. Chapters 27–29 discuss database and LINQ to SQL fundamentals, presented in the context of an **Address-Book** desktop app, a **Guestbook** web app and a **Password-Protected Book Information** web app, respectively. Chapter 27 also demonstrates using the Visual Studio tools to build a GUI that uses LINQ to SQL to access the database.

■ *Windows Presentation Foundation (WPF) GUI and Graphics.* Graphics make apps fun to create and use. In our introduction to graphics, Chapter 25, we discuss Graphical Device Interface (GDI+)—the Windows service that provides the graphical features used by Windows Forms apps in Visual Studio 2010—to teach students to print a personalized bank check. We extend our coverage of GUI and graphics in Chapter 26 with an introduction to Windows Presentation Foundation (WPF)—Microsoft's framework that integrates GUI, graphics and multimedia capabilities. We present a WPF-based painting app to demonstrate WPF GUI and graphics capabilities.

■ *ASP.NET 4.* Microsoft's .NET server-side technology, ASP.NET 4, enables you to create robust, scalable web-based applications. In Chapters 27–29, you'll build several applications, including a web-based **Guestbook** application that uses ASP.NET, LINQ and a LinqDataSource to store data in a database and display data in a web page. The chapter also discusses the ASP.NET Development Server for testing your web applications on your local computer. Chapter 29 adds for this new edition a password-protected, web-based books database app and an ASP.NET Ajax validation app that demonstrates how Ajax technology can give web-based apps the responsiveness and look-and-feel of desktop apps.

■ *Conditional If Expressions.* Visual Basic provides a new conditional If expression (introduced in Chapter 7), which consists of a condition, a true expression and a false expression. It tests its condition, then evaluates to its true or false expression based on the truth or falsity of the condition. This can be used as shorthand notation for some If...Then...Else statements.

■ *Local Type Inference.* When you initialize a local variable in its declaration, you can now omit the variable's type—the compiler infers it from the variable's initializer value (introduced in Chapter 11).

■ *Optional Parameters.* You can specify method parameters with default values—if a corresponding method argument isn't provided in the method call, the compiler inserts the optional parameter's default value in the call (introduced in Chapter 13).

■ *Object Initializers.* When creating a new object, you can use the new object initializer syntax to assign values to the new object's properties (introduced in Chapter 23).

■ *"Quick Fix" Window.* The IDE now provides an **Error Correction Options** window that enables you to quickly fix certain common programming errors (introduced in Chapter 5).

■ *We emphasize the IDE's* **IntelliSense** *feature* that helps you write code faster and with fewer errors.

Pedagogic Features in Simply Visual Basic 2010, Fourth Edition

This book is loaded with pedagogic features for students and instructors including:

■ *APP-DRIVEN Approach.* Each chapter uses a contemporary, real-world app to teach programming concepts. The examples and exercises are up-to-the-minute with common desktop, Internet and web apps. An alphabetical list of these apps appears in Fig. 1. All of the chapter examples have a business, home or personal focus. At the beginning of each chapter, students "test-drive" the completed app so they can see how it works. Then they build the app by following detailed, step-by-step instructions. The book concentrates on the principles of good software engineering and stresses program clarity.

■ *LIVE-CODE Approach.* This book emphasizes LIVE-CODE examples. Each chapter ends with the complete, working program code, and the students can run the app that they just created. We call this method of teaching and writing the *Live-Code Approach*.

■ *Real-World Technologies.* This text incorporates contemporary technologies to develop useful apps. For example, we use the Unified Modeling Language® (UML) to replace flowcharts—an older standard. The UML has become the preferred graphical modeling language for designing object-oriented apps. In *Simply Visual Basic 2010, 4/e* we use the UML to show the flow of control for several control statements, so students gain practice reading the type of diagrams that are used in industry.

■ *Visual Programming and Graphical User Interfaces (GUIs).* From the first chapter, we immerse students in visual programming techniques, which students use to create and modify GUI-based programs quickly and easily. The early chapters provide students with a foundation for designing GUIs—concepts that they'll apply throughout the book. Many chapters contain GUI Design Tips that are summarized at the end of the chapter for easy reference. Appendix C compiles the GUI Design Tips.

■ *Windows Forms vs. Windows Presentation Foundation (WPF).* Microsoft recommends that developers use Windows Forms rather than WPF for line-of-business apps, which is the primary market for students and professionals reading this book. We implement most of our GUIs with Windows Forms, but we also introduce WPF, which Microsoft recommends for more advanced GUI, graphics and multimedia apps.

Apps in *Simply Visual Basic 2010, 4/e*

Account Information	Encryption	Photo Album
Address Book	Enhanced Dental Payment	Pig Latin
Address Book GUI	Factorial	Present Value Calculator
Advanced Painter	Fee Calculator	Prime Numbers
Airline Reservation	File Scrape	Quiz Average
Alarm	Flag Quiz	Radio GUI
Alarm Clock GUI	Food Survey	Restaurant Bill
Anagram Game	Form Painter	Road Sign Test
Arithmetic Calculator	Fund Raiser	Salary Survey
Average Three Numbers	Fuzzy Dice Order Form	Sales Commission
Birthday Saver	Gas Pump	Sales Report
Bookstore	Grade Calculator	Savings Calculator
Bouncing Ball Game	Guess the Number	Schedule Book
Cafeteria Survey	Guest Book	Screen Saver
Calculator GUI	Income Tax Calculator	Screen Scraping
Car Payment Calculator	Interest Calculator	Security Panel
Car Reservation	Inventory	Shipping Hub
Cash Register	Inventory Enhancement	Shipping Time
"Cat and Mouse" Painter	Length/Distance Converter	Sibling Survey
Cell Phone GUI	Letterhead Designer	Simple Calculator
Check Writer	Line Length	Simple Encryption
Circle Painter	Lottery Picker	Student Grades
Class Average	Maximum	Supply Cost Calculator
Company Logo Designer	Microwave Oven	Task List
Compound Interest	Microwave Oven GUI	Temperature Converter
Counter	Miles Per Gallon	Ticket Information
Craps Game	Monitor Invoice GUI	To-Do List
Currency Converter	Mortgage Calculator	Typing Tutor
Charge Account Analyzer	Multiplication Teacher	Vending Machine GUI
Dental Payment	Odd Numbers	Wage Calculator
Dice Simulator	Office Supplies	Weather Viewer
Digit Extraction	Password GUI	Welcome
Discount Calculator	Pay Raise Calculator	
Display Square	Phone Book	

Figure 1   Apps in Simply Visual Basic 2010's examples and exercises.

- ***Syntax Shading.*** For readability, we syntax shade the code, similar to the way most integrated-development environments and code editors syntax color the code. Our syntax-shading conventions are:

```
comments appear like this
keywords appear like this
literal values appear like this
text, class, method, variable and property names appear in black
```

- ***Object-Oriented Programming.*** Object-oriented programming is the most widely employed technique for developing robust, reusable software, and

Visual Basic 2010 offers substantial object-oriented programming features. This book introduces students to defining classes and using objects, laying a foundation for more advanced programming courses.

■ **Visual Studio 2010 Debugger.** Debuggers are software tools that help programmers find and correct logic errors in program code. Visual Studio 2010 contains a powerful debugger that allows you to analyze your programs line-by-line as they execute. Throughout the book, we teach the Visual Studio 2010 Debugger; we explain how to use its key features and offer many debugging exercises.

To the Instructor

Focus of the Book

Simply Visual Basic 2010, 4/e is intended for introductory-level courses and course sequences in computer programming for students with little or no programming experience. This book teaches computer programming principles and the Visual Basic 2010 language, including data types, control statements, object-oriented programming, .NET Framework Class Library classes, GUI concepts, event-driven programming, database and web apps development, and more. After mastering the material in this book, students will be able to program in Visual Basic 2010 and to employ many key capabilities of the .NET 4.0 platform.

The book is up-to-date with Microsoft's Visual Studio 2010, which includes Visual Basic 2010. We rebuilt every app in the book using the 2010 software. All apps and solutions have been fully tested on this platform.

A Note Regarding Software for the Book

This book includes the Microsoft® Visual Studio® 2010 Express Editions All-in-One DVD, which contains the Visual Basic® 2010 Express Edition (and other Microsoft development tools). These tools are also downloadable from

```
www.microsoft.com/express/Windows
```

We wrote *Simply Visual Basic 2010* using Visual Basic® Express Edition. You can learn more about Visual Basic® at `msdn.microsoft.com/en-us/vstudio/default.aspx`. For more information about setting up your computer to work with the examples and exercises in this book, see the Before You Begin section that follows this Preface.

A Note Regarding Terminology Used in the Book

In Chapter 13, we discuss methods as Sub procedures (sometimes called subroutines) and Function procedures (sometimes called functions). We use this terminology for two reasons. First, the keywords Sub and Function are used in procedure and method definitions, so this naming is logical for students. Second, Visual Basic professionals have used this terminology for years and will continue to do so. We also use the term "function" at certain points in this text to refer to Visual Basic 6 Function procedures that remain in Visual Basic 2010 (such as Pmt). When we introduce object-oriented programming concepts in Chapter 19, we discuss the difference between procedures and methods and indicate that the procedures defined throughout the text are, in fact, methods.

Objectives

Each chapter begins with objectives that inform students of what to expect and give them an opportunity, after reading the chapter, to determine whether they've met the intended goals.

Outline

The chapter outline enables students to approach the material in top-down fashion. Along with the chapter objectives, the outline helps students anticipate topics and set an appropriate learning pace.

Example Apps (with Outputs)

We present Visual Basic 2010 features in the context of complete, working programs. All examples are available as downloads from:

> www.deitel.com/books/SimplyVB2010/

Illustrations/Figures/"ACE" Tables

Abundant charts, line drawings and app outputs are included. The control-statements discussion, for example, features carefully drawn UML activity diagrams. [*Note:* We do not teach UML diagramming as an app-development tool, but we do use UML diagrams to explain the precise operation Visual Basic 2010's control statements.] Most chapters include our "ACE" tables that list the actions, controls and events that are crucial to implementing object-oriented apps.

Programming Tips

Hundreds of programming tips help students focus on important aspects of app development. These tips and practices represent the best the authors have gleaned from a combined seven decades of programming and teaching experience.

Good Programming Practice

Good Programming Practices call attention to techniques that will help students produce programs that are clearer, more understandable and more maintainable.

Common Programming Error

Students tend to make certain errors frequently. Pointing out these *Common Programming Errors* reduces the likelihood that they'll make these same mistakes.

Error-Prevention Tip

These tips contain suggestions for exposing bugs and removing them from students' programs; many describe aspects of Visual Basic 2010 that prevent bugs from getting into programs in the first place.

Portability Tip

We include *Portability Tips* to help students write code that will run on a variety of platforms and to explain how Visual Basic 2010 achieves its high degree of portability among .NET 4.0 platforms.

Software Design Tip

The *Software Design Tips* highlight architectural and design issues that affect the construction of software systems.

GUI Design Tip

The *GUI Design Tips* highlight graphical-user-interface conventions to help students design attractive, intuitive, user-friendly GUIs.

Skills Summary

Most chapters include a bullet-list-style summary of the new programming concepts presented. This reinforces key actions taken to build the app in each chapter.

Key Terms

Each chapter includes a list of important terms defined in the chapter. These terms and definitions also appear in the index and in a bookwide glossary, so the student can locate terms and their definitions quickly.

Self-Review Questions and Answers

Self-review multiple-choice questions and answers are included after most sections to build students' confidence with the material and prepare them for the regular exercises. Students should be encouraged to attempt all the self-review exercises and check their answers.

Exercises (Solutions in Instructor Solutions Manual)

Each chapter concludes with exercises. Typical exercise sections include 10 multiple-choice questions, a "What does this code do?" exercise, a "What's wrong with this code?" exercise, three programming exercises and a programming challenge. [*Note:* In the "What does this code do?" and "What's wrong with this code?" exercises, we show only portions of the code in the text.]

   The questions involve simple recall of important terminology and concepts, writing individual Visual Basic 2010 statements, writing small portions of Visual Basic 2010 apps and writing complete Visual Basic 2010 methods, classes and apps. Every programming exercise uses a step-by-step methodology to suggest how to solve the problems. The solutions for the exercises are *available only to instructors* through their Prentice-Hall representatives.

GUI Design Guidelines

Consistent and proper graphical-user-interface design is crucial to visual programming. In each chapter, we summarize the GUI design guidelines that were introduced. Appendix C presents a cumulative list of these GUI design guidelines for easy reference.

Controls, Events, Properties & Methods Summaries

Most chapters include a summary of the controls, events, properties and methods covered in the chapter. The summary includes a picture of each control, shows the control "in action" and lists the control's properties, events and methods that were discussed up to and including that chapter.

Thousands of Index Entries

We have included an extensive index which is especially useful when you use the book as a reference.

Double Indexing of Visual Basic 2010 Code Examples

For every source-code program in the book, we index the figure caption both alphabetically and as a subindex item under "Examples." This makes it easier to find examples using particular features.

Microsoft DreamSpark™

Microsoft DreamSpark— Professional Developer and Designer Tools for Students

Microsoft provides many of its developer tools to students for free via a program called DreamSpark (https://www.dreamspark.com/). Students can visit the website to create an account. Once verified by Microsoft, students can obtain this software.

Instructor Resources for Simply Visual Basic 2010, Fourth Edition

The following supplements are available to *qualified instructors only* through Pearson Education's Instructor Resource Center (www.pearsonhighered.com/irc):

- *PowerPoint® slides* containing all the code and figures in the text, plus bulleted items that summarize key points.
- *Test Item File* of multiple-choice questions (approximately two per book section)
- *Solutions Manual* with solutions to many of the end-of-chapter exercises. Please check the Instructor Resource Center to determine which exercises have solutions.

Please do not write to us requesting access to the Pearson Instructor's Resource Center. Access is restricted to college instructors teaching from the book. Instructors may obtain access only through their Pearson representatives. If you're not a registered faculty member, contact your Pearson representative or visit

www.pearsonhighered.com/educator/replocator/

Solutions are *not* provided for "project" exercises. Check out our Programming Projects Resource Center for lots of additional exercise and project possibilities (www.deitel.com/ProgrammingProjects/).

CourseSmart Web Books

Students and instructors have increasing demands on their time and money. Pearson has responded by offering digital texts and course materials online through CourseSmart. Faculty can now review course materials online. Students can access a digital version of a text for less than the cost of a print book and can see the same content as in the print textbook enhanced by search, note-taking and printing tools. For detailed information on the CourseSmart version of *Simply Visual Basic 2010, 4/e*, visit www.coursesmart.com.

Deitel Online Resource Centers

Our website www.deitel.com provides Resource Centers on various topics of interest to our readers—see the list of Resource Centers in the first few pages of this book and visit www.deitel.com/ResourceCenters.html. We've found many exceptional resources online, including tutorials, documentation, software downloads, articles, blogs, podcasts, videos, code samples, books, e-books and more—most are free. Some of the Resource Centers you might find helpful while studying this book are Visual Basic, ASP.NET, ASP.NET AJAX, LINQ, .NET, SQL Server, Web Services, Windows Presentation Foundation, Windows 7, UML, Code Search Engines and Code Sites, Game Programming and Programming Projects.

Acknowledgments

Thanks to Barbara Deitel for long hours devoted to this project—she created all of our Java and Android Resource Centers, and patiently researched hundreds of technical details. We're fortunate to have worked with the dedicated team of publishing professionals at Pearson. We appreciate the guidance, savvy and energy of Tracy Johnson (Computer Science Executive Editor), Michael Hirsch (former Editor-in-Chief of Computer Science) and Marcia Horton (Vice President and Editorial Director, ECS). Carole Snyder and Bob Engelhardt have done a marvelous job managing the review and production processes, respectively.

Recent Editions Reviewers

We wish to acknowledge the efforts of our recent editions reviewers. Adhering to tight schedules, they scrutinized the text and the programs, providing countless suggestions for improving the accuracy and completeness of the presentation. ***Microsoft reviewers:*** Adrian "Spotty" Bowles (Microsoft Corporation), Marcelo Guerra Hahn (Microsoft Corporation), Huanhui Hu (Microsoft Corporation), Timothy Ng

(Microsoft Corporation), Akira Onishi (Microsoft Corporation), April Reagan (Microsoft Corporation), Steve Stein (Microsoft Corporation) and Scott Wisniewski (Microsoft Corporation). *Academic reviewers:* Dr. Douglas B. Bock (Southern Illinois University Edwardsville, and a Microsoft Certified Solution Developer for .NET technologies (MCSD.NET)), Dr. Laurence Boxer (Niagara University and SUNY at Buffalo), Edward Hunter (Chapman University College), Christopher J. Olson (Dakota State University) and Josh Pauli (Dakota State University). *Industry reviewers:* Jeff Certain (Colorado CustomWare, Inc.), Matthew Kleinwaks (Abby Rating Systems, Inc.; Microsoft Visual Basic MVP), Éric Moreau (Moer, Inc.; Microsoft Visual Basic MVP), José Antonio González Seco (Parliament of Andalusia), Rod Stephens (President, Rocky Mountain Computer Consulting, Inc.) and Chris Williams (Magenic; Microsoft Visual Basic MVP).

Well, there you have it! Visual Basic 2010 is a powerful programming language that will help you write programs quickly and effectively. It scales nicely into the realm of enterprise systems development to help organizations build their business-critical and mission-critical information systems. As you read the book, we would sincerely appreciate your comments, criticisms, corrections and suggestions for improving the text. Please address all correspondence to:

deitel@deitel.com

We'll respond promptly, and post corrections and clarifications on:

www.deitel.com/books/SimplyVB2010/

We hope you enjoy reading *Simply Visual Basic 2010, Fourth Edition* as much as we enjoyed writing it!

Paul J. Deitel
Dr. Harvey M. Deitel
Abbey S. Deitel

About the Authors   **Paul J. Deitel**, CEO and Chief Technical Officer of Deitel & Associates, Inc., is a graduate of MIT, where he studied Information Technology. Through Deitel & Associates, Inc., he has delivered hundreds of Visual Basic, Java, C++, C, C# and Internet programming courses to industry clients, including Cisco, IBM, Siemens, Sun Microsystems (now Oracle), Dell, Lucent Technologies, Fidelity, NASA at the Kennedy Space Center, Digital Equipment Corporation (now Hewlett-Packard), the National Severe Storm Laboratory, White Sands Missile Range, Rogue Wave Software, Boeing, SunGard Higher Education, Stratus, Cambridge Technology Partners, One Wave, Hyperion Software, Adra Systems, Entergy, CableData Systems, Nortel Networks, Puma, iRobot, Invensys and many more. He and his co-author, Dr. Harvey M. Deitel, are the world's best-selling programming-language textbook authors.

Dr. Harvey M. Deitel, Chairman and Chief Strategy Officer of Deitel & Associates, Inc., has 50 years of experience in the computer field. Dr. Deitel earned B.S. and M.S. degrees from MIT and a Ph.D. from Boston University. He has extensive college teaching experience, including earning tenure and serving as the Chairman of the Computer Science Department at Boston College before founding Deitel & Associates, Inc., with his son, Paul J. Deitel. He and Paul are the co-authors of dozens of books and *LiveLessons* video packages and they are writing many more. The Deitels' texts have earned international recognition, with translations published in Japanese, German, Russian, Chinese, Spanish, Korean, French, Polish, Italian, Portuguese, Greek, Urdu and Turkish. Dr. Deitel has delivered hundreds of professional programming seminars to major corporations, academic institutions, government organizations and the military.

Abbey S. Deitel, President of Deitel & Associates, Inc., is a graduate of Carnegie Mellon University's Tepper School of Management where she received a B.S. in Industrial Management. Abbey has been managing the business operations of Deitel & Associates, Inc. for 14 years. She has contributed to numerous Deitel & Associates publications and is the co-author of *Internet & World Wide Web How to Program, 5/e*; *iPhone for Programmers: An App-Driven Approach*; *Android for Programmers: An App-Driven Approach* and *Android How to Program*.

Corporate Training from Deitel & Associates, Inc.

Deitel & Associates, Inc., is an internationally recognized corporate training and authoring organization. The company provides instructor-led courses delivered at client sites worldwide on major programming languages and platforms, such as Visual Basic®, Visual C#®, Visual C++®, Java™, C, C++, XML®, Python®, object technology, Internet and web programming, Android™ and iPhone® app development, and a growing list of additional programming and software-development courses. The founders of Deitel & Associates, Inc., are Paul J. Deitel and Dr. Harvey M. Deitel. The company's clients include many of the world's largest companies, government agencies, branches of the military, and academic institutions. Through its 36-year publishing partnership with Prentice Hall/Pearson, Deitel & Associates, Inc., publishes leading-edge programming textbooks, professional books and *LiveLessons* video courses. Deitel & Associates, Inc., and the authors can be reached via e-mail at:

deitel@deitel.com

To learn more about the company, its publications and its *Dive Into*® *Series* Corporate Training curriculum delivered at client locations worldwide, visit:

www.deitel.com/training/

subscribe to the *Deitel*® *Buzz Online* e-mail newsletter at:

www.deitel.com/newsletter/subscribe.html

and join the authors' communities on Facebook (www.facebook.com/DeitelFan), Twitter (@deitel) and Google+ (gplus.to/deitel).

Individuals wishing to purchase Deitel books, and *LiveLessons* video training courses can do so through www.deitel.com. Bulk orders by corporations, the government, the military and academic institutions should be placed directly with Pearson. For more information, visit

www.pearsonhighered.com

This section contains information you should review before using this book and instructions to ensure that your computer is set up properly for use with this book. We'll post updates to this Before You Begin section (if any) on the book's website:

www.deitel.com/books/vb2010htp/

Font and Naming Conventions

We use fonts to distinguish between features, such as menu names, menu items, and other elements that appear in the program-development environment. Our convention is to emphasize IDE features in a sans-serif bold **Helvetica** font (for example, **Properties** window) and to emphasize program text in a sans-serif Lucida font (for example, Private x As Boolean = True).

A Note Regarding Software for the Book

This textbook includes a DVD which contains the Microsoft® Visual Studio® 2010 Express Edition Integrated Development Environments for Visual Basic 2010, Visual C# 2010, Visual C++ 2010, Visual Web Developer 2010 and SQL Server 2008. (You do not need Visual C# or Visual C++ for use with this book.) These IDEs are also downloadable from www.microsoft.com/express. The Express Editions are fully functional, and there is no time limit for using the software. We discuss the setup of this software shortly. The system requirements for these editions can be found at:

www.microsoft.com/express/Support/

Viewing File Extensions

Several screenshots in *Visual Basic 2010 How to Program* display file names with file-name extensions (for example, .txt, .vb or .png). Your system's settings may need to be adjusted to display file-name extensions. Follow these steps to configure your computer:

1. In the **Start** menu, select **All Programs**, then **Accessories**, then **Windows Explorer**.

2. In Windows Vista and Windows 7, press *Alt* to display the menu bar, then select **Folder Options...** from **Windows Explorer**'s **Tools** menu. In Windows XP, simply select **Folder Options...** from **Windows Explorer**'s **Tools** menu.

3. In the dialog that appears, select the **View** tab.

4. In the **Advanced settings:** pane, uncheck the box to the left of the text **Hide extensions for known file types**. [*Note*: If this item is already unchecked, no action needs to be taken.]

Obtaining the Code Examples

The examples for *Simply Visual Basic 2010, 4/e* are available for download at

> www.deitel.com/books/simplyvb2010/

If you're not already registered at our website, go to www.deitel.com and click the **Register** link below our logo in the upper-left corner of the page. Fill in your information. There is no charge to register, and we do not share your information with anyone. After registering, you'll receive a confirmation e-mail with your verification code. You need this code to sign in at www.deitel.com for the first time.

Next, go to www.deitel.com and sign in using the **Login** link below our logo in the upper-left corner of the page. Then, go to www.deitel.com/books/simplyvb2010/. Click the **Examples** link to download the Examples.zip file to your computer. Write down the location where you choose to save the file on your computer.

We assume the examples are located at C:\Examples on your computer. Extract the contents of Examples.zip using a tool such as WinZip (www.winzip.com) or the built-in capabilities of Windows Explorer.

Installing the Software

Before you can run the applications in *Simply Visual Basic 2010, 4/e* or build your own applications, you must install a development environment. We used Microsoft's free Visual Basic 2010 Express Edition in the examples for most chapters and Visual Web Developer 2010 Express Edition for Chapters 28–29. Chapters 27–29 require SQL Server Express Edition, which is installed with Visual Basic 2010 Express. The Visual Studio Express Editions are included on the DVD bundled with this book and can also be downloaded from:

> www.microsoft.com/express/

To install the Visual Basic 2010 and Visual Web Developer 2010 Express Editions, insert the DVD that accompanies this book into your computer's DVD drive to launch the software installer, then click the name of the product you wish to install and follow the on-screen instructions. If the setup window does not appear, use Windows Explorer to view the contents of the DVD drive and double click Setup.exe to launch the installer.

Differences Between Visual Studio 2010 and the Express Editions

There are differences between the full versions of Visual Studio 2010 and the Express Editions we use in this book—for example, there are often more options in the Visual Studio 2010 menus and dialogs. One key difference is that the **Database Explorer** we refer to in Chapters 27–29 is called the **Server Explorer** in the full Visual Studio 2010 products.

Creating Your Working Directory

You should create a working directory on your C: drive in which you'll save the apps you'll create. Throughout the book, we assume the folder you'll use is C:\SimplyVB2010. If you choose a different location for your working directory, you must substitute that location in chapter steps that refer to C:\SimplyVB2010.

You're now ready to begin your Visual Basic studies with *Simply Visual Basic 2010, 4/e*. We hope you enjoy the book!

1

Test-Driving a Painter App

Introducing Computers, the Internet and Visual Basic

Welcome to Visual Basic 2010, which, from this point forward, we'll refer to simply as Visual Basic. In use today are more than a billion *general-purpose computers*, and billions more *embedded computers* are used in cell phones, smartphones, tablet computers, home appliances, automobiles and more—and many of these devices are connected to the Internet. According to a study by Cisco Internet Business Solutions Group, there were 12.5 billion Internet-enabled devices in 2010, and the number is predicted to reach 25 billion by 2015 and 50 billion by 2020.[1] This book focuses on building a wide range of business and personal desktop apps—short for applications. The *portable* Internet and web technologies you'll learn later in the book allow you to design web pages and apps that run on the desktop *as well as* smartphones and tablet devices.

The core of the book teaches Visual Basic using our **app-driven approach**, which provides step-by-step instructions for creating and interacting with useful, real-world computer applications. With this approach and our signature **live-code approach**, which shows dozens of *complete, working* Visual Basic apps and depicts their *actual inputs and outputs*, you'll learn the basic skills that underlie good programming. You'll also study chapters on graphics, multimedia, database and web programming.

Be sure to read both the Preface and the Before You Begin section to learn about the book's coverage and how to set up your computer to run the example apps. The apps are available at www.deitel.com/books/simplyVB2010 and www.pearsonhighered.com/deitel. *Run every app* as you study it.

1.1 Computing in Business, Industry and Research

These are exciting times in the computer field. Many of the most influential and successful businesses of the last two decades are technology companies, including Microsoft, Apple, IBM, Hewlett Packard, Dell, Intel, Motorola, Cisco, Google, Amazon, Facebook, Twitter, Groupon, Foursquare, Yahoo!, eBay and many more. These companies are major employers of people who study information systems, computer science or related disciplines.

---

1. www.cisco.com/web/about/ac79/docs/innov/IoT_IBSG_0411FINAL.pdf.

In the past, most computer applications ran on computers that were not connected to one another, whereas today's Internet apps can be written to communicate among computers throughout the world. Figure 1.1 lists examples of how computers and the Internet are being used to improve health care.

Name	Description
Electronic health records	These might include a patient's medical history, prescriptions, immunizations, lab results, allergies, insurance information and more. Making this information available to health care providers across a secure network improves patient care, reduces errors and increases overall efficiency of the health care system.
Human Genome Project	The Human Genome Project was founded to identify and analyze the 20,000+ genes in human DNA. The project used computer programs to analyze complex genetic data, determine the sequences of the billions of chemical base pairs that make up human DNA and store the information in databases that are available over the Internet to researchers worldwide.

Figure 1.1   Computers and the Internet in health care.

Figure 1.2 provides examples of how computers and the Internet are being used for social good. The exercises at the end of this chapter ask you to propose other projects that would use computers and the Internet to "make a difference."

Name	Description
AMBER™ Alert	The AMBER (America's Missing: Broadcast Emergency Response) Alert System is used to find abducted children. Law enforcement notifies TV and radio broadcasters and state transportation officials, who then broadcast alerts on TV, radio, computerized highway signs, the Internet and wireless devices. AMBER Alert recently partnered with Facebook, whose users can "Like" AMBER Alert pages by location to receive alerts in their news feeds.
World Community Grid	People worldwide can donate their unused computer processing power by installing a free secure software program that allows the World Community Grid (www.worldcommunitygrid.org) to harness unused capacity. This computing power, accessed over the Internet, is used in place of expensive supercomputers to conduct scientific research projects that are making a difference, providing clean water to third-world countries, fighting cancer, growing more nutritious rice for regions fighting hunger and more.
One Laptop Per Child (OLPC)	One Laptop Per Child (one.laptop.org) is providing low-power, inexpensive, Internet-enabled laptops to children in third-world countries—enhancing learning and reducing the digital divide.

Figure 1.2   Projects that use computers and the Internet for social good.

We rely on computers and the Internet to communicate, navigate, collaborate and more. Figure 1.3 gives examples of how computers and the Internet provide the infrastructure for these tasks.

Name	Description
Microsoft's Windows Embedded Automotive	Microsoft's Windows Embedded Automotive operating system is used by automobile manufacturers to provide capabilities such as speech synthesis (for reading text messages to you) and speech recognition (for allowing you to use voice commands to browse music, request traffic alerts and more). Auto manufacturers Ford, Fiat and Kia offer systems based on Windows Embedded Automotive.

Figure 1.3   Examples of computers and the Internet in infrastructure. (Part 1 of 2.)

Name	Description
Cloud computing	**Cloud computing** allows you to use software, hardware and information stored in the "cloud"—i.e., accessed on remote computers via the Internet and available on demand—rather than having it stored on your personal computer. Amazon is one of the leading providers of public cloud computing services. You can rent extra storage capacity using the Amazon Simple Storage Service (Amazon S3), or augment processing capabilities with Amazon's EC2 (Amazon Elastic Compute Cloud). These services, allowing you to increase or decrease resources to meet your needs at any given time, are generally more cost effective than purchasing expensive hardware to ensure that you have enough storage and processing power to meet your needs at their peak levels. Business applications are often expensive, require significant hardware to run them and knowledgeable support staff to ensure that they're running properly and securely. Using cloud computing services shifts the burden of managing these apps from the business to the service provider, saving businesses money.
GPS	Global Positioning System (GPS) devices use a network of satellites to retrieve location-based information. Multiple satellites send time-stamped signals to the GPS device, which calculates the distance to each satellite based on the time the signal left the satellite and the time the signal arrived. This information is used to determine the exact location of the device. GPS devices can provide step-by-step directions and help you easily find nearby businesses (restaurants, gas stations, etc.) and points of interest. GPS is used in numerous location-based Internet services such as check-in apps to help you find your friends (e.g., Foursquare and Facebook), exercise apps such as RunKeeper that track the time, distance and average speed of your outdoor jog, dating apps that help you find a match nearby and apps that dynamically update changing traffic conditions.
Robots	Robots can be used for day-to-day tasks (e.g., iRobot's Roomba vacuuming robot), entertainment (e.g., robotic pets), military combat, deep sea and space exploration (e.g., NASA's Mars rover) and more. RoboEarth (www.roboearth.org) is "a World Wide Web for robots." It allows robots to learn from each other by sharing information and thus improving their abilities to perform tasks, navigate, recognize objects and more.
E-mail, Instant messaging, Video chat and FTP	Internet-based servers support all of your online messaging. E-mail messages go through a mail server that also stores the messages. Instant messaging (IM) and Video chat apps, such as AIM, Skype and Yahoo! Messenger allow you to communicate with others in real time by sending your messages and live video through servers. FTP (file transfer protocol) allows you to exchange files over the Internet between multiple computers (e.g., a client computer such as your desktop and a file server).

Figure 1.3 Examples of computers and the Internet in infrastructure. (Part 2 of 2.)

Figure 1.4 lists a few of the ways in which computers and the Internet are used in entertainment.

Name	Description
Internet TV	Internet TV set-top boxes (such as Apple TV, Google TV and TiVo) allow you to access an enormous amount of content on demand, such as games, news, movies, television shows and more.

Figure 1.4 Examples of computers and the Internet in entertainment. (Part 1 of 2.)

Name	Description
iTunes and the App Store	iTunes is Apple's media store where you can buy and download digital music, movies, television shows, e-books, ringtones and apps (for iPhone, iPod and iPad) over the Internet. Apple's iCloud service allows you to store your media purchases "in the cloud" and access them from any iOS (Apple's mobile operating system) device. In June 2011, Apple announced at their World Wide Developer Conference (WWDC) that 15 billion songs had been downloaded through iTunes, making Apple the leading music retailer. As of July 2011, 15 billion apps had been downloaded from the App Store (`www.apple.com/pr/library/2011/07/07Apples-App-Store-Downloads-Top-15-Billion.html`).
Game programming	Analysts expect global video game revenues to reach $91 billion by 2015 (`www.vg247.com/2009/06/23/global-industry-analysts-predicts-gaming-market-to-reach-91-billion-by-2015/`). The most sophisticated games can cost as much as $100 million to develop. Activision's *Call of Duty: Black Ops*—one of the best-selling game of all time—earned $360 million in just one day (`www.forbes.com/sites/insertcoin/2011/03/11/call-of-duty-black-ops-now-the-best-selling-video-game-of-all-time/`)! Online *social gaming*, which enables users worldwide to compete with one another over the Internet, is growing rapidly. Zynga—creator of popular online games such as *Farmville* and *Mafia Wars*—was founded in 2007 and already has over 200 million monthly users. To accommodate the growth in traffic, Zynga is adding nearly 1,000 servers each week (`techcrunch.com/2010/09/22/zynga-moves-1-petabyte-of-data-daily-adds-1000-servers-a-week/`).

Figure 1.4   Examples of computers and the Internet in entertainment. (Part 2 of 2.)

Figure 1.5 lists some of the most popular categories of business apps.

Software app	Description
Accounting	Software such as QuickBooks and Sage Peachtree that allows businesses and individuals to do invoicing, bank-account management, bill payment, financial planning and more.
Blogging	Software tools that allow you to create and maintain blogs. Popular blogging tools include Wordpress, Blogger and MoveableType.
CRM	Customer Relationship Management (CRM) tools, such as Salesforce.com and Oncontact (which operate in the cloud), enable businesses to keep track of customer information.
Backup and recovery	Backup and recovery software such as Norton Ghost and NovaBACKUP helps companies protect their files and systems from data loss.
Collaboration	Tools such as Microsoft SharePoint and Cisco's WebEx that enable teams of people to collaborate on projects.
Database	An electronic collection of data that's organized for easy access and manipulation. Some key database management systems are Oracle and SQL Server.
e-Commerce	Tools such as Shopify and Yahoo Merchant that help business manage online sales including a shopping cart, payment processing and more.

Figure 1.5   Popular categories of business apps. (Part 1 of 2.)

Software app	Description
e-mail	Software such as Microsoft Outlook, Mac Mail and Mozilla Thunderbird that's used to manage e-mail communications.
Office suite	Office suites such as Microsoft Office and Google Docs include software such as word processors, spreadsheets, e-mail, presentation software (for slides, etc.) and more.
Security	Security software helps protect valuable data such as financial information, intellectual property and customer data from viruses and theft. Popular security apps include Norton AntiVirus, McAfee and Microsoft Security Essentials.
Project management	Project Management software, such as Clarizen and AtTak, helps businesses manage project deadlines and tasks and communicate and collaborate with team members.
Enterprise resource planning	Enterprise resource planning (ERP) software integrates software services across an organization including financial and accounting systems, human resources, project management, CRM, supply-chain management and more. Leading providers of ERP software include SAP and Oracle.

Figure 1.5   Popular categories of business apps. (Part 2 of 2.)

SELF-REVIEW

1. _____ allows people worldwide to donate their unused computer processing power to be harnessed and used in place of expensive supercomputers to conduct scientific research projects.
   a) Enterprise resource planning   b) The World Community Grid
   c) Cloud computing   d) The Human Genome Project

2. _____ allows you to use software, hardware and information accessed on remote computers via the Internet and available on demand—rather than having it stored on your personal computer.
   a) Project management   b) Blogging
   c) Cloud computing   d) Enterprise resource planning

Answers: 1) b. 2) c.

1.2 Hardware and Software

A computer is a device that can perform computations and make logical decisions phenomenally faster than human beings can. Many of today's personal computers can perform billions of calculations in one second—more than a human can perform in a lifetime. *Supercomputers* are already performing *thousands of trillions (quadrillions)* of instructions per second! To put that in perspective, a quadrillion-instruction-per-second computer can perform in one second more than 100,000 calculations *for every person on the planet!* And—these "upper limits" are growing quickly! As of 2011, the world's fastest supercomputer was the Fujitsu K, which can perform over 10 quadrillion calculations per second.[2]

Computers process data under the control of sets of instructions called **computer programs**. These programs guide the computer through orderly sets of actions specified by people called computer **programmers**. The programs that run on a computer are referred to as **software**. In this book, you'll learn today's key programming methodology that's enhancing programmer productivity, thereby reducing software-development costs—**object-oriented programming**.

---

2. techcrunch.com/2011/11/03/fujitsu-k-the-worlds-fastest-supercomputer-is-now-even-faster/.

A computer consists of various devices referred to as **hardware** (e.g., the keyboard, screen, mouse, hard disks, memory, DVDs and processing units). Owing to rapid developments in hardware and software technologies, computing costs are *dropping dramatically*. Computers that might have filled large rooms and cost millions of dollars decades ago are now inscribed on silicon chips smaller than a fingernail, costing perhaps a few dollars each. Ironically, silicon is one of the most abundant materials—it's an ingredient in common sand. Silicon-chip technology has made computing economical.

Computer chips (*microprocessors*) control countless devices such as anti-lock brakes in cars, navigation systems, smart home appliances, home security systems, cell phones and smartphones, robots, intelligent traffic intersections, collision avoidance systems, video game controllers and more. The vast majority of the microprocessors produced each year are embedded in devices other than general-purpose computers.

Moore's Law

Every year, you probably expect to pay at least a little more for most products and services. The opposite has been the case in the computer and communications fields, especially with regard to the costs of hardware supporting these technologies. For many decades, hardware costs have fallen rapidly. Every year or two, the capacities of computers have approximately *doubled* inexpensively. This remarkable trend often is called **Moore's Law**, named for the person who identified it, Gordon Moore, co-founder of Intel—the leading manufacturer of the processors in today's computers and embedded systems. Moore's Law and related observations apply especially to the amount of memory that computers have for programs, the amount of secondary storage (such as disk storage) they have to hold programs and data over longer periods of time, and their processor speeds—the speeds at which computers execute their programs (i.e., do their work). Similar growth has occurred in the communications field, in which costs have plummeted as enormous demand for communications **bandwidth** (i.e., information-carrying capacity) has attracted intense competition. We know of no other fields in which technology improves so quickly and costs fall so rapidly. Such phenomenal improvement is truly fostering the *Information Revolution*.

SELF-REVIEW

1. Computers process data, using sets of instructions called _____.

   a) hardware b) computer programs

   c) processing units d) programmers

2. The devices that make up a computer are called _____.

   a) hardware b) software

   c) programs d) programmers

   Answers: 1) b. 2) a.

1.3 Data Hierarchy

Data items processed by computers form a **data hierarchy** that becomes larger and more complex in structure as we progress from bits to characters to fields, and so on. Figure 1.6 illustrates a portion of the data hierarchy. Figure 1.7 summarizes the data hierarchy's levels.

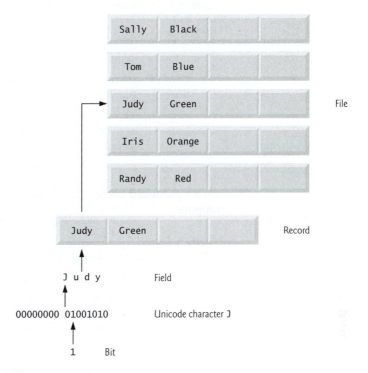

Figure 1.6   Data hierarchy.

Level	Description
Bits	The smallest data item in a computer can assume the value 0 or the value 1. Such a data item is called a **bit** (short for "binary digit"—a digit that can assume one of two values). It's remarkable that the impressive functions performed by computers involve only the simplest manipulations of 0s and 1s—*examining a bit's value*, *setting a bit's value* and *reversing a bit's value* (from 1 to 0 or from 0 to 1).
Characters	It's tedious for people to work with data in the low-level form of bits. Instead, they prefer to work with *decimal digits* (0–9), *letters* (A–Z and a–z), and *special symbols* (e.g., $, @, %, &, *, (,), –, +, ", :, ? and /). Digits, letters and special symbols are known as **characters**. The computer's **character set** is the set of all the characters used to write programs and represent data items. Computers process only 1s and 0s, so a computer's character set represents every character as a pattern of 1s and 0s. Visual Basic uses **Unicode**® characters that are composed of two **bytes**, each composed of eight bits. Unicode contains characters for many of the world's languages. The **ASCII (American Standard Code for Information Interchange)** character set is the popular subset of Unicode that represents uppercase and lowercase letters, digits and some common special characters.
Fields	Just as characters are composed of bits, **fields** are composed of characters or bytes. A field is a group of characters or bytes that conveys meaning. For example, a field consisting of uppercase and lowercase letters can be used to represent a person's name, and a field consisting of decimal digits could represent a person's age.

Figure 1.7   Levels of the data hierarchy. (Part 1 of 2.)

Level	Description
Records	Several related fields can be used to compose a **record** (implemented as a class in Visual Basic). In a payroll system, for example, the record for an employee might consist of the following fields (possible types for these fields are shown in parentheses):
	■ Employee identification number (a whole number)
	■ Name (a string of characters)
	■ Address (a string of characters)
	■ Hourly pay rate (a number with a decimal point)
	■ Year-to-date earnings (a number with a decimal point)
	■ Amount of taxes withheld (a number with a decimal point)
	Thus, a record is a group of related fields. In the preceding example, all the fields belong to the same employee. A company might have many employees and a payroll record for each one.
Files	A **file** is a group of related records. [*Note:* More generally, a file contains arbitrary data in arbitrary formats. In some operating systems, a file is viewed simply as a *sequence of bytes*—any organization of the bytes in a file, such as organizing the data into records, is a view created by the application programmer.] It's not unusual for an organization to have many files, some containing billions, or even trillions, of characters of information.

Figure 1.7 Levels of the data hierarchy. (Part 2 of 2.)

1. _____, the smallest data items in a computer, can assume the value 0 or the value 1.

   a) Characters   b) Bits
   c) Bytes   d) Fields

2. A _____ is a group of related records.

   a) file   b) class
   c) character   d) program

Answers: 1) b. 2) a.

1.4 Computer Organization

Regardless of differences in physical appearance, computers can be envisioned as divided into various **logical units** or sections (Fig. 1.8).

Logical Unit	Description
Input unit	This "receiving" section obtains information (data and computer programs) from **input devices** and places it at the disposal of the other units for processing. Most information is entered into computers through keyboards, touch screens and mouse devices. Other forms of input include speaking to your computer, scanning images and barcodes, reading from secondary storage devices (such as hard drives, DVD drives, Blu-ray Disc™ drives and USB flash drives—also called "thumb drives" or "memory sticks"), receiving video from a webcam and having your computer receive information from the Internet (such as when you download videos from YouTube™ or e-books from Amazon). Newer forms of input include reading position data from a GPS device, and motion and orientation information from an accelerometer in a smartphone or game controller.

Figure 1.8 Logical units of a computer. (Part 1 of 2.)

Logical Unit	Description
Output unit	This "shipping" section takes information that the computer has processed and places it on various **output devices** to make it available for use outside the computer. Most information that's output from computers today is displayed on screens, printed on paper, played as audio or video on portable media players (such as Apple's popular iPods) and giant screens in sports stadiums, transmitted over the Internet or used to control other devices, such as robots and "intelligent" appliances.
Memory unit	This rapid-access, relatively low-capacity "warehouse" section retains information that's been entered through the input unit, making it immediately available for processing when needed. The memory unit also retains processed information until it can be placed on output devices by the output unit. Information in the memory unit is *volatile*—it's typically lost when the computer's power is turned off. The memory unit is often called either **memory** or **primary memory**. Typical main memories on desktop and notebook computers contain between 1 and 8 GB (GB stands for gigabytes; a gigabyte is approximately one billion bytes).
Arithmetic and logic unit (ALU)	This "manufacturing" section performs *calculations*, such as addition, subtraction, multiplication and division. It also contains the *decision* mechanisms that allow the computer, for example, to compare two items from the memory unit to determine whether they're equal. Today's systems usually implement the ALU as part of the next logical unit, the CPU.
Central processing unit (CPU)	This "administrative" section coordinates and supervises the operation of the other sections. The CPU tells the input unit when information should be read into the memory unit, tells the ALU when information from the memory unit should be used in calculations and tells the output unit when to send information from the memory unit to certain output devices. Many of today's computers have multiple CPUs and, hence, can perform many operations simultaneously. A **multi-core processor** implements multiple processors on a single integrated-circuit chip—a *dual-core processor* has two CPUs and a *quad-core processor* has four CPUs. Today's desktop computers have processors that can execute billions of instructions per second.
Secondary storage unit	This is the long-term, high-capacity "warehousing" section. Programs or data not actively being used by the other units normally are placed on secondary storage devices (e.g., your *hard drive*) until they're again needed, possibly hours, days, months or even years later. Information on secondary storage devices is *persistent*—it's preserved even when the computer's power is turned off. Secondary storage information takes much longer to access than information in primary memory, but the cost for a unit of secondary storage is much less than for a unit of primary memory. Examples of secondary storage devices include CD drives, DVD drives and flash drives, some of which can hold up to 256 GB. Typical hard drives on desktop and notebook computers can hold up to 2 TB (TB stands for terabytes; a terabyte is approximately one trillion bytes).

Figure 1.8   Logical units of a computer. (Part 2 of 2.)

SELF-REVIEW   1. The _____ is responsible for performing calculations and contains decision-making mechanisms.

    a) output unit   b) memory unit

    c) arithmetic and logic unit   d) input unit

    2. Information stored in _____ is normally erased when the computer is turned off.

    a) primary memory   b) secondary storage

    c) CD-ROM drives   d) hard drives

Answers: 1) c. 2) a.

1.5 Machine Languages, Assembly Languages and High-Level Languages

Programmers write instructions in various programming languages, some directly understandable by computers and others requiring intermediate *translation* steps. Hundreds of such languages are in use today. These may be divided into three general types:

1. Machine languages
2. Assembly languages
3. High-level languages

Any computer can directly understand only its own **machine language,** defined by its hardware design. Machine languages generally consist of strings of numbers (ultimately reduced to 1s and 0s) that instruct computers to perform their most elementary operations one at a time. Machine languages are *machine dependent* (a particular machine language can be used on only one type of computer). Such languages are cumbersome for humans. For example, here's a section of an early machine-language program that adds overtime pay to base pay and stores the result in gross pay:

```
+1300042774
+1400593419
+1200274027
```

Programming in machine language was simply too slow and tedious for most programmers. Instead of using the strings of numbers that computers could directly understand, programmers began using English-like abbreviations to represent elementary operations. These abbreviations formed the basis of **assembly languages.** *Translator programs* called **assemblers** were developed to convert early assembly-language programs to machine language at computer speeds. The following section of an assembly-language program also adds overtime pay to base pay and stores the result in gross pay:

```
load    basepay
add     overpay
store   grosspay
```

Although such code is clearer to humans, it's incomprehensible to computers until translated to machine language.

Computer usage increased rapidly with the advent of assembly languages, but programmers still had to use many instructions to accomplish even the simplest tasks. To speed the programming process, **high-level languages** were developed in which single statements could be written to accomplish substantial tasks. Translator programs called **compilers** convert high-level language programs into machine language. High-level languages allow you to write instructions that look almost like everyday English and contain commonly used mathematical notations. A payroll program written in a high-level language might contain a *single* statement such as

```
grossPay = basePay + overTimePay
```

From these examples, it's clear why programmers prefer high-level languages. Visual Basic is one of the world's most popular high-level programming languages.

SELF-REVIEW   1. The only programming language that a computer can directly understand is its own
_____.

a) high-level language   b) assembly language
c) machine language   d) English

2. Programs that translate high-level language programs into machine language are called
   _____.

    a) assemblers   b) compilers
    c) programmers   d) converters

Answers: 1) c. 2) b.

1.6 Object Technology

Building software quickly, correctly and economically remains an elusive goal at a time when demands for new and more powerful software are soaring. **Objects, or more precisely the** *classes* **objects come from, are essentially** *reusable* **software components.** There are date objects, time objects, audio objects, video objects, automobile objects, people objects, etc. Almost any *noun* can be reasonably represented as a software object in terms of *attributes* (e.g., name, color and size) and *behaviors* (e.g., calculating, moving and communicating). Software developers have discovered that using a modular, object-oriented design and implementation approach can make software-development groups much more productive than was possible with earlier techniques—object-oriented programs are often easier to understand, correct and modify.

The Automobile as an Object

Let's begin with a simple analogy. Suppose you want to *drive a car and make it go faster by pressing its accelerator pedal.* What must happen before you can do this? Well, before you can drive a car, someone has to *design* it. A car typically begins as engineering drawings, similar to the *blueprints* that describe the design of a house. These drawings include the design for an accelerator pedal. The pedal *hides* from the driver the complex mechanisms that actually make the car go faster, just as the brake pedal hides the mechanisms that slow the car, and the steering wheel hides the mechanisms that turn the car. This enables people with little or no knowledge of how engines, braking and steering mechanisms work to drive a car easily.

Before you can drive a car, it must be *built* from the engineering drawings that describe it. A completed car has an *actual* accelerator pedal to make the car go faster, but even that's not enough—the car won't accelerate on its own (we hope), so the driver must *press* the pedal to accelerate the car.

Methods and Classes

Let's use our car example to introduce some key object-oriented programming concepts. Performing a task in a program requires a **method**. The method houses the program statements that actually perform its tasks. It hides these statements from its user, just as a car's accelerator pedal hides from the driver the mechanisms of making the car go faster. In object-oriented programming languages, we create a program unit called a **class** to house the set of methods that perform the class's tasks. For example, a class that represents a bank account might contain one method to *deposit* money to an account, another to *withdraw* money from an account and a third to *inquire* what the account's current balance is. A class is similar in concept to a car's engineering drawings, which house the design of an accelerator pedal, steering wheel and so on.

Making Objects from Classes

Just as someone has to *build a car* from its engineering drawings before you can actually drive a car, you must *build an object* from a class before a program can perform the tasks that the class's methods define. The process of doing this is called *instantiation*. An object is then referred to as an **instance** of its class.

Software Design Tip

Use a building-block approach to creating your programs. Avoid reinventing the wheel—use existing pieces wherever possible. This software reuse is a key benefit of object-oriented programming.

Reuse

Just as a car's engineering drawings can be *reused* many times to build many cars, you can *reuse* a class many times to build many objects. Reuse of existing classes when building new classes and programs saves time and effort. Reuse also helps you build more reliable and effective systems, because existing classes and components often have gone through extensive *testing*, *debugging* and *performance tuning*. Just as the notion of *interchangeable parts* was crucial to the Industrial Revolution, reusable classes are crucial to the software revolution that's been spurred by object technology.

Messages and Method Calls

When you drive a car, pressing its gas pedal sends a *message* to the car to perform a task—that is, to go faster. Similarly, you *send messages to an object*. Each message is implemented as a **method call** that tells a method of the object to perform its task. For example, a program might call a particular bank-account object's *deposit* method to increase the account's balance.

Attributes and Instance Variables

A car, besides having capabilities to accomplish tasks, also has *attributes*, such as its color, its number of doors, the amount of gas in its tank, its current speed and its record of total miles driven (i.e., its odometer reading). Like its capabilities, the car's attributes are represented as part of its design in its engineering diagrams (which, for example, include an odometer and a fuel gauge). As you drive an actual car, these attributes are carried along with the car. Every car maintains its *own* attributes. For example, each car knows how much gas is in its own gas tank, but *not* how much is in the tanks of *other* cars.

An object, similarly, has attributes that it carries along as it's used in a program. These attributes are specified as part of the object's class. For example, a bank-account object has a *balance attribute* that represents the amount of money in the account. Each bank-account object knows the balance in the account it represents, but *not* the balances of the *other* accounts in the bank. Attributes are specified by the class's **instance variables**.

Encapsulation

Classes **encapsulate** (i.e., wrap) attributes and methods into objects—an object's attributes and methods are intimately related. Objects may communicate with one another, but normally they're not allowed to know how other objects are implemented—implementation details are *hidden* within the objects themselves. This **information hiding** is crucial to good software engineering.

Inheritance

A new class of objects can be created quickly and conveniently by **inheritance**—the new class absorbs the characteristics of an existing class, possibly customizing them and adding unique characteristics of its own. In our car analogy, an object of class "convertible" certainly *is an* object of the more *general* class "automobile," but more *specifically*, the roof can be raised or lowered.

SELF-REVIEW

1. The _____ houses the program statements that actually perform its tasks.
   a) object
   b) instance variable
   c) class
   d) method

2. The process of building an object from a class before a program can perform the tasks that the class's methods define is called _____.
   a) instantiation
   b) inheritance
   c) encapsulation
   d) information hiding

Answers: 1) d. 2) a.

1.7 Microsoft's Windows® Operating System

Microsoft became the dominant software company in the 1980s and 1990s. In the mid-1980s, Microsoft developed the **Windows operating system**, consisting of a graphical user interface built on top of DOS (Disk Operating System; a personal-computer operating system that users interacted with by typing commands). The Windows operating system became incredibly popular after the 1993 release of Windows 3.1, whose successors, Windows 95 and Windows 98, virtually cornered the desktop operating systems market by the late 1990s. These operating systems, which borrowed from many concepts (such as icons, menus and windows) popularized by early Apple Macintosh operating systems, enabled users to navigate multiple apps simultaneously. Microsoft entered the corporate operating systems market with the 1993 release of Windows NT. Windows XP was released in 2001 and combined Microsoft's corporate and consumer operating system lines. Windows Vista, released in 2007, offered the attractive new Aero user interface, many powerful enhancements and new apps. A key focus of Windows Vista was enhanced security. Windows 7 is Microsoft's latest operating system—its features include enhancements to the Aero user interface, faster startup times, further refinement of Vista's security features, touch-screen and multi-touch support, and more. This book is intended for Windows XP, Windows Vista and Windows 7 users. At the time of this publication, Windows 8 was about to be released. Windows is by far the world's most widely used operating system.

SELF-REVIEW

1. The _____ consists of a graphical user interface built on top of DOS (a personal-computer operating system that users interacted with by typing commands).
   a) Apple Macintosh operating system   b) Windows operating system
   c) Linux operating system   d) Apache web server

2. Windows Vista and Windows 7 feature the _____ user interface.
   a) XP   b) Aero
   c) DOS   d) NT

Answers: 1) b. 2) b.

1.8 Programming Languages

In this section we provide brief comments on several popular programming languages (Fig. 1.9). In the next section we introduce Visual Basic.

Programming language	Description
C	C was implemented in 1972 by Dennis Ritchie at Bell Laboratories. It initially became widely known as the UNIX operating system's development language. Today, most of the code for general-purpose operating systems is written in C or C++.
C++	C++, an extension of C, was developed by Bjarne Stroustrup in the early 1980s at Bell Laboratories. C++ provides a number of features that "spruce up" the C language, but more important, it provides capabilities for object-oriented programming.
Objective-C	Objective-C is another object-oriented language based on C. It was developed in the early 1980s and later acquired by NeXT, which in turn was acquired by Apple. It has become the key programming language for Apple's Mac OS X operating system and all of Apple's iOS-based devices (such as iPods, iPhones and iPads).

Figure 1.9 Popular programming languages. (Part 1 of 2.)

Programming language	Description
Java	Sun Microsystems in 1991 funded an internal corporate research project led by James Gosling, which resulted in the C++-based object-oriented programming language called Java. A key goal of Java is to enable the writing of programs that will run on a great variety of computer systems and computer-controlled devices. This is sometimes called "write once, run anywhere." Java is used to develop large-scale enterprise applications, to enhance the functionality of web servers (the computers that provide the content we see in our web browsers), to provide applications for consumer devices (smartphones, television set-top boxes and more) and for many other purposes. Sun was acquired by Oracle in 2010.
Visual C#	Microsoft's three primary object-oriented programming languages are Visual Basic, Visual C++ (based on C++) and Visual C# (based on C++ and Java, and developed for integrating the Internet and the web into computer applications).
PHP	PHP—an object-oriented, "open-source" scripting language supported by a community of users and developers—is used by numerous websites including Wikipedia and Facebook. PHP also supports many databases, including MySQL. Two other popular languages similar in concept to PHP are Perl and Python. The term "LAMP" describes four key technologies for building open-source software—Linux (operating system), Apache (web server), MySQL (database) and PHP or Perl or Python (server-side scripting languages).
JavaScript	JavaScript—developed by Brendan Eich at Netscape in 1995—is the most widely used scripting language. It's primarily used to add programmability to web pages—for example, animations and interactivity with the user. It's provided with all major web browsers.

Figure 1.9   Popular programming languages. (Part 2 of 2.)

SELF-REVIEW 1. _____ is an extension of C and offers object-oriented capabilities.
    a) Visual Basic   b) C++
    c) assembly language   d) Windows

2. _____ is a C++-based object-oriented programming language developed by Sun Microsystems that enables you to write programs that will run on a great variety of computer systems and computer-controlled devices.
    a) C#   b) Java
    c) C++   d) Visual Basic

Answers: 1) b. 2) b.

1.9 Visual Basic

Visual Basic evolved from **BASIC** (Beginner's All-purpose Symbolic Instruction Code), developed in the mid-1960s at Dartmouth College as a language for introducing novices to fundamental programming techniques.

When Bill Gates co-founded Microsoft Corporation in the 1970s, he implemented BASIC on several early personal computers. In the late 1980s and the early 1990s, Microsoft developed the Microsoft Windows **graphical user interface (GUI)**—the *visual* part of the operating system with which users interact. With the creation of the Windows GUI, the natural evolution of BASIC was to **Visual Basic**, introduced by Microsoft in 1991 to make programming Windows apps easier.

Until Visual Basic appeared, developing Microsoft Windows-based apps was a difficult process. Visual Basic programs are created with the use of a collection of software tools called an **Integrated Development Environment (IDE).** With Microsoft's **Visual Studio 2010** IDE, you can write, run, test and debug Visual Basic programs quickly and conveniently.

The latest versions of Visual Basic are fully *object oriented*—you'll study a rich treatment of object-oriented programming later in the book. Visual Basic is **event driven**—you'll write programs that respond to **events** such as mouse clicks, keystrokes and timer expirations. It's a *visual programming language*—in addition to writing program statements to build portions of your apps, you'll also use Visual Studio's graphical user interface to conveniently *drag and drop* predefined objects, such as buttons and textboxes, into place on your screen, and label and resize them. Visual Studio will write much of the GUI program code for you.

SELF-REVIEW

1. Microsoft created _____ in 1991 to make it easier to program Windows apps.
   a) Windows   b) BASIC
   c) Visual Basic   d) C#

2. Visual Basic evolved from _____, which was created as a language for writing simple programs quickly and easily.
   a) C++   b) Windows
   c) Java   d) BASIC

Answers: 1) c. 2) d.

1.10 The Internet and the World Wide Web

In the late 1960s, ARPA—the Advanced Research Projects Agency of the Department of Defense—rolled out plans to network the main computer systems of approximately a dozen ARPA-funded universities and research institutions. The computers were to be connected with communications lines operating at a then-stunning 56 Kbps (1 Kbps is equal to 1,024 bits per second), at a time when most people (of the few who even had networking access) were connecting over telephone lines to computers at a rate of 110 bits per second. Academic research was about to take a giant leap forward. ARPA proceeded to implement what quickly became known as the **ARPAnet**, the grandparent of today's **Internet**.

Things worked out differently from the original plan. Although the ARPAnet enabled researchers to network their computers, its main benefit proved to be the capability for quick and easy communication via what came to be known as **electronic mail (e-mail)**. This is true even on today's Internet, with e-mail, instant messaging, file transfer and social media such as Facebook and Twitter, allowing billions of people worldwide to communicate with each other.

The protocol (in other words, the set of rules) for communicating over the ARPAnet became known as the **Transmission Control Protocol (TCP)**. TCP ensured that messages, consisting of pieces called "packets," were properly routed from sender to receiver, arrived intact and were assembled in the correct order.

In parallel with the early evolution of the Internet, organizations worldwide were implementing their own networks for both intraorganization (that is, within an organization) and interorganization (that is, between organizations) communication. A huge variety of networking hardware and software appeared. One challenge was to enable these different networks to communicate with each other. ARPA accomplished this by developing the **Internet Protocol (IP)**, which created a true "network of networks," the current architecture of the Internet. The combined set of protocols is now called **TCP/IP**.

Businesses rapidly realized that by using the Internet, they could improve their operations and offer new and better services to their clients. Companies started spending large amounts of money to develop and enhance their Internet presence. This generated fierce competition among communications carriers and hardware and software suppliers to meet the increased infrastructure demand. As a result, **bandwidth**—the information-carrying capacity of communications lines—on the Internet has increased tremendously, while hardware costs have plummeted.

World Wide Web

The **World Wide Web** is a collection of hardware and software associated with the Internet that allows computer users to locate and view multimedia-based documents (documents with various combinations of text, graphics, animations, audios and videos) on almost any subject. The introduction of the World Wide Web (WWW) was a relatively recent event. In 1989, Tim Berners-Lee of CERN (the European Organization for Nuclear Research) began to develop a technology for sharing information via "hyperlinked" text documents. Berners-Lee called his invention the **HyperText Markup Language (HTML)**. He also wrote communication protocols such as **HyperText Transfer Protocol (HTTP)** to form the backbone of his new hypertext information system, which he referred to as the World Wide Web.

In October 1994, Berners-Lee founded an organization, called the **World Wide Web Consortium (W3C**, www.w3.org), devoted to developing technologies for the World Wide Web. One of the W3C's primary goals is to make the web universally accessible to everyone regardless of disabilities, language or culture.

The Internet and the web will surely be listed among the most important creations of humankind. In the past, most computer applications ran on "stand-alone" computers (not connected to one another). Today's applications can be written with the aim of communicating among the world's computers. In fact, as you'll see, this is the focus of Microsoft's .NET strategy. The Internet and the World Wide Web make information instantly and conveniently accessible to large numbers of people, enabling even individuals and small businesses to achieve worldwide exposure. This is profoundly changing the way we do business and conduct our personal lives. To highlight the importance of Internet and web programming, we include two chapters at the end of the book in which you'll build and run web-based applications.

SELF-REVIEW   1. Today's Internet evolved from the _____, which was a Department of Defense project.

a) ARPAnet   b) HTML
c) CERN   d) WWW

2. The combined set of protocols for communicating over the Internet is called _____.

a) HTML   b) TCP/IP
c) ARPA   d) TCP

Answers: 1) a. 2) b.

1.11 Microsoft .NET

In 2000, Microsoft announced its **.NET initiative** (www.microsoft.com/net), a broad new vision for using the Internet and the web in the development, engineering, distribution and use of software. Developers can create .NET applications in any .NET-compatible language (such as Visual Basic, Visual C++, Visual C# and others). Part of the initiative includes Microsoft's **ASP.NET** technology, which enables you to create web applications. You use ASP.NET to build the web-based bookstore application later in the book.

The .NET strategy extends the idea of **software reuse** to the Internet by allowing programmers to concentrate on their specialties without having to implement every component of every application. Visual programming (which you'll learn throughout this book) has become popular because it enables you to create Win-

dows and web applications easily, using such prepackaged graphical components as
buttons, **textboxes** and **scrollbars**.

The Microsoft **.NET Framework** is at the heart of the .NET strategy. This
framework executes applications and web services, contains a class library (called
the **Framework Class Library**) and provides many other programming capabilities
that you'll use to build Visual Basic applications. In this book, you'll develop .NET
software with Visual Basic. Steve Ballmer, Microsoft's CEO, has stated that Microsoft was "betting the company" on .NET. Such a dramatic commitment surely indicates a bright future for Visual Basic 2010 programmers.

SELF-REVIEW

1. _____ is a technology specifically designed for the .NET platform and intended for
   programmers to create web-based applications.

   a) Visual Basic   b) C++
   c) HTML   d) ASP.NET

2. Programmers use the _____, a part of the .NET Framework, to build Visual Basic
   applications.

   a) Visual Basic Library   b) Framework Class Library
   c) Microsoft Class Library   d) Visual Basic Framework

Answers: 1) d. 2) b.

1.12 Web 2.0: Going Social

In 2003 there was a noticeable shift in how people and businesses were using the
web and developing web-based apps. The term **Web 2.0** was coined by **Dale Dough-
erty** of **O'Reilly Media**[3] in 2003 to describe this trend. Generally, Web 2.0 companies use the web as a platform to create collaborative, community-based sites (e.g.,
social networking sites, blogs, wikis).

Web 1.0 versus Web 2.0

Web 1.0 (the state of the web through the 1990s and early 2000s) was focused on a relatively small number of companies and advertisers producing content for users to
access (some people called it the "brochure web"). Web 2.0 *involves* the users—not
only do they often create content, but they help organize it, share it, remix it, critique
it, update it, etc. One way to look at Web 1.0 is as a *lecture*, a small number of professors informing a large audience of students. In comparison, Web 2.0 is a *conversation*,
with everyone having the opportunity to speak and share views. Companies that
understand Web 2.0 realize that their products and services are conversations as well.

Architecture of Participation

Web 2.0 is providing new opportunities and connecting people and content in
unique ways. Web 2.0 embraces an **architecture of participation**—a design that
encourages user interaction and community contributions. You, the user, are the
most important aspect of Web 2.0—so important, in fact, that in 2006, *TIME* magazine's "Person of the Year" was "you."[4] The article recognized the social phenome-
non of Web 2.0—the shift away from a *powerful few* to an *empowered many*. Several
popular blogs now compete with traditional media powerhouses, and many Web 2.0
companies are built almost entirely on user-generated content. For websites like
Facebook®, Twitter™, YouTube, eBay® and Wikipedia®, users create the *content*,

---

3. T. O'Reilly, "What is Web 2.0: Design Patterns and Business Models for the Next
   Generation of Software." September 2005 <http://www.oreillynet.com/pub/a/or-
   eilly/tim/news/2005/09/30/what-is-web-20.html?page=1>.
4. L. Grossman, "TIME's Person of the Year: You." *TIME*, December 2006 <http://
   www.time.com/time/magazine/article/0,9171,1569514,00.html>.

while the companies provide the *platforms* on which to enter, manipulate and share the information. These companies *trust their users*—without such trust, users cannot make significant contributions to the sites.

The architecture of participation has influenced software development as well. **Open-source software** departs from the proprietary software-development style that dominated software's early years. With open-source development, individuals and companies contribute their efforts in developing, maintaining and evolving software in exchange for the right to use that software for their own purposes, typically at no charge. Open-source code is often scrutinized by a much larger audience than proprietary software, so errors often get removed faster. Open source also encourages more innovation.

Some key organizations in the open-source community are the Eclipse Foundation (the Eclipse Integrated Development Environment helps programmers conveniently develop software), the Mozilla Foundation (creators of the Firefox web browser), the Apache Software Foundation (creators of the Apache web server used to develop web-based applications) and SourceForge (which provides the tools for managing open-source projects—it has over 300,000 of them under development). Rapid improvements to computing and communications, decreasing costs and open-source software have made it much easier and more economical to create a software-based business now than just a decade ago. A great example is Facebook, which was launched from a college dorm room and built with open-source software.

Using **collective intelligence**—the concept that a large diverse group of people will create smart ideas—communities collaborate to develop software that many people believe is better and more robust than proprietary software. Rich Internet Applications (RIAs) are being developed (using technologies such as Ajax) that have the look and feel of desktop software, enhancing a user's overall experience.

Search Engines and Social Media

Search engines, including Google™, Microsoft Bing™, and many more, have become essential to sifting through the massive amount of content on the web. Social bookmarking sites such as Delicious.com allow users to share their favorite sites with others. Social media sites such as Digg™ enable the community to decide which news articles are the most significant. The way we find the information on these sites is also changing—people are **tagging** (i.e., labeling) web content by subject or keyword in a way that helps anyone locate information more effectively. Photo-sharing sites like Flickr and video-sharing sites like YouTube count on their users to tag the elements they share or visit to help future users find content quickly.

Semantic Web

In the future, computers will learn to understand the meaning of the data on the web—the beginnings of the **Semantic Web** are already appearing. Continual improvements in hardware, software and communications technologies will enable exciting new types of apps. Search engines, in particular, would be able to deliver far more precise results.

Google

In 1996, Stanford computer science Ph.D. candidates Larry Page and Sergey Brin began collaborating on a new search engine. In 1997, they chose the name Google—a play on the mathematical term *googol*, a quantity represented by the number "one" followed by 100 "zeros" (or 10^{100})—a staggeringly large number. Google's ability to return extremely accurate search results quickly helped it become the most widely used search engine and one of the most popular websites in the world.

Google continues to be an innovator in search technologies. For example, Google Goggles is a fascinating mobile app (available on Android and iPhone) that allows you to perform a Google search using a photo rather than entering text. You simply take a picture of a landmark, book (covers or barcodes), logo, art or wine bottle label, and Google Goggles scans the photo and returns search results. You can also take a picture of text (for example, a restaurant menu or a sign) and Google Goggles will translate it for you.

Web Services and Mashups

Web services and the applications-development methodology of *mashups* can help you rapidly develop powerful and intriguing apps by combining (often free) complementary web services and other forms of information feeds (Fig. 1.10). One of the first mashups was www.housingmaps.com, which combines the real estate listings provided by www.craigslist.org with the mapping capabilities of Google Maps to offer maps that show the locations of apartments for rent in a given area.

Web services source	How it's used
Google Maps	Mapping services
Facebook	Social networking
Foursquare	Mobile check-in
LinkedIn	Social networking for business
YouTube	Video search
Twitter	Microblogging
Groupon	Social commerce
Netflix	Movie rentals
eBay	Internet auctions
Wikipedia	Collaborative encyclopedia
PayPal	Payments
Last.fm	Internet radio
Amazon eCommerce	Shopping for books and more
Salesforce.com	Customer Relationship Management (CRM)
Skype	Internet telephony (both voice and video)
Microsoft Bing	Search
Flickr	Photo sharing
Zillow	Real estate pricing
Yahoo Search	Search
WeatherBug	Weather

Figure 1.10 Some popular web services that you can use to build web apps (www.programmableweb.com/apis/directory/1?sort=mashups).

Web services, inexpensive computers, abundant high-speed Internet access, open-source software and many other elements have inspired new, exciting, *lightweight business models* that people can launch with only a small investment. Some types of websites with rich and robust functionality that might have required hundreds of thousands or even millions of dollars to build in the 1990s can now be built for nominal sums.

Ajax

Ajax is one of the premier Web 2.0 software technologies. Ajax helps Internet-based apps perform like desktop apps—a difficult task, given that Internet apps suffer transmission delays as data is shuttled back and forth between your computer and server computers on the Internet. Using Ajax, applications such as Google Maps have achieved excellent performance and approach the look-and-feel of desktop apps. We show in Chapter 29 how to build Ajax-enabled applications using ASP.NET Ajax-enabled components.

Social Apps

Over the last several years, there's been a tremendous increase in the number of social apps on the web. Even though the computer industry is mature, these sites were still able to become phenomenally successful in a relatively short period. Figure 1.11 discusses a few of the social apps that are making an impact.

Company	Description
Facebook	Facebook was launched in 2004 and is already worth an estimated $100 billion. By January 2011, Facebook was the most active site on the Internet with more than 800 million users (www.facebook.com/press/info.php?statistics). At its current growth rate (about 5% per month), Facebook could reach one billion users in 2012, out of two billion Internet users! The activity on the site makes it extremely attractive for app developers. Each day, over 20 million apps are installed by Facebook users (www.facebook.com/press/info.php?statistics).
Twitter	Twitter (founded in 2006) has revolutionized *microblogging*. Users post tweets—messages up to 140 characters long. Approximately 200 million tweets are posted per day. You can follow the tweets of friends, celebrities, businesses, government representatives (including Barack Obama, who has nearly 11 million followers), and so on, or you can follow tweets by subject to track news, trends and more. At the time of this writing, Lady Gaga had the most followers (over 15 million). Twitter has become the point of origin for many breaking news stories worldwide.
LinkedIn	LinkedIn, founded by Reid Hoffman in 2002, is the world's largest online professional social network with more than 135 million members. LinkedIn allows you to connect with other users with whom you have relationships, building up your professional network. You can use your network to find jobs, find candidates for open positions at your organization, find new business opportunities, participate in industry groups and more.
Groupon	Groupon, a *social commerce* site, was launched in 2008. The company was valued at $12.7 billion at the time of its initial public offering in November 2011, making it the fastest-growing company ever! Groupon offers daily deals in each market for restaurants, retailers, services, attractions and more. Deals are activated only after a minimum number of people sign up to buy the product or service. If you sign up for a deal and it has yet to meet the minimum, you might be inclined to tell others about the deal via e-mail, Facebook, Twitter, etc. One of the most successful national Groupon deals to date was a certificate for $50 worth of merchandise from a major retailer for $25. More than 620,000 vouchers were sold in one day (www.huffingtonpost.com/2011/06/30/the-most-successful-group_n_887711.html)!
Foursquare	Foursquare, launched in 2009, is a mobile *check-in* app that allows you to notify your friends of your whereabouts. You can download the app to your smartphone and link it to your Facebook and Twitter accounts so your friends can follow you from multiple platforms. If you do not have a smartphone, you can check in by text message. Foursquare uses GPS to determine your location. Businesses use Foursquare to send offers to users in the area. Launched in March 2009, Foursquare already has over 10 million users worldwide (foursquare.com/about).

Figure 1.11 Social apps. (Part 1 of 2.)

Company	Description
Skype	Skype (founded in 2003) allows you to make mostly free voice and video calls over the Internet using a technology called *VoIP (Voice over IP*; IP stands for "Internet Protocol"). The company was sold to Microsoft in 2011 for $8.5 billion. There are over 660 million registered users.
YouTube	YouTube is a video-sharing site that was founded in 2005. Within one year, the company was purchased by Google for $1.65 billion. YouTube now accounts for 10% of all Internet traffic (techcrunch.com/2011/05/17/netflix-largest-internet-traffic/). Within one week of the release of Apple's iPhone 3GS—the first iPhone model to offer video—mobile uploads to YouTube grew 400% (www.hypebot.com/hypebot/2009/06/youtube-reports-1700-jump-in-mobile-video.html). YouTube has over three billion views per day (www.youtube.com/t/press).

Figure 1.11   Social apps. (Part 2 of 2.)

SELF-REVIEW

1. With _____, individuals and companies contribute their efforts in developing, maintaining and evolving software in exchange for the right to use that software for their own purposes, typically at no charge.

    a) proprietary software   b) tagging
    c) social networking   d) open-source software

2. Web services can be used to create _____, in which you can rapidly develop powerful and intriguing apps by combining (often free) complementary web services and other forms of information feeds.

    a) tags   b) business models
    c) mashups   d) Ajax

Answers: 1) d. 2) c.

1.13 Test-Driving the Visual Basic Advanced Painter App

In each chapter throughout the book, you're given a chance to "test-drive" that chapter's featured app—you'll actually run and interact with the completed app. Then, you'll learn the Visual Basic features you need to build the app. Finally, you'll "put it all together," creating your own working version of the app. You begin here in Chapter 1 by running an existing app that allows the user to draw with "brushes" of four different colors and three different sizes. You'll actually build a part of this app in Chapter 26, then finish the app in the Chapter 26 exercises.

The following box, *Test-Driving the **Advanced Painter** App*, will show you how the app allows the user to draw with different brush styles. The elements and functionality you see in this app are typical of what you'll learn to program in this text. [*Note:* We use fonts to distinguish between IDE features such as menu names and menu items and other elements that appear in the IDE. Our convention is to emphasize IDE features (such as the **File** menu) in a semibold **sans-serif Helvetica** font and to emphasize other elements, such as filenames (for example, `Form1.cs`), in a `sans-serif Lucida` font.

Test-Driving the
Advanced Painter App

1. ***Checking your setup.*** Confirm that you've set up your computer properly by reading the Before You Begin section located after the Preface.

2. ***Locating the app directory.*** Open a Windows Explorer window and navigate to the `C:\Examples\ch01` directory (Fig. 1.12).

(cont.)

Double click this filename to run the application

Figure 1.12 Contents of `C:\Examples\ch01` directory.

3. ***Running the* Advanced Painter *app.*** Now that you're in the proper directory, double click the filename `AdvancedPainter.exe` (Fig. 1.12) to run the app (Fig. 1.13).

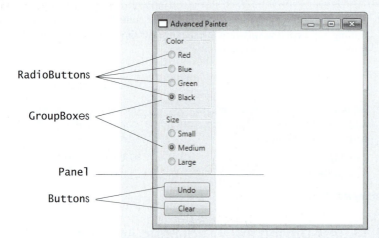

RadioButtons

GroupBoxes

Panel

Buttons

Figure 1.13 Visual Basic **Advanced Painter** app.

In Fig. 1.13, several graphical elements—called **controls**—are labeled. The controls include `GroupBoxes`, `RadioButtons`, a `Panel` and `Buttons` (these controls are discussed in depth later in the text). The app allows you to draw with a red, blue, green or black brush of small, medium or large size. You'll explore these options in this test-drive. You can also undo your previous operation (the last brush stroke) or clear the drawing to start from scratch.

By using existing controls—which are *objects*—you can create powerful apps in Visual Basic much faster than if you had to write all the code yourself. In this text, you'll learn how to use many preexisting controls, as well as how to write your own program code to customize your apps.

The brush's properties, selected in the `RadioButtons` labeled **Black** and **Medium**, are default settings—the initial settings you see when you first run the app. You include default settings to provide visual cues for users to choose their own settings. Now you'll choose your own settings.

4. ***Changing the brush color.*** Click the `RadioButton` labeled **Red** to change the color of the brush and **Small** to change the size of the brush. Position the mouse over the white `Panel`, then press and hold down the left mouse button to draw with the brush. Draw flower petals, as shown in Fig. 1.14. Then click the `RadioButton` labeled **Green** to change the color of the brush again.

(cont.)

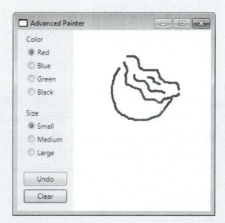

Figure 1.14   Drawing with a new brush color.

5. ***Changing the brush size.*** Click the RadioButton labeled **Large** to change the size of the brush. Draw grass and a flower stem, as shown in Fig. 1.15.

Figure 1.15   Drawing with a new brush size.

6. ***Finishing the drawing.*** Click the RadioButton labeled **Blue**. Then click the RadioButton labeled **Medium**. Draw raindrops, as shown in Fig. 1.16, to complete the drawing.

Close box

Figure 1.16   Finishing the drawing.

7. ***Closing the app.*** Close your running app by clicking its **close box**, (Fig. 1.16).

1.14 Web Resources

The Internet and the web are extraordinary resources. This section includes links to interesting and informative websites. Reference sections like this one are included throughout the book where appropriate.

msdn.microsoft.com/vbasic
This is Microsoft's Visual Basic website with links to code samples, starter kits, tutorials, blogs, webcasts and other valuable resources.

www.deitel.com/visualbasic2010/
Our Visual Basic Resource Center focuses on the enormous amount of Visual Basic content available online. Search for resources, downloads, tutorials, documentation, books, e-books, journals, articles, blogs, forums and more that will help you develop Visual Basic apps.

www.deitel.com
Visit this site for code downloads, updates, corrections and additional resources for Deitel & Associates publications, including *Simply Visual Basic 2010*, Frequently Asked Questions (FAQs), hot links, errata and code downloads.

www.pearsonhighered.com/deitel/
The Deitel & Associates page on the Pearson website contains information about all Deitel publications and code downloads for this book.

1.15 Wrap-Up

In this chapter, you learned how computers are organized. You studied the levels of programming languages and which kinds of languages, including Visual Basic, require translators. You became familiar with some of the most popular programming languages. You learned the importance of object-oriented programming. You were introduced to Microsoft's .NET initiative and learned some key aspects of .NET.

You took a working Visual Basic app out for a "test-drive." In the process of doing this, you learned that Visual Basic provides lots of prebuilt controls that perform useful functions, and that by familiarizing yourself with the capabilities of these controls, you can develop powerful apps much faster than if you tried to build them completely yourself. You were encouraged to explore several websites with additional information on this book, computers, the Internet, the web, .NET and Visual Basic.

In the next chapter, you'll learn about the Visual Basic 2010 Integrated Development Environment (IDE). This will help you prepare to create your own Visual Basic apps. You'll continue to learn with our app-driven approach, in which you'll see Visual Basic features in useful apps and will

1. study the user requirements for each app,
2. test-drive a working version of the app,
3. learn the technologies you'll need to build the app yourself, and
4. study the complete Visual Basic code for the working app.

As you work through the book, if you have any questions about Visual Basic 2010, just send an e-mail to deitel@deitel.com, and we'll respond promptly. We sincerely hope you enjoy learning the latest version of Microsoft's powerful Visual Basic language—one of the most widely used programming languages in the world—with *Simply Visual Basic 2010, Fourth Edition*. Good luck!

KEY TERMS **arithmetic and logic unit (ALU)**—The "manufacturing" section of the computer. The ALU performs calculations and makes decisions.

ASP.NET—.NET software that helps you create web apps.

attribute—Describe the properties of an object (e.g., name, color and size).

BASIC (Beginner's All-purpose Symbolic Instruction Code)—A programming language for writing simple programs. Developed in the mid-1960s at Dartmouth College, its primary purpose was to familiarize novices with programming techniques.

central processing unit (CPU)—The part of the computer's hardware that's responsible for supervising the operation of the other sections of the computer.

class—The type of a group of related objects. A class specifies the general format of its objects; the properties and actions available to an object depend on its class. An object is to its class much as a house is to the blueprint from which a house is constructed.

compiler—A translator program that converts high-level-language programs into machine language.

computer program—A set of instructions that guides a computer through an orderly series of actions.

computer programmer—A person who writes computer programs.

control—A reusable GUI component.

C#—A programming language that was designed specifically for the .NET platform. It has roots in C, C++ and Java, adapting the best features of each. Like Visual Basic, C# is object oriented and has access to .NET's powerful library of prebuilt components, enabling you to develop apps quickly.

Framework Class Library—.NET's collection of "prepackaged" classes and methods for performing mathematical calculations, string manipulations, character manipulations, input/output operations, error checking and many other useful operations.

graphical user interface (GUI)—The visual part of an app with which users interact.

hardware—The various devices that make up a computer, including the keyboard, screen, mouse, hard drive, memory, CD-ROM, DVD, printer and processing units.

high-level language—A type of programming language in which a single program statement accomplishes a substantial task. High-level languages use instructions that look almost like everyday English and contain common mathematical notations.

input device—Devices that are used to interact with a computer, such as keyboards, mice, microphones, scanners and digital cameras.

Integrated Development Environment (IDE)—A software tool that enables you to write, run, test and debug programs quickly and conveniently.

Internet—A worldwide computer network. Most people today access the Internet through the web.

Java—A popular programming language that's used to create web pages with dynamic content, to build large-scale enterprise applications, to enhance the functionality of web servers, to provide apps for consumer devices and for many other purposes.

memory—Stores data temporarily while an app is running.

method—Houses the program statements that actually perform tasks, hiding the statements from the user.

.NET Framework—Microsoft-provided software that executes apps, provides the Framework Class Library and supplies many other programming capabilities.

.NET Framework Class Library—.NET's collection of "prepackaged" classes and methods for performing mathematical calculations, string manipulations, character manipulations, input/output operations, error checking and many other useful operations.

.NET Initiative—Microsoft's vision for using the Internet and the web in the development, engineering, distribution and use of software.

.NET Platform—The set of software components that enables .NET programs to run—allows apps to be distributed to a variety of devices as well as to desktop computers. Offers a programming model that allows software components created in different programming languages (such as Visual Basic and C#) to communicate with one another.

object—Software component that models an item in the real world. There are date objects, time objects, paycheck objects, file objects and the like.

object-oriented programming (OOP)—Models real-world objects with software counterparts.

output device—A device to which information that's processed by the computer can be sent.

primary memory—Another name for the memory unit.

secondary storage unit—The long-term, high-capacity "warehouse" section of the computer.

software—The programs that run on a computer.

software reuse—The reuse of existing pieces of software, an approach that enables you to avoid "reinventing the wheel" and to develop apps faster.

Transmission Control Protocol/Internet Protocol (TCP/IP)—The combined set of communications protocols for the Internet.

Visual Basic—Programming language introduced by Microsoft in 1991 to make programming Windows apps easier. It has evolved into an object-oriented language.

visual programming with Visual Basic—You use Visual Studio's graphical user interface to conveniently drag and drop predefined controls into place on the screen, and label and resize them. Visual Studio writes much of the Visual Basic code, saving you considerable effort.

Visual Studio—Integrated development environment (IDE) for developing apps using Visual Basic (and other languages).

World Wide Web (WWW)—A communications system that allows computer users to locate and view multimedia documents (such as documents with text, graphics, animations, audios and videos) and allows programmers to build full web-based apps.

MULTIPLE-CHOICE QUESTIONS

1.1 The web was developed _____.

a) by ARPA   b) at CERN by Tim Berners-Lee

c) before the Internet   d) as a replacement for the Internet

1.2 Microsoft's _____ initiative integrates the Internet and the web into software development.

a) .NET   b) BASIC

c) Windows   d) W3C

1.3 `TextBoxes`, `Buttons` and `RadioButtons` are examples of _____.

a) platforms   b) high-level languages

c) IDEs   d) controls

1.4 _____ devices use a network of satellites to retrieve location-based information.

a) GPS   b) CRM

c) Cloud-computing   d) Internet TV

1.5 Visual Basic is an example of a(n) _____ language, in which single program statements accomplish substantial tasks.

a) machine   b) intermediate-level

c) high-level   d) assembly

1.6 The _____ that objects come from are essentially reusable software components.

a) attributes   b) classes

c) methods   d) instance variables

1.7 A major benefit of _____ programming is that the software it produces is more understandable and better organized than software produced with earlier techniques.

a) object-oriented   b) centralized

c) procedural   d) HTML

1.8 .NET's collection of prepackaged classes and methods is called the _____.

a) NCL   b) WCL

c) .NET Framework Class Library   d) PPCM

1.9 _____ is a design embraced by Web 2.0 that encourages user interaction and community contributions.

a) Cloud computing
b) Mashup
c) Architecture of participation
d) The semantic web

1.10 Which of these programming languages was specifically created for .NET?

a) C#
b) C++
c) BASIC
d) Visual Basic

EXERCISES

1.11 Fill in the blanks in each of the following:

a) The company that popularized personal computing was _____.

b) Computers process data under the control of sets of instructions called computer _____.

c) The three types of languages discussed in the chapter are _____, _____ and _____.

d) _____, or labeling content, is another key part of the collaborative theme of Web 2.0.

e) With _____ development, individuals and companies contribute their efforts in developing, maintaining and evolving software in exchange for the right to use that software for their own purposes, typically at no charge.

f) The _____ was the predecessor to the Internet.

1.12 Fill in the blanks in each of the following statements (based on Section 1.6):

a) Objects have the property of _____—although objects may know how to communicate with one another across well-defined interfaces, they normally are not allowed to know how other objects are implemented.

b) In object-oriented programming languages, we create _____ to house the set of methods that perform tasks.

c) With _____, new classes of objects are derived by absorbing characteristics of existing classes, then adding unique characteristics of their own.

d) The size, shape, color and weight of an object are considered _____ of the object's class.

1.13 Categorize each of the following items as either hardware or software:

a) CPU
b) Compiler
c) Input unit
d) A word-processor program
e) A Visual Basic program

1.14 Computers can be thought of as being divided into six units.

a) Which unit can be thought of as the "boss" of the other units?

b) Which unit is the high-capacity "warehouse" and retains information even when the computer is powered off?

c) Which unit might determine whether two items stored in memory are identical?

d) Which unit obtains information from devices like the keyboard and the mouse?

1.15 Expand each of the following acronyms:

a) W3C
b) TCP/IP
c) OOP
d) HTML

1.16 What are the advantages to using object-oriented programming techniques?

1.17 _(Cloud Computing)_ Describe three benefits of the cloud-computing model.

1.18 _(Web Services)_ In Fig. 1.10 we listed several web services that can be used to create your own web applications. Using two different web services—either from the table or that you find online—describe a type of mashup web application that you would like to create. How does it use the content provided by each of the web services?

1.19 (*Internet Negatives*) Besides their numerous benefits, the Internet and the web have several downsides, such as privacy issues, identity theft, SPAM and malware. Research some of the negative aspects of the Internet. List five problems and describe what could possibly be done to help solve each.

1.20 (*Web 2.0*) In this chapter, we discussed a few popular Web 2.0 businesses, including Facebook, Twitter, Groupon, Foursquare, Skype and YouTube. Identify three other Web 2.0 businesses and describe why they fit the Web 2.0 business model.

1.21 (*Watch as an Object*) You're probably wearing on your wrist one of the world's most common types of objects—a watch. Discuss how each of the following terms and concepts applies to the notion of a watch: object, attributes, behaviors, class, messages, encapsulation and information hiding.

Making a Difference

1.22 (*Privacy*) Some online e-mail services save all e-mail correspondence for some period of time. Suppose a disgruntled employee were to post all of the e-mail correspondences for millions of people, including yours, on the Internet. Discuss the issues.

1.23 (*Programmer Responsibility and Liability*) As a programmer in industry, you may develop software that could affect people's health or even their lives. Suppose a software bug in one of your programs caused a cancer patient to receive an excessive dose during radiation therapy and that the person was severely injured or died. Discuss the issues.

1.24 (*2010 "Flash Crash"*) An example of the consequences of our dependence on computers was the so-called "flash crash" that occurred on May 6, 2010, when the U.S. stock market fell precipitously in a matter of minutes, wiping out trillions of dollars of investments, and then recovered within minutes. Research online the causes of this crash and discuss the issues it raises.

1.25 (*Making a Difference Projects*) The following is a list of just a few worldwide organizations that are working to make a difference. Visit these sites and our Making a Difference Resource Center at www.deitel.com/makingadifference. Prepare a top-10 list of programming projects that you think could indeed "make a difference."

■ www.imaginecup.com/
The *Microsoft Imagine Cup* is a global competition in which students use technology to try to solve some of the world's most difficult problems, such as environmental sustainability, ending hunger, emergency response, literacy and combating HIV/AIDS. Visit www.imaginecup.com/about for more information about the competition and to learn about the projects developed by previous winners. You can also find several project ideas submitted by worldwide charitable organizations at www.imaginecup.com/students/imagine-cup-solve-this.

■ www.un.org/millenniumgoals
The United Nations Millennium Project seeks solutions to major worldwide issues such as environmental sustainability, gender equality, child and maternal health, universal education and more.

■ www.ibm.com/smarterplanet/
The IBM® Smarter Planet website discusses how IBM is using technology to solve issues related to business, cloud computing, education, sustainability and more.

■ www.gatesfoundation.org/Pages/home.aspx
The Bill and Melinda Gates Foundation provides grants to organizations that work to alleviate hunger, poverty and disease in developing countries. In the United States, the foundation focusses on improving public education, particularly for people with few resources.

■ www.nethope.org/
NetHope is a collaboration of humanitarian organizations worldwide working to solve technology problems such as connectivity, emergency response and more.

■ www.rainforestfoundation.org/home
The Rainforest Foundation works to preserve rainforests and to protect the rights of the

indigenous people who call the rainforests home. The site includes a list of things you can do to help.

■ www.undp.org/
The United Nations Development Programme (UNDP) seeks solutions to global challenges such as crisis prevention and recovery, energy and the environment and democratic governance.

■ www.unido.org
The United Nations Industrial Development Organization (UNIDO) seeks to reduce poverty, give developing countries the opportunity to participate in global trade, and promote energy efficiency and sustainability.

■ www.usaid.gov/
USAID promotes global democracy, health, economic growth, conflict prevention, humanitarian aid and more.

■ www.toyota.com/ideas-for-good/
Toyota's Ideas for Good website describes several Toyota technologies that are making a difference—including their Advanced Parking Guidance System, Hybrid Synergy Drive®, Solar Powered Ventilation System, T.H.U.M.S. (Total Human Model for Safety) and Touch Tracer Display. You can participate in the Ideas for Good challenge by submitting a short essay or video describing how these technologies can be used for other good purposes.

2

Welcome App

Introducing the Visual Basic 2010 Express IDE

Visual Studio 2010 is Microsoft's Integrated Development Environment (IDE) for creating, running and debugging **apps** written in various .NET programming languages. This chapter overviews the Visual Studio 2010 IDE and shows how to create a simple Visual Basic app by dragging and dropping predefined building blocks into place—a technique known as **visual app development**.

2.1 Test-Driving the **Welcome** App

In this section, you'll continue learning with our app-driven approach as you prepare to build an app that displays a welcome message and an image. This app must meet the following requirements:

> **App Requirements**
>
> *A software company (Deitel & Associates) has asked you to develop a Visual Basic app that displays the message "Welcome to Visual Basic 2010!" and a picture of the company's bug mascot.*

In this chapter, you'll familiarize yourself with the Visual Basic 2010 Express Edition IDE and begin to develop the **Welcome** app. Then, in Chapter 3, you'll "put it all together" and create the working **Welcome** app by following our step-by-step boxes. [*Note*: Our convention is to display app names in the **Helvetica** font.] You'll begin by test-driving the completed app. Then you'll learn the Visual Basic capabilities you'll need to create your own version of this app.

Test-Driving the
Welcome App

1. ***Checking your setup.*** Confirm that you've set up your computer properly by reading the Before You Begin section just after the Preface.

2. ***Locating the app directory.*** Open Windows Explorer and navigate to the C:\Examples\ch02 directory (Fig. 2.1).

Contents of
c:\Examples\ch02

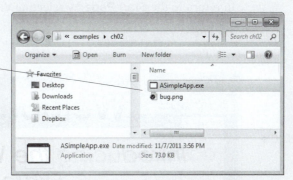

Figure 2.1   Contents of C:\Examples\ch02.

3. ***Running the app.*** Double click ASimpleApp.exe (Fig. 2.1) to run it (Fig. 2.2).

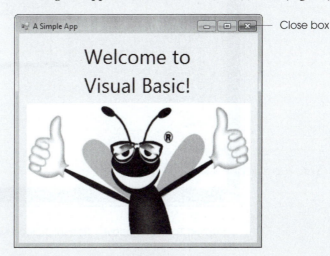

Close box

Figure 2.2   **Welcome** app executing.

4. ***Closing the app.*** Close your running app by clicking its close box, ▣.

2.2 Overview of the Visual Studio 2010 IDE

There are several versions of Visual Studio. This book's examples are based on **Microsoft Visual Basic 2010 Express**, which supports only the Visual Basic programming language. See the Before You Begin section that follows the Preface for information on installing the software. Microsoft also offers a full version of Visual Studio 2010, which includes support for Visual Basic and other languages, such as Visual C# and Visual C++. Our screen captures and discussions focus on Visual Basic 2010 Express. The examples will work on full versions of Visual Studio 2010 as well. We assume that you're familiar with Windows.

Introduction to Microsoft Visual Basic 2010 Express

We use the **>** character to indicate that you should select a menu item from a menu. For example, **File > Open File...** indicates that you should select the **Open File...** menu item from the **File** menu.

To start Microsoft Visual Basic 2010 Express Edition, select **Start > All Programs > Microsoft Visual Studio 2010 Express > Microsoft Visual Basic 2010**

Express. Once the Express Edition begins execution, the Start Page displays (Fig. 2.3). Depending on your version of Visual Studio, your **Start Page** may look different. The **Start Page** contains a list of links to Visual Studio 2010 IDE resources and web-based resources. From this point forward, we'll refer to the Visual Studio 2010 IDE simply as "Visual Studio" or "the IDE." At any time, you can return to the **Start Page** by selecting **View > Start Page**.

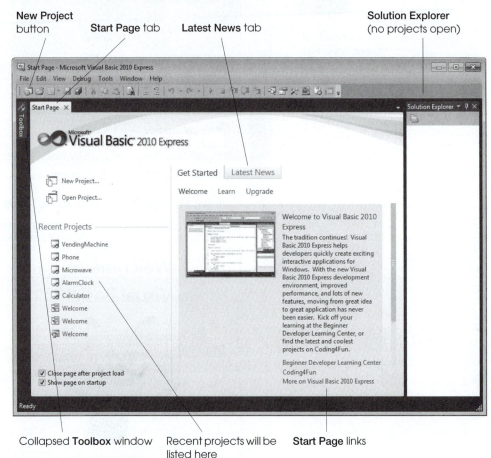

Figure 2.3   **Start Page** in Visual Basic 2010 Express Edition.

Links on the Start Page

The **Start Page** links are organized into sections—**Recent Projects**, **Get Started** and **Latest News**—that contain links to helpful app-development resources. Clicking any link on the **Start Page** displays relevant information associated with that link. [*Note:* An Internet connection is required for the IDE to access some of this information.] We refer to single clicking with the left mouse button as *selecting* or *clicking*. We refer to double clicking with the left mouse button simply as *double clicking*.

The **Recent Projects** section contains information on projects you've recently created or modified. You can also open existing projects or create new ones by clicking the links above this section. The **Get Started** section focuses on using the IDE for creating apps and learning Visual Basic.

The **Latest News** tab provides links to the latest Visual Basic developments (such as updates and bug fixes) and to information on advanced app-development topics. To access more extensive information on Visual Studio, you can browse the **MSDN (Microsoft Developer Network)** library at msdn.microsoft.com/en-us/ library/default.aspx. The MSDN site contains articles, downloads and chapters on technologies of interest to Visual Studio developers. You can also browse the web from the IDE by selecting **View > Other Windows > Web Browser** or by typing *<Ctrl> <Alt> R*. To request a web page, type its URL into the location bar (Fig. 2.4) and press the *Enter* key—your computer, of course, must be connected to the Internet. The web page that you wish to view appears in the web browser tab in the IDE (Fig. 2.4).

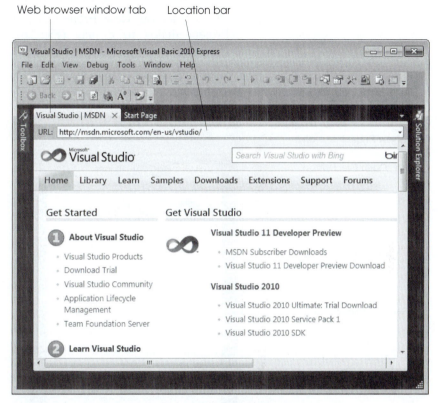

Figure 2.4   Displaying a web page in Visual Studio.

SELF-REVIEW

1. When you first open the Visual Basic 2010 Express Edition, the _____ displays.
   a) **What's New Page**   b) **Start Page**
   c) **Welcome Page**   d) None of the above.

2. The _____ section in the **Start Page** contains a listing of projects opened or created in Visual Basic.
   a) **MSDN**   b) **Getting Started**
   c) **Recent Projects**   d) **Visual Basic Express Headlines**

Answers: 1) b. 2) c.

2.3 Creating a Project for the Welcome App

In this section, you'll create a simple Visual Basic Windows Forms app. Visual Basic organizes apps into projects and solutions. A **project** is a group of related files, such as the Visual Basic code and any images that might make up an app. A **solution** may contain one or more projects. Multiple-project solutions are used to create large-scale apps. Each app we create in this book consists of a single project.

Creating a Project for the Welcome App

1. *Creating a new project.* If you've not already done so, start Visual Basic. There are several ways to create a new project or open an existing one, including:

(cont.)

- Select either **File > New Project...** to create a new project or **File > Open Project...** to open an existing project.
- From the **Start Page**, above the **Recent Projects** section, you can also click the links **New Project...** or **Open Project...**.
- Click either the **New Project** Button (Fig. 2.5), causing the **New Project** dialog to display (Fig. 2.6), or the **Open File** Button (Fig. 2.5), which displays the **Open File** dialog.

Dialogs are windows that facilitate user–computer communication. Like other windows, a dialog is identified by the text in its **title bar**.

Title bar ——
New Project button ——
Open File button ——
New Project link ——
Recent Projects listing ——

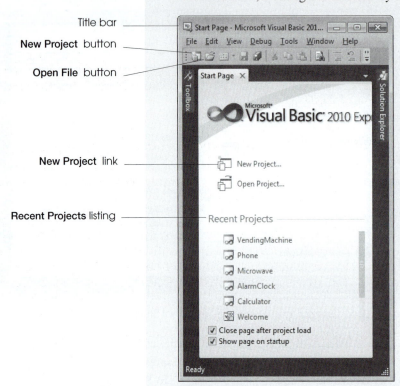

Figure 2.5   **New Project** button and **Recent Projects** listing.

2. ***Selecting the project type.*** Visual Basic provides several templates (Fig. 2.6). **Templates** are the project types you can create in Visual Basic—Windows Forms apps, console apps and others. In this chapter, we build a **Windows Forms Application**. You can also create your own custom app templates. [*Note*: Depending on your version of Visual Studio, the names and number of items shown in the list of templates could differ.]

3. ***Selecting the template.*** Select **Windows Forms Application** (Fig. 2.6). A **Windows Forms app** is an app that executes within a Windows operating system and typically has a **graphical user interface (GUI)**—the visual part of the app with which the user interacts. Windows apps include Microsoft software products such as Microsoft Word, Internet Explorer and Visual Studio; software products created by other vendors; and customized software that you and other programmers create. You'll create many Windows apps in this text.

(cont.)

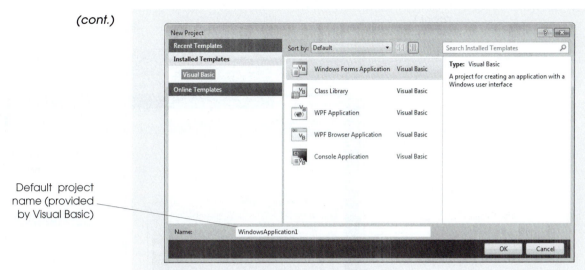

Figure 2.6   **New Project** dialog.

4. ***Changing the name of the project.*** By default, Visual Basic assigns the name **WindowsApplication1** to a new **Windows Forms Application** project and solution (Fig. 2.6). To rename the project, type ASimpleApp in the **Name:** TextBox. Then click **OK**. Changing the project's name to ASimple-App also changes its folder's name to ASimpleApp.

5. ***Changing the project's location.*** Save this project in your C:\SimplyVB2010 directory. Select **File > Save All**, which causes the **Save Project** dialog to appear (Fig. 2.7). In this dialog, click **Browse...** to locate your Simply-VB2010 directory, and click **Select Folder** (Fig. 2.8). Specify the project's name and location in the **Save Project** dialog, then click **Save**. This displays the IDE in **Design view** (Fig. 2.9), which enables you to design GUIs. The IDE's **Design** view is also known as the **Windows Forms Designer**.

Figure 2.7   **Save Project** dialog.

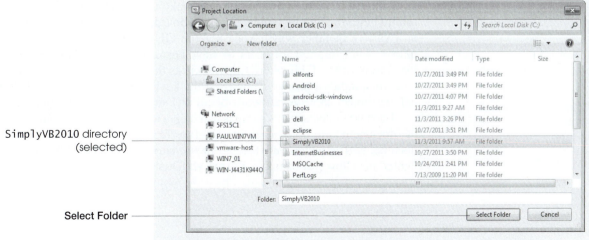

Figure 2.8   **Project Location** dialog.

(cont.)

Menu in the menu bar

Active tab

Form (Windows Forms app)

Properties window   Solution Explorer window

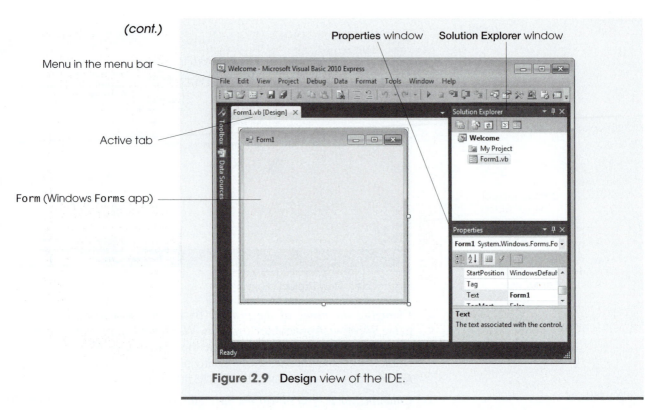

Figure 2.9 **Design** view of the IDE.

The rectangle in the **Design** area titled **Form1** (called a **Form**) represents the main window of the app you're creating. Visual Basic apps can have multiple Forms—however, most apps you'll create in this text will use only one. You'll learn how to customize the Form by adding GUI **controls**—in this example, you'll add a Label and a PictureBox (as you'll see in Chapter 3). A Label typically contains descriptive text (for example, "Welcome to Visual Basic!"), and a **PictureBox** displays an image, such as the Deitel bug mascot. Visual Basic Express has many *preexisting controls* and other components you can use to build and customize your apps. Many of these controls are discussed and used throughout the book. Other controls are available from third parties.

In this chapter, you'll work with preexisting controls from the .NET Framework Class Library. As you place controls on the Form, you'll be able to modify their properties (discussed in Section 2.5). For example, Fig. 2.10 shows where the Form's title can be modified and Fig. 2.11 shows a dialog in which a control's font properties can be modified.

Collectively, the Form and controls make up the app's GUI. Users enter data (**inputs**) into the app by typing at the keyboard, by clicking the mouse buttons and in a variety of other ways. Apps use the GUI to display instructions and other information (**outputs**) for users to view. For example, the **New Project** dialog in Fig. 2.6 presents a GUI where the user clicks the mouse button to select a template type, then inputs a project name from the keyboard (the figure is still showing the default project name **WindowsApplication1** supplied by Visual Studio).

Each open document's name is listed on a tab. To view a document when multiple documents are open, click its tab. Tabs facilitate easy access to multiple open documents. The **active tab** (the tab of the currently displayed document) is highlighted in yellow (for example, **Form1.vb [Design]** in Fig. 2.9).

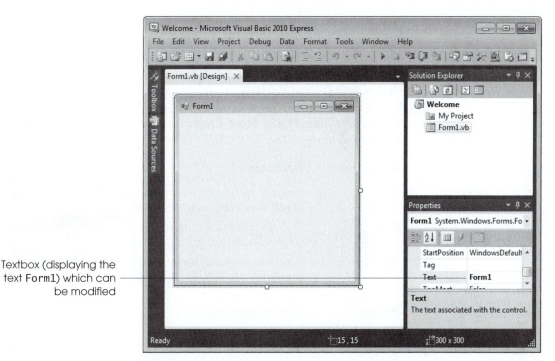

Figure 2.10   Textbox control for modifying a property in the Visual Studio IDE.

Textbox (displaying the text **Form1**) which can be modified

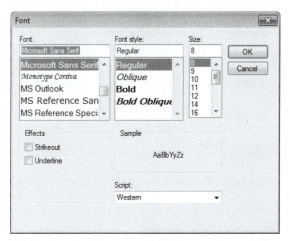

Figure 2.11   Dialog for modifying a control's font properties.

SELF-REVIEW   1. The visual part of the app with which users interact is the app's _____.

    a) graphical user interface   b) project

    c) solution   d) title bar

2. A _____ contains one or more projects that collectively form an app.

    a) dialog   b) Form

    c) solution   d) GUI

Answers: 1) a. 2) c.

2.4 Menu Bar and Toolbar

Commands for managing the IDE and for developing, maintaining and executing apps are contained in **menus**, which are located on the **menu bar** of the IDE (Fig. 2.12). The set of menus displayed depends on what you're currently doing in the IDE.

File   Edit   View   Project   Debug   Data   Format   Tools   Window   Help

Figure 2.12   Visual Studio menu bar.

Menus contain groups of related commands (also called **menu items**) that, when selected, cause the IDE to perform specific actions (for example, open a window, save a file, print a file and execute an app). For example, new projects are created by selecting **File > New Project...**. The menus depicted in Fig. 2.12 are summarized in Fig. 2.13.

Menu	Description
File	Contains commands for opening, closing, adding and saving projects, as well as printing project data and exiting Visual Studio.
Edit	Contains commands for editing programs, such as cut, copy, paste, undo, redo, delete, find and select.
View	Contains commands for displaying IDE windows (for example, **Solution Explorer**, **Toolbox**, **Properties** window) and for adding toolbars to the IDE.
Project	Contains commands for managing projects and their files.
Debug	Contains commands for compiling, debugging (that is, identifying and correcting problems in apps) and running apps.
Data	Contains commands for interacting with databases (that is, organized collections of data stored on computers), which we discuss in Chapter 27.
Format	Contains commands for arranging and modifying a Form's controls. The **Format** menu appears only when a GUI component is selected in **Design** view.
Tools	Contains commands for accessing additional IDE tools and options for customizing the IDE.
Window	Contains commands for hiding, opening, closing and displaying IDE windows.
Help	Contains commands for accessing the IDE's help features.

Figure 2.13   Summary of Visual Studio 2010 IDE menus.

You can access many of the more common menu commands from the **toolbar** (Fig. 2.14), which contains graphics, called **icons**, that graphically represent commands. By default, the standard toolbar is displayed when you run Visual Studio for the first time—it contains icons for the most commonly used commands, such as opening a file, adding an item to a project, saving files and running apps (Fig. 2.14). The icons that appear on the standard toolbar may vary, depending on the version of Visual Studio you're using. Some commands are initially disabled (grayed out or unavailable to use). These commands are enabled by Visual Studio only when they're necessary. For example, Visual Studio enables the command for saving a file once you begin editing a file.

You can customize the IDE's toolbars. Select **View > Toolbars** (Fig. 2.15). Each toolbar you select is displayed with the other toolbars at the top of the Visual Studio window. To execute a command via the toolbar, click its icon. Some icons contain a down arrow that you can click to display related commands, as shown in Fig. 2.16.

It can be difficult to remember what each toolbar icon represents. Hovering the mouse pointer over an icon highlights it and, after a brief pause, displays a description of the icon called a tool tip (Fig. 2.17). **Tool tips** help you become familiar with the IDE's features and serve as useful reminders for each toolbar icon's functionality.

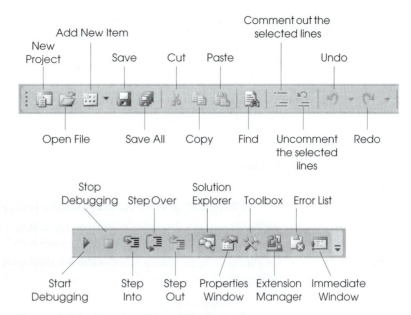

Figure 2.14   Standard Visual Studio toolbar.

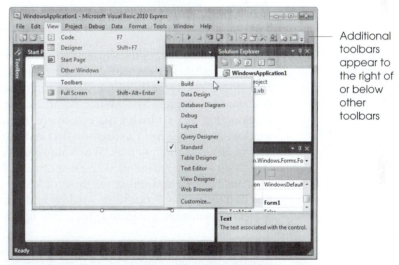

Figure 2.15   Adding the **Build** toolbar to the IDE.

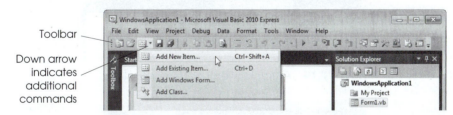

Figure 2.16   IDE toolbar icon showing additional commands.

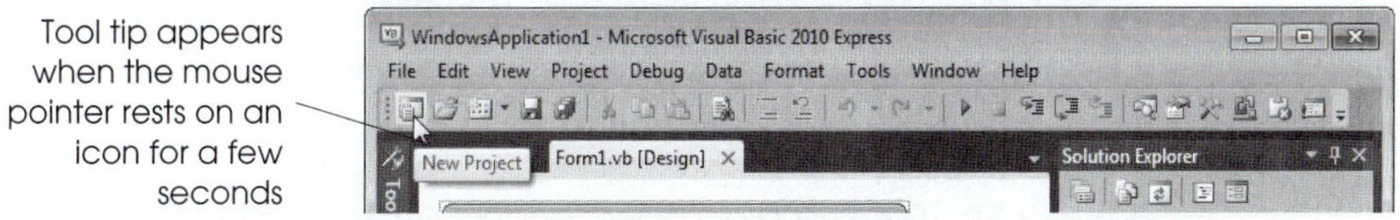

Tool tip appears when the mouse pointer rests on an icon for a few seconds

Figure 2.17   Tool tip demonstration.

SELF-REVIEW
1. _____ contain groups of related commands.

   a) Menu items   b) Menus
   c) Tool Tips   d) Icons

2. When the mouse pointer is positioned over an IDE toolbar icon for a few seconds, a _____ is displayed.

   a) toolbox   b) toolbar
   c) menu   d) tool tip

Answers: 1) b. 2) d.

2.5 Navigating the Visual Studio IDE; Auto-Hide

The IDE provides windows for accessing project files and customizing controls. This section introduces several windows that you'll use frequently when developing Visual Basic apps. These windows can be accessed via the toolbar icons (Fig. 2.18) or by selecting the desired window's name in the **View** menu.

Figure 2.18   Toolbar icons for three Visual Studio windows.

Visual Studio provides a space-saving feature called **auto-hide**. When auto-hide is enabled, a tab appears along either the left, right or bottom edge of the IDE window (Fig. 2.19). This tab contains one or more icons, each of which identifies a hidden window. Placing the mouse pointer over one of these icons displays that window (Fig. 2.20). Moving the mouse pointer outside the window's area hides the window. To "pin down" a window (that is, to disable auto-hide and keep the window open), click the pin icon. When auto-hide is enabled, the pin icon is horizontal (Fig. 2.20)—when a window is "pinned down," the pin icon is vertical (Fig. 2.21).

The next few sections cover three of Visual Studio's main windows—the **Solution Explorer**, the **Properties** window and the **Toolbox**. These windows display project information and include tools that help you build your apps.

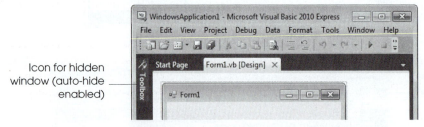

Figure 2.19   Auto-hide feature demonstration.

Figure 2.20   Displaying a hidden window when auto-hide is enabled.

Toolbox   Vertical orientation for pin icon
"pinned down"   when window is "pinned down"

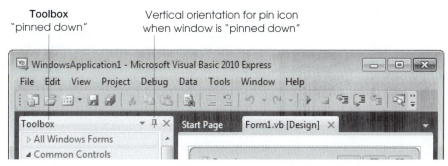

Figure 2.21   Disabling auto-hide ("pinning down" a window).

Solution Explorer

The **Solution Explorer** window (Fig. 2.22) provides access to all of a solution's files. If the window is not shown in the IDE, click the **Solution Explorer** icon in the IDE (Fig. 2.18), select **View > Other Windows > Solution Explorer** or type *<Ctrl> <Alt> L*. When you open a new or existing solution, the **Solution Explorer** displays the solution's contents.

Show All Files icon ————   ——— Toolbar
                                                            Startup project

Figure 2.22   Solution Explorer window with an open project.

The solution's **startup project** is the one that runs when you select **Debug > Start Debugging** (or press the *F5* key). For a single-project solution like the examples in this book, the startup project is the *only* project (in this case, **WindowsApplication1**) and the project name appears in bold text in the **Solution Explorer** window. When you create an app for the first time, the **Solution Explorer** window lists only the project's My Project and Form1.vb files (Fig. 2.22). The Visual Basic file that corresponds to the Form shown in Fig. 2.1 is named Form1.vb (selected in Fig. 2.22). Visual Basic files use the .vb filename extension, which is short for "Visual Basic." By default, the IDE displays *only* files that you may need to edit—other files that the IDE generates are hidden. The **Solution Explorer** window includes a toolbar that contains several icons.

Navigating a Project with the Solution Explorer

1. ***Expanding a node.*** After clicking the **Show All Files** icon (Fig. 2.22), click the arrow to the left of **References** to display items grouped under that heading. The **Solution Explorer** window should look like Fig. 2.23.

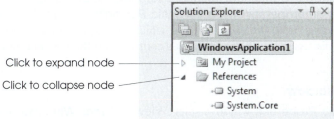

Click to expand node ————
Click to collapse node ————

Figure 2.23   Expanded node.

2. ***Collapsing a node.*** Click the arrow again to collapse the tree. Other Visual Studio windows also use this convention.

Toolbox

The **Toolbox** (**View > Other Windows > Toolbox**) contains icons representing controls used to customize Forms (Fig. 2.24). With visual app development, you can "drag and drop" controls onto the Form and the IDE will write the code that creates the controls for you. This is faster and simpler than writing this code yourself. Just as you do not need to know how to build an engine to drive a car, you do not need to know how to build controls to use them. Reusing preexisting controls saves time and money when you develop apps. You'll use the **Toolbox** when you create your first app in the next chapter.

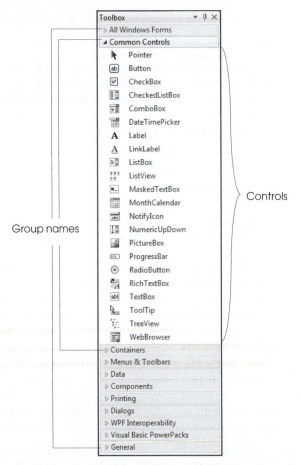

Figure 2.24   **Toolbox** window displaying controls for the **Common Controls** group.

The **Toolbox** groups the prebuilt controls into categories—**All Windows Forms, Common Controls, Containers, Menus & Toolbars, Data, Components, Printing, Dialogs, WPF Interoperability, Visual Basic PowerPacks** and **General** are listed in Fig. 2.24. Again, note the use of arrows, which can expand or collapse a group of controls. We discuss many of the **Toolbox**'s controls and their functionality throughout the book.

Properties Window

To display the **Properties** window, select **View > Other Windows > Properties Window**, click the **Properties** window toolbar icon shown in Fig. 2.18, or press the *F4* key. The **Properties window** displays the properties for the currently selected Form (Fig. 2.25), control or file in **Design** view. **Properties** specify information about the Form or control, such as its size, color and position. Each Form or control has its own set of properties—a property's description is displayed at the bottom of the **Properties** window whenever that property is selected.

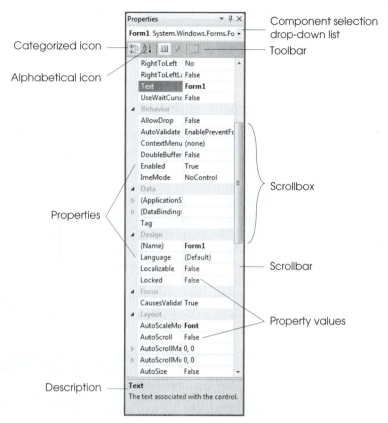

Figure 2.25   Properties window.

Figure 2.25 shows `Form1`'s **Properties** window. The left column lists the `Form`'s properties—the right column displays the current value of each property. You can sort the properties either alphabetically (by clicking the **Alphabetical icon**) or categorically (by clicking the **Categorized icon**) according to their use (that is, **Appearance**, **Behavior**, **Design**, etc.). Depending on the size of the **Properties** window, some of the properties may be hidden from view on the screen. Users can scroll through the list of properties by **dragging** the **scrollbox** up or down inside the **scrollbar**, or by clicking the arrows at the top and bottom of the scrollbar. We'll soon show how to set individual properties.

The **Properties** window is crucial to visual app development—it allows you to modify a control's properties visually, *without writing code.* You can see which properties are available for modification and, in many cases, can learn the range of acceptable values for a given property. The **Properties** window displays a brief description of the selected property, helping you understand its purpose. A property can be set quickly using this window, and no code needs to be written.

At the top of the **Properties** window is the **component selection drop-down list**, which allows you to select the `Form` or control to display its properties in the **Properties** window (Fig. 2.25). Using the component selection drop-down list is an alternative way to display a `Form`'s or control's properties without clicking the actual `Form` or control in the GUI.

SELF-REVIEW   1. The _____ allows you to add controls to the `Form` in a visual manner.

   a) **Solution Explorer**   b) **Properties** window

   c) **Toolbox**   d) **Dynamic Help** window

2. The _____ window allows you to view a solution's files.
   a) **Properties**
   b) **Solution Explorer**
   c) **Toolbox**
   d) None of the above

Answers: 1) c. 2) b.

2.6 Using Help

Microsoft provides extensive help documentation via the **Help menu**. Using **Help** is an excellent way to get information quickly about Visual Studio, Visual Basic and more.

Context-Sensitive Help

Visual Studio provides **context-sensitive help** pertaining to the "current content" (that is, the items around the location of the mouse cursor). To use context-sensitive help, click an item, such as the Form, then press the *F1* key. The help documentation is displayed in a web browser window. To return to the IDE, either close the browser window or select the icon for the IDE in your Windows task bar. Figure 2.26 shows the help page for a Form's Text property. You can view this help by selecting the Form, clicking its Text property in the **Properties** window and pressing the *F1* key.

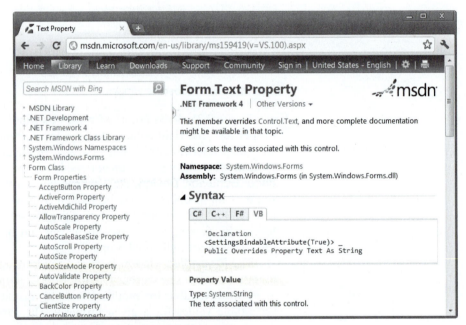

Figure 2.26 Using context-sensitive help.

1. _____ displays relevant help articles, based on the selected object.
   a) Internal help
   b) Context-sensitive help
   c) External help
   d) Context-driven help

2. The _____ gives you access to the most up-to-date documentation, as well as tutorials, downloads, support, forums and more.
   a) **Recent Projects**
   b) Windows Forms Designer
   c) **Tools** menu
   d) online help

Answers: 1) b. 2) d.

2.7 Saving and Closing Projects in Visual Basic

Once you're finished with a project, you should save the project's files and close the project.

Closing the Project for the Welcome App

1. ***Saving the project's files.*** Before closing the project for the **Welcome** app, you should save its files, ensuring that any changes made to the project are not lost. Although you did not make any changes to the project's files for this particular chapter, you'll be making such changes in most of the others, so for practice, save your project files by selecting **File > Save All**.

2. ***Closing the project.*** Select **File > Close Project**.

2.8 Web Resources

The Internet and the web are extraordinary resources. This section includes links to interesting and informative websites.

`msdn.microsoft.com/vstudio`
This site is the home page for Microsoft Visual Studio. It includes news, documentation, downloads and other resources.

`msdn.microsoft.com/en-us/vbasic/default.aspx`
This site provides information on the newest release of Visual Basic, including downloads, community information and resources.

`social.msdn.microsoft.com/forums/en-US/category/visualbasic/`
This site provides access to the Microsoft Visual Basic forums, which you can use to get your Visual Basic language and IDE questions answered.

`msdn.microsoft.com/en-us/magazine/default.aspx`
This is the Microsoft Developer Network Magazine site. It provides articles and code on many Visual Basic and .NET programming topics. There's also an archive of past issues.

`www.deitel.com/VisualBasic2010/`
This site lists many of the key web resources we used as we were preparing to write this book. There's lots of great stuff here to help you become familiar with the world of Visual Basic 2010.

2.9 Wrap-Up

In this chapter, we introduced key features of the Visual Studio Integrated Development Environment (IDE). You used the technique of visual app development to create a working Visual Basic app without writing any code. Visual Basic app development is a mixture of the two styles: Visual app development allows you to develop GUIs easily. Conventional app development (which we introduce in Chapter 3) allows you to specify the behavior of your apps.

You created a Visual Basic Windows Forms app with one Form. You worked with the **Solution Explorer**, **Toolbox** and **Properties** windows, which are essential to developing Visual Basic apps. The **Solution Explorer** window allows you to manage your solution's files visually.

You explored Visual Studio's help features. We demonstrated context-sensitive help, which displays help topics related to selected controls or text.

In the next chapter, you begin creating Visual Basic apps. You follow step-by-step instructions for completing the **Welcome** app by using visual app development and the IDE features you learned in this chapter.

SKILLS SUMMARY

Creating a New Project
- Select **File > New Project....**
- Click the link **New Project...** on the **Start Page**.
- Select **Windows Forms App** in from the list of templates.
- Provide the project's name in the **Name:** TextBox.
- Click the **OK** Button.

Saving a Project
- Select **File > Save All**.
- Provide the project's name in the **Name:** TextBox.
- Provide the project's directory information in the **Location:** TextBox.

Viewing a Tool Tip for a Visual Basic Icon
- Place the mouse pointer on the icon, and keep it there until the tool tip appears.

Collapsing a Node in the Solution Explorer
- Click the arrow to the left of the node.

Expanding a Node in the Solution Explorer
- Click the arrow to the left of the node.

Scrolling Through the List of Controls in the Toolbox
- Click the scroll arrows.

Viewing the Properties Window
- Select **View > Other Windows > Properties Window** or press *F4*.

Viewing the Solution Explorer
- Select **View > Other Windows > Solution Explorer**.

Viewing the Toolbox
- Select **View > Other Windows > Toolbox**.

Displaying a Hidden Window
- Place the mouse pointer over the hidden window's tab.

Disabling Auto-Hide and "Pinning Down" a Window
- Click the window's horizontal pin icon to change it to a vertical pin icon.

Enabling Auto-Hide
- Click the window's vertical pin icon to change it to a horizontal pin icon.

Opening the Help Window
- Select an item on which you want help and press the *F1* key.

KEY TERMS

active tab—The tab of the document displayed in the IDE.

Alphabetical icon—The icon in the **Properties** window that, when clicked, sorts properties alphabetically.

auto-hide—A space-saving IDE feature used for windows such as **Toolbox**, **Properties** and **Solution Explorer** that hides a window until the mouse pointer is placed on the hidden window's tab.

Categorized icon—The icon in the **Properties** window that, when clicked, sorts properties categorically.

component selection drop-down list—The drop-down list at the top of the **Properties** window that allows you to select the Form or control object whose properties you want set.

context-sensitive help—A help option (launched by pressing *F1*) that provides links to articles that apply to the current content (that is, the item selected with the mouse pointer).

database—Stores information for access by apps.

Data menu—The menu of the IDE that contains commands for interacting with databases.

Debug menu—The menu of the IDE that contains commands for debugging and running an app.

Design view—The IDE view that contains the Windows Forms designer to allow you to lay out controls in a Windows Forms app.

dialog—A window that can display and gather information.

Form—The object that represents the Windows app's graphical user interface (GUI).

graphical user interface (GUI)—The visual part of the app with which the user interacts.

icon—The graphical representation of commands in the Visual Studio 2010 IDE.

Integrated Development Environment (IDE)—The software used to create, document, run and debug apps.

input—Data that the user enters into an app.

internal web browser—The web browser included in Visual Basic 2010 Express, with which you can browse the web.

location bar—The drop-down list in Visual Basic's internal web browser where you can enter the name of a website to visit.

menu—A group of related commands that, when selected, cause the IDE to perform specific actions, such as opening windows, saving files, printing files and executing apps.

menu bar—Contains the menus for a window.

menu item (or command)—A command located in a menu that, when selected, causes an app to perform a specific action.

Microsoft Developer Network (MSDN)—An online library that contains articles, downloads and chapters on technologies of interest to Visual Basic developers.

New Project dialog—A dialog that allows you to choose what type of app you wish to create.

output—The results of an app.

pin icon—An icon that enables or disables the auto-hide feature.

project—A group of related files that compose an app.

Properties window—The window that displays the properties for a Form, control object or file.

property—Specifies a control or Form object's attributes, such as size, color and position.

scroll arrows—Arrows at the ends of a scrollbar that enable you to scroll through items.

solution—Contains one or more projects.

Solution Explorer—A window that provides access to all the projects and their files in a solution.

Start Page—The initial page displayed when Visual Studio 2010 is opened.

templates—Starting points for the projects you create in Visual Basic.

title bar—The top of a window in which the title of the window is displayed.

toolbar—A bar containing buttons that, when clicked, execute commands.

toolbar icon—A picture on a toolbar button.

Toolbox—A window that contains controls used to build and customize Forms.

Tools menu—A menu of the IDE that contains commands for accessing additional IDE tools and options that enable customization of the IDE.

tool tip—The description of an icon that appears when the mouse pointer is held over that icon for a few seconds.

Visual Studio—Microsoft's integrated development environment (IDE), which allows developers to create apps in a variety of .NET programming languages.

Windows Forms app—An app that executes on a Windows operating system and has a graphical user interface (GUI)—the visual part of the app with which the user interacts.

Windows Form Designer—Used to design the GUI of a Windows Forms app.

MULTIPLE-CHOICE QUESTIONS

2.1 The _____ integrated development environment is used for creating apps written in programming languages such as Visual Basic.
a) **Solution Explorer**   b) Gates
c) Visual Studio   d) Microsoft

2.2 The .vb filename extension indicates a _____.
a) Visual Basic file   b) dynamic help file
c) help file   d) very big file

2.3 The pictures on toolbar buttons are called _____.
a) prototypes   b) icons
c) tool tips   d) tabs

2.4 The _____ allows you to configure controls visually, without writing code.
a) **Properties** window   b) **Solution Explorer**
c) menu bar   d) **Toolbox**

2.5 The _____ hides the **Toolbox** when the mouse pointer is moved outside the **Toolbox**'s area.
a) component-selection feature   b) auto-hide feature
c) pinned command   d) minimize command

2.6 A _____ appears when the mouse pointer is positioned over an IDE toolbar icon for a few seconds.
a) drop-down list   b) menu
c) tool tip   d) down arrow

2.7 The Visual Basic IDE provides _____.
a) help documentation   b) toolbars
c) windows for accessing project files   d) All of the above

2.8 The _____ contains a list of helpful links, such as **Get Started** and **Latest News**.
a) **Solution Explorer** window   b) **Properties** window
c) **Start Page**   d) **Toolbox** link

2.9 The **Properties** window contains _____.
a) the component selection drop-down list   b) a **Solution Explorer**
c) menus   d) a menu bar

2.10 A _____ can be enhanced by adding reusable components such as Buttons.
a) control   b) Form
c) tab   d) property

2.11 An app's GUI can include _____.
a) toolbars   b) icons
c) menus   d) All of the above

2.12 The _____ does not contain a pin icon.
a) **Properties** window   b) **Solution Explorer** window
c) **Toolbox** window   d) active tab

2.13 Form _____ specify attributes such as size and position.
a) nodes   b) inputs
c) properties   d) title bars

EXERCISES

2.14 *(Closing and Opening the Start Page)* In this exercise, you learn how to close and reopen the **Start Page**. To accomplish this task, perform the following steps:

a) Close Visual Basic if it's open by selecting **File > Exit** or by clicking its close box.

b) Start Visual Basic 2010 Express Edition.

c) Close the **Start Page** by clicking its close box (Fig. 2.27).

d) Select **View > Start Page** to display the **Start Page**.

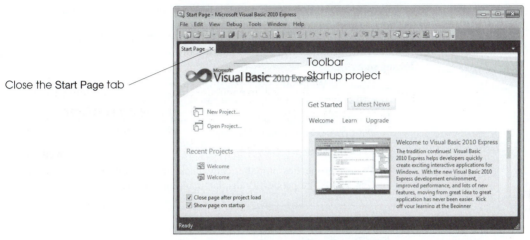

Close the Start Page tab

Figure 2.27   Closing the **Start Page**.

2.15 *(Enabling Auto-Hide for the Solution Explorer Window)* In this exercise, you learn how to use the **Solution Explorer** window's auto-hide feature by performing the following steps:

a) Open the **Start Page**.

b) In the **Start Page**, click the **Open Project** Button to display the **Open Project** dialog. You can skip to *Step e* if the **Welcome** app is already open.

c) In the **Open Project** dialog, navigate to C:\SimplyVB2010\ASimpleApp, and click **Open**.

d) In the **Open Project** dialog, select ASimpleApp (this might display as ASimple-App.sln), and click **Open**.

e) Position the mouse pointer on the vertical pin icon in the **Solution Explorer** window's title bar (Fig. 2.28).

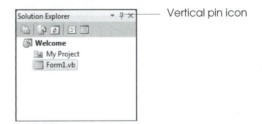

Vertical pin icon

Figure 2.28   Enabling auto-hide.

f) Click the vertical pin icon. This action causes a **Solution Explorer** tab to appear on the right side of the IDE and changes the vertical pin icon to a horizontal pin icon (Fig. 2.29). Auto-hide has now been enabled for the **Solution Explorer** window.

g) Position the mouse pointer on the **Solution Explorer** tab to view the **Solution Explorer** window.

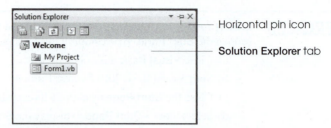

Horizontal pin icon

Solution Explorer tab

Figure 2.29 Solution Explorer window with auto-hide enabled.

2.16 *(Sorting Properties Alphabetically in the Properties Window)* In this exercise, you learn how to sort the **Properties** window's properties alphabetically by performing the following steps:

a) Open the **Welcome** app by performing steps *a* through *d* of Exercise 2.15. If the **Welcome** app is already open, you can skip this step.

b) Locate the **Properties** window. If it's not visible, display it by selecting **View > Other Windows > Properties Window**.

c) Click the Form.

d) To sort properties alphabetically, click the **Properties** window's **Alphabetical** icon (Fig. 2.30). The properties display in alphabetic order.

Alphabetical icon

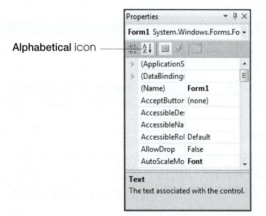

Figure 2.30 Sorting properties alphabetically.

Objectives

In this chapter, you'll learn to:
- Set the text in the Form's title bar.
- Change the Form's background color.
- Place a Label control on the Form.
- Display text in a Label control.
- Place a PictureBox control on the Form.
- Display an image in a PictureBox control.
- Execute an app.

Outline

Welcome App

Introduction to Visual App Development

Today, users prefer software with interactive graphical user interfaces (GUIs) that respond to actions such as Button clicks, data input and much more. As a result, most Windows apps, such as Microsoft Word and Internet Explorer, are GUI based. With Visual Basic, you can create Windows apps that input and output information in a variety of ways, which you learn throughout the book.

In this chapter, you'll use visual app development to complete the **Welcome** app you began creating in Chapter 2. You'll build the app's GUI by placing two controls—a Label and a PictureBox—on the Form. You'll use the Label control to display text and the PictureBox control to display an image. You'll customize the appearance of the Form, Label and PictureBox objects by setting values in the **Properties** window. You'll set many property values, including the Form's background color, the PictureBox's image and the Label's text. You'll also learn how to execute your app in the Visual Basic 2010 IDE.

3.1 Test-Driving the Welcome App

The last chapter introduced you to the Visual Basic 2010 IDE. In this chapter, you'll use the IDE to build the **Welcome** app you started in Chapter 2. This app must meet the following requirements:

> **App Requirements**
>
> *Recall that a software company (Deitel & Associates) has asked you to develop a simple **Welcome** app that includes the greeting "Welcome to Visual Basic 2010!" and a picture of the company's bug mascot. Now that you're familiar with the Visual Basic IDE, your task is to develop this app to satisfy the company's request.*

You'll begin by test-driving the completed app. Then you'll learn the additional Visual Basic capabilities that you'll need to create your own version of this app.

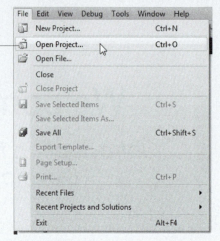

Test-Driving the Welcome App

Open Project... command (selected) opens an existing project

1. ***Opening the completed app.*** Start Visual Basic and select **File > Open Project...** (Fig. 3.1) to display the **Open Project** dialog (Fig. 3.2). Select the C:\Examples\ch03\CompletedApp\ASimpleApp directory. Select the solution file (ASimpleApp.sln) and click the **Open** Button.

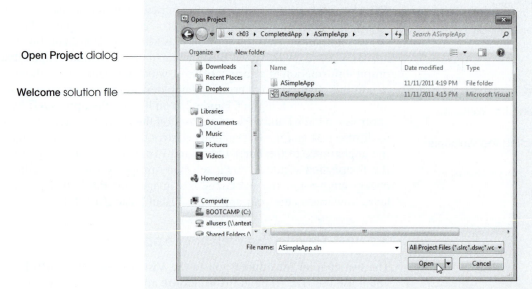

Figure 3.1 Opening an existing project with the **File** menu's **Open Project...** command.

Open Project dialog

Welcome solution file

Figure 3.2 **Open Project** dialog displaying the contents of the **ASimpleApp** solution.

2. ***Opening the Form in Design view.*** Double click ASimpleApp.vb in the **Solution Explorer** to open the app's Form in **Design** view (Fig. 3.3).

3. ***Running the app.*** Select **Debug > Start Debugging** (Fig. 3.4). The **Start Debugging** command runs the app. The Form shown in Fig. 3.5 appears.

4. ***Closing the app.*** Close the running app by clicking its close box (⬛).

5. ***Closing the project.*** Close the project by selecting **File > Close Project**.

(cont.)

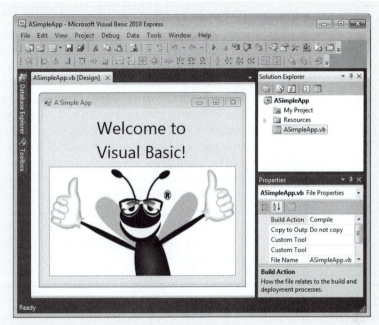

Figure 3.3   The app's Form in **Design** view.

Start Debugging command
(selected) runs the app ——————

Figure 3.4   Running the app using the **Debug** menu's **Start Debugging** command.

Close box

Figure 3.5   The running app.

3.2 Constructing the Welcome App

In this section, you'll perform the steps necessary to develop the app, which consists of a single `Form` that uses a `Label` and a `PictureBox`. The app and the bug image are available with this chapter's examples. You can download the examples from `www.deitel.com/books/simplyvb2010/`. We assume that you've installed the examples at `C:\Examples` on your computer.

You won't write any code. Instead, you'll use visual app-development techniques. Visual Studio processes your actions (such as *mouse clicking*, *dragging* and *dropping*) to generate app code. Chapter 5 begins our discussion of writing app code. Throughout the book, you'll produce increasingly substantial and powerful apps that usually include a combination of code written by you and code generated by Visual Studio. The generated code can be difficult for novices to understand— but you'll rarely need to look at it.

Visual app development is useful for building GUI-intensive apps that require a significant amount of user interaction. The following box shows you how to begin constructing the app.

Changing the Form's Filename and Title Bar Text	1. **Closing the open project.** If a project is already open, close it by selecting **File > Close Project**. A dialog asking whether to save the current project might appear. If you have not saved the project previously, click **Save** to save your changes or **Discard** to ignore them. If you have saved it previously, click **Yes** to save your changes or **No** to ignore them

2. **Creating the new project.** To create a new Windows Forms application, select **File > New Project...** to display the **New Project** dialog (Fig. 3.6). Select **Windows Forms Application**. Name the project **ASimpleApp** and click **OK**.

Select the **Windows Forms Application** template

Type the project name here

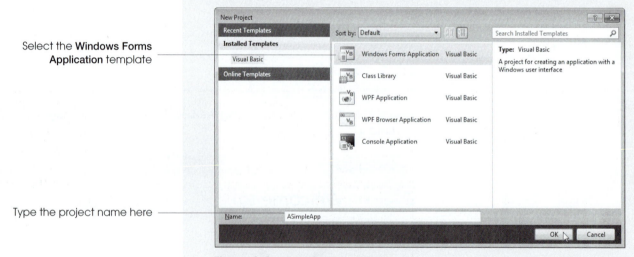

Figure 3.6 **New Project** dialog.

3. **Saving the project.** We mentioned in the last chapter that you must set the directory in which the project is saved. To specify the directory in Visual Basic 2010 Express, select **File > Save All** to display the Save Project **dialog** (Fig. 3.7). By default, projects are saved to your user directory in the folder `Documents\Visual Studio 2010\Projects`. To change the project location, click the **Browse...** button, which opens the Project Location **dialog** (Fig. 3.8). Navigate through the directories, select one in which to place the project (in our example, we use the directory **C:\SimplyVB2010**) and click **Select Folder** to close the dialog. Click **Save** in the **Save Project** dialog (Fig. 3.7) to save the project and close the dialog.

(cont.)

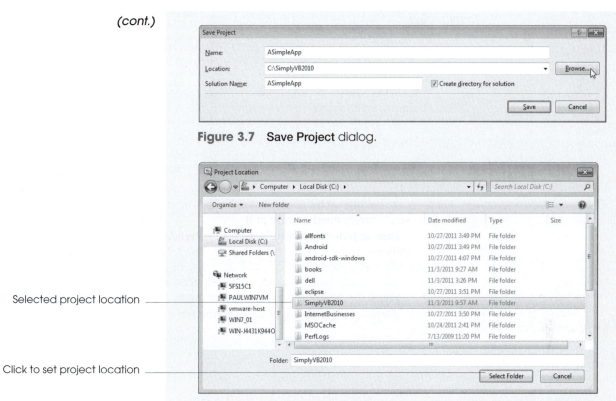

Figure 3.7   **Save Project** dialog.

Selected project location ——————

Click to set project location ——————

Figure 3.8   Setting the project location in the **Project Location** dialog.

When you first begin working in the IDE, it's in **design mode** (that is, the app is being *designed* and is *not executing*). This provides access to all the environment windows (for example, **Toolbox**, **Properties**), menus and toolbars, as you'll see shortly.

Setting the Form's Text Property and Resizing the Form

1. ***Setting the text in the Form's title bar.*** The text in the Form's title bar is determined by the Form's **Text property** (Fig. 3.9). If the **Properties** window isn't open, click the properties icon in the toolbar or select **View > Other Windows > Properties Window**. Click anywhere in the Form to display the Form's properties in the Properties window. In the textbox to the right of the Text property, type "A Simple App", as in Fig. 3.9. Press the *Enter* key—the Form's title bar is updated immediately (Fig. 3.10).

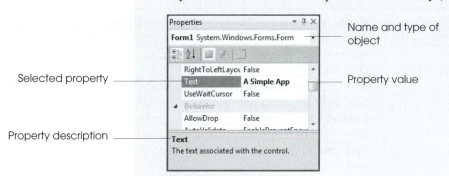

Selected property ——————

Property description ——————

Name and type of object

Property value

Figure 3.9   Setting the Form's Text property in the **Properties** window.

(cont.)

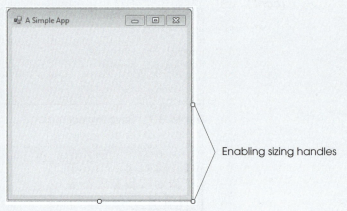

Enabling sizing handles

Figure 3.10 Form with enabled sizing handles.

2. *Resizing the Form.* Click and drag one of the Form's enabled **sizing handles** (the small white squares that appear around the Form, as shown in Fig. 3.10). Using the mouse, select the bottom-right sizing handle and drag it down and to the right to make the Form larger (Fig. 3.11).

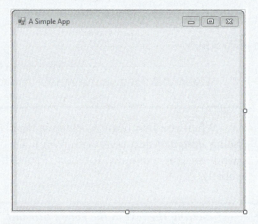

Figure 3.11 Resized Form.

Now that you've resized the Form, you'll customize it further by changing its background color from gray to light blue.

Setting the Form's Background Color

1. *Changing the Form's background color.* The **BackColor property** specifies a Form's or control's background color. Clicking BackColor in the **Properties** window causes a down-arrow button to appear next to the property value (Fig. 3.12). When clicked, the down-arrow button displays other options, which vary depending on the property. In this case, the arrow displays the tabs **Custom**, **Web** and **System** (the default) for selecting colors. Click the **Custom tab** to display the **palette** (a grid of colors). Select the box that represents light blue. Once you select the color, the palette closes and the Form's background color changes to light blue (Fig. 3.13).

(cont.)

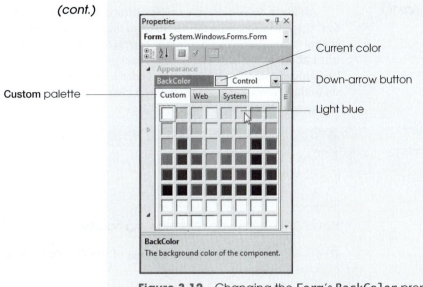

Figure 3.12   Changing the Form's BackColor property.

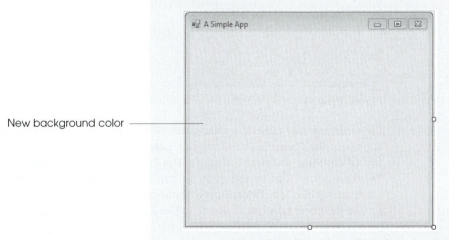

Figure 3.13   Form with new BackColor property applied.

Now that you've finished customizing the Form, you can add a control to the Form—a customized Label that displays a greeting.

Adding a Label to the Form	1. ***Adding a Label control to the Form.*** If the **Toolbox** isn't already open, select **View > Other Windows > Toolbox** to display the set of controls you'll use for creating your apps. For the type of app we're creating in this chapter, the typical controls we use are located in either the **All Windows Forms** group of the **Toolbox** or the **Common Controls** group. If either group name is collapsed, expand it by clicking the arrow to the left of the group name (the **All Windows Forms** and **Common Controls** groups are shown in Fig. 2.24). Next, double click the Label control in the **Toolbox**. This action causes a Label to appear in the upper-left corner of the Form (Fig. 3.14). If the Form is behind the **Toolbox**, you may need to hide the **Toolbox** to see the Label.

(cont.)
Although double clicking any **Toolbox** control places it on the `Form`, you also can "drag" controls from the **Toolbox** to the `Form`—you may prefer dragging the control because you can position it wherever you want. The `Label` displays the text **Label1** by default. The `Label`'s background color is the same as the `Form`'s background color. When a control is added to the `Form`, its `BackColor` property is set to the `Form`'s `BackColor`. You can change the `Label`'s background color by changing its `BackColor` property.

Label control

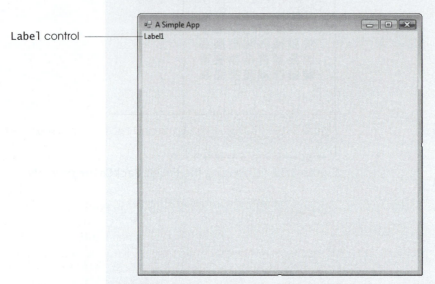

Figure 3.14 Adding a `Label` to the `Form`.

2. ***Customizing the Label's appearance.*** Select the `Label`. Its properties now appear in the **Properties** window. The `Label`'s `Text` property determines the text (if any) that the `Label` displays. The `Form` and `Label` each have their own `Text` property—`Form`s and controls can have the same types of properties (such as `BackColor`, `Text`, etc.) without conflict. Set the `Label`'s `Text` property to `Welcome to Visual Basic!`. The `Label` resizes to fit all the typed text on one line.

By default, the **AutoSize property** of the `Label` is set to `True`, which allows the `Label` to update its size to fit all of the text if necessary. Set the `AutoSize` property to `False` (Fig. 3.15) so that you can resize the `Label` on your own. Resize the `Label` (using the sizing handles) so that the text fits. Move the `Label` to the top center of the `Form` by dragging it or by using the keyboard's left and right arrow keys to adjust its position (Fig. 3.16). Alternatively, when the `Label` is selected, you can center the `Label` control horizontally by selecting **Format > Center In Form > Horizontally**.

AutoSize property

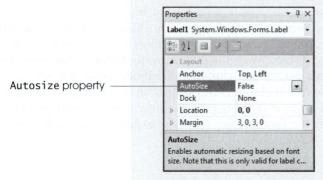

Figure 3.15 Changing the `Label`'s `AutoSize` property to `False`.

(cont.)

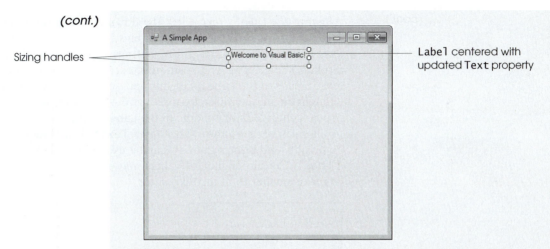

Sizing handles

Label centered with updated **Text** property

Figure 3.16　GUI after the **Form** and **Label** have been customized.

3. ***Setting the Label's font size.*** To change the font and appearance of the **Label**'s text, select the value of the **Font property**, then click the **ellipsis button** that appears next to the value (Fig. 3.17). The IDE displays a dialog containing additional values—in this case, the **Font dialog** (Fig. 3.18). You can select the font name (the font options may be different, depending on your system), font style (**Regular**, *Italic*, **Bold**, etc.) and font size (**16**, **18**, **20**, etc.). The **Sample** text (Fig. 3.18) shows the selected font settings. Under **Font**, select **Segoe UI**, Microsoft's recommended font for user interfaces. Under **Size**, select **24** points, then click **OK**. If the **Label**'s text does not fit on a single line, it wraps to the next line. Resize the **Label** vertically if it's not large enough to hold the text. You may need to center the **Label** horizontally again after resizing.

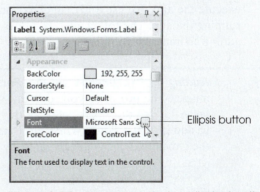

Ellipsis button

Figure 3.17　**Properties** window displaying the **Label**'s **Font** property.

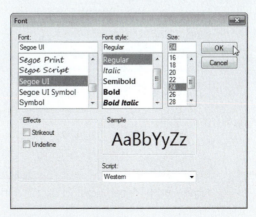

Figure 3.18　**Font** dialog for selecting fonts, styles and sizes.

(cont.) 4. *Aligning the Label's text.* Click the down arrow to the right of the Label's TextAlign property, which determines how the text is aligned within the Label. A three-by-three grid of buttons representing alignment choices is displayed (Fig. 3.19). The position of each button corresponds to where the text appears in the Label. For this app, set the TextAlign property to MiddleCenter in the three-by-three grid—this selection causes the text to appear centered in the middle of the Label, with equal spacing from the text to all sides of the Label. The other TextAlign values, such as TopLeft, TopRight, and BottomCenter, can be used to position the text anywhere in a Label. Certain alignment values may require that you resize the Label larger or smaller to fit the text better.

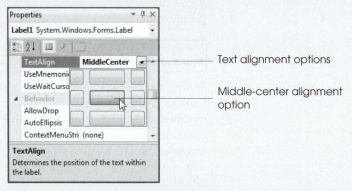

Text alignment options

Middle-center alignment option

Figure 3.19 Centering the Label's text.

5. *Saving the project.* Select **File > Save All** to save your modified project.

To finish this first Visual Basic Windows app, you need to insert an image and execute the app. We use a PictureBox control to add an image to the Form before running the app. The following box guides you step by step through the process of adding an image to your Form.

Inserting an Image and Running the App

1. *Adding a PictureBox to the Form.* The PictureBox control displays images. The process involved in this step is similar to adding a Label to the Form. Locate the PictureBox in the **Toolbox** (Fig. 2.24) and double click it to add it to the Form. When the PictureBox appears, move it underneath the Label, either by dragging it or by using the arrow keys (Fig. 3.20).

Updated Label

PictureBox

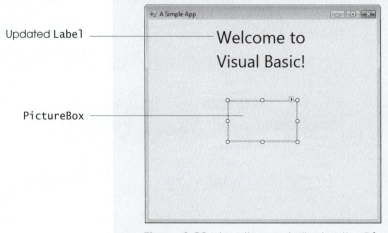

Figure 3.20 Inserting and aligning the PictureBox.

(cont.)   2.   ***Inserting an image.*** Click the PictureBox to display its properties in the
            Properties window (Fig. 3.21). Locate the **Image property**, which displays a
            preview of the selected image or **(none)** if no image is selected. Click the ellip-
            sis (**...**) button to display the **Select Resource dialog** (Fig. 3.22), which is
            used to import files, such as images, for use in a app. Click the **Import...** but-
            ton to browse for an image to insert, select the image file and click **OK**. We
            used bug.png from this chapter's examples folder. The image is previewed
            in the **Select Resource** dialog (Fig. 3.23). Click **OK** to use the image. Sup-
            ported image formats include PNG (Portable Network Graphics), GIF
            (Graphic Interchange Format), JPEG (Joint Photographic Experts Group)
            and BMP (Windows bitmap). To scale the image to the PictureBox's size,
            change the **SizeMode property** to **StretchImage** (Fig. 3.24). Resize the Pic-
            tureBox, making it larger (Fig. 3.25).

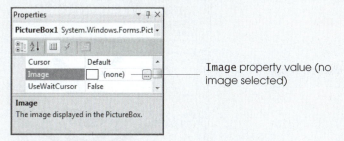

Image property value (no image selected)

Figure 3.21   Image property of the PictureBox.

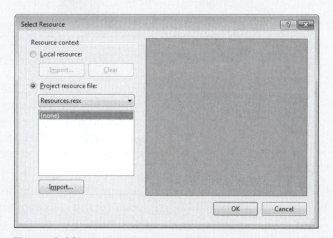

Figure 3.22   **Select Resource** dialog to select an image for the PictureBox.

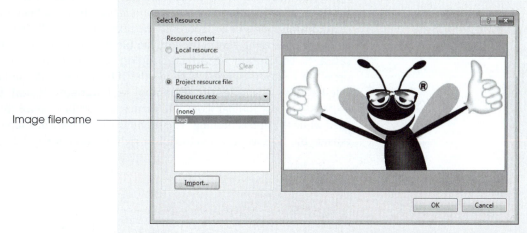

Image filename

Figure 3.23   **Select Resource** dialog displaying a preview of selected image.

(cont.)

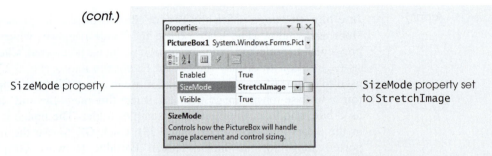

SizeMode property ———

SizeMode property set to StretchImage

Figure 3.24   Scaling an image to the size of the PictureBox.

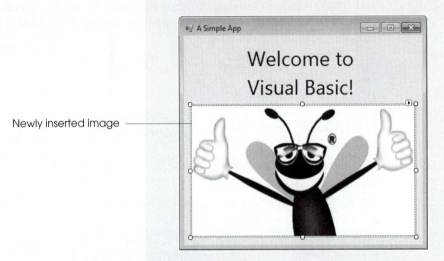

Newly inserted image ———

Figure 3.25   PictureBox displaying an image.

3. *Saving the project.* Select **File > Save All** to save the entire solution. The solution file (which has the filename extension .sln) contains the name and location of its project, and the project file (which has the filename extension .vbproj) contains the names and locations of all the files in the project. If you want to reopen your project at a later time, simply open its .sln file.

4. *Running the project.* Recall that up to this point we've been working in the IDE *design mode* (that is, the app being created is *not* executing). In **run mode**, the app *is* executing, and you can interact with only a few IDE features—features that are not available are disabled (grayed out). The text **Form1.vb [Design]** in the project tab (Fig. 3.26) means that we're designing the Form *visually* rather than *programmatically*. If we had been writing code, the tab would have contained only the text **Form1.vb**. If there's an asterisk (*) at the end of the text in the tab, the file has been changed and should be saved. Select **Debug > Start Debugging** to execute the app (or you can press the *F5* key). Figure 3.27 shows the IDE in run mode (indicated by the title-bar text **ASimpleApp (Running) – Microsoft Visual Basic 2010 Express**). Many toolbar icons and menus are disabled, since they cannot be used while the app is running. The running app appears in a separate window outside the IDE as shown in the lower-right portion of Fig. 3.27.

(cont.)

Newly inserted image

Figure 3.26 Debugging a solution.

IDE displays text **Running** to indicate that the app is executing

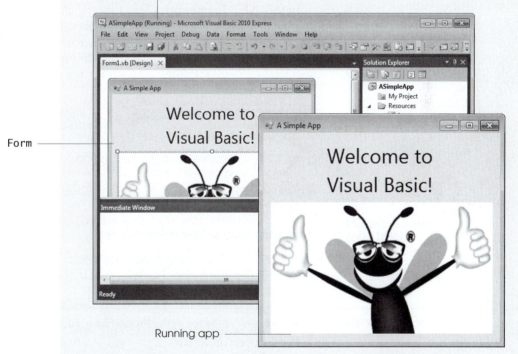

Form

Running app

Figure 3.27 IDE in run mode, with the running app in the foreground.

5. ***Terminating execution.*** Click the running app's close box ( ). This action stops the app's execution and returns the IDE to *design mode.* You can also select Debug > Stop Debugging to terminate the app.

6. ***Closing the IDE.*** Close the IDE by clicking its close box.

SELF-REVIEW

1. The Form's _____ property specifies the text that's displayed in the Form's title bar.

    a) `Title`   b) `Text`

    c) `(Name)`   d) `Name`

2. Property _____ specifies how text is aligned within a `Label`'s boundaries.

    a) `Alignment`   b) `AlignText`

    c) `Align`   d) `TextAlign`

Answers: 1) b. 2) d.

3.3 Objects Used in the App

In Chapters 1 and 2, you learned that controls are *reusable* software components called *objects*. The app used a `Form` object, a `Label` object and a `PictureBox` object to create a GUI that displayed text and an image. Each of these objects is an instance of a class defined in the .NET Framework Class Library. The `Form` object was created by the Visual Basic IDE. The `Label` and `PictureBox` objects were created when you *double clicked* their respective icons in the **Toolbox**.

We used the **Properties** window to set the properties (attributes) for each object. Recall that the `ComboBox` at the top of the **Properties** window—also called the *component object box*—displays the names and class types of `Form` and control objects (Fig. 3.28). In Fig. 3.29, the component object box displays the name (`ASimpleApp`) and class type (`Form`) of the `Form` object. You can rename the `Form` by selecting `Form1.vb` in the Solution Explorer window and changing its filename to `ASimpleApp.vb`. This will also change the name of the `Form` to `ASimpleApp`.

In the .NET Framework Class Library, classes are organized by functionality into directory-like entities called **namespaces**. The class types used in this app have namespace `System.Windows.Forms`. This namespace contains control classes and the `Form` class. You'll be introduced to additional namespaces in later chapters.

Figure 3.28 Component object box expanded to show the app's objects.

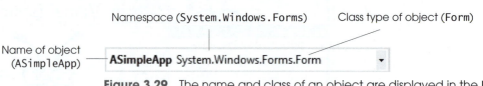

Figure 3.29 The name and class of an object are displayed in the **Properties** window's component object box.

SELF-REVIEW

1. The `ComboBox` at the top of the **Properties** window is the _____.

    a) component object box   b) control box

    c) control object box   d) component box

2. The .NET Framework Class Library organizes classes into _____.

    a) collections   b) name boxes

    c) namespaces   d) class spaces

Answers: 1) a. 2) c.

3.4 Wrap-Up

This chapter introduced you to visual app development in Visual Basic. You learned that visual app development helps you to design and create the graphical user interface portions of apps quickly and easily, by dragging and dropping controls onto Forms. You used visual app development to design the GUI portions of an app quickly and easily, by dragging and dropping controls (a Label and a PictureBox) onto a Form or by double clicking controls in the **Toolbox**.

In creating the app, you used the **Properties** window to set the Text and BackColor properties of the Form. You learned that Label controls display text and that PictureBoxes display images. You displayed text in a Label and added an image to a PictureBox. You also worked with the AutoSize, TextAlign and Font properties of a Label and the Image and SizeMode properties of a PictureBox.

You also examined the relationship between controls and classes. You learned that .NET Framework Class Library classes are grouped into directory-like entities called namespaces and that controls are instances (objects) of .NET Framework Class Library classes. The .NET Framework Class Library classes used in this chapter (Form, Label and PictureBox) belong to namespace System.Windows.Forms. You used the **Properties** window's component object box to view an object's name, namespace and class type.

In the next chapter, you continue learning visual app development. In particular, you'll create an app with controls that are designed to accept user input.

SKILLS SUMMARY

Creating GUIs Quickly and Efficiently

■ Use visual app-development techniques.

Placing a Control on the Form

■ Double click the control in the **Toolbox** to place the control in the upper-left corner of the Form, or drag the control from the **Toolbox** onto the Form.

Resizing the Form or Control with Sizing Handles

■ Click and drag one of the object's enabled sizing handles.

Setting the Form's Background Color

■ Use the **Properties** window to set the Form's BackColor property.

Adding a Label Control to the Form

■ Double click the Label control in the **Toolbox** to place the control in the upper-left corner of the Form, or drag the Label from the **Toolbox** onto the Form.

Setting a Label's Text Property

■ Use the **Properties** window to set the Label's Text property.

Setting a Label's Font Property

■ Click the value of the Font property in the **Properties** window, which causes an ellipsis Button to appear next to the value. Click the ellipsis Button to display the **Font** dialog. Change the font name, style and size of the Label's text.

Aligning Text in a Label

■ Use the **Properties** window to set the Label's TextAlign property.

Resizing a Label

■ Use the **Properties** window to set the AutoSize property to False, then use the sizing handles in the Form Designer.

Adding an Image to the Form

■ Use a PictureBox control to display the image. In the **Properties** window, click the ellipsis Button next to the PictureBox Image property's value or the **Choose Image** link in the property description to browse for an image to insert using the **Select Resource** dialog.

- Scale the image to the size of the `PictureBox` by setting property `SizeMode` to value `StretchImage`.

Displaying a Form or Control's Properties in the Properties Window

- Click the `Form` or a control on the `Form`.

KEY TERMS

AutoSize property of a Label—Determines whether a `Label` is automatically sized based on its content.

BackColor property—Specifies the background color of the `Form` or a control.

design mode—IDE mode that allows you to create apps using Visual Studio 2010's windows, toolbars and menu bar.

Font property—Specifies the font name, style and size of any displayed text in the `Form` or one of its controls.

Image property—Indicates the filename of the image displayed in a `PictureBox`.

Label—Control that displays text the user can't modify.

namespace—Classes in the .NET Framework Class Library are organized by functionality into these directory-like entities.

palette—A set of colors.

PictureBox—Control that displays an image.

run mode—IDE mode indicating that the app is executing.

Select Resource dialog—Used to import files, such as images, to any app.

SizeMode property—Property that specifies how an image is displayed in a `PictureBox`.

sizing handle—Square that, when enabled, can be used to resize the `Form` or one of its controls.

StretchImage—Value of `PictureBox` property `SizeMode` that scales an image to fill the `PictureBox`.

Text property—Specifies the text displayed by the `Form` or a `Label`.

TextAlign property—Specifies how text is aligned within a `Label`.

visual app development—Technique in which Visual Basic processes your actions (such as clicking, dragging and dropping controls) and writes code for you.

GUI DESIGN GUIDELINES

Overall Design

- Use colors in your apps, but not to the point of distracting the user.

Forms

- Choose short, descriptive `Form` titles. Capitalize words that are not articles, prepositions or conjunctions. Do not use punctuation.
- Use 9pt Segoe UI font to improve readability for controls that display text.

Labels

- Use `Label`s to display text that users cannot change.
- Ensure that all `Label` controls are large enough to display their text. You can do this by setting `AutoSize` to `True`, or by setting `AutoSize` to `False` and resizing the `Label` manually.

PictureBoxes

- Use `PictureBox`es to enhance GUIs with graphics that users cannot change.
- Images should fit inside their `PictureBox`es. This can be achieved by setting `PictureBox` property `SizeMode` to `StretchImage`.

CONTROLS, EVENTS,   **Label**   **A** Label   This control displays on the Form text that the user can't modify.
PROPERTIES &
METHODS   ■ *In action*

Welcome to
Visual Basic!

■ *Properties*

Text—Specifies the text displayed in the Label.

Font—Specifies the font name, style and size of the text displayed in the Label.

TextAlign—Determines how the text is aligned in the Label.

AutoSize—Allows for automatic resizing of the Label to fit its text.

PictureBox PictureBox   This control displays an image on the Form.

■ *In action*

■ *Properties*

Image—Specifies the image that's displayed in the PictureBox.

SizeMode—Specifies how the image is displayed in the PictureBox.

Form   Represents the main window of a GUI app.

■ *In action*

■ *Properties*

BackColor—Specifies the background color of the Form.

Font—Specifies the font name, style and size of any displayed text in the Form. The Form's controls use this font by default.

Text—Specifies the text displayed in the title bar of a Form.

MULTIPLE-CHOICE   **3.1** Property _____ determines the Form's background color.
QUESTIONS

    a) BackColor   b) BackgroundColor

    c) FormBackgroundColor   d) Color

3.2 To save all the project's files, select _____.

    a) **Save > Solution > Save Files**   b) **File > Save**

    c) **File > Save All**   d) **File > Save As...**

3.3 When the ellipsis `Button` to the right of the **Font** property value is clicked, the _____ is displayed.

    a) **Font Property** dialog   b) **New Font** dialog

    c) **Font Settings** dialog   d) **Font** dialog

3.4 `PictureBox` property _____ contains a preview of the image displayed in the `PictureBox`.

    a) `Picture`   b) `ImageName`

    c) `Image`   d) `PictureName`

3.5 When setting the `BackColor` property, the _____ tab allows you to create your own color.

    a) **Custom**   b) **Web**

    c) **System**   d) **User**

3.6 `PictureBox` property _____ specifies how an image is displayed in a `PictureBox`.

    a) `Size`   b) `Height`

    c) `Width`   d) `SizeMode`

3.7 A `Label` control displays the text specified by property _____.

    a) `Caption`   b) `Data`

    c) `Text`   d) `Name`

3.8 In _____ mode, the app is executing.

    a) start   b) run

    c) break   d) design

3.9 The text that appears at the top of the `Form` is specified in the `Form`'s _____ property.

    a) `Text`   b) `PictureName`

    c) `Label`   d) `FileName`

3.10 The _____ value of `PictureBox` property `SizeMode` scales an image to fill the `PictureBox`.

    a) `FullSize`   b) `StretchImage`

    c) `SpanPicture`   d) `FillBox`

EXERCISES *For Exercises 3.11–3.16, you're asked to create the GUI shown in each exercise. You'll use the visual app-development techniques presented in this chapter to create a variety of GUIs. You'll be creating only the GUIs, so your apps will not be fully operational. For example, the* **Calculator** *GUI in Exercise 3.11 does not behave like a calculator when its* `Buttons` *are clicked. You'll learn how to make your apps fully operational in later chapters. Create each app as a separate project. If you accidentally double click a control in* **Design** *view, the IDE displays the* `Form`'s *source code. To return to* **Design** *view, select* **View > Designer***.*

3.11 *(Calculator GUI)* Create the GUI for the calculator shown in Fig. 3.30.

    a) ***Creating a new project.*** Create a new **Windows Forms Application** named `Calculator`.

    b) ***Renaming the Form file.*** Name the `Form` file `Calculator.vb`.

    c) ***Manipulating the Form's properties.*** Change the `Text` property of the `Form` to `Calculator`. Change the `Font` property to 9pt Segoe UI. Change the `Size` property of the `Form` to 272, 206. Note that Visual Studio resizes a `Form` when you change its font size. *Be sure to set the font size before setting the* `Form`'s *size.*

    d) ***Adding a TextBox to the Form.*** Add a `TextBox` control by double clicking it in the **Toolbox**. A `TextBox` control enables the user to enter input into apps. Set the `Text-`

Box's Text property to 0. Change the Size property to 240, 23. [*Note:* You cannot change the height of a single-line TextBox. You'll learn how to create multiline TextBoxes in Chapter 11.] Set the TextAlign property to Right; this right aligns text displayed in the TextBox. Finally, set the TextBox's Location property to 8, 16—this property specifies where the upper-left corner of the control is placed on the form.

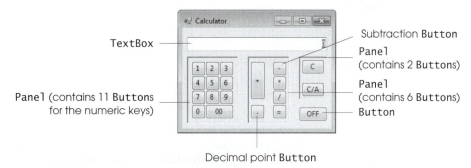

Figure 3.30   Calculator GUI.

e) *Adding the first Panel to the Form.* Panel controls are used to group other controls. Double click the Panel icon (🔲 Panel) in the **Containers** category of the **Toolbox** to add a Panel to the Form. Change the Panel's BorderStyle property to Fixed3D to make the inside of the Panel appear recessed. Change the Size property to 88, 112. Finally, set the Location property to 8, 48. This Panel will contain the calculator's numeric keys.

f) *Adding the second Panel to the Form.* Click the Form. Double click the Panel icon in the **Toolbox** to add another Panel to the Form. Change the Panel's BorderStyle property to Fixed3D. Change the Size property to 72, 112. Finally, set the Location property to 112, 48. This Panel will contain the calculator's operator keys.

g) *Adding the third (and last) Panel to the Form.* Click the Form. Double click the Panel icon in the **Toolbox** to add another Panel to the Form. Change the Panel's BorderStyle property to Fixed3D. Change the Size property to 48, 72. Finally, set the Location property to 200, 48. This Panel will contain the calculator's **C** (clear) and **C/A** (clear all) keys.

h) *Adding Buttons to the Form.* There are 20 Buttons on the calculator. To add a Button to a Panel, drag a Button (🔲 Button) from the **Toolbox** and drop it on the appropriate Panel. Change the Text property of each Button to the calculator key it represents. The value you enter in the Text property appears on the face of the Button. Finally, resize the Buttons, using their Size properties. Each Button labeled 0–9, *, /, -, = and . (decimal point) should have a size of 24, 24. The **00** and **OFF** Buttons have size 48, 24. The **+** Button is sized 25, 64. The **C** (clear) and **C/A** (clear all) Buttons are sized 38, 24.

i) *Aligning the Buttons.* To align the numeric Buttons as they appear in Fig. 3.30, select the **1** Button and set its Location property to 6, 6. Place the **2** and **3** Buttons to the right of the **1** Button. Select the three Buttons in the top row (**1**, **2** and **3**) by clicking the **1** Button, then holding the *Shift* key while you select the **2** and **3** Buttons. The formatting you do next is based on the Button you selected first (that is, the **1** Button). Use the **Format > Horizontal Spacing > Remove** option to place the Buttons directly next to each other. Use the **Format > Align > Middles** option to place them in a straight row. Repeat the process to vertically align Buttons **1**, **4**, **7** and **0** using the **Format > Vertical Spacing > Remove** and **Format > Align > Centers** options. You can drag and drop the rest of the numeric Buttons into position—the IDE "snaps" each Button into alignment with those around it. The **Format** menu contains many useful options. [*Note:* You can display many of the **Format** menu options in a Visual Studio toolbar—right click the toolbar in the IDE and select **Layout**.]

j) *Saving and closing the project.* Select **File > Save All** to save your changes. Then select **File > Close Project** to close the project for this app.

3.12 *(Alarm Clock GUI)* Create the GUI for the alarm clock in Fig. 3.31.

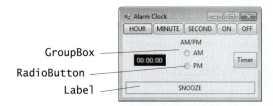

GroupBox

RadioButton

Label

Figure 3.31 Alarm Clock GUI.

a) *Creating a new project.* Create a new **Windows Forms Application** named `AlarmClock`.

b) *Renaming the Form file.* Name the Form file `AlarmClock.vb`.

c) *Manipulating the Form's properties.* Change the Font property of the Form to 9pt Segoe UI. Change the Text property to `Alarm Clock`. Change the Size property of the Form to 281, 176. Remember to change the Font property's size before you set the Form's Size property.

d) *Adding Buttons to the Form.* Add six Buttons to the Form. Change the Text property of each Button to the appropriate text. Change the Size properties of the **Hour** and **Minute** Buttons to 60, 23. Change the Size of the **Second** Button to 65, 23. Change the Size of the **ON** and **OFF** Buttons to 40, 23. The **Timer** Button gets size 48, 32. Use the **Format > Horizontal Spacing > Remove** option to align the Buttons in the top row so the Buttons appear as shown in Fig. 3.31.

e) *Adding a Label to the Form.* Add a Label to the Form. Change the Text property to **SNOOZE**. Set its AutoSize property to `False` and its Size to 254, 23. Set the Label's TextAlign property to `MiddleCenter`. Finally, to draw a border around the edge of the **SNOOZE** Label, change the BorderStyle property of the **SNOOZE** Label to `FixedSingle`.

f) *Adding a GroupBox to the Form.* GroupBoxes are like Panels, except that GroupBoxes can display a title. To add a GroupBox to the Form, double click the GroupBox control (GroupBox) in the **Containers** tab of the **Toolbox**. Change the Text property to AM/PM, and set the Size property to 72, 72. To place the GroupBox in the correct location on the Form, set the Location property to 104, 29.

g) *Adding AM/PM RadioButtons to the GroupBox.* Add two RadioButtons to the Form by dragging the RadioButton control (RadioButton) in the **Toolbox** and dropping it onto the GroupBox twice. Change the Text property of one RadioButton to AM and the other to PM. Then place the RadioButtons as shown in Fig. 3.31 by setting the Location of the **AM** RadioButton to 16, 16 and that of the **PM** RadioButton to 16, 40. Set the AutoSize property to `False` and set their Size properties to 48, 24.

h) *Adding the time Label to the Form.* Add a Label to the Form and change its Text property to `00:00:00`. Change the BorderStyle property to `Fixed3D` and the Back-Color to `Black`. Set the AutoSize property to `False` and set the Size property to 64, 23. Use the Font property to make the time bold. Change the ForeColor to `Silver` (located in the **Web** tab) to make the time stand out against the black background. Set TextAlign to `MiddleCenter` to center the text in the Label. Position the Label as shown in Fig. 3.31.

i) *Saving and closing the project.* Select **File > Save All** to save your changes. Then select **File > Close Project** to close the project for this app.

3.13 *(Microwave Oven GUI)* Create the GUI for the microwave oven shown in Fig. 3.32.

a) *Creating a new project.* Create a new **Windows Forms Application** named `Microwave`.

b) *Renaming the Form file.* Name the Form file `Microwave.vb`.

c) *Manipulating the Form's properties.* Change the Form's Font property to 9pt Segoe UI and the Text property to `Microwave Oven`. Change the Size property to 552, 290.

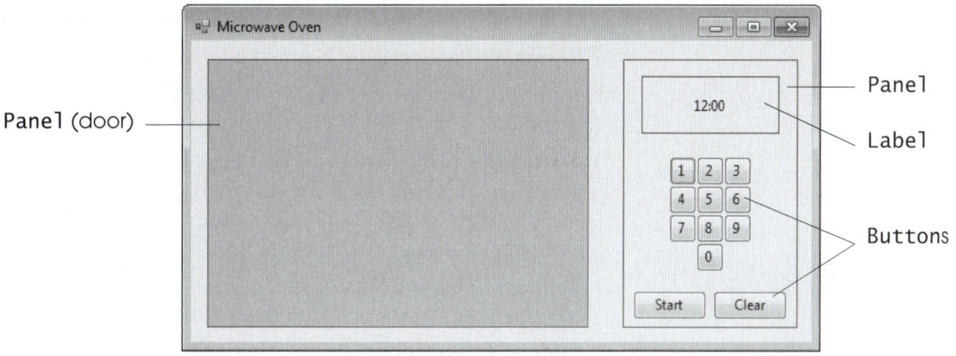

Figure 3.32   Microwave Oven GUI.

d) *Adding the microwave oven door.* Add a Panel to the Form by double clicking the Panel control (☐ Panel) in the **Toolbox**. Select the Panel and change the BackColor property to Silver (located in the **Web** tab) in the **Properties** window. Then change the Size to 328, 224. Next, change the BorderStyle property to FixedSingle. Position the Panel as shown in Fig. 3.32 by using the four-way arrow icon (⊕) in the upper-left corner of the selected Panel.

e) *Adding another Panel.* Add another Panel and change its Size to 152, 224 and its BorderStyle to FixedSingle. Place the Panel to the right of the door Panel, as shown in Fig. 3.32.

f) *Adding the microwave oven clock.* Add a Label to the right Panel by clicking the Label in the **Toolbox** once, then clicking once inside the right Panel. Change the Label's Text to 12:00, BorderStyle to FixedSingle, AutoSize to False and Size to 120, 48. Change TextAlign to MiddleCenter. Place the clock as shown in Fig. 3.32.

g) *Adding a keypad to the microwave oven.* Place a Button in the right Panel by clicking the Button control in the Toolbox once, then clicking inside the Panel. Change the Text to 1 and the Size to 24, 24. Repeat this process for nine more Buttons, changing the Text property in each to the next number in the keypad. Then add the **Start** and **Clear** Buttons, each of Size 64, 24. Don't forget to set the Text properties for each of these Buttons. Finally, arrange the Buttons as shown in Fig. 3.32. The **1** Button is located at 39, 80 and the **Start** Button at 8, 192.

h) *Saving and closing the project.* Select **File > Save All** to save your changes. Then select **File > Close Project** to close the project for this app.

3.14 *(Cell Phone GUI)* Create the GUI for the cell phone shown in Fig. 3.33.

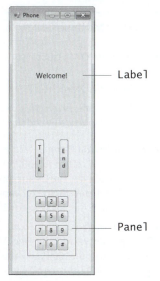

Figure 3.33   Cell Phone GUI.

a) *Creating a new project.* Create a new **Windows Forms Application** named Phone.

b) *Renaming the Form file.* Name the Form file Phone.vb.

c) *Manipulating the Form's properties.* Change the Form's Font property to 9pt Segoe UI. Change the Text property to Phone and the Size to 184, 560.

d) *Adding the display Label.* Add a Label to the Form. Change its BackColor property to NavajoWhite (in the **Web** tab palette), the Text to Welcome!, AutoSize to False and the Size to 156, 210. Change the TextAlign property to MiddleCenter. Then place the Label as shown in Fig. 3.33.

e) *Adding the keypad Panel.* Add a Panel to the Form. Change its BorderStyle property to FixedSingle and its Size to 104, 136.

f) *Adding the Buttons.* Add the keypad Buttons to the Form (12 Buttons in all). Each Button on the number pad should be of Size 24, 24 and should be placed in the Panel. Change the Text property of each Button such that numbers 0–9, the pound (#) and the star (*) keys are represented. Then add the final two Buttons such that the Text property for one is Talk and for the other is End. Change the Size of each Button to 20, 80, and notice how the small Size causes the Text to align vertically.

g) *Placing the controls.* Arrange all the controls so that your GUI looks like Fig. 3.33.

h) *Saving and closing the project.* Select **File > Save All** to save your changes. Then select **File > Close Project** to close the project for this app.

3.15 *(Vending Machine GUI)* Create the GUI for the vending machine in Fig. 3.34.

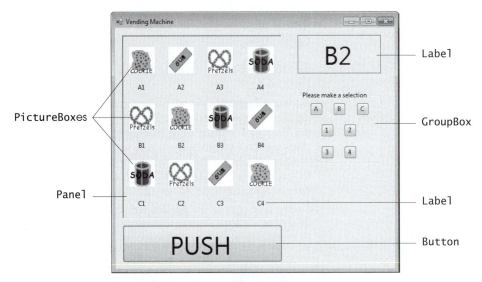

Figure 3.34   Vending Machine GUI.

a) *Creating a new project.* Create a new **Windows Forms Application** named VendingMachine.

b) *Renaming the Form file.* Name the Form file VendingMachine.vb.

c) *Manipulating the Form's properties.* Set the Font property of the Form to 9pt Segoe UI, the Text property to Vending Machine and the Size to 560, 490.

d) *Adding the food-selection Panel.* Add a Panel to the Form, and change its Size to 312, 344 and BorderStyle to Fixed3D. Add a PictureBox to the Panel, and change its Size to 50, 50. Then set the Image property by clicking the **Choose Image** link and choosing a file from the C:\Examples\ch03\ExerciseImages\VendingMachine directory. Repeat this process for 11 more PictureBoxes.

e) *Adding Labels for each vending item.* Add a Label under the first PictureBox. Change its Text property to A1, its TextAlign property to MiddleCenter, AutoSize to False and Size to 50, 16. Place the Label so that it's located as in Fig. 3.34. Repeat this process for A2 through C4 (11 Labels).

f) *Creating the vending machine door (as a Button).* Add a Button to the Form by dragging the Button control in the **Toolbox** and dropping it below the Panel. Change the Button's Text property to PUSH, its Font Size to 36 and its Size to 312, 70. Then place the Button on the Form as shown in Fig. 3.34.

g) *Adding the selection-display Label.* Add a Label to the Form, and change the Text property to B2, BorderStyle to FixedSingle, Font Size to 36, TextAlign to MiddleCenter, AutoSize to False and Size to 160, 72.

h) *Grouping the input Buttons.* Add a GroupBox below the Label, and change the Text property to Please make a selection and the Size to 160, 136.

i) *Adding the input Buttons.* Finally, add Buttons to the GroupBox. For the seven Buttons, change the Size property to 24, 24. Then change the Text property of the Buttons such that each Button has one of the values A, B, C, 1, 2, 3 or 4, as shown in Fig. 3.34. When you're done, move the controls on the Form so that they're aligned as shown in the figure.

j) *Saving and closing the project.* Select **File > Save All** to save your changes. Then select **File > Close Project** to close the project for this app.

Programming Challenge ▶   **3.16 (Radio GUI)** Create the GUI for the radio in Fig. 3.35. [*Note:* All colors used in this exercise are from the **Web** palette.] In this exercise, you'll create this GUI on your own. Feel free to experiment with different control properties. For the image in the PictureBox, use the file (MusicNote.gif) found in the C:\Examples\ch03\ExerciseImages\Radio directory.

a) *Creating a new project.* Create a new **Windows Forms Application** named Radio.

b) *Renaming the Form file.* Name the Form file Radio.vb.

c) *Manipulating the Form's properties.* Change the Form's Font property to 9pt Segoe UI, the Text property to Radio and the Size to 576, 242. Set BackColor to PeachPuff.

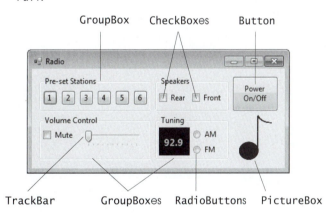

Figure 3.35   Radio GUI.

d) *Adding the Pre-set Stations GroupBox and Buttons.* Add a GroupBox to the Form. Set its Size to 232, 64, its Text to Pre-set Stations, its ForeColor to Black and its BackColor to RosyBrown. Change its Font to bold. Finally, set its Location to 24, 16. Add six Buttons to the GroupBox. Set each BackColor to PeachPuff and each Size to 24, 24. Change the Buttons' Text properties to 1, 2, 3, 4, 5, 6, respectively.

e) *Adding the Speakers GroupBox and CheckBoxes.* Add a GroupBox to the Form. Set its Size to 160, 64, its Text to Speakers and its ForeColor to Black. Set its Location to 280, 16. Add two CheckBoxes to the Form. Set each CheckBox's AutoSize property to False and Size to 56, 24. Set the Text properties for the CheckBoxes to Rear and Front.

f) *Adding the Power On/Off Button.* Add a Button to the Form. Set its Text to Power On/Off, its BackColor to RosyBrown, its ForeColor to Black and its Size to 72, 64. Change its Font style to Bold.

g) *Adding the Volume Control GroupBox, the Mute CheckBox and the Volume Track-Bar.* Add a GroupBox to the Form. Set its Text to Volume Control, its BackColor to RosyBrown, its ForeColor to Black and its Size to 200, 80. Set its Font style to Bold. Add a CheckBox to the GroupBox. Set its Text to Mute and its Size to 56, 19. Add a TrackBar (◦− TrackBar)—found in the **All Windows Forms** category—to the GroupBox.

h) *Adding the Tuning GroupBox, the radio station Label and the AM/FM RadioButtons.* Add a GroupBox to the Form. Set its Text to Tuning, its ForeColor to Black and its BackColor to RosyBrown. Set its Font style to Bold and its Size to 216, 80. Add a Label to the GroupBox. Set its BackColor to PeachPuff, its BorderStyle to FixedSingle, its TextAlign to MiddleCenter and its Size to 56, 24. Set its Text to 92.9. Place the Label as shown in Fig. 3.35. Add two RadioButtons to the GroupBox. Change the BackColor to PeachPuff and change the Size to 45,24. Set one's Text to AM and the other's Text to FM.

i) *Adding the image.* Add a PictureBox to the Form. Set its BackColor to Transparent, its SizeMode to StretchImage and its Size to 56, 72. Set its Image property to C:\Examples\ch03\ExerciseImages\Radio\MusicNote.gif.

j) *Saving and closing the project.* Select **File > Save All** to save your changes. Then select **File > Close Project** to close the project for this app.

Objectives

In this chapter, you'll:

■ Program visually, using GUI design guidelines.
■ Rename the Form.
■ Add TextBoxes and a Button to the Form.
■ Use the BorderStyle property for Labels.

Outline

Designing the Inventory App

Introducing *TextBoxes and Buttons*

This chapter introduces you to GUI design. You'll design the graphical user interface for a simple inventory app. Through each set of steps, you'll enhance the app's user interface by adding controls. You'll design a Form on which you place Labels, TextBoxes and a Button. You'll learn new properties for Labels and TextBoxes. At the end of the chapter, you'll find a list of GUI design guidelines to help you create appealing and easy-to-use graphical user interfaces.

4.1 Test-Driving the Inventory App

In this chapter, you'll create an inventory app that calculates the number of textbooks received by a college bookstore. This app must meet the following requirements:

> **App Requirements**
>
> *A college bookstore receives cartons of textbooks. In each shipment, all cartons contain the same number of textbooks. The inventory manager wants to use a computer to calculate the total number of textbooks arriving at the bookstore for each shipment. The inventory manager will enter the number of cartons received and the fixed number of textbooks in each carton for each shipment; then the app will calculate the total number of textbooks in the shipment.*

This app performs a simple calculation. The user (the inventory manager) inputs into TextBoxes the number of cartons and the number of items in each carton. The user then clicks a Button, which causes the app to multiply the two numbers and display the result—the total number of textbooks received. You'll begin by test-driving the completed app. Then you'll learn the additional Visual Basic capabilities needed to create your own version of this app.

Test-Driving the Inventory App

1. **Opening the completed app.** Open the directory C:\Examples\ch04\Com-pletedApp\Inventory to locate the **Inventory** app. Double click Inventory.sln to open the app in the Visual Basic IDE. Depending on your system configuration, you may not see the .sln filename extension. In this case, double click the file named Inventory that contains a solution file icon, ▣.

2. **Running the Inventory app.** Select **Debug > Start Debugging** to run the app. The **Inventory** Form shown in Fig. 4.1 will appear.

Labels
TextBoxes
Label

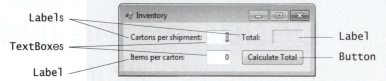

Label
Button

Figure 4.1 **Inventory** app Form with default data displayed by the app.

Note that there are two controls that you did not use in the **Welcome** app—the TextBox and Button controls. A **TextBox** is a control that the user can enter data into from the keyboard and that can display data to the user. A **Button** is a control that causes the app to perform an action when clicked.

3. **Entering quantities in the app.** Some controls (such as TextBoxes) do not display self-descriptive text—we refer to these controls by using the Labels that identify them. For example, we refer to the TextBox to the right of the **Cartons per shipment:** Label as the **Cartons per shipment:** TextBox. Enter 3 in the **Cartons per shipment:** TextBox. Enter 15 in the **Items per carton:** TextBox. Figure 4.2 shows the Form after these values have been entered.

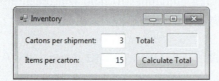

Figure 4.2 **Inventory** app with new quantities entered.

4. **Calculating the total number of items received.** Click the **Calculate Total** Button. The app multiplies the two numbers you entered and displays the result (45) in the Label to the right of **Total:** (Fig. 4.3).

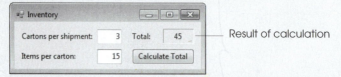

Result of calculation

Figure 4.3 Result of clicking the **Calculate Total** Button in the **Inventory** app.

5. **Closing the app.** Close your running app by clicking its close box.

6. **Closing the project.** Select **File > Close Project**.

4.2 Constructing the Inventory App

Now that you've test-driven the completed app, you'll begin creating your own version of the app. You'll create a new project that contains the Form on which you place the controls required for the **Inventory** app. Then you'll save the solution containing the Form to your working directory, C:\SimplyVB2010. [*Note:* We assume you've created this directory as per the instructions in the Before You Begin section. If you chose to use a different directory, save the solution to that directory.] Finally, the initial steps conclude with instructions for renaming the Form.

Creating a New App

1. ***Creating the new project.*** To create a Windows app, select **File > New Project...** to display the **New Project** dialog (Fig. 4.4). From the list of templates, select **Windows Forms Application**. Type `Inventory` in the **Name:** Text-box, and click the **OK** Button.

List of templates with **Windows Forms Application** selected

Name: TextBox

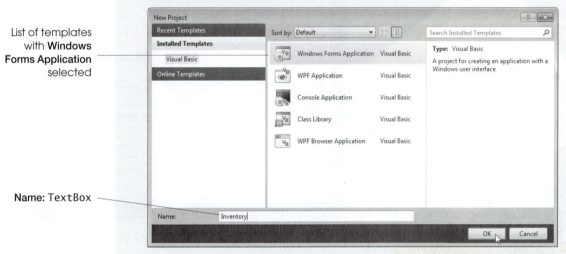

Figure 4.4   **New Project** dialog for creating new apps.

2. ***Saving the project to your working directory.*** Now that a blank workspace has loaded, select **File > Save All,** to display the **Save Project** dialog (Fig. 4.5). Ensure that the **Location:** is set to `C:\SimplyVB2010`.

Figure 4.5   **Save Project** dialog for saving the newly created app.

3. ***Viewing the Form.*** Click the **Save** Button (Fig. 4.5) to close the **Save Project** dialog. The IDE then returns to the app, containing a Form named **Form1** (Fig. 4.6). If the Form does not appear as in Fig. 4.6, select **View > Designer**. Then click the Form in the IDE to select it.

4. ***Renaming the Form file.*** It's a good practice to change the Form's filename to a name more meaningful for your app. To do so, click the Form's filename (`Form1.vb`) in the **Solution Explorer**. Then select `File Name` in the **Properties** window, and type `Inventory.vb` in the field to the right. Press *Enter* to update the filename. Unless otherwise noted, you need to press *Enter*, or select another property, for changes made in the **Properties** window to take effect.

(cont.)

Form title bar (for **Form1**)
Form filename (**Form1.vb**)

Form

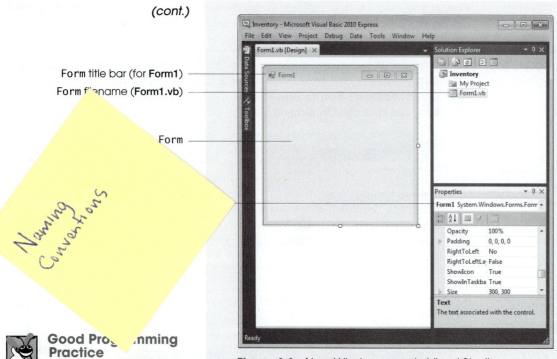

Figure 4.6   New Windows app in Visual Studio.

Good Programming Practice

Change the **Form** name to a unique and meaningful name for easy identification.

Good Programming Practice

Use standard suffixes for names of objects (controls and **Forms**) so that you can easily tell them apart. Append the suffix "Form" to **Form** names. Capitalize the first letter of the **Form** name because **Form** is a class. Objects (such as controls) should begin with lowercase letters.

5. ***Renaming the Form object.*** Each **Form** object needs a unique and meaningful name for easy identification. In the Visual Basic IDE, you set the **Form**'s name by using the **Name** property. By default, the Visual Basic IDE names the **Form** **Form1**. When you change the **Form**'s filename, the Visual Basic IDE updates the **Form**'s **Name** property automatically to the name of the file without the .vb extension—in this case, **Inventory**. Click the **Form** in the Windows Form Designer. In the **Properties** window (Fig. 4.7), locate and double click the field to the right of the **Name** property, listed as (**Name**). Type the name **InventoryForm**, then press *Enter* to update the name.

Name property

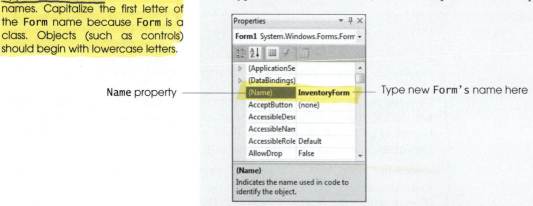

Type new **Form**'s name here

Figure 4.7   Renaming a **Form** in the **Properties** windows.

6. ***Saving the project.*** Select **File > Save All** to save your changes. Saving your work helps you avoid losing changes to the app.

GUI Design Tip

Change the **Form**'s font to 9pt **Segoe UI** to be consistent with Microsoft's recommended font for Windows 7.

Next, you learn how to modify your **Form** by setting its font. As in all our examples, you should set the **Form**'s font to 9pt **Segoe UI**, the Microsoft-recommended font for Windows 7 GUIs. By default, the controls added to the **Form** use the same font as the **Form** itself. You'll also learn how to change the **Form**'s title and size.

Although you've already changed the filename to Inventory.vb, you still need to change the title-bar text to help users identify the Form's purpose. Changing the Form's size to suit its content improves its appearance.

Customizing the Form

1. **Setting the Form's font.** In the preceding chapter, you used the **Font** dialog to change the font. You now use the **Properties** window to change the Form's font. Select the Form in the Windows Form Designer. If the **Properties** window isn't already open, click the **Properties** icon in the IDE toolbar or select **View > Other Windows > Properties Window**. To change the Form's font to 9pt Segoe UI, click the arrow ▷ to the left of the Font property in the **Properties** window (Fig. 4.8). This causes other properties related to the Form's Font to be displayed. In the list that appears, select the font's Name property, then click the down arrow to the right of the property value. In the list that appears, select Segoe UI. [*Note*: The list may contain fonts other than those shown in Fig. 4.9, depending on the fonts that are installed on your system.] Then set the font's Size property to 9.

   Notice that several properties, such as Font, have an arrow next to the property name to indicate that additional properties are available for this node. For example, when you expand the Font node, you'll see that the Name, Size and Bold properties of a Font each have their own listings in the **Properties** window.

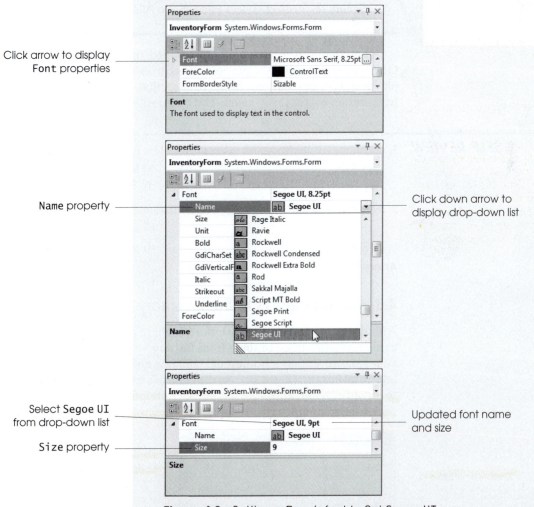

Figure 4.8 Setting a Form's font to 9pt Segoe UI.

(cont.)

GUI Design Tip

Changing the Form's title allows users to identify the Form's purpose.

GUI Design Tip

Form titles should use book-title capitalization.

Form titles book-title

2. **Setting the text in the Form's title bar.** The text in the Form's title bar is determined by the Form's **Text** property. To display the Form's properties in the **Properties** window, click the Form in the Windows Form Designer. Double-click the field to the right of the **Text** property in the **Properties** window, type Inventory and press *Enter*. Form titles should use book-title capitalization. **Book-title capitalization** is a style that capitalizes the first letter of each significant word in the text (for example, *Capitalization in a Book Title*). The updated title bar is shown in Fig. 4.9.

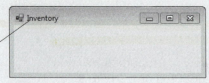

Figure 4.9   Resized Form displaying new title-bar text.

3. **Resizing the Form.** Double click the field to the right of the **Size** property in the **Properties** window, then type 320, 114 (which represent the *width* and the *height* of the Form, respectively) and press *Enter* (Fig. 4.9). The Form is now the same size as the completed app you test-drove at the beginning of the chapter.

4. **Saving the project.** Select **File > Save All** to save your changes.

Now that you've created and modified the Form, you'll add controls to the GUI. Labels describe the purpose of controls on the Form and can be used to display results of calculations. In the next section, you'll learn how to add Label controls and set each Label's name, text and position on the Form.

SELF-REVIEW

1. _____ is the Microsoft-recommended font for GUIs in Windows 7.
   a) Arial   b) Microsoft Sans Serif
   c) Segoe UI   d) Times New Roman

2. Form titles should use _____ capitalization.
   a) book-title   b) complete
   c) no   d) sentence-style

Answers: 1) c. 2) a.

4.3 Adding Labels to the Inventory App

Although you might not have noticed it, there are four Labels in this app. You can easily recognize three of them from the app you designed in Chapter 3. The fourth Label, however, has a border and contains no text until the user clicks the **Calculate Total** Button (Fig. 4.10). As the control's name indicates, Labels are often used to identify other controls on the Form. **Descriptive Labels** help the user understand each control's purpose, and **output Labels** are used to display program output.

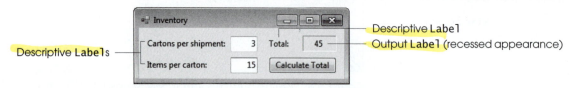

Figure 4.10   Labels used in the **Inventory** app.

Adding Labels to the Form

Location value 0, 0 ───

Label control ───

1. ***Adding a Label control to the Form.*** Click the **All Windows Forms** group in the **Toolbox**. Then, double click the Label control in the **Toolbox** to place a Label on the Form (Fig. 4.11).

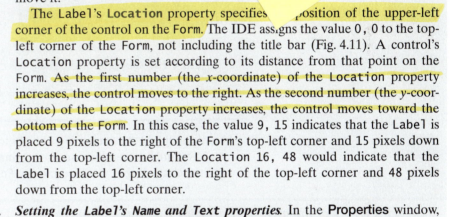

Figure 4.11   Adding a Label

[handwritten note: X - Y coordinate]

2. ***Setting the Label's location.*** I... ...elect **View > Properties Window**. In ... ...l's Location property to 9, 15. Using ... ...pace between the Label and the edges of t... ...preceding chapter, you can drag a control from ... ...rm. You can also fine tune a control's position by sele... ...he arrow keys to move it.

   The Label's **Location** property specifies ... position of the upper-left corner of the control on the Form. The IDE assigns the value 0, 0 to the top-left corner of the Form, not including the title bar (Fig. 4.11). A control's Location property is set according to its distance from that point on the Form. As the first number (the *x*-coordinate) of the Location property increases, the control moves to the right. As the second number (the *y*-coordinate) of the Location property increases, the control moves toward the bottom of the Form. In this case, the value 9, 15 indicates that the Label is placed 9 pixels to the right of the Form's top-left corner and 15 pixels down from the top-left corner. The Location 16, 48 would indicate that the Label is placed 16 pixels to the right of the top-left corner and 48 pixels down from the top-left corner.

3. ***Setting the Label's Name and Text properties.*** In the **Properties** window, double click the field to the right of the Text property, then type Cartons per shipment:. Set the Name property to cartonsLabel.

   When entering values for a Label's Text property, you should use sentence-style capitalization. **Sentence-style capitalization** means that you capitalize the first letter of the first word in the text. Every other letter in the text is lowercase unless it's the first letter of a proper noun (for example, *Deitel*).

4. ***Modifying the Label's text alignment.*** Select the TextAlign property in the **Properties** window; then, in the field to the right, click the down arrow (Fig. 4.12). Property TextAlign sets the alignment of text within a control such as a Label. Clicking the down arrow opens a window in which you can select the alignment of the text in the Label (Fig. 4.12). In this window, select the middle-left rectangle, which indicates that the Label's text aligns to the middle, vertically, and to the left, horizontally, in the control. The value of the property changes to MiddleLeft. Figure 4.13 displays the Label

[handwritten note: Sentence-style Append "label"]

(cont.)

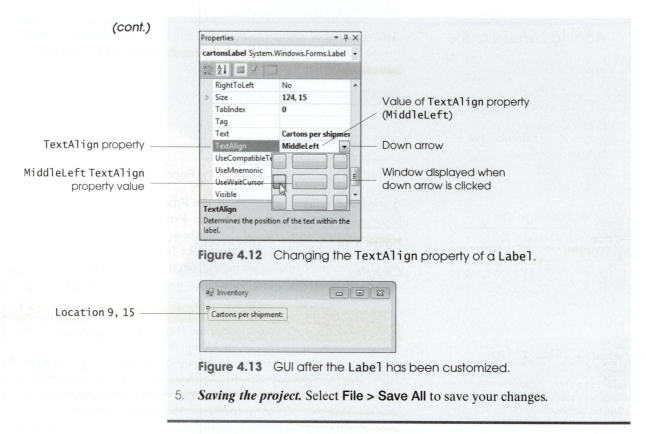

Figure 4.12   Changing the `TextAlign` property of a `Label`.

Value of `TextAlign` property
(`MiddleLeft`)

`TextAlign` property

`MiddleLeft` `TextAlign`
property value

Down arrow

Window displayed when
down arrow is clicked

Location 9, 15

Figure 4.13   GUI after the `Label` has been customized.

5. *Saving the project.* Select **File > Save All** to save your changes.

Now you'll add the remaining `Label`s to the `Form`. They help the user understand what inputs to provide and how to interpret the app's output. These `Label`s identify the controls that you'll add to the `Form` later.

Placing Additional Labels on the Form

GUI Design Tip

Align the left or right sides of a group of descriptive `Label`s if the `Label`s are arranged vertically.

GUI Design Tip

Use a descriptive `Label` to identify an output `Label`.

GUI Design Tip

Place an app's output below and/or to the right of the `Form`'s input controls.

1. *Adding a second descriptive Label.* Double click the `Label` control on the **Toolbox** to add a second `Label`. Set the `Label`'s `Location` property to 9, 46. Set the `Label`'s `Text` property to `Items per carton:`, and change the `Name` property of this `Label` to `itemsLabel`. Then set the `Label`'s `TextAlign` property to `MiddleLeft`.

2. *Adding a third descriptive Label.* Double click the `Label` control on the **Toolbox** to add a third `Label`. Set the `Label`'s `Location` property to 190, 15. Set the `Label`'s `Text` property to `Total:` and change its `Name` property to `totalLabel`. Then set the `Label`'s `TextAlign` property to `MiddleLeft`.

3. *Adding an output Label.* Add the fourth `Label` by double clicking the `Label` control on the **Toolbox**. Set the `Label`'s `AutoSize` property to `False`. Then, set the `Label`'s `Size` property to 50, 23 and its `Location` property to 243, 11. These settings cause the text in the output label to align with the text in its corresponding descriptive label. Then name this `Label` `totalResultLabel`. Set the `Label`'s `TextAlign` property to `MiddleCenter`. For the previous `Label`s, you set this property to `MiddleLeft`. To select value `MiddleCenter`, follow the same actions as in *Step 2*, but select the center rectangle shown in Fig. 4.14. You should use `MiddleCenter` text alignment to display results of calculations because it distinguishes the value in the output `Label` from the values in the descriptive `Label`s (whose `TextAlign` property is set to `MiddleLeft`).

(cont.)

GUI Design Tip

If output Labels are arranged vertically to display numbers used in a mathematical calculation (such as in an invoice), use the MiddleRight value for the TextAlign property.

GUI Design Tip

Output Labels should be distinguishable from descriptive Labels. This can be done by setting the Border-Style property of an output Label to Fixed3D.

Good Programming Practice

Clear an output Label's value initially or provide a default value. When the app performs the calculation for that value, the Label's Text property should be updated to the new value. You'll learn how to do this in the next chapter.

Clear label

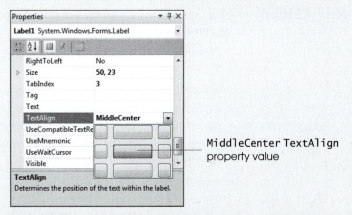

MiddleCenter TextAlign property value

Figure 4.14 Setting the TextAlign property to MiddleCenter.

4. *Changing a Label's BorderStyle property.* The totalResultLabel displays the result of the app's calculation; therefore, you should make this Label appear different from the other Labels. To do this, you'll change the appearance of the Label's border by changing the value of the **BorderStyle** property. Assign the value Fixed3D (Fig. 4.15) to totalResultLabel's BorderStyle property to make the Label seem three dimensional (Fig. 4.16). [*Note*: If selected, FixedSingle displays a single dark line as a border.]

Fixed3D BorderStyle property value highlighted

Figure 4.15 Changing a Label's BorderStyle property to Fixed3D.

5. *Clearing a Label's Text property.* When a Label is added to a Form, the Text property is assigned the default name of the Label. In this case, you should clear the text of the Label, because you will not be adding meaningful text to totalResultLabel until later. To do this, delete the text to the right of the Text property in the **Properties** window and press *Enter*. Figure 4.16 displays the GUI with all Labels added.

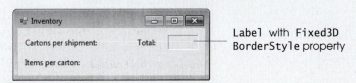

Label with Fixed3D BorderStyle property

Figure 4.16 GUI with all Labels added.

6. *Saving the project.* Select **File > Save All** to save your changes.

SELF-REVIEW

1. The value _____ for the Location property indicates the top-left corner (not including the title bar) of the Form.

   a) 1, 1
   b) 0, 0
   c) 1, 0
   d) 0, 1

2. An output Label should _____.

   a) be distinguishable from other Labels
   b) initially have an empty Text property or a default value (e.g., 0)
   c) use Fixed3D for the BorderStyle property
   d) All of the above

Answers: 1) b. 2) d.

4.4 Adding TextBoxes and a Button to the Form

The **Inventory** app requires user input to calculate the total number of textbooks that have arrived per shipment. The user enters the number of cartons and the fixed number of books per carton. Because data of this type is entered from the keyboard, you use a TextBox control. Next, you'll learn how to add TextBoxes to your Form and set their properties. Then, you'll add a Button control to complete your GUI.

1. *Adding a TextBox to the Form*. Double click the TextBox control,

       [abl] TextBox

   in the **Toolbox** to add a TextBox to the Form. Setting properties for a Text-Box is similar to setting the properties for a Label. To name the TextBox, select its Name property in the **Properties** window, and enter cartonsText-Box in the field to the right of the property (Fig. 4.17). Set the TextBox's Width property (found inside the Size property) to 40 and its Location property to 136, 12. These size and location properties cause the baseline of the text in the TextBox to align with the baseline of the text in the Label that describes it. Set the TextBox's Text property to 0 (Fig. 4.18). This causes the value for your TextBox to be initially 0 when the app runs.

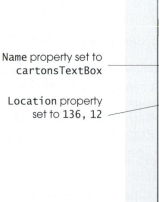

Append the TextBox suffix to the name of every TextBox control.

GUI Design Tip

Use TextBoxes to input data from the keyboard.

(handwritten note: Append textbox)

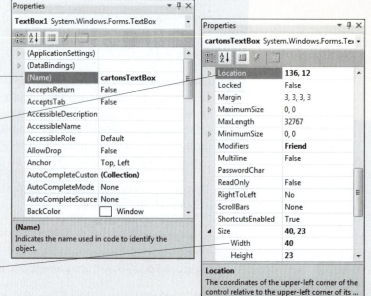

Name property set to cartonsTextBox

Location property set to 136, 12

Width property set to 40

Figure 4.17   **Properties** window for the cartonsTextBox TextBox.

(cont.)

GUI Design Tip

Each TextBox should have a descriptive Label indicating the input expected from the user.

GUI Design Tip

Place each descriptive Label either above or to the left of the control (for instance, a TextBox) that it identifies.

GUI Design Tip

Make TextBoxes wide enough for their expected inputs.

GUI Design Tip

A descriptive Label and the control it identifies should be aligned on the left if they're arranged vertically.

GUI Design Tip

The text in a descriptive Label and the text in the control it identifies should be aligned on the bottom if they're arranged horizontally.

2. ***Changing the TextAlign property of a TextBox.*** Change cartonsText-Box's TextAlign property to Right. Note that, when you click the down arrow to the right of this property, the window in Fig. 4.12 does not appear. This is because TextBoxes have fewer TextAlign options, which are displayed simply as a list. Select Right from this list (Fig. 4.18). Generally, when multiple TextBoxes used for numeric input are stacked vertically, their text should be right aligned.

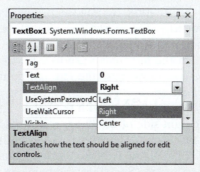

Figure 4.18 Selecting value Right of the TextAlign property of a Text-Box control.

3. ***Adding a second TextBox to the Form.*** Double click the TextBox control in the **Toolbox**. Name the TextBox itemsTextBox. Set the Width property (found inside the Size property) to 40 and the Location property to 136, 43. These settings ensure that the left sides of the two TextBoxes align. The settings also align the baseline of the text in the TextBox and the baseline of the text in the Label that describes it. Set the Text property to 0 and the TextAlign property to Right. Figure 4.19 shows the Form after the Text-Boxes have been added and their properties have been set.

Many of the second TextBox's properties match those of the first Text-Box (e.g., Width, Text and TextAlign). When creating multiple controls of the same type with many of the same property values, it's often easier to copy the original control. To do this, select the control you wish to copy and press *Ctrl + C*. Then press *Ctrl + V* to paste it onto the Form. Reposition the new control and adjust its properties as needed.

Figure 4.19 GUI after TextBoxes have been added and modified.

4. ***Saving the project.*** Select **File > Save All** to save your changes.

Your controls align horizontally and vertically. In general, you should place each descriptive Label above or to the left of the control it describes (for instance, a TextBox). If you're arranging your controls on the same line, the text of the descriptive Label and the text of the control it describes should be aligned. However, if you arrange your controls vertically, the Label should be placed above the control it describes and the left sides of the controls should align. Following these simple guidelines will make your apps more appealing visually and easier to use by making the controls on the app less crowded.

Now that the user can enter data using a TextBox, you need a way for the user to command the app to perform the calculation and display the result. The most common way for a user to do this is by clicking a Button. The following box explains how to add a Button to the **Inventory** app.

Adding a Button to the Form

GUI Design Tip

Buttons are often stacked downward from the top right of a Form or arranged on the same line starting from the bottom right of a Form.

Good Programming Practice

Append the Button suffix to Button control names.

GUI Design Tip

As you drag controls, the IDE displays blue and purple lines called snaplines. The blue lines help you position controls relative to one another. The purple lines help you position controls relative to the control text.

GUI Design Tip

Buttons are labeled using their **Text** property. These labels should use book-title capitalization and be brief while still being meaningful to the user.

1. ***Adding a Button to the Form.*** Add a Button to the Form by double clicking the Button control,

  Button

in the **Toolbox**. Setting the properties for a Button is similar to setting the properties for a Label or a TextBox. Enter `calculateButton` in the Button's Name property.

Set the Button's Size to 100, 24 and Location to 193, 42. Note that these settings cause the left and right sides of the Button to align with the Labels above it (Fig. 4.20). You also can accomplish this by aligning the left side of the Button with the Label above it. Then drag the sizing handle on the right side of the Button until the blue **snapline** appears to indicate that the Button is aligned with the right side of the Label above it. (Earlier in the chapter we referred to "adequate space" between a Label and the Form's edges. Snaplines also help you maintain adequate space between controls and between a control and the Form's border.) Enter `Calculate Total` in the Button's Text property. A Button's Text property displays its value on the face of the Button. You should use book-title capitalization in a Button's Text property. When labeling Buttons, keep the text brief while still clearly indicating the Button's function.

2. ***Running the app.*** Select **Debug > Start Debugging** to run the app (Fig. 4.20). Note that no action occurs if you click the **Calculate Total** Button because you haven't written code that tells the app how to respond to your click. In Chapter 5, you'll write code to display the total number of books in the shipment when the Button is clicked.

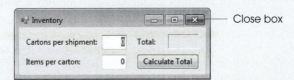
  — Close box

Figure 4.20 Running the app after completing its design.

3. ***Closing the app.*** Close your running app by clicking its close box.

4. ***Closing the IDE.*** Close the Visual Basic IDE by clicking its close box.

SELF-REVIEW

1. A Button's _____ property sets the text on the face of the Button.
   a) Name
   b) Text
   c) Title
   d) Face

2. Buttons are often _____ of the Form.
   a) on the same line, from the bottom right
   b) aligned with the title-bar text
   c) stacked from the top right
   d) Either a or c

Answers: 1) b. 2) d.

4.5 Wrap-Up

In this chapter, you began constructing your **Inventory** app by designing its graphical user interface. You learned how to use Labels to describe controls and how to set a Label's TextAlign and BorderStyle properties. You used these properties to distinguish between descriptive and output Labels.

After labeling your Form, you added TextBoxes to allow users to input data from the keyboard. Finally, you added a Button to the **Inventory** app, allowing a user to signal the app to perform an action (in this case, to multiply two numbers and display the result). While adding controls to the Form, you also learned some GUI design tips to help you create appealing and intuitive graphical user interfaces.

The next chapter teaches you to program code in Visual Basic that runs when the user clicks the **Calculate Total** Button. When the Button is clicked, the app receives a signal called an *event*. You'll learn how to program your app to respond to that event by performing the multiplication calculation and displaying the result.

SKILLS SUMMARY

Creating a New Project

- Select **File > New Project...** to create a project.
- In the **New Project** dialog, select the **Windows Forms Application** template and provide a descriptive name in the **Name:** TextBox.
- Select **File > Save All** to save a project to your working directory (C:\SimplyVB2010) by selecting it from the **Project Location** dialog.

Setting the App's Font to Segoe UI

- Select Segoe UI from the Font Name property ComboBox in the Form's **Properties** window. Set the Font Size property to 9.

Creating a Descriptive Label

- Add a Label to your Form, then change the TextAlign property to MiddleLeft.
- Use sentence-style capitalization in the label and end the label's text with a colon (:).

Creating an Output Label

- Add a Label to your Form, and change the BorderStyle property to Fixed3D and the TextAlign property to MiddleCenter.

Enabling User Input from the Keyboard

- Add a TextBox control to your Form.

Signaling That the App Should Perform an Action

- Add a Button to the Form, and write program code to perform that action. (You'll learn how to add program code in Chapter 5.)

KEY TERMS

book-title capitalization—A style that capitalizes the first letter of each significant word in the text (for example, **Calculate Total**).

BorderStyle property—Specifies the appearance of a Label's border, which allows you to distinguish one control from another visually. The BorderStyle property can be set to None (no border), FixedSingle (a single dark line as a border), or Fixed3D (giving the Label a "sunken" appearance).

Button control—When clicked, commands the app to perform an action.

descriptive Label—A Label used to describe another control on the Form. This helps users understand a control's purpose.

Location property—Specifies the location (*x*- and *y*-coordinates) of the upper-left corner of a control. This property is used to place a control on the Form precisely.

Name property—Assigns a unique and meaningful name to a control for easy identification.

output Label—A Label used to display results.

sentence-style capitalization—A style that capitalizes the first letter of the first word in the text. Every other letter in the text is lowercase, unless it's the first letter of a proper noun (for example, **Cartons per shipment**).

Segoe UI font—The Microsoft-recommended font for use in Windows 7 apps.

Size property—Property that specifies the width and height, in pixels, of the Form or one of its controls.

snaplines—The IDE displays blue and purple lines called snaplines as you drag controls around a Form. The blue lines help you position controls relative to one another. The purple lines help you position controls relative to the control text.

Text property—Sets the text displayed on a control.

TextAlign property—Specifies how text is aligned within a Label.

TextBox control—Retrieves user input from the keyboard.

GUI DESIGN GUIDELINES

Overall Design

- Leave space between the edges of the Form and its controls.
- Although you can drag a Label control to a location on the Form, the Location property can be used to specify a precise position.
- Place an app's output below and/or to the right of the Form's input controls.
- As you drag controls, the IDE displays blue and purple lines called snaplines. The blue lines help you position controls relative to one another. The purple lines help you position controls relative to the control text.

Buttons

- Buttons are labeled using their Text property. These labels should use book-title capitalization and be brief while still being meaningful to the user.
- Buttons should be stacked downward from the top right of a Form or arranged on the same line starting from the bottom right of a Form.

Forms

- Changing the Form's title allows users to identify the Form's purpose.
- Form titles should use book-title capitalization.
- Change the Form font to 9pt Segoe UI to be consistent with Microsoft's recommended font for Windows 7.
- Microsoft recommends using italic fonts only to emphasize text and bold fonts only to focus the user's attention on text that the user must read. (For more information, see msdn.microsoft.com/en-us/library/windows/desktop/aa511282.aspx.)

Labels

- A Label used to describe the purpose of a control should use sentence-style capitalization and end with a colon. These types of Labels are called descriptive Labels.
- The TextAlign property of a descriptive Label should be set to MiddleLeft. This ensures that text within groups of Labels aligns.
- Place each descriptive Label above or to the left of the control (for instance, a TextBox) that it identifies.
- Align the left or right sides of a group of descriptive Labels if the Labels are arranged vertically.
- Use a descriptive Label to identify an output Label.
- Output Labels should be distinguishable from descriptive Labels. This can be done by setting the BorderStyle property of an output Label to Fixed3D.
- If several output Labels are arranged vertically to display numbers used in a mathematical calculation (such as in an invoice), use the MiddleRight value for the TextAlign property.
- A descriptive Label and the control it identifies should be aligned on the left if they're arranged vertically.
- The text in a descriptive Label and the text in the control it identifies should be aligned if they're arranged horizontally.

TextBoxes

- Use TextBoxes to input data from the keyboard.

- Each TextBox should have a descriptive Label indicating the input expected from the user.
- Make TextBoxes wide enough for their expected inputs.

CONTROLS, EVENTS,
PROPERTIES &
METHODS

Button   When clicked, commands the app to perform an action.

- *In action*

- *Properties*

  Location—Specifies the location of the Button relative to the container's top-left corner.

  Name—Specifies the name used to identify the Button. The name should include the Button suffix.

  Size—Specifies the width and height (in pixels) of the Button.

  Text—Specifies the text displayed on the Button.

Form   Represents the main window of a GUI app.

- *In action*

- *Properties*

  BackColor—Specifies the background color of the Form.

  Font—Specifies the font name, style and size of any displayed text in the Form. The Form's controls use this font by default.

  Name—Specifies the name used to identify the Form. The name should include the Form suffix.

  Size—Specifies the width and height (in pixels) of the Form.

  Text—Specifies the text displayed in the title bar of a Form.

Label   A Label   This control displays text that the user cannot modify.

- *In action*

  Total: 45

- *Properties*

  AutoSize—Allows for automatic resizing of the Label to fit its contents.

  BorderStyle—Specifies the appearance of the Label's border.

  Font—Specifies the font name, style and size of the text displayed in the Label.

  Location—Specifies the location of the Label on the Form relative to the Form's top-left corner.

  Name—Specifies the name used to identify the Label. The name should include the Label suffix.

  Size—Specifies the width and height (in pixels) of the Label.

  Text—Specifies the text displayed in the Label.

  TextAlign—Determines how the text is aligned within the Label.

TextBox   [abl] TextBox   This control allows the user to input data from the keyboard.

■ *In action*

> | 0 |

■ *Properties*

Location—Specifies the location of the TextBox on the Form relative to the Form's top-left corner.

Name—Specifies the name used to identify the TextBox. The name should include the TextBox suffix.

Size—Specifies the width and height (in pixels) of the TextBox.

Text—Specifies the initial text displayed in the TextBox.

TextAlign—Specifies how the text is aligned within the TextBox.

Width—Specifies the width (in pixels) of the TextBox.

MULTIPLE-CHOICE QUESTIONS

4.1 A new Windows app is created by selecting _____ from the **File** menu.

   a) **New Program**
   b) **New File...**
   c) **New Project...**
   d) **New App**

4.2 A Label's BorderStyle property can be set to _____.

   a) Fixed3D
   b) Single
   c) 3D
   d) All of the above

4.3 When creating a Label, you can specify the Label's _____.

   a) text alignment
   b) border style
   c) size
   d) All of the above

4.4 Changing the value stored in the _____ property changes the name of the Form's file.

   a) Name
   b) File
   c) File Name
   d) Full Path

4.5 _____ should be appended as a suffix to all TextBox names.

   a) Text Box
   b) Text
   c) Box
   d) TextBox

4.6 A(n) _____ helps the user understand a control's purpose.

   a) Button
   b) descriptive Label
   c) output Label
   d) title bar

4.7 A _____ is a control in which the user can enter data from a keyboard.

   a) Button
   b) TextBox
   c) Label
   d) PictureBox

4.8 A descriptive Label should use _____.

   a) sentence-style capitalization
   b) book-title capitalization
   c) a colon at the end of its text
   d) Both a and c

4.9 You should use the _____ font in your Windows 7 apps.

   a) Segoe UI
   b) MS Sans Serif
   c) Times
   d) Palatino

4.10 _____ should be appended as a suffix to all Button names.

   a) Press
   b) Label
   c) Click
   d) Button

EXERCISES   *At the end of each chapter, you'll find a summary of new GUI design tips listed in the GUI Design Guidelines section. A cumulative list of GUI design guidelines, organized by control, appears in Appendix C. In these exercises, you'll find Visual Basic Forms that do not follow the GUI design guidelines presented in this chapter. For each exercise, modify control properties so that your end result is consistent with the guidelines presented in the chapter. Note that these apps do not provide any functionality.*

4.11 *(Address Book GUI)* In this exercise, you apply the GUI design guidelines you've learned to a graphical user interface for an address book (Fig. 4.21).

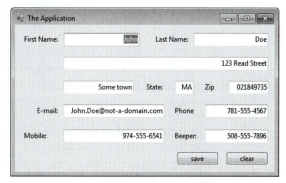

Figure 4.21   **Address Book** app without GUI design guidelines applied.

a) *Copying the template to your working directory.* Copy the directory `C:\Examples\ch04\Exercises\AddressBook` to your `C:\SimplyVB2010` directory.

b) *Opening the app's template file.* Double click `AddressBook.sln` in the AddressBook directory to open the app.

c) *Applying GUI design guidelines.* Rearrange the controls and modify properties so that the GUI conforms to the design guidelines you've learned.

d) *Saving the project.* Select **File > Save All** to save your changes.

4.12 *(Mortgage Calculator GUI)* In this exercise, you apply the GUI design guidelines you've learned to a graphical user interface for a mortgage calculator (Fig. 4.22).

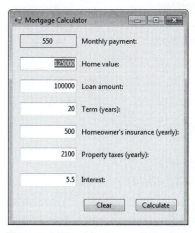

Figure 4.22   **Mortgage Calculator** app without GUI design guidelines applied.

a) *Copying the template to your working directory.* Copy the directory `C:\Examples\ch04\Exercises\MortgageCalculator` to your `C:\SimplyVB2010` directory.

b) *Opening the app's template file.* Double click `MortgageCalculator.sln` in the MortgageCalculator directory to open the app.

c) *Applying GUI design guidelines.* Rearrange the controls and modify properties so that the GUI conforms to the design guidelines you've learned.

d) *Saving the project.* Select **File > Save All** to save your changes.

4.13 *(Password GUI)* In this exercise, you apply the GUI design guidelines you've learned to a graphical user interface for a password-protected message app (Fig. 4.23).

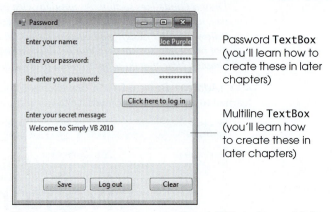

Figure 4.23 **Password** app without GUI design guidelines applied.

a) *Copying the template to your working directory.* Copy the directory C:\Examples\ch04\Exercises\Password to your C:\SimplyVB2010 directory.

b) *Opening the app's template file.* Double click Password.sln in the Password directory to open the app.

c) *Applying GUI design guidelines.* Rearrange the controls and modify properties so that the GUI conforms to the design guidelines you've learned.

d) *Saving the project.* Select **File > Save All** to save your changes.

Programming Challenge ▶

4.14 *(Monitor Invoice GUI)* In this exercise, you apply the GUI design guidelines you've learned to a graphical user interface for an invoice app (Fig. 4.24).

Figure 4.24 **Invoice** app without GUI design guidelines applied.

a) *Copying the template to your working directory.* Copy the directory C:\Examples\ch04\Exercises\MonitorInvoice to your C:\SimplyVB2010 directory.

b) *Opening the app's template file.* Double click the MonitorInvoice.sln file to open the app.

c) *Applying GUI design guidelines.* Rearrange the controls and modify properties so that the GUI conforms to the design guidelines you've learned.

d) *Saving the project.* Select **File > Save All** to save your changes.

Objectives

In this chapter, you'll learn to:
- Add an event handler for a `Button` control.
- Insert code into an event handler.
- Access a property's value by using Visual Basic code.
- Use the assignment and multiplication operators.
- Use the Visual Basic IDE to fix compilation errors.

Outline

Completing the Inventory App

Introducing Programming

This chapter introduces fundamentals of programming to create an app with which users can interact. You'll learn these concepts as you add functionality (with Visual Basic program code) to the **Inventory** app you designed in Chapter 4. The term **functionality** describes the actions an app can execute. In this chapter, you'll examine GUI events, which represent user actions, such as clicking a `Button` or altering a value in a `TextBox`, and **event handlers**, which are pieces of code that execute when such events occur (that is, when the events are "raised"). You'll learn why events and event handlers are crucial to programming Windows apps.

5.1 Test-Driving the Inventory App

In this chapter, you'll complete the **Inventory** app you designed in Chapter 4. Recall that the app must meet the following requirements:

> **App Requirements**
>
> *A college bookstore receives cartons of textbooks. In each shipment, all cartons contain the same number of textbooks. The inventory manager wants to use a computer to calculate the total number of textbooks arriving at the bookstore for each shipment. The inventory manager will enter the number of cartons received and the fixed number of textbooks in each carton for each shipment; then the app will calculate the total number of textbooks in the shipment.*

The inventory manager has reviewed and approved your design. Now you must add program code that, when the user clicks a `Button`, makes the app multiply the number of cartons by the number of textbooks per carton and display the result—the total number of textbooks received. You'll begin by test-driving the completed app. Then you'll learn the additional Visual Basic capabilities needed to create your own version of this app.

1. ***Opening the completed app.*** Open the directory C:\Examples\ch05\Com-pletedApp\Inventory2 to locate the **Inventory** app. Double click Inventory2.sln to open the app in the Visual Basic IDE.

2. ***Running the Inventory app.*** Select **Debug > Start Debugging** to run the app (Fig. 5.1). Enter 3 in the **Cartons per shipment:** TextBox. Enter 15 in the **Items per carton:** TextBox. Figure 5.1 shows the Form after these values have been entered.

Figure 5.1 **Inventory** app with quantities entered.

3. ***Calculating the total number of items received.*** Click the **Calculate Total** Button. The app multiplies the two numbers you entered and displays the result (45) in the Label to the right of **Total:** (Fig. 5.2).

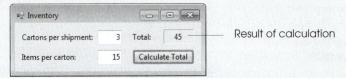

Result of calculation

Figure 5.2 Result of clicking the **Calculate Total** Button in the **Inventory** app.

4. ***Closing the app.*** Close your running app by clicking its close box.

5. ***Closing the IDE.*** Select **File > Exit**.

5.2 Introduction to Visual Basic Program Code

In Chapter 3 and Chapter 4, you were introduced to visual programming, which allows you to create GUIs without writing any program code. In this section, you combine visual programming with conventional programming techniques to enhance the **Inventory** app.

Before you begin to view and edit code, you should customize the way the IDE displays and formats your code. In the following box, you open the template app and change the display and format settings to make it easy for you to work with code and follow our discussions. Adding line numbers, adjusting tab sizes and setting fonts and colors help you navigate your code more easily.

Customizing the IDE

1. ***Copying the template to your working directory.*** Copy the C:\Examples\ch05\TemplateApp\Inventory2 directory to C:\SimplyVB2010. This directory contains the app created by following the steps in Chapter 4.

2. ***Opening the Inventory app's template file.*** Double click Inventory2.sln in the Inventory2 directory to open the app in the Visual Basic IDE. If an error occurs when you try to copy or modify the template, please consult your system administrator to ensure that you have proper privileges to edit these apps.

(cont.)   3. ***Displaying line numbers.*** In our programming discussions, we refer to specific code elements by line number. To help you locate where to insert code in the examples, you need to enable the IDE's capability to show line numbers in your code. Select **Tools > Options…**, and, in the **Options** dialog that appears (Fig. 5.3), expand the **Text Editor Basic** category by clicking the triangle next to it. [*Note:* Make sure the **Show all settings** CheckBox is *not* selected—otherwise the dialog displays different categories.] Select the **Editor** category that subsequently appears (Fig. 5.4) and locate the **Interaction** group of CheckBoxes in this category. If the CheckBox next to **Line numbers** isn't checked, click inside the box to add a checkmark. If the box is already checked, you need not do anything; however, do not close the dialog.

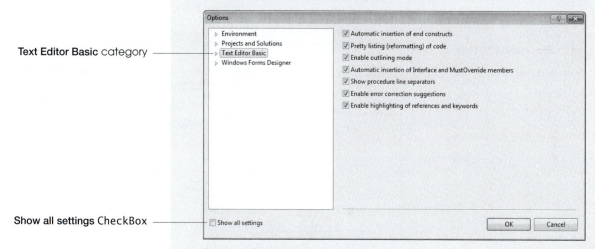

Text Editor Basic category

Show all settings CheckBox

Figure 5.3   **Options** dialog.

4. ***Setting the tab size.*** Just as you indent the first line of each paragraph when writing a letter, it's important to use proper spacing when writing code. Indenting code improves program readability. You can control indents with tabs. In the **Options** dialog that you opened in the preceding step (Fig. 5.4), enter 3 for both the tab size and indent size fields.

The tab size setting indicates the number of spaces each tab character represents. The **Indent size:** setting determines the number of spaces each indent inserted by the Visual Basic IDE represents. The IDE inserts three spaces for you if you're using the **Smart** indenting feature (Fig. 5.4)—you can insert them yourself with one keystroke by pressing the *Tab* key.

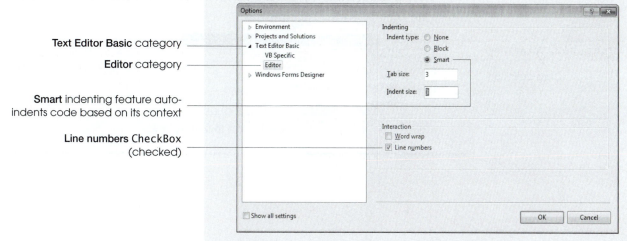

Text Editor Basic category

Editor category

Smart indenting feature auto-indents code based on its context

Line numbers CheckBox (checked)

Figure 5.4   **General** settings page for the Visual Basic text editor.

(cont.)

**Good Programming
Practice**

You can change the font and color settings if you prefer a different appearance for your code. To remain consistent with this book, however, we recommend that you not change the default font and color settings.

5. ***Exploring fonts and colors.*** Some people prefer to work with fonts and colors that differ from the IDE's defaults. If you wish to change the default fonts and colors, click the triangle next to the **Environment** category; then click the **Fonts and Colors** category that appears. The subsequent screen allows you to customize fonts and colors used to display code. The Visual Basic IDE can apply colors and fonts to make it easier for you to read and edit code. Note that, if your settings are not consistent with the default settings, what you see on your screen will appear different from what is presented in this book. If you need to reset your settings to the default for fonts and colors, click the **Use Defaults** Button (Fig. 5.5).

6. ***Applying your changes.*** Click the **OK** Button to apply your changes and dismiss the **Options** dialog.

Use Defaults Button

Fonts and Colors category

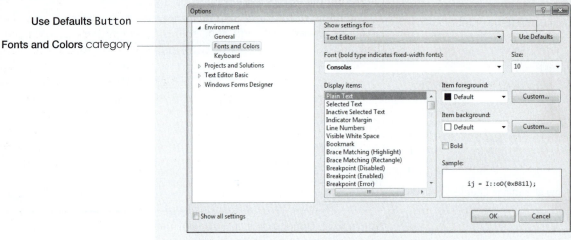

Figure 5.5 Examining the **Fonts and Colors** page.

Next, you'll take your first peek at Visual Basic code.

Introducing Visual Basic Code

1. ***Viewing app code.*** If the Windows Form Designer isn't open, double click the Inventory.vb file in the **Solution Explorer** window. Then switch to Code view (where the app's code is displayed in an editor window) by selecting **View > Code** or pressing *F7*. The tabbed window (Inventory.vb) in Fig. 5.6, also called a **code editor**, appears. When you're asked to select **View > Code**, the Inventory.vb file must be selected in the **Solution Explorer**.

Inventory.vb tabbed window

Class definition

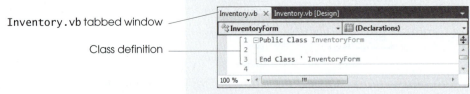

Figure 5.6 IDE showing code for the **Inventory** app.

(cont.)

Most Visual Basic programs consist of pieces called *classes*, which simplify app organization. Recall from Chapter 1 that classes contain groups of code statements that perform tasks and return information when the tasks are completed. The code in this app defines your **Inventory** app class. These lines collectively are called a **class definition**. Most apps consist of a combination of code written by programmers (like you) and preexisting classes written and provided by Microsoft in the .NET Framework Class Library. Again, the key to successful Visual Basic app development is achieving the right mix of the two. You'll learn how to use both techniques in your programs.

2. *Examining class definitions.* Line 1 (Fig. 5.6) begins the class definition. The **Class keyword** introduces a class definition in Visual Basic and is immediately followed by the **class name** (InventoryForm in this app, the value you entered in the Form's Name property).

The name of the class is an **identifier**, which is a series of characters consisting of letters, digits and underscores (_). Identifiers cannot begin with a digit and cannot contain spaces. Examples of valid identifiers are value1, label_Value and exitButton. The name 7welcome isn't a valid identifier, because it begins with a digit, and the name input field isn't a valid identifier, because it contains a space. The class definition ends at line 3 with the keywords **End Class**. **Keywords** are *reserved* for use by Visual Basic (you'll learn the various keywords throughout the text). Reserved words cannot be used as identifiers. Note that keywords appear in blue by default in the IDE. A complete list of Visual Basic keywords can be found in Appendix D, Keyword Chart.

The Class keyword is preceded by the Public keyword. The code for every Form you design in the Visual Basic IDE begins with the Public keyword. You'll learn about this keyword in Chapter 19.

Visual Basic keywords and identifiers are *not* **case sensitive**. This means that uppercase and lowercase letters are considered to be identical in identifiers; this practice causes InventoryForm and inventoryform to be understood by Visual Basic as the same identifier. Although the first letter of every keyword is capitalized, keywords are nevertheless not case sensitive. The IDE applies the correct case to each letter of a keyword and identifier, so when you type clasS, it changes to Class when you press the *Enter* key.

Good Programming Practice

Capitalize the first letter of each class identifier, such as the Form name.

SELF-REVIEW

1. Identifiers _____.
   a) can begin with any character, but cannot contain spaces
   b) must begin with a digit, but cannot contain spaces
   c) cannot begin with a digit and cannot contain spaces
   d) cannot begin with a digit, but can contain spaces

2. Visual Basic keywords are _____.
   a) case sensitive   b) comments
   c) not reserved words   d) not case sensitive

Answers: 1) c. 2) d.

5.3 Inserting an Event Handler

Now that you've finalized the GUI, you're ready to modify the app to respond to user input. You'll do this by inserting code manually. Most of the Visual Basic apps in this book provide functionality in the form of event handlers. Recall that an event handler executes when the event (such as clicking a Button) with which it is associated occurs. The next box shows you how to add an event handler to your app.

**Adding a Button's
Click Event Handler**

Asterisks indicate unsaved
changes to app

Empty event handler

1. **Adding an event handler for the Button.** In this step, you use the Windows Form Designer to create an event handler and enter **Code** view. Begin by clicking the Inventory.vb [Design] tab to view the Windows Form Designer. Then double click the Form's **Calculate Total** Button to enter **Code** view. Note that the code for the app, which now includes the new event handler in lines 3–5 of Fig. 5.7, is displayed.

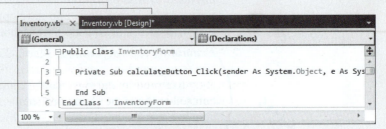

Figure 5.7 Adding event handler `calculateButton_Click` before you add your program code.

Double clicking the **Calculate Total** Button in **Design** view caused the IDE to generate the Button's `Click` event handler—the code that executes when the user clicks the **Calculate Total** Button. When you double click a control, the IDE inserts an event handler for that control (or displays the event handler, if it already exists). [*Note:* If you accidentally create an event handler, you can simply delete the generated code.] The type of event that's handled differs based on the control. For instance, double clicking a Button control creates a `Click` event handler. Double clicking other controls generates other types of event handlers. Each control has a default type of event handler that's generated when you double click the control in **Design** view.

At the end of each event handler's first line, Visual Basic inserts a Handles clause. Scroll to the right in **Code** view to see the Handles clause for the **Calculate Total** Button's `Click` event handler (line 3)

```
Handles calculateButton.Click
```

This **Handles clause** indicates that the event handler is called when the `calculateButton`'s `Click` event occurs.

In Visual Basic, event handlers by convention follow the naming scheme *controlName_eventName*. This *convention* mimics the event handler's Handles clause. The word *controlName* refers to the name of the control provided in its Name property (in this case, `calculateButton`) and *eventName* represents the name of the event (in this case, `Click`) raised by the control. When event *eventName* occurs on the control *controlName*, event handler *controlName_eventName* executes. In this app, `calculateButton_Click` handles the **Calculate Total** Button's `Click` event, so the code in `calculateButton_Click` executes when the user clicks the **Calculate Total** Button.

2. **Running the app.** Select **Debug > Start Debugging** to run the app (Fig. 5.8). The IDE automatically saves your work before running the app. Click the **Calculate Total** Button.

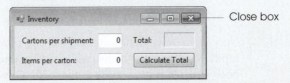

Close box

Figure 5.8 Running the app without functionality.

(cont.)

Although you've added an event handler for the Button's Click event, no action occurs when you click the Button because you have not yet added any code to the event handler. In the next box, you add code so that, when a user clicks the Button, text displays in the output Label (totalResultLabel).

3. ***Closing the app.*** Close the running app by clicking its close box—you cannot edit the app's code while it's running.

Now that you've created an event handler for the **Calculate Total** Button, you need to insert code to perform an action. Specifically, you need to make the app multiply the number of cartons in a shipment by the fixed number of items per carton when a user clicks the **Calculate Total** Button. You write your first Visual Basic statement in the following box.

Adding Code to an Empty Event Handler

Good Programming Practice

You may spread a lengthy statement over several lines. When doing so, choose breaking points that make sense, such as after an operator, and indent all subsequent lines with one "level" of indentation.

Common Programming Error

Placing nonwhitespace characters, to the right of a line-continuation character is a compilation error. Compilation errors are introduced in the box, *Using the IDE to Eliminate Compilation Errors* in Section 5.5.

1. ***Changing to Code view.*** If you're not already in **Code** view, select **View > Code** to view the app's code.

2. ***Reformatting the event handler.*** Line 3 of Fig. 5.7 is too long to fit on a single line in our book, so we split it into two lines as shown in lines 3–4 of Fig. 5.9. To improve readability, long statements may be split over several lines. Earlier versions of Visual Basic required you to use the **line-continuation character** (_) to do split lines as follows:

```
Private Sub calculateButton_Click(sender As System.Object, _
    e As System.EventArgs) Handles calculateButton.Click
```

The _ character at the end of the first line above indicates that the next line is a *continuation* of the previous line. A single statement can contain as many line-continuation characters as necessary. However, at least one space character must precede each line-continuation character and only whitespace characters (i.e., spaces, tabs and newlines) may appear to the right of a line-continuation character.

As of Visual Basic 2010, line-continuation characters are not required in most cases, so we'll use them only when necessary. For the few cases in which they're still required, the compiler will tell you if you do not include them.

```
1   Public Class InventoryForm
2
3       Private Sub calculateButton_Click(sender As System.Object,
4           e As System.EventArgs) Handles calculateButton.Click
5
6       End Sub
7   End Class ' InventoryForm
```

Figure 5.9   Code after reformatting calculateButtons_click's first line.

3. ***Adding code to the event handler.*** In the event handler, insert lines 6–7 of Fig. 5.10 by typing the text on the screen. Add the text in line 8 following the keywords End Sub.

Event handler ⎯⎯

```
3       Private Sub calculateButton_Click(sender As System.Object,
4           e As System.EventArgs) Handles calculateButton.Click
5
```

Type this code ⎯⎯

```
6       ' display cartonsTextBox input in totalResultLabel
7       totalResultLabel.Text = cartonsTextBox.Text
8       End Sub ' calculateButton_Click
```

Figure 5.10   Code added to the **Calculate Total** Button's event handler.

(cont.)

Good Programming Practice

Comments written at the end of a line should be preceded by a space, to enhance program readability.

Line 6 of Fig. 5.10 begins with a **single-quote character** (`'`), which indicates that the remainder of the line is a **comment**. You insert comments in programs to improve the readability of your code. These comments explain the code so that other programmers who need to work with the app can understand it more easily. By default, comments are displayed in green.

Comments also help you read your own code, especially when you haven't looked at it for a while. Comments can be placed either on their own lines (these are called "full-line comments") or at the end of a line of Visual Basic code (these are called "end-of-line comments").

The Visual Basic compiler *ignores* comments—they do *not* cause the computer to perform any actions when your apps run. The comment in line 6 simply indicates that the next line displays the value entered into the **Cartons per shipment:** TextBox in the **Total:** Label. Comments appear in green when displayed in the code editor of the Visual Basic IDE.

Line 7 of Fig. 5.10 presents your first executable Visual Basic **statement**, which performs an action. This statement (line 7) accesses the `Text` properties of `cartonsTextBox` and `totalResultLabel`. In Visual Basic, properties are accessed in code by placing a period between the control name (for example, `totalResultLabel`) and the property name (for example, `Text`). This period, which is placed to the right of the control name, is called the **member-access operator** (`.`), or the **dot operator**. When the control name and member-access operator are typed, a window appears listing that object's members (Fig. 5.11). This convenience feature, known as *IntelliSense*, displays items that are available in the program and can be used in the current context, such as all the members in an object. The *IntelliSense* window can also be opened by pressing *Ctrl + Space*. You scroll to the member you're interested in and select it. You also can continue typing to narrow down the choices. Click the member name once to display a description of that member; double click it to add the member's name to your app. You can also press *Enter* or *Tab* to insert the member—*Tab* inserts the member, *Enter* inserts the member and a new line. *IntelliSense* can be useful in discovering a class's members and their purpose. The *IntelliSense* window in Fig. 5.11 shows two tabs—**Common** and **All**. The **Common** tab shows the *most commonly used* members that can appear to the right of the dot operator. The **All** tab shows *every* member that can appear there. You can close the *IntelliSense* window by pressing *Esc*.

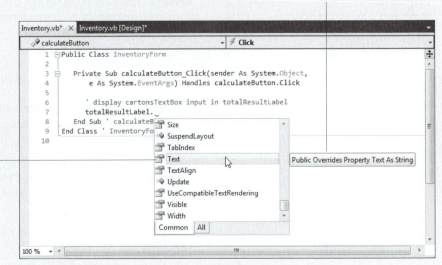

Figure 5.11 *IntelliSense* activating while entering code.

(cont.)

Let's examine line 7 of Fig. 5.10 more closely. Reading the line from left to right, we see `totalResultLabel`'s `Text` property, followed by an "equals" sign (=), followed by `cartonsTextBox`'s `Text` property value. The "=" symbol, as used here, is known as the **assignment operator**. The expressions on either side of the assignment operator are referred to as its **operands**. This assignment operator assigns the value on the right of the operator (the **right operand**) to the variable on the left of the operator (the **left operand**). The assignment operator is known as a **binary operator** because it has *two* operands—`totalResultLabel.Text` and `cartonsTextBox.Text`.

The entire statement is called an **assignment statement** because it assigns a value to the left operand. In this example, you're assigning the value of `cartonsTextBox`'s `Text` property to `totalResultLabel`'s `Text` property. The statement is read as, "The `Text` property of `totalResultLabel` *gets* the value of `cartonTextBox`'s `Text` property." The right operand is unchanged by the assignment statement.

When the user clicks the **Calculate Total** `Button`, the event handler executes, displaying the value the user entered in the **Cartons per shipment:** `TextBox` in the output `Label` `totalResultLabel`. Clearly, this is *not* the correct result—the correct result is the number of items per carton times the number of cartons per shipment. In the box *Completing the **Inventory** App*, you correct this error. We've added a comment in line 8 of Fig. 5.10, indicating the end of our event handler.

> ![Good Programming Practice icon] **Good Programming Practice**
>
> Add comments following the **End Sub** keywords to indicate the end of an event handler.

4. ***Running the app.*** Select **Debug > Start Debugging** to run the app (Fig. 5.12). Type 5 into the **Cartons per shipment:** `TextBox` and 10 into the **Items per carton:** `TextBox`, then click the **Calculate Total** `Button`. The text of `totalResultLabel` now incorrectly displays the data, 5, that was entered into the **Cartons per shipment:** `TextBox`, rather than the correct result, 50. You'll fix this in the next box.

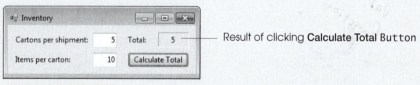

Result of clicking **Calculate Total** `Button`

Figure 5.12 Running the app with the event handler.

5. ***Closing the app.*** Close the running app by clicking its close box.

SELF-REVIEW   1. Event handlers generated by the Visual Basic IDE follow the naming convention
_____.

   a) *controlName_eventName*   b) *eventName_controlName*
   c) *eventNameControlName*   d) *controlNameEventName*

2. The expressions on either side of the assignment operator are referred to as its
_____.

   a) operator values   b) results
   c) operands   d) arguments

Answers: 1) a. 2) c.

5.4 Performing a Calculation and Displaying the Result

Now that you're familiar with displaying output in a `Label`, you'll complete the **Inventory** app by displaying the product of the number of cartons per shipment and the number of items per carton. In the following box, you'll learn how to perform mathematical operations in Visual Basic.

**Completing the
Inventory App**

1. ***Performing the calculation.*** Replace the body of `calculateButton_Click` with the code in lines 6–8. The comment in line 6 indicates that you'll be multiplying the two values entered by the user and displaying the result in a `Label`.

```
1   Public Class InventoryForm
2
3      Private Sub calculateButton_Click(sender As System.Object,
4         e As System.EventArgs) Handles calculateButton.Click
5
6         ' multiply values input and display result in Label
7         totalResultLabel.Text =
8            Val(cartonsTextBox.Text) * Val(itemsTextBox.Text)
9      End Sub ' calculateButton_Click
10  End Class ' InventoryForm
```

Figure 5.13   Using multiplication in the **Inventory** app.

2. ***Adding multiline code.*** The statement in lines 7–8 performs the multiplication and assignment. We use the assignment operator to assign a value to `totalResultLabel.Text` in line 7. The Visual Basic compiler knows that the statement continues past the current line, because an assignment (=) must always have a right operand.

The assignment operator in line 7 assigns the result of multiplying the numbers entered by the user to `totalResultLabel.Text`. In line 8, the expression `Val(cartonsTextBox.Text)` is followed by an asterisk (*), then the expression `Val(itemsTextBox.Text)`. The asterisk is known as the **multiplication operator**—the operator's left and right operands are multiplied together.

Your **Inventory** app cannot prevent users from accidentally entering nonnumeric input, such as letters and special characters like $ and @. Line 8 uses the **Val function** to prevent inputs like this from terminating the app. A function is a piece of code that performs a task when called (executed) and sends, or returns, a value to the location from which it was called. In this case, the values returned by `Val` become the values used in the multiplication expression (line 8). You call functions (as in line 8) by typing their name followed by parentheses. Any values inside the parentheses (for example, `cartonsTextBox.Text`) are known as function **arguments**. Arguments are inputs to the function that provide information the function needs to perform its task. In this case, the argument specifies which value you want to send to function `Val`. You'll learn how to create your own functions in Chapter 13.

Function `Val` obtains a value from a string of characters (keyboard input). The value obtained is *guaranteed* to be a number. We use `Val` because this app isn't intended to perform arithmetic calculations with characters that are not numbers. `Val` reads its argument from left to right one character at a time until it either processes the right-most character or it reads a character that makes no sense as a number. Once the end of the character string or a nonsense character is read, `Val` returns the number it has read up to that point. `Val` ignores whitespace characters (for example, "33 5" will be converted to 335). Figure 5.14 presents samples of `Val` calls and their results. `Val` recognizes the decimal point as a numeric character, and recognizes the plus and minus signs when they appear at the beginning of the string (to indicate that a number is positive or negative). `Val` does not recognize such symbols as commas and dollar signs. If function `Val` receives an argument that cannot be converted to a number (for example, "b35", which begins with a nonnumeric character), it returns 0. The result of the calculation is assigned to `totalResultLabel.Text` (line 7), to display the result to the user.

(cont.)

   Be careful when using Val—although the value returned is a number, it's not always the value the user intended (see Fig. 5.14). If incorrect data is entered by the user, Val makes no indication of the error. The function returns a value (usually not the value intended by the user) and the app continues, possibly using the incorrect input in calculations. For example, someone entering a monetary amount may enter the text $10.23, which Val evaluates to 0. Note how a common mistake causes an app to execute incorrectly. Visual Basic provides two ways to handle invalid input. One is to use Visual Basic's *string-processing* capabilities to examine input. You'll learn about such capabilities as you read this book. The other form of handling invalid input is called *exception handling*, where you write code to handle errors that may be raised as the app executes. You'll learn about exception handling in Chapter 24.

3. ***Running the app.*** Select **Debug > Start Debugging** to run your app. Now you can enter data in both TextBoxes. When the **Calculate Total** Button is clicked, the app multiplies the two numbers entered and displays the result in totalResultLabel.

4. ***Closing the app.*** Close the running app by clicking its close box.

5. ***Saving the project.*** Select **File > Save All** to save your modified code.

Val function call examples	Results
Val("16")	16
Val("-3")	-3
Val("1.5")	1.5
Val("67a4")	67
Val("8+5")	8
Val("14 Main St.")	14
Val("+1 2 3 4 5")	12345
Val("hello")	0

Figure 5.14 Val function call examples.

Figure 5.15 presents the **Inventory** app's code. The lines of code that contain new programming concepts you learned in this chapter are highlighted.

```
1  Public Class InventoryForm
2
3     Private Sub calculateButton_Click(sender As System.Object,
4        e As System.EventArgs) Handles calculateButton.Click
5
6        ' multiply values input and display result in Label
7        totalResultLabel.Text =
8           Val(cartonsTextBox.Text) * Val(itemsTextBox.Text)
9     End Sub ' calculateButton_Click
10 End Class ' InventoryForm
```

Figure 5.15 **Inventory** app code.

SELF-REVIEW 1. _____ provide information that functions need to perform their tasks.
   a) Comments   b) Arguments
   c) Outputs   d) Both a and b

2. What is the result of `Val("%5")`?

    a) 5   b) 0

    c) 500   d) 0.05

Answers: 1) b. 2) b.

5.5 Using the IDE to Eliminate Compilation Errors

So far in this book, you've executed apps by selecting **Debug > Start Debugging**. This compiles and runs the app. If you do not write your code correctly, errors appear in a window known as the **Error List**. **Debugging** is the process of fixing errors in an app. There are two types of errors—compilation errors and logic errors. Compilation errors occur when code statements violate the grammatical rules of the programming language or when code statements are simply incorrect in the current context. Some examples of compilation errors include misspellings of keywords or identifiers, failure to include a parenthesis where one is required or using an identifier in the wrong context. An app cannot be executed until *all* of its compilation errors are corrected. Some compilation errors are known as **syntax errors**. These are specifically the errors that violate the grammatical rules of the programming language, such as lack of a parenthesis where one is required.

    Logic errors do not prevent the app from compiling successfully, but do cause the app to produce erroneous results. The Visual Basic IDE contains a **debugger** that allows you to analyze the behavior of your app to determine whether it's executing correctly and help you locate and remove logic errors.

    You can compile an app without executing it by selecting **Debug > Build** *ProjectName*, where *ProjectName* appears as the name of your current project. Programmers frequently do this when they wish to determine whether there are any compilation errors in their code. Using either **Debug > Start Debugging** or **Debug > Build** *ProjectName* will display any compilation errors in the **Error List** window.

    For each error displayed in the **Error List** window, the IDE provides a description of the error. Figure 5.16 displays the errors that appear when the keyword `Class` is missing from `End Class` at the end of the code (line 10 in Fig. 5.15). Typically, when more than one error message is displayed (as in this case), the first error listed could be the cause of one or more of the remaining errors (which is the case here). Double click the first error in the **Error List** window to go the location of the error in the code. Sometime the IDE will display an **Error Correction** window with additional information about the error and possible ways to fix it. In the next box, you'll create the compilation error we just discussed, view the results and fix the errors.

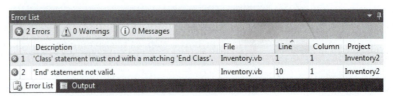

Figure 5.16   **Error List** lists compilation errors.

Using the IDE to Eliminate Compilation Errors

1. *Opening the completed app.* If the **Inventory** app isn't currently open, locate the `Inventory2.sln` file, then double click it to load your app in the IDE.

2. *Creating your own compilation errors.* Now you'll create your own compilation errors, for demonstration purposes. If you're not in **Code** view, select **View > Code**. Open the **Error List** window by selecting **View > Other Windows > Error List**. Remove the keyword Class in line 10. Note the changes to the IDE (Fig. 5.17).

(cont.)

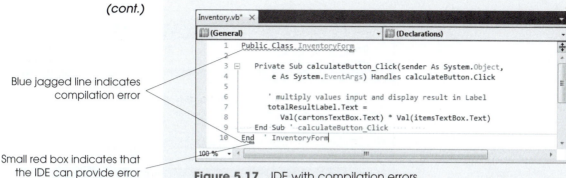

Blue jagged line indicates compilation error

Small red box indicates that the IDE can provide error correction suggestions

Figure 5.17   IDE with compilation errors.

The Visual Basic IDE provides **real-time error checking**. While manipulating the code in the code editor, you may have noticed that compilation errors are immediately reported in the **Error List**. The precise location of the error in your code is also emphasized by a blue jagged line. Together, the blue jagged lines and **Error List** notify you of possible errors and give you a chance to fix them. The IDE will not run your modified app until *all* compilation errors have been corrected.

3. *Locating and correcting the compilation errors.* Double clicking an error in the **Error List** window moves the cursor in the editor to the code containing that error. Double click the first error to jump to the error in line 10. Placing the cursor over the blue jagged line displays the error message. If the blue jagged line ends with a small red rectangle as in Fig. 5.17, double clicking the error message in the **Error List** will also display the **Error Correction** window (Fig. 5.18). In this case, the **Error Correction Options** window provides the exact correction to fix the error. If you click the link (do not do this yet), the IDE performs the correction. In some cases, the **Error Correction Options** window displays several possible corrections.

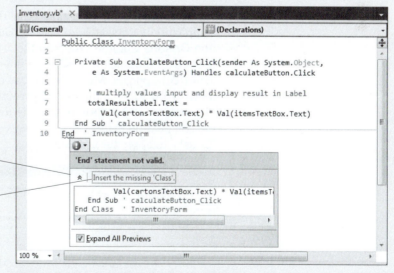

Error Correction window showing the error message

Click this suggested correction link to perform the correction

Figure 5.18   Viewing possible compilation error corrections in the **Error Correction Options** window.

4. *Getting additional help.* Additional help regarding the compilation error is also available through the **Error List** item's context menu, which you can access by right clicking an error. Right click the second error in the **Error List**, and select **Show Error Help** (Fig. 5.19). This displays a reference page in your web browser with information regarding the error message (Fig. 5.20) if information is available, or a general Visual Basic help page if there's no additional information.

(cont.)

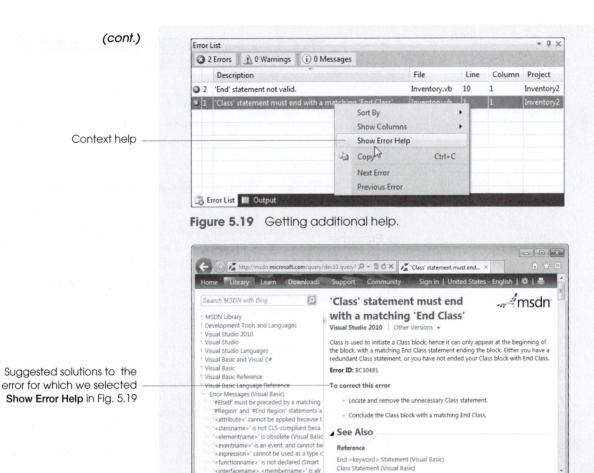

Figure 5.19 Getting additional help.

Context help

Suggested solutions to the
error for which we selected
Show Error Help in Fig. 5.19

Figure 5.20 Additional help shown in a web browser window.

5. ***Fixing the compilation errors.*** Now that you know how to locate and fix
compilation errors, let's go back to **Code** view and use the **Error Correction Options** window to correct the error you created in *Step 2*. To do this,
hover over the small red rectangle in line 10. The **Error Correction Options**
icon ( ) appears. Move the mouse cursor over this icon, then click the
down arrow to open the **Error Correction Options** window (Fig. 5.21). The
blue link toward the top of this window provides a possible correction for
the compilation error. Click the suggested correction—**Insert the missing
'Class'**—to apply the correction.

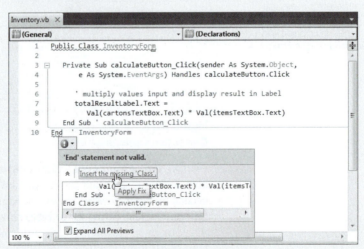

Figure 5.21 Using the **Error Correction** window to fix a compilation error.

(cont.)

6. ***Saving the project.*** Select **File > Save All** to save your modified code. The app is now ready to be compiled and executed.

7. ***Closing the IDE.*** Close the Visual Basic IDE by clicking its close box.

In this section, you learned about compilation errors and how to find and correct them. In later chapters, you'll learn to detect and remove logic errors by using the Visual Basic IDE runtime debugger.

SELF-REVIEW

1. If there are compilation errors in an app, they appear in a window known as the _____.

     a) **Task List**   b) **Output**

     c) **Properties**   d) **Error List**

2. A compilation error occurs when _____.

     a) a keyword is spelled incorrectly   b) a parenthesis is omitted

     c) a keyword is missing   d) All of the above

Answers: 1) d. 2) d.

5.6 Wrap-Up

In this chapter, you were introduced to Visual Basic programming. You learned how to use a `TextBox` control to allow users to input data and how to use a `Button` control to signal to your running app that it's to perform a particular action. You learned that a key to good programming is to achieve the right balance between employing visual programming (in which the IDE writes code for you) and writing your own code.

You added an event handler to your app to perform a simple multiplication calculation. You used the `Val` function to obtain a value from the user input and used that value in the calculation. You then displayed the result to the user by assigning it to a `Label`'s `Text` property. You also used comments to improve the readability of your code. You learned that placing code in an event handler allows an app to respond to that type of event, such as clicking a `Button`.

Finally, you learned about compilation errors and how to use the Visual Basic IDE to locate and fix them. In the next chapter, you'll continue developing your **Inventory** app by using identifiers to create variables. You'll also enhance your **Inventory** app by using the `TextChanged` event, which is raised when the user changes the value in a `TextBox`. After applying your knowledge of variables, you'll use the debugger while an app runs to remove a logic error from that app.

SKILLS SUMMARY

Accessing a Property's Value by Using Visual Basic Code

■ To access a control's property, place the property name after the control name and the member-access operator (`.`). For example, to access the `Text` property of a `TextBox` named `cartonsTextBox`, use `cartonsTextBox.Text`.

Inserting Visual Basic Comments in Code

■ Begin the comment with a single-quote character (`'`). A comment can be placed either on its own line (full-line comment) or at the end of a line of code (end-of-line comment).

Continuing a Code Statement Over More Than One Line

■ Though no longer required in most cases, you can insert a line-continuation character (`_`), preceded by one or more space characters, to indicate that the next line is a continuation of the preceding line. Only whitespace characters may follow a line-continuation character.

Naming an Event Handler

■ Use the format for an event handler, *controlName_eventName*, where *controlName* is the name of the control that the event is related to and *eventName* is the name of the event.

Inserting an Event Handler for a `Button` Control's `Click` Event

■ Double click the `Button` in **Design** view to create an empty event handler; then insert the code that executes when the event occurs.

Using an Assignment Statement

■ Use the = ("equals" sign) to assign the value of its right operand to its left operand.

Using the Multiplication Operator

■ Use an asterisk (*) between the two expressions to be multiplied. The operator multiplies the right and left operands if both operands contain numeric values. It's a compilation error to use the multiplication operator on values of nonnumeric data types.

Obtaining a Numeric Value from a `TextBox`

■ Pass the value of the `TextBox`'s `Text` property to function `Val`.

Finding a Compilation Error in the Code

■ Double click the error message in the **Error List** window.

Obtaining Help for a Compilation Error

■ Right click the error message in the **Error List** window, and select **Show Error Help** from the context menu.

KEY TERMS

argument—Inputs to a function that provide information the function needs to perform its task.

assignment operator—The "=" symbol used to assign values in an assignment statement.

assignment statement—A statement that copies one value to another. An assignment statement contains an "equals" sign (=) operator that causes the value of its right operand to be copied to its left operand.

binary operator—An operator that requires two operands.

case sensitive—The instance where two words that are spelled identically are treated differently if their capitalization differs.

class definition—The code that belongs to a class, beginning with keywords `Public Class` and ending with keywords `End Class`. [You'll learn later that not all class definitions need to begin with the keyword `Public`.]

class name—The identifier used to identify the name of a class in code.

`Class` keyword—The keyword that begins a class definition.

`Click` event—An event raised when a user clicks a control.

code editor—A window where a user can create, view or edit an app's code.

Code view—A mode of the Visual Basic IDE where the app's code is displayed in an editor window.

comment—Text that follows a single-quote character (') and is inserted to improve an app's readability.

compilation error—An error that occurs when program statements violate the grammatical rules of a programming language or when statements are simply incorrect in the current context.

debugger—A tool that allows you to analyze the behavior of your app to determine whether it's executing correctly and to help you locate and remove errors.

debugging—The process of finding and fixing errors in an app.

dot operator—See member-access operator.

`End Class` keywords—Mark the end of a class definition.

Error List window—A window which displays compilation errors in your code.

event—A user action such as clicking a button that can trigger an event handler. [You'll learn later that not all events are initiated by user actions.]

event handler—A section of code that's executed (called) when a certain event is raised (occurs).

functionality—The actions an app can execute.

Handles clause—Specifies the event handled by an event handler and the object to which the event corresponds.

identifier—A series of characters consisting of letters, digits and underscores used to name program units such as classes, controls and variables.

IntelliSense—Visual Basic IDE feature that aids you during development by providing windows that list program items that are available in the current context.

keyword—A word in code reserved by the compiler for a specific purpose. By default, these words appear in blue in the IDE and cannot be used as identifiers.

left operand—The expression on the left side of a binary operator.

line-continuation character—An underscore character (_) preceded by one or more space characters, used to continue a statement to the next line of code.

logic error—An error that does not prevent the app from compiling successfully but does cause the app to produce erroneous results.

member-access operator—Also known as the dot operator (.). Allows you to access a control's properties using code.

multiplication operator—The asterisk (*) used to multiply two operands, producing their product as a result.

operand—An expression on which an operator performs its task.

real-time error checking—Feature of the Visual Basic IDE that provides immediate notification of possible errors in your code. For example, unrecognized identifier errors are indicated by blue, jagged underlines in code.

right operand—The expression on the right side of a binary operator.

reserved words (keywords)—Words that are reserved by the Visual Basic compiler.

single-quote character(')—Indicates the beginning of a code comment.

statement—A unit of code that, when compiled and executed, performs an action.

syntax error—An error that occurs when program statements violate the grammatical rules of a programming language. Syntax errors are a subset of compilation errors.

Val function—Filters a number from its argument if possible. This avoids errors introduced by entering nonnumeric data when only numbers are expected. However, the result of the Val function isn't always what you intended.

whitespace character—A space, tab or newline character.

CONTROLS, EVENTS, PROPERTIES & METHODS

Button   ab Button   This control allows the user to raise an action or event.

- *In action*

  Calculate Total

- *Event*

  Click—Raised when the user clicks the Button.

- *Properties*

  Location—Specifies the location of the Button on the Form relative to the Form's top-left corner.

  Name—Specifies the name used to identify the Button. The name should include the Button suffix.

  Size—Specifies the width and height (in pixels) of the Button.

  Text—Specifies the text displayed on the Button.

MULTIPLE-CHOICE QUESTIONS

5.1 A user action, such as clicking a Button is an example of a(n) _____ . ,

a) statement   b) event

c) app   d) function

5.2 To switch to **Code** view, select _____.

a) **Code > View**   b) **Design > Code**

c) **View > Code**   d) **View > File Code**

5.3 Code that performs the functionality of an app _____.

a) normally is provided by the programmer

b) can never be in the form of an event handler

c) always creates a graphical user interface

d) is always generated by the IDE

5.4 Comments _____.

a) help improve program readability

b) are preceded by the single-quote character

c) are ignored by the compiler

d) All of the above

5.5 The _____ allows a statement to continue past one line (when that character is preceded by one or more space characters).

a) single-quote (') character   b) hyphen (-) character

c) underscore (_) character   d) plus (+) character

5.6 A(n) _____ causes an app to produce erroneous results.

a) logic error   b) event

c) assignment statement   d) compilation error

5.7 A(n) _____ is a portion of code that performs a specific task and returns a value.

a) variable   b) function

c) operand   d) identifier

5.8 Visual Basic keywords are _____.

a) identifiers   b) reserved words

c) case sensitive   d) properties

5.9 The Visual Basic IDE will not to run your app until all _____ errors are corrected.

a) logical   b) serious

c) compilation   d) runtime

5.10 An example of a whitespace character is a _____ character.

a) space   b) tab

c) newline   d) All of the above

EXERCISES

5.11 *(Inventory Enhancement)* Extend the **Inventory** app to include a `TextBox` in which the user can enter the number of shipments received in a week. Assume that every shipment has the same number of cartons (each of which has the same number of items). Then modify the code so that the **Inventory** app uses that value in its calculation.

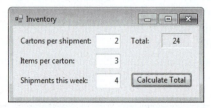

Figure 5.22 Enhanced **Inventory** app GUI.

a) *Copying the template app to your working directory.* Copy the directory `C:\Examples\ch05\Exercises\InventoryEnhancement` to your `C:\SimplyVB2010` directory.

b) *Opening the app's template file.* Double click InventoryEnhancment.sln in the InventoryEnhancement directory to open the app.

c) *Resizing the Form.* Resize the Form you used in this chapter by setting the Size property to 320, 149. Move the Button toward the bottom of the Form, as shown in Fig. 5.22. Its new location should be 193, 72.

d) *Adding a Label.* Add a Label to the Form and change the Text property to Shipments this week:. Set the Location property to 9, 77. Set the Label's Name property to shipmentsLabel.

e) *Adding a TextBox.* Add a TextBox to the right of the Label. Set its Text property to 0 and the Location property to 136, 74. Set the TextAlign and Size properties to the same values as for the other TextBoxes in this chapter's example. Set the TextBox's Name property to shipmentsTextBox.

f) *Modifying the code.* Modify the **Calculate Total** Button's Click event handler so that it multiplies the number of shipments per week with the product of the number of cartons in a shipment and the number of items in a carton.

g) *Running the app.* Select **Debug > Start Debugging** to run your app. Enter values for the number of cartons per shipment, items per carton and shipments in the current week. Click the **Calculate Total** Button and verify that the total displayed is equal to the result when the three values entered are multiplied together. Enter a few sets of input and verify the total each time.

h) *Closing the app.* Close your running app by clicking its close box.

i) *Closing the IDE.* Close the Visual Basic IDE by clicking its close box.

5.12 (*Counter App*) Create a counter app that consists of a Label and Button on the Form. The Label initially displays 0, but, each time a user clicks the Button, the value in the Label is increased by 1. When incrementing the Label, you need to write a statement such as countTotalLabel.Text = Val(countTotalLabel.Text) + 1.

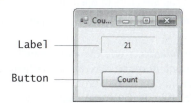

Label
Button

Figure 5.23   Counter GUI.

a) *Creating the app.* Create a new project named Counter.

b) *Changing the name of the Form file.* Change the name of Form1.vb to Counter.vb.

c) *Modifying the Form.* Change your Form's Font property to 9pt Segoe UI and the Size property to 176, 146. Modify the Form so that the title reads **Counter**. Change the name of the Form to CounterForm.

d) *Adding a Label.* Add a Label to the Form, and place it as shown in Fig. 5.23. Make sure that the Label's Text property is set to 0 and that TextAlign property is set so that any text will appear in the middle (both horizontally and vertically) of the Label. This can be done by using the TextAlign property's MiddleCenter value. Set the BorderStyle property to Fixed3D. Set the Label's Name property to countTotalLabel.

e) *Adding a Button.* Add a Button to the Form so that it appears as shown in Fig. 5.23. Set the Button's Text property to contain the text **Count**. Set the Button's Name property to countButton.

f) *Creating an event handler.* Add an event handler to the **Count** Button such that the value in the Label increases by 1 each time the user clicks the **Count** Button.

g) *Running the app.* Select **Debug > Start Debugging** to run your app. Click the **Count** Button several times and verify that the output value is incremented each time.

h) *Closing the app.* Close your running app by clicking its close box.

i) *Closing the IDE.* Close the Visual Basic IDE by clicking its close box.

5.13 *(Account Information App)* Create an app that allows a user to enter a name, account number and deposit amount. The user then clicks the **Enter** Button, which causes the name and account number to be copied and displayed in two output Labels. The deposit amount entered will be added to the balance amount displayed in another output Label. The result is displayed in the same output Label. Every time the **Enter** Button is clicked, the deposit amount entered is added to the balance amount displayed in the output Label, keeping a cumulative total. When updating the Label, you need to write a statement such as

```
balanceAmountLabel.Text =
   Val(depositAmountTextBox.Text) + Val(balanceAmountLabel.Text)
```

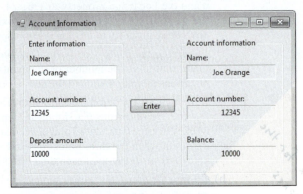

Figure 5.24 Account Information GUI.

a) *Copying the template app to your working directory.* Copy the directory `C:\Examples\ch05\Exercises\AccountInformation` to your `C:\SimplyVB2010` directory.

b) *Opening the app's template file.* Double click `AccountInformation.sln` in the `AccountInformation` directory to open the app.

c) *Creating an event handler.* Add an event handler for the **Enter** Button's `Click` event.

d) *Coding the event handler.* Code the event handler to copy information from the **Name:** and **Account number:** TextBoxes to their corresponding output Labels. Then add the value in the **Deposit amount:** TextBox to the **Balance:** output Label, and display the result in the **Balance:** output Label.

e) *Running the app.* Select **Debug > Start Debugging** to run your app. Enter the values in Fig. 5.24 and click the **Enter** Button. Verify that the account information is displayed in the Labels on the right. Enter varying deposit amounts and click the **Enter** Button after each. Verify that the balance amount on the right has the new values added.

f) *Closing the app.* Close your running app by clicking its close box.

g) *Closing the IDE.* Close the Visual Basic IDE by clicking its close box.

What does this code do? ▶ **5.14** After entering 10 in `priceTextBox` and 1.05 in `taxTextBox`, a user clicks the Button named `enterButton`. What is the result of the click, given the following code?

```
1   Private Sub enterButton_Click(sender As System.Object,
2      e As System.EventArgs) Handles enterButton.Click
3
4      outputLabel.Text = Val(priceTextBox.Text) * Val(taxTextBox.Text)
5   End Sub ' enterButton_Click
```

What's wrong with this code? ▶ **5.15** The following event handler should execute when the user clicks a **Calculate** Button. Identify the error(s) in its code.

```
1   Private Sub calculateButton_Click(sender As System.Object,
2      e As System.EventArgs) Handles calculateButton.Click
3
4      resultLabel.Text = priceTextBox.Text * taxTextBox.Text
5   End Sub ' calculateButton_Click
```

Using the Debugger ▶ **5.16** *(Account Information Debugging Exercise)* Copy the directory `C:\Examples\ ch05\Exercises\DebuggingExercise` to your `C:\SimplyVB2010` directory, then run the **Account Information** app. Remove any compilation errors, so that the app runs correctly.

Programming Challenge ▶ **5.17** *(Account Information Enhancement)* Modify Exercise 5.13 so that it no longer asks for the user's name and account number, but now asks the user for a withdrawal or deposit amount. The user can enter both a withdrawal and deposit amount at the same time. When the **Enter** Button is clicked, the balance is updated appropriately.

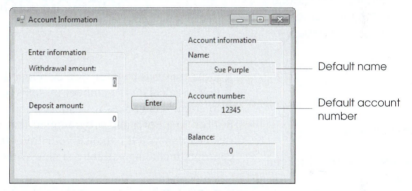

Figure 5.25   Enhanced **Account Information** GUI.

a) *Copying the template app to your working directory.* If you have not already done so, copy the `C:\Examples\ch05\Exercises\AccountInformation` directory to your `C:\SimplyVB2010` directory.

b) *Opening the app's template file.* Double click `AccountInformation.sln` in the `AccountInformation` directory to open the app.

c) *Modifying the GUI.* Modify the GUI so that it appears as in Fig. 5.25.

d) *Setting the default values.* Set the default name and account number to the values shown in Fig. 5.25 using the **Properties** window.

e) *Writing code to add functionality.* Update the account balance for every withdrawal (which decreases the balance) and every deposit (which increases the balance). When the balance is updated, reset the TextBoxes to "0".

f) *Running the app.* Select **Debug > Start Debugging** to run your app. Enter various withdrawal and deposit amounts; click the **Enter** Button after each. Verify that the balance on the right of the app is updated appropriately after each click of the **Enter** Button.

g) *Closing the app.* Close your running app by clicking its close box.

h) *Closing the IDE.* Close the Visual Basic IDE by clicking its close box.

Enhancing the Inventory App

Introducing Variables, Memory Concepts and Arithmetic

In the previous chapter, you developed an **Inventory** app that used multiplication to calculate the number of items received into inventory. You learned how to create TextBoxes to read user input from the keyboard. You also added a Button to a Form and programmed that Button to respond to a user's click. In this chapter, you'll enhance your **Inventory** app using additional programming concepts, including variables, a new event and arithmetic.

6.1 Test-Driving the Enhanced Inventory App

In this chapter, you'll enhance the previous chapter's **Inventory** app by inserting code rather than dragging and dropping Visual Basic controls. You'll use variables to perform arithmetic in Visual Basic, and you'll study memory concepts to help you understand how apps run on computers. Recall that your **Inventory** app from Chapter 5 calculated the number of items received from information supplied by the user—the number of cartons and the number of textbooks per carton. The enhanced app must meet the following requirements:

> ### App Requirements
>
> *The inventory manager notices a flaw in your **Inventory** app. Although the app calculates the correct result, that result continues to display even after new data is entered. The only time the output changes is when the inventory manager clicks the **Calculate Total** Button again. You need to alter the **Inventory** app to clear the result as soon as the user enters new information into either of the TextBoxes, to avoid any confusion over the accuracy of your calculated result.*

You'll begin by test-driving the completed app. Then you'll learn the additional Visual Basic technologies needed to create your own version of this app. At first glance, the app does not seem to operate any differently from the one in the previous chapter. However, you should notice that the **Total:** Label clears when you enter new data into either of the TextBoxes.

*Test-Driving the
Enhanced Inventory App*

1. *Opening the completed app.* Open the C:\Examples\Ch06\Completed-App\Inventory3 directory to locate the enhanced **Inventory** app. Double click Inventory3.sln to open the app in the Visual Basic IDE.

2. *Running the Inventory app.* Select **Debug > Start Debugging** to run the app (Fig. 6.1).

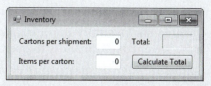

Figure 6.1   **Inventory** app GUI displayed when the app runs.

3. *Calculating the number of items in the shipment.* Enter 5 in the **Cartons per shipment:** TextBox and 6 in the **Items per carton:** TextBox. Click the **Calculate Total** Button. The result (30) displays in the **Total:** output Label (Fig. 6.2).

Figure 6.2   Running the **Inventory** app.

4. *Entering new quantities.* After you modify the app, the result displayed in the **Total:** Label will be removed when the user enters a new quantity in either TextBox. Enter 13 as the new number of cartons—the last calculation's result is cleared (Fig. 6.3). This is explained later in this chapter.

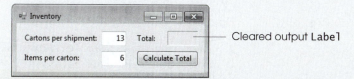

Cleared output Label

Figure 6.3   Enhanced **Inventory** app clears output Label after new input.

5. *Closing the app.* Close your running app by clicking its close box.

6. *Closing the IDE.* Close the Visual Basic IDE by clicking its close box.

6.2 Variables

A **variable** holds data for your app, much as the Text property of a Label holds the text to be displayed to the user. Unlike the Text property of a Label, however, variable values are not shown to the user by default. Using variables in an app allows you to store and manipulate data without necessarily showing it to the user and to store data without adding or using controls. Variables store data such as numbers, the date, the time and so on. However, each variable used in Visual Basic corresponds to exactly one type of information. For example, a variable of a numeric data type cannot be used to store text.

In Visual Basic, you must must **declare**, or report, all variables to the compiler by using program code. All **declarations** that you'll make within event handlers begin with the keyword **Dim**. Recall that keywords are reserved for use by Visual Basic. The complete list of Visual Basic keywords can be found at

msdn.microsoft.com/en-us/library/dd409611(VS.100).aspx

The following box introduces programming with variables. A variable name can be any valid identifier, which, as you learned in Chapter 5, is a name that the compiler can recognize (and is not a keyword). As you also learned in the previous chapter, there are many valid characters for identifiers.

Using Variables in the Inventory App

Good Programming Practice

Use only letters and digits as characters for your variable names.

Good Programming Practice

Typically, variable-name identifiers begin with a lowercase letter. Every word in the name after the first word should begin with a capital letter—for example, `firstNumber`. This is often called camel case.

1. *Copying the template to your working directory.* Copy the `C:\Examples\Ch06\TemplateApp\Inventory3` directory to `C:\SimplyVB2010`.

2. *Opening the Inventory app's template file.* Double click `Inventory3.sln` in the `Inventory3` directory to open the app in the Visual Basic IDE.

3. *Adding variable declarations to event handler `calculateButton_Click`.* If you're in **Design** view, enter **Code** view by selecting **View > Code**. Add lines 6–9 of Fig. 6.4 to event handler `calculateButton_Click`. Lines 7–9 are declarations, which begin with keyword `Dim`. Note that, when you type the word `Dim`, as with all keywords, the IDE colors it blue by default. The words `cartons`, `items` and `result` are variable names. Lines 7–9 declare that variables `cartons`, `items` and `result` store data of type *Integer*, using the `As` keyword. The `As` keyword indicates that the following word (in this case `Integer`) is the variable type. `Integer` variables store **integer** values (whole numbers such as 919, 0 and –11). Notice that the IDE initially underlines the variables to indicate that they have *not* been referenced in the app. This is to safeguard against including any unnecessary variables in your app.

```
2       ' handles Click event
3       Private Sub calculateButton_Click(sender As System.Object,
4           e As System.EventArgs) Handles calculateButton.Click
5
6           ' declare variables
7           Dim cartons As Integer
8           Dim items As Integer
9           Dim result As Integer
```

Click event handler — (line 3)
Variable declarations — (lines 7–9)

Figure 6.4 Declaring variables in event handler `calculateButton_Click`.

4. *Retrieving input from TextBoxes.* Skip one line after the variable declarations, and add lines 11–13 (Fig. 6.5) in event handler `calculateButton_Click`. Once the user enters numbers and clicks **Calculate Total**, the values found in the `Text` property of each `TextBox` control are converted to numerical values by the `Val` function. Then the numbers are assigned to variables `cartons` (line 12) and `items` (line 13) with the assignment operator, =. Line 12 is read as "`cartons` *gets* the result of the `Val` function applied to `cartonsTextBox.Text`."

```
11      ' retrieve numbers from TextBoxes
12      cartons = Val(cartonsTextBox.Text)
13      items = Val(itemsTextBox.Text)
```

Assigning user input to variables — (lines 12–13)

Figure 6.5 Retrieving numerical input from TextBoxes.

5. *Saving the project.* Select **File > Save All** to save your modified code.

The `Val` function returns a numerical value as data type **Double** when converting a value retrieved from a `TextBox`'s `Text` property. Data type `Double` is used to store both whole and fractional numbers. Normally, `Doubles` store floating-point numbers, which are numbers with decimal points such as 2.3456 and –845.4680. Variables of data type `Double` can hold much larger (and much smaller) values than variables of data type `Integer`.

After `Val` converts the two values input by the user to `Doubles`, lines 12–13 implicitly convert the `Doubles` to `Integer` values. The integer value obtained by converting the Double in line 12 is assigned to variable cartons, which is of type Integer. Likewise, the integer value obtained by converting the Double in line 13 is assigned to variable items. Because Doubles and Integers are different types, Visual Basic performs a conversion from one type to the other. This process is called **implicit conversion,** because the conversion is performed by Visual Basic without any additional code. Implicit conversions from Double to Integer are generally considered poor programming practice due to the potential loss of information. In Chapter 15, you'll learn how to perform *explicit* conversions. Now that you've assigned values to your new variables, use the variables to calculate the number of textbooks received.

Visual Basic defines 15 **primitive data types** (listed in Fig. 6.6), such as Integer. Primitive data type names are also keywords. In addition to the primitive types, Visual Basic also defines the type Object. Together, the primitive data types and type Object are known as **built-in data types.** You'll use some of these data types throughout the book. Appendix E lists the primitive types and their value ranges.

Built-in (primitive) data types				
Boolean	Date	Integer	Long	Short
Byte	Decimal	Single	Char	Double
SByte	String	UInteger	ULong	UShort

Figure 6.6   Visual Basic built-in data types.

Using Variables in a Calculation

1. ***Performing the multiplication operation.*** Skip one line from the end of the last statement you inserted and insert lines 15–16 in event handler calculateButton_Click (Fig. 6.7). The statement in line 16 multiplies the Integer variable cartons by items and assigns the result to variable result, using the assignment operator =. The statement is read as, "result *gets* the value of cartons * items." (Most calculations are performed in assignment statements.)

```
15        ' multiply two numbers
16        result = cartons * items
17
18        ' display result in Label
19        totalResultLabel.Text = result
20    End Sub ' calculateButton_Click
```

Calculating and displaying the result

Figure 6.7   Multiplication, using variables in calculateButton_Click.

2. ***Displaying the result.*** Add lines 18–19 of Fig. 6.7 to event handler calculateButton_Click. After the calculation is completed, line 19 displays the result of the multiplication operation. The number is assigned to totalResultLabel's Text property. Once the property is updated, the Label displays the result of the multiplication operation (Fig. 6.8).

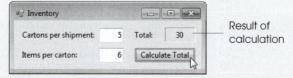

Result of calculation

Figure 6.8   Displaying the multiplication result using variables.

3. ***Running the app.*** Select **Debug > Start Debugging** to run your app. Enter 5 in the **Cartons per shipment:** TextBox and 6 in the **Items per carton:** TextBox. Then click the **Calculate Total** Button to test your app.

4. ***Closing the app.*** Close your running app by clicking its close box.

SELF-REVIEW

1. When Visual Basic converts a `Double` to an `Integer` without requiring any code, this is referred to as a(n) _____.

   a) explicit conversion   b) implicit conversion

   c) data-type change   d) transformation

2. Data types already defined in Visual Basic, such as `Integer`, are known as _____ data types.

   a) provided   b) existing

   c) defined   d) primitive

Answers: 1) b. 2) d.

6.3 Handling the TextChanged Event

You may have noticed that the flaw, or **bug**, mentioned in the app requirements at the beginning of this chapter remains in your app. Although `totalResultLabel` displays the current result, once you enter a new number into a TextBox, that result is no longer valid—the result displayed does *not* change again until you click the **Calculate Total** Button, potentially confusing the app user. In the next box, you'll add event handlers to clear the output whenever new data is entered.

Handling the TextChanged Event

1. ***Adding an event handler for cartonsTextBox's TextChanged event.*** Switch to the IDE's **Design** view and double click the **Cartons per shipment:** TextBox to generate an event handler for the **TextChanged** event, which is raised when the TextBox's text changes. This is the *default* event for Text-Boxes. The IDE generates an event handler with an *empty* body (no additional code) and places the cursor in the body. Insert line 28 of Fig. 6.9 into your code. Note that we split the first line of the event handler into three lines and added a line-continuation character (_) at the end of line 25 of this code—this line-continuation character is necessary because the `Handles` clause cannot appear on a line by itself otherwise. We also added the comment in line 22, before the event handler. Recall from Chapter 5 that the line-continuation character is typically unnecessary in Visual Basic 2010.

   According to the app requirements for this chapter, the app should clear the value in `totalResultLabel` every time users change the text in either TextBox. Line 28 clears the value in `totalResultLabel` by assigning `String.Empty` to the Label's Text property. `String.Empty` represents an empty string—that is, one that does not contain any characters. This empty string replaces whatever is stored in `totalResultLabel.Text`. You can also represent an empty string as "".

Good Programming Practice

If a statement is wider than the code editor window, use the line-continuation character to continue it on the next line.

TextChanged event handler ———

```
22      ' handles TextChanged event for cartonsTextBox
23      Private Sub cartonsTextBox_TextChanged(
24         sender As System.Object,
25         e As System.EventArgs) _
26         Handles cartonsTextBox.TextChanged
27
28         totalResultLabel.Text = String.Empty ' clear output label
29      End Sub ' cartonsTextBox_TextChanged
```

Figure 6.9 TextChanged event handler for **Cartons per shipment:** TextBox.

(cont.)

2. ***Adding an event handler for* itemsTextBox's *TextChanged event.*** You want the result cleared regardless of which TextBox changes value first. Return to **Design** view by clicking the **Inventory.vb [Design]** tab. Then double click the **Items per carton:** TextBox, and insert line 36 from Fig. 6.10 into the new event handler. Note that this line performs the same task as line 28—you want the same action to occur, namely, clearing `totalResultLabel`.

```
31      ' handles TextChanged event for itemsTextBox
32      Private Sub itemsTextBox_TextChanged(
33          sender As System.Object,
34          e As System.EventArgs) Handles itemsTextBox.TextChanged
35
36          totalResultLabel.Text = String.Empty ' clear output label
37      End Sub ' itemsTextBox_TextChanged
```

Figure 6.10 TextChanged event handler for **Items per carton:** TextBox.

3. ***Running the app.*** Select **Debug > Start Debugging** to run your app. To test the app, enter 8 in the **Cartons per shipment:** TextBox and 7 in the **Items per carton:** TextBox. When you click the **Calculate Total** Button, the number 56 should appear in the output Label. Then enter 9 in the **Items per carton:** TextBox to ensure that the TextChanged event handler clears the output Label.

4. ***Closing the app.*** Close your running app by clicking its close box.

Figure 6.11 presents the source code for the enhanced **Inventory** app. The lines of code that contain new programming concepts you learned in this chapter are highlighted.

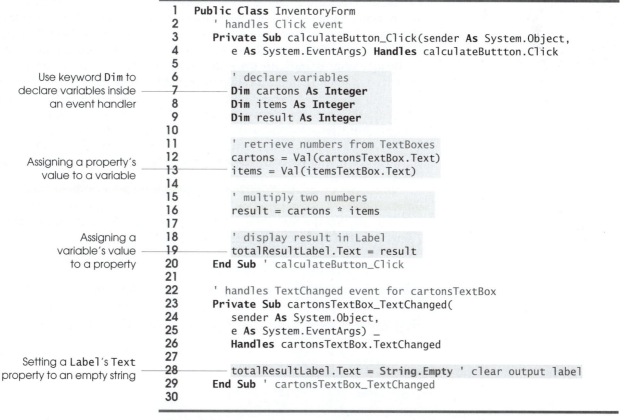

```
 1      Public Class InventoryForm
 2          ' handles Click event
 3          Private Sub calculateButton_Click(sender As System.Object,
 4              e As System.EventArgs) Handles calculateButtton.Click
 5
 6              ' declare variables
 7              Dim cartons As Integer
 8              Dim items As Integer
 9              Dim result As Integer
10
11              ' retrieve numbers from TextBoxes
12              cartons = Val(cartonsTextBox.Text)
13              items = Val(itemsTextBox.Text)
14
15              ' multiply two numbers
16              result = cartons * items
17
18              ' display result in Label
19              totalResultLabel.Text = result
20          End Sub ' calculateButton_Click
21
22          ' handles TextChanged event for cartonsTextBox
23          Private Sub cartonsTextBox_TextChanged(
24              sender As System.Object,
25              e As System.EventArgs) _
26              Handles cartonsTextBox.TextChanged
27
28              totalResultLabel.Text = String.Empty ' clear output label
29          End Sub ' cartonsTextBox_TextChanged
30
```

Use keyword `Dim` to declare variables inside an event handler

Assigning a property's value to a variable

Assigning a variable's value to a property

Setting a `Label`'s `Text` property to an empty string

Figure 6.11 **Inventory** app code. (Part 1 of 2.)

```
31         ' handles TextChanged event for itemsTextBox
32         Private Sub itemsTextBox_TextChanged(
33            sender As System.Object,
34            e As System.EventArgs) Handles itemsTextBox.TextChanged
35
36            totalResultLabel.Text = String.Empty ' clear output label
37         End Sub ' itemsTextBox_TextChanged
38      End Class ' InventoryForm
```

Figure 6.11 **Inventory** app code. (Part 2 of 2.)

SELF-REVIEW

1. One way to represent the _____ in Visual basic is with "".
   a) empty value
   b) empty string
   c) Both of the above
   d) None of the above

2. Assign `String.Empty` to a Label's _____ property to remove its text.
   a) `ClearText`
   b) `Remove`
   c) `Display`
   d) `Text`

Answers: 1) b. 2) d.

6.4 Memory Concepts

Variable names—such as `cartons`, `items` and `result`—correspond to actual locations in the computer's memory. Every variable has a **name**, **type**, **size** (the number of bytes required to store a value of the variable's type) and a **value**. In the **Inventory** app code listing in Fig. 6.11, when the statement (line 12)

```
cartons = Val(cartonsTextBox.Text)
```

executes, the user input stored in `cartonsTextBox.Text` is implicitly converted to an `Integer`. Suppose that the user enters the characters 12 in the **Cartons per shipment:** TextBox. This input is stored in `cartonsTextBox.Text`. When the user clicks **Calculate Total**, line 12 converts the user input to a `Double` using `Val`, then the `Double` value is implicitly converted to an `Integer`. The assignment then places the `Integer` value 12 in the location for variable `cartons`, as shown in Fig. 6.12.

Figure 6.12 Memory location showing name and value of variable `cartons`.

Whenever a value is placed in a memory location, this value *replaces* the value previously stored in that location. The previous value is *overwritten* (lost).

Suppose that the user then enters the characters 10 in the **Items per carton:** TextBox and clicks **Calculate Total**. Line 13 of Fig. 6.11

```
items = Val(itemsTextBox.Text)
```

converts `itemsTextBox.Text` to a `Double` using `Val`; then the `Double` value is implicitly converted to an `Integer`. The assignment then places the `Integer` value 10 in the location of variable `items`, and memory appears as shown in Fig. 6.13.

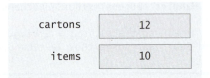

Figure 6.13 Memory locations after values for `cartons` and `items` have been input.

Once the **Calculate Total** Button is clicked, line 16 multiplies these values and places their total into variable `result`. The statement

```
result = cartons * items
```

multiplies the values and replaces `result`'s previous value. After `result` is calculated, memory appears as shown in Fig. 6.14. The values of `cartons` and `items` appear exactly as they did before they were used in the calculation of `result`. Although these values were used when the computer performed the calculation, they were not destroyed. This illustrates that when a value is read from a memory location, the process is **nondestructive** (meaning that the value is not overwritten).

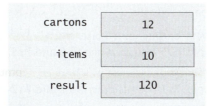

cartons	12
items	10
result	120

Figure 6.14 Memory locations after a multiplication operation.

1. When a value is placed into a memory location, the value _____ the previous value in that location.

    a) copies   b) replaces

    c) adds itself to   d) moves

2. When a value is read from memory, that value is _____.

    a) overwritten   b) replaced with a new value

    c) moved to a new location in memory   d) not overwritten

Answers: 1) b. 2) d.

6.5 Arithmetic

Most programs perform arithmetic calculations. In the last chapter, you performed the arithmetic operation multiplication by using the multiplication operator (`*`). The **arithmetic operators** are summarized in Fig. 6.15. Note the use of various special symbols not used in algebra. For example, the **asterisk** (`*`) indicates multiplication, the keyword **Mod** represents the **modulus operator**, the **backslash** (`\`) represents *integer division* and the **caret** (`∧`) represents exponentiation. Most of the arithmetic operators in Fig. 6.15 are **binary operators**, each requiring two operands.

Visual Basic .NET operation	Arithmetic operator	Algebraic expression	Visual Basic 2010 expression
Addition	+	$f + 7$	f + 7
Subtraction	−	$p - c$	p - c
Multiplication	*	bm	b * m
Division (float)	/	x/y or $\frac{x}{y}$ or $x \div y$	x / y
Division (integer)	\	none	v \ u
Modulus	Mod	$r \bmod s$	r Mod s
Exponentiation	∧	q^p	q ∧ p
Unary Negative	−	$-e$	-e
Unary Positive	+	$+g$	+g

Figure 6.15 Arithmetic operators.

For example, the expression `sum + value` contains the *binary* operator + and the *two* operands `sum` and `value`. Visual Basic also provides **unary operators**, which are operators that take only *one* operand. For example, unary versions of plus (+) and minus (–) are provided so that you can write expressions such as +9 (a positive number) and –19 (a negative number).

Visual Basic has separate operators for **integer division** (the backslash, \) and **floating-point division** (the forward slash, /). Floating-point division divides two numbers (whole or fractional) and returns a floating-point number (a number with a decimal point). The operator for integer division treats its operands as integers and returns an integer result. When floating-point numbers (numbers with decimal points) are used with the integer-division operator, the numbers are *first rounded* as follows:

- numbers ending in `.5` are rounded to the nearest *even* integer—for example, `6.5` rounds *down* to 6 and `7.5` rounds *up* to 8

- all other floating-point numbers are rounded to the nearest integer—for example, `7.1` rounds *down* to 7 and `7.7` rounds *up* to 8

then divided. This means that, although `4.5 \ 2` evaluates to 2 as expected, the statement `5.5 \ 2` evaluates to 3, because `5.5` is rounded to 6 *before* the division occurs. Similarly, although `7.1 \ 4` evaluates to 1 as expected, the statement `7.7 \ 4` evaluates to 2, because `7.7` is rounded to 8 *before* the division occurs. Note that any fractional part in the integer division result simply is *truncated (discarded)—no rounding occurs. Neither division operator allows division by zero.* If your code divides by zero, a runtime error known as an "exception" occurs. By default, this error terminates the execution of the app. You'll learn about exception handling in Chapter 24.

The **modulus operator, Mod, yields** the *remainder* after division. The expression `x Mod y` yields the remainder after `x` is divided by `y`. Thus, `7 Mod 4` yields 3, and `17 Mod 5` yields 2. This operator is used most commonly with `Integer` operands, but also can be used with other types. The modulus operator can be applied to several interesting problems, such as discovering whether one number is a *multiple* of another. If a and b are numbers, `a Mod b` yields 0 if a is a multiple of b. `8 Mod 3` yields 2, so 8 is not a multiple of 3. But `8 Mod 2` and `8 Mod 4` each yield 0, because 8 is a multiple both of 2 and of 4.

Arithmetic expressions in Visual Basic must be written in **straight-line form** so that you can type them into a computer easily. For example, `7.1` divided by `4.3` cannot be written

$$\frac{7.1}{4.3}$$

but is written in straight-line form as `7.1 / 4.3`. Raising 3 to the second power cannot be written as 3^2 but is written in straight-line form as `3 ^ 2`.

Parentheses are used in Visual Basic expressions to *group* operations in the same manner as in algebraic expressions. To multiply *a* times the quantity *b + c*, you write

```
a * (b + c)
```

Visual Basic applies the operators in arithmetic expressions in a precise sequence, determined by the **rules of operator precedence,** which are generally the same as those followed in algebra. These rules enable Visual Basic to apply operators in the correct order.

Common Programming Error

Attempting to divide by zero is a **runtime error** (that is, an error that has its effect while the app executes). Dividing by zero terminates an app by default.

Rules of Operator Precedence

1. ***Operators in expressions contained within a pair of parentheses are evaluated first***. Thus, *parentheses can be used to force the order of evaluation to occur in any sequence you desire.* Parentheses are at the highest level of precedence. With **nested** (or **embedded**) parentheses, the operators contained in the *innermost* pair of parentheses are applied *first*.

2. ***Exponentiation is applied next***. If an expression contains several exponentiation operations, operators are applied from *left to right*.

3. ***Unary positive and negative, + and -, are applied next***. If an expression contains several sign operations, operators are applied from *left to right*.

4. ***Multiplication and floating-point division operations are applied next***. If an expression contains several multiplication and floating-point division operations, operators are applied from left to right.

5. ***Integer division is applied next***. If an expression contains several `Integer` division operations, operators are applied from *left to right*.

6. ***Modulus operations are applied next***. If an expression contains several modulus operations, operators are applied from *left to right*.

7. ***Addition and subtraction operations are applied last***. If an expression contains several addition and subtraction operations, operators are applied from *left to right*.

Note that we mention *nested* parentheses. Not all expressions with several pairs of parentheses contain nested parentheses. For example, although the expression

    a * (b + c) + c * (d + e)

contains multiple pairs of parentheses, none of the parentheses are nested. These sets of parentheses are referred to as being "on the same level" and are evaluated from *left to right*.

Let's consider several expressions in light of the rules of operator precedence. Each example lists an algebraic expression and its Visual Basic equivalent.

The following calculates the average of three numbers:

Algebra: $m = \dfrac{(a + b + c)}{3}$

Visual Basic: m = (a + b + c) / 3

The parentheses are *required* because floating-point division has *higher* precedence than addition. The entire quantity (a + b + c) is to be divided by 3. If the parentheses are omitted, erroneously, we obtain a + b + c / 3, which evaluates as

$a + b + \dfrac{c}{3}$

The following is the equation of a straight line:

Algebra: $y = mx + b$

Visual Basic: y = m * x + b

No parentheses are required. The multiplication is applied first, because multiplication has a *higher* precedence than addition. The assignment occurs *last* because it has a *lower* precedence than multiplication and addition.

To develop a better understanding of the rules of operator precedence, consider how the expression $y = ax^2 + bx + c$ is evaluated:

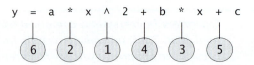

$$y = a * x \wedge 2 + b * x + c$$

The circled numbers under the statement indicate the order in which Visual Basic applies the operators. Remember that in Visual Basic x^2 is represented as $x \wedge 2$. Also, note that the assignment operator is applied *last* because it has a *lower* precedence than any of the arithmetic operators.

As in algebra, it's acceptable to place *unnecessary* parentheses in an expression to make the expression easier to read—these are called **redundant parentheses**. For example, the preceding assignment statement might use redundant parentheses to emphasize terms:

$$y = (a * (x \wedge 2)) + (b * x) + c$$

Good Programming Practice

Using redundant parentheses in complex arithmetic expressions can make the expressions easier to read.

SELF-REVIEW

1. Arithmetic expressions in Visual Basic must be written _____ to facilitate entering apps into the computer.

    a) using parentheses   b) on multiple lines

    c) in straight-line form   d) None of the above

2. The expression to the right of the assignment operator (=) is always evaluated _____ the assignment occurs.

    a) before   b) after

    c) at the same time as   d) None of the above

Answers: 1) c. 2) a.

6.6 Using the Debugger: Breakpoints

The debugger will be one of your most important tools in developing apps, once you become familiar with its features. You were introduced to some of Visual Studio's capabilities for finding and eliminating errors in Chapter 5, where you used it to locate and eliminate compilation errors. In this chapter, you'll study the debugger, learning about breakpoints, which allow you to examine what your app is doing while it's running. A **breakpoint** is a marker that can be set at any *executable* line of code. When app execution reaches a breakpoint, execution *pauses*, allowing you to peek inside your app and ensure that there are no logic errors, such as an incorrect calculation. In the next box, *Using the Debugger: Breakpoints*, you'll learn how to use breakpoints in the Visual Basic IDE debugger.

Using the Debugger: Breakpoints

1. ***Inserting breakpoints in the Visual Basic IDE.*** Ensure that the `Inventory3` project is open in the IDE's **Code** view. To insert a breakpoint in the IDE, either click inside the **margin indicator bar** (the gray margin indicator at the left of the code window, Fig. 6.16) next to the line of code at which you wish to break, or *right click* that line of code and select **Breakpoint > Insert Breakpoint**. You can set as many breakpoints as necessary. Set breakpoints at lines 16 and 19 of your code. A *solid circle* appears in the margin indicator bar next to the line of code, indicating that a breakpoint has been set (Fig. 6.16). When the app runs, it *suspends execution* at any line that contains a breakpoint. The app is said to be in **break mode** when the debugger pauses the app's execution. Breakpoints can be set during design mode, break mode and run mode.

(cont.)

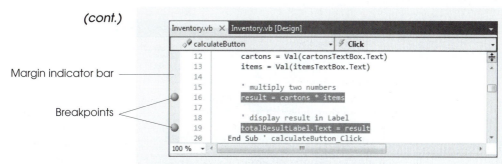

Figure 6.16 Setting two breakpoints.

Margin indicator bar

Breakpoints

2. ***Beginning the debugging process.*** After setting breakpoints in the code editor, select **Debug > Start Debugging** to begin the debugging process. During debugging of a Windows app, the app window appears (Fig. 6.17), allowing app interaction (input and output). Enter 10 and 7 into the Textboxes and click **Calculate Total** to continue. The title bar of the IDE displays **(Debugging)** (Fig. 6.18), indicating that the IDE is in break mode.

Figure 6.17 **Inventory** app running.

Title bar displays **(Debugging)**

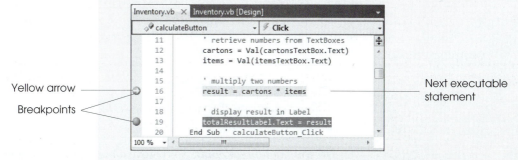

Figure 6.18 Title bar of the IDE displaying **(Debugging)**.

3. ***Examining app execution.*** App execution suspends at the first breakpoint, and the IDE becomes the **active window** (Fig. 6.19). The yellow arrow to the left of line 16 indicates that this line contains the next statement to execute.

Yellow arrow

Breakpoints

Next executable statement

Figure 6.19 App execution suspended at the first breakpoint.

4. ***Using the Continue command to resume execution.*** To resume execution, select **Debug > Continue** (or press *F5*). The app executes until it stops at the next breakpoint, in line 19. Note that when you place your mouse pointer over the variable name result, the value that the variable stores is displayed in a **Quick Info** box (Fig. 6.20). In a sense, you're peeking inside the computer at the value of one of your variables. As you'll see, this can help you spot logic errors in your apps.

(cont.)

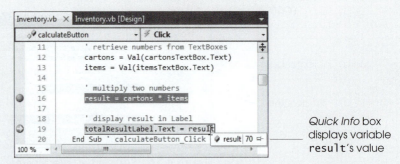

Figure 6.20 Displaying a variable value by placing the mouse pointer over a variable name.

Quick Info box displays variable **result**'s value

5. *Finishing app execution.* Use the **Debug > Continue** command to complete the app execution. When there are no more breakpoints at which to suspend execution, the app executes to completion and the output appears in the **Total:** Label (Fig. 6.21).

Figure 6.21 App output.

6. *Closing the app.* Close your running app by clicking its close box.

7. *Disabling a breakpoint.* To disable a breakpoint, right click in a line of code in which a breakpoint has been set, and select **Breakpoint > Disable Breakpoint**. The disabled breakpoint is indicated by a hollow maroon circle (Fig. 6.22). Disabling rather than removing a breakpoint allows you to see where the breakpoint was previously and to reenable the breakpoint (by clicking inside the hollow circle). This also can be done by *right clicking* the line marked by the hollow maroon circle and selecting **Breakpoint > Enable Breakpoint**.

Disabled breakpoint

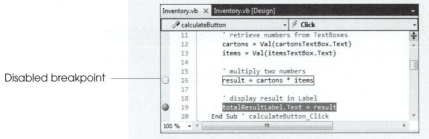

Figure 6.22 Disabled breakpoint.

8. *Removing a breakpoint.* To remove a breakpoint that you no longer need, *right click* a line of code in which a breakpoint has been set and select **Breakpoint > Delete Breakpoint**. You also can remove a breakpoint by clicking the maroon circle in the margin indicator bar.

9. *Saving the project.* Select **File > Save All** to save your modified code.

10. *Closing the IDE.* Close the Visual Basic IDE by clicking its close box.

In this section, you learned how to use the debugger to set breakpoints so that you can examine the results of code while an app is running. You also learned how to continue execution after an app suspends execution at a breakpoint and how to disable and remove breakpoints.

---

1. A _____ is a marker that can be set at any executable line of code. .

      a) stoppoint   b) suspendpoint

      c) breakpoint   d) None of the above

2. When app execution suspends at a breakpoint, the next statement to be executed is the statement _____ the breakpoint.

      a) before   b) after

      c) at   d) None of the above

Answers: 1) c. 2) c.

6.7 Wrap-Up

You've now added variables to your **Inventory** app. You began by using variables to produce the same results as your previous **Inventory** app. Then you enhanced the **Inventory** app, using the `TextChanged` event, which allowed you to execute code that cleared the value in the output `Label` when the user changed a value in either `TextBox`.

You learned about memory concepts, including how variables are read and written. You'll apply these concepts to the apps that you build in later chapters, which rely heavily on variables. You learned how to perform arithmetic in Visual Basic, and you studied the rules of operator precedence to evaluate mathematical expressions correctly. Finally, you learned how to insert breakpoints in the debugger. Breakpoints allow you to pause app execution and examine variable values. This capability will prove useful to you in finding and fixing logic errors.

In the next chapter, you'll design a graphical user interface and write code to create a wage calculator. You'll use pseudocode, an informal language that helps you design the app. You'll learn to use the debugger's **Watch** window, another useful tool that helps you remove logic errors.

SKILLS SUMMARY

Declaring a Variable
- Use the keyword `Dim`.
- Use a valid identifier as a variable name.
- Use the keyword `As` to indicate that the following word specifies the variable's data type.
- Specify a type such as `Integer` or `Double`.

Handling a TextBox's TextChanged Event
- Double click a `TextBox` on a `Form` to generate an empty `TextChanged` event handler.
- Insert code into the event handler that executes when the text in a `TextBox` changes.

Reading a Value from a Memory Location
- Use the variable's name (as declared in the variable's `Dim` statement) at the point in the code where the variable's value is needed.

Replacing a Value in a Memory Location
- Use the variable name, followed by the assignment operator (=), followed by an expression giving the new value.

Representing Positive and Negative Numbers
- Use the unary versions of plus (+) and minus (-).

Performing Arithmetic Operations
- Write arithmetic expressions in straight-line form.

- Use the operator precedence rules to determine the order in which operators are applied.
- Use operator + to perform addition.
- Use operator – to perform subtraction.
- Use operator * to perform multiplication.
- Use operator / to perform floating-point division.
- Use operator \ (backslash) to perform integer division, which treats the operands as Integers and returns an Integer result.
- Use operator ∧ to perform exponentiation.
- Use the modulus operator, Mod, to report the remainder after division.
- Use parentheses to manage the order of operations and to clarify expressions.

Setting a Breakpoint

- Click the margin indicator bar (the gray margin indicator at the left of the code window) next to the line at which you wish to break, or right click a line of code and select **Breakpoint > Insert Breakpoint**.

Resuming App Execution after Entering Break Mode During Debugging

- Select **Debug > Continue**.

Disabling a Breakpoint

- Right click a line of code containing a breakpoint, and select **Breakpoint > Disable Breakpoint**.

Enabling a Breakpoint

- Enable a disabled breakpoint by clicking inside the hollow circle in the margin indicator bar.
- You also can enable a disabled breakpoint by right clicking the line marked by the hollow maroon circle and selecting **Breakpoint > Enable Breakpoint**.

Removing a Breakpoint

- Right click a line of code containing a breakpoint, and select **Breakpoint > Delete Breakpoint**.
- You also can remove a breakpoint by clicking the maroon circle in the margin indicator bar.

KEY TERMS

active window—The frontmost window on your screen.

arithmetic operators—The operators +, -, *, /, \, ∧ and Mod.

As keyword—Used in variable declarations. Indicates that the following word (such as Integer) is the variable type.

asterisk (*)—Multiplication operator. The operator's left and right operands are multiplied together.

backslash (\)—Integer division operator. The operator divides its left operand by its right and returns an Integer result.

binary operators—An operator that takes two operands.

break mode—The IDE mode when app execution is suspended. This mode is entered through the debugger.

breakpoint—A location where execution is to suspend, indicated by a solid maroon circle.

bug—A flaw in a program that prevents it from executing correctly.

built-in data type—The primitive data types and type Object.

caret (∧)—Exponentiation operator. This operator raises its left operand to a power specified by the right operand.

declaration—The reporting of a new variable to the compiler. The variable can then be used in the Visual Basic code.

declare a variable—Report the name and type of a variable to the compiler.

Dim keyword—Indicates the declaration of a variable.

Double data type—Stores both whole and fractional numbers. Normally, `Doubles` store floating-point numbers.

embedded parentheses—Another term for nested parentheses.

empty string—A string that does not contain any characters.

exponentiation operator (^)—Raises its left operand to a power specified by the right operand.

floating-point division—Divides two numbers and returns a floating-point number.

implicit conversion—A conversion from one data type to another performed by Visual Basic.

integer—A whole number, such as 919, -11, 0 and 138624.

Integer data type—Variables of this type store integer values.

integer division—Integer division takes two `Integer` operands and yields an `Integer` quotient. The fractional portion of the result is discarded.

margin indicator bar—A margin in the IDE where breakpoints are displayed.

Mod (modulus operator)—Yields the remainder after division.

name of a variable—The identifier used in an app to access or modify a variable's value.

nested parentheses—These occur when an expression in parentheses is found within another expression surrounded by parentheses. With nested parentheses, the operators contained in the innermost pair of parentheses are applied first.

nondestructive memory operation—A process that does not overwrite a value in memory.

primitive data type—A data type already defined in Visual Basic, such as `Integer`.

Quick Info **box**—Displays the value of a variable during debugging.

redundant parentheses—Unnecessary parentheses used in an expression to make it easier to read.

rules of operator precedence—Rules that determine the precise order in which operators are applied in an expression.

runtime error—An error that has its effect at execution time.

size of a variable—The number of bytes required to store a value of the variable's type.

straight-line form—The manner in which arithmetic expressions must be written to be represented in Visual Basic code.

TextChanged event—Occurs when the text in a `TextBox` changes.

type of a variable—Specifies the kind of data that can be stored in a variable and the range of values that can be stored.

unary operator—An operator that takes only one operand.

value of a variable—The piece of data that's stored in a variable's location in memory.

variable—A location in the computer's memory where a value can be stored.

CONTROLS, EVENTS, PROPERTIES & METHODS

TextBox   `abl` TextBox   This control allows the user to input data from the keyboard.

■ *In action*

■ *Event*

TextChanged—Raised when the text in the `TextBox` is changed.

■ *Properties*

Location—Specifies the location of the `TextBox` relative to its container's top-left corner.

Name—Specifies the name used to identify the `TextBox`. The name should include the `TextBox` suffix.

Size—Specifies the width and height (in pixels) of the `TextBox`.

Text—Specifies the text displayed in the `TextBox`.

TextAlign—Specifies how the text is aligned within the `TextBox`.

MULTIPLE-CHOICE QUESTIONS

6.1 _____ parentheses are added to an expression simply to make it easier to read.
   a) necessary   b) redundant
   c) embedded   d) nested

6.2 The _____ operator performs integer division.
   a) \   b) +
   c) Mod   d) ^

6.3 Every variable has a _____.
   a) name   b) value
   c) type   d) All of the above

6.4 To resume app execution after entering break mode during debugging, select _____.
   a) Debug > Continue   b) Continue > Execution
   c) Resume > Execution   d) Debug > Resume

6.5 Arithmetic expressions are evaluated _____.
   a) from right to left   b) from left to right
   c) according to the rules of operator precedence
   d) Both b and c

6.6 Variable declarations in event handlers begin with the keyword _____.
   a) Declare   b) Dim
   c) Sub   d) Integer

6.7 Modifying a value in a TextBox raises the _____ event.
   a) TextAltered   b) ValueChanged
   c) ValueEntered   d) TextChanged

6.8 The _____ function converts user input from a TextBox to a value of type Double.
   a) Convert   b) MakeDouble
   c) Val   d) WriteDouble

6.9 Variables that store integer values should be declared as _____.
   a) Integer   b) Int
   c) IntVariable   d) None of the above

6.10 The data type in a variable declaration is immediately preceded by keyword _____.
   a) IsA   b) Type
   c) Dim   d) As

EXERCISES

6.11 *(Simple Encryption App)* This app uses a simple technique to encrypt a number. Encryption is the process of modifying data so that only those intended to receive the data can undo the changes and view the original data. The user enters the data to be encrypted via a TextBox. The app then multiplies the number by 7 and adds 5. The app displays the encrypted number in a Label as shown in Fig. 6.23.

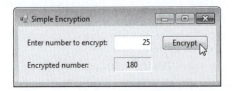

Figure 6.23   Result of completed **Simple Encryption** app.

a) *Copying the template to your working directory.* Copy the directory `C:\Examples\Ch06\Exercises\SimpleEncryption` to your `C:\SimplyVB2010` directory.

b) *Opening the app's template file.* Double click `SimpleEncryption.sln` in the `SimpleEncryption` directory to open the app.

c) *Coding the `Click` event handler.* Encrypt the number in the `Click` event handler for the **Encrypt** `Button` by using the preceding technique. The user input should be stored in an `Integer` variable (`number`) before it's encrypted. The event handler then should display the encrypted number.

d) *Clearing the result.* Add an event handler for the **Enter number to encrypt:** Text-Box's `TextChanged` event. This event handler should clear the **Encrypted number:** output `Label` whenever the user enters new input.

e) *Running the app.* Select **Debug > Start Debugging** to run your app. Enter the value 25 into the **Enter number to encrypt:** TextBox and click the **Encrypt** `Button`. Verify that the value 180 is displayed in the **Encrypted number:** output `Label`. Enter other values and click the **Encrypt** `Button` after each. Verify that the appropriate encrypted value is displayed each time.

f) *Closing the app.* Close your running app by clicking its close box.

g) *Closing the IDE.* Close the Visual Basic IDE by clicking its close box.

6.12 *(Temperature Converter App)* Write an app that converts a Celsius temperature, *C*, to its equivalent Fahrenheit temperature, *F*. Figure 6.24 displays the completed app. Use the following formula:

$$F = \frac{9}{5}C + 32$$

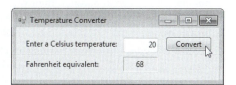

Figure 6.24 Completed **Temperature Converter**.

a) *Copying the template to your working directory.* Copy the directory `C:\Examples\Ch06\Exercises\TemperatureConversion` to your `C:\SimplyVB2010` directory.

b) *Opening the app's template file.* Double click `TemperatureConversion.sln` in the `TemperatureConversion` directory to open the app.

c) *Coding the `Click` event handler.* Perform the conversion in the **Convert** `Button`'s `Click` event handler. Define `Integer` variables to store the user-input Celsius temperature and the result of the conversion. Display the Fahrenheit equivalent of the Celsius temperature.

d) *Clearing user input.* Clear the result in the **Enter a Celsius temperature:** TextBox's `TextChanged` event.

e) *Running the app.* Select **Debug > Start Debugging** to run your app. Enter the value 20 into the **Enter a Celsius temperature:** TextBox and click the **Convert** `Button`. Verify that the value 68 is displayed in the output `Label`. Enter other Celsius temperatures; click the **Convert** `Button` after each. Use the formula provided above to verify that the proper Fahrenheit equivalent is displayed each time.

f) *Closing the app.* Close your running app by clicking its close box.

g) *Closing the IDE.* Close the Visual Basic IDE by clicking its close box.

6.13 *(Simple Calculator App)* In this exercise, you'll add functionality to a simple calculator app. The calculator allows a user to enter two numbers in the TextBoxes. There are four Buttons labeled +, -, / and *. When the user clicks the Button labeled as addition, subtraction, multiplication or division, the app performs that operation on the numbers in the TextBoxes and displays the result. The calculator also should clear the calculation result when the user enters new input. Figure 6.25 displays the completed calculator.

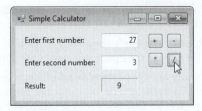

Figure 6.25 Result of **Calculator** app.

a) *Copying the template to your working directory.* Copy the directory C:\Examples\ Ch06\Exercises\SimpleCalculator to your C:\SimplyVB2010 directory.

b) *Opening the app's template file.* Double click SimpleCalculator.sln in the SimpleCalculator directory to open the app.

c) *Coding the addition Click event handler.* This event handler should add the two numbers and display the result.

d) *Coding the subtraction Click event handler.* This event handler should subtract the second number from the first and display the result.

e) *Coding the multiplication Click event handler.* This event handler should multiply the two numbers and display the result.

f) *Coding the division Click event handler.* This event handler should divide the first number by the second and display the result.

g) *Clearing the result.* Write event handlers for the TextBoxes' TextChanged events. Write code to clear resultLabel after the user enters new input into either TextBox.

h) *Running the app.* Select **Debug > Start Debugging** to run your app. Enter a first number and a second number, then verify that each Button works by clicking it and viewing the output. Repeat this process with two new values and again verify that the proper output is displayed based on which Button is clicked.

i) *Closing the app.* Close your running app by clicking its close box.

j) *Closing the IDE.* Close the Visual Basic IDE by clicking its close box.

What does this code do? ▶ **6.14** This code modifies variables number1, number2 and result. What are the final values of these variables?

```
1   Dim number1 As Integer
2   Dim number2 As Integer
3   Dim result As Integer
4
5   number1 = 5 * (4 + 6)
6   number2 = 2 ^ 2
7   result = number1 \ number2
```

What's wrong with this code? ▶ **6.15** Find the error(s) in the following code, which uses variables to perform a calculation.

```
1   Dim number1 As Integer
2   Dim number2 As Integer
3   Dim result As Integer
4
5   number1 = (4 * 6 ^ 4) / (10 Mod 4 - 2)
6   number2 = (16 \ 3) ^ 2 * 6 + 1
7   result = number1 - number2
```

Using the Debugger ▶ **6.16** *(Average Three Numbers)* You've just written an app that takes three numbers as input in TextBoxes, stores the three numbers in variables, then finds the average of the numbers (note that the average is *rounded* to the nearest integer value). The output is displayed in a Label (Fig. 6.26, which displays the incorrect output). You soon realize, however, that the number displayed in the Label is not the average, but rather a number that does not make sense given the input. Use the debugger to help locate and remove this error.

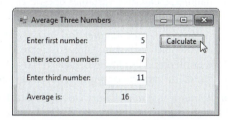

Figure 6.26   Average Three Numbers app.

a) *Copying the template to your working directory.* Copy the directory C:\Examples\ Ch06\Exercises\AverageDebugging to your C:\SimplyVB2010 directory.

b) *Opening the app's template file.* Double click AverageDebugging.sln in the AverageDebugging directory to open the app.

c) *Running the app.* Select **Debug > Start Debugging** to run your app. View the output to observe that the output is incorrect.

d) *Closing the app.* Close the app, and view the Average.vb file in **Code** view.

e) *Setting breakpoints.* Set a breakpoint in the calculateButton_Click event handler. Run the app again, and use the debugger to help find the error(s).

f) *Finding and correcting the error(s).* Once you've found the error(s), modify the app so that it correctly calculates the average of three numbers.

g) *Running the app.* Select **Debug > Start Debugging** to run your app. Enter the three values from Fig. 6.26 into the input TextBoxes provided and click the **Calculate** Button. Verify that the output now accurately reflects the average of these values, which is 8.

h) *Closing the app.* Close your running app by clicking its close box.

i) *Closing the IDE.* Close the Visual Basic IDE by clicking its close box.

Programming Challenge ▶   **6.17** (*Digit Extraction*) Write an app that allows the user to enter a five-digit number into a TextBox. The app then separates the number into its individual digits and displays each digit in a Label. The app should look and behave similarly to Fig. 6.27. [*Hint:* You can use the Mod operator to extract the ones digit from a number. For instance, 12345 Mod 10 is 5. You can use integer division (\) to "peel off" digits from a number. For instance, 12345 \ 100 is 123. This allows you to treat the 3 in 12345 as a ones digit. Now you can isolate the 3 by using the Mod operator. Apply this technique to the rest of the digits.]

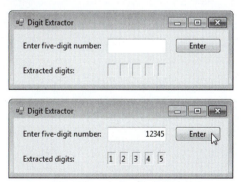

Figure 6.27   Digit Extractor app GUI.

a) *Creating the app.* Create a new project named DigitExtractor. Change the name of the Form1.vb file to DigitExtractor.vb. Change the name of the Form to DigitExtractorForm. Add Labels, a TextBox and a Button to the app's Form. Name the TextBox inputTextBox and name the Button enterButton. Name the other controls logically based on the tips provided in earlier chapters.

b) *Adding an event handler for enterButton's Click event.* In **Design** view, double click enterButton to create the enterButton_Click event handler. In this event handler, create five variables of type Integer. Use integer division and the Mod operator to extract each digit. Store the digits in the five variables created.

c) *Adding an event handler for inputTextBox's TextChanged event.* In **Design** view, double click inputTextBox to create the inputTextBox_TextChanged event handler. In this event handler, clear the five Labels used to display each digit. This event handler clears the output whenever new input is entered.

d) *Running the app.* Select **Debug > Start Debugging** to run your app. Enter a five-digit number and click the **Enter** Button. Enter a new five-digit number and verify that the previous output is cleared.

e) *Closing the app.* Close your running app by clicking its close box.

f) *Closing the IDE.* Close the Visual Basic IDE by clicking its close box.

7

Wage Calculator App

Introducing Algorithms, Pseudocode and Program Control

Before writing an app, you must have a thorough understanding of the problem you need to solve. This allows you to design a carefully planned approach to solving the problem. When writing an app, it's equally important to recognize the types of building blocks that are available and to use proven app-construction principles. In this chapter, you'll learn the theory and principles of **structured programming**. Structured programming is a technique for organizing program control that helps you develop apps that are clear and easier to debug and modify.

7.1 Test-Driving the Wage Calculator App

In this section, we preview the **Wage Calculator** app. This app must meet the following requirements:

App Requirements

A payroll company calculates the employees' earnings per week. Employees' weekly salaries are based on the number of hours they worked and their hourly wages. Create an app that accepts this information and calculates each employee's total (gross) earnings. The app assumes a standard work week of 40 hours. The wages for 40 or fewer hours are calculated by multiplying the employee's hourly wage by the number of hours worked. Any time worked over 40 hours in a week is considered "overtime" and earns time and a half. Salary for time and a half is calculated by multiplying the employee's hourly wage by 1.5 and multiplying the result of that calculation by the number of overtime hours worked. The total overtime earned is added to the user's gross earnings for the regular 40 hours of work to calculate the total earnings for that week.

This app calculates earnings from the hourly wage and the hours worked per week. Normally, an employee who has worked 40 or fewer hours is paid regular wages. The calculation differs if the employee has worked more than the standard 40-hour work week. In this chapter, we introduce a programming construct known as a control structure that allows you to make this distinction and perform different calculations based on different user inputs. You begin by test-driving

135

the completed app. Then you learn the additional Visual Basic capabilities needed to create your own version of this app.

Test-Driving the Wage Calculator App

GUI Design Tip

When using multiple TextBoxes vertically, align them on their right sides, and where possible make them the same size. Left align the descriptive Labels for such Text-Boxes.

1. *Opening the completed app.* Open the directory C:\Examples\ch07\CompletedApp\WageCalculator to locate the **Wage Calculator** app. Double click WageCalculator.sln to open the app in the Visual Basic IDE.

2. *Running the app.* Select **Debug > Start Debugging** to run the app (Fig. 7.1). To organize the GUI, we vertically aligned the TextBoxes on their right sides and made the TextBoxes the same size. We also left aligned the Text-Boxes' descriptive Labels.

Figure 7.1 **Wage Calculator** app.

3. *Entering the employee's hourly wage.* Enter **10** in the **Hourly wage:** TextBox.

4. *Entering the number of hours the employee worked.* Enter **45** in the **Weekly hours:** TextBox.

5. *Calculating the employee's gross earnings.* Click the **Calculate** Button. The result ($475.00) is displayed in the **Gross earnings:** TextBox (Fig. 7.2). Note that the employee's earnings are the sum of the wages for the standard 40-hour work week (40 * 10) and the overtime pay (5 * 10 * 1.5).

Figure 7.2 Calculating wages by clicking the **Calculate** Button.

6. *Closing the app.* Close your running app by clicking its close box.

7. *Closing the IDE.* Close the Visual Basic IDE by clicking its close box.

7.2 Algorithms

Computing problems can be solved by executing a series of actions in a specific order. A procedure for solving a problem, in terms of:

    1. the *actions* to be executed and

    2. the *order* in which these actions are to be executed

is called an **algorithm**. The following example demonstrates the importance of correctly specifying the order in which the actions are to be executed. Consider the "rise-and-shine algorithm" followed by one junior executive for getting out of bed and going to work: (1) get out of bed, (2) take off pajamas, (3) take a shower, (4) get dressed, (5) eat breakfast and (6) carpool to work. This routine prepares the executive for a productive day at the office.

However, suppose that the same steps are performed in a slightly *different* order: (1) get out of bed, (2) take off pajamas, (3) get dressed, (4) take a shower, (5) eat breakfast, (6) carpool to work. In this case, our junior executive shows up for work soaking wet.

Indicating the appropriate sequence in which to execute actions is equally crucial in computer programs. **Program control** refers to the task of *ordering* an app's statements correctly. In this chapter, you'll begin to investigate the program-control capabilities of Visual Basic.

SELF-REVIEW

1. _____ refer(s) to the task of ordering an app's statements correctly.

   a) Actions   b) Program control
   c) Control structures   d) Visual programming

2. A(n) _____ is a plan for solving a problem in terms of the actions to be executed and the order in which these actions are to be executed.

   a) chart   b) control structure
   c) algorithm   d) ordered list

   Answers: 1) b. 2) c.

7.3 Pseudocode

Pseudocode is an *informal* language that helps you formulate algorithms. The pseudocode we present is particularly useful in the development of algorithms that will be converted to structured portions of Visual Basic apps. Pseudocode resembles everyday English—it's convenient and user friendly, but it's *not* an actual computer-programming language.

Pseudocode statements are *not* executed on computers. Rather, pseudocode helps you think out an app before attempting to write it in a programming language, such as Visual Basic. In this chapter, we provide several examples of pseudocode.

Software Design Tip

Pseudocode helps you conceptualize an app during the app-design process. Pseudocode statements can be converted to Visual Basic at a later point.

The pseudocode that we present consists solely of characters, so that you can create and modify the pseudocode by using editor programs, such as the Visual Basic code editor or Notepad. A carefully prepared pseudocode program can be converted easily to a corresponding Visual Basic app. Much of this conversion is as simple as replacing pseudocode statements with their Visual Basic equivalents. Let's look at an example of a pseudocode statement:

Assign 0 to the counter

This pseudocode statement provides an easy-to-understand task. You can put several such statements together to form an algorithm that can be used to meet app requirements. When you complete the pseudocode algorithm, you can then convert pseudocode statements to their equivalent Visual Basic statements. The pseudocode statement above, for instance, can be converted to the following Visual Basic statement:

```
counter = 0
```

Pseudocode normally describes only **executable statements**—the actions performed when the corresponding Visual Basic app is run. An example of a programming statement that's not executed is a declaration. The declaration

```
Dim number As Integer
```

informs the compiler of `number`'s type and instructs the compiler to reserve space in memory for this variable. The declaration does *not* cause any action, such as input, output or a calculation, to occur when the app executes, so we would not include this information in the pseudocode.

1. _____ is an informal language that helps you develop algorithms.

    a) Pseudocode   b) VB-Speak

    c) Notation   d) None of the above

2. Pseudocode _____.

    a) usually describes only declarations   b) is executed on computers

    c) usually describes only executable lines of code

    d) usually describes declarations and executable lines of code

Answers: 1) a. 2) c.

7.4 Control Statements

Normally, statements in an app are executed one after another in the order in which they're written. This is called **sequential execution**. Visual Basic allows you to *alter the order* in which statements are executed. A **transfer of control** occurs when an executed statement does *not* directly follow the previously executed statement in the written app. This is common in computer programs.

Sequence Statement, Activity Diagrams, the UML

All programs can be written in terms of only three types of control statements: the *sequence statement*, the *selection statement* and the *repetition statement*. The **sequence statement** is *built into* Visual Basic—unless directed to act otherwise, the computer executes Visual Basic statements *sequentially*—that is, one after the other in the order in which they appear in the app. The **activity diagram** in Fig. 7.3 illustrates a typical sequence statement, in which two calculations are performed in order.

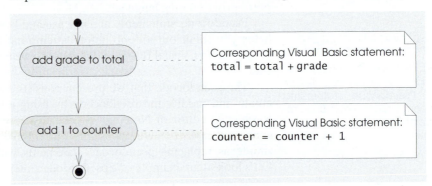

Figure 7.3   Sequence statement activity diagram.

Activity diagrams are part of the **Unified Modeling Language (UML)**—an industry standard for modeling software systems. An activity diagram models the activity (also called the **workflow**) of a portion of a software system. Such activities may include a portion of an algorithm, such as the sequence structure in Fig. 7.3. Activity diagrams are composed of special-purpose symbols, such as the **action-state symbol** (a rectangle with its left and right sides replaced with arcs curving outward), the **diamond symbol** and the **small circle symbol**; these symbols are connected by **transition arrows**, which represent the *flow* of the activity. Figure 7.3 does not include any diamond symbols—these are used in later activity diagrams.

Like pseudocode, activity diagrams help you develop and represent algorithms, although many programmers prefer pseudocode because it's easy to type into a text editor and tune it. Activity diagrams clearly show how control structures operate.

Consider the activity diagram for the sequence structure in Fig. 7.3. The activity diagram contains two **action states** that represent actions to perform. Each action state contains an **action expression**—for example, "add grade to total" or "add 1 to counter"—that specifies a particular action to perform. Other actions might include calculations or input/output operations. The arrows in the activity diagram are called *transition arrows*. These arrows represent **transitions**, indicating the *order* in which the actions represented by the action states occur—the app that implements the activities illustrated by the activity diagram in Fig. 7.3 first adds `grade` to `total`, then adds `1` to `counter`.

The **solid circle** located at the top of the activity diagram represents the activity's **initial state**—the *beginning* of the workflow *before* the app performs the modeled activities. The solid circle surrounded by a hollow circle that appears at the bottom of the activity diagram represents the **final state**—the *end* of the workflow *after* the app performs its activities.

Notice, in Fig. 7.3, the rectangles with the upper-right corners folded over. They look like sheets of paper and are called **notes** in the UML. Notes are like *comments* in Visual Basic apps—they're explanatory remarks that describe the purpose of symbols in the diagram. Figure 7.3 uses UML notes to show the Visual Basic code that you might associate with each action state in the activity diagram. A dotted line connects each note with the element that the note describes. Activity diagrams normally do *not* show the Visual Basic code that implements the activity, but we use notes here to show you how the diagram relates to Visual Basic code.

Selection Statements

Visual Basic provides three types of **selection statements**, which we discuss in this chapter and in Chapter 12. The `If...Then` selection statement performs (selects) an action (or sequence of actions) based on a condition. A **condition** is an expression with a **true** or **false** value that's used to make a *decision*. Conditions are **evaluated** (that is, *tested*) to determine whether their value is true or false. These values are of data type `Boolean`, and we specify them in Visual Basic code by using the keywords `True` and `False`. Sometimes we refer to a condition as a `Boolean` expression.

If the condition evaluates to `True`, the actions specified by the `If...Then` statement are executed. If the condition evaluates to `False`, those actions are skipped. The `If...Then...Else` selection statement performs an action (or sequence of actions) if a condition is true and a different action (or sequence of actions) if the condition is false. The `Select Case` statement, discussed in Chapter 12, performs one of many actions (or sequences of actions), depending on an expression's value.

The `If...Then` statement is called a **single-selection statement** because it selects or ignores a single action (or a sequence of actions). The `If...Then...Else` statement is called a **double-selection statement** because it selects between two different actions (or sequences of actions). The `Select Case` statement is called a **multiple-selection statement** because it selects among many different actions (or sequences of actions).

Repetition Statements

Visual Basic provides seven types of **repetition statements** (also called *loops*) for performing a statement or group of statements repeatedly. These are listed below with the chapters in which they're introduced:

- `While...End While`[1]
- `Do While...Loop` (Chapter 9)
- `Do Until...Loop` (Chapter 9)
- `Do...Loop While` (Chapter 10)
- `Do...Loop Until` (Chapter 10)
- `For...Next` (Chapter 11)
- `For Each...Next` (Chapter 20)

---

1. We do not discuss the `While...End While` loop in this book. This repetition statement behaves identically to the `Do While...Loop` and is provided for programmers familiar with previous versions of Visual Basic.

Keywords

The words If, Then, Else, End, Select, Case, While, Do, Until, Loop, For, Next and Each are all Visual Basic *keywords*—Appendix D includes a complete list of Visual Basic keywords. We'll discuss many of Visual Basic's keywords and their respective purposes.

Control Statement Notes

Visual Basic has 11 control statements—the sequence statement, three types of selection statements and seven types of repetition statements. All Visual Basic apps are formed by combining as many of each type of control statement as is necessary. As with the sequence statement in Fig. 7.3, each control statement is drawn with two small circle symbols—a solid black one to represent the entry point to the control statement, and a solid black one surrounded by a hollow circle to represent the exit point.

All Visual Basic control statements are **single-entry/single-exit control statements**—each has exactly one entry point and one exit point. Such control statements make it easy to build apps—the control statements are attached to one another by connecting the exit point of one to the entry point of the next. This is similar to stacking building blocks, so we call it **control-statement stacking**. The only other way to connect control statements is through **control-statement nesting**, whereby one control statement can be placed inside another. Thus, algorithms in Visual Basic apps are constructed from only 11 different types of control statements combined in only two ways—this is a model of simplicity.

SELF-REVIEW

1. All Visual Basic apps can be written in terms of _____ types of control statements.
   a) one   b) two
   c) three   d) four

2. The process of statements executing one after another in the order in which they're written is called _____.
   a) transfer of control   b) sequential execution
   c) workflow   d) None of the above

Answers: 1) c. 2) b.

7.5 If...Then Selection Statement

A selection statement chooses among alternative courses of action in an app. For example, suppose that the passing grade on a test is 60 (out of 100). The pseudocode statement

> *If student's grade is greater than or equal to 60*
>   *Display "Passed"*

Common Programming Error

Omitting the Then keyword in an If...Then statement is a syntax error. The IDE helps prevent this error by inserting the Then keyword after you write the condition.

determines whether the condition "student's grade is greater than or equal to 60" is true or false. If the condition is true, then "Passed" is displayed, and the next pseudocode statement in order is "performed." (Remember that pseudocode is *not* a real programming language.) If the condition is false, the display statement is *ignored*, and the next pseudocode statement in order is performed.

The preceding pseudocode *If* statement may be written in Visual Basic as

```
If studentGrade >= 60 Then
    displayLabel.Text = "Passed"
End If
```

The Visual Basic code corresponds closely to the pseudocode, demonstrating the usefulness of pseudocode as an app-development tool. The body (sometimes called a **block**) of the If...Then statement displays the string "Passed" in a Label. The keywords End If close an If...Then statement.

The indentation in the If...Then statement enhances code readability. The Visual Basic compiler *ignores* whitespace characters, such as spaces, tabs and newlines used for indentation and vertical spacing, unless the whitespace characters are contained in strings.

The condition between keywords If and Then determines whether the statement(s) within the If...Then statement will execute. If true, the body of the If...Then statement executes. If the condition is false, the body is *not* executed. Conditions in If...Then statements can be formed by using the **equality operators** and **relational operators** (also called **comparison operators**), which are summarized in Fig. 7.4. The relational and equality operators all have the *same* level of precedence.

Algebraic equality or relational operator	Visual Basic equality or relational operator	Example of Visual Basic condition	Meaning of Visual Basic condition
Relational operators			
>	>	x > y	x is greater than y
<	<	x < y	x is less than y
≥	>=	x >= y	x is greater than or equal to y
≤	<=	x <= y	x is less than or equal to y
Equality operators			
=	=	x = y	x is equal to y
≠	<>	x <> y	x is not equal to y

Figure 7.4 Equality and relational operators.

Figure 7.5 shows the syntax of the If...Then statement. A statement's **syntax** specifies how the statement must be formed to compile without syntax errors. Let's look closely at the syntax of an If...Then statement. The first line of Fig. 7.5 specifies that the statement must begin with the keyword If and be followed by a condition and the keyword Then. Note that we've italicized *condition*. This indicates that, when creating your own If...Then statement, you should replace the text *condition* with the *actual* condition that you would like evaluated. The second line indicates that you should replace *statements* with the actual statements that you want to be included in the body of the If...Then statement. Note that the text *statements* is placed within square brackets. These brackets do *not* appear in the actual If...Then statement. Instead, the square brackets indicate that certain portions of the statement are *optional*. In this example, the square brackets indicate that all statements in the If...Then statement's body are *optional*. Of course, if there are *no* statements in the body of the If...Then statement, then *no* actions will occur as part of that statement, regardless of the condition's value. The final line indicates that the statement ends with the End If keywords.

Syntax

```
If condition Then
    [ statements ]
End If
```

Figure 7.5 If...Then statement syntax.

Figure 7.6 illustrates the single-selection If...Then statement. This activity diagram contains what is perhaps the most important symbol in an activity diagram—the *diamond*, or **decision symbol**, which indicates that a *decision* is to be made. Note the two sets of square brackets above or next to the arrows leading from the decision symbol; these are called **guard conditions**. A decision symbol indicates that the workflow continues along a path determined by the symbol's associated guard conditions, which can be true or false. Each transition arrow emerging from a decision symbol has a guard condition (specified in square brackets above or next to the transition arrow). If a particular guard condition is true, the workflow enters the action state to which that transition arrow points. For example, in Fig. 7.6, if the grade is greater than or equal to 60, the app displays "Passed," then transitions to the final state of this activity. If the grade is less than 60, the app immediately transitions to the final state without displaying a message. Only one guard condition associated with a particular decision symbol can be true at once.

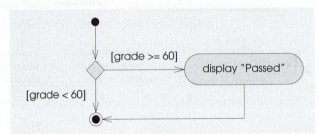

Figure 7.6 If...Then single-selection statement activity diagram.

Note that the If...Then statement (Fig. 7.6) is a *single-entry/single-exit statement*. The activity diagrams for the remaining control statements contain (aside from small circle symbols and transition arrows) only action-state symbols, indicating actions to be performed, and diamond symbols, indicating decisions to be made. This is the **action/decision model of programming** we've been emphasizing.

SELF-REVIEW

1. Which of the following If...Then statements correctly displays that a student received an A on an exam if the score was 90 or above?

   a) ```
If studentGrade <> 90 Then
    displayLabel.Text = "Student received an A"
End If
```

   b) ```
If studentGrade > 90 Then
    displayLabel.Text = "Student received an A"
End If
```

   c) ```
If studentGrade = 90 Then
    displayLabel.Text = "Student received an A"
End If
```

   d) ```
If studentGrade >= 90 Then
    displayLabel.Text = "Student received an A"
End If
```

2. The symbol _____ is not a Visual Basic operator.

   a) *   b) ^

   c) %   d) <>

Answers: 1) d. 2) c.

7.6 If...Then...Else Selection Statement and Conditional If Expressions

As you've learned, the If...Then selection statement performs an indicated action (or sequence of actions) only when the condition evaluates to True; otherwise, the action (or sequence of actions) is skipped. The If...Then...Else selection statement allows you to specify that a *different* action (or sequence of actions) is to be performed when the condition is true than when the condition is false. For example, the pseudocode statement

> If student's grade is greater than or equal to 60
>   Display "Passed"
> Else
>   Display "Failed"

displays "Passed" if the student's grade is greater than or equal to 60, but displays "Failed" if the student's grade is less than 60. In either case, after output occurs, the next pseudocode statement in sequence is "performed." The preceding pseudocode may be written in Visual Basic as

```
If studentGrade >= 60 Then
    displayLabel.Text = "Passed"
Else
    displayLabel.Text = "Failed"
End If
```

Good Programming Practice

It's important to indent both body statements of an If...Then...Else statement to improve readability and emphasize the structure of the code.

Note that the body of the `Else` clause is indented so that it lines up with the indented body of the `If` clause. A standard indentation convention should be applied consistently throughout your apps. It's difficult to read programs that do not use uniform spacing conventions. The IDE helps you maintain consistent indentation with its "smart indenting" feature, which is enabled by default for Visual Basic.

The `If...Then...Else` selection statement follows the same general syntax as the `If...Then` statement. The `Else` keyword and any related statements are placed between the `If...Then` and closing `End If` keywords, as in Fig. 7.7.

Good Programming Practice

Applying a standard indentation convention consistently throughout your apps enhances readability. Visual Basic's "smart indenting" feature helps you do this.

Syntax

```
If condition Then
    [ statements ]
Else
    [ statements ]
End If
```

Figure 7.7 If...Then...Else statement syntax.

The preceding `If...Then...Else` statement can also be written using a **conditional If expression**, as in

```
displayLabel.Text = If(studentGrade >= 60, "Passed", "Failed")
```

A conditional `If` expression starts with the keyword `If` and is followed by three expressions in parentheses—a condition, the value of the conditional expression if the condition is true and the value if the condition is false.

Figure 7.8 illustrates the flow of control in the `If...Then...Else` double-selection statement. Once again, aside from the initial state, transition arrows and final state, the only symbols in the activity diagram represent action states and decisions. In this example, the grade is either less than 60 or greater than or equal to 60. If the grade is less than 60, the app displays `"Failed"`. If the grade is greater than or equal to 60, the app displays `"Passed"`.

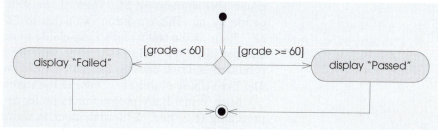

Figure 7.8 If...Then...Else double-selection statement activity diagram.

Nested If...Then...Else statements test for multiple conditions by placing If...Then...Else statements inside other If...Then...Else statements. For example, the following pseudocode displays "A" for exam grades greater than or equal to 90, "B" for grades in the range 80–89, "C" for grades in the range 70–79, "D" for grades in the range 60–69 and "F" for all other grades:

> If student's grade is greater than or equal to 90
>> Display "A"
> Else
>> If student's grade is greater than or equal to 80
>>> Display "B"
>> Else
>>> If student's grade is greater than or equal to 70
>>>> Display "C"
>>> Else
>>>> If student's grade is greater than or equal to 60
>>>>> Display "D"
>>>> Else
>>>>> Display "F"

The preceding pseudocode may be written in Visual Basic as shown in Fig. 7.9.

Good Programming Practice

If there are several levels of indentation, each level should be indented farther to the right by the same amount of space.

```
1   If studentGrade >= 90 Then
2       displayLabel.Text = "A"
3   Else
4       If studentGrade >= 80 Then
5           displayLabel.Text = "B"
6       Else
7           If studentGrade >= 70 Then
8               displayLabel.Text = "C"
9           Else
10              If studentGrade >= 60 Then
11                  displayLabel.Text = "D"
12              Else
13                  displayLabel.Text = "F"
14              End If
15          End If
16      End If
17  End If
```

Figure 7.9 Visual Basic code converted from pseudocode.

If studentGrade is greater than or equal to 90, the first condition evaluates to True and the statement displayLabel.Text = "A" is executed. With a value for studentGrade greater than or equal to 90, the remaining three conditions will evaluate to True. These conditions, however, are *never* evaluated, because they're placed within the Else portion of the *outer* If...Then...Else statement. The first condition is True, so all statements within the Else clause are skipped. Let's now assume that studentGrade contains the value 75. The first condition is False, so the app executes the statements within the Else clause of this statement. This Else clause also contains an If...Then...Else statement, with the condition studentGrade >= 80. This condition evaluates to False, causing the statements in this If...Then...Else statement's Else clause to execute. This Else clause contains yet another If...Then...Else statement, with the condition studentGrade >= 70. This condition is True, causing the statement displayLabel.Text = "C" to execute. The Else clause of this If...Then...Else statement is then skipped.

Most Visual Basic programmers prefer to use the **ElseIf keyword** to write the preceding If...Then...Else statement, as shown in Fig. 7.10.

```
1   If studentGrade >= 90 Then
2       displayLabel.Text = "A"
3   ElseIf studentGrade >= 80 Then
4       displayLabel.Text = "B"
5   ElseIf studentGrade >= 70 Then
6       displayLabel.Text = "C"
7   ElseIf studentGrade >= 60 Then
8       displayLabel.Text = "D"
9   Else
10      displayLabel.Text = "F"
11  End If
```

Figure 7.10   If...Then...Else statement using the ElseIf keyword.

The two statements are equivalent, but you should use the latter statement—it avoids deep indentation of the code. Such deep indentation often leaves little room on a line, forcing lines to be split and decreasing code readability. Note that the final portion of the If...Then...Else statement uses the Else keyword to handle all the remaining possibilities. The Else clause must always be last in an If...Then...Else statement—following an Else clause with another Else or ElseIf clause is a syntax error. You should also note that the latter statement requires only one End If.

SELF-REVIEW

1. If...Then...Else is a _____ -selection statement.

   a) single   b) double
   c) triple   d) nested

2. Placing an If...Then...Else statement inside another If...Then...Else statement is an example of _____ .

   a) nesting If...Then...Else statements   b) stacking If...Then...Else statements
   c) creating sequential If...Then...Else   d) None of the above
      statements

Answers: 1) b. 2) a.

7.7 Constructing the Wage Calculator App

This section builds the **Wage Calculator** by using the If...Then...Else statement. The If...Then...Else statement allows you to select between calculating regular wages and including overtime pay based on the number of hours worked. The following pseudocode describes the basic operation of the **Wage Calculator** app.

> When the user clicks the Calculate Button
>> Retrieve the number of hours worked and hourly wage from the TextBoxes
>>
>> If the number of hours worked is less than or equal to 40 hours
>>> Gross earnings equals hours worked times hourly wage
>>
>> Else
>>> Gross earnings equals 40 times hourly wage plus
>>> hours above 40 times wage and a half
>>
>> Display gross earnings

Now that you've test-driven the **Wage Calculator** app and studied its pseudocode representation, you'll use an **Action/Control/Event (ACE) table** to help you convert the pseudocode to Visual Basic. Figure 7.11 lists the actions, controls and events that help you complete your own version of this app.

Visual Studio provides many programming tools to help you create powerful and effective apps. With so many tools available, it's often helpful to create a table to organize and choose the best GUI elements. Like pseudocode, these tables simplify the task of creating the app by outlining the app's actions. The table also assigns controls and events to the actions described in the pseudocode.

The Labels in the first row display information about the app to the user. These Labels guide the user through the app. The Button control, calculateButton, is used to calculate the employee's wages. Note that the third column of the table specifies that we'll be using this control's Click event to perform the calculations. The TextBoxes contain input from the user. The final control, earningsResultLabel, is a Label that displays the app's output.

	Action	Control	Event
Action/Control/Event (ACE) Table for the Wage Calculator App	Label the app's controls	wageLabel, hoursLabel, earningsLabel	App is run
		calculateButton	Click
	Retrieve the number of hours worked and hourly wage from the TextBoxes	wageTextBox, hoursTextBox	
	If the number of hours worked is less than or equal to 40 hours Gross earnings equals hours worked times hourly wage		
	Else Gross earnings equals 40 times hourly wage plus hours above 40 times wage and a half		
	Display gross earnings	earningsResult-Label	

Figure 7.11 Action/Control/Event table for the **Wage Calculator** app.

We now apply our pseudocode and the ACE table to complete the **Wage Calculator** app. The following box guides you through the process of adding a Click event to the **Calculate** Button and declaring the variables you need to calculate the employee's wages. If you forget to add code to this Click event, the app won't respond when the user clicks the **Calculate** Button.

Declaring Variables in the Calculate *Button's* Click *Event Handler*

1. ***Copying the template to your working directory.*** Copy the C:\Examples\ ch07\TemplateApp\WageCalculator directory to your C:\SimplyVB2010 directory.

2. ***Opening the Wage Calculator app's template file.*** Double click WageCalculator.sln in the WageCalculator directory to open the app in the Visual Basic IDE. If the app does not open in **Design** view, double click the **WageCalculator.vb** file in the **Solution Explorer**. If the **Solution Explorer** is not open, select **View > Other Windows > Solution Explorer**.

3. ***Adding the Calculate Button Click event handler.*** In this example, the event handler calculates the gross earnings when the **Calculate** Button's Click event occurs. Double click the **Calculate** Button. An event handler is generated, and the IDE switches to **Code** view. Lines 3–6 of Fig. 7.12 display the generated event handler.

(cont.)

```
1  Public Class WageCalculatorForm
2     ' handles Click event
3     Private Sub calculateButton_Click(sender As System.Object,
4        e As System.EventArgs) Handles calculateButton.Click
5
6     End Sub ' calculateButton_Click
7  End Class ' WageCalculatorForm
```

Figure 7.12   **Calculate Button** event handler.

The **End Sub** keywords (line 6) indicate the end of event handler `calculateButton_Click`. The **End Class** keywords (line 7) indicate the end of class `WageCalculatorForm`. We often add comments so that you can easily determine which event handler or class is being closed without having to search for the beginning of that event handler or class in the file.

4. *Declaring variables.* This app uses the primitive data types `Double` and `Decimal`. A `Double` holds numbers with decimal points. Because hours and wages are often fractional numbers, `Integers` are not appropriate for this app. Add lines 6–9 of Fig. 7.13 into the body of event handler `calculateButton_Click`. Line 7 contains a variable declaration for the `Double hours`, which holds the number of hours entered by the user.

```
2     ' handles Click event
3     Private Sub calculateButton_Click(sender As System.Object,
4        e As System.EventArgs) Handles calculateButton.Click
5
6        ' declare variables
7        Dim hours As Double
8        Dim wage As Decimal
9        Dim earnings As Decimal
10
11    End Sub ' calculateButton_Click
```

Variable declarations ⟵ 7, 8, 9

Figure 7.13   Declaring variables of type `Double` and `Decimal`.

Type **Decimal** is used to store *monetary amounts* because this data type minimizes rounding errors in arithmetic calculations involving monetary amounts. Lines 8–9 declare `wage`, which stores the hourly wage entered by the user, and `earnings`, which stores the total amount of earnings for the week.

Good Programming Practice

Constants (also called named constants) help make programs more readable by providing names for constant values.

5. *Declaring a constant.* Add line 11 of Fig. 7.14 to the end of event handler `calculateButton_Click`. Line 11 contains a **constant**, an identifier whose value cannot be changed after its initial declaration. Constants are declared with keyword **Const**. In this case, we assign to the constant `HOUR_LIMIT` the maximum number of hours worked before mandatory overtime pay (40). Note that we capitalize the constant's name to emphasize that it's a constant.

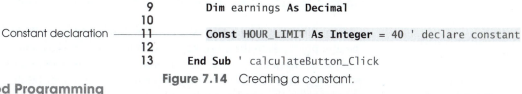

```
9        Dim earnings As Decimal
10
11       Const HOUR_LIMIT As Integer = 40 ' declare constant
12
13    End Sub ' calculateButton_Click
```

Constant declaration ⟵ 11

Figure 7.14   Creating a constant.

6. *Saving the project.* Select **File > Save All** to save your modified code.

Good Programming Practice

Capitalize each letter in the name of a constant and separate each word in the name with an underscore.

Now that you've declared variables, you can use them to retrieve values entered by the user, then use those values to compute and display the user's earnings. The following box walks you through using an If...Then...Else statement to determine the user's earnings.

Determining the User's Wages

1. **Obtaining inputs from the TextBoxes.** Add lines 13–15 of Fig. 7.15 to the end of event handler calculateButton_Click. ==Lines 14–15 assign values to hours and wage from the TextBoxes into which the user enters data. The Val function returns the user input as Doubles (lines 14–15).== Visual Basic implicitly converts the Double result of Val to data type Decimal before assigning the result to wage (line 15).

```
11        Const HOUR_LIMIT As Integer = 40 ' declare constant
12
13        ' assign values from user input
14        hours = Val(hoursTextBox.Text)
15        wage = Val(wageTextBox.Text)
16
17      End Sub ' calculateButton_Click
```

Variable assignment → (lines 14–15)

Figure 7.15 Assigning data to variables.

Error-Prevention Tip

To reduce errors, the IDE sometimes adds keywords for you. One example is the adding of End If when an If...Then or an If...Then...Else statement is created. This eliminates the possibility that such keywords will be forgotten or misspelled.

2. **Determining wages based on hours worked.** Begin to add the If...Then...Else statement shown in lines 17–28 of Fig. 7.16 to the end of event handler calculateButton_Click. First type lines 17–18, then press *Enter*. Note that the keywords End If are added for you by the IDE. Continue by adding lines 19–27 to the If...Then...Else statement. You might need to indent as you go. This If...Then...Else statement determines whether employees earn overtime in addition to their usual wages. Line 18 determines whether the value stored in hours is less than or equal to HOUR_LIMIT. If it is, then line 20 assigns the product of hours and wage to earnings. ==When you multiply a variable of data type Double by a variable of data type Decimal, Visual Basic implicitly converts the Decimal variable to a Double.== The Double result is then implicitly converted to a Decimal when it's assigned to Decimal variable earnings.

```
17        ' determine earnings
18      If hours <= HOUR_LIMIT Then
19          ' if less than or equal to 40 hours, regular wages
20          earnings = hours * wage
21      Else
22          ' if over 40 hours, regular wages for first 40
23          earnings = HOUR_LIMIT * wage
24
25          ' time and a half for the additional hours
26          earnings = earnings +
27              (hours - HOUR_LIMIT) * (1.5 * wage)
28      End If
```

If...Then...Else statement →

Figure 7.16 If...Then...Else statement to determine wages.

Good Programming Practice

Place a blank line before and after each control statement to make it stand out in the code.

If, on the other hand, hours is not less than or equal to HOUR_LIMIT, then the app proceeds to the Else keyword in line 21. Line 23 computes the earnings for the hours worked up to the limit set by HOUR_LIMIT and assigns it to earnings. Lines 26–27 determine how many hours over HOUR_LIMIT there are (by using the expression hours - HOUR_LIMIT), then multiplies that by 1.5 times the user's hourly wage. This calculation results in the user's time-and-a-half pay for overtime hours, which is then added to earnings, and the result is assigned to earnings.

(cont.)   3. ***Displaying the result.*** Add lines 30–31 of Fig. 7.17 to the end of event handler `calculateButton_Click`. Line 31 assigns the value in `earnings` to the
Text property of the `Label` `earningsResultLabel`, implicitly converting
`earnings` from a `Decimal` to a string.

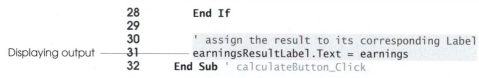

```
28          End If
29
30          ' assign the result to its corresponding Label
31          earningsResultLabel.Text = earnings
32       End Sub ' calculateButton_Click
```

Displaying output — 31

Figure 7.17   Assigning the result to `earningsResultLabel`.

4. ***Running the app.*** Select **Debug > Start Debugging** to run your app. Note
that the output is not yet formatted as it should be in the completed app
(Fig. 7.18). You learn how to add this functionality in Section 7.9.

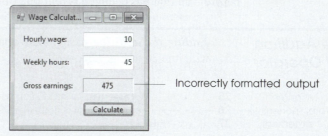

Incorrectly formatted output

Figure 7.18   **Wage Calculator** with incorrectly formatted output.

5. ***Closing the app.*** Close your running app by clicking its close box.

SELF-REVIEW   1. The `Decimal` data type is used to store _____ .
     a) letters and digits   b) integers
     c) strings   d) monetary amounts

2. Constants are declared with keyword _____ .
     a) `Fixed`   b) `Constant`
     c) `Final`   d) `Const`

Answers: 1) d. 2) d.

7.8 Assignment Operators

Visual Basic provides several assignment operators for abbreviating assignment
statements. For example, the statement

```
number = number + 3
```

which adds 3 to the value in `number`, can be abbreviated with the addition assignment operator `+=` as

```
number += 3
```

The `+=` operator adds the value of the right operand to the value of the left operand
and stores the result in the left operand. Visual Basic provides assignment operators for several binary operators, including +, -, *, ^, / and \. When an assignment
statement is evaluated, the expression to the right of the operator is always evaluated first, then the appropriate assignment is made to the variable on the left.
Figure 7.19 show some of the assignment operators, sample expressions using these
operators and explanations.

Assignment operators	Sample expression	Explanation	Assigns
Assume: c = 4			
+=	c += 7	c = c + 7	11 to c
-=	c -= 3	c = c - 3	1 to c
*=	c *= 4	c = c * 4	16 to c
/=	c /= 2	c = c / 2	2 to c
\=	c \= 3	c = c \ 3	1 to c
^=	c ^= 2	c = c ^ 2	16 to c

Figure 7.19   Assignment operators.

The following box demonstrates abbreviating our time-and-a-half calculation with the += operator. When you run the app again, notice that it runs the same as before—all that has changed is that one of the longer statements was made shorter.

Using the Addition Assignment Operator

1. ***Adding the addition assignment operator.*** Replace lines 26–27 of Fig. 7.16 with line 26 of Fig. 7.20.

Addition assignment operator shortens statement

```
25          ' time and a half for the additional hours
26          earnings += (hours - HOUR_LIMIT) * (1.5 * wage)
27       End If
```

Figure 7.20   Using the addition assignment operator in a calculation.

In this step, we've used the addition assignment operator to make our statement shorter. Note that the statement still performs the same action—the time-and-a-half pay for the user is calculated and added to the regular wages earned.

2. ***Running the app.*** Select **Debug > Start Debugging** to run your app. Note that the app still does not format the output properly. The functionality of the app is the same as it was in the last box—we're now simply using the += operator to abbreviate a statement.

3. ***Closing the app.*** Close your running app by clicking its close box.

SELF-REVIEW

1. The *= operator _____.
   a) squares the value of the right operand and stores the result in the left operand
   b) adds the value of the right operand to the value of the left operand and stores the result in the left operand
   c) creates a new variable and assigns the value of the right operand to that variable
   d) multiplies the value of the left operand by the value of the right operand and stores the result in the left operand

2. If number is initialized with the value 5, what value will number contain after the expression number -= 3 is executed?
   a) 3   b) 5
   c) 7   d) 2

Answers: 1) d. 2) d.

7.9 Formatting Text

There are several ways to format output in Visual Basic. In this section, we introduce method **String.Format** to control how text displays. Modifying the appearance of text for display purposes is known as **text formatting**. This method takes as an argument a **format control string**, followed by arguments that indicate the values to be formatted. The format control string argument specifies *how* the remaining arguments are to be formatted.

Recall that your **Wage Calculator** does not display the result of its calculation with the appropriate decimal and dollar sign that you saw when test-driving the app. Next, you learn how to apply currency formatting to the value in the **Gross earnings:** TextBox.

Formatting the Gross Earnings

GUI Design Tip

Format monetary amounts using the C (currency) format specifier.

Formatting output as currency

1. *Modifying the Calculate Button's Click event.* If the IDE is not already in **Code** view, select **View > Code**. Replace line 31 of Fig. 7.17 with line 30 of Fig. 7.21. Line 30 sends the format control string, `"{0:C}"`, and the value to be formatted, earnings, to the String.Format method. The number zero indicates that argument 0 (earnings—the first argument after the format control string) should take the format specified by the letter after the colon; this letter is called the **format specifier**. In this case, we use the format defined by the uppercase letter C, which represents the **currency format**, used to display values as monetary amounts. The effect of the C format specifier varies, depending on the locale setting of your computer. In our case, the result is preceded with a dollar sign ($), uses a comma as the thousands separator and displays with two decimal places (representing cents) because we're in the United States. You may also specify the locale to use, but that's beyond the scope of this chapter.

```
27            End If
28
29            ' assign the result to its corresponding Label
30            earningsResultLabel.Text = String.Format("{0:C}", earnings)
31        End Sub ' calculateButton_Click
```
Figure 7.21 Using the Format method to display the result as currency.

---

2. *Running the app.* Select **Debug > Start Debugging** to run your app. The app should now output gross earnings as currency.

3. *Closing the app.* Close your running app by clicking its close box.

4. *Saving the project.* Select **File > Save All** to save your modified code.

Figure 7.22 shows several format specifiers. These are *case insensitive*, so the uppercase letters may be used interchangeably with their lowercase equivalents. Note that format code D must be used only with *integer* types (such as Integer, Byte, Short and Long).

Format Specifier	Description
C	*Currency*. Formats the currency based on the computer's locale setting. For U.S. currency, precedes the number with $, separates every three digits with commas and sets the number of decimal places to two.
E	*Scientific notation*. Displays one digit to the left of the decimal point and six digits to the right of the decimal point, followed by the character E and a three-digit integer representing the exponent of a power of 10. For example, 956.2 is formatted as 9.562000E+002.
F	*Fixed point*. Sets the number of decimal places to two.

Figure 7.22 Format specifiers for strings. (Part 1 of 2.)

Format Specifier	Description
G	*General*. Visual Basic chooses either E or F for you, depending on which representation generates a shorter string.
D	*Decimal integer*. Displays an integer as a whole number in standard base 10 format.
N	*Number*. Separates every three digits with a comma and sets the number of decimal places to two. (Varies by locale.)

Figure 7.22 Format specifiers for strings. (Part 2 of 2.)

Figure 7.23 presents the source code for the **Wage Calculator** app. When you compile and run this app now, it formats the gross earnings exactly as in the test drive (Fig. 7.2). The lines of code that contain new programming concepts you learned in this chapter are highlighted.

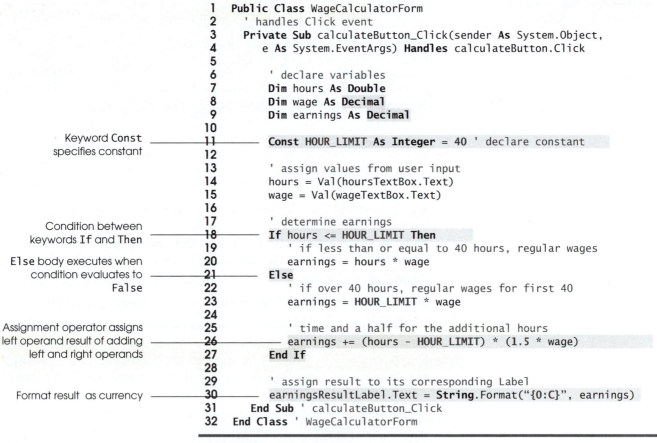

```
1    Public Class WageCalculatorForm
2      ' handles Click event
3      Private Sub calculateButton_Click(sender As System.Object,
4        e As System.EventArgs) Handles calculateButton.Click
5
6        ' declare variables
7        Dim hours As Double
8        Dim wage As Decimal
9        Dim earnings As Decimal
10
11       Const HOUR_LIMIT As Integer = 40 ' declare constant
12
13       ' assign values from user input
14       hours = Val(hoursTextBox.Text)
15       wage = Val(wageTextBox.Text)
16
17       ' determine earnings
18       If hours <= HOUR_LIMIT Then
19         ' if less than or equal to 40 hours, regular wages
20         earnings = hours * wage
21       Else
22         ' if over 40 hours, regular wages for first 40
23         earnings = HOUR_LIMIT * wage
24
25         ' time and a half for the additional hours
26         earnings += (hours - HOUR_LIMIT) * (1.5 * wage)
27       End If
28
29       ' assign result to its corresponding Label
30       earningsResultLabel.Text = String.Format("{0:C}", earnings)
31     End Sub ' calculateButton_Click
32   End Class ' WageCalculatorForm
```

Keyword Const specifies constant — line 11

Condition between keywords If and Then — line 18

Else body executes when condition evaluates to False — line 21

Assignment operator assigns left operand result of adding left and right operands — line 26

Format result as currency — line 30

Figure 7.23 **Wage Calculator** app code.

SELF-REVIEW

1. Method `String.Format` is used to _____.

a) create constants

b) control how text is formatted

c) format Visual Basic statements

d) All of the above

2. The _____ format displays values as monetary amounts.
   a) decimal integer   b) number
   c) currency   d) fixed point

Answers: 1) b. 2) c.

7.10 Using the Debugger: The Watch Window

Visual Studio includes several debugging windows that are accessible from the **Debug > Windows** submenu. The **Watch window**, which is available only in *break mode*, allows you to examine the value of a variable or expression. You can use the **Watch** window to *view changes in a variable's value as the app executes,* or you can change a variable's value yourself by entering the new value directly into the **Watch** window. Each expression or variable that's added to the **Watch** window is called a watch. In the following box, we demonstrate how to add, remove and manipulate watches by using the **Watch** window.

Using the Debugger: The Watch Window

1. ***Starting debugging.*** If the IDE is not in **Code** view, switch to **Code** view now. Set breakpoints in lines 15 and 20 (Fig. 7.24). Select **Debug > Start Debugging** to run the app. The **Wage Calculator** Form appears. Enter 12 into the **Hourly wage:** TextBox and 40 into the **Weekly hours:** TextBox (Fig. 7.25). Click the **Calculate** Button.

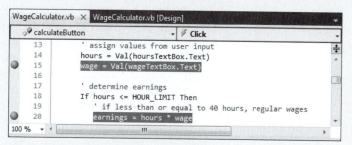

Figure 7.24   Breakpoints added to **Wage Calculator** app.

Figure 7.25   **Wage Calculator** app.

2. ***Suspending app execution.*** Clicking the **Calculate** Button causes event handler `calculateButton_Click` to execute until the breakpoint is reached. At that point, app execution is paused, and the IDE switches into *break mode*. Note that the active window has been changed from the running app to the IDE. The **active window** is the window that's currently being used and is sometimes referred to as the window that has the **focus**. The **Wage Calculator** app is still running, but it may be hidden behind the IDE.

(cont.)   3. ***Examining data.*** Once the app has entered *break mode*, you're free to explore the values of various variables, using the debugger's **Watch** window. To display the **Watch** window, select **Debug > Windows > Watch**. The **Watch** window is initially empty. To add a watch, you can type an expression into the **Name** column. Single click in the first field of the **Name** column. Type hours, then press *Enter*. The value and type are added by the IDE (Fig. 7.26). Note that this value is 40.0 — the value assigned to hours in line 14. Type wage in the next row, then press *Enter*. The value displayed for wage is 0D. The D indicates that the number stored in wage is of type Decimal. You can also highlight a variable name in the code and drag-and-drop that variable into the **Watch** window or right click the variable in the code and select **Add Watch**.

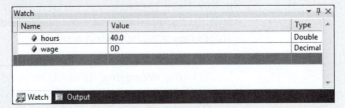

Figure 7.26   **Watch** window.

4. ***Examining different expressions.*** Add the expression (wage + 3) * 5 into the **Watch** window. The **Watch** window can evaluate arithmetic expressions, returning the value 15D. Add the expression wage = 3 into the **Watch** window — expressions containing the = symbol are treated as Boolean expressions instead of assignment statements. The value returned is False, because wage does not currently contain the value 3. Add the expression variableThatDoesNotExist into the **Watch** window. This identifier does not exist in the current app and therefore cannot be evaluated. An appropriate message is displayed in the **Value** field. Your **Watch** window should look similar to Fig. 7.27.

Complex expression ———
Boolean expression ———
Invalid expression ———
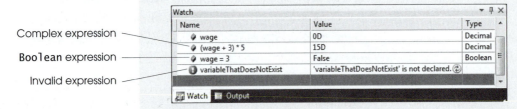

Figure 7.27   Examining expressions.

5. ***Removing an expression from the Watch window.*** At this point, we'd like to clear the final expressions from the **Watch** window. To remove an expression, simply right click the expression in the **Watch** window and select **Delete Watch** (Fig. 7.28). Alternatively, you can click a variable in the **Watch** window and press the *Delete* key to remove the expression. Remove all the expressions that you added in *Step 4*.

6. ***Viewing modified values in a Watch window.*** Continue debugging by selecting **Debug > Continue**. The app continues to execute until the next breakpoint (line 20). Line 15 executes, assigning the wage value entered (12) to wage. The If...Then condition evaluates to True in line 18, and the app is once again suspended in line 20. Note that the value of wage has changed not only in the app, but also in the **Watch** window. Because the value has changed since the last time the app was suspended, the modified value is displayed in *red* in Visual Studio (Fig. 7.29).

(cont.)

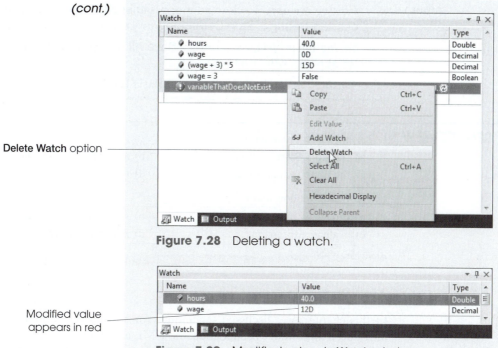

Figure 7.28   Deleting a watch.

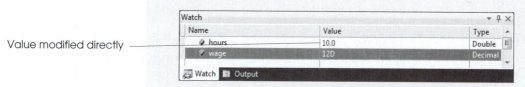

Figure 7.29   Modified values in **Watch** window.

7. ***Modifying values directly in a Watch window.*** The **Watch** window can be used to *change the value of a variable* by entering the new value in the **Value** column. Double click in the **Value** field for hours, replace 40.0 with 10.0, then press *Enter*. The modified value appears in red in Visual Studio (Fig. 7.30). This option enables you to test various values to confirm the behavior of your app.

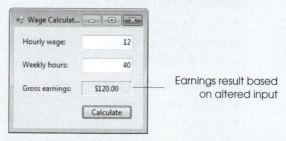

Figure 7.30   Modifying values in a **Watch** window.

8. ***Viewing the app result.*** Select **Debug > Continue** to continue app execution. Once the event handler calculateButton_Click finishes execution, the focus is returned to the **Wage Calculator** window and the final result is displayed (Fig. 7.31). The result is $120.00, because we changed hours to 10.0 in the last step. The TextBox to the right of **Weekly hours:** still displays the value **40**, because we changed the value of hours, but not the Text property of either TextBox.

Figure 7.31   Output displayed after the debugging process.

(cont.)

9. ***Closing the app.*** To close your app, either click the running app's close box or select **Debug > Stop Debugging**.

10. ***Saving the project.*** Select **File > Save All** to save your modified code. [*Note:* Breakpoints will also be saved.]

11. ***Closing the IDE.*** Close the Visual Basic IDE by clicking its close box.

SELF-REVIEW

1. An app enters break mode when _____.
   a) **Debug > Start** is selected
   b) a breakpoint is reached
   c) the **Watch** window is used
   d) there's a syntax error

2. The **Watch** window allows you to _____.
   a) change variable values
   b) view variable type information
   c) evaluate expressions
   d) All of the above

Answers: 1) b. 2) d.

7.11 Wrap-Up

In this chapter, we discussed techniques for solving programming problems. We introduced algorithms, pseudocode, the UML and control statements. We discussed different types of control statements and when each should be used.

You began by test-driving an app that used the If...Then...Else statement to determine an employee's weekly pay. You studied different control statements and used the UML to diagram the decision-making processes of the If...Then and the If...Then...Else statements.

You learned how to format text by using the method String.Format and how to abbreviate assignment statements by using the assignment operators.

In the Using the Debugger section, you learned how to use the **Watch** window to view an app's data. You learned how to add watches, remove watches and change variable values.

In the next chapter you'll learn how to display message dialogs based on user input. You'll study the logical operators, which give you more expressive power for forming the conditions in your control statements, and you'll use the CheckBox control to allow the user to select from various options in an app.

SKILLS SUMMARY

Choosing Among Alternate Courses of Action
- Use the If...Then or If...Then...Else control statements.

Conceptualizing the App Before Using Visual Studio 2010
- Use pseudocode.
- Create an Action/Control/Event (ACE) table.

Understanding Control Statements
- View the control statement's corresponding UML diagram.

Performing Comparisons
- Use the equality and relational operators.

Creating a Constant
- Use the Const keyword.
- Assign a value to the constant in the declaration.

Abbreviating Assignment Expressions
- Use the assignment operators.

Formatting a Value as a Monetary Amount

■ Use the format code C in method String.Format.

Examining Data During App Execution

■ Use the debugger to set a breakpoint, and examine the **Watch** window.

KEY TERMS

action/decision model of programming—Creating apps that consist of *actions* to be performed and *decisions* to be made.

action expression (in the UML)—Used in an action state within a UML activity diagram to specify a particular action to perform.

action state—An action to perform in a UML activity diagram that's represented by an action-state symbol.

action-state symbol—A rectangle with its left and right sides replaced with arcs curving outward that represents an action to perform in a UML activity diagram.

active window—The window that's currently being used—sometimes referred to as the window that has the focus.

activity diagram—A UML diagram that models the activity (also called the workflow) of a portion of a software system.

algorithm—A procedure for solving a problem, specifying the actions to be executed and the order in which they're to be executed.

block—A group of code statements.

Boolean data type—A data type whose variables can have the value True or False.

condition—An expression with a True or False value that's used to make a decision.

conditional If expression—A shorthand representation of an If...Then...Else statement.

Const keyword—Used to declare a named constant.

control statement—An app component that specifies the order in which statements execute (also known as the flow of control).

control-statement nesting—Placing one control statement in the body of another control statement.

control-statement stacking—A set of control statements in sequence. The exit point of one control statement is connected to the entry point of the next control statement in sequence.

constant—An identifier whose value cannot be changed after its initial declaration.

currency format—Used to display values as monetary amounts.

Decimal data type—Used to store monetary amounts and other precise floating-point values.

decision symbol—The diamond-shaped symbol in a UML activity diagram that indicates that a decision is to be made.

diamond symbol—A symbol (also known as the decision symbol) in a UML activity diagram; this symbol indicates that a decision is to be made.

double-selection statement—A statement, such as If...Then...Else, that selects between two different actions or sequences of actions.

Else keyword—Indicates the statements to be executed if the condition of the If...Then...Else statement is false.

equality operators—Operators = (is equal to) and <> (is not equal to) that compare two values.

executable statements—Statements that are performed when the corresponding Visual Basic app is run.

final state—Represented by a solid circle surrounded by a hollow circle in a UML activity diagram; the end of the workflow.

focus—Designates the window currently in use.

format control string—A string that specifies how data should be formatted.

format specifier—Code that specifies the type of format that should be applied to a string for output.

formatting text—Modifying the appearance of text for display purposes.

guard condition—An expression contained in square brackets above or next to the arrows leading from a decision symbol in a UML activity diagram that determines whether workflow continues along a path.

If...Then statement—Selection statement that performs an action (or sequence of actions) based on a condition. This is also called the single-selection statement.

If...Then...Else statement—Selection statement that performs an action (or sequence of actions) if a condition is true and performs a different action (or sequence of actions) if the condition is false. This is also called the double-selection statement.

initial state—Represented by a solid circle in a UML activity diagram; the beginning of the workflow before the app performs the modeled activities.

multiple-selection statement—A statement that selects among many different actions or sequences of actions.

nested statement—A statement that's placed inside another control statement.

note (in a UML diagram)—An explanatory remark (represented by a rectangle with a folded upper-right corner) in a UML activity diagram.

program control—Specifying the order in which control statements should be executed.

pseudocode—An informal, English-like language that helps you develop algorithms.

relational operators—Operators < (less than), > (greater than), <= (less than or equal to) and >= (greater than or equal to) that compare two values.

repetition structure (or repetition statement)—Allows you to specify that an action or sequence of actions should be repeated, depending on the value of a condition.

selection structure (or selection statement)—Selects among alternative courses of action.

sequence structure (or sequence statement)—Built into Visual Basic—unless directed to act otherwise, the computer executes Visual Basic statements sequentially.

sequential execution—Statements in an app are executed one after another in the order in which they're written.

single-entry/single-exit control statement—A control statement that has one entry point and one exit point. All Visual Basic control statements are single-entry/single-exit control statements.

single-selection statement—The If...Then statement, which selects or ignores a single action or sequence of actions.

small circles (in the UML)—The solid circle in an activity diagram represents the activity's initial state, and the solid circle surrounded by a hollow circle represents the activity's final state.

solid circle (in the UML)—A UML activity diagram symbol that represents the activity's initial state.

String.Format method—Formats a string.

structured programming—A technique for organizing program control using sequence, selection and repetition structures to help you develop apps that are easy to understand, debug and modify.

syntax—The rules for forming the correct statements.

transfer of control—Occurs when an executed statement does not directly follow the previously executed one in a running app.

transition—A change from one action state to another that's represented by transition arrows in a UML activity diagram.

UML (Unified Modeling Language)—An industry standard for modeling software systems graphically.

Watch window—A Visual Basic IDE window that allows you to view and modify variable values while an app is being debugged.

workflow—The activity of a portion of a software system.

GUI DESIGN GUIDELINES

Overall Design

- Format all monetary amounts using the C (currency) format specifier.

TextBox

■ When using multiple TextBoxes vertically, align them on their right sides, and where possible make the TextBoxes the same size. Leftalign the descriptive Labels for such TextBoxes.

CONTROLS, EVENTS, PROPERTIES & METHODS

String This class represents a series of characters treated as a single unit.

■ *Method*

Format—Arranges the String in a specified format.

MULTIPLE-CHOICE QUESTIONS

7.1 In a condition, the _____ operator returns False if the left operand is larger than the right operand.

a) =   b) <

c) <=   d) All of the above

7.2 A _____ occurs when an executed statement does not directly follow the previously executed statement in the written app.

a) transition   b) flow

c) logical error   d) transfer of control

7.3 You can interact with the **Watch** window in _____.

a) run mode   b) debug mode

c) break mode   d) All of the above

7.4 The If...Then statement is called a _____ statement because it selects or ignores one action.

a) single-selection   b) multiple-selection

c) double-selection   d) repetition

7.5 The three types of control statements are the sequence statement, the selection statement and the _____ statement.

a) repeat   b) replay

c) redo   d) repetition

7.6 In an activity diagram, a rectangle with curved sides represents _____.

a) a complete algorithm   b) a comment

c) an action   d) the termination of the app

7.7 The If...Then...Else selection statement ends with the keywords _____.

a) End If Then Else   b) End If Else

c) End Else   d) End If

7.8 A variable of data type Boolean can be assigned keyword _____ or keyword _____.

a) True, False   b) Off, On

c) True, NotTrue   d) Yes, No

7.9 An identifier whose value cannot be changed after its initial declaration is called a _____.

a) Double   b) constant

c) standard   d) Boolean

7.10 The _____ operator assigns the result of adding the left and right operands to the left operand.

a) +   b) =+

c) +=   d) None of the above

EXERCISES   **7.11** *(Currency Converter App)* Develop an app that functions as a currency converter, as shown in Fig. 7.32. Users must provide a number in the **Dollars to convert:** TextBox and a currency name (as text) in the **Convert from dollars to:** TextBox. Clicking the **Convert** Button converts the specified amount into the indicated currency and displays it in a Label. Limit yourself to the following currencies as user input: euros, yen and pesos. Use the following exchange rates: 1 dollar = .74 euros, 76.9 yen and 14 pesos.

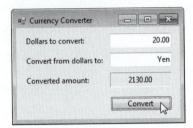

Figure 7.32   **Currency Converter** GUI.

a) *Copying the template to your working directory.* Copy the directory C:\Examples\ ch07\Exercises\CurrencyConverter to your C:\SimplyVB2010 directory.

b) *Opening the app's template file.* Double click CurrencyConverter.sln in the CurrencyConverter directory to open the app.

c) *Adding an event handler for the Convert Button's Click event.* Double click the **Convert** Button to generate an empty event handler for the Button's Click event. The code for *Steps d–f* belongs in this event handler.

d) *Obtaining the user input.* Define a Decimal variable named amount. Use the Val function to convert the user input from the **Dollars to convert:** TextBox to a Double. Assign the result to variable amount. Visual Basic implicitly performs this conversion from Double to Decimal.

e) *Performing the conversion.* Use nested If...Then...Else statements to determine which currency the user entered. Assign the result of the conversion to amount. Display the result using method String.Format with format specifier F.

f) *Running the app.* Select **Debug > Start Debugging** to run your app. Enter a value in dollars to be converted and the name of the currency you wish to convert to. Click the **Convert** Button and, using the exchange rates above, verify that the correct output displays.

g) *Closing the app.* Close your running app by clicking its close box.

h) *Closing the IDE.* Close the Visual Basic IDE by clicking its close box.

7.12 *(Wage Calculator That Performs Tax Calculations)* Develop an app that calculates an employee's earnings, as shown in Fig. 7.33. The user should provide the hourly wage and number of hours worked per week. When the **Calculate** Button is clicked, the employee's gross earnings should display in the **Gross earnings:** TextBox. The **Less FWT:** TextBox should display the amount deducted for federal taxes and the **Net earnings:** TextBox should display the difference between the gross earnings and the federal tax amount. Assume that overtime wages are 1.5 times the hourly wage and federal taxes are 15% of gross earnings. The **Clear** Button should clear all fields.

a) *Copying the template to your working directory.* Copy the directory C:\Examples\ ch07\Exercises\ExpandedWageCalculator to your C:\SimplyVB2010 directory.

b) *Opening the app's template file.* Double click WageCalculator.sln in the ExpandedWageCalculator directory to open the app.

c) *Modifying the Calculate Button's Click event handler.* Add the code for *Steps d–f* to calculateButton_Click.

d) *Adding a new variable and a new constant.* Declare variable federalTaxes to store the amount deducted for federal taxes. Declare constant TAX_RATE and assign it the value 0.15 (that is, 15%).

Figure 7.33   Wage Calculator GUI.

e) *Calculating and displaying the federal taxes deducted.* Multiply the total earnings (earnings) by the federal tax rate (TAX_RATE) to determine the amount to be removed for taxes. Assign the result to federalTaxes. Display this value using method String.Format with format specifier C.

f) *Calculating and displaying the employee's net pay.* Subtract federalTaxes from earnings to calculate the employee's net earnings. Display this value using method String.Format with format specifier C.

g) *Creating an event handler for the Clear Button.* Double click the **Clear** Button to generate an empty event handler for the Click event. This event handler should clear user input from the two TextBoxes and the results from the three output Labels.

h) *Running the app.* Select **Debug > Start Debugging** to run your app. Enter an hourly wage and the number of hours worked. Click the **Calculate** Button and verify that the appropriate output is displayed for gross earnings, amount taken out for federal taxes and net earnings. Click the **Clear** Button and check that all fields are cleared.

i) *Closing the app.* Close your running app by clicking its close box.

j) *Closing the IDE.* Close the Visual Basic IDE by clicking its close box.

7.13 *(Customer Charge Account Analyzer App)* Develop an app (as shown in Fig. 7.34) that determines whether a department-store customer has exceeded the credit limit on a charge account. Each customer enters an account number (an Integer), a balance at the beginning of the month (a Decimal), the total of all items charged this month (a Decimal), the total of all credits applied to the customer's account this month (a Decimal), and the customer's allowed credit limit (a Decimal). The app should input each of these facts, calculate the new balance (= *beginning balance – credits + charges*), display the new balance and determine whether the new balance exceeds the customer's credit limit. If the credit limit is exceeded, the app should display a message (in a Label at the bottom of the Form) informing the customer of this fact. If the user changes the account number, the app should clear the other TextBoxes, the error message Label and the result Label.

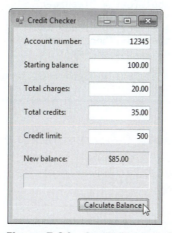

Figure 7.34   Credit Checker GUI.

a) *Copying the template app to your working directory.* Copy the directory `C:\Examples\ch07\Exercises\CreditChecker` to `C:\SimplyVB2010`.

b) *Opening the app's template file.* Double click `CreditChecker.sln` in the CreditChecker directory to open the app.

c) *Adding the Calculate Balance Button's `Click` event handler.* Double click the **Calculate Balance** Button to generate the empty event handler for the `Click` event. The code for *Steps d–g* is added to this event handler.

d) *Declaring variables.* Declare four `Decimal` variables to store the starting balance, charges, credits and credit limit. Declare a fifth `Decimal` variable to store the new balance in the account after the credits and charges have been applied.

e) *Obtaining user input.* Obtain the user input from the TextBoxes' Text properties.

f) *Calculating and displaying the new balance.* Calculate the new balance by subtracting the total credits from the starting balance and adding the charges. Assign the result to the fifth variable in part d). Display the result formatted as currency.

g) *Determining whether the credit limit has been exceeded.* If the new balance exceeds the specified credit limit, a message should be displayed in `errorLabel`.

h) *Handling the Account number: TextBox's TextChanged event.* Double click the **Account number:** TextBox to generate its TextChanged event handler. This event handler should clear the other TextBoxes, the error message Label and the result Label.

i) *Running the app.* Select **Debug > Start Debugging** to run your app. Enter an account number, your starting balance, the amount charged to your account, the amount credited to your account and your credit limit. Click the **Calculate Balance** Button and verify that the new balance displayed is correct. Enter an amount charged that exceeds your credit limit. Click the **Calculate Balance** Button and ensure that a message is displayed in the lower Label. Change the account number and check that all fields are cleared.

j) *Closing the app.* Close your running app by clicking its close box.

k) *Closing the IDE.* Close the Visual Basic IDE by clicking its close box.

What does this code do? ▶

7.14 Assume that `ageTextBox` is a TextBox control and that the user has entered the value 27 into this TextBox. Determine the action performed by the following code:

```
1   Dim age As Integer
2
3   age = Val(ageTextBox.Text)
4
5   If age < 0 Then
6       ageLabel.Text = "Enter a value greater than or equal to zero."
7   ElseIf age < 13 Then
8       ageLabel.Text = "Child"
9   ElseIf age < 20 Then
10      ageLabel.Text = "Teenager"
11  ElseIf age < 30 Then
12      ageLabel.Text = "Young Adult"
13  ElseIf age < 65 Then
14      ageLabel.Text = "Adult"
15  Else
16      ageLabel.Text = "Senior Citizen"
17  End If
```

What's wrong with this code? ▶   **7.15** Assume that `ampmLabel` is a `Label` control. Find the error(s) in the following code:

```
1   Dim hour As Integer
2
3   hour = 14
4
5   If hour < 11 Then
6       If hour > 0 Then
7           ampmLabel.Text = "AM"
8       End If
9   Else
10      ampmLabel.Text = "PM"
11  ElseIf hour > 23 Then
12      ampmLabel.Text = "Time Error."
13  End If
```

Using the Debugger ▶   **7.16** *(Grade Calculator App)* Copy the `C:\Examples\ch07\Debugger` directory to your working directory. This directory contains the `Grades` app, which takes a number from the user and displays the corresponding letter grade. For values 90–100 it should display **A**; for 80–89, **B**, for 70–79, **C**, for 60–69, **D** and for anything lower, an **F**. Run the app. Enter the value 85 in the `TextBox` and click **Calculate**. Note that the app displays **D** when it ought to display **B**. Select **View > Code** to enter the code editor and set as many breakpoints as you feel are necessary. Select **Debug > Start Debugging** to use the debugger to help you find the error(s). Figure 7.35 shows the incorrect output when the value 85 is input.

Figure 7.35   Incorrect output for **Grade** app.

Programming Challenge ▶   **7.17** *(Encryption App)* A company transmits data over the telephone, but it's concerned that its phones could be tapped. All its data is transmitted as four-digit `Integers`. The company has asked you to write an app that encrypts its data so that it may be transmitted more securely. Encryption is the process of transforming data for security reasons. Create a `Form` similar to Fig. 7.36. Your app should read four digits entered by the user and encrypt the information. Assume that the user inputs a single digit in each `TextBox`. Use the following technique to encrypt the number:

a) Replace each digit by (*the sum of that digit and 7*) Mod 10.

b) Swap the first digit with the third, and swap the second digit with the fourth.

Figure 7.36   Encryption app.

Objectives

In this chapter, you'll:

- Use **CheckBox**es to allow users to select options.
- Use dialogs to display messages.
- Use logical operators to form more powerful conditions.

Outline

Dental Payment App

Introducing CheckBoxes and Message Dialogs

Many Visual Basic apps use **message dialogs** that display messages to users. You encounter many dialogs while using a computer, from those that instruct you to select files or enter passwords to others that notify you of problems while using an app. In this chapter, you'll use message dialogs to inform users of input problems.

You might have noticed that **TextBox**es allow users to enter nearly any value as input. In some cases, you may want to use controls that provide users with predefined options. One way to do this is by providing **CheckBox**es in your app. You'll also learn about logical operators, which you can use in your apps to make more involved decisions based on user input.

8.1 Test-Driving the Dental Payment App

There are many procedures that dentists can perform. The office assistant may present the patient with a computer-generated bill listing services rendered. In this chapter, you'll program an app that prepares a bill for some basic dental procedures. This app must meet the following requirements:

> **App Requirements**
>
> *A dentist's office administrator wishes to create an app that employees can use to bill patients. The app must allow the user to enter the patient's name and specify which services were performed during the visit. The app will then calculate the total charges. If a user attempts to calculate a bill before any services are specified, or before the patient's name is entered, an error message will be displayed informing the user that necessary input is missing.*

In the **Dental Payment** app, you'll use CheckBox controls and a message dialog to assist the user in entering data. You'll begin by test-driving the completed app. Then you'll learn the additional Visual Basic capabilities needed to create your own version of this app.

Test-Driving the Dental Payment App

1. **Opening the completed app.** Open the directory C:\Examples\ch08\CompletedApp\DentalPayment to locate the **Dental Payment** app. Double click DentalPayment.sln to open the app in the Visual Basic IDE.

2. **Running the Dental Payment app.** Select **Debug > Start Debugging** to run the app (Fig. 8.1).

   There are three square-shaped controls—known as **CheckBox**es—in the Form's left column. A CheckBox is a small square that either is blank or contains a check mark. When a CheckBox is selected, a check mark appears in the box (☑). A CheckBox can be selected simply by clicking within its small square or by clicking on its text. A selected CheckBox can be *unchecked* using the same technique. You'll learn how to add CheckBox controls to a Form shortly.

CheckBox controls
(unchecked)

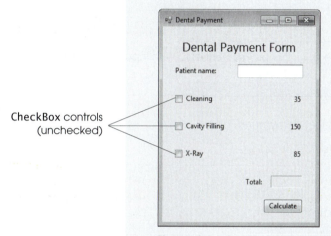

Figure 8.1   Running the completed **Dental Payment** app.

3. **Attempting to calculate a total without entering input.** Leave the **Patient name:** field blank, and *deselect* any CheckBoxes that you've selected. Click the **Calculate** Button. A message dialog appears (Fig. 8.2) indicating that you must enter data. Close this dialog by clicking its **OK** Button.

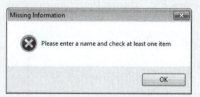

Figure 8.2   Message dialog appears when no name is entered and/or no CheckBoxes are selected.

4. **Entering quantities in the app.** Type Bob Jones in the **Patient name:** field. Check all three CheckBoxes by clicking each one. A check mark appears in each CheckBox (Fig. 8.3).

5. **Unchecking the Cavity Filling CheckBox.** Click the **Cavity Filling** CheckBox to remove its check mark. Only the **Cleaning** and **X-Ray** CheckBoxes should now be selected (Fig. 8.4).

6. **Determining the bill.** Click the **Calculate** Button. This causes the app to total the price of the services performed during the dentist visit. The result is displayed in the **Total:** field (Fig. 8.5).

(cont.)

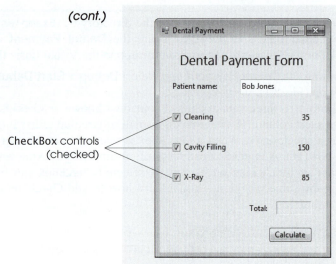

Figure 8.3   **Dental Payment** app with input entered.

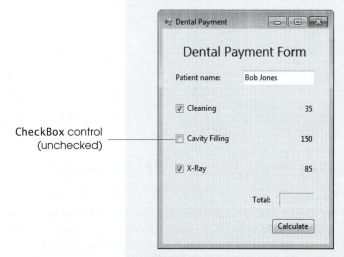

Figure 8.4   **Dental Payment** app with input changed.

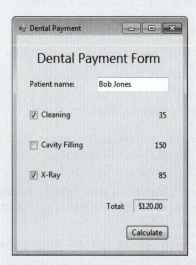

Figure 8.5   **Dental Payment** app with total calculated.

7. *Closing the app.* Close your running app by clicking its close box.
8. *Closing the project.* Close the project by selecting **File > Close Project**.

8.2 Designing the Dental Payment App

Recall that pseudocode is an *informal* English-like language that helps you develop algorithms. The following pseudocode describes the basic operation of the **Dental Payment** app, which runs when the user clicks **Calculate**:

*When the user clicks the "Calculate" **Button***
    Clear previous output

    *If user has not entered a patient name or has not selected any **CheckBoxes***
        Display message in dialog
    Else
        Initialize the total to zero

        *If "Cleaning" **CheckBox** is selected*
            Add cost of a cleaning to the total

        *If "Cavity Filling" **CheckBox** is selected*
            Add cost of receiving a cavity filling to the total

        *If "X-Ray" **CheckBox** is selected*
            Add cost of receiving an x-ray to the total

        Format total to be displayed as currency
        Display total

Walk through [handwritten annotation]

Now that you've test-driven the **Dental Payment** app and studied its pseudocode representation, you'll use an ACE table to help you convert the pseudocode to Visual Basic. Figure 8.6 lists the *actions*, *controls* and *events* that will help you complete your own version of this app. Data is input using a `TextBox` (`nameTextBox`) and Check-Boxes (`cleanCheckBox`, `cavityCheckBox` and `xrayCheckBox`). Output is displayed in the `Label` `totalResultLabel` when a `Button` (`calculateButton`) is clicked.

Action/Control/Event (ACE) Table for the Dental Payment App	**Action**	**Control/Class/Object**	**Event**

	Label all the app's controls	`titleLabel,`
		`nameLabel,`
		`totalLabel,`
		`cleanCostLabel,`
		`fillingCostLabel,`
		`xrayCostLabel`
			App is run

		`calculateButton`	`Click`
	Clear previous output	`totalResultLabel`	

	If user has not entered a patient name or has not selected any **CheckBoxes**	`nameTextBox,`
		`cleanCheckBox,`
		`cavityCheckBox,`
		`xrayCheckBox`	

	Display message in dialog	`MessageBox`	
	Else Initialize the total to zero		
	If "Cleaning" **CheckBox** is selected Add cost of a cleaning to the total	`cleanCheckBox`	
	If "Cavity Filling" **CheckBox** is selected Add cost of receiving a cavity filling to the total	`cavityCheckBox`	
	If "X-Ray" **CheckBox** is selected Add cost of receiving an x-ray to the total	`xrayCheckBox`	
	Format total to be displayed as currency	`String`	
	Display total	`totalResultLabel`	

Figure 8.6   ACE table for **Dental Payment** app.

8.3 Using CheckBoxes

A CheckBox is known as a **state button** because it can be in the "on" or "off" [true/false] state. When a CheckBox is selected, a check mark appears in the box. Any number of CheckBoxes can be selected at a time, including *none* at all. The text that appears alongside a CheckBox is called the **CheckBox label**.

You can determine whether a CheckBox is on (that is, checked) by using the **Checked property**. If the CheckBox is checked, the Checked property contains the Boolean value True; otherwise, it contains False. [*Note:* A CheckBox can also have an *indeterminate state* if its ThreeState property is set to True. We do not discuss such CheckBoxes in this book.]

You'll now create the **Dental Payment** app from the template provided. The box that follows demonstrates how to add the CheckBoxes to your app. The app you build in the next two boxes does not display a dialog if the TextBox is empty and/or all the CheckBoxes are unchecked when the **Calculate** Button is clicked. You'll learn how to display that dialog in Section 8.4.

Adding CheckBoxes to the Form

1. *Copying the template app to your working directory.* Copy the C:\Examples\ch08\TemplateApp\DentalPayment directory to C:\SimplyVB2010.

2. *Opening the Dental Payment app's template file.* Double click DentalPayment.sln in the DentalPayment directory to open the app in the Visual Basic IDE. Double click DentalPayment.vb in the **Solution Explorer** if the form does not appear.

3. *Adding CheckBox controls to the Form.* Add a CheckBox to the Form by double clicking the

   ☑ CheckBox

   icon in the **Toolbox**. Repeat this process until three CheckBoxes have been added to the Form.

4. *Customizing the CheckBoxes.* For this app, you'll modify the AutoSize, Location, Text, Size and Name properties of each CheckBox. First, set the AutoSize property of all three CheckBoxes to False, so that you can specify their exact sizes. Next, change the Size property of all three to 122, 24. Change the first CheckBox's Name property to cleanCheckBox and set its Location property to 22, 113 and its Text property to Cleaning. Change the second CheckBox's Name property to cavityCheckBox, its Location property to 22, 160 and its Text property to Cavity Filling. Change the final CheckBox's Name property to xrayCheckBox, its Location property to 22, 207 and its Text property to X-Ray.

5. *Saving the project.* Select **File > Save All** to save your changes.

After placing the CheckBoxes on the Form and setting their properties, you need to code an event handler to enhance the app's functionality when users select CheckBoxes and click **Calculate**.

Adding the Calculate Button's Event Handler

1. *Adding an event handler for calculateButton's Click event.* Double click the **Calculate** Button on the Form to create an event handler for that control's Click event.

(cont.)   2. ***Adding If...Then statements to calculate the patient's bill.*** Add lines 6–28
of Fig. 8.7 to your app. Be sure to include all blank lines shown in Fig. 8.7 to
improve code readability and to ensure that your line numbers correspond
to the figure's.

Line 7 clears any text in the output Label that may remain from a previous calculation. Line 10 declares Decimal variable total, which stores the
total charges for the patient. This variable is initialized to 0. Lines 12–25
define three If...Then statements that determine whether the user has
checked any of the Form's CheckBoxes. Each If...Then statement's condition compares a CheckBox's Checked property to True. For each If...Then
statement, the dollar value of the service is added to total if the current
CheckBox is checked. For example, if CheckBox cleanCheckBox is selected
(line 13), line 14 uses the Val function to obtain the value from the clean-
CostLabel and adds it to total. Line 28 displays the total (formatted as a
currency amount) in totalResultLabel.

```
2      ' handles Click event
3      Private Sub calculateButton_Click(sender As System.Object,
4          e As System.EventArgs) Handles calculateButton.Click
5
6          ' clear text displayed in Label
7          totalResultLabel.Text = String.Empty
8
9          ' total contains amount to bill patient
10         Dim total As Decimal = 0
11
12         ' if patient had a cleaning
13         If cleanCheckBox.Checked = True Then
14             total += Val(cleanCostLabel.Text)
15         End If
16
17         ' if patient had a cavity filled
18         If cavityCheckBox.Checked = True Then
19             total += Val(fillingCostLabel.Text)
20         End If
21
22         ' if patient had an X-ray taken
23         If xrayCheckBox.Checked = True Then
24             total += Val(xrayCostLabel.Text)
25         End If
26
27         ' display the total
28         totalResultLabel.Text = String.Format("{0:C}", total)
29     End Sub ' calculateButton_Click
```

Figure 8.7   Using the **Checked** property.

3. ***Running the app.*** Select **Debug > Start Debugging** to run your app. Note
that the user is *not* required to enter a name or select any CheckBoxes before
clicking the **Calculate** Button. If no CheckBoxes are selected, the bill displays the value **$0.00** (Fig. 8.8).

4. ***Selecting a CheckBox.*** Select the **Cleaning** CheckBox and click the **Calculate** Button. The **Total:** field now displays **$35.00**.

5. ***Closing the app.*** Close your running app by clicking its close box.

(cont.)

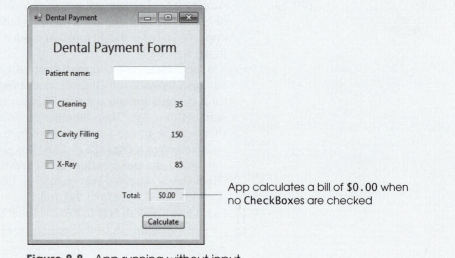

Figure 8.8   App running without input.

SELF-REVIEW

1. The _____ property sets a **CheckBox**'s label.

    a) `Text`
                      b) `Value`

    c) `Label`
                    d) `Checked`

2. Which property specifies whether a **CheckBox** is selected?

    a) `Selected`
                  b) `Checked`

    c) `Clicked`
                  d) `Check`

Answers: 1.) a. 2.) b.

8.4 Using a Dialog to Display a Message

In the completed app, a message is displayed in a dialog if the user attempts to calculate the total charges without specifying which services were performed or without entering a name. In this section, you learn how to display a dialog when a patient name is not input. When the dialog is closed, control returns to the app's **Form**. The message dialog used in your app is displayed in Fig. 8.9.

Title bar ⎯

Icon indicates the tone
of the message ⎯

Close box

Dialog sized to accommodate contents

OK Button allows the
user to close the dialog

Figure 8.9   Dialog displayed by the app.

The message dialog contains a *title bar* and a *close box*. This dialog also contains a *message* (`Please enter a name and check at least one item`), an **OK** Button that allows the user to **dismiss** (close) the dialog (which the user must do to proceed) and an *icon* that indicates the tone of the message. (In this case,  indicates that a problem has occurred.)

Message dialogs are defined by class **MessageBox** and can be displayed by using method **MessageBox.Show**. The message dialog is customized by the arguments passed to **MessageBox.Show**. The box that follows demonstrates displaying a message dialog based on a condition.

GUI Design Tip

Text displayed in a dialog should be descriptive and brief.

Displaying a Message Dialog Using MessageBox.Show

1. **Adding an If...Then statement to calculateButton's Click event handler.** The message should display only if the user does not enter the patient's name. Later, you'll add the code to determine if no CheckBoxes have been marked. Place the cursor in line 8, press *Enter*, then insert lines 9–12 of Fig. 8.10 into your event handler. Be sure to include a blank line after the End If keywords.

   Line 10 tests whether data was entered in the **Patient name:** TextBox. If no data has been entered, the expression nameTextBox.Text = String.Empty evaluates to True. You'll add the body of this If...Then statement in *Step 2*.

```
6          ' clear text displayed in Label
7          totalResultLabel.Text = String.Empty
8
9          ' if no name entered, display an error message
10         If nameTextBox.Text = String.Empty Then
11
12         End If
```

Figure 8.10   Adding an If...Then statement to the calculateButton Click event handler.

(cont.)

2. **Adding code to display a message dialog.** Insert lines 12–16 from Fig. 8.11 into the body of the If...Then statement you created in the preceding step. Change the End If (line 12 of Fig. 8.10) to Else (line 17 of Fig. 8.11). The code you added to the Click event earlier (Fig. 8.7) now comprises the body of the Else portion of your If...Then...Else statement. The Else is marked as a syntax error because the If...Then...Else statement is now missing the End If keywords. You'll add these keywords in *Step 3*.

```
6          ' clear text displayed in Label
7          totalResultLabel.Text = String.Empty
8
9          ' if no name entered, display an error message
10         If nameTextBox.Text = String.Empty Then
11
12             ' display an error message in a dialog
13             MessageBox.Show(
14                 "Please enter a name and check at least one item",
15                 "Missing Information", MessageBoxButtons.OK,
16                 MessageBoxIcon.Error)
```
Change End If to Else ── 17   `Else ' add prices`

using a message box

Figure 8.11   Message dialog code that displays a message to users.

   Lines 13–16 call method MessageBox.Show using four arguments separated by commas. The first argument specifies the text that displays in the dialog, the second specifies the text that appears in its title bar, the third indicates which Button(s) to display at the bottom of the dialog and the fourth indicates which icon appears to the left of the dialog's text. We'll discuss the final two arguments in more detail shortly.

3. **Closing the If...Then...Else statement.** Scroll to the end of your event-handler code. Insert the keywords End If (line 39 of Fig. 8.12) to terminate the If...Then...Else statement. Figure 8.13 displays the entire method calculateButton_Click after the new code has been added. Compare this code to your own to ensure that you've added the new code correctly.

```
37             ' display the total
38             totalResultLabel.Text = String.Format("{0:C}", total)
39         End If
40     End Sub ' calculateButton_Click
```

Figure 8.12   Ending the If...Then...Else statement.

(cont.)

```
 2    ' handles Click event
 3    Private Sub calculateButton_Click(sender As System.Object,
 4       e As System.EventArgs) Handles calculateButton.Click
 5
 6       ' clear text displayed in Label
 7       totalResultLabel.Text = String.Empty
 8
 9       ' if no name entered, display an error message
10       If nameTextBox.Text = String.Empty Then
11
12          ' display an error message in a dialog
13          MessageBox.Show(
14             "Please enter a name and check at least one item",
15             "Missing Information", MessageBoxButtons.OK,
16             MessageBoxIcon.Error)
17       Else ' add prices
18
19          ' total contains amount to bill patient
20          Dim total As Decimal = 0
21
22          ' if patient had a cleaning
23          If cleanCheckBox.Checked = True Then
24             total += Val(cleanCostLabel.Text)
25          End If
26
27          ' if patient had a cavity filled
28          If cavityCheckBox.Checked = True Then
29             total += Val(fillingCostLabel.Text)
30          End If
31
32          ' if patient had an X-ray taken
33          If xrayCheckBox.Checked = True Then
34             total += Val(xrayCostLabel.Text)
35          End If
36
37          ' display the total
38          totalResultLabel.Text = String.Format("{0:C}", total)
39       End If
40    End Sub ' calculateButton_Click
```

Figure 8.13 `calculateButton_Click` event handler.

4. ***Running the app.*** Select **Debug > Start Debugging** to run your app.

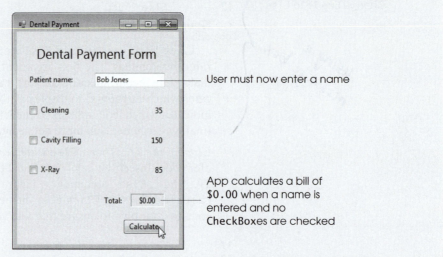

Figure 8.14 Total calculated without any **CheckBoxes** selected.

(cont.)

The user does *not* have to select any CheckBoxes before clicking the **Calculate** Button but *must* enter a name in the **Patient name:** TextBox. If none of the CheckBoxes is selected, the bill contains the value **$0.00** (Fig. 8.14). In the next section, you modify the code to test whether the user has selected any CheckBoxes. [*Note:* You cannot interact with the app's Form until you close the message dialog.]

5. ***Closing the app.*** Close your running app by clicking its close box.

In this example, you passed four arguments to method MessageBox.Show. As we discussed, the third argument specified the Button(s) to display in the dialog. You passed one of the **MessageBoxButtons** constants to method Message-Box.Show. You use only the MessageBoxButtons.OK constant in this book. Figure 8.15 lists the available MessageBoxButtons constants. Several Buttons can be displayed at once. The fourth argument specified the *icon* to display in the dialog. To set the icon to display, you passed one of the **MessageBoxIcon** constants to method MessageBox.Show. Some of the available icon constants are shown in Fig. 8.16.

MessageBoxButtons Constants	Description
OK	**OK** Button. Allows the user to *acknowledge* a message.
OKCancel	**OK** and **Cancel** Buttons. Allow the user to *continue* or *cancel* an operation.
YesNo	**Yes** and **No** Buttons. Allow the user to *respond* to a question.
YesNoCancel	**Yes**, **No** and **Cancel** Buttons. Allow the user to *respond* to a question or *cancel* an operation.
RetryCancel	**Retry** and **Cancel** Buttons. Allow the user to *retry* or to *cancel* an operation that has *failed*.
AbortRetryIgnore	**Abort**, **Retry** and **Ignore** Buttons. When one of a series of operations has *failed*, these Buttons allow the user to *abort* the entire sequence, *retry* the *failed* operation or *ignore* the *failed* operation and *continue*.

Figure 8.15 Message dialog MessageBoxButtons constants.

MessageBoxIcon Constants	Icon	Description
Exclamation	⚠	Icon containing an exclamation point. Typically used to caution the user against potential problems.
Information	 ⓘ	Icon containing the letter "i." Typically used to display information about the state of the app.
None		No icon is displayed.
Error	 ⊗	Icon containing an **×** in a red circle. Typically used to alert the user to errors or critical situations.

Figure 8.16 Some message dialog MessageBoxIcon constants.

SELF-REVIEW

1. Call the _____ method of class MessageBox to display a message dialog.
   a) Display   b) Message
   c) Open   d) Show

2. What is the message dialog icon containing the letter "i" typically used for?

   a) To display information about the state of the app

   b) To caution the user against potential problems

   c) To ask the user a question

   d) To alert the user to critical situations

Answers: 1.) d. 2.) a.

8.5 Logical Operators

So far, you've studied only **simple conditions**, such as `count <= 10`, `total > 1000`, and `number <> value`. Each selection statement that you've used evaluated only *one* condition with one of the operators >, <, >=, <=, = or <>.

Error-Prevention Tip

Always write the *simplest* condition possible by limiting the number of logical operators used. Conditions with many logical operators can be hard to read and can introduce subtle bugs into your apps.

To handle multiple conditions more efficiently, **logical operators** can be used to form complex conditions by combining simple ones. The logical operators are **And**, **AndAlso**, **Or**, **OrElse**, **Xor** and **Not**. We'll consider examples that use several of these operators. After you learn about logical operators, you'll use them to create a complex condition in your **Dental Payment** app to confirm that the user selected at least one CheckBox. See Appendix A for the complete operator precedence table.

Using AndAlso

Suppose that you wish to ensure that *two* conditions are *both* true in an app before choosing a certain path of execution. In that case, you can use the logical `AndAlso` operator as follows:

```
If genderTextBox.Text = "Female" AndAlso age >= 65 Then
    seniorFemales += 1
End If
```

This If...Then statement contains two simple conditions. The condition `gender-TextBox.Text = "Female"` determines whether a person is female, and the condition `age >= 65` determines whether a person is a senior citizen. The = and >= operators have a higher precedence than operator `AndAlso`. The If...Then statement considers the combined condition

```
genderTextBox.Text = "Female" AndAlso age >= 65
```

This condition evaluates to `True` *if and only if* both of the simple conditions are true—i.e., `genderTextBox.Text` contains the value `"Female"` and `age` contains a value greater than or equal to 65. When this combined condition is true, variable `seniorFemales` is incremented by 1. However, if either or both of the simple conditions are false, the app skips the increment and proceeds to the statement following the If...Then statement. The readability of the preceding combined condition can be improved by adding redundant (that is, unnecessary) parentheses:

```
(genderTextBox.Text = "Female") AndAlso (age >= 65)
```

Figure 8.17 illustrates the outcome of using the `AndAlso` operator with two expressions. The table lists all four possible combinations of `True` and `False` values for *expression1* and *expression2*, which represent the left operand and the right operand, respectively. Such tables are called **truth tables**. Expressions that include relational operators, equality operators and logical operators evaluate to `True` or `False`.

expression1	expression2	expression1 AndAlso expression2
False	False	False
False	True	False
True	False	False
True	True	True

Figure 8.17 Truth table for the `AndAlso` operator.

Using `OrElse`

Now let's consider the `OrElse` operator. Suppose that you wished to ensure that either *or* both of two conditions were true before you chose a certain path of execution. You would use the `OrElse` operator, as in the following app segment:

```
If (semesterAverage >= 90) OrElse (finalExam >= 90) Then
    MessageBox.Show("Student grade is A", "Student Grade",
        MessageBoxButtons.OK, MessageBoxIcon.Information)
End If
```

This statement also contains *two* simple conditions. The condition `semesterAverage >= 90` is evaluated to determine whether the student deserves an "A" in the course because of an outstanding performance throughout the semester. The condition `finalExam >= 90` is evaluated to determine whether the student deserves an "A" in the course because of an outstanding performance on the final exam. The If...Then statement then considers the combined condition

Error-Prevention Tip

When writing conditions that contain combinations of `AndAlso` and `OrElse` operators, use parentheses to ensure that the conditions evaluate properly. Otherwise, logic errors could occur because `AndAlso` has *higher* precedence than `OrElse`.

```
(semesterAverage >= 90) OrElse (finalExam >= 90)
```

and awards the student an "A" if either or both of the conditions are true, meaning that the student performed well during the semester, performed well on the final exam or *both*. Note that the text `"Student grade is A"` is displayed unless both of the conditions are false. Figure 8.18 provides a truth table for the `OrElse` operator. Note that the `AndAlso` operator has a higher precedence than the `OrElse` operator. See Appendix A for a complete listing of operator precedence in Visual Basic.

expression1	*expression2*	*expression1* OrElse *expression2*
False	False	False
False	True	True
True	False	True
True	True	True

Figure 8.18 Truth table for the `OrElse` operator.

Short-Circuit Evaluation

An expression containing operator `AndAlso` is evaluated only until truth or falsity is known. For example, evaluation of the expression

```
(genderTextBox.Text = "Female") AndAlso (age >= 65)
```

stops immediately if `genderTextBox.Text` is not equal to `"Female"` (which means that the entire expression is false). In this case, the evaluation of the second expression is irrelevant; once the first expression is known to be false, the whole expression *must* be false. Evaluation of the second expression occurs *if and only if* `genderTextBox.Text` is equal to `"Female"` (which means that the entire expression can still be true if the condition `age >= 65` is true).

Similarly, an expression containing `OrElse` is evaluated *only* until its truth or falsity is known. For example, evaluation of the expression

```
If (semesterAverage >= 90) OrElse (finalExam >= 90) Then
```

stops immediately if `semesterAverage` is greater than or equal to 90 (which means that the entire expression is true). In this case, the evaluation of the second expression is *irrelevant*; once the first expression is known to be true, the whole expression *must* be true.

This way of evaluating logical expressions requires fewer operations and therefore takes less time. This performance feature for the evaluation of `AndAlso` and `OrElse` expressions is called **short-circuit evaluation**. Visual Basic also provides the

And and Or operators, which do *not* short-circuit. (They always evaluate their right operand regardless of whether or not the condition's truth or falsity is already known.) One potential problem of using AndAlso/OrElse instead of And/Or arises when the right operand contains a *side effect*, such as a function call that modifies a variable. Because such side effects might not occur when using short-circuit evaluation, subtle logic errors could occur. As a good programming practice, most Visual Basic programmers try to avoid writing conditions that contain side effects.

Using Xor

A condition containing the **logical exclusive OR (Xor)** operator is True *if and only if one of its operands results in a True value and the other results in a False value.* If *both* operands are True or *both* are False, the entire condition is false. Figure 8.19 presents a truth table for the logical exclusive OR operator (Xor). This operator *always* evaluates both of its operands (that is, there's *no* short-circuit evaluation).

expression1	expression2	expression1 Xor expression2
False	False	False
False	True	True
True	False	True
True	True	False

Figure 8.19 Truth table for the logical exclusive OR (Xor) operator.

Using Not

Visual Basic's **Not (logical negation)** operator enables you to "reverse" the meaning of a condition. Unlike the logical operators AndAlso, OrElse and Xor, each of which combines *two* expressions (that is, these are all *binary* operators), the Not operator is a *unary* operator, requiring only *one* operand. The Not operator is placed before a condition to choose a path of execution if the original condition (without the Not operator) is False. The Not operator is demonstrated by the following app segment:

```
If Not (grade = value) Then
    displayLabel.Text = "They are not equal!"
End If
```

The parentheses around the condition grade = value improve the readability of the condition. Most programmers prefer to write

```
Not (grade = value)
```

as

```
(grade <> value)
```

Figure 8.20 provides a truth table for the Not operator. In the box that follows you'll modify your **Dental Payment** app to use a complex expression.

expression	Not expression
False	True
True	False

Figure 8.20 Truth table for the Not operator (logical negation).

Using Logical Operators in Complex Expressions

1. *Inserting a complex expression into the Click event handler.* Replace lines 9–10 in DentalPayment.vb with lines 9–13 of Fig. 8.21.

(cont.)

Add the highlighted code ──────

```
8
9        ' if no name entered or no CheckBox checked, display message
10       If (nameTextBox.Text = String.Empty) OrElse
11          (cleanCheckBox.Checked = False AndAlso
12           xrayCheckBox.Checked = False AndAlso
13           cavityCheckBox.Checked = False) Then
```

Figure 8.21 Using the AndAlso and OrElse logical operators.

Lines 10–13 define a more sophisticated logical expression than others we've used in this book. Note the use of OrElse and AndAlso. If the name is blank or if no CheckBox is checked, a dialog should appear. After the original expression (nameTextBox.Text = String.Empty) you use OrElse to indicate that either the expression "on the left" (nameTextBox.Text = String.Empty) or the expression "on the right" (which ensures that no CheckBoxes have been checked) needs to be true in order for the entire expression to evaluate to True and execute the body of the If...Then statement. The complex expression "on the right" uses AndAlso twice to determine whether all three of the CheckBoxes are unchecked. Note that because AndAlso has a higher precedence than OrElse, the parentheses in lines 10, 11 and 13 are redundant (unnecessary) but they do improve readability.

2. ***Running the app.*** Select **Debug > Start Debugging** to run your app. Note that users must enter a name and select at least one **CheckBox** before they click the **Calculate** Button. The app appears the same as in Figs. 8.1 and 8.4. You've now corrected the weakness from your earlier implementation of the **Dental Payment** app.

3. ***Closing the app.*** Close your running app by clicking its close box.

Figure 8.22 presents the source code for the **Dental Payment** app. The lines of code containing new app-development concepts that you learned in this chapter are highlighted.

```
1   Public Class DentalPaymentForm
2       ' handles Click event
3       Private Sub calculateButton_Click(sender As System.Object,
4          e As System.EventArgs) Handles calculateButton.Click
5
6          ' clear text displayed in Label
7          totalResultLabel.Text = String.Empty
8
9          ' if no name entered or no CheckBox checked, display message
10         If (nameTextBox.Text = String.Empty) OrElse
11            (cleanCheckBox.Checked = False AndAlso
12             xrayCheckBox.Checked = False AndAlso
13             cavityCheckBox.Checked = False) Then
14
15            ' display an error message in a dialog
16            MessageBox.Show( _
17               "Please enter your name and check at least one item",
18               "Missing Information", MessageBoxButtons.OK
19                MessageBoxIcon.Error)
20         Else ' add prices
21
22            ' total contains amount to bill patient
23            Dim total As Decimal = 0
24
```

Using logical operators and the Checked property of a CheckBox ────── (points to lines 10–13)

Displaying a MessageBox ────── (points to lines 16–19)

Figure 8.22 Code for the **Dental Payment** app. (Part 1 of 2.)

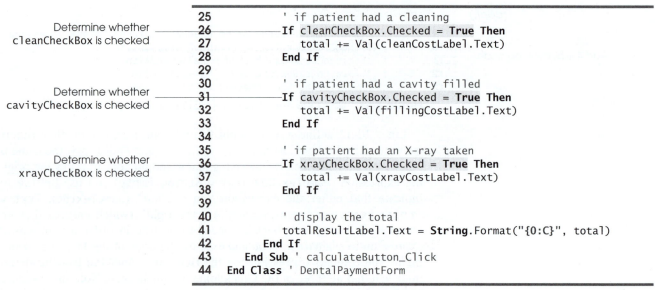

```
Determine whether          25            ' if patient had a cleaning
cleanCheckBox is checked    26           If cleanCheckBox.Checked = True Then
                            27               total += Val(cleanCostLabel.Text)
                            28           End If
                            29
                            30            ' if patient had a cavity filled
Determine whether          31            If cavityCheckBox.Checked = True Then
cavityCheckBox is checked   32               total += Val(fillingCostLabel.Text)
                            33           End If
                            34
                            35            ' if patient had an X-ray taken
Determine whether          36            If xrayCheckBox.Checked = True Then
xrayCheckBox is checked     37               total += Val(xrayCostLabel.Text)
                            38           End If
                            39
                            40            ' display the total
                            41            totalResultLabel.Text = String.Format("{0:C}", total)
                            42         End If
                            43      End Sub ' calculateButton_Click
                            44   End Class ' DentalPaymentForm
```

Figure 8.22   Code for the **Dental Payment** app. (Part 2 of 2.)

SELF-REVIEW   1. A unary operator _____.

   a) requires exactly one operand   b) requires two operands
   c) must use the `AndAlso` keyword   d) can have no operands

2. The _____ operator is used to ensure that two conditions are both true.

   a) `Xor`   b) `AndAlso`
   c) `Also`   d) `OrElse`

Answers: 1.) a. 2.) b.

8.6 Designer-Generated Code

In Chapter 6, you learned that every variable must be declared with a name and a type before you can use it in an app. Like the variables you've declared, GUI controls also *must* be declared before they're used. You might be wondering where these declarations are, since you've not seen them in any of the examples so far. A nice aspect of Visual Basic is that when you work in **Design** view to build and configure your app's GUI, Visual Basic *automatically* declares the controls for you. It also generates code that creates each control and configures its properties—including any changes that you make to the properties through the **Properties** window or by dragging and resizing controls on the `Form`.

   To improve the readability of your app code, Visual Basic "hides" the GUI declarations and other GUI code it generates in a separate file that starts with the same name as the `Form`'s `.vb` file but ends with **Designer.vb**—in this chapter, the file is named `DentalPayment.Designer.vb`. By placing this code in a *separate* file, Visual Basic allows you to focus on your app's logic rather than the tedious details of building the GUI.

   You can view these separate files and even edit them—though editing is *not* recommended. To view the `Designer.vb` file for the **Dental Payment** app, click the **Show All Files** icon (discussed in Section 2.5) in the **Solution Explorer**, then click the arrow sign next to `DentalPayment.vb` to expand its node. Double click `DentalPayment.Designer.vb` to view the code.

   Figure 8.23 shows the declarations that the IDE generated for all of the controls used in the **Dental Payment** app (lines 170–181). Note that the IDE declares each control's type with its fully qualified type name—that is, the namespace `System.Windows.Forms` followed by the type of the control. The controls declared in

Fig. 8.23 are created by lines 25–36 in the completed app's DentalPayment-Form.Designer.vb file.

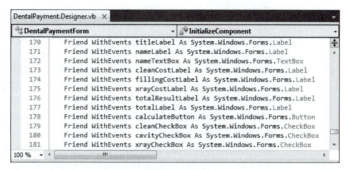

Figure 8.23   GUI declarations for the controls in the **Dental Payment** app.

In *Steps 3* and *4* of the box *Adding CheckBoxes to the Form* earlier in this chapter, you placed three CheckBoxes on the Form and configured several of their properties. Figure 8.24 shows some of the statements that the IDE created based on your actions. For example, you set the Size property of each CheckBox to 122,24. Lines 123, 132 and 141 are the generated statements that change the size of the CheckBoxes. Similarly, you changed the locations of the CheckBoxes. The statements that change their locations appear in lines 121, 130 and 139.

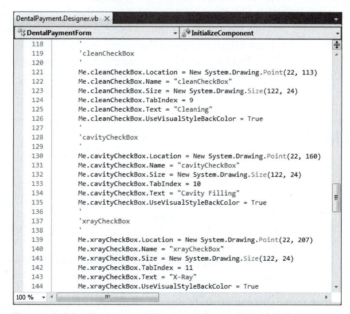

Figure 8.24   Statements that configure the CheckBox properties.

Everything you do with visual app development in **Design** view has consequences in the Designer.vb file, but the IDE handles the GUI code for you. This greatly simplifies the app-development process and makes you more productive. It also eliminates many common programming errors and typos.

GUIs are tremendous tools for interfacing with computers. However, they require lots of code. Visual app development in **Design** view enables the IDE to generate *most* of this code for you, and the *hidden* Designer.vb file gets the GUI "out of the way" so you can concentrate on the logic of your app.

8.7 Wrap-Up

In this chapter, you used CheckBox controls to provide a series of choices to users in the **Dental Payment** app. CheckBoxes provide options that can be selected by clicking them. When a CheckBox is selected, its square contains a check mark. You can determine whether a CheckBox is selected in your code by accessing its Checked property.

Your **Dental Payment** app also used a message dialog to display a message to the user when information was not entered appropriately. To implement the dialog in your app, you used the Show method of class MessageBox and constants provided by class MessageBoxButtons and MessageBoxIcon to display a message dialog containing Buttons and an icon. You used If...Then statements to calculate the cost of the dental visit or display a message dialog if the user was missing input. Later in this book you'll learn to disable a control (such as a Button) when its events should not cause any action to occur—for example, you might not want to allow a Button to be clicked until the user has provided input in a TextBox.

You learned to use the logical AndAlso operator when both conditions must be true for the overall condition to be true—if either condition is false, the overall condition is false. You also learned that the logical OrElse operator requires at least one of its conditions to be true for the overall condition to be true—if both conditions are false, the overall condition is false. The logical Xor operator requires that exactly one of its conditions be true for the overall condition to be true—if both conditions are false or if both conditions are true, the overall condition is false. The logical Not operator reverses the Boolean result of a condition—True becomes False, and False becomes True. You then used the AndAlso and OrElse operators to form a complex condition.

Finally, you learned about the Designer.vb file that the IDE generates to store the code that builds the controls in your GUI. This file also contains the statements that configure the controls based on your actions in **Design** mode.

In the next chapter, you'll learn more about Visual Basic's control structures. Specifically, you'll use repetition statements, which allow you to specify that an action or a group of actions should be performed many times.

SKILLS SUMMARY

Adding a CheckBox to a Form
- Double click the CheckBox in the **Toolbox**.

Selecting a CheckBox
- Click the CheckBox when the app is running, and a check mark appears in the box.

Deselecting a CheckBox
- Click a checked CheckBox when the app is running to remove its check mark.

Determining Whether a CheckBox Is Selected
- Access the CheckBox's Checked property.

Displaying a Dialog
- Use method MessageBox.Show.

Combining Multiple Conditions
- Use the logical operators to form complex conditions by combining simple ones.

KEY TERMS

And operator—A logical operator used to ensure that two conditions are *both* true before choosing a certain path of execution. Does not perform short-circuit evaluation.

AndAlso operator—A logical operator used to ensure that two conditions are *both* true before choosing a certain path of execution. Performs short-circuit evaluation.

CheckBox control—A small square GUI element that either is empty or contains a check mark.

CheckBox label—The text that appears next to a CheckBox.

Checked property of the CheckBox control—Specifies whether the CheckBox is checked (True) or unchecked (False).

Designer.vb file—The file containing the declarations and statements that build an app's GUI.

dismiss a dialog—Synonym for closing a dialog.

logical exclusive OR (Xor) operator—A logical operator that's True if and only if one of its operands is True and the other is False. Does not perform short-circuit evaluation.

logical operators—The operators (for example, AndAlso, OrElse, Xor and Not) that can be used to form complex conditions by combining simple ones.

message dialog—A window that displays messages to users or gathers input from users.

MessageBox class—Provides a method for displaying message dialogs.

MessageBoxButtons constants—Identifiers that specify the Buttons that can be displayed in a MessageBox dialog.

MessageBoxIcon constants—Identifiers that specify the icons that can be displayed in a MessageBox dialog.

MessageBox.Show method—Displays a message dialog.

Not (logical negation) operator—A logical operator that enables you to reverse the meaning of a condition: A True condition, when logically negated, becomes False, and a False condition, when logically negated, becomes True.

Or operator—A logical operator used to ensure that either *or* both of two conditions are true in an app before a certain path of execution is chosen. Does not perform short-circuit evaluation.

OrElse operator—A logical operator used to ensure that either *or* both of two conditions are true in an app before a certain path of execution is chosen. Performs short-circuit evaluation.

repetition statements—Statements that allow you to specify that an action or a group of actions should be performed many times.

short-circuit evaluation—The evaluation of the right operand in AndAlso and OrElse expressions occurs only if evaluation of the left operand is insufficient to determine the value of the expression.

simple condition—Contains one expression that evaluates to True or False.

state button—A button that can be in the "on" or "off" (True or False, respectively) state.

truth table—A table that displays the Boolean result of a logical operator for all possible combinations of True and False values for its operands.

Xor (logical exclusive OR) operator—A logical operator that's True if and only if one of its operands is True and the other is False. Does not perform short-circuit evaluation.

GUI DESIGN GUIDELINES

CheckBoxes

- A CheckBox's label should be descriptive and brief. When a CheckBox label contains more than one word, use book-title capitalization.
- Align groups of CheckBoxes either horizontally or vertically.

Message Dialogs

- Text displayed in a dialog should be descriptive and brief.

CONTROLS, EVENTS, PROPERTIES & METHODS

CheckBox ☑ CheckBox   This control allows the user to select an option.

- *In action*

- *Properties*

    AutoSize—Allows for automatic resizing of the CheckBox.

    Checked—Specifies whether the CheckBox is checked (True) or unchecked (False).

    Location—Specifies the location of the CheckBox on the Form.

Name—Specifies the name used to access the CheckBox control programmatically. We prefer to end the name with CheckBox.

Size—Specifies the width and height (in pixels) of the CheckBox.

Text—Specifies the text displayed next to the CheckBox.

MessageBox   This class allows the user to display a message dialog.

■ *In action*

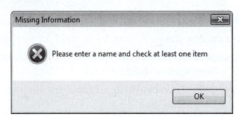

■ *Method*

Show—Displays a message dialog. The user cannot interact with the app's Form until the message dialog is closed.

MessageBoxButtons   This class provides constants used to specify the Buttons displayed in a message dialog.

■ *In action*

Button specified by MessageBoxButtons constant OK.

■ *Constants*

OK—**OK** Button. Allows the user to acknowledge a message.

OKCancel—**OK** and **Cancel** Buttons. Allow the user to either confirm or cancel an operation.

YesNo—**Yes** and **No** Buttons. Allow the user to respond to a question.

YesNoCancel—**Yes**, **No** and **Cancel** Buttons. Allow the user to respond to a question or cancel an operation.

RetryCancel—**Retry** and **Cancel** Buttons. Allow the user either to retry or to cancel an operation that has failed.

AbortRetryCancel—**Abort**, **Retry** and **Ignore** Buttons. When one of a series of operations has failed, these Buttons allow the user to abort the entire sequence, retry the failed operation or ignore the failed operation and continue.

MessageBoxIcon   This class provides constants used to specify the icon displayed in a message dialog.

■ *In action*

■ *Constants*

Exclamation—Icon containing an exclamation point. Typically used to caution the user against potential problems.

Information—Icon containing the letter "i." Typically used to display information about the state of the app.

None—No icon is displayed in the message dialog.

Error—Icon containing a white **x** in a red circle. Typically used to alert the user to errors or critical situations.

MULTIPLE-CHOICE QUESTIONS

8.1 How many CheckBoxes in a GUI can be selected at once?

a) 0   b) 1

c) 4   d) any number

8.2 The first argument passed to method MessageBox.Show is _____.

a) the text displayed in the dialog's title bar

b) a constant representing the Buttons displayed in the dialog

c) the text displayed inside the dialog

d) a constant representing the icon that appears in the dialog

8.3 You can specify the Button(s) and icon to be displayed in a message dialog by using the MessageBoxButtons and _____ constants.

a) MessageIcon   b) MessageBoxImages

c) MessageBoxPicture   d) MessageBoxIcon

8.4 _____ are used to create complex conditions.

a) Assignment operators   b) Activity diagrams

c) Logical operators   d) Formatting codes

8.5 Operator AndAlso _____.

a) performs short-circuit evaluation

b) is not a keyword

c) is a comparison operator

d) evaluates to False if both operands are True

8.6 A CheckBox is selected when its Checked property is set to _____.

a) On   b) True

c) Selected   d) Checked

8.7 The condition *expression1* AndAlso *expression2* evaluates to True if _____.

a) *expression1* is True and *expression2* is False

b) *expression1* is False and *expression2* is True

c) both *expression1* and *expression2* are True

d) both *expression1* and *expression2* are False

8.8 The condition *expression1* OrElse *expression2* evaluates to False if _____.

a) *expression1* is True and *expression2* is False

b) *expression1* is False and *expression2* is True

c) both *expression1* and *expression2* are True

d) both *expression1* and *expression2* are False

8.9 The condition *expression1* Xor *expression2* evaluates to True if _____.

a) *expression1* is True and *expression2* is False

b) *expression1* is False and *expression2* is True

c) both *expression1* and *expression2* are True

d) Both (a) and (b)

8.10 The condition Not(*expression1* AndAlso *expression2*) evaluates to True if _____.

a) *expression1* is True and *expression2* is False

b) *expression1* is False and *expression2* is True

c) Both (a) and (b).

d) Neither (a) nor (b).

EXERCISES

8.11 *(Enhanced Dental Payment App)* Modify the **Dental Payment** app from this chapter to include additional services, as shown in Fig. 8.25. Add the proper functionality (using

If...Then statements) to determine whether any of the new CheckBoxes are selected, and, if so, add the price of the service to the total bill. Display an error message in a dialog if the user selects the **Other** CheckBox but does not specify a price for the service.

Figure 8.25   Enhanced **Dental Payment** app.

a) *Copying the template to your working directory.* Copy the directory C:\Examples\ ch08\Exercises\DentalPaymentEnhanced to your C:\SimplyVB2010 directory.

b) *Opening the app's template file.* Double click DentalPaymentEnhanced.sln in the DentalPaymentEnhanced directory to open the app.

c) *Adding CheckBoxes, Labels and a TextBox.* Add two CheckBoxes and two Labels to the Form. The new CheckBoxes should be labeled **Fluoride** and **Root Canal**, respectively. Add these CheckBoxes and Labels beneath the X-Ray CheckBox and its price Label. The price for a fluoride treatment is $50; the price for a root canal is $800. Add a CheckBox labeled **Other** and a Label containing a dollar sign (**$**) to the Form, as shown in Fig. 8.25. Then add a TextBox to the right of the $ Label in which the user can enter the cost of the service performed.

d) *Modifying the Click event-handler code.* Add code to the calculateButton_Click event handler to determine whether the new CheckBoxes have been selected. This can be done by modifying the compound condition in the first If...Then statement in the event handler. Add an ElseIf clause to determine whether the user selected the **Other** CheckBox but did not specify a price—if so, display an error message in a dialog. Also, use If...Then statements to update the bill amount.

e) *Running the app.* Select **Debug > Start Debugging** to run your app. Test your app by checking one or more of the new services. Click the **Calculate** Button and verify that the proper total is displayed. Test the app again by checking some of the services, then checking the **Other** CheckBox and entering a dollar value for this service. Click the **Calculate** Button and verify that the proper total is displayed and that it includes the price for the "other" service.

f) *Closing the app.* Close your running app by clicking its close box.

g) *Closing the IDE.* Close the Visual Basic IDE by clicking its close box.

8.12 *(Fuzzy Dice Order Form App)* Write an app that allows users to process orders for fuzzy dice, as shown in Fig. 8.26. The app should calculate the total price of the order, including tax and shipping. TextBoxes for inputting the order number, the customer name and the shipping address are provided. Provide CheckBoxes for selecting the fuzzy dice color. The app should also contain a Button that, when clicked, calculates the subtotals for each type of fuzzy dice ordered and the total of the entire order (including tax and shipping). Use 5% for the tax rate. Shipping charges are $1.50 for up to 20 pairs of dice. If more than 20 pairs are ordered, shipping is free.

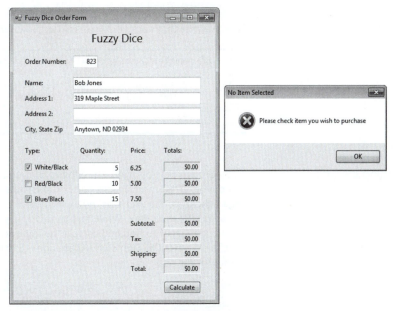

Figure 8.26   Fuzzy Dice Order Form app.

a) *Copying the template to your working directory.* Copy the directory `C:\Examples\ch08\Exercises\FuzzyDiceOrderForm` to your `C:\SimplyVB2010` directory.

b) *Opening the app's template file.* Double click `FuzzyDiceOrderForm.sln` in the `FuzzyDiceOrderForm` directory to open the app.

c) *Adding CheckBoxes to the Form.* Add three CheckBoxes to the Form. Label the first CheckBox **White/Black**, the second one **Red/Black** and the third **Blue/Black**.

d) *Adding a `Click` event handler and its code.* Create the `Click` event handler for the **Calculate** Button. The app should warn users if they specify an item's quantity without checking its corresponding CheckBox. For the total to be calculated, the user must enter an order number, a name and a shipping address. Use logical operators to ensure that these terms are met. If they aren't, display a message in a dialog.

e) *Calculating the total cost.* Calculate the subtotal, tax, shipping and total, and display the results in their corresponding `Labels`.

f) *Running the app.* Select **Debug > Start Debugging** to run your app. Test the app by providing quantities for checked items. Ensure that your app is calculating 5% sales tax. Verify that shipping is free if more than 20 pairs of dice are ordered. Also, determine whether your code containing the logical operators works correctly by specifying a quantity for an item that's not checked. For instance, in Fig. 8.26, a quantity is specified for **Red/Black** dice, but the corresponding CheckBox is not selected. This should cause the message dialog in Fig. 8.26 to appear.

g) *Closing the app.* Close your running app by clicking its close box.

h) *Closing the IDE.* Close the Visual Basic IDE by clicking its close box.

Assume that `nameTextBox` is a TextBox and that `otherCheckBox` is a CheckBox next to ...ch is another TextBox called `otherTextBox`, in which the user should specify a value. ...t does this code segment do?

```
If (nameTextBox.Text = String.Empty OrElse
    (otherCheckBox.Checked = True AndAlso
    otherTextBox.Text = String.Empty)) Then

    MessageBox.Show("Please enter a name or value",
        "Input Error", MessageBoxButtons.OK,
        MessageBoxIcon.Error)

End If
```

What's wrong with this code? ▶ **8.14** Assume that `nameTextBox` is a `TextBox`. Find the error(s) in the following code:

```
1   If nameTextBox.Text = "John Doe" Then
2
3       MessageBox.Show("Welcome, John!",
4           MessageBoxIcon.Exclamation)
5
6   End If
```

Using the Debugger ▶ **8.15** *(Sibling Survey App)* The **Sibling Survey** app displays the siblings selected by the user in a dialog. If the user checks either the **Brother(s)** or **Sister(s)** CheckBox and the **No Siblings** CheckBox, the user is asked to verify the selection. Otherwise, the user's selection is displayed in a MessageBox. While testing this app, you noticed that it does not execute properly. Use the debugger to find and correct the logic error(s) in the code. This exercise is located in `C:\Examples\ch08\Exercises\Debugger\SiblingSurvey`. Figure 8.27 shows the correct output for the app.

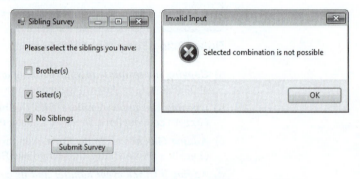

Figure 8.27   Correct output for the **Sibling Survey** app.

Programming Challenge ▶ **8.16** *(Modified Fuzzy Dice Order Form App)* Modify the **Fuzzy Dice Order Form** app from Exercise 8.12 to determine whether customers should receive a 7% discount on their purchase (Fig. 8.28). Customers ordering more than $500 (before tax and shipping) in fuzzy dice are eligible for this discount.

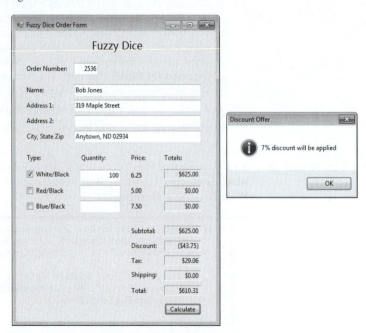

Figure 8.28   Modified **Fuzzy Dice Order Form** app.

a) *Opening the app*. Open the app you created in Exercise 8.12.

b) *Adding the discount Label*. Add two Labels to the Form to display the discount. Place the Labels below the **Subtotal** Label as shown in Fig. 8.28.

c) *Determining whether the total cost is over $500*. Use an If...Then statement to determine whether the subtotal is greater than $500.

d) *Displaying the discount and subtracting the discount from the total*. If a customer orders more than $500 in fuzzy dice, display a message dialog, as shown in Fig. 8.28, informing the user that the customer is entitled to a 7% discount. The message dialog should contain an Information icon and an **OK** Button. Calculate 7% of the total amount before taxes and shipping, and display the discount amount in the **Discount:** field. Subtract this amount from the subtotal, and update the **Total:** field.

e) *Running the app*. Select **Debug > Start Debugging** to run your app. Confirm that your app calculates and displays the discount properly.

f) *Closing the app.* Close your running app by clicking its close box.

g) *Closing the IDE.* Close the Visual Basic IDE by clicking its close box.

Car Payment Calculator App

Introducing the Do While...Loop and Do Until...Loop Repetition Statements

This chapter continues the discussion of structured programming that we began in Chapter 7. We introduce **repetition statements**, which are control statements that can repeat actions based on a condition's value. In everyday life you perform many repetitive tasks based on conditions. For example, each time you turn a page in this book (while there are more pages to read), you're repeating a simple task, namely turning a page, based on a condition, namely that there are more pages to read.

Performing tasks repeatedly is an important part of structured programming. Repetition statements are used in many types of apps. In this chapter, you learn to use the Do While...Loop and the Do Until...Loop repetition statements. You'll use a repetition statement in the **Car Payment Calculator** app that you build. Later chapters introduce additional repetition statements.

9.1 Test-Driving the Car Payment Calculator App

The problem stated below requires an app that repeats a calculation four times—you'll use a repetition statement to solve this problem. The app must meet the following requirements:

App Requirements

Typically, banks offer car loans for periods ranging from two to five years (24 to 60 months). Borrowers repay the loans in monthly installments. The amount of each monthly payment is based on the length of the loan, the amount borrowed and the interest rate. Create an app that allows the customer to enter the price of a car, the down-payment amount and the annual interest rate of the loan. The app should display the loan's duration in months and the monthly payments for two-, three-, four- and five-year loans. The variety of options allows the user to compare repayment plans and choose the most appropriate.

You begin by test-driving the completed app. Then you learn the additional Visual Basic capabilities needed to create your own version of this app, including the predefined Visual Basic function Pmt for calculating monthly payments.

Test-Driving the Car Payment Calculator App

1. ***Opening the completed app.*** Open the directory C:\Examples\ch09\CompletedApp\CarPaymentCalculator to locate the **Car Payment Calculator** app. Double click CarPaymentCalculator.sln to open the app in the Visual Basic IDE.

2. ***Running the app.*** Select **Debug > Start Debugging** to run the app (Fig. 9.1). Note the new GUI control—the ListBox control, which allows users to view and/or select from multiple items in a list. Users cannot add items to, or remove items from, a ListBox by interacting directly with it. The ListBox does *not* accept keyboard input—users cannot add or delete selected items. You must write code that adds items to, or removes items from, a ListBox.

ListBox control ——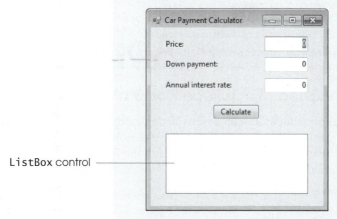

Figure 9.1   **Car Payment Calculator** app before data has been entered.

3. ***Entering quantities in the app.*** Enter 16900 in the **Price:** TextBox. Enter 6000 in the **Down payment:** TextBox. Enter 4.5 in the **Annual interest rate:** TextBox. The Form appears as in Fig. 9.2.

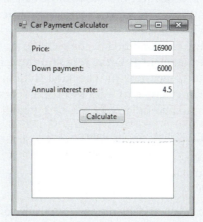

Figure 9.2   **Car Payment Calculator** app after data has been entered.

4. ***Calculating the monthly payment amounts.*** Click the **Calculate** Button. The app displays the monthly payment amounts in the ListBox (Fig. 9.3). The information is organized in tabular format.

5. ***Closing the app.*** Close your running app by clicking its close box.

6. ***Closing the IDE.*** Close the Visual Basic IDE by clicking its close box.

(cont.)

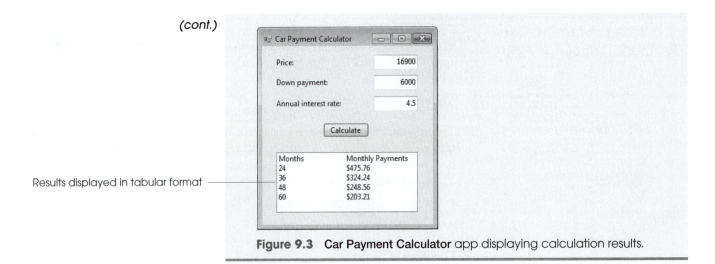

Figure 9.3 **Car Payment Calculator** app displaying calculation results.

9.2 `Do While`...`Loop` Repetition Statement

A repetition statement can repeat actions, depending on the value of a *condition* (which can be either true or false). For example, if you go to the grocery store with a list of items to purchase, you go through the list until you've put each item in your shopping cart. This process is described by the following pseudocode statements:

Do while there are more items on my shopping list
 Put next item in cart
 Cross it off my list

These statements describe the repetitive actions that occur during a shopping trip. The condition "there are more items on my shopping list" can be true or false. If it's true, then the actions "Put next item in cart" and "Cross it off my list" are performed in sequence. In an app, these actions execute repeatedly while the condition remains true. The statements indented in this repetition statement constitute its **body**. When the last item on the shopping list has been put in the cart and crossed off the list, the condition becomes false. At this point, the repetition terminates, and the first statement after the repetition statement executes. In the shopping example, you would proceed to the checkout station.

As an example of a `Do While`...`Loop` statement, let's look at an app segment designed to find the first power of 3 greater than 50.

Common Programming Error

Provide in the body of every `Do While`...`Loop` statement an action that eventually causes the condition to become false. If you do not, the repetition statement never terminates, causing an error called an **infinite loop**. Such an error causes the app to "hang up." When an infinite loop occurs in your app, return to the IDE and select **Debug > Stop Debugging**.

```
Dim product As Integer = 3

Do While product <= 50
    product *= 3
Loop
```

The app segment declares and initializes variable `product` to 3, taking advantage of a Visual Basic feature that allows *variable initialization* to be incorporated into a declaration. The condition in the `Do While`...`Loop` statement, `product <= 50`, is referred to as the **loop-continuation condition**. While the loop-continuation condition remains true, the `Do While`...`Loop` statement executes its body repeatedly. When the loop-continuation condition becomes false, the `Do While`...`Loop` statement terminates, and `product` contains the first power of 3 larger than 50.

Let's examine the execution of the preceding code in detail. When the `Do While`...`Loop` statement is entered, the value of `product` is 3 and the loop-continuation condition (3 <= 50) is true. Each time the loop executes, the variable `product` is multiplied by 3, taking on the values 9, 27 and 81, successively. When `product` becomes 81, the condition in the `Do While`...`Loop` statement, `product <= 50`, evaluates to `False`. When the repetition ends, the final value of `product` is 81, which is, indeed, the first power of 3 greater than 50. App execution continues with the next statement after the Do While...Loop statement. If a Do While...Loop statement's condition is *initially false*, the body does *not* execute and your app simply continues executing with the next statement after the keyword Loop. The following box describes each step as the preceding repetition statement executes.

Executing the Do While...Loop Repetition Statement	1. The app declares variable product and sets its value to 3.
	2. The app enters the Do While...Loop repetition statement.
	3. The loop-continuation condition is checked. The condition evaluates to True (product is less than or equal to 50), so the app continues executing at the next statement in the loop's body.
	4. The value (currently 3) stored in product is multiplied by 3 and the result is assigned to product; product now contains 9.
	5. The loop-continuation condition is checked. The condition evaluates to True (product is less than or equal to 50), so the app continues executing at the next statement in the loop's body.
	6. The value (currently 9) stored in product is multiplied by 3 and the result is assigned to product; product now contains 27.
	7. The loop-continuation condition is checked. The condition evaluates to True (product is less than or equal to 50), so the app continues executing at the next statement in the loop's body.
	8. The value (currently 27) stored in product is multiplied by 3 and the result is assigned to product; product now contains 81.
	9. The loop-continuation condition is checked. The condition evaluates to False (product is not less than or equal to 50), so the app exits the Do While...Loop repetition statement and continues executing at the first statement after keyword Loop.

Let's use a UML activity diagram to illustrate the flow of control in the preceding Do While...Loop repetition statement. The diagram in Fig. 9.4 contains an initial state, transition arrows, a merge, a decision, two guard conditions, an action state, three notes and a final state. The action state represents the statement that multiplies the value of product by 3.

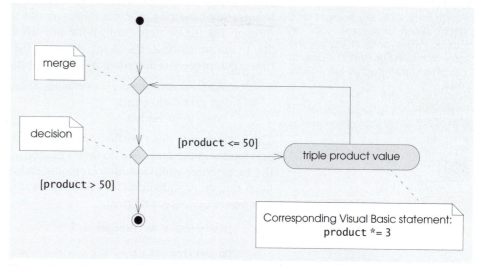

Figure 9.4 Do While...Loop repetition statement UML activity diagram.

The activity diagram clearly shows the repetition. The transition arrow emerging from the action state points back to the merge, creating a **loop**. The guard conditions are tested each time the loop iterates. Eventually, the guard condition `product > 50` becomes true. At this point the `Do While...Loop` statement terminates, and control passes to the next statement in the app following the loop.

Figure 9.4 introduces the UML's **merge symbol**. The UML represents *both* the merge symbol and the decision symbol as diamonds. The merge symbol *joins two flows of activity into one*. In this diagram, the merge symbol joins the transitions from the initial state and from the action state, so they both flow into the loop-continuation condition, which determines whether the loop body statement should begin (or continue) executing. In this case, the UML activity diagram enters its action state when the loop-continuation guard condition `product <= 50` is true.

Although the UML represents both the decision and the merge symbols with the diamond shape, the symbols can be distinguished by the number of "incoming" and "outgoing" transition arrows. A decision symbol has *one* transition arrow pointing to the diamond and *two* (or more) transition arrows pointing out from the diamond to indicate possible transitions from that point. In addition, each transition arrow pointing out of a decision symbol has a guard condition next to it. A merge symbol has *two* (or more) transition arrows pointing to the diamond and only *one* transition arrow pointing out from the diamond to indicate multiple activity flows merging.

SELF-REVIEW

1. The body of a `Do While...Loop` statement executes _____.
   a) at least once
   b) never
   c) while its condition is true
   d) while its condition is false

2. The UML represents both the merge symbol and the decision symbol as _____.
   a) rectangles with rounded sides
   b) diamonds
   c) small black circles
   d) ovals

Answers: 1) c. 2) b.

9.3 `Do Until...Loop` Repetition Statement

Common Programming Error

Failure to provide the body of a `Do Until...Loop` statement with an action that eventually causes the condition in the `Do Until...Loop` to become true creates an infinite loop.

Unlike the `Do While...Loop` repetition statement, the `Do Until...Loop` repetition statement determines whether its condition is *false* before repetition can continue, and the loop terminates when its condition becomes true. This is known as a **loop-termination condition**. For example, you can think of grocery shopping as looping through the list of items until none are left on the list. Note that the condition "there are no more items on my shopping list" must be false for the loop to continue. This process is described by the following pseudocode statements:

```
Do until there are no more items on my shopping list
    Put next item in cart
    Cross it off my list
```

These statements describe the repetitive actions that occur during a shopping trip. Statements in the body of a `Do Until...Loop` are executed repeatedly for as long as the loop-termination condition remains `False`. As an example of a `Do Until...Loop` repetition statement, let's look again at an app segment designed to find the first power of 3 larger than 50:

```
Dim product As Integer = 3

Do Until product > 50
    product *= 3
Loop
```

The following box describes each step as the repetition statement executes.

1. The app declares variable `product` and sets its value to 3.
2. The app enters the `Do Until...Loop` repetition statement.
3. The loop-termination condition is checked. The condition evaluates to `False` (product is not greater than 50), so the app continues executing at the next statement in the loop's body.
4. The value (currently 3) stored in `product` is multiplied by 3 and the result is assigned to `product`; product now contains 9.
5. The loop-termination condition is checked. The condition evaluates to `False` (product is not greater than 50), so the app continues executing at the next statement in the loop's body.
6. The value (currently 9) stored in `product` is multiplied by 3 and the result is assigned to `product`; product now contains 27.
7. The loop-termination condition is checked. The condition evaluates to `False` (product is not greater than 50), so the app continues executing at the next statement in the loop's body.
8. The value (currently 27) stored in `product` is multiplied by 3 and the result is assigned to `product`; product now contains 81.
9. The loop-termination condition is checked. The condition now evaluates to `True` (product is greater than 50), so the app exits the `Do Until...Loop` repetition statement and continues executing at the first statement after keyword `Loop`.

The UML activity diagram in Fig. 9.5 illustrates the flow of control for the Do Until...Loop repetition statement. This diagram is the same as the Do While...Loop repetition statement's activity diagram.

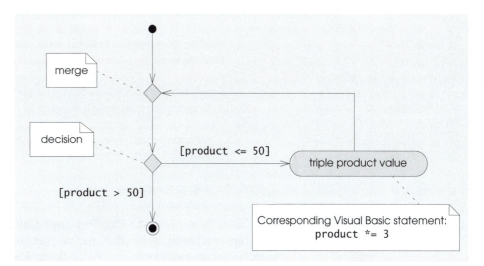

Figure 9.5 Do Until...Loop repetition statement UML activity diagram.

SELF-REVIEW

1. A Do Until...Loop repetition statement differs from a Do While...Loop repetition statement in _____.

   a) that a Do While...Loop repetition statement loops as long as the loop-continuation condition remains False, whereas a Do Until...Loop repetition statement loops as long as the loop-continuation condition remains True

   b) that a Do Until...Loop repetition statement loops as long as the loop-termination condition remains False, whereas a Do While...Loop repetition statement loops as long as the loop-continuation condition remains True

   c) that a Do Until...Loop repetition statement always executes at least once

   d) no way. There's no difference between the Do Until...Loop and Do While...Loop repetition statements

2. Statements in the body of a Do Until...Loop execute repeatedly for as long as the _____ remains False.

   a) loop-continuation condition   b) do-loop condition

   c) loop-termination condition   d) until-loop condition

   Answer: 1) b. 2) c.

9.4 Constructing the Car Payment Calculator App

Now that you've learned the Do While...Loop and Do Until...Loop repetition statements, you're ready to construct the **Car Payment Calculator** app.

The following pseudocode describes the basic operation of the **Car Payment Calculator** app that occurs when a user enters information and clicks the **Calculate Button**:

> When the user clicks the Calculate Button
>   Initialize loan length to two years
>   Clear the ListBox of any previous calculation results
>   Add a header to the ListBox
>
>   Get down payment from a TextBox
>   Get sticker price from a TextBox
>   Get annual interest rate from a TextBox
>
>   Calculate loan amount (sticker price – down payment)
>   Calculate monthly interest rate (annual interest rate / 12)
>
>   Do while loan length is less than or equal to five years
>   Convert the loan length in years to number of months
>
>   Calculate monthly payment based on loan amount, monthly interest rate and loan length in months
>
>   Insert result into ListBox
>   Increment loan length in years by one year

You've test-driven the **Car Payment Calculator** app and studied its pseudocode representation. Now you'll use an Action/Control/Event (ACE) table to help you convert the pseudocode to Visual Basic. Figure 9.6 lists the *actions*, *controls* and *events* that will help you complete your own version of this app.

Note in the pseudocode that the retrieval of the down payment, sticker price and annual interest rate and the calculation of the loan amount and monthly interest rate occur *before* the repetition statement because they need to be performed only *once*. Statements that have different results in each iteration are included *in the repetition statement*. The repetition statement's body includes: converting loan length in years to loan length in months, calculating the monthly payment amount, displaying the calculation's result and incrementing the loan length in years.

Action/Control/Event (ACE) Table for the Car Payment Calculator

Action	Control	Event
Label all the app's controls	`priceLabel`, `downPaymentLabel`, `interestLabel`	App is run
	`calculateButton`	Click
Initialize loan length to two years		
Clear the ListBox of any previous calculation results	`paymentsListBox`	
Add a header to the ListBox	`paymentsListBox`	
Get down payment from a TextBox	`downPaymentTextBox`	
Get sticker price from a TextBox	`priceTextBox`	
Get annual interest rate from a TextBox	`interestTextBox`	
Calculate loan amount		
Calculate monthly interest rate		
Do while loan length is less than or equal to five years Convert the loan length in years to number of months		
Calculate monthly payment based on loan amount, monthly interest rate and loan length in months		
Insert result into ListBox	`paymentsListBox`	
Increment loan length in years by one year		

Figure 9.6   **Car Payment Calculator** app ACE table.

The app displays the calculation results in a `ListBox`. Next, you add and customize the `ListBox` that displays the results.

Adding a ListBox to the Car Payment Calculator App

Good Programming Practice

Append the `ListBox` suffix to all `ListBox` control names.

GUI Design Tip

A `ListBox` should be large enough either to display all of its contents or to allow scrollbars to be used easily, if necessary.

1. ***Copying the template to your working directory.*** Copy the directory `C:\Examples\ch09\TemplateApp\CarPaymentCalculator` to the directory `C:\SimplyVB2010` directory.

2. ***Opening the Car Payment Calculator app's template file.*** Double click `CarPaymentCalculator.sln` in the `CarPaymentCalculator` directory to open the app in the Visual Basic IDE. The `TextBox`es for user input and the **Calculate** `Button` are provided for you.

3. ***Adding a ListBox control to the Form.*** Double click the `ListBox` control,

      `ListBox`

   in the **Toolbox**. Change the `ListBox`'s Name property to `paymentsListBox`. Set the Location property to 24, 166 and the Size property to 230, 94. Figure 9.7 shows the Form with the `ListBox` control. Note that the `ListBox` displays its Name property in **Design** view—the name is *not* displayed when the app is running.

4. ***Saving the project.*** Select **File > Save All** to save your changes.

(cont.)

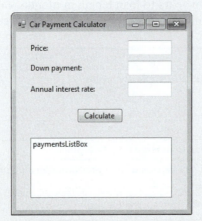

Figure 9.7   **ListBox** added to **Car Payment Calculator** app's Form.

After adding the ListBox, you must add an *event handler* to the app to respond when the user clicks the **Calculate** Button. Event handler calculateButton_Click updates the ListBox's contents. The following box describes how to add items to a ListBox and how to clear a ListBox.

Using Code to Change a ListBox's Contents

1. ***Adding the Calculate Button's event handler.*** Double click the **Calculate** Button to generate the empty event handler calculateButton_Click. Add the comment before the event handler and reformat the event handler as shown in lines 2–4 of Fig. 9.8.

```
2    ' handles Calculate Button's Click event
3    Private Sub calculateButton_Click(sender As System.Object,
4       e As System.EventArgs) Handles calculateButton.Click
5
6       ' remove text displayed in ListBox
7       paymentsListBox.Items.Clear()
8    End Sub ' calculateButton_Click
```

Figure 9.8   Clearing the contents of a ListBox.

2. ***Clearing the ListBox control.*** Add lines 6–7 of Fig. 9.8 to calculateButton_Click. Each time the user clicks the **Calculate** Button, any content previously displayed in the ListBox is removed to prepare to display the new results. To remove all content from the ListBox, call method **Clear** of the ListBox's **Items** property (line 7). This property enables you to add content to and remove content from the ListBox. The Items property returns an *object* that contains the list of items displayed in the ListBox. Add the comment in line 8 to indicate the end of the event handler.

 **GUI Design Tip**

Use headers in a ListBox when you're displaying tabular data. Adding headers improves readability by describing the information that's displayed in the ListBox.

3. ***Adding content to the ListBox control.*** Add lines 9–11 of Fig. 9.9 to calculateButton_Click. The ListBox displays the number of monthly payments and the amount per payment. To clarify the information that's being displayed, we add a line of text—called a **header**—to the ListBox using method **Add** (lines 10–11 of Fig. 9.9). In this case, the column headings "Months" and "Monthly Payment" are separated by two *tab* characters.

(cont.)

```
 6            ' remove text displayed in ListBox
 7            paymentsListBox.Items.Clear()
 8
 9            ' add header to ListBox
10            paymentsListBox.Items.Add("Months" & ControlChars.Tab &
11                ControlChars.Tab & "Monthly Payments")
12        End Sub ' calculateButton_Click
```

Figure 9.9   Adding a header to a ListBox.

The ampersand (&) is the **string-concatenation operator**—it *concatenates* (that is, combines) its two operands into one string value by appending the right operand's text to the end of the left operand's text. In lines 10–11, the header is created by joining the values "Months" and "Monthly Payments" with two **ControlChars.Tab** constants—each inserts a tab character in the string to separate the columns (Fig. 9.3). [*Note:* The .NET Framework Class Library type ControlChars provides constants for several special characters, including Tab, CrLf and Newline. Many of these constants have corresponding Visual Basic-specific constants, such as vbTab, vbCrLf and vbNewline.]

values

4. ***Saving the project.*** Select **File > Save All** to save your modified code.

Now that you've learned how to change a ListBox's contents, you need to declare variables and obtain user input for the calculation. The following box shows you how to initialize the **Car Payment Calculator** app's variables. The box also guides you through converting the annual interest rate to the monthly interest rate and shows you how to calculate the monthly loan amount.

Declaring Variables and Retrieving User Input

1. ***Declaring variables.*** Add lines 6–13 of Fig. 9.10 to the event handler calculateButton_Click above the code you added in the preceding box. Variables years and months store the length of the loan in years and months, respectively. The calculation requires the length in months, but the loop-continuation condition uses the number of years. Variables price, downPayment and interest store the user input from the TextBoxes. Variable monthlyPayment stores the result of the monthly payment calculation. Variables loanAmount and monthlyInterest store calculation results.

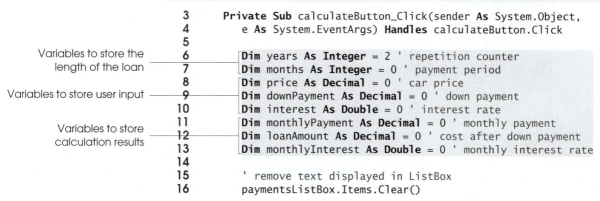

```
 3        Private Sub calculateButton_Click(sender As System.Object,
 4            e As System.EventArgs) Handles calculateButton.Click
 5
 6            Dim years As Integer = 2 ' repetition counter
 7            Dim months As Integer = 0 ' payment period
 8            Dim price As Decimal = 0 ' car price
 9            Dim downPayment As Decimal = 0 ' down payment
10            Dim interest As Double = 0 ' interest rate
11            Dim monthlyPayment As Decimal = 0 ' monthly payment
12            Dim loanAmount As Decimal = 0 ' cost after down payment
13            Dim monthlyInterest As Double = 0 ' monthly interest rate
14
15            ' remove text displayed in ListBox
16            paymentsListBox.Items.Clear()
```

Variables to store the length of the loan → (lines 6–7)

Variables to store user input → (lines 8–10)

Variables to store calculation results → (lines 11–13)

Figure 9.10   Variables for the **Car Payment Calculator** app.

2. ***Retrieving user input needed for the calculation.*** Add lines 22–26 of Fig. 9.11 below the code you added in the preceding box. Lines 24–26 retrieve the down payment (downPayment), price (price) and annual interest rate (interest) provided by the user. Line 26 divides the interest rate by 100—if the user enters 5, the interest rate is 0.05.

(cont.)

```
17
18        ' add header to ListBox
19        paymentsListBox.Items.Add("Months" & ControlChars.Tab &
20           ControlChars.Tab & "Monthly Payments")
21
22        ' retrieve user input and assign values
23        ' to their respective variables
24        downPayment = Val(downPaymentTextBox.Text)
25        price = Val(priceTextBox.Text)
26        interest = Val(interestTextBox.Text) / 100
```

Figure 9.11 Retrieving input in the **Car Payment Calculator** app.

3. ***Calculating values used in the calculation.*** The app computes the amount of the loan by subtracting the down payment from the price. Add lines 28–30 of Fig. 9.12 to calculate the amount borrowed (line 29) and the monthly interest rate (line 30). These calculations need to occur only *once*, so they're placed *before* the Do While…Loop statement that's added in the next box. Variables loanAmount and monthlyInterest are used in the monthly-payment calculation, which you'll add to your app shortly.

```
26        interest = Val(interestTextBox.Text) / 100
27
28        ' determine amount borrowed and monthly interest rate
29        loanAmount = price - downPayment
30        monthlyInterest = interest / 12
31
```

Figure 9.12 Determining amount borrowed and monthly interest rate.

4. ***Saving the project.*** Select **File > Save All** to save your modified code.

Next, you add a repetition statement to the app to calculate the monthly loan payments. The repetition statement performs this calculation for loans that last two, three, four and five years.

Calculating the Monthly Payment Amounts with a Do While…Loop Repetition Statement

1. ***Setting the loop-continuation condition.*** Add lines 32–33 of Fig. 9.13 below the lines you added in Fig. 9.12. After you type line 33 and press *Enter*, the IDE closes the repetition statement by adding the keyword Loop in line 35.

```
31
32        ' calculate payments for two, three, four and five year loans
33        Do While years <= 5
34
35        Loop
```

Figure 9.13 Do While…Loop to calculate payments.

Recall that the shortest loan in this app lasts two years, so you initialized years to 2 in line 6 (Fig. 9.10). The loop-continuation condition (years <= 5) in Fig. 9.13 specifies that the Do While…Loop statement executes while years remains less than or equal to 5. This loop is an example of **counter-controlled repetition**. This technique uses a variable called a **counter** (years) to control the number of times that a set of statements executes. Counter-controlled repetition also is called **definite repetition**, because the number of repetitions is known *before* the repetition statement begins executing. In this example, repetition terminates when the counter (years) exceeds 5.

(cont.)   2.   ***Calculating the payment period.*** Add lines 34–35 of Fig. 9.14 to the Do While...Loop repetition statement to calculate the number of payments (that is, the length of the loan in months). The number of months changes with each iteration of the loop, and the calculation result changes based on the length of the payment period. Variable months takes on the values 24, 36, 48 and 60, on successive iterations.

```
32          ' calculate payments for two, three, four and five year loans
33          Do While years <= 5
34             ' calculate payment period
35             months = 12 * years
36          Loop
```

Figure 9.14   Converting the loan duration from years to months.

3.   ***Computing the monthly payment.*** Add lines 37–39 of Fig. 9.15 to the Do While...Loop repetition statement. Lines 38–39 (Fig. 9.15) use the Pmt function to calculate the user's monthly payment. The built-in Visual Basic function Pmt returns a Double value that specifies the monthly payment amount on a loan for a constant interest rate (monthlyInterest) and a given time period (months). Line 39 passes to Pmt the interest rate, the total number of payments (equal to the number of months in the payment period) and the amount borrowed. Function Pmt's third argument—the amount borrowed in this example—is a *negative* value if it represents cash to be paid (as in this app) and a *positive* value if it represents cash to be received. The Double return value of Pmt is automatically converted to type Decimal when you assign it to Decimal variable monthlyPayment.

```
33          Do While years <= 5
34             ' calculate payment period
35             months = 12 * years
36
37             ' calculate monthly payment using Pmt
38             monthlyPayment =
39                Pmt(monthlyInterest, months, -loanAmount)
40          Loop
```

Figure 9.15   Pmt function returns monthly payment.

4.   ***Displaying the monthly payment amount.*** Add lines 41–44 of Fig. 9.16 to the app. The number of monthly payments and the monthly payment amounts are displayed beneath the header in the ListBox. To add this content to the ListBox, call method Add of the ListBox's Items property (lines 42–44 of Fig. 9.16). Lines 43–44 use method String.Format to display monthlyPayment in currency format. The *two* tab characters ensure that the monthly payment amount is placed in the second column. The space provided by the extra tab character makes the app's output more readable.

```
37             ' calculate monthly payment using Pmt
38             monthlyPayment =
39                Pmt(monthlyInterest, months, -loanAmount)
40
41             ' display payment value
42             paymentsListBox.Items.Add(months & ControlChars.Tab &
43                ControlChars.Tab & String.Format("{0:C}",
44                monthlyPayment))
45          Loop
```

Figure 9.16   Displaying the number of months and the amount of each monthly payment.

(cont.)

5. ***Incrementing the counter variable.*** Add line 46 of Fig. 9.17 before the closing Loop keyword of the repetition statement. Line 46 increments the counter variable (years). Variable years is incremented in each iteration until it equals 6. Then the loop-continuation condition (years <= 5) evaluates to False and the repetition ends.

```
41              ' display payment value
42              paymentsListBox.Items.Add(months & ControlChars.Tab &
43                 ControlChars.Tab & String.Format("{0:C}",
44                 monthlyPayment))
45
46              years += 1 ' increment counter
47           Loop
```

Figure 9.17   Incrementing the counter.

6. ***Running the app.*** Select **Debug > Start Debugging** to run your app. The app should calculate and display monthly payments. Enter values for a car's price, down payment and annual interest rate and click the **Calculate** Button to verify that the app is working correctly.

7. ***Closing the app.*** Close your running app by clicking its close box.

8. ***Closing the IDE.*** Close the Visual Basic IDE by clicking its close box.

Figure 9.18 presents the source code for the **Car Payment Calculator** app. The lines of code that contain new programming concepts you learned in this chapter are highlighted.

```
1    Public Class CarPaymentCalculatorForm
2       ' handles Calculate Button's Click event
3       Private Sub calculateButton_Click(sender As System.Object,
4          e As System.EventArgs) Handles calculateButton.Click
5
6          Dim years As Integer = 2 ' repetition counter
7          Dim months As Integer = 0 ' payment period
8          Dim price As Decimal = 0 ' car price
9          Dim downPayment As Decimal = 0 ' down payment
10         Dim interest As Double = 0 ' interest rate
11         Dim monthlyPayment As Decimal = 0 ' monthly payment
12         Dim loanAmount As Decimal = 0 ' cost after down payment
13         Dim monthlyInterest As Double = 0 ' monthly interest rate
14
15         ' remove text displayed in ListBox
16         paymentsListBox.Items.Clear()
17
18         ' add header to ListBox
19         paymentsListBox.Items.Add("Months" & ControlChars.Tab &
20            ControlChars.Tab & "Monthly Payments")
21
22         ' retrieve user input and assign values
23         ' to their respective variables
24         downPayment = Val(downPaymentTextBox.Text)
25         price = Val(priceTextBox.Text)
26         interest = Val(interestTextBox.Text) / 100
27
28         ' determine amount borrowed and monthly interest rate
29         loanAmount = price - downPayment
30         monthlyInterest = interest / 12
31
```

Clear the ListBox ——— 16

Add a header to the ListBox ——— 19

Figure 9.18   **Car Payment Calculator** app code. (Part 1 of 2.)

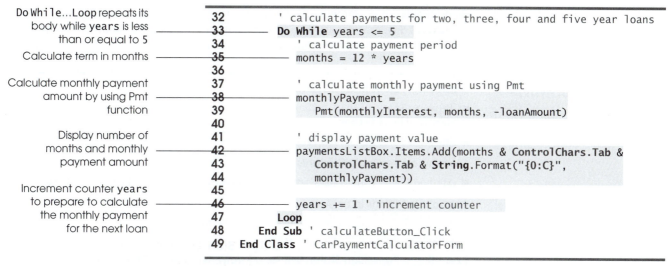

Do While...Loop repeats its
body while **years** is less
than or equal to 5

Calculate term in months

Calculate monthly payment
amount by using Pmt
function

Display number of
months and monthly
payment amount

Increment counter **years**
to prepare to calculate
the monthly payment
for the next loan

```
32          ' calculate payments for two, three, four and five year loans
33          Do While years <= 5
34              ' calculate payment period
35              months = 12 * years
36
37              ' calculate monthly payment using Pmt
38              monthlyPayment =
39                  Pmt(monthlyInterest, months, -loanAmount)
40
41              ' display payment value
42              paymentsListBox.Items.Add(months & ControlChars.Tab &
43                  ControlChars.Tab & String.Format("{0:C}",
44                  monthlyPayment))
45
46              years += 1 ' increment counter
47          Loop
48      End Sub ' calculateButton_Click
49  End Class ' CarPaymentCalculatorForm
```

Figure 9.18   **Car Payment Calculator** app code. (Part 2 of 2.)

SELF-REVIEW   1. Counter-controlled repetition is also called _____ because the number of repetitions
is known before the loop begins executing.

a) definite repetition   b) known repetition

c) sequential repetition   d) counter repetition

2. The line of text added to a ListBox to describe the information that will be displayed is
called a _____.

a) title   b) starter

c) header   d) clarifier

Answers: 1) a. 2) c.

9.5 Wrap-Up

In this chapter, you began using repetition statements. You used the Do While...
Loop and the Do Until...Loop statements to repeat actions in an app, depending on
a loop-continuation condition or a loop-termination condition, respectively.

The Do While...Loop repetition statement executes as long as its loop-continuation condition is True. When the condition becomes False, the repetition terminates. An infinite loop occurs if this condition never becomes False.

The Do Until...Loop repetition statement executes as long as its loop-termination condition is False. The repetition terminates when the condition becomes
True. An infinite loop occurs if this condition never becomes True.

You learned about counter-controlled repetition, in which a repetition statement "knows" in advance the number of times it will iterate, and a variable known
as a counter precisely counts that number of iterations. You used a repetition statement to develop the **Car Payment Calculator** app, in which you calculated the
monthly payments for a given loan amount and a given interest rate for loan dura-
tions of two, three, four and five years.

In the **Car Payment Calculator** app, you used the ListBox control to display
several payment options for a car loan. You learned about the ListBox control,
which is used to maintain a list of items. Items can be added to and removed from
the ListBox programmatically. Values are added to a ListBox control by invoking
method Add on the ListBox control's Items property. The Items property returns
an object that contains all the values displayed in the ListBox.

In the next chapter, you learn two other repetition statements, and you continue exploring counter-controlled repetition. The **Car Payment Calculator** app

demonstrated one common use of repetition statements—performing a calculation for several different values. The app in Chapter 10 introduces another common use of repetition statements—summing a series of numbers.

SKILLS SUMMARY

Displaying Values in a ListBox

■ Property Items of the ListBox control returns an object that contains the values to be displayed in a ListBox.

■ Invoke method Add to add values to the Items property.

Clearing a ListBox's Contents

■ Method Clear of the Items's property deletes (clears) all the values in the ListBox.

Repeating Actions in an App

■ Use a repetition statement that depends on the true or false value of a loop-continuation condition or a loop-termination condition.

Executing a Repetition Statement for a Known Number of Repetitions

■ Use counter-controlled repetition with a counter variable to determine the number of times that a set of statements will execute.

Using the Do While...Loop Repetition Statement

■ This repetition statement executes while the loop-continuation condition is True.

■ An infinite loop occurs if the condition never becomes False.

Using the Do Until...Loop Repetition Statement

■ This repetition statement executes until the loop-termination condition is True.

■ An infinite loop occurs if the condition never becomes True.

Concatenating Strings

■ Use the & operator to build a new string from two existing strings. The right operand's contents are appended to the left operand's contents to create the new string.

KEY TERMS

Add method of Items—Adds an item to a ListBox control.

body of a control statement—The set of statements that are enclosed in a control statement.

Clear method of Items—Deletes all the values in a ListBox control.

ControlChars.Tab constant—Represents a tab character.

counter—A variable used to determine the number of times the body of a repetition statement executes.

counter-controlled repetition—A technique that uses a counter variable to determine the number of times that the body of a repetition statement executes. Also called definite repetition.

definite repetition—See counter-controlled repetition.

Do Until...Loop repetition statement—A control statement that executes a set of body statements *until* its loop-termination condition becomes True.

Do While...Loop repetition statement—A control statement that executes a set of body statements *while* its loop-continuation condition is True.

header—A line of text at the top of a ListBox that clarifies the information being displayed.

infinite loop—An error in which a repetition statement never terminates.

Items property of the ListBox control—Returns an object containing all the values in the ListBox.

ListBox control—Allows the user to view items in a list. Items can be added to or removed from the list programmatically.

loop—Another name for a repetition statement.

loop-continuation condition—The condition used in a repetition statement (such as a Do While...Loop) that enables repetition to continue while the condition is True and causes repetition to terminate when the condition becomes False.

loop-termination condition—The condition used in a repetition statement (such as a Do Until...Loop) that enables repetition to continue while the condition is False and causes repetition to terminate when the condition becomes True.

merge symbol (in the UML)—A diamond symbol in the UML that joins two flows of activity into one flow of activity.

Pmt function—A built-in Visual Basic function that, given an interest rate, the total number of payments and a monetary loan amount, returns a Double value specifying the amount per payment. Function Pmt's third argument is a negative value if it represents cash to be paid and a positive value if it represents cash to be received.

repetition statement—Allows you to specify that an action or actions should be repeated, depending on the value of a condition.

string-concatenation operator (&)—This operator combines its two operands into one string value.

GUI DESIGN GUIDELINES

ListBox
- A ListBox should be large enough to display all of its content or to allow scrollbars, if necessary, to be used easily.
- Use headers in a ListBox when you're displaying tabular data. Adding headers improves readability by describing the information that's displayed in the ListBox.

CONTROLS, EVENTS, PROPERTIES & METHODS

ListBox   ListBox   This control allows the user to view and select from items in a list.

- *In action*

Months	Monthly Payments
24	$490.50
36	$339.06
48	$263.55
60	$218.41

- *Properties*

    Items—Returns an object that contains the items displayed in the ListBox.

    Location—Specifies the location of the ListBox on the Form.

    Name—Specifies the name used to access the properties of the ListBox programatically. The name should be appended with the ListBox suffix.

    Size—Specifies the width and height (in pixels) of the ListBox.

- *Methods*

    Items.Add—Adds an item to the Items property.

    Items.Clear—Deletes all the values in the ListBox's Items property.

MULTIPLE-CHOICE QUESTIONS

9.1 The _____ statement executes until its loop-termination condition becomes True.

    a) Do While...Loop   b) Do Until...Loop

    c) Do   d) Loop

9.2 The _____ statement executes until its loop-continuation condition becomes False.

    a) Do While...Loop   b) Do Until...Loop

    c) Do   d) Do While

9.3 A(n) _____ loop occurs when a condition in a Do While...Loop never becomes False.

    a) infinite   b) undefined

    c) nested   d) indefinite

9.4 A _____ is a variable that helps control the number of times that a set of statements executes.

    a) repeater   b) counter

    c) loop   d) repetition control statement

9.5 The _____ control allows users to add and view items in a list.

a) ListItems

b) SelectBox

c) ListBox

d) ViewBox

9.6 In a UML activity diagram, a(n) _____ symbol joins two flows of activity into one flow of activity.

a) merge

b) combine

c) action state

d) decision

9.7 Property _____ returns an object containing all the values in a ListBox.

a) All

b) List

c) ListItemValues

d) Items

9.8 Items's method _____ deletes all the values in a ListBox.

a) Remove

b) Delete

c) Clear

d) Del

9.9 Items's method _____ adds an item to a ListBox.

a) Include

b) Append

c) Add

d) None of the above

9.10 Function _____ calculates monthly payments on a loan based on a fixed interest rate.

a) MonPmt

b) Payment

c) MonthlyPayment

d) Pmt

EXERCISES

9.11 *(Table of Powers App)* Write an app that displays a table of numbers from 1 to an upper limit, along with each number's squared value (the number *n* to the power 2, or *n* ^ 2) and cubed value (the number *n* to the power 3, or *n* ^ 3). The user specifies the upper limit, and the results are displayed in a ListBox, as in Fig. 9.19.

a) *Copying the template to your working directory.* Copy the directory C:\Examples\ ch09\Exercises\TableOfPowers to your C:\SimplyVB2010 directory.

b) *Opening the app's template file.* Double click TableOfPowers.sln in the TableOf-Powers directory to open the app.

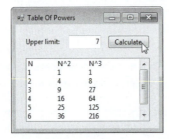

Figure 9.19 Table of Powers app's Form.

c) *Adding a ListBox.* Add a ListBox to the app, as shown in Fig. 9.19. Name the List-Box resultsListBox.

d) *Adding the Upper limit: TextBox event handler.* Double click the **Upper limit:** Text-Box to generate an event handler for this TextBox's TextChanged event. In this event handler, clear the ListBox.

e) *Adding the Calculate Button event handler.* Double click the **Calculate** Button to generate the empty event handler calculateButton_Click. Add the code specified by the remaining steps to this event handler.

f) *Clearing the ListBox.* Use method Clear on the Items property to clear the List-Box of any previous data.

g) *Obtaining the upper limit supplied by the user.* Assign the value entered by the user in the **Upper limit:** TextBox to a variable. Note that the TextBox's Name property is set to inputTextBox.

h) *Adding a header.* Use method Add on the Items property to insert a header in the ListBox. The header should label three columns—N, N^2 and N^3. Column headings should be separated by tab characters.

i) *Calculating the powers from 1 to the specified upper limit.* Use a Do Until...Loop to calculate the squared value and the cubed value of each number from 1 to the upper limit, inclusive. Add an item to the ListBox containing the current number being analyzed, its squared value and its cubed value.

j) *Incrementing the counter.* Remember to increment the counter appropriately each time through the loop.

k) *Running the app.* Select **Debug > Start Debugging** to run your app. Enter an upper limit and click the **Calculate** Button. Verify that the table of powers displayed contains the correct values.

l) *Closing the app.* Close your running app by clicking its close box.

m) *Closing the IDE.* Close the Visual Basic IDE by clicking its close box.

9.12 *(Mortgage Calculator App)* A bank offers mortgages that can be repaid in 5, 10, 15, 20, 25 or 30 years. Write an app that allows the user to enter the price of a house (the amount of the mortgage) and the annual interest rate. When the user clicks the **Calculate** Button, the app displays a table of the mortgage length in years together with the monthly payment, as shown in Fig. 9.20.

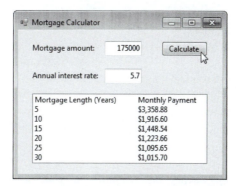

Figure 9.20   **Mortgage Calculator** app's Form.

a) *Copying the template to your working directory.* Copy the directory C:\Examples\ ch09\Exercises\MortgageCalculator to your C:\SimplyVB2010 directory.

b) *Opening the app's template file.* Double click MortgageCalculator.sln in the MortgageCalculator directory to open the app.

c) *Adding a ListBox.* Add a ListBox as shown in Fig. 9.20. Name it resultsListBox.

d) *Adding a Calculate Button event handler.* Double click the **Calculate** Button to generate the empty event handler calculateButton_Click. Add the code specified in the remaining steps to your event handler.

e) *Converting the annual interest rate to the monthly interest rate.* To convert the annual interest rate from a percent value into its Double equivalent, divide the annual rate by 100. Then divide the Double annual rate by 12 to obtain the monthly rate.

f) *Clearing the ListBox.* Use method Clear on the Items property to clear the List-Box of any previous data.

g) *Displaying a header.* Use method Add to display a header in the ListBox. The header should be the column headers "Mortgage Length (Years)" and "Monthly Payment", separated by a tab character.

h) *Using a repetition statement.* Add a Do While...Loop repetition statement to calculate six monthly payment options for the user's mortgage. Each option has a different number of years that the mortgage can last. For this exercise, use the following numbers of years: 5, 10, 15, 20, 25 and 30.

i) *Converting the length of the mortgage from years to months.* Convert the number of years to months.

j) *Calculating the monthly payments for six different mortgages.* Use the Pmt function to compute the monthly payments. Pass to the function the monthly interest rate, the number of months in the mortgage and the mortgage amount. Remember that the mortgage amount must be negative, because it represents an amount of money being paid out by the lender.

k) *Displaying the results.* Use method Add on the Items property to display the length of the mortgage in years and the monthly payment in the ListBox. Use three tab characters to ensure that the monthly payment appears in the second column.

l) *Running the app.* Select **Debug > Start Debugging** to run your app. Enter a mortgage amount and annual interest rate, then click the **Calculate** Button. Verify that the monthly payments displayed contain the correct values.

m) *Closing the app.* Close your running app by clicking its close box.

n) *Closing the IDE.* Close the Visual Basic IDE by clicking its close box.

9.13 *(Office Supplies App)* Create an app that allows the user to make a list of office supplies to buy, as shown in Fig. 9.21. The user should enter the supply item in a TextBox and click the **Buy** Button to add it to the ListBox. The **Clear** Button removes all the items from the ListBox.

Figure 9.21 Office Supplies app's Form.

a) *Copying the template to your working directory.* Copy the C:\Examples\ch09\Exercises\OfficeSupplies directory to your C:\SimplyVB2010 directory.

b) *Opening the app's template file.* Double click OfficeSupplies.sln in OfficeSupplies directory to open the app.

c) *Adding a ListBox.* Add a ListBox to the Form. Name the ListBox suppliesListBox. Place and size it as shown in Fig. 9.21.

d) *Adding an event handler for the Buy Button.* Double click the **Buy** Button to generate the event handler buyButton_Click. The event handler should obtain the user input from the TextBox. The user input is then added as an item into the ListBox. After the input is added to the ListBox, clear the **Supply:** TextBox.

e) *Adding an event handler for the Clear Button.* Double click the **Clear** Button to generate the event handler clearButton_Click. The event handler should use the Clear method on the Items property to clear the ListBox.

f) *Running the app.* Select **Debug > Start Debugging** to run your app. Enter several items into the **Supply:** TextBox and click the **Buy** Button after entering each item. Verify that each item is added to the ListBox. Click the **Clear** Button and verify that all items are removed from the ListBox.

g) *Closing the app.* Close your running app by clicking its close box.

h) *Closing the IDE.* Close the Visual Basic IDE by clicking its close box.

What does this code do? **9.14** What is the result of the following code?

```
1   Dim x As Integer = 1
2   Dim mysteryValue As Integer = 1
3
4   Do While x < 6
5      mysteryValue *= x
6      x += 1
7   Loop
8
9   displayLabel.Text = mysteryValue
```

What's wrong with this code? **9.15** Find the error(s) in the following code:

a) Assume that the variable x is declared and initialized to 1. The loop should total the numbers from 1 to 10.

```
1   Dim total As Integer = 0
2
3   Do Until x <= 10
4      total += x
5      x += 1
6   Loop
```

b) Assume that the variable counter is declared and initialized to 1. The loop should sum the numbers from 1 to 100. Assume total is initialized to 0.

```
1   Do While counter <= 100
2      total += counter
3   Loop
4
5   counter += 1
```

c) Assume that the variable counter is declared and initialized to 1000. The loop should iterate from 1000 to 1.

```
1   Do While counter > 0
2      numbersListBox.Items.Add(counter)
3      counter += 1
4   Loop
```

d) Assume that the variable counter is declared and initialized to 1. The loop should execute five times, adding the numbers 1–5 to a ListBox.

```
1   Do While counter < 5
2      numbersListBox.Items.Add(counter)
3      counter += 1
4   Loop
```

Using the Debugger **9.16** *(Odd Numbers App)* The **Odd Numbers** app should display all of the odd integers between 1 and the number entered by the user. Copy the **Odd Numbers** app from C:/Examples/ch09/Exercises/Debugger to your working directory. Run the app. Note that an infinite loop occurs after you enter a value into the **Upper limit:** TextBox and click the **View** Button. Select **Debug > Stop Debugging** to close the running app. Use the debugger to find and fix the error(s) in the app. Figure 9.22 displays the correct output for the app.

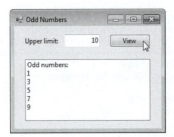

Figure 9.22 Correct output for the **Odd Numbers** app.

Programming Challenge ▶ **9.17** *(To-Do List App)* Use a `ListBox` as a to-do list. Enter each item in a `TextBox`, and add it to the `ListBox` by clicking a `Button`. The item should be displayed in a numbered list, as in Fig. 9.23. To do this, we introduce property `Count`, which returns the number of items in a `ListBox`'s `Items` property. The following is a sample call to assign the number of items displayed in `sampleListBox` to an `Integer` variable:

```
count = sampleListBox.Items.Count
```

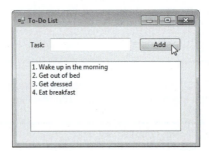

Figure 9.23 **To-Do List** app's `Form`.

Class Average App

Introducing the Do...Loop While and Do...Loop Until Repetition Statements

Objectives

In this chapter, you'll:
- Use the Do...Loop While statement.
- Use the Do...Loop Until statement.
- Access the items in a ListBox control.
- Further understand counter-controlled repetition.
- Transfer the focus to a control.
- Enable and disable Buttons.

Outline

This chapter continues the discussion of repetition statements that we began in Chapter 9. In that chapter we examined Do While...Loop and Do Until...Loop repetition statements, which test their loop-continuation and loop-termination conditions *before* an iteration. This chapter introduces two additional repetition statements, Do...Loop While and Do...Loop Until, which test their conditions *after* each iteration. As a result, the body statements contained in these repetition statements are performed *at least once*.

You'll also learn how to disable and enable controls on a Form. When a control, such as a Button, is disabled, it no longer responds to the user. You'll use this feature to prevent the user from causing errors in your apps. This chapter also introduces the concept of transferring the app's focus to a control. Proper use of the focus makes an app more intuitive and easier to use.

10.1 Test-Driving the Class Average App

This app must meet the following requirements:

> **App Requirements**
>
> *A teacher regularly gives quizzes to a class of 10 students. The grades on these quizzes are integers in the range from 0 to 100 (0 and 100 are both valid grades). The teacher would like you to develop an app that computes the class average for one quiz.*

The class average is equal to the sum of the grades divided by the number of students who took the quiz. The algorithm for solving this problem must input each grade, add it to the total, perform the averaging calculation and display the result. You'll begin by test-driving the completed app. Then you'll learn the additional Visual Basic capabilities needed to create your own version of this app.

Test-Driving the Class Average App

1. *Opening the completed app.* Open the directory C:\Examples\ch10\Com-pletedApp\ClassAverage to locate the **Class Average** app. Double click ClassAverage.sln to open the app in the Visual Basic IDE.

2. *Running the Class Average app.* Select **Debug > Start Debugging** to run the app (Fig. 10.1).

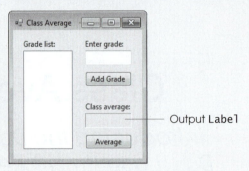

Figure 10.1 **Class Average** app's **Form** in run mode.

3. *Entering quiz grades.* Enter 85 as the first quiz grade in the **Enter grade:** TextBox, and click the **Add Grade** Button. The grade displays in the List-Box, as in Fig. 10.2. After you click the **Add Grade** Button, the cursor appears in the **Enter grade:** TextBox. When a control is selected (for example, the **Enter grade:** TextBox), it's said to have the **focus** of the app. You'll learn to set the focus to a control as you build this chapter's app. As a result of the app's focus being transferred to the **Enter grade:** TextBox, you can type another grade without navigating to the TextBox with the mouse or the *Tab* key. Transferring the focus to a particular control tells the user what information the app expects next. [*Note:* If you click the **Average** Button before 10 grades have been input, a runtime error occurs. Select **Debug > Stop Debugging** to close the running app. Repeat *Step 2*. You'll fix this problem in the exercises.]

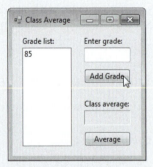

Figure 10.2 Entering grades in the **Class Average** app.

4. *Repeating* **Step 3** *nine times.* Enter nine other grades between 0 and 100, and click the **Add Grade** Button after each entry. After 10 grades are displayed in the **Grade list:** ListBox, the Form will look similar to Fig. 10.3. Note that the **Add Grade** Button is disabled once you've entered 10 grades. That is, its color is gray, and clicking the Button does not invoke its event handler.

5. *Calculating the class average.* Click the **Average** Button to calculate the average of the 10 quizzes. The class average is displayed in an output Label above the **Average** Button (Fig. 10.4). Note that the **Add Grade** Button is now enabled.

(cont.)

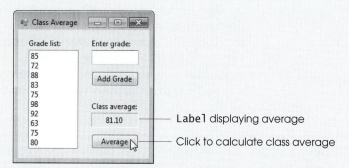

Ten quiz grades entered ——

Disabled **Add Grade** Button

Figure 10.3   **Class Average** app after 10 grades have been input.

Label displaying average

Click to calculate class average

Figure 10.4   Displaying the class average.

6. ***Entering another set of grades.*** You can calculate the class average for another set of 10 grades without restarting the app. Enter a grade in the TextBox and click the **Add Grade** Button. Note that the **Grade list:** List-Box and the **Class average:** field are cleared when you start entering another set of grades (Fig. 10.5).

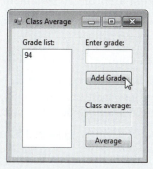

Figure 10.5   Entering a new set of grades.

7. ***Closing the app.*** Close your running app by clicking its close box.
8. ***Closing the IDE.*** Close the Visual Basic IDE by clicking its close box.

10.2 Do...Loop While Repetition Statement

The **Do...Loop While** repetition statement is similar to the Do While...Loop statement; both statements iterate while their loop-continuation conditions are True. In the Do While...Loop statement, the loop-continuation condition is tested at the *beginning* of the loop, *before* the loop body executes. The Do...Loop While statement tests the loop-continuation condition *after* the loop body executes, so the body *always* executes *at least once.* When a Do...Loop While statement terminates, execution continues with the statement after the Loop While keywords.

Common Programming Error

An infinite loop occurs when the loop-continuation condition in a Do...Loop While statement never becomes False.

To illustrate the Do...Loop While repetition statement, consider the example of packing a suitcase. Before you begin packing, the suitcase is empty. You place an item in the suitcase, then determine whether the suitcase is full. As long as the suitcase is not full, you continue to put items in it.

As an example of a Do...Loop While statement, let's look at the following app segment designed to display the numbers 1 through 3 in a ListBox:

```
Dim counter As Integer = 1

Do
    displayListBox.Items.Add(counter)
    counter += 1
Loop While counter <= 3
```

The app segment initializes counter to 1. The loop-continuation condition in the Do...Loop While statement is counter <= 3. While this condition is True, the Do...Loop While statement executes. When it becomes False (that is, when counter is greater than 3), the Do...Loop While statement finishes executing and displayListBox contains the numbers 1 through 3. The following box describes each step as the above repetition statement executes.

Executing the Do...Loop While Repetition Statement

1. The app declares variable counter and sets its value to 1.

2. The app enters the Do...Loop While repetition statement.

3. The number (currently 1) stored in counter is added to displayListBox's Items property.

4. The value of counter is increased by 1; counter now contains 2.

5. The loop-continuation condition is checked. The condition evaluates to True (counter is less than or equal to 3), so the app continues executing at the first statement after the Do statement.

6. The number (currently 2) stored in counter is added to displayListBox's Items property.

7. The value of counter is increased by 1; counter now contains 3.

8. The loop-continuation condition is checked. The condition evaluates to True (counter is less than or equal to 3), so the app continues executing at the first statement after the Do statement.

9. The number (currently 3) stored in counter is added to displayListBox's Items property.

10. The value of counter is increased by 1; counter now contains 4.

11. The loop-continuation condition is checked. The condition evaluates to False (counter is not less than or equal to 3), so the app exits the Do...Loop While repetition statement.

 Error-Prevention Tip

Including a final value in the condition of a repetition statement (and choosing the appropriate relational operator) can reduce the occurrence of off-by-one errors. For example, in a Do While...Loop statement used to print the values 1–10, the loop-continuation condition should be counter <= 10, rather than counter < 10 (which is an off-by-one error) or counter < 11 (which is correct, but less clear).

If you mistyped the loop-continuation condition as counter < 3 or counter <= 2, the ListBox would display only 1 and 2. Including an incorrect relational operator (such as the less-than sign in counter < 3) or an incorrect final value for a loop counter (such as the 2 in counter <= 2) in the condition of any repetition statement, or using an incorrect initial value (such as counter = 0), can cause **off-by-one errors**, which occur when a loop executes for one more or one less iteration than is necessary.

Figure 10.6 illustrates the UML activity diagram for a Do...Loop While statement. This diagram makes it clear that the loop-continuation guard condition ([counter <= 3]) does not evaluate until after the loop performs the action state at least once. Recall that action states can include one or more Visual Basic statements executed one after the other (sequentially) as in the preceding example. When you use a Do...Loop While repetition statement in building an app, you provide the appropriate action state and the guard conditions for your app.

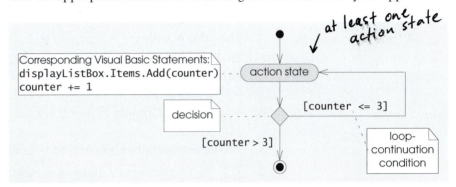

Figure 10.6   Do...Loop While repetition statement UML activity diagram.

1. The Do...Loop While statement repeats when the loop-continuation condition _____.
   a) is False after the loop body executes   b) is False before the loop body executes
   c) is True after the loop body executes   d) is True before the loop body executes

2. An infinite loop occurs when the loop-continuation condition in a Do While...Loop or Do...Loop While statement _____.
   a) never becomes True   b) never becomes False
   c) is False   d) is tested repeatedly

Answers: 1) c. 2) b.

10.3 Do...Loop Until Repetition Statement

The **Do...Loop Until** statement is similar to the Do Until...Loop statement, except that in the Do...Loop Until statement the loop-termination condition is tested *after* the loop body executes, so the body executes *at least* once. When a Do...Loop Until terminates, execution continues with the statement after the Loop Until keywords.

Common Programming Error

An infinite loop occurs when the loop-termination condition in a Do...Loop Until statement never becomes True.

Again, consider the suitcase-packing example. Before you begin packing, the suitcase is empty. You place an item in it, then determine whether the suitcase is full. As long as the condition "the suitcase is full" is False, you continue to put items into the suitcase.

As an example of a Do...Loop Until statement, let's look at another app segment designed to display the numbers 1 through 3 in a ListBox:

```
Dim counter As Integer = 1

Do
    displayListBox.Items.Add(counter)
    counter += 1
Loop Until counter > 3
```

The app segment initializes counter to 1, and the loop-termination condition in the Do...Loop Until statement is counter > 3. While the loop-termination condition is False, the Do...Loop Until statement executes. When the loop-termination condition becomes True, the Do...Loop Until statement finishes executing and displayListBox contains the numbers 1 through 3. The following box describes each step as the repetition statement executes.

Executing the Do...Loop Until Repetition Statement

1. The app declares variable counter and sets its value to 1.

2. The app enters the Do...Loop Until repetition statement.

3. The number (currently 1) stored in counter is added to displayListBox's Items property.

4. The value of counter is increased by 1; counter now contains 2.

5. The loop-termination condition is checked. The condition evaluates to False (counter is not greater than 3), so the app continues executing at the first statement after the Do statement.

6. The number (currently 2) stored in counter is added to displayListBox's Items property.

7. The value of counter is increased by 1; counter now contains 3.

8. The loop-termination condition is checked. The condition evaluates to False (counter is not greater than 3), so the app continues executing at the first statement after the Do statement.

9. The number (currently 3) stored in counter is added to displayListBox's Items property.

10. The value of counter is increased by 1; counter now contains 4.

11. The loop-termination condition is checked. The condition now evaluates to True (counter is greater than 3), so the app exits the Do...Loop Until repetition statement.

The Do...Loop Until UML activity diagram (Fig. 10.7) makes it clear that the loop-termination guard conditions are not evaluated until after the body is executed at least once. This UML diagram indicates exactly the same guard conditions as detailed in Fig. 10.6. The only difference for a Do...Loop Until repetition statement is that it continues to execute when the loop-termination guard condition is False. When the guard condition evaluates to True, the repetition ends and program control moves to the next statement following the Loop Until keywords.

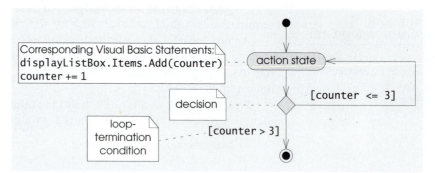

Figure 10.7 Do...Loop Until repetition statement UML activity diagram.

Start App

10.4 Creating the Class Average App

Now that you've learned the Do...Loop While and Do...Loop Until repetition statements, you can begin to develop the **Class Average** app. First, you use pseudocode to list the actions to execute and to specify the order of execution. You use counter-controlled repetition to calculate the class average. Recall that this technique uses a counter variable to determine how many times a set of statements executes. In this example, repetition terminates when the counter exceeds 10 because we're assuming, for simplicity, that the user enters only 10 grades. The following pseudocode describes the operation of the **Class Average** app when the **Add Grade** Button is clicked and when the **Average** Button is clicked:

> When the user clicks the Add Grade Button
> > If an average has already been calculated for a set of grades
> > > Clear the output Label and the ListBox
> >
> > Retrieve grade entered by user in the Enter grade: TextBox
> > Display the grade in the ListBox
> > Clear the Enter grade: TextBox
> > Transfer focus to the Enter grade: TextBox
> >
> > If the user has entered 10 grades
> > > Disable the Add Grade Button
> > > Transfer focus to the Average Button
>
> When the user clicks the Average Button
> > Set total to zero
> > Set grade counter to zero
> >
> > Do
> > > Read the next grade in the ListBox
> > > Add the grade to the total
> > > Add one to the grade counter
> > Loop While the grade counter is less than 10
> >
> > Calculate the class average by dividing the total by 10
> > Display the class average
> > Enable the Add Grade Button
> > Transfer focus to the Enter grade: TextBox

Now that you've test-driven the **Class Average** app and studied its pseudocode representation, you'll use an ACE table to help you convert the pseudocode to Visual Basic. Figure 10.8 lists the *actions*, *controls* and *events* that will help you complete your own version of this app.

Labels → We label the app's GUI, using Labels gradeLabel, averageLabel and gradeListLabel. The user enters grades in gradeTextBox and clicks the addButton. The Click event then Adds the value that the user entered in gradeTextBox to the ListBox, using method gradesListBox.Items.Add. When the user has entered 10 grades and clicked averageButton, the app retrieves each value from the ListBox, adds it to the total and computes the class average by dividing by 10. The class average is then displayed in averageResultLabel.

Action/Control/Event Table for the Class Average App

Action	Control	Event
Label all the app's controls	gradeLabel, gradeListLabel, averageLabel	App is run

Figure 10.8   ACE table for the **Class Average** app. (Part 1 of 2.)

Action	Control	Event
	addButton	Click
If an average has already been calculated for a set of grades	averageResultLabel	
Clear the output Label and the ListBox	averageResultLabel, gradesListBox	
Retrieve grade entered by user in the Enter grade: TextBox	gradeTextBox	
Display the grade in the ListBox	gradesListBox	
Clear the Enter grade: TextBox	gradeTextBox	
Transfer focus to the Enter grade: TextBox	gradeTextBox	
If the user has entered 10 grades	gradesListBox	
Disable the Add Grade Button	addButton	
Transfer focus to the Average Button	averageButton	
	averageButton	Click
Set total to zero		
Set grade counter to zero		
Do		
Read the next grade in the ListBox	gradesListBox	
Add the grade to the total		
Add one to the grade counter		
Loop While the grade counter is less than 10		
Calculate the class average by dividing the total by 10		
Display the class average	averageResultLabel	
Enable the Add Grade Button	addButton	
Transfer focus to the Enter grade: TextBox	gradeTextBox	

Figure 10.8   ACE table for the **Class Average** app. (Part 2 of 2.)

Now that we've formulated an algorithm for solving the **Class Average** problem, we can begin adding functionality to the template app. To display in the **Grade list:** ListBox a grade entered in the **Enter grade:** TextBox, the user clicks the **Add Grade** Button. If the app is already displaying grades in the **Grade list:** ListBox and the class average in the **Class average:** Label, the values are first cleared. The following box guides you through adding this functionality to the **Add Grade** Button's event handler.

Entering Grades in the
Class Average App

1. *Copying the template to your working directory.* Copy the directory C:\Examples\ch10\TemplateApp\ClassAverage to your C:\SimplyVB-2010 directory.

2. *Opening the Class Average app's template file.* Double click Class-Average.sln in the ClassAverage directory to open the app in the Visual Basic IDE. Double click ClassAverage.vb in the **Solution Explorer** to display the Form (Fig. 10.9).

(cont.)

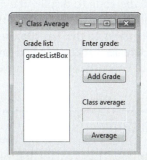

Figure 10.9 Class Average app's Form in Design view.

3. *Adding an event handler for the Add Grade Button.* Each time a grade in the **Class Average** app is entered, the user must click the **Add Grade** Button. Double click the Button labeled **Add Grade** to create event handler addButton_Click. Add the comment and reformat the empty event handler as shown in lines 2–4 of Fig. 10.10.

Clearing the grade list and class average

```
2     ' handles Add Grade Button's Click event
3     Private Sub addButton_Click(sender As System.Object,
4        e As System.EventArgs) Handles addButton.Click
5
6        ' clear previous grades and calculation result
7        If averageResultLabel.Text <> String.Empty Then
8           averageResultLabel.Text = String.Empty
9           gradesListBox.Items.Clear()
10       End If
```

Figure 10.10 Clearing the output Label and ListBox after a calculation.

4. *Clearing the ListBox and the Class average: Label of any output from a previous calculation.* Add lines 6–10 (Fig. 10.10) to event handler addButton_Click. To determine whether there was a previous calculation, test whether averageResultLabel displays any text by comparing the Text property's value to the empty string (line 7). If averageResultLabel displays the result of a previous calculation, set its Text property to the empty string (line 8). Line 9 clears the grades from the ListBox.

5. *Displaying each grade in the ListBox control.* Add lines 12–14 of Fig. 10.11 to event handler addButton_Click below the If...Then statement. Line 13 Adds the grade entered in gradeTextBox to gradesListBox's Items property. The grade is displayed in the ListBox.

Adding a numeric grade to the ListBox and clearing the user input from the TextBox

```
11
12       ' display grade in ListBox
13       gradesListBox.Items.Add(Val(gradeTextBox.Text))
14       gradeTextBox.Clear() ' clear grade from TextBox
```

Figure 10.11 Adding the grade input to the ListBox and clearing the Enter grade: TextBox.

6. *Preparing for the next grade to be entered.* Method Clear (line 14 of Fig. 10.11) deletes the grade from the TextBox to prepare the app for the next grade to be entered. Using this method is the same as assigning String.Empty to the TextBox's Text property.

7. *Saving the project.* Select **File > Save All** to save your modified code.

You've added the code to display the grade entered in the **Enter grade:** Text-Box in the ListBox when the user clicks the **Add Grade** Button. Next, you learn how to *transfer the focus* to the TextBox so the user can enter the next grade after clicking the **Add Grade** Button. The following box also shows you how to *disable* the **Add Grade** Button after 10 grades have been entered and its functionality is no longer needed.

Transferring the Focus to a Control and Disabling a Button

1. ***Transferring the focus to a control.*** Add line 15 (Fig. 10.12) to event handler addButton_Click. Line 15 calls gradeTextBox's **Focus** method to place the cursor in the TextBox for the next grade input. This process is called **transferring the focus**. Here the focus is transferred from the Button the user just clicked to the TextBox in which the user will input the next value.

Transferring the focus of the app to the TextBox

```
14    gradeTextBox.Clear() ' clear grade from TextBox
15    gradeTextBox.Focus() ' transfer focus to TextBox
```
Figure 10.12 Transferring the focus to the TextBox control.

GUI Design Tip

Transfer the focus to the control that should be used next.

GUI Design Tip

Disable Buttons when their function should not be available to users.

2. ***Disabling the Add Grade Button to prohibit users from entering more than 10 grades.*** Your app should accept exactly 10 grades. If the number of grades already entered by the user is equal to 10, then the app should prevent the user from entering more grades. Add lines 17–21 of Fig. 10.13 to event handler addButton_Click. Line 18 determines whether 10 grades have been entered, using the = comparison operator. Items's **Count** property returns the number of items displayed in the **Grade list:** ListBox. If 10 grades have been entered, line 19 disables addButton by setting its **Enabled** property to **False**. Clicking a disabled Button does *not* execute its event handler.

Disabling the **Add grade** Button and transferring the focus to the **Average** Button

```
17    ' prohibit users from entering more than 10 grades
18    If gradesListBox.Items.Count = 10 Then
19        addButton.Enabled = False ' disable Add Grade Button
20        averageButton.Focus() ' transfer focus to Average Button
21    End If
```
Figure 10.13 App accepts only 10 grades.

Common Programming Error

A control must be enabled in order to receive focus.

3. ***Transferring the focus to the Average Button after 10 grades have been entered.*** After 10 grades have been entered, line 20 transfers the focus to the **Average** Button, so the user can press *Enter* or *Space* to invoke the **Average** Button's event handler, without tabbing to the Button or using the mouse.

4. ***Saving the project.*** Select **File > Save All** to save your modified code.

After 10 grades have been entered and displayed in the ListBox, the **Add Grade** Button's event handler transfers the focus to the **Average** Button. When the user clicks the **Average** Button, the app calculates and displays the average of the 10 grades. The following box shows you how to sum the grades with a Do...Loop Until repetition statement before the average calculation. The box also covers displaying the result in the **Class average:** Label.

Calculating the Class Average

1. ***Adding an event handler for the Average Button.*** Double click the **Average** Button to generate event handler averageButton_Click. Add the comment and reformat the empty event handler as shown in lines 24–26 of Fig. 10.14.

(cont.)

2. ***Initializing variables used in the class average calculation.*** Add lines 28–32 of Fig. 10.14 to event handler averageButton_Click. Line 29 declares Integer total. You use total to calculate the sum of the 10 grades (you'll need this sum later when you calculate the average grade). Line 30 declares the counter (gradeCounter). It's important that variables used as totals and counters have appropriate *initial values* before they're used. If a numerical variable is not initialized before its first use, Visual Basic initializes it to a default value of 0. However, notice in Fig. 10.14 that we've manually initialized all of the variables to 0. This makes the program clearer. Variable grade (line 31) temporarily stores each grade read from the ListBox. Although the grades entered are Integers, the result of the averaging calculation can be a floating-point value (such as the 81.10 result in Fig. 10.4); therefore, you declare Double variable average (line 32) to store the class average.

```
24        ' handles Average Button's Click event
25        Private Sub averageButton_Click(sender As System.Object,
26            e As System.EventArgs) Handles averageButton.Click
27
28            ' initialization phase
29            Dim total As Integer = 0
30            Dim gradeCounter As Integer = 0
31            Dim grade As Integer = 0
32            Dim average As Double = 0
```

Initializing variables

Figure 10.14 Initialization phase of class average calculation.

3. ***Summing the grades displayed in the ListBox.*** Add lines 34–40 of Fig. 10.15 to event handler averageButton_Click. The Do...Loop Until statement (lines 35–40) sums the grades that it reads from the ListBox. Line 40 indicates that the statement should iterate until the value of gradeCounter is greater than or equal to 10. [*Note:* In Exercise 10.12 you modify the app to handle *any* number of grades.] Line 37 reads the current value from the ListBox, using the ListBox's Items collection, and stores that value in grade. The items in a ListBox are accessed by their *position number*, starting from position number 0 (i.e., Items(0) is the first element). Line 38 adds grade to the previous value of total and assigns the result to total, using the += assignment operator. Variable gradeCounter is incremented (line 39) to indicate that another grade has been processed. (Incrementing the counter ensures that the condition at line 40 eventually becomes True, terminating the loop.)

```
34        ' sum grades in ListBox
35        Do
36            ' read grade from ListBox
37            grade = gradesListBox.Items(gradeCounter)
38            total += grade ' add grade to total
39            gradeCounter += 1 ' increment counter
40        Loop Until gradeCounter >= 10
```

Using the Do...Loop Until repetition statement to sum grades in the ListBox

Figure 10.15 Do...Loop Until summing grades.

4. ***Calculating and displaying the average.*** Add lines 42–45 of Fig. 10.16 to event handler averageButton_Click. Line 42 assigns the result of the average calculation to variable average. Line 43 displays the value of variable average. Note the use of the F format specifier to display average in floating-point format. After the average is displayed, another set of 10 grades can be entered. To allow this, you need to enable the **Add Grade** Button by setting property Enabled to True (line 44). Line 45 transfers the focus to the **Enter grade:** TextBox.

GUI Design Tip

Enable a disabled Button when its function should be available to the user once again.

(cont.)

Calculating the class average, enabling the **Add Grade** Button and transferring the focus to the **Enter Grade:** TextBox

```
42      average = total / 10 ' calculate average
43      averageResultLabel.Text = String.Format("{0:F}", average)
44      addButton.Enabled = True ' enable Add Grade Button
45      gradeTextBox.Focus() ' reset focus to Enter grade: TextBox
46   End Sub ' averageButton_Click
```

Figure 10.16 Displaying the result of the average calculation.

5. *Running the app.* Select **Debug > Start Debugging** to run your app, which can now calculate and display the class average. Enter the 10 grades shown in Fig. 10.3 using the **Enter grade:** TextBox and the **Add Grade** Button. After entering 10 grades, click the **Average** Button and verify that the average displayed is correct.

6. *Closing the app.* Close your running app by clicking its close box.

7. *Closing the IDE.* Close the Visual Basic IDE by clicking its close box.

Figure 10.17 presents the source code for the **Class Average** app. The lines of code that contain the new programming concepts you learned in this chapter are highlighted.

```
1   Public Class ClassAverageForm
2      ' handles Add Grade Button's Click event
3      Private Sub addButton_Click(sender As System.Object,
4         e As System.EventArgs) Handles addButton.Click
5
6         ' clear previous grades and calculation result
7         If averageResultLabel.Text <> String.Empty Then
8            averageResultLabel.Text = String.Empty
9            gradesListBox.Items.Clear()
10        End If
11
12        ' display grade in ListBox
13        gradesListBox.Items.Add(Val(inputTextBox.Text))
14        gradeTextBox.Clear() ' clear grade from TextBox
15        gradeTextBox.Focus() ' transfer focus to TextBox
16
17        ' prohibit users from entering more than 10 grades
18        If gradesListBox.Items.Count = 10 Then
19           addButton.Enabled = False ' disable Add Grade Button
20           averageButton.Focus() ' transfer focus to Average Button
21        End If
22     End Sub ' addButton_Click
23
24     ' handles Average Button's Click event
25     Private Sub averageButton_Click(sender As System.Object,
26        e As System.EventArgs) Handles averageButton.Click
27
28        ' initialization phase
29        Dim total As Integer = 0
30        Dim gradeCounter As Integer = 0
31        Dim grade As Integer = 0
32        Dim average As Double = 0
33
34        ' sum grades in ListBox
35        Do
36           ' read grade from ListBox
37           grade = gradesListBox.Items(gradeCounter)
38           total += grade ' add grade to total
39           gradeCounter += 1 ' increment counter
40        Loop Until gradeCounter >= 10
```

Clearing gradeTextBox — 14

Transferring focus to gradeTextBox — 15

Disabling the **Add Grade** Button and transferring the focus to the **Average** Button — 19, 20

Accessing a grade in the ListBox via the Items property — 34, 37

Using a Do...Loop Until statement to total all the grades — 37, 38

Figure 10.17 **Class Average** app code. (Part 1 of 2.)

Enabling the **Add Grade** Button and transferring the focus to the **Enter grade:** TextBox

```
41
42            average = total / 10 ' calculate average
43            averageResultLabel.Text = String.Format("{0:F}", average)
44            addButton.Enabled = True ' enable Add Grade Button
45            gradeTextBox.Focus() ' reset focus to Enter grade: TextBox
46        End Sub ' averageButton_Click
47    End Class ' ClassAverageForm
```

Figure 10.17 **Class Average** app code. (Part 2 of 2.)

SELF-REVIEW

1. If you do not want a Button to call its event-handler method when the Button is clicked, set property _____ to _____

   a) Enabled, False   b) Enabled, True

   c) Disabled, True   d) Disabled, False

2. _____ a TextBox selects that TextBox to receive user input.

   a) Enabling   b) Clearing

   c) Transferring the focus to d) Disabling

Answers: 1) a. 2) c.

10.5 Wrap-Up

In this chapter, you learned how to use the Do...Loop While and the Do...Loop Until repetition statements. We provided the syntax and included UML activity diagrams that explained how each statement executes. You used the Do...Loop Until statement in the **Class Average** app that you developed.

The Do...Loop While repetition statement executes as long as its loop-continuation condition is True. This repetition statement always executes at least once. When the loop-continuation condition becomes False, the repetition terminates. This repetition statement enters an infinite loop if the loop-continuation condition never becomes False.

The Do...Loop Until repetition statement also executes at least once. It executes as long as its loop-termination condition is False. When the loop-termination condition becomes True, the repetition terminates. The Do...Loop Until statement enters an infinite loop if the loop-termination condition never becomes True.

You also learned more sophisticated techniques for creating polished graphical user interfaces for your apps. You now know how to invoke method Focus to transfer the focus to another control in an app, indicating that the next action the user takes should involve this control. You also learned how to disable Buttons that should not be available to a user at certain times during an app's execution, and you learned how to re-enable those Buttons.

In the next chapter, you'll continue studying repetition statements. You'll learn how to use the For...Next repetition statement, which makes counter-controlled repetition particularly convenient.

SKILLS SUMMARY

Do...Loop While Repetition Statement

- Iterates while its loop-continuation condition is True.
- Tests the loop-continuation condition after the loop body is performed.
- Always executes the loop body at least once.
- Becomes an infinite loop if the loop-continuation condition never becomes False.

Do...Loop Until Repetition Statement

- Iterates until its loop-termination condition becomes True.
- Tests the loop-termination condition after the loop body is performed.

- Always executes the loop body at least once.
- Becomes an infinite loop if the loop-termination condition never becomes True.

Disabling a Button

- Set Button property Enabled to False.

Enabling a Button

- Set Button property Enabled to True.

Accessing an Element in a ListBox

- Use the Items property followed by the element number in parentheses.

Determining the Number of Items in a ListBox

- Use the Count property of the ListBox's Items property.

Transferring the Focus to a Control

- Call method Focus.

KEY TERMS

Count property of Items—Returns the number of ListBox items.

Do...Loop Until repetition statement—Executes at least once and continues executing until its loop-termination condition becomes True.

Do...Loop While repetition statement—Executes at least once and continues executing until its loop-continuation condition becomes False.

Enabled property—Specifies whether a control such as a Button appears enabled (True) or disabled (False).

Focus method—Transfers the focus of the app to the control on which the method is called.

off-by-one error—The kind of logic error that occurs, for example, when a loop executes for one more or one less iteration than is intended.

transferring the focus—Preselects a control so the user knows which control to interact with next.

GUI DESIGN GUIDELINES

Overall Design

- Transfer the focus to the control that should be used next.

Button

- Disable a Button when its function should not be available to users.
- Enable a disabled Button when its function should once again be available to users.

CONTROLS, EVENTS, PROPERTIES & METHODS

Button   ab Button   When clicked, commands the app to perform an action.

- *In action*

  Calculate Total

- Event

  Click—Raised when the user clicks the Button.

- *Properties*

  Enabled—Determines whether the Button's event handler executes when the Button is clicked.

  Location—Specifies the location of the Button on the Form relative to the Form's top-left corner.

  Name—Specifies the name used to access the Button programmatically. The name should be appended with the Button suffix.

  Size—Specifies the width and height (in pixels) of the Button.

  Text—Specifies the text displayed on the Button.

- *Method*

  Focus—Transfers the focus of the app to the Button that calls it.

ListBox ListBox   This control allows the user to view and select from items in a list.

- ■ *In action*

Months	Monthly Payments
24	$490.50
36	$339.06
48	$263.55
60	$218.41

- ■ *Properties*

  Items—Returns an object that contains the items displayed in the ListBox.

  Items.Count—Returns the number of items in the ListBox.

  Location—Specifies the location of the ListBox on the Form relative to the Form's top-left corner.

  Name—Specifies the name used to access the ListBox programmatically. Append the ListBox suffix to the name.

  Size—Specifies the width and height (in pixels) of the ListBox.

- ■ *Methods*

  Items.Add—Adds an item to the Items property.

  Items.Clear—Deletes all the values in the ListBox's Items property.

TextBox abl TextBox   This control allows the user to input data from the keyboard.

- ■ *In action*

  | 0 |

- ■ *Event*

  TextChanged—Raised when the text in the TextBox is changed.

- ■ *Properties*

  Location—Specifies the location of the TextBox on the Form relative to the Form's top-left corner.

  Name—Specifies the name used to access the TextBox programmatically. The name should be appended with the TextBox suffix.

  Size—Specifies the width and height (in pixels) of the TextBox.

  Text—Specifies the initial text displayed in the TextBox.

  TextAlign—Specifies how the text is aligned within the TextBox.

  Width—Specifies the width (in pixels) of the TextBox.

- ■ *Methods*

  Clear—Removes the text from the TextBox on which it's called.

  Focus—Transfers the focus of the app to the TextBox on which it's called.

MULTIPLE-CHOICE QUESTIONS

10.1 A(n) _____ occurs when a loop-continuation condition in a Do...Loop While never becomes False.

    a) infinite loop   b) counter-controlled loop

    c) control statement   d) nested control statement

10.2 Set property _____ to True to enable a Button.

    a) Disabled   b) Focus

    c) Enabled   d) ButtonEnabled

10.3 The _____ statement executes at least once and continues executing until its loop-termination condition becomes True.

    a) Do While...Loop   b) Do...Loop Until

    c) Do...Loop While   d) Do Until...Loop

10.4 The _____ statement executes at least once and continues executing until its loop-continuation condition becomes `False`.

   a) `Do...Loop Until`   b) `Do Until...Loop`

   c) `Do While...Loop`   d) `Do...Loop While`

10.5 Method _____ transfers the focus to a control.

   a) `GetFocus`   b) `Focus`

   c) `Transfer`   d) `Activate`

10.6 A _____ contains the sum of a series of values.

   a) total   b) counter

   c) condition   d) loop

10.7 Property _____ of _____ contains the number of items in a `ListBox`.

   a) `Count, ListBox`   b) `ListCount, Items`

   c) `ListCount, ListBox`   d) `Count, Items`

10.8 A(n) _____ occurs when a loop executes for one more or one less iteration than is necessary.

   a) infinite loop   b) counter-controlled loop

   c) off-by-one error   d) nested control statement

10.9 A `Do...Loop Until` repetition statement's loop-termination condition is evaluated _____.

   a) only the first time the body executes   b) before the body executes

   c) after the body executes   d) None of the above

10.10 If its continuation condition is initially `False`, a `Do...Loop While` repetition statement _____.

   a) never executes   b) executes while the condition is `False`

   c) executes until the condition becomes True   d) executes only once

---

EXERCISES

10.11 *(Modified Class Average App)* Modify the **Class Average** app, as in Fig. 10.18, so that the **Average** Button is disabled until 10 grades have been entered.

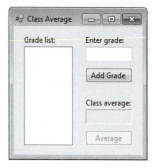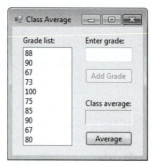

Figure 10.18   Modified **Class Average** app.

  a) *Copying the template to your working directory.* Copy the directory `C:\Examples\ch10\Exercises\ModifiedClassAverage` to your `C:\SimplyVB2010` directory.

  b) *Opening the app's template file.* Double click `ClassAverage.sln` in the Modified-ClassAverage directory to open the app.

  c) *Initially disabling the Average Button.* Use the **Properties** window to modify the **Average** Button in the Form so that it's disabled when the app first executes by setting its `Enabled` property to `False`.

d) *Enabling the Average Button after 10 grades have been entered.* Add code to the addButton_Click event handler so that the **Average** Button becomes enabled when 10 grades have been entered.

e) *Disabling the Average Button after the calculation has been performed.* Add code to the averageButton_Click event handler so that the **Average** Button is disabled once the calculation result has been displayed.

f) *Running the app.* Select **Debug > Start Debugging** to run your app. Enter 10 grades and ensure that the **Average** Button is disabled until all 10 grades are entered. Verify that the **Add Grade** Button is disabled after 10 grades are entered. Once the **Average** Button is enabled, click it and verify that the average displayed is correct. The **Average** Button should then become disabled again, and the **Add Grade** Button should be enabled.

g) *Closing the app.* Close your running app by clicking its close box.

h) *Closing the IDE.* Close the Visual Basic IDE by clicking its close box.

10.12 *(Class Average App That Handles Any Number of Grades)* Rewrite the **Class Average** app to handle any number of grades, as in Fig. 10.19. Note that the app does not know how many grades the user will enter, so the Buttons must be enabled at all times.

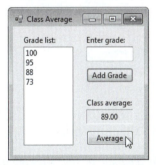

Figure 10.19 Modified **Class Average** app handling an unspecified number of grades.

a) *Copying the template to your working directory.* Copy the directory C:\Examples\ ch10\Exercises\UndeterminedClassAverage to your C:\SimplyVB2010 directory.

b) *Opening the app's template file.* Double click ClassAverage.sln in the UndeterminedClassAverage directory to open the app.

c) *Never disabling the Add Grade Button.* Remove code from the addButton_Click event handler so that the **Add Grade** Button is not disabled after entering 10 grades.

d) *Summing the grades in the ListBox.* Modify code in the averageButton_Click event handler so that gradeCounter increments until it's equal to the number of grades entered. Use gradesListBox.Items.Count to determine the number of items in the ListBox. The number returned by the Count property will be zero if no grades are entered. Use an If...Then selection statement to avoid division by zero and display a message dialog to the user if no grades are entered when the user clicks the **Average** Button.

e) *Calculating the class average.* Modify the code in the averageButton_Click event handler so that average is computed by using the actual number of grades rather than the value 10.

f) *Running the app.* Select **Debug > Start Debugging** to run your app. Enter 10 grades and click the **Average** Button. Verify that the average displayed is correct. Follow the same actions but this time for 15 grades, then for 5 grades. Each time, verify that the appropriate average is displayed.

g) *Closing the app.* Close your running app by clicking its close box.

h) *Closing the IDE.* Close the Visual Basic IDE by clicking its close box.

10.13 *(Arithmetic Calculator App)* Write an app that allows the user to enter a series of numbers and manipulate them. The app should provide users with the option of adding or multiplying the numbers. Users should enter each number in a TextBox. After entering the number, the user clicks a Button, and the number is inserted in a ListBox. The GUI should behave as in Fig. 10.20.

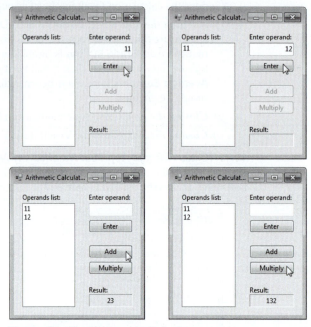

Figure 10.20 Arithmetic Calculator app.

a) *Copying the template to your working directory.* Copy the directory C:\Examples\ch10\Exercises\ArithmeticCalculator to your C:\SimplyVB2010 directory.

b) *Opening the app's template file.* Double click ArithmeticCalculator.sln in the ArithmeticCalculator directory to open the app.

c) *Adding a ListBox to display the entered numbers.* Add a ListBox. Place and size it as in Fig. 10.20.

d) *Creating an event handler for the Enter Button.* Create the Click event handler for the **Enter** Button. If the result of a previous calculation is displayed, this event handler should clear the result, clear the ListBox and disable the addition and multiplication Buttons. It should then insert the current number in the **Operands list:** ListBox. When the ListBox contains at least two numbers, the event handler should then enable the addition and multiplication Buttons.

e) *Summing the values in the ListBox.* Define the Click event handler for the **Add** Button. This event handler should compute the sum of all the values in the **Operands list:** ListBox and display the result in resultLabel.

f) *Multiplying the values in the ListBox.* Define the Click event handler for the **Multiply** Button. This event handler should compute the product of all the values in the **Operands list:** ListBox and display the result in resultLabel.

g) *Running the app.* Select **Debug > Start Debugging** to run your app. Enter two values, then click the **Add** and **Multiply** Buttons. Verify that the results displayed are correct. Also, make sure that the **Add** and **Multiply** Buttons are not enabled until two values have been entered. Enter a new value and verify that the previous result and the ListBox are cleared. Enter two more values, then click the **Add** and **Multiply** Buttons. Verify that the results displayed are correct.

h) *Closing the app.* Close your running app by clicking its close box.

i) *Closing the IDE.* Close the Visual Basic IDE by clicking its close box.

What does this code do? ▶ **10.14** What is the result of the following code?

```
1   Dim y As Integer
2   Dim x As Integer
3   Dim mysteryValue As Integer
4
5   x = 1
6   mysteryValue = 0
7
8   Do
9       y = x ^ 2
10      displayListBox.Items.Add(y)
11      mysteryValue += 1
12      x += 1
13  Loop While x <= 10
14
15      resultLabel.Text = mysteryValue
```

What's wrong with this code? ▶ **10.15** Find the error(s) in the following code. This code should add 10 to the value in y and store it in z. It then should reduce the value of y by one and repeat until y is less than 10. Last, resultLabel should display the final value of z.

```
1   Dim y As Integer = 10
2   Dim z As Integer = 2
3
4   Do
5       z = y + 10
6   Loop Until y < 10
7
8   y -= 1
9
10      resultLabel.Text = z
```

Using the Debugger ▶ **10.16** *(Factorial App)* The **Factorial** app calculates the factorial of an integer entered by the user. The factorial of an integer is the product of the integers from 1 to that number. For example, the factorial of 3 is 6 (1 × 2 × 3). Copy the **Factorial** app from C:\Examples\ch10\Exercises\Factorial to your working directory. While testing the app, you noticed that it did not execute correctly. Use the debugger to find and correct the logic error(s) in the app. Figure 10.21 displays the correct output for the **Factorial** app.

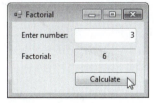

Figure 10.21   Correct output for the **Factorial** app.

Programming Challenge ▶ **10.17** *(Restaurant Bill App)* Develop an app that calculates a restaurant bill. The user should be able to enter the item ordered, the quantity of the item ordered and the price per item. When the user clicks the **Add Item** Button, your app should display the number ordered, the item ordered and the price per unit in three ListBoxes, as shown in Fig. 10.22. When the user clicks the **Total Bill** Button, the app should calculate the total cost. For each entry in the ListBox, multiply the cost of each item by the number of items ordered.

Figure 10.22   Restaurant Bill app's Form.

11

Interest Calculator App

Introducing the For...Next Repetition Statement and NumericUpDown Control

As you learned in Chapters 9 and 10, apps are often required to repeat actions. Using a Do repetition statement allowed you to specify a condition and test it either before entering the loop or after executing the body of the loop. In the **Car Payment Calculator** app and the **Class Average** app, a counter was used to determine the number of times the loop should iterate. In fact, the use of counters in repetition statements is so common in apps that Visual Basic provides an additional control statement specially designed for such cases—the For...Next repetition statement. In this chapter, you'll use this repetition statement to create an **Interest Calculator** app.

11.1 Test-Driving the Interest Calculator App

The **Interest Calculator** app calculates the amount of money in your savings account. You'll begin with a certain amount of money and will be paid interest for a period of time. The user specifies the principal amount (the initial amount of money in the account), the interest rate and the number of years for which interest will be calculated. The app then displays the results. This app must meet the following requirements:

App Requirements

You're considering investing $1,000.00 in a savings account that yields 2% interest compounded annually, and you want to forecast how your investment will grow. Assuming that you leave all interest on deposit, calculate and display the amount of money in the account at the end of each year over a period of n years. To compute these amounts, use the following formula:

$$a = p(1 + r)^n$$

where

p is the original amount of money invested (the principal)

r is the annual interest rate (for example, .02 is equivalent to 2%)

n is the number of years

a is the amount on deposit at the end of the nth year.

You'll begin by test-driving the completed app. Then you'll learn the additional Visual Basic capabilities needed to create your own version of this app.

Test-Driving the Interest Calculator App

1. **Opening the completed app.** Open C:\Examples\ch11\CompletedApp\ InterestCalculator to locate the **Interest Calculator** app. Double click InterestCalculator.sln to open the app in the IDE.

2. **Running the Interest Calculator app.** Select **Debug > Start Debugging** to run the app (Fig. 11.1).

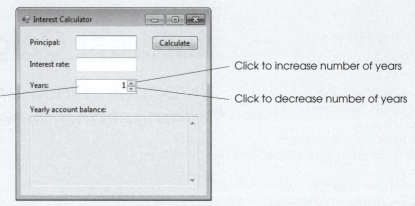

NumericUpDown control

Click to increase number of years

Click to decrease number of years

Figure 11.1 Completed **Interest Calculator** app.

3. **Providing a principal value.** Once the app is running, provide a value in the **Principal:** TextBox. Input 1000, as specified in the problem statement.

4. **Providing an interest-rate value.** Next, type a value in the **Interest Rate:** TextBox. We specified the interest rate 2% in the problem statement, so enter 2 in the **Interest Rate:** TextBox.

5. **Providing the duration of the investment.** Now, choose the number of years for which you want to calculate the amount in the savings account. In this case, select 10 by entering it using the keyboard or by clicking the up arrow in the **Years:** NumericUpDown control repeatedly until the value reads 10.

6. **Calculating the amount.** After you input the necessary information, click the **Calculate** Button. The amount of money in your account at the end of each year during a period of 10 years displays in the multiline TextBox. The app should look similar to Fig. 11.2.

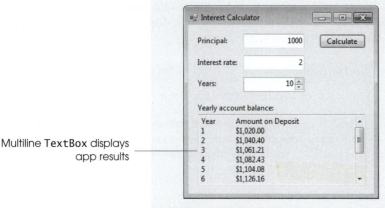

Multiline TextBox displays app results

Figure 11.2 Output of completed **Interest Calculator** app.

7. **Closing the app.** Close your running app by clicking its close box.

8. **Closing the IDE.** Close the Visual Basic IDE by clicking its close box.

11.2 Essentials of Counter-Controlled Repetition

In Chapters 9 and 10, you learned how to use counter-controlled repetition. Its four essential elements are:

1. the *name* of a *control variable* (or loop counter) that's used to determine whether the loop continues to iterate
2. the *initial value* of the control variable
3. the *increment* (or *decrement*) by which the control variable is modified during each iteration of the loop (that is, each time the loop is performed)
4. the *condition* that tests for the *final value* of the control variable (to determine whether looping should continue).

The example in Fig. 11.3 uses the four elements of counter-controlled repetition. This Do While...Loop statement is similar to the **Car Payment Calculator** app's loop in Chapter 9.

```
1   Dim years As Integer = 2 ' control variable
2
3   Do While years <= 5
4      months = 12 * years ' calculate payment period
5
6      ' calculate payment value
7      monthlyPayment =
8         Pmt(monthlyInterest, months, -loanAmount)
9
10      ' display payment value
11      paymentsListBox.Items.Add(months & ControlChars.Tab &
12         ControlChars.Tab & String.Format("{0:C}", monthlyPayment))
13
14      years += 1 ' increment counter
15   Loop
```

Figure 11.3   Counter-controlled repetition example.

Recall that the **Car Payment Calculator** app calculates and displays monthly car payments over periods of two to five years. The declaration in line 1 *names* the control variable (years) and indicates that it's of data type Integer. This declaration initializes the variable to an *initial value* of 2.

Consider the Do While...Loop statement (lines 3–15). Line 4 uses the years variable to calculate the number of months over which car payments are to be made. Lines 7–8 use the Pmt function to determine the monthly payment for the car. This value depends on the monthly interest rate, the duration of the loan in months and the loan amount. Lines 11–12 display the amount in a ListBox. Line 14 increments the control variable years by 1 for each iteration of the loop. The condition in the Do While...Loop statement (line 3) tests whether the value of the control variable is less than or equal to 5, meaning that 5 is the *final value* for which the condition is true. The body of this Do While...Loop is performed even when the control variable is 5. The loop terminates when the control variable exceeds 5 (that is, when years has a value of 6).

SELF-REVIEW

1. Counter-controlled repetition _____ the control variable after each iteration.

   a) increments   b) initializes

   c) decrements   d) Either a or c

2. What aspect of the control variable determines whether looping should continue?

   a) name   b) initial value

   c) type   d) final value

Answers: 1) d. 2) d.

11.3 Introducing the For...Next Repetition Statement

The For...Next repetition statement makes it easier for you to write code to perform counter-controlled repetition. This statement specifies all four essential elements. It takes less time to code and is easier to read than an equivalent Do repetition statement.

Let's examine the first line of the For...Next repetition statement (Fig. 11.4), which we call the For...Next header. It specifies all four essential elements for counter-controlled repetition. The line should be read "*for the values of counter starting at 2 and ending at 10, do the following statements, then add (step) two to counter.*"

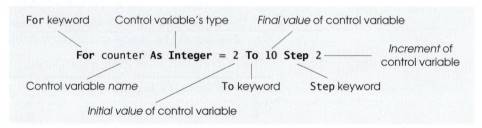

Figure 11.4   For...Next header components.

A For...Next statement such as

```
For counter As Integer = 2 To 10 Step 2
    body statement(s)
Next
```

begins with the keyword For. Then the statement declares and initializes a control variable (in this case, Integer control variable counter is declared and set to 2). Note that you do not use the Dim keyword to declare the control variable in a For...Next header. Following the initial value of the control variable is the keyword To, followed by the final value of the control variable. You can then use the Step keyword to specify the amount by which to increase (or decrease) the control variable each time the loop body completes execution. If you wish to *decrease* the variable each time through the loop, simply use a *negative* number after the Step keyword. In this case, the final value must be *less than* the starting value—otherwise the loop body *does not execute*. The Step keyword is optional. If you omit it, the control variable increments by *one* after each repetition, by default.

The body of a For...Next statement is placed after the For...Next header. The keyword Next marks the end of the For...Next repetition statement. Optionally, you can include the name of the control variable to the right of the Next keyword (e.g., Next counter). Some programmers like to do this to help make the program clearer, especially in nested For...Next statements.

When you declare the control variable in the For...Next header (as we did above), the control variable exists only until the loop terminates execution. The following box describes each step as the preceding repetition statement executes.

Common Programming Error

Attempting to access the control variable (when it's declared in a For...Next header) in code after the loop results in a compilation error, because the variable no longer exists.

Executing the For...Next Repetition Statement

1. The app declares variable counter and sets its value to 2.

2. The loop-continuation condition is checked. The condition evaluates to True (counter is 2, which is less than or equal to 10), so the app executes the body of the For...Next repetition statement.

3. The value of counter is increased by 2; counter now contains 4.

(cont.)

4. The loop-continuation condition is checked. The condition evaluates to True (counter is 4, which is less than or equal to 10), so the app executes the body of the For...Next repetition statement.

5. The value of counter is increased by 2; counter now contains 6.

6. The loop-continuation condition is checked. The condition evaluates to True (counter is 6, which is less than or equal to 10), so the app executes the body of the For...Next repetition statement.

7. The value of counter is increased by 2; counter now contains 8.

8. The loop-continuation condition is checked. The condition evaluates to True (counter is 8, which is less than or equal to 10), so the app executes the body of the For...Next repetition statement.

9. The value of counter is increased by 2; counter now contains 10.

10. The loop-continuation condition is checked. The condition evaluates to True (counter is 10, which is less than or equal to 10), so the app executes the body of the For...Next repetition statement.

11. The value of counter is increased by 2; counter now contains 12.

12. The loop-continuation condition is checked. The condition evaluates to False (counter is 12, which is not less than or equal to 10), so the app exits the For...Next repetition statement.

The For...Next statement can be represented by other repetition statements. For example, an equivalent Do While...Loop statement for Fig. 11.4 is

```
counter = 2

Do While counter <= 10
    body statement(s)
    counter += 2
Loop
```

Note that the For...Next statement's header (Fig. 11.4) implies the loop-continuation condition (counter <= 10), which is shown explicitly in the preceding Do While...Loop statement. The starting value, ending value and increment portions of a For...Next header can contain arithmetic expressions. The expressions are evaluated once (when the For...Next statement begins executing) and then used as the starting value, ending value and increment of the For...Next header. For example, assume that a = 2 and b = 10. The header

```
For i As Integer = a To (4 * a * b) Step (b \ a)
```

is equivalent to the header

```
For i As Integer = 2 To 80 Step 5
```

If the implied loop-continuation condition is initially False (for example, if the starting value is greater than the ending value and the increment value is positive), the For...Next statement's body is *not* performed. Instead, execution proceeds with the statement after the For...Next statement.

The control variable frequently is displayed or used in calculations in the For...Next body, but it does not have to be. It's common to use the control variable only to control repetition and not use it in the For...Next body.

The UML activity diagram for the For...Next statement is similar to that of the Do While...Loop statement. For example, the UML activity diagram of the For...Next statement

```
For counter As Integer = 1 To 10
    displayListBox.Items.Add(counter * 10)
Next
```

Error-Prevention Tip

Although the value of the control variable can be changed in the body of a For...Next loop, avoid doing so, because this practice can lead to subtle errors.

is shown in Fig. 11.5. This activity diagram shows that the initialization occurs only once and that incrementing occurs *after* each execution of the body statement. Note that, besides small circles and transition arrows, the activity diagram contains only action states, merge symbols and decision symbols.

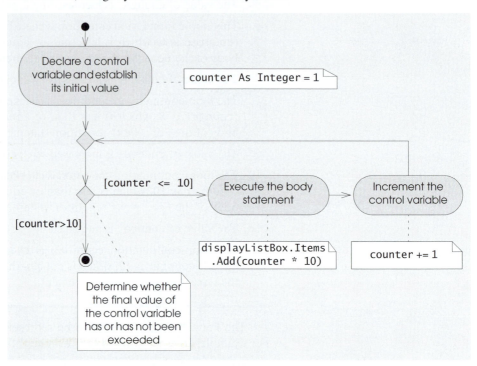

Figure 11.5 For...Next repetition statement UML activity diagram.

The For...Next header indicates each item needed to conduct counter-controlled repetition with a control variable. To help solidify your understanding of this new repetition statement, let's consider how the Do While...Loop statement of Fig. 11.3 can be replaced by a For...Next statement.

The converted code is shown in Fig. 11.6. When the For...Next statement begins execution, line 1 declares Integer control variable years and initializes it to 2.

The implied loop-continuation condition years <= 5 (which depends on the control variable's final value) is tested in line 1. Keyword To is required in the For...Next statement. The value before this keyword specifies the initial value of years; the value that follows it specifies the value tested for loop continuation (in this case, 5). Keyword Step is optional and is not used here. Step specifies the increment (the amount that's added to years each time the For...Next body is executed). If Step is omitted, then the increment is 1, by default.

```
1   For years As Integer = 2 To 5
2       months = 12 * years ' calculate payment period
3
4       ' calculate payment value
5       value = Pmt(monthlyRate, months, -loanAmount)
6
7       ' display payment value
8       paymentsListBox.Items.Add(months & ControlChars.Tab &
9           ControlChars.Tab & String.Format("{0:C}", value))
10  Next
```

Figure 11.6 Code segment for the **Car Payment Calculator** app that demonstrates the For...Next statement.

The initial value of years is 2, so the implied loop-continuation condition is satisfied and the payment calculations within the For...Next body are executed.

After execution of the For...Next body, the Next keyword is reached (line 10). This keyword marks the end of the For...Next repetition statement. When Next is reached, years is incremented by 1 (the default increment amount), and the loop begins again with the implied loop-continuation condition test.

This process repeats until the implied loop-continuation condition becomes False as years becomes greater than 5, then repetition terminates.

Local Type Inference

In each For...Next statement presented so far, we declared and initialized the control variable in the For...Next statement's header. Visual Basic provides a feature called **local type inference** that enables it to infer a local variable's type based on the context in which the variable is initialized. A local variable is any variable declared in the body of a method (such as an event handler). For example, in the declaration

```
Dim x = 7
```

the compiler infers that the variable x should be of type Integer, because the compiler assumes that whole-number values, like 7, are of type Integer. Similarly, in the declaration

```
Dim y = -123.45
```

the compiler infers that the variable y should be of type Double, because the compiler assumes that floating-point number values, like -123.45, are of type Double.

You can also use local type inference with control variables in the header of a For...Next statement. For example, in Fig. 11.6, line 1 could be written as

```
For years = 2 To 5
```

In this case, years is of type Integer because it's initialized with a whole-number value (2). We prefer to explicitly declare the type of a variable in our examples.

The local type inference feature is one of several Visual Basic features that support Language Integrated Query (LINQ). We'll use local type inference when we present LINQ examples in Chapters 20, 21, 23 and 27–29.

SELF-REVIEW

1. If the Step clause is omitted, the increment of a For...Next statement defaults to _____.
   a) 2   b) 1
   c) 0   d) –1

2. The value before the To keyword in a For...Next statement specifies the _____.
   a) initial value of the counter variable   b) final value of the counter variable
   c) increment   d) number of times the statement iterates

Answers: 1) b. 2) a.

11.4 Examples Using the For...Next Statement

The following examples demonstrate different ways of varying the control variable in a For...Next statement. In each case, we write the appropriate For...Next header:

a) Vary the control variable from 1 to 100 in increments of 1.

```
For i As Integer = 1 To 100
or
For i As Integer = 1 To 100 Step 1
```

b) Vary the control variable from 100 to 1 in increments of -1 (*decrements* of 1).

```
For i As Integer = 100 To 1 Step -1
```

c) Vary the control variable from 7 to 77 in increments of 7.

```
For i As Integer = 7 To 77 Step 7
```

d) Vary the control variable from 20 to -20 in increments of -2 (*decrements* of 2).

```
For i As Integer = 20 To -20 Step -2
```

e) Vary the control variable over the sequence of the following values: 2, 5, 8, 11, 14, 17, 20.

```
For i As Integer = 2 To 20 Step 3
```

f) Vary the control variable over the sequence of the following values: 99, 88, 77, 66, 55, 44, 33, 22, 11, 0.

```
For i As Integer = 99 To 0 Step -11
```

SELF-REVIEW

1. Which of the following is the appropriate For...Next header for varying the control variable over the following sequence of values: 25, 20, 15, 10, 5?
   a) `For i As Integer = 5 To 25 Step 5`   b) `For i As Integer = 25 To 5 Step -5`
   c) `For i As Integer = 5 To 25 Step -5`   d) `For i As Integer = 25 To 5 Step 5`

2. Which of the statements below describes the following For...Next header?

```
For i As Integer = 81 To 102
```

   a) Vary the control variable from 81 to 102 in increments of 1.
   b) Vary the control variable from 81 to 102 in increments of 0.
   c) Vary the control variable from 102 to 81 in increments of -1.
   d) Vary the control variable from 81 to 102 in increments of 2.

Answers: 1) b. 2) a.

11.5 Constructing the Interest Calculator App

Our solution to this chapter's problem statement computes interest over a given number of years by using the For...Next statement. This repetition statement performs the calculation for every year that the money remains on deposit.

The following pseudocode describes the basic operation of the **Interest Calculator** app when the **Calculate** Button is clicked:

> When the user clicks the Calculate Button
>   Get the values for the principal, interest rate and years entered by the user
>   Store a header String to be added to the output TextBox
>
>   For each year (starting at 1 and ending with the number of years entered)
>   Calculate the current value of the investment
>   Append the year and the current value of the investment to the String
>   that will be displayed in the output TextBox
>
>   Display the final output in the output TextBox

The template app we provide for this chapter contains the **Calculate** Button plus two Labels and their corresponding TextBoxes—for **Principal:** and for **Interest Rate:**. The Form has a **Years:** Label, but you'll insert the NumericUpDown control for this input. The **NumericUpDown** control limits a user's choices for the number of years to a specific range. You'll then create a multiline TextBox with a scrollbar and add it to the app's GUI. Finally, you'll add functionality with a For...Next statement. Now that you've test-driven the **Interest Calculator** app and studied its pseudocode representation, you'll use an ACE table to help you convert the pseudocode to Visual Basic. Figure 11.7 lists the *actions*, *controls* and *events* that help you complete your own version of this app.

Action/Control/Event (ACE) Table for the Interest Calculator App

Action	Control	Event
Label the app's controls	`principalLabel, rateLabel, yearsLabel, yearlyAccountLabel`	App is run
	`calculateButton`	Click
Get the values for the principal, interest rate and years entered by user	`principalTextBox, rateTextBox, yearUpDown`	
Store a header to be added to the output TextBox		
For each year (starting at 1 and ending with the number of years entered) Calculate the current value of the investment Append the year and the current value of the investment to the String that will be displayed in the output TextBox		
Display the final output in the output TextBox	`resultTextBox`	

Figure 11.7   ACE table for **Interest Calculator** app.

In the following box, you'll begin building the **Interest Calculator** app. First, you'll add a `NumericUpDown` control to allow the user to specify the number of years. This control provides up and down arrows that allow the user to scroll through the control's range of values. The box shows you how to set the limits of the range (maximum and minimum values). We use 10 as the maximum value and 1 as the minimum value for this control. The **Increment** property specifies by how much the current number in the `NumericUpDown` control changes when the user clicks the control's up (for incrementing) or down (for decrementing) arrow. This app uses the **Increment** property's default value, 1.

Adding and Customizing a NumericUpDown Control

1. ***Copying the template to your working directory.*** Copy the `C:\Examples\ch11\TemplateApp\InterestCalculator` directory to your `C:\SimplyVB2010` directory.

2. ***Opening the Interest Calculator app's template file.*** Double click `InterestCalculator.sln` in the `InterestCalculator` directory to open the app in the Visual Basic IDE (Fig. 11.8). Double click the `InterestCalculator.vb` file in the **Solution Explorer** if the Form is not already visible.

3. ***Adding a NumericUpDown control.*** Double click `NumericUpDown`

   🔢 NumericUpDown

   in the **Toolbox** to add it to the Form. Change the control's Name property to `yearUpDown`. To improve code readability, append the UpDown suffix to `NumericUpDown` control names.

(cont.)

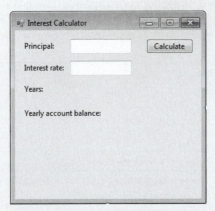

Figure 11.8 The **Interest Calculator** app in **Design** view.

4. ***Setting the NumericUpDown control's location and size.*** Set yearUpDown's Location property to 91, 82 and its Width property to 100 so that it aligns horizontally and vertically with the TextBoxes above it.

5. ***Setting property TextAlign.*** Set property TextAlign to Right. The number now appears right aligned in the control.

Good Programming Practice

Append the UpDown suffix to NumericUpDown control names.

6. ***Setting range limits for the NumericUpDown control.*** By default, this control sets 0 as the minimum and 100 as the maximum. To change these values, set the Maximum property of the **Years:** NumericUpDown control to 10. Then set its Minimum property to 1. This limits users to selecting values between 1 and 10 for the number of years. If the user inputs a value less than Minimum or greater than Maximum, the value is automatically set to the minimum or maximum value, respectively, when the control loses focus. Note that the NumericUpDown control displays 1, the value of its Minimum property. Your Form should now look like Fig. 11.9.

GUI Design Tip

Use a NumericUpDown control to limit the range of user input.

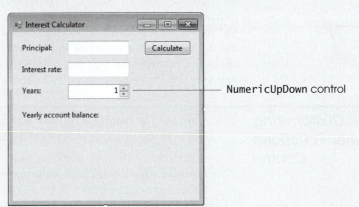

NumericUpDown control

GUI Design Tip

A NumericUpDown control should follow the same GUI Design Guidelines as a TextBox.

Figure 11.9 NumericUpDown control added to **Interest Calculator** app.

7. ***Saving the project.*** Select **File > Save All** to save your modified code.

The **Interest Calculator** app displays the results of its calculations in a **multiline TextBox**, which is simply a TextBox that can display more than one line of text. You can configure the TextBox to have a scrollbar, so that, if the TextBox is too small to display its contents, the user can scroll up and down to view the entire contents of the box. Next, you'll create this TextBox.

Adding and Customizing a Multiline TextBox with a Scrollbar

GUI Design Tip

If a TextBox will display multiple lines of output, set the Multiline property to True and left align the output by setting the TextAlign property to Left (its default value).

GUI Design Tip

If a TextBox is used to display output, set the ReadOnly property to True to ensure that the user cannot change the output.

GUI Design Tip

If a multiline TextBox will display many lines of output, limit the Text-Box height and use a vertical scroll-bar to allow users to view additional lines of output.

1. *Adding a TextBox to the Form.* Double click the TextBox control in the **Toolbox** to add a TextBox to the Form. Name it resultTextBox.

2. *Creating a multiline TextBox.* Select the TextBox's **Multiline** property, and change its value from False to True. Doing so allows the TextBox to contain multiple lines.

3. *Setting the size and location of the TextBox.* Set the TextBox's Location property to 16, 140 and the Size property to 274, 111, so that it aligns horizontally with the controls above it.

4. *Setting property ReadOnly.* To ensure that the user cannot change the output in the **Yearly account balance:** TextBox, set the **ReadOnly** property to True.

5. *Inserting a vertical scrollbar.* Using scrollbars allows you to keep the size of a TextBox small while still allowing the user to view all the information in that TextBox. The length of the text could exceed the height of the TextBox, so enable the vertical scrollbar by setting resultTextBox's **ScrollBars** property to **Vertical**. A vertical scrollbar appears on the right side of the TextBox. By default, property ScrollBars is set to **None**. You can also set property ScrollBars to **Horizontal** or **Both**. A horizontal scrollbar appears at the bottom of the TextBox. The value Both indicates that horizontal and vertical scrollbars should be displayed—the horizontal scroll bar is displayed only if the text exceeds the width of the TextBox. Note that, even without scrollbars, the user can scroll through the text by using the arrow keys. The scrollbar is initially disabled on your Form. A scrollbar is enabled only when it's needed (that is, when there's too much text in the TextBox). Your Form should look like Fig. 11.10.

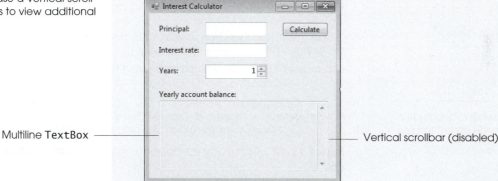

Multiline TextBox ⎯⎯⎯⎯⎯⎯⎯⎯⎯⎯⎯⎯⎯⎯⎯⎯⎯⎯⎯⎯⎯ Vertical scrollbar (disabled)

Figure 11.10   Multiline TextBox with vertical scrollbar added to the Form.

6. *Saving the project.* Select **File > Save All** to save your modified code.

Now that you've finished designing the GUI, you'll add functionality to your app. When the user clicks the **Calculate** Button, you want the app to retrieve the input, then output a table containing the amount on deposit at the end of each year. You do this by adding code to the Button's Click event handler.

Adding a Click Event Handler

1. *Creating the event handler.* Double click the **Calculate** Button. The **Calculate** Button Click event handler appears in the app's code. Add the comment and reformat the empty event handler as shown in lines 2–4 of Fig. 11.11.

(cont.)

2. ***Adding code to event handler calculateButton_Click.*** Add lines 6–14 of Fig. 11.11 to the calculateButton_Click event handler. Lines 7–10 declare the variables needed to store user inputs, calculation results and the output. Variable principal stores the amount of the principal as entered by the user and rate stores the interest rate. Variable amount stores the result of the interest calculation.

   Line 10 declares a String variable output. **String** variables store a series of characters. The characters most commonly used are letters and numbers, although there are also many special characters, such as $, *, ^, tabs and newlines. A list of characters you're likely to use is found in Appendix B. You actually have been using Strings all along—Labels and TextBoxes both store values in the Text property as values of type String. In fact, when you assign a numeric data type, such as an Integer, to the Text property of a Label, the Integer value is implicitly converted to a String. Lines 13–14 retrieve the principal and the interest rate from TextBoxes.

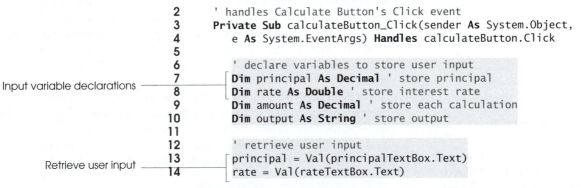

```
 2        ' handles Calculate Button's Click event
 3        Private Sub calculateButton_Click(sender As System.Object,
 4           e As System.EventArgs) Handles calculateButton.Click
 5
 6           ' declare variables to store user input
 7           Dim principal As Decimal ' store principal
 8           Dim rate As Double ' store interest rate
 9           Dim amount As Decimal ' store each calculation
10           Dim output As String ' store output
11
12           ' retrieve user input
13           principal = Val(principalTextBox.Text)
14           rate = Val(rateTextBox.Text)
```

Input variable declarations — (lines 7–8)

Retrieve user input — (lines 13–14)

Figure 11.11   App code for retrieving and storing user input.

The multiline TextBox displays the results in two columns. Add lines 16–18 of Fig. 11.12 to assign the header to output. The header labels the two columns as Year and Amount on Deposit, respectively.

```
16           ' set output header
17           output = "Year" & ControlChars.Tab &
18              "Amount on Deposit" & ControlChars.CrLf
```

Appending header text to the output String — (lines 16–18)

Figure 11.12   App code for appending the header text to the String variable.

Recall that you clear values in a Label by setting its Text property to String.Empty. When assigning new text to a String variable, you must begin and end the text with a double quotation mark ("). The opening and closing double quotation marks must appear on the same line; otherwise, a syntax error occurs. For example, if you wanted to store the word Year in the String variable year, you would use the following statement:

```
year = "Year"
```

You can append a String or a character to the end of another String by using the concatenation operator (&). In lines 17–18 of Fig. 11.12, you use the ControlChars.Tab constant to insert a tab character between the word Year and the text Amount on Deposit. You then insert a newline character (ControlChars.CrLf), so that the next series of text will appear in the *next line* of output.

3. ***Saving the project.*** Select **File > Save All** to save your modified code.

The For...Next statement in lines 21–26 of Fig. 11.13 performs the interest calculations for the specified number of years. You'll create the For...Next statement in the next box.

Calculating Cumulative Interest with a For...Next Statement	1. ***Declaring and initializing the control variable and establishing the loop-continuation test.*** Add lines 20–26 of Fig. 11.13 to the calculateButton_Click event handler. Note that the keyword Next appears once you press *Enter* at the end of line 21. Line 21 is the For...Next header which declares the control variable yearCounter and initializes it to 1. The value after the keyword To sets the implied loop-continuation condition. This loop continues while the control variable is less than or equal to the number of years specified by the user.

Using the For...Next statement to format and append text to the output String

```
20    ' calculate amount after each year and append to string
21    For yearCounter As Integer = 1 To yearUpDown.Value
22        amount =
23            principal * ((1 + rate / 100) ^ yearCounter)
24        output &= (yearCounter & ControlChars.Tab &
25            String.Format("{0:C}", amount) & ControlChars.CrLf)
26    Next
```

Figure 11.13 App code for the For...Next statement.

2. ***Performing the interest calculation.*** The For...Next statement executes its body once for each year up to the value of yearUpDown's **Value** property, which contains the number of years selected by the user. The control variable yearCounter increases from 1 to yearUpDown.Value in increments of 1. Lines 22–23 of Fig. 11.13 to perform the calculation from the formula

$$a = p(1 + r)^n$$

where a is amount, p is principal, r is rate and n is yearCounter. Note that the calculation in line 23 also divides rate by 100. This implies that the user must enter an interest-rate value in percentage format (for example, the user should enter the number 5.5 to represent 5.5%).

3. ***Appending the calculation to the output string.*** Add lines 24–25 of Fig. 11.13. These lines append additional text to the end of output, using the &= operator. The &= operator (which behaves much like the += operator) appends the right operand to the text in the left operand. This new value is then assigned to the variable in the left operand. The text includes the current yearCounter value, a tab character (ControlChars.Tab) to position to the second column, the result of the call String.Format("{0:C}", amount) and, finally, a newline character (ControlChars.CrLf) to start the next output on the next line. Recall that the C (for "currency") formatting code indicates that its corresponding argument (amount) should be displayed in monetary format.

4. ***Reaching the Next keyword.*** After the body of the loop is performed, app execution reaches keyword Next, which is now in line 26. The counter (yearCounter) is incremented by 1, and the loop begins again with the implied loop-continuation test.

5. ***Terminating the For...Next statement.*** The For...Next statement executes until the control variable exceeds the number of years specified by the user.

(cont.)

6. ***Displaying the result of the calculations.*** After exiting the For…Next statement, output is ready to be displayed to the user in resultTextBox. Add line 28 of Fig. 11.14 to display the header and the results in the multiline TextBox.

Displaying in the multiline TextBox the result of the calculations performed in the For…Next statement

```
28          resultTextBox.Text = output ' display result
29        End Sub ' calculateButton_Click
30      End Class ' InterestCalculatorForm
```

Figure 11.14   App code for displaying calculation results.

7. ***Running the app.*** Select **Debug > Start Debugging** to run your app. Your app can now calculate and display the amount on deposit for each year. Enter 1000 in the **Principal:** TextBox, 2 in the **Interest Rate:** TextBox and 10 in the **Years:** NumericUpDown control. Click the **Calculate** Button and verify that the results are the same as those displayed in Fig. 11.2.

8. ***Closing the app.*** Close your running app by clicking its close box.

9. ***Closing the IDE.*** Close the Visual Basic IDE by clicking its close box.

Figure 11.15 presents the source code for the **Interest Calculator** app. The lines of code that contain new programming concepts you learned in this chapter are highlighted.

Declare a variable of type String

Construct a header for the TextBox as a String

Loop from 1 to the value specified by the user in the yearUpDown control

Append result of calculation to the String named output

Display results in resultTextBox

```
1   Public Class InterestCalculatorForm
2     ' handles Calculate Button's Click event
3     Private Sub calculateButton_Click(sender As System.Object,
4       e As System.EventArgs) Handles calculateButton.Click
5
6       ' declare variables to store user input
7       Dim principal As Decimal ' store principal
8       Dim rate As Double ' store interest rate
9       Dim amount As Decimal ' store each calculation
10      Dim output As String ' store output
11
12      ' retrieve user input
13      principal = Val(principalTextBox.Text)
14      rate = Val(rateTextBox.Text)
15
16      ' set output header
17      output = "Year" & ControlChars.Tab &
18        "Amount on Deposit" & ControlChars.CrLf
19
20      ' calculate amount after each year and append to string
21      For yearCounter = 1 To yearUpDown.Value
22        amount =
23          principal * ((1 + rate / 100) ^ yearCounter)
24        output &= (yearCounter & ControlChars.Tab &
25          String.Format("{0:C}", amount) & ControlChars.CrLf)
26      Next
27
28      resultTextBox.Text = output ' display result
29    End Sub ' calculateButton_Click
30  End Class ' InterestCalculatorForm
```

Figure 11.15   Interest Calculator app.

SELF-REVIEW   1. The _____ property determines by how much the current number in a NumericUp-
Down control changes when the user clicks the up arrow or the down arrow.

    a) Amount   b) Step

    c) Increment   d) Next

2. Which For…Next header alters the control variable from 1 to 50 in increments of 5?

    a) **For** i = 1 **To** 50 **Step** 50   b) **For** 1 **To** 50 **Step** 5

    c) **For** i = 1 **To** 50 **Step** = 5   d) **For** i = 1 **To** 50 **Step** 5

Answers: 1) c. 2) d.

11.6 Wrap-Up

In this chapter, you learned that the essential elements of counter-controlled repetition are the name of a control variable, the initial value of the control variable, the increment (or decrement) by which the control variable is modified each time through the loop and the condition that tests the current value of the control variable against its final value. We then explored the For…Next repetition statement, which combines these essentials of counter-controlled repetition in its header.

You then changed the **Car Payment Calculator** app's Do While…Loop statement into a For…Next statement. You built an **Interest Calculator** after analyzing the pseudocode and the ACE table for this app. In the **Interest Calculator**'s GUI, you added new design elements, including a NumericUpDown control, useful for handling numeric input, and a multiline TextBox that contained a scrollbar.

In the next chapter, you'll learn to use the Select Case multiple-selection statement. You've learned that the If…Then…Else selection statement can be used in code to select between two courses of action, based on the value of a condition. The Select Case multiple-selection statement can save development time and improve code readability if the number of conditions is large. You'll use a Select Case multiple-selection statement to build a **Security Panel** app.

SKILLS SUMMARY

Using the For…Next Repetition Statement

- Declare a control variable and specify its initial value before keyword To.
- Specify the value tested for loop continuation after keyword To.
- Use optional keyword Step to specify the increment (or decrement).
- Use keyword Next to mark the end of the statement.
- Use the For…Next statement to help eliminate off-by-one errors.

Creating a Multiline TextBox with a Vertical Scrollbar

- Insert a TextBox onto the Form.
- Set the TextBox property Multiline to True.
- Set the TextBox property ScrollBar to Vertical.

Specifying a NumericUpDown Control's Maximum Value

- Use the NumericUpDown property Maximum.

Specifying a NumericUpDown Control's Minimum Value

- Use the NumericUpDown property Minimum.

Changing the Current Number in a NumericUpDown Control

- Click the NumericUpDown control's up or down arrow or type a new value.

Specifying by How Much the Current Number in a NumericUpDown Control Changes When the User Clicks an Arrow

- Use the NumericUpDown property Increment.

Obtaining the Value of a NumericUpDown Control

■ Use the NumericUpDown property Value.

KEY TERMS

&= operator—Modifies the String on its left side by appending the value on its right side to the end of the String.

For...Next header—The first line of a For...Next repetition statement. The For...Next header specifies all four essential elements for counter-controlled repetition.

For...Next repetition statement—Repetition statement that conveniently handles the details of counter-controlled repetition. The For...Next statement uses all four elements essential to counter-controlled repetition in one line of code (the name of a control variable, the initial value, the increment or decrement value and the final value).

For keyword—Begins the For...Next statement.

Horizontal value of ScrollBars property—Used to display a horizontal scrollbar on the bottom of a TextBox.

Increment property of a NumericUpDown control—Specifies by how much the current number in the NumericUpDown control changes when the user clicks the control's up (for incrementing) or down (for decrementing) arrow.

local type inference—Enables the compiler to infer a local variable's type based on the context in which the variable is initialized.

Maximum property of a NumericUpDown control—Determines the maximum input value in a particular NumericUpDown control.

Minimum property of a NumericUpDown control—Determines the minimum input value in a particular NumericUpDown control.

Multiline property of a TextBox control—Specifies whether the TextBox is capable of displaying multiple lines of text. If the property value is True, the TextBox may contain multiple lines of text; if the value of the property is False, the TextBox can contain only one line of text.

None value of ScrollBars property—Used to display no scrollbars on a TextBox.

NumericUpDown control—Allows you to specify maximum and minimum numeric input values. Also allows you to specify an increment (or decrement) when the user clicks the up (or down) arrow.

ReadOnly property of a TextBox control—Determines whether the user can change the value of a TextBox.

ScrollBars property of a TextBox control—Specifies whether a TextBox has a scrollbar and, if so, of what type. By default, the ScrollBars property is set to None.

Step keyword—Optional component of the For...Next header that specifies the increment or decrement (that is, the amount added to or subtracted from the control variable each time the loop is executed); if Step is not specified, the compiler assumes it's one.

String data type—Stores a series of characters.

To keyword—Used to specify a range of values. Commonly used in For...Next headers to specify the initial and final values of the statement's control variable.

Vertical value of ScrollBars property—Used to display a vertical scrollbar on the right side of a TextBox.

GUI DESIGN GUIDELINES

TextBox

■ If a TextBox will display multiple lines of output, set the Multiline property to True and left align the output by setting the TextAlign property to Left.

■ If a TextBox is used to display output, set the ReadOnly property to True to ensure that the user cannot change the output.

■ If a multiline TextBox will display many lines of output, limit the TextBox height and use a vertical scrollbar to allow users to view additional lines of output.

NumericUpDown

■ A NumericUpDown control should follow the same GUI Design Guidelines as a TextBox.

■ Use a NumericUpDown control to limit the range of numeric user input.

CONTROLS, EVENTS, PROPERTIES & METHODS

NumericUpDown   NumericUpDown   This control allows you to specify maximum and minimum numeric input values.

■ *In action*

■ *Properties*

Increment—Specifies by how much the current number in the NumericUpDown control changes when the user clicks the control's up (for incrementing) or down (for decrementing) arrow.

Location—Specifies the location of the NumericUpDown control on the Form relative to the Form's top-left corner.

Maximum—Determines the maximum input value in a particular NumericUpDown control.

Minimum—Determines the minimum input value in a particular NumericUpDown control.

Name—Specifies the name used to access the NumericUpDown control programmatically. The name should be appended with the UpDown suffix.

Size—Specifies the width and height (in pixels) of the NumericUpDown control.

TextAlign—Specifies how the text is aligned within the NumericUpDown control.

Value—Specifies the value in the NumericUpDown control.

Width—Specifies the width (in pixels) of the NumericUpDown.

TextBox   abl TextBox   This control allows the user to input data from the keyboard.

■ *In action*

0

■ *Event*

TextChanged—Raised when the text in the TextBox is changed.

■ *Properties*

Location—Specifies the location of the TextBox on the Form relative to the Form's top-left corner.

Multiline—Specifies whether the TextBox is capable of displaying multiple lines of text.

Name—Specifies the name used to access the TextBox programmatically. The name should be appended with the TextBox suffix.

ReadOnly—Determines whether the value of a TextBox can be changed by the user.

ScrollBars—Specifies whether the multiline TextBox contains a vertical and/or horizontal scrollbar.

Size—Specifies the width and height (in pixels) of the TextBox.

Text—Specifies the text displayed in the TextBox.

TextAlign—Specifies how the text is aligned within the TextBox.

Width—Specifies the width (in pixels) of the TextBox.

■ *Methods*

Clear—Removes the text from the TextBox on which it's called.

Focus—Transfers the focus of the app to the TextBox on which it's called.

MULTIPLE-CHOICE QUESTIONS

11.1 "Hello" has data type _____.

    a) String   b) StringLiteral

    c) Character   d) StringText

11.2 A _____ provides the ability to enter or display multiple lines of text in the same control.

    a) TextBox   b) NumericUpDown

    c) MultilineTextBox   d) multiline NumericUpDown

11.3 The For...Next header specifies _____.

a) the control variable and its initial value   b) the increment or decrement

c) the loop-continuation condition   d) all four essentials of counter-controlled repetition

11.4 _____ is optional in a For...Next header when the control variable's increment is 1.

a) Keyword To   b) The initial value of the control variable

c) Keyword Step   d) The final value of the control variable

11.5 Setting TextBox property ScrollBars to _____ creates only a vertical scrollbar.

a) True   b) Vertical

c) Up   d) Both

11.6 _____ is used to determine whether a For...Next loop continues to iterate.

a) The initial value of the control variable   b) Keyword For

c) Keyword Step   d) The final value of the control variable

11.7 In a For...Next statement, the control variable is incremented (or decremented) _____.

a) after the body of the loop executes   b) when keyword To is reached

c) while the loop-continuation condition is False   d) while the body of the loop executes

11.8 In a For...Next statement, the body executes _____.

a) zero or more times   b) one or more times

c) exactly one time   d) None of the above.

11.9 The _____ and _____ properties limit the values users can select in the NumericUpDown control.

a) Maximum, Minimum   b) Top, Bottom

c) High, Low   d) Max, Min

11.10 The For...Next header _____ can be used to vary the control variable over the odd numbers in the range 1–9.

a) For i As Integer = 1 To 10 Step 1   b) For i As Integer = 1 To 10 Step 2

c) For i As Integer = 1 To 10 Step -1   d) For i As Integer = 1 To 10 Step -2

EXERCISES

11.11 *(Present Value Calculator App)* A bank wants to show its customers how much they would need to invest now (i.e., the "present value") to achieve a specified financial goal (i.e., the "future value") in 5, 10, 15, 20, 25 or 30 years. Users must provide their financial goal (the amount of money desired after the specified number of years have elapsed), an interest rate and the length of the investment in years. Create an app that calculates and displays the principal (initial amount to invest) needed to achieve the user's financial goal. Your app should allow the user to invest money for 5, 10, 15, 20, 25 or 30 years. For example, a customer who wants to reach the financial goal of $15,000 over a period of 5 years when the interest rate is 6.6% will need to invest $10,896.96, as shown in Fig. 11.16. Use the &= operator and a For...Next loop to accomplish this.

    a) *Copying the template to your working directory.* Copy the directory C:\Examples\ch11\Exercises\PresentValue to your C:\SimplyVB2010 directory.

    b) *Opening the app's template file.* Double click PresentValue.sln in the PresentValue directory to open the app.

    c) *Adding the NumericUpDown control.* Place and size the NumericUpDown control so that it follows the GUI Design Guidelines. Set the NumericUpDown control's Name property to yearUpDown. Set the NumericUpDown control's Mimimum and Maximum properties to 5 and 30, respectively, and its Increment to 5. To allow the user to select only a duration that's in the specified range of values, set the yearUpDown control's

ReadOnly property to True. This forces the user to select a value using the yearUp-Down control's up and down arrows, which select values in intervals of 5.

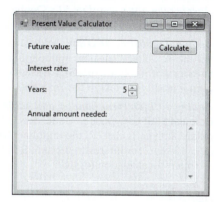 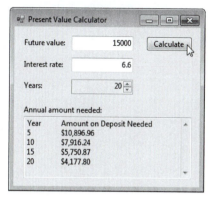

Figure 11.16   Present Value Calculator GUI.

d) *Adding a multiline TextBox.* Add a TextBox to the Form below the NumericUpDown control and set its Name property to resultTextBox. Set the TextBox to display multiple lines and a vertical scrollbar. Resize and position the TextBox on the Form so that it follows the GUI Design Guidelines. Ensure that the user cannot modify the text in the TextBox.

e) *Adding a Click event handler and adding code.* Add a Click event handler for the **Calculate** Button. Once in **Code** view, add code to the app such that, when the **Calculate** Button is clicked, the multiline TextBox displays the necessary principal for each five-year interval. Use the following version of the present-value calculation formula:

$$p = a / (1 + r)^n$$

where
   p is the amount needed to achieve the future value
   a is the future-value amount
   r is the annual interest rate (for example, .05 is equivalent to 5%)
   n is the number of years.

f) *Running the app.* Select **Debug > Start Debugging** to run your app. Enter amounts for the future value, interest rate and number of years. Click the **Calculate** Button and verify that the year intervals and the amount on deposit needed for each are correct. Test the app again, this time entering 30 for the number of years. Verify that the vertical scrollbar appears to display all of the output.

g) *Closing the app.* Close your running app by clicking its close box.

h) *Closing the IDE.* Close the Visual Basic IDE by clicking its close box.

11.12 *(Compound Interest: Comparing Rates App)* Write an app that calculates the amount of money in an account after 10 years for interest-rate amounts of 5–10%. For this app, users must provide the initial principal.

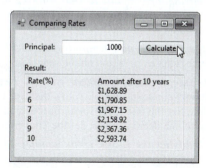

Figure 11.17   Comparing Rates GUI.

a) *Copying the template to your working directory.* Copy the directory C:\Examples\ ch11\Exercises\ComparingRates to your C:\SimplyVB2010 directory.

b) *Opening the app's template file.* Double click ComparingRates.sln in the ComparingRates directory to open the app.

c) *Adding a multiline TextBox.* Add a TextBox to the Form below the **Result:** Label. Set the TextBox to display multiple lines. Resize and position the TextBox on the Form so that it follows the GUI Design Guidelines (Fig. 11.17). Ensure that the user cannot modify the text in the TextBox.

d) *Adding a Click event handler and adding code.* Add a Click event handler for the **Calculate** Button. Once in **Code** view, add code to the app such that, when the **Calculate** Button is clicked, the multiline TextBox displays the amount in the account after 10 years for interest rates of 5, 6, 7, 8, 9 and 10%. Use the following version of the interest-calculation formula:

$$a = p \, (1 + r)^{\,n}$$

where

a is the investment's value at the end of the nth year

p is the original amount invested (the principal)

r is the annual interest rate (for example, .05 is equivalent to 5%)

n is the number of years (always 10 in this exercise).

e) *Running the app.* Select **Debug > Start Debugging** to run your app. Enter the principal amount for an account and click the **Calculate** Button. Verify that the correct amounts after 10 years are displayed, based on interest-rate amounts of 5–10%.

f) *Closing the app.* Close your running app by clicking its close box.

g) *Closing the IDE.* Close the Visual Basic IDE by clicking its close box.

11.13 *(Validating Input to the Interest Calculator App)* Enhance the **Interest Calculator** app with error checking. Test whether the user has entered valid values for the principal and interest rate. If the user enters an invalid value, display a message in the multiline TextBox. Figure 11.18 demonstrates the app handling an invalid input.

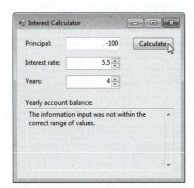

Figure 11.18 Interest Calculator app with error checking.

a) *Copying the template to your working directory.* Copy the directory C:\Examples\ ch11\Exercises\InterestCalculatorEnhancement to your C:\SimplyVB2010 directory.

b) *Opening the app's template file.* Double click InterestCalculator.sln in the InterestCalculatorEnhancement directory to open the app.

c) *Adding a NumericUpDown control.* Replace the **Interest rate:** TextBox with a NumericUpDown control. Allow the user to enter values in the range of 0.0 to 100.0 only. Set the DecimalPlaces property to 1. This allows users to specify a value with up to one decimal place. Set the Increment to 0.1.

d) *Modifying the Click event handler.* Modify the code in the **Calculate** Button's Click event handler to validate the input. The principal must be a positive amount. Also, retrieve the interest rate from the **Interest rate:** NumericUpDown.

e) *Displaying the error message.* Display the text "The information input was not within the correct range of values." in resultTextBox if the principal value is not valid.

f) *Running the app.* Select **Debug > Start Debugging** to run your app. Enter invalid data for the principal and interest rate. The invalid data for the interest rate is automatically adjusted to be within the minimum and maximum values allowed by the NumericUpDown control. The invalid data for the principal can include negative numbers or values that start with letters. Verify that entering invalid data for the principal and clicking the **Calculate** Button results in the error message displayed in Fig. 11.18.

g) *Closing the app.* Close your running app by clicking its close box.

h) *Closing the IDE.* Close the Visual Basic IDE by clicking its close box.

What does this code do? ▶ **11.14** What is the value of result after the following code executes? Assume that power, result and number are all declared as Integers.

```
1  power = 5
2  number = 10
3  result = number
4
5  For i As Integer = 1 To (power - 1)
6      result *= number
7  Next
```

What's wrong with this code? ▶ **11.15** Identify and correct the error(s) in each of the following:

a) This statement should display in a ListBox all numbers from 100 to 1 in descending order.

```
1  For counter As Integer = 100 To 1
2      displayListBox.Items.Add(counter)
3  Next
```

b) The following code should display in a ListBox the odd Integers from 19 to 1 in descending order.

```
1  For counter As Integer = 19 To 1 By -1
2      displayListBox.Add(counter)
3  Next
```

Using the Debugger ▶ **11.16** *(Savings Calculator App)* The **Savings Calculator** app calculates the amount that the user will have on deposit after one year. The app gets the initial amount on deposit from the user and assumes that the user will add $100 to the account every month for the entire year. No interest is added to the account. While testing the app, you noticed that the amount calculated by the app was incorrect. Use the debugger to locate and correct any logic error(s). Figure 11.19 displays the correct output for this app.

Figure 11.19   Correct output for the **Savings Calculator** app.

Programming Challenge ▶

11.17 *(Pay Raise Calculator App)* Develop an app that computes the amount of money an employee makes each year over a user-specified number of years. The employee receives an hourly wage and a pay raise once every year. For simplicity, assume that employees work 40 hours a week, 52 weeks a year. The user specifies the hourly wage and the amount of the raise (in percent per year).

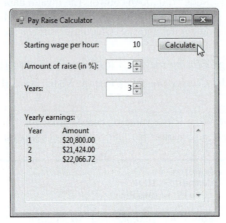

Figure 11.20   Pay Raise GUI.

a) *Copying the template to your working directory.* Copy the directory `C:\Examples\ch11\Exercises\PayRaise` to your `C:\SimplyVB2010` directory.

b) *Opening the app's template file.* Double click `PayRaise.sln` in the `PayRaise` directory to open the app.

c) *Adding controls to the Form.* Add two `NumericUpDown` controls to the Form. The first `NumericUpDown` control should allow the user to specify the pay-raise percentage. The user should be able to specify percentages only in the range of 3–8%. Create the second `NumericUpDown` control for users to select the number of years in the range 1–50. Then add a multiline `TextBox` control to the app. Set its `ScrollBar` property to display a vertical scrollbar. Ensure that the user cannot modify the text in the `NumericUpDown` and `TextBox` controls. Resize and move the controls you created so that they follow the GUI Design Guidelines as in Fig. 11.20.

d) *Adding a `Click` event handler and adding code.* Add a `Click` event handler for the **Calculate** Button. Once in **Code** view, add code to use the `For...Next` statement to compute the yearly salary amounts, based on the yearly pay raise.

e) *Running the app.* Select **Debug > Start Debugging** to run your app. Enter a starting wage per hour, the size of the yearly raise and the number of years worked. Click the **Calculate** Button and verify that the correct amount after each year is displayed in the **Yearly earnings:** TextBox.

f) *Closing the app.* Close your running app by clicking its close box.

g) *Closing the IDE.* Close the Visual Basic IDE by clicking its close box.

Objectives

In this chapter, you'll:

- Use the Select Case multiple-selection statement.
- Use Case statements.
- Use the Is keyword.
- Use the Items property's Insert method to insert an item into a ListBox at a specified position.
- Obtain the current date and time.
- Display the date and time.
- Use TextBox property PasswordChar.

Outline

Security Panel App

Introducing the Select Case Multiple-Selection Statement

In the last chapter, you learned to use the For...Next statement, which is the most concise statement for performing counter-controlled repetition. In this chapter, you'll learn about the Select Case multiple-selection statement. It's used to simplify code that otherwise would use several ElseIf statements sequentially when an app must choose among many possible actions to perform.

12.1 Test-Driving the Security Panel App

In this chapter, you'll use the Select Case multiple-selection statement to construct a **Security Panel** app. This app must meet the following requirements:

App Requirements

A lab wants to install a security panel outside a laboratory room. Only authorized personnel may enter the lab, using their security codes. The following are valid security codes (also called access codes) and the groups of employees they represent:

Values	Group
1645–1689	Technicians
8345	Custodians
9998, 1006–1008	Scientists

Once a security code is entered, access is either granted or denied. All access attempts are written to a window below the keypad. If access is granted, the date, time and group (scientists, custodians, etc.) are written to the window. If access is denied, the date, the time and the message "Access Denied" are written to the window. Furthermore, the user can enter any one-digit access code to summon a security guard for assistance. The date, the time and the message "Assistance Requested" are then written to the window to indicate that the request has been received.

You'll begin by test-driving the completed app. Then you'll learn the additional Visual Basic capabilities needed to create your own version of this app.

Test-Driving the Security Panel App

1. **Opening the completed app.** Open the directory `C:\Examples\ch12\CompletedApp\SecurityPanel` to locate the **Security Panel** app. Double click `SecurityPanel.sln` to open the app in the Visual Basic IDE.

2. **Running the Security Panel app.** Select **Debug > Start Debugging** to run the app (Fig. 12.1). At the top of the `Form`, you're provided with a `TextBox` that displays an asterisk for each digit in the security code entered using the GUI keypad. Note that the GUI keypad looks much like a real-world keypad. The **C** `Button` clears your current input, and the **#** `Button` causes the app to process the security code entered. Results are displayed in the `List-Box` at the bottom of the `Form`.

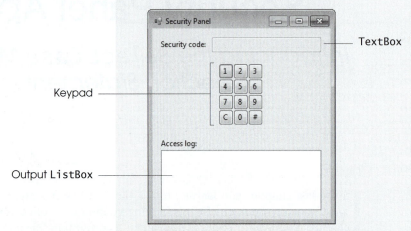

Keypad

Output `ListBox`

Figure 12.1   **Security Panel** app executing.

3. **Entering an invalid security code.** Use the keypad to enter the invalid security code 1212. Note that an asterisk (*) is displayed in the `TextBox` (Fig. 12.2) for each numeric key you click on the `Form`. These characters prevent other people from seeing the code you enter. Next, click the **#** `Button`. A message indicating that access is denied appears in the `ListBox`, as in Fig. 12.3. Note that the `TextBox` is cleared when the **#** `Button` is pressed.

GUI Design Tip

If your GUI is modeling a real-world object, its design should mimic the physical appearance of the object.

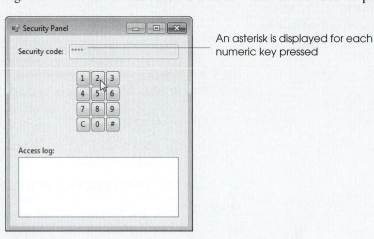

An asterisk is displayed for each numeric key pressed

Figure 12.2   Asterisks displayed in **Security code:** field.

(cont.)

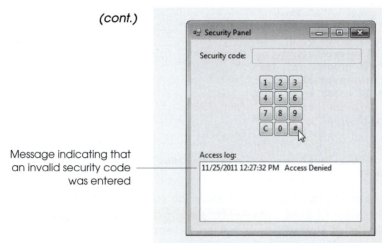

Figure 12.3   **Security Panel** displaying **Access Denied** message.

Message indicating that
an invalid security code
was entered

4. ***Using the C Button.*** Press a few numeric keys, then click the **C** Button. Note that all the asterisks displayed in the TextBox disappear. Users often make mistakes when keystroking or when clicking Buttons, so the **C** Button allows users to make a "fresh start."

5. ***Entering a valid security code.*** Use the keypad to enter 1006, then click the # Button. Note that a second message appears in the ListBox, as in Fig. 12.4.

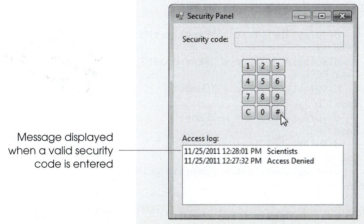

Figure 12.4   **Security Panel** app confirming a valid security-code entry.

Message displayed
when a valid security
code is entered

6. ***Closing the app.*** Close your running app by clicking its close box.

7. ***Closing the IDE.*** Close the Visual Basic IDE by clicking its close box.

12.2 Introducing the Select Case Multiple-Selection Statement

In this section, you'll learn how to use the **Select Case multiple-selection statement**. For comparison purposes, we provide an If...Then...Else multiple-selection statement that displays a text message based on a student's grade:

```
If grade = "A" Then
    displayLabel.Text = "Excellent!"
ElseIf grade = "B" Then
    displayLabel.Text = "Very good!"
ElseIf grade = "C" Then
    displayLabel.Text = "Good."
ElseIf grade = "D" Then
    displayLabel.Text = "Poor."
ElseIf grade = "F" Then
    displayLabel.Text = "Failure."
Else
    displayLabel.Text = "Invalid grade."
End If
```

This statement can be used to produce the correct output when selecting among multiple values of grade. [*Note:* String comparisons are case sensitive—"A" is not equal to "a".] However, by using the `Select Case` statement, you can simplify every instance like

```
If grade = "A" Then
```

to one like

```
Case "A"
```

and eliminate the `If` and `ElseIf` keywords.

The following `Select Case` multiple-selection statement performs the same functionality as the preceding `If...Then...Else` statement:

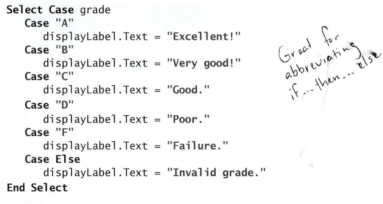

```
Select Case grade
    Case "A"
        displayLabel.Text = "Excellent!"
    Case "B"
        displayLabel.Text = "Very good!"
    Case "C"
        displayLabel.Text = "Good."
    Case "D"
        displayLabel.Text = "Poor."
    Case "F"
        displayLabel.Text = "Failure."
    Case Else
        displayLabel.Text = "Invalid grade."
End Select
```

Great for abbreviating if...then...else

Good Programming Practice

Visual Basic automatically indents the statements in the body of each `Case` to improve readability.

The `Select Case` statement begins with the keywords `Select Case` followed by a **test expression** (also called a **controlling expression**) and terminates with keywords **End Select**. The test expression is specified once, in the first line of the `Select Case` statement, and is used in each `Case` statement. The preceding `Select Case` statement contains five **Case statements** and the optional **Case Else statement**. Each `Case` statement contains the keyword `Case` followed by an **expression list**. The expression list can contain any built-in data type, such as strings ("A") or numeric values (707 and 9.9). Each `Case` statement's expression list is compared to grade—the `Select Case` statement's controlling expression. Although a `Select Case` statement can have *any* number of Cases, only one `Case Else` is allowed.

Common Programming Error

When using the optional `Case Else` statement in a `Select Case` statement, failing to place the `Case Else` as the last `Case` is a syntax error.

Figure 12.5 shows the UML activity diagram for this `Select Case` multiple-selection statement. The first condition to be evaluated is grade = "A". If this condition is True, the text "Excellent!" is displayed, and control proceeds to the first statement after the `Select Case` statement. If the condition evaluates to False (that is, grade <> "A"), the statement continues by testing the next condition, grade = "B". If this condition is True, the text "Very good!" is displayed, and control proceeds to the first statement after the `Select Case` statement. If the condition is False (that is, grade <> "B"), the statement continues to test the *next* condition. This process continues until a *matching* Case is found or until the final

Common Programming Error

`Case` statements that have the same value in their expression lists result in logic errors. At runtime, only the body of the first matching `Case` executes.

condition evaluates to False (grade <> "F"). If the latter occurs, the Case Else's body is executed, and the text "Invalid grade." is displayed. The app then continues with the first statement after the Select Case statement.

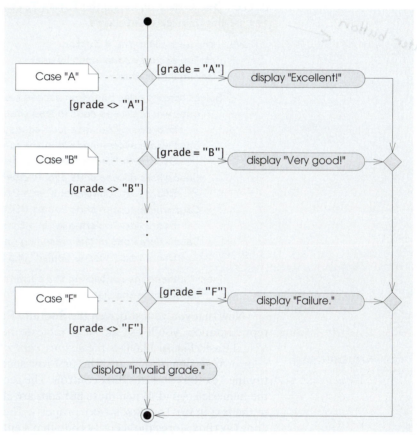

Figure 12.5 Select Case multiple-selection statement UML activity diagram.

SELF-REVIEW

1. Select Case is a _____-selection statement.
   a) multiple   b) double
   c) single   d) None of the above

2. When does the Case Else body execute?
   a) Every time a Select Case statement executes
   b) When more than one Case is matched
   c) When all Cases are matching Case statements in a Select Case statement
   d) None of the above

Answers: 1) a. 2) d.

12.3 Constructing the Security Panel App

The **Security Panel** app contains 10 Buttons that display digits. (We call these numeric Buttons.) You'll create an event handler for each Button's Click event. These Buttons make up the GUI keypad. The following pseudocode describes the Click event handler for each of these numeric Buttons:

> If a numeric Button is clicked
>   Concatenate Button's digit to the TextBox's Text property value

Combine w/ Current input ←

Later in this chapter, you'll convert this pseudocode into Visual Basic code and create the Click event handlers for each numeric Button. The user then can use the numeric Buttons to enter digits and have them concatenated to the text in a Text-Box.

In addition to the numeric Buttons, this app also contains a **C** Button and a **#** Button. The **C** Button clears the Form's TextBox. The pseudocode for the **#** Button's event handler is as follows:

Enter button ←

```
When the user clicks the # Button
    Retrieve security code input by user
    Clear input TextBox

    Select correct Case based on access code
        Case where access code is less than 10
            Store text "Assistance Requested" in a String variable
        Case where access code is in the range 1645 to 1689
            Store text "Technicians" in a String variable
        Case where access code equals 8345
            Store text "Custodians" in a String variable
        Case where access code equals 9998 or is in the range 1006 to 1008
            Store text "Scientists" in a String variable
        Case where none of the preceding Cases match
            Store text "Access Denied" in a String variable

    Insert a message containing the current time and the String variable's
        contents in the ListBox
```

Now that you've test-driven the **Security Panel** app and studied its pseudocode representation, you'll use an ACE table to help you convert the pseudocode to Visual Basic. Figure 12.6 lists the *actions*, *controls* and *events* that help you complete your own version of this app. The first row specifies that you'll use Labels to identify the TextBox and ListBox controls. The second row introduces the Buttons for the numeric keypad. When these Buttons are clicked, their values are concatenated to the text in the TextBox's Text property. The next row indicates that securityCodeTextBox stores the security code that's entered by the user. The next two rows specify that the user can click the **Clear** Button to clear the TextBox. The rest of the table indicates the functionality of the enterButton (i.e., the **#** Button in the GUI).

Action/Control/Event (ACE) Table for the Security Panel App

Action	Control	Event
Label the app's fields	securityCodeLabel, accessLogLabel	App is run
	oneButton, twoButton, threeButton, fourButton, fiveButton, sixButton, sevenButton, eightButton, nineButton, zeroButton	Click
Concatenate Button's digit to the TextBox's Text property value	securityCodeTextBox	
	clearButton	Click
Clear input TextBox	securityCodeTextBox	

Figure 12.6   ACE table for **Security Panel** app. (Part 1 of 2.)

Action	Control	Event
	enterButton	Click
Retrieve security code input by user	securityCodeTextBox	
Clear input TextBox	securityCodeTextBox	

Select correct Case based on access code
  Case where access code is less than 10
    Store text "Assistance Requested"
  Case where access code is in the range 1645
  to 1689
    Store text "Technicians"
  Case where access code equals 8345
    Store text "Custodians"
  Case where access code equals 9998 or is
  in the range 1006 to 1008
    Store text "Scientists"
  Case where none of preceding Cases match
    Store text "Access Denied"		

Insert a message containing the current time and the String variable's contents in the ListBox	logEntryListBox	

Figure 12.6   ACE table for **Security Panel** app. (Part 2 of 2.)

Now that you're familiar with the Select Case multiple-selection statement, you'll use it to build the **Security Panel** app.

Using the PasswordChar Property

1. *Copying the template to your working directory.* Copy the C:\Examples\ ch12\Templateapp\SecurityPanel directory to C:\SimplyVB2010.

2. *Opening the Security Panel app's template file.* Double click Security-Panel.sln in the SecurityPanel directory.

GUI Design Tip

Mask passwords or other sensitive pieces of information in TextBoxes.

3. *Displaying the * character in the TextBox.* Select the **Security code:** Text-Box at the top of the Form, and set its PasswordChar property to * in the **Properties** window. Text in a TextBox can be hidden or **masked** with the character specified in property **PasswordChar. Masking characters** are displayed rather than the actual text that the user types. However, the Text-Box's Text property does contain the text the user typed. For example, if a user enters 5469, the TextBox displays ****, yet stores "5469" in its Text property. Now any character entered in this TextBox displays as the *.

4. *Disabling the TextBox.* The primary reason for using a TextBox instead of a Label to display the access code is to use the PasswordChar property. To prevent users from modifying the text in the TextBox, set its **Enabled** property to **False**. You can also accomplish this using the ReadOnly property.

5. *Creating the enterButton_Click event handler.* Double click the # Button to create the enterButton_Click event handler. Add the comment and reformat the empty event handler as shown in lines 2–4 of Fig. 12.7.

6. *Declaring and initializing variables.* Add lines 6–10 of Fig. 12.7 to the enter-Button_Click event handler. Lines 6–7 declare accessCode and message to store the user's security code (access code) and the message displayed to the user (based on the access code entered), respectively. Line 9 sets accessCode to the code entered by the user. Initially, the securityCodeTextBox contains the empty string. If the user clicks the # Button without entering a code, the Val function returns 0. Line 10 clears the **Security code:** TextBox.

(cont.)

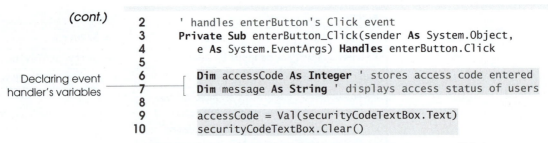

```
 2    ' handles enterButton's Click event
 3    Private Sub enterButton_Click(sender As System.Object,
 4       e As System.EventArgs) Handles enterButton.Click
 5
 6       Dim accessCode As Integer ' stores access code entered
 7       Dim message As String ' displays access status of users
 8
 9       accessCode = Val(securityCodeTextBox.Text)
10       securityCodeTextBox.Clear()
```

Declaring event handler's variables — *(pointing to lines 6–7)*

Figure 12.7   Variable declarations for `enterButton_Click`.

7. *Saving the project.* Select **File > Save All** to save your modified code.

Now that you've designed the GUI for your app, declared the variables for your event handler and obtained a value for variable `accessCode`, let's continue by creating your `Select Case` statement, as shown in the following box. This statement determines the user's access level based on the code input.

Adding a `Select Case` Statement to the App

1. *Adding a `Select Case` statement to `enterButton_Click`.* Add line 12 from Fig. 12.8 to the `enterButton_Click` event handler and press *Enter*. Visual Basic adds the keywords `End Select` (line 14) below the `Select Case` line that you just added. Line 12 begins the `Select Case` statement, which contains the *controlling expression* `accessCode`—the access code entered by the user. Recall that this expression (the value of `accessCode`) is compared *sequentially* with each `Case` until either a match occurs or the `End Select` statement is reached. If a matching `Case` is found, the body of the `Case` executes and program control proceeds to the first statement after the `End Select` statement.

```
10       securityCodeTextBox.Clear()
11
12       Select Case accessCode ' check access code input
13
14       End Select
```

Creating a `Select Case` statement — *(pointing to lines 12–14)*

Figure 12.8   `Select Case` statement.

2. *Adding a `Case` to the `Select Case` statement.* Add lines 13–14 from Fig. 12.9 to the `Select Case` statement. The first `Case` statement tests whether `accessCode` is less than 10. Keyword `Is` followed by a relational or equality operator can be used to compare the controlling expression and the value to the right of the operator. In this case, if the value in `accessCode` is *less than* 10, the code in the body of the `Case` statement executes and `message` is assigned the text `"Assistance Requested"`, which is displayed after the body of the `Select Case` statement completes.

```
12       Select Case accessCode ' check access code input
13          Case Is < 10 ' access code less than 10
14             message = "Assistance Requested"
15       End Select
```

Is keyword can be used for relational and equality comparisons — *(pointing to lines 12–15)*

Figure 12.9   First `Case` added to `Select Case` statement.

3. *Specifying `Case`s for the remaining access codes.* Add lines 15–20 from Fig. 12.10 to the `Select Case` statement.

(cont.)

To keyword can be used to
specify a range of values to test

Comma used to separate
multiple expressions in a Case

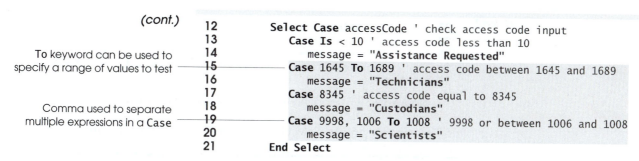

```
12      Select Case accessCode ' check access code input
13         Case Is < 10 ' access code less than 10
14            message = "Assistance Requested"
15         Case 1645 To 1689 ' access code between 1645 and 1689
16            message = "Technicians"
17         Case 8345 ' access code equal to 8345
18            message = "Custodians"
19         Case 9998, 1006 To 1008 ' 9998 or between 1006 and 1008
20            message = "Scientists"
21      End Select
```

Figure 12.10 Cases specified for remaining access codes.

**Common
Programming Error**

If the value on the left side of the To
keyword in a Case statement is
larger than the value on the right
side, the Case is ignored during app
execution, potentially causing a
logic error.

The Case statement in lines 15–16 determines whether the value of accessCode is in the *range* 1645 to 1689, inclusive. Keyword To is used to specify the range. If the user enters an access code in this range, the body of the Case statement sets message to "Technicians".

The next Case statement (lines 17–18) checks for a specific number. If accessCode matches the value 8345, then the statement in that Case is executed. Specifying a single value in a Case statement is common.

The next Case statement (lines 19–20) determines whether accessCode is 9998 or a number in the *range* 1006 to 1008, inclusive. Note that when multiple values or value ranges are provided in a Case statement, they're separated by commas.

4. ***Adding a Case Else to the Select Case statement***. Add lines 21–22 from Fig. 12.11 to the Select Case statement. These lines contain the optional Case Else, which is executed when the controlling expression does *not* match any of the previous Cases. If used, the Case Else must *follow* all other Case statements. In your app, the body of the Case Else statement sets variable message to "Access Denied". The required keywords End Select (line 23 of Fig. 12.11) terminate the Select Case statement.

Case Else statement
executes when no
other Case matches

```
19         Case 9998, 1006 To 1008 ' 9998 or between 1006 and 1008
20            message = "Scientists"
21         Case Else ' if no other Case is True
22            message = "Access Denied"
23      End Select
```

Figure 12.11 Case Else of the Select Case statement.

5. ***Displaying results in the ListBox***. Insert lines 25–26 of Fig. 12.12 after the Select Case statement. The statement at line 26 uses the Items property's Insert method to insert an item into the ListBox at a specified position. The Insert method takes two arguments—the first specifies the position at which to insert the item (starting at 0 for the first item), the second specifies the item to insert. Line 26 inserts a String in logEntryListBox consisting of the current system date and time, followed by three spaces and the value assigned to message. This item, the String, is inserted as the first item (as specified by the first argument, 0) in the ListBox, so the messages are displayed in *reverse chronological order*. The first part of method Insert's second argument contains the expression Date.Now. The .NET Framework Class Library provides a Date type that can be used to store and display date and time information. The Date property Now returns the system time and date. Passing this value as part of a String in the second argument to method Insert (line 26) causes this value to be converted and displayed as a String. [*Note:* The format used to display the Date as a String varies depending on your *locale*.] You'll learn about how a date is stored using the Date type in Chapter 14.

(cont.)

```
23          End Select
24
25          ' display time and message in ListBox
26          logEntryListBox.Items.Insert(0, Date.Now & "    " & message)
27      End Sub ' enterButton_Click
```

Figure 12.12 Updating the **Security Panel** app's `ListBox`.

6. *Saving the project.* Select **File > Save All** to save your modified code.

Now that you've defined the `enterButton_Click` event handler, you'll focus on the numeric `Button`s. You'll create event handlers for each numbered `Button` and for the **C** `Button`.

Programming the Remaining Event Handlers

1. *Creating the `zeroButton_Click` event handler.* In **Design** view, double click the **0** `Button` (`zeroButton`) to create the `zeroButton_Click` event handler. Add the comment and reformat the empty event handler as shown in lines 29–31 of Fig. 12.13.

2. *Coding the `zeroButton_Click` event handler.* Add line 33 of Fig. 12.13 to the event handler. Line 33 appends the `String` `"0"` to the end of `securityCodeTextBox`'s `Text` property value. You do this to append the numeric `Button`'s value to the access code in the `TextBox`.

```
29          ' handles zeroButton's Click event
30          Private Sub zeroButton_Click(sender As System.Object,
31              e As System.EventArgs) Handles zeroButton.Click
32
33              securityCodeTextBox.Text &= "0" ' concatenate "0" to display
34          End Sub ' zeroButton_Click
```

Figure 12.13 Event handler `zeroButton_Click`.

3. *Defining the other numeric `Button`s' event handlers.* Repeat *Steps 1–2* for the remaining numeric `Button`s (**1** through **9**). Be sure to substitute the `Button`'s number for the quoted value (for example, `oneButton_Click` sets `securityCodeTextBox`'s number as `&= "1"`). Figure 12.14 shows the event handlers for `Button`s `oneButton` and `twoButton`.

```
36          ' handles oneButton's Click event
37          Private Sub oneButton_Click(sender As System.Object,
38              e As System.EventArgs) Handles oneButton.Click
39
40              securityCodeTextBox.Text &= "1" ' concatenate "1" to display
41          End Sub ' oneButton_Click
42
43          ' handles twoButton's Click event
44          Private Sub twoButton_Click(sender As System.Object,
45              e As System.EventArgs) Handles twoButton.Click
46
47              securityCodeTextBox.Text &= "2" ' concatenate "2" to display
48          End Sub ' twoButton_Click
```

Figure 12.14 Event handlers `oneButton_Click` and `twoButton_Click`.

4. *Defining the `clearButton_Click` event handler.* Double click the **C** `Button` and add line 103 as shown in Fig. 12.15 to clear the **Security code:** `TextBox`.

(cont.)

```
99     ' handles clearButton's Click event
100    Private Sub clearButton_Click(sender As System.Object,
101       e As System.EventArgs) Handles clearButton.Click
102
103       securityCodeTextBox.Clear() ' clear text from TextBox
104    End Sub ' clearButton_Click
```

Figure 12.15   Event handler `clearButton_Click` defined.

5. *Running the app.* Select **Debug > Start Debugging**. Enter several security codes and verify that the correct output is displayed in the **ListBox**.

6. *Closing the app.* Close your running app by clicking its close box.

7. *Closing the IDE.* Close the Visual Basic IDE by clicking its close box.

Figure 12.16 presents the source code for the **Security Panel** app. The lines of code that contain new programming concepts you learned in this chapter are highlighted. Look over the code carefully to make sure that you've added all of the event handlers correctly.

```
1    Public Class SecurityPanelForm
2      ' handles enterButton's Click event
3      Private Sub enterButton_Click(sender As System.Object,
4         e As System.EventArgs) Handles enterButton.Click
5
6         Dim accessCode As Integer ' stores access code entered
7         Dim message As String ' displays access status of users
8
9         accessCode = Val(securityCodeTextBox.Text)
10        securityCodeTextBox.Clear()
11
12        Select Case accessCode ' check access code input
13           Case Is < 10 ' access code less than 10
14              message = "Assistance Requested"
15           Case 1645 To 1689 ' access code between 1645 and 1689
16              message = "Technicians"
17           Case 8345  ' access code equal to 8345
18              message = "Custodians"
19           Case 9998, 1006 To 1008 ' 9998 or between 1006 and 1008
20              message = "Scientists"
21           Case Else ' if no other Case is True
22              message = "Access Denied"
23        End Select
24
25        ' display time and message in ListBox
26        logEntryListBox.Items.Insert(0, Date.Now & "   " & message)
27     End Sub ' enterButton_Click
28
29     ' handles zeroButton's Click event
30     Private Sub zeroButton_Click(sender As System.Object,
31        e As System.EventArgs) Handles zeroButton.Click
32
33        securityCodeTextBox.Text &= "0" ' concatenate "0" to display
34     End Sub ' zeroButton_Click
35
36     ' handles oneButton's Click event
37     Private Sub oneButton_Click(sender As System.Object,
38        e As System.EventArgs) Handles oneButton.Click
39
40        securityCodeTextBox.Text &= "1" ' concatenate "1" to display
41     End Sub ' oneButton_Click
```

Using a **Select Case** statement to determine user access level — *(line 12)*

Obtain the current date and time using `Date.Now` — *(line 26)*

Appending text to a **TextBox** for output purposes — *(lines 33, 40)*

Figure 12.16   Security Panel app. (Part 1 of 2.)

```
42
43        ' handles twoButton's Click event
44        Private Sub twoButton_Click(sender As System.Object,
45           e As System.EventArgs) Handles twoButton.Click
46
47           securityCodeTextBox.Text &= "2" ' concatenate "2" to display
48        End Sub ' twoButton_Click
49
50        ' handles threeButton's Click event
51        Private Sub threeButton_Click(sender As System.Object,
52           e As System.EventArgs) Handles threeButton.Click
53
54           securityCodeTextBox.Text &= "3" ' concatenate "3" to display
55        End Sub ' threeButton_Click
56
57        ' handles fourButton's Click event
58        Private Sub fourButton_Click(sender As System.Object, _
59           e As System.EventArgs) Handles fourButton.Click
60
61           securityCodeTextBox.Text &= "4" ' concatenate "4" to display
62        End Sub ' fourButton_Click
63
64        ' handles fiveButton's Click event
65        Private Sub fiveButton_Click(sender As System.Object,
66           e As System.EventArgs) Handles fiveButton.Click
67
68           securityCodeTextBox.Text &= "5" ' concatenate "5" to display
69        End Sub ' fiveButton_Click
70
71        ' handles sixButton's Click event
72        Private Sub sixButton_Click(sender As System.Object,
73           e As System.EventArgs) Handles sixButton.Click
74
75           securityCodeTextBox.Text &= "6" ' concatenate "6" to display
76        End Sub ' sixButton_Click
77
78        ' handles sevenButton's Click event
79        Private Sub sevenButton_Click(sender As System.Object,
80           e As System.EventArgs) Handles sevenButton.Click
81
82           securityCodeTextBox.Text &= "7" ' concatenate "7" to display
83        End Sub ' sevenButton_Click
84
85        ' handles eightButton's Click event
86        Private Sub eightButton_Click(sender As System.Object,
87           e As System.EventArgs) Handles eightButton.Click
88
89           securityCodeTextBox.Text &= "8" ' concatenate "8" to display
90        End Sub ' eightButton_Click
91
92        ' handles nineButton's Click event
93        Private Sub nineButton_Click(sender As System.Object,
94           e As System.EventArgs) Handles nineButton.Click
95
96           securityCodeTextBox.Text &= "9" ' concatenate "9" to display
97        End Sub ' nineButton_Click
98
99        ' handles clearButton's Click event
100       Private Sub clearButton_Click(sender As System.Object,
101          e As System.EventArgs) Handles clearButton.Click
102
103          securityCodeTextBox.Clear() ' clear text from TextBox
104       End Sub ' clearButton_Click
105    End Class ' SecurityPanelForm
```

Figure 12.16   **Security Panel** app. (Part 2 of 2.)

1. A Case that handles all values larger than a specified value must precede the > operator with keyword _____.

      a) Select   b) Is

      c) Case   d) All

2. Use a(n) _____ to separate multiple conditions in a Case statement.

      a) period   b) asterisk

      c) comma   d) colon

Answers: 1) b. 2) c.

12.4 Wrap-Up

In this chapter, you learned how to use the Select Case multiple-selection statement and discovered its similarities to the If...Then...Else statement. You studied a UML activity diagram that illustrates the flow of control in Select Case statements.

    You then applied what you learned to create your **Security Panel** app. You set a TextBox's PasswordChar property to * in the **Properties** window to mask the text in the TextBox. You used a Select Case statement to determine whether the user entered a correct security code. You also defined a Case Else statement, which executes if a valid security code is not provided. You used Date.Now to obtain the system time and date. Finally, you learned how to insert an item at a specified position in a ListBox using the Items.Insert method.

    In the next chapter, you'll learn how to construct apps from small, manageable pieces of reusable code called procedures. You'll use this capability to enhance an example you created earlier in the book.

SKILLS SUMMARY

Creating a Select Case Statement

- Use the keywords Select Case followed by a controlling expression.
- Use the keyword Case followed by an expression to compare with the controlling expression.
- Define the statements that execute if the Case's expression matches the controlling expression.
- Use the keywords Case Else followed by statements to execute if the controlling expression does not match any of the provided Cases. Case Else, if used, must be the last Case statement.
- Use the keywords End Select to end the Select Case statement.

Masking User Input in a TextBox

- Set the TextBox's PasswordChar property to the desired character, typically the asterisk (*), to mask the user input.
- Retrieve the value typed by the user in the Text property.

Retrieving the Current Date and Time

- Use property Now of type Date, which, when converted to a String, displays the current date in the format 12/31/2002 11:59:59 P.M. (depending on locale).

Inserting an Item at the Beginning of a ListBox

- Use the Items property's Insert method with the first argument 0.

KEY TERMS

Case Else statement—Optional statement whose body executes if the Select Case's test expression does not match an expression of any Case.

Case statement—Statement whose body executes if the Select Case's test expression matches the Case's expression.

controlling expression—Value compared sequentially with each `Case` until either a match occurs or the `End Select` statement is reached. Also known as a test expression.

Date type—A type whose properties can be used to store and display date and time information.

Enabled property of a TextBox—Determines whether the `TextBox` responds to user input.

End Select keywords—Terminates the `Select Case` statement.

expression list—Multiple expressions separated by commas. Used for `Case`s in `Select Case` statements, when certain statements should execute based on more than one condition.

Insert method of a ListBox's Items property—Inserts an item in a `ListBox` at the location specified by its first argument.

Is keyword—A keyword that, when followed by a comparison operator, can be used to compare the controlling expression of a `Select Case` statement and a value.

masking—Hiding text such as passwords or other sensitive pieces of information that should not be observed by other people as they're typed. Masking is achieved by using the `PasswordChar` property of the `TextBox` for which you would like to hide data. The actual data entered is retained in the `TextBox`'s `Text` property.

masking character—Used to replace each character displayed in a `TextBox` when the `TextBox`'s data is masked for privacy.

multiple-selection statement—Performs one of many actions (or sequences of actions) depending on the value of the controlling expression.

Now property of Date type—Returns the current system time and date.

PasswordChar property of a TextBox—Specifies the masking character for a `TextBox`.

Select Case statement—The multiple-selection statement used to make a decision by comparing an expression to a series of conditions. The algorithm then takes different actions based on those values.

GUI DESIGN GUIDELINES

Overall Design

- If your GUI is modeling a real-world object, its design should mimic the physical appearance of the object.

TextBox

- Mask passwords or other sensitive pieces of information in `TextBox`es.

CONTROLS, EVENTS, PROPERTIES & METHODS

TextBox   abl TextBox   This control allows the user to input data from the keyboard.

- *In action*

  | 0 |

- *Event*

  `TextChanged`—Raised when the text in the `TextBox` is changed.

- *Properties*

  `Enabled`—Determines whether the user can enter data (`True`) in the `TextBox` or not (`False`).

  `Location`—Specifies the location of the `TextBox` on the `Form` relative to the `Form`'s top-left corner.

  `Multiline`—Specifies whether the `TextBox` is capable of displaying multiple lines of text.

  `Name`—Specifies the name used to access the `TextBox` programmatically. The name should be appended with the `TextBox` suffix.

  `PasswordChar`—Specifies the masking character to be used when displaying data in the `TextBox`.

  `ReadOnly`—Determines whether the value of a `TextBox` can be changed by the user.

  `ScrollBars`—Specifies whether the `TextBox` contains scrollbars.

  `Size`—Specifies the width and height (in pixels) of the `TextBox`.

  `Text`—Specifies the text displayed in the `TextBox`.

TextAlign—Specifies how the text is aligned within the TextBox.

Width—Specifies the width (in pixels) of the TextBox.

- *Methods*

Clear—Removes text from the TextBox that calls it.

Focus—Transfers the focus of the app to the TextBox that calls it.

ListBox [icon] ListBox   This control allows the user to view and select from items in a list.

- *In action*

```
1/6/2012 12:09:57 PM  Scientists
1/6/2012 12:09:34 PM  Access Denied
```

- *Properties*

Items—Returns an object that contains the items displayed in the ListBox.

Items.Count—Returns the number of items in the ListBox.

Location—Specifies the location of the ListBox on the Form relative to the Form's top-left corner.

Name—Specifies the name used to access the ListBox programmatically. The name should be appended with the ListBox suffix.

Size—Specifies the width and height (in pixels) of the ListBox.

- *Methods*

Items.Add—Adds an item to the end of the Items property.

Items.Clear—Deletes all the values in the ListBox's Items property.

Items.Insert—Inserts the item specified by its second argument into the Items property at the location (starting at 0 for the first item) specified by its first argument.

MULTIPLE-CHOICE QUESTIONS

12.1 The _____ keywords signify the end of a Select Case statement.

a) End Case
b) End Select
c) End Select Case
d) Case End

12.2 The expression _____ returns the current system time and date.

a) Date.DateTime
b) Date.SystemDateTime
c) Date.Now
d) Date.SystemTimeDate

12.3 You can hide information entered into a TextBox by setting the TextBox's _____ property to a character that will be displayed for every character the user enters.

a) PrivateChar
b) Mask
c) MaskingChar
d) PasswordChar

12.4 Which of the following is a syntax error?

a) Having duplicate Case statements in the same Select Case statement
b) Having a Case statement in which the value to the left of a To keyword is larger than the value to the right
c) Preceding a Case statement with the Case Else statement in a Select Case statement
d) Using keyword Is in a Select Case statement

12.5 Keyword _____ is used to specify a range in a Case statement.

a) Also
b) Between
c) To
d) From

12.6 _____ separates multiple values tested in a Case statement.

  a) A comma   b) An underscore

  c) Keyword Also   d) A semicolon

12.7 The _____ method inserts a value at a specified location in a ListBox.

  a) Append   b) Items.Insert

  c) InsertAt   d) Items.Add

12.8 If the value on the left of the To keyword in a Case statement is larger than the value on the right, _____.

  a) a syntax error occurs

  b) the body of the Case statement executes

  c) the body of the Case statement never executes

  d) the statement causes a runtime error

12.9 The expression following the keywords Select Case is called a _____.

  a) guard condition   b) controlling expression

  c) selection expression   d) case expression

12.10 To prevent a user from modifying text in a TextBox, set its _____ property to False.

  a) Enabled   b) Text

  c) TextChange   d) Editable

EXERCISES

12.11 *(Sales Commission Calculator App)* Develop an app that calculates a salesperson's commission from the number of items sold (Fig. 12.17). Assume that all items have a fixed price of $10 per unit. Use a Select Case statement to implement the following sales commission schedule:

    Fewer than 10 items sold = 1% commission
    Between 10 and 40 items sold = 2% commission
    Between 41 and 100 items sold = 4% commission
    More than 100 items sold = 8% commission

Figure 12.17   Sales Commission Calculator GUI.

a) *Copying the template to your working directory.* Copy the directory C:\Examples\ch12\Exercises\SalesCommissionCalculator to your C:\SimplyVB2010 directory.

b) *Opening the app's template file.* Double click SalesCommissionCalculator.sln in the SalesCommissionCalculator directory to open the app.

c) *Defining an event handler for the Button's Click event.* Create an event handler for the Calculate Button's Click event.

d) *Displaying the salesperson's gross sales.* In your new event handler, multiply the number of items that the salesperson has sold by 10, and display the resulting gross sales as a monetary amount.

e) *Calculating the salesperson's commission percentage.* Use a Select Case statement to compute the salesperson's commission percentage from the number of items sold. The rate that's selected is applied to all the items the salesperson sold.

f) *Displaying the salesperson's earnings.* Multiply the salesperson's gross sales by the commission percentage determined in the preceding step to calculate the salesperson's earnings. Remember to divide by 100 to obtain the percentage.

g) *Running the app.* Select **Debug > Start Debugging** to run your app. Enter a value for the number of items sold and click the **Calculate** Button. Verify that the gross sales displayed is correct, that the percentage of commission is correct and that the earnings displayed is correct based on the commission assigned.

h) *Closing the app.* Close your running app by clicking its close box.

i) *Closing the IDE.* Close the Visual Basic IDE by clicking its close box.

12.12 *(Cash Register App)* Use the numeric keypad from the **Security Panel** app to build a **Cash Register** app (Fig. 12.18). In addition to numbers, the cash register should include a decimal-point Button. Apart from this numeric operation, there should be **Enter**, **Delete**, **Clear** and **Total** Buttons. For simplicity, sales tax should be calculated based on the total amount purchased. Use a Select Case statement to compute sales tax. Add the tax amount to the subtotal to calculate the total. Display the subtotal, tax and total for the user. Use the following sales-tax percentages, which are based on the amount of money spent:

Amounts under $100 = 10% (.10) sales tax
Amounts between $100 and $500 = 7.5% (.075) sales tax
Amounts above $500 = 5% (.05) sales tax

Figure 12.18   Cash Register GUI.

a) *Copying the template to your working directory.* Copy the directory C:\Examples\ch12\Exercises\CashRegister to your C:\SimplyVB2010 directory.

b) *Opening the app's template file.* Double click CashRegister.sln in the CashRegister directory to open the app.

c) *Defining event handlers for the numeric Buttons and decimal point in the keypad.* Create event handlers for each Button's Click events. Have each event handler concatenate the proper value to the TextBox at the top of the Form.

d) *Defining an event handler for the Enter Button's Click event.* Create an event handler for the enterButton's Click event. Have this event handler add the current amount to the subtotal, display the new subtotal and clear the current price entered.

e) *Defining an event handler for the Total Button's Click event.* Create an event handler for totalButton's Click event. Have this event handler use the subtotal to compute the tax amount and then the total. Display this information in the appropriate Labels.

f) *Defining an event handler for the Clear Button's Click event.* Create an event handler for the clearButton's Click event. Have this event handler clear the user input and display the value 0.00 for the subtotal, sales tax and total.

g) *Defining an event handler for the Delete Button's Click event.* Create an event handler for the deleteButton's Click event. Have this event handler clear only the data in the TextBox.

h) *Running the app.* Select **Debug > Start Debugging** to run your app. Use the keypad to enter various dollar amounts, clicking the **Enter** Button after each. Verify that the **Subtotal:** field updates after each new entry. After several amounts have been entered, click the **Total** Button and verify that the appropriate sales tax and total are displayed. Enter several values again and click the **Delete** Button to clear the current input. Click the **Clear** Button to clear all the output values.

i) *Closing the app.* Close your running app by clicking its close box.

j) *Closing the IDE.* Close the Visual Basic IDE by clicking its close box.

12.13 *(Income Tax Calculator App)* Create an app that computes the amount of income tax that a person must pay, depending upon salary. Income tax should be calculated for each portion of income in each range. For example, a user who earns $25,000 pays 10% on the first $7,825 and 15% on the remaining $17,175. Your app should perform as shown in Fig. 12.19. Use the following income ranges and corresponding tax rates:

Not over $7,825 = 10% income tax
$7,826–31,850 = 15% income tax
$31,851–77,100 = 25% income tax
$77,101–160,850 = 28% income tax
$160,850–349,700 = 33% income tax
Over $349,700 = 35% income tax

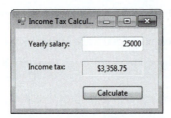

Figure 12.19 Income Tax Calculator GUI.

a) *Copying the template to your working directory.* Copy the directory `C:\Examples\ch12\Exercises\IncomeTaxCalculator` to your `C:\SimplyVB2010` directory.

b) *Opening the app's template file.* Double click `IncomeTaxCalculator.sln` in the `IncomeTaxCalculator` directory to open the app.

c) *Defining an event handler for the Calculate Button's Click event.* Use the designer to create an event handler for the `calculateButton`'s `Click` event. Have this event handler use a `Select Case` statement to determine the user's income-tax percentage. Display the result in the output `Label`.

d) *Using the TextChanged event to clear the output.* Double click the **Yearly salary:** TextBox to create its `TextChanged` event. Clear the output `Label` when the user changes the value in the TextBox.

e) *Running the app.* Select **Debug > Start Debugging** to run your app. Enter a yearly salary and click the **Calculate** Button. Verify that the appropriate income tax is displayed, based on the ranges listed in the exercise description.

f) *Closing the app.* Close your running app by clicking its close box.

g) *Closing the IDE.* Close the Visual Basic IDE by clicking its close box.

What does this code do? ▶ **12.14** What is output by the following code? Assume that `donationButton` is a `Button`, `donationTextBox` is a `TextBox` and `messageLabel` is an output `Label`.

```
1  Private Sub donationButton_Click(sender As System.Object,
2     e As System.EventArgs) Handles donationButton.Click
3
4     Select Case Val(donationTextBox.Text)
5        Case 0
6           messageLabel.Text = "Please consider donating to our cause."
7        Case 1 To 100
8           messageLabel.Text = "Thank you for your donation."
9        Case Is > 100
10          messageLabel.Text = "Thank you very much for your donation!"
11       Case Else
12          messageLabel.Text = "Please enter a valid amount."
13    End Select
14 End Sub
```

What's wrong with this code? **12.15** This Select Case statement should determine whether the Integer value is even or odd. Find the error(s) in the following code:

```
1   Select Case value Mod 2
2      Case 0
3         outputLabel.Text = "Odd Integer"
4      Case 1
5         outputLabel.Text = "Even Integer"
6   End Select
```

Using the Debugger **12.16** *(Discount Calculator App)* Copy the C:\Examples\ch12\DiscountCalculator directory to your C:\SimplyVB2010 directory. The **Discount Calculator** app determines the discount the user receives, based on how much money the user spends. A 15% discount is received for purchases over $200, a 10% discount for purchases between $150 and $200, a 5% discount for purchases between $100 and $149 and a 2% discount for purchases between $50 and $99. While testing your app, you notice that it's not calculating the discount properly for some values. Use the debugger to find and fix the logic error(s) in the app. Figure 12.20 displays the correct output for the app.

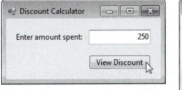

Figure 12.20   Correct output for the **Discount Calculator** app.

Programming Challenge **12.17** *(Enhanced Cash Register App)* A store is holding a sale. Modify the **Cash Register** app (Exercise 12.12) to calculate the discount received based on the total amount spent after taxes. The discount should be displayed in a dialog box as well as in the **Discount:** Label. Figure 12.21 displays the enhanced **Cash Register** app GUI. The store offers the following discounts based on the total amount spent:

> Under $200 = 10% discount
> $200–500 = 20% discount
> Over $500 = 30% discount

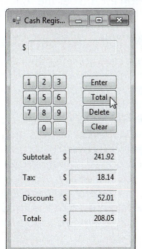

Figure 12.21   Enhanced **Cash Register** GUI.

13

Enhancing the Wage Calculator App

Introducing *Function Procedures and Sub Procedures*

Most software apps that solve real-world problems are much larger than the apps presented in the first few chapters of this text. Experience has shown that the best way to develop and maintain a large app is to construct it from smaller, more manageable pieces. This technique is known as **divide and conquer**. These manageable pieces include program components—known as **procedures**—that simplify the design, implementation and maintenance of large apps. In this chapter, you learn how to create two kinds of procedures—namely, **Function** procedures and Sub procedures.

13.1 Test-Driving the Enhanced Wage Calculator App

Use procedures to enhance the **Wage Calculator** app that you created in Chapter 7. This app must meet the following requirements:

App Requirements

Recall the problem statement from Chapter 7: A payroll company calculates the gross earnings per week of employees. Employees' weekly salaries are based on the number of hours they worked and their hourly wages. Create an app that accepts this information and calculates each employee's total (gross) earnings. The app assumes a standard work week of 40 hours. The wages for 40 or fewer hours are calculated by multiplying the employee's hourly wage by the number of hours worked. Any time worked over 40 hours in a week is considered "overtime" and earns time and a half. Salary for time and a half is calculated by multiplying the employee's hourly wage by 1.5 and multiplying the result of that calculation by the number of overtime hours worked. The total overtime earned is added to the user's gross earnings for the regular 40 hours of work to calculate the total earnings for that week.

The completed app has the same functionality as the app in Chapter 7 but uses procedures to organize the code better. This app calculates earnings based on an employee's hourly wage and the number of hours worked per week. An employee who works 40 or fewer hours earns the hourly wage multiplied by the number of hours worked. The calculation differs if the employee has worked more than the standard 40-hour work week. In this chapter, you'll learn about procedures that perform calculations based on input values that may differ with each execution of the app. You'll begin by test-driving the completed app. Then you'll learn the additional Visual Basic technologies needed to create your own version of this app.

Test-Driving the Enhanced Wage Calculator App

1. ***Opening the completed app.*** Open the directory C:\Examples\Ch13\CompletedApp\WageCalculator2 to locate the **Wage Calculator** app. Double click WageCalculator2.sln to open the app in the Visual Basic IDE.

2. ***Running the Wage Calculator app.*** Select **Debug > Start Debugging** to run the app.

3. ***Entering the employee's hourly wage.*** Enter 10 in the **Hourly wage:** Text-Box (Fig. 13.1).

Figure 13.1   **Wage Calculator** running.

4. ***Entering the number of hours the employee worked.*** Enter 45 in the **Weekly hours:** TextBox.

5. ***Calculating wages earned.*** Click the **Calculate** Button. The result ($475.00) is displayed in the **Gross earnings:** Label.

6. ***Closing the app.*** Close the running app by clicking its close box.

7. ***Closing the IDE.*** Close the Visual Basic IDE by clicking its close box.

13.2 Classes and Procedures

The key to creating large apps is to break them into smaller pieces. In object-oriented programming, these pieces consist primarily of *classes*, which can be further broken down into **methods**. In Visual Basic programming, methods are implemented by writing procedures. We frequently refer to procedures as methods.

Programmers typically combine **programmer-defined** classes and methods with preexisting code available in the .NET Framework Class Library. Using preexisting code saves time, effort and money. The concept of **reusing code** increases efficiency for app developers. Figure 13.2 lists several preexisting Visual Basic methods.

You've already used several preexisting classes and methods in the .NET Framework Class Library. For example, all of the GUI controls you've used in your apps are defined in the .NET Framework Class Library as classes. You've also used .NET Framework Class Library class methods, such as method Format of class String, to display output properly in your apps. Without method String.Format, you would have needed to code this functionality yourself—a task that would have included many lines of code as well as programming techniques that have not been introduced yet. You'll learn many more .NET Framework Class Library classes and methods in this book.

Procedure	Description	Examples
`Math.Max(x, y)`	Returns the larger of x and y	`Math.Max(2.3, 12.7)` is `12.7` `Math.Max(-2.3, -12.7)` is `-2.3`
`Math.Min(x, y)`	Returns the smaller of x and y	`Math.Min(2.3, 12.7)` is `2.3` `Math.Min(-2.3, -12.7)` is `-12.7`

`Math.Sqrt(x)`	Returns the square root of x	`Math.Sqrt(9)` is `3.0`
		`Math.Sqrt(2)`
		    is `1.4142135623731`

`Pmt(x, y, z)`	Calculates payments where x specifies the interest rate, y the number of payment periods and z the principal value of the loan—a negative value if it represents cash to be paid or a positive value if it represents cash to be received	`Pmt(0.05, 12, -4000)` is `451.301640083261`
`Val(x)`	Returns the numeric value of x	`Val("5")` is 5 `Val("5a8")` is 5 `Val("a5")` is 0
`String.Format(` *formatString*, *listOfArguments*)	Returns a formatted `String`. The first parameter, *formatString*, specifies the formatting and *listOfArguments* specifies the values to format	`String.Format("{0:C}", 1.23)` is `"$1.23"`

Figure 13.2   Some predefined Visual Basic methods.

The .NET Framework Class Library cannot provide every conceivable feature that you might want, so Visual Basic allows you to create your own programmer-defined procedures to meet the unique requirements of your apps. Two types of procedures exist: **Function procedures** and **Sub procedures**. In the next section, you'll learn about `Function` procedures; in Section 13.4, you'll learn about Sub procedures. Throughout this chapter, the term "procedure" refers to both `Function` procedures and Sub procedures, unless otherwise noted.

SELF-REVIEW

1. _____ provides you with preexisting classes that perform common tasks.

   a) The Framework Class Library   b) The `PreExisting` keyword
   c) The Framework Code Library   d) The `Library` keyword

2. Programmers normally use _____.

   a) programmer-defined procedures   b) preexisting procedures
   c) both programmer-defined and preexisting procedures
   d) neither programmer-defined nor preexisting procedures

Answers: 1) a. 2) c.

13.3 Function Procedures

Software Design Tip

Use procedures to increase the clarity and organization of your apps. This not only helps others understand your apps, but it also helps you develop, test and debug your apps.

The apps presented earlier in this book call .NET Framework Class Library methods (such as `String.Format`) to help accomplish the apps' tasks. You'll now learn how to write your own programmer-defined procedures. You'll first learn how to create procedures in the context of two small apps, before you create the enhanced **Wage Calculator** app. The first app uses the *Pythagorean theorem* to calculate the length of the *hypotenuse of a right triangle*, and the second app determines the maximum of three numbers. Let's begin by reviewing the Pythagorean theorem. A right triangle (a triangle with a 90-degree angle) always satisfies the following relationship—the sum of the squares of the two smaller sides of the triangle equals the square of the largest side of the triangle, which is known as the hypotenuse. In this app, the two smaller sides are called sides A and B, and their lengths are used to calculate the length of the hypotenuse. Follow the steps in the next box to create the app.

Creating the *Hypotenuse* **Calculator** *App*

1. ***Copying the template to your working directory.*** Copy the C:\Examples\ Ch13\TemplateApp\HypotenuseCalculator directory to your C:\Simply-VB2010 directory.

2. ***Opening the Hypotenuse Calculator app's template file.*** Double click HypotenuseCalculator.sln in the HypotenuseCalculator directory to open the app in the Visual Basic IDE. When you open the Form in **Design** view, you'll see the GUI shown in Fig. 13.3. When this app is running, the user enters the lengths of a triangle's two shorter sides into the **Length of side A:** and **Length of side B:** TextBoxes, then clicks the **Calculate Hypotenuse** Button. The completed app calculates the length of the hypotenuse and displays the result in the **Length of hypotenuse:** output Label.

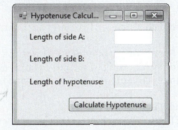

Figure 13.3   **Hypotenuse Calculator** GUI.

3. ***Viewing the template app code.*** Switch to **Code** view, and examine the code provided in the template, shown in Fig. 13.4. Initially, lines 8–11 are underlined by the IDE because they are not yet used.

```
1   Public Class HypotenuseCalculatorForm
2       ' handles Calculate Button's Click event
3       Private Sub calculateButton_Click(sender As System.Object,
4           e As System.EventArgs) Handles calculateButton.Click
5
6       Dim sideA As Double ' length of side A
7       Dim sideB As Double ' length of side B
8       Dim hypotenuse As Double ' length of hypotenuse
9       Dim squareSideA As Double ' value of side A squared
10      Dim squareSideB As Double ' value of side B squared
11      Dim squareHypotenuse As Double ' value of hypotenuse squared
12
13          sideA = Val(sideATextBox.Text)
14          sideB = Val(sideBTextBox.Text)
15
16          ' if input received is less than or equal to zero
17          If (sideA <= 0) OrElse (sideB <= 0) Then
18              MessageBox.Show("You must enter a non-negative number",
19                  "Invalid Input Entered", MessageBoxButtons.OK,
20                  MessageBoxIcon.Error)
21          Else
22
23          End If
24      End Sub ' calculateButton_Click
25  End Class ' HypotenuseCalculatorForm
```

Lengths for sides A, B and hypotenuse — (lines 6–8)

Square of lengths for sides A, B and hypotenuse — (lines 9–11)

Message dialog displays if a negative value, zero or a non-numeric value is entered — (lines 18–20)

Figure 13.4   **Hypotenuse Calculator** template code.

(cont.)

Good Programming Practice

Add comments at the beginning of a procedure to indicate its purpose.

Good Programming Practice

Add comments at the end of your procedures, indicating which procedure is being terminated.

We've provided an incomplete event handler for the **Calculate Hypotenuse** Button. This event handler contains six declarations (lines 6–11). Variables `sideA` and `sideB` contain the lengths of sides A and B, entered by the user. Variable `hypotenuse` will contain the length of the hypotenuse, which will be calculated later. Variable `squareSideA` will store side A's length squared. Similarly, variables `squareSideB` and `squareHypotenuse` will store the squares of the lengths of side B and the hypotenuse, respectively. Lines 13–14 store the user input for the lengths of sides A and B. Lines 17–23 contain an `If...Then...Else` statement. The `If` statement's body displays a message dialog if a negative value, zero or a non-numeric value is input as the length of side A, side B or both. The `Else`'s body, which executes only if you enter values greater than zero, should calculate the length of the hypotenuse. You'll soon fill it in.

4. ***Creating an empty Function procedure.*** Add lines 26–28 of Fig. 13.5 after event handler `calculateButton_Click` and before the `End Class` keywords, then press *Enter*. The keywords `End Function` are added by the IDE (line 30) when you press *Enter*. You learn about these keywords shortly. We added a comment in line 30 to identify the procedure being terminated.

Function procedure header ⟶

End Function keywords mark the end of a ⟶ Function procedure

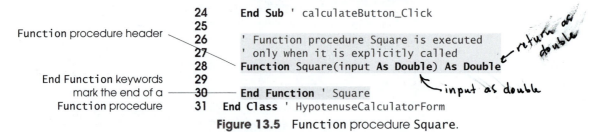

```
24    End Sub ' calculateButton_Click
25
26    ' Function procedure Square is executed
27    ' only when it is explicitly called
28    Function Square(input As Double) As Double
29
30    End Function ' Square
31  End Class ' HypotenuseCalculatorForm
```
(handwritten annotations: "← return as double", "← input as double")

Figure 13.5 `Function` procedure `Square`.

5. ***Understanding the Function procedure.*** The procedure begins in line 28 (Fig. 13.5) with keyword **Function** followed by a **procedure name** (in this case, `Square`). The procedure name can be any valid identifier and is followed by a set of parentheses containing the parameter declarations, if any.

The declaration in the parentheses is known as the **parameter list**, where variables (called **parameters**) are declared. Parameters enable a procedure to receive data that helps it perform its task. The parameter list can contain zero or more declarations separated by commas. It declares each parameter's name and type. Parameters may be used only in the `Function` procedure body.

Software Design Tip

To promote reusability, each procedure should perform a single well-defined task, and the procedure name should express that task effectively and concisely.

A `Function` procedure returns one value after it performs its task. To specify the type of the returned value, the parameter list is followed by the keyword As, which is in turn followed by a data type (`Double` in this example). The type that follows `As`, known as the **return type**, indicates the type of the result returned from the `Function` (in this case, `Double`). The first line of a procedure (including the keyword `Function`, the procedure name, the parameter list and the return type) is often called the **procedure header**. The procedure header for `Square` declares *one* parameter, `input`, to be of type `Double` and sets the return type of `Square` to be `Double`.

Good Programming Practice

Procedure names should begin with an uppercase first letter. Each subsequent word in the name should begin with an uppercase first letter.

The `Function` procedure of Fig. 13.5 ends on line 30 with the keywords `End Function`. The declarations and statements that appear after the procedure header but before the keywords `End Function` form the **procedure body**, which contains code that performs actions—generally by manipulating the parameters from the parameter list—and returns a result. In the next step, you add statements to `Square`'s body. The procedure header, the body and the keywords `End Function` are collectively known as a **procedure definition**.

(cont.)

6. ***Adding code to the body of a Function procedure.*** Your Function procedure should perform the squaring functionality needed in this app. Add lines 30–31 of Fig. 13.6 to Square's body.

```
28      Function Square(input As Double) As Double
29
30          ' return square of parameter variable
31          Return input ^ 2
32      End Function ' Square
```

Calculate the square using the ∧ operator

Figure 13.6 Square procedure definition.

Line 31 uses the ∧ operator to calculate the square of input—the parameter of this procedure—and uses a **Return statement** to return this value. This statement begins with the keyword **Return**, followed by an expression. The Return statement returns the result of the expression following keyword Return, in this case input ∧ 2, and terminates execution of the procedure. This value is returned to the point at which the procedure was called. You'll write the code to call the procedure in the next step.

7. ***Invoking procedure Square.*** Now that you've created your procedure, you can **call** it—that is, make it perform its designated task—from your event handler. This is also known as **invoking** the procedure. Add lines 22–24 of Fig. 13.7 to your app, in the Else block of the event handler's If...Then...Else statement. These lines call Square by using the procedure name followed by a set of parentheses that contain the procedure's **argument(s)**—information that the **callee** (the procedure being called) requires to do its job. Each argument is assigned to one of the procedure's parameters when the procedure is called. The number of arguments in the call must match the number of parameters in the definition. In this case, each call to Square receives one argument—sideA (line 23) and sideB (line 24). These variables contain the user input. In each call, the argument's value is passed to procedure Square and stored in its parameter input.

```
21          Else
22              ' calculate squares of sides A and B
23              squareSideA = Square(sideA)
24              squareSideB = Square(sideB)
25
26          End If
```

Calling procedure Square

Figure 13.7 Invoking procedure Square.

Good Programming Practice

Placing a blank line between procedure definitions enhances app readability.

Good Programming Practice

Selecting descriptive parameter names makes the information provided by the *Parameter Info* feature more meaningful.

Good Programming Practice

Placing a blank line between procedure definitions enhances app readability.

When program control reaches line 23 of Fig. 13.7, the app calls Function procedure Square. At this point, the app makes a copy of the value stored in variable sideA (the user input), and program control transfers to the first line of Square.

Square receives the copy of the value entered by the user and stores it in the parameter input. When the Return statement in Square is reached, the value to the right of keyword Return is returned to the **caller** (the **calling procedure**) in line 23 where Square was called. Square's execution is now complete and the parameter that held the *copy* of the argument value is discarded.

Program control also transfers to line 23 at this point, and the app continues by assigning the return value of Square to variable squareSideA. These same actions occur again when program control reaches the second call to Square in line 24. With this call, the value passed to Square is the value stored in variable sideB, and the value returned is assigned to variable squareSideB. In the next step, you'll determine the hypotenuse using the values of squareSideA and squareSideB.

(cont.)

When you typed the opening parenthesis after the procedure name, you probably noticed that the Visual Basic IDE displays a window containing the procedure's argument names and types (Fig. 13.8). This is the *Parameter Info* feature of the IDE, which provides you with information about procedures and their arguments. The *Parameter Info* feature displays information for programmer-defined procedures as well as for .NET Framework Class Library methods.

Parameter Info window ———————

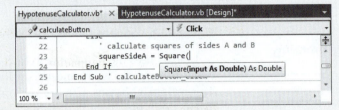

Figure 13.8 *Parameter Info window.*

8. *Calling a preexisting method of the .NET Framework Class Library.* Add lines 26–34 of Fig. 13.9 to the `Else`'s body of the `If...Then...Else` statement in your app. Line 28 adds the square of side A and the square of side B, resulting in the square of the hypotenuse, which is assigned to variable `squareHypotenuse`. Line 32 then calls .NET Framework Class Library method `Sqrt` of class `Math` (by using the dot operator). This method calculates the square root of the square of the hypotenuse to find the length of the hypotenuse, then formats the result and displays it in the `outputLabel`.

```
24          squareSideB = Square(sideB)
25
26          ' use Pythagorean Theorem to calculate
27          ' length of side squared
28          squareHypotenuse = squareSideA + squareSideB
29
30          ' use Math.Sqrt method to calculate
31          ' square root of hypotenuse squared
32          hypotenuse = Math.Sqrt(squareHypotenuse)
33
34          outputLabel.Text = String.Format("{0:F}", hypotenuse)
35       End If
36    End Sub ' calculateButton_Click
```

Figure 13.9 Completing the `calculateButton_Click` event handler.

Error-Prevention Tip

Small procedures are easier to test, debug and understand than large ones.

9. *Running the app.* Select **Debug > Start Debugging** to run your app. Enter 3 into the **Length of side A:** TextBox and 4 into the **Length of side B:** TextBox. Click the **Calculate Hypotenuse** Button. The output is shown in Fig. 13.10.

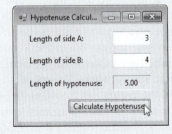

Figure 13.10 Hypotenuse Calculator app running.

10. *Closing the app.* Close your running app by clicking its close box.

11. *Closing the IDE.* Close the Visual Basic IDE by clicking its close box.

You've now successfully created a Function procedure and tested it by running the app to confirm that it works correctly. This Function procedure can now be used in any Visual Basic app where you wish to calculate the square of a Double. All you need to do is include the procedure definition in your app. This is an example of code reuse, which helps you create apps faster.

As demonstrated in the **Hypotenuse Calculator** app, the procedure call used to call a Function procedure follows the format

name(*argument list*)

There must be one argument in the argument list of the procedure call for each parameter in the parameter list of the procedure header. The arguments also must be compatible with the parameters' types (that is, Visual Basic must be able to assign the value of the argument to its corresponding parameter). For example, a parameter of type Double could receive the value of 53547.350009, 22 or -.03546, but not "hello", because a Double variable cannot contain a String. If a procedure does not receive any values, the parameter list is empty (that is, the procedure name is followed by an empty set of parentheses).

As you saw in the preceding example, the statement

Return *expression*

can occur anywhere in a Function procedure body and returns the value of *expression* to the caller. If necessary, Visual Basic attempts to convert the value of *expression* to the Function procedure's return type. Functions Return *exactly one value*. When a Return statement executes, control returns immediately to the point at which that Function procedure was called.

You now create another Function procedure. This procedure, which is part of the **Maximum** app, returns the largest of three numbers entered by the user. In the following box, you'll create the **Maximum** app.

Software Design Tip

The procedure header and procedure calls must agree with regard to the number, types and order of parameters and arguments.

Common Programming Error

Calling a procedure that does not exist or misspelling the procedure name in a procedure call results in a compilation error.

Creating a Function Procedure That Returns the Largest of Three Numbers

1. *Copying the template to your working directory.* Copy the C:\Examples\Ch13\TemplateApp\Maximum directory to C:\SimplyVB2010.

2. *Opening the Maximum app's template file.* Double click Maximum.sln in the Maximum directory to open the app in the Visual Basic IDE. Switch to **Design** view (Fig. 13.11).

3. *Creating an event handler for the Maximum Button.* Double click the **Maximum** Button to create an event handler for this Button's Click event. Add the comment in line 2 of Fig. 13.12 and split the header over two lines, as shown in lines 3–4. Add lines 6–7 to the event handler. Lines 6–7 call Function procedure Maximum and pass it the three values the user has entered into the app's TextBoxes. The IDE underlines Maximum in blue on your screen—indicating a compilation error—because Function procedure Maximum has not yet been defined. You'll define Maximum in the next step. This compilation error occurs whenever you call a procedure that's not recognized by the Visual Basic IDE. Misspelling the name of a procedure in a procedure call also causes a compilation error. Finally, add the comment after keywords End Sub in line 8.

(cont.)

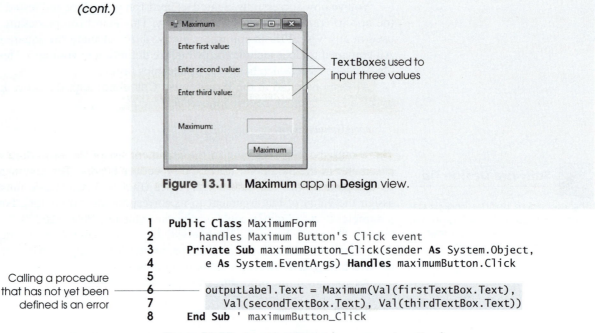

Figure 13.11   **Maximum** app in **Design** view.

Calling a procedure that has not yet been defined is an error

```
1   Public Class MaximumForm
2       ' handles Maximum Button's Click event
3       Private Sub maximumButton_Click(sender As System.Object,
4           e As System.EventArgs) Handles maximumButton.Click
5
6           outputLabel.Text = Maximum(Val(firstTextBox.Text),
7               Val(secondTextBox.Text), Val(thirdTextBox.Text))
8       End Sub ' maximumButton_Click
```

Figure 13.12   Invoking **Function** procedure **Maximum**.

4. ***Creating Function procedure Maximum.*** Add lines 10–12 of Fig. 13.13 after event handler **maximumButton_Click**, then press *Enter*. Note that the keywords End Function are added for you by the IDE. The parameter list specifies that the values of the three arguments passed to **Maximum** are stored in parameters **one**, **two** and **three**. The parameter list is followed by the keyword As and the return type **Double**.

Empty **Function** procedure **Maximum**

```
8       End Sub ' maximumButton_Click
9
10      ' find maximum of three parameter values
11      Function Maximum(one As Double, two As Double,
12          three As Double) As Double
13
14      End Function ' Maximum
15  End Class ' MaximumForm
```

Figure 13.13   Maximum **Function** procedure.

5. ***Adding functionality to Function procedure Maximum.*** Add lines 14–20 of Fig. 13.14 to the body of **Maximum**. Line 14 creates a variable that contains the maximum of the first two numbers passed to this procedure. This maximum is determined in line 17 by using the **Max** method of .NET Framework Class Library class **Math**. This method takes two **Doubles** and returns the maximum of these two values. The value returned is assigned to variable **temporaryMaximum** in line 17. You then compare that value to **Function** procedure **Maximum**'s third parameter, **three**, in line 18. The maximum determined in this line, **finalMaximum**, is the maximum of the three values. Line 20 uses a **Return** statement to return this value. The **Return** statement terminates the procedure's execution and returns the result (the value of **finalMaximum**) to the calling procedure. The result is returned to the point (line 6 of Fig. 13.12) where **Maximum** was called and is assigned to **outputLabel**'s **Text** property.

(cont.)

```
11        Function Maximum(one As Double, two As Double,
12           three As Double) As Double
13
14           Dim temporaryMaximum As Double
15           Dim finalMaximum As Double
16
17           temporaryMaximum = Math.Max(one, two)
18           finalMaximum = Math.Max(temporaryMaximum, three)
19
20           Return finalMaximum
21        End Function ' Maximum
22     End Class ' MaximumForm
```

Calling `Math.Max` to determine the maximum of two values

Figure 13.14   `Math.Max` returns the larger of its two arguments.

6. ***Running the app.*** Select **Debug > Start Debugging** to run your app (Fig. 13.15). Enter a numeric value into each TextBox, and click the **Maximum** Button. Note that the largest of the three values is displayed in the output Label.

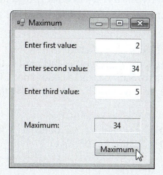

Figure 13.15   **Maximum** app running.

7. ***Closing the app.*** Close your running app by clicking its close box.

8. ***Closing the IDE.*** Close the Visual Basic IDE by clicking its close box.

SELF-REVIEW

1. A procedure is invoked by a(n) _____.

    a) callee
    b) caller
    c) argument
    d) parameter

2. The _____ statement in a `Function` procedure sends a value back to the calling procedure.

    a) `Return`
    b) `Back`
    c) `End`
    d) None of the above

Answers: 1) b. 2) a.

13.4 Using Procedures in the Wage Calculator App

The **Calculate** Button's `Click` event handler in the original version of the **Wage Calculator** app (Chapter 7) calculated wages and displayed the result in a Label. In the following box, you'll write Sub procedure `DisplayPay` to perform these tasks. **Sub procedures** are similar to `Function` procedures, with one important difference—Sub procedures do not return a value to the caller. When the user clicks the **Calculate** Button, event handler `calculateButton_Click` calls Sub procedure `DisplayPay`.

Creating a Sub Procedure within the Wage Calculator App

1. *Copying the template to your working directory.* Copy the C:\Examples\ Ch13\TemplateApp\WageCalculator2 directory to C:\SimplyVB2010.

2. *Opening the Wage Calculator app's template file.* Double click WageCalculator2.sln in the WageCalculator2 directory to open the app in the Visual Basic IDE.

3. *Creating the calculateButton_Click event handler.* View the app's Form in **Design** view. Double click the **Calculate** Button to generate the Click event handler. Add the comment and reformat the empty event handler as shown in lines 2–4 of Fig. 13.16.

4. *Entering functionality to calculateButton_Click.* Add lines 6–15 of Fig. 13.16 to the empty event handler. This code calls DisplayPay to calculate and display the wages. Lines 11–12 retrieve the user input from the TextBoxes and assign the values to variables declared in lines 7–8. Line 15 calls procedure DisplayPay, which you define shortly. This procedure call takes *two* arguments: the hours worked (userHours) and the hourly wage (wage). Note that the call to DisplayPay is underlined in blue on your screen because the procedure has not yet been defined; for the moment, this is a compilation error.

```
1   Public Class WageCalculatorForm
2       ' handles Calculate Button's Click event
3       Private Sub calculateButton_Click(sender As System.Object,
4          e As System.EventArgs) Handles calculateButton.Click
5
6          ' declare variables
7          Dim userHours As Double ' hours worked
8          Dim wage As Decimal ' hourly wages
9
10         ' assign values from user input
11         userHours = Val(hoursTextBox.Text)
12         wage = Val(wageTextBox.Text)
13
14         ' call DisplayPay Sub procedure
15         DisplayPay(userHours, wage)
16      End Sub ' calculateButton_Click
```

Call to DisplayPay ⟶ line 15

Figure 13.16 calculateButton_Click calls DisplayPay.

5. *Creating a Sub procedure.* After event handler calculateButton_Click, add Sub procedure DisplayPay to your app (lines 18–39 of Fig. 13.17).

   Procedure DisplayPay receives the argument values and stores them in the parameters hours and rate. The syntax of a Sub procedure is the same as that of a Function procedure, with a few small changes. In particular, the Function and End Function keywords are replaced with the **Sub** and **End Sub** keywords (lines 19 and 39 of Fig. 13.17), respectively. Another difference is that there's no return type, because Sub procedures do *not* return values.

   Note that the variable earnings and the constant HOUR_LIMIT are now in procedure DisplayPay. In Fig. 7.14, they were located in the calculateButton_Click event handler—they're no longer needed there, so they've been removed from that event handler.

   Lines 26–35 define the If...Then...Else statement that determines whether overtime must be calculated. The condition for this statement determines whether hours is less than or equal to constant HOUR_LIMIT. If it is, then the employee's earnings *without* overtime are calculated. Otherwise, the employee's earnings *including* overtime are calculated. Line 38 displays the result (formatted as currency) in a Label.

   When control reaches the End Sub statement, control returns to the calling procedure, calculateButton_Click (line 15 of Fig. 13.16).

Common Programming Error

Declaring a variable in a procedure's body with the same name as a parameter in the procedure header is a compilation error.

(cont.)

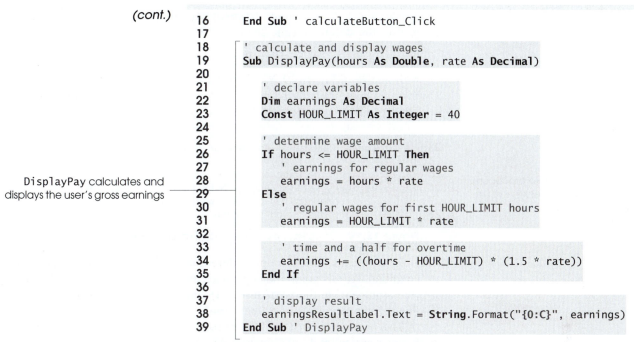

```
16        End Sub ' calculateButton_Click
17
18          ' calculate and display wages
19          Sub DisplayPay(hours As Double, rate As Decimal)
20
21             ' declare variables
22             Dim earnings As Decimal
23             Const HOUR_LIMIT As Integer = 40
24
25             ' determine wage amount
26             If hours <= HOUR_LIMIT Then
27                ' earnings for regular wages
28                earnings = hours * rate
29             Else
30                ' regular wages for first HOUR_LIMIT hours
31                earnings = HOUR_LIMIT * rate
32
33                ' time and a half for overtime
34                earnings += ((hours - HOUR_LIMIT) * (1.5 * rate))
35             End If
36
37             ' display result
38             earningsResultLabel.Text = String.Format("{0:C}", earnings)
39          End Sub ' DisplayPay
```

DisplayPay calculates and displays the user's gross earnings

Figure 13.17   Sub procedure DisplayPay definition.

6. ***Saving the project***. Select **File > Save All** to save your modified code.

The following box shows you how to add Function procedure CheckOvertime to the app. The Function determines whether an employee has worked overtime.

Creating a Function Procedure within the Wage Calculator App

Common Programming Error

Failure to return a value from a Function procedure causes the procedure to return the default value for the *return-type* (0 for numeric types, False for Booleans, Nothing for so-called reference types), often resulting in logic errors.

1. ***Creating a Function procedure header***. Add Function procedure Check-Overtime (lines 41–50 of Fig. 13.18) to your app, after the DisplayPay procedure definition. Note that the return type of the procedure is Boolean—the value returned by the procedure must be a Boolean (that is, a constant, variable or expression that evaluates to True or False).

    When CheckOvertime is called, control transfers to line 42. The arguments passed to this procedure (passed in the procedure call, which you write in the next step) are stored in the parameters total (the total hours worked) and limit (the maximum hours before overtime is paid). Line 46 returns the Boolean value True, to indicate that the employee has worked overtime; line 48 returns the Boolean value False, to indicate that the employee has not worked overtime. Program control and the value (either True or False) are returned to the line where CheckOvertime was initially called.

```
39        End Sub ' DisplayPay
40
41          ' determine whether overtime pay has been earned
42          Function CheckOvertime(total As Double,
43             limit As Integer) As Boolean
44
45             If total > limit Then
46                Return True ' return True if over limit
47             Else
48                Return False ' return False otherwise
49             End If
50          End Function ' CheckOvertime
51     End Class ' WageCalculatorForm
```

CheckOvertime determines whether the user has worked overtime

Figure 13.18   Function procedure CheckOverTime definition.

(cont.)   2. ***Modifying Sub procedure DisplayPay.*** In Sub procedure DisplayPay, replace the statement (line 26 of Fig. 13.17)

```
If hours <= HOUR_LIMIT Then
```

with line 26 of Fig. 13.19. We modify DisplayPay so that it now calls Function procedure CheckOvertime to determine whether the employee qualifies for overtime pay.

```
23          Const HOUR_LIMIT As Integer = 40
24
25          ' determine wage amount
26          If CheckOvertime(hours, HOUR_LIMIT) = False Then
27              ' earnings for regular wages
28              earnings = hours * rate
```

Call to procedure CheckOvertime — *(points to line 26)*

Figure 13.19 DisplayPay calls Function procedure CheckOvertime.

Line 26 calls Function procedure CheckOvertime in the If statement's condition. At this point, the app copies the values of hours and HOUR_LIMIT (the arguments in the procedure call), and control transfers to the header of Function procedure CheckOvertime.

The parameters in CheckOvertime's header are initialized to copies of hours's and HOUR_LIMIT's values. The Function's return value is compared to the value False in line 26. Note that this line can also be written as

```
If Not CheckOvertime(hours, HOUR_LIMIT) Then
```

Now when the **Calculate** Button is clicked, DisplayPay is called and executed. Recall that Function procedure CheckOvertime is called by the DisplayPay Sub procedure. This sequence of calls is repeated every time the user clicks the **Calculate** Button.

3. ***Running the app.*** Select **Debug > Start Debugging** to run your app. Enter an hourly wage and number of hours worked (less than *or equal to* 40), then click the **Calculate** Button. Verify that the appropriate earnings are displayed. Change the number of hours worked to a value over 40 and click the **Calculate** Button again. Verify that the appropriate output is displayed.

4. ***Closing the app.*** Close your running app by clicking its close box.

Figure 13.20 presents the source code for the **Wage Calculator** app. The lines of code that contain new programming concepts you learned in this chapter are highlighted.

```
1    Public Class WageCalculatorForm
2        ' handles Calculate Button's Click event
3        Private Sub calculateButton_Click(sender As System.Object,
4            e As System.EventArgs) Handles calculateButton.Click
5
6            ' declare variables
7            Dim userHours As Double ' hours worked
8            Dim wage As Decimal ' hourly wages
9
10           ' assign values from user input
11           userHours = Val(hoursTextBox.Text)
12           wage = Val(wageTextBox.Text)
13
14           ' call DisplayPay Sub procedure
15           DisplayPay(userHours, wage)
16       End Sub ' calculateButton_Click
```

Call to Sub procedure that calculates and displays wages — *(points to line 15)*

Figure 13.20 Code for **Wage Calculator** app. (Part 1 of 2.)

Sub procedure header specifies parameter names and types

Call to **Function** procedure that determines whether user has worked overtime

End Sub keywords indicate the end of **Sub** procedure definition

Function procedure header specifies parameter names and types as well as a return type

End Function keywords indicate the end of **Function** procedure definition

```
17
18       ' calculate and display wages
19       Sub DisplayPay(hours As Double, rate As Decimal)
20
21           ' declare variables
22           Dim earnings As Decimal
23           Const HOUR_LIMIT As Integer = 40
24
25           ' determine wage amount
26           If CheckOvertime(hours, HOUR_LIMIT) = False Then
27               ' earnings for regular wages
28               earnings = hours * rate
29           Else
30               ' regular wages for first HOUR_LIMIT hours
31               earnings = HOUR_LIMIT * rate
32
33               ' time and a half for overtime
34               earnings += ((hours - HOUR_LIMIT) * (1.5 * rate))
35           End If
36
37           ' display result
38           earningsResultLabel.Text = String.Format("{0:C}", earnings)
39       End Sub ' DisplayPay
40
41       ' determine whether overtime pay has been earned
42       Function CheckOvertime(total As Double,
43           limit As Integer) As Boolean
44
45           If total > limit Then
46               Return True ' return True if over limit
47           Else
48               Return False ' return False otherwise
49           End If
50       End Function ' CheckOvertime
51   End Class ' WageCalculatorForm
```

Figure 13.20   Code for **Wage Calculator** app. (Part 2 of 2.)

SELF-REVIEW   1. Arguments passed to a procedure can be _____.

    a) constants   b) expressions

    c) variables   d) All of the above

2. The _____ is a comma-separated list of declarations in a procedure header.

    a) argument list   b) parameter list

    c) value list   d) variable list

Answers: 1) d. 2) b.

13.5 Using the Debugger: Debugging Controls

Now you continue your study of the debugger by learning about the debugging controls on the **Standard** toolbar (Fig. 13.21). These ToolStripButtons provide convenient access to commands in the **Debug** menu. If the **Standard** toolbar isn't visible in the IDE, select **View > Toolbars > Standard**. In this section, you learn how to use the debug toolbar buttons to verify that a procedure's code is executing correctly. In the following box, we use the debug toolbar buttons to examine the **Wage Calculator** app.

Start Debugging   Step Into   Step Over

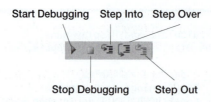

Stop Debugging   Step Out

Figure 13.21   Debugging controls (known as **ToolStripButton**s) on the **Standard** toolbar.

Using the Debugger:
Debugging Controls

1. ***Opening the completed app.*** If your completed **Wage Calculator** app is not open, double click the `WageCalculator2.sln` file in the directory `C:\SimplyVB2010\WageCalculator2` to open it.

2. ***Setting a breakpoint.*** Set a breakpoint in line 15 by clicking in the margin indicator bar (Fig. 13.22).

3. ***Starting the debugger.*** To start the debugger, select **Debug > Start Debugging**. The **Wage Calculator** app executes. Enter the value 7.50 in the **Hourly wage:** TextBox, and enter 35 in the **Weekly hours:** TextBox. Click the **Calculate** Button.

Breakpoint set at a line
containing a procedure call

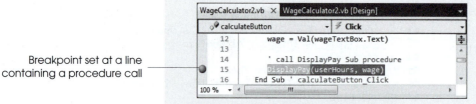

Figure 13.22   Setting a breakpoint.

4. ***Using the Step Into ToolStripButton.*** The **Step Into** ToolStripButton ( ) executes the app's next statement (the yellow highlighted line on your screen). If the next statement to execute is a procedure call (Fig. 13.23) and you click the **Step Into** ToolStripButton, control transfers to the called procedure so you can execute the procedure's statements and confirm that they execute properly. Click the **Step Into** ToolStripButton to enter procedure `DisplayPay` (Fig. 13.24).

Next statement to execute
is a procedure call

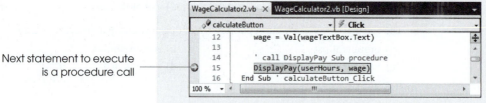

Figure 13.23   Statement calls procedure `DisplayPay`.

Control transfers to the
procedure definition

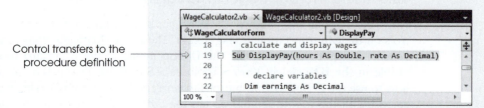

Figure 13.24   Using the **Standard** toolbar's **Step Into** `ToolStripButton`.

5. ***Clicking the Step Over ToolStripButton.*** Click the **Step Over** ToolStripButton ( ) to execute the current statement (line 19 in Fig. 13.24) without stepping into it and transfer control to line 26 (Fig. 13.25).

(cont.)

Procedure `CheckOverTime` executes the current statement without stepping into it when you click the **Step Over** `ToolStripButton`

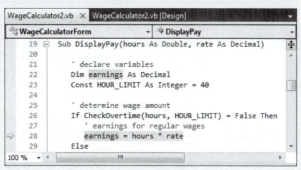

Figure 13.25   Using the **Standard** toolbar's **Step Over** `ToolStripButton`.

6. *Clicking the Step Over ToolStripButton again*. Click the **Step Over** `ToolStripButton`. **Step Over** behaves like the **Step Into** when the next statement to execute *does not* contain a procedure call. If the next statement to execute contains a procedure call, the called procedure executes in its entirety (without showing you the procedure's statements), and the yellow arrow advances to the next executable line in the current procedure (Fig. 13.26).

```vb
19 ⊟    Sub DisplayPay(hours As Double, rate As Decimal)
20
21          ' declare variables
22          Dim earnings As Decimal
23          Const HOUR_LIMIT As Integer = 40
24
25          ' determine wage amount
26          If CheckOvertime(hours, HOUR_LIMIT) = False Then
27              ' earnings for regular wages
28              earnings = hours * rate
29          Else
```

Figure 13.26   Using the **Standard** toolbar's **Step Over** `ToolStripButton` again.

7. *Setting a breakpoint*. Set a breakpoint at the end of procedure `Display-Pay` in line 39 (End Sub) of Fig. 13.27. You'll make use of this breakpoint in the next step.

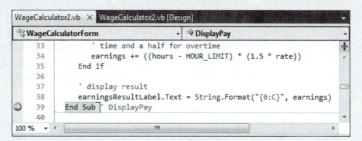

Figure 13.27   Using the **Standard** toolbar's **Continue** `ToolStripButton`.

8. *Using the* **Continue** `ToolStripButton`. Clicking the **Continue** `ToolStrip-Button` (▶) executes any statements between the next executable statement and the next breakpoint or simply continues program execution if there are no more breakpoints. Note that there's one executable statement (line 38) before the breakpoint that was set in *Step 7*. Click the **Continue** `Tool-StripButton`. The next executable statement is now line 39 (Fig. 13.27). This feature is particularly useful when you have many lines of code before the next breakpoint that you do not want to step through line by line.

(cont.)

9. ***Using the Stop Debugging* ToolStripButton**. Click the **Stop Debugging** ToolStripButton (⬛) to end the debugging session and return the IDE to design mode.

10. ***Starting the debugger.*** We have one last feature to present that requires you to start the debugger again. Start the debugger, as you did in *Step 3*, entering the same values as input, then click the app's **Calculate** Button. Keep the breakpoint in line 15 (Fig. 13.22) and remove the breakpoint from line 39.

11. ***Using the Step Into* ToolStripButton**. Repeat *Step 4*.

12. ***Clicking the Step Out* ToolStripButton**. Often, in lengthy procedures, you want to look at a few key lines of code and then continue debugging the caller's code. The **Step Out** feature is useful for such situations, where you do not want to continue stepping through the entire procedure line by line.

   After you've stepped into the DisplayPay procedure, click the **Step Out** ToolStripButton (⬛) to execute the statements in the procedure and return control to line 15, which contains the procedure call.

13. ***Clicking the Stop Debugging* ToolStripButton**. Click the **Stop Debugging** ToolStripButton to end the debugging session.

14. ***Closing the IDE.*** Close the Visual Basic IDE by clicking its close box.

SELF-REVIEW

1. During debugging, the _____ ToolStripButton executes the remaining statements in the current procedure call and returns program control to the place where the procedure was called.

   a) **Step Into**   b) **Step Out**

   c) **Step Over**   d) **Steps**

2. The _____ ToolStripButton behaves like the **Step Into** ToolStripButton when the next statement to execute does not contain a procedure call.

   a) **Step Into**   b) **Step Out**

   c) **Step Over**   d) **Steps**

Answers: 1) b. 2) c.

13.6 Optional Parameters

It's not uncommon for a program to invoke a procedure repeatedly with the same argument value for a particular parameter. In such cases, you can specify that such a parameter is an **Optional parameter** that has a default value. In a procedure call, when the argument for an Optional parameter is omitted, the compiler rewrites the procedure call and inserts the Optional parameter's default value. There are three rules for using Optional parameters:

■ Each Optional parameter must have a default value.

■ The default value must be a constant expression (typically a literal value, such as a numeric value or a string literal).

■ All parameters that appear after an Optional parameter in the parameter list, must also be Optional parameters.

Consider the Function BoxVolume that calculates the volume of a box (i.e., length times width times height):

```
Function BoxVolume(Optional length As Integer = 1,
   Optional width As Integer = 1,
   Optional height As Integer = 1) As Integer

   Return length * width * height
End Function ' BoxVolume
```

In this case, all three parameters are optional, as specified by the `Optional` keyword before each parameter's declaration. Notice that each parameter has a default value specified with an = and a literal value (1). If `BoxVolume` is invoked with fewer than three `Integer` arguments, the value 1 will be specified for each omitted argument. You can now invoke `Function BoxVolume` several different ways:

```
BoxVolume() ' returns 1; default values used for length, width, height
BoxVolume(10) ' returns 10; default values used for width, height
BoxVolume(10, 20) ' returns 200; default value used for height
BoxVolume(10, 20, 30) ' returns 6000; no default values used
BoxVolume(, 20, 30) ' returns 600; default value used for length
BoxVolume(10, , 30) ' returns 300; default value used for width
```

Arguments can be omitted for any parameter. For example, the last two method calls omitted the `length` and `width` parameters, respectively. Notice that comma placeholders are used when an omitted argument is not the last argument in the call.

13.7 Wrap-Up

In this chapter, you learned about the difference between `Function` and `Sub` procedures, and you learned how procedures can be used to organize an app better. From this point forward, we frequently refer to `Function` and `Sub` procedures simply as methods. This chapter introduced you to the concept called code reuse, showing how time and effort can be saved by using preexisting code. You used preexisting code provided by the .NET Framework Class Library and learned to create your own code that can be used in other apps.

You learned the syntax for creating and invoking the two types of procedures. You learned the components of a procedure, including the procedure header, parameter list, and (in the case of `Function` procedures) the return type and `Return` statement. After learning how to develop and write procedures, you learned about the order of execution that occurs from the line where a procedure is called (invoked) to the procedure definition, and about returning control back to the point of invocation. In this chapter's apps, you created three `Function` procedures—`Square`, `Maximum` and `CheckOvertime`—and a `Sub` procedure (`DisplayPay`).

After creating the procedures in this chapter, you learned how to debug the procedures in the app by using the `ToolStripButtons` in the **Standard** toolbar. These `ToolStripButtons` (including **Step Into**, **Step Out** and **Step Over**) can be used to determine whether a procedure is executing correctly. Finally, you learned how to declare and use `Optional` parameters.

In the next chapter, you'll learn about such controls as `GroupBoxes` and `DateTimePickers` and use them to build a **Shipping Time** app. This app controls information about a package being shipped from one location to another.

SKILLS SUMMARY

Creating a `Function` Procedure

- Use keyword `Function` to begin the procedure.
- Specify a parameter list in parentheses declaring each parameter's name and type.
- Place the keyword `As` and the return type after the parenthesis that terminates the parameter list.
- Press *Enter* to generate the terminating `End Function` statement.
- Add code to the procedure's body to perform a specific task.
- Return a value with the `Return` statement.

Using a `Function` Procedure

- Use a `Function` procedure when a value needs to be returned to the caller.

Returning a Value from a `Function` Procedure

- Use the `Return` keyword followed by the value to be returned.

Creating a Sub Procedure

- Start the procedure header with keyword Sub.
- Specify a parameter list in parentheses declaring each parameter's name and type.
- Press *Enter* to generate the terminating End Sub statement.
- Add code to the procedure's body to perform a specific task.

Invoking a Procedure

- Specify the procedure name and any arguments in parentheses.
- Ensure that the arguments passed match the procedure definition's parameters in number, type and order.

Using the Debugging Controls in the Standard Toolbar

- To execute a procedure while stepping through your code in the debugger, click the **Step Into** ToolStripButton if you'd like to view the execution of that procedure's body statements.
- To step out of a procedure in the debugger, click the **Step Out** ToolStripButton to return to the caller.
- When you wish to execute a procedure in your code without stepping through it in the debugger, click the **Step Over** ToolStripButton.

Specifying Optional Parameters in a Procedure Definition

- Place the keyword Optional before the declaration of each parameter that should have a default value.
- Follow the parameter's type with an = and its default value.

KEY TERMS

argument—Information provided to a procedure call.

callee—The procedure being called.

caller—The procedure that calls another procedure. Also known as the calling procedure.

divide-and-conquer technique—Constructing large apps from small, manageable pieces to make development and maintenance of large apps easier.

End Function keywords—Indicate the end of a Function procedure.

End Sub keywords—Indicate the end of a Sub procedure.

Function keyword—Begins the definition of a Function procedure.

Function procedure—A procedure similar to a Sub procedure, with one important difference: Function procedures return a value to the caller, whereas Sub procedures do not.

invoking a procedure—Causing a procedure to perform its designated task.

Max method of class Math—A method of class Math which returns the greater of its two arguments.

method—A procedure contained in a class.

Min method of class Math—A method of class Math which returns the lesser of its two arguments.

Optional parameter—A parameter that's specified with a default value. If the corresponding argument is omitted in the procedure call, the default value is supplied by the compiler.

Parameter Info **feature of the IDE**—Provides information about procedures and their arguments.

parameter—A variable declared in a procedure's parameter list that can be used in the body of the procedure.

parameter list—A comma-separated list in which the procedure declares each parameter's name and type.

procedure—A set of instructions for performing a particular task.

procedure body—The declarations and statements that appear after the procedure header but before the keywords End Sub or End Function. The procedure body contains Visual Basic code that performs actions, generally by manipulating or interacting with the parameters from the parameter list.

procedure call—Invokes a procedure, specifies the procedure name and provides arguments that the callee (the procedure being called) requires to perform its task.

procedure definition—The procedure header, body and ending statement.

procedure header—The first line of a procedure (including the keyword Sub or Function, the procedure name, the parameter list and the Function procedure return type).

procedure name—Follows the keyword Sub or Function and distinguishes one procedure from another. A procedure name can be any valid identifier.

programmer-defined procedure—A procedure created by a programmer to meet the unique needs of a particular app.

Return keyword—Signifies the return statement that sends a value back to the procedure's caller.

Return statement—Used to return a value from a Function procedure.

return type—Data type of the result returned from a Function procedure.

reusing code—The practice of using existing code to build new code. Reusing code saves time, effort and money.

Sqrt method of class Math—A method of class Math which returns the square root of its argument.

Sub keyword—Begins the definition of a Sub procedure.

Sub procedure—A procedure similar to a Function procedure, with one important difference: Sub procedures do not return a value to the caller, whereas Function procedures do.

CONTROLS, EVENTS, PROPERTIES & METHODS

Math   This class provides methods used to perform common arithmetic calculations.

■ *Methods*

Min—Returns the lesser of two numeric values.

Max—Returns the greater of two numeric values.

Sqrt—Returns the square root of a numeric value.

MULTIPLE-CHOICE QUESTIONS

13.1 A procedure defined with keyword Sub _____.

a) must specify a return type   b) does not accept arguments

c) returns a value   d) does not return a value

13.2 The technique of developing large apps from small, manageable pieces is known as _____.

a) divide and conquer   b) returning a value

c) click and mortar   d) a building-block algorithm

13.3 What is the difference between Sub and Function procedures?

a) Sub procedures return values, Function procedures do not.

b) Function procedures return values, Sub procedures do not.

c) Sub procedures accept parameters, Function procedures do not.

d) Function procedures accept parameters, Sub procedures do not.

13.4 What occurs after a procedure call is made?

a) Control is given to the called procedure. After the procedure is run, the app continues execution at the point where the procedure call was made.

b) Control is given to the called procedure. After the procedure is run, the app continues execution with the statement after the called procedure's definition.

c) The statement before the procedure call is executed.

d) The app terminates.

13.5 Functions can return _____ value(s).

a) zero   b) exactly one

c) one or more   d) any number of

13.6 Which of the following must be true when making a procedure call to a procedure that does not have Optional parameters?

   a) The number of arguments in the procedure call must match the number of parameters in the procedure header.

   b) The argument types must be compatible with their corresponding parameter types.

   c) Both (a) and (b)   d) None of the above

13.7 Which of the following statements correctly returns the variable value from a Function procedure?

   a) `Return Dim value`   b) `Return value As Integer`

   c) `value Return`   d) `Return value`

13.8 The _____ ToolStripButton executes the next statement in the app. If the next statement to execute contains a procedure call, the called procedure executes in its entirety.

   a) **Step Into**   b) **Step Out**

   c) **Step Over**   d) **Steps**

13.9 The first line of a procedure (including the keyword Sub or Function, the procedure name, the parameter list and the Function procedure return type) is known as the procedure _____.

   a) body   b) title

   c) caller   d) header

13.10 Method _____ of class Math calculates the square root of the value passed as an argument.

   a) `SquareRoot`   b) `Root`

   c) `Sqrt`   d) `Square`

EXERCISES

13.11 *(Temperature Converter App)* Write an app that performs temperature conversions (Fig. 13.28). The app should perform two types of conversions: degrees Fahrenheit to degrees Celsius, and degrees Celsius to degrees Fahrenheit.

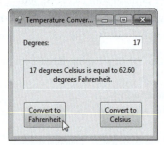 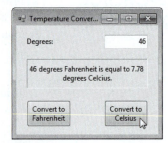

Figure 13.28 Temperature Converter GUI.

   a) *Copying the template to your working directory.* Copy the directory `C:\Examples\Ch13\Exercises\TemperatureConversion` to your `C:\SimplyVB2010` directory.

   b) *Opening the app's template file.* Double click `TemperatureConversion.sln` in the `TemperatureConversion` directory to open the app.

   c) *Converting Fahrenheit to Celsius.* To convert degrees Fahrenheit to degrees Celsius, use this formula:

```
celsius = (5 / 9) * (fahrenheit - 32)
```

   d) *Converting Celsius to Fahrenheit.* To convert degrees Celsius to degrees Fahrenheit, use this formula:

```
fahrenheit = (9 / 5) * celsius + 32
```

   e) *Adding event handlers to your app.* Double click each Button to add the proper event handlers to your app. These event handlers call procedures (that you define in the next step) to convert the degrees entered to either Fahrenheit or Celsius. Each event handler displays the result in the app's output Label.

f) *Adding `Function` procedures to your app.* Create Function procedures to perform each conversion, using the formulas above. The user should provide the temperature to convert.

g) *Formatting the temperature output.* To format the temperature information, use the String.Format method. Use F as the formatting code to limit the temperature to two decimal places.

h) *Running the app.* Select **Debug > Start Debugging** to run your app. Enter a temperature value. Click the **Convert to Fahrenheit** Button and verify that the correct output is displayed based on the formula given. Click the **Convert to Celsius** Button and again verify that the output is correct.

i) *Closing the app.* Close your running app by clicking its close box.

j) *Closing the IDE.* Close the Visual Basic IDE by clicking its close box.

13.12 *(Display Square App)* Write an app that displays a solid square composed of a character entered by the user (Fig. 13.29). The user also should input the size.

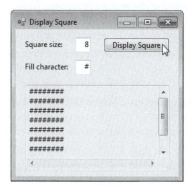

Figure 13.29   Display Square app.

a) *Copying the template to your working directory.* Copy the directory C:\Examples\Ch13\Exercises\DisplaySquare to your C:\SimplyVB2010 directory.

b) *Opening the app's template file.* Double click DisplaySquare.sln in the DisplaySquare directory to open the app.

c) *Adding a Sub procedure.* Write a Sub procedure DisplaySquare to display the solid square. The size (the length of each side) should be specified by the Integer parameter size. The character that fills the square should be specified by the String parameter fillCharacter. Use a For...Next statement nested within another For...Next statement to create the square. The outer For...Next specifies what row is currently being displayed. The inner For...Next appends all the characters that form the row to a display String. Use the multiline TextBox provided to display the square. For example, if size is 8 and fillCharacter is #, the app should look similar to Fig. 13.29.

d) *Adding an event handler for your Button's `Click` event.* Double click the **Display Square** Button to create the event handler. Program the event handler to call procedure DisplaySquare.

e) *Running the app.* Select **Debug > Start Debugging** to run your app. Enter a size for the square (that is, the length of each side) and a fill character. Click the **Display Square** Button. A square should be displayed of the size you specified, using the character you specified.

f) *Closing the app.* Close your running app by clicking its close box.

g) *Closing the IDE.* Close the Visual Basic IDE by clicking its close box.

13.13 *(Miles Per Gallon App)* Drivers often want to know the miles per gallon their cars get so they can estimate gasoline costs. Develop an app that allows the user to input the number of miles driven and the number of gallons used for a tank of gas and that displays the corresponding miles per gallon.

Figure 13.30 Miles Per Gallon app.

a) *Copying the template to your working directory.* Copy the directory C:\Examples\ Ch13\Exercises\MilesPerGallon to your C:\SimplyVB2010 directory.

b) *Opening the app's template file.* Double click MilesPerGallon.sln in the Miles-PerGallon directory to open the app.

c) *Calculating the miles per gallon.* Write a Function procedure MilesPerGallon that takes the number of miles driven and gallons used (entered by the user), calculates the amount of miles per gallon and returns the miles per gallon for a tankful of gas.

d) *Displaying the result.* Create a Click event handler for the **Calculate MPG** Button that invokes the Function procedure MilesPerGallon and displays the result returned from the procedure as in Fig. 13.30.

e) *Running the app.* Select **Debug > Start Debugging** to run your app. Enter a value for the number of miles driven and the number of gallons used. Click the **Calculate MPG** Button and verify that the correct output is displayed.

f) *Closing the app.* Close your running app by clicking its close box.

g) *Closing the IDE.* Close the Visual Basic IDE by clicking its close box.

What does this code do? ▶ **13.14** What does the following code do? Assume that this procedure is invoked by using Mystery(70, 80).

```
1  Sub Mystery(number1 As Integer, number2 As Integer)
2      Dim x As Integer
3      Dim y As Double
4
5      x = number1 + number2
6      y = x / 2
7
8      If y <= 60 Then
9          resultLabel.Text = "<= 60"
10     Else
11         resultLabel.Text = "Result is " & y
12     End If
13 End Sub ' Mystery
```

What's wrong with this code? ▶ **13.15** Find the error(s) in the following code, which should take an Integer value as a parameter and return the value of the parameter multiplied by 2.

```
1  Function TimesTwo(number As Integer) As Integer
2      Dim result As Integer
3
4      result = number * 2
5  End Function ' TimesTwo
```

Using the Debugger ▶ **13.16** *(Gas Pump App)* The **Gas Pump** app (Fig. 13.31) calculates the cost of gas at a local gas station. This gas station charges $3.13 per gallon for **Regular** grade gas, $3.33 per gallon for **Special** grade gas and $3.45 per gallon for **Super +** grade gas. The user enters the number of gallons to purchase and clicks the desired grade. The app calls a Sub procedure to compute the total cost from the number of gallons entered and the selected grade, then displays the result. While testing the app, you noticed that one of your totals was incorrect, given the input.

Figure 13.31   **Gas Pump** app executing correctly.

a) *Copying the template to your working directory*. Copy the directory C:\Examples\ Ch13\GasPump to your C:\SimplyVB2010 directory.

b) *Opening the app's template file.* Double click GasPump.sln in the GasPump directory to open the app.

c) *Running the app*. Select **Debug > Start Debugging** to run your app. Determine which total is incorrect.

d) *Setting a breakpoint*. Set a breakpoint at the beginning of the event handler that's providing incorrect output. For instance, if the **Regular** Button is providing incorrect output when clicked, add a breakpoint at the beginning of that Button's Click event handler. Use the debugger to help find any logic error(s) in the app.

e) *Modifying the app*. Once you've located the error(s), modify the app so that it behaves correctly.

f) *Running the app*. Select **Debug > Start Debugging** to run your app. Enter a number of gallons and click the **Regular**, **Special** and **Super +** Buttons. After each Button is clicked, verify that the total displayed is correct based on the prices given in this exercise's description.

g) *Closing the app.* Close your running app by clicking its close box.

h) *Closing the IDE.* Close the Visual Basic IDE by clicking its close box.

Programming Challenge ▶ **13.17** (*Prime Numbers App*) An Integer greater than 1 is said to be prime if it's divisible by only 1 and itself. For example, 2, 3, 5 and 7 are prime numbers, but 4, 6, 8 and 9 are not. Write an app that takes two numbers (representing a lower bound and an upper bound) and determines all of the prime numbers within the specified bounds, inclusive.

a) *Creating the app*. Create an app named PrimeNumbers and have its GUI appear as shown in Fig. 13.32. Add an event handler for the **Calculate Primes** Button's Click event.

b) *Checking for prime numbers*. Write a Function procedure Prime that returns True if a number is prime, False otherwise. To determine whether a number is prime, write a For...Next statement that counts from 2 to the square root of the number. In the body of the loop, use the Mod operator (Chapter 6) to determine whether the number is divisible by the counter variable's value (that is, the remainder is 0). If so, the number is not prime.

c) *Limiting user input*. Allow users to enter a lower bound (lower) and an upper bound (upper). Prevent the user from entering bounds less than or equal to 1, or an upper bound that's smaller than the lower bound.

d) *Displaying the prime numbers*. Call Function procedure Prime from your event handler to determine which numbers between the lower and upper bounds are prime. Then have the event handler display the prime numbers in a multiline, scrollable TextBox, as in Fig. 13.32.

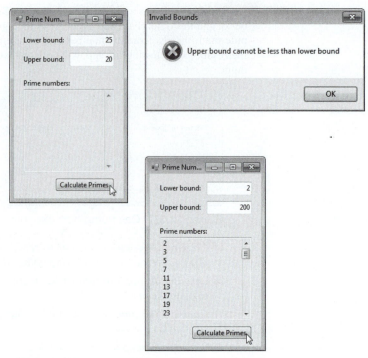

Figure 13.32 **Prime Numbers** app.

e) *Running the app.* Select **Debug > Start Debugging** to run your app. Enter a lower bound and an upper bound that's smaller than the lower bound. Click the **Calculate Primes** Button. You should receive an error message. Enter negative bounds and click the **Calculate Primes** Button. Again, you should receive an error message. Enter valid bounds and click the **Calculate Primes** Button. This time, the primes within that range should be displayed.

f) *Closing the app.* Close your running app by clicking its close box.

g) *Closing the IDE.* Close the Visual Basic IDE by clicking its close box.

Objectives

In this chapter, you'll:

- Create and manipulate **Date** variables.
- Execute code at regular intervals using a **Timer** control.
- Retrieve **Date** input with a **DateTimePicker** control.
- Group controls using a **GroupBox** control.

Outline

Shipping Time App

Using Dates and Timers

Many companies, from airlines to shipping companies, rely on date and time information in their daily operations and often require apps that reliably perform date and time calculations. In this chapter, you'll create an app that performs calculations using the Date primitive type, which enables you to store and manipulate date and time information. You'll also learn how to use a DateTimePicker control to retrieve date and time information from the user and how to group sets of controls using GroupBoxes. Finally, you'll learn how to use a Timer—a Windows Forms control that executes code at specified time intervals.

14.1 Test-Driving the Shipping Time App

In this chapter, you'll build the **Shipping Time** app. This app must meet the following requirements:

> **App Requirements**
>
> *A seafood distributor has asked you to create an app that calculates the delivery time for fresh seafood shipped from Portland, Maine, to its distribution center in Las Vegas, Nevada, where only the freshest seafood is accepted. The distributor has arrangements with local airlines to guarantee that seafood ships on flights that leave either at noon or at midnight. However, for security reasons, the airport requires the distributor to drop off the seafood at the airport at least one hour before each flight. When the distributor specifies the drop-off time, the app should display the delivery time in Las Vegas. This app should take into account the three-hour time difference (it's three hours earlier in Las Vegas) and the six-hour flight time between the two cities. The app should allow the user to select drop-off times within the current day (seafood must be shipped within a day to guarantee freshness). The app should also include a running clock that displays the current time.*

This app calculates the shipment's delivery time from the user's drop-off time, taking into account such factors as transit time and time zones. You'll use the DateTimePicker control to enable the user to enter the drop-off time. You'll use the Date properties and methods to calculate the delivery time. You'll begin by test-driving the completed app. Then you'll learn the additional Visual Basic capabilities needed to create your own version of this app.

Test-Driving the Shipping Time App

1. *Opening the completed app.* Open the directory C:\Examples\ch14\CompletedApp\ShippingTime to locate the **Shipping Time** app. Double click ShippingTime.sln to open the app in the Visual Basic IDE.

2. *Running the Shipping Time app.* Select **Debug > Start Debugging** to run the app (Fig. 14.1).

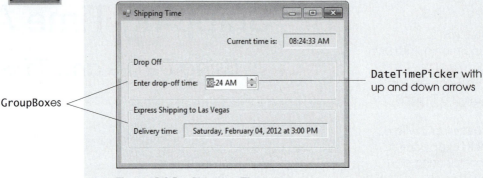

DateTimePicker with up and down arrows

GroupBoxes

Figure 14.1 **Shipping Time** app.

3. *Entering a drop-off time.* The default drop-off time is set to your computer's current time when you execute the app. When you change the drop-off time, the **Delivery time:** Label displays the delivery time based on the new time. If you select a time before 11:00 AM, the shipment arrives in Las Vegas at 3:00 PM If you specify a time between 11:00 AM and 11:00 PM, the shipment arrives in Las Vegas at 3:00 AM the following day. Finally, if you specify a time after 11:00 PM, the shipment arrives at 3:00 PM on the following day.

   The time displayed in the **Current time is:** Label updates to the current time once each second. However, the drop-off time displayed in the DateTimePicker changes only if you select different values by using the up and down arrows or by typing in a new value.

4. *Closing the app.* Click your running app's close box.

5. *Closing the IDE.* Close the Visual Basic IDE by clicking its close box.

14.2 Date Variables

Importance of correct data type

Error-Prevention Tip

Always store dates in a Date variable. Storing dates in variables of other types can lead to conversion errors and loss of data.

Choosing the correct data type in which to store information can decrease development time by simplifying code. For example, if you're using whole numbers, variables of type Integer are your best choice; if you need to store monetary values, you should use variables of type Decimal. If you want to store date information (such as the day, month, year and time), you could use separate variables to keep track of the month, day of the week, year and other date-related information. This would be a complicated task and could slow the development of apps that require date and time information.

Declaring a Date Variable

The primitive type Date simplifies manipulation, storage and display of date (and time) information. Date is the Visual Basic keyword that corresponds to the Date-Time type in the .NET Framework Class Library—the types Date and DateTime can be used interchangeably. A Date variable stores information about a point in time (for example, 12:00:00 AM on January 1, 2012). Using code, you can access a Date's properties, including the year, month, day, the hour and the minute. Your

Shipping Time app requires calculations involving time, so you use Date variables to store and manipulate this information.

You use the New keyword when creating a Date value. In the code, the statement

Date constructor ─────────────────┐

```
Dim delivery As New Date(2012, 1, 1, 0, 0, 0)
```

Date variable ─────────

declares a Date variable named delivery. The New keyword calls the Date's **constructor**—a procedure that initializes an object when it's created. You'll learn how to write your own constructors in Chapter 19. The constructor used here requires six arguments—year, month, day, hour, minute and second—which are described in Fig. 14.2. The preceding statement is the preferred alternative to initializing an object in its declaration, as in

Six arguments

```
Dim delivery As Date = New Date(2012, 1, 1, 0, 0, 0)
```

which you'll see used in older Visual Basic code.

Argument	Range	Description
Initializing a Date variable using **New Date**(*year*, *month*, *day*, *hour*, *minute*, *second*)		
year	Integer values 1–9999	Specifies the year.
month	Integer values 1–12	Specifies the month of the year.
day	Integer values 1–*number of days in month*	Specifies the day of the month. Each month has 28 to 31 days depending on the month and year.
hour	Integer values 0–23	Specifies the hour of the day on a 24-hour clock. The value 0 represents 12:00 AM (midnight).
minute	Integer values 0–59	Specifies the minute of the hour.
second	Integer values 0–59	Specifies the number of elapsed seconds in the current minute.

Figure 14.2   Date constructor arguments.

Type Date actually has many so-called overloaded constructors. **Method overloading** allows you to create multiple methods with the *same name* but *different signatures*—that is, with different numbers and types of parameters, or with parameters ordered differently (by type). When an overloaded method is called, the compiler selects the proper one by examining the number, types and order (by type) of the arguments. Often, method overloading is used to create several methods with the same name that perform similar tasks on different sets of parameters (e.g., multiple constructors that enable you to initialize objects in different ways). If a type provides overloaded constructors or methods, *IntelliSense* shows a tooltip containing one of the available overloads and you can cycle through the others by clicking the tooltip. This tooltip appears when you type the opening left parenthesis after the constructor or method name. For example:

```
Dim currentTime As New Date(
```

Figure 14.3 shows an overloaded Date constructor that takes only three arguments—year, month and day. As you can see in the tooltip, this is one of Date's 11 overloaded constructors.

▲ 3 of 11 ▼ New(**year As Integer**, month As Integer, day As Integer)
Initializes a new instance of the System.DateTime structure to the specified year, month, and day.
year: *The year (1 through 9999).*

Figure 14.3   *IntelliSense* showing overloaded Date constructors.

Using Date Members

After assigning a value to a Date variable, you can access its properties using the member-access (dot) operator, as follows:

```
Dim year = delivery.Year ' retrieves Date delivery's year
Dim month = delivery.Month ' retrieves Date delivery's month
Dim day = delivery.Day ' retrieves Date delivery's day
Dim hour = delivery.Hour ' retrieves Date delivery's hour
Dim minute = delivery.Minute ' retrieves Date delivery's minute
Dim second = delivery.Second ' retrieves Date delivery's second
```

In this chapter, you'll use several Date properties and methods that can be accessed through the member-access operator.

Values in Dates cannot be added like numeric-primitive data types such as Integers and Decimals—though you can compare Dates with relational operators as you would numeric data. To add or subtract values in Date variables, you must call the correct method, using the member-access operator. Figure 14.4 demonstrates how to perform various calculations with Date variables.

Statement	Result
Assume delivery has been initialized with a Date value.	
delivery = delivery.AddHours(3)	Add 3 hours.
delivery = delivery.AddMinutes(-5)	Subtract 5 minutes.
delivery = delivery.AddDays(1)	Add 1 day.
delivery = delivery.AddMinutes(30)	Add 30 minutes.
delivery = delivery.AddHours(-12)	Subtract 12 hours.

Figure 14.4 Date methods that perform various calculations.

Common Programming Error

Date methods do not modify the Date value on which they're called. You must assign the result of the method to a variable of type Date.

The Date methods do *not* actually change the value of the Date variable on which they're called. Instead, each method returns a Date value containing the calculation's result. To change the value of Date variable delivery, you must *assign* variable delivery the value returned by the "add" method.

Visual Basic provides a simple way to assign the current date and time to a Date variable. You can use Date's Now property to assign your computer's current date and time to a Date variable:

```
Dim currentTime As Date = Date.Now
```

This assignment does not require keyword New, because the Date.Now property returns a Date value. Much like methods MessageBox.Show and String.Format, you can access the Now property of the Date type by following the type name with the member-access operator and the property name. Methods and properties accessible through the type's name, rather than a variable of that type, are known as **Shared** members. The MSDN online documentation uses the **s** symbol to indicate a Shared member.

Now that you're familiar with Date variables, you design the **Shipping Time** app by using two new controls—the GroupBox control and the DateTimePicker control. A **GroupBox** groups related controls visually by drawing a labeled box around them. GroupBoxes are especially useful for grouping controls, such as CheckBoxes, that represent related choices. A **DateTimePicker** allows users to enter date and time information efficiently.

(handwritten margin notes) use "add" to change date even subtract · using a groupbox

---

SELF-REVIEW

1. You can use the _____ method to subtract 2 days from a Date value.
   a) SubtractDays   b) AddDays
   c) SubDays   d) SubtractTime

2. The Date methods that perform calculations using Date values _____.

   a) return a new Date value   b) modify the Date value(s)
   c) do not return values   d) Either (a) or (b)

Answers: 1) b. 2) a.

14.3 Creating the Shipping Time App: Design Elements

You're now ready to begin analyzing the problem statement and developing pseudo-code. The following pseudocode describes the the **Shipping Time** app's operation:

> When the Form loads:
>   Set range of possible drop-off times to any time in the current day
>   Call sub procedure DisplayDeliveryTime to determine and display the
>   shipment's delivery time
>
> When the user changes the drop-off time:
>   Call sub procedure DisplayDeliveryTime to determine and display the
>   shipment's delivery time
>
> After one second has elapsed:
>   Update and display the current time
>
> When the DisplayDeliveryTime procedure gets called:
>   Call function DepartureTime to determine the time the shipment's flight
>   departs
>   Add 3 hours to determine the delivery time (takes into account 6 hours
>   for time of flight minus 3 hours for the time difference)
>   Display the delivery time
>
> When the DepartureTime procedure gets called:
>   Select correct Case based on the hour the shipment was dropped off
>
>   Case where the drop-off hour is 0–10 (midnight to 10:59 AM)
>   Delivery set to depart on noon flight of current day
>
>   Case where the drop-off hour is 23 (11:00–11:59 PM)
>   Delivery set to depart on noon flight of next day
>
>   Case where none of the preceding Cases match
>   Delivery set to depart on midnight flight of current day

Now that you've test-driven the **Shipping Time** app and studied its pseudocode representation, you use an ACE table to help you convert the pseudocode to Visual Basic. Figure 14.5 lists the *actions*, *controls* and *events* that help you complete your own version of this app.

Action/Control/Event (ACE) Table for the Shipping Time App

Action	Control	Event/Method
Label the app's controls	currentTimeIsLabel, dropOffLabel, deliveryTimeLabel, dropOffGroupBox, deliveryTime-GroupBox	App is run
	ShippingTimeForm	Load
Set range of possible drop-off times to any time in the current day	dropOff-DateTimePicker	
Call sub procedure DisplayDeliveryTime to determine and display the shipment's delivery time	dropOff-DateTimePicker, lasVegasTimeLabel	

Figure 14.5 ACE table for the **Shipping Time** app. (Part 1 of 2.)

(cont.)

Action	Control	Event/Method
	dropOff- DateTimePicker	ValueChanged
Call sub procedure DisplayDeliveryTime to determine and display the shipment's delivery time	dropOff- DateTimePicker, lasVegasTimeLabel	
	clockTimer	Tick
Update and display the current time	currentTimeLabel	
		Display- DeliveryTime
Call function DepartureTime to determine the time the shipment's flight departs	dropOff- DateTimePicker	
Add three hours to determine the delivery time		
Display the delivery time	lasVegasTimeLabel	
		DepartureTime
Select correct Case based on the hour the shipment was dropped off	dropOff- DateTimePicker	
Case where drop-off hour is 0–10 Delivery set to depart on noon flight		

Case where drop-off hour is 23
    Delivery set to depart on noon flight
    of next day		

Case where none of the preceding Cases match
    Delivery set to depart on midnight
    flight of current day		

Figure 14.5   ACE table for the **Shipping Time** app. (Part 2 of 2.)

The following box demonstrates how to insert a GroupBox control into your app.

Placing Controls in a GroupBox

1. ***Copying the template to your working directory.*** Copy the C:\Examples\ ch14\TemplateApp\ShippingTime to your C:\SimplyVB2010 directory.

2. ***Opening the Shipping Time app's template file.*** Double click Shipping-Time.sln in the ShippingTime directory to open the app in the Visual Basic IDE.

3. ***Displaying the template Form.*** Double click ShippingTime.vb in the **Solution Explorer** window to display the Form in the IDE.

4. ***Inserting a GroupBox control in the Form.*** The template includes a Group-Box that displays the seafood-shipment delivery time. Add a second Group-Box to contain the drop-off time by double clicking the GroupBox control,

    GroupBox

   in the **Containers** tab of the **Toolbox**. Change the Text property to Drop Off and the Name property to dropOffGroupBox. Place the GroupBox above the provided GroupBox and make them the same size. After these modifications, your Form should look like Fig. 14.6.

 **GUI Design Tip**

GroupBox titles should be concise and should use book-title capitalization.

Good Programming Practice

Append the GroupBox suffix to GroupBox control names.

(cont.)

Newly created GroupBox displaying the text **Drop Off**

GroupBoxes

Figure 14.6   GroupBox controls on the **Shipping Time** Form.

5. ***Creating Labels inside the GroupBox.*** To place a Label inside the Group-Box, click the Label control in the **Toolbox** then click inside the GroupBox (Fig. 14.7)—you can also drag any control from the **Toolbox** and drop it inside a GroupBox. Change the Label's Text property to Enter drop-off time: and its Name property to dropOffLabel. Then change the position of the Label by setting its Location property to 6, 33—this value aligns it with the **Delivery time:** Label.

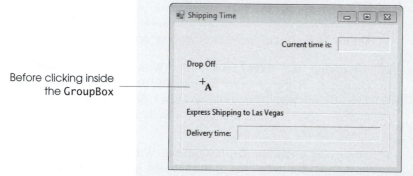

Before clicking inside the GroupBox

Figure 14.7   Adding a Label to a GroupBox.

GUI Design Tip

Use GroupBoxes to group related controls in a box with a title.

The Location values you entered are measured from the top-left corner of the GroupBox, not the Form. Objects that contain controls, such as Forms, GroupBoxes and Panels (which you'll use in Chapter 19) are called **containers.** The Location of a control is measured from the *top-left* corner of its container object.

If a GroupBox is placed over a control that's already on the Form, the control will be behind the GroupBox (that is, the GroupBox hides the control by covering it). To avoid this problem, remove all controls from the area in which you wish to place the GroupBox control before inserting it. You can then either drag and drop existing controls into the GroupBox or add new controls as needed as described earlier.

6. ***Saving the project.*** Select **File > Save All** to save your changes.

You've now added a GroupBox and a Label to the **Shipping Time** app to display the drop-off time. In the following box, you add a DateTimePicker control to retrieve the drop-off time from the user.

Recall that the DateTimePicker retrieves date and time information from the user. The DateTimePicker allows you to select from several predefined date and time formats (for example, date formats like 12/31/2012 and Monday, December 31, 2012; and time formats like 2:00:00 PM), or you can create your own format. The date and time information is then stored in a variable of type Date, which you can manipulate using Date methods. The format limits the date and/or time information the user can see, but does not alter the Date value stored in the DateTimePicker.

Creating and Customizing the DateTimePicker

GUI Design Tip

Each DateTimePicker should have a corresponding descriptive Label.

Good Programming Practice

Append the DateTimePicker suffix to DateTimePicker control names.

GUI Design Tip

Use a DateTimePicker to retrieve date and time information from the user.

Error-Prevention Tip

Be cautious when using the Custom-Format property to specify a Date-TimePicker's display. The format may be interpreted differently based on your locale.

Error-Prevention Tip

If the user is to specify a date and/or time, use a DateTimePicker control to prevent the user from entering invalid date or time values.

1. **Adding the DateTimePicker.** To add a DateTimePicker to your app, drag a DateTimePicker control

from the **Toolbox** and drop it to the right of the **Enter drop-off time:** Label to place it in the GroupBox. Your Form should look similar to Fig. 14.8. (Your control contains your computer's current date.)

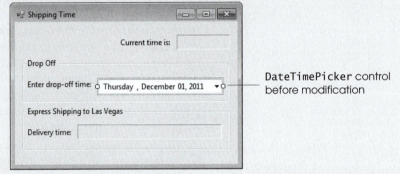

Figure 14.8 DateTimePicker control on the Form.

2. **Modifying the DateTimePicker.** With the DateTimePicker selected, change its Name property to dropOffDateTimePicker. Align the Date-TimePicker with its descriptive Label. Next, change its **Format** property to Custom. This indicates that you'll specify how the date appears in the Date-TimePicker.

3. **Specifying a custom display format.** When the DateTimePicker's Format property is set to Custom, it displays the date and time using the custom format that you specify in the **CustomFormat** property. The DateTimePicker now displays the date in the format 12/1/2011, the default format when the Format property is set to Custom and you have not set CustomFormat property.

   Set the CustomFormat property to hh:mm tt. This property is case sensitive. The "hh" displays the hour as a number from 01 to 12, the ":" inserts a colon and the "mm" indicates that the number of minutes from 00 to 59 should follow the colon. The "tt" indicates that AM or PM should appear, depending on the time of day. You can find an extensive list of date and time formats at msdn2.microsoft.com/en-us/library/8kb3ddd4.aspx. The Format property eliminates the problem of a user's entering a letter or symbol when the app expects a number—the DateTimePicker does *not* allow values in any format other than what you specify in the Format or Custom-Format properties. The DateTimePicker also prevents the user from specifying an invalid time, such as 32:15. Resize the DateTimePicker to a size appropriate for this time-only format.

(cont.)

4. ***Using up and down arrows in the DateTimePicker.*** Set the DateTime-Picker's **ShowUpDown** property to True. This allows the user to select the date or time by clicking the up or down arrows that appear on the control's right side, much like a NumericUpDown control. When the property is set to False (the default), a down arrow appears on the control's right side (Fig. 14.8). Clicking the down arrow causes a month calendar to appear, allowing the user to select a date (but not a time). A demonstration of the month calendar is shown in the Controls, Events, Properties & Methods section at the end of this chapter. For this app, the user needs to enter only the time of day, so you use up and down arrows to allow the user to select the time (Fig. 14.9).

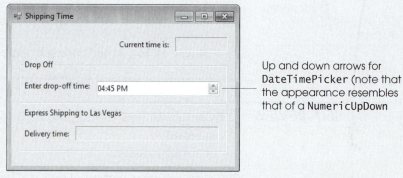

Up and down arrows for DateTimePicker (note that the appearance resembles that of a NumericUpDown

Figure 14.9   Customized DateTimePicker control on the Form.

5. ***Saving the project.*** Select **File > Save All** to save your modified code.

The final control you add to the Form is a Timer. You use the Timer control to generate events that help you display the current time of day on the Form.

Creating a Timer Control

1. ***Adding a Timer control.*** A Timer control is an object that can run code at a specified time interval in milliseconds (1/1000s of a second) by generating a Tick event. By default, the Timer runs code every 100 milliseconds (1/10 of a second). Each time the Tick event occurs, its event handler executes. You can customize the "wake period" (the amount of time between Timer Tick events) and the code it executes (the event handler for the Tick event) so that a certain task is performed once every "wake up" period.

   Add a Timer to the Form by dragging and dropping the Timer control

    Timer

   from the **Toolbox**'s **Components** tab onto the Form. The Timer does *not* actually appear on the Form—rather, it appears below the Form designer in an area called the **component tray** (Fig. 14.10). The Timer control is placed there because it's not part of the graphical user interface—it's a control that operates in the background to generate events.

2. ***Customizing the Timer control.*** Rename the Timer by setting its Name property to clockTimer. To allow the Timer to generate Tick events, set the Timer's Enabled property to True. Then set its **Interval** property to 1000, which specifies the number of milliseconds between Tick events (1,000 milliseconds = 1 second).

3. ***Saving the project.*** Select **File > Save All** to save your modified code.

(cont.)

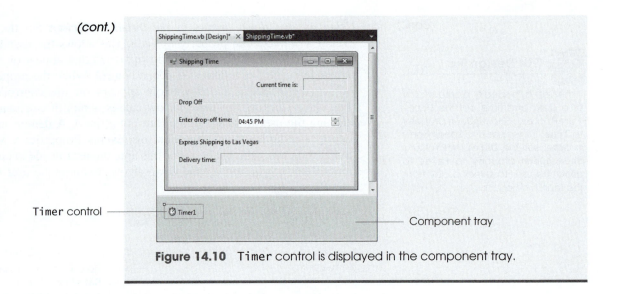

Timer control ——

—— Component tray

Figure 14.10 Timer control is displayed in the component tray.

SELF-REVIEW

1. By default, the Timer control generates a Tick event every _____.

   a) second   b) 100 seconds

   c) 100 milliseconds   d) half a second

2. Setting the Format property of the DateTimePicker control to _____ allows you to specify how the date and/or time appears in the DateTimePicker.

   a) Custom   b) Unique

   c) User   d) Other

Answers: 1) c. 2) a.

14.4 Creating the Shipping Time App: Inserting Code

Now that you've completed the **Shipping Time** app's visual design, you'll complete the app by inserting code. You'll begin coding the app's functionality by creating a clock in the app that updates the current time every second. You'll then write code that displays the delivery time from Portland to Las Vegas. You'll implement this feature by inserting code that runs when the Form loads or whenever the user specifies a new drop-off time. In the following box, you'll write the code to create the clock.

Coding the Shipping Time App's Clock

1. **Inserting code to handle the Timer's Tick event.** Double click the Timer control in the component tray to generate the empty event handler for the Tick event. Add the comment and reformat the empty event handler as shown in lines 2–4 of Fig. 14.11. Add lines 6–8 of Fig. 14.11 to the body of the event handler. Be sure to format the event handler as shown in Fig. 14.11 to ensure that your line numbers match those in the text.

```
2    ' handles clockTimer's Tick event
3    Private Sub clockTimer_Tick(sender As System.Object,
4        e As System.EventArgs) Handles clockTimer.Tick
5
6        ' print current time
7        currentTimeLabel.Text = String.Format("{0:hh:mm:ss tt}",
8            Date.Now)
9    End Sub ' clockTimer_Tick
```

Printing the current time —— (lines 7)

Figure 14.11 Inserting code for a Tick event.

(cont.)

Lines 3–9 define the `Tick` event handler, which executes every second. Date property `Now` retrieves your computer's current time. The event handler takes this information and formats it to match the format you specify, `"{hh:mm:ss tt}"`. The Text property of `currentTimeLabel` is then set to the formatted `String` for display to the user. Recall that in the method `String.Format` the 0 corresponds to the argument that will be formatted (that is, `Date.Now`) and the text following the colon contains the format information for that argument's value. You're already familiar with the purpose of `hh:mm` and `tt`. The `:ss` following mm indicates that a colon followed by the number of seconds (00–59) should be displayed.

2. ***Saving the project.*** Select **File > Save All** to save your modified code.

Now that you've coded your app's clock, using the `Timer`'s `Tick` event handler, you insert code to display a delivery time when the app opens. You begin by creating a Load event handler for your app.

Using Code to Display a Delivery Time

1. ***Adding the ShippingTimeForm_Load event handler.*** When an app runs, the Form is displayed. However, sometimes you also want a specific action to occur when the app opens but before the Form displays. To run code when the app first opens, create an event handler for the Form's **Load** event. To create a Load event handler, return to the Windows Form Designer by clicking the **ShippingTime.vb [Design]** tab. Double click an empty area in the Form to generate the Load event handler and enter **Code** view. Be careful not to double click a control on the Form; this generates the control's event handler instead. You can double click the Form's title bar to ensure that you don't accidentally create an event handler for another control. Add the comment and reformat the empty event handler as shown in lines 11–13 of Fig. 14.12.

2. ***Storing the current date.*** Add line 15 from Fig. 14.12 into the Load event handler to store the current date in variable `currentTime`. (You store the date as a variable so that you can preserve information about the current date for use later in the event handler.)

```
11        ' initialize DateTimePicker status when Form loads
12        Private Sub ShippingTimeForm_Load(sender As System.Object,
13           e As System.EventArgs) Handles MyBase.Load
14
15           Dim currentTime As Date = Date.Now ' store current time
16        End Sub ' ShippingTimeForm_Load
```

Storing the current time in `currentTime` —— 15

Figure 14.12   Storing the current time.

3. ***Setting the drop-off hours.*** Add lines 17–22 of Fig. 14.13 to the ShippingTimeForm_Load event handler. These lines set the `MinDate` and `MaxDate` properties for `dropOffDateTimePicker`. The **MinDate** property specifies the earliest value that the `DateTimePicker` allows the user to enter. The **MaxDate** property specifies the latest value that the `DateTimePicker` allows the user to enter. Together, these two properties set the range of drop-off times from which the user can select.

(cont.)

Setting the range of
drop-off times

```
17     ' set range of possible drop-off times
18     dropOffDateTimePicker.MinDate = New Date(currentTime.Year,
19        currentTime.Month, currentTime.Day, 0, 0, 0)
20
21     dropOffDateTimePicker.MaxDate =
22        dropOffDateTimePicker.MinDate.AddDays(1)
23  End Sub ' ShippingTimeForm_Load
```

Figure 14.13 Setting the `MinDate` and `MaxDate` properties.

To guarantee freshness, the seafood shipment should be dropped off at the airline within the current day; therefore, the earliest drop-off time (`Min-Date`) is set to 12:00 A.M (midnight). of the current day (lines 18–19), and the latest drop-off time (`MaxDate`) is set to 12:00 AM the following day (lines 21–22). The `MaxDate` value is calculated by adding one day to the `MinDate` value using method `AddDays`. Recall that the `AddDays` method does not change the `Date` value on which it operates—it returns a new `Date` value. This value is assigned to the `MaxDate` property in line 21.

The `Date` constructor (called in line 18) creates a value that stores a date and a time of midnight. Recall that the first parameter is the year, the second is the month and the third is the day. The last three parameters specify the hour, minute and number of seconds. A `Date` variable's `Year` property returns the value of its year as an `Integer` (for example, 2012). Its `Month` property returns the value of the `Date` variable's month as an `Integer` (for example, 6 for June). Finally, the `Date` variable's `Day` property returns the day of the month (an `Integer` between 1 and 31, depending on the month and year).

The `Date` type also provides property **Today**, which returns the current date with the time set to `00:00:00` (midnight). You can use this property to return the current date when you do not need any information about the time. You could have used property `Today` rather than `Now` in the Form's Load event handler. The `DateTimePicker`'s `MinDate` property would be set to the value returned by `Date.Today` (midnight of the current day). The `MaxDate` property would be set by adding one day to the `MinDate` property. We used the `Now` property to give you more practice using the `Date` constructor and to demonstrate the `Year`, `Month` and `Day` properties.

4. ***Calling the `DisplayDeliveryTime` procedure.*** Add lines 24–25 of Fig. 14.14 to call the `DisplayDeliveryTime` procedure. The IDE underlines the call to `DisplayDeliveryTime` in blue due to the compilation error you introduce by calling a procedure that has not yet been written. You write this procedure later in this chapter. The `DisplayDeliveryTime` procedure calculates the delivery time in Las Vegas and displays the result in the **Delivery time:** `Label`.

Displaying the delivery time

```
24     ' display the delivery time
25     DisplayDeliveryTime()
26  End Sub ' ShippingTimeForm_Load
```

Figure 14.14 Calling the `DisplayDeliveryTime` procedure.

5. ***Saving the project.*** Select **File > Save All** to save your modified code.

So far, you've added functionality that calls `DisplayDeliveryTime` to display the delivery time when the app runs initially. However, you should allow a user to select any drop-off time and to determine when the shipment will be delivered. In the following box, you'll learn how to handle the `DateTimePicker`'s **ValueChanged** event, which occurs when the user changes the `DateTimePicker`'s value.

<table>
<tr><td>

Coding the
ValueChanged Event
Handler

</td><td>

1. ***Creating the ValueChanged event handler.*** Click the **ShippingTime.vb [Design]** tab. Double click the DateTimePicker control dropOffDateTimePicker to generate its ValueChanged event handler. Add the comment and reformat the empty event handler as shown in lines 28–31 of Fig. 14.15 so that the line numbers in your code match those presented in this chapter.

2. ***Inserting code in the event handler.*** Insert lines 33–34 of Fig. 14.15 into the event handler. This code runs when the user changes the time in the DateTimePicker. The ValueChanged event handler also calls procedure DisplayDeliveryTime to calculate and display the delivery time in Las Vegas. As in the previous box, the IDE underlines the call to DisplayDeliveryTime in blue because the procedure is not yet defined. In the next box, you write the DisplayDeliveryTime procedure, after which the compilation error no longer appears.

</td></tr>
</table>

```
28        ' handles the DateTimePicker's ValueChanged event
29        Private Sub dropOffDateTimePicker_ValueChanged(
30           sender As System.Object, e As System.EventArgs) _
31           Handles dropOffDateTimePicker.ValueChanged
32
33           ' display the delivery time
34           DisplayDeliveryTime()
35        End Sub ' dropOffDateTimePicker_ValueChanged
```

Calculating and displaying the delivery time → (lines 33–34)

Figure 14.15   Inserting code in the **ValueChanged** event handler.

3. ***Saving the project.*** Select **File > Save All** to save your modified code.

Next, you'll define the DisplayDeliveryTime procedure that was called by two event handlers. You'll use Date methods to calculate and display the delivery time in an output Label.

<table>
<tr><td>

Coding the
DisplayDeliveryTime
Procedure

</td><td>

1. ***Creating the DisplayDeliveryTime procedure.*** Add lines 37–46 of Fig. 14.16 below the ValueChanged event handler. Line 40 calls the procedure DepartureTime. Note that DepartureTime is underlined in blue in the IDE. This is due to the compilation error you introduce when you call a procedure that has not yet been written. You'll write this procedure in the next box. The DepartureTime procedure determines which flight (midnight or noon) the seafood shipment will use. It returns a Date value representing the flight's departure time. Line 40 stores this value in the Date variable delivery.

</td></tr>
</table>

```
37        ' calculates and displays the delivery time
38        Sub DisplayDeliveryTime()
39           ' obtain initial delivery time
40           Dim delivery As Date = DepartureTime()
41
42           ' add 3 hours to departure and display result
43           delivery = delivery.AddHours(3)
44           lasVegasTimeLabel.Text = delivery.ToLongDateString &
45              " at " & delivery.ToShortTimeString
46        End Sub ' DisplayDeliveryTime
```

Determining the departure time → 40
Adding the travel time → 43
Displaying the delivery time → 44

Figure 14.16   DisplayDeliveryTime procedure.

(cont.)

2. ***Calculating and displaying the delivery time.*** Line 43 calculates the delivery time by adding three hours to the departure time (see the discussion following this box). Lines 44–45 display the Las Vegas delivery time by calling the Date types's ToLongDateString and ToShortTimeString methods. A Date variable's **ToLongDateString** method returns the date as a String in the format "Wednesday, October 30, 2012." A Date variable's **ToShort-TimeString** returns the time as a String in the format "4:00 PM."

3. ***Saving the project.*** Select **File > Save All** to save your modified code.

When calculating the shipment's delivery time, you must account for the time-zone difference and the flight time. For instance, if you send a shipment from Portland, Maine, to Las Vegas, it travels west three time zones (the time in Las Vegas is three hours earlier) and spends six hours in transit. If you drop off the shipment at 5:00 PM in Portland, the shipment leaves on the midnight flight and arrives in Las Vegas at

$$12\text{:}00 \text{ AM } + (\textit{time zone change } + \textit{flight time}) = 12\text{:}00 \text{ AM } + (\text{-}3 + 6) \textit{ hours}$$

which is 3:00 AM Las Vegas time. Similarly, if the shipment takes the noon flight to Las Vegas, it arrives at 3:00 PM

To complete the app, you'll need to code the DepartureTime Function procedure. You'll use a Select Case statement and Date methods to return a Date containing the departure time (noon or midnight) for the seafood shipment's flight.

Coding the DepartureTime Procedure

1. ***Writing the DepartureTime procedure.*** Insert lines 48–52 of Fig. 14.17 into your code below the DisplayDeliveryTime procedure. Line 50 stores the current date in the Date variable currentDate. Line 51 declares the Date variable departTime, the variable you use to store the DepartureTime Function procedure's return value.

```
48    ' return flight departure time for selected drop-off time
49    Function DepartureTime() As Date
50       Dim currentDate As Date = Date.Now ' store current date
51       Dim departTime As Date ' store departure time
52    End Function ' DepartureTime
53  End Class ' ShippingTimeForm
```

Declaring variables — lines 50, 51

Figure 14.17 Inserting procedure DepartureTime into the app.

2. ***Determining which flight the shipment uses.*** Insert lines 53–66 of Fig. 14.18 after the variable declarations and before the End Function statement in Fig. 14.17. The Select Case statement that begins at line 54 uses the hour specified by the user in the DateTimePicker as the controlling expression. The DateTimePicker's **Value** property (which is of type Date) contains the value selected by the user. The Date's Hour property returns the hour of the Date stored in the DateTimePicker's Value property. Recall that the Hour property stores the hour value as an Integer in the range of 0 to 23.

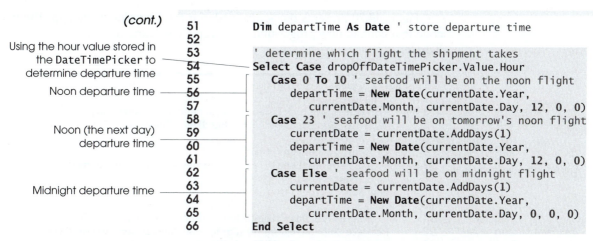

Figure 14.18 Determining the seafood shipment's flight departure time.

The first `Case` statement's expression list (line 55) determines whether the `DateTimePicker`'s value is between midnight (`Hour = 0`) and 10:59 AM (`Hour = 10`). If so, the seafood shipment takes the noon flight to Las Vegas. (Recall that the shipment must arrive at the airport at least one hour before the flight leaves.) The first `Case` statement's body (lines 56–57) stores the departure time of noon on the current day in the variable `departTime`.

The next `Case` statement's expression list (line 58) determines whether the value in the `DateTimePicker` is between 11:00 PM and 11:59 PM (`Hour = 23`). If the drop-off time occurs between 11:00 PM and 11:59 P.M, the seafood shipment takes the noon flight to Las Vegas the next day. The body of this `Case` (lines 59–61) stores the departure time of noon on the next day in the variable `departTime`.

The `Case Else`'s body executes if the controlling expression matches neither of the other two `Cases` (the value in the `DateTimePicker` is between 11:00 AM and 10:59 PM). In this case, the seafood shipment takes the midnight flight to Las Vegas. The `Case Else` (lines 63–65) stores the departure time of midnight in the variable `departTime`. Note that because midnight occurs on the following day, the `Date` variable representing midnight should contain a `Day` property value corresponding to the next day (line 63).

3. ***Returning the delivery time.*** Insert line 68 of Fig. 14.19 into the `Departure-Time` procedure following the `End Select` statement. Line 68 returns the `Date` value containing the flight departure time.

```
66            End Select
67
68            Return departTime ' return the flight's departure time
69        End Function ' DepartureTime
70    End Class ' ShippingTimeForm
```

Returning the departure time

Figure 14.19 Returning the flight departure time.

4. ***Running the app.*** Select **Debug > Start Debugging** to run your app.

5. ***Closing the app.*** Close your running app by clicking its close box.

6. ***Closing the IDE.*** Close the Visual Basic IDE by clicking its close box.

Figure 14.20 presents the source code for the **Shipping Time** app. The lines of code that contain new programming concepts you learned in this chapter are highlighted.

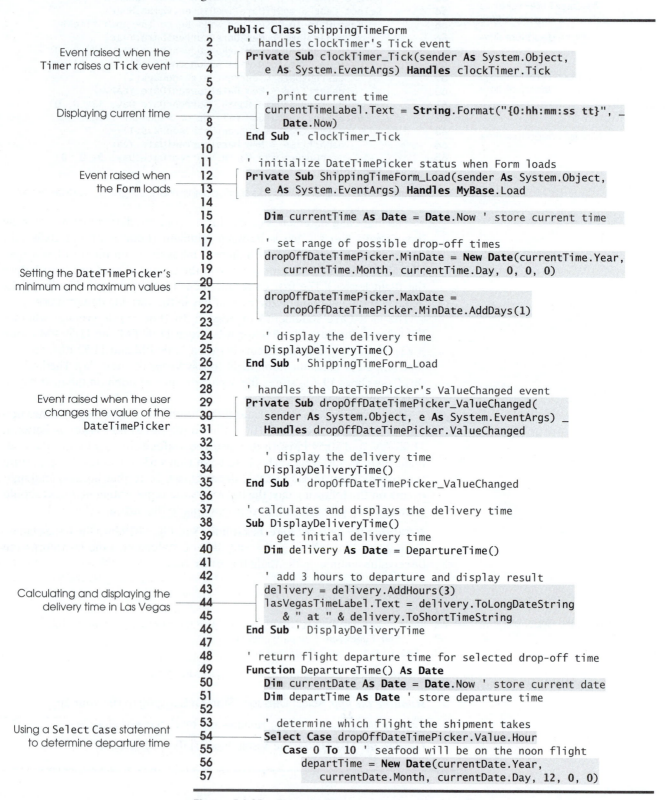

```
 1   Public Class ShippingTimeForm
 2      ' handles clockTimer's Tick event
 3      Private Sub clockTimer_Tick(sender As System.Object,
 4         e As System.EventArgs) Handles clockTimer.Tick
 5
 6         ' print current time
 7         currentTimeLabel.Text = String.Format("{0:hh:mm:ss tt}", _
 8            Date.Now)
 9      End Sub ' clockTimer_Tick
10
11      ' initialize DateTimePicker status when Form loads
12      Private Sub ShippingTimeForm_Load(sender As System.Object,
13         e As System.EventArgs) Handles MyBase.Load
14
15         Dim currentTime As Date = Date.Now ' store current time
16
17         ' set range of possible drop-off times
18         dropOffDateTimePicker.MinDate = New Date(currentTime.Year,
19            currentTime.Month, currentTime.Day, 0, 0, 0)
20
21         dropOffDateTimePicker.MaxDate =
22            dropOffDateTimePicker.MinDate.AddDays(1)
23
24         ' display the delivery time
25         DisplayDeliveryTime()
26      End Sub ' ShippingTimeForm_Load
27
28      ' handles the DateTimePicker's ValueChanged event
29      Private Sub dropOffDateTimePicker_ValueChanged(
30         sender As System.Object, e As System.EventArgs) _
31         Handles dropOffDateTimePicker.ValueChanged
32
33         ' display the delivery time
34         DisplayDeliveryTime()
35      End Sub ' dropOffDateTimePicker_ValueChanged
36
37      ' calculates and displays the delivery time
38      Sub DisplayDeliveryTime()
39         ' get initial delivery time
40         Dim delivery As Date = DepartureTime()
41
42         ' add 3 hours to departure and display result
43         delivery = delivery.AddHours(3)
44         lasVegasTimeLabel.Text = delivery.ToLongDateString
45            & " at " & delivery.ToShortTimeString
46      End Sub ' DisplayDeliveryTime
47
48      ' return flight departure time for selected drop-off time
49      Function DepartureTime() As Date
50         Dim currentDate As Date = Date.Now ' store current date
51         Dim departTime As Date ' store departure time
52
53         ' determine which flight the shipment takes
54         Select Case dropOffDateTimePicker.Value.Hour
55            Case 0 To 10 ' seafood will be on the noon flight
56               departTime = New Date(currentDate.Year,
57                  currentDate.Month, currentDate.Day, 12, 0, 0)
```

Lines with marginal annotations:

- Lines 3–4: Event raised when the Timer raises a Tick event
- Lines 7–8: Displaying current time
- Lines 12–13: Event raised when the Form loads
- Lines 18–22: Setting the DateTimePicker's minimum and maximum values
- Lines 29–31: Event raised when the user changes the value of the DateTimePicker
- Lines 43–45: Calculating and displaying the delivery time in Las Vegas
- Lines 54: Using a Select Case statement to determine departure time

Figure 14.20 **Shipping Time** app code. (Part 1 of 2.)

```
58              Case 23 ' seafood will be on tomorrow's noon flight
59                 currentDate = currentDate.AddDays(1)
60                 departTime = New Date(currentDate.Year,
61                    currentDate.Month, currentDate.Day, 12, 0, 0)
62              Case Else ' seafood will be on midnight flight
63                 currentDate = currentDate.AddDays(1)
64                 departTime = New Date(currentDate.Year,
65                    currentDate.Month, currentDate.Day, 0, 0, 0)
66           End Select
67
68           Return departTime ' return the flight's departure time
69        End Function ' DepartureTime
70     End Class ' ShippingTimeForm
```

Figure 14.20   **Shipping Time** app code. (Part 2 of 2.)

SELF-REVIEW

1. The ToShortTimeString method is called on a Date variable to return its value in the format _____.

   a) 11 o'clock   b) 23:00

   c) 11:00   d) 11:00 PM

2. DateTimePicker properties _____ and _____ specify the earliest and latest dates that can be selected, respectively.

   a) MinDate, MaxDate   b) Now, Later

   c) Minimum, Maximum   d) Early, Late

Answers: 1) d. 2) a.

14.5 Wrap-Up

In this chapter, you learned how to use the Date type to manipulate date and time information. You used variables of this type to calculate and display delivery times in your **Shipping Time** app. To help users enter date and time information, you used a DateTimePicker control. You observed how this control can display custom date and time formats and limit user input. To help you group controls on the Form visually, you used the GroupBox control. You also learned how to use the Timer control to execute code at fixed intervals specified in milliseconds.

You then used three new event handlers to help you complete the **Shipping Time** app. You learned that the Form's Load event handler executes code when the app is opened initially. You used this event to set initial values in your app. You then learned how to use the DateTimePicker control's ValueChanged event handler to execute code when the control's value changes. You used this event handler to update the delivery time each time the user entered a new time. Finally, you learned about the Timer's Tick event handler, which you used to update and display the current time in a Label that serves as a clock.

In the next chapter, you'll use the **Fund Raiser** app to introduce scope rules. This will help you understand how Visual Basic keeps track of variables throughout your app.

SKILLS SUMMARY

Executing Code When the App Opens

■ Use the Form's Load event handler to execute code when the app first opens.

Storing and Manipulating Date and Time Information

■ Use a Date variable (which corresponds to the DateTime built-in type) to store and manipulate date and time information. A Date variable stores information about a point in time (e.g., 12:00:00 AM on January 1, 2012). This information can be formatted for display in predefined long or short formats or in custom (programmer-defined) formats.

Using Date Variables

- Use keyword New to create a new Date value.

- Use property Date.Now to obtain your computer's current date and time for the local time zone.

- Use the member-access operator (.) to access properties of a Date variable, such as Years, Hours, etc.

- Use Date methods, such as AddHours and AddDays, to add or subtract time from values in Date variables. Then assign the value returned by the method to a Date variable.

Using a GroupBox Control

- Use a GroupBox control to group related controls visually. To add a GroupBox to the Form, double click the GroupBox control in the **Toolbox** or drag a GroupBox control from the **Toolbox** onto a Form.

- Use property Text to configure the title of a GroupBox.

Placing Controls Inside a GroupBox

- Place a control inside the GroupBox by clicking the control's name in the **Toolbox**, then clicking inside the GroupBox. You also can drag the control from the **Toolbox** or the Form and drop it inside the GroupBox.

Using the DateTimePicker Control

- Use a DateTimePicker control to get date and time information from the user.

- Set property Format to Custom to indicate that you'll specify how the date appears in the DateTimePicker. Specify the format in property CustomFormat.

- Set property ShowUpDown to True to allow the user to select the date or time by clicking an up or down arrow. If this property's value is False, a monthly calendar drops down, allowing the user to pick a date.

- Use the DateTimePicker's ValueChanged event handler to execute code when the value in the DateTimePicker changes.

Using the Timer Control

- Use a Timer control to execute code (the Tick event handler) at specified intervals.

- To add a Timer control to the Form, click the Timer in the **Toolbox**, then click anywhere on the Form. You also can double click the Timer in the **Toolbox**. The Timer control appears in the component tray.

- Specify the number of milliseconds between Tick events using the Interval property.

- Set the Enabled property to True so that the Tick event is raised once per Interval.

KEY TERMS

component tray—The area below the Windows Form Designer that contains controls, such as Timers, that are not part of the graphical user interface.

constructor—A procedure that initializes an object when it's created.

container—An object, such as a GroupBox or Form, that contains other controls.

CustomFormat property of a DateTimePicker control—The DateTimePicker property that contains your format string with which to display the date and/or time when DateTimePicker Format property is set to Custom.

DateTime primitive type—The .NET Framework Class Library type that corresponds to the Date keyword.

Date variable—A variable of type Date, capable of storing date and time data.

DateTimePicker control—Retrieves date and time information from the user.

Format property of a DateTimePicker control—The DateTimePicker property that allows you to specify a predefined or custom format with which to display the date and/or time.

GroupBox control—Groups related controls visually.

Interval property of a Timer control—The Timer property that specifies the number of milliseconds between Tick events.

Load event of a Form—Raised when an app initially executes.

MaxDate property of a DateTimePicker control—The DateTimePicker property that specifies the latest value that the DateTimePicker allows the user to enter.

method overloading—Allows you to create multiple methods with the same name but different signatures.

MinDate property of a DateTimePicker control—Specifies the earliest value that the control allows the user to enter.

New keyword—Used to call a constructor when creating an object.

Now property of type Date—The Date property that retrieves your computer's current time and date.

signature—Specifies a procedure's parameters and their types.

ShowUpDown property of a DateTimePicker control—The DateTimePicker property that, when True, allows the user to specify the time using up and down arrows, and, when False, allows the user to specify the date using a calendar.

Tick event of a Timer control—Raised after the number of milliseconds specified in the Timer control's Interval property has elapsed (if Enabled is True).

Timer control—Generates Tick events to run code at specified intervals.

Today property of type Date—Returns the current date with the time set to midnight.

ToLongDateString method of type Date—Returns a String containing the date in the format "Wednesday, October 30, 2002."

ToShortTimeString method of type Date—Returns a String containing the time in the format "4:00 PM."

Value property of a DateTimePicker control—Stores the value (such as a time) in a DateTimePicker control.

ValueChanged event of a DateTimePicker control—Raised when a user selects a new day or time in the DateTimePicker control.

GUI DESIGN GUIDELINES

DateTimePicker

- Use a DateTimePicker to retrieve date and time information from the user.
- Each DateTimePicker should have a corresponding descriptive Label.
- If the user is to specify a time of day or a date and time, set the DateTimePicker's ShowUpDown property to True. If the user is to specify only a date, set the Date-TimePicker's ShowUpDown property to False to allow the user to select a day from the month calendar.

GroupBox

- GroupBox titles should be concise and should use book-title capitalization.
- Use GroupBoxes to group related controls in a box with a title.

CONTROLS, EVENTS, PROPERTIES & METHODS

Date   This type provides properties and methods to store and manipulate date and time information.

- *Properties*

  Day—Returns the day stored in a Date variable.

  Hour—Returns the hour stored in a Date variable.

  Minute—Returns the minute stored in a Date variable.

  Month—Returns the month stored in a Date variable.

  Now—Returns the system's current date and time.

  Second—Returns the second stored in the Date variable.

  Today—Returns the system's current date with the time set to 00:00:00 (midnight).

  Year—Returns the year stored in a Date variable.

- *Methods*

  AddDays—Creates a new Date value that's the specified number of days later (or earlier) in time.

AddHours—Creates a new Date value that's the specified number of hours later (or earlier) in time.

AddMinutes—Creates a new Date value that's the specified number of minutes later (or earlier) in time.

ToLongDateString—Returns a String containing the date in the format "Wednesday, October 30, 2002."

ToShortTimeString—Returns a String containing the time in the format "4:00 PM."

DateTimePicker   🖮 DateTimePicker   This control is used to retrieve date and time information from the user.

■ *In action*

DateTimePicker
using default format

■ *Event*

ValueChanged—Raised when the Value property is changed.

■ *Properties*

CustomFormat—Sets a custom format string to use when displaying the date and/or time.

Format—Specifies the format in which the date and time are displayed on the control. Long specifies that the date is to be displayed in the format "Monday, December 31, 2012." Short specifies that the date is to be displayed in the format "12/31/2012." Time specifies that the time is to be displayed in the format "8:39:53 PM." Custom allows you to specify a custom format in which to display the date and/or time.

Location—Specifies the location of the DateTimePicker control relative to the top-left corner of the container (e.g., a Form or a GroupBox).

MinDate—Specifies the minimum date and/or time that can be selected.

MaxDate—Specifies the maximum date and/or time that can be selected.

Name—Specifies the name used to access the DateTimePicker control programmatically. The name should be appended with the DateTimePicker suffix.

ShowUpDown—Specifies whether the up and down arrows (True) are displayed on the control for time values. If False, a down arrow is displayed for accessing a drop-down calendar.

Size—Specifies the width and height (in pixels) of the DateTimePicker control.

Value—Stores the date and/or time in the DateTimePicker control.

GroupBox   ⌗ GroupBox   This control groups related controls visually in a box with a title.

■ *In action*

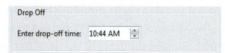

■ *Properties*

Location—Specifies the location of the GroupBox control relative to the top-left corner of the container (e.g., a Form or a GroupBox).

Name—Specifies the name used to access the GroupBox control programmatically. The name should be appended with the GroupBox suffix.

Size—Specifies the width and height (in pixels) of the GroupBox control.

Text—Specifies the text displayed on the GroupBox.

***

Timer   ⏲ Timer   This control wakes up at specified intervals of time to execute code in its `Tick` event handler.

- *Event*

  `Tick`—Raised after the number of milliseconds specified in the `Interval` property has elapsed.

- *Properties*

  `Enabled`—Determines whether the `Timer` is running (`True`). The default is `False`.

  `Interval`—Specifies the time interval (in milliseconds) between `Tick` events.

  `Name`—Specifies the name used to access the `Timer` control programmatically. The name should be appended with the `Timer` suffix.

***

MULTIPLE-CHOICE QUESTIONS

14.1 The _____ allows you to store and manipulate date information easily.

a) `Date` type

b) `DatePicker` control

c) `GroupBox` control

d) `Now` property

14.2 You can _____ a `Date` variable.

a) add hours to

b) add days to

c) subtract hours from

d) All of the above

14.3 To subtract one day from `Date` variable day's value, assign the value returned by _____ to day.

a) `day.AddHours(-24)`

b) `day.SubtractDays(1)`

c) `day.AddDays(-1)`

d) Both (a) and (c)

14.4 The time 3:45 and 35 seconds in the afternoon would be formatted as 03:45:35 PM according to the format string _____.

a) `"hh:mm:ss"`

b) `"hh:mm:ss tt"`

c) `"hh:mm:ss am:pm"`

d) `"h:m:s tt"`

14.5 A(n) _____ event occurs before the `Form` is displayed.

a) `LoadForm`

b) `InitializeForm`

c) `Load`

d) `FormLoad`

14.6 `Timer` property `Interval` sets the rate at which `Tick` events occur in _____.

a) nanoseconds

b) microseconds

c) milliseconds

d) seconds

14.7 To set `Date` variable time five hours earlier, use _____.

a) `time = time.SubtractHours(5)`

b) `time = time.AddHours(-5)`

c) `time = time.AddHours(5)`

d) `time.AddHours(-5)`

14.8 A _____ is a container.

a) `GroupBox`

b) `Form`

c) `Timer`

d) Both a and b

14.9 A `Date` variable stores hour values in the range _____.

a) 1 to 12

b) 0 to 12

c) 0 to 24

d) 0 to 23

14.10 A `DateTimePicker`'s _____ property specifies the format string with which to display the date.

a) `CustomFormat`

b) `FormatString`

c) `Format`

d) `Text`

EXERCISES

14.11 *(World Clock App)* Create an app that displays the current time in Los Angeles, Atlanta, London and Tokyo. Use a Timer to update the clock every second. Assume that your local time is the time in Atlanta. Atlanta is three hours later than Los Angeles. London is five hours later than Atlanta. Tokyo is nine hours later than London. The app should look similar to Fig. 14.21.

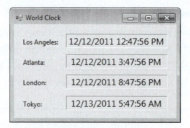

Figure 14.21   World Clock GUI.

a) *Copying the template to your working directory*. Copy the directory `C:\Examples\ch14\Exercises\WorldClock` to your `C:\SimplyVB2010` directory.

b) *Opening the app's template file.* Double click `WorldClock.sln` in the `WorldClock` directory to open the app.

c) *Adding a Timer to the Form*. Add a Timer control to the **World Clock** app. Set the Timer control's Name property to `clockTimer`. The Timer should generate a Tick event every 1,000 milliseconds (one second). Remember to set the Enabled property to True to start generating events.

d) *Adding a Tick event handler for clockTimer*. Add a Tick event handler for `clockTimer`. The event handler should calculate and display the current times for Los Angeles, Atlanta, London and Tokyo.

e) *Running the app.* Select **Debug > Start Debugging** to run your app. Look at the clock on your machine to verify that the time for Los Angeles is three hours earlier, the time in Atlanta is the same as what your clock says, the time in London is five hours later, and the time in Tokyo is 14 hours later (nine hours later than London).

f) *Closing the app.* Close your running app by clicking its close box.

g) *Closing the IDE.* Close the Visual Basic IDE by clicking its close box.

14.12 *(Shipping Time App Enhancement)* During the winter, a distribution center in Denver, Colorado, needs to receive seafood shipments to supply the local ski resorts. Enhance the **Shipping Time** app by adding Denver, Colorado, as another shipping destination. Denver is two time zones west of Portland, Maine, meaning that the time is two hours earlier than Portland. Because there are no direct flights to Denver, shipments from Portland take eight hours.

Figure 14.22   Enhanced Shipping Time GUI.

a) *Copying the template to your working directory*. Copy the directory `C:\Examples\ch14\Exercises\ShippingTimeEnhanced` to your `C:\SimplyVB2010` directory.

b) *Opening the app's template file.* Double click ShippingTime.sln in the ShippingTimeEnhanced directory to open the app.

c) *Inserting a GroupBox.* Resize the Form to fit the **Express Shipping to Denver** GroupBox as shown in Fig. 14.22. Add a GroupBox to the Form. Change the Text property of the GroupBox to indicate that it contains the delivery time in Denver. Resize and position the GroupBox so that it resembles the GUI shown in Fig. 14.22.

d) *Inserting Labels.* In the GroupBox you just created, add an output Label to display the delivery time for a seafood shipment to Denver and a corresponding descriptive Label.

e) *Inserting code to the DisplayDeliveryTime procedure.* Add code to DisplayDeliveryTime procedure to compute and display the delivery time in Denver.

f) *Running the app.* Select **Debug > Start Debugging** to run your app. Select various drop-off times, and ensure that the delivery times are correct for both Las Vegas and Denver.

g) *Closing the app.* Close your running app by clicking its close box.

h) *Closing the IDE.* Close the Visual Basic IDE by clicking its close box.

14.13 *(Alarm App)* Create an app that allows the user to set an alarm clock. The user should be able to set the time of the alarm by using a DateTimePicker. While the alarm is set, the user should not be able to modify the DateTimePicker. If the alarm is set and the current time matches or exceeds the time in the DateTimePicker, play the computer's "beep" sound. (Your computer must have the necessary hardware for sound enabled.) The user should be able to cancel an alarm by using a **Reset** Button. This Button is disabled when the app starts.

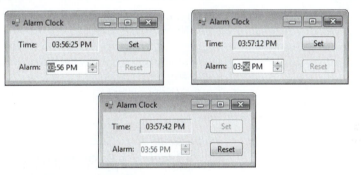

Figure 14.23 Alarm GUI.

a) *Copying the template to your working directory.* Copy the directory C:\Examples\ch14\Exercises\AlarmClock to your C:\SimplyVB2010 directory.

b) *Opening the app's template file.* Double click AlarmClock.sln in the AlarmClock directory to open the app.

c) *Inserting a DateTimePicker.* Add a DateTimePicker control to the Form. Set the DateTimePicker to display only the time, as shown in Fig. 14.23. Resize and position the DateTimePicker control so that it appears as it does in Fig. 14.23.

d) *Coding the Set Button's Click event handler.* Add a Click event handler for the **Set** Button. This event handler should disable the **Set** Button and the DateTimePicker and enable the **Reset** Button.

e) *Coding the Timer's Tick event handler.* Define the Tick event handler for the Timer. A Tick event should occur every 1,000 milliseconds (one second). Update the current time once a second. If the alarm is set and the current time matches or exceeds the time in the DateTimePicker, play the computer's "beep" sound by calling the Beep function. To do so, type Beep() on its own line in your code. Recall that you can use relational operators with Date values.

f) *Coding the Reset Button's Click event handler.* Define the Click event handler for the **Reset** Button. When the **Reset** Button is clicked, the GUI should be set back to its original state.

g) *Running the app.* Select **Debug > Start Debugging** to run your app. Use the Date-TimePicker and the **Set** Button to set a time for the alarm to go off. Wait for that time to verify that the alarm makes beeping sounds. Click the **Reset** Button to set a new time for the alarm to go off.

h) *Closing the app.* Close your running app by clicking its close box.

i) *Closing the IDE.* Close the Visual Basic IDE by clicking its close box.

What does this code do? ▶ **14.14** This code creates a Date variable. What date does this variable contain?

```
Dim day As New Date(2012, 1, 2, 3, 4, 5)
```

What's wrong with this code? ▶ **14.15** The following lines of code are supposed to create a Date variable and increment its hour value by two. Find the error(s) in the code.

```
Dim currentDay As Date = Date.Now
currentDay.AddHours(2)
```

Programming Challenge ▶ **14.16** (*Fee Calculator*) Create an app that computes the fee for parking a car in a parking garage (Fig. 14.24). The user should provide the **Time In:** and **Time Out:** values by using Date-TimePickers. The app should calculate the cost of parking in the garage for the specified amount of time. Assume that parking costs $3 an hour. When calculating the total time spent in the garage, you can ignore the seconds value, but treat the minutes value as a fraction of an hour (1 minute is 1/60 of an hour). For simplicity, assume that no overnight parking is allowed, so each car leaves the garage on the same day in which it arrives.

Figure 14.24　Fee Calculator GUI.

a) *Copying the template to your working directory.* Copy the directory C:\Examples\ch14\Exercises\FeeCalculator to your C:\SimplyVB2010 directory.

b) *Opening the app's template file.* Double click FeeCalculator.sln in the FeeCalculator directory to open the app.

c) *Inserting the DateTimePicker controls.* Add two DateTimePicker controls to the Form. Set the DateTimePickers so that they show the time only. Set the Size and Location properties of each DateTimePicker control so that they appear as in Fig. 14.24.

d) *Writing the Function procedure Fee.* Define a Function procedure Fee that accepts two Dates as parameters—the value of the **Time In:** DateTimePicker and the value of the **Time Out:** DateTimePicker. Using this information, procedure Fee should calculate the fee for parking in the garage. The Function procedure should then return this value as a Decimal.

e) *Coding the Calculate Button's Click event handler.* Add the Click event handler for the **Calculate** Button. This event handler should call Fee to obtain the amount due. It should then display the amount (formatted as currency) in a Label.

f) *Running the app.* Select **Debug > Start Debugging** to run your app. Use the Date-TimePickers' up and down arrows to select the time the car was placed in the garage and the time the car was taken out of the garage. Click the **Calculate** Button and verify that the correct fee is displayed.

g) *Closing the app.* Close your running app by clicking its close box.

h) *Closing the IDE.* Close the Visual Basic IDE by clicking its close box.

Fund Raiser App

Introducing Scope, Pass-by-Reference and *Option Strict*

Objectives

In this chapter, you'll:

- Create variables that can be used in all the Form's procedures.
- Distinguish between value types and reference types.
- Pass arguments by reference, using **ByRef**, so that the called procedure can modify the caller's variables.
- Eliminate subtle data-type errors by enabling **Option Strict** in your projects.
- Change a value from one data type to another, using methods of class **Convert**.

Outline

15.1 Test-Driving the **Fund Raiser** App

15.2 Constructing the **Fund Raiser** App

15.3 Passing Arguments: Pass-by-Value vs. Pass-by-Reference

15.4 **Option Strict**

15.5 Wrap-Up

In this chapter, you'll learn several important Visual Basic concepts. First, you'll learn how to declare variables *outside* a class's procedure definitions. These variables can be referenced from *any* procedure within your class's code. Next, you'll learn another technique for passing arguments to procedures. In the procedures that you've created so far, the app has made *a copy* of each argument's value, and any changes the called procedure made to the copy did *not* affect the original variable's value. You'll learn how to pass an argument to a procedure—using a technique called pass-by-reference—so that changes made to the parameter's value in the procedure are made to the *original variable* in the caller. You'll learn how the Visual Basic compiler handles conversions between different data types and how to enable a feature called **Option Strict** to avoid subtle errors that can occur when a value of one type is assigned to a variable of an *incompatible* type. In addition, you'll become familiar with methods from class **Convert** that allow you to convert data from one type to another *explicitly*.

15.1 Test-Driving the **Fund Raiser** App

In this chapter, you'll create a fund raiser app that determines how much donated money is available after operating costs. This app must meet the following requirements:

App Requirements

An organization is hosting a fund raiser to collect donations. A portion of each donation is used to cover the operating expenses of the organization—the rest of the donation goes to the charity. Create an app that allows the organization to keep track of the total amount of money raised. The app should deduct 17% of each donation for operating costs—the remaining 83% is given to the charity. The app should display the amount of each donation after the 17% for operating expenses is deducted—it also should display the total amount raised for the charity (that is, the total amount donated less operating costs) for all donations up to that point.

The user enters a donation amount into a `TextBox` and clicks a `Button` to calculate the net donation amount that the charity receives after its operating expenses have been deducted. In addition, the total amount of money raised for the charity is updated and displayed. You'll begin by test-driving the completed app. Then you'll learn the additional Visual Basic technologies needed to create your own version of this app.

Test-Driving the Fund Raiser App

1. ***Opening the completed app.*** Open the directory `C:\Examples\ch15\CompletedApp\FundRaiser` to locate the **Fund Raiser** app. Double click `FundRaiser.sln` to open the app in the Visual Basic IDE.

2. ***Running the Fund Raiser app.*** Select **Debug > Start Debugging** to run the app (Fig. 15.1).

Figure 15.1   **Fund Raiser** app's `Form`.

3. ***Entering a donation in the app.*** Enter 1500 in the **Donation:** `TextBox`. Click the **Make Donation** `Button`. The app calculates the amount of the donation after the operating expenses have been deducted and displays the result ($1,245.00) in the **After expenses:** field. Because this is the first donation entered, this amount is repeated in the **Total raised:** field (Fig. 15.2).

Figure 15.2   **Fund Raiser** app's `Form` with first donation entered.

4. ***Entering additional donations.*** Enter more donations, and click the **Make Donation** `Button`. Note that the total raised increases with each additional donation (Fig. 15.3).

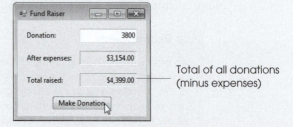

Total of all donations (minus expenses)

Figure 15.3   Making further donations.

5. ***Closing the app.*** Close your running app by clicking its close box.

6. ***Closing the IDE.*** Close the Visual Basic IDE by clicking its close box.

15.2 Constructing the Fund Raiser App

The following pseudocode statements describe the basic operation of the **Fund Raiser** app:

> When the user changes the current donation amount in the TextBox:
>> Clear Label that displays amount of current donation that goes toward charity
>
> When the user clicks the Make Donation Button:
>> Obtain amount of current donation from TextBox
>> Call function CalculateDonation to calculate amount of current donation that goes toward charity (amount after operating costs)
>> Display amount of current donation that goes toward charity
>> Update total amount raised for charity (from all donations received)
>> Display total amount raised for charity
>
> When the CalculateDonation procedure gets called:
>> Calculate operating costs (multiply the donated amount by the operating-cost percentage)
>> Calculate amount of donation that goes toward charity (subtract operating costs from donated amount)

Now that you've test-driven the **Fund Raiser** app and studied its pseudocode representation, you'll use an ACE table to help you convert the pseudocode to Visual Basic. Figure 15.4 lists the *actions*, *controls* and *events* that help you complete your own version of this app.

Action/Control/Event Table for the Fund Raiser App

Action	Control	Event/Method
Label all the app's controls	donationLabel, donatedLabel, totalLabel	App is run
	donationTextBox	TextChanged
Clear Label that displays amount of current donation that goes toward charity	donatedValueLabel	
	donateButton	Click
Obtain amount of current donation from TextBox Call function CalculateDonation to calculate amount of current donation that goes toward charity	donationTextBox	
Display amount of current donation that goes toward charity Update total amount raised for charity	donatedValueLabel	
Display total amount raised for charity	totalValueLabel	
Calculate operating costs Calculate amount of donation that goes toward charity		Calculate-Donation

Figure 15.4 Fund Raiser app's ACE table.

You're now ready to begin programming the **Fund Raiser** app. First, you'll declare the variables needed in the app. In this discussion, you'll learn a new concept—scope. The **scope** of a variable's identifier is the portion of an app in which the identifier can be referenced. Some identifiers can be referenced *throughout* an app—others can be referenced only from *limited portions* of an app (such as within a single procedure). You'll now add code to your app to illustrate these various scopes.

Examining Scope with the *Fund Raiser* App

1. ***Copying the template.*** Copy the `C:\Examples\ch15\TemplateApp\Fund-Raiser` directory to your `C:\SimplyVB2010` directory.

2. ***Opening the Fund Raiser app's template file.*** Double click `Fund-Raiser.sln` in the `FundRaiser` directory to open the app in the Visual Basic IDE (Fig. 15.5).

Figure 15.5   **Fund Raiser** template app's **Form**.

3. ***Placing declarations in the code file.*** Select **View > Code**, and add lines 2–3 of Fig. 15.6 to class `FundRaiserForm` in `FundRaiser.vb`. In this app, you need a variable that stores the total amount of money raised for charity.

```
1   Public Class FundRaiserForm
2       ' instance variable stores total raised for charity
3       Dim totalRaised As Decimal = 0
```

Figure 15.6   Declaring an instance variable in class `FundRaiserForm`.

This variable is initialized when the Form first loads and must retain its value while the app executes (that is, it cannot be created each time a procedure is invoked). Variable `totalRaised` stores the total amount of money raised. This variable is an **instance variable**—a variable declared inside a class, but outside any of the class's procedure definitions. *All* procedures in class `FundRaiserForm` have access to this variable and can modify its value.

[handwritten annotation: any procedure can access this variable]

Instance variables have **module scope**. Module scope begins at the identifier after keyword `Class` and terminates at the `End Class` statement. This scope enables *any* procedure in a class to access *all* instance variables defined in the same class. A Form's module-scope instance variables are created when the Form is created (normally, when the app begins executing).

4. ***Creating the Click event handler for the Make Donation Button.*** Select **View > Designer** to return to **Design** view. Double click the **Make Donation** Button to generate its `Click` event handler `donateButton_Click`. Split the procedure header over two lines, as in lines 26–27 of Fig. 15.7, and place the comments in lines 25 and 29 around the event handler.

```
23      End Sub ' donationTextBox_TextChanged
24
25      ' handles Make Donation Button's Click event
26      Private Sub donateButton_Click(sender As System.Object,
27          e As System.EventArgs) Handles donateButton.Click
28
29      End Sub ' donateButton_Click
30   End Class ' FundRaiserForm
```

Figure 15.7   Adding a `Click` event handler to the app.

Chapter 15   **Fund Raiser** App   **323**

(cont.)

5. ***Declaring local variables in event handler donateButton_Click.*** Add lines 29–30 of Fig. 15.8 to event handler donateButton_Click. Variable donation (line 29) stores the donation amount. Variable afterCosts (line 30) stores the donation amount after the operating expenses have been deducted.

```
25    ' handles Make Donation Button's Click event
26    Private Sub donateButton_Click(sender As System.Object,
27       e As System.EventArgs) Handles donateButton.Click
28
29       Dim donation As Decimal ' amount donated
30       Dim afterCosts As Decimal ' amount for charity
31
32    End Sub ' donateButton_Click
```

Figure 15.8 Declaring local variables in the donateButton_click event handler.

In Visual Basic, identifiers, such as donation and afterCosts, that are declared *inside* a procedure (but *outside* a control statement, such as a Do While…Loop) have **procedure scope**. Procedure scope begins at the identifier's declaration in the procedure and ends at the last statement of the procedure. Procedure-scope identifiers *cannot* be referenced *outside* of the procedure in which they're declared. A procedure's parameters also have procedure scope.

Identifiers declared *inside* control statements (such as inside an If…Then statement) have **block scope**, which begins at the identifier's declaration and ends at the enclosing block's final statement (for example, Else or End If).

Variables with procedure scope or block scope are called **local variables**, because they cannot be referenced *outside* the procedure or block in which they're declared. If a local variable has the *same* name as an instance variable (that is, a variable with module scope), the instance variable is *hidden* in the block or procedure by the local variable. Any expression containing the variable name uses the local variable's value and *not* the instance variable's value. The instance variable's value is not destroyed, though—you can still access the instance variable by preceding its name with the keyword Me and a dot (.).

6. ***Examining the CalculateDonation procedure.*** The template app provides Function procedure CalculateDonation (lines 5–15 of Fig. 15.9). Line 8 declares the constant COSTS, which stores the operating-cost percentage. This constant also is local to the procedure and cannot be used elsewhere. CalculateDonation accepts one parameter—the total donation amount (donatedAmount). The amount of the donation that goes toward operating costs is 17% of the initial donation. The net donation (the amount that goes toward charity) is calculated by multiplying local constant COSTS (with the value 0.17) by the donation amount and subtracting this result from the donation amount.

Procedure CalculateDonation subtracts the operating cost from the donation amount (donatedAmount) and assigns the result to netDonation (line 12). The Function procedure then returns the Decimal result (line 14).

Error-Prevention Tip

Hidden variable names can sometimes lead to subtle logic errors. Use unique names for all variables, regardless of scope, to prevent an instance variable from becoming hidden.

(cont.)

Parameter `donatedAmount` has procedure scope because it's declared in the procedure header

Local variable `netDonation` has procedure scope because it's declared in the procedure body

```
 5      ' returns donation amount after operating expenses
 6      Function CalculateDonation(donatedAmount As Decimal) As Decimal
 7
 8         Const COSTS As Double = 0.17
 9         Dim netDonation As Decimal
10
11         ' calculate amount of donation for charity
12         netDonation = donatedAmount - (donatedAmount * COSTS)
13
14         Return netDonation
15      End Function ' CalculateDonation
```

Figure 15.9   `Function` procedure `CalculateDonation` provided in the template app.

7. ***Demonstrating the difference between module scope and procedure scope.*** Now we demonstrate the limits of procedure scope. In line 12 of Fig. 15.9, temporarily replace the constant COSTS with the variable donation (Fig. 15.10), which is declared as a local variable in donateButton_Click (line 29 in Fig. 15.8). In the IDE, note the jagged line under donation to indicate an error. Variables with procedure scope can be accessed and modified *only* in the procedure in which they're defined. The error message displayed when the mouse pointer rests on donation indicates that donation is not declared. This variable is "local" to donateButton_Click, so Function CalculateDonation cannot "see" the declaration of donation. Replace donation with COSTS in line 12.

```
11      ' calculate amount of donation for charity
12      netDonation = donatedAmount - (donatedAmount * donation)
```

Figure 15.10   Demonstrating procedure scope.

8. ***Obtaining the donation amount.*** Add lines 31–32 of Fig. 15.11 to event handler donateButton_Click. You obtain the donation amount from the donationTextBox (line 32).

```
24      ' handles Make Donation Button's Click event
25      Private Sub donateButton_Click(sender As System.Object,
26         e As System.EventArgs) Handles donateButton.Click
27
28         Dim donation As Decimal ' amount donated
29         Dim afterCosts As Decimal ' amount for charity
30
31         ' get donation amount
32         donation = Val(donationTextBox.Text)
33
34      End Sub ' donateButton_Click
```

Figure 15.11   Obtaining the donation amount.

9. ***Calculating and displaying the donation amount after the operating expenses.*** Add lines 34–38 of Fig. 15.12 to the event handler. Line 35 invokes procedure CalculateDonation with the amount of the donation (donation). The result of this procedure—the net amount that goes to charity after the deduction for operating costs—is assigned to variable afterCosts. This amount is formatted as a currency string and displayed in the **After expenses:** Label (line 38).

(cont.)

```
31              ' get donation amount
32              donation = Val(donationTextBox.Text)
33
34              ' obtain donation amount after operating costs deduction
35              afterCosts = CalculateDonation(donation)
36
37              ' display amount of donation after costs
38              donatedValueLabel.Text = String.Format("{0:C}", afterCosts)
39
40          End Sub ' donateButton_Click
```

Figure 15.12 Calculating and displaying the donation amount after operating expenses.

10. ***Updating and displaying the fund raiser total.*** Add lines 40–44 of Fig. 15.13 to the event handler. Line 41 updates instance variable `totalRaised`, which stores the total amount given to the charity after the operating costs have been deducted. Line 44 displays the total amount raised for charity.

```
37              ' display amount of donation after costs
38              donatedValueLabel.Text = String.Format("{0:C}", afterCosts)
39
40              ' update total amount of donations received
41              totalRaised += afterCosts
42
43              ' display total amount collected for charity
44              totalValueLabel.Text = String.Format("{0:C}", totalRaised)
45          End Sub ' donateButton_Click
```

Figure 15.13 Updating and displaying the total amount raised for charity.

Note that `totalRaised` is *not* declared as a local variable in this event handler and does *not* have a jagged line beneath it. Recall that `totalRaised` is an instance variable, declared in line 3 of Fig. 15.6. Instance variables may be used in any of the class's procedures.

Instance variable `totalRaised` has *module scope* and therefore maintains its value between procedure calls. Local variables with procedure scope, such as `donation`, do *not* retain their values between procedure calls and are reinitialized each time their procedure is invoked.

11. ***Clearing the After expenses: Label to display the next result.*** The template app includes event handler donationTextBox_TextChanged (lines 17–22 of Fig. 15.14) for the **Donation:** TextBox's TextChanged event. When the user enters data into the TextBox, the TextChanged event occurs and line 21 clears the previous donation from the **After expenses:** Label.

```
17          ' handles Donation: TextBox's TextChanged event
18          Private Sub donationTextBox_TextChanged(sender As System.Object,
19              e As System.EventArgs) Handles donationTextBox.TextChanged
20
21              donatedValueLabel.Text = String.Empty ' clear Label
22          End Sub ' donationTextBox_TextChanged
```

Figure 15.14 Clearing the **Donation:** TextBox.

12. ***Running the app.*** Select **Debug > Start Debugging** to run your app. Enter several donation values to see that they're added to the total donation amount each time the **Make Donation** Button is clicked. The app now runs and displays the correct output.

13. ***Closing the app.*** Close your running app by clicking its close box.

1. Instance variables have _____ scope.

   a) block   b) procedure

   c) module   d) None of the above

2. Variables with either procedure scope or block scope are called _____.

   a) instance variables   b) local variables

   c) class variables   d) hidden variables

Answers: 1) c. 2) b.

15.3 Passing Arguments: Pass-by-Value vs. Pass-by-Reference

Arguments are passed to procedures in one of two ways—**pass-by-value** or **pass-by-reference**. The keyword `ByVal` indicates that an argument will be passed by value. When this is done, the app makes a copy of the argument's value and passes the copy to the called procedure. Changes made to the copy in the called procedure do *not* affect the original variable's value in the calling procedure.

In contrast, when an argument is passed by reference (using keyword `ByRef`), the original variable in the calling procedure *can* be *accessed* and *modified directly* by the called procedure. This is useful in some situations, such as when a procedure needs to return more than one result.

Pass-by-value is the default in Visual Basic. The IDE implicitly uses `ByVal` for any parameter that is not preceded by `ByVal` or `ByRef`—as has been the case in all of our previous apps.

In the following box, you'll use keyword `ByRef` to pass an argument by reference to the procedure that calculates the donation amount after operating costs.

Passing Arguments with `ByRef` in the Fund Raiser App

1. ***Passing variable afterCosts by reference.*** Replace line 35 in the event handler `donateButton_Click` with line 35 of Fig. 15.15. We now pass two variables to procedure `CalculateDonation`. This procedure currently accepts only one argument, so the second argument (`afterCosts`) is flagged as a compilation error. In the following steps, we resolve this error by rewriting procedure `CalculateDonation` so that it accepts two arguments. The first argument (in this case, `donation`) is passed by value. The second argument (in this case, `afterCosts`) is passed by reference. When the `CalculateDonation` procedure returns, variable `afterCosts` contains the portion of the donation that the charity receives. Therefore, no assignment statement is necessary.

```
24      ' handles Make Donation Button's Click event
25      Private Sub donateButton_Click(sender As System.Object,
26         e As System.EventArgs) Handles donateButton.Click
27
28         Dim donation As Decimal ' amount donated
29         Dim afterCosts As Decimal ' amount for charity
30
31         ' get donation amount
32         donation = Val(donationTextBox.Text)
33
34         ' obtain donation amount after operating costs deduction
35         CalculateDonation(donation, afterCosts)
```

Figure 15.15 Passing variable `afterCosts` by reference.

2. ***Removing the old CalculateDonation Function procedure.*** Delete the `CalculateDonation` Function procedure (lines 5–15 of Fig. 15.16) from `FundRaiser.vb`.

(cont.)

```
 5      ' returns donation amount after operating expenses
 6      Function CalculateDonation(donatedAmount As Decimal) As Decimal
 7
 8          Const COSTS As Double = 0.17
 9          Dim netDonation As Decimal
10
11          ' calculate amount of donation for charity
12          netDonation = donatedAmount - (donatedAmount * COSTS)
13
14          Return netDonation
15      End Function ' CalculateDonation
```

Delete these lines of code ⟶ 10

Figure 15.16 Function procedure `CalculateDonation` to be removed.

3. ***Coding the new CalculateDonation Sub procedure.*** Add lines 5–9 of Fig. 15.17 to your code. Lines 6–7 specify procedure `CalculateDonation`'s header. Keyword `ByRef` (line 7) indicates that variable `netDonation` is passed by reference. This means that any changes made to variable `net-Donation` in `CalculateDonation` are actually made to the argument variable in the caller—in this case, `donateButton_Click`'s local variable `afterCosts`. Since it's no longer necessary for `CalculateDonation` to return a value, you define it as a Sub procedure rather than a Function procedure.

```
 5      ' calculates donation amount after operating expenses
 6      Sub CalculateDonation(donatedAmount As Decimal,
 7          ByRef netDonation As Decimal)
 8
 9      End Sub ' CalculateDonation
```

Figure 15.17 `CalculateDonation` Sub procedure.

4. ***Calculating the donation amount for charity after operating costs.*** Add lines 9–12 of Fig. 15.18 to Sub procedure `CalculateDonation`. Line 12 uses the same calculation as the original Function procedure `CalculateDonation` (Fig. 15.16). The only difference is that assigning the calculation result to variable `netDonation` actually assigns the value to a variable in the caller—local variable `afterCosts` in `donateButton_Click`. You do *not* need to return the calculation result.

```
 5      ' calculates donation amount after operating expenses
 6      Sub CalculateDonation(donatedAmount As Decimal,
 7          ByRef netDonation As Decimal)
 8
 9          Const COSTS As Double = 0.17
10
11          ' calculate amount of donation for charity
12          netDonation = donatedAmount - (donatedAmount * COSTS)
13      End Sub ' CalculateDonation
```

Figure 15.18 Calculating the net donation after operating costs.

5. ***Running the app.*** Select **Debug > Start Debugging** to run your app. Again, the app displays the correct results, adding to the total donation amount for each input. This solution, however, uses pass-by-reference rather than pass-by-value.

6. ***Closing the app.*** Close your running app by clicking its close box.

In the next section you'll improve upon this app again by using `Option Strict`, which helps you write cleaner code.

Value Types and Reference Types

Data types in Visual Basic are divided into two categories—**value types** and **reference types.** A variable of a value type (such as `Integer`) simply contains *a value* of that type. For example, the declaration

```
Dim count As Integer = 7
```

places the value 7 into the `Integer` variable `count`.

By contrast, a variable of a *reference type* contains the *address* where an object is stored in memory. Such a variable is said to *refer to* an object. For example, the variables you'll use to interact with the controls in a GUI are all reference-type variables that refer to objects of the various control types (e.g., `Button`, `TextBox`). Reference-type instance variables are initialized by default to the value `Nothing`—indicating that the variable does *not* yet refer to an object. Except for type `String`, Visual Basic's primitive types are *value types*—`String` is a *reference type*. Value types are defined in Visual Basic using the keyword `Structure` (or Enum). All other types are reference types.

To interact with an object, you must use a variable that references the object to invoke (i.e., call) the object's methods and access its properties. For example, the statement

```
currentTimeLabel.Text = String.Format("{0:hh:mm:ss tt}", Date.Now)
```

uses the variable `currentTimeLabel` (of reference type `Label`) to access the `Label`'s `Text` property and assign it a formatted `String`.

The distinction between value types and reference types is important when arguments are passed to methods. By *default*, arguments are passed by *value*. When a reference-type variable is passed to a procedure *by value*, a *copy* of the variable's value is passed. Because the procedure receives a copy of an object's *address*, the procedure can modify the object at that address in memory. The reference-type variable is passed by value, so you *cannot* make it refer to a *different* object. However, the object to which the variable refers is effectively passed by reference. If you want to change the object to which a reference-type variable refers, you can declare the corresponding parameter with `ByRef` to pass that variable to a procedure by reference.

SELF-REVIEW

1. Keyword _____ indicates pass-by-reference.

    a) `Reference`   b) `ByRef`

    c) `ByReference`   d) `PassByRef`

2. When an argument is passed by reference, the called procedure can access and modify _____.

    a) the caller's original data directly   b) a copy of the caller's data

    c) Both (a) and (b)   d) Neither (a) nor (b)

Answers: 1) b. 2) a.

15.4 Option Strict

When accessing data, a computer needs to know the data's *type* in order to make sense of it. Imagine that you're purchasing a book from an online store that ships internationally. You notice that the book's price is 20, but no currency is associated with the price—it could be dollars, euros, pesos, yen or something else. Therefore, it's important to know what type of currency is being used. If the currency is not the one that you normally use, you need to perform a conversion to get the price.

Similar conversions occur many times in an app. The Visual Basic compiler determines a data type, and, with that knowledge, it can add two `Integer`s or combine two `String`s of text. Visual Basic can *convert* one data type to another, as long as the conversion "makes sense." For example, you're allowed to assign an `Integer` value to a `Decimal` variable without writing code that tells the app how to do the conversion. Such assignments perform so-called **implicit conversions**. When an attempted conversion does *not* make sense, such as assigning `"hello"` to an `Integer` variable, an error occurs. Figure 15.19 lists some of Visual Basic's data types and their allowed *implicit* conversions. [*Note*: We do not discuss every data type in this book. Consult the Visual Basic documentation to learn more about Visual Basic data types.]

Data Type	Can be implicitly converted to these (larger) types
`Boolean`	`Object`
`Byte`	`Short`, `Integer`, `Long`, `Decimal`, `Single`, `Double` or `Object`
`Char`	`String` or `Object`
`Date`	`Object`
`Decimal`	`Single`, `Double` or `Object`
`Double`	`Object`
`Integer`	`Long`, `Decimal`, `Single`, `Double` or `Object`
`Long`	`Decimal`, `Single`, `Double` or `Object`
`Object`	none
`Short`	`Integer`, `Long`, `Decimal`, `Single`, `Double` or `Object`
`Single`	`Double` or `Object`
`String`	`Object`

Figure 15.19   Some data types and their allowed implicit conversions.

The types listed in the right column are "larger" in that they can store more data than the types in the corresponding lines of the left column. For example, `Integer` types (left column) can be converted to `Long` types (right column, which includes four other data types). An `Integer` variable can store values in the approximate range ±2.1 billion—a `Long` variable can store numbers in the approximate range $\pm 9 \times 10^{18}$ (9 followed by 18 zeros). This means that any `Integer` value can be assigned to a `Long` variable without losing data. These are called *implicit* **widening conversions**, because the value of a "smaller" type (`Integer`) is being assigned to a variable of a "larger" type (`Long`) that can represent a wider range of values.

When a "larger" type, such as `Double`, is assigned to a "smaller" type, such as `Integer`, either a runtime error occurs because the value being assigned is too large to be stored in the smaller type or the assignment is permitted. Consider the following code:

```
Dim value1 As Double = 4.6
Dim value2 As Integer = value1
```

Common Programming Error

Narrowing conversions can result in loss of data, which can cause subtle logic errors.

Variable `value2` will be assigned 5—the result of implicitly converting the `Double` value 4.6 to an `Integer`. Such conversions are called implicit **narrowing conversions**. They can introduce subtle errors in apps, because the actual value being assigned could have been altered *without* your being aware of it—a dangerous practice. For example, if you were expecting variable `value2` to be assigned a value other than 5 (such as 4.6 or 4), a logic error would occur.

Visual Basic provides a *project setting* called **Option Strict** that, when set to **On**, disallows implicit narrowing conversions. If you attempt an implicit narrowing conversion, the compiler issues a compilation error. Later, we show how you can override this by performing narrowing conversions explicitly. First, however, you'll learn how to enable Option Strict, which is set to Off by default. The following box demonstrates how to set Option Strict to On through the Visual Basic IDE.

Enabling Option Strict

1. *Opening the project's property pages.* In the **Solution Explorer**, right click the project name (FundRaiser) to display a context menu. Select **Properties** to open the **FundRaiser** property pages tab (Fig. 15.20). You also can double click the project's My Project folder in the **Solution Explorer**.

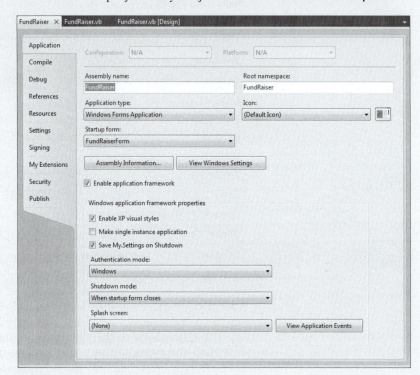

Figure 15.20 **FundRaiser**'s property pages tab.

2. *Selecting the Compile category.* On the left side of the **FundRaiser** property pages tab, select the **Compile** category (Fig. 15.21). Toward the top of the **Compile** category's page is a ComboBox labeled **Option Strict:**. By default, the option is set to Off.

Compile category ——

ComboBox containing value for Option Strict, which is set to Off by default ——

Figure 15.21 Selecting **Compile** in the **FundRaiser**'s property pages.

3. *Setting Option Strict to On.* Select **On** in the ComboBox labeled **Option Strict:** (Fig. 15.22). Option Strict is now set to On for this app.

(cont.)

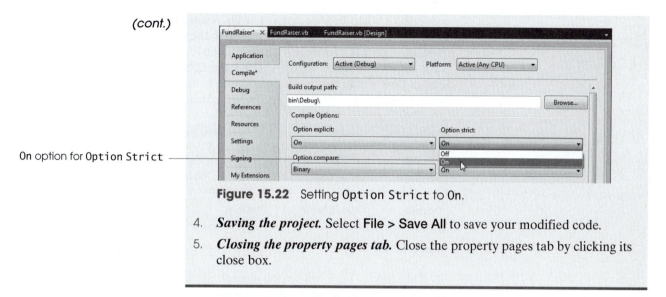

Figure 15.22 Setting `Option Strict` to On.

On option for `Option Strict` ———

4. *Saving the project.* Select **File > Save All** to save your modified code.

5. *Closing the property pages tab.* Close the property pages tab by clicking its close box.

As an alternative to setting `Option Strict` to On through the app's property pages, you can set `Option Strict` to On *programmatically* by adding the statement

```
Option Strict On
```

as the first line of code in a source-code file. This statement must appear *before* any other code in the file, including the class definition. When set programmatically, `Option Strict` is turned on only for the file(s) in which the statement appears. When set through the IDE, `Option Strict` is turned on for all files in the project. From this point forward, *all* code examples in the remainder of this book have had `Option Strict` set to On through the IDE. `Option Strict` should be set to On for all of your apps unless turning it off is absolutely necessary.

You can set `Option Strict` to On by default for each new app you create. Select **Tools > Options...**, then expand the **Projects and Solutions** node and select **VB Defaults**. Select **On** in the ComboBox labeled **Option Strict:** (Fig. 15.23). `Option Strict` will be set to On by default for all new apps you create.

Error-Prevention Tip

Set `Option Strict` to On in *every* app to avoid subtle errors that can be introduced by implicit narrowing conversions.

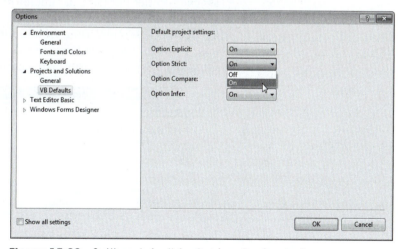

Figure 15.23 Setting default for `Option Strict` to On.

Performing Narrowing Conversions with **Option Strict** *Set to* **On**

When `Option Strict` is On, you must write code to perform narrowing conversions *explicitly*. At first this may seem like a nuisance, but it helps you create more robust apps and avoid subtle errors that could result from implicit conversions. The .NET framework provides methods in class **Convert** (Fig. 15.24) that help you perform conversions when `Option Strict` is `On`. Visual Basic also provides keywords that perform similar conversions. For example, the conversions performed by `Convert` methods `ToInt32`, `ToDecimal` and `ToDouble` also can be done using the Visual Basic conversion functions `CInt`, `CDec` and `CDbl`, respectively. We use the methods of class `Convert` in this book. In addition to these methods, every object in Visual Basic defines a `ToString` method, which converts the object to a `String`.

Convert To	Convert Method	Sample Statement
`Integer`	`ToInt32`	`value = Convert.ToInt32(inputTextBox.Text)`
`Decimal`	`ToDecimal`	`value = Convert.ToDecimal(` `    Pmt(monthlyInterest, months, -loanAmount))`
`Double`	`ToDouble`	`rate =` `    Convert.ToDouble(rateTextBox.Text) / 100`

Figure 15.24 Three of class `Convert`'s methods.

The name of each conversion method in class `Convert` begins with the word `To`, followed by the name of the data type to which the method converts its argument. For example, to convert a `String` entered by the user in `inputTextBox` to an `Integer`, use the statement

```
number = Convert.ToInt32(inputTextBox.Text)
```

`Int32` is the .NET type that Visual Basic's `Integer` keyword represents. Conversions in statements that call `Convert` methods or Visual Basic's conversion functions are called **explicit conversions**. In the following box, you'll learn to use explicit conversions.

Using Class Convert in the Fund Raiser App

1. ***Converting a Double amount to a Decimal value.*** Note that line 12 in Fig. 15.25 is underlined. Place the mouse pointer over the jagged line. An error message displays, indicating that `Option Strict` *prohibits* an implicit conversion from `Double` to `Decimal`. Multiplying a `Decimal` (donated-Amount) and a `Double` (`COSTS`) results in a `Double` value. The result is then assigned to the `Decimal` parameter `netDonation`, causing an *implicit* conversion from `Double` to `Decimal`. This conversion is *not* allowed by `Option Strict` because converting from `Double` to `Decimal` could result in data loss. You can also view this error by selecting **View > Other Windows > Error List** to open the **Error List** window.

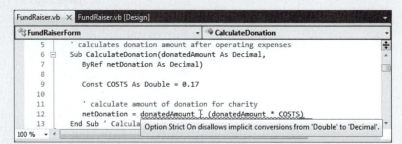

Figure 15.25 `Option Strict` prohibits implicit narrowing conversions.

(cont.)

Replace the underlined expression with lines 12–13 of Fig. 15.26. Method Convert.ToDecimal converts the Double value to a Decimal value. When the conversion is performed explicitly with a call to method Convert.ToDecimal, the jagged lines disappear. This error also could be corrected by declaring the COSTS constant as a Decimal. We declared it as a Double to demonstrate converting a Double value to a Decimal using method Convert.ToDecimal.

```
 6    Sub CalculateDonation(donatedAmount As Decimal,
 7       ByRef netDonation As Decimal)
 8
 9       Const COSTS As Double = 0.17
10
11       ' calculate amount of donation for charity
12       netDonation = Convert.ToDecimal(donatedAmount -
13          (donatedAmount * COSTS))
14    End Sub ' CalculateDonation
```

Figure 15.26   Explicitly performing a narrowing conversion with Convert.ToDecimal.

2. ***Converting the user input from a String to a Decimal.*** Line 31 of Fig. 15.27 is underlined. The error message that appears when the mouse pointer rests on this line indicates that Option Strict prohibits an implicit conversion from Double to Decimal.

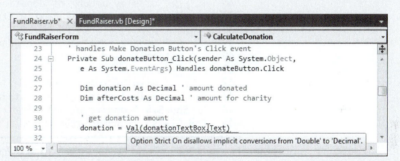

Figure 15.27   Option Strict prohibits a narrowing conversion from type Double to type Decimal.

Replace the underlined expression with line 31 of Fig. 15.28. Method Convert.ToDecimal explicitly converts donationTextBox.Text to a Decimal. After this change is made, the jagged line disappears. Recall that the Val function returns 0 if its argument *cannot* be converted to a Double. The methods of class Convert generate exceptions if their argument cannot be converted. Chapter 24 discusses exceptions in detail.

Figure 15.28 presents the source code for the **Fund Raiser** app. The lines of code that contain new programming concepts you learned in this chapter are highlighted.

```
1    Public Class FundRaiserForm
2       ' instance variable stores total raised for charity
3       Dim totalRaised As Decimal = 0
4
5       ' calculates donation amount after operating expenses
6       Sub CalculateDonation(donatedAmount As Decimal,
7          ByRef netDonation As Decimal)
8
```

Instance variable declaration

Procedure CalculateDonation determines the amount of donation after operating costs— parameter netDonation is modified directly (using ByRef)

Figure 15.28   **Fund Raiser** app's code. (Part 1 of 2.)

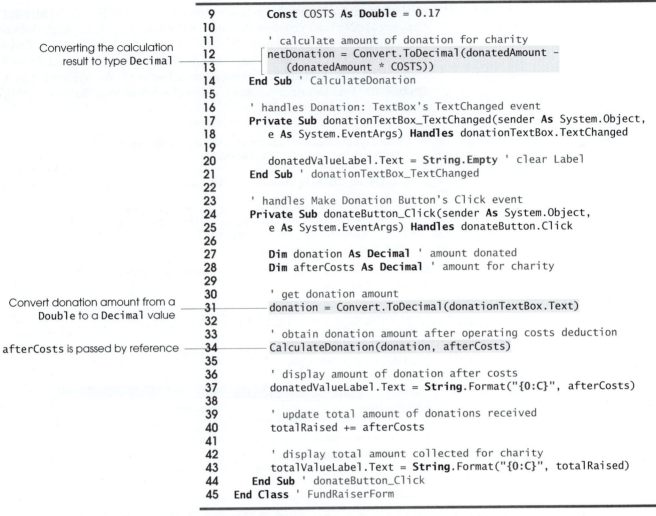

```
 9          Const COSTS As Double = 0.17
10
11          ' calculate amount of donation for charity
12          netDonation = Convert.ToDecimal(donatedAmount -
13             (donatedAmount * COSTS))
14       End Sub ' CalculateDonation
15
16       ' handles Donation: TextBox's TextChanged event
17       Private Sub donationTextBox_TextChanged(sender As System.Object,
18          e As System.EventArgs) Handles donationTextBox.TextChanged
19
20          donatedValueLabel.Text = String.Empty ' clear Label
21       End Sub ' donationTextBox_TextChanged
22
23       ' handles Make Donation Button's Click event
24       Private Sub donateButton_Click(sender As System.Object,
25          e As System.EventArgs) Handles donateButton.Click
26
27          Dim donation As Decimal ' amount donated
28          Dim afterCosts As Decimal ' amount for charity
29
30          ' get donation amount
31          donation = Convert.ToDecimal(donationTextBox.Text)
32
33          ' obtain donation amount after operating costs deduction
34          CalculateDonation(donation, afterCosts)
35
36          ' display amount of donation after costs
37          donatedValueLabel.Text = String.Format("{0:C}", afterCosts)
38
39          ' update total amount of donations received
40          totalRaised += afterCosts
41
42          ' display total amount collected for charity
43          totalValueLabel.Text = String.Format("{0:C}", totalRaised)
44       End Sub ' donateButton_Click
45    End Class ' FundRaiserForm
```

Converting the calculation result to type `Decimal` — (lines 12–13)

Convert donation amount from a `Double` to a `Decimal` value — (line 31)

`afterCosts` is passed by reference — (line 34)

Figure 15.28   **Fund Raiser** app's code. (Part 2 of 2.)

SELF-REVIEW

1. When `Option Strict` is set to `On`, you must explicitly perform _____.

    a) narrowing conversions   b) widening conversions

    c) all type conversions   d) no conversions

2. The methods in _____ are used to change data types explicitly.

    a) class `Strict`   b) class `Change`

    c) class `Convert`   d) class `Conversion`

Answers: 1) a. 2) c.

15.5 Wrap-Up

In this chapter, you learned concepts about data types and variables, and you built the **Fund Raiser** app to demonstrate these concepts.

You learned how to create instance variables, which are declared inside a class but outside any of the class's procedure definitions. Instance variables have module scope—they're accessible to all procedures in the class in which they're declared. In this chapter, you declared your instance variable in the `FundRaiserForm` class. In Chapter 19, you'll learn how to create your own classes and how to declare instance variables in them. Before this chapter, all the variables you declared were local variables—that is, variables with either procedure scope or block scope. Variables with procedure scope are accessible only within the procedure in which they're declared. Variables with block scope are accessible only within the block (such as the body of an If...Then statement) in which they're declared.

You learned the difference between passing arguments by value and by reference. When passing by value, the calling procedure makes a copy of the argument's value and passes the copy to the called procedure. Changes to the called procedure's copy do not affect the original variable value in the calling procedure. When passing by reference, the original data can be accessed and modified directly by the called procedure. You know that all arguments are passed by value by default, so it's never necessary to use keyword ByVal. Use keyword ByRef to pass arguments by reference. You learned to distinguish between value types and reference types.

You also learned about data-type conversions. You learned that narrowing conversions (such as converting a Double to a Decimal) can result in data loss and that widening conversions (such as a conversion from Integer to Double) don't have this problem. You learned that setting Option Strict to On causes the Visual Basic compiler to flag implicit narrowing conversions as compilation errors and forces you to perform such conversions explicitly.

In the next chapter, you'll learn about random-number generation, and you'll create an app that simulates the dice game called craps.

SKILLS SUMMARY

Setting Option Strict to On in the Current Project

- Right click the project name in the **Solution Explorer** and select **Properties**.
- Select **Compile** from the categories in the property pages.
- Set the **Option Strict:** ComboBox to On.

Setting Option Strict to On by Default for All New Apps

- Select **Tools > Options...**.
- Expand the **Projects and Solutions** node and select **VB Defaults**.
- Set the **Option Strict:** ComboBox to On.

Passing Arguments

- Arguments can be passed by value (ByVal, the default) or by reference (ByRef).

Passing Arguments by Value

- Keyword ByVal is not required—arguments are passed by value by default unless keyword ByRef is specified in the corresponding parameter's declaration.
- The app makes a copy of the argument's value and passes the copy to the called procedure.
- Changes to the called procedure's copy do not affect the original argument's value.

Passing Arguments by Reference

- In the procedure header, place keyword ByRef before the name of each parameter that's to be passed by reference.
- Called procedures can access and modify original arguments directly.

Understanding Scope

- Instance variables have module scope and can be accessed by all procedures in the same class.
- Local variables have either procedure scope or block scope.
- Variables with procedure scope cannot be referenced outside the procedure in which they're declared.
- Variables with block scope cannot be referenced outside the block (such as the body of an If...Then statement) in which they're declared.

Converting Between Data Types

- Use the appropriate method of class Convert to perform an explicit conversion from one data type to another.

KEY TERMS

block scope—Variables declared inside control statements, such as an `If...Then` statement, have block scope. Block scope begins at the identifier's declaration and ends at the block's final statement (for example, `Else` or `End If`).

ByRef keyword—Used to pass an argument by reference.

ByVal keyword—Used to pass an argument by value, but you never need to use this keyword because arguments are passed by value by default.

Convert class—Provides methods for converting data types.

explicit conversion—An operation that converts a value of one type to another type using code to (explicitly) tell the app to do the conversion. An example of an explicit conversion is to convert a value of type `Double` to type `Decimal` using a `Convert` method.

implicit conversion—An operation that converts a value of one type to another type without writing code to (explicitly) tell the app to do the conversion.

instance variable—Declared inside a class but outside any procedure of that class. Instance variables have module scope.

local variable—Declared inside a procedure or block, such as the body of an `If...Then` statement. Local variables have either procedure scope or block scope.

module scope—Variables declared inside a class definition but outside any of the classes procedures have module scope. Module scope begins at the identifier after keyword `Class` and terminates at the `End Class` statement; it enables all procedures in the same class to access all instance variables defined in that class.

narrowing conversion—A conversion where the value of a "larger" type is being assigned to a variable of a "smaller" type, where the larger type can store more data than the smaller type. Narrowing conversions can result in loss of data, which can cause subtle logic errors.

Option Strict—When set to `On`, disallows implicit narrowing conversions (for example, conversion from `Double` to `Decimal`). If you attempt an implicit narrowing conversion, the compiler issues a compilation error.

pass-by-reference—When an argument is passed by reference, the called procedure can access and modify the caller's argument value directly. Keyword `ByRef` indicates pass-by-reference.

pass-by-value—When an argument is passed by value, the app makes a copy of the argument's value and passes the copy to the called procedure. With pass-by-value, changes to the called procedure's copy do not affect the caller's argument value. Keyword `ByVal` indicates pass-by-value, but you never need to use this keyword because all arguments are passed by value by default.

procedure scope—Variables declared inside a procedure but outside a control statement have procedure scope. Variables with procedure scope cannot be referenced outside the procedure in which they're declared.

reference type—A type that stores the address of an object. Any type that's not a value type is a reference type. Primitive type `String` is a reference type.

scope—The portion of an app in which an identifier (such as a variable name) can be referenced. Some identifiers can be referenced throughout an app, others only from limited portions of an app (such as within a single procedure or block).

widening conversion—A conversion in which the value of a "smaller" type is assigned to a variable of a "larger" type—that is, a type that can store more data than the smaller type.

value type—A type that's defined as a `Structure` (or, as we'll see in the next chapter, an `Enum`). A variable of a value type contains a value of that type. The primitive types (other than `String`) are value types.

MULTIPLE-CHOICE QUESTIONS

15.1 In the property pages tab, _____ must be selected to access `Option Strict`.
a) Compile
b) Designer Defaults
c) General
d) Imports

15.2 When `Option Strict` is set to `On`, variables _____.
   a) are passed by value
   b) are passed by reference
   c) might need to be converted explicitly to a different type to avoid errors
   d) cannot be used within the block in which they're declared

15.3 A variable declared inside a class, but outside a procedure, is called a(n) _____.
   a) local variable
   b) hidden variable
   c) instance variable
   d) constant variable

15.4 Visual Basic provides methods in class _____ to convert from one data type to another.
   a) `ChangeTo`
   b) `Convert`
   c) `ConvertTo`
   d) `ChangeType`

15.5 When `Option Strict` is _____, the implicit conversion from a `Decimal` to an `Integer` results in an error.
   a) `On`
   b) `True`
   c) `Off`
   d) `False`

15.6 Keyword _____ indicates pass-by-reference.
   a) `ByReference`
   b) `ByRef`
   c) `Ref`
   d) `Reference`

15.7 With _____, changes made to a parameter variable's value do not affect the value of the variable in the calling procedure.
   a) `Option Strict`
   b) pass-by-value
   c) pass-by-reference
   d) None of the above

15.8 Instance variables _____.
   a) can be accessed by a procedure in the same class
   b) have module scope
   c) Neither of the above
   d) Both of the above

15.9 Assigning a "smaller" type to a "larger" type is a _____ conversion.
   a) narrowing
   b) shortening
   c) widening
   d) lengthening

15.10 A value of type `Single` can be implicitly converted to _____ when `Option Strict` is `On`.
   a) `Integer`
   b) `Double`
   c) Neither of the above
   d) Both of the above

EXERCISES

15.11 *(Task List App)* Create an app that allows the user to add items to a daily task list. The app should also display the number of tasks to be performed. Use method `ToString` to display the number of tasks in a `Label`. The app's GUI should look like the one in Fig. 15.29.

Figure 15.29   **Task List** app's GUI.

a) *Copying the template to your working directory.* Copy the directory `C:\Examples\ch15\Exercises\TaskList` to your `C:\SimplyVB2010` directory.

b) *Opening the app's template file.* Double click `TaskList.sln` in the `TaskList` directory to open the app.

c) *Setting* `Option Strict` *to* `On`. Use the directions provided in the box, *Enabling* `Option Strict`, to set `Option Strict` to `On`.

d) *Creating an instance variable.* Declare `numberOfTasks` as an instance variable of class `TaskListForm`. This variable is used to keep track of how many tasks have been entered.

e) *Adding the Add Task Button's* `Click` *event handler.* Double click the **Add Task** Button to generate the empty event handler `addButton_Click`. This event handler should display the user input in the `ListBox` and clear the user input from the `Text-Box`. The event handler should also update the `Label` that displays the number of tasks. Use method `ToString` to display the number of tasks in the `Label`. Finally, the event handler should transfer the focus to the `TextBox`.

f) *Running the app.* Select **Debug > Start Debugging** to run your app. Enter several tasks, and click the **Add Task** Button after each. Verify that each task is added to the **Task list:** `ListBox`, and that the number of tasks is incremented with each new task.

g) *Closing the app.* Close your running app by clicking its close box.

h) *Closing the IDE.* Close the Visual Basic IDE by clicking its close box.

15.12 *(Quiz Average App)* Develop an app that computes a student's average quiz score for all of the quiz scores entered. The app should look like the GUI in Fig. 15.30. Use method `Convert.ToInt32` to convert the user input to an `Integer`. Use instance variables with module scope to keep track of the sum of all the quiz scores entered and the number of quiz scores entered.

Figure 15.30   **Quiz Average** app's GUI.

a) *Copying the template to your working directory.* Copy the directory `C:\Examples\ch15\Exercises\QuizAverage` to your `C:\SimplyVB2010` directory.

b) *Opening the app's template file.* Double click `QuizAverage.sln` in the `QuizAverage` directory to open the app.

c) *Setting* `Option Strict` *to* `On`. Use the directions provided in the box, *Enabling* `Option Strict`, to set `Option Strict` to `On`.

d) *Adding instance variables.* Add two instance variables—`totalScore`, which keeps track of the sum of all the quiz scores entered, and `taken`, which keeps track of the number of quiz scores entered.

e) *Adding the Submit Score Button's event handler.* Double click the **Submit Score** Button to generate the empty event handler `submitButton_Click`. The code required by *Steps f–k* should be placed in this event handler.

f) *Obtaining user input.* Use method `Convert.ToInt32` to convert the user input from the `TextBox` to an `Integer`.

g) *Updating the number of quiz scores entered.* Increment the number of quiz scores entered.

h) *Updating the sum of all the quiz scores entered.* Add the current quiz score to the current total to update the sum of all the quiz scores entered.

i) *Calculating the average score.* Divide the sum of all the quiz scores entered by the number of quiz scores entered to calculate the average score.

j) *Displaying the average score.* Use method `ToString` to display the average quiz grade in the **Average:** field.

k) *Displaying the number of quizzes taken.* Use method `ToString` to display the number of quiz scores entered in the **Number taken:** field.

l) *Running the app.* Select **Debug > Start Debugging** to run your app. Enter several quiz scores, clicking the **Submit Score** Button after each. With each new score, verify that the **Number taken:** field is incremented and that the average is updated correctly.

m) *Closing the app.* Close your running app by clicking its close box.

n) *Closing the IDE.* Close the Visual Basic IDE by clicking its close box.

15.13 *(Modified Maximum App)* Modify the **Maximum** app from Chapter 13 (Fig. 15.31) to use keyword `ByRef` to pass a fourth argument to procedure `Maximum` by reference. Use methods from class `Convert` to perform any necessary type conversions.

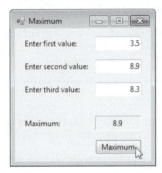

Figure 15.31   Modified **Maximum** app's GUI.

a) *Copying the template to your working directory.* Copy the directory `C:\Examples\ch15\Exercises\Maximum` to your `C:\SimplyVB2010` directory.

b) *Opening the app's template file.* Double click `Maximum.sln` in the `Maximum` directory to open the app.

c) *Setting `Option Strict` to `On`.* Use the directions provided in the box, *Enabling Option Strict*, to set `Option Strict` to `On`.

d) *Adding a local variable.* Add local variable max of type `Double` to event handler `maximumButton_Click`. The code required in *Steps d–f* should be placed in this event handler. Variable max stores the result of procedure `Maximum`.

e) *Passing four arguments to procedure `Maximum`.* Use method `Convert.ToDouble` to convert the user input from the TextBoxes to `Doubles`. Pass these three values as the first three arguments to procedure `Maximum`. Pass local variable max as the fourth argument to procedure `Maximum`.

f) *Displaying the maximum value.* Use method `ToString` to display local variable max in the **Maximum:** field.

g) *Changing procedure `Maximum` to a Sub procedure.* Change procedure `Maximum` to a Sub procedure. Make sure that Sub procedure `Maximum` no longer returns a value and does not specify a return type. The modifications required in *Steps g–h* should be performed on this Sub procedure.

h) *Adding a fourth parameter to procedure `Maximum`.* Add a fourth parameter finalMaximum of type `Double` to `Maximum`'s procedure header. Use keyword `ByRef` to specify that this argument is passed by reference. Remove the declaration of variable finalMaximum from the body of procedure `Maximum`.

i) *Running the app.* Select **Debug > Start Debugging** to run your app. Enter three different values into the input fields and click the **Maximum** Button. Verify that the largest value is displayed in the **Maximum:** field.

j) *Closing the app.* Close your running app by clicking its close box.

k) *Closing the IDE.* Close the Visual Basic IDE by clicking its close box.

What does this code do? ▶ **15.14** What is displayed in `displayLabel` when the user clicks the `enterButton`?

```
1  Public Class ScopeTestForm
2     Dim value2 As Integer = 5
3
4     Private Sub enterButton_Click(sender As System.Object,
5        e As System.EventArgs) Handles enterButton.Click
6
7        Dim value1 As Integer = 10
8        Dim value2 As Integer = 3
9
10       Test(value1)
11       displayLabel.Text = value1.ToString()
12    End Sub ' enterButton_Click
13
14    Sub Test(ByRef value1 As Integer)
15       value1 *= value2
16    End Sub ' Test
17 End Class ' ScopeTestForm
```

What's wrong with this code? ▶ **15.15** Find the error(s) in the following code (the procedure should assign the value 14 to variable `result`). Assume that `Option Strict` is set to `On`.

```
1  Sub Sum()
2     Dim numberWords As String = "4"
3     Dim number As Integer = 10
4     Dim result As Integer
5
6     result = numberWords + number
7  End Sub ' Sum
```

Programming Challenge ▶ **15.16** (*Schedule Book App*) Develop an app that allows the user to enter a schedule of appointments and their respective times. Create the Form in Fig. 15.32 and name the app **Schedule Book**. Add a `Function` procedure called `TimeTaken` that returns a `Boolean` value. Each time a user enters a new appointment, `Function` procedure `TimeTaken` determines whether the user has scheduled more than one appointment at the same time. If `TimeTaken` returns `True`, the user is notified via a message dialog. Otherwise, the appointment is added to the `ListBoxes`. Set `Option Strict` to `On`, and use methods from class `Convert` as necessary.

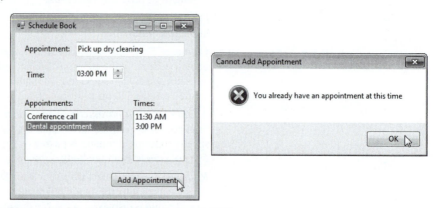

Figure 15.32 Schedule Book app's GUI.

Objectives

In this chapter, you'll learn to:

- Code simulation techniques that employ random-number generation.
- Use class **Random** methods to generate random numbers.
- Use enumerations to enhance code readability.
- Read images from files.

Outline

Craps Game App

Introducing Random-Number Generation and Enum

You'll now learn a popular type of app—simulation and game playing. In this chapter, you'll develop a **Craps Game** app. Something in the air of a casino invigorates many people—from the quarter-poppers at the one-armed bandits to the high rollers at the plush mahogany-and-felt craps tables. Many of these individuals are drawn by the element of chance—the possibility that luck will convert a pocketful of money into a mountain of wealth.

You can introduce the element of chance into computer apps using random numbers. This chapter's **Craps Game** app introduces several new concepts, including random-number generation and enumerations. It also uses important concepts that you learned previously, including instance variables, procedures and the Select Case multiple-selection control statement.

16.1 Test-Driving the Craps Game App

The dice game known as "craps" is a popular game of chance played in casinos worldwide. The **Craps Game** app must meet the following requirements:

App Requirements

Create an app that simulates playing the game of craps. In this game, a player rolls two dice. Each die has six faces. Each face contains one, two, three, four, five or six spots. After the dice have come to rest, the sum of the spots on the two top faces is calculated. If the sum is 7 or 11 on the first throw, the player wins. If the sum is 2, 3 or 12 on the first throw (called "craps"), the player loses (the "house" wins). If the sum is 4, 5, 6, 8, 9 or 10 on the first throw, that sum becomes the player's "point." To win, a player must continue rolling the dice until the point value is rolled. The player loses by rolling a 7 before rolling the point.

Creating this app teaches you two important concepts—random-number generation and enumerations. You'll begin by test-driving the completed app. Then you'll learn the additional Visual Basic capabilities needed to create your own version of this app.

341

Test-Driving the Craps Game App

1. ***Opening the completed app.*** Open the directory C:\Examples\ch16\CompletedApp\CrapsGame to locate the **Craps Game** app. Double click CrapsGame.sln to open the app in the Visual Basic IDE.

2. ***Running the Craps Game app.*** Select **Debug > Start Debugging** to run the app (Fig. 16.1).

Figure 16.1 **Craps Game** app's initial appearance.

3. ***Starting the game.*** Click the **Play** Button. There are three possible outcomes at this point.

   ■ The player wins by rolling 7 or 11 (Fig. 16.2).

Figure 16.2 Player wins on first roll by rolling 7 or 11 (11 in this case).

   ■ The player loses by rolling 2, 3 or 12 (Fig. 16.3).

Figure 16.3 Player loses on first roll by rolling 2, 3 or 12 (2 in this case).

   ■ Otherwise, the roll becomes the player's point (4, 5, 6, 8, 9 or 10), which is then displayed for the remainder of the game (Fig. 16.4).

Note that in this app, unlike the real game of craps, the value of the roll is computed using the forward-facing die faces instead of the top faces. This makes reading the die faces easier.

(cont.)

Figure 16.4   First roll sets the point that the player must match to win.

4.   ***Continuing the game.*** If the app displays **Roll again!**, as in Fig. 16.4, click the **Roll** Button repeatedly until either you win by matching your point value (Fig. 16.5) or you lose by rolling a 7 (Fig. 16.6). When the game ends, you can click **Play** to start over.

Figure 16.5   Winning the game by matching your point before rolling a 7.

Figure 16.6   Losing by rolling a 7 before matching your point.

5.   ***Closing the app.*** Close your running app by clicking its close box.

6.   ***Closing the IDE.*** Close the Visual Basic IDE by clicking its close box.

16.2 Random-Number Generation

Now you'll learn how to use an object of class **Random** to introduce the element of chance into your apps. You'll learn more about working with objects of existing classes over the next few chapters; then you'll learn to create your own classes and objects of those classes in Chapter 19. Consider the following statements:

```
Dim randomObject As New Random()
Dim randomNumber As Integer = randomObject.Next()
```

The first statement declares `randomObject` as a reference of type Random and initializes it with a New Random object. A reference-type variable contains a **reference** to an object. Recall that keyword New creates a new object in memory. When you create an object, New returns a reference to that object, which you typically store in a reference-type variable so you can interact with the object.

The second statement declares Integer variable randomNumber and assigns it the value returned by calling Random's **Next** method on randomObject, which generates a positive Integer value from zero and up to, but not including, the largest possible Integer, which is the constant **Int32.MaxValue** (the value 2,147,483,647). To generate random values of type Double, you can use method **NextDouble**, which returns a positive Double value from 0.0 up to, but not including, 1.0.

If the Next method were to produce truly random values, then every value in this range would have an *equal* chance (or probability) of being chosen when Next is called. The values returned by Next are actually **pseudorandom numbers**—a sequence of values produced by a complex mathematical calculation. This mathematical calculation comes close, but it's *not* exactly random in choosing numbers.

The range of values produced by Next is often different from the range needed in a particular app. For example, an app that simulates coin tossing might require only 0 for heads and 1 for tails. An app that simulates the rolling of a six-sided die would require random Integers from 1 to 6. Similarly, an app that randomly predicts the next type of spaceship (out of four possibilities) that flies across the horizon in a video game might require random Integers from 1 to 4.

By passing an argument to the Next method as follows

```
value = 1 + randomObject.Next(6)
```

you can produce integers in the range from 1 to 6. When a single argument is passed to Next, the values returned by Next are in the range from 0 up to, but not including, the value of that argument. In the preceding statement, Next produces values in the range 0–5. You can change the range of numbers produced by adding 1 to the previous result, so that the returned values are in the range 1–6. This new range corresponds nicely with the roll of a six-sided die, for example.

You may also pass two arguments to Next to produce a range of numbers. For example, the preceding statement also could be written as

```
value = randomObject.Next(1, 7) ' from 1 up to, but not including, 7
```

Note that you must use 7 as the second argument to the Next method to produce integers in the range 1–6. The first argument indicates the minimum value in the desired range. The second is equal to *one more than the maximum value desired*.

The range of values produced by method NextDouble is also usually different from the range needed in a particular app. By multiplying the value returned from method NextDouble as follows

```
value = 6 * randomObject.NextDouble()
```

you can produce Double values in the range from 0.0 to 6.0 (not including 6.0). Figure 16.7 shows sample ranges returned by calls to Next and NextDouble.

Method call	Resulting range
randomObject.Next()	0 to one less than Int32.MaxValue
randomObject.Next(30)	0 to 29
10 + randomObject.Next(10)	10 to 19
randomObject.Next(10, 20)	10 to 19
randomObject.Next(5, 100)	5 to 99
randomObject.NextDouble()	0.0 to less than 1.0
8 * randomObject.NextDouble()	0.0 to less than 8.0

Figure 16.7　Next and NextDouble method calls with corresponding ranges.

1. The statement _____ returns a number in the range from 8 to 300.
   a) `randomObject.Next(8, 300)`   b) `randomObject.Next(8, 301)`
   c) `1 + randomObject.Next(8, 300)`   d) None of the above

2. The statement _____ returns a number in the range 15 to 35.
   a) `randomObject.Next(15, 36)`   b) `randomObject.Next(15, 35)`
   c) `10 + randomObject.Next(5, 26)`   d) Both (a) and (c)

Answers: 1) b. 2) d.

16.3 Constructing the Craps Game App

The following pseudocode describes the operation of the **Craps Game** app:

> When the player clicks the Play Button:
>   Roll the dice using random numbers
>   Display images corresponding to the numbers on the rolled dice
>   Calculate the sum of both dice
>
>   Select correct case based on the sum of the two dice:
>   Case where first roll is 7 or 11
>   Display the winning message
>   Case where first roll is 2, 3 or 12
>   Display the losing message
>   Case where none of the preceding Cases are true
>   Set the value of the point to the sum of the dice
>   Display point value
>   Display message to roll again
>   Display images for user's point
>   Disable the Play Button
>   Enable the Roll Button
>
> When the player clicks the Roll Button:
>   Roll the dice using random numbers
>   Display images corresponding to the numbers on the rolled dice
>   Calculate the sum of both dice
>
>   If the player rolls the same value as the point
>   Display the winning message
>   Disable the Roll Button
>   Enable the Play Button
>   Else If the player rolls a 7
>   Display the losing message
>   Disable the Roll Button
>   Enable the Play Button

Now that you've test-driven the **Craps Game** app and studied its pseudocode representation, you'll use an ACE table to help you convert the pseudocode to Visual Basic. Figure 16.8 lists the *actions*, *controls* and *events* that will help you complete your own version of this app.

Action/Control/Event (ACE) Table for the Craps Game App

Action	Control/Object	Event
Label the app's controls	`resultLabel`, `pointDiceGroupBox`	App is run
Roll the dice using random numbers	`randomObject`	

Figure 16.8 ACE table for the **Craps Game** app. (Part 1 of 2.)

(cont.)

Action	Control/Object	Event
	playButton	Click
Display images corresponding to the numbers on the rolled dice	die1Picture, die2Picture	
Calculate the sum of both dice		
Select correct case based on sum:		
Case where first roll is 7 or 11 Disable the Roll Button	rollButton	
Display the winning message	statusLabel	
Case where first roll is 2, 3 or 12 Disable the Roll Button	rollButton	
Display the losing message	statusLabel	

Case where none of the preceding Cases are true
    Set the value of the point to the
      sum of the dice		

Display the point value	pointDiceGroupBox	
Display message to roll again	statusLabel	
Display images for user's point	pointDie1Picture, pointDie2Picture	
Disable the Play Button	playButton	
Enable the Roll Button	rollButton	
	rollButton	Click
Display images corresponding to the numbers on the rolled dice	die1Picture, die2Picture	
Calculate the sum of both dice		
If the player rolls the same value as the point Display the winning message	statusLabel	
Disable the Roll Button	rollButton	
Enable the Play Button	playButton	
Else if the player rolls a 7 Display the losing message	statusLabel	
Disable the Roll Button	rollButton	
Enable the Play Button	playButton	

Figure 16.8 ACE table for the **Craps Game** app. (Part 2 of 2.)

In the following boxes, you'll create an app to simulate playing the game of craps. The numbers 2, 3, 7, 11 and 12 have special meanings during the game. You'll use these numbers (as constants) quite often. In this case, it would be helpful to create a group of related constants and assign them meaningful names for use in your app. You can do this by using an **enumeration** to create constant identifiers that describe various significant dice combinations in craps, such as SNAKE_EYES (2), TREY (3), CRAPS (7), LUCKY_SEVEN (7), YO_LEVEN (11) and BOX_CARS (12). By providing descriptive identifiers for a group of related constants, enumerations enhance program readability and ensure that numbers are consistent throughout the app. In the following box you'll learn how to use enumerations.

enumeration for group of identifiers

Introducing
Enumerations and
Declaring Instance
Variables

1. ***Copying the template to your working directory.*** Copy the C:\Examples\ch16\TemplateApp\CrapsGame directory to C:\SimplyVB2010.

2. ***Opening the app's template file.*** Double click CrapsGame.sln in the CrapsGame directory to open the app in the Visual Basic IDE. Figure 16.9 displays the Form in **Design** view. Remember to follow the steps in Chapter 15 to turn Option Strict On before going any further.

Figure 16.9   Template **Craps Game** Form in **Design** view.

3. ***Declaring an enumeration.*** Add lines 2–3 of Fig. 16.10 to your app, then press *Enter*. The IDE inserts the keywords End Enum automatically. Enumerations begin with the keyword **Enum** (line 3) and end with the keywords **End Enum** (line 10). The name of the enumeration (DiceNames) follows the keyword Enum (line 3). Now add lines 4–9 of Fig. 16.10 into your app between the lines containing keywords Enum and End Enum.

Defining an enumeration

```
1   Public Class CrapsGameForm
2       ' die-roll constants
3       Enum DiceNames
4           SNAKE_EYES = 2
5           TREY = 3
6           CRAPS = 7
7           LUCKY_SEVEN = 7
8           YO_LEVEN = 11
9           BOX_CARS = 12
10      End Enum
```

Figure 16.10   Enumeration DiceNames in the **Craps Game** app.

Good Programming Practice

Use enumerations to group related constants and enhance code readability.

We use an enumeration in this app to make the code easier to read, especially for someone who is unfamiliar with the game. You can refer to the numbers using the enumeration name and the member-access operator. For instance, use DiceNames.SNAKE_EYES for the number 2, DiceNames.TREY for 3, DiceNames.CRAPS and DiceNames.LUCKY_SEVEN for 7, DiceNames.YO_LEVEN for 11 and DiceNames.BOX_CARS for 12. You can assign the same value to multiple enumeration constants, as in lines 6 and 7. You're not required to provide values for the constants in an enumeration. If no values are specified, the constants are automatically assigned consecutive values starting from 0.

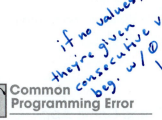

if no values, they're given consecutive values beg. w/ ⓪

Common Programming Error

You can specify an enumeration's type after its name by using the keyword As followed by Byte, SByte, Short, UShort, Integer, UInteger, Long, or ULong. If no type is specified, enumeration constants are of type Integer by default. Attempting to create enumerations of other types results in compilation errors.

4. ***Declaring constants and instance variables.*** Several methods require the use of the same variables and constants throughout the lifetime of the app. As you learned in Chapter 15, you declare instance variables for this purpose. Add lines 12–18 of Fig. 16.11 below the enumeration definition.

(cont.)

Declaring constants ──────

Declaring a variable
to store point value ──

Creating a **Random** object ──

```
10        End Enum
11
12        ' filename and directory constants
13        Const FILE_PREFIX As String = "images\die"
14        Const FILE_SUFFIX As String = ".png"
15
16        ' instance variables
17        Dim myPoint As Integer = 0
18        Dim randomObject As New Random()
```

Figure 16.11   Instance variables added to the **Craps Game** app.

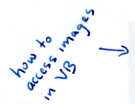

how to access images in VB →

In this app, you need to access images for the six die faces. For convenience, each image file has a name that differs only by one character—e.g.,
the image for the die face displaying 1 is named `die1.png`, and the image for
the die face displaying 6 is named `die6.png`. Recall that `png` is an image-file-
name extension that's short for Portable Network Graphic. These images are
stored in the folder named `images` in your project's `bin\Debug` directory. As
such, the `String` `"images\die1.png"` would correctly indicate the location
of the die face displaying 1 relative to the `bin\Debug` directory. To help create a `String` representing the path to the image, `Strings` `FILE_PREFIX`
(`images\die`) and `FILE_SUFFIX` (`.png`) are used (as constants) to store the
prefix and suffix of the filename (lines 13–14).

The game of craps requires that you store the user's point, once established on the first roll, for the game's duration. Therefore, variable `myPoint`
(line 17 of Fig. 16.11) is declared as an `Integer` to store the value of the dice
on the first roll. You use the `Random` object referenced by `randomObject`
(line 18) to "roll" the dice and generate those values. These variables are
declared outside of any methods (giving them module scope) so that they
can be accessed by any of the methods in the class.

5. ***Saving the project.*** Select **File > Save All** to save your modified code.

SELF-REVIEW

1. Use keyword _____ to define groups of related constants.

    a) `ReadOnly`   b) `Enum`
    c) `Constants`   d) `Enumeration`

2. The constants defined in an `Enum` _____.

    a) may use repeated names
    b) can be accessed using the `Enum`'s name followed by the member-access operator
    c) cannot be accessed in the block in which they're declared
    d) All of the above

    Answers: 1) b. 2) b.

16.4 Using Random Numbers in the Craps Game App

Now that you've declared an enumeration and instance variables, you'll add code to
execute when the user clicks the **Craps Game** app's `Buttons`. The following box
explains how to add the code that executes when the user clicks **Play**.

---

*Coding the Play
Button's Click Event
Handler*

1. ***Creating the Play Button's Click event handler.*** Return to the **Design** view
    to display the Form. Double click the **Play** Button to generate the **Play** But-
    ton's Click event handler and view the code file. (The **Play** Button is used
    to begin a new game of craps.)

(cont.)   2. ***Removing Images from a PictureBox and rolling dice.*** Begin coding the
Click event handler by adding lines 24–33 from Fig. 16.12 into the
playButton_Click event handler. Be sure to add the comments and format
the lines, as shown in Fig. 16.12, so that the line numbers in your code match
those presented in this chapter. [*Note:* RollDice is underlined in blue in the
IDE because the procedure is not yet defined.]

```
20        ' begin new game and determine point
21        Private Sub playButton_Click(sender As System.Object,
22           e As System.EventArgs) Handles playButton.Click
23
24           ' initialize variables for new game
25           myPoint = 0
26           pointDiceGroupBox.Text = "Point"
27           statusLabel.Text = String.Empty
28
29           ' remove point-die images
30           pointDie1Picture.Image = Nothing
31           pointDie2Picture.Image = Nothing
32
33        Dim sum As Integer = RollDice() ' roll dice
34
```

Initializing values for a new game — lines 25–27

Removing images from PictureBoxes — lines 30–31

"Rolling" the dice — line 33

a keyword (handwritten annotation pointing to line 30)

Figure 16.12 playButton_Click event handler definition.

Lines 25–27 initialize variables for a new game. Line 25 sets variable
myPoint, the craps game point value, to 0. Line 26 changes the text displayed on the GroupBox to Point, using the GroupBox's Text property. As
you saw in the test-drive, the GroupBox's Text property is used to display
the point value. Finally, line 27 clears the value of the output Label because
the user is starting a new game.

Lines 30–31 remove any images from the PictureBoxes used to display
the point die. Though there are no images when the app is first run, if the
user chooses to continue playing after completing a game, the images from
the previous game must be cleared. Setting the Image property to keyword
Nothing indicates that there's no image to display. Keyword Nothing is
used to indicate that a variable does not refer to an object.

Line 33 declares the variable sum and assigns it the value returned by rolling the dice. This is accomplished by calling the RollDice procedure, which
you'll define later in this chapter. [*Note:* Again, RollDice is underlined in
blue because the procedure is not yet defined.] The RollDice Function
procedure not only rolls dice and returns the sum of their values, but also
displays the die images in the lower two PictureBoxes.

3. ***Using a Select Case statement to determine the result of rolling the dice.***
Recall that if the player rolls 7 or 11 on the first roll, the player wins, but if
the player rolls 2, 3 or 12 on the first roll, the player loses. Add lines 35–36 of
Fig. 16.13 to the playButton_Click event handler beneath the code you
added in the previous step, then press *Enter*. Note that the keywords End
Select are autogenerated. Now add lines 37–46 of Fig. 16.13 into the
playButton_Click event handler between the Select and End Select
keywords.

(cont.)

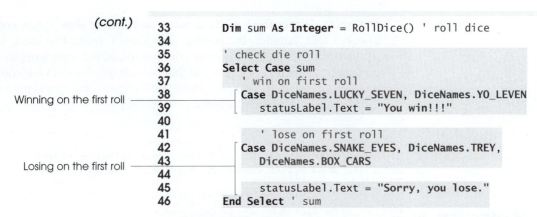

```
33          Dim sum As Integer = RollDice() ' roll dice
34
35          ' check die roll
36          Select Case sum
37              ' win on first roll
38          Case DiceNames.LUCKY_SEVEN, DiceNames.YO_LEVEN
39              statusLabel.Text = "You win!!!"
40
41              ' lose on first roll
42          Case DiceNames.SNAKE_EYES, DiceNames.TREY,
43              DiceNames.BOX_CARS
44
45              statusLabel.Text = "Sorry, you lose."
46          End Select ' sum
```

Winning on the first roll — (lines 38–39)

Losing on the first roll — (lines 42–45)

Figure 16.13   `Select Case` statement in `playButton_Click`.

The first `Case` statement (lines 38–39) selects values 7 and 11, using the enumeration values `DiceNames.LUCKY_SEVEN` and `DiceNames.YO_LEVEN`. Recall that several values can be specified in the same `Case` statement with a comma-separated list. If the sum of the dice is 7 or 11, the code in line 39 displays "You win!!!" in the output `statusLabel`. If the dice total is 2 (`Dice-Names.SNAKE_EYES`), 3 (`DiceNames.TREY`) or 12 (`DiceNames.BOX_CARS`), the code in the second `Case` statement executes (lines 42–45). This code displays a message in `statusLabel` indicating that the player has lost.

4. ***Using the Case Else statement to continue the game.*** If the player did not roll a 2, 3, 7, 11 or 12, then the value of the dice becomes the point and the player must roll again. Add lines 46–53 of Fig. 16.14 within the `Select Case` statement to implement this rule.

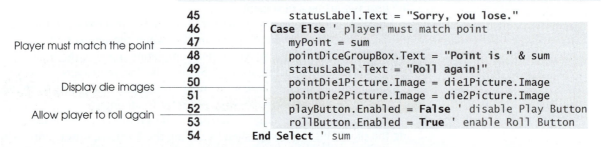

```
45              statusLabel.Text = "Sorry, you lose."
46          Case Else ' player must match point
47              myPoint = sum
48              pointDiceGroupBox.Text = "Point is " & sum
49              statusLabel.Text = "Roll again!"
50              pointDie1Picture.Image = die1Picture.Image
51              pointDie2Picture.Image = die2Picture.Image
52              playButton.Enabled = False ' disable Play Button
53              rollButton.Enabled = True ' enable Roll Button
54          End Select ' sum
```

Player must match the point — (lines 47–49)

Display die images — (lines 50–51)

Allow player to roll again — (lines 52–53)

Figure 16.14   `Case Else` statement in `playButton_Click`.

The first line of the `Case Else` statement's body (line 47) sets the instance variable `myPoint` to the sum of the die values. Next, line 48 changes the text in the `GroupBox`, using its `Text` property to display the value of the current point. Line 49, changes the `statusLabel` to notify the user to roll again.

If the user must match the point, you display the die images corresponding to the result of the dice roll. In Chapter 3, you learned how to insert an image into a `PictureBox`. To set the image for a `PictureBox`, you used its `Image` property. You can also use code to set this property. To display the die faces for the point in the `GroupBox`, set the `Image` property of each `PictureBox` in the `GroupBox` to the same `Image` property value as its corresponding `PictureBox` below the `GroupBox` (lines 50–51).

(cont.)   Recall that the `RollDice` method (which you'll define shortly) sets the `Image` properties of the lower `PictureBoxes`. Finally, the **Play** `Button` is disabled (line 52) and the **Roll** `Button` is enabled (line 53), limiting users to clicking the **Roll** `Button` for the rest of the game. Line 54 ends the `Select Case` statement.

5. ***Saving the project.*** Select **File > Save All** to save your modified code.

The **Roll** `Button` is enabled after the user clicks **Play** and does not win or lose on the first roll, so you must code an event handler for it. You'll define the event handler in the following box.

Coding the Roll Button's Click Event Handler

1. ***Generating the Roll Button's Click event handler.*** Return to **Design** view, and double click the **Roll** `Button` to generate the **Roll** `Button`'s `Click` event handler and open the code window. Add the comment and reformat the empty event handler as shown in lines 57–59 of Fig. 16.15.

2. ***Rolling the dice.*** The user clicks the **Roll** `Button` to try to match the point, which requires rolling dice. Add line 61 of Fig. 16.15, which rolls the dice, displays the die images and stores the sum of the dice in variable `sum`. [*Note:* `RollDice` is underlined in blue because the procedure is not yet defined. You'll define it to roll the dice and display the die images shortly.]

```
57      ' determine outcome of next roll
58      Private Sub rollButton_Click(sender As System.Object,
59         e As System.EventArgs) Handles rollButton.Click
60
61         Dim sum As Integer = RollDice() ' roll dice
62      End Sub ' rollButton_Click
```

Rolling the dice ⟶ 61

Figure 16.15   Rolling the dice in `rollButton_Click`.

3. ***Determining the output of the roll.*** If the roll matches the point, the user wins and the game ends. However, if the user rolls a 7 (`DiceNames.CRAPS`), the user loses and the game ends. Add lines 63–72 of Fig. 16.16 into the `rollButton_Click` event handler to incorporate this processing into your **Craps Game** app.

     The `If...Then` statement (lines 64–67) determines whether the sum of the dice in the current roll matches the point. If so, the program displays a winning message in `statusLabel`. It then allows the user to start a new game, by disabling the **Roll** `Button` and enabling the **Play** `Button`.

```
61         Dim sum As Integer = RollDice() ' roll dice
62
63         ' determine outcome of roll
64         If sum = myPoint Then ' player matches point
65            statusLabel.Text = "You win!!!"
66            rollButton.Enabled = False ' disable Roll Button
67            playButton.Enabled = True ' enable Play Button
68         ElseIf sum = DiceNames.CRAPS Then ' player loses
69            statusLabel.Text = "Sorry, you lose."
70            rollButton.Enabled = False ' disable Roll Button
71            playButton.Enabled = True ' enable Play Button
72         End If
73      End Sub ' rollButton_Click
```

Display winning message ⟶ 66

Display losing message ⟶ 70

Figure 16.16   Determining the outcome of a roll.

(cont.)

The ElseIf statement (lines 68–71) determines whether the sum of the dice in the current roll is 7 (DiceNames.CRAPS). If so, the app displays a message that the user has lost (in statusLabel) and ends the game by disabling the **Roll** Button and enabling the **Play** Button. If the player neither matches the point nor rolls a 7, then the player is allowed to roll again by clicking the **Roll** Button.

4. ***Saving the project.*** Select **File > Save All** to save your modified code.

In the following box, you'll add code to the app to simulate rolling dice and to display the dice in the appropriate PictureBoxes.

Using Random Numbers to Simulate Rolling Dice

1. ***Simulating die rolling.*** This app will roll and display dice many times as it executes. Therefore, it's a good idea to create two procedures: one to roll the dice (RollDice) and one to display a die (DisplayDie). Define Function procedure RollDice first, by adding lines 75–86 of Fig. 16.17.

```
73      End Sub ' rollButton_Click
74
75      ' generate random die rolls
76      Function RollDice() As Integer
77          ' roll the dice
78          Dim die1 As Integer = randomObject.Next(1, 7)
79          Dim die2 As Integer = randomObject.Next(1, 7)
80
81          ' display image corresponding to each die
82          DisplayDie(die1Picture, die1)
83          DisplayDie(die2Picture, die2)
84
85          Return (die1 + die2) ' return sum of dice values
86      End Function ' RollDice
```

Getting two random numbers — 78, 79

Displaying die images — 82

Returning sum of dice — 85

Figure 16.17 RollDice procedure definition.

This code sets the values of die1 and die2 to the values returned by randomObject.Next(1, 7), which is an Integer random number between 1 and 6 (lines 78 and 79). Remember that the number returned is always less than the second argument.

The procedure then calls DisplayDie (lines 82 and 83), a procedure that displays the image of the die face corresponding to each number. The first parameter in DisplayDie is the PictureBox that displays the image, and the second parameter is the number that appears on the face of the die. The calls to DisplayDie are underlined in blue as compilation errors because the procedure has not yet been defined. You'll define the DisplayDie procedure in *Step 2*. Finally, the procedure returns the sum of the values of the dice (line 85), which the app uses to determine the outcome of the craps game.

2. ***Displaying the dice images.*** You now define procedure DisplayDie to display the die images corresponding to the random numbers generated in procedure RollDice. Add lines 88–92 of Fig. 16.18 (after the RollDice procedure) to create the DisplayDie procedure.

Line 91 sets the Image property for the specified PictureBox. Because the Image property must be set using an object of type Image, you must create an Image object.

```
(cont.)   86        End Function ' RollDice
          87
          88          ' display die image
          89        Sub DisplayDie(die As PictureBox, face As Integer)
          90            ' assign die images to PictureBox
Displaying a die image ─ 91            die.Image = Image.FromFile(FILE_PREFIX & face & FILE_SUFFIX)
          92        End Sub ' DisplayDie
          93      End Class ' CrapsGameForm
```

Figure 16.18 `DisplayDie` procedure definition.

Class Image's **FromFile** method helps create Image objects. It returns an Image containing the image located at the specified path. In this case, you concatenate FILE_PREFIX & face & FILE_SUFFIX to create the file's path. If the value of face is 1, the concatenated string is images\die1.png—the image in the images folder of a die face showing 1. The app searches for the specified file in the directory in which its executable file (.exe) is located, in this case C:\SimplyVB2010\CrapsGame\bin\Debug\. This starting location combined with the file path created using the String constants indicates that the image is located at C:\SimplyVB2010\CrapsGame\bin\Debug\images\die1.png. If the image cannot be found at the location you specify, an exception is raised. You'll learn how to handle exceptions in Chapter 24. You can use Windows Explorer to verify that this is the correct location. This image is then displayed in the PictureBox by using its Image property.

3. **Running the app.** Select **Debug > Start Debugging** to run your completed app and enjoy the game!

4. **Closing the app.** Close your running app by clicking its close box.

5. **Closing the IDE.** Close the Visual Basic IDE by clicking its close box.

Figure 16.19 presents the source code for the **Craps Game** app. The lines of code that contain new programming concepts you learned in this chapter are highlighted. As part of the project settings, Option Strict is set to On (to prevent implicit narrowing conversions).

```
 1    Public Class CrapsGameForm
 2        ' die-roll constants
 3        Enum DiceNames
 4            SNAKE_EYES = 2
 5            TREY = 3
 6            CRAPS = 7
 7            LUCKY_SEVEN = 7
 8            YO_LEVEN = 11
 9            BOX_CARS = 12
10        End Enum
11
12        ' filename and directory constants
13        Const FILE_PREFIX As String = "images\die"
14        Const FILE_SUFFIX As String = ".png"
15
16        ' instance variables
17        Dim myPoint As Integer = 0
18        Dim randomObject As New Random()
19
20        ' begin new game and determine point
21        Private Sub playButton_Click(sender As System.Object,
22            e As System.EventArgs) Handles playButton.Click
23
```

Defining an enumeration ─ (lines 3–10)

Creating a Random object ─ (line 18)

Figure 16.19 **Craps Game** app's code. (Part 1 of 3.)

```
24          ' initialize variables for new game
25          myPoint = 0
26          pointDiceGroupBox.Text = "Point"
27          statusLabel.Text = String.Empty
28
29          ' remove point-die images
30          pointDie1Picture.Image = Nothing
31          pointDie2Picture.Image = Nothing
32
33          Dim sum As Integer = RollDice() ' roll dice
34
35          ' check die roll
36          Select Case sum
37             ' win on first roll
38             Case DiceNames.LUCKY_SEVEN, DiceNames.YO_LEVEN _
39                statusLabel.Text = "You win!!!"
40
41             ' lose on first roll
42             Case DiceNames.SNAKE_EYES, DiceNames.TREY, _
43                DiceNames.BOX_CARS
44
45                statusLabel.Text = "Sorry, you lose."
46             Case Else ' player must match point
47                myPoint = sum
48                pointDiceGroupBox.Text = "Point is " & sum
49                statusLabel.Text = "Roll again!"
50                pointDie1Picture.Image = die1Picture.Image
51                pointDie2Picture.Image = die2Picture.Image
52                playButton.Enabled = False ' disable Play Button
53                rollButton.Enabled = True ' enable Roll Button
54          End Select ' sum
55       End Sub ' playButton_Click
56
57       ' determine outcome of next roll
58       Private Sub rollButton_Click(sender As System.Object,
59          e As System.EventArgs) Handles rollButton.Click
60
61          Dim sum As Integer = RollDice() ' roll dice
62
63          ' determine outcome of roll
64          If sum = myPoint Then ' player matches point
65             statusLabel.Text = "You win!!!"
66             rollButton.Enabled = False ' disable Roll Button
67             playButton.Enabled = True ' enable Play Button
68          ElseIf sum = DiceNames.CRAPS Then ' player loses
69             statusLabel.Text = "Sorry, you lose."
70             rollButton.Enabled = False ' disable Roll Button
71             playButton.Enabled = True ' enable Play Button
72          End If
73       End Sub ' rollButton_Click
74
75       ' generate random die rolls
76       Function RollDice() As Integer
77          ' roll the dice
78          Dim die1 As Integer = randomObject.Next(1, 7)
79          Dim die2 As Integer = randomObject.Next(1, 7)
80
81          ' display image corresponding to each die
82          DisplayDie(die1Picture, die1)
83          DisplayDie(die2Picture, die2)
84
85          Return (die1 + die2) ' return sum of dice values
86       End Function ' RollDice
87
```

Labels (margin annotations):
- Removing the images from both point PictureBoxes → lines 30–31
- Using Enum constants → line 38
- Using Enum constants → lines 42–43
- Generating random numbers → lines 78–79

Figure 16.19 Craps Game app's code. (Part 2 of 3.)

Using code to display an image

```
88        ' display die image
89        Sub DisplayDie(die As PictureBox, face As Integer)
90           ' assign die images to PictureBox
91           die.Image = Image.FromFile(FILE_PREFIX & face & FILE_SUFFIX)
92        End Sub ' DisplayDie
93     End Class ' CrapsGameForm
```

Figure 16.19 **Craps Game** app's code. (Part 3 of 3.)

SELF-REVIEW

1. Use the _____ method of class `Image` to create an `Image` object from a file.
   a) `Image`
   b) `ImageFile`
   c) `Image.ImageFile`
   d) `Image.FromFile`

2. To clear the image in a `PictureBox`, set its `Image` property to _____.
   a) `String.Empty`
   b) `Nothing`
   c) `None`
   d) `Empty`

Answers: 1) d. 2) b.

16.5 Wrap-Up

In this chapter, you created the **Craps Game** app to simulate playing the popular dice game called craps. You learned about the Random class and how it can be used to generate random numbers by creating a Random object and calling method Next on it. You then learned how to specify the range of values within which random numbers should be generated by passing various arguments to method Next. You also learned about enumerations, which enhance program readability by using descriptive identifiers to represent constants in an app.

Using your knowledge of random-number generation and event handlers, you wrote code that added functionality to your **Craps Game** app. You used random-number generation to simulate the element of chance. In addition to "rolling dice" in code, you learned how to use a PictureBox to display an image by using code. In the next chapter, you learn how to use arrays, which allow you to use one name to store many values. You apply your knowledge of random numbers and arrays to create a **Flag Quiz** app that tests your knowledge of various nations' flags.

SKILLS SUMMARY

Generating Random Numbers

- Create an object of class Random, and call this object's Next or NextDouble methods.

Generating Random Numbers within a Specified Range

- Call the Random class's Next method with one argument to produce values from 0 up to, but not including, the argument's value.

- Call the Random class's Next method with two arguments to produce values from the first argument's value up to, but not including, the second argument's value.

Using Enumerations

- Begin the declaration of an enumeration with keyword Enum. Then use a list of descriptive names and set each one to the value it represents. End the enumeration with keywords End Enum.

- You can refer to the enumeration values using the enumeration name and the member-access operator followed by the name of the constant.

Creating an Image Object

- Pass a String representing the image's location to the Image.FromFile method.

Clearing a Reference's Value

- Assign the Nothing keyword to the variable storing the reference you wish to clear.

KEY TERMS

End Enum keywords—Ends an enumeration.

Enum keyword—Begins an enumeration.

enumeration—A group of related, named constants.

Image.FromFile—A Shared method of class Image that returns an Image object containing the image located at the specified path.

Int32.MaxValue constant—The largest possible 32-bit Integer (2,147,483,647).

Next method of class Random—A method of class Random that, when called with no arguments, generates a positive Integer value from zero, up to but not including, the value of the constant Int32.MaxValue. When called with arguments, the method generates an Integer value in a range constrained by those arguments.

NextDouble method of class Random—A method of class Random that generates a positive Double value that's greater than or equal to 0.0 and less than 1.0.

Nothing keyword—Used to clear a reference's value.

pseudorandom numbers—A sequence of values produced by a complex mathematical calculation that simulates random-number generation.

Random class—Contains methods to generate pseudorandom numbers.

reference—Keyword New creates a new object in memory and returns a reference to that object. You typically store an object's reference in a reference-type variable so that you can interact with the object.

CONTROLS, EVENTS, PROPERTIES & METHODS

Image This class provides functionality to manipulate images.

■ *Method*

FromFile—Used to specify the image to load and where it's located.

Random This class is used to generate random numbers.

■ *Methods*

Next—When called with no arguments, generates a positive Integer value between zero and the largest possible Integer, which is the constant Int32.MaxValue (2,147,483,647). When called with one argument, generates a positive Integer value from zero up to, but not including, the argument passed to it. When called with two arguments, generates a positive Integer value in the range from the first argument's value up to, but not including, the second argument's value.

NextDouble—Generates a positive Double value that's greater than or equal to 0.0 and less than 1.0.

MULTIPLE-CHOICE QUESTIONS

16.1 A Random object can generate pseudorandom numbers of type _____.

a) Integer   b) Single

c) Double   d) Both (a) and (c)

16.2 Constant identifiers within enumerations (e.g. SNAKE_EYES, TREY, CRAPS) _____ be assigned the same numeric value.

a) cannot   b) can

c) must   d) should

16.3 The Next method of class Random can be called using _____.

a) one argument   b) no arguments

c) two arguments   d) All of the above

16.4 The statement _____ assigns value a random number in the range 5–20.

a) value = randomObject.Next(5, 21)   b) value = randomObject.Next(4, 20)

c) value = randomObject.Next(5, 20)   d) value = randomObject.Next(4, 21)

16.5 The _____ method takes a parameter that specifies the file from which an image is loaded.

a) `Next` in class `Random`

b) `FromFile` in class `Image`

c) `File` in class `Image`

d) None of the above

16.6 The values returned by the methods of class `Random` are _____ numbers.

a) pseudorandom

b) completely random

c) ordered

d) None of the above

16.7 When creating random numbers, the second argument passed to the `Next` method is _____.

a) equal to the maximum value you wish to be generated

b) equal to one more than the maximum value you wish to be generated

c) equal to one less than the maximum value you wish to be generated

d) equal to the minimum value you wish to be generated

EXERCISES

16.8 *(Guess the Number App)* Develop an app that generates a random number and prompts the user to guess the number (Fig. 16.20). When the user clicks the **New Game** Button, the app chooses a number in the range 1 to 100 at random. The user enters guesses into the **Guess:** TextBox and clicks the **Enter** Button. If the guess is correct, the game ends, and the user can start a new game. If the guess is not correct, the app should indicate whether the guess is higher or lower than the correct number.

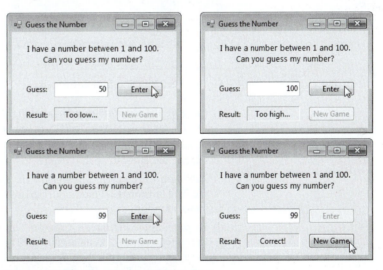

Figure 16.20 Guess the Number app.

a) *Copying the template to your working directory.* Copy the directory `C:\Examples\ch16\Exercises\GuessNumber` to your `C:\SimplyVB2010` directory.

b) *Opening the app's template file.* Double click `GuessNumber.sln` in the `GuessNumber` directory to open the app.

c) *Creating a Random object.* Create two instance variables. The first variable should reference a Random object, and the second variable should store a randomly generated number in the range of 1 to 100.

d) *Adding a `Click` event handler for the Enter Button.* Add a `Click` event handler for the **Enter** Button that retrieves the value entered by the user and compares it to the random number. If the guess is correct, display **Correct!** in the output Label. Then disable the **Enter** Button and enable the **New Game** Button. If the user's guess is higher than the correct answer, display **Too high...** in the output Label. If the user's guess is lower than the correct answer, display **Too low...** in the output Label. Place the focus on the **Guess:** TextBox.

e) *Adding a Click event handler for the New Game Button.* Add a Click event handler for the **New Game** Button that generates a new random number for the instance variable. The event handler should then disable the **New Game** Button, enable the **Enter** Button and clear the **Result:** Label and the **Guess:** TextBox. Move the focus to the **Guess:** TextBox.

f) *Adding a TextChanged event handler for the Guess: TextBox.* Add a TextChanged event handler for the **Guess:** TextBox that clears the **Result:** Label.

g) *Running the app.* Select **Debug > Start Debugging** to run your app. Enter guesses (clicking the **Enter** Button after each) until you've successfully determined the answer. Click the **New Game** Button and test the app again.

h) *Closing the app.* Close your running app by clicking its close box.

i) *Closing the IDE.* Close the Visual Basic IDE by clicking its close box.

16.9 *(Dice Simulator App)* Develop an app that simulates rolling two six-sided dice. Your app should have a **Roll** Button that, when clicked, displays two die images corresponding to random numbers. It should also display the number of times each face has appeared. Your app should look like Fig. 16.21.

Figure 16.21   Dice Simulator app.

a) *Copying the template to your working directory.* Copy the directory C:\Examples\ch16\Exercises\DiceSimulator to your C:\SimplyVB2010 directory.

b) *Opening the app's template file.* Double click DiceSimulator.sln in the DiceSimulator directory to open the app.

c) *Adding a Click event handler for the Roll Button.* Add a Click event handler for the **Roll** Button. Call method DisplayDie twice in this event handler to display the images for both dice.

d) *Displaying the die image.* Create a Sub procedure named DisplayDie that takes a PictureBox control as an argument. This method should generate a random number to simulate a die roll, then display the die image in the corresponding PictureBox control on the Form. The die image should correspond to the random number that was generated. To set the image, refer to the code presented in Fig. 16.19.

e) *Displaying the frequency.* Add a Sub procedure called DisplayFrequency to be called from DisplayDie that uses a Select Case statement to update the number of times each face has appeared. Create an enumeration for the die faces which will be used in the Select Case statement.

f) *Running the app.* Select **Debug > Start Debugging** to run your app. Click the **Roll** Button several times. Each time, two die faces are displayed. Verify after each roll that the appropriate face values on the left are incremented. You can perform several hundred rolls quickly by placing the focus on the **Roll Button** (by clicking it) and holding down the *Enter* key. The frequency of each face should be similar.

g) *Closing the app.* Close your running app by clicking its close box.

h) *Closing the IDE.* Close the Visual Basic IDE by clicking its close box.

16.10 *(Lottery Picker App)* A lottery commission offers four different lottery games to play: Three-number, Four-number, Five-number and Five-number + one lotteries. Each game has independent numbers. Develop an app that randomly picks numbers for all four games and displays the generated numbers in a GUI (Fig. 16.22). You should use two digits to display all numbers by using the D2 format specifier in a call to String.Format. The games are played as follows:

- Three-number lotteries require players to choose three numbers in the range 0–9.
- Four-number lotteries require players to choose four numbers in the range 0–9.
- Five-number lotteries require players to choose five numbers in the range 1–39.
- Five-number + 1 lotteries require players to choose five numbers in the range 1–49 and an additional number in the range of 1–42.

Figure 16.22   Lottery Picker app.

a) *Copying the template to your working directory.* Copy the directory C:\Examples\ ch16\Exercises\LotteryPicker to your C:\SimplyVB2010 directory.

b) *Opening the app's template file.* Double click LotteryPicker.sln in the LotteryPicker directory to open the app.

c) *Generating random numbers.* Create a Function procedure that generates a random number within a given range and returns it as a String. Create another Function procedure which generates a specified number of digits within a given range and returns the digits as a String. Use the previous Function to help implement this Function.

d) *Drawing numbers for the games.* Add code into your app to call the previously created procedure in order to generate numbers for all four games. To make the app simple, allow repetition of numbers.

e) *Running the app.* Select **Debug > Start Debugging** to run your app. Click the **Generate** Button multiple times. Make sure the values displayed are within the ranges described in the exercise description.

f) *Closing the app.* Close your running app by clicking its close box.

g) *Closing the IDE.* Close the Visual Basic IDE by clicking its close box.

What does this code do? ▶ **16.11** What does the following code do?

```
1   Sub PickRandomNumbers()
2
3       Dim number1 As Integer
4       Dim number As Double
5       Dim number2 As Integer
6       Dim randomObject As New Random()
7
8       number1 = randomObject.Next()
9       number = 5 * randomObject.NextDouble()
10      number2 = randomObject.Next(1, 10)
11      integer1Label.Text = Convert.ToString(number1)
12      double1Label.Text = Convert.ToString(number)
13      integer2Label.Text = Convert.ToString(number2)
14  End Sub ' PickRandomNumbers
```

16.12 *(Multiplication Teacher App)* Develop an app that helps children learn multiplication. Use random-number generation to produce two positive one-digit integers that display in a question, such as "How much is 6 times 7?" The student should type the answer into a TextBox. If the answer is correct, then the app randomly displays one of three messages in a Label, **Very Good!**, **Excellent!** or **Great Job!**. If the student is wrong, the Label displays the message **No. Please try again.** The GUI and sample user interactions are shown in Fig. 16.23.

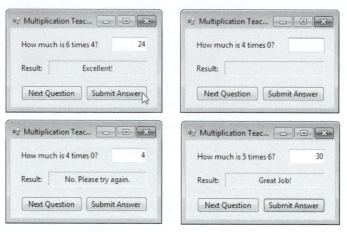

Figure 16.23 **Multiplication Teacher** app.

a) *Copying the template to your working directory.* Copy the directory C:\Examples\ch16\Exercises\MultiplicationTeacher to your C:\SimplyVB2010 directory.

b) *Opening the app's template file.* Double click MultiplicationTeacher.sln in the MultiplicationTeacher directory to open the app.

c) *Generating the questions.* Add a procedure into your app to generate each new question.

d) *Displaying a new question.* Add code into your app to call the procedure created in the preceding step when the user clicks the **Next Question** Button, as well as when the Form loads.

e) *Determining whether the right answer was entered.* When the user clicks the **Submit Answer** Button, determine whether the student answered the question correctly, and display the appropriate message.

f) *Displaying a random message.* Add a procedure GenerateOutput that displays a random message congratulating the student for answering correctly. This method should be called if the student answered the question correctly.

g) *Running the app.* Select **Debug > Start Debugging** to run your app. Enter several correct answers and at least one incorrect answer. Verify that **No. Please try again.** is displayed when you're incorrect, and one of the other responses is displayed at random when you're correct.

h) *Closing the app.* Close your running app by clicking its close box.

i) *Closing the IDE.* Close the Visual Basic IDE by clicking its close box.

Objectives

In this chapter, you'll learn to:
- Create and initialize arrays.
- Store information in an array.
- Refer to individual elements of an array.
- Sort arrays.
- Use **ComboBox**es to display options in a drop-down list.
- Replace characters in a **String**.

Outline

Flag Quiz App

Introducing One-Dimensional Arrays and ComboBoxes

This chapter introduces basic concepts and features of **data structures**. Data structures group and organize related data. **Arrays** are data structures that consist of data items of the same type. You'll learn how to create arrays and how to access the information they contain. You'll also learn how to sort a `String` array's information alphabetically.

This chapter's **Flag Quiz** app includes a ComboBox control. A ComboBox presents user options in a drop-down list that opens when you click the down arrow at the right side of the control. You may also type into the ComboBox control to locate an item. This is the first time that you'll add a ComboBox to an app, but you've used them many times before in the Visual Studio environment. For example, when you activated `Option Strict` in Chapter 15, you selected **On** from a ComboBox.

17.1 Test-Driving the Flag Quiz App

You'll now create an app that tests a student's knowledge of the flags of various countries. The app uses arrays to store information, such as the country names and `Boolean` values that determine whether a country name has been previously selected by the app as a correct answer. This app must meet the following requirements:

App Requirements

A geography teacher would like to quiz students on their knowledge of the flags of various countries. The teacher has asked you to write an app that displays a flag and allows the student to select the corresponding country from a list. The app should inform the user of whether the answer is correct and display the next flag. The app should display five flags randomly chosen from the flags of Australia, Brazil, China, Italy, Russia, South Africa, Spain and the United States. When the app is run, a given flag should be displayed only once.

You'll begin by test-driving the completed app. Then you'll learn the additional Visual Basic capabilities needed to create your own version of this app.

Test-Driving the Flag Quiz App

1. ***Opening the completed app.*** Open the directory C:\Examples\ch17\Com-pletedApp\FlagQuiz to locate the **Flag Quiz** app. Double click FlagQuiz.sln to open the app in the Visual Basic IDE.

2. ***Running the Flag Quiz app.*** Select **Debug > Start Debugging** to run the app (Fig. 17.1). Note that you might see a different flag when you run the app, because the app randomly selects which flag to display.

PictureBox displays flag

ComboBox contains answers (country names)

Figure 17.1   **Flag Quiz** app running.

3. ***Selecting an answer.*** The ComboBox contains eight country names. One country name corresponds to the displayed flag and is the correct answer. The scrollbar allows you to browse through the ComboBox's drop-down list. Select an answer from the ComboBox, as shown in Fig. 17.2.

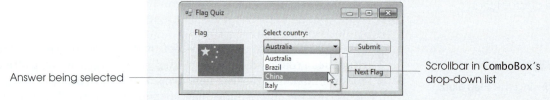

Answer being selected

Scrollbar in ComboBox's drop-down list

Figure 17.2   Selecting an answer from the ComboBox.

4. ***Submitting a correct answer.*** Click the **Submit** Button to check your answer. If it's correct, the message "Correct!" is displayed in an output Label (Fig. 17.3). Note that the **Submit** Button is now *disabled* and the **Next Flag** Button is *enabled*.

Figure 17.3   Submitting the correct answer.

5. ***Displaying the next flag.*** Click the **Next Flag** Button to display a different flag (Fig. 17.4). Note that the **Submit** Button is now *enabled*, the **Next Flag** Button is *disabled*, the ComboBox displays **Australia** (the first country listed in the ComboBox) and the output Label is cleared.

Figure 17.4   Displaying the next flag.

(cont.)   6. ***Submitting an incorrect answer.*** To demonstrate the app's response, select an incorrect answer and click **Submit**, as in Fig. 17.5. The app displays `"Sorry, incorrect."` in the output `Label`.

Figure 17.5   Submitting an incorrect answer.

7. ***Finishing the quiz.*** After the app displays five flags and the user has submitted five answers, the quiz ends (Fig. 17.6). Note that the two `Buttons` and the `ComboBox` are *disabled*.

ComboBox is disabled when the quiz ends

Figure 17.6   Finishing the quiz.

8. ***Closing the app***. Click your running app's close box.

9. ***Closing the IDE***. Close the Visual Basic IDE by clicking its close box.

17.2 Introducing Arrays

An array is a group of variables that all contain data items of the same array name and "element" type. Array names follow the same conventions that apply to other identifiers. To refer to a particular location in an array, you specify the name of the array and the **position number** of the location, which is a value that indicates a specific location within an array. Position numbers begin at 0 (zero).

Figure 17.7 depicts an `Integer` array named `netUnitsSold`. This array contains 13 items, also called **elements.** Each array element represents the net number of "units sold" of a particular book in one month at a bookstore. For example, `netUnitsSold(1)` is the net sales of that book for January (month 1), `netUnitsSold(2)` is the net sales for February, and so on. In this example, you simply ignore the first element of the array, because there's no month zero.

Each array element is referred to by providing the name of the array followed by the position number of the element in parentheses (). The position numbers for the elements in an array begin with 0. Thus, the element 0 of array `netUnitsSold` is referred to as `netUnitsSold(0)`, element 1 of array `netUnitsSold` is referred to as `netUnitsSold(1)`, element 6 of array `netUnitsSold` is referred to as `netUnitsSold(6)` and so on. Element *i* of array `netUnitsSold` is referred to as `netUnitsSold(i)`. The position number in parentheses is called an **index.** An index must be either zero, a positive integer or an integer expression that yields a nonnegative result. If an app uses an expression as an index, the expression is evaluated *first to* determine the index. For example, if variable `value1` is equal to 5, and variable `value2` is equal to 6, then the following statement adds 2 to `netUnitsSold(11)`

```
netUnitsSold(value1 + value2) += 2
```

Note that an **indexed array name** (the array name followed by an index enclosed in parentheses)—like any other variable name—can be used on the left side of an assignment to place a new value into an array element.

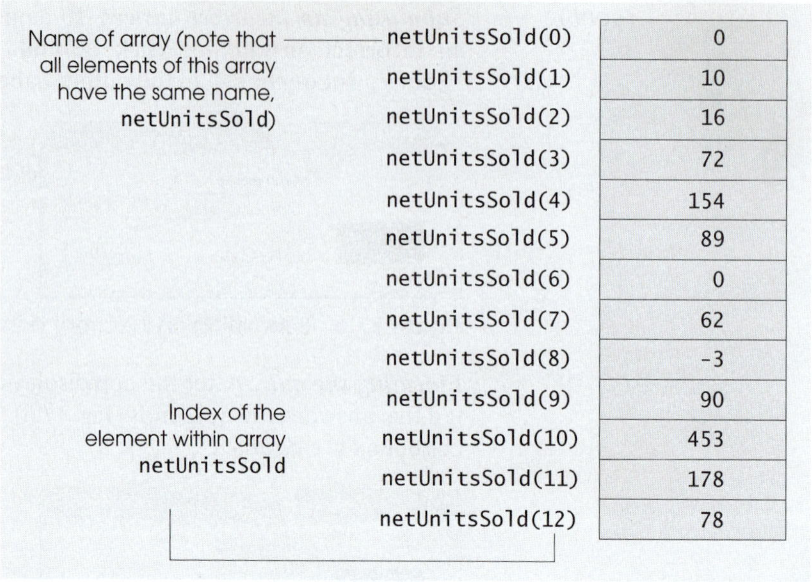

Name of array (note that all elements of this array have the same name, netUnitsSold)	netUnitsSold(0)	0
	netUnitsSold(1)	10
	netUnitsSold(2)	16
	netUnitsSold(3)	72
	netUnitsSold(4)	154
	netUnitsSold(5)	89
	netUnitsSold(6)	0
	netUnitsSold(7)	62
	netUnitsSold(8)	-3
Index of the element within array netUnitsSold	netUnitsSold(9)	90
	netUnitsSold(10)	453
	netUnitsSold(11)	178
	netUnitsSold(12)	78

Figure 17.7   Array consisting of 13 elements.

Let's examine array `netUnitsSold` in Fig. 17.7 more closely. The name of the array is `netUnitsSold`. The 13 elements of the array are referred to as `netUnitsSold(0)` through `netUnitsSold(12)`. The value of `netUnitsSold(1)` is 10, the value of `netUnitsSold(2)` is 16, the value of `netUnitsSold(3)` is 72, the value of `netUnitsSold(7)` is 62 and the value of `netUnitsSold(11)` is 178. A positive value for an element in this array indicates that more books were sold than were returned. A negative value for an element in this array indicates that more books were returned than were sold. A value of zero indicates that the number of books sold was equal to the number of books returned.

Values stored in arrays can be used in various calculations and apps. For example, to determine the net units sold in the first three months of the year, then store the result in variable `firstQuarterUnits`, we'd write

```
firstQuarterUnits =
    netUnitsSold(1) + netUnitsSold(2) + netUnitsSold(3)
```

You'll use **one-dimensional** arrays, such as `netUnitsSold`, in this chapter. The indexed array names of one-dimensional arrays use only one index. In the next chapter, you'll study two-dimensional arrays—their indexed array names use two indices.

SELF-REVIEW   1. The number that refers to a particular element of an array is called its _____.

    a) value   b) size

    c) indexed array name   d) index

2. The indexed array name of one-dimensional array `units`'s element 2 is _____.

    a) `units{2}`   b) `units(2)`

    c) `units[0,2]`   d) `units[2]`

Answers: 1) d. 2) b.

17.3 Declaring and Allocating Arrays

To declare an array, you'll provide its name and data type. Either of the following statements declares the array in Fig. 17.7:

```
Dim netUnitsSold As Integer()
Dim netUnitsSold() As Integer
```

The parentheses that follow the data type indicate that `netUnitsSold` is an array. Arrays can be declared to contain any data type. In an array of a primitive data type, every element contains one value of the declared type. For example, every element of an `Integer` array contains an `Integer` value.

Before you can use an array, you must specify its *size* and allocate *memory* for it. Arrays are represented as objects in Visual Basic, and all objects are typically allocated by using keyword New. The value stored in the array variable is actually a reference to the array object. To allocate memory for the array `netUnitsSold` *after* it's been declared, use the statement

```
netUnitsSold = New Integer(0 To 12) {}
```

Common Programming Error

Attempting to access elements in the array by using an index *outside* the array bounds results in an `IndexOutOfRangeException`. We discuss exceptions in Chapter 24.

Array bounds determine what indices can be used to access an element in the array. Here, the array bounds are 0 and 12 (one less than the number of elements in the array). Because array indices begin at 0, the actual number of array elements (13) is one larger than the upper bound specified in the allocation (12).

The required braces ({ and }) are called an **initializer list** and specify the initial element values. When the initializer list is *empty*, as it is here, the array elements are initialized to the *default value* for the array's data type—0 for numeric primitive-data-type variables (such as `Integer`), `False` for `Boolean` variables and `Nothing` for references. Recall that keyword `Nothing` denotes an *empty reference* (that is, a value indicating that a reference variable has not been assigned an object).

If you know the number of elements at the time you declare the array, you can write the array declaration as

```
Dim netUnitsSold(0 To 12) As Integer
```

which creates a 13-element array. In this case, the compiler implicitly uses the New keyword for you.

An initializer list may also contain a comma-separated list specifying the initial values of the elements in the array. For example, the statements

```
Dim salesPerDay As Integer()
salesPerDay = New Integer() {0, 2, 3, 6, 1, 4, 5, 6}
```

Common Programming Error

If you specify an upper bound when initializing an array, it's a compilation error if you provide too many or too few values in the initializer list.

declare and allocate an array of eight `Integer` values. The compiler determines the array bounds from the number of elements in the initializer list. Thus, it's *not* necessary to specify the size of the array when you use a nonempty initializer list.

You can specify *both* the array bounds and an initializer list, as in:

```
Dim temperatures As Double() =
    New Double(0 To 3) {23.45, 34.98, 78.98, 53.23}
```

The upper bound is one less than the number of items in the array. The preceding statement can also be written as

```
Dim temperatures As Double() = {23.45, 34.98, 78.98, 53.23}
```

In this case, the compiler determines the array bounds from the number of elements in the initializer list and *implicitly* uses the New keyword for you.

You can simplify the preceding statement further by using local type inference to determine the array's type as follows:

```
Dim temperatures = {23.45, 34.98, 78.98, 53.23}
```

In this case, the compiler infers from the initializer list that temperatures is an array of `Double`s.

Arrays can also be initialized using implicit lower bounds. For example, the preceding statement could have been written as follows:

```
Dim temperatures As Double() =
    New Double(3) {23.45, 34.98, 78.98, 53.23}
```

In this case the value 0 and the keyword To are not included in the parentheses.

Often, the elements of an array are used in a calculation. The following box demonstrates declaring and initializing an array and accessing its elements.

Computing the Sum of an Array's Elements

1. *Copying the template to your working directory.* Copy the C:\Examples\ ch17\TemplateApp\SumArray directory to C:\SimplyVB2010.

2. *Opening the Sum Array app's template file.* Double click SumArray.sln in the SumArray directory to open the app in the Visual Basic IDE.

3. *Adding the Button's Click event handler.* Double click the **Sum Array** Button in **Design** view (Fig. 17.8) to generate the empty event handler sumButton_Click. Add a comment in line 2 of Fig. 17.9 and split the header over two lines, as shown in lines 3–4.

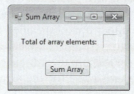

Figure 17.8 **Sum Array** app's Form in **Design** view.

4. *Combining the declaration and allocation of an array.* Add lines 6–8 of Fig. 17.9 to the event handler. Line 7 combines the declaration and allocation of an array into one statement. Variable values is a reference to an array of Integers containing 10 elements that are initialized with the values from 1 to 10. Line 8 declares and initializes variable total, which will be used to sum the values in the array.

```
1   Public Class SumArrayForm
2       ' handles Sum Array Button's Click event
3       Private Sub sumButton_Click(sender As System.Object,
4           e As System.EventArgs) Handles sumButton.Click
5
6           ' declare and initialize array
7           Dim values As Integer() = {1, 2, 3, 4, 5, 6, 7, 8, 9, 10}
8           Dim total As Integer = 0
```

Creating an array of Integers

Figure 17.9 Declaring an array in the event handler.

Error-Prevention Tip

Use method GetUpperBound when you need to find an array's highest index. Using an actual numerical value for the upper bound instead could lead to errors if you change the number of array elements.

Error-Prevention Tip

It's important to note the difference between the "seventh element of the array" and "array element seven." Array indices begin at 0, which means that the former has the index 6, whereas the latter has the index 7. This confusion is a common source of "off-by-one" errors.

5. *Calculating the sum.* Add lines 10–16 (Fig. 17.10) to the event handler. The For...Next loop (lines 11–14) retrieves each element's value (one at a time) and adds it to the total (line 13). Method **GetUpperBound** (line 11) returns the index of the array's last element. GetUpperBound takes one argument, indicating a dimension of the array. For one-dimensional arrays, such as values in this example, GetUpperBound's argument is always 0, to indicate the first (and only) dimension of the array. In this case, values.GetUpperBound(0) returns 9. We discuss arrays with *two* dimensions in Chapter 18.

Every array in Visual Basic "knows" its own length. The **length** (or the number of elements) of the array (10 in this case) is returned by the expression values.Length.

We could have set the upper bound in the For...Next loop as

```
values.Length - 1
```

which returns 9. The value returned by method GetUpperBound is the last index in the array—one less than the value of the array's **Length** property.

(cont.)

Retrieve the value of each
element and add it to the
total, one at a time

```
 8        Dim total As Integer = 0
 9
10        ' loop through indices 0 to 9 (the upper bound)
11        For index As Integer = 0 To values.GetUpperBound(0)
12           ' add the array elements to the total
13           total += values(index)
14        Next
15
16        resultLabel.Text = Convert.ToString(total) ' display result
17     End Sub ' sumButton_Click
18  End Class ' SumArrayForm
```

Figure 17.10   Calculating the sum of the values of an array's elements.

6. *Displaying the result.* Line 16 displays the sum of the array element values.

7. *Running the app.* Select **Debug > Start Debugging** to run your app. The result of adding the integers from 1 to 10, inclusive, is displayed when you click the **Sum Array** Button (Fig. 17.11).

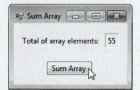

Figure 17.11   Displaying the sum of the values of an array's elements.

8. *Closing the app.* Close your running app by clicking its close box.

9. *Closing the IDE.* Close the Visual Basic IDE by clicking its close box.

SELF-REVIEW   1. Arrays can be allocated using keyword _____.

a) `Declare`   b) `Create`

c) `New`   d) `Allocate`

2. An array's length is _____.

a) one more than the array's last index   b) one less than the array's last index

c) the same as the array's last index   d) returned by method `GetUpperBound`

Answers: 1) c. 2) a.

17.4 Constructing the Flag Quiz App

Before you begin building the **Flag Quiz** app, you need to develop it using pseudocode and an ACE table. The following pseudocode describes the basic operation of the **Flag Quiz** app:

> When the Form loads:
>   Sort the country names alphabetically
>   Place country names in the ComboBox
>   Call DisplayFlag to randomly select a flag and display it

When the user clicks the Submit Button:
    Retrieve the selected country name
    If the selected value matches the correct answer
        Display "Correct!" in the Label
    Else
        Display "Sorry, incorrect." in the Label

    If five images have been displayed
        Append "Done!" to the Label's text
        Disable the Next Flag Button and the ComboBox
    Else
        Enable Next Flag Button

    Disable Submit Button

When the user clicks the Next Flag Button:
    Call DisplayFlag to randomly select a flag and display it
    Clear the Label's text
    Set ComboBox to display its first item
    Update the number of flags shown
    Enable Submit Button
    Disable Next Flag Button

When DisplayFlag is called:
    Call GetUniqueRandomNumber to obtain the index of a flag that has not yet
        been used
    Obtain the name of the country from the countries array
    Call BuildPathName to get the image's path and filename
    Display the flag in a PictureBox

When GetUniqueRandomNumber is called:
    Create a Random object
    Select the index of a flag that has not been used
    Set the corresponding element of the used array to true
    Return the index

When BuildPathName is called:
    Use String method Replace to remove spaces from the country String
    Return a String containing the corresponding image's path and filename

Now that you've test-driven the **Flag Quiz** app and studied its pseudocode representation, you'll use an ACE table to help you convert the pseudocode to Visual Basic. Figure 17.12 lists the *actions*, *controls* and *events* that help you complete your own version of this app.

Action/Control/Event (ACE) Table for the Flag Quiz App	Action	Control/Class/Object	Event or Method
	Label the app's controls	`flagGroupBox`, `selectLabel`	App is Run
		`FlagQuizForm`	Load
	Sort the countries alphabetically	`Array`, `countries` (array)	
	Place country names in the ComboBox	`countriesCombo-Box`	
	Call DisplayFlag to randomly select a flag and display it		

Figure 17.12   **Flag Quiz** app's ACE table. (Part 1 of 3.)

Action	Control/Class/ Object	Event or Method
	submitButton	Click
Retrieve the selected country name	countriesCombo-Box	
If the selected value matches the correct answer Display "Correct!" in the Label	feedbackLabel	
Else Display "Sorry, incorrect." in Label	feedbackLabel	
If five images have been displayed Append "Done!" to Label's text	feedbackLabel	
Disable the Next Flag Button and the ComboBox	nextButton, countriesCombo-Box	
Else Enable Next Flag Button	nextButton	
Disable Submit Button	submitButton	
	nextButton	Click
Call DisplayFlag to randomly select a flag and display it		
Clear the Label's text	feedbackLabel	
Set ComboBox to display its first item	countriesCombo-Box	
Update the number of flags shown		
Enable Submit Button	submitButton	
Disable Next Flag Button	nextButton	
		Display-Flag
Call GetUniqueRandomNumber to obtain the index of a flag that has not yet been used		
Obtain the name of the country from the countries array	countries (array)	
Call BuildPathName to get the image's path and filename		
Enable Submit Button	submitButton	
Display the flag in a PictureBox	flagPicture	
		Get-Unique-Random-Number
Create a Random object	randomObject	
Select the index of a flag that has not been used	randomObject, used (array)	
Set the corresponding element of the used array to true	used (array)	
Return the index		

Figure 17.12   **Flag Quiz** app's ACE table. (Part 2 of 3.)

Action	Control/Class/ Object	Event or Method
		Build- PathName
Use String method Replace to remove spaces from the country String	country	
Return a String containing the corresponding image's path and filename		

Figure 17.12 **Flag Quiz** app's ACE table. (Part 3 of 3.)

The following box shows you how to initialize the variables used in the app. In particular, the app requires two one-dimensional arrays.

Initializing Important Variables

1. *Copying the template to your working directory.* Copy the C:\Examples\ ch17\TemplateApp\FlagQuiz directory to C:\SimplyVB2010.

2. *Opening the Flag Quiz app's template file.* Double click FlagQuiz.sln in the FlagQuiz directory to open the app in the Visual Basic IDE.

3. *Declaring the array of country names.* Add lines 2–4 of Fig. 17.13 to the app. Lines 3–4 declare and initialize array countries as an instance variable of class FlagQuizForm. Each element is a String containing the name of a country. These lines assign the initializer list to the array, combining the declaration and initialization into one statement. The compiler determines the array's size (in this case, 8) based on the number of values in the initializer list.

```
1    Public Class FlagQuizForm
2        ' String array stores country names
3        Dim countries As String() = {"Russia", "China", "Australia",
4            "United States", "Italy", "South Africa", "Brazil", "Spain"}
```

Creating an array of Strings to store country names — (lines 3–4)

Figure 17.13 String array that stores country names.

4. *Creating a Boolean array.* The app should display each flag once. Since the app uses random-number generation to pick a flag, the same flag could be selected multiple times—just as, when you roll a six-sided die many times, a die face could be repeated. You'll use a Boolean array to keep track of which flags have been displayed. Add lines 6–8 of Fig. 17.14 to Flag-Quiz.vb. Lines 7–8 declare and create Boolean array named used.

```
4            "United States", "Italy", "South Africa", "Brazil", "Spain"}
5
6        ' Boolean array tracks displayed flags
7        Dim used As Boolean() =
8            New Boolean(0 To countries.GetUpperBound(0)) {}
```

Creating an array of Boolean values with the same number of elements as the array of country names — (lines 7–8)

Figure 17.14 Boolean array that keeps track of displayed flags.

Method GetUpperBound returns array countries's highest index, which is used as the upper bound of used. Therefore, array used has the same size as array countries. The elements of used correspond to the elements of countries—used(0) specifies whether the flag corresponding to the country name in countries(0) (Russia) has been displayed. By default, each uninitialized element in a Boolean array is False. The app will set an element of used to True if its corresponding flag has been displayed.

(cont.)   5.   ***Initializing a counter and a variable to store the answer.*** Add lines 10–11 of
                   Fig. 17.15 to `FlagQuiz.vb`. The app ensures that only five flags are displayed
                   by incrementing variable `count`, which is initialized to 1 (line 10). The cor-
                   rect answer (the name of the country whose flag is displayed) will be stored
                   in `country` (line 11).

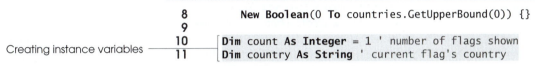

```
 8              New Boolean(0 To countries.GetUpperBound(0)) {}
 9
10    Dim count As Integer = 1 ' number of flags shown
11    Dim country As String ' current flag's country
```

Creating instance variables

Figure 17.15   Instance variables used throughout the app.

6.   ***Saving the project.*** Select **File > Save All** to save your modified code.

GUI Design Tip

Each **ComboBox** should be accompanied by a descriptive **Label** describing the **ComboBox**'s contents.

Now you'll add another control to the **Flag Quiz** app template. The **Flag Quiz**
app allows students to select answers from a ComboBox. The **ComboBox** control combines features of a `TextBox` and a `ListBox`. A ComboBox usually appears as a Text-
Box with a down arrow to its right. The user can click the down arrow to display a
list of predefined items. If a user chooses an item from this list, that item is displayed in the ComboBox. If the list contains more items than the drop-down list can
display at one time, a vertical scrollbar appears. The following box shows you how
to assign an array's elements to a ComboBox before the `Form` is displayed to the user.

Adding and Customizing a ComboBox

1.   ***Adding a ComboBox to the Form.*** Double click `FlagQuiz.vb` in the **Solution**
     Explorer to display the app's Form (Fig. 17.16). Add a ComboBox to the Form
     by double clicking the

          📇 ComboBox

     control in the **Toolbox**.

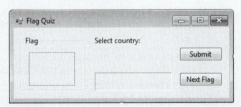

Figure 17.16   **Flag Quiz** template app's Form.

2.   ***Customizing the ComboBox.*** Change the Name property of the ComboBox to
     `countriesComboBox`. Position the ComboBox just below the **Select country:**
     Label and match its width with that of the output Label below it. The Form
     should look like Fig. 17.17.

Good Programming Practice

Append the **ComboBox** suffix to ComboBox control names.

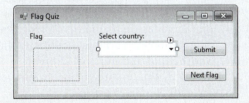

Figure 17.17   ComboBox added to **Flag Quiz** app's Form.

(cont.)

GUI Design Tip

If a ComboBox's content should not be editable, set its DropDownStyle property to DropDownList.

3. **Setting the appearance of the ComboBox.** Property `DropDownStyle` determines the ComboBox's appearance. Value `DropDownList` specifies that the ComboBox is not editable (the user cannot type text in its `TextBox`). You can click the arrow button to display a drop-down list from which you can select an item. In this ComboBox style, if you press the key that corresponds to the first letter of an item in the ComboBox, that item is selected and displayed in the ComboBox's TextBox. Set the DropDownStyle property of the ComboBox to DropDownList. Then, set the `MaxDropDownItems` property of the countriesComboBox to 4, so that the drop-down list displays a maximum of four items at one time. A vertical scrollbar is added to the drop-down list to allow users to scroll through the remaining items.

4. **Generating an event handler to add items to the ComboBox during the Load event.** The ComboBox should contain a list of country names when the Form is displayed. The Form's Load event occurs before the Form is displayed—as a result, you should add the items to the ComboBox in the Form's Load event handler. Double click the Form to generate the empty event handler FlagQuizForm_Load.

5. **Displaying items in the ComboBox.** Add a comment and format the FlagQuizForm_Load event handler as shown in lines 13–15 of Fig. 17.18, then add lines 17–18. ComboBox property `DataSource` (line 18) specifies the source of the items displayed in the ComboBox. In this case, the source is array countries.

```
13      ' handles Flag Quiz Form's Load event
14      Private Sub FlagQuizForm_Load(sender As System.Object,
15         e As System.EventArgs) Handles MyBase.Load
16
17         ' display country names in ComboBox
18         countriesComboBox.DataSource = countries
19      End Sub ' FlagQuizForm_Load
```

Specifying the source of the ComboBox items ⎯⎯ (pointing to line 18)

Figure 17.18   Assigning the `String` elements of an array to a ComboBox.

6. **Saving the project.** Select **File > Save All** to save your modified code.

Recall that to specify the image displayed in a `PictureBox`, you need to set its Image property to the image's filename. The flag images are located at `C:\Simply-VB2010\FlagQuiz\bin\Debug\images`. The name of each flag-image file is of the form *countryname*`.png`, where *countryname* has no whitespace. The following box shows how the app constructs the full path name needed to locate and display each flag.

Building a Flag-Image File's Path Name

1. **Creating a procedure to build the flag-image file's path name.** Add lines 21–25 of Fig. 17.19 to the **Flag Quiz** app after event handler FlagQuizForm_Load. Function BuildPathName constructs and returns a relative path that includes the name of a flag-image's file. The country name is retrieved from instance variable country (the correct answer). Line 23 uses the String.Format method to create a String that begins with images\ followed by the country name (which is substituted at for {0}) and the .png image filename extension.

(cont.)

Removing whitespace from a country name

```
21      ' return full path name of image file as a String
22      Function BuildPathName() As String
23          Return String.Format("images\{0}.png",
24                      country.Replace(" ", String.Empty))
25      End Function ' BuildPathName
```

Figure 17.19   Removing whitespace from the country name.

Some countries—for example, South Africa and the United States—have space characters in their names, but the flag-image filenames do *not* contain spaces. Line 24 uses `String` method **Replace** to replace occurrences of the space character with an empty `String`. The `Replace` method takes two arguments—a `String` to replace in the original `String` and a `String` with which to replace all occurrences of the first argument. Method `Replace` returns a new `String` with the specified replacements. If there are no occurrences of the first argument in the `String`, the method returns a *copy* of the original `String`. [*Note:* `String` methods, such as `Replace`, do *not* modify the `String` object for which they're called. The `String` object returned by these methods contains a *copy* of the modified `String`.]

2. ***Saving the project.*** Select **File > Save All** to save your modified code.

To ensure that the user is not asked the same question twice, a flag must be displayed no more than once when running the app. The app uses the `Boolean` array `used` to track which flags have been displayed. The following box shows you how to ensure that the app displays a flag no more than *once*.

Selecting a Unique Flag to Display

1. ***Creating the GetUniqueRandomNumber procedure.*** Add lines 27–28 of Fig. 17.20 to the **Flag Quiz** app after procedure `BuildPathName`. Line 28 is the header for the `GetUniqueRandomNumber` procedure. `GetUniqueRandomNumber` returns the index of a country name whose flag has not been displayed.

Determining whether a country's flag has been displayed previously

```
25      End Function ' BuildPathName
26
27      ' return an unused random number
28      Function GetUniqueRandomNumber() As Integer
29          Dim randomObject As New Random()
30          Dim randomNumber As Integer
31
32          Do ' generate random numbers until unused flag is found
33              randomNumber = randomObject.Next(0, used.Length)
34          Loop Until used(randomNumber) = False
```

Figure 17.20   Generating a unique index.

2. ***Generating a random index.*** Add line 29 of Fig. 17.20 to the procedure `GetUniqueRandomNumber`. To select the next flag to display, you'll create a `Random` object that you'll use to select random flags.

3. ***Ensuring that each flag displays only once.*** Add lines 30–34 of Fig. 17.20 to `GetUniqueRandomNumber`. Method `Next` (line 33) of class `Random` generates a random index between 0 and `used.Length` (the number of country names). If the index has been selected previously, the element of `used` at the generated index is `True`. The `Do...Loop Until` statement (lines 32–34) iterates until it finds an *unused* flag (that is, until `used(randomNumber)` is `False`).

(cont.)

4. ***Indicating that the index has been used.*** Add lines 36–37 of Fig. 17.21 to the `GetUniqueRandomNumber` procedure. Line 37 sets the element at the selected index of `used` to `True`. This indicates that the flag has been used. Checking the values in this array ensures that the index will *not* be used again in the app.

```
34         Loop Until used(randomNumber) = False
35
36         ' indicate that flag has been used
37         used(randomNumber) = True
38
39         Return randomNumber ' return index for new flag
40      End Function ' GetUniqueRandomNumber
```

Indicate that the unused flag will be displayed, then return the flag's index for use → (lines 36–37, 39)

Figure 17.21 Returning the unique index.

5. ***Returning the unique random number.*** Add line 39 of Fig. 17.21 to the `GetUniqueRandomNumber` procedure to return the unique random index.

6. ***Saving the project.*** Select **File > Save All** to save your modified code.

With the full path name and a unique flag selected, the app can display that flag. The following box shows how to display the selected flag.

Displaying a Flag

1. ***Creating the `DisplayFlag` procedure.*** Add lines 42–43 of Fig. 17.22 to the **Flag Quiz** app after procedure `GetUniqueRandomNumber`. Procedure `DisplayFlag` selects a random country name and displays that country's flag.

```
40      End Function ' GetUniqueRandomNumber
41
42      ' display random flag in PictureBox
43      Sub DisplayFlag()
44         ' unique index ensures that a flag is used no more than once
45         Dim randomNumber As Integer = GetUniqueRandomNumber()
46
47         ' retrieve country name from array countries
48         country = countries(randomNumber)
```

Getting the index of an unused flag → (line 45)

Retrieving the flag's corresponding country name → (line 48)

Figure 17.22 Choosing a random country name.

2. ***Obtaining a unique index.*** Add lines 44–45 of Fig. 17.22 to the `DisplayFlag` procedure. Line 45 invokes `GetUniqueRandomNumber` to find an index of a flag that has not been displayed during the app's execution and assigns the index to `randomNumber`.

3. ***Retrieving a country name.*** Add lines 47–48 of Fig. 17.22 to the `DisplayFlag` procedure. Line 48 obtains the flag's corresponding country name from index `randomNumber` of `String` array `countries` and assigns it to instance variable `country`, which represents the correct answer.

4. ***Building the flag image's path name.*** Add lines 50–51 of Fig. 17.23 to the `DisplayFlag` procedure. Line 51 invokes procedure `BuildPathName`. The procedure returns the flag image's path name, which is assigned to `path`.

(cont.)

Getting the path name of
the flag and displaying
the flag image

```
48        country = countries(randomNumber)
49
50        ' get image's full path name
51        Dim path As String = BuildPathName()
52        flagPicture.Image = Image.FromFile(path) ' display image
53     End Sub ' DisplayFlag
```

Figure 17.23 Displaying a flag image.

5. ***Displaying the flag image.*** Add line 52 of Fig. 17.23 to the DisplayFlag
   procedure. Line 52 sets flagPicture's Image property to the Image object
   returned by method Image.FromFile. Recall that method Image.FromFile
   returns an Image object from the specified file.

6. ***Displaying a flag when the app is run.*** When the Form loads, the first flag
   image in the quiz is displayed. The Form's Load event handler should invoke
   procedure DisplayFlag. Add line 20 of Fig. 17.24 to the event handler
   FlagQuizForm_Load.

```
13     ' handles Flag Quiz Form's Load event
14     Private Sub FlagQuizForm_Load(sender As System.Object,
15        e As System.EventArgs) Handles MyBase.Load
16
17        ' display country names in ComboBox
18        countriesComboBox.DataSource = countries
19
20        DisplayFlag() ' display first flag in PictureBox
21     End Sub ' FlagQuizForm_Load
```

Displaying a flag when app is
first run

Figure 17.24 Displaying a flag when the **Form** is loaded.

7. ***Saving the project.*** Select **File > Save All** to save your modified code.

The user submits an answer by selecting a country name from the ComboBox
and clicking the **Submit** Button. The app displays whether the user's answer is correct. If the app is finished (that is, five flags have been displayed), the app informs
the user that the quiz is done—otherwise, the app enables the user to view the next
flag. The following box implements this functionality.

Processing a User's
Answer

1. ***Adding the Submit Button's Click event handler.*** Double click the **Submit**
   Button to generate the Click event handler submitButton_Click. Format
   it as shown in lines 57–59 of Fig. 17.25.

```
57     ' handles Submit Button's Click event
58     Private Sub submitButton_Click(sender As System.Object,
59        e As System.EventArgs) Handles submitButton.Click
60
61        ' retrieve answer from ComboBox
62        Dim response As String = countriesComboBox.Text
63
64        ' verify answer
65        If response = country Then
66           feedBackLabel.Text = "Correct!"
67        Else
68           feedBackLabel.Text = "Sorry, incorrect."
69        End If
```

Retrieving the user's answer

Determining whether the
user's answer is correct

Figure 17.25 Submit Button Click event handler.

(cont.)

2. ***Retrieving the selected ComboBox item.*** Add lines 61–62 of Fig. 17.25 to the empty event handler. Line 62 retrieves the user's answer by using the ComboBox's Text property. Property **Text** returns the String that's currently selected in the ComboBox. Variable response contains the selected country's name.

3. ***Verifying the user's answer.*** Add lines 64–69 of Fig. 17.25 to submitButton_Click. The If...Then...Else statement (lines 65–69) determines whether the user's response matches the correct answer and displays "Correct!" in the Label if the user's response matches the correct answer (line 66); otherwise, it displays "Sorry, incorrect." (line 68).

4. ***Informing the user that the quiz is over when five flags have been displayed.*** Add lines 71–80 of Fig. 17.26 to the submitButton_Click event handler. If five flags have been displayed, the Label displays text informing the user that the quiz is over (line 73), the nextButton is disabled (line 74) and the countriesComboBox is disabled (line 75)—by setting its **Enabled** property to False.

```
69          End If
70
71          ' inform user if quiz is over
72          If count >= 5 Then ' quiz is over
73              feedBackLabel.Text &= "  Done!"
74              nextButton.Enabled = False
75              countriesComboBox.Enabled = False
76          Else ' quiz is not over
77              nextButton.Enabled = True
78          End If
79
80          submitButton.Enabled = False
81      End Sub ' submitButton_Click
```

Determining whether the quiz is over → 75

Figure 17.26 Testing whether the quiz is finished.

5. ***Continuing the quiz when fewer than five flags have been shown.*** If the quiz is not finished (that is, count is less than 5), the app enables the **Next Flag** Button (line 77). The functionality of the **Next Flag** Button will be discussed in the next box. Line 80 disables the submitButton.

6. ***Saving the project.*** Select **File > Save All** to save your modified code.

The user requests the next flag in the quiz by clicking the **Next Flag** Button. The app then displays the next flag and increments the number of flags shown. In the following box, you'll implement this functionality.

Displaying the Next Flag

1. ***Adding the Next Flag Button's Click event handler to the app.*** Return to **Design** view (**View > Designer**). Double click the **Next Flag** Button to generate the Click event handler nextButton_Click. Add the comment and format the event handler as shown in lines 83–85 of Fig. 17.27.

(cont.)

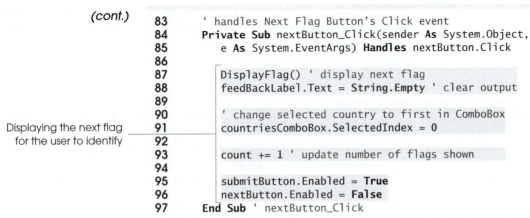

Displaying the next flag
for the user to identify

```
83        ' handles Next Flag Button's Click event
84        Private Sub nextButton_Click(sender As System.Object,
85           e As System.EventArgs) Handles nextButton.Click
86
87           DisplayFlag() ' display next flag
88           feedBackLabel.Text = String.Empty ' clear output
89
90           ' change selected country to first in ComboBox
91           countriesComboBox.SelectedIndex = 0
92
93           count += 1 ' update number of flags shown
94
95           submitButton.Enabled = True
96           nextButton.Enabled = False
97        End Sub ' nextButton_Click
```

Figure 17.27 Next Flag Button Click event handler.

2. *Displaying the next flag.* Add line 87 of Fig. 17.27 to the empty event handler. This line calls procedure DisplayFlag to place the next flag in the PictureBox.

3. *Clearing the previous results.* Add line 88 of Fig. 17.27 to the event handler to clear the output Label, deleting the results of the previous question.

4. *Resetting the ComboBox.* Add lines 90–91 of Fig. 17.27 to the event handler. Line 91 sets property SelectedIndex of countriesComboBox to 0, which selects and displays the first item in the ComboBox's drop-down list.

5. *Updating the number of flags shown.* Add line 93 of Fig. 17.27 to the event handler to update instance variable count to indicate that one more flag has been shown.

6. *Enabling the Submit Button and disabling the Next Flag Button.* Add lines 95–96 of Fig. 17.27 to the event handler. Line 95 enables the **Submit Button** and line 96 disables the **Next Flag Button**. This is a visual reminder to the user that an answer must be submitted before another flag can be displayed.

7. *Saving the project.* Select **File > Save All** to save your modified code.

SELF-REVIEW

1. Property _____ specifies the source of the data displayed in the ComboBox.

   a) ComboData   b) Source

   c) DataList   d) DataSource

2. ComboBox property _____ is 0 when the first ComboBox item is selected.

   a) SelectedIndex   b) SelectedValue

   c) Index   d) SelectedNumber

Answers: 1) d. 2) a.

17.5 Sorting Arrays

Sorting data refers to arranging the data into some particular order, such as ascending or descending order. Sorting is one of the most popular computing capabilities. For example, a bank sorts checks by account number so that it can prepare individual bank statements at the end of each month. Telephone companies sort account information by last name and, within last-name listings, by first name, to make it easy to find phone numbers. Virtually every organization must sort some data, and often, massive amounts of it. In this section, you'll learn how to sort the values in an array so that you can alphabetize the list of countries in the **Flag Quiz** app.

Users are able to find a country name in the ComboBox faster if the country names are alphabetized. [*Note:* Class ComboBox contains property **Sorted**, which, when set to True, sorts the items in the ComboBox alphabetically. We do not use this property because this chapter focuses on arrays and we wanted to show how to sort an array.] The following box shows you how to sort an array.

Sorting an Array

1. ***Sorting the array of country names.*** Add line 17 of Fig. 17.28 to event handler FlagQuizForm_Load. Line 17 passes array **countries** to method **Array.Sort**, which sorts the values in the array into *ascending* alphabetical order. This line is placed prior to assigning array **countries** to the Combo-Box's DataSource property to ensure that the items in the ComboBox are displayed in alphabetical order.

Alphabetizing country names in the array

```
13        ' handles Flag Quiz Form's Load event
14        Private Sub FlagQuizForm_Load(sender As System.Object,
15          e As System.EventArgs) Handles MyBase.Load
16
17            Array.Sort(countries) ' alphabetize country names
18
19            ' display country names in ComboBox
20            countriesComboBox.DataSource = countries
21
22            DisplayFlag() ' display first flag in PictureBox
23        End Sub ' FlagQuizForm_Load
```

Figure 17.28   Sorting the array of country names.

2. ***Running the app.*** Select **Debug > Start Debugging** to run your app. The country names should now be alphabetized. Enter different answers and make sure that the proper message is displayed based on whether the answer is correct. Make sure that after five answers have been entered, the text **Done!** is appended to the current message displayed.

3. ***Closing the app.*** Close your running app by clicking its close box.

4. ***Closing the IDE.*** Close the Visual Basic IDE by clicking its close box.

Figure 17.29 presents the source code for the **Flag Quiz** app. The lines of code that contain new programming concepts you learned in this chapter are highlighted.

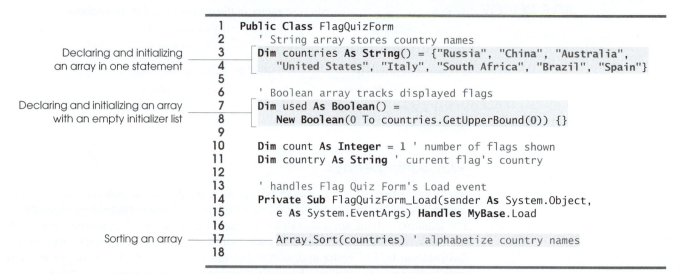

```
1   Public Class FlagQuizForm
2       ' String array stores country names
3       Dim countries As String() = {"Russia", "China", "Australia",
4           "United States", "Italy", "South Africa", "Brazil", "Spain"}
5
6       ' Boolean array tracks displayed flags
7       Dim used As Boolean() =
8           New Boolean(0 To countries.GetUpperBound(0)) {}
9
10      Dim count As Integer = 1 ' number of flags shown
11      Dim country As String ' current flag's country
12
13      ' handles Flag Quiz Form's Load event
14      Private Sub FlagQuizForm_Load(sender As System.Object,
15          e As System.EventArgs) Handles MyBase.Load
16
17          Array.Sort(countries) ' alphabetize country names
18
```

Declaring and initializing an array in one statement

Declaring and initializing an array with an empty initializer list

Sorting an array

Figure 17.29   **Flag Quiz** app's code. (Part 1 of 3.)

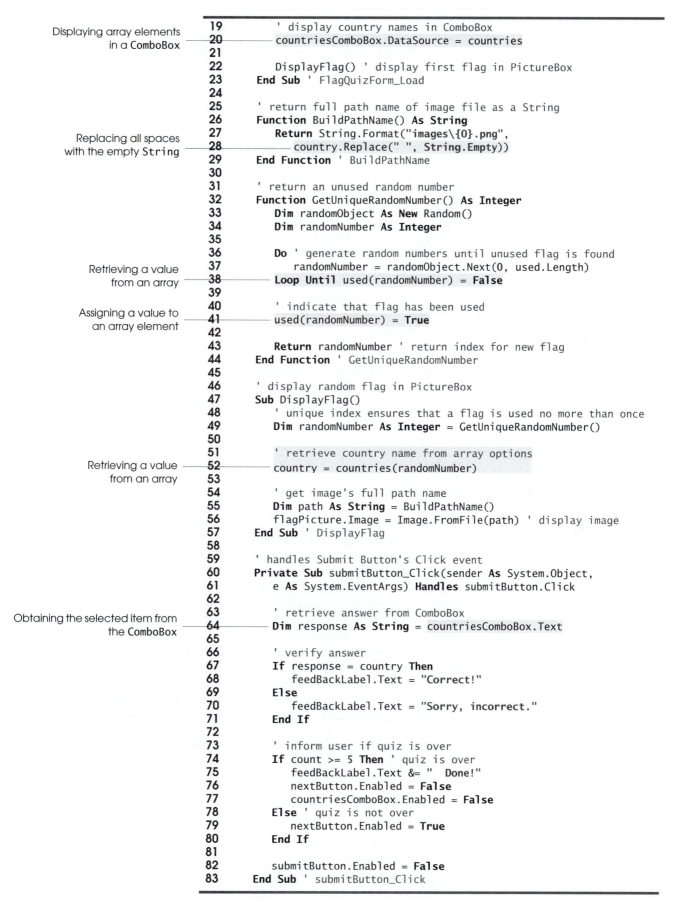

```
Displaying array elements     19          ' display country names in ComboBox
          in a ComboBox       20          countriesComboBox.DataSource = countries
                              21
                              22          DisplayFlag() ' display first flag in PictureBox
                              23      End Sub ' FlagQuizForm_Load
                              24
                              25      ' return full path name of image file as a String
                              26      Function BuildPathName() As String
                              27        Return String.Format("images\{0}.png",
     Replacing all spaces     28            country.Replace(" ", String.Empty))
 with the empty String        29      End Function ' BuildPathName
                              30
                              31      ' return an unused random number
                              32      Function GetUniqueRandomNumber() As Integer
                              33        Dim randomObject As New Random()
                              34        Dim randomNumber As Integer
                              35
                              36        Do ' generate random numbers until unused flag is found
                              37            randomNumber = randomObject.Next(0, used.Length)
      Retrieving a value      38        Loop Until used(randomNumber) = False
         from an array        39
                              40        ' indicate that flag has been used
   Assigning a value to       41        used(randomNumber) = True
     an array element         42
                              43        Return randomNumber ' return index for new flag
                              44      End Function ' GetUniqueRandomNumber
                              45
                              46      ' display random flag in PictureBox
                              47      Sub DisplayFlag()
                              48          ' unique index ensures that a flag is used no more than once
                              49        Dim randomNumber As Integer = GetUniqueRandomNumber()
                              50
                              51          ' retrieve country name from array options
      Retrieving a value      52        country = countries(randomNumber)
         from an array        53
                              54          ' get image's full path name
                              55        Dim path As String = BuildPathName()
                              56        flagPicture.Image = Image.FromFile(path) ' display image
                              57      End Sub ' DisplayFlag
                              58
                              59      ' handles Submit Button's Click event
                              60      Private Sub submitButton_Click(sender As System.Object,
                              61          e As System.EventArgs) Handles submitButton.Click
                              62
                              63          ' retrieve answer from ComboBox
Obtaining the selected item from 64     Dim response As String = countriesComboBox.Text
              the ComboBox    65
                              66          ' verify answer
                              67        If response = country Then
                              68            feedBackLabel.Text = "Correct!"
                              69        Else
                              70            feedBackLabel.Text = "Sorry, incorrect."
                              71        End If
                              72
                              73          ' inform user if quiz is over
                              74        If count >= 5 Then ' quiz is over
                              75            feedBackLabel.Text &= "  Done!"
                              76            nextButton.Enabled = False
                              77            countriesComboBox.Enabled = False
                              78        Else ' quiz is not over
                              79            nextButton.Enabled = True
                              80        End If
                              81
                              82        submitButton.Enabled = False
                              83      End Sub ' submitButton_Click
```

Figure 17.29   **Flag Quiz** app's code. (Part 2 of 3.)

```
84
85        ' handles Next Flag Button's Click event
86        Private Sub nextButton_Click(sender As System.Object,
87           e As System.EventArgs) Handles nextButton.Click
88
89           DisplayFlag() ' display next flag
90           feedBackLabel.Text = String.Empty ' clear output
91
92           ' change selected country to first in ComboBox
93           countriesComboBox.SelectedIndex = 0
94
95           count += 1 ' update number of flags shown
96
97           submitButton.Enabled = True
98           nextButton.Enabled = False
99        End Sub ' nextButton_Click
100    End Class ' FlagQuizForm
```

Setting the selected ComboBox item ——— (points to line 93)

Figure 17.29 Flag Quiz app's code. (Part 3 of 3.)

SELF-REVIEW

1. The process of ordering the elements of an array is called _____ the array.
   a) allocating
   b) sorting
   c) declaring
   d) initializing

2. Which of the following sorts array averageRainfall?
   a) `Array(averageRainfall).Sort()`
   b) `Sort.Array(averageRainfall)`
   c) `Sort(averageRainfall)`
   d) `Array.Sort(averageRainfall)`

Answers: 1) b. 2) d.

17.6 Wrap-Up

In this chapter, you learned about data structures called arrays, which contain elements of the same type. You then learned how to create, initialize and access one-dimensional arrays. You created a simple app called **Sum Array**, which calculated the sum of the Integer values stored in an array. You studied pseudocode and an ACE table to help you begin creating the **Flag Quiz** app.

In building the **Flag Quiz** app, you were introduced to the ComboBox control. You learned how to add a ComboBox to the Form and modify the ComboBox's appearance. You then populated the ComboBox with data from an array. You reviewed how to display images in a PictureBox and how to generate random numbers by using an object of class Random.

You were introduced to String method Replace (for replacing characters in a String). You learned how to sort an array by using method Array.Sort.

In the next chapter, you'll learn how to create more sophisticated arrays with two dimensions, and you'll use them to implement the **Student Grades** app. Two-dimensional arrays are like tables organized in rows and columns.

SKILLS SUMMARY

Creating an Array

- Declare the array using one of the two following formats:

      Dim *arrayName* As *arrayType*()
      Dim *arrayName*() As *arrayType*

  where *arrayName* is the reference name of the array, and *arrayType* is the type of data that will be stored in the array.

- If you know the number of elements in advance you can use

      Dim *arrayName*(0 To *maxIndex*) As *arrayType*

or

$$\text{Dim } arrayName \text{ As } arrayType() = \textbf{New } arrayType(0 \text{ To } maxIndex) \text{ \{\}}$$

to specify an array with a high index of *maxIndex*.

Assigning an Array Object to an Array Variable
- Use keyword New as in the statement:

$$arrayName = \textbf{New } arrayType() \text{ \{}arrayInitializerList\text{\}}$$

where *arrayInitializerList* is a comma-separated list of the items that initialize the elements of the array.

Declaring and Initializing an Array with an Initializer List
- Use keyword New as in the statement:

$$\text{Dim } arrayName \text{ As } arrayType() = \textbf{New } arrayType() \text{ \{}arrayInitializerList\text{\}}$$

or use the shorthand notation

$$\text{Dim } arrayName \text{ As } arrayType() = \text{\{}arrayInitializerList\text{\}}$$

in which the compiler implicitly uses the keyword New or use implicit type inference as in

$$\text{Dim } arrayName = \text{\{}arrayInitializerList\text{\}}$$

Referring to Element *n* of an Array
- Enclose the index *n* in parentheses after the array name.

Obtaining the Number of Elements in an Array
- Use property Length.

Obtaining the Index of the Last Element in a One-Dimensional Array
- Invoke method GetUpperBound with 0 as its argument, or use *arrayName*.Length - 1.

Combining TextBox Features with ListBox Features
- Use a ComboBox control.

Setting the Maximum Number of Drop-Down Items a ComboBox's List Displays
- Use property MaxDropDownItems.

Specifying the Source of Data Displayed in a ComboBox
- Use property DataSource.

Obtaining the Selected Text in a ComboBox
- Use ComboBox property Text.

Changing the Style of a ComboBox
- Use property DropDownStyle.

Sorting an Array into Ascending Order
- Pass the array to be sorted as the argument to method Array.Sort.

Replacing Characters in a String
- Use method Replace with two String arguments—the substring to locate and replace, and the replacement String.
- The method returns a copy of the original String with appropriate replacements (if any).

KEY TERMS   **array**—A data structure containing data items of the same type.

array bounds—Integers that determine what indices can be used to access an element in an array. The lower bound is 0; the upper bound is the length of the array minus one.

Array.Sort method—Sorts the values of an array into ascending order.

ComboBox control—Combines a TextBox with a ListBox.

DataSource property of class ComboBox—Specifies the source of items listed in a ComboBox.

data structure—Groups and organizes related data.

DropDownList value of DropDownStyle property —Specifies that a ComboBox is not editable.

DropDownStyle property of class ComboBox—Property of the ComboBox control that specifies the appearance of the ComboBox.

element—An item in an array.

Enabled property of class ComboBox—Specifies whether a user can select an item from a ComboBox.

GetUpperBound method of class Array—Returns an array's highest index.

index—An array element's position number. An index must be zero, a positive integer or an integer expression that yields a nonnegative result. If an app uses an expression as an index, the expression is evaluated first, to determine the index.

indexed array name—The array name followed by an index enclosed in parentheses. The indexed array name can be used on the left side of an assignment statement to place a new value into an array element. The indexed array name can be used in the right side of an assignment to retrieve the value of that array element.

initializer list—The required braces ({ and }) and the optional comma-separated list (that the braces enclose) of the initial values of the elements in an array. When the initializer list is empty, the elements in the array are initialized to the default value for the array's data type.

length of an array—The number of elements in an array.

Length property of class Array—Contains the length of (or number of elements in) an array.

MaxDropDownItems property of class ComboBox—Property of the ComboBox control that specifies how many items can be displayed in the drop-down list. If the ComboBox has more elements than this, it provides a scrollbar to access all of them.

one-dimensional array—An array that uses only one index.

position number—A value that indicates a specific location within an array. Position numbers begin at 0 (zero).

Replace method of class String—Returns a copy of the String for which it's called. Replaces all occurrences of the characters in its first String argument with the characters in its second String argument.

SelectedIndex property of class ComboBox—Specifies the index of the selected item. Returns –1 if no item is selected.

Sorted property of class ComboBox—When set to True, sorts the items in a ComboBox alphabetically.

Text property of class ComboBox—Returns the currently selected String in the ComboBox.

GUI DESIGN GUIDELINES

ComboBoxes

- Each ComboBox should have a descriptive Label that describes its contents.
- If a ComboBox's content should not be editable, set its DropDownStyle property to Drop-DownList.

CONTROLS, EVENTS, PROPERTIES & METHODS

ComboBox   🔲 ComboBox   This control allows the user to select from a drop-down list of options.

- *In action*

- *Properties*

  DataSource—Specifies the source of the items listed in a ComboBox.

  DropDownStyle—Specifies a ComboBox's appearance.

`Enabled`—Specifies whether a user can select an item from the `ComboBox`.

`Location`—Specifies the location of the `ComboBox` control relative to the top-left corner of the container (e.g., a `Form` or a `GroupBox`).

`MaxDropDownItems`—Specifies the maximum number of items the `ComboBox` can display in its drop-down list. If the `ComboBox` has more elements than this, it provides a scrollbar to access all of them.

`Name`—Specifies the name used to access the `ComboBox` control programmatically. The name should be appended with the `ComboBox` suffix.

`SelectedIndex`—Specifies the index of the selected item. Returns –1 if no item is selected.

`Size`—Specifies the width and height (in pixels) of the `ComboBox` control.

`Sorted`—When set to `True`, displays the `ComboBox` options in alphabetical order.

`Text`—The currently selected `String` in the `ComboBox`.

Array   This data structure stores a fixed number of elements of the same type.

■ *Property*

`Length`—Specifies the number of elements in the array.

■ *Methods*

`GetUpperBound`—Returns the array's highest index.

`Sort`—Orders an array's elements. An array of numerical values would be organized in ascending order, and an array of `Strings` in alphabetical order.

String   The `String` class represents a series of characters treated as a single unit.

■ *Methods*

`Format`—Arranges a `String` in a specified format.

`Replace`—Returns a copy of the `String` for which it's called. Replaces all occurrences of the characters in its first `String` argument with the characters in its second `String` argument.

MULTIPLE-CHOICE QUESTIONS

17.1 Arrays can be declared to hold values of _____.

a) type `Double`
b) type `Integer`
c) type `String`
d) any data type

17.2 An array's elements are related by the fact that they have the same array name and _____.

a) constant value
b) index
c) type
d) value

17.3 Method _____ returns an array's highest index.

a) `GetUpperBound`
b) `GetUpperLimit`
c) `GetHighestIndex`
d) `Length`

17.4 The first element in every array is the _____.

a) index
b) zeroth element
c) length of the array
d) smallest value in the array

17.5 Arrays _____.

a) are controls
b) always have one dimension
c) keep data in sorted order at all times
d) are objects

17.6 The array initializer list can _____.

a) be used to determine the size of the array
b) contain a comma-separated list of initial values for the array elements
c) be empty
d) All of the above

17.7 Which method call sorts array words in ascending order?

a) `Array.Sort(words)`   b) `words.SortArray()`

c) `Array.Sort(words, 1)`   d) `Sort(words)`

17.8 The `ComboBox` control combines a `TextBox` control with a _____ control.

a) `DateTimePicker`   b) `ListBox`

c) `NumericUpDown`   d) `Label`

17.9 The _____ property of the `ComboBox` control specifies how many items can be displayed in the drop-down list.

a) `ItemsMax`   b) `ScrollLimit`

c) `MaxDropDownItems`   d) `MaxDropDownItems`

17.10 Property _____ contains the size of an array.

a) `Elements`   b) `ArraySize`

c) `Length`   d) `Size`

EXERCISES

17.11 *(Enhanced Flag Quiz App)* Enhance the **Flag Quiz** app by counting the number of questions that were answered correctly (Fig. 17.30). After all the questions have been answered, display a message in a `Label` that describes how well the user performed. The following table shows which messages to display:

Number of correct answers	Message
5	Excellent!
4	Very good
3	Good
2	Poor
1 or 0	Fail

Figure 17.30 Enhanced **Flag Quiz** app's GUI.

a) *Copying the template to your working directory.* Copy the directory `C:\Examples\ch17\Exercises\FlagQuiz2` to your `C:\SimplyVB2010` directory.

b) *Opening the app's template file.* Double click `FlagQuiz2.sln` in the `FlagQuiz2` directory to open the app.

c) *Adding a variable to count the number of correct answers.* Add an instance variable `numberCorrect`, and initialize it to 0. You use this variable to count the number of correct answers submitted by the user.

d) *Counting the correct answers.* Increment `numberCorrect` in the **Submit** Button's event handler whenever the submitted answer is correct.

e) *Displaying the message.* Write a procedure `DisplayScore` that displays a message in `scoreLabel` depending on the value of `numberCorrect`. Call this procedure from the **Submit** Button's event handler when the quiz is completed.

f) *Running the app.* Select **Debug > Start Debugging** to run your app. The finished app should behave as in Fig. 17.30. Run the app a few times and enter a different number of correct answers each time to verify that the correct feedback is displayed.

g) *Closing the app.* Close your running app by clicking its close box.

h) *Closing the IDE.* Close the Visual Basic IDE by clicking its close box.

17.12 *(Salary Survey App)* Use a one-dimensional array to solve the following problem: A company pays its salespeople on a commission basis. The salespeople receive $200 per week, plus 9% of their gross sales for that week. For example, a salesperson who grosses $5,000 in sales in a week receives $200 plus 9% of $5,000, a total of $650. Write an app (using an array of counters) that determines how many of the salespeople earned compensation in each of the following ranges (assuming that each salesperson's salary is truncated to an integer amount): $200–299, $300–399, $400–499, $500–599, $600–699, $700–799, $800–899, $900–999 and over $999.

Allow the user to enter the sales for each employee in a TextBox. The user clicks the **Calculate** Button to calculate the salesperson's salary. When the user is done entering this information, clicking the **Show Totals** Button displays how many of the salespeople earned salaries in each of the above ranges. The finished app should behave like Fig. 17.31.

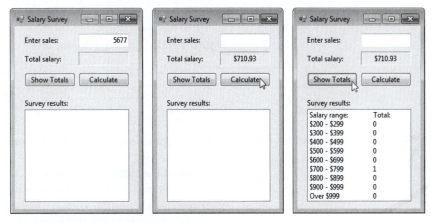

Figure 17.31   Salary Survey app's GUI.

a) *Copying the template to your working directory.* Copy the directory C:\Examples\ ch17\Exercises\SalarySurvey to your C:\SimplyVB2010 directory.

b) *Opening the app's template file.* Double click SalarySurvey.sln in the Salary-Survey directory to open the app.

c) *Creating an array of salary ranges.* Create a String array salaries, and initialize it to contain the salary ranges (the Strings displayed in the ListBox's first column).

d) *Creating an array that represents the number of salaries in each range.* Create an empty Integer array to store the number of employees who earn salaries in each range.

e) *Creating an event handler for the Calculate Button.* Write event handler calculateButton_Click. Obtain the user input from the **Enter sales:** TextBox. Calculate the commission due to the employee and add that amount to the base salary. Increment the element in array salaries that corresponds to the employee's salary range. This event handler should also display the employee's salary in the **Total salary:** Label.

f) *Writing an event handler for the Show Totals Button.* Create event handler totalsButton_Click to display the salary distribution in the ListBox. Use a For...Next statement to display the range (an element in array salaryRanges) and the number of employees whose salary falls in that range (an element in array salaries).

g) *Running the app.* Select **Debug > Start Debugging** to run your app. Enter several sales amounts using the **Calculate** Button. Click the **Show Totals** Button and verify that the proper amounts are displayed for each salary range, based on the salaries calculated from your input.

h) *Closing the app.* Close your running app by clicking its close box.

i) *Closing the IDE.* Close the Visual Basic IDE by clicking its close box.

17.13 *(Cafeteria Survey App)* Twenty students were asked to rate, on a scale from 1 to 10, the quality of the food in the student cafeteria, with 1 being "awful" and 10 being "excellent." Allow the user input to be entered using a ComboBox. Use an Integer array to store the frequency of each rating. Display the frequencies as a histogram in a multiline, scrollable Text-Box. Figure 17.32 demonstrates the completed app.

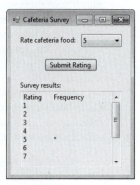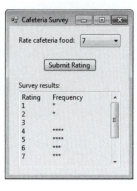

Figure 17.32 Cafeteria Survey GUI.

a) *Copying the template to your working directory.* Copy the directory `C:\Examples\ch17\Exercises\CafeteriaSurvey` to your `C:\SimplyVB2010` directory.

b) *Opening the app's template file.* Double click `CafeteriaSurvey.sln` in the `CafeteriaSurvey` directory.

c) *Creating an array of the possible ratings.* Create an array of 10 integers, called `choices`, to contain the integers in the range 1–10, inclusive.

d) *Adding a ComboBox.* Add a ComboBox to the GUI as in Fig. 17.32. The ComboBox will display the possible ratings. Set property `DropDownStyle` to `DropDownList`.

e) *Displaying the possible ratings when the app starts.* Write the event handler for the Load event so that the `DataSource` of the ComboBox is set to `choices` when the app starts.

f) *Creating an array to store the responses.* Create an `Integer` array of length 11 named `responses`. This will be used to store the number of responses in each of the 10 categories (element 0 will not be used).

g) *Counting the number of responses.* Create an `Integer` variable named `responseCounter` to keep track of how many responses have been input.

h) *Storing the responses.* Write the event handler `submitButton_Click` to increment `responseCounter`. Store the response in array `responses`. Call procedure `DisplayHistogram` to display the results. Disable the **Submit Rating** Button after 20 responses have been entered.

i) *Creating procedure `DisplayHistogram`.* The procedure template is already provided for you in the app template. Add a header to the TextBox. Use nested For...Next loops to display the ratings in the first column. The second column uses asterisks to indicate how many students surveyed submitted the corresponding rating.

j) *Running the app.* Select **Debug > Start Debugging** to run your app. Enter 20 responses using the **Submit Rating** Button. Verify that the resulting histogram displays the responses entered.

k) *Closing the app.* Close your running app by clicking its close box.

l) *Closing the IDE.* Close the Visual Basic IDE by clicking its close box.

What does this code do? **17.14** This function declares `numbers` as its parameter. What does it return?

```
1  Function Mystery(numbers As Integer()) As Integer()
2     Dim length As Integer = numbers.Length - 1
3     Dim tempArray As Integer() = New Integer(0 To length) {}
4
5     For i As Integer = length To 0 Step -1
6        tempArray(length - i) = numbers(i)
7     Next
8
9     Return tempArray
10 End Function ' Mystery
```

What's wrong with this code? ▶   **17.15** The code that follows uses a For...Next loop to sum the elements in an array. Find the error(s).

```
1   Sub SumArray()
2      Dim sum As Integer
3      Dim numbers As Integer() = {1, 2, 3, 4, 5, 6, 7, 8}
4
5      For counter As Integer = 0 To numbers.Length
6         sum += numbers(counter)
7      Next
8   End Sub ' SumArray
```

Programming Challenge ▶   **17.16** *(Road Sign Test App)* Write an app that tests the user's knowledge of road signs. Your app should display a random sign image and ask the user to select the sign name from a ComboBox. This app should look like Fig. 17.33. [*Hint:* The app is similar to the **Flag Quiz** app.] You can find the images in C:\Examples\ch17\Exercises\images. Remember to set Option Strict to On.

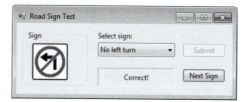

Figure 17.33   Road Sign Test GUI.

18

Objectives

In this chapter, you'll:

- Understand the similarities and differences between one-dimensional and two-dimensional arrays.
- Declare and manipulate two-dimensional arrays.
- Use two-dimensional arrays.
- Use nested **For…Next** loops.
- Use **RadioButton**s to enable users to select exactly one option out of several.

Outline

Student Grades App

Introducing Two-Dimensional Arrays and *RadioButtons*

In this chapter, you'll learn about two-dimensional arrays, which allow you to store multiple values of the same type organized into rows and columns. Two-dimensional arrays are useful for representing *tabular data*. For example, an instructor could use a two-dimensional array whose rows represent the students in a class and whose columns represent the grades the students received on each of the class's exams. You'll also learn about the RadioButton control, which enables users to choose only one of several options.

18.1 Test-Driving the Student Grades App

You'll implement the **Student Grades** app by using a two-dimensional array. This app must meet the following requirements:

App Requirements

A teacher issues three tests to a class of 10 students. The grades on these tests are integers in the range from 0 to 100. The teacher has asked you to develop an app to keep track of each student's average and the class average. The teacher has also asked that there be a choice to view the grades as either numbers or letters. Letter grades should be calculated according to the grading system:

A	*90–100*
B	*80–89*
C	*70–79*
D	*60–69*
F	*Below 60*

The app should allow a user to input the student's three test grades, then compute each student's average and the class average. The app should display number grades by default.

The student's average is equal to the sum of the student's three grades divided by three. The class average is equal to the sum of all of the students' grades divided by the number of tests taken. You'll begin by test-driving the completed app. Then you'll learn the additional Visual Basic capabilities needed to create your own version of this app.

Test-Driving the Student Grades App

1. ***Opening the completed app.*** Open the directory C:\Examples\ch18\CompletedApp\StudentGrades to locate the **Student Grades** app. Double click StudentGrades.sln to open the app in the Visual Basic IDE.

2. ***Running the Student Grades app.*** Select **Debug > Start Debugging** to run the app (Fig. 18.1).

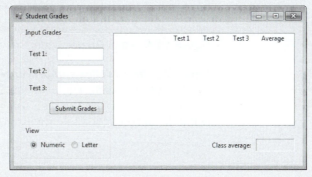

Figure 18.1   Running the completed **Student Grades** app.

3. ***Entering data.*** Type 87, 94 and 93 in the **Test 1:**, **Test 2:** and **Test 3:** Text-Boxes, respectively (Fig. 18.2). Click the **Submit Grades** Button to calculate the student's average and display the student's test scores and average in the ListBox (Fig. 18.3). Enter grades for nine more students, three at a time. Once 10 students have been entered, all the controls in the **Input Grades** GroupBox are *disabled* (Fig. 18.4).

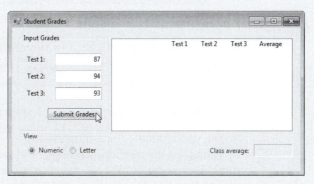

Figure 18.2   Inputting data to the **Student Grades** app.

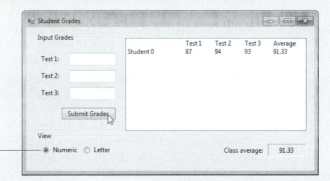

Numeric RadioButton selected by default

Figure 18.3   Displaying the student's numerical average.

(cont.)

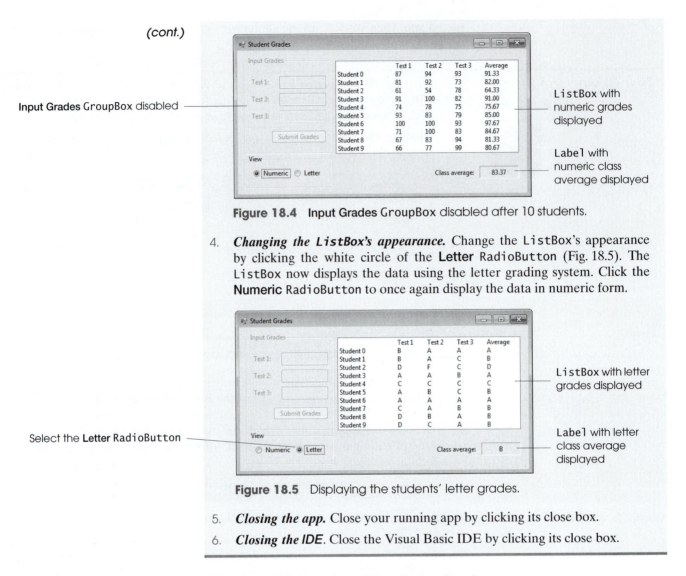

Figure 18.4 **Input Grades** `GroupBox` disabled after 10 students.

4. **Changing the `ListBox`'s appearance.** Change the `ListBox`'s appearance by clicking the white circle of the **Letter** `RadioButton` (Fig. 18.5). The `ListBox` now displays the data using the letter grading system. Click the **Numeric** `RadioButton` to once again display the data in numeric form.

Figure 18.5 Displaying the students' letter grades.

5. **Closing the app.** Close your running app by clicking its close box.

6. **Closing the IDE.** Close the Visual Basic IDE by clicking its close box.

18.2 Two-Dimensional Rectangular Arrays

So far, you've studied one-dimensional arrays, which contain one sequence (or row) of values. In this section, we introduce **two-dimensional arrays** (sometimes called **double-subscripted arrays**), which require two indices to identify particular elements. **Rectangular arrays** are two-dimensional arrays that are often used to represent **tables** of values consisting of information arranged in **rows** and **columns**. Each row is the same size and therefore has the same number of columns (hence, the term "rectangular"). To identify a particular table element, you specify two indices—by convention, the first identifies the element's row and the second the element's column. Figure 18.6 illustrates a two-dimensional rectangular array, named array, that contains three rows and four columns. A rectangular two-dimensional array with *m* rows and *n* columns is called an ***m*-by-*n* array**; therefore, the array in Fig. 18.6 is a 3-by-4 array.

Every element in array is identified in Fig. 18.6 by an element name of the form array(i, j), where array is the name of the array and i and j are the indices that uniquely identify the row and column of each element in array. All row numbers and column numbers in two-dimensional arrays begin with zero, so the elements in the first row each have a first index of 0; the elements in the last column each have a second index of 3 (Fig. 18.6).

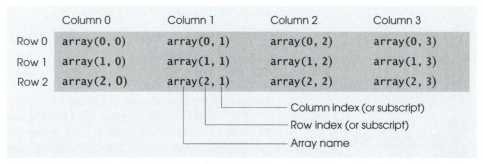

Figure 18.6 Two-dimensional rectangular array with three rows and four columns.

Two-dimensional arrays are initialized much like one-dimensional arrays. For example, a two-dimensional rectangular array, `numbers`, with two rows and two columns, could be declared and initialized with

```
Dim numbers As Integer(,) = New Integer(0 To 1, 0 To 1) {}
numbers(0, 0) = 1
numbers(0, 1) = 2
numbers(1, 0) = 3
numbers(1, 1) = 4
```

Note that a comma (,) is required inside the parentheses following the data type to indicate that the array is two-dimensional. Similar to one-dimensional arrays, if you know the number of rows and columns at the time you declare the two-dimensional array, you can write the declaration as

```
Dim numbers(0 To 1, 0 To 1) As Integer
```

which creates a two-dimensional array with two rows and two columns. In this case, the compiler *implicitly* uses the `New` keyword and initializes all the elements to 0.

Two-dimensional arrays also may be initialized using an initializer list. The preceding initialization could be written on one line as:

```
Dim numbers As Integer(,) = New Integer(,) {{1, 2}, {3, 4}}
```

The values in the initializer list are grouped by row using nested braces, with 1 and 2 initializing `numbers(0, 0)` and `numbers(0, 1)`, respectively, and 3 and 4 initializing `numbers(1, 0)` and `numbers(1, 1)`, respectively. The preceding declaration can also be written as

```
Dim numbers As Integer(,) = {{1, 2}, {3, 4}}
```

In this case, the compiler implicitly uses the `New` keyword to create the array object.

Recall from Chapter 17 that you can specify the lower bounds of an array implicitly or explicitly. The same is true for each dimension of a two-dimensional array. Accordingly, the array numbers also can be allocated as follows:

```
Dim numbers As Integer(,) = New Integer(1, 1) {}
```

or

```
Dim numbers(1, 1) As Integer
```

SELF-REVIEW   1. Arrays that use two indices are referred to as _____ arrays.

  a) single-subscripted   b) two-dimensional
  c) double   d) one-dimensional

  2. The expression _____ creates an `Integer` array of two rows and five columns.

  a) **New Integer**(0 To 2, 0 To 5) {}   b) **New Integer**(0 To 1, 0 To 5) {}
  c) **New Integer**(0 To 1, 0 To 4) {}   d) **New Integer**(0 To 2, 0 To 4) {}

Answers: 1) b. 2) c.

18.3 Using RadioButtons

A **RadioButton** is a normally small white circle that either is blank or contains a smaller dot. When a RadioButton is selected, a dot appears in the circle. A RadioButton is known as a *state button* because it can be in only the "on" (True) state or the "off" (False) state. (The other state button you've studied is the Check-Box, which was introduced in Chapter 8.)

RadioButtons are similar to CheckBoxes in that they're state buttons, but RadioButtons normally appear as a group—only one RadioButton in the group can be selected at a time. Like car-radio preset buttons, which can select only one station at a time, RadioButtons represent a set of **mutually exclusive options**—a set of options of which only one can be selected at a time. By default, all RadioButtons added directly to the Form become part of the same group. To separate RadioButtons into several groups, each RadioButton group must be in a different container (such as a GroupBox).

The RadioButton control's **Checked** property indicates whether the Radio-Button is *checked* (contains a small dot) or *unchecked* (blank). If the RadioButton is checked, the Checked property returns the Boolean value True. If the RadioButton is not checked, the Checked property returns False.

A RadioButton also generates an event when its checked state changes. Event **CheckedChanged** occurs when a RadioButton is either selected or deselected.

The following pseudocode describes the operation of the **Student Grades** app:

When the user clicks the Submit Grades Button:
    Retrieve the student's grades from the TextBoxes
    Add the student's test scores to the array
    Display the student's test scores and average in the ListBox
    Display the class's average in the Class average: Label
    Clear the student's test scores from the TextBoxes

    If 10 students have been entered
        Disable the input controls

When the user selects the Numeric RadioButton:
    Display each student's numeric test scores and average in the ListBox
    Display the class's numeric average in the Class average: Label

When the user selects the Letter RadioButton:
    Display each student's letter test scores and average in the ListBox
    Display the class's letter average in the Class average: Label

Your **Student Grades** app uses the RadioButton control's CheckedChanged event handler to update the ListBox and **Class average:** Label when the user selects either letter or numeric grades for display.

Now that you've test-driven the **Student Grades** app and studied its pseudo-code representation, you'll use an ACE table to help you convert the pseudocode to Visual Basic. Figure 18.7 lists the *actions, controls* and *events* that help you complete your own version of this app.

GUI Design Tip

Use RadioButtons when the user must choose only one option from a group.

GUI Design Tip

Always place each group of RadioButtons in a separate container (such as a GroupBox).

Action/Control/Event (ACE) Table for the Student Grades App

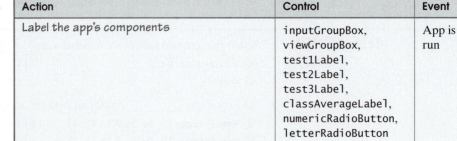

Action	Control	Event
Label the app's components	inputGroupBox, viewGroupBox, test1Label, test2Label, test3Label, classAverageLabel, numericRadioButton, letterRadioButton	App is run

Figure 18.7 ACE table for the **Student Grades** app. (Part 1 of 2.)

Action	Control	Event
	submitButton	Click
Retrieve the student's grades from the TextBoxes	test1TextBox, test2TextBox, test3TextBox	
Add the student's test scores to the array		
Display the student's test scores and average in the ListBox	gradesListBox	
Display the class's average in the Class average: Label	averageLabel	
Clear the student's test scores from the TextBoxes	test1TextBox, test2TextBox, test3TextBox	
If 10 students have been entered		
Disable the input controls	inputGroupBox	
	numericRadioButton	Check-Changed
Display each student's numeric test scores and average in the ListBox	gradesListBox	
Display the class's numeric average in the Class average: Label	averageLabel	
	letterRadioButton	Check-Changed
Display each student's letter test scores average in the ListBox	gradesListBox	
Display the class's letter average in the Class average: Label	averageLabel	

Figure 18.7   ACE table for the **Student Grades** app. (Part 2 of 2.)

Now you'll build your **Student Grades** app, using a two-dimensional array and RadioButtons. The RadioButtons allow the user to view the students' grades as letters or numbers.

Adding RadioButtons to the View GroupBox

1. *Copying the template to your working directory.* Copy the C:\Examples\ ch18\TemplateApp\StudentGrades directory to your C:\SimplyVB2010 directory.

2. *Opening the Student Grades app's template file.* Double click Student-Grades.sln in the StudentGrades directory to open the app in the Visual Basic IDE.

3. *Adding RadioButtons to the View GroupBox.* Select the **View** GroupBox on the Form. Add a RadioButton to the GroupBox by double clicking the **RadioButton** control,

     ⊙ RadioButton

in the **Toolbox**. Repeat this process so that two RadioButtons are added to the GroupBox. Note that, as with CheckBoxes, each RadioButton control contains a Text property.

(cont.)

4. **Customizing the RadioButtons.** Align the RadioButtons horizontally. Rename the left RadioButton by changing its Name property to numeric-RadioButton, and set its Text property to Numeric. Then set the right RadioButton control's Name property to letterRadioButton, and set its Text property to Letter. Set the Checked property of numericRadio-Button to True so that it will be selected when the app first executes. Your Form should look similar to Fig. 18.8.

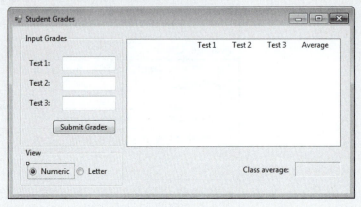

Figure 18.8 RadioButtons placed in the GroupBox.

5. **Saving the project.** Select **File > Save All** to save your modified code.

SELF-REVIEW

1. The _____ property determines whether a RadioButton is selected.
   a) Selected
   b) Clicked
   c) Checked
   d) Enabled

2. The _____ event is raised when a RadioButton is either selected or deselected.
   a) CheckedChanged
   b) Changed
   c) SelectedChanged
   d) None of the above

Answers: 1) c. 2) a.

18.4 Inserting Code into the Student Grades App

Now that you've placed the controls on the Form, you're ready to write code to interact with the data given by the user. First you'll declare a two-dimensional array to contain the student test scores.

Declaring a Two-Dimensional Array

1. **Declaring a two-dimensional array.** Add lines 2–3 of Fig. 18.9 to your code. Line 2 declares a 10-by-3 array of Integers to contain the test scores. Each row in the array represents a student. Each column represents a test. Note the studentCount instance variable (line 3), which contains the number of students entered by the user so far.

```
1  Public Class StudentGradesForm
2      Dim grades As Integer(,) = New Integer(0 To 9, 0 To 2) {}
3      Dim studentCount As Integer = 0 ' number of students entered
4
```

Figure 18.9 Declaring a two-dimensional array.

2. **Saving the project.** Select **File > Save All** to save your modified code.

The template code provides an incomplete version of the **Submit Grades** Button's Click event handler. You'll now use the two-dimensional array that you declared in the previous box to finish this event handler.

Finishing the Submit Grades Button's Click Event Handler

1. ***Retrieving the student's test scores.*** Double click the **Submit Grades** Button to display its Click event handler in **Code** view. Add lines 9–12 of Fig. 18.10 to your code. Lines 10–12 add the student's test scores to the grades array using the studentCount instance variable to add the scores to the appropriate row. You store each test score in a separate column of the array.

Store the student's test scores in the array

```
5      ' handles submit button click event
6      Private Sub submitButton_Click(sender As System.Object,
7         e As System.EventArgs) Handles submitButton.Click
8
9         ' retrieve the student's grades
10        grades(studentCount, 0) = Convert.ToInt32(test1TextBox.Text)
11        grades(studentCount, 1) = Convert.ToInt32(test2TextBox.Text)
12        grades(studentCount, 2) = Convert.ToInt32(test3TextBox.Text)
13     End Sub ' submitButton_Click
```

Figure 18.10   Storing the student's test scores.

2. ***Displaying the output.*** Insert lines 14–41 of Fig. 18.11 into your code. Lines 15–16 declare and initialize a String variable used to create the output that's added to the ListBox. Lines 19–30 use a For...Next statement to iterate over each of the student's test scores. Line 19 calls array method GetUpperBound to set the final value of the control variable. Recall from Chapter 17 that method GetUpperBound returns the highest index of the dimension specified by the argument passed to the method. In this case, you retrieve the highest index of the array's second dimension, indicated by passing 1 as the argument to GetUpperBound. This returns the index of the last column in the grades array. Line 21 uses the Checked property of letterRadioButton to determine how the user wants to view the student's grades. Line 24 calls the LetterGrade method to determine the letter grade corresponding to a given numeric grade retrieved from the array—this method has been provided for you in the template. Line 23 adds the letter grade to the output String. The Else branch of the decision (lines 25–29) adds the information to the output String in numeric form.

   Lines 33–34 add the student's test average to the output String, adding a Tab character for proper formatting. Line 34 passes the number of the row containing the current student's grades to method CalculateStudentAverage, which returns the student's test average as a String. Note that the CalculateStudentAverage method is underlined in blue, indicating a compilation error. This occurs because the method has not been defined yet—you'll create it in later steps. Line 38 increments the number of students for whom grades have been entered. Line 41 displays the class's test average in the **Class average:** Label. Note that method CalculateClassAverage is underlined in blue, again indicating a compilation error. You'll create this method in later steps.

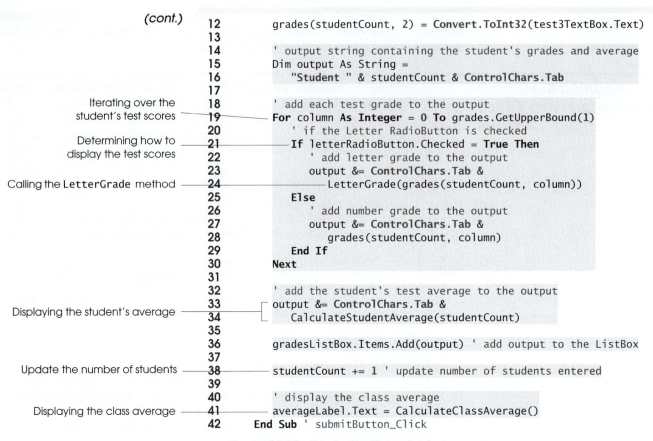

(cont.)

```
12          grades(studentCount, 2) = Convert.ToInt32(test3TextBox.Text)
13
14          ' output string containing the student's grades and average
15          Dim output As String =
16             "Student " & studentCount & ControlChars.Tab
17
18          ' add each test grade to the output
19          For column As Integer = 0 To grades.GetUpperBound(1)
20             ' if the Letter RadioButton is checked
21             If letterRadioButton.Checked = True Then
22                ' add letter grade to the output
23                output &= ControlChars.Tab &
24                   LetterGrade(grades(studentCount, column))
25             Else
26                ' add number grade to the output
27                output &= ControlChars.Tab &
28                   grades(studentCount, column)
29             End If
30          Next
31
32          ' add the student's test average to the output
33          output &= ControlChars.Tab &
34             CalculateStudentAverage(studentCount)
35
36          gradesListBox.Items.Add(output) ' add output to the ListBox
37
38          studentCount += 1 ' update number of students entered
39
40          ' display the class average
41          averageLabel.Text = CalculateClassAverage()
42       End Sub ' submitButton_Click
```

Labels:
- Iterating over the student's test scores — line 19
- Determining how to display the test scores — line 21
- Calling the LetterGrade method — line 24
- Displaying the student's average — lines 33–34
- Update the number of students — line 38
- Displaying the class average — line 41

Figure 18.11 Displaying the output.

3. *Clearing the input and disabling the input controls.* Insert lines 43–52 of Fig. 18.12. Lines 44–46 remove the user's input from each TextBox. Line 47 moves the focus to the **Test 1:** TextBox. If the grades array is full (line 50), line 51 disables the **Input Grades** GroupBox so that no more grades can be entered—disabling a GroupBox disables all the controls it contains. Line 50 adds one to the result of grades.GetUpperBound(0) to obtain the number of rows in the array. Recall from Chapter 17 that arrays provide a Length property which returns the number of elements in an array. You cannot use the Length property here because grades is a two-dimensional array. The Length property of a rectangular two-dimensional array returns the total number of elements in the array, in this case 30 (10 rows times 3 columns).

```
41          averageLabel.Text = CalculateClassAverage()
42
43          ' clear the input TextBoxes and set focus to first TextBox
44          test1TextBox.Clear()
45          test2TextBox.Clear()
46          test3TextBox.Clear()
47          test1TextBox.Focus()
48
49          ' limit number of students
50          If studentCount = grades.GetUpperBound(0) + 1 Then
51             inputGroupBox.Enabled = False ' disable GroupBox controls
52          End If
53       End Sub ' submitButton_Click
```

Label:
- Disable the input controls when the grades array is full — lines 50–51

Figure 18.12 App does not allow more than 10 data entries.

4. *Saving the project.* Select **File > Save All** to save your modified code.

In the previous box, you called methods CalculateStudentAverage and CalculateClassAverage, which are not yet defined, to display the appropriate data. You'll create these methods in the next box.

Coding Methods to Average Test Grades

1. *Coding the CalculateStudentAverage method.* Add lines 55–76 of Fig. 18.13 above the LetterGrade method. Lines 60–62 use a For...Next statement to sum the grades contained in the row of the grades array specified by the argument passed to the method. Line 67 uses the letterRadioButton's Checked property to determine how the user wants to view the average. Lines 69 and 72 calculate the student's average test score by dividing the sum of the test scores by the number of tests taken. Line 69 also calls method LetterGrade. Recall that the first column in a two-dimensional array has index 0. You must add one to the last column's index (GetUpperBound(1)) to determine the number of columns in each row. Line 71 calls String.Format with the format control string "{0:F}" to format the test average with exactly two digits following the decimal point. You can follow the F format specifier with a number to set a different **precision**—the number of digits following the decimal point. The default precision is two. Line 75 returns the String containing the student's test average.

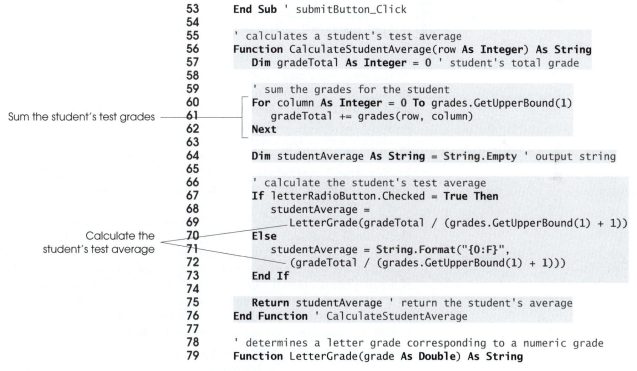

```
53      End Sub ' submitButton_Click
54
55      ' calculates a student's test average
56      Function CalculateStudentAverage(row As Integer) As String
57          Dim gradeTotal As Integer = 0 ' student's total grade
58
59          ' sum the grades for the student
60          For column As Integer = 0 To grades.GetUpperBound(1)
61              gradeTotal += grades(row, column)
62          Next
63
64          Dim studentAverage As String = String.Empty ' output string
65
66          ' calculate the student's test average
67          If letterRadioButton.Checked = True Then
68              studentAverage =
69                  LetterGrade(gradeTotal / (grades.GetUpperBound(1) + 1))
70          Else
71              studentAverage = String.Format("{0:F}",
72                  (gradeTotal / (grades.GetUpperBound(1) + 1)))
73          End If
74
75          Return studentAverage ' return the student's average
76      End Function ' CalculateStudentAverage
77
78      ' determines a letter grade corresponding to a numeric grade
79      Function LetterGrade(grade As Double) As String
```

Sum the student's test grades — (lines 60–62)

Calculate the student's test average — (lines 70–72)

Figure 18.13 Calculating a student's test average.

2. *Coding the CalculateClassAverage method.* Add lines 78–102 of Fig. 18.14 below the CalculateStudentAverage method. Method CalculateClassAverage calculates the class's test average and returns it as a String. Lines 83–88 use **nested For...Next statements** to iterate over the columns in each row. The outer For...Next statement's header (line 83) declares the row control variable and sets the initial value to 0 (the first row) and the final value to studentCount - 1 (the last row in which grades have been entered). Notice that you must subtract 1 from studentCount because the first row's index is 0. This For...Next statement iterates over each row containing student grades.

(cont.)

```
76      End Function ' CalculateStudentAverage
77
78      ' calculates the class average
79      Function CalculateClassAverage() As String
80         Dim classTotal As Integer = 0 ' class's total grade
81
82         ' loop through all rows
83         For row As Integer = 0 To studentCount - 1
84            ' loop through all columns
85            For column As Integer = 0 To grades.GetUpperBound(1)
86               classTotal += grades(row, column) ' add grade to total
87            Next column
88         Next row
89
90         Dim classAverage As String = String.Empty ' output string
91
92         ' if the Letter RadioButton is checked, return letter grade
93         If letterRadioButton.Checked = True Then
94            classAverage = LetterGrade(classTotal /
95               (studentCount * (grades.GetUpperBound(1) + 1)))
96         Else ' return number grade
97            classAverage = String.Format("{0:F}", (classTotal /
98               (studentCount * (grades.GetUpperBound(1) + 1))))
99         End If
100
101        Return classAverage ' return the class average
102     End Function ' CalculateClassAverage
```

Outer For...Next statement iterates over each row → (line 83)

Inner For...Next statement iterates over each column → (line 85)

Calculate the class's test average → (lines 96, 97)

Figure 18.14 Calculating the class's test average.

The inner For...Next statement (lines 85–87) sums all the grades in the current row. This is similar to the For...Next statement used in lines 60–62 of the CalculateStudentAverage method (Fig. 18.13) which sums a single student's test grades. Each time the body of the outer For...Next statement executes, the inner For...Next statement sums all the grades for the current row. These nested For...Next statements sum all the grades contained in the grades array. Note that you followed the Next keyword of each For...Next statement with the name of the statement's control variable. This greatly improves readability of nested For...Next statements.

Lines 94–95 and 97–98 calculate the class's average test score by dividing the summed grades (classTotal) by the number of grades. The number of grades is determined by multiplying the number of students (student-Count) by the number of grades for each student (the number of columns). If the user has selected the **Letter** RadioButton, line 94 formats the average as a letter grade; otherwise line 97 displays the average as a number with exactly two digits after the decimal point. Line 101 returns the String containing the class's test average in the desired format (letter or numeric).

3. ***Saving the project.*** Select **File > Save All** to save your modified code.

You'll now code event handlers to enhance the app's functionality by allowing the user to select whether the results are presented as letter grades or numeric grades.

Coding Event Handlers for the RadioButtons

4. *Creating the numericRadioButton_CheckedChanged event handler.* In **Design** view, double click the **Numeric** RadioButton to generate its CheckedChanged event handler. Add the comment and reformat the empty event handler as shown in lines 125–128 of Fig. 18.15. Add lines 130–135 of Fig. 18.15 to the event handler. Recall that a RadioButton's CheckedChanged event occurs both when it's selected and when it's deselected. Line 131 tests whether the numericRadioButton is selected. If so, and the number of students entered is greater than 0 (line 132), the event handler calls method DisplayClassGrades to display the grades in the proper form. Note that DisplayClassGrades is underlined in blue, indicating a compilation error, because you have not yet defined it. You'll define this method later in this box.

```
123    End Function ' LetterGrade
124
125    ' handles Numeric RadioButton's CheckChanged event
126    Private Sub numericRadioButton_CheckedChanged(
127       sender As System.Object, e As System.EventArgs) _
128       Handles numericRadioButton.CheckedChanged
129
130       ' if Numeric RadioButton is checked, display number grades
131       If numericRadioButton.Checked = True AndAlso
132          studentCount > 0 Then
133
134          DisplayClassGrades()
135       End If
136    End Sub ' numericRadioButton_CheckedChanged
```

Displaying the class's grades — 134

Figure 18.15 Method numericRadioButton_CheckedChanged.

5. *Creating the letterRadioButton_CheckedChanged event handler.* In **Design** view, double click the **Letter** RadioButton to generate its CheckedChanged event handler. Add the comment and reformat the empty event handler as shown in lines 138–141 of Fig. 18.16. Add lines 143–148 of Fig. 18.16 to the event handler. This event handler performs checks and actions similar to those of the numericRadioButton's CheckChanged event handler.

```
136    End Sub ' numericRadioButton_CheckedChanged
137
138    ' handles Letter RadioButton's CheckChanged event
139    Private Sub letterRadioButton_CheckedChanged(
140       sender As System.Object, e As System.EventArgs) _
141       Handles letterRadioButton.CheckedChanged
142
143       ' if the Letter RadioButton is checked, display letter grades
144       If letterRadioButton.Checked = True AndAlso
145          studentCount > 0 Then
146
147          DisplayClassGrades()
148       End If
149    End Sub ' letterRadioButton_CheckedChanged
```

Displaying the class's grades — 147

Figure 18.16 Method letterRadioButton_CheckedChanged.

6. *Creating the DisplayClassGrades method.* Add lines 151–186 of Fig. 18.17 below the **Letter** RadioButton's CheckedChanged event handler. Method DisplayClassGrades displays each student's grades and test average, as well as the class average, in the format selected by the user (numeric or letter). Line 153 clears the ListBox using its Clear method. Lines 156–159 replace the header displayed at the top of the ListBox.

(cont.)

```vbnet
149   End Sub ' letterRadioButton_CheckedChanged
150
151   ' display the grades for all students entered
152   Sub DisplayClassGrades()
153      gradesListBox.Items.Clear() ' clear the ListBox
154
155      ' add the header to the ListBox
156      gradesListBox.Items.Add(ControlChars.Tab & ControlChars.Tab &
157         "Test 1" & ControlChars.Tab &
158         "Test 2" & ControlChars.Tab &
159         "Test 3" & ControlChars.Tab & "Average")
160
161      ' loop through all the rows
162      For row As Integer = 0 To studentCount - 1
163         Dim output As String = "Student " & row & ControlChars.Tab
164
165         ' loop through all the columns
166         For column As Integer = 0 To grades.GetUpperBound(1)
167            If letterRadioButton.Checked = True Then
168               ' add letter grade to output string
169               output &= ControlChars.Tab &
170                  LetterGrade(grades(row, column))
171            Else
172               ' add number grade to output string
173               output &= ControlChars.Tab & (grades(row, column))
174            End If
175         Next column
176
177         ' add the student's average to the output
178         output &= ControlChars.Tab & CalculateStudentAverage(row)
179
180         ' add the output to the ListBox
181         gradesListBox.Items.Add(output)
182      Next row
183
184      ' update the class average
185      averageLabel.Text = CalculateClassAverage()
186   End Sub ' DisplayClassGrades
187 End Class ' StudentGradesForm
```

Outer For…Next statement iterates over each row of the array — (line 162)

Inner For…Next statement adds the grades in each column of the current row to the output String — (lines 166–175)

Displaying the class's average — (line 185)

Figure 18.17 Method `DisplayClassGrades`.

Lines 162–182 use nested For…Next statements to iterate over each grade in the grades array, displaying it in the chosen format. As in the Calculate-ClassAverage method (Fig. 18.14), the outer For…Next statement iterates over the rows of the array while the inner For…Next statement iterates over the columns. The inner For…Next statement uses the output String (declared in the body of the outer For…Next statement) to create each item that's added to the ListBox, much as you did in the **Submit Grades** Button's Click event handler. The If…Then…Else statement (lines 167–174) in the body of the inner For…Next statement determines how the user wishes to view the grades (numeric or letter) and adds the grade, in the appropriate form, to the output String. The inner For…Next statement ends at the Next keyword in line 175. Note that you place the name of the statement's control variable after the Next keyword to improve readability. The body of the outer For…Next statement then adds the current student's average to the output String (line 178) and adds the String to the gradesListBox. Line 182 marks the end of the outer For…Next statement with keyword Next, followed by the name of the statement's control variable to increase readability. Line 185 displays the class's average in the averageLabel.

7. ***Running the app***. Select **Debug > Start Debugging** to run your app. Test your app to ensure that it functions as the completed app does.

(cont.)   8. ***Closing the app.*** Close your running app by clicking its close box.

9. ***Closing the IDE.*** Close the Visual Basic IDE by clicking its close box.

Figure 18.18 presents the source code for the **Student Grades** app. The lines of code that contain new programming concepts you learned in this chapter are highlighted.

```
 1   Public Class StudentGradesForm
 2       Dim grades As Integer(,) = New Integer(0 To 9, 0 To 2) {}
 3       Dim studentCount As Integer = 0 ' number of students entered
 4
 5       ' handles submit button click event
 6       Private Sub submitButton_Click(sender As System.Object,
 7          e As System.EventArgs) Handles submitButton.Click
 8
 9          ' retrieve the student's grades
10          grades(studentCount, 0) = Convert.ToInt32(test1TextBox.Text)
11          grades(studentCount, 1) = Convert.ToInt32(test2TextBox.Text)
12          grades(studentCount, 2) = Convert.ToInt32(test3TextBox.Text)
13
14          ' output string containing the student's grades and average
15          Dim output As String =
16             "Student " & studentCount & ControlChars.Tab
17
18          ' add each test grade to the output
19          For column As Integer = 0 To grades.GetUpperBound(1)
20             ' if the Letter RadioButton is checked
21             If letterRadioButton.Checked = True Then
22                ' add letter grade to the output
23                output &= ControlChars.Tab &
24                   LetterGrade(grades(studentCount, column))
25             Else
26                ' add number grade to the output
27                output &= ControlChars.Tab &
28                   grades(studentCount, column)
29             End If
30          Next
31
32          ' add the student's test average to the output
33          output &= ControlChars.Tab &
34             CalculateStudentAverage(studentCount)
35
36          gradesListBox.Items.Add(output) ' add output to the ListBox
37
38          studentCount += 1 ' update number of students entered
39
40          ' display the class average
41          averageLabel.Text = CalculateClassAverage()
42
43          ' clear the input TextBoxes and set focus to first TextBox
44          test1TextBox.Clear()
45          test2TextBox.Clear()
46          test3TextBox.Clear()
47          test1TextBox.Focus()
48
49          ' limit number of students
50          If studentCount = grades.GetUpperBound(0) + 1 Then
51             inputGroupBox.Enabled = False ' disable GroupBox's controls
52          End If
53       End Sub ' submitButton_Click
54
```

Labels pointing to code lines:

- Creating a two-dimensional array → (line 2)
- Assigning values to elements of a two-dimensional array → (lines 10–12)
- Iterating over the columns in a row of a two-dimensional array → (line 19)
- Using the **Checked** property of a **RadioButton** control → (line 21)
- Calling the **LetterGrade** method with an element of a two-dimensional array → (line 24)
- Accessing an element of a two-dimensional array → (line 28)
- Determining the number of rows in a two-dimensional array → (line 50)
- Disabling all the controls in a **GroupBox** → (line 51)

Figure 18.18   **Student Grades** app code. (Part 1 of 4.)

```vb
55      ' calculates a student's test average
56      Function CalculateStudentAverage(row As Integer) As String
57          Dim gradeTotal As Integer = 0 ' student's total grade
58
59          ' sum the grades for the student
60          For column As Integer = 0 To grades.GetUpperBound(1)
61              gradeTotal += grades(row, column)
62          Next
63
64          Dim studentAverage As String = String.Empty ' output string
65
66          ' calculate the student's test average
67          If letterRadioButton.Checked = True Then
68              studentAverage =
69                  LetterGrade(gradeTotal / (grades.GetUpperBound(1) + 1))
70          Else
71              studentAverage = String.Format("{0:F}",
72                  (gradeTotal / (grades.GetUpperBound(1) + 1)))
73          End If
74
75          Return studentAverage ' return the student's average
76      End Function ' CalculateStudentAverage
77
78      ' calculates the class average
79      Function CalculateClassAverage() As String
80          Dim classTotal As Integer = 0 ' class's total grade
81
82          ' loop through all rows
83          For row As Integer = 0 To studentCount - 1
84              ' loop through all columns
85              For column As Integer = 0 To grades.GetUpperBound(1)
86                  classTotal += grades(row, column) ' add grade to total
87              Next column
88          Next row
89
90          Dim classAverage As String = String.Empty ' output string
91
92          ' if the Letter RadioButton is checked, return letter grade
93          If letterRadioButton.Checked = True Then
94              classAverage = LetterGrade(classTotal /
95                  (studentCount * (grades.GetUpperBound(1) + 1)))
96          Else ' return number grade
97              classAverage = String.Format("{0:F}", (classTotal /
98                  (studentCount * (grades.GetUpperBound(1) + 1))))
99          End If
100
101         Return classAverage ' return the class average
102     End Function ' CalculateClassAverage
103
104     ' determines a letter grade corresponding to a numeric grade
105     Function LetterGrade(ByVal grade As Double) As String
106         Dim output As String ' the letter grade to return
107
108         ' determine the correct letter grade
109         Select Case grade
110             Case Is >= 90
111                 output = "A"
112             Case Is >= 80
113                 output = "B"
114             Case Is >= 70
115                 output = "C"
116             Case Is >= 60
117                 output = "D"
```

Iterating over the columns in a row of a two-dimensional array — *(lines 60–62)*

Using the **Checked** property of a **RadioButton** control — *(line 67)*

Calculating the student's average and formatting it as a number with two digits after the decimal point — *(lines 71–72)*

Using nested **For...Next** statements to iterate over the columns in each row of a two-dimensional array — *(lines 83–88)*

Using the **Checked** property of a **RadioButton** control — *(line 93)*

Calculating the class's average and formatting it as a number with two digits after the decimal point — *(lines 97–98)*

Figure 18.18 **Student Grades** app code. (Part 2 of 4.)

```
118              Case Else
119                 output = "F"
120           End Select
121
122           Return output ' return the letter grade
123        End Function ' LetterGrade
124
125        ' handles Numeric RadioButton's CheckChanged event
126        Private Sub numericRadioButton_CheckedChanged(
127           sender As System.Object, e As System.EventArgs) _
128           Handles numericRadioButton.CheckedChanged
129
130           ' if Numeric RadioButton is checked, display number grades
131           If numericRadioButton.Checked = True AndAlso
132              studentCount > 0 Then
133
134              DisplayClassGrades()
135           End If
136        End Sub ' numericRadioButton_CheckedChanged
137
138        ' handles Letter RadioButton's CheckChanged event
139        Private Sub letterRadioButton_CheckedChanged(
140           sender As System.Object, e As System.EventArgs) _
141           Handles letterRadioButton.CheckedChanged
142
143           ' if the Letter RadioButton is checked, display letter grades
144           If letterRadioButton.Checked = True AndAlso
145              studentCount > 0 Then
146
147              DisplayClassGrades()
148           End If
149        End Sub ' letterRadioButton_CheckedChanged
150
151        ' display the grades for all students entered
152        Sub DisplayClassGrades()
153           gradesListBox.Items.Clear() ' clear the ListBox
154
155           ' add the header to the ListBox
156           gradesListBox.Items.Add(ControlChars.Tab & ControlChars.Tab &
157              "Test 1" & ControlChars.Tab &
158              "Test 2" & ControlChars.Tab &
159              "Test 3" & ControlChars.Tab & "Average")
160
161           ' loop through all the rows
162           For row As Integer = 0 To studentCount - 1
163              Dim output As String = "Student " & row & ControlChars.Tab
164
165              ' loop through all the columns
166              For column As Integer = 0 To grades.GetUpperBound(1)
167                 If letterRadioButton.Checked = True Then
168                    ' add letter grade to output string
169                    output &= ControlChars.Tab &
170                       LetterGrade(grades(row, column))
171                 Else
172                    ' add number grade to output string
173                    output &= ControlChars.Tab & (grades(row, column))
174                 End If
175              Next column
176
177              ' add the student's average to the output
178              output &= ControlChars.Tab & CalculateStudentAverage(row)
179
180              ' add the output to the ListBox
181              gradesListBox.Items.Add(output)
182           Next row
```

Handling the CheckedChanged event of a RadioButton control

Handling the CheckedChanged event of a RadioButton control

Outer For...Next statement iterates over the rows of a two-dimensional array

Inner For...Next statement iterates over the columns of a row in a two-dimensional array

Using the control variable's name to improve readability of nested For...Next statements

Using the control variable's name to improve readability of nested For...Next statements

Figure 18.18   Student Grades app code. (Part 3 of 4.)

```
183
184          ' update the class average
185          averageLabel.Text = CalculateClassAverage()
186      End Sub ' DisplayClassGrades
187 End Class ' StudentGradesForm
```

Figure 18.18   Student Grades app code. (Part 4 of 4.)

SELF-REVIEW

1. A container can contain _____ RadioButton(s).

   a) exactly two   b) no more than one
   c) no more than three   d) any number of

2. When one RadioButton in a container is selected, _____.

   a) others can be selected at the same time   b) a logic error will occur
   c) all others in the container will be deselected   d) Both (a) and (c)

3. Typically, _____ statements are used to iterate over each element in a two-dimensional array.

   a) Do While...Loop   b) nested For...Next
   c) Do...Loop Until   d) nested Do...Loop While

Answers: 1.) d. 2.) c. 3.) b.

18.5 Wrap-Up

In this chapter, you learned how to declare and assign values to a two-dimensional array. You used code to store user input in a two-dimensional array. You also learned how to use For...Next statements to iterate over the rows or columns in a two-dimensional array. You used nested For...Next statements to iterate over every element in the two-dimensional array.

To help you complete the **Student Grades** app, you used RadioButtons. You learned that you must group related RadioButtons in separate containers. Initially, zero or one RadioButton in a container is selected, and only one can be selected at a time. You learned how to determine a RadioButton's state by examining its Checked property. You also learned that selecting or deselecting a RadioButton calls its CheckedChanged event handler.

In the next chapter, you'll learn about classes. (Recall that you've been using classes all along, from the Form class that represents the app's GUI to the Random class that you'll use to generate random numbers.) You'll create your own classes for use in your apps.

SKILLS SUMMARY

Creating a Two-Dimensional Array

■ Declare the array using the format:

> Dim *arrayName* As *arrayType*(,)

where *arrayName* is the reference name of the array, and *arrayType* is the type of data that will be stored in the array. The comma (,) in the parentheses indicates that the array is two-dimensional.

Assigning an Object to an Array Variable

■ Use keyword New as in the statement:

> *arrayName* = **New** *arrayType*(,) {{*arrayInitializerList*}, {*arrayInitializerList*},…}

where *arrayInitializerList* is a comma-separated list of the items that initialize the elements of one row in the array. You can also use

> *arrayName* = **New** *arrayType*(,) {}

to create the array and initialize its elements to the default value for *arrayType*.

Referring to Element *m, n* of a Two-Dimensional Array

■ Follow the array name by (*m, n*), where *m* is the row index and *n* is the column index.

Obtaining the Number of Rows and Columns in a Two-Dimensional Array

■ Pass 0 (the first dimension of the array) to method GetUpperBound to retrieve the index of the last row.

■ Pass 1 (the second dimension of the array) to method GetUpperBound to retrieve the index of the last column.

Using Two-Dimensional Arrays

■ Declare a rectangular array to create a table of values (each row contains the same number of columns).

■ Use a For...Next statement to iterate over the rows or columns of the two-dimensional array.

■ Use nested For...Next statements to iterate over every element in the two-dimensional array.

Using a RadioButton

■ Use a RadioButton in an app to present the user with mutually exclusive options.

Selecting a RadioButton at Runtime

■ Click the white circle of the RadioButton. A small dot appears inside the white circle.

Determining Whether a RadioButton Is Selected

■ Access the RadioButton's Checked property.

Executing Code When a RadioButton's State Has Changed

■ Use the CheckedChanged event handler, which executes when a RadioButton is selected or deselected.

■ Inspect the RadioButton's Checked property to determine whether it was selected or deselected.

KEY TERMS

Checked property of RadioButton control—When True, the control displays a small dot. When False, the control displays an empty white circle.

CheckedChanged event—Raised when a RadioButton's state changes.

column—The second dimension of a two-dimensional array.

double-subscripted array—See two-dimensional array.

Enabled property of GroupBox control—When False, disables all controls contained in the GroupBox.

m-by-n array—A two-dimensional array with *m* rows and *n* columns.

mutually exclusive options—A set of options of which only one can be selected at a time.

nested For...Next statements—A For...Next statement defined in the body of another For...Next statement; commonly used to iterate over the elements of a two-dimensional array.

precision—Specifies the number of digits to the right of the decimal point in a formatted floating-point value.

RadioButton control—Appears as a small circle that's either blank (unchecked) or contains a smaller dot (checked). Usually these controls appear in groups of two or more. Exactly one RadioButton in a group is selected at one time.

rectangular array—A type of two-dimensional array that can represent tables of values consisting of information arranged in rows and columns. Each row contains the same number of columns.

row—The first dimension of a two-dimensional array.

table—A two-dimensional array used to contain information arranged in rows and columns.

two-dimensional array—An array that contains multiple rows of values.

GUI DESIGN GUIDELINES

RadioButton

- Use `RadioButtons` when the user must choose only one option from a group.
- Always place each group of `RadioButtons` in a separate container (such as a `GroupBox`).
- Align groups of `RadioButtons` either horizontally or vertically.

CONTROLS, EVENTS, PROPERTIES & METHODS

RadioButton   ⦿ RadioButton   This control allows the user to select only one of several options.

- *In action*

    ⦿ Numeric

- *Event*

    `CheckedChanged`—Raised when the control is either selected or deselected.

- *Properties*

    `Checked`—Set to `True` if the control is selected and `False` if it's not selected.

    `Location`—Specifies the location of the `RadioButton` control relative to the top-left corner of the container (e.g., a `Form` or a `GroupBox`).

    `Name`—Specifies the name used to access the `RadioButton` control programmatically. The name should be appended with the `RadioButton` suffix.

    `Size`—Specifies the width and height (in pixels) of the `RadioButton` control.

    `Text`—Specifies the text displayed in the label to the right of the `RadioButton`.

GroupBox   [ᵡʸ] GroupBox   This control groups related controls visually in a box with a title.

- *In action*

    Drop Off

    Enter drop-off time: 10:44 AM   ⬍

- *Properties*

    `Location`—Specifies the location of the `GroupBox` control relative to the top-left corner of the container (e.g., a `Form` or a `GroupBox`).

    `Enabled`—When set to `False`, disables all controls contained in the `GroupBox`.

    `Name`—Specifies the name used to access the `GroupBox` control programmatically. The name should be appended with the `GroupBox` suffix.

    `Size`—Specifies the width and height (in pixels) of the `GroupBox` control.

    `Text`—Specifies the text displayed on the `GroupBox`.

MULTIPLE-CHOICE QUESTIONS

18.1 When declaring an array, a(n) _____ is required inside parentheses in order to indicate that the array is two-dimensional.

    a) comma   b) asterisk

    c) period   d) apostrophe

18.2 A two-dimensional array in which each row contains the same number of columns is called a _____ array.

    a) data   b) rectangular

    c) tabular   d) All of the above

18.3 In an *m*-by-*n* array, the *m* stands for _____.

    a) the number of columns in the array   b) the total number of array elements

    c) the number of rows in the array   d) the number of elements in each row

18.4 Which of the following statements assigns an array of five rows and three columns to a two-dimensional Integer array named array?

    a) array = **New Integer**(0 To 5, 0 To 3) {}

    b) array = **New Integer**(0 To 4, 0 To 2){}

    c) array = **New Integer**(0 To 4, 0 To 3) {}

    d) array = **New Integer**(0 To 5, 0 To 2) {}

18.5 A RadioButton is a type of _____ control.

    a) check   b) change

    c) state   d) action

18.6 Use a _____ to group RadioButtons on the Form.

    a) GroupBox control   b) ComboBox control

    c) ListBox control   d) None of the above

18.7 The _____ event handler is invoked when the user selects a RadioButton.

    a) Selected   b) CheckedChanged

    c) ButtonChanged   d) CheckSelected

18.8 The _____ property is set to True when a RadioButton is selected.

    a) Selected   b) Chosen

    c) On   d) Checked

18.9 Two-dimensional arrays are often used to represent _____.

    a) a pie chart   b) distances

    c) lines   d) tables

18.10 Which of the following statements assigns an array of three rows and three columns to a two-dimensional array of integers array?

    a) **Dim** array **As Integer**()() =
        New Integer()() {{1, 2, 3}, {4, 5, 6}, {7, 8, 9}}

    b) **Dim** array **As Integer**() =
        {{1, 2, 3}, {4, 5, 6}, {7, 8, 9}}

    c) **Dim** array **As Integer**(,) =
        New Integer(,) {{1, 2, 3}, {4, 5, 6}, {7, 8, 9}}

    d) All of the above

EXERCISES

18.11 *(Food Survey App)* A school cafeteria is giving an electronic survey to its students to improve their lunch menu. Create an app that uses a two-dimensional array to store votes for the survey. Provide RadioButtons to allow students to indicate whether they like or dislike a particular food (Fig. 18.19).

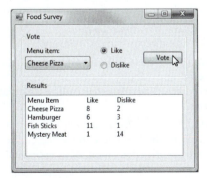

Figure 18.19 Food Survey app.

    a) *Copying the template to your working directory.* Copy the directory C:\Examples\ ch18\Exercises\FoodSurvey to your C:\SimplyVB2010 directory.

b) *Opening the app's template file.* Double click FoodSurvey.sln in the FoodSurvey directory to open the app.

c) *Adding RadioButtons to the Vote GroupBox.* Add two RadioButtons to the **Vote** GroupBox. Name one likeRadioButton and the other dislikeRadioButton. Change their Text properties to Like and Dislike, respectively. Set the Checked property of likeRadioButton to True.

d) *Declaring a two-dimensional Integer array.* Declare a two-dimensional Integer array named votes, with four rows and two columns. Each row corresponds to a menu item in the ComboBox. The columns store the number of "like" and "dislike" votes, respectively. The items in the ComboBox provided in the template app were added through the IDE using the ComboBox's Items property.

e) *Creating event handler voteButton_Click.* Generate the Click event handler for the **Vote** Button. Create a local Integer variable index. This variable should contain the index of the selected item in the **Menu item:** ComboBox. Use the Checked property to determine whether the student likes or dislikes the selected menu item and update the votes array accordingly.

f) *Displaying the data.* Create a Sub procedure named DisplayVotes. Add a header to the resultsListBox as in Fig. 18.19. Use a For...Next statement to iterate through each row in the votes array. Add the menu item, the number of "like" votes and the number of "dislike" votes to the ListBox. Call this procedure from the **Vote** Button's Click event handler.

g) *Running the app.* Select **Debug > Start Debugging** to run your app. Choose either the **Like** or **Dislike** RadioButton. Click the **Vote** Button and verify that the displayed information is updated correctly. Make several more votes and make sure that the numbers are correct.

h) *Closing the app.* Close your running app by clicking its close box.

i) *Closing the IDE.* Close the Visual Basic IDE by clicking its close box.

18.12 *(Enhanced Gas Pump App)* Enhance the **Gas Pump** app from Exercise 13.16 by allowing the user to choose the grade of gasoline using RadioButtons (Fig. 18.20). The total should be cleared when the user changes the number of gallons or the gasoline grade.

Figure 18.20   Enhanced **Gas Pump** app.

a) *Copying the template to your working directory.* Copy the directory C:\Examples\ch18\Exercises\EnhancedGasPump to your C:\SimplyVB2010 directory.

b) *Opening the app's template file.* Double click GasPump.sln in the Enhanced-GasPump directory to open the app.

c) *Modifying the GUI.* The GUI provided in the template is that of the original **Gas Pump** app. Modify this GUI to appear as in Fig. 18.20. Replace the three Buttons with three RadioButtons. Add a **Calculate** Button. Reposition and resize the controls.

d) *Modifying the Total method.* Modify the Select Case statement provided in the Total method template to use the Checked property of each RadioButton to determine the price per gallon. Also, use a Double instance variable to store the number of gallons instead of an Integer.

e) *Adding a ResetPump method.* Create the ResetPump method to reset the **Gas Pump** app. Clear the TextBox and output Label and set the gallons instance variable to 0.

f) *Coding the Calculate Button's Click event handler.* Double click the **Calculate** Button to generate its Click event handler. Use an If...Then statement to determine whether the user entered a number of gallons to purchase. If so, retrieve the number of gallons from the TextBox and store it in the gallons instance variable. Call Sub procedure Total to display the total cost of the purchase.

g) *Coding the CheckedChanged event handlers.* Double click each of the RadioButtons to generate their CheckedChanged event handlers. These event handlers should reset the app.

h) *Coding the TextChanged event handler.* Double click the **Number of gallons:** Text-Box to generate its TextChanged event handler. To ensure that the price displayed is always relative to the number of gallons in the TextBox, the TextChanged event handler should reset the **Total:** Label and the gallons instance variable.

i) *Running the app.* Select **Debug > Start Debugging** to run your app. Test your app to ensure that it displays the correct total according to the grade selected.

j) *Closing the app.* Close your running app by clicking its close box.

k) *Closing the IDE.* Close the Visual Basic IDE by clicking its close box.

What does this code do? ▶ **18.13** What is returned by the following code? Assume that GetStockPrices is a Function procedure that returns a 2-by-31 array, with the first row containing the stock price at the beginning of the day and the last row the stock price at the end of the day, for each day of the month.

```
1   Function Mystery() As Integer()
2      Dim prices As Integer(,) = New Integer(0 To 1, 0 To 30) {}
3
4      prices = GetStockPrices()
5
6      Dim result As Integer() = New Integer(30) {}
7
8      For i As Integer = 0 To 30
9         result(i) = prices(1, i) - prices(0, i)
10     Next
11
12     Return result
13  End Function ' Mystery
```

What's wrong with this code? ▶ **18.14** Find the error(s) in the following code. The TwoDArrays procedure should create a two-dimensional array and initialize all its values to one.

```
1   Sub TwoDArrays()
2      Dim array As Integer(,)
3
4      array = New Integer(0 To 3, 0 To 3) {}
5
6      ' assign 1 to all cell values
7      For i As Integer = 0 To 3
8         array(i, i) = 1
9      Next
10  End Sub ' TwoDArrays
```

Programming Challenge ▶ **18.15** *(Sales Report App)* A clothing manufacturer has asked you to create an app that calculates its total sales for a week. Sales values should be input separately for each clothing item, but the amount of sales for each of the five weekdays should be input all at once. The app should calculate the total amount of sales for each item in the week and also the total sales for the manufacturer for all the items in the week. Because the manufacturer is a small company, it produces at most 10 items in any week. The app is shown in Fig. 18.21.

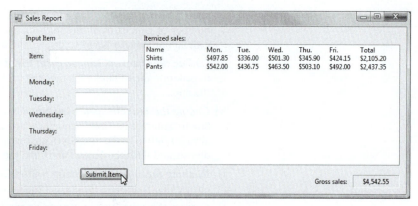

Figure 18.21 Sales Report app.

a) *Copying the template to your working directory.* Copy the directory C:\Examples\ch18\Exercises\SalesReport to your C:\SimplyVB2010 directory.

b) *Opening the app's template file.* Double click SalesReport.sln in the SalesReport directory to open the app.

c) *Declaring a two-dimensional Decimal array.* Declare a two-dimensional Decimal array named itemSales, with 10 rows and five columns.

d) *Inputting data from the user.* Add code to the beginning of the **Submit Item** Button's Click event handler to retrieve the data entered by the user. Assign the item name to the one-dimensional itemNames array, indexed with itemCount (which stores the number of items added). Assign the daily sales data to the two-dimensional itemSales array. The first index in this array is itemCount, and the second ranges from 0 to 4 depending on the day of the week (Monday–Friday). Increment variable itemCount to record that another item's sales data has been added. Disable the **Submit Item** Button after 10 items have been entered.

e) *Iterating over all the items added.* Add a For...Next statement after the output variable's declaration in the DisplaySales procedure. Iterate over each item added by the user. For each item, assign its name to String ouput. Append two tab characters to format the output properly.

f) *Iterating over the days in the week.* Add a nested For...Next statement to the body of the For...Next statement from the previous step. This For...Next statement iterates over the daily sales (the columns in the itemSales array). Append the daily sales (formatted as currency) followed by a tab character to the output String. Add the daily sales amount to the weekly total.

g) *Calculating the total sales and outputting an item's sales.* After iterating over the daily sales, add the weekly sales to the gross sales. Format the gross sales as currency and display it in the **Gross sales:** Label. Add code to append the weekly sales to output. Then add output to the ListBox using the Add method of ListBox property Items.

h) *Running the app.* Select **Debug > Start Debugging** to run your app. Test your app to ensure that it runs correctly, as in Fig. 18.21.

i) *Closing the app.* Close your running app by clicking its close box.

j) *Closing the IDE.* Close the Visual Basic IDE by clicking its close box.

Objectives

In this chapter, you'll learn to:

- Create your own classes.
- Create and use objects of your own classes.
- Control access to object instance variables.
- Use keyword `Private`.
- Create your own properties.
- Use the `Panel` control.
- Use `String` methods `PadLeft` and `Substring`.

Outline

Microwave Oven App

Building Your Own Classes and Objects

In earlier chapters, you used the following app-development methodology: You analyzed many typical problems that required apps to be built and determined what classes from the .NET Framework Class Library were needed to implement each app. You then selected appropriate methods from these classes and created any necessary procedures to complete each app.

You've now seen several .NET classes. Each GUI control is defined as a class. When you add a control to your app from the **Toolbox**, an object (also known as an *instance*) of that class is created and added to your app. You've also seen .NET classes that are *not* GUI controls. Classes String and Random, for example, have been used to create String objects (for textual data) and Random objects (for generating random numbers), respectively. When you create and use an object of a class in an app, your app is known as a **client** of that class.

In this chapter, you'll learn to create and use your own classes (sometimes known as **programmer-defined classes** or **programmer-defined types**). Creating your own classes is a key part of object-oriented programming (OOP). As with procedures, classes can be *reused*. Visual Basic apps typically are created by using a combination of .NET classes and methods and programmer-defined classes and methods. You've already created several procedures in this book. Note that they all were created within classes, because all of your apps have been defined as classes (each Form you've created is a class). In this chapter (and for the remainder of the book), you'll refer to a class's procedures as *methods*, which is the industry-preferred term for procedures located within a class.

You'll create a microwave oven simulator where the user will enter an amount of time for the microwave to cook food. To handle the time data, you'll create a class called Time. This class stores a number of minutes and seconds (which your **Microwave Oven** app will use to keep track of the remaining cook time) and provides properties whereby clients of the class can change the number of minutes and seconds.

19.1 Test-Driving the Microwave Oven App

In this chapter you'll build your own class as you construct your **Microwave Oven** app. This app must meet the following requirements:

411

App Requirements

An electronics company is considering building microwave ovens. The company has asked you to develop an app that simulates a microwave oven. The oven contains a keypad that allows the user to specify the microwave cook time, which is displayed for the user. Once a time is entered, the user clicks the **Start Button** *to begin the cooking process. The microwave's glass window changes color (from gray to yellow) to simulate the oven's light that remains on while the food is cooking, and a timer counts down one second at a time. Once the time expires, the color of the microwave's glass window returns to gray (indicating that the microwave's light is now off) and the microwave displays the text "Done!" The user can click the* **Clear Button** *at any time to stop the microwave and enter a new time. The user should be able to enter a number of minutes no larger than 59 and a number of seconds no larger than 59; otherwise, the invalid portion of the cook time is set to zero. A beep is sounded whenever a* **Button** *is clicked and when the microwave oven has finished a countdown.*

You'll begin by test-driving the completed app. Then you'll learn the additional Visual Basic technologies that you'll need to create your own version of this app.

Test-Driving the Microwave Oven App

1. ***Opening the completed app.*** Open the directory C:\Examples\ch19\CompletedApp\MicrowaveOven to locate the **Microwave Oven** app. Double click MicrowaveOven.sln to open the app in the Visual Basic IDE.

2. ***Running the Microwave Oven app.*** Select **Debug > Start Debugging** to run the app (Fig. 19.1). The app contains a large rectangle on the left (representing the microwave oven's glass window) and a keypad on the right, including a Label with the text **Microwave Oven**. The numeric Buttons are used to enter the cook time, which is displayed in the Label on the top right. Note that the keypad Buttons appear flat, to give the app a more "real-world" appearance. To create this appearance, the Buttons' FlatStyle property has been set to Flat. Similarly, the Label's BorderStyle property has been set to FixedSingle.

Microwave's glass window ———

Microwave Oven

1 2 3
4 5 6
7 8 9
0

Start   Clear

——— Label

——— Numeric keypad (Buttons appear flat)

Figure 19.1 **Microwave Oven** app's Form.

3. ***Entering a time.*** Click the following numeric Buttons in order: **1, 2, 3, 4** and **5.** Each time you click a keypad Button, you'll hear a beeping sound. (If you don't hear a beeping sound, please check your computer's settings to ensure that the volume of your machine's speaker has not been lowered or muted.)

(cont.)   Note that you can enter no more than four digits (the first two for the minutes and the second two for the seconds)—any extra digits will not appear (Fig. 19.2). The number of minutes and the number of seconds must each be 59 or less. If the user enters an invalid number of minutes or seconds (such as 89), the invalid amount is set to zero.

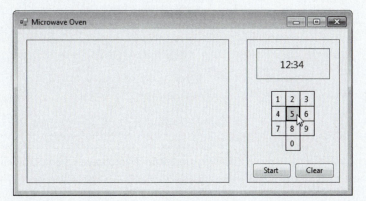

Figure 19.2   **Microwave Oven** app accepts only four digits.

4. ***Entering invalid data.*** Click the **Clear** Button to clear your input. Click the following numeric Buttons in order: **7**, **2**, **3** and **5** (Fig. 19.3). This input is invalid because the number of minutes, 72, is larger than the maximum allowed value, 59, so the number of minutes is reset to zero when the **Start** Button is clicked. Click the **Start** Button now. Note that the number of minutes is reset to **00** (Fig. 19.4). Also note that the microwave oven's window has changed to yellow, to simulate the light that goes on inside the oven so that the user can watch the food cooking.

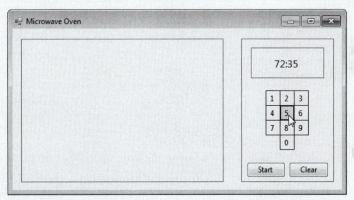

Figure 19.3   **Microwave Oven** app with invalid input.

Color yellow simulates
microwave light
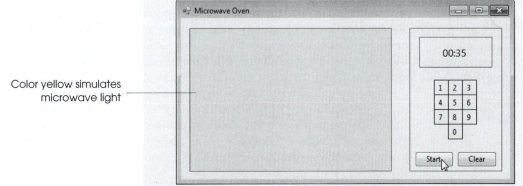

Figure 19.4   **Microwave Oven** app after the user enters 7, 2, 3 and 5 and presses the **Start** Button.

(cont.)

5. ***Entering valid data.*** Click the **Clear** Button to enter a new cook time. Click Button **5** (to indicate five seconds); then, click **Start** (Fig. 19.5).

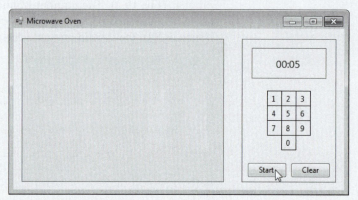

Figure 19.5   **Microwave Oven** app with valid time entered and inside light turned on (it's now cooking).

6. ***Viewing the app after the cooking time has expired.*** Wait five seconds. Note that the display Label shows the time counting down by 1 each second. When the time has reached zero, the oven beeps, the display Label changes to contain the text **Done!** and the microwave oven's window changes back to the same color as the Form (Fig. 19.6).

Label displays **Done!** when cooking is finished

Color returns to default color to simulate that cooking has finished

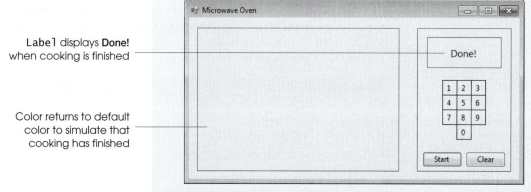

Figure 19.6   **Microwave Oven** app after the cooking time has elapsed.

7. ***Closing the app.*** Close your running app by clicking its close box.

8. ***Closing the project.*** Close the project by selecting **File > Close Project**.

GUI Design Tip

Use Panels to organize groups of related controls where their purpose is obvious. If the controls' purpose is not obvious, use a GroupBox rather than a Panel, because GroupBoxes can contain captions.

19.2 Designing the Microwave Oven App

In Chapter 14, you learned to use GroupBoxes to group various controls. The **Microwave Oven** app groups controls using a **Panel control**. The main difference between Panels and GroupBoxes is that GroupBoxes can display a caption. The **Microwave Oven** app requires two Panels—one to contain the controls of the app, and the other to represent the microwave oven's glass window. The template app provided for you contains one of these Panels.

The **Microwave Oven** app contains a class (called Time) whose objects store the cook time in minutes and seconds. All the controls you've used (including the Form itself) are defined as classes. You'll begin by creating the Time class. The following pseudocode describes the basic operation of class Time:

When the time object is created:

  Assign input to variables for number of minutes and number of seconds

When setting the number of minutes:

    If the number of minutes is less than 60
        Set the number of minutes to specified value
    Else
        Set the number of minutes to 0

When setting the number of seconds:

    If the number of seconds is less than 60
        Set the number of seconds to specified value
    Else
        Set the number of seconds to 0

When an object of class `Time` is created, the number of minutes and number of seconds are initialized. Any invalid number (minutes or seconds) is set to 0. The following pseudocode describes the basic operation of your **Microwave Oven** class:

When the user clicks a numeric Button:
    Sound beep
    Display the formatted time

When the user clicks the Start Button:
    Store the minutes and seconds
    Display the formatted time
    Begin countdown—Start timer
    Turn the microwave light on

When the timer ticks (once per second):
    Decrease time by one second
    Display new time

    If new time is zero
        Stop the countdown
        Sound beep
        Display text "Done!"
        Turn the microwave light off

When the user clicks the Clear Button:
    Display the text "Microwave Oven"
    Clear input and time data
    Stop the countdown
    Turn the microwave light off

The user enters input by clicking the numeric `Button`s. Each time a numeric `Button` is clicked, the number on it is appended to the end of the cook time displayed in the GUI's `Label`. At most, four digits can be displayed. After entering the cook time, the user can click the **Start** `Button` to begin the cooking process or click the **Clear** `Button` and enter a new time. Each `Button` makes a beeping sound when clicked. If the **Start** `Button` is clicked, a countdown using a `Timer` control begins, and the microwave oven's window changes to yellow, indicating that the oven's light is on (so that the user can watch the food cook). Each second, the display is updated to show the remaining cooking time. When the countdown finishes, another beep is sounded, the display `Label` displays the text **Done!** and the microwave oven's light is turned off by changing the window's color back to its default gray.

Now that you've test-driven the **Microwave Oven** app and studied its pseudocode representation, you'll use an ACE table to help you convert the pseudocode to Visual Basic. Figure 19.7 lists the *actions*, *controls* and *events* that will help you complete your own version of this app.

Action	Control/Object	Event
	All GUI components created	App is run
	oneButton, twoButton, three-Button, fourButton, fiveButton, sixButton, sevenButton, eightButton, nineButton, zeroButton	Click
Sound beep		
Display the formatted time	displayLabel	
	startButton	Click
Store the minutes and seconds	timeObject	
Display the formatted time	displayLabel	
Begin countdown—Start timer	clockTimer	
Turn microwave light on	windowPanel	
	clockTimer	Tick
Decrease time by one second	timeObject	
Display new time	displayLabel	
If new time is zero	timeObject	
Stop the countdown	clockTimer	
Sound beep		
Display text "Done!"	displayLabel	
Turn the microwave light off	windowPanel	
	clearButton	Click
Display the text "Microwave Oven"	displayLabel	
Clear input and time data	timeIs (time entered String) timeObject	
Stop the countdown	clockTimer	
Turn microwave light off	windowPanel	

Figure 19.7   ACE table for the **Microwave Oven** app.

Input is sent to the app when the user clicks one of the numeric Buttons. Values are displayed in displayLabel as they're entered. Once all input has been entered, the user clicks the **Start** Button to begin the countdown. The Form's windowPanel background color is set to yellow to simulate the microwave oven's light being turned on, and clockTimer updates displayLabel each second during the countdown. To clear the input and start over, the user can click the **Clear** Button. In the following box, you'll begin creating your **Microwave Oven** app by adding the second Panel to the Form and viewing the template code.

Adding a Panel Control to the Microwave Oven App

1. ***Copying the template to your working directory.*** Copy the C:\Examples\ ch19\TemplateApp\MicrowaveOven directory to your C:\SimplyVB2010 directory.

2. ***Opening the Microwave Oven app's template file.*** Double click MicrowaveOven.sln in the MicrowaveOven directory to open the app in the Visual Basic IDE.

(cont.)

When a number is entered, play a beep, append the number to timeIs and display the new time

3. ***Adding a Panel to the Form.*** Add a Panel control to the Form by double clicking the Panel control (Panel) in the **Containers** tab of the **Toolbox**. Name the control windowPanel because this Panel represents your microwave oven's window. Set the Panel's Size property to 328, 224 and its Location property to 14, 16. Set the BorderStyle property to FixedSingle, to display a thin black rectangle surrounding your Panel.

4. ***Viewing the template code.*** Before you add code to this app, switch to code view and examine the code provided. Line 4 of Fig. 19.8 declares instance variable timeIs, a String that will store user input.

```
1   Public Class MicrowaveOvenForm
2
3       ' contains time entered as a String
4       Dim timeIs As String = String.Empty
```

Figure 19.8   Variable timeIs contains the user's input.

The template code also contains event handlers for the numeric Buttons' Click events. Each Button is clicked when the user wants to append the current Button's digit to the amount of cooking time. Let's look at one of these event handlers closely (Fig. 19.9). Line 10 calls function **Beep**, which causes your computer to make a beeping sound. Each event handler for the numeric keypad Buttons begins with a call to Beep, appends the current Button's number to timeIs (line 11) and calls method DisplayTime (line 12), which displays the current cooking time in the app's Label. There are 10 of these event handlers—one for each digit from 0 to 9.

```
6       ' event handler appends 1 to time string
7       Private Sub oneButton_Click(sender As System.Object,
8           e As System.EventArgs) Handles oneButton.Click
9
10          Beep() ' sound beep
11          timeIs &= "1" ' append digit to time input
12          DisplayTime() ' display time input properly
13      End Sub ' oneButton_Click
```

Figure 19.9   Typical numeric event handler.

MicrowaveOven.vb contains four more methods that you'll define in this chapter. The first is the startButton_Click event handler in lines 96–100 of Fig. 19.10. This event handler starts the microwave oven's cooking process, which in this simulation consists of a time countdown and a change of the window's color to yellow, simulating the oven's light being on.

Event handler clearButton_Click (lines 102–106) clears the time entered. The **Clear** Button is used to change the time entered or terminate cooking early. The event handler resets the time to all zeros and displays the text **Microwave Oven**. Method DisplayTime (lines 108–111) displays the cooking time as it's being entered. Event handler clockTimer_Tick (lines 113–117) changes the app's Label during the countdown.

5. ***Saving the project.*** Select **File > Save All** to save your modified code.

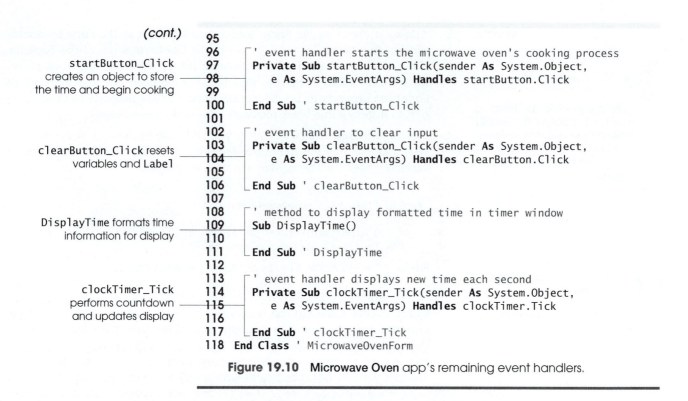

(cont.)

startButton_Click creates an object to store the time and begin cooking

clearButton_Click resets variables and Label

DisplayTime formats time information for display

clockTimer_Tick performs countdown and updates display

```
 95
 96     ' event handler starts the microwave oven's cooking process
 97     Private Sub startButton_Click(sender As System.Object,
 98         e As System.EventArgs) Handles startButton.Click
 99
100     End Sub ' startButton_Click
101
102     ' event handler to clear input
103     Private Sub clearButton_Click(sender As System.Object,
104         e As System.EventArgs) Handles clearButton.Click
105
106     End Sub ' clearButton_Click
107
108     ' method to display formatted time in timer window
109     Sub DisplayTime()
110
111     End Sub ' DisplayTime
112
113     ' event handler displays new time each second
114     Private Sub clockTimer_Tick(sender As System.Object,
115         e As System.EventArgs) Handles clockTimer.Tick
116
117     End Sub ' clockTimer_Tick
118 End Class ' MicrowaveOvenForm
```

Figure 19.10   **Microwave Oven** app's remaining event handlers.

SELF-REVIEW   1. A Panel is different from a GroupBox in that a _____.

    a) GroupBox can be used to organize controls, whereas a Panel cannot

    b) Panel contains a caption, whereas a GroupBox does not

    c) GroupBox contains a caption, whereas a Panel does not

    d) Panel can be used to organize controls, whereas a GroupBox cannot

2. Function Beep causes the computer to _____.

    a) make three beeping sounds in sequence b) make a beeping sound

    c) display a message dialog and make a   d) set off the system alarm and pause the
       beeping sound   app

Answers: 1) c. 2) b.

19.3 Adding a New Class to the Project

Next, you'll learn how to add a class to your app. This class is used to create objects that contain the time in minutes and seconds.

Adding a Class to the Microwave Oven App

1. *Adding a new class to the project.* Select **Project > Add Class**. In the dialog that appears (Fig. 19.11), enter the class name (Time) in the **Name:** field and click **Add**. Note that the class name (ending with the .vb file extension) appears in the **Solution Explorer** below the project name (Fig. 19.12).

(cont.)

Select **Class** as new item ——————

Name of new class ——————

Figure 19.11   **Add New Item** dialog allows you to create a new class.

2. *Viewing the code that has been added to this class.* If Time.vb does not open for you when it's created, double click the file in the **Solution Explorer**. Note that a few lines of code have been added for you (Fig. 19.13). Line 1, which begins the Time class definition, contains the keywords Public and Class, followed by the name of the class (in this case, Time). Keyword Class indicates that what follows is a class definition. You'll learn about keyword Public in Section 19.7. The keywords End Class (line 3) indicate the end of the class definition. Any code placed between these two lines forms the class definition's body. Any methods or variables defined in the body of a class are considered to be **members** of that class.

New file displayed in
Solution Explorer ——————

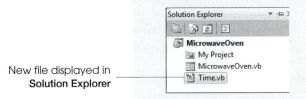

Figure 19.12   **Solution Explorer** displaying the new class file.

Empty class definition
added by the IDE ——————

```
1   Public Class Time
2
3   End Class
```

Figure 19.13   Empty class definition.

3. *Adding instance variables to your app.* Add lines 1–2 of Fig. 19.14 to Time.vb, above the class definition. Always add comments indicating the name and purpose of your class files. Add lines 6–8 to the Time class definition.

Lines 7–8 declare each of the two Integer instance variables—minute-Value and secondValue. The Time class stores a time value containing minutes and seconds—the value for minutes is stored in minuteValue and the value for seconds in secondValue. Finally, be sure to add a comment in line 10 where the class definition is terminated.

Good Programming Practice

Add comments at the beginning of your classes to increase readability. The comments should indicate the name of the file that contains the class and the purpose of the class being defined.

(cont.)

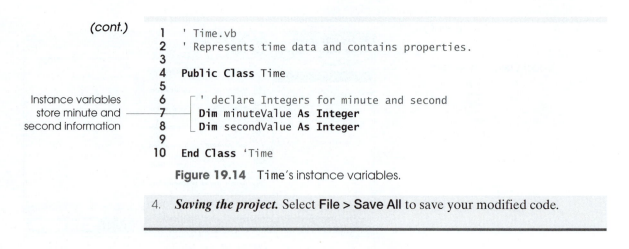

Instance variables store minute and second information

```
1   ' Time.vb
2   ' Represents time data and contains properties.
3
4   Public Class Time
5
6       ' declare Integers for minute and second
7       Dim minuteValue As Integer
8       Dim secondValue As Integer
9
10  End Class 'Time
```

Figure 19.14 Time's instance variables.

4. **Saving the project.** Select **File > Save All** to save your modified code.

SELF-REVIEW

1. To add a class to a project in the Visual Basic IDE, select _____.

   a) **File > Add Class**

   b) **File > Add File > Add Class**

   c) **Project > Add Class**

   d) **Project > Add File > Add Class**

2. A class definition ends with the keyword(s) _____.

   a) `Class End`

   b) `End Class`

   c) `EndClass`

   d) `End`

Answers: 1) c. 2) b.

19.4 Initializing Class Objects: Constructors

A class can contain methods as well as instance variables. You've already used method `Format` from class `String` and method `Next` from class `Random`. A **constructor** is a special method within a class definition that's used to initialize a class's instance variables. The constructor is always named `New`. In the following box, you'll create a constructor for your `Time` class that allows clients to create `Time` objects and initialize their data.

Defining a Constructor

1. **Adding a constructor to a class.** Add lines 10–11 of Fig. 19.15 to the body of class `Time`, then press *Enter*. The keywords `End Sub` are added for you, just as with the other `Sub` procedures you've created in this text.

   `New` is the constructor method. You write code for the constructor that's invoked whenever an object of that class is **instantiated** (created). This constructor method then performs the actions in its body, which you'll add in the next few steps. A constructor's actions consist mainly of statements that initialize the class's instance variables.

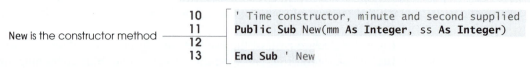

New is the constructor method

```
10      ' Time constructor, minute and second supplied
11      Public Sub New(mm As Integer, ss As Integer)
12
13      End Sub ' New
```

Figure 19.15 Empty constructor.

(cont.)

Common Programming Error

Attempting to declare a constructor as a Function procedure instead of as a Sub procedure and attempting to Return a value from a constructor are both syntax errors.

Error-Prevention Tip

Providing a constructor to ensure that every object is initialized with meaningful values can help eliminate logic errors.

Constructors *can* take arguments (you'll see how to provide arguments to constructors momentarily) but cannot return values. An important difference between constructors and other methods is that constructors *cannot* specify a return data type—for this reason, Visual Basic constructors are implemented as Sub procedures rather than Function procedures, because Sub procedures cannot return values. A class's instance variables can be initialized in the constructor or when they're defined in the class definition. Variable secondValue, for instance, can be initialized where it's declared (line 8 of Fig. 19.14) or it can be initialized in Time's constructor.

2. ***Initializing variables in a constructor.*** Add lines 13–14 of Fig. 19.16 to the constructor. These lines initialize Time's instance variables to the values of the constructor's parameter variables (line 11 of Fig. 19.15). When a client of a class creates an object of that class, values are often specified for that object. A Time object can now be created with the statement

```
timeObject = New Time(5, 3)
```

which appears in the client. The Time object is created and the constructor executes. The constructor's parameters, the values 5 and 3, are used to initialize secondValue and minuteValue.

```
10      ' Time constructor, minute and second supplied
11      Public Sub New(mm As Integer, ss As Integer)
12
13          minuteValue = mm ' initialize minuteValue
14          secondValue = ss ' initialize secondValue
15      End Sub ' New
```
Initialize instance variables ⎯ (lines 13–14)

Figure 19.16   Constructor initializing instance variables.

3. ***Creating a Time object.*** After defining the class, you can use it as a type (just as you would use Integer or Double) in declarations. View Microwave-Oven.vb by selecting the **MicrowaveOven.vb** tab above the code editor. Add lines 6–7 of Fig. 19.17 to your app. Note the use of the class name, Time, as a type. Just as you can create *many* variables from a data type, such as Integer, you can create *many* objects from class types. You can create your own class types as needed; this is one reason why Visual Basic is known as an **extensible language**—the language can be "extended" with new data types. Note that, after you type As in line 7, *IntelliSense* displays a window of available types. Your Time class is displayed in the *IntelliSense* window (Fig. 19.18).

```
4      Dim timeIs As String = String.Empty
5
6          ' contains time entered
7      Dim timeObject As Time
```
Declare timeObject of programmer-defined ⎯ type Time (lines 6–7)

Figure 19.17   Declaring an object of type Time.

(cont.)

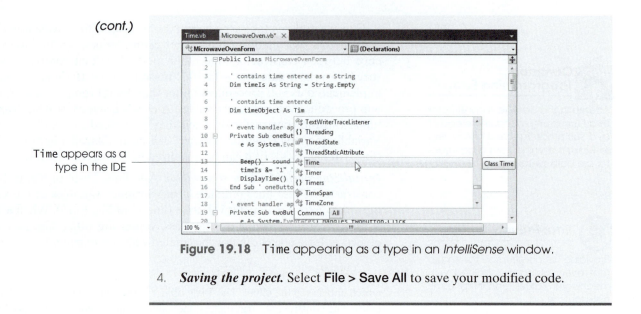

Time appears as a type in the IDE

Figure 19.18 Time appearing as a type in an *IntelliSense* window.

4. ***Saving the project.*** Select **File > Save All** to save your modified code.

SELF-REVIEW

1. A(n) _____ language is one that can be "extended" with new data types.
   a) data   b) extensible
   c) typeable   d) extended

2. Variables can be initialized _____.
   a) when they're declared   b) to their default values
   c) in a constructor   d) All of the above

Answers: 1) b. 2) d.

19.5 Properties

Clients of a class usually want to manipulate that class's instance variables. For example, assume a class (Person) that stores information about a person, including age information (stored in Integer instance variable age). Clients who create an object of class Person might want to modify age—perhaps incorrectly, by assigning a negative value to age, for example. Classes often provide **properties** to allow clients to access and modify instance variables safely. The syntax used to access properties is the same as the syntax used to access instance variables. You've already seen and used several properties in previous chapters. For instance, many GUI controls contain a Text property, used to *get* or *set* the text displayed by a control. When a value is assigned to a property, the code in the property definition is executed. The code in the property typically checks the value to be assigned and rejects invalid data. In this chapter, you'll learn how to create your own properties to help clients of a class read and modify the class's instance variables. You'll create two properties, Minute and Second, for your Time class. Minute allows clients to access variable minuteValue safely, and Second allows clients to access variable second-Value safely.

Good Programming Practice

Capitalize the first letter of a property's name.

A **property definition** may consist of two **accessors**—methodlike code units that handle the details of modifying and returning data. The **Set accessor** allows clients to set (that is, assign values to) properties. For example, when the code

```
timeObject.Minute = 35
```

executes, the Set accessor of the Minute property executes. Set accessors typically provide *data-validation* capabilities (such as *range checking*) to ensure that the value of each instance variable is set properly. In your **Microwave Oven** app, users can specify an amount of minutes only in the range 0 to 59. Values not in this range are discarded by the `Set` accessor, and `minuteValue` is assigned the value 0. The **Get accessor** allows clients to get (that is, obtain the value of) a property. When the code

```
minuteValue = timeObject.Minute
```

executes, the `Get` accessor of the `Minute` property executes and returns the value of the `minuteValue` instance variable.

Each property is typically defined to perform validity checking—to ensure that the data assigned to the property is valid. Keeping an object's data valid is also known as keeping that data in a **consistent state**. Property `Minute` keeps instance variable `minuteValue` in a consistent state. In the following box, you'll create properties `Minute` and `Second` for class `Time`, defining `Get` and `Set` accessors for each.

Defining Properties

1. ***Adding property `Minute` to class `Time`.*** View `Time.vb` by selecting the **Time.vb** tab above the code editor. Add lines 17–19 of Fig. 19.19 below the constructor, then press *Enter* to add property `Minute` to class `Time`. Lines 20–25 are added for you automatically by the IDE.

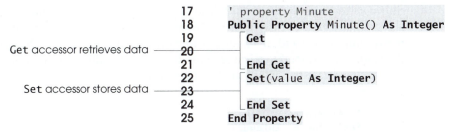

```
17          ' property Minute
18          Public Property Minute() As Integer
19              Get
20
21              End Get
22              Set(value As Integer)
23
24              End Set
25          End Property
```

Get accessor retrieves data ——— 19, 20

Set accessor stores data ——— 22, 23

Figure 19.19 Empty `Minute` property.

Good Programming Practice

Name each property with a capital first letter.

Note the syntax used in a property definition. You begin in line 18 with the keyword `Public` (which is discussed in Section 19.7), followed by the keyword **Property**, which indicates that you're defining a property. The keyword `Property` is followed by the name of the property (in this case, `Minute`) and a set of parentheses, which is similar to the way you define methods. The first line of the property concludes with the keyword `As` followed by a data type (in this case, `Integer`), indicating the data type of any value assigned to, or read from, this property.

The keyword **Get** in line 19 indicates the beginning of this property's `Get` accessor. The keywords **End Get** in line 21 indicate the end of the `Get` accessor. Any code that you insert between these two lines makes up the `Get` accessor's body and is executed when a client of this class attempts to read a value from the `Minute` property, as with the code

```
minutes = timeObject.Minute
```

Typically, the `Get` property simply returns the value, but could also calculate a value as well.

The keyword **Set** in line 22 indicates the beginning of this property's `Set` accessor. The keywords **End Set** in line 24 indicate the end of the `Set` accessor. Any code that you insert between these two lines makes up the `Set` accessor's body and is executed automatically (that's the beauty of properties) when a client of this class attempts to assign a value to the `Minute` property, as with the code `timeObject.Minute = 35`. The value assigned is stored in the parameter specified in line 22, which by default uses the identifier `value`. This identifier is used to access the value assigned to property `Minute`. The property ends in line 25 with the keywords **End Property**.

(cont.)   2. ***Defining the Get accessor.*** Add line 21 of Fig. 19.20 to your `Get` accessor.
Also add a comment (line 19) above the `Get` accessor, to increase readabil-
ity. When property `Minute` is referenced, you want your `Get` accessor to
return the value of `minuteValue` just as a method (function) would return a
value, so you use the keyword `Return` in line 21, followed by the identifier
`minuteValue`. Finally, add a comment in line 22 to indicate the end of the
`Get` accessor.

```
17      ' property Minute
18      Public Property Minute() As Integer
19         ' return Minute value
20         Get
21            Return minuteValue
22         End Get ' end of Get accessor
```

Returning data from a property ——— 21 (points to line 21)

Figure 19.20   `Get` accessor definition.

3. ***Defining the Set accessor.*** Add lines 26–31 of Fig. 19.21 to your `Set` accessor. Also add a comment (line 24) above the `Set` accessor, to increase readability. When property `Minute` is assigned a value, you want to test whether
the value to be assigned is valid. You do not want to accept a minute value
less than 0 or greater than 59, a condition that's tested in line 27. If the number of minutes is valid, it's assigned to `minuteValue` in line 28. Otherwise,
the value 0 is assigned to `minuteValue` in line 30. Finally, add a comment at
line 32 to indicate the end of the `Set` accessor.

```
24      ' set Minute value
25      Set(value As Integer)
26         'if minute value entered is valid
27         If (value >= 0 AndAlso value < 60) Then
28            minuteValue = value
29         Else
30            minuteValue = 0 ' set invalid input to 0
31         End If
32      End Set ' end of Set accessor
```

Validate minute data ——— (points to lines 27–31)

Figure 19.21   `Set` accessor definition.

4. ***Adding property Second to class Time.*** Add lines 35–37 of Fig. 19.22 to your
app, then press *Enter*. Lines 38–43 are added for you by the IDE.

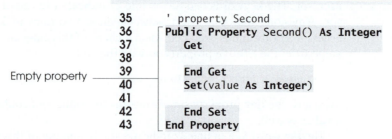

```
35      ' property Second
36      Public Property Second() As Integer
37         Get
38
39         End Get
40         Set(value As Integer)
41
42         End Set
43      End Property
```

Empty property ——— (points to lines 36–43)

Figure 19.22   `Second` property.

5. ***Defining the Second property's accessors.*** Add comments above each accessor (lines 37 and 42 of Fig. 19.23). Add line 39 to property `Second`'s `Get` accessor and lines 44–49 to property `Second`'s `Set` accessor. Note that this property
is similar to `Minute`, except that variable `secondValue` is being modified and
read, as opposed to variable `minuteValue`. Finally, you should add comments
at the end of each accessor (lines 40 and 50) to increase readability.

(cont.)

```
33     End Property ' Minute
34
35     ' property Second
36     Public Property Second() As Integer
37         ' return Second value
38         Get
39             Return secondValue
40         End Get ' end of Get accessor
41
42         ' set Second Value
43         Set(value As Integer)
44             ' if second value entered is valid
45             If (value >= 0 AndAlso value < 60) Then
46                 secondValue = value
47             Else
48                 secondValue = 0 ' set invalid input to 0
49             End If
50         End Set ' end of Set accessor
51     End Property ' Second
```

Second property performs similar data manipulations to `Minute` property

Figure 19.23   Second property definition.

6. ***Assigning values to properties.*** Change lines 13–14 of Fig. 19.16 to lines 13–14 of Fig. 19.24. Now that you've defined properties to ensure that only *valid* data is assigned to `minuteValue` and `secondValue`, you can use these properties to safely initialize instance variables in the class's constructor. When a client calls `New` and passes values for `mm` and `ss`, the constructor calls the `Set` accessors to validate the values. You should not bypass a class's properties to assign values to or retrieve values from the class's instance variables. The properties ensure the data is valid, keeping the data in a consistent state. Accessing the instance variables directly bypasses this validation.

```
10     ' Time constructor, minute and second supplied
11     Public Sub New(mm As Integer, ss As Integer)
12
13         Minute = mm ' invokes Minute set accessor
14         Second = ss ' invokes Second set accessor
15     End Sub ' New
```

It's safer to assign data to properties rather than instance variables, because Set accessors perform validity checking

Figure 19.24   Constructor using properties to initialize variables.

7. ***Saving the project.*** Select **File > Save All** to save your modified code.

SELF-REVIEW

1. A(n) _____ can ensure that a value is appropriate for a data member before the data member is assigned that value.

    a) `Get` accessor   b) `Access` accessor
    c) `Modify` accessor   d) `Set` accessor

2. Properties can contain both _____ accessors.

    a) `Return` and `Value`   b) `Get` and `Value`
    c) `Get` and `Set`   d) `Return` and `Set`

Answers: 1) d. 2) c.

19.6 Completing the Microwave Oven App

Now that you've completed your `Time` class, you'll use an object of this class to maintain the cooking time in your app. Follow the steps in the next box to add this functionality to your app.

Completing the Microwave Oven App

1. **Formatting user input.** View MicrowaveOven.vb in the code editor. Add lines 103–107 of Fig. 19.25 to event handler startButton_Click. Variables second and minute (lines 103–104) store the second and minute values entered by the user. Line 107 uses String method **PadLeft**, which appends characters to the beginning of a String based on its length. This method can be used to guarantee the length of a String—if the String has fewer characters than desired, method PadLeft adds characters to the beginning until the String has the proper number of characters. You want timeIs to contain four characters (for example, "0325" rather than "325" for a time of "3:25", representing 3 minutes and 25 seconds). Having four digits makes the conversion to minutes and seconds easier. You can now simply convert the first two digits (03) to a minute value and the last two digits (25) to a second value. Class String also provides method **PadRight**, which appends characters to the end of a String based on its length.

```
99      ' event handler starts the microwave oven's cooking process
100     Private Sub startButton_Click(sender As System.Object,
101        e As System.EventArgs) Handles startButton.Click
102
103        Dim second As Integer
104        Dim minute As Integer
105
106        ' ensure that timeIs has 4 characters
107        timeIs = timeIs.PadLeft(4, "0"c)
108
109     End Sub ' startButton_Click
```

Ensure timeIs has four characters for conversion purposes — (points to lines 106–107)

Figure 19.25 Declaring variables for second and minute values.

The first argument in the PadLeft call, 4, specifies the desired length of timeIs. If timeIs already contains four or more characters, PadLeft has *no* effect. The second argument (the character 0) specifies the character that's appended to the beginning of the String. Note that specifying only "0" as the second argument causes an error, because "0" is of type String. Method PadLeft expects the second argument to be a single character of data type **Char**. You obtain the character 0 by using the literal value "0"c to indicate that 0 is a Char, not a String. The letter c following the closing double quote is Visual Basic's syntax for a **character literal**. If you do not specify the second argument, PadLeft uses *spaces* by default.

2. **Converting user input to Integers.** Add lines 109–111 of Fig. 19.26 to event handler startButton_Click. Line 110 calls method Convert.ToInt32 to convert the last two characters of timeIs to an Integer and assign this value to second. The last two characters are selected from timeIs by using method **Substring**, which returns part of a String. The argument passed to Substring, 2, indicates that the subset of characters returned from this method should begin with the character at position 2 and continue to the end of the String. Remember that the character at position 2 is actually the third character in the String, because the position values of a String begin at 0. In the example "0325", calling Substring with the argument 2 returns "25". Line 111 selects the first two characters of timeIs, converts the value to an Integer, and assigns this value to minute. The call to Substring in line 111 takes two arguments. The first argument, 0, indicates that the characters returned from this method start with the first character (at position 0) of timeIs. The second argument, 2, indicates that only two characters from the starting position are to be returned. In the example "0325", calling Substring with the arguments 0 and 2 returns "03".

(cont.)

Convert input to
seconds and minutes

```
108
109       ' extract seconds and minutes
110       second = Convert.ToInt32(timeIs.Substring(2))
111       minute = Convert.ToInt32(timeIs.Substring(0, 2))
112
113    End Sub ' startButton_Click
```

Figure 19.26   Form minute and second values from input.

3. ***Creating a Time object.*** Add lines 113–114 of Fig. 19.27 to start-
   Button_Click. Line 114 creates an object of type Time. When the object is
   instantiated, operator New allocates the memory in which the Time object
   will be stored; then the Time constructor (which must be named New) is
   called with the values of minute and second to initialize the Time object's
   instance variables. The New operator then returns a reference to the newly
   created object; this reference is assigned to timeObject.

Use keyword New to
create a new object

```
111       minute = Convert.ToInt32(timeIs.Substring(0, 2))
112
113       ' create Time object to contain time entered by user
114       timeObject = New Time(minute, second)
115
116    End Sub ' startButton_Click
```

Figure 19.27   Creating a Time object.

4. ***Accessing a Time object's properties.*** Add lines 116–117 of Fig. 19.28 to
   startButton_Click. These lines use the newly created Time object and
   method String.Format to display the cooking time properly. You want the
   resulting String to contain two digits (for the minute), a colon (:) and
   finally another two digits (for the second). For example, if the time entered
   was 3 minutes and 20 seconds, the String that will display for the user is
   "03:20". To achieve this result, you pass to the method the format control
   string "{0:D2}:{1:D2}", which indicates that arguments 0 and 1 (the first
   and second arguments after the format String argument) take the format
   D2 (base-10 decimal number format using two digits) for display purposes—
   thus, 8 would be converted to 08. The colon between the curly braces } and {
   is included in the output, separating the minutes from the seconds. The arguments after the format-control string access timeObject's minute and second values, using the Minute and Second properties. Note that Time's
   properties appear in the *IntelliSense* window (Fig. 19.29) when you try to
   access the object's members (using the dot operator).

Display cooking time

```
113       ' create Time object to contain time entered by user
114       timeObject = New Time(minute, second)
115
116       displayLabel.Text = String.Format("{0:D2}:{1:D2}",
117          timeObject.Minute, timeObject.Second)
118
119    End Sub ' startButton_Click
```

Figure 19.28   Displaying time information with separating colon.

(cont.)

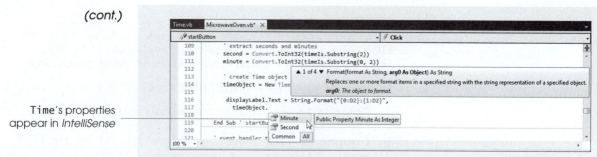

Time's properties appear in *IntelliSense*

Figure 19.29   Properties of a programmer-defined type also appear in *IntelliSense*.

5. *Starting the cooking process.* Add lines 119–123 of Fig. 19.30 to your app. Line 119 clears the user's input, so that the user can enter new input at any time. Line 121 starts the `Timer` by setting its `Enabled` property to `True`. The `Timer`'s `Tick` event is now raised once per second—its `Interval` property is set to 1000 (milliseconds) in the template. You'll implement the event handler for this event shortly. Line 123 sets the `Panel`'s `BackColor` property to yellow to simulate the light inside the microwave oven. The color yellow is assigned to property `BackColor` using property `Yellow` of structure `Color`. The **Color** structure contains several predefined colors as properties.

```
118
119          timeIs = String.Empty ' clear timeIs for future input
120
121          clockTimer.Enabled = True ' start timer
122
123          windowPanel.BackColor = Color.Yellow ' turn "light" on
124
125       End Sub ' startButton_Click
```

Start timer and turn light on to indicate microwave oven is cooking

Figure 19.30   Starting the microwave oven countdown.

6. *Clearing the cook time.* Add lines 131–136 of Fig. 19.31 to event handler `clearButton_Click`. Line 132 sets the app's `Label` to **Microwave Oven**. Line 133 clears the input values stored in `timeIs`, and line 134 resets `timeObject` to `Nothing`. Line 135 disables the `Timer`, which stops the countdown. Line 136 sets the `Panel`'s background back to the `Panel`'s original color to simulate turning off the light inside the microwave oven. Note that we set the `Panel`'s color using the **DefaultBackColor** property. This property contains the default background color for a control. When a `Panel` is added to a `Form`, its background takes on the default background color of the `Form`.

```
127       ' event handler to clear input
128       Private Sub clearButton_Click(sender As System.Object,
129          e As System.EventArgs) Handles clearButton.Click
130
131          ' reset each property or variable to its initial setting
132          displayLabel.Text = "Microwave Oven"
133          timeIs = String.Empty
134          timeObject = Nothing
135          clockTimer.Enabled = False
136          windowPanel.BackColor = Control.DefaultBackColor
137       End Sub ' clearButton_Click
```

Resetting **Microwave Oven** app

Figure 19.31   Clearing the **Microwave Oven** input.

(cont.)   7. ***Displaying data as it's being input.*** Add lines 142–150 of Fig. 19.32 to
              method `DisplayTime`. This method is called each time the user enters
              another digit for the cooking time. Lines 142–143 declare variables `second`
              and `minute`, which store the current number of seconds and minutes. Line
              145 declares `display`, which stores the user's current input in the proper dis-
              play format. Lines 148–150 remove any extra digits entered by the user.
              (Recall that the user may enter a maximum of four digits.) Line 148 uses
              `String` property **Length**, which returns the number of characters in a
              `String`, to determine whether `timeIs` has more than four digits. If it does,
              line 149 uses `String` method `Substring` to remove the extra digits. The
              arguments (0 followed by 4) indicate that the substring returned should
              begin with the first character in `timeIs` and continue for four characters.
              The result is assigned back to `timeIs`, ensuring that any characters
              appended past the first four are removed.

```
139        ' method to display formatted time in timer window
140        Sub DisplayTime()
141
142           Dim second As Integer
143           Dim minute As Integer
144
145           Dim display As String ' String displays current input
146
147           ' if too much input entered
148           If timeIs.Length > 4 Then
149              timeIs = timeIs.Substring(0, 4)
150           End If
```

Figure 19.32 Modifying invalid user input.

8. ***Completing the `DisplayTime` method.*** Add lines 152–160 of Fig. 19.33 to
   method `DisplayTime`. These lines are similar to those of event handler
   `startButton_Click`. Line 152 appends zeros to the front of `timeIs` if fewer
   than four digits were entered. Lines 155–156 use method `Substring` to isolate the number of seconds and minutes currently entered. Lines 159–160
   then use method `Format` to display the input correctly.

```
151
152           display = timeIs.PadLeft(4, "0"c)
153
154           ' extract seconds and minutes
155           second = Convert.ToInt32(display.Substring(2))
156           minute = Convert.ToInt32(display.Substring(0, 2))
157
158           ' display number of minutes, ":" and number of seconds
159           displayLabel.Text = String.Format("{0:D2}:{1:D2}",
160              minute, second)
161        End Sub ' DisplayTime
```

Figure 19.33 Display current input.

9. ***Performing the countdown.*** Add lines 167–182 of Fig. 19.34 to event handler
   `clockTimer_Tick`. Remember that this event handler executes approximately every second for as long as the `Timer` is enabled. Lines 168–182 modify the display `Label` once per second so that the time remaining is shown to
   the user.

(cont.)

```
163         ' event handler displays new time each second
164         Private Sub clockTimer_Tick(sender As System.Object,
165            e As System.EventArgs) Handles clockTimer.Tick
166
167            ' perform countdown, subtract one second
168            If timeObject.Second > 0 Then
169               timeObject.Second -= 1
170               displayLabel.Text = String.Format("{0:D2}:{1:D2}",
171                  timeObject.Minute, timeObject.Second)
172            ElseIf timeObject.Minute > 0 Then
173               timeObject.Minute -= 1
174               timeObject.Second = 59
175               displayLabel.Text = String.Format("{0:D2}:{1:D2}",
176                  timeObject.Minute, timeObject.Second)
177            Else ' countdown finished
178               clockTimer.Enabled = False ' stop timer
179               Beep()
180               displayLabel.Text = "Done!" ' inform user time is finished
181               windowPanel.BackColor = Control.DefaultBackColor
182            End If
183         End Sub ' clockTimer_Tick
```

Modify time appropriately during countdown

Figure 19.34 Modifying the display during countdown.

If the value of seconds is greater than zero (line 168), the number of seconds is decremented by one (line 169). If the value of seconds is zero but the value of minutes is greater than zero (line 172), the number of minutes is decremented by one (line 173) and the number of seconds is reset to 59 for the new minute (line 174). If the number of seconds is zero and the number of minutes is zero, the cooking process is stopped—the Timer is disabled (line 178), a beep is sounded (line 179), the display Label is set to **Done!** (line 180) and the window Panel's background color is set back to its default background color (line 181).

10. ***Running the app***. Select **Debug > Start Debugging** to run your app. Enter a cook time and click the **Start** Button. The app should now count down correctly, as you've defined the Tick event handler for clockTimer. Click the **Clear** Button and verify that the input is cleared and the countdown is stopped.

11. ***Closing the app***. Close your running app by clicking its close box.

1. The _____ property returns the number of characters in a String.

   a) Length   b) Size

   c) Char   d) Width

2. The expression example.Substring(0, 7) returns the character(s) _____.

   a) that begin at position seven and run backward to position zero

   b) that begin at position zero and continue for seven characters

   c) at position zero and position seven

   d) at position zero, repeated seven times

Answers: 1) a. 2) b.

Common Programming Error

Attempting to access a Private class member from outside its class is a compilation error.

19.7 Controlling Access to Members

Keywords **Public** and **Private** are called **access modifiers**. You defined properties with access modifier Public earlier in this chapter. Class members that are declared with access modifier Public are available to any client of the class. Declaring instance variables, properties or methods with access modifier Private

Software Design Tip

Declare all instance variables of a class as Private. When necessary, provide Public properties to set and get instance-variable values.

makes them available only to members of the class. Attempting to access a class's Private data from outside the class definition is a compilation error. Normally, instance variables are declared Private, whereas methods and properties are declared Public. There are advanced access modifiers (Protected and Friend) that are beyond the scope of this book. In the following box, you'll declare this app's instance variables as Private.

Controlling Access to Members

1. *Declaring Time's instance variables as Private.* View Time.vb by selecting the **Time.vb** tab above the code editor. Replace keyword Dim in lines 7–8 with keyword Private (as in Fig. 19.35), indicating that these instance variables are accessible only to members of class Time. A class's Private instance variables may be accessed only by methods and properties of the class.

Good Programming Practice

Group all Private class members in a class definition, followed by all Public class members to enhance clarity and readability.

```
4   Public Class Time
5
6       ' declare Integers for minute and second
7       Private minuteValue As Integer
8       Private secondValue As Integer
```
Figure 19.35   Time's instance variables are Private.

2. *Declaring MicrowaveOvenForm's instance variables as Private.* View MicrowaveOven.vb by selecting the **MicrowaveOven.vb** tab above the code editor. Replace keyword Dim in lines 4 and 7 with keyword Private (as in Fig. 19.36), indicating that these instance variables are accessible only to members of class MicrowaveOvenForm.

```
1   Public Class MicrowaveOvenForm
2
3       ' contains time entered as a String
4       Private timeIs As String = String.Empty
5
6       ' contains time entered
7       Private timeObject As Time
```
Figure 19.36   Microwave Oven's instance variables are Private.

Software Design Tip

It's possible to declare the Get and Set accessors with different access modifiers. One of the accessors must have the *same* access as the property, and the other must be *more restrictive* than the property. For example, in a Public property, the Get accessor could be Public and the Set accessor could be Private to create a property that's "read-only" to the class's clients.

3. *Setting method DisplayTime as Private.* Add keyword Private to the beginning of method DisplayTime (line 140 of Fig. 19.37). As with variables, methods are declared Private to make them accessible only to other members of the current class. In this example only the class that defines your **Microwave Oven** uses method DisplayTime, so you should make this method Private.

Note that the event handlers you've created throughout this book have the keyword Private automatically added to their headers. You'll now know that this occurs because event handlers are specific to the Form's class, and not the entire app, which includes class Time.

```
139     ' method to display formatted time in timer window
140     Private Sub DisplayTime()
141
142         Dim second As Integer
143         Dim minute As Integer
```
Figure 19.37   Microwave Oven's methods are Private.

(cont.)

4. ***Running the app.*** Select **Debug > Start Debugging** to run your app. Note that the app performs exactly as it did at the end of the last box. This occurs because when instance variables are declared by using keyword Dim, they're by default Private variables. For example, recall that the instance variables of Time did not appear in the *IntelliSense* window of Fig. 19.29. These variables were Private by default and therefore not accessible outside of class Time. Inaccessible variables do not appear in the *IntelliSense* window. It's a good practice always to precede instance variables with a member-access modifier (usually Private). Changing DisplayTime to be Private did not affect the app either, because your code does not attempt to access this method from outside the class in which it's defined. Note that you cannot use the Private access modifier to declare local variables in a method; you must use Dim.

5. ***Closing the app.*** Close your running app by clicking its close box.

Good Programming Practice

For clarity, every instance variable or property definition should be preceded by a member-access modifier.

Figures 19.38 and 19.39 present the source code for the **Microwave Oven** app. The lines of code that contain new programming concepts that you learned in this chapter are highlighted.

Declaring a variable of a programmer-defined type

Make a "beep" sound by calling method Beep

```
1    Public Class MicrowaveOvenForm
2
3        ' contains time entered as a String
4        Private timeIs As String = String.Empty
5
6        ' contains time entered
7        Private timeObject As Time
8
9        ' event handler appends 1 to time string
10       Private Sub oneButton_Click(sender As System.Object,
11           e As System.EventArgs) Handles oneButton.Click
12
13           Beep() ' sound beep
14           timeIs &= "1" ' append digit to time input
15           DisplayTime() ' display time input properly
16       End Sub ' oneButton_Click
17
18       ' event handler appends 2 to time string
19       Private Sub twoButton_Click(sender As System.Object,
20           e As System.EventArgs) Handles twoButton.Click
21
22           Beep() ' sound beep
23           timeIs &= "2" ' append digit to time input
24           DisplayTime() ' display time input properly
25       End Sub ' twoButton_Click
26
27       ' event handler appends 3 to time string
28       Private Sub threeButton_Click(sender As System.Object,
29           e As System.EventArgs) Handles threeButton.Click
30
31           Beep() ' sound beep
32           timeIs &= "3" ' append digit to time input
33           DisplayTime() ' display time input properly
34       End Sub ' threeButton_Click
35
36       ' event handler appends 4 to time string
37       Private Sub fourButton_Click(sender As System.Object,
38           e As System.EventArgs) Handles fourButton.Click
39
```

Figure 19.38 **Microwave Oven** app code. (Part 1 of 4.)

```
40          Beep() ' sound beep
41          timeIs &= "4" ' append digit to time input
42          DisplayTime() ' display time input properly
43       End Sub ' fourButton_Click
44
45       ' event handler appends 5 to time string
46       Private Sub fiveButton_Click(sender As System.Object,
47          e As System.EventArgs) Handles fiveButton.Click
48
49          Beep() ' sound beep
50          timeIs &= "5" ' append digit to time input
51          DisplayTime() ' display time input properly
52       End Sub ' fiveButton_Click
53
54       ' event handler appends 6 to time string
55       Private Sub sixButton_Click(sender As System.Object,
56          e As System.EventArgs) Handles sixButton.Click
57
58          Beep() ' sound beep
59          timeIs &= "6" ' append digit to time input
60          DisplayTime() ' display time input properly
61       End Sub ' sixButton_Click
62
63       ' event handler appends 7 to time string
64       Private Sub sevenButton_Click(sender As System.Object,
65          e As System.EventArgs) Handles sevenButton.Click
66
67          Beep() ' sound beep
68          timeIs &= "7" ' append digit to time input
69          DisplayTime() ' display time input properly
70       End Sub ' sevenButton_Click
71
72       ' event handler appends 8 to time string
73       Private Sub eightButton_Click(sender As System.Object,
74          e As System.EventArgs) Handles eightButton.Click
75
76          Beep() ' sound beep
77          timeIs &= "8" ' append digit to time input
78          DisplayTime() ' display time input properly
79       End Sub ' eightButton_Click
80
81       ' event handler appends 9 to time string
82       Private Sub nineButton_Click(sender As System.Object,
83          e As System.EventArgs) Handles nineButton.Click
84
85          Beep() ' sound beep
86          timeIs &= "9" ' append digit to time input
87          DisplayTime() ' display time input properly
88       End Sub ' nineButton_Click
89
90       ' event handler appends 0 to time string
91       Private Sub zeroButton_Click(sender As System.Object,
92          e As System.EventArgs) Handles zeroButton.Click
93
94          Beep() ' sound beep
95          timeIs &= "0" ' append digit to time input
96          DisplayTime() ' display time input properly
97       End Sub ' zeroButton_Click
98
99       ' event handler starts the microwave oven's cooking process
100      Private Sub startButton_Click(sender As System.Object,
101         e As System.EventArgs) Handles startButton.Click
102
```

Figure 19.38   Microwave Oven app code. (Part 2 of 4.)

```
103        Dim second As Integer
104        Dim minute As Integer
105
106        ' ensure that timeIs has 4 characters
107        timeIs = timeIs.PadLeft(4, "0"c)
108
109        ' extract seconds and minutes
110        second = Convert.ToInt32(timeIs.Substring(2))
111        minute = Convert.ToInt32(timeIs.Substring(0, 2))
112
113        ' create Time object to contain time entered by user
114        timeObject = New Time(minute, second)
115
116        displayLabel.Text = String.Format("{0:D2}:{1:D2}",
117           timeObject.Minute, timeObject.Second)
118
119        timeIs = String.Empty ' clear timeIs for future input
120
121        clockTimer.Enabled = True ' start timer
122
123        windowPanel.BackColor = Color.Yellow ' turn "light" on
124
125     End Sub ' startButton_Click
126
127     ' event handler to clear input
128     Private Sub clearButton_Click(sender As System.Object,
129        e As System.EventArgs) Handles clearButton.Click
130
131        ' reset each property or variable to its initial setting
132        displayLabel.Text = "Microwave Oven"
133        timeIs = String.Empty
134        timeObject = Nothing
135        clockTimer.Enabled = False
136        windowPanel.BackColor = Control.DefaultBackColor
137     End Sub ' clearButton_Click
138
139     ' method to display formatted time in timer window
140     Private Sub DisplayTime()
141
142        Dim second As Integer
143        Dim minute As Integer
144
145        Dim display As String ' String displays current input
146
147        ' if too much input entered
148        If timeIs.Length > 4 Then
149           timeIs = timeIs.Substring(0, 4)
150        End If
151
152        display = timeIs.PadLeft(4, "0"c)
153
154        ' extract seconds and minutes
155        second = Convert.ToInt32(display.Substring(2))
156        minute = Convert.ToInt32(display.Substring(0, 2))
157
158        ' display number of minutes, ":" and number of seconds
159        displayLabel.Text = String.Format("{0:D2}:{1:D2}",
160           minute, second)
161     End Sub ' DisplayTime
162
163     ' event handler displays new time each second
164     Private Sub clockTimer_Tick(sender As System.Object,
165        e As System.EventArgs) Handles clockTimer.Tick
166
```

Figure 19.38 Microwave Oven app code. (Part 3 of 4.)

```
167        ' perform countdown, subtract one second
168        If timeObject.Second > 0 Then
169           timeObject.Second -= 1
170           displayLabel.Text = String.Format("{0:D2}:{1:D2}",
171              timeObject.Minute, timeObject.Second)
172        ElseIf timeObject.Minute > 0 Then
173           timeObject.Minute -= 1
174           timeObject.Second = 59
175           displayLabel.Text = String.Format("{0:D2}:{1:D2}",
176              timeObject.Minute, timeObject.Second)
177        Else ' no more seconds
178           clockTimer.Enabled = False ' stop timer
179           Beep()
180           displayLabel.Text = "Done!" ' inform user time is finished
181           windowPanel.BackColor = Control.DefaultBackColor
182        End If
183     End Sub ' clockTimer_Tick
184 End Class ' MicrowaveOvenForm
```

Figure 19.38   **Microwave Oven** app code. (Part 4 of 4.)

```
 1  ' Time.vb
 2  ' Represents time data and contains properties.
 3
 4  Public Class Time
 5
 6     ' declare Integers for minute and second
 7     Private minuteValue As Integer
 8     Private secondValue As Integer
 9
10     ' Time constructor, minute and second supplied
11     Public Sub New(mm As Integer, ss As Integer)
12
13        Minute = mm ' invokes Minute Set accessor
14        Second = ss ' invokes Second Set accessor
15     End Sub ' New
16
17     ' property Minute
18     Public Property Minute() As Integer
19        ' return Minute value
20        Get
21           Return minuteValue
22        End Get ' end of Get accessor
23
24        ' set Minute value
25        Set(value As Integer)
26           ' if minute value entered is valid
27           If (value >= 0 AndAlso value < 60) Then
28              minuteValue = value
29           Else
30              minuteValue = 0 ' set invalid input to 0
31           End If
32        End Set ' end of Set accessor
33     End Property ' Minute
34
35     ' property Second
36     Public Property Second() As Integer
37        ' return Second value
38        Get
39           Return secondValue
40        End Get ' end of Get accessor
41
```

Keyword **Class** used to define a class → line 4

New is the constructor → line 11

Assign data to properties, rather than directly to instance variables → lines 13–14

End Sub keywords end the constructor definition → line 15

Keyword **Property** used to define a property → line 36

Get accessor returns data → lines 39

Figure 19.39   Class **Time**. (Part 1 of 2.)

```
42          ' set Second value
43          Set(value As Integer)
44             ' if second value entered is valid
45             If (value >= 0 AndAlso value < 60) Then
46                secondValue = value
47             Else
48                secondValue = 0 ' set invalid input to 0
49             End If
50          End Set ' end of Set accessor
51       End Property ' Second
52    End Class ' Time
```

Set accessor modifies and validates data → (lines 43–50)

End Property keywords end property definition → (line 51)

End Class keywords end class definition → (line 52)

Figure 19.39 Class Time. (Part 2 of 2.)

SELF-REVIEW

1. Instance variable declarations should be preceded by which of the following keywords:
   a) `Dim`
   b) `Private`
   c) `Public`
   d) Any of the above

2. Instance variables are considered _____ by default.
   a) `Private`
   b) `Public`
   c) `Dimensional`
   d) None of the above

Answers: 1) b. 2) a.

19.8 Auto-Implemented Properties

The properties we declared in class `Time` each perform validation to ensure that the minute and second always contain valid values. For properties that do not have any additional logic in their `Set` and `Get` accessors, there is a new feature in Visual Basic 2010—called **auto-implemented properties**—that allows you to write one line of code and have the compiler generate the property's code for you. These can be helpful when you're quickly creating a new class definition—you can replace them with full property definitions if you need to add validation. For example, if the `Time` class's `Minute` property did not require validation, we could have replaced line 7 and lines 18–33 in Fig. 19.39 with

```
Public Property Minute As Integer
```

The compiler would then generate a `Private` instance variable of type `Integer` named `_Minute` and the following property code:

```
Public Property Minute As Integer
   Get
      Return _Minute
   End Get

   Set(ByVal value As Integer)
      _Minute = value
   End Set
End Property
```

You can also assign an initial value to an auto-implemented property in its declaration, just as you can for a class's instance variables, as in

```
Public Property Minute As Integer = 30 ' set Minute to 30
```

Auto-implemented properties are provided as a convenience feature for "simple" properties like the one described above. In general, however, you should perform validation in a property's `Set` accessor. Doing so requires *you* to define the property *and* its corresponding instance variable.

19.9 Using the Debugger: The Locals Window

Now you'll enhance your knowledge of the debugger by studying the capabilities of the **Locals** window. This window allows you to view the values stored in an object's instance variables. In this section, you'll learn how to view the contents of time-Object's instance variables to verify that your app is executing correctly. In the following box, you'll use this window to examine the state of the Time object in the **Microwave Oven** app.

Using the Debugger:
Using the Locals Window

1. ***Viewing the app code.*** View MicrowaveOven.vb by selecting the **Micro-waveOven.vb** tab above the code editor.

2. ***Setting breakpoints.*** Set breakpoints in lines 168 and 181 by clicking in the margin indicator bar (Fig. 19.40). You can set breakpoints in your app to examine an object's instance variables at certain places during execution. In the **Microwave Oven** app, clockTimer's Tick event handler modifies the properties of timeObject. Setting breakpoints in lines 168 and 181 allows you to suspend execution before and after certain properties have been modified, ensuring that data is being modified properly.

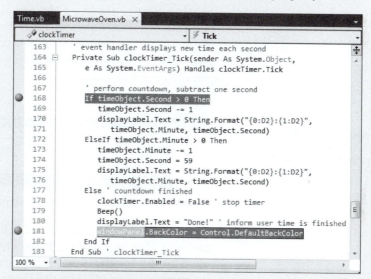

Figure 19.40 **Microwave Oven** app with breakpoints added.

3. ***Starting the debugger.*** Start the debugger by selecting **Debug > Start Debugging**.

4. ***Opening the Locals window.*** Open the **Locals** window (Fig. 19.41) by selecting **Debug > Windows > Locals** while the debugger is running. The **Locals** window allows you to view the state of the variables in the current scope. Recall that the scope of a variable's identifier is the portion of an app in which the identifier can be referenced. The Timer's Tick event is a method of the Form class, so all the instance variables and controls of the Form are viewable in the **Locals** window. This means that you can view the values of the properties of timeObject, because timeObject is an instance variable of the Form class.

(cont.)

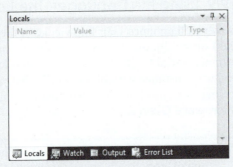

Figure 19.41 Empty **Locals** window.

5. ***Setting the time.*** Set the microwave oven's time to `1:01`, and click the **Start** Button.

6. ***Using the Locals window.*** While execution is still halted, look at the **Locals** window. If it's now hidden, reselect **Debug > Windows > Locals**. The **Locals** window lists all the variables that are in the scope of clockTimer's `Tick` event handler. To view the contents of `timeObject`, click the plus box next to the word **Me**. Scroll down until you reach `timeObject`, and click the plus box next to it. This shows all the members of `timeObject`, their current values and their types (Fig. 19.42). Note that it displays different icons for the object's instance variables and properties.

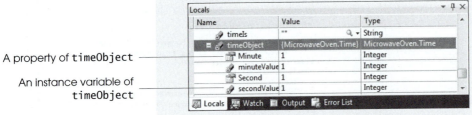

A property of `timeObject`

An instance variable of `timeObject`

Figure 19.42 **Locals** window displaying the state of `timeObject`.

7. ***Continuing program execution.*** Click the debug toolbar's **Continue** Button, and view the values of the `timeObject`'s members. Note that the value for the amount of seconds (as represented by variable `secondValue` and property `Second`) (Fig. 19.43) appears in red to indicate it has changed. Click the **Continue** Button again.

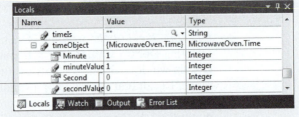

Changed values are displayed in red by the IDE

Figure 19.43 **Locals** window displaying changed variables.

8. ***Changing the value of a variable.*** In the **Locals** window, double click the value for property `Second`. Type 0 and press *Enter* to set the microwave oven's time to zero (Fig. 19.44). The **Locals** window allows you to change the values of variables to verify that program execution is correct at certain points without having to run the program again for each value. Now set the value of the `Second` property to 100. Note that the `Second` property validates the data and sets the value to 0.

(cont.)

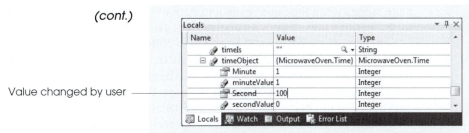

Value changed by user

Figure 19.44 Changing the value of a variable in the **Locals** window.

9. *Continuing execution.* Click the **Continue** Button. Execution continues until the breakpoint in line 181 is reached.

10. *Stopping the debugger.* Click the **Stop Debugging** Button to end the debugging session.

11. *Closing the app.* Close your running app by clicking its close box.

12. *Clearing the breakpoints.* Clear the breakpoints you set in the app.

13. *Closing the IDE.* Close the Visual Basic IDE by clicking its close box.

In this section, you learned how to use the **Locals** window to view the state of an object and verify that your app is executing correctly.

SELF-REVIEW

1. The **Locals** window allows you to _____.
   a) change the value stored in an instance variable of an object
   b) view all of the variables in the current scope
   c) view the values stored in all of the variables in the current scope
   d) All of the above

2. When a variable's value changes, it becomes _____ in the **Locals** window.
   a) red   b) italic
   c) blue   d) bold

Answers: 1) d. 2) a.

19.10 Wrap-Up

In earlier chapters, you used .NET classes and methods to add functionality to your apps. In this chapter, you learned how to create your own classes, also known as programmer-defined classes, to provide functionality not available in the .NET Framework Class Library. Visual Basic apps typically are created by using a combination of .NET classes and methods and programmer-defined classes and methods.

You created a microwave-oven simulator using a programmer-defined class called Time. You added a class definition file to your app to create the Time class; then you added instance variables, a constructor, and properties to that class. You defined your constructor to initialize the class's instance variables. For each property, you defined Get and Set accessors that allow the class's instance variables to be safely accessed and modified. You then applied what you learned about classes and properties to create a Time object. You used the properties of class Time to access and display the number of minutes and number of seconds that the user specified as the microwave oven's cook time. You also learned how to control access to the members of class Time through the use of Public and Private member-access modifiers. You learned how Panels can organize controls (much like GroupBoxes), and used a Panel to simulate the microwave oven's door. You learned how to create a beeping sound. You even learned some new ways to manipulate strings using the `Substring` and `PadLeft` methods. You concluded the chapter by learning how to view an app's values using the debugger's **Locals** window.

In the next chapter, you'll learn about collections. The .NET Framework Class Library provides several collection classes that enable you to store collections of data in an organized way. A collection can be thought of as a group of items. You'll use collections to create a **Shipping Hub** app that stores information about several packages that are being shipped to various states. Each package is defined by using a `Package` programmer-defined class. Several `Package` objects are maintained by using collections.

SKILLS SUMMARY

Defining a `Public` Property

- Use keywords `Public Property` followed by the property name and a set of parentheses.
- After the parentheses, specify the property's type with the `As` keyword.
- Press *Enter*. Empty `Get` and `Set` accessors are added for you by the IDE, followed by the keywords `End Property`. The `Get` accessor begins with keyword `Get` and ends with keywords `End Get`. The `Set` accessor begins with keyword `Set` and ends with keywords `End Set`.
- In the `Get` accessor, provide code to return the requested data.
- In the `Set` accessor, provide code to modify the relevant data. Be sure to validate the data.

Adding a Class File to Your Project

- Select **Project > Add Class**.
- Enter a name for the class.

Creating a Constructor

- Use keywords `Public Sub New`, followed by a set of parentheses enclosing any constructor parameters.
- Press *Enter*. The keywords `End Sub` are added by the IDE.
- Add code to initialize the object's data.

Adding a `Panel` to Your App

- Double click the `Panel` control in the **Containers** tab of the **Toolbox**, or drag the `Panel` control from the **Toolbox** to the `Form`. We recommend appending `Panel` to `Panel` control names.

KEY TERMS

access modifier—Keywords used to specify what members of a class a client may access. Includes keywords `Public` and `Private`.

accessors—Methodlike code units that handle the details of modifying and returning data.

Beep function—Causes your computer to make a beep sound.

Char data type—Primitive type that represents a character.

Class keyword—Reserved word required to begin a class definition.

character literal—A single character represented as a value of type `Char`. Create a character literal by placing a single character in double quotes followed by the letter c (e.g., "0"c).

client—When an app creates and uses an object of a class, the app is known as a client of the class.

Color structure—Contains several predefined colors as properties.

consistent state—A way to maintain the values of an object's instance variables such that the values are always valid.

constructor—A special class method that initializes a class's variables.

DefaultBackColor property—Contains the default background color for a control.

End Class keywords—Reserved words required to end a class definition.

extensible language—A language that can be "extended" with new data types. Visual Basic is an extensible language.

FixedSingle value of the BorderStyle property of a Label—Specifies that the Label will display a thin, black border.

Flat value of the FlatStyle property of a Button—Specifies that a Button will appear flat.

FlatStyle property of a Button—Determines whether the Button will appear flat or three-dimensional.

Get accessor—Used to retrieve a value of a property.

Get/End Get keywords—Reserved words that define a property's Get accessor.

instantiate an object—Create an object (or instance) of a class.

Length property of class String—Returns the number of characters in a String.

Locals window—Allows you to view the state of the variables and properties in the current scope during debugging.

members of a class—Methods, variables and properties declared within the body of a class.

PadLeft method of class String—Adds characters to the beginning of a string until the length of the string equals the specified length.

PadRight method of class String—Adds characters to the end of a string until the length of the string equals the specified length.

Panel control—Used to group controls. Unlike GroupBoxes, Panels do not have captions.

Private keyword—Member-access modifier that makes members accessible only to the class that defines the members.

programmer-defined class (programmer-defined type)—A class defined by a programmer, as opposed to classes predefined in the Framework Class Library.

property—Contains accessors—portions of code that handle the details of modifying and returning data.

property definition—Defines the accessors for a property.

Property/End Property keywords—Reserved words indicating the definition of a class property.

Public keyword—Member-access modifier that makes instance variables or methods accessible wherever the app has a reference to that object.

Set accessor—Provides data-validation capabilities to ensure that the value is set properly.

Set/End Set keywords—Reserved words that define a property's Set accessor.

Substring method of class String—Returns characters from a string, corresponding to the arguments passed by the user, that indicate the start position within a String and the number of characters to return.

GUI DESIGN GUIDELINES

Panel

- Use Panels to organize groups of related controls where their purpose is obvious. If the controls' purpose is not obvious, use a GroupBox rather than a Panel, because GroupBoxes can contain captions.

- Although it's possible to have a Panel without a border (by setting the BorderStyle property to None), use borders on your Panels to improve user interface readability and organization.

- A Panel can display scrollbars when it's not large enough to display all of its controls. To increase usability, we suggest avoiding the use of scrollbars on Panels. If a Panel is not large enough to display all of its contents, make it larger.

CONTROLS, EVENTS, PROPERTIES & METHODS

Button   ⒶⒷ Button   This control allows the user to raise an action or event.

- *In action*

- *Event*

  Click—Raised when the user clicks the Button.

- *Properties*

  Enabled—Determines whether the Button's event handler is executed when the Button is clicked.

  FlatStyle—Determines whether the Button appears flat or three-dimensional.

  Location—Specifies the location of the Button on the Form relative to the top-left corner of its container.

  Name—Specifies the name used to access the Button programmatically. The name should be appended with the Button suffix.

  Size—Specifies the height and width (in pixels) of the Button.

  Text—Specifies the text displayed on the Button.

- *Method*

  Focus—Transfers the focus of the app to the Button that calls it.

Label   A   This control displays text on the Form that the user cannot modify.

- *In action*

  > Microwave
  > Oven

- *Properties*

  BorderStyle—Specifies the appearance of the Label's border.

  Font—Specifies the font name, style and size of the text displayed in the Label.

  Location—Specifies the location of the Label on the Form relative to the top-left corner of its container.

  Name—Specifies the name used to access the Label programmatically. The name should be appended with the Label suffix.

  Size—Specifies the width and height (in pixels) of the Label.

  Text—Specifies the text displayed on the Label.

  TextAlign—Specifies how the text is aligned within the Label.

Panel   ▨ Panel   This control is used to organize various controls. Unlike a GroupBox control, the Panel control does not display a caption.

- *In action*

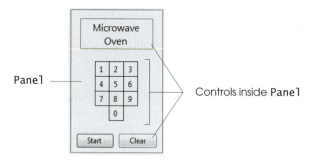

- *Properties*

  Name—Specifies the name of the Panel.

  Size—Specifies the size of the Panel.

  Location—Specifies the Panel's location on the Form relative to the top-left corner of its container.

  BorderStyle—Specifies the Panel's border style. Options include None (displaying no border), FixedSingle (a single-line border) and Fixed3D (a three-dimensional border).

  None—Specifies that the Panel will not display a border.

  FixedSingle—Specifies that the Panel will display a thin, black border.

  Fixed3D—Specifies that the Panel will display a three-dimensional border.

  BackColor—Specifies the background color of the Panel.

String The String class represents a series of characters treated as a single unit.

- *Property*

  Length—Returns the number of characters in the String.

- *Methods*

  Format—Arranges the string in a specified format.

  IndexOf—Returns the index of the specified character(s) in a String.

  Insert—Returns a copy of the String for which it's called with the specified character(s) inserted.

  PadLeft—Returns a copy of a String with padding characters inserted at the beginning.

  Remove—Returns a copy of the String for which it's called with the specified character(s) removed.

  Substring—Returns a substring from a String.

  ToLower—Returns a copy of the String for which it's called with any uppercase letters converted to lowercase letters.

MULTIPLE-CHOICE QUESTIONS

19.1 A Button appears flat if its _____ property is set to Flat.

    a) BorderStyle   b) FlatStyle

    c) Style   d) BackStyle

19.2 Keyword _____ introduces a class definition.

    a) NewClass   b) ClassDef

    c) VBClass   d) Class

19.3 Keyword _____ is used to create an object.

    a) CreateObject   b) Instantiate

    c) Create   d) New

19.4 String characters are of data type _____.

    a) Char   b) StringCharacter

    c) Character   d) strCharacter

19.5 The _____ is used to retrieve the value of an instance variable.

    a) Get accessor of a property   b) Retrieve method of a class

    c) Client method of a class   d) Set accessor of a property

19.6 When you enter the header for a constructor in the Visual Basic IDE, then press *Enter*, the keywords _____ are created for you.

    a) End Public Class   b) End Procedure

    c) End Sub   d) End

19.7 An important difference between constructors and other methods is that _____.

    a) constructors cannot specify a return data type

    b) constructors cannot specify any parameters

    c) other methods are implemented as Sub procedures

    d) constructors can assign values to instance variables

19.8 A class can yield many _____, just as a primitive data type can yield many values.

    a) names   b) objects (instances)

    c) values   d) types

19.9 The Set accessor enables you to _____.

    a) provide range checking   b) modify data

    c) provide data validation   d) All of the above

19.10 Instance variables declared Private are not accessible _____.

    a) outside the class   b) by other methods of the same class

    c) inside the same class   d) None of the above

EXERCISES

19.11 *(Triangle Creator App)* Create an app that allows the user to enter the lengths for the three sides of a triangle as Integers. The app should then determine whether the triangle is a right triangle (two sides of the triangle form a 90-degree angle), an equilateral triangle (all sides of equal length) or neither. The app's GUI is completed for you (Fig. 19.45). You must create a class to represent a triangle object and define the event handler for the **Create** Button.

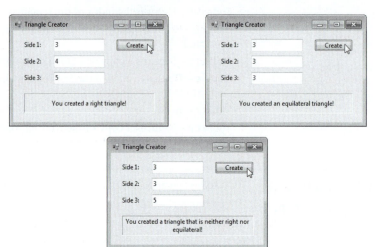

Figure 19.45 **Triangle Creator** app with all possible outputs.

a) *Copying the template to your working directory.* Copy the directory C:\Examples\ ch19\Exercises\Triangle to your C:\SimplyVB2010 directory.

b) *Opening the app's template file.* Double click Triangle.sln in the Triangle directory to open the app.

c) *Creating the Triangle class.* Add a class to the project, and name it Triangle. This is where you define the properties of the Triangle class.

d) *Defining the necessary constructor and properties.* Define a constructor that takes the lengths of the three sides of the triangle as arguments. Create three properties that enable clients to access and modify the lengths of the three sides. If the user enters a negative value, that side should be assigned the value zero and the display updated.

e) *Adding additional features.* Create two more properties in the Triangle class—one determining whether the sides form a right triangle, the other an equilateral triangle. Use the Pythagorean theorem ($a^2 + b^2 = c^2$) to test for a right triangle. These properties are considered **read-only**, because you would naturally define only the Get accessor. There's no simple Set accessor that can make a triangle a right triangle or an equilateral triangle without first modifying the lengths of the triangle's sides. To create a read-only property (where the Set accessor is omitted), precede keyword Property with the keyword ReadOnly.

f) *Adding code to event handler.* Now that you've created your Triangle class, you can use it to create objects in your app. Double click the **Create** Button in **Design** view to generate the event handler. Create new variables to store the three lengths from the TextBoxes; then use those values to create a new Triangle object.

g) *Displaying the result.* Use an If...ElseIf statement to determine whether the triangle is a right triangle, an equilateral triangle or neither. Display the result in a Label.

h) *Running the app.* Select **Debug > Start Debugging** to run your app. Add various inputs until you've created an equilateral triangle, a right triangle and a triangle that's neither right nor equilateral. Verify that the proper output is displayed for each.

i) *Closing the app.* Close your running app by clicking its close box.

j) *Closing the IDE.* Close the Visual Basic IDE by clicking its close box.

19.12 *(Modified Microwave Oven App)* Modify the chapter's **Microwave Oven** app to include an additional digit to represent the hour. Allow the user to enter up to 9 hours, 59 minutes and 59 seconds (Fig. 19.46).

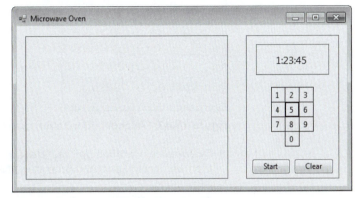

Figure 19.46 Modified **Microwave Oven** app's GUI.

a) *Copying the template to your working directory.* Copy the directory `C:\Examples\ch19\Exercises\MicrowaveOven2` to your `C:\SimplyVB2010` directory.

b) *Opening the app's template file.* Double click `MicrowaveOven2.sln` in the `MicrowaveOven2` directory to open the app.

c) *Adding the hour variable.* To allow cooking time that includes the hour digit, you need to modify the `Time` class. Define a new `Private` instance variable to represent the hour. Change `Time`'s constructor to receive the hour as its first argument (now the constructor should have three arguments). You also have to modify other methods to include an hour variable.

d) *Adding the Hour property.* Use the `Minute` and `Second` properties as your template to create the property for the hour. Remember, the hour must be less than 10.

e) *Changing the padding amount.* Change the calls to the `PadLeft` method to be consistent with the new time format.

f) *Extracting the hour.* Add a call to the `Substring` method so that hour gets the first digit in the `timeIs` String. Also, change the calls to the `Substring` method for minute and second so that they extract the proper digits from the `timeIs` String.

g) *Accessing the first five digits.* Change the If...Then statement from the `Display-Time` method to take and display the first five digits entered by the user.

h) *Edit the Timer object.* Edit the `clockTimer_Tick` event handler to provide changes to hours and its corresponding minutes and seconds.

i) *Displaying the time.* Edit the Format String so that the display `Label` includes the hour.

j) *Running the app.* Select **Debug > Start Debugging** to run your app. Enter various times and verify that the app counts down properly.

k) *Closing the app.* Close your running app by clicking its close box.

l) *Closing the IDE.* Close the Visual Basic IDE by clicking its close box.

19.13 *(Account Information App)* The local bank wants you to create an app that allows it to view clients' information. The interface is created for you (Fig. 19.47); you need to implement the `Client` class. Once the app is completed, the bank manager should be able to click the **Next** or **Previous** Button to run through each client's information. The information is stored in four arrays containing first names, last names, account numbers and account balances, respectively.

a) *Copying the template to your working directory.* Copy the directory `C:\Examples\ch19\Exercises\AccountInformation` to your `C:\SimplyVB2010` directory.

b) *Opening the app's template file.* Double click `AccountInformation.sln` in the `AccountInformation` directory to open the app.

Figure 19.47 Account Information app GUI.

c) *Determining variables for the class.* Examine the code from `AccountInforma-tion.vb`, including all the properties that the `Client` object uses to retrieve the information.

d) *Creating the Client class.* Create a new class and call it `Client`. Add this class to the project. Define four `Private` instance variables to represent each value the `Client` class should contain. Create properties that allow clients to get and set these values. Use the properties in a constructor to initialize the instance variables.

e) *Defining each property.* Each `Private` variable should have a corresponding property allowing the user to set or get the `Private` variable's value. Note that the account number should not be negative.

f) *Adding more information.* In the `AccountInformationForm_Load` event handler, add one more value to each array to create another account.

g) *Running the app.* Select **Debug > Start Debugging** to run your app. Click the **Previous** and **Next** Buttons to ensure that each account's information is displayed properly.

h) *Closing the app.* Close your running app by clicking its close box.

i) *Closing the IDE.* Close the Visual Basic IDE by clicking its close box.

What does this code do? ▶ **19.14** What does the following code do? The first code listing contains the definition of class Shape. Each Shape object represents a closed shape with a number of sides. The second code listing contains a method (Mystery) created by a client of class Shape. What does this method do?

```vb
 1  Public Class Shape
 2
 3      Private sides As Integer
 4
 5      ' constructor with number of sides
 6      Public Sub New(value As Integer)
 7          Side = value
 8      End Sub ' New
 9
10      ' set and get side value
11      Public Property Side() As Integer
12          ' return sides
13          Get
14              Return sides
15          End Get ' end of Get accessor
16
17          ' set sides
18          Set(value As Integer)
19              If value > 0 Then
20                  sides = value
21              Else
22                  sides = 0
23              End If
24          End Set ' end of Set accessor
25      End Property ' Side
26  End Class ' Shape
```

```
1  Public Function Mystery(shapeObject As Shape) As String
2     Dim shape As String
3
4     ' determine case with shapeObject.Side
5     Select Case shapeObject.Side
6        Case Is < 3
7           shape = "Not a Shape"
8        Case 3
9           shape = "Triangle"
10       Case 4
11          shape = "Square"
12       Case Else
13          shape = "Polygon"
14    End Select
15
16    Return shape
17 End Function ' Mystery
```

What's wrong with this code? ▶ **19.15** Find the error(s) in the following code. The following method should create a new Shape object with numberSides sides. Assume the Shape class from Exercise 19.14.

```
1  Private Sub ManipulateShape(numberSides As Integer)
2     Dim shapeObject As New Shape(3)
3
4     shape.sides = numberSides
5  End Sub ' ManipulateShape
```

Using the Debugger ▶ **19.16** *(View Name App)* The **View Name** app allows the user to enter the user's first and last names. When the user clicks the **View Name** Button, a MessageBox that displays the user's first and last names appears. The app creates an instance of Class Name. This class uses its property definitions to set the first-name and last-name instance variables. Copy the ViewNames folder from C:\Examples\ch19\Exercises\Debugger to C:\SimplyVB2010. Open and run the app. While testing your app, you noticed that the MessageBox did not display the correct output. Use the debugger to find the logic error(s) in the app. The correct output is displayed in Fig. 19.48.

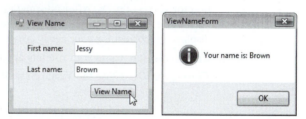

Figure 19.48 View Name app with correct output.

Programming Challenge ▶ **19.17** *(DVD Burner App)* Create an app that simulates a DVD burner. Users create a DVD with their choice of title and bonus materials. The GUI is provided for you (Fig. 19.49). You'll create a class (DVD) to represent the DVD object and another class (Bonus) to represent bonus materials for a DVD object.

 a) *Copying the template to your working directory.* Copy the directory C:\Examples\ch19\Exercises\DVDBurner to your C:\SimplyVB2010 directory.

 b) *Opening the app's template file.* Double click DVDBurner.sln in the DVDBurner directory to open the app.

 c) *Creating the bonus material object.* Create a class, and name it Bonus. The class's objects each represent one bonus-material item on the DVD. Each Bonus object should have a name (description) and a length (in minutes).

Figure 19.49   **DVD Burner** app's GUI.

d) *Creating the DVD class.* Create a class and name it DVD. This class contains the movie title and the length of the movie. The class should also include an array of three Bonus items. Create properties that allow clients to get and set the movie's title and length. Create a ReadOnly property to get the movie's bonus material as a String containing each bonus item's name and length.

e) *Creating the necessary variables.* Before you define the **Create** Button's event handler, create a DVD class instance variable. Inside the **Create** Button's event handler, create the necessary variables to store the information from the TextBoxes on the GUI. This is also where you need to create the array of Bonus objects to store the bonus materials.

f) *Adding bonus-material information.* Add the description and length of each specified bonus item to the Bonus array you created in the preceding step.

g) *Creating a DVD object.* Use information about the movie, its title, length and the array of bonus materials to make your DVD object.

h) *Displaying the output.* The **Information** Button's Click event handler is already defined for you. Locate the event handler, add a String containing the complete information on the DVD object that you created earlier and display this String to a MessageBox.

i) *Running the app.* Select **Debug > Start Debugging** to run your app. Enter information for several DVDs. After information is entered for each, click the **Create** Button. Then click the **Information** Button and verify that the information being displayed is correct for your newly created DVD.

j) *Closing the app.* Close your running app by clicking its close box.

k) *Closing the IDE.* Close the Visual Basic IDE by clicking its close box.

Objectives

In this chapter, you'll learn to:
- Use generic collections.
- Create and manipulate a `List(Of T)` object.
- Use Language Integrated Query (LINQ) to select elements from a collection.
- Set the `MaxLength` property of a `TextBox`.
- Specify the tab order in a GUI using the `TabStop` and `TabIndex` properties of the controls.
- Create an access key for a control.
- Use a `For Each...Next` loop to iterate through a collection.
- Obtain a `String` representation of an object.

Outline

Shipping Hub App

Introducing Generic Collections, LINQ, For Each...Next and Access Keys

Though most business can be conducted over phone lines and using e-mail messages, often it's necessary to send packages by a shipping company. As the pace of business increases, shipping companies seek an efficient means to transfer packages from one location to another. One approach is to send packages to a central location (a hub) before they reach their final destination. In this chapter, you'll develop a **Shipping Hub** app to simulate package processing at a shipping warehouse. You'll use collections, which provide a quick and easy way to organize and manipulate the data used by your app. The chapter focuses on the `List` collection, which provides data-storage capabilities similar to an array, but with much greater flexibility. You'll learn to use the `For Each...Next` repetition statement to iterate through the objects in a collection. You'll also learn to use part of Visual Basic's Language-Integrated Query (LINQ) capabilities to select elements from a collection based on a condition—known as filtering the collection.

20.1 Test-Driving the Shipping Hub App

In this section, you'll test-drive the **Shipping Hub** app, which must meet the following requirements:

App Requirements

*A shipping company receives packages at its headquarters, which functions as its shipping hub. The company then ships them to a distribution center in one of the following states: Alabama, Florida, Georgia, Kentucky, Mississippi, North Carolina, South Carolina, Tennessee, West Virginia or Virginia. The company needs an app to track the packages that pass through its shipping hub. For each package that arrives at the hub, the user clicks the app's **Scan New Button** to generate a package ID number. Once a package has been scanned, the user should be able to enter the shipping address for it. The user should be able to navigate through the list of scanned packages by using* **< BACK** *or* **NEXT >** *Buttons and by viewing a list of all packages destined for a particular state.*

This app stores a list of packages in a List(Of Packages) object. You'll use the For Each...Next repetition statement to access the objects stored in the List. You'll begin by test-driving the completed app. Then you'll learn the additional Visual Basic technologies needed to create your own version of the app.

Test-Driving the Shipping Hub App

1. *Opening the completed app.* Open the directory C:\Examples\ch20\CompletedApp\ShippingHub to locate the **Shipping Hub** app. Double click ShippingHub.sln to open the app in the Visual Basic IDE.

2. *Running the Shipping Hub app.* Select **Debug > Start Debugging** to run the app (Fig. 20.1).

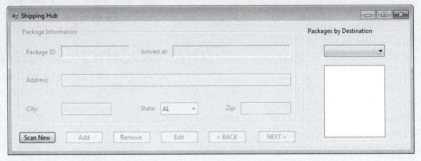

Figure 20.1 **Shipping Hub** app when first run.

3. *Scanning a new package.* Click the **Scan New** Button. The app displays a package ID number and the arrival time, enables the TextBoxes and allows the user to enter the package information (Fig. 20.2). The package ID number for your first package will most likely be different than the one shown here because it's randomly generated each time the app executes.

Figure 20.2 Scanning a new package.

4. *Using the Tab key.* Type 318 Some Street in the **Address:** TextBox, then press the *Tab* key. Note that the cursor moves to the **City:** TextBox (Fig. 20.3).

GUI Design Tip

Using the Tab key is an efficient way for users to navigate through the controls in a GUI.

Cursor now appears
in the **City:** TextBox

Figure 20.3 Pressing the *Tab* key moves the cursor to the next TextBox.

(cont.)   5. ***Adding a package to the list of packages.*** Type Point Pleasant in the **City:** field, then press the *Tab* key. Select **WV** from the **State:** ComboBox, then press the *Tab* key. Type 25550 in the **Zip:** field, and click the **Add** Button to add the package to the app's List.

Note that you *cannot* enter more than five numbers in the **Zip:** field because the **Zip:** TextBox's MaxLength property is set to 5. The **MaxLength** property determines the maximum number of characters that the user can enter into a TextBox. The values in the **State:** ComboBox were added using its **Items** property in the Windows Form Designer. When the program is not running, you can switch to **Design** view and select the **State:** ComboBox. Then, click the **Edit Items...** link at the bottom of the **Properties** window. The dialog that opens allows you to edit the items in the ComboBox's drop-down list.

6. ***Removing, editing and browsing packages.*** The app's **NEXT >** and **< BACK** Buttons allow the user to navigate the list of packages. The user can click on the **Remove** Button to delete packages and on the **Edit** Button to update a particular package's information. Experiment with the various Buttons by adding, removing and editing packages. Use the following sample data:

- 9 Some Road, Goose Creek, SC, 29445
- 234 Some Place, Tamassee, SC, 29686
- 46 Some Avenue, Mammoth Cave, KY, 42259
- 3 Some Street, Yazoo City, MS, 39194

7. ***Viewing all packages going to a state.*** The ComboBox on the right side of the app allows the user to select a state. When a state is selected, all of the package ID numbers of packages destined for that state are displayed in the ListBox (Fig. 20.4). If the ListBox contains more package numbers than it can display, a vertical scrollbar appears automatically.

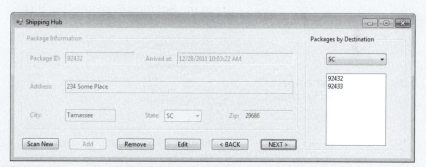

Figure 20.4   Viewing all packages going to South Carolina.

8. ***Closing the app.*** Close your running app by clicking its close box.
9. ***Closing the IDE.*** Close the Visual Basic IDE by clicking its close box.

20.2 Package Class

Your app must store each package's shipping information. Each package ships to one location with an address, city, state and zip code. Since multiple packages can be shipped to the same location, each package needs a *unique identification number* to distinguish it from other packages. As you learned in Chapter 19, a convenient way to group related information is by creating instances of a class. The Package class that we included with this example's template app (but did not add to the project) provides properties for keeping track of package information. Figure 20.5 describes the properties for class Package. You must add the Package class to the **Shipping Hub** app before you can use it to create objects of this class. You'll learn how to add the Package class to the **Shipping Hub** app in the next box.

Property	Description
Address	Provides access to instance variable `addressValue`, which represents the package's address as a `String`.
City	Provides access to instance variable `cityValue`, which represents the package's city as a `String`.
State	Provides access to instance variable `stateValue`, which stores the package's state as a `String`. It uses the standard two-letter state abbreviations. For example, NC is used for North Carolina.
Zip	Provides access to instance variable `zipValue`. Represents the zip code as a `String`.
PackageNumber	Provides access to instance variable `packageNumberValue`, which stores the package's identification number as an `Integer`.
ArrivalTime	Provides access to instance variable `timeValue`, which stores the package's arrival time as a `Date`.

Figure 20.5   Properties of class `Package`.

Adding a Class to an App

1. *Copying the template to your working directory.* Copy the `C:\Examples\ch20\TemplateApp\ShippingHub` directory to `C:\SimplyVB2010`.

2. *Opening the Shipping Hub app's template file.* Double click `Shipping-Hub.sln` in the `ShippingHub` directory to open the app in the Visual Basic IDE.

3. *Adding class Package.* In the **Solution Explorer**, right click the **Shipping-Hub** project. Select **Add > Existing Item...** from the context menu that appears. When the **Add Existing Item** dialog appears, select the `Package.vb` file and click **Add**. The `Package` class is now included in the app and shown in the **Solution Explorer** (Fig. 20.6).

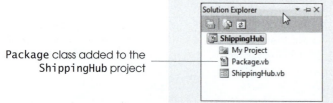

Package class added to the
ShippingHub project

Figure 20.6   **Solution Explorer** with `Package.vb` added.

20.3 Using Properties TabIndex and TabStop

Many apps require users to enter information into multiple `TextBox`es. It's awkward for users to have to select each `TextBox` using the mouse. Most apps allow the user to press the *Tab* key to navigate between the controls on the `Form`. To ensure ease of use, the focus must be transferred to the proper control when the *Tab* key is pressed. The **TabIndex** property allows you to specify the order in which focus transfers between controls when *Tab* is pressed. However, some controls, such as a read-only `TextBox`, should not be selected using the *Tab* key. The **TabStop** property specifies whether the user can select the control using the *Tab* key. Setting this property to `False` prevents the control from being selected by using the *Tab* key. You'll set both of these properties in the following box.

Setting Properties TabIndex and TabStop

GUI Design Tip

Set a control's TabStop property to True only if the control is used to receive user input.

GUI Design Tip

Use the TabIndex property to define the logical order in which the user should enter data. Usually the order transfers the focus of the app from top to bottom and left to right.

1. *Opening ShippingHub.vb.* Double click ShippingHub.vb in the **Solution Explorer** to open the file in **Design** view. The **Shipping Hub** app requires that the user enter the package information into its TextBoxes. To make it easy for the user to enter the data, you'll allow the user to press the *Tab* key to access the proper control.

2. *Setting property TabStop.* The TabStop property defaults to True for controls that receive user input. Make sure that the TabStop property is set to True for the **Address:**, **City:**, and **Zip:** TextBoxes, the **State:** and **Packages by Destination** ComboBoxes and the six Buttons.

3. *Using the Tab Order view in the Windows Form Designer.* The IDE provides a view called **Tab Order** to help visualize the tab order. To use the **Tab Order** view, first ensure that the **Layout** toolbar is displayed by right clicking in the gray area to the right of the existing toolbars at the top of the IDE and selecting **Layout** if it's not already selected. Next, select the Form by clicking it, then click the **Tab Order** icon ([🔲]) on the toolbar. You can also select **Tools > Settings > Expert Settings**, then use the **View > Tab Order** menu option. Visual Studio displays white numbers indicating the TabIndex appear in blue boxes in the upper-left corner of each control (Fig. 20.7). The first time you click a control in this view, its TabIndex value is set to zero, as displayed in the TabIndex box (Fig. 20.7). Subsequent clicks will increment the value by one.

TabIndex box set to zero ——

TabIndex boxes (not modified) ——

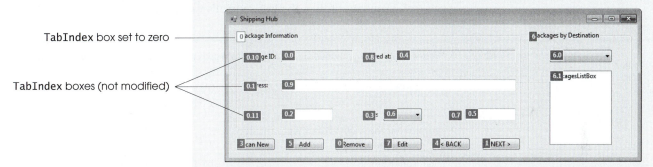

Figure 20.7 Setting the TabIndex properties using the **Tab Order** view of the **Shipping Hub** app.

Begin by clicking the **Package Information** GroupBox. Note that its value becomes 0 and the background of the surrounding box changes to white (Fig. 20.7). Then click the **Address:** TextBox. Now the value changes to 0.0. The first zero refers to the TabIndex of the container (in this case, the GroupBox) and the second to the TabIndex for that control within the container.

Continue setting the tab indices by clicking the **City:** TextBox, then the **State:** ComboBox and finally the **Zip:** TextBox. Finish setting the tab indices for the GroupBox by clicking each control that has not been changed. Controls that have not been changed display a box with a blue background.

4. *Setting the TabIndex properties for the rest of the app.* Continue setting the TabIndex properties by clicking the **Scan New** Button. Then click the remaining unchanged controls in the order indicated in Fig. 20.8. When all the app's controls have been ordered, the TabIndex boxes will once again display a blue background. Exit the **Tab Order** view by selecting **View > Tab Order** or by pressing the *Esc* key.

(cont.)

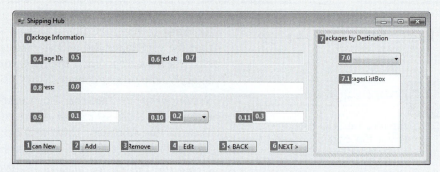

Figure 20.8   **Tab Order** view of the **Shipping Hub** app.

5. *Saving the project.* Select **File > Save All** to save your modified code.

Designing your GUI with the tab order in mind helps you add the controls in the order they should receive the focus. If this is not possible, proper use of the `TabIndex` and `TabStop` properties enables users to enter data into an app more efficiently. Most controls have `TabIndex` and `TabStop` properties. `TabIndex` values on a `Form` or within a `GroupBox` should be unique—two controls cannot receive the focus at the same time. For its `TabIndex` property, by default, the first control added to the `Form` has a value of 0, the second control a value of 1, the third control a value of 2 (one more than the last control's value), and so on.

SELF-REVIEW

1. Property _____ specifies the order in which controls receive the focus when *Tab* is pressed.

    a) `Text`   b) `TabStop`

    c) `Index`   d) `TabIndex`

2. To prevent the focus from being transferred to a control using the *Tab* key, set property _____ to _____.

    a) `TabIndex, 0`   b) `TabStop, False`

    c) `TabControl, True`   d) `TabIndex, Nothing`

Answers: 1) d. 2) b.

20.4 Using Access Keys

Many apps allow users to interact with controls such as `Button`s and menus via the keyboard. **Access keys** (or keyboard shortcuts) allow the user to perform an action on a control using the keyboard.

To specify an access key for a control, insert an & (ampersand) symbol in the control's `Text` property before the letter you wish to use as an access key. If you wish to use "s" as the access key on the **Scan New** `Button`, set its `Text` property to `&Scan New`. You can specify many access keys in an app, but each letter used as an access key in a container should be unique. To use the access key, you must press and hold the *Alt* key, then press the access-key character on the keyboard (release both keys after pressing the access-key character). In this case of the **Scan New** `Button`, you would press and hold the *Alt* key, then press the *S* key (also written as *Alt+S*). You would then release both keys. The effect of using the access key is the same as clicking the button.

Access keys are often used on `Button` controls and on the `MenuStrip` control, which will be introduced in Chapter 21. To display an ampersand character on a control, type **&&** in its `Text` property. Follow the steps in the next box to use access keys in your **Shipping Hub** app.

Creating Access Keys

Using the & symbol to create an access key (there's no space between & and S)

1. ***Creating an access key for the Scan New Button.*** Insert an & symbol before the letter S in the Text property of the **Scan New** Button (Fig. 20.9). Press *Enter* or click outside the field to update the property. Note that the letter S is now underlined on the Button (Fig. 20.9). If the user presses *Alt*, then *S*, during execution, this has the same effect as "clicking" the **Scan New** Button—the Click event is raised. Depending on your system configuration, you may need to press the *Alt* key to display the underline under the access-key character at execution time.

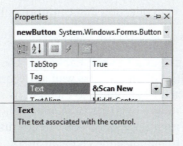 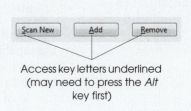

Access key letters underlined (may need to press the *Alt* key first)

Figure 20.9 Creating an access key, and showing Buttons with access keys.

2. ***Inserting access keys for the remaining Buttons.*** Use the Text properties of the remaining Buttons to create access keys. Precede the B on the **< BACK** Button with an ampersand. Repeat this process for the A on the **Add** Button, the R on the **Remove** Button, the E on the **Edit** Button and the N on the **NEXT >** Button. Note that the access key does *not* have to be the first letter in the control's text.

3. ***Saving the project.*** Select **File > Save All** to save your modified code.

SELF-REVIEW

1. When creating an access key, the _____ the ampersand is/are underlined.
   a) character preceding
   b) character following
   c) characters following
   d) characters preceding

2. Press the _____ key, then the underlined character on a Button, to use the access key.
   a) *Control*
   b) *Shift*
   c) *Alt*
   d) *Tab*

Answers: 1) b. 2) c.

20.5 Collections

The .NET Framework Class Library provides several classes, called **collections**, which you can use to store groups of related objects. These classes provide methods that facilitate the storage and organization of your data without requiring any knowledge of the details of how the objects are being stored. This capability improves your app-development time because you do not have to write code to organize your data efficiently—the methods in the collection classes are proven to be reliable and efficient.

In Chapters 17 and 18, you learned how to declare and use arrays in your apps. You may have noticed a limitation to arrays—once an array is declared, its size does *not* change automatically to match its data set. This poses a problem if the number of items in the array needs to change repeatedly over time.

Class List(Of T) (from namespace System.Collections.Generic) provides a convenient solution to this problem. List(Of T) is a generic collection. Generic classes specify a set of related classes with a single class declaration. The generic class List(Of T) specifies a set of classes which provide the functionality for a List of any data type. The identifier T is a placeholder (known as a type parameter) which you replace with an actual type (known as the type argument) when you declare an instance of the generic List(Of T) collection. For example,

```
Dim list As List(Of Integer)
```

declares a List collection that can store only Integer values, and

```
Dim list2 As List(Of Package)
```

declares list2 as a List of Packages. The generic List collection provides all of the capabilities of an array, as well as dynamic resizing capabilities. **Dynamic resizing** enables the List object to increase its size to accommodate new elements and to decrease its size to conserve memory when elements are removed.

As of Visual Basic 2010, you can now use **collection initializers** (similar to array initializers) to initialize the elements in a collection, as in

```
Dim list2 As New List(Of Integer) From {1, 2, 3, 4, 5}
```

SELF-REVIEW
1. Collections _____.
   a) force you to focus on how your data is stored
   b) speed up app development
   c) allow you to focus on the details of your app
   d) Both (b) and (c)

2. One limitation of arrays is that _____.
   a) their size cannot change automatically   b) they can store only primitive data types
   c) Strings cannot be placed in them   d) All of the above

Answers: 1) d. 2) a.

20.6 Shipping Hub App: Using Class List(Of T)

By now, you're familiar with designing GUIs and writing methods and event handlers. This chapter's template file provides much of the app's functionality so that you can concentrate on using a List. You're encouraged to study the full source code at the end of the chapter to understand how the app is implemented. The following pseudocode statements describe the basic operation of your **Shipping Hub** app:

```
When the Form loads:
     Generate a random initial package ID number
     Set the SelectedIndex of the State ComboBox to 0
     Create an empty List of Packages

When the user clicks the Scan New Button:
     Generate the next package ID number
     Create a new Package object
     Display the new Package's package number and arrival time
     Enable the TextBoxes, the ComboBox and the Add Button

When the user clicks the Add Button:
     Retrieve address, city, state and zip code values; and disable input controls
     Add the package to the List
     Disable the Package Information GroupBox and the appropriate Buttons
     Disable the Add Button
     Add the package number to the ListBox
```

Change the Packages by Destination ComboBox value to the package's
   destination state
Enable the New Button

When the user clicks the < BACK Button:
   Display the previous package in the List

When the user clicks the NEXT > Button:
   Display the next package in the List

When the user clicks the Remove Button:
   Remove the package from the Packages by Destination ListBox
   Remove the package from the List

When the user clicks the Edit Button:
   Change the Button to read Update
   Allow the user to modify package address information

When the user clicks the Update Button:
   Update the package's information in the List
   Disable controls that allow user input, and change the
      Update Button to read Edit

When a different state is selected in the Packages by Destination ComboBox:
   Display the package number for each package destined for that
      state in the ListBox

The **Shipping Hub** app must store a list of packages through which the user can navigate using the **NEXT >** and **< BACK** Buttons. Each time the app runs, it must allow for any number of packages to be added. Since arrays don't resize automatically, you'd be limited by the number of values that you could store in the array. [*Note:* You can manually resize an array with the Visual Basic keywords ReDim and Preserve, which we do not cover in this book.] The List collection solves this problem by combining the functionality of an array with dynamic resizing capabilities.

Now that you've test-driven the **Shipping Hub** app and studied its pseudocode representation, you'll use an ACE table to help you convert the pseudocode to Visual Basic. Figure 20.10 lists the *actions*, *controls* and *events* that help you complete your own version of this app.

Action/Control/Event (ACE) Table for the Shipping Hub App	Action	Control/Object	Event
	Label the app's controls	informationGroupBox, listByGroupBox, arrivedLabel, packageIDLabel, addressLabel, cityLabel, stateLabel, zipLabel	App is run
		ShippingHubForm	Load
	Generate a random initial package ID number	randomObject	
	Set the SelectedIndex of the State ComboBox to 0	stateComboBox	
	Create an empty List of Packages	list	

Figure 20.10 ACE table for the **Shipping Hub** app. (Part 1 of 3.)

Action	Control/Object	Event
	`newButton`	`Click`
Generate the next package ID number		
Create a new Package object	`packageObject`	
Display the new Package's package number and arrival time	`packageNumberLabel`, `arrivalTimeLabel`	
Enable the TextBoxes, the ComboBox and the Add Button	`informationGroupBox`	
	`addButton`	`Click`
Disable the Package Information GroupBox and the appropriate Buttons	`informationGroup-Box` (call SetButtons with True as an argument for the Buttons)	
Disable the Add Button	`addButton`	
Add the package to the List	`list`	
Add the package number to the ListBox	`packagesListBox`	
Change the Packages by Destination ComboBox value to the package's destination state	`viewPackagesCombo-Box`	
Enable the New Button	`newButton`	
	`backButton`	`Click`
Display the previous package in the List	`list`, `packageNumberLabel`, `arrivalTimeLabel` `addressTextBox`, `cityTextBox`, `stateComboBox`, `zipTextBox`	
	`nextButton`	`Click`
Display the next package in the List	`list`, `packageNumberLabel`, `arrivalTimeLabel` `addressTextBox`, `cityTextBox`, `stateComboBox`, `zipTextBox`	
	`removeButton`	`Click`
Remove the package from the Packages by Destination ListBox	`packagesListBox`	
Remove the package from the List	`list`	
	`editUpdateButton`	`Click`
Change the Button to read Update	`editUpdateButton`	
Allow the user to modify package address information	`informationGroupBox`	

Figure 20.10   ACE table for the **Shipping Hub** app. (Part 2 of 3.)

Action	Control/Object	Event
	editUpdateButton	Click
Update the package's information in the List	list	
Disable controls that allow user input, and change the Update Button to read Edit	informationGroupBox	
	viewPackages-ComboBox	Selected-Index-Changed
Display the package number for each package destined for that state in the ListBox	packagesListBox, list	

Figure 20.10   ACE table for the **Shipping Hub** app. (Part 3 of 3.)

In this chapter, you'll focus on using a List in the **Shipping Hub** app. You'll begin by creating a List(Of Package) object. The List class is located in namespace **System.Collections.Generic**.

Creating a List of Packages

1. ***Declaring a List(Of Package).*** Insert line 3 of Fig. 20.11 in the Shipping-Hub class to declare the List(Of Package) named list.

Declaring a
List(Of Package)
reference

```
2
3      Private list As List(Of Package)
4      Private packageObject As Package ' current package
```

Figure 20.11   Declaring the List(Of Package) reference.

2. ***Initializing the List(Of Package).*** To use the List instance variable declared in *Step 1*, you must create a new List(Of Package) object. You then assign a reference to the List(Of Package) object to the instance variable. Insert line 20 (Fig. 20.12) to the Form's Load event handler. This line uses the New keyword to create an empty List(Of Package) object when the app loads. Note that line 18 uses stateComboBox's SelectedIndex property to show the first state in the list.

Initializing the
List(Of Package)
reference

```
16
17         ' show first state in ComboBox
18         stateComboBox.SelectedIndex = 0
19
20         list = New List(Of Package)() ' create the List
21     End Sub ' ShippingHubForm_Load
```

Figure 20.12   Creating a List(Of Package) object.

3. ***Saving the project.*** Select **File > Save All** to save your modified code.

Now that you've created a List object, you'll insert code that allows the user to add Packages to the List. To accomplish this, you'll create a reference to an object of class Package and use List's Add method to store the reference in the List. Recall that you've already added the Package class to your app. You'll now create Packages and add them to your List.

Adding and Removing Packages

1. ***Creating a package.*** The user clicks the **Scan New** Button when a new package arrives at the shipping hub. When this occurs, the app creates a package number and allows the user to enter the shipping address. Insert lines 29–30 from Fig. 20.13 into the **Scan New** Button's Click event handler. Line 29 increments packageID (declared at line 7) to ensure that all packages have a *unique* identification number. Line 30 passes the package number as an argument to the constructor for class Package. The value that you pass to the Package constructor can then be accessed using its PackageNumber property. Every time line 30 executes, it uses the same reference, packageObject, to refer to a new Package object. However, the previous Package object is *not* lost each time a new Package is created. This is because each Package reference will be stored in the List.

```
23    ' Scan New Button Click event
24    Private Sub newButton_Click(sender As System.Object,
25        e As System.EventArgs) Handles newButton.Click
26
27        ClearControls() ' clear fields
28
29        packageID += 1 ' increment package ID
30        packageObject = New Package(packageID) ' create package
31
```

Create a new **Package** object with a unique ID — lines 29–30

Figure 20.13 Creating a Package object.

2. ***Displaying the package number and arrival time.*** After the package has been "scanned," the app should display the package's arrival time and package number. In the newButton_Click event handler, insert lines 32–35 of Fig. 20.14. Lines 32–33 use the Package's PackageNumber property to display the package identification number in a Label. The **ToString** method returns a String representation of an object and is available for all types. For instance, a Date structure's ToString method returns the date as a String, in the format 11/29/2010 9:34:00 AM (recall that this depends on the user's locale). However, be aware that for some .NET classes, ToString merely returns the class name. Lines 34–35 use the Package's ArrivalTime property to display the arrival time (the current time) in a Label. The Package's ArrivalTime property is set to the current time in the Package class's constructor. Recall that the ArrivalTime property is already defined for you in the Package class.

```
31
32    packageNumberLabel.Text =
33        packageObject.PackageNumber.ToString() ' package number
34    arrivalTimeLabel.Text =
35        packageObject.ArrivalTime.ToString() ' show arrival time
36
```

Displaying arrival time and package ID number in Labels — lines 32–35

Figure 20.14 Displaying the package's number and arrival time.

3. ***Adding a package to the List.*** The user clicks the **Add** Button to add the package to the List after entering the package's information. Add line 50 of Fig. 20.15 to the **Add** Button's Click event handler. This line stores the package information by adding the Package object to list using the List's Add method.

(cont.)

```
45        ' Add Button Click event
46        Private Sub addButton_Click(sender As System.Object,
47           e As System.EventArgs) Handles addButton.Click
48
49           SetPackage() ' set Package properties from TextBoxes
50           list.Add(packageObject) ' add package to the List
51
```

Adding a Package object to a List ⎯⎯⎯ *(pointing to line 50)*

Figure 20.15   Adding a package to the List.

Each time you add a Package to the List by calling the Add method, the Package is placed at the end of the List. With arrays, you refer to a value's location by its index. Similarly, in a List, you can refer to an element's location in the List as the element's **index**. Like an array, the index of an element at the beginning of the List is zero, and the index of an element at the end of the List is one less than the number of elements in the List.

4. *Removing a package from the List.* When the user selects a package and clicks the **Remove** Button, the app should remove the Package from the List. The List class provides a simple way to remove elements from the List. Insert line 104 (Fig. 20.16) into the **Remove** Button's Click event handler. This line uses the **RemoveAt** method to remove a package from the List. The argument passed to the method RemoveAt is the index (stored in variable position) of the Package in the List. Variable position keeps track of the index and is incremented or decremented each time the user clicks the **NEXT >** or **< BACK** Buttons.

```
102          End If
103
104          list.RemoveAt(position) ' remove package from list
105
106          ' load next package in list if there is one
107          If List.Count > 0 Then
```

Removing the current Package from the List ⎯⎯⎯ *(pointing to line 104)*

Figure 20.16   Removing a Package from the List.

If a Package at index 3 is removed from the List, the Package that was previously at index 4 will then be located at index 3. Whenever an object is removed from a List, the indices update accordingly. Note that line 107 of Fig. 20.16 uses the Count property of class List. Like the Length property of an array, the **Count** property returns the number of elements currently stored in the List.

5. *Saving the project.* Select **File > Save All** to save your modified code.

Once a Package has been added to the List, the **Shipping Hub** app disables the TextBoxes so that the user does *not* accidentally modify the package information. An **Edit** Button is provided to allow users to modify the package information (except for the arrival time and the package identification number). When the user clicks **Edit**, its event handler should enable the controls that allow the user to modify the package data. You'll add functionality to accomplish this in the following box.

Updating Package Information

1. *Changing the Edit Button's Text property.* Add lines 132–133 of Fig. 20.17 before the Else clause in the editUpdateButton_Click event handler. When the **Edit** Button is clicked, line 133 changes the text on the **Edit** Button to &Update (using U as the access key). This indicates that the user should click the same Button, which now is labeled **Update**, to submit changes to the package information.

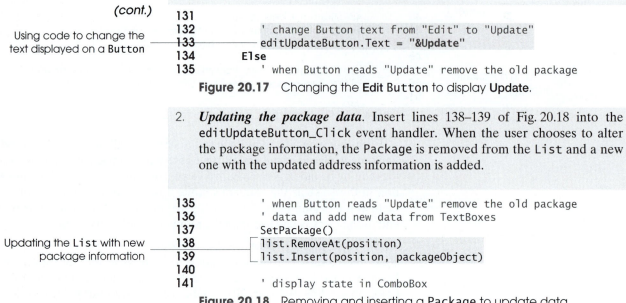

(cont.)

Using code to change the text displayed on a **Button**

```
131
132         ' change Button text from "Edit" to "Update"
133         editUpdateButton.Text = "&Update"
134     Else
135         ' when Button reads "Update" remove the old package
```

Figure 20.17   Changing the **Edit Button** to display **Update**.

2. *Updating the package data.* Insert lines 138–139 of Fig. 20.18 into the `editUpdateButton_Click` event handler. When the user chooses to alter the package information, the `Package` is removed from the `List` and a new one with the updated address information is added.

Updating the **List** with new package information

```
135         ' when Button reads "Update" remove the old package
136         ' data and add new data from TextBoxes
137         SetPackage()
138         list.RemoveAt(position)
139         list.Insert(position, packageObject)
140
141         ' display state in ComboBox
```

Figure 20.18   Removing and inserting a **Package** to update data.

Line 138 removes the old `Package` object from the `List`. Line 139 uses class `List`'s `Insert` method to add the package to the `List`. The `Insert` method is like the Add method, but `Insert` allows you to specify the index in the `List` at which to insert the `Package`. The first argument to the `Insert` method is the index at which to insert the `Package` (in this case, `position`), and the second argument contains the `Package` to insert into the `List` (package). Using the `Insert` method allows you to place the updated `Package` object at the same index in the `List` as the `Package` object you just removed, thus maintaining the package IDs in sequential order. [*Note:* We could have modified the existing `Package` object, but we chose to introduce other methods of the `List` collection here.]

3. *Changing the Button's Text property to Edit.* After the user clicks the **Update** Button, the TextBoxes are once again disabled. Since the user's changes have been applied, you should reset the text on the **Update** Button to read **Edit**. Insert line 149 of Fig. 20.19 into the event handler to reset the text on the **Button** to **Edit**. Note once again the use of the & to enable the **Button**'s access key.

4. *Saving the project.* Select **File > Save All** to save your modified code.

Using code to display the text on the **Button**

```
146         SetButtons(True) ' enable appropriate Buttons
147
148         ' change Button text from "Update" to "Edit"
149         editUpdateButton.Text = "&Edit"
150     End If
151 End Sub ' editUpdateButton_Click
```

Figure 20.19   Setting the **Button**'s **Text** property back to **Edit**.

The user navigates the `List` by clicking the **NEXT >** and **< BACK** Buttons. Each time the user chooses to view a different package in the `List`, the package information displayed in the Form's controls must be updated. To display a package's information, you must retrieve the information from the `List` that contains the `Package` objects. You'll learn how to do this in the following box.

Displaying a Package

1. *Retrieving package data.* Insert lines 165–166 from Fig. 20.20 into your app's LoadPackage method. To display the information, you must retrieve the data from the List using the elements index enclosed in parentheses, as you did with arrays. Line 166 assigns to packageObject the Package stored at index position.

```
162     ' load package information into Form
163     Private Sub LoadPackage()
164
165         ' retrieve package from List
166         packageObject = list(position)
167
168     End Sub ' LoadPackage
```

Retrieving a Package object from a List

Figure 20.20 Retrieving a Package from the List.

2. *Displaying the package information.* Insert lines 168–176 of Fig. 20.21 into your app. These lines retrieve the package information from package-Object and display the data in the corresponding controls on the Form. Lines 174 and 176 use the ToString method to convert the arrival time and package number to their String representations.

Displaying data stored in the Package object

```
168     ' display package data
169     addressTextBox.Text = packageObject.Address
170     cityTextBox.Text = packageObject.City
171     stateComboBox.Text = packageObject.State
172     zipTextBox.Text = packageObject.Zip
173     arrivalTimeLabel.Text =
174         packageObject.ArrivalTime.ToString()
175     packageNumberLabel.Text =
176         packageObject.PackageNumber.ToString()
177     End Sub ' LoadPackage
```

Figure 20.21 Displaying the package data in the Form's controls.

3. *Saving the project.* Select **File > Save All** to save your modified code.

In this section, you learned that a generic List collection stores references to any single type. The complete details of generics are beyond the scope of this book. If you plan to continue your Visual Basic studies, we provide a thorough treatment of generics and generic collections in *Visual Basic 2010 How to Program, Fourth Edition*. We also provide chapters and Resource Centers with additional Visual Basic 2010 information at www.deitel.com. Our Visual Basic Resource Center

www.deitel.com/visualbasic

includes articles on many Visual Basic 2010 features, including generics. Check our Resource Centers for lots of additional information on the subjects in this book and new developments in VB.

SELF-REVIEW

1. Method _____ of class List can be used to add an object at a specific location in the List.

   a) AddAt   b) Insert

   c) AddObjectAt   d) Add

2. The **Shipping Hub** app uses a List because class List _____.

   a) can store a variable number of objects

   b) allows the addition and removal of packages

c) allows the insertion of items into any index in the List

d) All of the above

Answers: 1) b. 2) d.

20.7 For Each...Next Repetition Statement

Visual Basic provides the **For Each...Next** repetition statement for iterating through all the elements in an array or a collection. Instead of setting initial, final and increment values for a counter variable, the For Each...Next statement uses a control variable that can be assigned each element in the collection. Assuming that you've created a List called list that contains Package objects, the code

```
For Each packageObject As Package In list
    packagesListBox.Items.Add(packageObject.PackageNumber)
Next
```

Good Programming Practice

Use a For Each...Next repetition statement to iterate through values in an array or collection without using a counter variable.

adds each package's ID number to a ListBox. The For Each...Next statement requires both a group and an element. The **group** specifies the array or collection (in this case, list) through which you wish to iterate. The **element** (in this case, packageObject) is used to store a reference to an object in the group (for reference types) or to store a value (for value types). The For Each...Next statement assigns the current element in the collection to the element variable (in this case, packageObject). The body of the For Each...Next statement then executes. When the body completes execution, the next element in the collection is assigned to the element variable and the body executes again. This continues until there are no more items in the collection. Note that the For Each...Next statement does not require you to specify initial and final counter values, and thus it simplifies access to groups of values. Note that body statement in the preceding For Each...Next statement uses packagesListBox's Items property (a collection). The **Items** property stores the items displayed in a ListBox or ComboBox.

Common Programming Error

If the element in a For Each...Next statement cannot be converted to the same type as the groups's objects, a compilation error occurs. For example, if a List contained Date values, declaring a reference to a Package object as the element would cause a compilation error.

Figure 20.22 shows the UML activity diagram for the preceding For Each...Next statement. It's similar to the UML diagram for the For...Next statement in Chapter 11. The difference is that the For Each...Next continues to execute the body until *all* elements in the array or collection have been accessed.

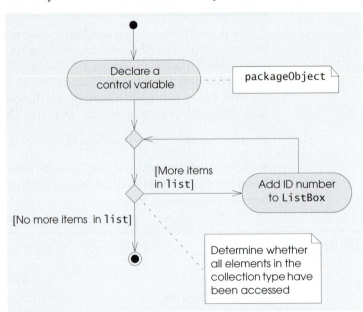

Figure 20.22   UML activity diagram for a **For Each...Next** repetition statement.

When the user selects a state from the viewPackagesComboBox, the app displays the package number for each package destined for that state. You'll now use the For Each...Next statement in the **Shipping Hub** app to add this functionality.

Inserting a For Each...Next Statement

1. *Inserting a For Each...Next statement.* Add lines 219–220 of Fig. 20.23 to the viewPackagesComboBox_SelectedIndexChanged event handler, then press *Enter*. Note that the Next keyword is added for you by the IDE. Line 220 is the header of the repetition statement. This line declares control variable viewPackage of type Package. The loop iterates through list, assigning the next element in the List (beginning with the first Package object) to control variable viewPackage before executing the body of the loop during each iteration. Note that you've added this code to a ComboBox's Selected-IndexChanged event handler. The **SelectedIndexChanged** event occurs when the value selected in the ComboBox changes.

```
217        packagesListBox.Items.Clear() ' clear ListBox
218
219        ' list all packages for current state in ListBox
220    For Each viewPackage As Package In list
221
222        Next
```

For Each...Next header ⎯ points to line 220

Figure 20.23   Writing a For Each...Next statement.

2. *Determining a package's destination state.* Insert lines 221–226 of Fig. 20.24 into your app. These lines contain an If...Then statement that tests each package's destination state against the state name displayed in the **Packages by Destination** ComboBox. If these state names match, line 225 displays the package number in the ListBox.

```
217        packagesListBox.Items.Clear() ' clear ListBox
218
219        ' list all packages for current state in ListBox
220    For Each viewPackage As Package In list
221            ' determine whether state package is being shipped to
222            ' matches the state selected in the ComboBox
223        If viewPackage.State = state Then
224            ' add Package number to the ListBox
225            packagesListBox.Items.Add(viewPackage.PackageNumber)
226        End If
227        Next
```

Displaying package ID numbers only for packages destined for the specified state ⎯ points to lines 223–226

Figure 20.24   Displaying all packages going to selected state.

3. *Running the app.* Select **Debug > Start Debugging** to run your app. Enter information for several packages going to the same state. Select that state in the **Packages by Destination** GroupBox and verify that the correct packages are listed. Click the app's Buttons and make sure that you can remove, cycle through or modify the packages.

4. *Closing the app.* Close your running app by clicking its close box.

20.8 Language-Integrated Query (LINQ)

In the previous section, you used a For Each...Next repetition statement to iterate through a List of Packages to find those destined for a selected state. This technique is sometimes known as *filtering* a collection based on certain criteria (i.e., conditions). This is typical of how many older apps perform search operations. **Language-Integrated Query (LINQ)** capabilities can be used to filter collections.

A **query** retrieves specific information from a data source, such as a collection. LINQ enables you to write queries directly in your Visual Basic code. With LINQ, you can query arrays, collections and other data sources such as XML documents and SQL databases. In this chapter, we use LINQ to Objects to query collections. We discuss LINQ to SQL in Chapter 27.

A typical LINQ query contains three clauses—a `From` clause, a `Where` clause and a `Select` clause. The `From` clause, which must appear first in a LINQ query, specifies a **range variable** and the data source to query. The range variable represents each item in the data source, much like the control variable in a `For Each...Next` statement. The `Where` clause specifies the conditions that must be met for the item to be included in the results. The expression in the `Where` clause must evaluate to a `Boolean`. If the expression evaluates to `True`, the item is included in the results. The `Select` clause specifies the value(s) placed in the results. For example, assuming that you've created a `List` of `Package` objects called `list`, the LINQ to Objects query

```
Dim cityQuery = From p In list
                Where p.City = "Boston"
                Select p
```

selects all the `Packages` in `list` that are destined for Boston. The query iterates through each `Package` in `list` and checks whether the `Package`'s `City` property equals `"Boston"`. If the expression in the `Where` clause evaluates to `True`, the `Select` clause includes the corresponding `Package` in the result, which is a collection of 0 or more `Packages` (because we're querying a `List(Of Package)`). LINQ uses **deferred execution**—the query does *not* execute until you attempt to iterate through the query results.

Notice that there are *no* type declarations in this sample query. To implement some of the advanced features of LINQ, Visual Basic 2010 can use *local type inference* to infer the type of a variable based on the context in which it's initialized. The compiler knows that `list` contains `Package` objects. So it infers that `p` is of the type `Package`. We discuss the type of `cityQuery` in the following box.

This example query is similar to the `For Each...Next` statement you wrote in the previous box. In the following box you'll learn to use LINQ to select from the `List` all the `Packages` destined for a specified state.

Using LINQ to Select Packages from a List

1. ***Declaring a LINQ query.*** Add lines 219–222 of Fig. 20.25 to your app. These lines declare a LINQ query that selects from `list` all the `Packages` destined for the specified state (local variable `state`). Recall that the compiler infers the type of the range variable (`p`). In this case, the type is `Package` because the compiler knows that `list` contains `Package` objects. The `Where` clause determines whether the `Package`'s `State` property is equal to the state selected in the `viewPackagesComboBox`.

```
217        packagesListBox.Items.Clear() ' clear ListBox
218
219        ' LINQ query to select packages destined for specified state
220        Dim stateQuery = From p In list
221                               Where p.State = state
222                               Select p
```

Declaring a LINQ query to select Packages destined for specified state

Figure 20.25 Declaring a LINQ query.

(cont.)

2. ***Using a For Each...Next statement to iterate through the query results.***
Replace the For Each...Next statement from Fig. 20.24 with lines 225–228 of
Fig. 20.26. This For Each...Next statement iterates over the results from the
stateQuery. The query results are contained in an IEnumerable(Of
Package) object. **IEnumerable** is an **interface**—a set of methods that can be
called on an object to tell it to perform some task or return some piece of
information. The IEnumerable interface provides methods to iterate
through a set of objects, such as an array or a collection. Arrays and collections implement the IEnumerable interface—you can call any IEnumerable
method on an array or collection object to iterate through its elements. The
For Each...Next statement *implicitly* calls these IEnumerable methods. As
such, a For Each...Next statement can iterate over any object that implements the IEnumerable interface. This means you can use a For
Each...Next statement to iterate over the results of any LINQ query. The
For Each...Next statement in lines 225–228 adds the PackageNumber of
each Package returned by stateQuery to the packagesListBox. Note that
execution of the stateQuery is deferred until program control reaches line
225, where we begin iterating through the results.

Use a For Each...Next
statement to display the results
of the query

```
224        ' list all packages for current state in ListBox
225        For Each viewPackage In stateQuery
226           ' display the package id in the ListBox
227           packagesListBox.Items.Add(viewPackage.PackageNumber)
228        Next
```

Figure 20.26   Iterating through query results using a For Each...Next statement.

3. ***Closing the app.*** Close your running app by clicking its close box.

1. ***Closing the IDE.*** Close Visual Basic IDE by clicking its close box.

Figure 20.27 presents the source code for the **Shipping Hub** app. The lines of
code containing new programming concepts that you learned in this chapter are
highlighted.

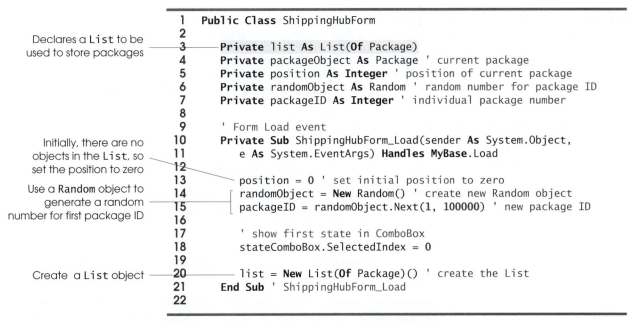

Declares a List to be
used to store packages

Initially, there are no
objects in the List, so
set the position to zero

Use a Random object to
generate a random
number for first package ID

Create a List object

```
 1    Public Class ShippingHubForm
 2
 3        Private list As List(Of Package)
 4        Private packageObject As Package ' current package
 5        Private position As Integer ' position of current package
 6        Private randomObject As Random ' random number for package ID
 7        Private packageID As Integer ' individual package number
 8
 9        ' Form Load event
10        Private Sub ShippingHubForm_Load(sender As System.Object,
11           e As System.EventArgs) Handles MyBase.Load
12
13           position = 0 ' set initial position to zero
14           randomObject = New Random() ' create new Random object
15           packageID = randomObject.Next(1, 100000) ' new package ID
16
17           ' show first state in ComboBox
18           stateComboBox.SelectedIndex = 0
19
20           list = New List(Of Package)() ' create the List
21        End Sub ' ShippingHubForm_Load
22
```

Figure 20.27   Complete code listing for the **Shipping Hub** app. (Part 1 of 5.)

```
23    ' Scan New Button Click event
24    Private Sub newButton_Click(sender As System.Object,
25       e As System.EventArgs) Handles newButton.Click
26
27       ClearControls() ' clear fields
28
29       packageID += 1 ' increment package ID
30       packageObject = New Package(packageID) ' create package
31
32       packageNumberLabel.Text =
33          packageObject.PackageNumber.ToString() ' package number
34       arrivalTimeLabel.Text =
35          packageObject.ArrivalTime.ToString() ' show arrival time
36
37       ' only allow user to add package
38       informationGroupBox.Enabled = True ' enable GroupBox
39       SetButtons(False) ' enable/disable Buttons
40       addButton.Enabled = True ' enable Add Button
41       newButton.Enabled = False ' disable Scan New Button
42       addressTextBox.Focus() ' transfer the focus to addressTextBox
43    End Sub ' newButton_Click
44
45    ' Add Button Click event
46    Private Sub addButton_Click(sender As System.Object,
47       e As System.EventArgs) Handles addButton.Click
48
49       SetPackage() ' set Package properties from TextBoxes
50       list.Add(packageObject) ' add package to the List
51
52       informationGroupBox.Enabled = False ' disable GroupBox
53       SetButtons(True) ' enable appropriate Buttons
54
55       ' package cannot be added until Scan New is clicked
56       addButton.Enabled = False ' disable Add Button
57
58       ' if package's state displayed, add ID to ListBox
59       If stateComboBox.Text = viewPackagesComboBox.Text Then
60          packagesListBox.Items.Add(packageObject.PackageNumber)
61       End If
62
63       viewPackagesComboBox.Text = packageObject.State ' list package
64       newButton.Enabled = True ' enable Scan New Button
65    End Sub ' addButton_Click
66
67    ' Back Button Click event
68    Private Sub backButton_Click(sender As System.Object,
69       e As System.EventArgs) Handles backButton.Click
70
71       ' move backward one package in the list
72       If position > 0 Then
73          position -= 1
74       Else ' wrap to end of list
75          position = list.Count - 1
76       End If
77
78       LoadPackage() ' load package data from item in list
79    End Sub ' backButton_Click
80
81    ' Next Button Click event
82    Private Sub nextButton_Click(sender As System.Object,
83       e As System.EventArgs) Handles nextButton.Click
84
```

Use ToString to convert values

When the user clicks the **< BACK** Button, decrement the position. If the position was zero, set the position to the last object in the List

Figure 20.27 Complete code listing for the **Shipping Hub** app. (Part 2 of 5.)

When the user clicks the
NEXT > Button, increment
the position. If the position
was the last object in the
array, set the position to zero

Set the position to the
previous package in the List

Using & in the Text property of a
Button to create an access key

Removing and inserting
items from/into a List

```
85        ' move forward one package in the list
86        If position < list.Count - 1 Then
87           position += 1
88        Else
89           position = 0 ' wrap to beginning of list
90        End If
91
92        LoadPackage() ' load package data from item in list
93     End Sub ' nextButton_Click
94
95     ' Remove Button click event
96     Private Sub removeButton_Click(sender As System.Object,
97        e As System.EventArgs) Handles removeButton.Click
98
99        ' remove ID from ListBox if state displayed
100       If stateComboBox.Text = viewPackagesComboBox.Text Then
101          packagesListBox.Items.Remove(packageObject.PackageNumber)
102       End If
103
104       list.RemoveAt(position) ' remove package from list
105
106       ' load next package in list if there is one
107       If list.Count > 0 Then
108          ' if not at first position, go to previous one
109          If position > 0 Then
110             position -= 1
111          End If
112
113          LoadPackage() ' load package data from item in list
114       Else
115          ClearControls() ' clear fields
116       End If
117
118       SetButtons(True) ' enable appropriate Buttons
119    End Sub ' removeButton_Click
120
121    ' Edit/Update Button Click event
122    Private Sub editUpdateButton_Click(sender As System.Object,
123       e As System.EventArgs) Handles editUpdateButton.Click
124
125       ' when Button reads "Edit", allow user to
126       ' edit package information only
127       If editUpdateButton.Text = "&Edit" Then
128          informationGroupBox.Enabled = True ' enable GroupBox
129          SetButtons(False)
130          editUpdateButton.Enabled = True
131
132          ' change Button text from "Edit" to "Update"
133          editUpdateButton.Text = "&Update"
134       Else
135          ' when Button reads "Update" remove the old package
136          ' data and add new data from TextBoxes
137          SetPackage()
138          list.RemoveAt(position)
139          list.Insert(position, packageObject)
140
141          ' display state in ComboBox
142          viewPackagesComboBox.Text = packageObject.State
143
144          ' when done, return to normal operating state
145          informationGroupBox.Enabled = False ' disable GroupBox
146          SetButtons(True) ' enable appropriate Buttons
147
```

Figure 20.27   Complete code listing for the **Shipping Hub** app. (Part 3 of 5.)

Using & in the **Text** property of a **Button** to create an access key

```
148            ' change Button text from "Update" to "Edit"
149            editUpdateButton.Text = "&Edit"
150         End If
151      End Sub ' editUpdateButton_Click
152
153      ' set package properties
154      Private Sub SetPackage()
155         packageObject.Address = addressTextBox.Text
156         packageObject.City = cityTextBox.Text
157         packageObject.State =
158            stateComboBox.SelectedItem.ToString()
159         packageObject.Zip = zipTextBox.Text
160      End Sub ' SetPackage
161
162      ' load package information into Form
163      Private Sub LoadPackage()
164
165         ' retrieve package from list
166         packageObject = list(position)
167
168         ' display package data
169         addressTextBox.Text = packageObject.Address
170         cityTextBox.Text = packageObject.City
171         stateComboBox.Text = packageObject.State
172         zipTextBox.Text = packageObject.Zip
173         arrivalTimeLabel.Text =
174            packageObject.ArrivalTime.ToString()
175         packageNumberLabel.Text =
176            packageObject.PackageNumber.ToString()
177      End Sub ' LoadPackage
178
179      ' clear all the input controls on the Form
180      Private Sub ClearControls()
181         addressTextBox.Clear()
182         cityTextBox.Clear()
183         zipTextBox.Clear()
184         stateComboBox.SelectedText = String.Empty
185         arrivalTimeLabel.Text = String.Empty
186         packageNumberLabel.Text = String.Empty
187      End Sub ' ClearControls
188
189      ' enable/disable Buttons
190      Private Sub SetButtons(state As Boolean)
191         removeButton.Enabled = state
192         editUpdateButton.Enabled = state
193         nextButton.Enabled = state
194         backButton.Enabled = state
195
196         ' disable navigation if not multiple packages
197         If list.Count < 2 Then
198            nextButton.Enabled = False
199            backButton.Enabled = False
200         End If
201
202         ' if no items, disable Remove and Edit/Update Buttons
203         If list.Count = 0 Then
204            editUpdateButton.Enabled = False
205            removeButton.Enabled = False
206         End If
207      End Sub ' SetButtons
208
```

Retrieve data from user, and store it in the **Package** object

Using **ToString** to convert values

Enable or disable **Buttons** depending on value of **state**

Figure 20.27   Complete code listing for the **Shipping Hub** app. (Part 4 of 5.)

```
209      ' event raised when user selects a new state in ComboBox
210      Private Sub viewPackagesComboBox_SelectedIndexChanged(
211         sender As System.Object, e As System.EventArgs)
212         Handles viewPackagesComboBox.SelectedIndexChanged
213
214         Dim state As String =
215            viewPackagesComboBox.SelectedItem.ToString()
216
217         packagesListBox.Items.Clear() ' clear ListBox
218
219         ' LINQ query to select packages destined for specified state
220         Dim stateQuery = From p In list
221                          Where p.State = state
222                          Select p
223
224         ' list all packages for current state in ListBox
225         For Each viewPackage As Package In stateQuery
226            ' display the Package's id in the ListBox
227            packagesListBox.Items.Add(viewPackage.PackageNumber)
228         Next
229      End Sub ' viewPackagesComboBox_SelectedIndexChanged
230   End Class ' ShippingHubForm
```

Declare a LINQ query to select **Packages** destined for specified state *(annotation pointing to lines 220–222)*

Figure 20.27   Complete code listing for the **Shipping Hub** app. (Part 5 of 5.)

SELF-REVIEW

1. The group in a For Each...Next repetition statement represents _____.
   a) the counter used for iteration   b) the reference used for iteration
   c) an array or collection   d) the guard condition

2. The _____ statement provides a convenient way to iterate through values in an array or collection.
   a) Do While...Loop   b) For...Next
   c) For Each...Next   d) None of the above

Answers: 1) c. 2) c.

20.9 Wrap-Up

In this chapter, you learned how to use the TabStop and TabIndex properties to enhance the **Shipping Hub** app's usability. You learned how to determine which controls receive the app's focus when the *Tab* key is pressed using the TabStop property. You then specified the order in which controls receive the focus when the *Tab* key is pressed. To further enhance the user interface, you created access keys to allow the user to "click" Buttons in the **Shipping Hub** app by pressing the *Alt* key and then the access key for the particular Button.

You learned about using the List collection. You used List methods to add a Package object to a List and delete the Package from a specific index in a List. You then wrote code to insert a Package object into the List at a specific index. These methods helped you store, edit and navigate a List of Packages in the **Shipping Hub** app.

You learned about the For Each...Next repetition statement. You declared a control variable for use in the repetition statement and used that reference in the For Each...Next statement to iterate through each element in a group (which can be an array or a collection). Then you used the For Each...Next statement to iterate through Package objects in the List in your **Shipping Hub** app.

Finally, you learned to use LINQ to Objects to create queries that selected objects from a collection based on specified conditions. You also learned how to use a For Each...Next statement to iterate through the results of the query.

In the next chapter, you'll learn about keyboard events, which are events raised when the user presses and releases keys on the keyboard. You'll also learn the Dictionary collection and use LINQ to Objects to filter the collection of controls on a Form.

SKILLS SUMMARY

Using the TabIndex and TabStop Properties

- Set the TabIndex properties of controls on your Form using numbers to specify the order in which to transfer the focus of the app when the user presses the *Tab* key. Using **View > Tab Order** helps in configuring the order of this process. (If **View > Tab Order** is not available, select **Tools > Settings > Expert Settings**.)

- Set the TabStop property of a control to False if a control is not used by the user to input data. Set the TabStop property of a control to True if focus should be transferred to the control using the *Tab* key.

Creating Access Keys

- Insert the & symbol in a control's Text property before the character you wish to use as an access key (keyboard shortcut).

Creating a List

- Assign a reference to a List to an object of type System.Collections.Generic.List using keyword New.

```
Dim list As New List(Of Integer)()
```

Using a Collection Initializer

- Follow the new collection object with keyword From and a comma-separated list of initializers in curly braces, as in

```
Dim list As New List(Of Integer) From {1, 2, 3, 4, 5}
```

Limiting the Number of Characters that Can Be Typed in a TextBox

- Set the TextBox's MaxLength property.

Using a List

- Call List method Add to add the method's argument to the end of the List.

- Call List method RemoveAt on a List object to remove the object from the List at the index specified by the method's argument.

- Call List method Insert on a List object to add the object specified by the second argument to the List at the index specified by the first argument.

- Use List property Count on a List object to obtain the number of its elements.

Using a For Each...Next Repetition Statement

- Declare a variable of the same type as the elements you wish to access in a group (that is, an array or a collection).

- Specify the variable as the control variable in the For Each...Next repetition statement and the array or collection through which you wish to iterate. The loop repeats and the body of the For Each...Next repetition statement executes for each element in the group. The value accessed at the beginning of each iteration is stored in the control variable for the body of the loop.

Using Language-Integrated Query (LINQ) to Select Objects

- Declare a variable and assign a LINQ query to it. A basic LINQ query consists of a From clause, a Where clause and a Select clause.

- Specify in the From clause an element variable name and the array or collection from which to select elements.

- Specify in the Where clause the conditions that must be met to include an element in the results.

- Specify in the Select clause the information to select from the element.

- To execute the LINQ query, iterate over its results.

KEY TERMS   **access key**—Keyboard shortcut that allows the user to perform an action on a control using the keyboard.

Add method of class `List`—Adds a specified object to the end of a `List`.

collection—A class used to store groups of related objects.

`Count` property of `List`—Returns the number of objects contained in the `List`.

deferred execution—A LINQ query is not executed until you begin to iterate over its results.

dynamic resizing—A capability that allows certain objects (such as `List`s) to increase or decrease in size based on the addition or removal of elements from that object. Enables the `List` object to increase its size to accommodate new elements and to decrease its size when elements are removed.

element of a `For Each...Next` statement—Used to store a reference to the current value of the collection being iterated.

`For Each...Next` repetition statement—Iterates through elements in an array or collection.

`From` clause (of a LINQ query)—Specifies a range variable and the data source to query.

group (of a `For Each...Next` statement)—Specifies the array or collection through which you wish to iterate.

index of a `List`—The value with which you can refer to a specific element in a `List`, based on the element's location in the `List`.

`IEnumerable` interface—Provides methods to iterate through a set of objects, such as an array or a collection.

`Insert` method of class `List`—Inserts a specified object into the specified location of a `List`.

interface—Specifies a set of methods that can be called on an object which implements the interface to perform certain tasks.

`Items` property of `ComboBox`—Collection containing the values displayed in a `ComboBox`.

Language-Integrated Query (LINQ)—Provides support for writing queries in Visual Basic.

`List(Of T)` class—Has the same capabilities as an array, as well as dynamic resizing and more.

`MaxLength` property of `TextBox`—Specifies the maximum number of characters that can be input into a `TextBox`.

query (LINQ)—Retrieves specific information from a data source, such as a collection.

range variable (LINQ)—The control variable for a LINQ query.

`RemoveAt` method of class `List`—Removes the object located at a specified location of a `List`.

`Select` clause (of a LINQ query)—Specifies the value(s) placed in the results of the query.

`SelectedIndexChanged` event of `ComboBox`—Raised when a new value is selected in a `ComboBox`.

`System.Collections.Generic` namespace—Contains collection classes such as `List`.

`TabIndex` property—A control property that specifies the order in which focus is transferred to controls on the `Form` when the *Tab* key is pressed.

`TabStop` property—A control property that specifies whether a control can receive the focus when the *Tab* key is pressed.

`ToString` method—Returns a `String` representation of the object or data type on which the method is called.

`Where` clause (of a LINQ query)—Specifies the conditions that must be met for an item to be included in the results.

GUI DESIGN GUIDELINES   **Overall Design**

- Set a control's `TabStop` property to `True` only if the control is used to receive user input.
- Use the `TabIndex` property to define the logical order in which the user should enter data. Usually the order transfers the focus of the app from top to bottom and left to right.
- Use access keys to allow users to "click" a control using the keyboard.
- Using the *Tab* key is an efficient way for users to navigate through the controls in a GUI.

CONTROLS, EVENTS, PROPERTIES & METHODS

List   This class is used to store a variable number of objects of any specified type.

- *Property*

  Count—Returns the number of objects contained in the List.
- *Methods*

  Add—Adds an object to the end of a List.

  Insert—Adds an object to the List object at a specific index.

  RemoveAt—Removes an object from the List object at the specified index.

ComboBox   ▣ ComboBox   This control allows users to select options from a drop-down list.

- *In action*

- *Event*

  SelectedIndexChanged—Raised when a new value is selected in the ComboBox.
- *Properties*

  DataSource—Specifies the source of the items displayed in a ComboBox.

  DropDownStyle—Determines the ComboBox's style.

  Enabled—Determines whether the user can enter data (True) in the ComboBox or not (False).

  Items—Collection containing the values displayed in a ComboBox.

  Location—Specifies the location of the ComboBox control relative to the top-left corner of the container (e.g., a Form or a GroupBox).

  MaxDropDownItems—Determines the maximum number of items to be displayed when the user clicks the drop-down arrow.

  Name—Specifies the name used to access the ComboBox control programmatically. The name should be appended with the ComboBox suffix.

  SelectedItem—Contains the item selected by the user.

  TabIndex—Specifies the order in which focus is transferred to controls when *Tab* is pressed.

  TabStop—Specifies whether the user can select the control using the *Tab* key.

  Text—Specifies the text displayed in the ComboBox.

TextBox   ▣ TextBox   This control allows the user to input data from the keyboard.

- *In action*

  | 0 |

- *Event*

  TextChanged—Raised when the text in the TextBox is changed.
- *Properties*

  Enabled—Determines whether the user can enter data in the TextBox or not.

  Location—Specifies the location of the TextBox control relative to the top-left corner of the container (e.g., a Form or a GroupBox).

  MaxLength—Specifies the maximum number of characters that can be input into the TextBox.

  Multiline—Specifies whether the TextBox is capable of displaying multiple lines of text.

  Name—Specifies the name used to access the TextBox programmatically. The name should be appended with the TextBox suffix.

PasswordChar—Specifies the masking character to be used when displaying data in the TextBox.

ReadOnly—Determines whether the value of a TextBox can be changed.

ScrollBars—Specifies whether a multiline TextBox contains a scrollbar.

Size—Specifies the width and height (in pixels) of the TextBox.

TabIndex—Specifies the order in which focus is transferred to controls when *Tab* is pressed.

TabStop—Specifies whether the user can select the control using the *Tab* key.

Text—Specifies the text displayed in the TextBox.

TextAlign—Specifies how the text is aligned within the TextBox.

■ *Methods*

Focus—Transfers the focus of the app to the TextBox that calls it.

Clear—Empties the TextBox on which it's called.

MULTIPLE-CHOICE QUESTIONS

20.1 _____ are specifically designed to store groups of values.

a) Collections

b) Properties

c) Accessors

d) None of the above

20.2 The _____ key provides a quick and convenient way to navigate through controls on a Form.

a) *Tab*

b) *Enter*

c) *Caps Lock*

d) *Alt*

20.3 A List differs from an array in that a List can _____.

a) store objects of any type

b) resize itself dynamically

c) be accessed programmatically

d) Both (b) and (c)

20.4 The element in a For Each...Next statement _____.

a) must be of type Integer

b) must be of (or convertible to) the same type as the group elements

c) must be of type List

d) None of the above

20.5 The control that receives the focus the first time *Tab* is pressed has a TabIndex property set to _____.

a) First

b) the lowest value

c) Next

d) None of the above

20.6 Users should be able to use the *Tab* key to transfer the focus to _____.

a) only Buttons

b) only TextBoxes

c) only controls that have an AcceptTab property

d) only the controls that receive user input

20.7 To ensure that the proper controls obtain the focus when the *Tab* key is pressed, use the _____.

a) TabIndex property

b) TabStop and TabIndex properties

c) TabStop property

d) Focus property

20.8 To add a value to the end of a List, call the _____ method.

a) Add

b) AddToEnd

c) AddAt

d) InsertAt

20.9 To remove a value from a specific index in the List, use method _____.

a) Remove

b) RemoveAt

c) Delete

d) DeleteAt

20.10 A LINQ query can be used _____ .

a) to select elements from a collection   b) in a For Each...Next statement

c) to select elements from an array   d) All of the above

EXERCISES

20.11 (*Modified Shipping Hub App*) Modify the **Shipping Hub** app created in this chapter, so that the user can double click a package in the packagesListBox. When a package number is double clicked, the package's information should be displayed in a MessageBox (Fig. 20.28).

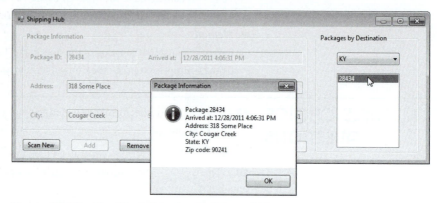

Figure 20.28   Modified **Shipping Hub** app GUI.

a) *Copying the template to your working directory.* Copy the directory C:\Examples\ ch20\Exercises\ShippingHubModified to your C:\SimplyVB2010 directory.

b) *Opening the app's template file.* Double click ShippingHubModified.sln in the ShippingHubModified directory to open the app.

c) *Viewing the event handler.* Click **ShippingHub.vb** in the **Solution Explorer** and select **View > Code**. Scroll to the end of the code listing to locate the ListBox's DoubleClick event handler. A ListBox's DoubleClick event is raised when the control is double clicked.

d) *Initializing necessary variables.* Create a reference of type Package to hold the Package selected from the List. Create a String variable to store the information about the given package. Write code in the DoubleClick event handler to declare the Package tempPackage and the String packageInfo.

e) *Writing a LINQ query.* Create a LINQ query that selects from list the Package with the PackageNumber that's selected in the ListBox. Create an Integer variable to store the number selected in the ListBox and use that variable in your LINQ query. Do *not* initialize the Integer variable yet.

f) *Checking whether the user has selected a valid item.* To determine whether the user has selected a valid item (and not an empty element in the ListBox), write an If...Then statement to make sure that an item is selected in the ListBox. [*Hint:* A SelectedIndex value of -1 means that no item is currently selected.]

g) *Retrieving the correct Package.* If a valid item is selected from the ListBox, assign the selected package ID number to the Integer variable you created in *Step e*. Assign to tempPackage the first element in the query results. Use the query's First property to access this element. Each Package has a unique PackageNumber—only one Package is returned by the query. However, the query returns an IEnumerable from which you must explicitly select the first item to assign it to a reference of type Package. Place all the package information in the String you declared in *Step d*.

h) *Inserting the Else statement.* Create an Else statement to notify the user if an invalid item has been selected from the ListBox. If this occurs, add a message to the packageInfo String displayed in the MessageBox.

i) *Displaying the MessageBox.* Call the MessageBox's Show method to display the text you've added to the packageInfo String. This displays either the information for the package selected or a message stating that an invalid package has been selected.

j) *Running the app.* Select **Debug > Start Debugging** to run your app. Add several packages. In the **Packages by Destination** GroupBox, select a state for which there are packages being sent. Double click one of the packages listed in the **Packages by Destination** ListBox, and verify that the correct information is displayed in a MessageBox.

k) *Closing the app.* Close your running app by clicking its close box.

l) *Closing the IDE.* Close the Visual Basic IDE by clicking its close box.

20.12 *(Controls Collection App)* Visual Basic provides many different types of collections. One such collection is the Controls collection, which provides access to all of the controls on a Form. Create an app that uses the Controls collection and a For Each...Next loop to iterate through each control on the Form. As each control is encountered, add its name to a ListBox, and change the control's background color.

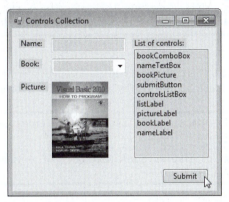

Figure 20.29   Controls Collection GUI.

a) *Copying the template to your working directory.* Copy the directory C:\Examples\ ch20\Exercises\ControlsCollection to your C:\SimplyVB2010 directory.

b) *Opening the app's template file.* Double click ControlsCollection.sln in the ControlsCollection directory to open the app.

c) *Generating an event handler.* Switch to **Design** view. Double click the **Submit** Button to create an event handler for the Click event.

d) *Declaring a control variable.* Declare a reference of type Control. This reference represents each element in the For Each...Next statement as it iterates through each Control on the Form.

e) *Clearing the ListBox.* To ensure that the information in the ListBox is updated each time the **Submit** Button is clicked, clear the ListBox of all items.

f) *Writing a For Each...Next statement.* To create the For Each...Next statement, use the control variable that you created to iterate through the Form's Controls collection.

g) *Adding each control's name to the ListBox.* Use the ListBox's Items.Add method to insert the name of each control on the Form. Recall that a control's Name property contains the name of the control.

h) *Changing the control's background color.* Use the Control's BackColor property to change its background color. Set the property to a new color using a member of the Color structure. [*Hint:* Type the word Color followed by the member-access operator to display a list of predefined colors using the *IntelliSense* feature.] Note that the color of the PictureBox does not appear to change, because its image displays in the control's foreground.

i) *Running the app.* Select **Debug > Start Debugging** to run your app. Click the **Submit** Button. Verify that the controls' background colors change, and that all the controls are listed in the **List of controls:** ListBox.

j) *Closing the app.* Close your running app by clicking its close box.

k) *Closing the IDE.* Close the Visual Basic IDE by clicking its close box.

What does this code do? ▶ **20.13** What is the result of executing the following code?

```
1  Dim listItem As Integer
2  Dim output As String = String.Empty
3
4  Dim list As New System.Collections.Generic.List(Of Integer)()
5  list.Add(1)
6  list.Add(3)
7  list.Add(5)
8
9  For Each listItem In list
10     output &= (" " & listItem)
11  Next
12
13  MessageBox.Show(output, "Mystery", _
14     MessageBoxButtons.OK, MessageBoxIcon.Information)
```

What's wrong with this code? ▶ **20.14** This code should iterate through an array of Packages in list and display each package's number in displayLabel. Find the error(s) in the following code.

```
1  Dim value As System.Collections.Generic.List(Of Package)
2
3  For Each value In list
4     displayLabel.Text &= (" " & value.PackageNumber)
5  Next
```

Programming Challenge ▶ **20.15** *(Enhanced Shipping Hub App)* Enhance the **Shipping Hub** app created in Exercise 20.11 to allow the user to move a maximum of five packages from the warehouse to a truck for shipping (Fig. 20.30). If you have not completed Exercise 20.11, follow the steps in Exercise 20.11 before proceeding with this exercise. If you've completed Exercise 20.11, copy the code you added to the packagesListBox DoubleClick event handler to the same event handler in this app before beginning this exercise.

a) *Copying the template to your working directory.* Copy the directory C:\Examples\ch20\Exercises\ShippingHubEnhanced to your C:\SimplyVB2010 directory.

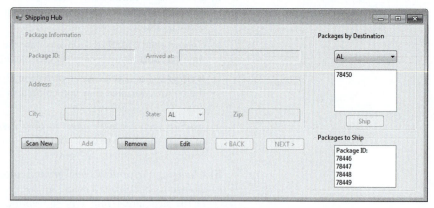

Figure 20.30 Enhanced **Shipping Hub** GUI.

b) *Opening the app's template file.* Double click ShippingHubEnhanced.sln in the ShippingHubEnhanced directory to open the app.

c) *Enabling the Ship Button.* The **Ship** Button should not be enabled until a package is selected in packageListBox. Double click packageListBox in **Design** view to define its SelectedIndexChanged event handler. Use the Button's Enabled property to enable the Button if the SelectedIndex of the ListBox is not -1. This means that when the user selects a package from the ListBox, the user can send it to the truck by clicking the **Ship** Button. Also, insert a line of code after the For Each...

Next statement in the viewPackagesComboBox_SelectedIndexChanged event handler to disable the **Ship** Button when a user chooses a different state.

d) *Defining the Ship Button's Click Event.* Double click the **Ship** Button in **Design** view to define the Click event handler.

e) *Creating temporary variables.* Create two temporary Package references to store the correct package's information. Use tempPackage as the reference to the element in the collection of a For Each...Next statement, and truckPackage as a reference to the package added to the truck.

f) *Using the If...Then...Else statement.* Use an If...Then...Else statement to allow packages to be placed onto the truck if the number of packages on the truck is less than five.

g) *Using a LINQ query.* Use a LINQ query to select from list the Package whose PackageNumber is selected in the ListBox. Assign the selected Package to the truckPackage reference.

h) *Adding the package to the truck.* Add the selected Package to the truck by adding the reference to truckPackage to the truck's List, truckList.

i) *Removing the package.* Use List's Remove method to delete the Package meant for the truck from list. Also remove the Package's PackageNumber from packagesListBox.

j) *Displaying the Packages in the **Packages to Ship** ListBox.* Clear the truckListBox, then add "Package ID:" as a header. Use a For Each...Next statement that iterates through each Package in truckList and displays each Package's PackageNumber in truckListBox.

k) *Refreshing the GUI.* Call the ClearControls and SetButtons methods to clear the TextBoxes and enable the appropriate Buttons. Set the **Ship** Button's Enabled property to False.

l) *Coding the Else statement.* Display a MessageBox that notifies the user if the number of packages on the truck is already five. Then disable the **Ship** Button.

m) *Running the app.* Select **Debug > Start Debugging** to run your app. Add several packages. Add several Packages to the **Packages to Ship** ListBox. Verify that you can add only five Packages to this ListBox.

n) *Closing the app.* Close your running app by clicking its close box.

o) *Closing the IDE.* Close the Visual Basic IDE by clicking its close box.

21

Typing App

Introducing Keyboard Events, Menus, Dialogs and the Dictionary Collection

Text-editor apps enable you to perform many tasks, from writing e-mails to creating business proposals. These apps often use menus and dialogs to help you customize the appearance of your document. They also respond to keys pressed on the keyboard either by displaying characters or by performing *actions* (such as accessing menus or dialogs). In this chapter, you'll learn how to handle **keyboard events**, which occur when keys on the keyboard are pressed and released. Handling keyboard events allows you to specify the action that the app is to take when a particular key is pressed. When you handle the key events in this app, you'll use LINQ to Objects, the Form's Controls collection and a Dictionary collection to locate the correct Button to highlight on the GUI. You'll then learn how to add menus to your app. By now, you're familiar with using various menus and dialogs provided by Windows apps. You'll learn to create menus that group related commands and allow the user to select various actions to perform in the app. Finally, you'll learn about the **Font** and **Color** dialogs, which allow the user to change the appearance of text in the app.

21.1 Test-Driving the Typing App

In this chapter, you'll create a **Typing** App to help students learn how to type. This app must meet the following requirements:

> ### App Requirements
>
> *A high-school course teaches students how to type. The instructor would like to use a Windows app that allows students to watch what they're typing on the screen without looking at the keyboard. You've been asked to create an app that displays what the student types. The app has to display a virtual keyboard that highlights any key the student presses on the real keyboard. This app must also contain menu commands for selecting the font style and color of the text displayed, clearing the text displayed and inverting the background and foreground colors of the display.*

This app allows the user to type text. As the user presses each key, the app highlights the corresponding key on the GUI and adds the character to a TextBox. The user can select the color and style of the characters typed, invert the background and foreground colors and clear the TextBox. You'll begin by test-driving the completed app. Then you'll learn the additional Visual Basic capabilities that you'll need to create your own version of this app.

Test-Driving the Typing App

1. **Opening the completed app.** Open the directory C:\Examples\ch21\CompletedApp\Typing to locate the **Typing** app. Double click Typing.sln to open the app in the Visual Basic IDE.

2. **Running the Typing App.** Select **Debug > Start Debugging** to run the app. Once the app has loaded, type the sentence "Programming in Visual Basic is simple." As you type, the corresponding keys light up on the Form's virtual keyboard and the text is displayed in the TextBox (Fig. 21.1). [*Note:* This app assumes that only one key is pressed at a time; however, capital letters do work.]

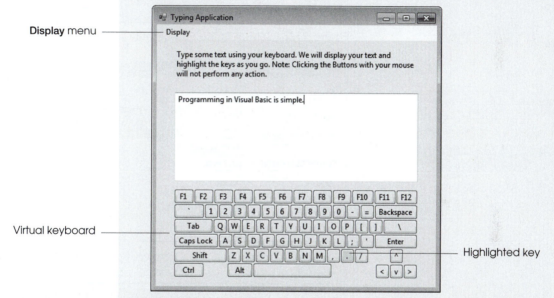

Figure 21.1 **Typing** app with key pressed.

3. **Changing the font.** Select **Display > Text > Font...** (Fig. 21.2) to open the **Font** dialog shown in Fig. 21.3. Note that the access keys for the menu items are *not* underlined by default. As you learned in Section 20.4, you can press the *Alt* key to display the access keys. The **Font** dialog allows you to choose the font style for the app's output. Select Segoe UI from the **Font:** ComboBox, select Bold from the **Font style:** ComboBox and select 11 from the **Size:** ComboBox. Click the **OK** Button. The text you typed in *Step 2* is now bold and bigger.

4. **Changing the color of the font.** Select **Display > Text > Color...** to display the **Color** dialog (Fig. 21.4). This dialog allows you to choose the color of the text displayed. Select a color, and click **OK**.

(cont.)

Menu item ——————

Submenu ——————

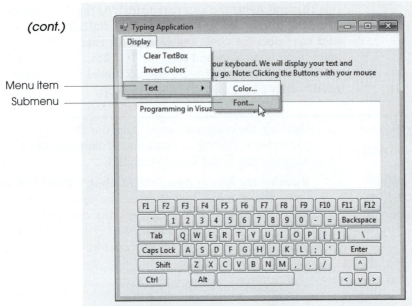

Figure 21.2   Selecting the **Font...** menu item.

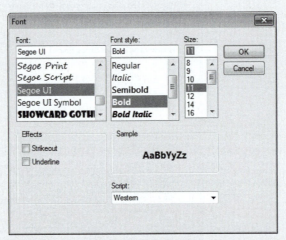

Figure 21.3   **Font** dialog displayed when **Display > Text > Font...** is selected.

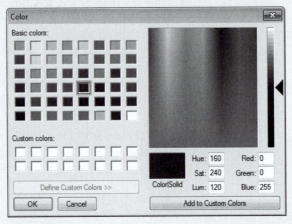

Figure 21.4   **Color** dialog displayed when **Display > Text > Color...** is selected.

(cont.)   5. ***Inverting the background and foreground colors.*** Select **Display > Invert Colors** (Fig. 21.5). This option allows you to swap the background and foreground colors. The result is shown in Fig. 21.6.

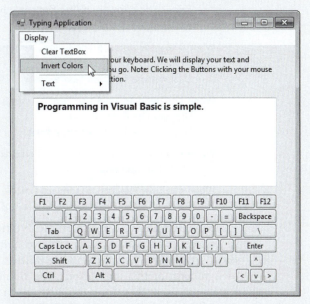

Figure 21.5   Selecting the **Invert Colors** menu item.

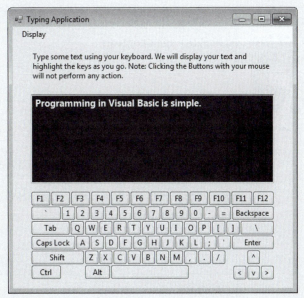

Figure 21.6   Output with colors inverted.

6. ***Clearing the TextBox.*** Select **Display > Clear TextBox** to remove all the text from the TextBox.

7. ***Closing the app.*** Close your running app by clicking its close box.

8. ***Closing the IDE.*** Close the Visual Basic IDE by clicking its close box.

21.2 Analyzing the Typing App

Before you begin building the **Typing** app, you should analyze the app's components. The following pseudocode describes the basic operation of the **Typing** app:

> When the user presses a key while the TextBox has the focus:
>> Highlight the corresponding Button on the GUI
>
> When the user releases a key:
>> Reset the corresponding Button's background color to the Button's default background color
>
> When the user selects the Color... menu item:
>> Display the Color dialog
>> Update the TextBox text's color
>
> When the user selects the Font... menu item:
>> Display the Font dialog
>> Update the TextBox text's font
>
> When the user selects the Clear TextBox menu item:
>> Clear the TextBox
>
> When the user selects the Invert Colors menu item:
>> Swap the TextBox's background and foreground colors

Now that you've test-driven the **Typing** app and studied its pseudocode representation, you'll use an ACE table to help you convert the pseudocode to Visual Basic. Figure 21.7 lists the *actions*, *controls* and *events* that help you complete your own version of this app. [*Note:* The number of `Buttons` is large and no `Button` events are used; therefore, the `Buttons` in the virtual keyboard are *not* included in the ACE table.]

Action/Control/Event (ACE) Table for the Typing App	Action	Control	Event
	Label the app's controls	`promptLabel`, keyboard `Buttons`	App is run
		`outputTextBox`	`KeyPress`, `KeyDown`
	Highlight the corresponding Button on the GUI	keyboard `Buttons`	
		`outputTextBox`	`KeyUp`
	Reset the corresponding Button's background color to the Button's default background color	keyboard `Buttons`	
		`colorMenuItem`	`Click`
	Display the Color dialog	`dialog`	
	Update the TextBox text's color	`outputTextBox`	
		`fontMenuItem`	`Click`
	Display the Font dialog	`dialog`	
	Update the TextBox text's font	`outputTextBox`	
		`clearMenuItem`	`Click`
	Clear the TextBox	`outputTextBox`	
		`invertMenuItem`	`Click`
	Swap the TextBox's background and foreground colors	`outputTextBox`	

Figure 21.7 ACE table for the **Typing** App.

21.3 Keyboard Events

You'll now learn to handle keyboard events, which occur when keys on the keyboard are pressed and released. All keyboard events are raised by the control that currently has the focus. In the **Typing** app, these events are raised by the TextBox control. You'll first learn about the outputTextBox's **KeyDown** event, which occurs when a key is pressed while the outputTextBox has the focus. In the following box, you'll insert the code to handle the event when the user presses a key. This event handler processes control keys (e.g., *Shift*, *Enter*, *Tab*), function keys (e.g., *F1*, *F2*) and the arrow keys only. You'll learn to process the letter, digit and symbol keys in a subsequent box.

Coding the KeyDown Event Handler	1. ***Copying the template to your working directory.*** Copy the C:\Examples\ch21\TemplateApp\Typing directory to your working directory C:\SimplyVB2010.
	2. ***Opening the Typing app's template file.*** Double click Typing.sln in the Typing directory to open the app in the Visual Basic IDE.
	3. ***Determining whether the pressed key is a control key, function key or arrow key.*** Add lines 10–11 of Fig. 21.8 to your code, then press *Enter* to add the End If keywords.

Determine whether the pressed key is a control key, function key or arrow key

```
5     ' handles TextBox's KeyDown Event
6     Private Sub outputTextBox_KeyDown(sender As Object,
7        e As System.Windows.Forms.KeyEventArgs) _
8        Handles outputTextBox.KeyDown
9
10       If Char.IsControl(Convert.ToChar(e.KeyCode)) OrElse
11          IsFunctionOrArrowKey(e.KeyCode) Then
12
13       End If
14    End Sub ' OutputTextBox_KeyDown
```

Figure 21.8 Determining whether the pressed key is a control key, function key or arrow key.

When a key is pressed, the KeyDown event is raised for the control that has the focus. As you've seen in previous chapters, event handlers specify two parameters—sender and e. The **sender** Object is the GUI component that raised the event (this is also known as the source of the event), and e contains data for the event. In this case, e (which is of type **KeyEventArgs**) contains a **KeyCode** property (used in lines 10–11) that specifies which key was pressed as a value from the Keys enumeration.

The **Keys enumeration** represents keyboard keys using meaningful names. Recall that enumerations are used to assign meaningful names to constant values. In this case, each value in the Keys enumeration is an Integer that represents a key. In the method IsFunctionOrArrowKey (lines 69–82 of Fig. 21.9), Keys.F1 and Keys.F12 (line 73) represent the *F1* and *F12* keys, respectively. Similarly, Keys.Up, Keys.Down, Keys.Left and Keys.Right (line 75) represent the four arrow keys. You can find a listing of the constants in the Keys enumeration at http://msdn.microsoft.com/en-us/library/system.windows.forms.keys.aspx.

Line 10 uses the Char structure's **IsControl** method to determine whether the pressed key is a control character. This method receives a Char as an argument, so you convert e.KeyCode to a Char with Convert method ToChar. Line 11 calls method IsFunctionOrArrowKey in the template code to determine whether the key pressed is a function or arrow key.

(cont.)

```
68        ' determine whether pressed key is a function or arrow key
69        Function IsFunctionOrArrowKey(code As Keys) As Boolean
70           Dim result As Boolean
71
72           Select Case code
73              Case Keys.F1 To Keys.F12
74                 result = True
75              Case Keys.Up, Keys.Down, Keys.Left, Keys.Right
76                 result = True
77              Case Else
78                 result = False ' not a match
79           End Select
80
81           Return result
82        End Function ' IsFunctionOrArrowKey
```

Figure 21.9 Method `IsFunctionOrArrowKey` provided in the template.

4. ***Determining which Button to highlight using LINQ to Objects***. Add lines 13–21 of Fig. 21.10 to the `If` statement in Fig. 21.8. Line 14 declares variable `pressed`. Visual Basic *infers* the type of this variable from the result of the LINQ expression (lines 15–21).

Using LINQ to Objects to query the Form's `Controls` collection and locate the `Button` that matches the pressed key

```
10        If Char.IsControl(Convert.ToChar(e.KeyCode)) OrElse
11           IsFunctionOrArrowKey(e.KeyCode) Then
12
13           ' locate the Button representing the pressed key with LINQ
14           Dim pressed =
15              From currentControl In Me.Controls
16              Where TypeOf currentControl Is Button AndAlso
17                 keyDictionary.ContainsKey(
18                    e.KeyCode.ToString()) AndAlso
19                 keyDictionary(e.KeyCode.ToString()) =
20                    CType(currentControl, Button).Text
21              Select currentControl
22        End If
```

Figure 21.10 Using LINQ to locate the `Button` that matches the pressed key.

Line 15 iterates through the controls in the `Form`'s `Controls` collection. Recall that Visual Basic infers the type of the LINQ query's range variable (`currentControl`). Lines 16–20 specify the criteria for selecting a control from the collection. The expression

```
TypeOf currentControl Is Button
```

uses a `TypeOf...Is` expression (line 16)—which determines whether `currentControl` is a `Button`. The `Controls` collection contains the controls placed directly on the `Form`, but the app changes the background color of only the `Button` controls. The preceding expression ensures that only `Button`s are selected. [*Note:* A control is part of the `Controls` collection of the container in which the control is placed. The LINQ query assumes that all of the controls are placed directly on the `Form`, not in nested containers (e.g., `GroupBox`es or `Panel`s).]

(cont.)   The rest of the condition (lines 17–20) uses a `Dictionary` collection to help map the pressed key's `KeyCode` to the `Text` of a `Button` in the GUI. A `Dictionary` is a collection of key/value pairs. The key in the pair is used to determine the storage location for the corresponding value and to locate that value when it's required later for use in the app. In the template code for this app, we provided you with a predefined `Dictionary` named `keyDictionary` that maps the `String` representations of various control-key, function-key and arrow-key `KeyCodes` to the `Strings` that appear on the `Buttons` representing those keys in the GUI.

Line 3 in the code

```
Private keyDictionary As New Dictionary(Of String, String)
```

defines instance variable `keyDictionary` and assigns it a new `Dictionary` that stores pairs of `Strings`. When you define a `Dictionary`, you must specify the types of its keys and its values, similar to how you declared the type of elements stored in a `List` in Chapter 20. The keys and values are not required to be the same type.

The Form's `Load` event handler (Fig. 21.11) uses `Dictionary` method **Add** to insert *key/value pairs* in `keyDictionary`. Lines 59–61 add pairs of `Strings` representing the function keys. The `String` representation of a function key's `KeyCode` is the same as the text on the function key and the text on the GUI's corresponding `Button`. So, the key/value pair for the *F1* key consists of the `Strings` "F1" and "F1". Lines 64–74 add key/value pairs for the control keys and arrow keys in the GUI. The first argument to each call to `Add` is the `String` representation of the `KeyCode` and the second is the text on the corresponding `Button` in the GUI.

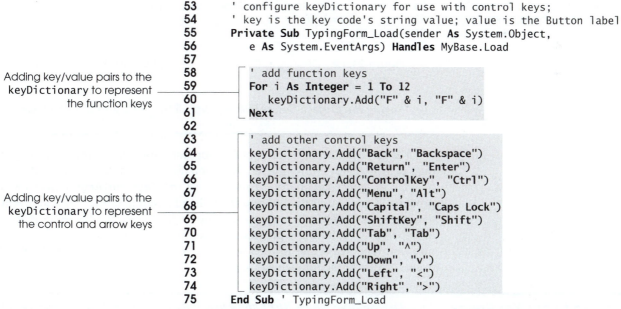

Adding key/value pairs to the `keyDictionary` to represent the function keys

Adding key/value pairs to the `keyDictionary` to represent the control and arrow keys

```
53      ' configure keyDictionary for use with control keys;
54      ' key is the key code's string value; value is the Button label
55      Private Sub TypingForm_Load(sender As System.Object,
56         e As System.EventArgs) Handles MyBase.Load
57
58         ' add function keys
59         For i As Integer = 1 To 12
60            keyDictionary.Add("F" & i, "F" & i)
61         Next
62
63         ' add other control keys
64         keyDictionary.Add("Back", "Backspace")
65         keyDictionary.Add("Return", "Enter")
66         keyDictionary.Add("ControlKey", "Ctrl")
67         keyDictionary.Add("Menu", "Alt")
68         keyDictionary.Add("Capital", "Caps Lock")
69         keyDictionary.Add("ShiftKey", "Shift")
70         keyDictionary.Add("Tab", "Tab")
71         keyDictionary.Add("Up", "^")
72         keyDictionary.Add("Down", "v")
73         keyDictionary.Add("Left", "<")
74         keyDictionary.Add("Right", ">")
75      End Sub ' TypingForm_Load
```

Figure 21.11   Adding key/value pairs to the `keyDictionary`.

Lines 17–18 in the LINQ expression's `Where` clause (Fig. 21.10) use the `Dictionary`'s **ContainsKey** method to determine whether the `KeyCode`'s `String` representation appears as a key in the `Dictionary`, in which case the method returns `True`. Lines 19–20

```
keyDictionary(e.KeyCode.ToString()) =
   CType(currentControl, Button).Text
```

(cont.)

get the `String` representation of the `KeyCode` and use it as a key in the `Dictionary` to obtain the corresponding value. Next, the value is compared with the `currentControl`'s `Text` property. If they match, the LINQ expression selects the control (line 21). For example, if the user presses *F5* and the `String "F5"` matches the text on one of the `Buttons` in the GUI, the LINQ query selects the control. The **`CType`** operator (line 20) converts a variable to another type. The `Controls` collection represents each control as a reference of type `Control`, so variable `currentControl`'s type is `Control`. The expression `CType(currentControl, Button)` converts the variable's type to `Button`, so the `Button`'s `Text` property can be used in the code. An exception is raised if `CType` cannot convert the specified object to the specified type (we discuss exceptions in detail in Chapter 24). However, you know this conversion will succeed because the `Where` clause has already checked that `currentControl` is of type `Button`.

5. ***Changing the color of a Button.*** Add lines 23–25 of Fig. 21.12 inside the end of the `If` statement in Fig. 21.10. Line 23 determines whether the collection returned by the LINQ expression (`pressed`) contains any elements. If it does, line 24 calls method `ChangeColor` (provided in the template code) to change the `Button`'s background color to yellow. The expression `pressed.First` represents the first item in the LINQ result. Recall from Chapter 20 that a LINQ query returns a collection of items that match the criteria in the `Where` clause. Again, the type of this item is `Control`, so `CType` is used to convert it to a `Button`.

If there's a **Button** that matches
the pressed key, change the
Button's background color

```
21              Select currentControl
22
23            If pressed.Count > 0 Then
24                ChangeColor(CType(pressed.First, Button))
25            End If
26        End If
27    End Sub ' outputTextBox_KeyDown
```

Figure 21.12   Changing the color of the **Button** that corresponds to the pressed key.

6. ***Saving the project.*** Select **File > Save All** to save your modified code.

The KeyDown event handler in this app does not test whether any of the letter, digit or symbol keys were pressed. It's often inconvenient to use the KeyDown event handler to detect keyboard events because the KeyEventArgs object's KeyCode property is case insensitive. If you try to handle letters in the KeyDown event handler, the event's KeyCode property does not indicate whether the letter is lowercase or uppercase. Visual Basic provides the **KeyPress** event handler, which can recognize both uppercase and lowercase letters. You'll learn how to use the KeyPress event handler in the following box.

Coding to the KeyPress Event Handler

1. ***Determining which Button to highlight using LINQ to Objects.*** Add lines 34–40 of Fig. 21.13 to the KeyPress event handler. Line 35 declares variable `pressed`. Once again, Visual Basic infers the type of this variable from the result of the LINQ expression (lines 36–40).

(cont.)

Using LINQ to Objects to query the Form's Controls collection and locate the Button that matches the pressed key

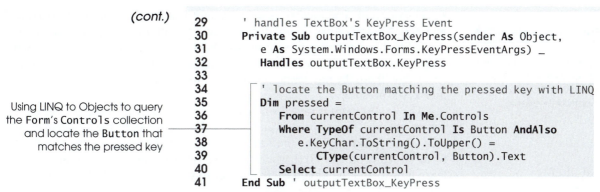

```
29        ' handles TextBox's KeyPress Event
30        Private Sub outputTextBox_KeyPress(sender As Object,
31           e As System.Windows.Forms.KeyPressEventArgs) _
32           Handles outputTextBox.KeyPress
33
34           ' locate the Button matching the pressed key with LINQ
35           Dim pressed =
36              From currentControl In Me.Controls
37              Where TypeOf currentControl Is Button AndAlso
38                 e.KeyChar.ToString().ToUpper() =
39                    CType(currentControl, Button).Text
40              Select currentControl
41        End Sub ' outputTextBox_KeyPress
```

Figure 21.13 Determining the Button that matches the pressed key.

Line 36 iterates through the Form's Controls collection. Lines 37–39 specify the criteria for selecting a control from the collection. The first part of the condition (line 37) determines whether the currentControl is a Button. Lines 38–39 determine whether the uppercase version of the pressed key matches the currentControl's Text property. Variable e refers to the KeyPressEventArgs object that's passed as an argument to the event handler. Property KeyChar is a Char that represents the character on the key that was pressed. Method ToUpper converts the String representation of the KeyChar property to uppercase. This conversion is necessary because the Text properties of the Buttons are uppercase and String comparisons are case sensitive in Visual Basic by default. If both parts of the condition are true, the currentControl is selected (line 40).

2. ***Changing the color of a Button.*** Add lines 42–48 of Fig. 21.14 to your code. Line 42 determines whether the KeyChar contains a space. If so, the space bar was pressed and line 43 calls ChangeColor with spaceButton as an argument. Line 45 determines whether the collection returned by the LINQ expression contains any elements. If so, line 46 calls method ChangeColor to change the corresponding Button's background color to yellow. Recall that a LINQ query does *not* execute until you access its results (line 45).

If the KeyChar is a space, change the background color of the Button that represents the space bar

If there's a Button that matches the pressed key, change the Button's background color

```
40                 Select currentControl
41
42           If e.KeyChar = " " Then ' if user pressed spacebar
43              ChangeColor(spaceButton)
44           Else
45              If pressed.Count > 0 Then
46                 ChangeColor(CType(pressed.First, Button))
47              End If
48           End If
49        End Sub ' outputTextBox_KeyPress
```

Figure 21.14 Changing the color of the Button that corresponds to the pressed key.

3. ***Running the app.*** Select **Debug > Start Debugging** to run your app. As you type, the Button corresponding to the key you press on the keyboard is highlighted and the text is added to the TextBox. The characters typed are added to the TextBox as part of its built-in key processing. Notice that the Button remains highlighted until another key is pressed.

4. ***Saving the project.*** Select **File > Save All** to save your modified code.

You may be wondering why you could not just use the KeyPress event handler to test for all of the keys on the keyboard. Control keys, such as *F1*, do not raise the

Software Design Tip

Use the `KeyPress` event handler for letter and number key events. Use the `KeyDown` event handler for modifier and control key events.

`KeyPress` event. The `KeyPress` event cannot test for the modifier keys (*Ctrl*, *Shift* and *Alt*). **Modifier keys** do *not* display characters on the keyboard but can be used to modify the way that apps respond to a keyboard event. For instance, pressing the *Shift* key while pressing a letter in a text editor displays the uppercase form of the letter. You'll use the `KeyDown` event handler to handle the event raised when a modifier key is pressed.

The **KeyUp** event is raised when a key is released by the user. It's raised regardless of whether the key press is handled by the `KeyPress` or the `KeyDown` event handler. The **Typing** app uses the `KeyUp` event handler to remove the highlight color from `Button`s on the GUI when the user releases the corresponding key. You'll learn how to add the `KeyUp` event handler to your app in the following box.

Creating the KeyUp Event Handler

1. ***Creating the KeyUp event handler.*** An empty `KeyUp` event handler is provided, to maintain clarity in the template app. However, if you want to generate `KeyUp`, `KeyDown` or `KeyPress` event handlers for other controls, begin by selecting the control for which you wish to add the event handler. In the **Typing** app select `outputTextbox` from the **Class Name** ComboBox in the top-left corner of the code editor. Then select the appropriate event handler from the **Method Name** ComboBox in the top-right corner of the code editor, as shown in Fig. 21.15. When you select an event name from the **Method Name** ComboBox, that event handler is generated in your code if it does not exist; otherwise, the IDE displays the existing event handler.

Class Name ComboBox ————

Method Name ComboBox drop-down list ————

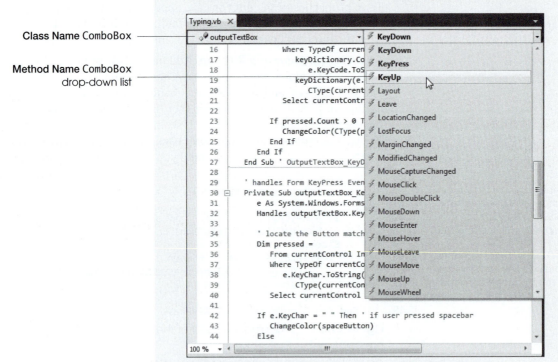

Figure 21.15 Generating the `KeyUp` event handler.

2. ***Writing code in the KeyUp event handler.*** Insert line 56 of Fig. 21.16 in your app. The `KeyUp` event handler executes whenever a key is released—therefore, you need to change the color of the released `Button` back to that `Button`'s default color. Line 56 calls `ResetColor`, provided for you in the template, to perform this action.

3. ***Running the app.*** Select **Debug > Start Debugging** to run your app. Notice that the highlighting is removed when the key is released.

(cont.)

Resetting a **Button**'s color
after a key is released —

```
52        Private Sub outputTextBox_KeyUp(sender As Object,
53            e As System.Windows.Forms.KeyEventArgs) _
54            Handles outputTextBox.KeyUp
55
56            ResetColor()
57        End Sub ' outputTextBox_KeyUp
```

Figure 21.16   Resetting a **Button**'s color when its key is released.

4. **Saving the project.** Select **File > Save All** to save your modified code.

Next, you'll examine the `ResetColor` method that we provided for you in the template. This method uses the `IsNot` operator—a helpful tool for determining whether a reference type variable refers to an object or contains the `Nothing` reference.

SELF-REVIEW   1. A _____ event is raised when a key on the keyboard is pressed or released.

a) keyboard   b) `KeyDownEvent`

c) `KeyChar`   d) `KeyUpEvent`

2. The _____ event is raised when a key is released.

a) `KeyEventUp`   b) `KeyRelease`

c) `KeyUp`   d) None of the above

Answers: 1) a. 2) c.

21.4 IsNot Operator

In Chapter 19, you learned how to create classes and objects of those classes. You also learned that you can use variables that store references to objects, known as reference type variables, to interact with those objects. Sometimes it's useful to know whether a reference type variable contains a reference to an object or it currently contains a `Nothing` reference, so that you can determine whether the variable can be used to manipulate an object. You can use the `IsNot` operator to compare a reference type variable's value to the value `Nothing`. Such a condition evaluates to `True` if the variable refers to an object—otherwise, the condition evaluates to `False`. You can also use `IsNot` to compare two reference type variables to determine whether or not they refer to the same object. If they do not, the condition evaluates to `True`; otherwise, `False`.

Figure 21.17 shows the `ResetColor` method that you called to restore the color of a `Button` when the corresponding key is released. Line 68 uses the `IsNot` operator to ensure that `lastButton`—an instance variable used to store the previously pressed `Button`—actually refers to a `Button`. If `lastButton` does not refer to a `Button` object, line 69 will not execute.

```
66        ' changes lastButton's color if it refers to a Button
67        Private Sub ResetColor()
68            If lastButton IsNot Nothing Then
69                lastButton.BackColor = SystemColors.Control
70            End If
71        End Sub ' ResetColor
```

Figure 21.17   `IsNot` operator inside the `ResetColor` method

Your app highlights the corresponding `Button`s, displays the output in a Text-Box, and changes the `Button`s back to their normal color, so that the user can see what they're typing. Now you'll allow the user to alter the appearance of the text in the TextBox. To do this, you'll use the **MenuStrip** control, which creates a menu that allows the user to select various options to format the TextBox.

21.5 Menus

Menus allow you to group related commands for GUI apps. Although most menus and commands vary among apps, some—such as **Open** and **Save**—are common to many apps. Menus are an important part of GUIs because they organize commands without cluttering the GUI. In this section, you'll learn how to enhance the **Typing** app by adding menus that allow the user to control how to display text in the Text-Box.

Creating a Menu

1. *Creating a MenuStrip control*. Switch to **Design** view. Double click Menu-Strip in the **Menus & Toolbars** tab of the **Toolbox** to add a MenuStrip to your app (Fig. 21.18). When you do this, a MenuStrip control appears in the component tray. Also, a box that reads **Type Here** appears on the top of your Form. This represents a **menu item**—an item that the user can select in a menu. When you type text in the **Type Here** field, Visual Studio creates a `ToolStripMenuItem` to represent the menu item. To edit menu items, click the **MenuStrip** icon in the component tray, the menu on the Form, or a menu item. This puts the IDE in **Menu Designer mode**, which allows you to create and edit menus and menu items. Change the Name property of the Menu-Strip control to menuBar.

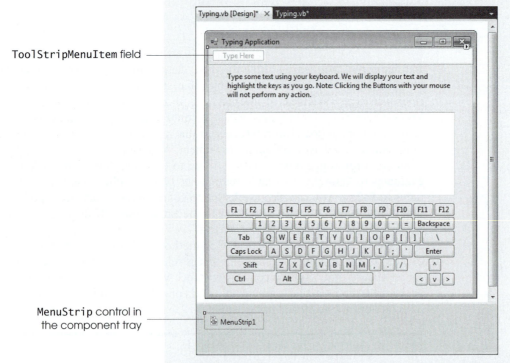

ToolStripMenuItem field

MenuStrip control in the component tray

Figure 21.18   MenuStrip control added to the **Typing** app.

(cont.)

Good Programming Practice

We suggest appending the `Menu-Item` suffix to `ToolStripMenuItem` controls.

GUI Design Tip

Use book-title capitalization in menu-item text.

2. ***Creating the first menu item.*** Click in the **Type Here** box, type `&Display` and press *Enter* (Fig. 21.19). This sets the text to be displayed in that menu item and indicates that the letter D is the access key. Then change the `Name` property of the `ToolstripMenuItem` to `displayMenuItem`. Note that when you click the **Type Here** field, two more fields appear. The field on the right represents a new menu item that can be created to the right of the **Display** menu item. The field below the **Display** menu item represents a menu item that appears when the **Display** menu item is selected. You'll use the **Display** menu item to display all of the options that allow the user to customize the output displayed in the `TextBox`.

Menu item ⎯⎯⎯⎯

Figure 21.19 Creating the **Display** menu.

3. ***Creating additional menu items.*** In the box below the **Display** menu, type `&Clear TextBox`. Set the `Name` property of this menu item to `clearMenu-Item`. Once again, two more boxes appear. Every time you add an item to a menu, these two boxes appear (Fig. 21.20). Entering text in the right box turns the menu item on the left into a submenu. The right box is now a menu item in that submenu. A **submenu** is a menu within another menu. The box that appears on the bottom of the menu allows you to add another item to that menu. Type `&Invert Colors` in the bottom box to add another menu item to the **Display** menu. Set the `Name` property of this menu item to `invertMenuItem`.

4. ***Inserting a separator bar.*** Click the small arrow on the right side of the **Type Here** box to display a drop-down list containing items that may be added to the menu. Select **Separator** from the drop-down list (Fig. 21.21). Note that a **separator bar**, which is a recessed horizontal rule, appears below the **Invert Colors** menu item (Fig. 21.22). Separator bars are used to group submenus and menu items. A separator bar also can be created by typing a hyphen (-) in the `Text` property of a menu item.

5. ***Creating a submenu.*** In the box under the separator bar, type `&Text`. This menu item will contain options to format the appearance of the text displayed in the `TextBox`. Set the `Name` property of this menu item to `text-MenuItem`. All menu items can contain both menu items and submenus. Insert `&Color...` and `&Font...` as menu items in the **Text** submenu, naming them `colorMenuItem` and `fontMenuItem`, respectively (Fig. 21.22).

GUI Design Tip

Use separator bars in a menu to group related menu items.

GUI Design Tip

If clicking a menu item opens a dialog, an ellipsis (...) should follow the menu item's text.

(cont.)

Submenu ———

Submenu item ———

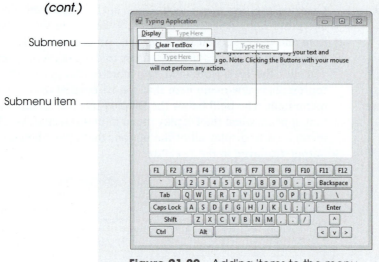

Figure 21.20 Adding items to the menu.

Select **Separator** to
insert a separator bar ———

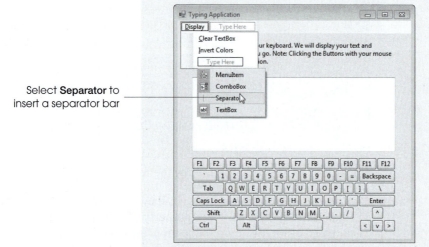

Figure 21.21 Adding a separator bar to group menu items.

Separator bar ———

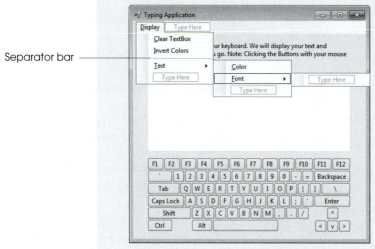

Figure 21.22 Adding a submenu to a menu item.

(cont.)   6. ***Running the app.*** Select **Debug > Start Debugging** to run your app, and select a menu item. At this point, nothing happens, because you have not created event handlers for the menu items.

7. ***Closing the app.*** Close the app by clicking its close box.

Like any other control, a menu item requires an event handler to perform an action when it's clicked. The **Typing** app introduces the **Font** and **Color** dialogs to allow users to customize the appearance of what is being typed. Dialogs allow you to receive input from and display messages to users. You'll learn how to use the **Font** dialog in the following box by displaying it from a menu item's event handler.

Coding the *Font... Menu Item's Click* Event Handler

1. ***Creating an event handler for the Font... menu item.*** In the Windows Form designer, double click the **Font...** menu item that you created to generate its `Click` event handler. Add a comment and reformat the event handler as shown in lines 113–115 of Fig. 21.23.

2. ***Declaring the dialog variables.*** Add lines 117–118 of Fig. 21.23 to your code. Line 117 creates a new `FontDialog` object that allows the user to select the font style to apply to the text. Line 118 declares a variable of type `DialogResult` that stores information indicating which `Button` the user clicked to exit the dialog.

```
113    ' handles Font menu item's Click event
114    Private Sub fontMenuItem_Click(sender As System.Object,
115       e As System.EventArgs) Handles fontMenuItem.Click
116
117    Dim dialog As New FontDialog
118    Dim result As DialogResult ' stores Button clicked
119    End Sub ' fontMenuItem_Click
```

Declaration for the `FontDialog` and its result *(pointing to lines 117–118)*

Figure 21.23 Declarations for the **FontDialog** and its **DialogResult**.

3. ***Displaying the dialog.*** Add lines 120–121 of Fig. 21.24 to your event handler. These lines call the `ShowDialog` method to display the **Font** dialog to the user and assign the return value of `ShowDialog` to variable `result`.

```
118       Dim result As DialogResult ' stores Button clicked
119
120       ' show dialog and get result
121       result = dialog.ShowDialog()
122    End Sub ' fontMenuItem_Click
```

Showing the dialog and assigning the result *(pointing to lines 120–121)*

Figure 21.24 Opening the **Font** dialog.

4. ***Exiting the event handler if the user clicks Cancel.*** Add lines 123–126 of Fig. 21.25 to your app. These lines determine whether the user has clicked the **Font** dialog's **Cancel** Button. Line 124 compares the value stored in `result` with the enumeration value `DialogResult.Cancel`. The `DialogResult` enumeration contains values corresponding to standard dialog `Button` names. This provides a convenient way to determine which `Button` the user has clicked. If the user clicks the **Cancel** Button, no action takes place and the method exits, using the `Return` statement (line 125). Since this method is a Sub procedure, you could also use `Exit Sub` in place of `Return` to exit the method.

(cont.)

Take no action if user cancels ───────

```
121            result = dialog.ShowDialog()
122
123            ' do nothing if user clicked dialog's Cancel Button
124            If result = System.Windows.Forms.DialogResult.Cancel Then
125              Return
126            End If
127         End Sub ' fontMenuItem_Click
```

Figure 21.25   Exit the event handler if the user clicks **Cancel**.

5. ***Setting the font.*** Add lines 128–129 of Fig. 21.26 to give the text the style that the user has selected from the `FontDialog`. This statement immediately updates the font displayed in `outputTextBox`.

Assigning the new font value ─────────

```
126            End If
127
128            ' assign new font value to TextBox
129            outputTextBox.Font = dialog.Font
130         End Sub ' fontMenuItem_Click
```

Figure 21.26   Changing the display font.

6. ***Saving the project.*** Select **File > Save All** to save your modified code.

The user of the **Typing** app should also be able to select the color of the font displayed in the TextBox. You'll learn how to display the **Color** dialog from an event handler in the following box.

***Coding the Color...
Menu Item's `Click`
Event Handler***

1. ***Creating an event handler for the Color... menu item.*** Double click the **Color...** menu item to generate its `Click` event handler. Add a comment and reformat the event handler as shown in lines 132–134 of Fig. 21.27.

2. ***Declaring the dialog variables.*** Add lines 136–137 of Fig. 21.27 to your app. Line 136 creates a new `ColorDialog` object that allows the user to select the color of the text. Line 137 declares a `DialogResult` variable to store the value of the **Button** clicked by the user.

Declarations for the
`ColorDialog` and its result ─────────

```
132         ' handles Color menu item's Click event
133         Private Sub colorMenuItem_Click(sender As System.Object,
134           e As System.EventArgs) Handles colorMenuItem.Click
135
136            Dim dialog As New ColorDialog
137            Dim result As DialogResult ' stores Button clicked
138         End Sub ' colorMenuItem_Click
```

Figure 21.27   Declarations for the **Color** dialog and its `DialogResult`.

3. ***Setting the ColorDialog's open mode.*** Add lines 139–140 of Fig. 21.28 to your app. The `ColorDialog` object allows you to specify which color options the dialog presents to the user of your app. To display the **Color** dialog as shown in Fig. 21.4, the `FullOpen` option must be set to `True` (line 139). If this option is set to `False`, only the left half of the dialog is displayed. Line 140 opens the **Color** dialog using the `ShowDialog` method.

(cont.)

Displaying the `ColorDialog` with a complete color selection

```
137          Dim result As DialogResult ' stores Button clicked
138
139        ⎡ dialog.FullOpen = True ' show all colors
140        ⎣ result = dialog.ShowDialog()
141        End Sub ' colorMenuItem_Click
```

Figure 21.28 Displaying the **Color** dialog.

4. *Setting the font color.* Add lines 142–148 of Fig. 21.29 to your app. The If...Then statement on lines 143–145 prevents the color from being changed if the user clicks **Cancel**. Line 148 sets the text's color to the color the user selected in the **Color** dialog.

Take no action if user cancels

Change text color in the TextBox

```
140          result = dialog.ShowDialog()
141
142          ' do nothing if user clicked dialog's Cancel Button
143        ⎡ If result = System.Windows.Forms.DialogResult.Cancel Then
144        |     Return
145        ⎣ End If
146
147          ' assign new color value to TextBox
148          outputTextBox.ForeColor = dialog.Color
149        End Sub ' colorMenuItem_Click
```

Figure 21.29 Changing the display text's color.

5. *Saving the project.* Select **File > Save All** to save your modified code.

The user should be able to clear all of the text in the TextBox using the **Clear TextBox** menu item. You'll learn how to do this in the following box.

Clearing the TextBox

1. *Generating an event handler for the Clear TextBox menu item.* Double click the **Clear TextBox** menu item to generate its `Click` event. Add a comment and reformat the event handler as shown in lines 151–153 of Fig. 21.30.

2. *Clearing the text.* Add line 155 of Fig. 21.30 to the clearMenuItem_Click event handler. This line calls the `Clear` method to erase the text in the TextBox. Calling the `Clear` method on a TextBox has the same effect as setting its `Text` property to the empty string.

```
151          ' handles Clear TextBox menu item's Click Event
152          Private Sub clearMenuItem_Click(sender As System.Object,
153              e As System.EventArgs) Handles clearMenuItem.Click
154
155              outputTextBox.Clear() ' clear TextBox
156          End Sub ' clearMenuItem_Click
```

Figure 21.30 Calling the `Clear` method of class `TextBox` to erase the text.

3. *Saving the project.* Select **File > Save All** to save your modified code.

The user should be able to swap the foreground and background colors of the TextBox. You'll learn how to accomplish this in the following box.

Inverting Colors

1. *Creating an event handler for the Invert Colors menu item.* Double click the **Invert Colors** menu item in **Design** view to create its `Click` event handler. Add a comment and reformat the event handler as shown in lines 158–160 of Fig. 21.31.

```
158        ' handles Invert Colors menu item's Click Event
159        Private Sub invertMenuItem_Click(sender As System.Object,
160           e As System.EventArgs) Handles invertMenuItem.Click
161
162        End Sub ' invertMenuItem_Click
```

Figure 21.31 Empty event handler for **Invert Color** menu item.

2. ***Inverting the colors***. Insert lines 162–166 of Fig. 21.32 to your app. Line 162 declares a `Color` variable to store a color value. To swap colors, you must use a temporary variable to hold one of the colors that you want to swap. A **temporary variable** is used to store data when swapping values. Such a variable is no longer needed after the swap occurs. Without a temporary variable, you would lose the value of one color property (by reassigning its value) before you could assign its color to the other property.

   Line 164 assigns the temporary `Color` variable the background color of the `TextBox`. Line 165 then sets the background color to the foreground color. Finally, line 166 assigns the text color the value stored in the temporary `Color` variable, which contains the `TextBox`'s background color from before the swap.

```
158        ' handles Invert Colors menu item's Click Event
159        Private Sub InvertMenuItem_Click(sender As System.Object,
160           e As System.EventArgs) Handles InvertMenuItem.Click
161
162           Dim temporaryColor As Color ' temporary Color value
163
164           temporaryColor = outputTextBox.BackColor
165           outputTextBox.BackColor = outputTextBox.ForeColor
166           outputTextBox.ForeColor = temporaryColor
167        End Sub ' invertMenuItem_Click
```

Using a temporary variable to swap color values *(annotation pointing to lines 164–166)*

Figure 21.32 Swapping the background and foreground colors.

3. ***Running the app***. Select **Debug > Start Debugging** to run your app. Enter text using your keyboard. The keys you press should be highlighted in the virtual keyboard on the Form. Use the menu to change the color of the text, then invert the colors of the text and the `TextBox`. Finally, use the menus to change the text's font, then clear the `TextBox`.

4. ***Closing the app***. Close your running app by clicking its close box.

5. ***Closing the IDE***. Close the Visual Basic IDE by clicking its close box.

Figure 21.33 presents the source code for the **Typing** app. The lines of code that contain new programming concepts you learned in this chapter are highlighted.

```
1     Public Class TypingForm
2        Private lastButton As Button ' reference to last Button pressed
3        Private keyDictionary As New Dictionary(Of String, String)
4
5        ' handles TextBox's KeyDown Event
6        Private Sub outputTextBox_KeyDown(sender As Object,
7           e As System.Windows.Forms.KeyEventArgs) _
8           Handles outputTextBox.KeyDown
9
10          If Char.IsControl(Convert.ToChar(e.KeyCode)) OrElse
11             IsFunctionOrArrowKey(e.KeyCode) Then
12
```

Instance variable to store which **Button** the user pressed *(annotation pointing to line 2)*

Converting a KeyCode to a Char using `Convert.ToChar` *(annotation pointing to line 10)*

Figure 21.33 **Typing** app code listing. (Part 1 of 4.)

Determining a `Control`'s type using `TypeOf`

Determining whether the `Dictionary` contains a key matching the `KeyCode`'s `String` representation

Converting a Control to a Button using `CType`

```
13          ' locate the Button representing the pressed key with LINQ
14          Dim pressed =
15             From currentControl In Me.Controls
16             Where TypeOf currentControl Is Button AndAlso
17                keyDictionary.ContainsKey(
18                   e.KeyCode.ToString()) AndAlso
19                keyDictionary(e.KeyCode.ToString()) =
20                   CType(currentControl, Button).Text
21             Select currentControl
22
23          If pressed.Count > 0 Then
24             ChangeColor(CType(pressed.First, Button))
25          End If
26       End If
27    End Sub ' outputTextBox_KeyDown
28
29    ' handles TextBox's KeyPress Event
30    Private Sub outputTextBox_KeyPress(sender As Object,
31       e As System.Windows.Forms.KeyPressEventArgs) _
32       Handles outputTextBox.KeyPress
33
34       ' locate the Button matching the pressed key with LINQ
35       Dim pressed =
36          From currentControl In Me.Controls
37          Where TypeOf currentControl Is Button AndAlso
38             e.KeyChar.ToString().ToUpper() =
39                CType(currentControl, Button).Text
40          Select currentControl
41
42       If e.KeyChar = " " Then ' if user pressed spacebar
43          ChangeColor(spaceButton)
44       Else
45          If pressed.Count > 0 Then
46             ChangeColor(CType(pressed.First, Button))
47          End If
48       End If
49    End Sub ' outputTextBox_KeyPress
50
51    ' handles the TextBox's KeyUp event
52    Private Sub outputTextBox_KeyUp(sender As Object,
53       e As System.Windows.Forms.KeyEventArgs) _
54       Handles outputTextBox.KeyUp
55
56       ResetColor()
57    End Sub ' outputTextBox_KeyUp
58
59    ' highlight Button passed as argument
60    Private Sub ChangeColor(buttonPassed As Button)
61       ResetColor()
62       buttonPassed.BackColor = Color.Yellow
63       lastButton = buttonPassed ' save Button to reset color later
64    End Sub ' ChangeColor
65
66    ' changes lastButton's color if it refers to a Button
67    Private Sub ResetColor()
68       If lastButton IsNot Nothing Then
69          lastButton.BackColor = SystemColors.Control
70       End If
71    End Sub ' ResetColor
72
73    ' configure keyDictionary for use with control keys;
74    ' key is the key code's string value; value is the Button label
75    Private Sub TypingForm_Load(sender As System.Object,
76       e As System.EventArgs) Handles MyBase.Load
```

Using the `IsNot` operator to determine whether `lastButton` refers to `Nothing`

Figure 21.33   Typing app code listing. (Part 2 of 4.)

```
77
78           ' add function keys
79           For i As Integer = 1 To 12
80              keyDictionary.Add("F" & i, "F" & i)
81           Next
82
83           ' add other control keys
84           keyDictionary.Add("Back", "Backspace")
85           keyDictionary.Add("Return", "Enter")
86           keyDictionary.Add("ControlKey", "Ctrl")
87           keyDictionary.Add("Menu", "Alt")
88           keyDictionary.Add("Capital", "Caps Lock")
89           keyDictionary.Add("ShiftKey", "Shift")
90           keyDictionary.Add("Tab", "Tab")
91           keyDictionary.Add("Up", "^")
92           keyDictionary.Add("Down", "v")
93           keyDictionary.Add("Left", "<")
94           keyDictionary.Add("Right", ">")
95        End Sub ' TypingForm_Load
96
97        ' determine whether pressed key is a function or arrow key
98        Function IsFunctionOrArrowKey(code As Keys) As Boolean
99           Dim result As Boolean
100
101          Select Case code
102             Case Keys.F1 To Keys.F12
103                result = True
104             Case Keys.Up, Keys.Down, Keys.Left, Keys.Right
105                result = True
106             Case Else
107                result = False ' not a match
108          End Select
109
110          Return result
111       End Function ' isFunctionOrArrowKey
112
113       ' handles Font menu item's Click event
114       Private Sub fontMenuItem_Click(sender As System.Object,
115          e As System.EventArgs) Handles fontMenuItem.Click
116
117          Dim dialog As New FontDialog()
118          Dim result As DialogResult ' stores Button clicked
119
120          ' show dialog and get result
121          result = dialog.ShowDialog()
122
123          ' do nothing if user clicked dialog's Cancel Button
124          If result = System.Windows.Forms.DialogResult.Cancel Then
125             Return
126          End If
127
128          ' assign new font value to TextBox
129          outputTextBox.Font = dialog.Font
130       End Sub ' fontMenuItem_Click
131
132       ' handles Color menu item's Click event
133       Private Sub colorMenuItem_Click(sender As System.Object,
134          e As System.EventArgs) Handles colorMenuItem.Click
135
136          Dim dialog As New ColorDialog()
137          Dim result As DialogResult ' stores Button clicked
138
139          dialog.FullOpen = True ' show all colors
140          result = dialog.ShowDialog()
```

Adding items to a Dictionary — (lines 84–94)

Create `FontDialog` and `DialogResult` variables — (lines 117–118)

Display dialog and get `Button` clicked to exit the dialog — (line 121)

Change the text's font to the value the user selected — (line 129)

Show all color options in the dialog — (line 139)

Display dialog and get `Button` clicked to exit the dialog — (line 140)

Figure 21.33 Typing app code listing. (Part 3 of 4.)

```
141
142          ' do nothing if user clicked dialog's Cancel Button
143          If result = System.Windows.Forms.DialogResult.Cancel Then
144             Return
145          End If
146
147          ' assign new color value to TextBox
148          outputTextBox.ForeColor = dialog.Color
149       End Sub ' colorMenuItem_Click
150
151       ' handles Clear TextBox menu item's Click Event
152       Private Sub clearMenuItem_Click(sender As System.Object,
153          e As System.EventArgs) Handles clearMenuItem.Click
154
155          outputTextBox.Clear() ' clear TextBox
156       End Sub ' clearMenuItem_Click
157
158       ' handles Invert Colors menu item's Click Event
159       Private Sub invertMenuItem_Click(sender As System.Object,
160          e As System.EventArgs) Handles invertMenuItem.Click
161
162          Dim temporaryColor As Color ' temporary Color value
163
164          temporaryColor = outputTextBox.BackColor
165          outputTextBox.BackColor = outputTextBox.ForeColor
166          outputTextBox.ForeColor = temporaryColor
167       End Sub ' invertMenuItem_Click
168    End Class ' Typing
```

Change the text's color to the value the user selected → (lines 147–148)

Swap text color and background color → (lines 164–166)

Figure 21.33   **Typing** app code listing. (Part 4 of 4.)

SELF-REVIEW

1. Menus can contain _____.

   a) commands that the user can select   b) submenus

   c) separator bars   d) All of the above

2. _____ allow you to receive input from and display messages to users.

   a) Dialogs   b) Enumerations

   c) Separator bars   d) All of the above

Answers: 1) d. 2) a.

21.6 Wrap-Up

In this chapter, you learned how to process keyboard events by using the KeyDown and KeyPress event handlers that are invoked when the user presses various keys on the keyboard. You used LINQ to Objects and a Dictionary collection to help map the key that was pressed to a specific Button in the GUI. You learned how to use the TypeOf...Is expression to determine whether a control is a Button. You then learned how to use the KeyUp event handler to handle the event raised when the user releases a key. You also learned how to use the IsNot operator to determine whether a reference variable contains a reference to an object or Nothing.

You added menus to the **Typing** app. You learned that menus allow you to add controls to your app without cluttering the GUI. You also learned how to code a menu item's Click event handler to alter the displayed text in the **Typing** app. You learned how to display the **Color** and **Font** dialogs so that the user could specify the font style and color of the text in the TextBox. You also learned how to use the DialogResult enumeration to determine which Button the user pressed to exit a dialog.

In the next chapter, you learn about the methods in the String class that allow you to manipulate Strings. These methods help you build a screen-scraper app that can search text for a particular value.

SKILLS SUMMARY

Adding Keyboard Event Handlers to a Control

- Select the control from the **Class Name** ComboBox.
- Select the desired event handler from the **Method Name** ComboBox.

Executing Code When the User Presses a Letter Key on the Keyboard

- Use the KeyPress event handler.
- Use property KeyChar to determine which key was pressed.

Executing Code When the User Presses a Key That Is Not a Letter

- Use the KeyDown event handler.
- Use property KeyCode to determine which key was pressed.

Executing Code When the User Releases a Key

- Use the KeyUp event handler.

Using the `Dictionary` Collection

- Call `Dictionary` method Add on a `Dictionary` object to add the key/value pair to the `Dictionary`.
- Use the `Dictionary`'s name followed by an item's key in parentheses to retrieve the key's value from the `Dictionary`, much like an array.

Converting an Object to a Different Type

- Use the CType method to convert the object to the desired type. An exception is raised if the conversion fails.

Adding Menus to Your App

- Double click the MenuStrip control in the **Toolbox**.
- Add menu items to the menu by typing the item's name in the **Type Here** boxes that appear in Menu Designer mode.
- Add submenus by typing a menu item's name in the **Type Here** box that appears to the right of the submenu's name.
- Use a menu item's Click event handler to perform an action when that menu item is selected by the user.

Adding a Font Dialog to Your App

- Use keyword New to create a new FontDialog object.
- Use a DialogResult variable to store the Button the user clicked to exit the dialog.
- Use method ShowDialog to display the dialog and obtain the Button the user selected to exit the dialog.

Adding a Color Dialog to Your App

- Use keyword New to create a new ColorDialog object.
- Use a DialogResult variable to store the Button the user clicked to exit the dialog.
- Set the FullOpen option to True to provide the user with the full range of colors.
- Use method ShowDialog to display the dialog and obtain the Button the user selected to exit the dialog.

KEY TERMS

Add method of class `Dictionary`—Adds a key/value pair to a `Dictionary` collection.

Cancel value of `DialogResult` enumeration—Used to determine whether the user clicked the **Cancel** Button of a dialog.

Char structure—Stores characters (such as letters and symbols).

ColorDialog class—Used to display a dialog from which the user can select colors.

ContainsKey method of class `Dictionary`—Determines whether the `Dictionary` contains the key specified as an argument.

CType operator—Converts the object passed as the first argument to the type passed as the second argument.

DialogResult enumeration—An enumeration that contains values corresponding to standard dialog `Button` names.

Dictionary collection—A collection of key/value pairs.

FontDialog class—Used to display a dialog from which the user can choose a font and its style.

FullOpen property of class ColorDialog—Property that, when `True`, enables the Color-Dialog to provide a full range of color options when displayed.

IsControl method of structure Char—Determines whether the `Char` passed as an argument represents a control key.

IsNot operator—Determines whether two reference variables contain references to different objects or whether a single reference variable refers to an object.

keyboard event—Raised when a key on the keyboard is pressed or released.

KeyChar property of class KeyPressEventArgs—Contains data about the key that raised the KeyPress event.

KeyCode property of class KeyEventArgs—Contains data about the key that raised the KeyDown event.

KeyDown event—Generated when a key is initially pressed. Used to handle the event raised when a key that's not a letter key is pressed.

KeyEventArgs class—Stores information about special modifier keys.

KeyPress event—Generated when a key is pressed.

KeyPressEventArgs class—Stores information about character keys.

Keys enumeration—Contains values representing keyboard keys.

KeyUp event—Generated when a key is released.

menu—Design element that groups related commands for GUI apps. Although these commands depend on the app, some—such as **Open** and **Save**—are common to many apps. Menus are an integral part of GUIs, because they organize commands without cluttering the GUI.

Menu Designer mode in the Visual Basic IDE—Design mode in the IDE that allows you to create and edit menus and menu items.

menu item—Command located in a menu that, when selected, causes the app to perform an action.

MenuStrip control—Allows you to add menus to your app.

modifier key—Key such as *Shift*, *Alt* or *Control* that modifies the way that an app responds to a keyboard event.

sender event argument—Event argument that contains a reference to the object that raised the event (also called the source of the event).

separator bar—Bar placed in a menu to separate related menu items.

ShowDialog method of class FontDialog or ColorDialog—The method that displays the dialog on which it's called.

submenu—Menu within another menu.

temporary variable—Used to store data when swapping values.

ToUpper method of class String—Returns the uppercase representation of a `String`. Similarly, `ToLower` returns the lowercase representation of a `String`.

ToolStripMenuItem class—Class which represents an individual menu item in a `MenuStrip`.

TypeOf...Is expression—Returns `True` if the object referenced by the variable is of the specified type.

GUI DESIGN GUIDELINES

MenuStrip
- Use book-title capitalization in menu-item text.
- Use separator bars in a menu to group related menu items.
- If clicking a menu item opens a dialog, an ellipsis (...) should follow the menu item's text.

CONTROLS, EVENTS, PROPERTIES & METHODS

Char This structure represents a character.

- *Method*

    `IsControl`—Determines whether the `Char` represents a control character.

ColorDialog   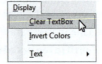 ColorDialog   This control allows the user to select a color.

- *Properties*

    `Color`—Contains the color selected by the user. The default color is black.

    `FullOpen`—When `True`, displays an extended color palette. If this property is set to `False`, a dialog with fewer options is displayed.

- *Method*

    `ShowDialog`—Displays the **Color** dialog to the user.

FontDialog   FontDialog   This control allows the user to select a font and customize its size and style.

- *Property*

    `Font`—Contains the font specified by the user.

- *Method*

    `ShowDialog`—Displays the **Font** dialog to the user.

KeyEventArgs This class represents arguments passed to the `KeyDown` event handler.

- *Property*

    `KeyCode`—Contains data about the key that raised the `KeyDown` event.

KeyPressEventArgs This class represents arguments passed to the `KeyPress` event handler.

- *Property*

    `KeyChar`—Contains data about the key that raised the `KeyPress` event.

ToolStripMenuItem   MenuStrip   This control allows you to create a menu item.

- *In action*

    Display
    | Clear TextBox |
    | Invert Colors |
    | Text ▶ |

- *Event*

    `Click`—Raised when the user clicks a menu item or presses an access key that represents an item.

Dictionary This class is used to store a variable number of key/value pairs.

- *Methods*

    `Add`—Adds a key/value pair to the `Dictionary` object.

    `ContainsKey`—Returns `True` if the `Dictionary` contains the specified key.

TextBox   abl TextBox   This control allows the user to input data from the keyboard.

- *In action*

■ *Events*

KeyDown—Raised when a key is pressed. KeyDown is case insensitive. It cannot recognize lowercase letters.

KeyPress—Raised when a key is pressed. KeyPress cannot handle modifier keys.

KeyUp—Raised when a key is released by the user.

TextChanged—Raised when the text in the TextBox is changed.

■ *Properties*

Enabled—Determines whether the user can enter data in the TextBox or not.

Font—Specifies the font used to display text in the TextBox.

ForeColor—Specifies color of the text in the TextBox.

Location—Specifies the location of the TextBox control relative to the top-left corner of the container (e.g., a Form or a GroupBox).

MaxLength—Specifies the maximum number of characters that can be input into the TextBox.

Multiline—Specifies whether the TextBox is capable of displaying multiple lines of text.

Name—Specifies the name used to access the TextBox programmatically. The name should be appended with the TextBox suffix.

PasswordChar—Specifies the masking character to be used when displaying data in the TextBox.

ReadOnly—Determines whether the value of a TextBox can be changed.

ScrollBars—Specifies whether a multiline TextBox contains a scrollbar.

Size—Specifies the width and height (in pixels) of the TextBox.

TabIndex—Specifies the order in which focus is transferred to controls when *Tab* is pressed.

TabStop—Specifies whether the user can select the control using the *Tab* key.

Text—Specifies the text displayed in the TextBox.

TextAlign—Specifies how the text is aligned within the TextBox.

■ *Methods*

Clear—Removes the text from the TextBox that calls it.

Focus—Transfers the focus of the app to the TextBox that calls it.

MULTIPLE-CHOICE QUESTIONS

21.1 When creating a menu, typing a(n) _____ in front of a menu-item name creates an access key for that item.

   a) &
   b) !
   c) $
   d) #

21.2 *Alt*, *Shift* and *Control* are _____ keys.

   a) modifier
   b) special
   c) function
   d) None of the above

21.3 KeyChar is a property of _____.

   a) KeyEventArgs
   b) Key
   c) KeyArgs
   d) KeyPressEventArgs

21.4 Typing a hyphen (-) as a menu item's Text property will create a(n) _____.

   a) separator bar
   b) access shortcut
   c) new submenu
   d) keyboard shortcut

21.5 A _____ provides a group of related commands for GUI apps.

   a) separator bar
   b) hot key
   c) menu
   d) margin indicator bar

21.6 The _____ enumeration specifies key codes and modifiers.

   a) Keyboard
   b) Key
   c) KeyboardTypes
   d) Keys

21.7 The _____ event is raised when a key is pressed by the user.

a) `KeyPress`
b) `KeyHeld`
c) `KeyDown`
d) Both (a) and (c)

21.8 Which of the following is not a keyboard event?

a) `KeyPress`
b) `KeyDown`
c) `KeyUp`
d) `KeyClicked`

21.9 Which of the following is not a structure?

a) `Char`
b) `Color`
c) `String`
d) `Date`

21.10 The _____ type allows you to determine which `Button` the user clicked to exit a dialog.

a) `DialogButtons`
b) `DialogResult`
c) `Buttons`
d) `ButtonResult`

EXERCISES

21.11 *(Inventory App with Keyboard Events)* Enhance the **Inventory** app that you developed in Chapter 4 to prevent the user from entering input that's not a number. Use keyboard events to allow the user to press the number keys, the left and right arrows and the *Backspace* keys. If any other key is pressed, display a `MessageBox` instructing the user to enter a number (Fig. 21.34).

Figure 21.34 **Inventory** app with key events.

a) *Copying the template to your working directory.* Copy the directory `C:\Examples\ch21\Exercises\KeyEventInventory` to your `C:\SimplyVB2010` directory.

b) *Opening the app's template file.* Double click `KeyEventInventory.sln` in the `KeyEventInventory` directory to open the app.

c) *Adding the KeyDown event handler for the first TextBox.* Use the **Class Name** and **Method Name** ComboBoxes to add an empty `KeyDown` event handler for the **Cartons per shipment:** `TextBox`.

d) *Adding a Select Case statement.* Add a `Select Case` statement to the `KeyDown` event handler that uses the `Keys` enumeration to determine whether a number key, a left or right arrow, *Enter* or the *Backspace* key was pressed.

e) *Adding the Case Else statement.* Add a `Case Else` statement that executes when a key other than a valid one for this app was pressed. If an invalid key was pressed, clear the `TextBox` and display a `MessageBox` that instructs the user to enter a number.

f) *Adding the KeyDown event handler for the second TextBox.* Repeat *Steps c–e*, but this time create a `KeyDown` event handler for the **Items per carton:** `TextBox`. This event handler should have the same functionality as the one for the **Cartons per shipment:** `TextBox`.

g) *Running the app.* Select **Debug > Start Debugging** to run your app. Try entering letters or pressing the up- and down-arrow keys in the `TextBox`es. A `MessageBox` should be displayed. Enter valid input and click the **Calculate Total** `Button`. Verify that the correct output is displayed.

h) *Closing the app.* Close your running app by clicking its close box.

i) *Closing the IDE.* Close the Visual Basic IDE by clicking its close box.

21.12 *(Bouncing Ball Game)* Write an app that allows the user to play a game, in which the goal is to prevent a bouncing ball from falling off the bottom of the Form. When the user presses the *S* key, a blue ball bounces off the top, left and right sides (the "walls") of the Form. A horizontal bar on the bottom of the Form serves as a paddle to prevent the ball from hitting the bottom of the Form. (The ball can bounce off the paddle but not off the bottom of the Form.) The user can move the paddle using the left and right arrow keys. If the ball hits the paddle, it bounces up, and the game continues. If the ball hits the bottom of the Form, the game ends. The paddle's width decreases every 20 seconds to make the game more challenging. The GUI and the bouncing ball are provided for you (Fig. 21.35).

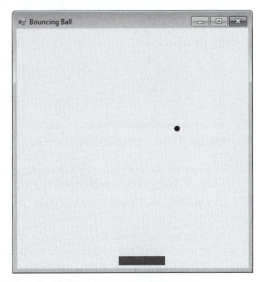

Figure 21.35   Bouncing Ball app.

a) *Copying the template to your working directory.* Copy the directory C:\Examples\ ch21\Exercises\BouncingBall to your C:\SimplyVB2010 directory.

b) *Opening the app's template file.* Double click BouncingBall.sln in the Bouncing-Ball directory to open the app.

c) *Creating the KeyDown event handler.* Insert a KeyDown event handler for the Form.

d) *Writing code to start the game.* Write an If...Then statement in the KeyDown event handler that tests whether the user presses the *S* key. You can use the KeyDown event handler for the *S* key in this case because you do not care whether the user presses an uppercase *S* or a lowercase *S*. If the user presses the *S* key, start the two Timers provided in the template (set their Enabled properties to True).

e) *Inserting code to move the paddle left.* Add an ElseIf statement that tests whether the user pressed the left-arrow key and whether the paddle's horizontal position (rectangleX) is greater than zero. If the paddle's horizontal position equals zero, the left edge of the paddle is touching the left wall and the paddle should not be allowed to move farther to the left. If both the conditions in the If...Then are true, decrease the paddle's *x*-position by 10.

f) *Inserting code to move the paddle right.* Add an ElseIf statement that tests whether the user pressed the right-arrow key and whether the paddle's *x*-coordinate is less than the width of the Form minus the width of the paddle (rectangleWidth). If the paddle's *x*-coordinate equals the Form's width minus the width of the paddle, the paddle's right edge is touching the right wall and the paddle should not be allowed to move farther to the right. If both the conditions in the If...Then statement are true, increase the paddle's *x*-coordinate by 10.

g) *Running the app.* Select **Debug > Start Debugging** to run your app. Press the *S* key to begin the game and use the paddle to keep the bouncing ball from dropping off the Form. Continue doing this until 20 seconds have passed, and verify that the paddle is decreased in size at that time.

h) *Closing the app.* Close your running app by clicking its close box.

i) *Closing the IDE.* Close the Visual Basic IDE by clicking its close box.

21.13 *(Form Painter App)* Create a menu for the **Form Painter** app that allows the user to select the size and color of the paint and the color of the Form (Fig. 21.36). The **Form Painter** app is provided for you.

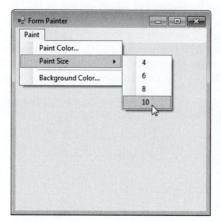

Figure 21.36 Modified **Painter** GUI.

a) *Copying the template to your working directory.* Copy the directory `C:\Examples\ch21\Exercises\FormPainter` to your `C:\SimplyVB2010` directory.

b) *Opening the app's template file.* Double click `FormPainter.sln` in the `FormPainter` directory to open the app.

c) *Creating the menus.* Create a menu titled **Paint** that contains a **Paint Color...** menu item, a **Paint Size** submenu that contains menu items **4**, **6**, **8** and **10**, a separator bar and a **Background Color...** menu item.

d) *Changing the paint color.* Add an event handler for the **Paint Color...** menu item. This event handler should display a **Color** dialog that allows the user to change the value stored in `paintColor`.

e) *Changing the paint size.* Add an event handler for each of the **Paint Size** submenu's menu items. Each event handler should change the value stored in `diameter` to the value displayed on the menu (that is, clicking the **4** menu item changes the value of `diameter` to 4).

f) *Changing the background color.* Add an event handler for the **Background Color...** menu item. This event handler should display a **Color** dialog that allows the user to change the value stored in `backgroundColor` and also change the `BackColor` property of the Form. To change the background color of the Form, assign the value specifying the background color to `BackColor`. For instance, the statement `BackColor = Color.White` changes the background color of the Form to white.

g) *Running the app.* Select **Debug > Start Debugging** to run your app. Use the menus to draw shapes of various colors and brush sizes. Use the other menu option to change the color of the Form.

h) *Closing the app.* Close your running app by clicking its close box.

i) *Closing the IDE.* Close the Visual Basic IDE by clicking its close box.

What does this code do? ▶ **21.14** What is the result of the following code?

```
1   Private Sub colorMenuItem_Click(sender As System.Object,
2      e As System.EventArgs) Handles colorMenuItem.Click
3
4      Dim dialog As New ColorDialog()
5      Dim result As DialogResult
6
7      dialog.FullOpen = True
8
9      result = dialog.ShowDialog()
10
```

```
11        If result = System.Windows.Forms.DialogResult.Cancel Then
12           Return
13        End If
14
15        BackColor = dialog.Color
16     End Sub ' colorMenuItem_Click
```

What's wrong with this code? ▶ **21.15** This code should allow a user to pick a font from a **Font** dialog and set the text in `displayTextBox` to that font. Find the error(s) in the following code, assuming that a `TextBox` named `displayTextBox` exists on a `Form`.

```
1   Private Sub Fonts()
2      Dim dialog As FontDialog
3
4      dialog = New FontDialog()
5      dialog.ShowDialog()
6      displayTextBox.Font = dialog.Font
7   End Sub
```

Programming Challenge ▶ **21.16** *(Dvorak Keyboard App)* Create an app that simulates the letters on the Dvorak keyboard. A Dvorak keyboard allows faster typing by placing the most commonly used keys in the most accessible locations. Use keyboard events to create an app similar to the **Typing** app that simulates the Dvorak keyboard instead of the standard keyboard. The correct Dvorak key should be highlighted on the virtual keyboard, and the correct character should be displayed in the `TextBox`. The keys and characters map as follows:

- On the top row, the *P* key of the Dvorak keyboard maps to the *R* key on a standard keyboard, and the *L* key of the Dvorak keyboard maps to the *P* key on a standard keyboard.
- On the middle row, the *A* key remains in the same position, and the *S* key on the Dvorak keyboard maps to the semicolon key on the standard keyboard.
- On the bottom row, the *Q* key on the Dvorak keyboard maps to the *X* key on the standard keyboard, and the *Z* key maps to the question-mark key.
- All of the other keys on the Dvorak keyboard map to the locations shown in Fig. 21.37.

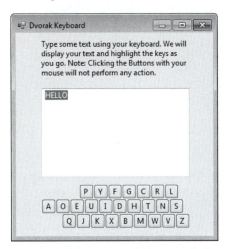

Figure 21.37   Dvorak Keyboard GUI.

a) *Copying the template to your working directory*. Copy the directory `C:\Examples\ch21\Exercises\DvorakKeyboard` to your `C:\SimplyVB2010` directory.

b) *Opening the app's template file*. Double click `DvorakKeyboard.sln` in the DvorakKeyboard directory to open the app.

c) *Creating the Dvorak key mapping*. Use a `Dictionary` to map the text of the key pressed to the text of its corresponding Dvorak key. Initialize this `Dictionary` in the Form's Load event.

d) *Creating the KeyPress event handler*. Use the **Class Name** and **Method Name** ComboBoxes to add a KeyPress event handler for the `TextBox`.

e) *Creating a LINQ statement*. Add a LINQ query statement to the KeyPress event handler. The LINQ query statement should select the `Button` in the Dvorak keyboard which corresponds to the key pressed on the user's keyboard. If a Dvorak key was pressed, highlight it on the GUI and display the character in the `TextBox` by appending the `Button`'s text to the `TextBox`'s `Text` property. Note that the `TextBox` does not display the actual key pressed on the keyboard. The `ReadOnly` property has been set to `True` to prevent user input from displaying in the `TextBox`. The `Back-Color` property has been set to `White` to maintain a familiar appearance.

f) *Running the app.* Select **Debug > Start Debugging** to run your app. Use your keyboard to enter text. Verify that the text entered is correct based on the rules in the exercise description. Make sure that the correct `Buttons` on the `Form` are highlighted as you enter text.

g) *Closing the app.* Close your running app by clicking its close box.

h) *Closing the IDE.* Close the Visual Basic IDE by clicking its close box.

Objectives

In this chapter, you'll learn to:
- Manipulate `String` objects.
- Use properties and methods of class `String`.
- Search for substrings within `Strings`.
- Extract substrings within `Strings`.
- Replace substrings within `Strings`.

Outline

Screen Scraping App
Introducing `String` Processing

This chapter introduces Visual Basic's `String`-processing capabilities. The techniques presented here can be used to create apps that manipulate text. Earlier chapters introduced class `String` from the `System` namespace and several of its methods. In this chapter, you'll learn how to search `Strings`, retrieve characters from `String` objects and replace characters in a `String`. You'll create an app that uses these `String`-processing capabilities to manipulate a `String` containing **HTML (HyperText Markup Language)**. HTML is a technology for describing web pages. Extracting desired information from the HTML that composes a web page is called **screen scraping**. Apps that perform screen scraping can be used to extract specific information, such as weather conditions or stock prices, from web pages so that the information can be formatted and manipulated more easily by computer apps. In this chapter, you'll create a simple **Screen Scraping** app.

22.1 Test-Driving the Screen Scraping App

This app must meet the following requirements:

App Requirements

An online European auction house wants to expand its business to include bidders from the United States. However, all its web pages currently display their prices in euros, not dollars. The auction house wants to generate separate web pages for American bidders that display the prices of auction items in dollars. These new web pages will be generated by using screen-scraping techniques on the already existing web pages. You've been asked to build a prototype app that tests the screen-scraping functionality. The app must search a sample string of HTML and extract information about the price of a specified auction item. For testing purposes, a ComboBox should be provided that contains auction items listed in HTML. The selected item's amount must then be converted to dollars. Assume the exchange rate is one euro to 1.58 dollars (that is, one euro is equivalent to $1.58). The price (in dollars) and sample HTML are displayed in Labels.

The **Screen Scraping** app searches for the name of a specified auction item in a string of HTML. Users select the item for which to search from a `ComboBox`. The app then extracts and displays the price in dollars of this item. You'll begin by test-driving the completed app. Then, you'll learn the additional Visual Basic capabilities needed to create your own version of the app.

Test-Driving the Screen Scraping *App*

1. *Opening the completed app.* Open the directory C:\Examples\ch22\CompletedApp\ScreenScraping to locate the **Screen Scraping** app. Double click ScreenScraping.sln to open the app in the Visual Basic IDE.

2. *Running the app.* Select **Debug > Start Debugging** to run the app (Fig. 22.1). Note that the HTML string is displayed in a `Label` at the bottom of the `Form`.

Label containing HTML ———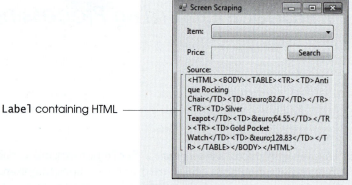

Figure 22.1 Screen Scraping app's Form.

3. *Selecting an item name.* The ComboBox contains three item names. Select an item name from the ComboBox, as shown in Fig. 22.2.

ComboBox's drop-down list ———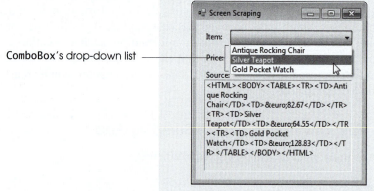

Figure 22.2 Selecting an item name from the ComboBox.

4. *Searching for an item's price.* Click the **Search** Button to display the price for the selected item. The extracted price is displayed in a `Label` (Fig. 22.3).

5. *Closing the app.* Close your running app by clicking its close box.

6. *Closing the IDE.* Close the Visual Basic IDE by clicking its close box.

(cont.)

Extracted price
(converted to dollars)

Price located in HTML string
(specified in Euros)

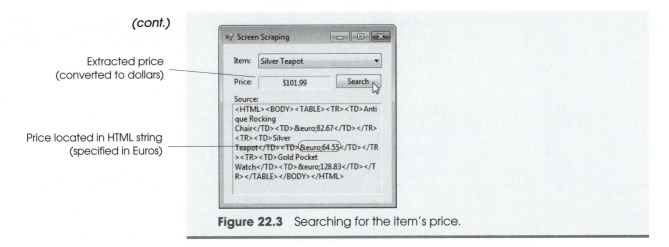

Figure 22.3 Searching for the item's price.

22.2 Fundamentals of Strings

A string is a series of characters treated as a single unit. These characters can be uppercase letters, lowercase letters, digits and various **special characters**, such as +, -, *, /, $ and others. A string is an object of class `String` in the `System` namespace. You write **string literals**, or **string constants** (often called **literal String objects**), as sequences of characters in double quotation marks, as follows:

```
"This is a string!"
```

You've already created and used `String`s in previous chapters. You know that a declaration can assign a `String` literal to a `String` variable. For example, the declaration

```
Dim myColor As String = "blue"
```

initializes `myColor` to refer to the literal `String` object `"blue"`.

Like arrays, `String`s always know their own size. `String` property **Length** returns the length of the `String` (that is, the number of characters in the `String`). For example, the expression `myColor.Length` evaluatess to 4 for the `String` `"blue"`.

Another useful property of class `String` is **Chars**, which returns the character located at a specific index in a `String`. Property `Chars` takes an `Integer` argument specifying the index and returns the character at that index. As in arrays, the *first* element of a `String` is located at *index 0*. For example, the following code

```
If string1.Chars(0) = string2.Chars(0) Then
    messageLabel.Text = "The first characters are the same."
End If
```

compares the character at index 0 (that is, the first character) of `string1` with the character at index 0 of `string2`. Expressions like `string1.Chars(0)` may also be written as `string1(0)`.

In earlier chapters, you used several methods of class `String` to manipulate `String` objects. Figure 22.4 lists some of these methods. Note that the example expression `" My String"` intentionally begins with a blank space. You'll learn new `String` methods later in this chapter.

Any `String` method or operator that appears to modify a `String` actually returns a new `String` that contains the results. For example, `String` method `ToUpper` does *not* actually modify the original `String`, but instead returns a new `String` in which each lowercase letter has been converted to uppercase. This occurs because `String`s are **immutable** objects—that is, characters in `String`s cannot be changed after the `String`s are created.

Method	Description	Sample Expression (assume text = " My String")
PadLeft(*length*, *char*)	Returns a copy of a String with character *char* inserted at the beginning until the String is *length* characters long.	text.PadLeft(12, "!"c) Returns: "!! My String"
PadRight(*length*, *char*)	Returns a copy of a String with character *char* inserted at the end until the String is *length* characters long.	text.PadRight(12, "!"c) Returns: " My String!!"
ToLower()	Returns a copy of the String with all upper-case letters converted to lowercase.	text.ToLower() Returns: " my string"
ToUpper()	Returns a copy of the String with all lower-case letters converted to uppercase.	text.ToUpper() Returns: " MY STRING"

Figure 22.4 String methods introduced in earlier chapters.

SELF-REVIEW

1. The _____ property of the class String returns the number of characters in the String.

   a) MaxChars   b) Length
   c) CharacterCount   d) TotalLength

2. A String can be composed of _____.

   a) digits   b) lowercase letters
   c) special characters   d) All of the above

Answers: 1) b. 2) d.

22.3 Analyzing the Screen Scraping App

Before building the **Screen Scraping** app, you must analyze its components. The following pseudocode describes the basic operation of the **Screen Scraping** app.

> When the Form loads:
>   Display the HTML that contains the items' prices in a Label
>
> When the user clicks the Search Button:
>   Search the HTML for the item the user selected from the ComboBox
>   Extract the item's price
>   Convert the item's price from euros to dollars
>   Display the item's price in a Label

Now that you've test-driven the **Screen Scraping** app and studied its pseudocode representation, you'll use an ACE table to help you convert the pseudocode to Visual Basic. Figure 22.5 lists the *actions*, *controls* and *events* that help you complete your own version of this app.

*Action/Control/Event
(ACE) Table for the
Screen Scraping App*

Action	Control/Object	Event

Label the app's controls	`itemLabel`
	`priceLabel`
	`sourceLabel`
		App is run

	`ScreenScraping-` `Form`	Load
Display the HTML that contains the items' prices in a Label	`htmlLabel`	
	`searchButton`	`Click`
Search the HTML for the item the user selected from the ComboBox	`itemsComboBox`	
Extract the item's price		
Convert the item's price from euros to dollars		
Display the item's price in a Label	`resultLabel`	

Figure 22.5   ACE table for **Screen Scraping** app.

Now that you've analyzed the **Screen Scraping** app's components, you'll learn about the `String` methods that you'll need to construct the app.

22.4 Locating Substrings in `Strings`

Many apps search for a character or set of characters in a `String`. For example, a word-processing app allows users to search their documents. Class `String` provides methods that make it possible to search for **substrings** (or sequences of characters) in a `String`. In the following box, you'll begin building the **Screen Scraping** app.

*Locating the Selected
Item's Price*

1. ***Copying the template to your working directory.*** Copy the `C:\Examples\ch22\TemplateApp\ScreenScraping` directory to your `C:\SimplyVB2010` directory.

2. ***Opening the Screen Scraping app's template file.*** Double click Screen-Scraping.sln in the ScreenScraping directory to open the app in the Visual Basic IDE. Double click ScreenScraping.vb in the **Solution Explorer** to display the app's Form in **Design** view.

3. ***Creating a `Click` event handler for the Search Button.*** Double click the **Search** Button on the app's Form to generate the event handler `searchButton_Click`. Reformat the event handler and add the comments as shown in lines 13–17 of Fig. 22.6.

```
11          "</TABLE></BODY></HTML>"
12
13      ' handles Search Button's Click event
14      Private Sub searchButton_Click(sender As System.Object,
15          e As System.EventArgs) Handles searchButton.Click
16
17      End Sub ' searchButton_Click
18   End Class ' ScreenScrapingForm
```

Figure 22.6   `searchButton_Click` event handler.

4. ***Declaring three Integer variables, a String reference and a Decimal variable.*** Add lines 17–21 of Fig. 22.7 to the `searchButton_Click` event handler. These lines declare `Integer` variables `itemLocation`, `priceBegin` and `priceEnd`, `String` variable `price` and `Decimal` variable `dollars`.

```
(cont.)  15              e As System.EventArgs) Handles searchButton.Click
         16
         17          Dim itemLocation As Integer ' index of desired item
         18          Dim priceBegin As Integer ' starting index of price
         19          Dim priceEnd As Integer ' ending index of price
         20          Dim price As String ' extracted price
         21          Dim dollars As Decimal ' price in dollars
         22      End Sub ' searchButton_Click
```

Figure 22.7   `searchButton_Click` event-handler declarations.

5. *Locating the specified item name.* Add lines 23–25 of Fig. 22.8 to event handler `searchButton_Click`. Lines 24–25 call `String` method `IndexOf` to locate the first occurrence of the specified item name in the HTML string stored in the `html` instance variable. There are several overloaded versions of `IndexOf` that search for substrings in a `String`. Lines 24–25 use the version of `IndexOf` that takes a single argument—the substring for which to search. (The specified item name is the `String` representation of the `SelectedItem` in `itemsComboBox`.)

```
         21          Dim dollars As Decimal ' price in dollars
         22
         23          ' locate desired item
         24          itemLocation = html.IndexOf(
         25              itemsComboBox.SelectedItem.ToString())
         26      End Sub ' searchButton_Click
```

Search for the `SelectedItem` in the `String html` — lines 23–25

Figure 22.8   Locating the desired item name.

`Option Strict` is set to `On`, so you must convert `SelectedItem` (which is of type `Object`) to a `String`, by using method `ToString`, before passing the selected item to method `IndexOf`. If `IndexOf` finds the specified substring (in this case, the item name), `IndexOf` returns the index at which the substring begins in the `String`. For example, the return value 0 means that the substring begins at the *first* character of the `String`. If `IndexOf` does not find the substring, it returns –1. The result is stored in variable `itemLocation`.

6. *Locating the start of the price.* Add lines 27–29 of Fig. 22.9 to event handler `searchButton_Click`. Lines 28–29 locate the index at which the item's price begins. Lines 28–29 use a version of method `IndexOf` that takes two arguments—the substring to find and the starting index in the `String` at which the search begins. The method does not examine any characters prior to the starting index (specified by `itemLocation`). A third version of method `IndexOf` takes three arguments—the substring to find, the index at which to start searching and the number of characters to search. You do *not* use this version of `IndexOf` in the **Screen Scraping** app.

The first price that follows the specified item name in the HTML is the desired price; therefore, you can begin the search at `itemLocation`. The substring to find is `"&euro;"`. This is the HTML representation of the euro symbol, which appears before every price value in the HTML. The index returned from method `IndexOf` is stored in variable `priceBegin`.

```
         25              itemsComboBox.SelectedItem.ToString())
         26
         27          ' locate price of item
         28          priceBegin = html.IndexOf("&euro;",
         29              itemLocation)
         30      End Sub ' searchButton_Click
```

Locate the beginning of the price in `html` — lines 27–29

Figure 22.9   Locating the desired item price.

(cont.)   7.   ***Locating the end of the price.*** Add line 30 of Fig. 22.10 to event handler `searchButton_Click` to find the index at which the desired price ends. Line 30 calls method `IndexOf` with the substring `"</TD>"` and the starting index `priceBegin`. A `</TD>` tag directly follows every price (excluding any spaces) in the HTML string, so the index of the first `</TD>` tag after `priceBegin` marks the end of the current price.

       The index returned from the method `IndexOf` is stored in the variable `priceEnd`. In the next box, you'll use `priceBegin` and `priceEnd` to obtain the price substring from the `String html`.

Locate the end of the
price in `html`

```
27              ' locate price of item
28              priceBegin = html.IndexOf("&euro;",
29                 itemLocation)
30              priceEnd = html.IndexOf("</TD>", priceBegin)
31        End Sub ' searchButton_Click
```

Figure 22.10   Locating the end of the item's price.

8.   ***Saving the project.*** Select **File > Save All** to save your modified code.

The **LastIndexOf** method is similar to method `IndexOf`. Method `LastIndexOf` locates the *last* occurrence of a substring in a `String`—it performs the search starting from the end of the `String` and searches toward the beginning. If method `LastIndexOf` finds the substring, it returns the starting index of the specified substring in the `String`; otherwise, `LastIndexOf` returns –1.

There are several overloaded versions of `LastIndexOf` that search for substrings in a `String`. The first version takes a single argument—the substring for which to search. The second version takes two arguments—the substring for which to search and the highest index from which to begin searching backward for the substring. The third version of method `LastIndexOf` takes three arguments—the substring for which to search, the starting index from which to start searching backward and the number of characters to search. Figure 22.11 shows examples of the three versions of `LastIndexOf`. Note that the example expression `" My String"` intentionally begins with a blank space.

Method	Example Expression (assume text = " My String")	Returns
LastIndexOf(*string*)	text.LastIndexOf("n")	8
LastIndexOf(*string, integer*)	text.LastIndexOf("n", 6)	-1
	text.LastIndexOf("y", 6)	2
LastIndexOf(*string, integer, integer*)	text.LastIndexOf("m", 7, 3)	-1
	text.LastIndexOf("r", 7, 3)	6

Figure 22.11   `LastIndexOf` examples.

SELF-REVIEW

1. Method _____ locates the first occurrence of a substring.
   a) `IndexOf`   b) `FirstIndexOf`
   c) `FindFirst`   d) `Locate`

2. The third argument passed to the `LastIndexOf` method is _____.
   a) the starting index from which to start searching backward
   b) the starting index from which to start searching forward
   c) the length of the substring to locate
   d) the number of characters to search

Answers: 1) a. 2) d.

22.5 Extracting Substrings from `Strings`

Once you've located a substring in a `String`, you might want to retrieve it. The following box uses the `Substring` method to retrieve the price of the selected item from the HTML string.

Retrieving the Desired Item's Price

1. ***Extracting the price.*** Add lines 32–34 of Fig. 22.12 to the `search-Button_Click` event handler. Recall from Chapter 19 that class `String` provides two versions of the `Substring` method, each of which returns a new `String` object that contains a copy of a part of an existing `String` object.

```
30          priceEnd = html.IndexOf("</TD>", priceBegin)
31
32            ' extract the price
33            price = html.Substring(priceBegin,
34               (priceEnd - priceBegin))
35        End Sub ' searchButton_Click
```

Extract price from `html` ──── 33

Figure 22.12   Retrieving the desired price.

Lines 33–34 extract the price, using the version of the `Substring` method that takes two `Integer` arguments. The first argument (`priceBegin`) specifies the starting index from which the method copies characters from the original `String`.

The second argument (`priceEnd - priceBegin`) specifies the length of the substring to be copied. The substring returned (`price`) contains a copy of the specified characters from the original `String`. In this case, the substring returned is the item's price (in euros).

The other version of method `Substring` takes one `Integer` argument. The argument specifies the starting index from which the method copies characters in the original `String`. The substring returned contains a copy of the characters from the starting index to the end of the `String`.

2. ***Saving the project.*** Select **File > Save All** to save your modified code.

SELF-REVIEW

1. The `Substring` method _____.
   a) accepts either one or two arguments
   b) returns a new `String` object
   c) creates a `String` object by copying part of an existing `String` object
   d) All of the above

2. The second argument passed to method `Substring` specifies _____.
   a) the last index of the `String` to copy
   b) the length of the substring to copy
   c) the index from which to begin copying backward
   d) a character which, when reached, signifies that copying is to stop

Answers: 1) d. 2) b.

22.6 Replacing Substrings in `Strings`

Perhaps you want to replace certain characters in `Strings`. Class `String` provides the **`Replace`** method to replace occurrences of one substring with a different substring. The `Replace` method takes as arguments a `String` to replace in the original `String` and a `String` with which to replace all occurrences of the first argument. Method `Replace` returns a new `String` with the specified replacements. The original `String` remains unchanged. If there are no occurrences of the first argument in the `String`, the method returns a copy of the original `String`. The following box uses method `Replace` to convert the extracted price from euros to dollars.

Converting the Price to Dollars

1. *Converting the price.* Add lines 36–39 of Fig. 22.13 to `searchButton_Click`. Line 37 uses `String` method `Replace` to return a new `String` object in which every occurrence in `price` of substring `"&euro;"` (the euro currency symbol) is replaced with substring `String.Empty` (the empty `String`)—there's one replacement in this example. Note that you assign the value returned from method `Replace` to `price`. This is required because method `Replace` returns a new `String`—it does *not* modify the original `String`. Line 38 calls method `Convert.ToDecimal` to retrieve the `price` as a `Decimal` and multiplies it by the conversion rate (`1.58D`). (You can find current exchange rates at `www.xe.com/ucc/`.) The D in line 38 indicates that `1.58` is a `Decimal` value rather than a `Double`. Recall that a `Decimal` multiplied by a `Double` results in a `Double`. Specifying `1.58` as a `Decimal` removes the need to convert the result of the multiplication. The price in dollars is assigned to `Decimal` variable `dollars`. Line 39 calls `String` method `Format` to display the price in `resultLabel` as currency.

Replace `"&euro;"` with `String.Empty` and convert the amount to dollars

(cont.)

```
34              (priceEnd - priceBegin))
35
36          ' convert price to dollars and display
37          price = price.Replace("&euro;", String.Empty)
38          dollars = Convert.ToDecimal(price) * 1.58D
39          resultLabel.Text = String.Format("{0:C}", dollars)
40      End Sub ' searchButton_Click
```

Figure 22.13 Converting the price to dollars.

2. *Saving the project.* Select **File > Save All** to save your modified code.

Method `Replace` also is used when the `Form` for the **Screen Scraping** app first loads. The following box uses method `Replace` to ensure that the HTML string displays correctly in a `Label`.

Displaying the HTML String

1. *Creating a Load event handler for the Form.* In **Design** view, double click the `Form` to generate an empty `Load` event handler. This event handler executes when the app runs.

2. *Formatting the Load event handler.* Add the comments in lines 42 and 46 of Fig. 22.14 around event handler `ScreenScrapingForm_Load`. Also, split the procedure header over two lines, as in lines 43–44 of Fig. 22.14, to improve its readability.

```
40      End Sub ' searchButton_Click
41
42      ' handles load event procedure for the Form
43      Private Sub ScreenScrapingForm_Load(sender As System.Object,
44          e As System.EventArgs) Handles MyBase.Load
45
46      End Sub ' ScreenScrapingForm_Load
47  End Class ' ScreenScrapingForm
```

Figure 22.14 `Load` event for the `Form`.

3. ***Displaying the HTML string in a Label.*** Add lines 46–47 of Fig. 22.15 to `ScreenScrapingForm_Load`. Line 47 calls `String` method `Replace` to replace every occurrence of `"&euro;"` in the HTML string with `"&&euro;"`. As explained previously, the substring `"&euro;"` is the HTML for the euro symbol. For this text to display in a `Label` correctly, you must prefix it with an additional ampersand (&) so that the "e" in "euro" is not confused with an access key. The value returned from `Replace` is displayed in `htmlLabel`.

```
42      ' handles load event procedure for the Form
43      Private Sub ScreenScrapingForm_Load(sender As System.Object,
44          e As System.EventArgs) Handles MyBase.Load
45
46          ' display the HTML string in a Label
47          htmlLabel.Text = html.Replace("&euro;", "&&euro;")
48      End Sub ' ScreenScrapingForm_Load
```

Replace all occurrences of "&euro" with "&&euro" → (lines 46–47)

Figure 22.15 Displaying the HTML string in a `Label`.

4. ***Running the app.*** Select **Debug > Start Debugging** to run your app. Select the different items from the **Item** ComboBox, clicking the **Search** Button after each selection. Make sure that in each case, the proper price is extracted and converted to dollars.

5. ***Closing the app.*** Close your running app by clicking its close box.

6. ***Closing the IDE.*** Close the Visual Basic IDE by clicking its close box.

SELF-REVIEW

1. If there are no occurrences of the substring in the `String`, method `Replace` returns _____.

    a) 0   b) -1

    c) nothing   d) a copy of the original `String`

2. `String` method `Replace` replaces _____ occurrence(s) of the substring in the `String`.

    a) the first   b) the last

    c) all of the   d) None of the above

Answer: 1) d. 2) c.

22.7 Other `String` Methods

Class `String` provides several additional methods that allow you to manipulate `String`s. Figure 22.16 lists some of these methods and provides a description of what each method does.

Method	Description	Sample Expression (assume text = " My String")
`EndsWith(`*`string`*`)`	Returns `True` if a `String` ends with argument *string*; otherwise, returns `False`.	`text.EndsWith("ing")` Returns: **True**
`Insert(`*`index`*`,` *`string`*`)`	Returns a copy of the `String` with the argument *string* inserted at *index*.	`text.Insert(0, "This is")` Returns: `"This is My String"`

Figure 22.16 Description of some other `String` methods. (Part 1 of 2.)

Method	Description	Sample Expression (assume text = " My String")

Join(*separator, array*)	Concatenates the elements in a String array, separated by the first argument. A new String containing the concatenated elements is returned.	`Dim array As String() =`
		`  New String() _`
		`    {"a", "b", "c"}`
		`String.Join(";", array)`
		
		Returns: `"a;b;c"`

Split()	Splits the words in a String whenever a space is reached.	`Dim array As String() =`
		`  text.Split()`
		
		Returns: A String array containing `""`, `"My"` and `"String"`

StartsWith(*string*)	Returns True if a ' starts with argument *string*; otherwise, returns False.	`text.StartsWith("Your")` Returns: **False**
Trim()	Removes any whitespace (that is, blank lines, spaces and tabs) from the beginning and end of a String. Methods TrimStart and TrimEnd are similar.	`text.Trim()` Returns: `"My String"`

Figure 22.16 Description of some other `String` methods. (Part 2 of 2.)

Figure 22.17 presents the source code for the **Screen Scraping** app. The lines of code that contain new programming concepts you learned in this chapter are highlighted.

```
1   Public Class ScreenScrapingForm
2
3       ' String of HTML to extract prices from
4       Dim html As String = "<HTML><BODY><TABLE>" &
5           "<TR><TD>Antique Rocking Chair</TD>" &
6           "<TD>&euro;82.67</TD></TR>" &
7           "<TR><TD>Silver Teapot</TD>" &
8           "<TD>&euro;64.55</TD></TR>" &
9           "<TR><TD>Gold Pocket Watch</TD>" &
10          "<TD>&euro;128.83</TD></TR>" &
11          "</TABLE></BODY></HTML>"
12
13      ' handles Search Button's Click event
14      Private Sub searchButton_Click(sender As System.Object,
15          e As System.EventArgs) Handles searchButton.Click
16
17          Dim itemLocation As Integer ' index of desired item
18          Dim priceBegin As Integer ' starting index of price
19          Dim priceEnd As Integer ' ending index of price
20          Dim price As String ' extracted price
21          Dim dollars As Decimal ' price in dollars
22
23          ' locate desired item
24          itemLocation = html.IndexOf(
25              itemsComboBox.SelectedItem.ToString())
26
27          ' locate price of item
28          priceBegin = html.IndexOf("&euro;",
29              itemLocation)
30          priceEnd = html.IndexOf("</TD>", priceBegin)
```

Search for the `SelectedItem` in the String html *(lines 24–25)*

Locate the beginning of the price in `html` *(lines 28–29)*

Locate the end of the price in `html` *(line 30)*

Figure 22.17 **Screen Scraping** app's code listing. (Part 1 of 2.)

```
31
32              ' extract the price
33      ┌─ price = html.Substring(priceBegin,
34      └─    (priceEnd - priceBegin))
35
36              ' convert price to dollars and display
37              price = price.Replace("&euro;", String.Empty)
38              dollars = Convert.ToDecimal(price) * 1.58D
39              resultLabel.Text = String.Format("{0:C}", dollars)
40          End Sub ' searchButton_Click
41
42          ' handles load event procedure for the Form
43          Private Sub ScreenScrapingForm_Load(sender As System.Object,
44              e As System.EventArgs) Handles MyBase.Load
45
46              ' display the HTML string in a Label
47              htmlLabel.Text = html.Replace("&euro;", "&&euro;")
48          End Sub ' ScreenScrapingForm_Load
49      End Class ' ScreenScrapingForm
```

Extract the price from `html` ── 33, 34

Replace "€" with the ── 37
empty `String`

Replace "€" with "&&euro" ── 47

Figure 22.17 **Screen Scraping** app's code listing. (Part 2 of 2.)

SELF-REVIEW

1. The _____ method removes all whitespace characters that appear at the beginning and end of a String.

   a) RemoveSpaces
   b) NoSpaces
   c) Trim
   d) Truncate

2. The StartsWith method returns _____ if a String begins with the method's String argument.

   a) True
   b) False
   c) 1
   d) the index of the substring

Answers: 1) c. 2) a.

22.8 Wrap-Up

In this chapter, you studied class `String` from the `System` namespace. You learned how to create and manipulate `String` objects. You learned how to locate, retrieve and replace substrings in `Strings`. You reviewed several methods from class `String` that were used in earlier chapters and learned several additional methods. You applied your knowledge of `Strings` in Visual Basic to create a simple **Screen Scraping** app that retrieves the price of an item in euros from an HTML `String` and converts it to dollars.

In the next chapter, you'll learn how data is represented in a computer, you're introduced to the concepts of files and streams, and you'll learn how to store data in sequential files.

SKILLS SUMMARY

Determining the Size of a String

■ Use String property Length.

Locating Substrings in Strings

■ Use String method IndexOf to locate the first occurrence of a substring.

■ Use String method LastIndexOf to locate the last occurrence of a substring.

Retrieving Substrings from Strings

■ Use String method Substring with one argument to obtain a substring that begins at the specified starting index and contains the remainder of the original String.

■ Use String method Substring with two arguments to specify the starting index and the length of the substring.

Replacing Substrings in `Strings`

■ Use `String` method `Replace` to replace occurrences of one substring with another substring.

Comparing Substrings to the Beginning or End of a `String`

■ Use `String` method `StartsWith` to determine whether a `String` starts with a particular substring.

■ Use `String` method `EndsWith` to determine whether a `String` ends with a particular substring.

Removing Whitespace from a `String`

■ Use `String` method `Trim` to remove all whitespace characters that appear at the beginning and end of a `String`.

KEY TERMS

Chars property of class `String`—Returns the character located at a specific index in a `String`.

EndsWith method of class `String`—Determines whether a `String` ends with a particular substring.

HTML (HyperText Markup Language)—A technology for describing web pages.

immutable—Describes an object that cannot be changed after it's created. In Visual Basic, `Strings` are immutable.

IndexOf method of class `String`—Returns the index of the first occurrence of a substring in a `String`. Returns -1 if the substring is not found.

Insert method of class `String`—Returns a new `String` object with the specified substring inserted at the given index of the original `String`.

Join method of class `String`—Concatenates the elements in a `String` array, separated by the first argument. A new `String` containing the concatenated elements is returned.

LastIndexOf method of class `String`—Returns the index of the last occurrence of a substring in a `String`. Returns -1 if the substring is not found.

Length property of class `String`—Returns the number of characters in the `String` for which it's called.

literal `String` object—A `String` constant written as a sequence of characters in double quotation marks (also called a string literal).

Replace method of class `String`—Returns a new `String` object in which every occurrence of a substring is replaced with a different substring.

special characters—Characters that are neither digits nor letters.

Split method of class `String`—Splits the words in a `String` whenever a space is reached.

StartsWith method of class `String`—Determines whether a `String` starts with a particular substring.

string constant—A `String` constant written as a sequence of characters in double quotation marks (also called a string literal).

string literal—A `String` constant written as a sequence of characters in double quotation marks (also called a literal `String` object).

substring—A sequence of characters in a `String`.

Substring method of class `String`—Creates a new `String` object by copying part of an existing `String` object.

Trim method of class `String`—Removes all whitespace characters from the beginning and end of a `String`.

CONTROLS, EVENTS, PROPERTIES & METHODS

`String`   The `String` class represents a series of characters treated as a single unit.

■ *Properties*

`Chars`—Returns the character located at a specific index in the `String`.

`Length`—Returns the number of characters in the `String`.

■ *Methods*

`EndsWith`—Determines whether a `String` ends with a particular substring.

`Format`—Arranges the string in a specified format.

`IndexOf`—Returns the index of the specified character(s) in a `String`. Returns `-1` if the substring is not found.

`Insert`—Returns a copy of the `String` for which it's called with the specified character(s) inserted.

`Join`—Concatenates the elements in a `String` array, separated by the first argument. A new `String` containing the concatenated elements is returned.

`LastIndexOf`—Returns the index of the last occurrence of a substring in a `String`. Returns `-1` if the substring is not found.

`PadLeft`—Inserts characters at the beginning of a `String`.

`Remove`—Returns a copy of the `String` for which it's called with the specified character(s) removed.

`Replace`—Returns a new `String` object in which every occurrence of a substring is replaced with a different substring.

`StartsWith`—Determines whether a `String` starts with a particular substring.

`Substring`—Returns a substring from a `String`.

`ToLower`—Returns a copy of the `String` for which it's called with any uppercase letters converted to lowercase letters.

`ToUpper`—Returns a copy of the `String` for which it's called with any lowercase letters converted to uppercase letters.

`Trim`—Removes all whitespace characters from the beginning and end of a `String`.

MULTIPLE-CHOICE QUESTIONS

22.1 Extracting desired information from web pages is called _____.

   a) web crawling   b) screen scraping

   c) querying   d) redirection

22.2 If method `IndexOf` does not find the specified substring, it returns _____.

   a) `False`   b) `0`

   c) `-1`   d) None of the above

22.3 The `String` class allows you to _____ `Strings`.

   a) search   b) retrieve characters from

   c) replace characters in   d) All of the above

22.4 _____ is a technology for describing web content.

   a) Class `String`   b) A string literal

   c) HTML   d) A screen scraper

22.5 The `String` class is located in the _____ namespace.

   a) `String`   b) `System.Strings`

   c) `System.IO`   d) `System`

22.6 The _____ method creates a new `String` object by copying part of an existing `String` object.

   a) `StringCopy`   b) `Substring`

   c) `CopyString`   d) `CopySubString`

22.7 All `String` objects are _____.

   a) the same size

   b) always equal to each other

   c) preceded by at least one whitespace character

   d) immutable

22.8 The IndexOf method with two arguments does not examine any characters that occur prior to the _____.

a) starting index
b) first match
c) last character of the String
d) None of the above

22.9 The _____ method determines whether a String ends with a particular substring.

a) CheckEnd
b) StringEnd
c) EndsWith
d) EndIs

22.10 The _____ method returns an array of Strings.

a) Join
b) Split
c) Replace
d) None of the above

EXERCISES

22.11 *(Supply Cost Calculator App)* Write an app that calculates the cost of all the supplies added to the user's shopping list (Fig. 22.18). The app should contain two ListBoxes. The first contains all the supplies offered and their respective prices. Users should be able to select the desired supplies from the first ListBox and add them to the second ListBox. Provide a **Calculate** Button that displays the total price for the user's shopping list (the contents of the second ListBox).

Figure 22.18 Supply Cost Calculator app's GUI.

a) *Copying the template to your working directory.* Copy the directory C:\Examples\ch22\Exercises\SupplyCalculator to your C:\SimplyVB2010 directory.

b) *Opening the app's template file.* Double click SupplyCalculator.sln in the SupplyCalculator directory to open the app.

c) *Adding code to the Add >> Button.* Double click the **Add >>** Button to create an empty event handler. Insert code in the event handler that adds the selected item from the first ListBox to shoppingListBox. Be sure to check that an item is selected in the first ListBox before attempting to add an item to shoppingListBox.

d) *Enabling the Buttons.* Once the user adds something to the shoppingListBox, set the Enabled properties of the **<< Remove** and **Calculate** Buttons to True.

e) *Deselecting the items.* Once the item is added to the shoppingListBox, make sure that it's deselected in the stockListBox. Also, clear the **Total:** Label to indicate to the user that a new total price must be calculated.

f) *Adding code to the << Remove Button.* Double click the **<< Remove** Button to create an empty event handler. The **Items in your list:** ListBox's SelectionMode property has been set to MultiExtended to allow the user to select multiple items. Use a Do While loop to remove any selected items in the shoppingListBox. Be sure to check that at least one item is selected before attempting to remove an item. [*Hint:* Method shoppingListBox.Items.RemoveAt(index) will remove the item located at index from the shoppingListBox. When an item is removed, the SelectedIndex property points to the next selected item, if there is one.] If there are no items remaining in the shoppingListBox, disable the **<< Remove** and **Calculate** Buttons. Also, clear the **Total:** Label to indicate to the user that a new total price must be calculated.

g) *Adding code to the Calculate `Button`*. Double click the **Calculate** `Button` to create an empty event handler. Use a For...Next statement to loop through all the items in the `shoppingListBox`. Convert each item from the `ListBox` into a `String`. Then use the `String` method `Substring` to extract the price of each item.

h) *Displaying the total*. Convert the `String` representing each item's price to a `Decimal`, and add this to the overall total (of type `Decimal`). Remember to output the value in currency format.

i) *Running the app*. Select **Debug > Start Debugging** to run your app. Use the **Add >>** and **<< Remove** `Buttons` to add and remove items from the **Items in your list:** `List-Box`. Click the **Calculate** `Button` and verify that the total price displayed is correct.

j) *Closing the app*. Close your running app by clicking its close box.

k) *Closing the IDE*. Close the Visual Basic IDE by clicking its close box.

22.12 *(Encryption App)* Write an app that encrypts a message from the user (Fig. 22.19). The app should be able to encrypt the message in two different ways: substitution cipher and transposition cipher (both described below). The user should be able to enter the message in a `TextBox` and select the desired method of encryption. Display the encrypted message in a `Label`.

Figure 22.19 Encryption app's GUI.

In a substitution cipher, every character in the English alphabet is represented by a different character in the substitution alphabet. Every time a letter occurs in the English sentence, it's replaced by the letter at the corresponding index of the substitution alphabet. In a transposition cipher, two `Strings` are created. The first new `String` contains all characters at the even indices of the input `String`. The second new `String` contains all characters at the odd indices. The new `Strings` are concatenated, with a space between them, to form the encrypted text. For example, a transposition cipher for the word "code" would be "cd oe."

a) *Copying the template to your working directory*. Copy the directory `C:\Examples\ ch22\Exercises\Encryption` to your `C:\SimplyVB2010` directory.

b) *Opening the app's template file*. Double click `Encryption.sln` in the `Encryption` directory to open the app.

c) *Adding code to the Encrypt `Button`*. Double click the **Encrypt** `Button` to create an empty event handler.

d) *Determining the cipher method*. Use If...Then...Else statements to determine which method of encryption the user has selected and call the appropriate procedure.

e) *Locating the `SubstitutionCipher` method*. Locate the `SubstitutionCipher` procedure. The English and substitution alphabet `Strings` are defined for you in this procedure.

f) *Converting the text input to lowercase*. Add code to the `SubstitutionCipher` method that uses the `ToLower` method of class `String` to make all the characters in the input `String` (`plainTextBox.Text`) lowercase.

g) *Performing the substitution encryption*. Use a For...Next statement to iterate through each character of the input `String`. Use `String` method `IndexOf` to find the index of the input character in the `String` holding the English alphabet. Attach the character from the `cipherAlphabet` at the corresponding index to the cipher text.

h) *Displaying the `String`*. Now that the `String` has been substituted with all the corresponding cipher characters, assign the cipher `String` to `cipherTextLabel`.

i) *Locating the TranspositionCipher method.* Locate the TranspositionCipher method. Define two String variables, each representing a word.

j) *Extracting the first word.* Use a For...Next statement to retrieve all the "even" indices (starting from 0) from the input String. Increment the control variable by 2 each time, and add the characters located at even indices to the first String created in *Step i*.

k) *Extracting the second word.* Use another For...Next statement to retrieve all the "odd" indices (starting from 1) from the same input String. Increment the control variable by 2, and add the characters at odd indices to the second String that you created in *Step i*.

l) *Outputting the result.* Add the two Strings together with a space in between, and output the result to cipherTextLabel.

m) *Running the app.* Select **Debug > Start Debugging** to run your app. Enter text into the **Enter text to encrypt:** TextBox. Select the **Substitution Cipher** RadioButton and click the **Encrypt** Button. Verify that the output is the properly encrypted text using the substitution cipher. Select the **Transposition Cipher** RadioButton and click the **Encrypt** Button. Verify that the output is the properly encrypted text using the transposition cipher.

n) *Closing the app.* Close your running app by clicking its close box.

o) *Closing the IDE.* Close the Visual Basic IDE by clicking its close box.

22.13 *(Anagram Game App)* Write an **Anagram Game** that contains an array of 20 pre-set words (Fig. 22.20). The game randomly selects a word and scrambles its letters. A Label displays the scrambled word for the user to guess. If the user guesses correctly, display a message, then repeat the process with a different word. If the guess is incorrect, display a message and let the user try again.

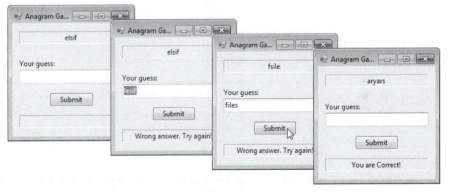

Figure 22.20 Anagram Game app's GUI.

a) *Copying the template to your working directory.* Copy the directory C:\Examples\ch22\Exercises\Anagram to your C:\SimplyVB2010 directory.

b) *Opening the app's template file.* Double click Anagram.sln in the Anagram directory to open the app.

c) *Locating the GenerateAnagram method.* Locate the GenerateAnagram method. It's the first method after the AnagramForm_Load event handler.

d) *Picking a random word.* Generate a random number to use as the index of the word in the anagram array. Retrieve a word from the anagram array, using the random number as an index. Store the word in another String variable.

e) *Generating the scrambled word.* Generate a second random number to store the index of a character to be moved. Use a For...Next statement to iterate through the word 20 times. In the body of the loop, pass the second random number to the Chars property of class String. Append the character returned by Chars to the end of the String, and remove it from its original position. Next, generate a new random number to move a different character during the next iteration of the loop. Remember to output the final word to anagramLabel.

f) *Defining the Submit Button.* Double click the **Submit** Button to generate an empty event handler.

g) *Testing the user's input.* Use an If...Then...Else statement to determine whether the user's input matches the actual word. If the user is correct, clear the TextBox, place the focus on the TextBox and generate a new word. Otherwise, select the user's text (using the TextBox's SelectAll method) and place the focus on the TextBox.

h) *Running the app.* Select **Debug > Start Debugging** to run your app. Submit correct answers and incorrect answers, and verify that the appropriate message is displayed each time.

i) *Closing the app.* Close your running app by clicking its close box.

j) *Closing the IDE.* Close the Visual Basic IDE by clicking its close box.

What does this code do? ▶ **22.14** What is assigned to result when the following code executes?

```
1   Dim word1 As String = "CHORUS"
2   Dim word2 As String = "d i n o s a u r"
3   Dim word3 As String = "The theme is string."
4   Dim result As String
5
6   result = word1.ToLower()
7   result = result.Substring(4)
8   word2 = word2.Replace(" ", String.Empty)
9   word2 = word2.Substring(4, 4)
10  result = word2 & result
11
12  word3 = word3.Substring(word3.IndexOf(" ") + 1, 3)
13
14  result = word3.Insert(3, result)
```

What's wrong with this code? ▶ **22.15** This code should remove all commas from test and convert all lowercase letters to uppercase letters. Find the error(s) in the following code.

```
1   Dim test As String = "Bug,2,Bug"
2
3   test = test.ToUpper()
4   test = test.Replace(String.Empty)
```

Programming Challenge ▶ **22.16** *(Pig Latin App)* Write an app that encodes English-language phrases into pig Latin (Fig. 22.21). Pig Latin is a form of coded language often used for amusement. Many different methods are used to form pig Latin words and phrases. For simplicity, use the following method:

> To form a pig Latin word from an English-language phrase, the translation proceeds one word at a time. To translate an English word into a pig Latin word, place the first letter of the English word (if it's not a vowel) at the end of the English word and add the letters "ay." If the first letter of the English word is a vowel, place it at the end of the word and add "y." Using this method, the word "jump" becomes "umpjay," the word "the" becomes "hetay" and the word "ace" becomes "ceay." Blanks between words remain blanks.

Assume the following: The English phrase consists of words separated by blanks, there are no punctuation marks and all words have two or more letters. Enable the user to input a sentence. The TranslateToPigLatin method translates the sentence into pig Latin, word by word. [*Hint:* You need to use the Join and Split methods of class String demonstrated in Fig. 22.16 to form the pig Latin phrases.]

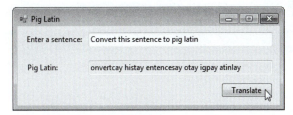

Figure 22.21 Pig Latin app.

a) *Copying the template to your working directory.* Copy the C:\Examples\ ch22\Exercises\PigLatin directory to your C:\SimplyVB2010 directory.

b) *Opening the app's template file.* Double click PigLatin.sln in the PigLatin directory to open the app.

c) *Splitting the sentence.* Use method Split on the String passed to the Translate-ToPigLatin method. Assign the result of this operation to words.

d) *Retrieving the word's first letter.* Declare a For...Next statement that iterates through your array of words. As you iterate through the array, store each word's first letter in temporary.

e) *Determining the suffix.* Use an If...Then...Else statement to determine whether the first letter is a vowel, then determine the suffix for each word. Store this suffix in suffix.

f) *Generating new words.* Generate the new words by arranging each word's pieces in the proper order.

g) *Returning the new sentence.* When the For...Next statement finishes, use method Join to combine all of the elements in words, and Return the new pig Latin sentence.

h) *Running the app.* Select **Debug > Start Debugging** to run your app. Enter a sentence and click the **Translate** Button. Verify that the sentence is correctly converted into pig Latin.

i) *Closing the app.* Close your running app by clicking its close box.

j) *Closing the IDE.* Close the Visual Basic IDE by clicking its close box.

23

Objectives

In this chapter, you'll learn to:

- Create, read from, write to and update files.
- Become familiar with sequential-access file processing.
- Use `StreamReader` and `StreamWriter` classes to read from, and write to, sequential-access files.
- Use the `OpenFileDialog` component.
- Use a `MonthCalendar` control.
- Use LINQ to query a sequential-access file.

Outline

Ticket Information App
Introducing Sequential-Access Files

Y ou studied the data hierarchy in Chapter 1. Storage of data in variables and arrays is temporary—such data is *lost* when a program terminates. To store data for a longer period of time, you can use files. A **file** is a collection of data that's given a name, such as `data.txt` or `Welcome.sln`. Data in files exists even after the app that created the data terminates—it's called **persistent data**. Computers store files on **secondary storage media**, including magnetic disks (for example, the hard drive of your computer), optical disks (for instance, CD-ROMs or DVDs), flash drives and magnetic tapes.

File processing—which includes creating, reading from, writing to and updating files—is an important capability of Visual Basic. It enables Visual Basic to support commercial apps that typically process massive amounts of persistent data. In this chapter, you'll learn about **sequential-access files**, which contain information that's read from a file in the order in which it was originally written to the file. You'll learn how to create, open and write to a sequential-access file by building a **Write Event** app. This app allows the user to create or open a **text file** (a file containing human-readable characters) and to input the date, time, price and description of a community event (such as a concert or a sporting match).

You'll then learn how to read data from a file by building the **Ticket Information** app. This app displays data from a text file named `calendar.txt` created by the **Write Event** app.

23.1 Test-Driving the Ticket Information App

Many communities and businesses use computer apps to allow their members and customers to view information about upcoming events, such as movies, concerts, sports and other activities. In Section 23.3, you'll first build a **Write Event** app that enables you to create a sequential-access file containing community-event information. The **Ticket Information** app that you'll build in this chapter displays the data stored in the file that the **Write Event** app generates. The **Ticket Information** app must meet the following requirements:

Your app allows a user to select a date from a **MonthCalendar** control. Then the app opens the `calendar.txt` file and reads its contents to display information about events scheduled for the selected date. You'll begin by test-driving the completed app. Then you'll learn the additional Visual Basic capabilities needed to create your own version of the app.

Test-Driving the Ticket Information App

1. **Opening the completed app.** Open the directory `C:\Examples\ch23\CompletedApp\TicketInformation` to locate the **Ticket Information** app. Double click `TicketInformation.sln` to open the app in the Visual Basic IDE.

2. **Running the Ticket Information app.** Select **Debug > Start Debugging** to run the app (Fig. 23.1). The calendar reflects the day and month on which you actually run the app. [*Note:* On Windows XP, the MonthCalendar control looks somewhat different from the version on Windows Vista in Fig. 23.1.] The MonthCalendar control is similar to the DateTimePicker control (Chapter 14), except that a MonthCalendar allows you to select a range of dates, whereas the DateTimePicker allows you to select the time, but no more than one date. For simplicity, you should select only one date. In addition, the app deals only with the current month, but the MonthCalendar control allows the user to view calendars of previous or future months by using the arrow buttons.

Arrow buttons allow user to scroll through months

MonthCalendar control

ComboBox lists any events

TextBox displays event details

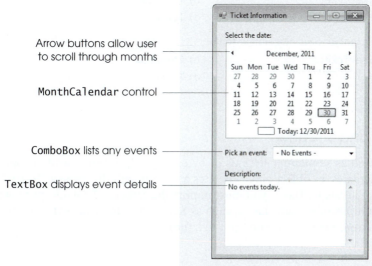

Figure 23.1 **Ticket Information** app's GUI.

(cont.)

3. *Getting event information.* Select the 13th day of the current month in the MonthCalendar. Note that the ComboBox displays "- No Events -" (Fig. 23.2). This is because no events are scheduled for the 13th. Select the 19th day of the month. The ComboBox now displays "- Events -". Click the ComboBox to view them and select **Comedy club**. The time, the price and description of the event appear in the **Description:** TextBox (Fig. 23.2).

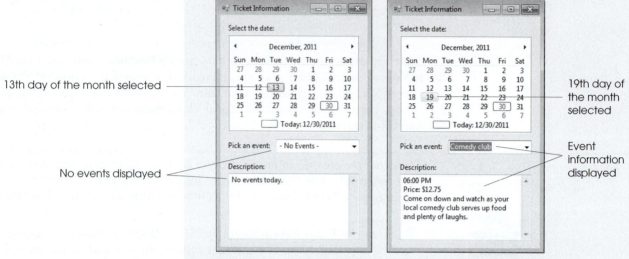

13th day of the month selected

No events displayed

19th day of the month selected

Event information displayed

Figure 23.2 **Ticket Information** app displaying event information.

4. *Testing the app.* Select other dates and view the results.

5. *Closing the app.* Close your running app by clicking its close box.

6. *Closing the IDE.* Close the Visual Basic IDE by clicking its close box.

1. The _____ control allows a user to select a range of dates.
   a) DateTimePicker   b) MonthCalendar
   c) ComboBox   d) TextBox

2. The MonthCalendar control is similar to the _____ control.
   a) DateTimePicker   b) ComboBox
   c) TextBox   d) Timer

Answers: 1) b. 2) a.

23.2 Files and Streams

Files are viewed as sequential **streams** of bytes (Fig. 23.3). When a file is opened, Visual Basic creates an object and associates a stream with that object. To perform file processing in Visual Basic, you must import the System.IO namespace, which includes definitions of stream classes, such as **StreamReader** (for text input from a file) and **StreamWriter** (for text output to a file).

0 1 2 3 4 5 6 7 8 9 ... $n-1$

end-of-file marker

Figure 23.3 Visual Basic's conceptual view of an n-byte file.

23.3 Writing to a File—Creating the Write Event App

An important aspect of the **Ticket Information** app is its ability to read data sequentially from a file. You need to create the file from which the **Ticket Information** app reads its data. Therefore, before you create the **Ticket Information** app, you must learn how to write to a sequential-access file.

The **Write Event** app enables the user to create a new file or open an existing file. The user might want to create a new file for events or update an existing file by adding more event information. You'll add this functionality in the following box.

Adding a Dialog to Open or Create a File

1. ***Copying the template to your working directory.*** Copy the `C:\Examples\ch23\TemplateApp\WriteEvent` directory to your `C:\SimplyVB2010` directory.

2. ***Opening the Write Event app's template file.*** Double click `WriteEvent.sln` in the `WriteEvent` directory to open the app in the Visual Basic IDE.

3. ***Adding a dialog to the Form.*** The app uses the `OpenFileDialog` component to customize the **Open** dialog. To add an `OpenFileDialog` to the app, double click the `OpenFileDialog` component

       📄 OpenFileDialog

   in the **All Windows Forms** category of the **Toolbox**. The control's name appears in the component tray at the bottom of the **Design** view. Change the control's Name property to `openFileDialog`. Change its `FileName` property to `calendar.txt`, which is the default filename displayed in the **Open** dialog. [*Note:* This is the name of the file from which the **Ticket Information** app retrieves information.] The **Open** dialog normally allows the user to open only existing files, but you also want the user to be able to create a file. For this reason, set property `CheckFileExists` to `False` so that the **Open** dialog allows the user to specify a new filename. If the user specifies a file that does not exist, the file is created and opened. Figure 23.4 shows the app in **Design** view after the `OpenFileDialog` component has been added and renamed.

   OpenFileDialog component ——

   Figure 23.4 `openFileDialog` added and renamed.

4. ***Saving the project.*** Select **File > Save All** to save your modified code.

The **Write Event** app stores the user-input information in a text file. It expects the user to open or create a file with the extension `.txt`. If the user does not do so, the app displays an error message. The following box guides you through adding this functionality.

Determining Whether a Filename Is Valid

1. ***Adding method `CheckValidity`.*** Add lines 3–6 of Fig. 23.5 to the app. Method `CheckValidity` receives a filename as a `String` and returns a `Boolean` value. If the filename is valid, the `Function` returns `True`; otherwise, `False`.

CheckValidity Function procedure header

```
1   Public Class WriteEventForm
2
3       ' determine validity of file type
4       Private Function CheckValidity(name As String) As Boolean
5
6       End Function ' CheckValidity
7   End Class ' WriteEventForm
```

Figure 23.5   Method `CheckValidity` header.

2. ***Displaying a `MessageBox` to indicate an invalid filename.*** Add lines 5–11 of Fig. 23.6 to method `CheckValidity`. String method `EndsWith` (line 6) returns `False` if the value of variable `name` does not end with `.txt`, the extension that indicates a text file. In this case, lines 7–9 display a `Message-Box` informing the user that the app expects a text file.

Displaying error message if incorrect file type is provided

```
3       ' determine validity of file type
4       Private Function CheckValidity(name As String) As Boolean
5           ' show error if user specified invalid file
6           If name.ToLower().EndsWith(".txt") = False Then
7               MessageBox.Show("Filename must end with .txt",
8                   "Invalid File Type",
9                   MessageBoxButtons.OK, MessageBoxIcon.Error)
10              Return False ' to indicate invalid file type
11          End If
12      End Function ' CheckValidity
```

Figure 23.6   Displaying an error message indicating an invalid filename.

3. ***Receiving a valid filename.*** Add lines 11–16 of Fig. 23.7 to the `If...Then` statement. If a valid filename is entered, the GUI should indicate that the user cannot create or open another file but may enter data into the file or close the file. For this reason, line 13 disables the **Open File...** Button, and lines 14–15 enable the **Enter** and **Close File** Buttons, respectively. The method returns `True` (line 16) to indicate that the user entered a valid filename.

Enabling and disabling Buttons

```
10              Return False ' to indicate invalid file type
11              ' change status of Buttons if filename is valid
12          Else
13              openFileButton.Enabled = False
14              enterButton.Enabled = True
15              closeFileButton.Enabled = True
16              Return True ' to indicate text file specified
17          End If
18      End Function ' CheckValidity
```

Figure 23.7   Changing the GUI if a valid filename is entered.

4. ***Saving the project.*** Select **File > Save All** to save your modified code.

You've added the `OpenFileDialog` component to allow users to open a file and a method that determines whether the user has entered a valid filename. Now you'll add code that associates the specified file with a stream.

Creating a
StreamWriter Object

1. *Importing namespace System.IO to enable file processing.* To access the classes that enable you to perform file processing with sequential-access files without preceding each class name with System.IO, add line 1 of Fig. 23.8 to import namespace System.IO.

Importing namespace System.IO ———

```
1   Imports System.IO
2
3   Public Class WriteEventForm
```

Figure 23.8   System.IO namespace imported into class `WriteEventForm`.

2. *Declaring a StreamWriter variable.* Namespace System.IO includes class StreamWriter, which we'll use to create an object for writing text to a file. Add line 5 of Fig. 23.9 to the WriteEventForm class definition to declare the variable that holds a StreamWriter object.

```
1   Imports System.IO
2
3   Public Class WriteEventForm
4
5       Private output As StreamWriter
6
7       ' determine validity of file type
```

Declaring StreamWriter variable ———

Figure 23.9   Declaring a `StreamWriter` variable.

3. *Creating the Open File... Button's Click event handler.* Switch to **Design** view and double click the **Open File...** Button on the **Write Event** app's Form to create the empty openFileButton_Click event handler. Add a comment and reformat the empty event handler as shown in lines 24–26 of Fig. 23.10.

```
24      ' handles Open File... Button's Click event
25      Private Sub openFileButton_Click(sender As System.Object,
26          e As System.EventArgs) Handles openFileButton.Click
27
28          ' display Open dialog
29          Dim result As DialogResult = openFileDialog.ShowDialog()
30
31          ' open specified file if user did not click Cancel Button
32          If result <> Windows.Forms.DialogResult.Cancel Then
33
34          End If
35      End Sub ' openFileButton_Click
```

Displaying **Open** dialog ———

If the user clicks **Cancel**, the
event handler exits without ———
performing any actions

Figure 23.10   Displaying the **Open** dialog and retrieving the result.

4. *Displaying the Open dialog.* Add lines 28–34 of Fig. 23.10 to the event handler. When the user clicks the **Open File...** Button, the **ShowDialog** method of the OpenFileDialog component displays the **Open** dialog to allow the user to open a file (line 29) and returns a value of type DialogResult. If the user specifies a file that does not exist, it's created. Line 29 assigns the return value of method ShowDialog to a DialogResult variable named `result`.

(cont.)

The value of the `DialogResult` variable specifies what `Button` the user clicked in the **Open** dialog. If the user clicked the **Cancel** `Button` (line 32), the event handler exits without performing the actions in the `If...Then` statement. At this point, the user can still open or create a file by clicking the enabled **Open File...** `Button` again. Be sure to add the comments, as shown in Fig. 23.10, so that the line numbers in your code match those presented in this chapter.

5. ***Retrieving the filename***. Add lines 33–34 of Fig. 23.11 to the `If` statement. Property `FileName` of `OpenFileDialog` specifies the full path of the file the user selected (line 34). The app stores the path and filename in `fileName`.

Setting variable to user-specified filename

```
31          ' open specified file if user did not click Cancel Button
32          If result <> Windows.Forms.DialogResult.Cancel Then
33              ' get specified filename
34              Dim fileName As String = openFileDialog.FileName
35          End If
```

Figure 23.11   Retrieving the name and path of selected file.

6. ***Checking for a valid file type***. Add lines 36–40 of Fig. 23.12 to the event handler. Line 37 invokes method `CheckValidity` (which you defined earlier in this chapter) to determine whether the specified file is a text file (that is, the filename ends with ".txt").

Check for valid filename

Create `StreamWriter` object

```
31          ' open specified file if user did not click Cancel Button
32          If result <> Windows.Forms.DialogResult.Cancel Then
33              ' get specified filename
34              Dim fileName As String = openFileDialog.FileName
35
36              ' validate filename
37              If CheckValidity(fileName) = True Then
38                  ' enable user to append data to file via StreamWriter
39                  output = New StreamWriter(fileName, True)
40              End If
41          End If
```

Figure 23.12   Validating the filename and initializing a `StreamWriter` object.

7. ***Initializing a StreamWriter object***. Line 39 creates and initializes `Stream-Writer` object `output`, which is used to write to the specified file. The `StreamWriter` constructor takes two arguments—the first indicates the name of the file (specified by variable `fileName`) to which you write information and the second is a `Boolean` value that determines whether the `StreamWriter` appends information to the end of the file. You pass value `True`, so that any information written to the file is *appended* to the end of the file if the file already exists. If you pass value `False`, any existing content in the file is deleted and replaced.

Common Programming Error

When you open an existing file by invoking the `StreamWriter` constructor with a `False` second argument, data previously contained in the file is lost.

8. ***Saving the project***. Select **File > Save All** to save your modified code.

Now that the app can open a file, the user can input information that's written to that file. In the following box, you'll add code that makes the **Enter** `Button`'s `Click` event handler write the data to the text file.

Writing Information to a Sequential-Access File

1. *Clearing user input from the TextBoxes and resetting the NumericUpDown control.* Add lines 44–50 of Fig. 23.13 to the app below the openFile-Button_Click event handler. After the user's input is processed, the **Enter** Button's event handler invokes method ClearUserInput to clear the Text-Boxes and reset the NumericUpDown control's value to 1 (the first day of the month).

```
42        End Sub ' openFileButton_Click
43
44        ' clear TextBoxes and reset NumericUpDown control
45        Private Sub ClearUserInput()
46            dayUpDown.Value = 1
47            priceTextBox.Clear()
48            eventTextBox.Clear()
49            descriptionTextBox.Clear()
50        End Sub ' ClearUserInput
51    End Class ' WriteEventForm
```

Clearing user input → (lines 46–49)

Figure 23.13   Clearing user input.

2. *Creating the enterButton_Click event handler.* In **Design** view, double click the **Enter** Button to create the enterButton_Click event handler. Add a comment and reformat the empty event handler as shown in lines 52–54 of Fig. 23.14.

3. *Defining the enterButton_Click event handler.* Add lines 56–62 of Fig. 23.14 to the event handler. Lines 57–60 write the user input to the file by using the StreamWriter's **Write** method. The Write method writes its argument to the file. Each field is separated by a *Tab* character—this makes it easier to extract the data from the file. Line 61 writes the last field using StreamWriter's **WriteLine** method. The WriteLine method writes its argument to the file, followed by a newline character. Each record in the file ends with a newline character—the delimiter we chose to mark the end of a record. The information is written to the file in the following order: day of the event, time, price, event name and description. Line 62 invokes the ClearUserInput procedure that you defined in *Step 1* of this box. Be sure to add the comments, as shown in Fig. 23.14, so that the line numbers in your code match those presented in this chapter.

```
52        ' handles Enter Button's Click event
53        Private Sub enterButton_Click(sender As System.Object,
54            e As System.EventArgs) Handles enterButton.Click
55
56            ' using StreamWriter to write data to file
57            output.Write(dayUpDown.Value & ControlChars.Tab)
58            output.Write(timeDateTimePicker.Text & ControlChars.Tab)
59            output.Write(priceTextBox.Text & ControlChars.Tab)
60            output.Write(eventTextBox.Text & ControlChars.Tab)
61            output.WriteLine(descriptionTextBox.Text)
62            ClearUserInput() ' prepare GUI for more user input
63        End Sub ' enterButton_Click
```

Writing information to a file → (lines 57–62)

Figure 23.14   StreamWriter writing to a file.

4. *Saving the project.* Select **File > Save All** to save your modified code.

You should always close the file after you've finished processing it to ensure that you don't lose any data. You'll add this capability to the **Close File** Button's `Click` event handler in the following box.

Closing the StreamWriter

1. **Create the `closeFileButton_Click` event handler.** In **Design** view, double click the **Close File** Button of the **Write Event** app's Form to create the `closeFileButton_Click` event handler. Add a comment and reformat the empty event handler as shown in lines 66–67 of Fig. 23.15.

2. **Defining the `closeFileButton_Click` event handler.** Add lines 69–74 of Fig. 23.15 to the event handler. Line 69 uses the StreamWriter's **Close** method to close the stream. Line 72 re-enables the **Open File...** Button in case the user would like to create or update another sequential-access file. Lines 73–74 disable the **Enter** and **Close File** Buttons, because users should not be able to click these Buttons when a file is not open.

```
65      ' handles Close File Button's Click event
66      Private Sub closeFileButton_Click(sender As System.Object,
67          e As System.EventArgs) Handles closeFileButton.Click
68
69      output.Close() ' close StreamWriter
70
71          ' allow user to open another file
72          openFileButton.Enabled = True
73          enterButton.Enabled = False
74          closeFileButton.Enabled = False
75      End Sub ' closeFileButton_Click
76  End Class ' WriteEventForm
```

Closing `StreamWriter` object ⟶ (line 69)

Figure 23.15 Closing the `StreamWriter`.

3. **Saving the project.** Select **File > Save All** to save your modified code.

You've now successfully created the **Write Event** app. You'll test this app to see how it works and view the file contents in the following box.

Writing Event Information to a File

1. **Running the Write Event app.** Select **Debug > Start Debugging** to run your app (Fig. 23.16).

Figure 23.16 **Write Event** app running.

2. **Creating a file.** Click the **Open File...** Button to display the **Open** dialog. To open the existing `calendar.txt` file, browse to `C:\Examples\ch23\TemplateApp\TicketInformation\TicketInformation\bin\Debug` (Fig. 23.17) and select `calendar.txt`.

(cont.)

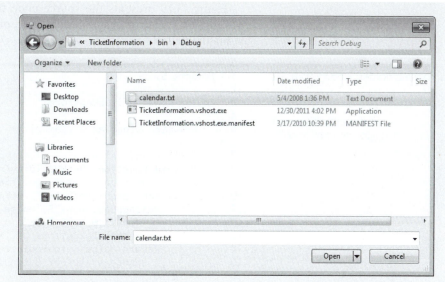

Figure 23.17   **Open** dialog displaying contents of the template **Ticket Information** app's **Debug** folder.

The filename `calendar.txt` should be displayed in the **File name:** field, as in Fig. 23.17. The **File name:** field may not display the extension (`.txt`), or `calendar` may be displayed with a capital "C" based on your computer's settings. Click the **Open** Button to open the existing `calendar.txt` file.

3. *Entering event information*. In the **Day:** NumericUpDown control, select 4 to indicate that the event is scheduled on the fourth day of the month. Enter 2:30 PM in the **Time:** DateTimePicker. Type 12.50 in the **Price:** TextBox. Enter Arts and Crafts Fair in the **Event:** TextBox. In the **Description:** TextBox, enter the information Take part in creating various types of arts and crafts at this fair. Click the **Enter** Button to add this event's information to the `calendar.txt` file.

4. *Entering more event information*. Write more event information to the file by repeating *Step 3* with your own set of events.

5. *Closing the file*. When you've entered all the events you wish, click the **Close File** Button. This closes the `calendar.txt` file and prevents any more events from being written.

6. *Closing the app*. Close your running app by clicking its close box.

7. *Opening and closing the sequential-access file*. Use the IDE to open `calendar.txt`. Select **File > Open File...** to display the **Open** dialog. Navigate to the folder C:\Examples\ch23_TicketInfo\TemplateApp\TicketInformation\TicketInformation\bin\Debug, select the `calendar.txt` file and click **Open**. Scroll through the file. The information you entered in *Steps 3* and *4* should appear in the file, similar to Fig. 23.18. Close the `calendar.txt` file.

Day and time of event, ticket price, event name and description

Figure 23.18   Sequential-access file generated by **Write Event** app.

8. *Closing the IDE*. Close the Visual Basic IDE by clicking its close box.

Figure 23.19 presents the source code for the **Write Event** app. The lines of code that contain new programming concepts you've learned so far in this chapter are highlighted.

```
Importing namespace System.IO ─── 1 ─ Imports System.IO
                                   2
                                   3   Public Class WriteEventForm
                                   4
              StreamWriter used ── 5 ─ Private output As StreamWriter
            to write text to a file 6
                                   7     ' determine validity of file type
                                   8     Private Function CheckValidity(name As String) As Boolean
                                   9       ' show error if user specified invalid file
                                  10       If name.EndsWith(".txt") = False Then
                                  11         MessageBox.Show("Filename must end with .txt",
                                  12           "Invalid File Type",
                                  13           MessageBoxButtons.OK, MessageBoxIcon.Error)
                                  14         Return False ' to indicate invalid file type
                                  15         ' change status of Buttons if filename is valid
                                  16       Else
                                  17         openFileButton.Enabled = False
                                  18         enterButton.Enabled = True
                                  19         closeFileButton.Enabled = True
                                  20         Return True ' to indicate text file specified
                                  21       End If
                                  22     End Function ' CheckValidity
                                  23
                                  24     ' handles Open File... Button's Click event
                                  25     Private Sub openFileButton_Click(sender As System.Object,
                                  26       e As System.EventArgs) Handles openFileButton.Click
                                  27
              Retrieve user input  28       ' display Open dialog
             from Open dialog ──── 29 ─── Dim result As DialogResult = openFileDialog.ShowDialog()
                                  30
     Checking the button pressed in 31       ' open specified file if user did not click Cancel Button
         the OpenFileDialog ────── 32 ─── If result <> Windows.Forms.DialogResult.Cancel Then
                                  33         ' get specified filename
 Storing filename entered by user ─ 34 ─── Dim fileName As String = openFileDialog.FileName
                                  35
                                  36         ' validate filename
                                  37         If CheckValidity(fileName) = True Then
     Create StreamWriter object    38           ' enable user to append data to file via StreamWriter
    to associate a stream with the 39 ───     output = New StreamWriter(fileName, True)
         user-specified text file  40         End If
                                  41       End If
                                  42     End Sub ' openFileButton_Click
                                  43
                                  44     ' clear TextBoxes and reset NumericUpDown control
                                  45     Private Sub ClearUserInput()
                                  46       dayUpDown.Value = 1
                                  47       priceTextBox.Clear()
                                  48       eventTextBox.Clear()
                                  49       descriptionTextBox.Clear()
                                  50     End Sub ' ClearUserInput
                                  51
                                  52     ' handles Enter Button's Click event
                                  53     Private Sub enterButton_Click(sender As System.Object,
                                  54       e As System.EventArgs) Handles enterButton.Click
                                  55
                                  56       ' using StreamWriter to write data to file
                                  57       output.Write(dayUpDown.Value & ControlChars.Tab)
         Append data to end of file 58       output.Write(timeDateTimePicker.Text & ControlChars.Tab)
                                  59       output.Write(priceTextBox.Text & ControlChars.Tab)
```

Figure 23.19   **Write Event** app's code. (Part 1 of 2.)

Append data to end of file
```
60          output.Write(eventTextBox.Text & ControlChars.Tab)
61          output.WriteLine(descriptionTextBox.Text)
62          ClearUserInput() ' prepare GUI for more user input
63    End Sub ' enterButton_Click
64
65    ' handles Close File Button's Click event
66    Private Sub closeFileButton_Click(sender As System.Object,
67       e As System.EventArgs) Handles closeFileButton.Click
68
```

Closing the file's
associated stream
```
69          output.Close() ' close StreamWriter
70
71          ' allow user to open another file
72          openFileButton.Enabled = True
73          enterButton.Enabled = False
74          closeFileButton.Enabled = False
75    End Sub ' closeFileButton_Click
76  End Class ' WriteEventForm
```

Figure 23.19   **Write Event** app's code. (Part 2 of 2.)

23.4 Building the Ticket Information App

Now that you've created the **Write Event** app to enable a user to write community-event information to a sequential-access text file, you'll create the **Ticket Information** app you test-drove at the beginning of the chapter. First you'll need to analyze the app. The following pseudocode describes the basic operation of the **Ticket Information** app:

> When the Form loads:
>   Display the current day's events
>
> When the user selects a date on the calendar:
>   Display the selected day's events
>
> When the user selects an event from the Pick an event: ComboBox:
>   Retrieve index of selected item in the Pick an event: ComboBox
>   Display event information in the Description: TextBox
>
> When procedure CreateEventList is called:
>   Extract data for the selected day from calendar.txt
>   Clear the Pick an event: ComboBox
>
>   If events are scheduled for that day
>   Add each event to the Pick an event: ComboBox
>   Display "- Events -" in the Pick an event: ComboBox
>   Display "Pick an event." in the Description: TextBox
>   Else
>   Display "- No Events -" in the Pick an event: ComboBox
>   Display "No events today." in the Description: TextBox
>
> When procedure ExtractData is called:
>   Clear the community-events collection
>   Open calendar.txt file for reading
>
>   Until there are no events left in the file
>   Read the next line of the file
>
>   If the current event is for the day selected by the user
>   Store the event information

Now that you've test-driven the **Ticket Information** app and studied its pseudocode representation, you'll use an ACE table to help you convert the pseudocode to Visual Basic. Figure 23.20 lists the *actions*, *controls* and *events* that help you complete your own version of this app.

Action/Control/Event (ACE) Table for the Ticket Information App	Action	Control	Event/Method
	Label the app's controls	dateLabel, eventLabel, description-Label	App is run
		TicketInfor-mationForm	Load
	Display the current day's events	eventComboBox, description-TextBox	
		dateMonth-Calendar	DateChanged
	Display the selected day's events	eventComboBox, description-TextBox	
		eventComboBox	Selected-IndexChanged
	Retrieve index of selected item in the Pick an event: ComboBox	eventComboBox	
	Display event information in the Description: TextBox	description-TextBox	
			Create-EventList
	Extract data for the selected day from calendar.txt	dateMonth-Calendar	
	Clear the Pick an event: ComboBox	eventComboBox	
	If events are scheduled for that day Add each event to the Pick an event: ComboBox	eventComboBox, community-Events	
	Display "- Events -" in the Pick an event: ComboBox	eventComboBox	
	Display "Pick an event." in the Description: TextBox	description-TextBox	
	Else Display "- No Events -" in the Pick an event: ComboBox	eventComboBox	
	Display "No events today." in the Description: TextBox	description-TextBox	
			ExtractData
	Clear the community-events collection	community-Events	
	Open calendar.txt file for reading	input	
	Until there are no events left in the file	input	
	Read the next line of the file	input	
	If the current event is for the day selected by the user Store the event information	community-Events	

Figure 23.20   ACE table for the **Ticket Information** app.

The **Ticket Information** app allows the user to view the information for a specific date by selecting the date from a MonthCalendar control. The following box guides you through configuring the MonthCalendar control.

Adding a MonthCalendar Control

1. ***Copying the template to your working directory.*** Copy the C:\Examples\ ch23\TemplateApp\TicketInformation directory to C:\SimplyVB2010.

2. ***Opening the Ticket Information template app.*** Double click Ticket-Information.sln in the TicketInformation directory to open the app in the Visual Basic IDE and view the template's Form. The template also provides the empty methods CreateEventList and ExtractData. You'll add code to these methods later.

3. ***Adding a MonthCalendar control to the Form.*** Double click the Month-Calendar control

 MonthCalendar

in the **All Windows Forms** group of the **Toolbox**. The **Properties** window displays the control's properties. Change the Name property to dateMonth-Calendar. Position the MonthCalendar control as in Fig. 23.21.

Figure 23.21 Ticket Information template app's Form after adding the MonthCalendar control.

4. ***Saving the project.*** Select **File > Save All** to save your modified code.

Now that you've added the MonthCalendar control, you can begin writing code for the **Ticket Information** app. For this app, you'll define two Sub procedures named CreateEventList and ExtractData. Before adding any functionality to the app, you'll import System.IO and create an instance variable in the next box.

Beginning to Build the Ticket Information App

1. ***Importing namespace System.IO.*** Switch to **Code** view. Add line 1 of Fig. 23.22 before the class definition to import namespace System.IO, so the app can use class StreamReader without its fully qualified class name.

```
1   Imports System.IO
2
3   Public Class TicketInformationForm
```

Figure 23.22 Importing the System.IO namespace.

(cont.)

2. ***Adding a List of CommunityEvents.*** Add lines 5–7 of Fig. 23.23 to the app. To keep track of information, you store the event information read from the file in `List(Of CommunityEvent) communityEvents` (lines 6–7). Note that the type `CommunityEvent` is underlined in the IDE, indicating a compilation error—the type is undefined. We provided this class for you with the template app. In the **Solution Explorer**, right click the **TicketInformation** project. Select **Add > Existing Item...** from the context menu that appears. When the **Add Existing Item** dialog appears, select the `CommunityEvent.vb` file and click **Add**. The `CommunityEvent` class stores the information about an event. The class includes properties `Day`, `Time`, `Price`, `Name` and `Description`. You can view the code for the `CommunityEvent` class by double clicking the `CommunityEvent.vb` file in the **Solution Explorer**.

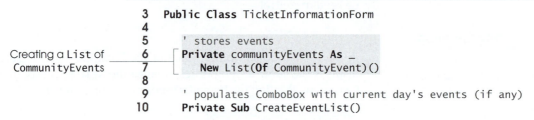

```
3    Public Class TicketInformationForm
4
5        ' stores events
6        Private communityEvents As _
7            New List(Of CommunityEvent)()
8
9        ' populates ComboBox with current day's events (if any)
10       Private Sub CreateEventList()
```

Creating a List of CommunityEvents

Figure 23.23 `List` declared to hold event information.

3. ***Saving the project.*** Select **File > Save All** to save your modified code.

When you run the **Ticket Information** app, by default, the current day is selected in the `MonthCalendar` control. The app shows the list of the day's events in the ComboBox. Recall that, if there are no events for the day, the ComboBox displays `"- No Events -"`. In the following box, you'll invoke a method from the Form's Load event handler to set the display in the ComboBox appropriately.

Handling the Form's Load Event

1. ***Defining the Form's Load event.*** Double click the Form in **Design** view to generate event handler `TicketInformationForm_Load`. Add the comment and reformat the empty event handler as shown in lines 19–21 of Fig. 23.24. Add lines 23–24 of Fig. 23.24 to the event handler. Line 24 invokes the `CreateEventList` method. You'll soon add code to `CreateEventList` to populate the ComboBox with any events scheduled for the current day.

```
19       ' handles Form's Load event
20       Private Sub TicketInformationForm_Load(sender As System.Object,
21           e As System.EventArgs) Handles MyBase.Load
22
23           ' display any events scheduled for today in ComboBox
24           CreateEventList() ' display events scheduled for today
25       End Sub ' TicketInformationForm_Load
```

You add code to the CreateEventList procedure later

Figure 23.24 Load event handler calling method `CreateEventList`.

2. ***Saving the project.*** Select **File > Save All** to save your modified code.

When the user selects a date in the `MonthCalendar` control, the **DateChanged** event is raised. You'll add code to the event handler to invoke the `CreateEventList` method in the following box.

Handling the *MonthCalendar's* *DateChanged Event*	1. ***Creating the MonthCalendar's DateChanged event handler.*** In **Design** view, double click the MonthCalendar to generate the empty event handler dateMonthCalendar_DateChanged. Add the comment and reformat the empty event handler as shown in lines 27–31 of Fig. 23.25. 2. ***Invoking the CreateEventList method.*** Add lines 33–34 of Fig. 23.25 to the dateMonthCalendar_DateChanged event handler. Line 34 invokes method CreateEventList, which you'll define in the next box.

```
27     ' handles MonthCalendar's DateChanged event
28     Private Sub dateMonthCalendar_DateChanged(
29        sender As System.Object,
30        e As System.Windows.Forms.DateRangeEventArgs) _
31        Handles dateMonthCalendar.DateChanged
32
33        ' display any events for the specified date in ComboBox
34        CreateEventList()
35     End Sub ' dateMonthCalendar_DateChanged
```

Calling method CreateEventList → lines 33–34

Figure 23.25 dateMonthCalendar's DateChanged event handler.

3. ***Saving the project.*** Select **File > Save All** to save your modified code.

The app invokes method CreateEventList from the Form's Load event and dateMonthCalendar's DateChanged event. The CreateEventList method populates the ComboBox with event names if there are any events for the day the user chooses—otherwise, it indicates that the event list is empty. You'll define this functionality in the following box.

Defining the *CreateEventList* *Method*	1. ***Setting variables and clearing the ComboBox in the CreateEventList method.*** Add lines 12–18 of Fig. 23.26 to the CreateEventList method. The method first declares a control variable, currentEvent (line 12), that's used to iterate through the events. Line 15 invokes the ExtractData method (which you'll define in the next box), passing the Date that's currently selected in the MonthCalendar. The ExtractData method stores event information in the List communityEvents that was created at lines 6–7. The date is specified by the MonthCalendar control's **SelectionStart** property. The MonthCalendar control allows you to select a range of dates. SelectionStart is the first date in the range selected. The Clear method of the ComboBox's Items property removes any events currently displayed in the ComboBox (line 18).

```
9      ' populates ComboBox with current day's events (if any)
10     Private Sub CreateEventList()
11
12        Dim currentEvent As CommunityEvent ' control variable
13
14        ' stores event information in List for selected day
15        ExtractData(dateMonthCalendar.SelectionStart)
16
17        ' remove any items in ComboBox
18        eventComboBox.Items.Clear()
19     End Sub ' CreateEventList
```

You add code to the ExtractData procedure in the next box → line 15

Figure 23.26 CreateEventList calls method ExtractData and clears the ComboBox.

(cont.)

2. ***Setting events displayed in the ComboBox.*** Add lines 20–34 of Fig. 23.27 to the CreateEventList method. If events are scheduled for the chosen day (i.e., Count is greater than 0, line 21), then the For Each…Next statement (lines 22–25) iterates through List communityEvents and adds the name of each event to the ComboBox. The CreateEventList method informs the user that events are scheduled for the specified day by using the Text properties of the ComboBox and TextBox (lines 28–29). If there are events for the chosen day, then the ComboBox displays "- Events -" and the Textbox displays "Pick an event."—otherwise, the ComboBox displays "- No events -" and the Textbox displays "No events today." (lines 32–33).

```
20          ' add each event's name to ComboBox
21          If communityEvents.Count > 0 Then
22             For Each currentEvent In communityEvents
23                ' extract and display event name
24                eventComboBox.Items.Add(currentEvent.Name)
25             Next
26
27          ' inform user that events are scheduled
28          eventComboBox.Text = " - Events - "
29          descriptionTextBox.Text = "Pick an event."
30
31          Else ' inform user that no events are scheduled
32          eventComboBox.Text = " - No Events - "
33          descriptionTextBox.Text = "No events today."
34          End If
35       End Sub ' CreateEventList
```

Extracting event name from currentEvent and displaying it in the ComboBox — lines 22-24

Indicating that events are scheduled for the day — lines 28-29

Indicating that no events are scheduled for the day — lines 32-33

Figure 23.27 Displaying the events scheduled for the specified day.

3. ***Saving the project.*** Select **File > Save All** to save your modified code.

As described in *Step 1* of the previous box, the ExtractData method uses a variable of type Date (currentDate) as its only parameter. The ExtractData method creates CommunityEvent objects from the information in calendar.txt and adds the CommunityEvents to the List. You'll define the ExtractData method in the following box.

Reading a Sequential-Access File

1. ***Adding variables to the ExtractData method.*** Add lines 39–44 of Fig. 23.28 to the ExtractData method. The Date selected in the MonthCalendar control is passed to the ExtractData method as the parameter currentDate. Line 40 assigns to chosenDay the selected day returned by the Day property of the currentDate parameter. The eventInfo variable (line 41) is an array of Strings used to store the event information retrieved from the file. The fileDay variable (line 42) stores the day of the event read from the file. Line 44 calls List method Clear to clear the List of CommunityEvents.

```
37       ' extracts event data for a specified day from calendar.txt
38       Private Sub ExtractData(currentDate As Date)
39          ' set to selected date in MonthCalendar control
40          Dim chosenDay As Integer = currentDate.Day
41          Dim eventInfo As String() ' array of event info
42          Dim fileDay As Integer ' day of event from file
43
44          communityEvents.Clear() ' clear the List of events
45       End Sub ' ExtractData
```

Figure 23.28 ExtractData method's variable declarations.

(cont.)

2. ***Creating a StreamReader to read from the file.*** Add lines 46–48 of Fig. 23.29 to the method. To read from the file, ExtractData creates a new Stream-Reader object (line 47), passing the name of the file to be read ("calen-dar.txt"). Recall that you wrote information to this file using the **Write Event** app earlier in this chapter. [*Note:* The data file is in the same directory as the app's executable (C:\SimplyVB2010\TicketInformation\Ticket-Information\bin\Debug), so you do not need to use the full path name.] String variable line (line 48) stores a line of text read from the file.

Creating a StreamReader object to read the calendar.txt file

```
44          communityEvents.Clear() ' clear the List of events
45
46          ' initialize StreamReader to read lines from file
47          Dim input As StreamReader = New StreamReader("calendar.txt")
48          Dim line As String ' holds a record from the file
49      End Sub ' ExtractData
```

Figure 23.29 Initializing the StreamReader used to read data from a sequential-access file.

3. ***Extracting the day from an event in the file.*** Add lines 50–58 of Fig. 23.30 to the ExtractData method. The Do Until...Loop statement determines whether the end of the file has been reached. When this condition becomes True, looping should stop. The StreamReader object's **EndOfStream** property returns True if the end of the file has been reached (line 51). The **Read-Line** method (line 52) of the StreamReader reads one line of text from the specified stream (input) and returns the characters as a String, or Nothing if the end of file is reached. Line 52 assigns the line read from the file to line. Recall that each field in the record is separated by a *Tab* character. Line 55 calls String method Split, passing the *Tab* character constant as an argument, and assigns the resulting array of Strings to array eventInfo. In Chapter 22 you used the Split method with no arguments to split a String wherever a space appeared. The argument passed to the Split method (in this case ControlChars.Tab) specifies the character (or characters) at which to split the String. This character (or characters) is called a **delimiter** and is used to mark the boundaries between fields in a record. Line 57 con-verts the first field in the record (that is, the day of the event) read from the file to an Integer and assigns that value to fileDay.

Verify that the end of the file has not been reached

Read a line of text from the file

Split the line of text into an array of Strings containing each field in the record

```
48          Dim line As String ' holds a record from the file
49
50          ' loop through lines in file
51          Do Until input.EndOfStream
52              line = input.ReadLine() ' read the next record in the file
53
54              ' return array of strings containing the record's fields
55              eventInfo = line.Split(ControlChars.Tab)
56
57              fileDay = Convert.ToInt32(eventInfo(0)) ' extract day
58          Loop
59      End Sub ' ExtractData
```

Figure 23.30 Extracting the day from an event entry in the file.

(cont.)

4. ***Storing event information read from the sequential-access file.*** Add lines 59–70 of Fig. 23.31 to the ExtractData method's Do Until…Loop statement. The loop reads each event sequentially from the file. If the day of the event read from the file (fileDay) and the specified day (chosenDay) are the same (line 60), then the event information (day, time, ticket price, name and description) is stored in a CommunityEvent object and added to the List (lines 62–69). Line 62 creates a new CommunityEvent object to store the event's information. Lines 63–67 assign each of the event's fields (stored in array eventInfo) to the corresponding property of class CommunityEvent. Line 69 adds the CommunityEvent object to the List.

```
57              fileDay = Convert.ToInt32(eventInfo(0)) ' extract day
58
59              ' if event scheduled for specified day, store information
60              If fileDay = chosenDay Then
61                 ' create the CommunityEvent object
62                 Dim newEvent As New CommunityEvent()
63                 newEvent.Day = fileDay
64                 newEvent.Time = eventInfo(1)
65                 newEvent.Price = Convert.ToDecimal(eventInfo(2))
66                 newEvent.Name = eventInfo(3)
67                 newEvent.Description = eventInfo(4)
68
69                 communityEvents.Add(newEvent) ' add event to the List
70              End If
71           Loop ' End Do Until
72        End Sub ' ExtractData
```

Store event information in a CommunityEvent object — (lines 62–67)

Add the event to the List — (line 69)

Figure 23.31 Storing event information in the List of CommunityEvents.

5. ***Saving the project.*** Select **File > Save All** to save your modified code.

The ComboBox displays the names of any events scheduled for the date specified in the MonthCalendar control. When the user selects the community event from the ComboBox, the SelectedIndexChanged event is raised and the description of the community event is displayed in the TextBox. The next box explains how to add this functionality.

Handling the SelectedIndexChanged Event

1. ***Creating the ComboBox's SelectedIndexChanged event handler.*** Double click the **Pick an event:** ComboBox in **Design** view to generate the empty event handler eventComboBox_SelectedIndexChanged. Add a comment and reformat the empty event handler as shown in lines 92–95 of Fig. 23.32.

2. ***Displaying event information.*** Add lines 97–105 of Fig. 23.32 to the event handler. When the user selects an event in the ComboBox, the eventComboBox_SelectedIndexChanged event handler displays information about the event in the descriptionTextBox. The SelectedIndex property of the ComboBox returns the index number of the selected event, which is equivalent to the index of the event in the communityEvents List. The event handler sets the TextBox's Text property to the time that the event starts (line 103), the ticket price (lines 104) and the event's description (line 105).

3. ***Running the app.*** Select **Debug > Start Debugging** to run your app. Select various dates and view the event information. Select the fourth day of the current month. You should be able to view the arts and crafts fair event added earlier in the chapter.

4. ***Closing the app.*** Close your running app by clicking its close box.

(cont.)

```
92         ' handles ComboBox's SelectedIndexChanged event
93         Private Sub eventComboBox_SelectedIndexChanged(
94            sender As System.Object, e As System.EventArgs) _
95            Handles eventComboBox.SelectedIndexChanged
96
97            ' get the event selected in the ComboBox
98            Dim selectedEvent As CommunityEvent =
99               communityEvents(eventComboBox.SelectedIndex)
100
101            ' place time, price and description of event in TextBox
102            descriptionTextBox.Text =
103               selectedEvent.Time & ControlChars.CrLf &
104               "Price: $" & selectedEvent.Price & ControlChars.CrLf &
105               selectedEvent.Description
106        End Sub ' eventComboBox_SelectedIndexChanged
```

Displaying event information in the **Description:** TextBox

Figure 23.32   Display information for selected event.

23.5 Using LINQ and Class `File` to Extract Data from a Text File

You've now completed the **Ticket Information** app using the `StreamReader` class to access the event data in `calendar.txt`. Next, you'll modify the `ExtractData` method using LINQ and class `File` to select the desired events from `calendar.txt`. As you've already learned, LINQ allows you to search an array or collection of data. In the next box, you'll use a LINQ query to replace the entire `Do Until…Loop` statement and several of the method's local variables. The following box guides you through creating the LINQ query.

Using LINQ to Select Events From a Text File

1. **Removing the `Do Until…Loop` and local variables.** Delete the `Do Until…Loop` statement from the `ExtractData` method. Also delete the local variables `eventInfo`, `fileDay`, `input` and `line` (Fig. 23.33).

```
37         ' extracts event data for a specified day from calendar.txt
38         Private Sub ExtractData(currentDate As Date)
39            ' set to selected date in MonthCalendar control
40            Dim chosenDay As Integer = currentDate.Day
41
42            communityEvents.Clear() ' clear the List of events
43         End Sub ' ExtractData
```

Figure 23.33   Removed `Do Until…Loop` and local variables.

2. **Writing the `From` clause.** Add lines 44–46 of Fig. 23.34. Line 45 declares local variable `eventQuery` to store the LINQ query used to search the data from `calendar.txt`. The `From` clause (line 46) specifies the range variable (`line`) and the data source. A LINQ data source can be any object that implements the `IEnumerable` interface, such as an array or collection. Class `File` provides methods for file manipulation including reading, creating, copying and deleting files. `File` method `ReadAllLines` returns an array of `Strings` in which each element is a line from the text file passed as an argument. Because an array implements interface `IEnumerable`, you can use LINQ to search the array. The query's range variable (`line`) is of type `String`. The compiler uses local type inference to determine the type. In this case, it infers type `String`, because we're querying the array of `Strings` returned by method `ReadAllLines`.

(cont.)

```
42        communityEvents.Clear() ' clear the List of events
43
44        ' select the events from the file scheduled for selected day
45        Dim eventQuery =
46            From line In File.ReadAllLines("calendar.txt")
```

Specifying the query's
data source ———— 45, 46

Figure 23.34 Specifying the data source.

3. ***Declaring a variable in the LINQ query***. Add lines 47–48 of Fig. 23.35. A
   `Let` clause (line 47) allows you to create and initialize a variable in a LINQ
   query. You can then use that variable later in the query. Line 47 declares an
   array of `String`s named `eventInfo` and assigns it the result of calling
   `String` method `Split` for the current `line` (which represents one record
   from the file). The `Where` clause (line 48) uses the array declared in the `Let`
   clause to determine whether the day of the event in the current record
   (`eventInfo(0)`) matches the day selected by the user (`chosenDay`).

```
42        communityEvents.Clear() ' clear the List of events
43
44        ' select the events from the file scheduled for selected day
45        Dim eventQuery =
46            From line In File.ReadAllLines("calendar.txt")
47            Let eventInfo As String() = line.Split(ControlChars.Tab)
48            Where Convert.ToInt32(eventInfo(0)) = chosenDay
```

Declaring variable eventInfo
inside the LINQ query ———— 47

Figure 23.35 Declaring a variable in a LINQ query.

4. ***Selecting the events for the specified day***. Add lines 49–56 of Fig. 23.36. As a
   LINQ query executes, it can create new objects which are returned as the
   query's result. Line 49 creates a new `CommunityEvent` object. The `With` keyword (line 49) specifies that the property names used in the expressions
   between the curly braces (lines 50–56) are from the new `CommunityEvent`
   object. Lines 51–55 assign values you read from the file (stored in `event-
   Info`) to the `CommunityEvent` object's corresponding properties. This use of
   the `With` keyword is called an **object initializer**. Object initializers can be
   used anywhere you can create an object using the normal syntax. The use of
   object initializers in a `Select` clause allows you to return any type of object
   from a LINQ query—you do not have to return the same type of object contained in the data source you're querying.

```
42        communityEvents.Clear() ' clear the List of events
43
44        ' select the events from the file scheduled for selected day
45        Dim eventQuery =
46            From line In File.ReadAllLines("calendar.txt")
47            Let eventInfo As String() = line.Split(ControlChars.Tab)
48            Where Convert.ToInt32(eventInfo(0)) = chosenDay
49            Select New CommunityEvent With
50            {
51                .Day = chosenDay,
52                .Time = eventInfo(1),
53                .Price = Convert.ToDecimal(eventInfo(2)),
54                .Name = eventInfo(3),
55                .Description = eventInfo(4)
56            } ' end LINQ query that creates CommunityEvent objects
```

Creates a new
CommunityEvent object ———— 49

Figure 23.36 Creating `CommunityEvent` objects in the `Select` clause.

(cont.)   5. ***Assigning the result to the List***. Add lines 58–59 below the LINQ query (Fig. 23.37). Line 59 uses interface IEnumerable's ToList method to assign the events selected from calendar.txt to the List object communityEvents. Method **ToList** returns a List of the items selected by the LINQ query—in this case, a List(Of CommunityEvent).

```
56              } ' end LINQ query that creates CommunityEvent objects
57
58              ' assign the selected events to the List
59              communityEvents = eventQuery.ToList()
60          End Sub ' ExtractData
```

Figure 23.37   Assigning the query result to the List.

6. ***Running the app.*** Select **Debug > Start Debugging** to run your app. Select various dates and view the event information. The app functions exactly as it did in the previous box.

7. ***Closing the app.*** Close your running app by clicking its close box.

8. ***Closing the IDE.*** Close the Visual Basic IDE by clicking its close box.

This example of using LINQ to query the content from a text file illustrates several important features of LINQ, including variable declarations (the Let clause) and object initializers (the With keyword). The most important feature, as noted earlier, is that you can use the same syntax to query different types of data sources. However, using LINQ to query a text file in the manner shown here does have some disadvantages. In particular, the query must first read the entire text file before continuing execution. This could be problematic for large files. The Stream-Reader is able to read one line of the file, then execute the remaining portion of the loop before reading the next line. Reading the entire file doesn't noticeably affect the **Ticket Information** app because the file being queried is quite small.

Imagine an app that searches a file for a single specific record. The Stream-Reader is required to read the file only until the point at which the desired record is found. If the record is located in the first line of the file, then one line only of the file must be read. The LINQ query reads the entire file no matter where the record is located in the file. It's not uncommon for a company to store hundreds, even thousands of records in a single file. Such a large file would cause the LINQ implementation to perform noticeably slower, or the program could run out of memory. Techniques are available that allow the LINQ query to read a single line of the file at a time, as the StreamReader does, but these techniques are beyond the scope of this book.

Figure 23.38 presents the source code for the **Ticket Information** app. The lines of code that contain new programming concepts you learned in this chapter are highlighted.

Importing namespace
System.IO
```
1   Imports System.IO
2
3   Public Class TicketInformationForm
4
5       ' stores events
6       Private communityEvents As _
7          New List(Of CommunityEvent)()
8
9       ' populates ComboBox with current day's events (if any)
10      Private Sub CreateEventList()
11
```

Figure 23.38   **Ticket Information** app's code. (Part 1 of 3.)

```
12          Dim currentEvent As CommunityEvent ' control variable
13
14          ' stores event information in List for selected day
15          ExtractData(dateMonthCalendar.SelectionStart)
16
17          ' remove any items in ComboBox
18          eventComboBox.Items.Clear()
19
20          ' add each new event name to ComboBox
21          If communityEvents.Count > 0 Then
22             For Each currentEvent In communityEvents
23                ' extract and display event name
24                eventComboBox.Items.Add(currentEvent.Name)
25             Next
26
27             ' inform user that events are scheduled
28             eventComboBox.Text = " - Events - "
29             descriptionTextBox.Text = "Pick an event."
30
31          Else ' inform user that no events are scheduled
32             eventComboBox.Text = " - No Events - "
33             descriptionTextBox.Text = "No events today."
34          End If
35       End Sub ' CreateEventList
36
37       ' extracts event data for a specified day from calendar.txt
38       Private Sub ExtractData(currentDate As Date)
39          ' set to selected date in MonthCalendar control
40          Dim chosenDay As Integer = currentDate.Day
41
42          communityEvents.Clear() ' clear the List of events
43
44          ' select the events from the file scheduled for selected day
45          Dim eventQuery =
46             From line In File.ReadAllLines("calendar.txt")
47             Let eventInfo As String() = line.Split(ControlChars.Tab)
48             Where Convert.ToInt32(eventInfo(0)) = chosenDay
49             Select New CommunityEvent With
50             {
51                .Day = chosenDay,
52                .Time = eventInfo(1),
53                .Price = Convert.ToDecimal(eventInfo(2)),
54                .Name = eventInfo(3),
55                .Description = eventInfo(4)
56             } ' end LINQ query that creates CommunityEvent objects
57
58          ' assign the selected events to the List
59          communityEvents = eventQuery.ToList()
60       End Sub ' ExtractData
61
62       ' handles Form's Load event
63       Private Sub TicketInformationForm_Load(sender As System.Object,
64          e As System.EventArgs) Handles MyBase.Load
65
66          ' display any events scheduled for today in ComboBox
67          CreateEventList()
68       End Sub ' TicketInformationForm_Load
69
70       ' handles MonthCalendar's DateChanged event
71       Private Sub dateMonthCalendar_DateChanged(
72          sender As System.Object,
73          e As System.Windows.Forms.DateRangeEventArgs) _
74          Handles dateMonthCalendar.DateChanged
75
```

Marginal annotations (left column):

Retrieve an array containing each line of `calendar.txt` → (line 46)

Split `line` into array of `Strings` → (line 47)

Check whether the `chosenDay` is the day from the line being processed → (line 48)

Creating a `CommunityEvent` object with an object initializer → (lines 49–56)

Retrieve a `List` containing each `CommunityEvent` object in the query result → (line 59)

Figure 23.38   **Ticket Information** app's code. (Part 2 of 3.)

```
76            ' display any events for the specified date in ComboBox
77            CreateEventList()
78        End Sub ' dateMonthCalendar_DateChanged
79
80        ' handles ComboBox's SelectedIndexChanged event
81        Private Sub eventComboBox_SelectedIndexChanged(
82            sender As System.Object, e As System.EventArgs) _
83            Handles eventComboBox.SelectedIndexChanged
84
85            ' get the event selected in the ComboBox
86            Dim selectedEvent As CommunityEvent =
87                communityEvents(eventComboBox.SelectedIndex)
88
89            ' place time, price and description of event in TextBox
90            descriptionTextBox.Text =
91                selectedEvent.Time & ControlChars.CrLf &
92                "Price: $" & selectedEvent.Price & ControlChars.CrLf &
93                selectedEvent.Description
94        End Sub ' eventComboBox_SelectedIndexChanged
95    End Class ' TicketInformationForm
```

Figure 23.38   Ticket Information app's code. (Part 3 of 3.)

23.6 Wrap-Up

In this chapter, you learned how to store data in sequential-access files. Data in files is called persistent data because it's maintained after the app that generated it terminates. Computers store files on secondary storage devices.

Sequential-access files store data items in the order in which they're written to the file. You learned how Visual Basic views each file as a sequential stream of bytes with an end-of-file marker. You learned how to create a sequential-access file in the **Write Event** app by associating a StreamWriter object with a specified filename. You used the StreamWriter to add information to that file. After creating a file of community events with the **Write Event** app, you developed the **Ticket Information** app using a StreamReader object to read information from that file sequentially. The user selects a date in the **Ticket Information** app's MonthCalendar control and extracts event information from a sequential-access file about any events scheduled for the specified date.

Next, you modified the **Ticket Information** app to use a LINQ query to select events scheduled for the specified date from the sequential-access file. You learned how to create a variable in a LINQ query using a Let clause. You also learned how to create objects in a LINQ query using object initializers.

SKILLS SUMMARY

Displaying an Open Dialog
- Add an OpenFileDialog component to your app by double clicking OpenFileDialog in the **Toolbox**.
- Invoke the OpenFileDialog's ShowDialog method.

Retrieving the Filename from an Open Dialog
- Use the FileName property of the OpenFileDialog object.

Writing Lines of Text to a Sequential-Access File
- Import namespace System.IO.
- Create a StreamWriter object by passing two arguments to the constructor—the name of the file to open for writing and a Boolean value that determines whether information is appended to the file or replaces the current contents of the file.
- Use the Write and WriteLine methods of class StreamWriter to write information to the file.
- Call the Close method of class StreamWriter to close the file.

Reading Lines of Text from a Sequential-Access File

- Import namespace `System.IO`.
- Create a `StreamReader` object by passing the name of the file to open for reading to the constructor.
- Use the `ReadLine` method of class `StreamReader` to read information from a file. You can also use `File` method `ReadAllLines`.
- Call the `Close` method of class `StreamReader` to close the file.

Adding a `MonthCalendar` Control

- Double click the `MonthCalendar` control in the **Toolbox** to add a `MonthCalendar` to the app.

Handling a `MonthCalendar` Control's `DateChanged` Event

- Double click the `MonthCalendar` control in **Design** view to generate the `DateChanged` event handler.
- Property `SelectionStart` returns the first (or only) date selected.

Retrieving Information from Text from a Sequential-Access File Using LINQ

- Import namespace `System.IO`.
- Specify the `String` array returned from method `ReadAllLines` of class `File` as the data source in the `From` clause.
- Declare a `String` array in a `Let` clause and assign it the `String` array returned from `String` method `Split` called on a `String` representing a record in the file.
- Use a `Where` clause to specify the constraints for selecting the record.
- Use a `Select` clause to specify the information returned by the query.

KEY TERMS

CheckFileExists property of class `OpenFileDialog`—Enables the user to display a warning if a specified file does not exist.

Close method of class `StreamWriter` or `StreamReader`—Used to close the stream.

DateChanged event of `MonthCalendar` control—Raised when a new date (or a range of dates) is selected.

delimiter—Marks the boundaries between fields in a record of a text file.

EndOfStream property of class `StreamReader`—Returns a `Boolean` value indicating whether the end of the file has been reached.

file—Collection of data that's assigned a name. Used for long-term persistence of large amounts of data, even after the app that created the data terminates.

File class—Provides methods for file manipulations including creating, copying and deleting files.

FileName property of class `OpenFileDialog`—Specifies the filename selected in the dialog.

MonthCalendar control—Displays a calendar from which a user can select a range of dates.

object initializer—Uses keyword `With` to assign property values to a newly created object.

OpenFileDialog component—Enables an app to use the **Open** dialog, which allows users to specify a file to be opened.

persistent data—Data maintained in files which exists after the app that created the data terminates.

ReadAllLines method of class `File`—Returns an array of `String`s containing each line of the file.

ReadLine method of class `StreamReader`—Reads a line from a file and returns it as a `String`.

secondary storage media—Devices such as magnetic disks, optical disks and magnetic tapes on which computers store files.

SelectionStart property of `MonthCalendar` control—Returns the first (or only) date selected.

sequential-access file—File containing data that's read in the order in which it was written to the file.

ShowDialog method of class OpenFileDialog—Displays the **Open** dialog and returns the result of the user interaction with the dialog.

stream—A sequence of characters.

StreamReader class—Provides methods for reading information from a file.

StreamWriter class—Provides methods for writing information to a file.

text file—A file containing human-readable characters.

ToList method of interface IEnumerable—Returns a List of the items contained in an IEnumerable object.

With keyword—Specifies that the subsequent property assignment statements contained between curly braces refer to the newly created object in an object initializer.

Write method of class StreamWriter—Writes a String to a file.

WriteLine method of class StreamWriter—Writes a String and a line terminator to a file.

CONTROLS, EVENTS, PROPERTIES & METHODS

ComboBox　　This control allows users to select options from a drop-down list.

- *In action*

- *Event*

  SelectedIndexChanged—Raised when a new value is selected in the ComboBox.

- *Properties*

  DataSource—Allows you to add items to the ComboBox.

  DropDownStyle—Determines the ComboBox's style.

  Enabled—Determines whether the user can select items from the ComboBox.

  Items(*index*)—Retrieves the value at the specified index.

  Items—Specifies the values the user can select from the ComboBox.

  Location—Specifies the location of the ComboBox control relative to the top-left corner of the container (e.g., a Form or a GroupBox).

  MaxDropDownItems—Determines the maximum number of items to be displayed when the user clicks the drop-down arrow.

  Name—Specifies the name used to access the ComboBox control programmatically. The name should be appended with the ComboBox suffix.

  SelectedValue—Contains the item selected by the user.

  TabIndex—Specifies the order in which focus is transferred to controls when *Tab* is pressed.

  TabStop—Specifies whether the user can select the control using the *Tab* key.

  Text—Specifies the text displayed in the ComboBox.

- *Methods*

  Items.Add—Adds an item to the ComboBox.

  Items.Clear—Deletes all the values in the ComboBox.

File　This class provides methods for file manipulations including creating, copying and deleting files.

- *Method*

  ReadAllLines—Returns an array of Strings containing each line of the file.

MonthCalendar  MonthCalendar   This control displays a calendar from which the user can select a date or a range of dates.

- *In action*

Select the date:

‹		April, 2008				›
Sun	Mon	Tue	Wed	Thu	Fri	Sat
30	31	1	2	3	4	5
6	7	8	9	10	11	12
13	14	15	16	17	18	19
20	21	22	23	24	25	26
27	28	29	30	1	2	3
4	5	6	7	8	9	10

Today: 4/9/2008

- *Event*

  DateChanged—Raised when a new date (or a range of dates) is selected.

- *Properties*

  Name—Specifies the name used to access the properties of the MonthCalendar control in the app code. The name should be appended with the MonthCalendar suffix.

  SelectionStart—Returns the first (or only) date selected.

OpenFileDialog   OpenFileDialog   This object enables an app to use the **Open** dialog.

- *Properties*

  CheckFileExists—Enables the user to display a warning if a specified file does not exist.

  FileName—Sets the default filename displayed in the dialog. It can also be used to retrieve the name of the file selected by the user.

  Name—Specifies the name used to access the OpenFileDialog component programmatically.

- *Method*

  ShowDialog—Displays the **Open** dialog and returns the result of the user interaction with the dialog.

StreamWriter   This class is used to write data to a file.

- *Methods*

  Close—Used to close the stream.

  Write—Writes the data specified in its argument.

  WriteLine—Writes the data specified in its argument, followed by a newline character.

StreamReader   This class is used to read data from a file.

- *Property*

  EndOfStream—Returns a Boolean value indicating whether the end of the file has been reached.

- *Methods*

  Close—Closes the stream.

  ReadLine—Reads a line of data from a particular file and returns it as a String (or Nothing if the end of the file is reached).

MULTIPLE-CHOICE QUESTIONS

23.1 Data maintained in a file is called _____.

a) persistent data   b) bits

c) secondary data   d) databases

23.2 Methods from the _____ class can be used to write data to a file.

a) `StreamReader`   b) `FileWriter`

c) `StreamWriter`   d) `WriteFile`

23.3 Namespace _____ provides the classes and methods you need to perform file processing.

a) `System.IO`   b) `System.Files`

c) `System.Stream`   d) `System.Windows.Forms`

23.4 Methods from the _____ class can be used to read data from a file.

a) `StreamWriter`   b) `FileReader`

c) `StreamReader`   d) `ReadFile`

23.5 A(n) _____ allows the user to select a file to open.

a) `CreateFileDialog`   b) `OpenFileDialog`

c) `MessageBox`   d) None of the above

23.6 Digits, letters and special symbols are referred to as _____. (See Section 1.3.)

a) constants   b) `Integers`

c) characters   d) None of the above

23.7 The _____ method reads a line from a file.

a) `ReadLine`   b) `Read`

c) `ReadAll`   d) `ReadToNewline`

23.8 A _____ contains information that's read in the order it was written.

a) sequential-access file   b) `StreamWriter`

c) `StreamReader`   d) None of the above

23.9 The smallest data item that a computer can support is called a _____. (See Section 1.3.)

a) character set   b) character

c) special symbol   d) bit

EXERCISES   **23.10** _(Birthday Saver App)_ Create an app that stores people's names and birthdays in a file (Fig. 23.39). The user creates a file and inputs each person's first name, last name and birthday on the Form. The information is then written to the file.

Figure 23.39 Birthday Saver app's GUI.

a) _Copying the template to your working directory._ Copy the directory `C:\Examples\ch23\Exercises\BirthdaySaver` to your `C:\SimplyVB2010` directory.

b) _Opening the app's template file._ Double click `BirthdaySaver.sln` in the BirthdaySaver directory to open the app (Fig. 23.39).

c) _Adding and customizing an `OpenFileDialog` component._ Add an `OpenFileDialog` component to the Form. Change its `Name` property to `openFileDialog`. Set the `CheckFileExists` property to `False`.

d) _Importing namespace `System.IO`._ Import `System.IO` to allow file processing.

e) _Declaring a `StreamWriter` object._ Declare a `StreamWriter` object that can be used throughout the entire class.

f) *Defining the Open File... Button's Click event handler.* Double click the **Open File...** Button to create the openButton_Click event handler. Write code to display the **Open** dialog. If the user clicks the **Cancel** Button in the dialog, the event handler performs no further actions. Otherwise, determine whether the user provided a filename that ends with the .txt extension. If not, display a MessageBox asking the user to select an appropriate file. If the user specified a valid filename, perform *Step g*.

g) *Initializing the StreamWriter.* Initialize the StreamWriter in the event handler openButton_Click, passing the user-input filename as an argument. Allow the user to append information to the file by passing the Boolean value True as the second argument to the StreamWriter. Enable the **Enter** and **Close File** Buttons. Disable the **Open File...** Button.

h) *Defining the Enter Button's Click event handler.* Double click the **Enter** Button to create the event handler enterButton_Click. This event handler writes the name of the person and the person's birthday on a line in the file. Finally, the TextBoxes on the Form are cleared, and the DateTimePicker's value is set back to the current date.

i) *Defining the Close File Button's Click event handler.* Double click the **Close File** Button to create the closeButton_Click event handler. Close the StreamWriter connection and reset the Buttons to their initial state in this event handler.

j) *Running the app.* Select **Debug > Start Debugging** to run your app. Open a file by clicking the **Open File...** Button. After a file has been opened, use the input fields provided to enter birthday information. After each person's name and birthday are typed in, click the **Enter** Button. When you're finished, close the file by clicking the **Close File** Button. Browse to the file and ensure that its contents contain the birthday information that you entered.

k) *Closing the app.* Close your running app by clicking its close box.

l) *Closing the IDE.* Close the Visual Basic IDE by clicking its close box.

23.11 *(Photo Album App)* Create an app that displays images for the user, as shown in Fig. 23.40. This app should display the current image in a large PictureBox and display the previous and next images in smaller PictureBoxes. A description of the book represented by the large image should be displayed in a multiline TextBox.

Figure 23.40 Photo Album app GUI.

a) *Copying the template to your working directory.* Copy the directory C:\Examples\ch23\Exercises\PhotoAlbum to your C:\SimplyVB2010 directory.

b) *Opening the app's template file.* Double click PhotoAlbum.sln in the PhotoAlbum directory to open the app.

c) *Importing System.IO namespace.* Import namespace System.IO to allow file processing.

d) *Creating instance variables.* Create instance variable current to represent the current image that's displayed, and set it to 0. Create the largeImage array (to store the

String path names of five large images), the smallImage array (to store the String path names of five small images) and the descriptions array (to store the descriptions of the six books represented by the images).

e) *Defining the RetrieveData procedure.* Create a Sub procedure named Retrieve-Data to store the path names of the larger images in largeImage and the path names of the smaller images in smallImage. (The images are placed in your app's bin\Debug folder in the subfolders images\large and images\small.) Sequential-access file books.txt (in the project's bin\Debug folder) stores the filename of each image. The file is organized such that the base part of each image's filename (not including the .jpg extension) and the book's description are on a single line, separated by a *Tab* character. The description of the book, which should be stored in array descriptions, follows the filename. Write code to read this data from the file and place it into arrays. [*Note:* There are only two fields in each record—the filename used for *both* images and the book description.]

f) *Defining the DisplayPicture procedure.* Create a Sub procedure named Display-Picture to display the current image in the large PictureBox, to display the previous and next images in the smaller PictureBoxes, and to place the description of the large image in the TextBox.

g) *Using If...Then...Else in the DisplayPicture procedure.* Use an If...Then...Else statement to display the images on the Form. If the Integer instance variable is 0, display the image of the first book. Also, display the next book's image in the next image PictureBox. However, since there's no previous image, nothing should be displayed in the previous image PictureBox, and the **Previous** Button should be disabled. If the last image is displayed in the large PictureBox, then disable the **Next** Button, and do not display anything in the next image PictureBox. Otherwise, all three PictureBoxes should display their corresponding images, and the **Previous** and **Next** Buttons should be enabled.

h) *Defining the PhotoAlbumForm_Load event handler.* Double click the Form to create the PhotoAlbumForm_Load event handler. Invoke methods RetrieveData and DisplayPicture in this event handler.

i) *Defining the previousButton_Click event handler.* Double click the **Previous Image** Button to create the previousButton_Click event handler. In this event handler, decrease the Integer instance variable by 1 and invoke procedure DisplayPicture.

j) *Defining the nextButton_Click event handler.* Double click the **Next** Button to create the nextButton_Click event handler. In this event handler, increment the Integer instance variable by 1 and invoke the DisplayPicture procedure.

k) *Running the app.* Select **Debug > Start Debugging** to run your app. Click the **Previous** and **Next** Buttons to ensure that the proper images and descriptions are displayed.

l) *Closing the app.* Close your running app by clicking its close box.

m) *Closing the IDE.* Close the Visual Basic IDE by clicking its close box.

23.12 *(Car Reservation App)* Create an app that allows a user to reserve a car for the specified day (Fig. 23.41). A small car-reservation company can rent out only four cars per day. Let the app allow the user to specify a certain day. If four cars have already been reserved for that day, then indicate to the user that no vehicles are available.

a) *Copying the template to your working directory.* Copy the directory C:\Examples\ch23\Exercises\CarReservation to your C:\SimplyVB2010 directory.

b) *Opening the app's template file.* Double click CarReservation.sln in the CarReservation directory to open the app.

c) *Adding a MonthCalendar control to the Form.* Drag and drop a MonthCalendar control on the Form. Set its Name property to dateMonthCalendar. Position the MonthCalendar control as shown in Fig. 23.41.

d) *Importing System.IO namespace.* Import namespace System.IO to allow file processing.

Figure 23.41 **Car Reservation** app GUI.

e) *Determining the number of reservations.* Create a method named NumberOfReser-vations that takes one argument of type Date. The procedure should use a LINQ that searches the reservations.txt file for reservations made for the selected date. The procedure should return the number of cars rented for the day selected. [*Hint:* Use the query result's Count method to determine the number of elements in the result.]

f) *Defining a Sub procedure.* Create a Sub procedure named CheckReservations. This procedure should invoke the NumberOfReservations method, passing in the user-selected day as an argument. The CheckReservations method should then retrieve the number returned by NumberOfReservations and determine whether four cars have been rented for that day. If four cars have been rented, then display a message dialog to the user stating that no cars are available that day for rental. If fewer than four cars have been rented for that day, create a StreamWriter object, passing res-ervations.txt as the first argument and True as the second argument to specify that data should be appended to any existing data. Write the day and the user's name to the reservations.txt file and display a message dialog to the user stating that a car has been reserved.

g) *Defining the reserveButton_Click event handler.* Double click the **Reserve Car** Button to create the reserveButton_Click event handler. In this event handler, invoke the CheckReservations procedure and clear the **Name:** TextBox.

h) *Running the app.* Select **Debug > Start Debugging** to run your app. Enter several reservations, including four reservations for the same day. Enter a reservation for a day that already has four reservations to ensure that a message dialog is displayed.

i) *Closing the app.* Close your running app by clicking its close box. Open reserva-tions.txt to ensure that the proper data has been stored (based on the reservations entered in *Step h*).

j) *Closing the IDE.* Close the Visual Basic IDE by clicking its close box.

What does this code do? ▶ **23.13** What is the result of the following code?

```
1   Dim path1 As String = "oldfile.txt"
2   Dim path2 As String = "newfile.txt"
3   Dim output As New StreamWriter(path2)
4   Dim input As New StreamReader(path1)
5
6   Dim line As String = input.ReadLine()
7
8   Do While line <> Nothing
9       output.WriteLine(line)
10      line = input.ReadLine()
11  Loop
12
13  output.Close()
14  input.Close()
```

What's wrong with this code? ▶ **23.14** Find the error(s) in the following code, which is supposed to read a line from some-file.txt, convert the line to uppercase and then append it to somefile.txt.

```
 1    Dim path As String = "somefile.txt"
 2    Dim output As New StreamWriter(path, True)
 3    Dim input As New StreamReader(path)
 4
 5    Dim contents As String = input.ReadLine()
 6
 7    contents = contents.ToUpper()
 8    output.Write(contents)
 9    output.Close()
10    input.Close()
```

Programming Challenge ▶ **23.15** *(File Scrape App)* Create an app, similar to the **Screen Scraping** app of Chapter 22, that opens a user-specified file and searches the file for the price of a book, returning it to the user (Fig. 23.42). [*Hint:* Use the ReadToEnd method of class StreamReader to retrieve the entire contents of a file as a single String. The book price appears, for example, in the sample booklist.htm file as Our Price: $59.99.]

Figure 23.42 **File Scrape** app GUI.

a) *Copying the template to your working directory.* Copy the directory C:\Examples\ ch23\Exercises\FileScrape to your C:\SimplyVB2010 directory. Note that two HTML files—booklist.htm and bookpool.htm—are provided for you in the project's bin\Debug folder.

b) *Opening the app's template file.* Double click FileScrape.sln in the FileScrape directory to open the app.

c) *Creating an event handler.* Create an event handler for the **Open...** Button that allows the user to select a file to search for prices. Once the file has been opened, enable the **Search** Button.

d) *Creating a second event handler.* Create an event handler for the **Search** Button. This event handler should search the specified HTML file for the book price. When the price is found, display it in the resultLabel.

e) *Running the app.* Select **Debug > Start Debugging** to run your app. Click the **Open...** Button and select one of the .htm files provided in the FileScrape directory. Click the **Search** Button and view the price of the book. For booklist.htm, the price should be $59.99, and for bookpool.htm the price should be $39.50.

f) *Closing the app.* Close your running app by clicking its close box.

g) *Closing the IDE.* Close the Visual Basic IDE by clicking its close box.

24

Enhanced Car Payment Calculator App

Introducing Exception Handling

In this chapter, you'll learn about **exception handling**. An **exception** is an indication of a problem that occurs during an app's execution. The name "exception" comes from the fact that such problems occur *infrequently*. Exception handling enables you to create apps that can resolve (or handle) exceptions while an app executes. In many cases, handling an exception allows an app to continue executing as if no problem had been encountered.

The chapter begins with a test-drive of the **Enhanced Car Payment Calculator** app, then overviews exception handling concepts and demonstrates basic exception-handling techniques. You'll learn the specifics of exception handling with the `Try`, `Catch` and `Finally` blocks.

24.1 Test-Driving the Enhanced Car Payment Calculator App

In this chapter, you'll enhance the **Car Payment Calculator** app from Chapter 9 by adding exception-handling statements. This app must meet the following requirements:

App Requirements

A bank wishes to accept only valid data from users on their car loans. Although the app you developed in Chapter 9 calculates a result when incorrect data is entered, this result does not correctly represent the user's input. Alter the Car Payment Calculator app to allow users to enter only Integers in the Price: TextBox and Down payment: TextBox. Similarly, allow users to enter only Double values in the Annual interest rate: TextBox. If the user enters anything besides an Integer for the price or down payment, or a Double for the interest rate, a message dialog should be displayed instructing the user to input proper data. The interest rate should be entered such that an input of 5 is interpreted by the app as 5%, 4 as 4%, etc.

The original **Car Payment Calculator** app used the `Val` function to set the value of the variables used in the app. This ensured that the payment calculation was always performed using numeric values. However, as discussed in Chapter 5, the value returned by `Val` is *not* always the value the user intended to enter. For example, if the user accidently enters a character in the middle of the down payment (e.g., 54a7), Val returns the numeric value from the beginning of the string until it reaches the first non-numeric character (54 in this case)—any number after the character is lost, and the calculation is incorrect. Also, Val does *not* prevent the user from entering a Double value for the price or down payment, for which Integer values are expected. You'll add exception handling to the **Car Payment Calculator** app so that when invalid input is entered, the app does *not* calculate monthly payments and the user is asked to enter valid input. If the user provides valid input, the app calculates the monthly payments for a car when financed for 24, 36, 48 and 60 months. Users input the car price, the down payment and the annual interest rate. You'll begin by test-driving the completed app. Then you'll learn the additional Visual Basic capabilities needed to create your own version of this app

Test-Driving the Enhanced Car Payment Calculator App

1. **Opening the completed app.** Open the directory C:\Examples\ch24\CompletedApp\EnhancedCarPaymentCalculator to locate the **Enhanced Car Payment Calculator** app. Double click EnhancedCarPaymentCalculator.sln to open the app in the IDE.

2. **Running the Enhanced Car Payment Calculator app.** Select **Debug > Start Debugging** to run the app (Fig. 24.1).

Figure 24.1   Running the completed **Enhanced Car Payment Calculator** app.

3. **Entering an invalid value in the Down payment: TextBox.** Enter 16900 in the **Price:** TextBox, 6000.50 in the **Down payment:** TextBox and 4.5 in the **Annual interest rate:** TextBox (Fig. 24.2).

Figure 24.2   Entering an invalid value in the **Down payment:** TextBox.

(cont.)

4. ***Attempting to calculate the monthly payment amounts.*** Click the **Calculate** Button to attempt to calculate the monthly payment. An error message dialog (Fig. 24.3) appears.

Displaying a message when an exception is thrown

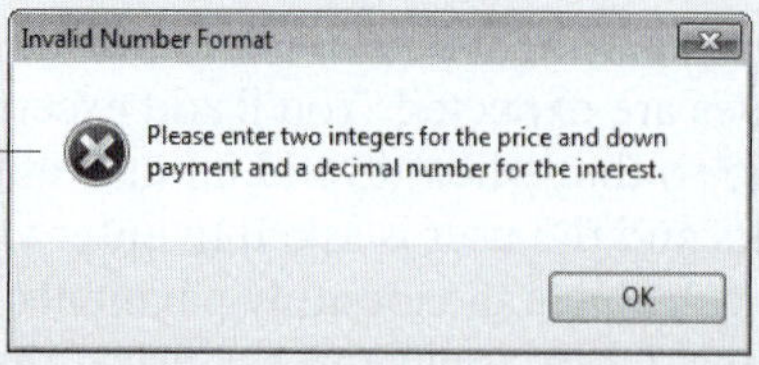

Figure 24.3 Message dialog displayed when incorrect input is entered.

5. ***Entering non-numeric data in the Down payment: TextBox.*** Change the value 6000.50 in the **Down payment:** TextBox to 600p (Fig. 24.4). Click the **Calculate** Button to attempt to display the monthly payment in the Text-Box. The message dialog shown in Fig. 24.3 appears again (a non-numeric character like p is not allowed where an Integer is expected). The same problem occurs when the user mistakenly includes a dollar sign in the input (e.g., $6000).

Figure 24.4 Entering non-numeric data in the **Down Payment:** TextBox.

6. ***Entering non-numeric data in the Annual interest rate: TextBox.*** Change the value 600p in the **Down payment:** TextBox to 6000. Enter 4.5% in the **Annual interest rate:** TextBox (Fig. 24.5). Click the **Calculate** Button to attempt to calculate the monthly payment. The message dialog shown in Fig. 24.3 appears again (4.5 is the correct input; entering the % character is incorrect).

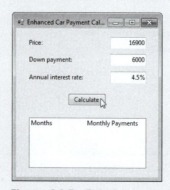

Figure 24.5 Entering non-numeric data in the **Annual interest rate:** TextBox.

7. ***Correcting the input.*** Change the value 4.5% in the **Annual interest rate:** TextBox to 4.5, and click the **Calculate** Button to display the monthly payments (Fig. 24.6).

(cont.)

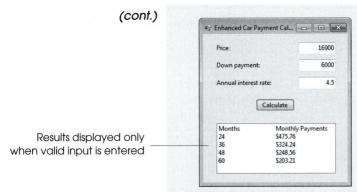

Figure 24.6 Displaying monthly payments after input is corrected.

8. **Closing the app.** Close your running app by clicking its close box.

9. **Closing the IDE.** Close the Visual Basic IDE by clicking its close box.

24.2 Introduction to Exception Handling

App logic frequently tests conditions that determine how app execution should proceed. Consider the following pseudocode:

Perform a task

If the preceding task did not execute correctly
    Perform error processing

Perform the next task

If the preceding task did not execute correctly
    Perform error processing

    ...

In this pseudocode, you begin by performing a task. Then you test whether the task executed correctly. If not, you perform error processing. Otherwise, you continue with the next task. Although this form of error checking works, intermixing app logic with error-handling logic can make the app difficult to read, modify, maintain and debug—especially in large apps. In fact, if problems occur infrequently, intermixing app and error-handling logic can degrade an app's performance, because the app must explicitly test for errors after each task to determine whether the next task can be performed.

Exception handling enables you to remove error-handling code from the code that implements your app's logic, thereby improving app clarity and enhancing modifiability. You can decide to handle only the exceptions you choose—all exceptions, all exceptions of a certain type or all exceptions in a group of related types. Such flexibility reduces the likelihood that errors will be overlooked and makes the app more robust.

A method **throws an exception** if a problem occurs during the method's execution and the method is unable to correct the problem. There's no guarantee that there will be an **exception handler**—code that executes when the app detects an exception—to process that kind of exception. If there is, the exception handler catches and handles the exception. If there is not, the exception is sent to the calling method, which may or may not handle it. An **uncaught** (or **unhandled**) **exception**—an exception that does not have an exception handler—likely causes app execution to terminate. This can actually help you locate problems in your code.

1. An _____ executes when the app detects an exception.
   a) exception code   b) exception processor
   c) exception handler   d) None of the above

2. A method _____ an exception if a problem occurs during the method execution but the method is unable to correct the problem.
   a) throws   b) catches
   c) returns   d) None of the above

Answers: 1) c. 2) a.

24.3 Exception Handling in Visual Basic

Visual Basic provides **Try statements** to enable exception handling. A Try statement consists of a Try block followed by at least one Catch block (or a Finally block, as you'll learn later) and is terminated with keywords **End Try**. A **Try block** consists of the Try keyword followed by a block of code in which exceptions might occur. The Try block encloses statements that might cause exceptions and statements that should *not* execute if an exception occurs.

Many of the methods in the .NET Framework Class Library throw exceptions when passed invalid input. An exception is thrown using the **Throw** keyword followed by the exception object to be thrown, as in:

```
Throw New Exception()
```

When a statement such as this executes, it creates an Exception object and passes it to the calling method.

Generally, at least one Catch block (also called an exception handler) appears after the Try block, before the End Try keywords. A **Catch block** contains code that *handles* an exception and allows the app to *continue* executing correctly. A Catch block can specify a parameter that identifies the type of exception the exception handler can process. A Catch block that does *not* specify a parameter catches *all* exceptions. A parameterless Catch block, if present, should be placed after all other Catch blocks.

If an exception occurs in a Try block, the Try block terminates *immediately*. As with any other block of code, when a Try block terminates, local variables declared in the block go out of scope. Next, the app searches for the first Catch block (immediately following the Try block) that can process the exception type that occurred. The app locates the matching Catch block by comparing the thrown exception's type with each Catch block's parameter type. A match occurs if the exception type matches the Catch block's parameter type. When a match occurs, the code in the Catch block executes. When a Catch block finishes processing the exception, local variables declared in the Catch block (and the Catch block's parameter) go out of scope. The Try statement's remaining Catch blocks are ignored, and execution resumes at the first line of code after the End Try keywords. (You'll learn another possibility when we introduce Finally blocks later in this chapter.)

If there's no Catch block that matches the exception thrown in the corresponding Try block, the exception is passed from the current method back to the calling method, which then attempts to handle the exception. If the calling method does not handle the exception, the exception is passed to the previous method in the call chain. This process continues until the exeception is caught or goes unhandled. If the exception goes unhandled by any method, Visual Basic displays a dialog with information about the exception. The user can then exit or continue running the app, although the app likely will not execute correctly due to the exception.

If no exceptions occur in a Try block, the app ignores the Catch block(s) for that Try block. App execution resumes with the next statement after the End Try keywords.

1. A Try statement typically contains a _____ block and at least one _____ block.
    a) `Catch`, `Try`   b) `Try`, `Catch`
    c) `Throw`, `Catch`   d) None of the above

2. If no exceptions occur in a Try block, the app ignores the _____ for that block.
    a) Catch block(s)   b) Return statement
    c) Both of the above   d) None of the above

Answers: 1) b. 2) a.

24.4 Constructing the Enhanced Car Payment Calculator App

Now that you've been introduced to exception handling, you'll construct your **Enhanced Car Payment Calculator** app. The following pseudocode describes the basic operation of the app:

> *When the user clicks the Calculate Button:*
> *Clear the ListBox of any previous text*
>
> *Try*
> *Get the car price from the Price: TextBox*
> *Get the down payment from the Down payment: TextBox*
> *Get the annual interest rate from the Annual interest rate: TextBox*
> *Calculate the loan amount (price minus down payment)*
> *Calculate the monthly interest rate (annual interest rate divided by 12)*
> *Calculate and display the monthly payments for 2, 3, 4 and 5 years*
> *Catch*
> *Display the error message dialog*

Now that you've test-driven the **Enhanced Car Payment Calculator** app and studied its pseudocode representation, you'll use an ACE table to help you convert the pseudocode to Visual Basic. Figure 24.7 lists the *actions*, *controls* and *events* that help you complete your own version of this app.

Action/Control/Event (ACE) Table for the Enhanced Car Payment Calculator App

Action	Control/Class/Object	Event

Label all the app's components	`priceLabel,`
	`downPaymentLabel,`
	`interestLabel`
		App is run

	`calculateButton`	`Click`
Clear the ListBox of any previous text	`paymentsListBox`	
Try Get the car price from the Price: TextBox	`priceTextBox`	
Get the down payment from the Down payment: TextBox	`downPayment-` `TextBox`	
Get the annual interest rate from the Annual interest rate: TextBox	`interestTextBox`	
Calculate the loan amount		
Calculate the monthly interest rate		
Calculate and display the monthly payments for 2, 3, 4 and 5 years	`paymentsListBox`	
Catch Display the error message dialog	`MessageBox`	

Figure 24.7 Enhanced Car Payment Calculator app ACE table.

Now that you've analyzed the **Enhanced Car Payment Calculator** app's components, you'll learn how to use exception handling in your app.

Handling a Format Exception	1. ***Copying the template to your working directory.*** Copy the C:\Examples\ ch24\TemplateApp\EnhancedCarPaymentCalculator directory to your C:\SimplyVB2010 directory.

2. ***Opening the Enhanced Car Payment Calculator app's template file.*** Double click EnhancedCarPaymentCalculator.sln in the EnhancedCarPaymentCalculator directory to open the app in the IDE.

3. ***Studying the code.*** View lines 25–27 of Fig. 24.8. Lines 25–26 read the Integer values from the **Down payment:** and **Price:** TextBoxes, respectively. Line 27 reads a Double value from the **Annual interest rate:** TextBox. These lines are different from the ones in the **Car Payment Calculator** app that you developed in Chapter 9. These three statements now must explicitly convert the data in the TextBoxes to Integer and Double values, using the methods of the Convert class, because **Option Strict** is set to On. However, these statements still use the Val function, which could cause the app to use incorrect data in its calculation, producing invalid results.

```
23        ' retrieve user input and assign values
24        ' to their respective variables
25        downPayment = Convert.ToInt32(Val(downPaymentTextBox.Text))
26        price = Convert.ToInt32(Val(priceTextBox.Text))
27        interest = Convert.ToDouble(Val(interestTextBox.Text) / 100)
```

Figure 24.8   Val ensures data is in numeric format.

Error-Prevention Tip

Before using a method, read its online documentation to determine whether it throws exceptions. If so, use the exception-handling techniques of this chapter to help make your code more robust. To access the online documentation for a method in the .NET Framework Class Library, you can click its name in the source-code editor and press *F1*.

Method Convert.ToInt32 throws a FormatException if it cannot convert its argument to an Integer. The **FormatException** class represents exceptions that occur when a method is passed an argument that's *not* in the expected format (e.g., an object of the wrong type, or a String containing non-numeric characters when only numeric characters are allowed). The call to the Convert.ToInt32 method does not currently throw an exception when the app is run because Val is *guaranteed* to convert its argument to a numeric value. This value is then passed to Convert.ToInt32, so an Integer value is *always* created. The Convert.ToDouble method performs in a similar manner by throwing a FormatException if it cannot convert its argument to a Double.

4. ***Changing the existing code.*** Change lines 25–27 of your template app to match lines 25–27 of Fig. 24.9 by removing the Val function call and the parentheses that designate its argument. Removing the Val function call causes Convert.ToInt32 and Convert.ToDouble to throw an exception if the user enters invalid input in one of the TextBoxes. This allows you to add code (later in this box) to catch the exception and ask the user to enter correct values.

Removing the Val function call allows exceptions to be thrown

```
23        ' retrieve user input and assign values
24        ' to their respective variables
25        downPayment = Convert.ToInt32(downPaymentTextBox.Text)
26        price = Convert.ToInt32(priceTextBox.Text)
27        interest = Convert.ToDouble(interestTextBox.Text) / 100
```

Figure 24.9   Removing the Val function call from the app.

(cont.)   5. *Causing a FormatException.* Select **Debug > Start Debugging** to run your
app. Enter invalid input as in Fig. 24.4 and click the **Calculate** Button. The
Exception Assistant shown in Fig. 24.10 appears, informing you that an
exception has occurred. The Exception Assistant indicates where the exception occurred and the exception's type, and provides links to helpful information on handling the exception. Close the Exception Assistant by clicking
its close box. Then, stop debugging by selecting **Debug > Stop Debugging**.

Type of thrown exception shown
at the top of the Exception
Assistant window

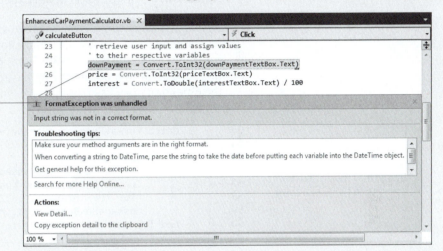

Figure 24.10   Exception Assistant showing a `FormatException`.

6. *Adding a Try block to your app.* Add lines 23–24 of Fig. 24.11 to your app,
but do not press *Enter* when you're done typing line 24. Instead, add line 51
of Fig. 24.12 to your app. The code currently contained between these two
lines is the code that *might* throw an exception *and* the code that you do *not*
want to execute if an exception occurs. The `Try` keyword in line 24 is *underlined*, indicating a syntax error. Adding the `Try` keyword to your app creates
a syntax error until a corresponding `Catch` (or `Finally`) block is added to
the app. In the next step, you'll add a `Catch` block to fix the error in line 24.

```
21              ControlChars.Tab & "Monthly Payments")
22
23              ' attempt to retrieve price, down payment and interest
24              Try
25              ' retrieve user input and assign values
```

Beginning a Try statement — 24

Figure 24.11   Enabling exception handling using a `Try` block.

```
50              Loop
51              End Try 'end Try...Catch statement
52          End Sub ' calculateButton_Click
53      End Class ' EnhancedCarPaymentCalculatorForm
```

Ending a Try statement — 51

Figure 24.12   Ending the `Try...Catch` block with the `End Try` keywords.

7. *Adding a Catch block to your app.* Insert a blank line before `End Try`, then
add lines 52–53 of Fig. 24.13. Keyword `Catch` begins a `Catch` block. A `Catch`
block ends when either another `Catch` block, a `Finally` block or the `End
Try` keywords are reached. Line 53 specifies that this `Catch` block executes if
a `FormatException` occurs. When an exception is caught here, it's assigned
to variable `formatExceptionParameter`. This code in this `Catch` block executes if the user enters invalid input in one of this app's `TextBoxes`. Note
that adding this `Catch` block fixed the error in line 24.

(cont.)

Catching a `FormatException`

```
50              Loop
51
52              ' process invalid number format
53          Catch formatExceptionParameter As FormatException
54
55          End Try 'end Try...Catch statement
56      End Sub ' calculateButton_Click
```

Figure 24.13 Handling a `FormatException`.

8. *Displaying an error message to the user.* Add lines 54–59 of Fig. 24.14 to the `Catch` handler to display a `MessageBox` instructing the user to enter valid input. Note that the `MessageBoxIcon.Error` icon is used because an exception is an error that occurs during the app's execution. If you'd like to access the exception object's error message, you can access its **Message** property.

Displaying a message when the `Catch` block executes

```
53          Catch formatExceptionParameter As FormatException
54              ' tell user data was invalid, and ask for new input
55          MessageBox.Show(
56              "Please enter two integers for the price and down" &
57              ControlChars.CrLf & "payment and a decimal number " &
58              "for the interest.", "Invalid Number Format",
59              MessageBoxButtons.OK, MessageBoxIcon.Error)
60      End Try 'end Try...Catch statement
```

Figure 24.14 Displaying a message dialog to the user.

9. *Running the app.* Select **Debug > Start Debugging** to run your app. Enter valid input, and verify that the output contains the correct payment amounts. Enter invalid input to ensure that the `MessageBox` is displayed. Test the app with invalid values in each `TextBox`.

10. *Closing the app.* Click your running app's close box.

11. *Closing the IDE.* Close the Visual Basic IDE by clicking its close box.

Figure 24.15 presents the source code for the **Enhanced Car Payment Calculator** app. The lines of code that contain new programming concepts you learned in this chapter are highlighted.

```
1   Public Class EnhancedCarPaymentCalculatorForm
2
3       ' handles Calculate Button's Click event
4       Private Sub calculateButton_Click(sender As System.Object,
5           e As System.EventArgs) Handles calculateButton.Click
6
7           Dim years As Integer = 2 ' repetition counter
8           Dim months As Integer = 0 ' payment period
9           Dim price As Integer = 0 ' car price
10          Dim downPayment As Integer = 0 ' down payment
11          Dim interest As Double = 0 ' interest rate
12          Dim monthlyPayment As Decimal = 0 ' monthly payment
13          Dim loanAmount As Integer = 0 ' cost after down payment
14          Dim monthlyInterest As Double = 0 ' monthly interest rate
15
16          ' remove text displayed in ListBox
17          paymentsListBox.Items.Clear()
18
19          ' add header to ListBox
20          paymentsListBox.Items.Add("Months" & ControlChars.Tab &
21              ControlChars.Tab & "Monthly Payments")
```

Figure 24.15 Enhanced Car Payment Calculator App. (Part 1 of 2.)

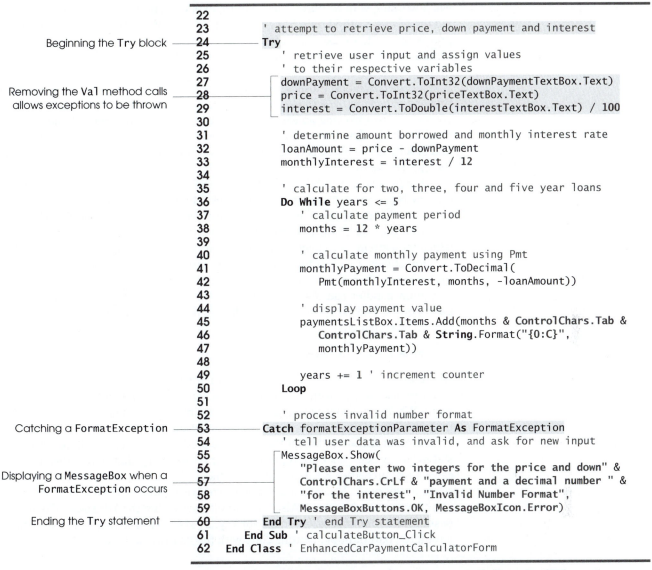

```
22
23            ' attempt to retrieve price, down payment and interest
24        Try
25            ' retrieve user input and assign values
26            ' to their respective variables
27            downPayment = Convert.ToInt32(downPaymentTextBox.Text)
28            price = Convert.ToInt32(priceTextBox.Text)
29            interest = Convert.ToDouble(interestTextBox.Text) / 100
30
31            ' determine amount borrowed and monthly interest rate
32            loanAmount = price - downPayment
33            monthlyInterest = interest / 12
34
35            ' calculate for two, three, four and five year loans
36            Do While years <= 5
37                ' calculate payment period
38                months = 12 * years
39
40                ' calculate monthly payment using Pmt
41                monthlyPayment = Convert.ToDecimal(
42                    Pmt(monthlyInterest, months, -loanAmount))
43
44                ' display payment value
45                paymentsListBox.Items.Add(months & ControlChars.Tab &
46                    ControlChars.Tab & String.Format("{0:C}",
47                    monthlyPayment))
48
49                years += 1 ' increment counter
50            Loop
51
52            ' process invalid number format
53        Catch formatExceptionParameter As FormatException
54            ' tell user data was invalid, and ask for new input
55            MessageBox.Show(
56                "Please enter two integers for the price and down" &
57                ControlChars.CrLf & "payment and a decimal number " &
58                "for the interest", "Invalid Number Format",
59                MessageBoxButtons.OK, MessageBoxIcon.Error)
60        End Try ' end Try statement
61    End Sub ' calculateButton_Click
62 End Class ' EnhancedCarPaymentCalculatorForm
```

Labels pointing to the code:
- Beginning the **Try** block → line 24
- Removing the **Val** method calls allows exceptions to be thrown → lines 27–29
- Catching a **FormatException** → line 53
- Displaying a **MessageBox** when a **FormatException** occurs → lines 55–59
- Ending the **Try** statement → line 60

Figure 24.15   Enhanced Car Payment Calculator App. (Part 2 of 2.)

SELF-REVIEW   1. If you're attempting to catch multiple errors, you may use several _____ blocks after the _____ block.

   a) `Try, Catch`   b) `Catch, Try`

   c) `Throw, Try`   d) None of the above

2. The exception you wish to handle should be declared as a parameter of the _____ block.

   a) `Try`   b) `Catch`

   c) `Throw`   d) None of the above

Answers: 1) b. 2) b.

24.5 Additional Exception Handling Capabilities

Visual Basic provides several additional exception handling capabilities not used in this book. An optional **Finally block** can be placed before the End Try keywords in a Try statement and allows you to specify code that *always* executes, whether or not an exception occurs in the corresponding Try block. This is particularly useful when working with resources that require explicit action to release them (e.g., calling the Close method on a StreamReader or StreamWriter object when finished processing a file or database connection). A Try statement containing a Finally block is *not* required to also contain a Catch block.

If an exception occurs in a Try block, the Try block terminates *immediately*. When a Catch block finishes processing the exception, execution resumes at the first line of code in the Finally block (if there is one). If the Try block finishes executing *without* throwing an exception, the Catch blocks are ignored and execution resumes at the first line of code in the Finally block (if there is one). When the end of a Finally block is reached, execution resumes at the first line of code after the End Try keywords.

If there's no Catch block that matches the exception thrown in the corresponding Try block (or if there's no Catch block whatsoever), execution resumes at the first line of code in the Finally block (if there is one). After the Finally block executes, the exception is passed to the method that called the current method, which then attempts to handle the exception.

Sometimes a Catch block may decide either that it cannot process a certain exception or that it can only partially process the exception. In such cases, the exception handler can *defer* the handling (or perhaps a portion of it) to another Catch block. The exception handler achieves this by **rethrowing the exception** using the Throw statement

> **Throw** *exceptionReference*

where *exceptionReference* is the parameter for the exception in the Catch block. You can also do this without specifying *exceptionReference* in the preceding statement. When a rethrow occurs, the next enclosing Try statement (if any)—normally in the calling method—detects the rethrown exception and attempts to catch it.

Another feature in Visual Basic 2010 related to exception handling is the Using statement, which concisely represents a Try...Finally that automatically deallocates a resource after it's used in the Try block. The Using statement is beyond the scope of this book. For information on Using, visit msdn2.microsoft.com/en-us/library/htd05whh.aspx. Also, you should investigate the IDisposable interface (msdn2.microsoft.com/en-us/library/system.idisposable.aspx), which is a required part of implementing code with the Using statement.

SELF-REVIEW   1. The _____ (if any) is/are always executed regardless of whether an exception occurs.

   a) Catch block   b) Finally block
   c) Catch and Finally blocks   d) None of the above

2. If an exception occurs in a Try block, the Finally block is executed _____.

   a) before the Catch block executes   b) instead of the Catch block
   c) after the Catch block executes   d) None of the above

Answers: 1) b. 2) c.

24.6 Wrap-Up

In this chapter, you learned exception-handling concepts and when to use exception handling in Visual Basic. You learned how to use a Try statement with Catch blocks to handle exceptions in your apps. You applied your knowledge of exception handling in Visual Basic to enhance your **Car Payment Calculator** app to check for input errors. You used a Try block to enclose the statements that might throw FormatExceptions and a Catch block to handle the FormatExceptions. This allows your app to recover from otherwise fatal errors.

Next, you learned about additional exception handling capabilities. You learned that a `Finally` block contains code that's always executed, regardless of whether or not an exception was thrown. You also learned that the `Throw` statement can be used to rethrow an exception that cannot be handled in the `Catch` block. In the next chapter, you'll learn about graphics and printing.

SKILLS SUMMARY

Handling an Exception

- Enclose in a `Try` block any code that might generate an exception and any code that should not execute if an exception occurs.
- Follow the `Try` block with one or more `Catch` blocks. Each `Catch` block is an exception handler that specifies the type of exception it can handle.
- Follow the `Catch` blocks with an optional `Finally` block that contains code that should always execute, regardless of whether or not an exception was thrown.

KEY TERMS

Catch block—Also called an exception handler, this block executes when the corresponding `Try` block in the app detects an exceptional situation and throws an exception of the type the `Catch` block declares.

End Try keywords—Indicates the end of a sequence of blocks containing a `Try` block, followed by zero or more `Catch` blocks and an optional `Finally` block. At least one `Catch` or `Finally` block must precede the `End Try` keywords

exception—An indication of a problem that occurs during an app's execution.

Exception Assistant—A window that appears in the IDE indicating where an exception has occurred, the type of exception, and information on handling the exception.

exception handler—A block that executes when the app detects an exceptional situation and throws an exception.

exception handling—Processing problems that occur during app execution.

Finally block—An optional block of code that follows the last `Catch` block in a sequence of `Catch` blocks or the `Try` block if there are no `Catches`. The `Finally` block provides code that always executes, whether or not an exception occurs.

FormatException class—An exception of this type is thrown when a method cannot convert its argument to a desired numeric type, such as `Integer` or `Double`.

Message property of an exception object—Provides access to the error message in an exception object.

rethrow an exception—The `Catch` block can defer the exception handling (or perhaps a portion of it) to another `Catch` block by using the `Throw` statement.

Throw statement—The statement used to throw an exception.

throws an exception—A method throws an exception if a problem occurs while the method is executing.

Try block—A block of statements that might cause exceptions and statements that should not execute if an exception occurs.

uncaught (unhandled) exception—An exception that does not have an exception handler. Uncaught exceptions might terminate app execution.

MULTIPLE-CHOICE QUESTIONS

24.1 Dealing with exceptional situations as an app executes is called _____.

a) exception detection

b) exception handling

c) exception resolution

d) exception debugging

24.2 A(n) _____ is always followed by at least one `Catch` block or a `Finally` block.

a) `if` statement

b) event handler

c) `Try` block

d) None of the above

24.3 The method call `Convert.ToInt32("123.4a")` will throw a _____.

    a) `FormatException`   b) `ParsingException`

    c) `DivideByZeroException`   d) None of the above

24.4 If no exceptions are thrown in a Try block, _____.

    a) the `Catch` block(s) are skipped   b) all `Catch` blocks are executed

    c) an error occurs   d) the default exception is thrown

24.5 A(n) _____ is an exception that does not have an exception handler.

    a) uncaught block   b) uncaught exception

    c) error handler   d) thrower

24.6 A Try statement must have at least _____.

    a) one or more `Catch` blocks   b) a `Finally` block

    c) (a) or (b)   d) None of the above

24.7 The _____ statement is used to rethrow an exception from inside a `Catch` block.

    a) `Rethrow`   b) `Throw`

    c) `Try`   d) `Catch`

24.8 _____ marks the end of a Try block and its corresponding `Catch` and `Finally` blocks.

    a) `End Try`   b) `End Finally`

    c) `End Catch`   d) `End Exception`

24.9 A `Finally` block is located _____.

    a) after the Try block, but before each `Catch` block

    b) before the Try block

    c) after the Try block and the Try block's corresponding `Catch` blocks

    d) Either (b) or (c)

24.10 A(n) _____ is executed if an exception is thrown from a Try block or if no exception is thrown.

    a) `Catch` block   b) `Finally` block

    c) exception handler   d) All of the above

EXERCISES

24.11 (*Enhanced Miles Per Gallon App*) Modify the **Miles Per Gallon** app (Exercise 13.13) to use exception handling to process the `FormatExceptions` that occur when converting the `Strings` in the `TextBoxes` to `Doubles` (Fig. 24.16). The original app allowed the user to input the number of miles driven and the number of gallons used for a tank of gas to determine the number of miles the user was able to drive on one gallon of gas.

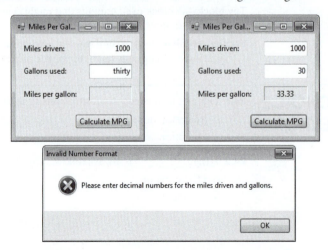

Figure 24.16 Enhanced **Miles Per Gallon** app's GUI.

a) *Copying the template to your working directory.* Copy the directory C:\Examples\ch24\Exercises\EnhancedMilesPerGallon to your C:\SimplyVB2010 directory.

b) *Opening the app's template file.* Double click EnhancedMilesPerGallon.sln in the EnhancedMilesPerGallon directory to open the app.

c) *Adding a Try block.* Find the calculateMPGButton_Click event handler. Enclose all of the code in this event handler in a Try block.

d) *Adding a Catch block.* After the Try block you added in *Step c*, add a Catch block to handle any FormatExceptions that may occur in the Try block. Inside the Catch block, add code to display an error message dialog.

e) *Running the app.* Select **Debug > Start Debugging** to run your app. Enter invalid data, as shown in Fig. 24.16, and click the **Calculate MPG** Button. A MessageBox will appear asking you to enter valid input. Enter valid input and click the **Calculate MPG** Button again. Verify that the correct output is displayed.

f) *Closing the app.* Close your running app by clicking its close box.

g) *Closing the IDE.* Close the Visual Basic IDE by clicking its close box.

24.12 (*Enhanced Prime Numbers App*) Modify the **Prime Numbers** app (Exercise 13.17) to use exception handling to process the FormatExceptions that occur when converting the Strings in the TextBoxes to Integers (Fig. 24.17). The original app took two numbers (representing a lower bound and an upper bound) and determined all of the prime numbers within the specified bounds, inclusive. An Integer greater than 1 is said to be prime if it's divisible by only 1 and itself. For example, 2, 3, 5 and 7 are prime numbers, but 4, 6, 8 and 9 are not.

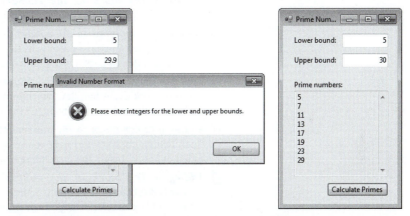

Figure 24.17   Enhanced **Prime Numbers** app's GUI.

a) *Copying the template to your working directory.* Copy the directory C:\Examples\ch24\Exercises\EnhancedPrimeNumbers to your C:\SimplyVB2010 directory.

b) *Opening the app's template file.* Double click EnhancedPrimeNumbers.sln in the EnhancedPrimeNumbers directory to open the app.

c) *Adding a Try block.* Find the calculatePrimesButton_Click event handler. Enclose all the code following the variable declarations in a Try block.

d) *Adding a Catch block.* Add a Catch block that catches any FormatExceptions that may occur in the Try block you added to calculatePrimesButton_Click in *Step c*. Inside the Catch block, add code to display an error message dialog.

e) *Running the app.* Select **Debug > Start Debugging** to run your app. Enter invalid data, as shown in Fig. 24.17, and click the **Calculate Primes** Button. A MessageBox should appear asking you to enter valid input. Enter valid input and click the **Calculate Primes** Button again. Verify that the correct output is displayed.

f) *Closing the app.* Close your running app by clicking its close box.

g) *Closing the IDE.* Close the Visual Basic IDE by clicking its close box.

24.13 (*Enhanced Simple Calculator App*) Modify the simple **Calculator** app (Exercise 6.13) to use exception handling to process the FormatExceptions that occur when converting the Strings in the TextBoxes to Integers and the DivideByZeroException that occurs when performing the division (Fig. 24.18). We define what a DivideByZeroException is shortly. The app should still perform simple addition, subtraction, multiplication and division.

Figure 24.18 Enhanced simple **Calculator** app.

a) *Copying the template to your working directory.* Copy the directory C:\Examples\ ch24\Exercises\EnhancedSimpleCalculator to your C:\SimplyVB2010 directory.

b) *Opening the app's template file.* Double click EnhancedSimpleCalculator.sln in the EnhancedSimpleCalculator directory to open the app.

c) *Adding a Try block to the addButton_Click event handler.* Find the add-Button_Click event handler. Enclose the body of addButton_Click in a Try block.

d) *Adding a Catch block to the addButton_Click event handler.* Add a Catch block that catches any FormatExceptions that may occur in the Try block that you added in *Step c*. Inside the Catch block, add code to display an error message dialog.

e) *Adding a Try block to the subtractButton_Click event handler.* Find the subtract-Button_Click event handler, which immediately follows addButton_Click. Enclose the body of the subtractButton_Click in a Try block.

f) *Adding a Catch block to the subtractButton_Click event handler.* Add a Catch block that catches any FormatExceptions that may occur in the Try block that you added in *Step e*. Inside the Catch block, add code to display an error message dialog.

g) *Adding a Try block to the multiplyButton_Click event handler.* Find the multiplyButton_Click event handler, which immediately follows subtract-Button_Click. Enclose the body of the multiplyButton_Click in a Try block.

h) *Adding a Catch block to the multiplyButton_Click event handler.* Add a Catch block that catches any FormatExceptions that may occur in the Try block that you added in *Step g*. Inside the Catch block, add code to display an error message dialog.

i) *Adding a Try block to the divideButton_Click event handler.* Find the divide-Button_Click event handler, which immediately follows multiplyButton_Click. Enclose the body of the divideButton_Click in a Try block.

j) *Adding a Catch block to the divideButton_Click event handler.* Add a Catch block that catches any FormatExceptions that may occur in the Try block that you added in *Step i*. Inside the Catch block, add code to display an error message dialog.

k) *Adding a second Catch block to the divideButton_Click event handler.* Immediately following the first Catch block inside the divideButton_Click event handler, add a Catch block to catch any DivideByZeroExceptions. A **DivideByZeroException** is thrown when division by zero in integer arithmetic occurs. Inside the Catch block, add code to display an error message dialog.

l) *Running the app.* Select **Debug > Start Debugging** to run your app. Enter valid input for the first number and 0 for the second number, then click the Button for division. A MessageBox should appear asking you not to divide by 0. Enter invalid input (such as letters) for the first and second numbers, then click each of the Buttons provided. This time a MessageBox should appear asking you to enter valid input. Enter valid input and click each of the Buttons provided. Verify that the correct output is displayed.

m) *Closing the app.* Close your running app by clicking its close box.

n) *Closing the IDE.* Close the Visual Basic IDE by clicking its close box.

What does this code do? ▶ **24.14** What does the following code do, assuming that value1 and value2 are both declared as Doubles?

```
1   Try
2       value1 = Convert.ToDouble(input1TextBox.Text)
3       value2 = Convert.ToDouble(input2TextBox.Text)
4
5       outputTextBox.Text = (value1 * value2).ToString()
6
7   Catch formatExceptionParameter As FormatException
8       MessageBox.Show(
9           "Please enter floating-point values.",
10          "Invalid Number Format",
11          MessageBoxButtons.OK, MessageBoxIcon.Error)
12  End Try
```

What's wrong with this code? ▶ **24.15** The following code should add integers from two TextBoxes and display the result in outputTextBox. Assume that value1 and value2 are declared as Integers. Find the error(s) in the following code:

```
1   Try
2       value1 = Convert.ToInt32(input1TextBox.Text)
3       value2 = Convert.ToInt32(input2TextBox.Text)
4
5       outputTextBox.Text = (value1 + value2).ToString()
6   End Try
7
8   Catch formatExceptionParameter As FormatException
9       MessageBox.Show(
10          "Please enter valid Integers.",
11          "Invalid Number Format",
12          MessageBoxButtons.OK, MessageBoxIcon.Error)
13  End Catch
```

25

CheckWriter App

Introducing Graphics and Printing

Graphics allow you to visually enhance Windows apps. In this chapter, you'll learn about tools for drawing two-dimensional shapes, and for controlling colors and fonts. To build the **CheckWriter** app, you'll use the GDI+ **Application Programming Interface (API)**. An API is the interface used by an app to access the operating system and various services on a computer. **GDI+ (Graphics Device Interface)** is a graphics API for creating and manipulating two-dimensional vector graphics, fonts and images. A **vector graphic** is not represented as a grid of pixels, but is instead represented by a set of mathematical properties called vectors, which describe a graphic's dimensions, attributes and position. Using the GDI+ API, you can create robust graphics without worrying about the specific details of graphics hardware.

The .NET `System.Drawing` namespace and the other namespaces that comprise GDI+ contain many sophisticated drawing capabilities. The `System.Drawing.Printing` namespace is used in the **CheckWriter** app to specify how a check is printed on the page.

GDI+ graphics capabilities help you preview and print a check using the **CheckWriter** app. To complete the app, you'll learn how to draw shapes, change the styles of the lines used to draw shapes and control the colors of filled shapes. You'll also learn how to specify a text style using fonts.

25.1 Test-Driving the CheckWriter App

This app must meet the following requirements:

App Requirements

A local business is responsible for distributing paychecks to its employees. The human-resources department needs a way to generate and print the paychecks. You've been asked to create an app that allows the human-resources department to input all the information necessary for a valid check, which includes the employee's name, the date, the amount that the employee should be paid and the company's address information. Your app should graphically draw the check so that it can be printed.

This app prints a paycheck. The user inputs the check number, the date, the numeric amount of the check, the employee's name, the amount of the check written in words and the company's address information. The user can press the **Preview** Button, which displays the format of the check. The user can then press the **Print** Button if the format is acceptable, causing the check to print from the printer. You'll begin by test-driving the completed app. Then you'll learn the additional Visual Basic capabilities needed to create your own version of this app.

Test-Driving the CheckWriter App

1. ***Opening the completed app.*** Open the directory C:\Examples\ch25\CompletedApp\CheckWriter to locate the **CheckWriter** app. Double click CheckWriter.sln to open the app in the Visual Basic IDE.

2. ***Running the CheckWriter app.*** Select **Debug > Start Debugging** to run the app (Fig. 25.1).

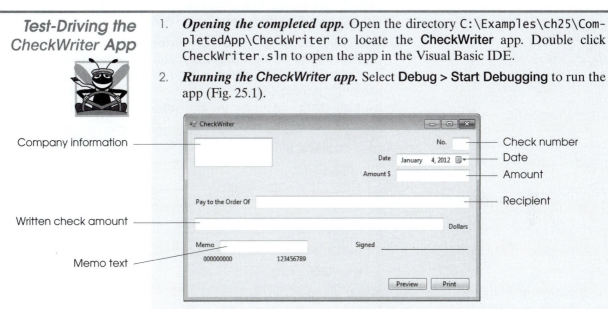

Figure 25.1 **CheckWriter** app displaying an empty check.

3. ***Providing inputs for the company information.*** In the company information TextBox, type The Company, then press *Enter* to proceed to the next line of the TextBox. Type 123 Fake Street. Press *Enter* to proceed to the third line of the TextBox. Type Any Town, MA 11111.

4. ***Providing values for the remaining information.*** For the **No.** field, input the check number 100. Leave the **Date** field (represented by a DateTimePicker control) as today's date, which is the default. Input 1,000.00 as the check amount. Enter John Smith as the recipient, and type One Thousand and 00/100 in the TextBox to the left of **Dollars**. In the **Memo** field, type Paycheck. The check should appear as shown in Fig. 25.2.

Figure 25.2 **CheckWriter** app displaying a completed check.

(cont.)

You may have noticed that at the bottom-left side of all bank checks is a string of numbers and symbols. These are called Magnetic Ink Character Recognition (MICR) numbers. MICR numbers are broken into three components. The first nine digits are the bank's routing number, followed by the account number then the check number. Banks have special machines that read these numbers and route the check to the appropriate account. Using the MICR font, you can create MICR numbers in your check-writing app. (We did not use the MICR font in this app.) To download the MICR font, visit www.newfreeware.com/graphics/696/.

5. *Previewing the check.* Click the **Preview** Button to display the completed check in a **Print preview** (Fig. 25.3). This dialog is actually a control of type PrintPreviewDialog, which is used to display how a document appears before it's printed. [*Note:* Printing or previewing the document is not possible when there's no printer installed on your computer.]

Figure 25.3 Preview of the completed check.

The **Print preview** dialog contains several toolbar Buttons. The first Button is the print Button (🖨), which allows the user to print the document. The next Button (🔍) zooms in and out, allowing the user to view the document at different sizes. The next five Buttons allow the user to specify the number of pages that can be displayed in the dialog at one time. The user can view one, two, three, four or six pages at a time in the dialog box. The **Close** Button closes the dialog box. Finally, the right-most control in the dialog box allows the user to specify which page of the document to view. The PrintPreviewDialog control is discussed in detail later in this chapter. The document that displays in this dialog box is the PrintDocument, an object that you'll create when coding the app.

6. *Closing the Print Preview dialog.* Click **Close** to close the **Print preview** dialog.

7. *Printing the check.* To print the check, your computer must be connected to a printer. Click the **Print** Button. The check prints from the default printer of your computer.

8. *Closing the app.* Close your app by clicking its close box.

9. *Closing the IDE.* Close the Visual Basic IDE by clicking its close box.

25.2 GDI+ Introduction

This section introduces the graphics classes and structures used in this chapter and discusses GDI+ graphics programming. Graphics typically consist of lines, shapes, colors and text drawn on the background of a control.

You'll use the methods of class **Graphics** to draw on the Form. Class **Graphics** contains methods used for drawing text, lines, rectangles and other shapes. Objects of the **Pen** and **Brush** classes affect the appearance of the lines and shapes you'll draw. A **Pen** specifies the line style used to draw a shape (for example, line thickness, solid lines, dashed lines, etc.). A **Brush** specifies how to fill a shape (for example, solid color or pattern). The drawing methods of class **Graphics** usually require a **Pen** or **Brush** object to render a specified shape.

The **Color** structure contains pre-defined colors and methods that allow you to create new colors. Objects of the **Font** class affect the appearance of text. The **Font** class contains properties (such as **Bold**, **Italic** and **Size**) that describe font characteristics. The **FontFamily** class contains methods for obtaining font information (such as **GetName**).

GDI+ uses a **coordinate system** (Fig. 25.4) to identify every point on the screen. A coordinate pair has both an *x*-**coordinate** (the horizontal coordinate) and a *y*-**coordinate** (the vertical coordinate). The *x*-coordinate is the horizontal distance from zero at the left of the drawing area, which increases as you move to the right. The *y*-coordinate is the vertical distance from zero at the top of the drawing area, which increases as you move down.

Portability Tip

Different computer monitors have different resolutions, so the density of pixels on various monitors will vary. This may cause graphics to appear in different sizes on different monitors.

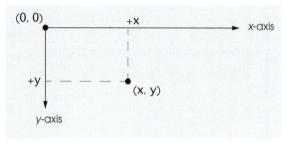

Figure 25.4   GDI+ coordinate system.

The **x-axis** defines every horizontal coordinate, and the **y-axis** defines every vertical coordinate. You position text and shapes on the screen by specifying their (*x*, *y*) coordinates. The upper-left corner of a GUI component (such as a **Panel** or the Form) has the coordinates (0, 0). In the diagram in Fig. 25.4, the point at position (*x*, *y*) is *x* pixels to the right of position (0, 0) along the *x*-axis and *y* pixels below position (0, 0) along the *y*-axis. Coordinate units are measured in pixels, which are the smallest units of resolution on a computer monitor.

SELF-REVIEW   1. The _____ class contains properties that describe font characteristics.

    a) `Font`   b) `GDIFont`
    c) `SystemFont`   d) `FontStyle`

2. The _____ corner of a GUI component has the coordinate (0, 0).

    a) lower-left   b) upper-right
    c) upper-left   d) lower-right

Answers: 1) a. 2) c.

25.3 Constructing the CheckWriter App

Now that you've learned about the features that you'll use in your **CheckWriter** app, you need to analyze the app. The following pseudocode describes the basic operation of the **CheckWriter** app:

```
When the user clicks the Preview Button
    Retrieve check information from the user
    Display the check in a Print Preview dialog
```

When the user clicks the Print Button
    Retrieve check information from the user
    Print the check on the printer

Now that you've test-driven the **CheckWriter** app and studied its pseudocode representation, you'll use an ACE table to help you convert the pseudocode to Visual Basic. Figure 25.5 lists the *actions*, *controls* and *events* that help you complete your own version of this app.

Action/Control/Event (ACE) Table for the CheckWriter App

Action	Control/Object	Event
Label the app's controls	checkNumberLabel, dateLabel, amountLabel, payeeLabel, dollarsLabel, memoLabel, signedLabel, underlineLabel, abaLabel, accountLabel	App is Run
	previewButton	Click
Retrieve check information from the user	checkNumberTextBox, dateTimePicker, amountTextBox, payeeTextBox, dollarTextBox, memoTextBox, payerTextBox	
Display the check in a Print preview dialog	previewObject, document	
	printButton	Click
Retrieve check information from the user	checkNumberTextBox, dateTimePicker, amountTextBox, payeeTextBox, dollarTextBox, memoTextBox, payerTextBox	
Print the check on the printer	document	

Figure 25.5   ACE table for the **CheckWriter** app.

Now that you've an understanding of the **CheckWriter** app, you can begin to create it. A template app is provided that contains many of the GUI's controls. You'll begin by creating a `PrintPreviewDialog` object in the following box.

Adding a PrintPreviewDialog in the CheckWriter App

1. ***Copying the template to your working directory.*** Copy the `C:\Examples\ch25\TemplateApp\CheckWriter` directory to `C:\SimplyVB2010`.

2. ***Opening the*** **CheckWriter** ***app's template file.*** Double click Check-Writer.sln in the CheckWriter directory to open the app in the Visual Basic IDE.

(cont.)   3. ***Adding the `PrintPreviewDialog`.*** In the **Toolbox**, locate the **PrintPreview-Dialog** control

> 🔲 PrintPreviewDialog

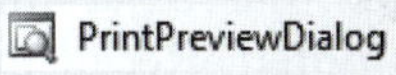

in the **All Windows Forms** group, and drag and drop it onto the Form. The control appears in the component tray as shown in Fig. 25.6.

`PrintPreviewDialog` in the component tray

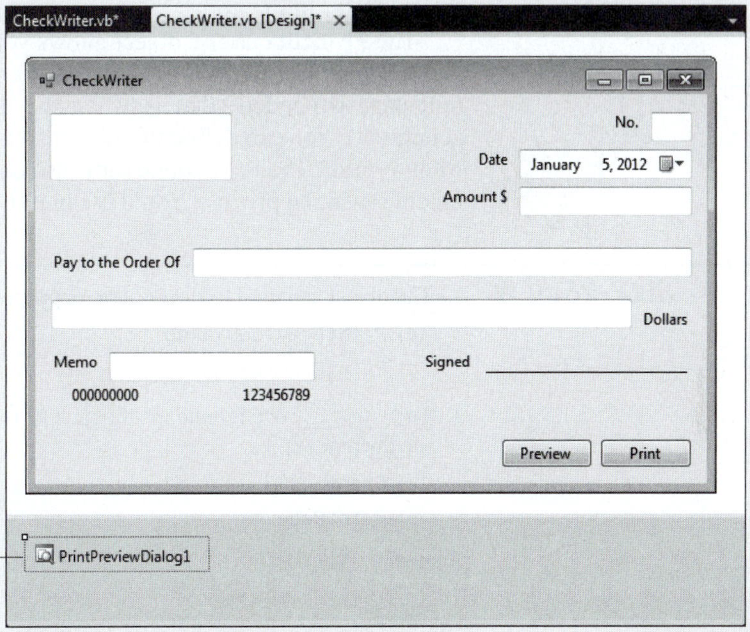

Figure 25.6   CheckWriter app in **Design** view with `PrintPreviewDialog`.

The `PrintPreviewDialog` control displays a dialog that allows users to view a document at different sizes, print a document and display multiple pages of a document before printing. Make sure the `PrintPreviewDialog` object that you just created is selected, and change its `Name` property to `previewObject`. This object has a `Document` property that specifies the document to preview. The document must be a `PrintDocument` object, as will be discussed later in the chapter. For now, do not specify the document.

4. ***Setting the `UseAntiAlias` property to `True`.*** The `PrintPreviewDialog` also contains the **`UseAntiAlias`** property, which makes the text in the dialog appear smoother on the screen. To accomplish this, set the `UseAntiAlias` property to `True`.

5. ***Saving the project.*** Select **File > Save All** to save your modified code.

SELF-REVIEW

1. Use a _____ control to preview a document before it's printed.

   a) `PrintDialog`   b) `PrintPreviewDialog`

   c) `PrintPreviewControl`   d) `PrintDocument`

2. A `PrintPreviewDialog` object has a _____ property that specifies the document to preview.

   a) `Preview`   b) `PreviewDocument`

   c) `View`   d) `Document`

Answers: 1) b. 2) d.

25.4 PrintPreviewDialogs and PrintDocuments

In the **CheckWriter** app, you'll use an object of the PrintPreviewDialog class. As previously mentioned, this object displays a dialog that shows a document as it appears when it's printed. Recall that the dialog object contains the **Document** property, which allows you to specify the document to preview, and that the object specified in the Document property must be of type PrintDocument. The PrintPreviewDialog's ShowDialog method displays the preview dialog. You'll use this method later in the app.

The **PrintDocument** object allows you to specify how to print a specified document. The object raises a **PrintPage** event when the data required to print the current page is needed (that is, when the document is printed or a print preview is generated). You can define this object's PrintPage event handler to specify what you want to print. The PrintDocument also contains a **Print** method that starts the document's printing process. You'll use method Print later in this chapter.

---

1. The object assigned to the Document property must be of type _____.
   a) PrintPreviewDialog b) PrintDocument
   c) PrintPreviewControl d) PrintDialog

2. The _____ event handler of object PrintDocument uses a Graphics object to print the document.
   a) Graphics b) Document
   c) PrintPage d) None of the above

Answers: 1) b. 2) c.

25.5 Creating an Event Handler for the CheckWriter App

Now that you've created the PrintPreviewDialog object in the **CheckWriter** app, you can begin to add functionality to the app. Before you can use print features, you must import the System.Drawing.Printing namespace. You'll implement these features in the following box.

Importing a Namespace

1. *Switching to Code view.* Select **View > Code** to view the CheckWriter.vb code.

2. *Importing namespaces.* Add line 1 before the class CheckWriterForm definition, as shown in Fig. 25.7 to import the **System.Drawing.Printing** namespace. This statement allows your app to access operating system services related to printing. After you import the namespace, the app can use PrintDocument objects. The namespace also enables access to the **PrintPageEventArgs** class. This class's Graphics property provides a Graphics object used to draw the graphics that appear on the printed page.

Importing namespace
System.Drawing.Printing

```
1  Imports System.Drawing.Printing
2
3  Public Class CheckWriterForm
```

Figure 25.7   Import System.Drawing.Printing namespace.

3. *Saving the project.* Select **File > Save All** to save your modified code.

Now that you've imported namespace System.Drawing.Printing, you can write code to enable printing and previewing. You'll begin by defining the document_PrintPage method, which specifies what to print. When printing the check, you want the printed document to resemble the app's Form. This can be accomplished using a For Each...Next statement that draws in a Graphics object the contents of each control. You can then print the check using this Graphics object. You'll begin writing code to perform these actions in the following box.

| *Defining an Event Handler to Print Pages* | 1. | ***Creating the document_PrintPage method.*** Add lines 5–9 into the app code, as in Fig. 25.8. These lines create the event handler for the PrintPage event. You need to type these lines to create the event handler because the PrintDocument object has not yet been created. You'll create this object later in the chapter. |

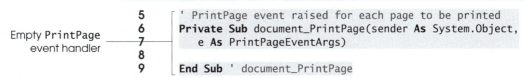

Empty PrintPage event handler

```
5    ' PrintPage event raised for each page to be printed
6    Private Sub document_PrintPage(sender As System.Object,
7       e As PrintPageEventArgs)
8
9    End Sub ' document_PrintPage
```

Figure 25.8 document_PrintPage event handler.

2. ***Declaring the variables.*** Add lines 9–22 of Fig. 25.9 to the event handler. Line 9 declares a Font variable named fontObject that's used to specify the text font. Lines 12–13 declare Single variables that represent the *x*- and *y*-coordinates where controls appear on the Form. **Single** is a type that stores floating-point values. Single is similar to Double, but is less precise and requires less memory. Lines 16 and 19 declare Single variables, which specify the coordinates of the left and top margins of the page to be printed. These values are determined by using the **MarginBounds.Left** and **MarginBounds.Top** properties of the PrintPageEventArgs object (e from line 7) that's passed when the PrintPage event is raised. Line 22 declares the String variable controlText, which is used to store text from the controls.

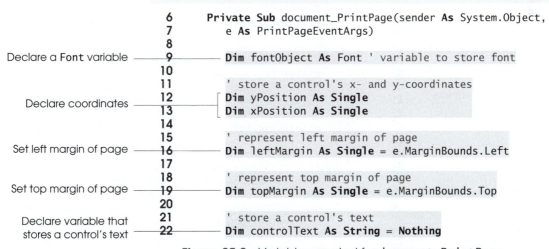

Declare a Font variable
Declare coordinates
Set left margin of page
Set top margin of page
Declare variable that stores a control's text

```
6    Private Sub document_PrintPage(sender As System.Object,
7       e As PrintPageEventArgs)
8
9    Dim fontObject As Font ' variable to store font
10
11   ' store a control's x- and y-coordinates
12   Dim yPosition As Single
13   Dim xPosition As Single
14
15   ' represent left margin of page
16   Dim leftMargin As Single = e.MarginBounds.Left
17
18   ' represent top margin of page
19   Dim topMargin As Single = e.MarginBounds.Top
20
21   ' store a control's text
22   Dim controlText As String = Nothing
```

Figure 25.9 Variables created for document_PrintPage.

3. ***Iterating through the controls on the Form.*** Add lines 24–28 of Fig. 25.10 to the PrintPage event handler. This For Each...Next statement iterates through the controls on the Form to print the check. You'll define this statement's body in the next box.

(cont.)

```
22        Dim controlText As String = Nothing
23
24        ' iterate over the controls on the Form,
25        ' printing the text displayed in each control
26        For Each controlObject As Control In Me.Controls
27
28        Next controlObject
```

Declaring a For Each...Next statement

Figure 25.10 For Each...Next statement used for iteration.

4. *Adding formatting lines and drawing the check's border.* Add lines 30–54 of Fig. 25.11 into the event handler. Checks contain lines for payee, payment amount, and memo information. To draw these lines, call the **DrawLine** method on the Graphics object (which is received by this event handler as part of the PrintPageEventArgs parameter). Method DrawLine takes five arguments, the first of which specifies the Pen to use to draw the line. A **Pen** specifies the characteristics of the line that's drawn. Lines 31, 38, 46 and 53 each use a value from the **Pens** class (Pens.Black) to specify that a solid black line should be drawn. The next four arguments are the coordinates of the line's endpoints in the following order: x1, y1, x2, y2. Lines 31–35 draw the payee line, using the Location property of the payeeTextBox control as arguments in the method call. Note that you add 15 to the *y*-coordinates for the line because the control's *y*-coordinate represents the *top* of the control—the line is now drawn at the bottom of the control. Lines 38–43 and lines 46–50 similarly use their respective control location properties to draw a line in the appropriate place on the check.

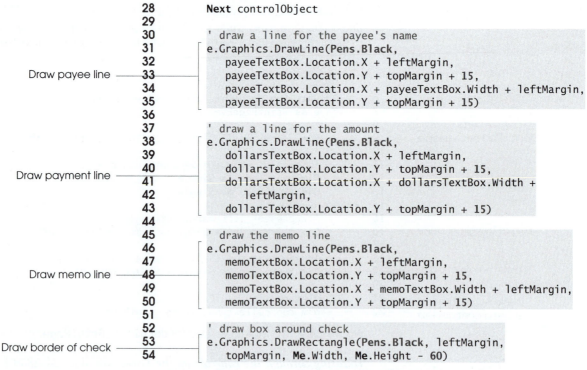

```
28        Next controlObject
29
30        ' draw a line for the payee's name
31        e.Graphics.DrawLine(Pens.Black,
32            payeeTextBox.Location.X + leftMargin,
33            payeeTextBox.Location.Y + topMargin + 15,
34            payeeTextBox.Location.X + payeeTextBox.Width + leftMargin,
35            payeeTextBox.Location.Y + topMargin + 15)
36
37        ' draw a line for the amount
38        e.Graphics.DrawLine(Pens.Black,
39            dollarsTextBox.Location.X + leftMargin,
40            dollarsTextBox.Location.Y + topMargin + 15,
41            dollarsTextBox.Location.X + dollarsTextBox.Width +
42                leftMargin,
43            dollarsTextBox.Location.Y + topMargin + 15)
44
45        ' draw the memo line
46        e.Graphics.DrawLine(Pens.Black,
47            memoTextBox.Location.X + leftMargin,
48            memoTextBox.Location.Y + topMargin + 15,
49            memoTextBox.Location.X + memoTextBox.Width + leftMargin,
50            memoTextBox.Location.Y + topMargin + 15)
51
52        ' draw box around check
53        e.Graphics.DrawRectangle(Pens.Black, leftMargin,
54            topMargin, Me.Width, Me.Height - 60)
```

Draw payee line

Draw payment line

Draw memo line

Draw border of check

Figure 25.11 Event handler document_PrintPage modified to draw formatting lines on the check.

(cont.)

The Form's border is not contained in a control—you must use a Graphics object to draw a rectangle around the check to be printed. To draw the rectangle around the check, use the PrintPageEventArgs object (e from line 7) that's passed when the PrintPage event is raised. The Graphics property of this object again allows you to specify what you want to print. By calling the **DrawRectangle** method (lines 53–54) on the Graphics object, you can specify the properties of the rectangle to draw.

The first argument you pass to the method is a Pen object that specifies how to draw the rectangle's border. The second argument specifies the *x*-coordinate of the upper-left corner of the rectangle you wish to draw. Use the leftMargin variable that you created in *Step 2* to represent the position of the left margin of the page on which the check prints. This value ensures that the rectangle aligns with the left margin. The third argument in the method specifies the *y*-coordinate of the upper-left corner of the rectangle. Use the topMargin variable that you created in *Step 2* to represent the position of the top margin of the page on which the check prints.

The fourth and fifth arguments specify the width and height of the rectangle. The width is set to Me.Width, which returns the width of the Form. Keyword Me references the current object—in this case, the Form. The height, on the other hand, is set to Me.Height - 60. This value is the height of the Form minus 60 pixels. You subtract 60 pixels because you do not want to print the space for the Buttons on the bottom of the Form. These Buttons were created to allow users to print and preview the checks. (They were not intended to be printed on the checks.)

5. *Saving the project*. Select **File > Save All** to save your modified code.

SELF-REVIEW

1. Importing the System._____ namespace gives you access to print-related functions.
   a) Windows   b) Printing
   c) Drawing.Printing   d) Drawing

2. The _____ keyword references the current object.
   a) Me   b) Current
   c) Form   d) None of the above

Answers: 1) c. 2) a.

25.6 Graphics Objects: Colors, Lines and Shapes

A Graphics object controls drawing in a Windows Forms app. In addition to providing methods for drawing various shapes, Graphics objects contain methods for font manipulation, color manipulation and other graphics-related actions. You can draw on many controls, such as Labels and Buttons, which have their own drawing areas. To draw on a control, first obtain a Graphics object for the control by invoking its CreateGraphics method, as in

```
Dim graphicsObject As Graphics = displayPanel.CreateGraphics()
```

Now you can use the methods provided in class Graphics to draw on the display-Panel. Many Graphics methods are used in this chapter.

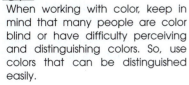

Good Programming Practice

When working with color, keep in mind that many people are color blind or have difficulty perceiving and distinguishing colors. So, use colors that can be distinguished easily.

Colors

Colors can enhance an app's appearance and help convey meaning. The **Color** structure defines methods and constants used to manipulate colors.

Every color can be created from a combination of alpha, red, green and blue components. The alpha value determines the **opacity** (amount of transparency) of the color. For example, the alpha value 0 specifies a transparent color, and the value 255 specifies an opaque color. Alpha values between 0 and 255 (inclusive) result in a blending of the color's RGB value with that of any background color, causing a semi-transparent effect. All three RGB components are `Bytes` that represent integer values in the range 0–255. The first number in the RGB value defines the amount of red in the color, the second defines the amount of green and the third defines the amount of blue. The larger the value for a particular color, the greater the amount of that color. Visual Basic enables you to choose from almost 17 million colors. If a screen can't display all of these colors, it displays the color closest to the one specified, or it attempts to imitate the color using **dithering** (using small dots of existing colors to form a pattern that simulates the desired color). Figure 25.12 summarizes some predefined `Color` constants. You can also find a list of various RGB values and their corresponding colors at `http://cloford.com/resources/colours/500col.htm`.

Constant	RGB value	Constant	RGB value
`Color.Orange`	255, 200, 0	`Color.White`	255, 255, 255
`Color.Pink`	255, 175, 175	`Color.Gray`	128, 128, 128
`Color.Cyan`	0, 255, 255	`Color.DarkGray`	64, 64, 64
`Color.Magenta`	255, 0, 255	`Color.Red`	255, 0, 0
`Color.Yellow`	255, 255, 0	`Color.Green`	0, 255, 0
`Color.Black`	0, 0, 0	`Color.Blue`	0, 0, 255

Figure 25.12 `Color` structure constants and their RGB values.

You can use pre-existing colors, or you can create your own by using the **FromArgb** method. The statement

```
Dim colorSilver As Color = Color.FromArgb(192, 192, 192)
```

creates a silver color and assigns it to variable `colorSilver`. Now you can use `colorSilver` whenever you need a silver color. The `Color` method `FromArgb` is used to create this color and other colors by specifying the RGB values as arguments. The version of the method shown above sets the alpha value to 255 (that is, opaque) by default. There are several overloaded versions of `FromArgb`.

Drawing Lines, Rectangles and Ovals

This section presents several `Graphics` methods for drawing lines, rectangles and ovals. To draw shapes and `Strings`, you must specify the type of `Brushes` and `Pens` to use. A `Pen`, which functions much like an ordinary pen, is used to specify such characteristics as the color and width of the shape's lines. Most drawing methods require a `Pen` object. To fill the interior of objects, you must specify a `Brush`. All classes derived from the abstract class `Brush` define objects that fill the interiors of shapes with color patterns or images. For example, a `SolidBrush` specifies the `Color` that fills the interior of a shape. The following statement creates a `Solid-Brush` with the color orange:

```
Dim brush As New SolidBrush(Color.Orange)
```

Many drawing methods have multiple versions. When employing methods that draw outlined hollow shapes, use versions that take a `Pen` argument. When employing methods that draw shapes filled with colors, patterns or images, use versions that take a `Brush` argument. Many of these methods require x, y, `width` and `height` arguments. The x and y arguments represent the shape's upper-left corner coordinate. The `width` and `height` arguments represent the width and height of the shape in pixels, respectively. Figure 25.13 summarizes several `Graphics` methods and their parameters.

Graphics Drawing Methods and Descriptions

Note: Many of these methods have multiple overloaded versions.

```
DrawLine(p As Pen, x1 As Single, y1 As Single,
    x2 As Single, y2 As Single)
```
Draws a line from the point (x1, y1) to the point (x2, y2). The Pen determines the color, style and width of the line.

```
DrawRectangle(p As Pen, x As Single, y As Single,
    width As Single, height As Single)
```
Draws a rectangle of the specified width and height. The top-left corner of the rectangle is at the point (x, y). The Pen determines the rectangle's color, style and border width.

```
FillRectangle(b As Brush, x As Single, y As Single,
    width As Single, height As Single)
```
Draws a solid rectangle of the specified width and height. The top-left corner of the rectangle is at the point (x, y). The Brush determines the fill pattern inside the rectangle.

```
DrawEllipse(p As Pen, x As Single, y As Single,
    width As Single, height As Single)
```
Draws an ellipse inside a rectangular area of the specified width and height. The top-left corner of the rectangular area is at the point (x, y). The Pen determines the color, style and border width of the ellipse.

```
FillEllipse(b As Brush, x As Single, y As Single,
    width As Single, height As Single)
```
Draws a filled ellipse inside a rectangular area of the specified width and height. The top-left corner of the rectangular area is at the point (x, y). The Brush determines the pattern inside the ellipse.

Figure 25.13 Graphics methods that draw lines, rectangles and ovals.

SELF-REVIEW

1. The RGB value of a Color represents _____.
   a) the index number of a color
   b) the amount of red, green and blue in a color
   c) the thickness of the drawing object
   d) the type of shape to draw

2. The _____ method is used to draw solid rectangles.
   a) DrawRectangle   b) FillRectangle
   c) SolidRectangle   d) OpaqueRectangle

Answers: 1) b. 2) b.

25.7 Printing Each Control of the CheckWriter App

Earlier, you created an empty For Each...Next statement to iterate through all the controls on the Form. Now you'll write code for the body of the For Each...Next statement to print all the controls on the Form, except for the Buttons.

Iterating through All the Objects of the Form to Print Each Control

1. *Checking for Buttons.* In the body of document_PrintPage's For Each...Next statement, add lines 27–30 of Fig. 25.14. Adding this If...Then statement determines whether the current control is a Button. If the control is not a Button, then the body of the If...Then statement executes. However, if the control is a Button, the For Each...Next statement continues to the next control on the Form.

(cont.)

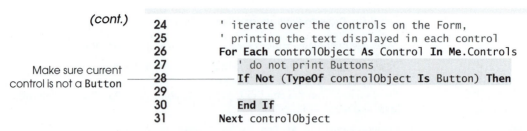

```
24      ' iterate over the controls on the Form,
25      ' printing the text displayed in each control
26      For Each controlObject As Control In Me.Controls
27          ' do not print Buttons
28          If Not (TypeOf controlObject Is Button) Then
29
30          End If
31      Next controlObject
```

Make sure current control is not a **Button**

Figure 25.14 Code to determine whether the current control is a **Button**.

2. ***Defining the body of the If...Then statement.*** Now you'll add code that properly prints the value that appears in each control on the check. Add lines 29–44 of Fig. 25.15 into the body of the If...Then statement.

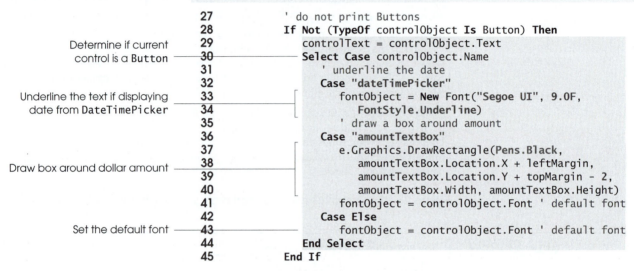

```
27          ' do not print Buttons
28          If Not (TypeOf controlObject Is Button) Then
29              controlText = controlObject.Text
30              Select Case controlObject.Name
31                  ' underline the date
32                  Case "dateTimePicker"
33                      fontObject = New Font("Segoe UI", 9.0F,
34                          FontStyle.Underline)
35                  ' draw a box around amount
36                  Case "amountTextBox"
37                      e.Graphics.DrawRectangle(Pens.Black,
38                          amountTextBox.Location.X + leftMargin,
39                          amountTextBox.Location.Y + topMargin - 2,
40                          amountTextBox.Width, amountTextBox.Height)
41                      fontObject = controlObject.Font ' default font
42                  Case Else
43                      fontObject = controlObject.Font ' default font
44              End Select
45          End If
```

Determine if current control is a **Button**

Underline the text if displaying date from **DateTimePicker**

Draw box around dollar amount

Set the default font

Figure 25.15 Select Case statement to print controls.

Line 29 sets the controlText variable that you created earlier to controlObject.Text. This contains the value of the control's Text property (text displayed to the user or entered by the user). The Select Case statement (lines 30–44) specifies how each control prints. The controlling expression is set to the value controlObject.Name. This is the Name property of the control. You can use the Name property to select specific controls that need to be treated differently when printed.

The first Case (lines 32–34) handles the dateTimePicker control. It sets fontObject to the date's font style—underlined 9pt Segoe UI font. The date is underlined and appears in 9pt in Segoe UI font. Fonts are discussed in detail later in this chapter.

The second Case (lines 36–41) executes if the control is amountTextBox. This Case draws the box that around the decimal check amount. Graphics method DrawRectangle is invoked via the e.Graphics property. The rectangle's outline prints in black as indicated by Pens.Black. The *x*- and *y*-coordinates are specified by adding the TextBox's *x-y* location on the Form to variables leftMargin and topMargin, respectively. Recall that you begin printing the check at the corner of the top and left margins. Adding the margin values to the Location properties ensures that amountTextBox prints in the same position as it appears on the Form. (Line 39 subtracts two points of space to center the box on the text.) Line 41 sets the font of the text to draw to the same value as the font used to display text in the control. The third *(cont.)*   Case (lines 42–43) executes for all the other controls. This Case sets the fontObject font style to the same value as the font used to display text in the control. Line 44 ends the Select Case statement.

3. ***Setting the positions of the text of each control.*** Add lines 46–55 of Fig. 25.16 to the body of the If...Then statement. Lines 47–48 set the xPosition variable to leftMargin + controlObject.Location.X. By adding the *x*-coordinate of the current control (represented by control-Object.Location.X) to the left margin, you ensure that the check will not draw outside the margins of the page.

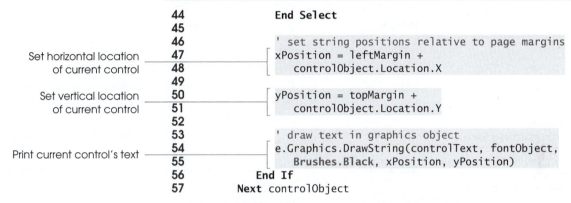

Set horizontal location of current control

Set vertical location of current control

Print current control's text

```
44              End Select
45
46              ' set string positions relative to page margins
47              xPosition = leftMargin +
48                  controlObject.Location.X
49
50              yPosition = topMargin +
51                  controlObject.Location.Y
52
53              ' draw text in graphics object
54              e.Graphics.DrawString(controlText, fontObject,
55                  Brushes.Black, xPosition, yPosition)
56          End If
57      Next controlObject
```

Figure 25.16 Code to set String positions of the controls.

Lines 50–51 perform a similar operation, setting yPosition to the sum of the top margin and *y*-coordinate of the control's location. Lines 54–55 call the DrawString method on the e.Graphics property. The **DrawString** method draws the specified String of text in the Graphics object. The first argument is the String to draw, in this case controlText. Recall that you set controlText to the Text property of the current control. The second argument is the font, which is specified by fontObject. The third argument specifies a Brush. You pass the value Brushes.Black, which creates a black brush object to draw the text. The **Brushes** class provides properties to access Brush objects of any standard color. The fourth and fifth arguments are the *x*- and *y*-coordinates where the first character of the String prints. Use the xPosition and yPosition variables that you set in lines 47–51 to print the text at the correct location on the page.

4. ***Saving the project.*** Select **File > Save All** to save your modified code.

SELF-REVIEW

1. The _____ method draws a specified String of text.

     a) String   b) PrintString

     c) DrawString   d) Draw

2. Typing Brushes.Black _____.

     a) obtains a black Brush object   b) retrieves the color of a brush

     c) paints the screen black   d) creates a Pen object

Answers: 1) c. 2) a.

25.8 Font Class

In the **CheckWriter** app, you used a Font object to specify the style of the text printed on a page. This section introduces the methods and constants contained in the Font class. Note that Fonts are *immutable*—once a Font has been created, its properties *cannot* be modified. That means that if you require a different Font, you must create a new Font object with the appropriate settings. That's the reason you created a new Font in lines 33–34 of Fig. 25.15 for the DateTimePicker control. There are many versions of the Font constructor for creating custom Fonts. Some properties of the Font class are summarized in Fig. 25.17.

Property	Description
Bold	Sets a font to a bold font style if value is set to True.
FontFamily	Represents the FontFamily of the Font (a grouping structure to organize fonts with similar properties).
Height	Represents the height of the font.
Italic	Sets a font to an italic font style if value is set to True.
Name	Sets the font's name to the specified String.
Size	Represents a Single value indicating the current font size measured in design units. (Design units are any specified units of measurement for the font.)
SizeInPoints	Represents a Single value indicating the current font size measured in points.
Strikeout	Sets a font to the strikeout font style if value is set to True (for example, ~~Strikeout~~).
Underline	Sets a font to the underline font style if the value is set to True.

Common Programming Error

Specifying a font that's not available on a system is a logic error. If this occurs, the system's default font is used instead.

Figure 25.17   Font class read-only properties.

The Size property returns the font size as measured in **design units**, whereas SizeInPoints returns the font size as measured in points (a more common measurement). The Size property can be specified in a variety of ways, such as inches or millimeters. Some versions of the Font constructor accept a GraphicsUnit argument—an enumeration that allows users to specify the unit of measurement used to describe the font size. Members of the GraphicsUnit enumeration include Point (1/72 inch), Display (1/100 inch), Document (1/300 inch), Millimeter, Inch and Pixel.

If the GraphicsUnit argument is provided, the Size property contains the size of the font as measured in the specified design unit, and the SizeInPoints property contains the size of the font in points. For example, if you create a Font having size 1 and specify that GraphicsUnit.Inch will be used to measure the font, the Size property will be 1, and the SizeInPoints property will be 72 because there are 72 points in an inch. If you create a new Font object without specifying a GraphicsUnit, the default measurement for the font size is GraphicsUnit.Point (thus, the Size and SizeInPoints properties will be equal).

The Font class has several overloaded constructors. Many of which require a font name, which is a String representing a font currently supported by the system. Common fonts include *Arial* and *Times New Roman*. Constructors also require the font size as an argument. Last, Font constructors usually require a font style, specified by an element of the **FontStyle** enumeration: FontStyle.Bold, FontStyle.Italic, FontStyle.Regular, FontStyle.Strikeout and FontStyle.Underline. You can specify multiple FontStyle elements by combining them using the Or operator (e.g., FontStyle.Bold **Or** FontStyle.Italic uses a bold italic font).

1. The most common measurement of font size is _____.

a) points b) inches

c) pixels d) millimeters

2. _____ is an example of a font style.

a) `Bold` b) `Italic`

c) `StrikeOut` d) All of the above

Answers: 1) a. 2) d.

25.9 Previewing and Printing the Check

After defining how objects are printed in the `document_PrintPage` event handler, you must define what occurs when each `Button` is clicked. You'll begin with the `printButton_Click` event handler to specify the functionality when clicking the **Print** `Button`. You'll write this event handler in the following box.

Defining the
`printButton_Click`
Event Handler

1. ***Creating the `printButton_Click` event handler.*** In the Windows Form Designer, double click the **Print** `Button`. The `printButton_Click` event handler appears in the `CheckWriter.vb` file. Add a comment and reformat the empty event handler as shown in lines 86–88 of Fig. 25.18.

2. ***Creating a `PrintDocument` object.*** Add lines 90–91 of Fig. 25.18 into the event handler. The `PrintDocument` object is used to help print the check. Be sure to add the comments and line-continuation characters as shown in Fig. 25.18 so that the line numbers in your code match those presented in this chapter.

Declaring a
`PrintDocument` object

```
86      ' print document
87      Private Sub printButton_Click(sender As System.Object,
88          e As System.EventArgs) Handles printButton.Click
89
90          ' create new object to assist in printing
91          Dim document As New PrintDocument()
92
93      End Sub ' printButton_Click
94
```

Figure 25.18 Code that creates the `PrintDocument` object.

3. ***Specifying the `PrintPage` event handler.*** Add lines 93–95 of Fig. 25.19 into the event handler. These lines specify the event handler called when the `PrintPage` event is raised. Lines 94–95 use the **`AddHandler`** statement to associate the `PrintPage` event of the `document` object with the event handler specified after the **`AddressOf`** operator (the `document_PrintPage` event handler that you created earlier in this chapter). To execute the code in the event handler, you must provide the name of the event handler you created to handle the event after operator `AddressOf`.

Adding an event handler for
the `PrintDocument` object

```
91          Dim document As New PrintDocument()
92
93          ' tell PrintDocument where to find PrintPage event handler
94          AddHandler document.PrintPage,
95              AddressOf document_PrintPage
```

Figure 25.19 Code that adds a `PrintPage` event handler to the `Print-Document` object.

(cont.)

4. ***Verifying that the user has a printer.*** Add lines 97–101 of Fig. 25.20 to the printButton_Click event handler. Line 98 uses the property **PrinterSettings.InstalledPrinters.Count** to determine how many printers are installed on the user's computer. This property is not limited to physical printers; it includes the Microsoft XPS Document Writer installed as part of recent .NET versions. If there are no printers (the Count property is 0), the user cannot print or preview the document. Line 99 in the body of the If...Then statement displays an error message by calling procedure ErrorMessage, which you'll define in the next box. Line 100 exits the event handler using the Return keyword.

```
95           AddressOf document_PrintPage
96
97           ' if no printers installed, display error message
98       If PrinterSettings.InstalledPrinters.Count = 0 Then
99           ErrorMessage()
100          Return ' exit event handler
101      End If
```

Take no action if there are no printers installed

Figure 25.20 Exiting the event handler if no printers are installed.

5. ***Printing the document.*** Add lines 103–104 of Fig. 25.21 to the printButton_Click event handler. Line 104 calls the PrintDocument's Print method. The Print method, in turn, raises the PrintPage event each time it needs output for printing. Your PrintPage event handler then executes and uses a Graphics object to draw. The Graphics object is obtained from the Graphics property of the PrintPageEventArgs class. In this case, the PrintPageEventArgs object was passed as argument e. The method document_PrintPage uses this PrintPageEventArgs' Graphics object to call the DrawRectangle, DrawLine and DrawString methods.

```
101      End If
102
103          ' print the document
104          document.Print()
105      End Sub ' printButton_Click
```

Print the check

Figure 25.21 Event handler printButton_Click modified to print the document.

6. ***Saving the project.*** Select **File > Save All** to save your modified code.

Now that you've defined the printButton_Click method, you'll complete the app by coding the Click event handler for the **Preview** Button. When this Button is clicked, a dialog appears allowing the user to preview the check before printing it. You'll create the previewButton_Click event handler to enable this feature in the following box.

Defining the previewButton_Click Event Handler

1. ***Creating the previewButton_Click event handler.*** In the Windows Form Designer, double click the **Preview** Button. The previewButton_Click event handler appears in the CheckWriter.vb file. Add a comment and reformat the empty event handler as shown in lines 107–109 of Fig. 25.22.

(cont.)   2. ***Creating the PrintDocument object and adding the PrintPage handler.***
Add lines 111–116 of Fig. 25.22 into the event handler. As in the print-
Button_Click event handler, line 112 creates a new PrintDocument object
named document. Lines 115–116 specify that the PrintDocument object's
PrintPage event handler is method document_PrintPage.

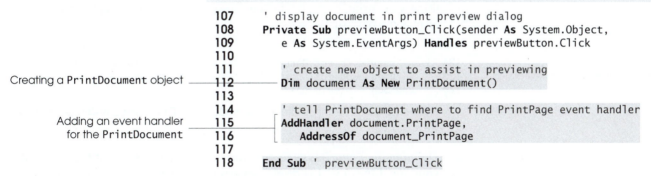

```
107         ' display document in print preview dialog
108         Private Sub previewButton_Click(sender As System.Object,
109            e As System.EventArgs) Handles previewButton.Click
110
111            ' create new object to assist in previewing
112            Dim document As New PrintDocument()
113
114            ' tell PrintDocument where to find PrintPage event handler
115            AddHandler document.PrintPage,
116               AddressOf document_PrintPage
117
118         End Sub ' previewButton_Click
```

Creating a PrintDocument object

Adding an event handler
for the PrintDocument

Figure 25.22   Event handler previewButton_Click modified to create
PrintDocument and add PrintPage event handler.

3. ***Verifying that the user has a printer.*** Add lines 118–122 of Fig. 25.23 to the
previewButton_Click event handler. These lines of code are exactly the
same as the code from *Step 4* of the previous box. An error message is displayed if there are no installed printers.

```
116               AddressOf document_PrintPage
117
118            ' if no printers installed, display error message
119            If PrinterSettings.InstalledPrinters.Count = 0 Then
120               ErrorMessage()
121               Return ' exit event handler
122            End If
123         End Sub ' previewButton_Click
```

Figure 25.23   Exiting the print preview event handler if no printers are
installed.

4. ***Specifying the PrintPreviewDialog object's Document property.*** Add line
124 of Fig. 25.24 into the event handler. Recall that when you created the
PrintPreviewDialog object, you learned that its Document property specifies the document to preview. This property requires that its value be of type
PrintDocument, the same class you use to print the check. This line sets
previewObject's Document property to document (the PrintDocument
you created at line 112).

```
122            End If
123
124            previewObject.Document = document ' specify document
125         End Sub ' previewButton_Click
```

Setting the document to preview

Figure 25.24   Event handler previewButton_Click modified to set the
PrintPreviewDialog object's Document property.

(cont.)

5. ***Showing the Print preview dialog.*** Add line 125 into the event handler, as shown in Fig. 25.25. This line invokes the `PrintPreviewDialog` object's `ShowDialog` method to display the **Print preview** dialog that displays how the `PrintDocument` appears when printed. To display the document, the `PrintPreviewControl`—a member of the `PrintPreviewDialog`—raises the `PrintPage` event. Rather than using the `Graphics` object to print a page using your printer, the `PrintPreviewDialog` uses the `Graphics` object to display the page on the screen.

Displaying the preview dialog

```
124        previewObject.Document = document ' specify document
125        previewObject.ShowDialog() ' show print preview
126      End Sub ' previewButton_Click
```

Figure 25.25   Event handler `previewButton_Click` modified to show preview dialog.

6. ***Defining the ErrorMessage procedure.*** Add lines 128–135 of Fig. 25.26 into your app. Lines 131–134 display an error message to the user indicating that printing and print previewing the check is not possible if there's no printer installed on the computer.

Method to display error message

```
126      End Sub ' previewButton_Click
127
128      ' display an error message to the user
129      Sub ErrorMessage()
130
131         MessageBox.Show("No printers installed. You must " &
132            "have a printer installed to preview or print " &
133            "the document.", "Print Error",
134            MessageBoxButtons.OK, MessageBoxIcon.Error)
135      End Sub ' ErrorMessage
136   End Class ' CheckWriterForm
```

Figure 25.26   Displaying an error message when no printer is installed.

7. ***Running the app.*** Select **Debug > Start Debugging** to run your app. Enter the information for the check, and click the **Preview** Button. The check is displayed in the print preview. Use the **Print** Button to print the check. Verify that the check prints out to your default printer (if you have a printer set up).

8. ***Closing the app.*** Close your running app by clicking its close box.

9. ***Closing the IDE.*** Close the Visual Basic IDE by clicking its close box.

Figure 25.27 presents the source code for the **CheckWriter** app. The lines of code that contain new programming concepts you learned in this chapter are highlighted.

Importing the necessary namespace

Event handler indicating what to print

Instance variable to store font

```
1   Imports System.Drawing.Printing
2
3   Public Class CheckWriterForm
4
5      ' PrintPage event raised for each page to be printed
6      Private Sub document_PrintPage(sender As System.Object,
7         e As PrintPageEventArgs)
8
9         Dim fontObject As Font ' variable to store font
```

Figure 25.27   **CheckWriter** app code. (Part 1 of 3.)

```
10
11          ' store a control's x- and y-coordinates
12          Dim yPosition As Single
13          Dim xPosition As Single
14
15          ' represent left margin of page
16          Dim leftMargin As Single = e.MarginBounds.Left
17
18          ' represent top margin of page
19          Dim topMargin As Single = e.MarginBounds.Top
20
21          ' store a control's text
22          Dim controlText As String = Nothing
23
24          ' iterate over the controls on the Form,
25          ' printing the text displayed in each control
26          For Each controlObject As Control In Me.Controls
27             ' do not print Buttons
28             If Not (TypeOf controlObject Is Button) Then
29                controlText = controlObject.Text
30                Select Case controlObject.Name
31                   ' underline the date
32                   Case "dateTimePicker"
33                      fontObject = New Font("Segoe UI", 9.0F,
34                         FontStyle.Underline)
35                   ' draw a box around amount
36                   Case "amountTextBox"
37                      e.Graphics.DrawRectangle(Pens.Black,
38                         amountTextBox.Location.X + leftMargin,
39                         amountTextBox.Location.Y + topMargin - 2,
40                         amountTextBox.Width, amountTextBox.Height)
41                      fontObject = controlObject.Font ' default font
42                   Case Else
43                      fontObject = controlObject.Font ' default font
44                End Select
45
46                ' set string positions relative to page margins
47                xPosition = leftMargin +
48                   controlObject.Location.X
49
50                yPosition = topMargin +
51                   controlObject.Location.Y
52
53                ' draw text in graphics object
54                e.Graphics.DrawString(controlText, fontObject,
55                   Brushes.Black, xPosition, yPosition)
56             End If
57          Next controlObject
58
59          ' draw a line for the payee's name
60          e.Graphics.DrawLine(Pens.Black,
61             payeeTextBox.Location.X + leftMargin,
62             payeeTextBox.Location.Y + topMargin + 15,
63             payeeTextBox.Location.X + payeeTextBox.Width + leftMargin,
64             payeeTextBox.Location.Y + topMargin + 15)
65
66          ' draw a line for the amount
67          e.Graphics.DrawLine(Pens.Black,
68             dollarsTextBox.Location.X + leftMargin,
69             dollarsTextBox.Location.Y + topMargin + 15,
70             dollarsTextBox.Location.X + dollarsTextBox.Width +
71                leftMargin,
72             dollarsTextBox.Location.Y + topMargin + 15)
73
```

Annotations (left margin):
- Using type Single to store coordinates (lines 12–13)
- Variable to store left margin value (line 16)
- Variable to store top margin value (line 19)
- Creating a Font object (lines 33–34)
- Drawing a rectangle using the DrawRectangle method (lines 37–40)
- Drawing text using the DrawString method (lines 54–55)
- Drawing a line using the DrawLine method (lines 60–64)

Figure 25.27   **CheckWriter** app code. (Part 2 of 3.)

```
74              ' draw the memo line
75              e.Graphics.DrawLine(Pens.Black,
76                 memoTextBox.Location.X + leftMargin,
77                 memoTextBox.Location.Y + topMargin + 15,
78                 memoTextBox.Location.X + memoTextBox.Width + leftMargin,
79                 memoTextBox.Location.Y + topMargin + 15)
80
81              ' draw box around check
82              e.Graphics.DrawRectangle(Pens.Black, leftMargin,
83                 topMargin, Me.Width, Me.Height - 60)
84           End Sub ' document_PrintPage
85
86           ' print document
87           Private Sub printButton_Click(sender As System.Object,
88              e As System.EventArgs) Handles printButton.Click
89
90              ' create new object to assist in printing
91              Dim document As New PrintDocument()
92
93              ' tell PrintDocument where to find PrintPage event handler
94              AddHandler document.PrintPage,
95                 AddressOf document_PrintPage
96
97              ' if no printers installed, display error message
98              If PrinterSettings.InstalledPrinters.Count = 0 Then
99                 ErrorMessage()
100                Return ' exit event handler
101             End If
102
103             ' print the document
104             document.Print()
105          End Sub ' printButton_Click
106
107          ' display document in print preview dialog
108          Private Sub previewButton_Click(sender As System.Object,
109             e As System.EventArgs) Handles previewButton.Click
110
111             ' create new object to assist in previewing
112             Dim document As New PrintDocument()
113
114             ' tell PrintDocument where to find PrintPage event handler
115             AddHandler document.PrintPage,
116                AddressOf document_PrintPage
117
118             ' if no printers installed, display error message
119             If PrinterSettings.InstalledPrinters.Count = 0 Then
120                ErrorMessage()
121                Return ' exit event handler
122             End If
123
124             previewObject.Document = document ' specify document
125             previewObject.ShowDialog() ' show print preview
126          End Sub ' previewButton_Click
127
128          ' display an error message to the user
129          Sub ErrorMessage()
130
131             MessageBox.Show("No printers installed. You must " &
132                "have a printer installed to preview or print " &
133                "the document.", "Print Error",
134                MessageBoxButtons.OK, MessageBoxIcon.Error)
135          End Sub ' ErrorMessage
136       End Class ' CheckWriterForm
```

Drawing a box around the check — (lines 82–83)

Create a **PrintDocument** object — (line 91)

Add an event handler for the **PrintDocument** object — (lines 94–95)

Display an error message if no printers are installed — (lines 98–100)

Printing the document — (line 104)

Create a **PrintDocument** object — (line 112)

Add an event handler for the **PrintDocument** object — (lines 115–116)

Display error message if no printers are installed — (lines 119–121)

Specifying the print document — (line 124)
Previewing the document to be printed — (line 125)

Figure 25.27 **CheckWriter** app code. (Part 3 of 3.)

SELF-REVIEW

1. When you associate an event with an event handler, keyword _____ is used to specify the location of the event handler.

    a) `AddHandler`   b) `AddressOf`

    c) `HandlerEvent`   d) Both a and b

2. The _____ object contains the `PrintPage` event.

    a) `PrintDocument`   b) `PrintPreviewDialog`

    c) `PrintPreviewControl`   d) `PrintDialog`

Answers: 1) b. 2) a.

25.10 Wrap-Up

In this chapter, you studied graphics and printing. You created a **CheckWriter** app that allows you to enter data in a check and print it using a printer installed on your computer. You learned how to use the `Graphics` object and its members. While building the **CheckWriter** app, you used these concepts to draw shapes and `Strings` using graphics objects such as `Pens` and `Brushes`. You also learned how to use code to create fonts to apply to text you wish to display or print.

You studied several new classes, including `PrintPreviewDialog` and `Print-Document`. You used the `PrintDocument` class to create a `PrintDocument` object. You then used its `PrintPage` event to execute code that draws and prints the check when the user clicks the **Print** Button. You also added a `PrintPreviewDialog` in your app, allowing the user to preview a check before printing it.

Microsoft has released a set of free Visual Basic Power Packs designed to make developing apps with Visual Basic even easier. The latest Power Pack includes several additional printing controls. You can download the Visual Basic Power Packs at `msdn.microsoft.com/en-us/vbasic/bb735936.aspx`.

In the next chapter, you'll learn about mouse events and Windows Presentation Foundation (WPF), Microsoft's framework for graphics, GUI and multimedia. You'll create an app that allows users to paint pictures on the screen using the mouse.

SKILLS SUMMARY

Printing a Line

- Use the `PrintPageEventArgs` object's `Graphics` property.
- Use the `Graphics` property to invoke the `DrawLine` method.
- Specify the five parameters—a `Pen` object, the first *x*-coordinate, the first *y*-coordinate, the second *x*-coordinate and the second *y*-coordinate.

Printing a Rectangle

- Use the `PrintPageEventArgs` object's `Graphics` property.
- Use the `Graphics` property to invoke the `DrawRectangle` method.
- Specify the five parameters—a `Pen` object, the top-left *x*-coordinate, the top-left *y*-coordinate, the width and the height.

Printing a `String`

- Use the `PrintPageEventArgs` object's `Graphics` property.
- Use the `Graphics` property to invoke the `DrawString` method.
- Specify the five parameters: the `String` to print, the font style, the `Brush` object, the *x*-coordinate and the *y*-coordinate of where to begin printing the `String`.

Associating an Event with a Defined Event Handler

- Follow the format `AddHandler` *objectName*.*eventName*, `AddressOf` *eventHandlerName,* where *objectName* represents the name of the object with which the event is associated, *eventName* represents the name of a valid event and *eventHandlerName* represents the name of the defined event handler to be associated with the specified event.

Printing a Document

- Create a new `PrintDocument` object.
- Define the `PrintDocument`'s `PrintPage` event handler to specify what to print.
- Use the `PrintDocument` to invoke the `Print` method.

Displaying a Print Preview Dialog

- Create a `PrintPreviewDialog` object.
- Specify the `PrintDocument` to preview in the `PrintPreviewDialog`'s `Document` property.
- Invoke the `PrintPreviewDialog`'s `ShowDialog` method.

KEY TERMS

AddHandler statement—Adds an event handler for a specific event.

AddressOf operator—Specifies the location of a method, which can be associated with an event.

API (app programming interface)—The interface used by a program to access the operating system and various services on the computer.

Brush object—An object used to specify drawing parameters when drawing solid shapes.

Brushes class—Provides easy access to `Brush` objects representing the standard colors.

Color structure—Represents a color and provides methods for creating custom colors.

Control class—A type that can be used to declare variables for referencing controls on the Form. Defines the common properties and methods of Windows Forms controls.

coordinate system—A scheme for identifying every possible point on the computer screen.

design units—Any specified units of measurement for the font.

dithering—Using small dots of existing colors to form a pattern that simulates a desired color.

Document property of class `PrintPreviewDialog`—Allows you to specify the document that's displayed in the dialog.

DrawLine method of class Graphics—Draws a line of a specified color between two specified points.

DrawRectangle method of class Graphics—Draws the outline of a rectangle of a specified size and color at a specified location.

DrawString method of class Graphics—Draws the specified `String` at the specified location.

Font class—Contains properties that define unique fonts.

FontFamily class—Represents the `FontFamily` of the Font (a grouping structure to organize fonts with similar properties).

FontStyle enumeration—Provides constants for specifying a font's style. These include `FontStyle.Bold`, `FontStyle.Italic`, `FontStyle.Regular`, `FontStyle.Strikeout` and `FontStyle.Underline`.

FromArgb method of Color structure—Creates a new `Color` object from RGB values and an alpha value.

GDI+ (Graphics Device Interface)—An app programming interface (API) that provides classes for creating two-dimensional vector graphics.

GetName method of class FontFamily—Returns the name of the `FontFamily` object.

MarginBounds.Left property of class PrintPageEventArgs—Specifies the left margin of a printed page.

MarginBounds.Top property of class PrintPageEventArgs—Specifies the top margin of a printed page.

Me keyword—References the current object.

opacity—Amount of transparency of the color.

Pen object—Specifies drawing parameters when drawing shape outlines.

Print method of class PrintDocument—Prints a document.

PrintDocument class—Allows the user to describe how to print a document.

PrintPage event—Occurs when the data required to print the current page is needed.

PrintPageEventArgs class—Contains data passed to a `PrintPage` event.

PrintPreviewDialog control—Previews a document in a dialog box before it prints.

PrinterSettings.InstalledPrinters.Count property—Determines how many printers are installed on the user's computer.

Single data type—Stores floating-point values. Single is similar to Double, but is less precise and requires less memory.

System.Drawing.Printing namespace—Allows your apps to access all services related to printing.

UseAntiAlias property of class PrintPreviewDialog—Makes the text in the PrintPreviewDialog appear smoother on the screen.

vector graphics—Graphics created by a set of mathematical properties called vectors, which include the graphics' dimensions, attributes and positions.

x-axis—Describes every horizontal coordinate.

x-coordinate—Horizontal distance (increasing to the right) from the left of the drawing area.

y-axis—Describes every vertical coordinate.

y-coordinate—Vertical distance (increasing downward) from the top of the drawing area.

CONTROLS, EVENTS, PROPERTIES & METHODS	**Font** Class used to define the font face, size and style of text throughout an app.

■ *Properties*

Bold—Sets the weight of the text.

FontFamily—Contains a FontFamily object, which is used to store font face information.

Italic—Sets the angle of the text.

Size—Sets the size of the text.

SizeInPoints—Returns the size of the text measured in points.

Graphics   The class that contains methods used to draw text, lines and shapes.

■ *Methods*

DrawLine—Draws a line of a specified size and color.

DrawRectangle—Draws the outline of a rectangle of a specified size and color at a specified location.

DrawString—Draws a String in a specified font and color at a specified position.

PrintDocument   This class allows you to specify how to print a document.

■ *Event*

PrintPage—Raised when data required to print a page is needed.

■ *Method*

Print—Begins the process of printing a page.

PrinterSettings   This class stores information about the system's printer settings.

■ *Property*

InstalledPrinters.Count—Returns the number of printers installed on the system.

PrintPageEventArgs   This class contains data passed to a PrintPage event.

■ *Properties*

MarginBounds—Specifies the margin of the printed page.

Left—Specifies the left margin of the page.

Top—Specifies the top margin of the page.

PrintPreviewDialog ☐ PrintPreviewDialog This control is used to display how a document will look when it's printed.

- ■ *Properties*

  Document—Specifies the document that the control previews. The document must be of type PrintDocument.

  Name—Specifies the name used to access the PrintPreviewDialog control programmatically.

  UseAntiAlias—Specifies whether the dialog displays a smoothed image.

- ■ *Method*

  ShowDialog—Used to display the PrintPreviewDialog to the user.

MULTIPLE-CHOICE QUESTIONS

25.1 The RGB value (0, 0, 255) is equivalent to _____.

a) Color.Red   b) Color.Green

c) Color.Blue   d) Color.Yellow

25.2 A PrintPreviewDialog object's _____ property makes text appear smoother.

a) AntiAlias   b) UseAntiAlias

c) Alias   d) UseAlias

25.3 Use a _____ object to allow the users to preview a document before it's printed.

a) PrintPreviewDialog   b) PrintDocument

c) Print   d) PrintPreview

25.4 The _____ event handler specifies what is printed.

a) OnPaint   b) Print

c) Document   d) PrintPage

25.5 To display the preview dialog of the _____ object, call method ShowDialog.

a) PrintPreviewDialog   b) PrintDocument

c) PrintDialog   d) Both a and b

25.6 The Print method sends a _____ object to the printer for printing.

a) Graphics   b) PrintDocument

c) PrintPreviewDialog   d) Brush

25.7 Keyword _____ references the current object.

a) This   b) Class

c) Me   d) Property

25.8 Opacity is the _____ value of a color.

a) red   b) transparency

c) dithering   d) blue

25.9 Design units are used to specify the _____ of a Font.

a) Size   b) Name

c) FontFamily   d) Style

25.10 The methods of class _____ are used to draw on the Form.

a) Graphics   b) Pen

c) Brush   d) Print

EXERCISES

25.11 (*CheckWriter Modified to Print Background Images*) Modify the **CheckWriter** app to display and print a background for the check. The GUI should look similar to Fig. 25.28. Users can select one of two background images. The image should appear in the **Print preview** dialog box and also should print as a background to the check.

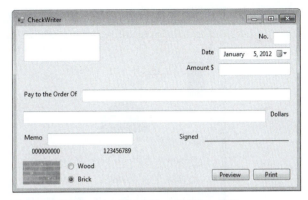

Figure 25.28 Modified **CheckWriter** GUI.

a) *Copying the template to your working directory.* Copy the directory C:\Examples\ ch25\Exercises\ModifiedCheckWriter to your C:\SimplyVB2010 directory.

b) *Opening the app's template file.* Double click CheckWriter.sln in the Modified-CheckWriter directory to open the app.

c) *Creating the CheckedChanged event handler.* Double click the **Wood** RadioButton to create its CheckedChanged event handler.

d) *Defining the CheckedChanged event handler.* Define the RadioButton's Checked-Changed event handler to notify the app when users have made a background selection. If the **Wood** RadioButton is selected, then a preview of the wooden background should display in previewPicture. Otherwise, if the **Brick** RadioButton is selected, then a preview of the brick background should display in previewPicture. To show the image preview, set the Image property of previewPicture to the selected image using the Image.FromFile method. The images are provided for you in the C:\Examples\ch25\Exercises\Images directory.

e) *Modifying the document_PrintPage event handler.* Modify event handler document_PrintPage to print the background image. [*Hint:* Use the DrawImage method to display the background image to print. DrawImage takes five arguments: The image file, the *x*-coordinate, the *y*-coordinate, the width and the height.] To print the image in the background, the DrawImage method must be the first method called on the Graphics object. Also be sure not to print the RadioButtons.

f) *Running the app.* Select **Debug > Start Debugging** to run your app. Enter data into the input fields and select either the **Wood** or **Brick** RadioButton. Verify that the appropriate image is displayed to the left of the RadioButtons. Click the **Preview** Button and verify that the check is displayed with the proper background. Close the preview and repeat this process selecting the background you had not selected before.

g) *Closing the app.* Close your running app by clicking its close box.

h) *Closing the IDE.* Close the Visual Basic IDE by clicking its close box.

25.12 (*Company Logo Designer App*) Develop a **Company Logo** app that allows users to design a company logo (Fig. 25.29). The app should provide the user with RadioButtons to allow the selection of the next shape to draw. TextBoxes should be provided to allow the user to enter the dimensions of the shapes.

a) *Copying the template to your working directory.* Copy the directory C:\Examples\ ch25\Exercises\CompanyLogo to your C:\SimplyVB2010 directory.

b) *Opening the app's template file.* Double click CompanyLogo.sln in the Company-Logo directory to open the app.

c) *Defining the Add Button's Click event handler.* Create the **Add** Button's Click event handler. Define the event handler so that the shape that users specify is drawn on the PictureBox. Use the CreateGraphics method on the PictureBox to retrieve the Graphics object used to draw on the PictureBox. Use the Graphics methods described in Fig. 25.13. Use method Color.FromName to create a color corresponding to the selected color in the ComboBox. [*Note:* The TextBoxes labeled **X1:, Y1:, X2:** and **Y2:** must contain integers to draw a line. Also, the TextBoxes labeled **X:, Y:, Width:** and **Height:** must contain integers to draw any other shape.]

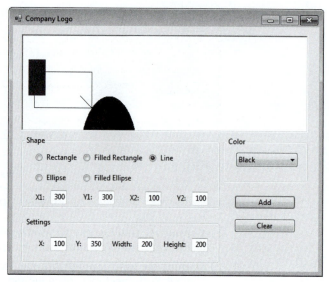

Figure 25.29   Company Logo GUI.

d) *Defining the Clear Button's `Click` event handler*. Create the **Clear** Button's `Click` event handler, and define it so that the `PictureBox` is cleared. [*Hint:* To clear the entire `PictureBox`, use the `PictureBox`'s `Invalidate` method. The `Invalidate` method is often used to refresh (update) graphics of a control. By using the `Invalidate` method without specifying a graphic to draw, the `PictureBox` clears.] Also ensure that all `TextBoxes` are cleared when the **Clear** Button is clicked.

e) *Running the app.* Select **Debug > Start Debugging** to run your app. Use the `RadioButtons` and `TextBoxes` to display at least one of each type of shape. Use different colors for the different shapes. Click the **Clear** Button to clear the shapes.

f) *Closing the app.* Close your running app by clicking its close box.

g) *Closing the IDE.* Close the Visual Basic IDE by clicking its close box.

25.13 (*Letterhead Designer App*) Create a **Letterhead** app that allows users to design stationery for company documents (Fig. 25.30). Allow users to specify the image that serves as the letterhead.

PictureBox displays image —

User enters contact information here —

Figure 25.30   Letterhead GUI.

a) *Copying the template to your working directory.* Copy the directory `C:\Examples\ch25\Exercises\LetterHead` to your `C:\SimplyVB2010` directory.

b) *Opening the app's template file.* Double click `LetterHead.sln` in the `LetterHead` directory to open the app.

c) *Adding an `OpenFileDialog`.* Double click the `OpenFileDialog` control in the **Dialogs** tab of the **Toolbox**. Name it `openImageFileDialog` and set the `FileName` property to `letterhead.png`.

d) *Defining the `browseButton_Click` event handler.* Double click the **Browse** Button in **Design** view to create its `Click` event handler. The `browseButton_Click` event handler should display an **Open** dialog allowing the user to browse to the desired image file. If the user clicks **OK** in the **Open** dialog, display the selected file's name in the **Image location:** TextBox. Use method Image.FromFile to display the image in the PictureBox. Method FromFile throws a System.IO.FileNotFoundException if the specified image file cannot be found.

e) *Creating a PrintPreviewDialog control.* Add a PrintPreviewDialog control to allow users to preview the letterhead before it's printed.

f) *Defining the PrintPage event handler.* Allow users to print the document by defining the PrintPage event handler as you did in the **CheckWriter** app. This method should draw the selected image at the top of the screen. The specified text should print below the image.

g) *Defining the printButton_Click event handler.* Double click the **Print** Button in **Design** view to create its Click event handler. The printButton_Click event handler should tell the PrintDocument where to find the PrintPage event handler, as in the **CheckWriter** app, and print the document.

h) *Defining the previewButton_Click event handler.* Double click the **Preview** Button in **Design** view to create its Click event handler. The previewButton_Click event handler should tell the PrintDocument where to find the PrintPage event handler, as in the **CheckWriter** app, and then show the preview dialog.

i) *Testing the app.* The Letterhead.png image file, located in C:\Examples\ch25\ Exercises\Images has been provided for you to test the app's letterhead image capability.

j) *Running the app.* Select **Debug > Start Debugging** to run your app. Enter your contact information and specify the location of an image. The image should be displayed in the PictureBox at the top of the Form. Click the **Preview** Button and verify that the image and contact information is displayed in the preview. Finally, click the **Print** Button to verify that the letterhead prints with the appropriate image and contact information.

k) *Closing the app.* Close your running app by clicking its close box.

l) *Closing the IDE.* Close the Visual Basic IDE by clicking its close box.

What does this code do? ▶ **25.14** What is the result of the following code? Assume that output_PrintPage is defined.

```
1   Private Sub printButton_Click(sender As System.Object,
2      e As System.EventArgs) Handles printButton.Click
3
4      Dim output As New PrintDocument()
5
6      AddHandler output.PrintPage,
7         AddressOf output_PrintPage
8
9      output.Print()
10  End Sub ' printButton_Click
```

What's wrong with this code? ▶ **25.15** Find the error(s) in the following code. This is the definition for a Click event handler for a Button. This event handler should draw a rectangle on a PictureBox control.

```
1   Private Sub drawImageButton_Click(sender As System.Object,
2      e As System.EventArgs) Handles drawImageButton.Click
3
4      ' create an orange colored brush
5      Dim brush As New SolidBrush(Orange)
6
7      ' create a Graphics object to draw on the PictureBox
8      Dim graphicsObject As Graphics = mainPicture.AcquireGraphics()
9
10     ' draw a filled rectangle
11     graphicsObject.FillRectangle(brush, 2, 3, 40, 30)
12  End Sub ' drawImageButton_Click
```

Programming Challenges ▶

25.16 (*Screen Saver App*) Develop a **Screen Saver** app. This app should add random-colored, random-sized, solid and hollow shapes at random positions on the screen (Fig. 25.31). Copy the C:\Examples\ch25\Exercises\ScreenSaver directory, and place it in C:\SimplyVB2010. The design of the Form has been created, which consists of a black Form and a Timer control. The DisplayShape method header has been provided and the Timer's tick event handler has been defined for you. You must write the rest of the DisplayShape method's code. Create the Graphics object for the Form using the Form's CreateGraphics method, and specify random colors, sizes and positions for the randomly chosen filled and hollow shapes that are displayed on the screen. The width and height of the shapes should be no larger than 100 pixels.

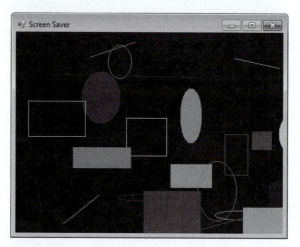

Figure 25.31   Screen Saver running.

25.17 (*Enhanced Screen Saver App*) Enhance the **Screen Saver** app from Exercise 25.16 by modifying the Timer control's Tick event handler. Add code to this event handler so that after a specified amount of time, the screen clears the displayed shapes. After the screen clears, random shapes should continue to display. Also, use the FromArgb method so that you can specify random opacity (alpha values) for the colors. You should pass four arguments to this method. The first argument is the alpha value, the second is the red value, the third is the green value and the fourth is the blue value.

"Cat and Mouse" Painter App

Introducing Graphics with Windows Presentation Foundation (WPF) and Mouse Events

Objectives

In this chapter, you'll:

- Create a GUI using WPF and XAML (Extensible Application Markup Language).
- Handle mouse events.
- Use mouse events to allow user interaction with an app.
- Use the `Ellipse` object to draw circles on the `Canvas`.

Outline

T he computer mouse is an important input device that's essential to interacting with the GUIs of Windows apps. With the mouse, the user can point to, click and drag items in apps. Clicking and releasing a mouse button and moving the mouse are associated with events. Every time you move the mouse, Windows receives that event and repositions the mouse pointer so its movement on the screen mimics the movement of the mouse.

In this chapter, you'll create a **Painter** app that handles mouse events. The user clicks the left mouse button and drags the mouse to create line drawings composed of small circles. You'll learn how to set the shape's color. You'll also learn how to stop drawing when the user releases the mouse button and how to enable the user to erase a drawing by moving the mouse while holding down the right mouse button. You'll create this app using Windows Presentation Foundation (WPF), Microsoft's newer framework for graphics, GUI and multimedia.

26.1 Test-Driving the Painter App

In this chapter, you'll create a **Painter** app using WPF. This app must meet the following requirements:

Application Requirements

The principal of an elementary school wants to introduce computers to children by appealing to their creative side. Many elementary-level apps test skills in arithmetic, but the principal wishes to use an app that allows children to express their artistic skills. Develop an app that allows the student to "paint" using the mouse. The app should draw when the user moves the mouse with the left mouse button held down and stop drawing when the left mouse button is released. The app draws many small circles side by side to trace out lines, curves and shapes. The user can select a color from the options presented as RadioButtons. An important part of any drawing app is the ability to erase mistakes or to clear the painting for more drawing room. The user can erase portions of the drawing by moving the mouse with the right mouse button held down.

You'll begin by test-driving the completed app. Then you'll learn the additional Visual Basic capabilities needed to create your own version of this app.

Test-Driving the Painter App

1. ***Opening the completed app***. Open the directory C:\Examples\ch27\CompletedApp\Painter to locate the **Painter** app. Double click Painter.sln to open the app in the Visual Basic IDE.

2. ***Running the Painter app***. Select **Debug > Start Debugging** to run the app (Fig. 26.1).

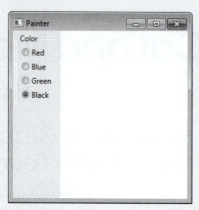

Figure 26.1   **Painter** app before drawing.

3. ***Drawing with the mouse***. To draw using the **Painter** app, press and hold down the left mouse button while the mouse pointer is anywhere over the white area of the app (Fig. 26.2). To stop drawing, release the mouse button. The app draws small black circles as you move the mouse while pressing the left mouse button. If you move the mouse slowly, these circles will appear to form a continuous line. The faster you move the mouse, the more space there will be between the circles.

Drawing lines composed of small colored circles

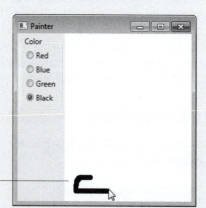

Figure 26.2   Drawing in the **Painter** app.

4. ***Changing the color***. Use the RadioButtons in the **Color** GroupBox to change the color of the circles you draw (Fig. 26.3).

5. ***Being creative***. Draw a cat and a computer mouse, as shown in Fig. 26.4. Be creative and have fun—your drawing need not look like the image shown.

6. ***Using the eraser***. Hold down the right mouse button and move the mouse pointer over part of your drawing. This "erases" the drawing wherever the mouse pointer comes into contact with colored areas by displaying white circles (Fig. 26.5).

(cont.)

Use the RadioButtons
to select a color

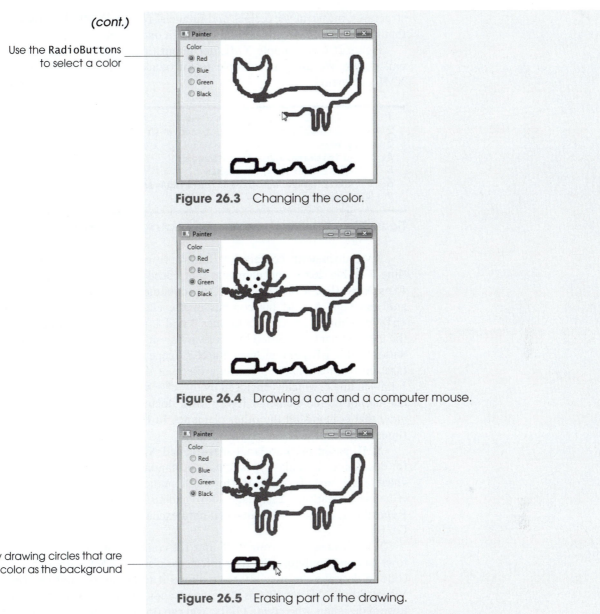

Figure 26.3   Changing the color.

Figure 26.4   Drawing a cat and a computer mouse.

Erasing by drawing circles that are
the same color as the background

Figure 26.5   Erasing part of the drawing.

7. *Closing the app*. Close your running app by clicking its close box.

8. *Closing the Project*. Select **File > Close Project**.

26.2 Windows Presentation Foundation (WPF)

Windows Presentation Foundation (WPF) is Microsoft's newer graphics framework that allows you to create more powerful and flexible GUIs than Windows Forms. You can also create media-rich experiences with animations, audio, video and graphics.

26.3 XAML (Extensible Application Markup Language)

WPF uses **XAML** (pronounced "zammel")—**Extensible Application Markup Language**—to describe the app's interface. XAML is a form of **XML** (**Extensible Markup Language**). XML permits document authors to create markup (i.e., a text-based notation for describing data) for virtually any type of information, such as mathematical formulas, software-configuration instructions, chemical molecular structures, music, news, recipes and financial reports. XML describes data in a way that both human beings and computers can understand.

Figure 26.6 is a simple XML document that describes information for a baseball player. We use this example to introduce basic XML syntax. Lines 1–2 are XML comments.

```
1   <!-- Fig. 26.6: player.xml -->
2   <!-- Baseball player structured with XML -->
3   <player>
4       <firstName>John</firstName>
5       <lastName>Doe</lastName>
6       <battingAverage>0.375</battingAverage>
7   </player>
```

Figure 26.6 XML that describes a baseball player's information.

XML documents contain text that represents content (i.e., data), such as John (line 4 of Fig. 26.6), and **elements** that specify the document's structure, such as firstName (line 4 of Fig. 26.6). XML documents delimit elements with **start tags** and **end tags**. A start tag consists of the element name in angle brackets (e.g., <player> and <firstName> in lines 3 and 4, respectively). An end tag consists of the element name preceded by a forward slash (/) in angle brackets (e.g., </first-Name> and </player> in lines 4 and 7, respectively). An element's start and end tags enclose text that represents a piece of data (e.g., the player's firstName—John—in line 4, which is enclosed by the <firstName> start tag and </firstName> end tag) or nested elements. Every XML document must have exactly one *root element* that contains all the other elements. In Fig. 26.6, the root element is player (lines 3–7).

XML-based markup languages—called **XML vocabularies**—provide a means for describing particular types of data in standardized, structured ways. Some XML vocabularies include MathML (for mathematics), VoiceXML™ (for speech), CML (Chemical Markup Language—for chemistry), XBRL (Extensible Business Reporting Language—for financial data exchange) and XAML (for creating WPF GUIs).

When you compile your WPF app, the computer interprets the XAML markup to create and configure the user interface. Using XAML rather than Visual Basic code to describe the user interface allows it to be interpreted by apps other than Visual Studio. Microsoft has developed apps, such as Expression Blend, geared toward designers who create GUIs. You can open the same solution in either Visual Studio or Expression Blend. This enables programmers to focus on the app's logic and enables designers to focus on the GUI's look-and-feel. It also allows designers and programmers to work together more efficiently. This is a big advantage of WPF over Windows Forms.

WPF provides many controls, some of which correspond directly to Windows Forms controls. In WPF, you can add Buttons, CheckBoxes, GroupBoxes, RadioButtons, Labels and TextBoxes among others, just as you would in a Windows Forms app. These basic WPF controls function much as their Windows Forms counterparts. WPF also includes controls for layout and multimedia. As you'll see in the next section, WPF takes a different approach to the layout of your user interface than Windows Forms.

26.4 Creating the Painter App's GUI in WPF

In this section, you'll create the **Painter** app's GUI using WPF. In Windows Forms, you place controls in specific locations on the Form using the Location property. By contrast, WPF *discourages* the use of absolute positioning. Instead, you use layout containers that *automatically* position the controls you place inside them. This allows WPF GUIs to adapt gracefully when the user resizes the window. Windows Forms apps can achieve this functionality through the use of more advanced controls not discussed in this book. The following box guides you through creating a WPF user interface.

Creating a WPF App	1. **Creating a WPF app.** To create a WPF app, select **File > New Project...** to open the **New Project** dialog. Select the **WPF Application** template and name the project Painter (Fig. 26.7). Click **OK** to create the project.

Select the **WPF App** template —

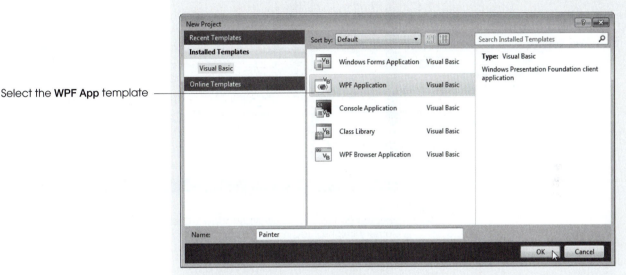

Figure 26.7   Creating a WPF app.

2. **Examining the WPF App project.** Figure 26.8 shows your newly created WPF app in Visual Basic. You see the familiar **Solution Explorer** and **Properties** windows. The **Properties** window looks different from the Windows Forms **Properties** window, but it serves the same purpose. Click anywhere in the design space. At the top of the WPF **Properties** window, you can set the name of the selected control by clicking the name of the control, which appears to the right of the control's type. There's also a **Search:** TextBox that you can use to help locate properties faster. The **Toolbox** contains only the WPF controls by default. We'll discuss these windows in more detail later in this chapter.

The most notable difference from the Windows Forms designer is the division of the design space into two sections, **Design** and **XAML**. The **Design** portion is similar to the **Designer** view in Windows Forms. However, instead of a Form, WPF uses a Window to contain the controls which make up the user interface. The WPF **Design** space also allows you to view your Window at different *zoom levels* using the slider in the top-left corner.

The **XAML** window contains the app's XAML markup. Recall that XAML describes the app's interface. The **XAML** window does not show line numbers by default. To display the line number, select **Tools > Options** to open the **Options** dialog (Fig. 26.9). Check the **Show all settings** CheckBox, then expand the **Text Editor** category. Select the **XAML** category and check the **Line numbers** CheckBox. Click **OK** to close the dialog and apply the new settings.

(cont.)

WPF `Window`

Zoom slider

WPF controls in the **Toolbox**

Name of currently
selected control

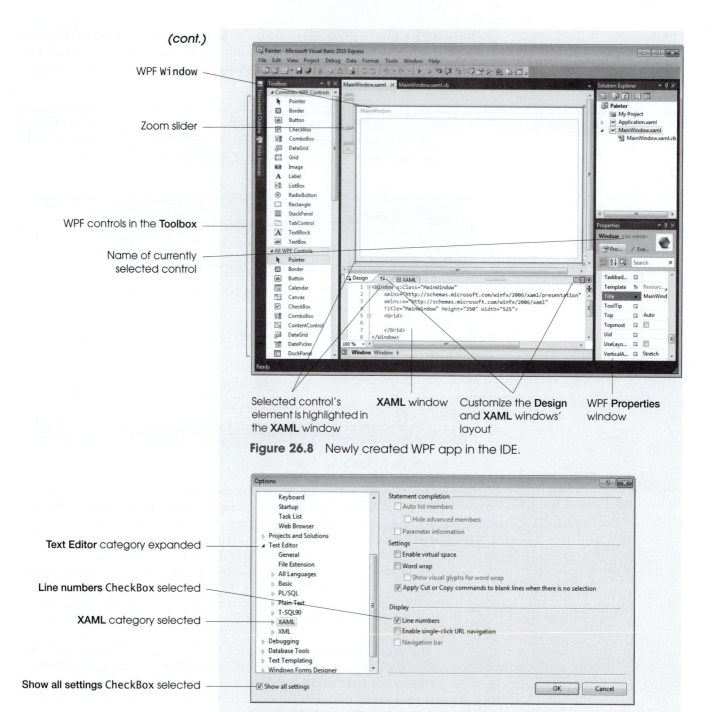

Selected control's
element is highlighted in
the **XAML** window

XAML window

Customize the **Design**
and **XAML** windows'
layout

WPF **Properties**
window

Figure 26.8 Newly created WPF app in the IDE.

Text Editor category expanded

Line numbers CheckBox selected

XAML category selected

Show all settings CheckBox selected

Figure 26.9 Displaying line numbers in the **XAML** window.

Every WPF control is represented by a XAML element (e.g., `<Window>`
in line 1 and `<Grid>` in line 5 of Fig. 26.10). When you select a control in the
designer, its corresponding XAML element is highlighted (Fig. 26.8). You
can also click an element in the XAML to select its corresponding control in
the designer. An element is delimited with a start tag (e.g., `<Window>` and
`<Grid>` in lines 1 and 5 of Fig. 26.10) and end tag (e.g., `</Grid>` and `</Win-
dow>` in lines 7–8). The start tag also specifies the element's **attributes** (e.g.,

(cont.) Title, Height and Width in line 4) which set the control's properties. We'll explore these attributes in more detail shortly. Lines 2–3 define the XML namespaces used in the XAML document. Every WPF app you'll create uses these namespaces, which provide access in the XAML to the WPF controls.

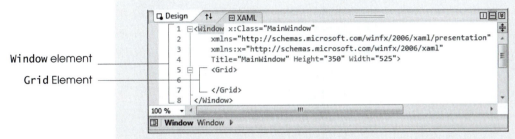

Window element

Grid Element

Figure 26.10   XAML representation of an empty WPF app.

3. *Saving the project*. Select **File > Save All** to save your new project.

In Windows Forms you placed a control on the Form and set the Location and Size properties (either manually or by using the mouse) to determine its position and size, respectively. When you run a typical Windows Forms app and resize the Form, the controls stay in place. Advanced controls and techniques are available that allow you to create resizable user interfaces with Windows Forms. In WPF, resizable controls and interfaces are the norm. You're discouraged from using fixed sizes and coordinates. Instead, controls are automatically sized based on their content. You place your controls in **layout containers** which position the controls based on their size and the amount of available space in the container.

The most flexible layout container is the **Grid**. Notice that a Grid is the default layout container in a WPF app (Fig. 26.10). The Grid control creates an invisible table of rows and columns to divide the Window into different regions. You place controls in these cells to determine where they appear on the screen. By default, the Grid consists of one row and one column.

Modifying the Window and Grid Controls

1. ***Changing the Window's properties.*** Recall from the previous box that an element's start tag specifies its property values as attributes. You can modify a control's properties by editing the attributes in the XAML directly. Line 4 of the **Painter** app's XAML sets the Window's Title, Height and Width attributes. Each attribute consists of a name (which corresponds to the property name in the control), an equal sign and a value in double quotes. Change the Window's title by setting the Title property to Painter in the XAML. The text in the Window's title bar updates accordingly (Fig. 26.11). You may also modify properties in the **Properties** window as you do for Windows Forms.

2. ***Selecting the Grid.*** The default Grid contains a single row and column. The **Painter** app uses a Grid with two columns. To create the two columns, first select the Grid control by clicking in the center of the Window or anywhere within the Grid's start and end tags in the XAML (Fig. 26.12). Note that when you select a control in the **Design** area, the control's start tag is highlighted.

(cont.)

Text updated in
`Window`'s title bar

Window's `Title` property

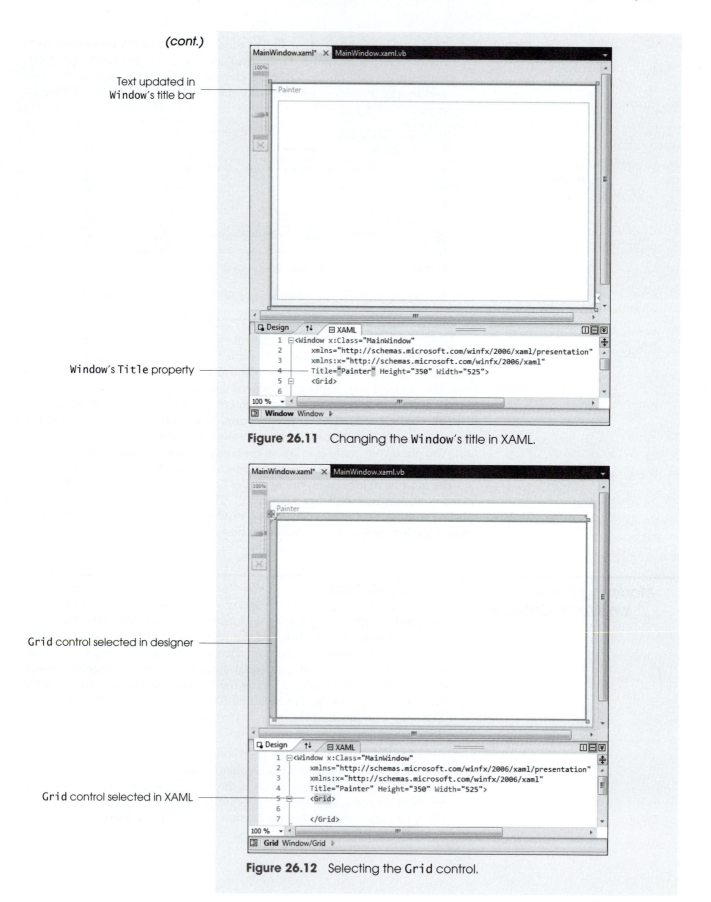

Figure 26.11 Changing the `Window`'s title in XAML.

Grid control selected in designer

Grid control selected in XAML

Figure 26.12 Selecting the `Grid` control.

(cont.)   3. ***Adding a column to the Grid.*** Locate the `Grid`'s `ColumnDefinitions` property in the **Properties** window. If you have trouble finding the property, use
the **Search:** box in the **Properties** window (Fig. 26.13). Start typing the
name of the property you want to set. The **Properties** window displays only
those properties that match what you've typed so far. Click the **X** Button at
the right of the search box to clear the search and display the full list of properties.

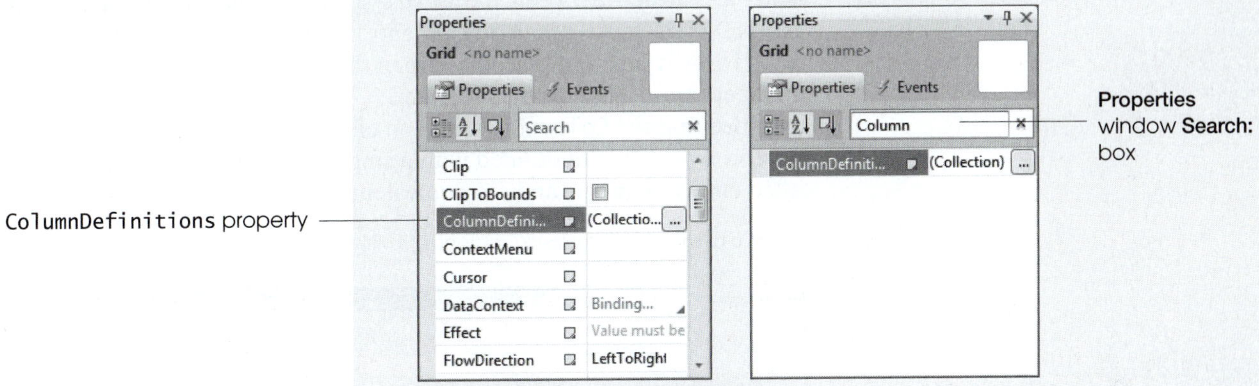

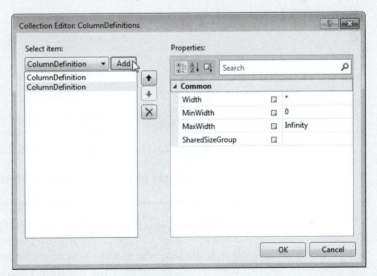

Figure 26.13   `Grid` properties.

Clicking the ellipsis to the right of the `ColumnDefinitions` property
opens the **Collection Editor** dialog (Fig. 26.14), which allows you to add columns to your `Grid` and set each column's properties. When this dialog opens,
the `ListBox` on the left is empty. The default single column (not shown in
the dialog's `ListBox`) is replaced by the first `ColumnDefinition` you add to
the `Grid`. Click the **Add** Button twice to add two `ColumnDefinitions` to
the `Grid`. For now, don't modify any other properties in this dialog. You'll
edit them in a later step. Click **OK** to close the dialog.

Figure 26.14   **Collection Editor** dialog for property `ColumnDefinitions`.

(cont.)

4. ***Examining the XAML.*** Figure 26.15 shows the effects of adding the two columns. The **Design** tab shows the two Grid columns separated by a thin blue line. When you modify a control's properties through the **Properties** window, the XAML is automatically updated to reflect those changes. Similarly, if you modify the XAML, the Window in the **Design** tab is updated to reflect the changes. Lines 6–9 were inserted by the IDE when you clicked **OK** in the **Collection Editor** dialog to add the two columns to the Grid. These elements are nested between the Grid's start and end tags to show that the ColumnDefinitions are **child elements** of the Grid control—they're part of the Grid. Any element placed between the start and end tags of another element becomes a child of that element.

   Notice that the ColumnDefinition elements (lines 7–8) do *not* have start and end tags—they're defined with a single tag that ends with />. These are called **empty elements** and are equivalent to:

   ```
   <ColumnDefinition></ColumnDefinition>
   ```

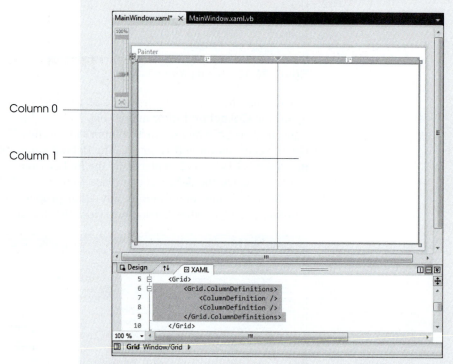

Figure 26.15 Two-column Grid layout container.

5. ***Saving the project.*** Select **File > Save All** to save your modified code.

In the next box you'll create the painting surface for the **Painter** app. The app allows the user to "paint" by drawing small circles at the mouse pointer's location. When drawing the circles, you must be able to place them in a specific location. WPF provides support for absolute positioning through the Canvas control. The **Canvas** is a layout container that allows you to position elements using absolute coordinates relative to the Canvas's top-left corner. This is the same layout concept you've used in Windows Forms.

Adding the Painting Canvas

1. ***Adding a Canvas to the Grid.*** As in Windows Forms apps, you can drag and drop controls from the **Toolbox** onto a WPF `Window`. Drag the `Canvas` control from the **Toolbox** and drop it in the right column of the `Grid` (Fig. 26.16). When you add a control to the `Grid`, the IDE automatically sets its `Name` and `Margin` properties. The `Margin` property specifies the amount of space to leave between a control's edge and any adjacent controls or its container. You can set margins for each side individually by setting the `Margin` property to a comma-separated list of four values. These values determine the spacing around the left, top, right and bottom sides, respectively. You also can use a single value to set the same spacing on all sides. The IDE sets the initial `Margin` value for a control so it appears exactly where you drop it and to match the default size of the control. This is contrary to WPF's layout philosophy and often yields unwanted results.

   Use the **Properties** window to set the `Margin` for the `Canvas` to 0 on all sides. Next, make the `Canvas` occupy the entire right column by changing the `Width` and `Height` properties to `Auto` and the `HorizontalAlignment` and `VerticalAlignment` properties to `Stretch`. The control now fills the `Grid` cell.

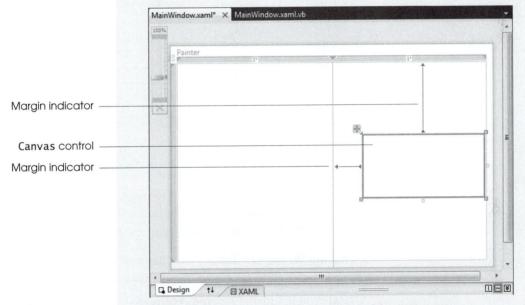

Figure 26.16 `Canvas` added to the `Grid`'s right column.

2. ***Naming the Canvas.*** At of the top of the **Properties** window is the type of object (`Canvas`) and the default name (`Canvas1`). Click the default name to make it editable then change the `Name` to `paintCanvas` (Fig. 26.17).

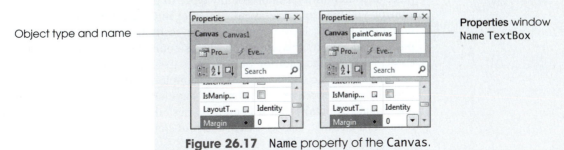

Figure 26.17 `Name` property of the `Canvas`.

(cont.)

Figure 26.18 shows the effects of setting the Margin, Height, Horizontal-Alignment, Width, VerticalAlignment and Name properties. Notice the **Grid.Column** attribute set in the Canvas's tag. This determines the column in which the element is placed in the enclosing Grid. Column numbers start at 0, so Grid.Column="1" places the Canvas in the second column (from left to right). Note that we added line breaks in the Canvas's XAML tag to improve readability. We'll continue to do this throughout the XAML presentation.

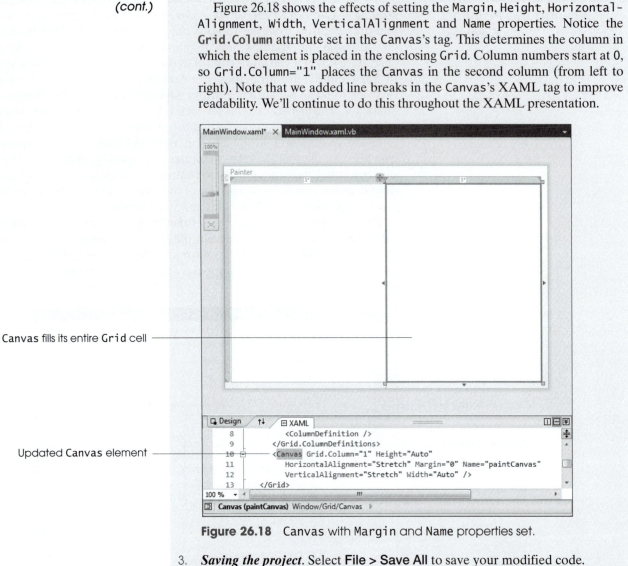

Canvas fills its entire Grid cell

Updated Canvas element

Figure 26.18 Canvas with Margin and Name properties set.

3. *Saving the project.* Select **File > Save All** to save your modified code.

Next, you'll add the RadioButtons that allow the user to choose a color in which to paint. The RadioButtons are placed in a GroupBox. In Windows Forms, you added controls to a GroupBox by dragging them from the **Toolbox** and dropping them into the GroupBox on the Form. In WPF, a GroupBox functions differently. A **GroupBox** is a type of content control. A **content control** can hold *only* one piece of content, which can be of any type. To place more than one item in a content control, you must place a layout container in the content control, then place additional items in the layout container. This restriction may seem unnecessarily complicated. However, this approach allows content controls to contain any type of content without the addition of properties to support different types of content.

The Window control is another example of a content control. As such, the nested element in a Window is almost always a layout container. The Window has the additional restriction that it cannot be nested in another control—it must be the outermost element, also known as the **root element** in the XAML.

Adding the Color Options

1. ***Adding a GroupBox to the Grid.*** Drag a GroupBox control from the **Toolbox** and drop it in the left column of the Grid. Again, the IDE sets the Margin property, attempting to position the control at the coordinates where you placed it (Fig. 26.19). Set the Margin property to 3 to leave a small amount of whitespace around the control. Note that the GroupBox expands across *both* columns of the Grid. When you added the GroupBox to the Grid, the Margin values created by the IDE caused it to overlap both columns. To allow for this, the IDE also set the **Grid.ColumnSpan** property to 2. To fix this, set the GroupBox's Grid.ColumnSpan property to 1. Next, change the Width and Height properties to Auto and the Horizontal-Alignment and VerticalAlignment properties to Stretch. The control now fills the Grid cell. Also set the Name property to colorGroupBox and the Header property to Color. The **Header** property sets the text displayed at the top of the GroupBox. Figure 26.20 shows the GroupBox with the properties set correctly (lines 13–15). Note that we added line breaks in the GroupBox's XAML tag to improve readability.

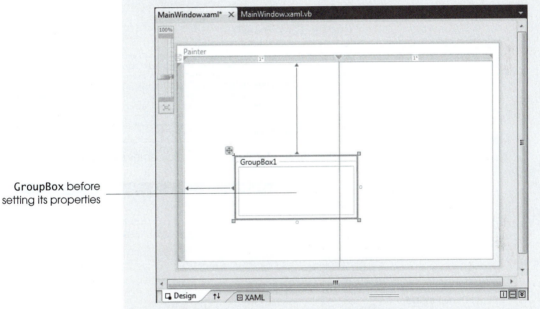

GroupBox before setting its properties

Figure 26.19 GroupBox added to the Grid spans both columns.

2. ***Adding a StackPanel to the GroupBox.*** Recall that the GroupBox is a content control and may contain only one element. To place the four RadioButtons in the GroupBox, you must first add a layout container. Drag a StackPanel control from the **Toolbox** and drop it into the GroupBox. A **StackPanel** arranges its child elements vertically (by default) or horizontally. The IDE sets the default size of a StackPanel to 200 by 100. Change the StackPanel's Width and Height properties to Auto. Do this by deleting the values in the fields to the right of each property in the **Properties** window—or you can delete the Width and Height attributes from the Stack-Panel's XAML tag. The StackPanel now fills the entire GroupBox (Fig. 26.21). Set the StackPanel's Name property to colorStackPanel and its Margin property to 3.

(cont.)

GroupBox after
setting its properties

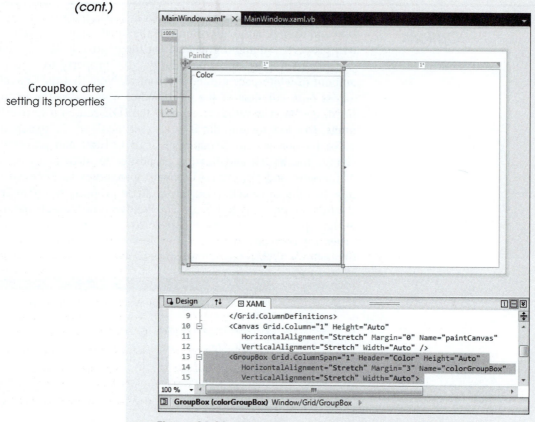

Figure 26.20 GroupBox with properties set correctly

StackPanel inside
a GroupBox

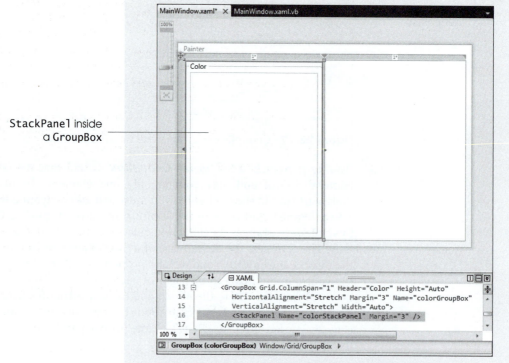

Figure 26.21 StackPanel added to the **Color** GroupBox.

(cont.)   3. ***Adding the RadioButtons.*** Drag four RadioButton controls from the
Toolbox and drop them into the StackPanel. Notice that no matter where
on the StackPanel you drop the RadioButton, it's positioned directly
below the RadioButtons previously added (Fig. 26.22). This demonstrates
how a StackPanel controls the layout of its children.

Set the Width and Height properties of each RadioButton to Auto and
the Margin to 3. Set the Content properties to Red, Blue, Green and Black
from top to bottom. Set their Name properties according to their colors (e.g.,
redRadioButton, blueRadioButton). Set the **Black** RadioButton's
IsChecked property to True to make it the default selection.

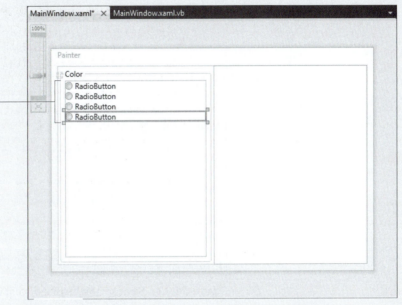

RadioButtons displayed in
the order in which they were
added to the StackPanel

Figure 26.22   RadioButtons added to a StackPanel.

Each RadioButton expands horizontally to fill the StackPanel. This provides more space than is needed. Select the StackPanel and change its HorizontalAlignment property to Left. The StackPanel shrinks to the width
of its largest element and aligns itself to the left side of its container. Change
the StackPanel's VerticalAlignment to Top—it shrinks to the height
required to fit its elements and aligns to the top of its container (Fig. 26.23).

4. ***Resizing the GroupBox.*** Set the GroupBox's HorizontalAlignment and
VerticalAlignment properties to Left and Top, respectively. This causes
the **Color** GroupBox to shrink to fit its content as the StackPanel did
(Fig. 26.24).

(cont.)

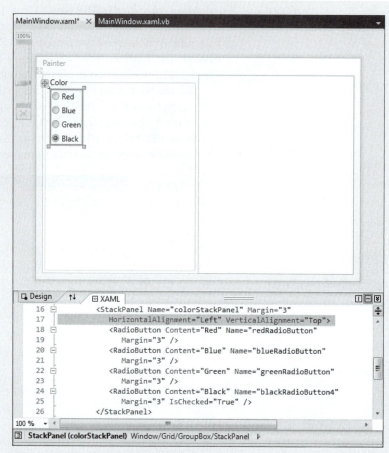

Figure 26.23 StackPanel resized to fit its elements.

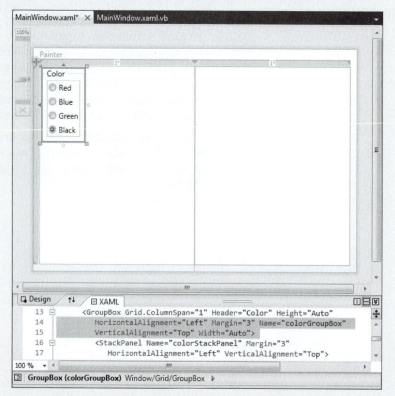

Figure 26.24 GroupBox resized to fit its elements.

(cont.)   5. ***Resizing the Grid column.*** Open the **Collection Editor** dialog for the Grid's ColumnDefinitions property by clicking the ellipsis next to the Grid's ColumnDefinitions property in the **Properties** window. Select the first ColumnDefinition in the ListBox on the left side of the dialog. In the **Properties** window on the right side of the dialog, set the Width property to Auto (Fig. 26.25)—this causes the column to resize automatically to fit its content. Note that you must type the value Auto. Select the second ColumnDefinition in the ListBox. By default, a ColumnDefinition's Width property is set to *, causing the column to resize proportionally to the other column(s). This enables the second column to occupy all remaining space in the Grid. Click **OK** to close the dialog. Because the first column is set to extend only far enough to fit its elements, the second column expands to fill the remaining available space (Fig. 26.26). Select the Canvas in the second column and notice that it still expands to fill the entire column, as in Fig. 26.18.

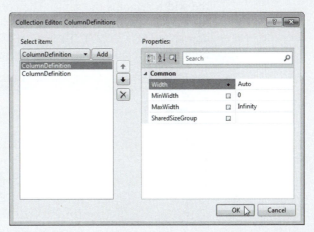

Figure 26.25   Setting column width with the **Collection Editor** dialog.

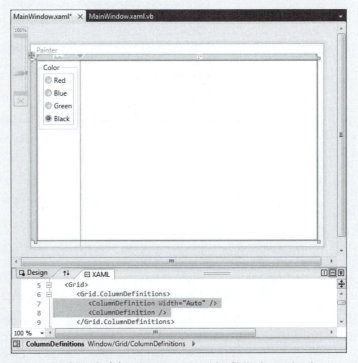

Figure 26.26   Grid columns resized to fit their content.

6. ***Saving the project.*** Select **File > Save All** to save your modified code.

An important advantage of WPF is the flexibility of the app's layout. You haven't set the size of any controls to a specific value—everything is sized relative to its content or the available space in the Window. This allows you to create GUIs which maintain their layout when content changes or the Window is resized. The next box demonstrates this flexibility.

Demonstrating Layout Flexibility in WPF

1. ***Setting background colors.*** Change the Background property of the Window to Beige. Set the Background property of the Canvas to White. This helps make the separate elements stand out and allows the user to clearly see the painting area.

2. ***Running the app.*** Select **Debug > Start Debugging** to run the **Painter** app.

3. ***Resizing the Window.*** Resize the running app's Window. The column containing the GroupBox expands and contracts in the vertical direction only—the width remains the same. The column containing the Canvas, as well as the Canvas itself, expands and contracts to fill the remaining available Window space (Fig. 26.27). To accomplish this flexibility with Windows Forms requires more advanced techniques and controls.

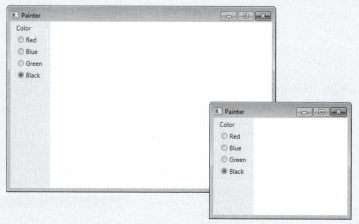

Figure 26.27 **Painter** app's GUI responding to Window resizing.

4. ***Closing the app.*** Close your running app by clicking its close box.

5. ***Saving the project.*** Select **File > Save All** to save your modified code.

1. The _____ is the most flexible layout container.

    a) Canvas
    b) StackPanel
    c) Grid
    d) GroupBox

2. A _____ can only contain one element.

    a) layout container
    b) content control
    c) Canvas
    d) flow container

Answers: 1) c. 2) b.

26.5 Constructing the Painter App

Before you begin programming the **Painter** app, you should review the app's functionality. The following pseudocode describes the basic operation of the **Painter** app and what happens when the user moves the mouse pointer over the app's Canvas:

> *When one of the color RadioButtons is selected:*
>   *Set the appropriate drawing color*

When the left mouse button is pressed:
  Enable drawing

When the left mouse button is released:
  Disable drawing

When the right mouse button is pressed:
  Enable erasing

When the right mouse button is released:
  Disable erasing

When the mouse is moved:
  If drawing is enabled
    Call method PaintCircle to draw a circle in the selected color at the
    position of the mouse pointer
  Else If erasing is enabled
    "Erase" by drawing a circle in the Canvas's background color at the
    position of the mouse pointer

Now that you've test-driven the **Painter** app and studied its pseudocode representation, you'll use an ACE table to help you convert the pseudocode to Visual Basic. Figure 26.28 lists the *actions*, *controls* and *events* that help you complete your own version of this app.

Action/Control/Event (ACE) Table for the Painter App

Action	Control/Object/Class	Event
	redRadioButton, blueRadioButton, greenRadioButton, blackRadioButton	Checked
Set the appropriate drawing color	brushColor	
	paintCanvas	MouseLeft-ButtonDown
Enable drawing		
	paintCanvas	MouseRight-ButtonDown
Enable erasing		
	paintCanvas	MouseLeft-ButtonUp
Disable drawing		
	paintCanvas	MouseRight-ButtonUp
Disable erasing		
	paintCanvas	MouseMove
If drawing is enabled Draw a circle in the selected color at the position of mouse pointer	Ellipse	
Else If erasing is enabled "Erase" by drawing a circle at the position of the mouse in the Canvas's background color	Ellipse	

Figure 26.28 **Painter** app's ACE table.

The next sections show you'll how to respond to mouse events. At first, your **Painter** app draws a circle when the user presses or releases the left mouse button. Next, you'll modify the app so that it draws when the user moves the mouse with the left button pressed. If the user moves the mouse without pressing a mouse button, nothing is drawn. To complete the **Painter** app, you'll add the eraser capability, which requires you to determine when the user presses the right mouse button.

26.6 Handling the `MouseLeftButtonDown` Event

This section begins our discussion of handling **mouse events**, which occur when the user interacts with the `Window` or the controls on the `Window` using the mouse. In the **Painter** app, the user interacts with the `Canvas` to draw.

A Canvas's `MouseLeftButtonDown` event occurs when the left mouse button is pressed while the mouse pointer is over the `Canvas`. You'll add a `MouseLeftButtonDown` event handler to your app in the following box. When you run your app after following the steps in this box, you can press the left mouse button to draw a circle on the `Canvas`. When you add the eraser capability to the **Painter** app in Section 26.9, you'll learn how to process right mouse button events.

Handling the
MouseLeftButtonDown
Event

1. ***Renaming the project files.*** Begin by renaming the **Painter** app's project files. Select the `MainWindow.xaml` file in the **Solution Explorer** and set its `File Name` property to `Painter.xaml`. This also renames the corresponding Visual Basic code file to `Painter.xaml.vb`. You must also change the app's **Startup URI**, the file in which the app begins executing. Right click the `Painter` project file in the **Solution Explorer** and select **Properties** to open the project's properties tab. You can also double click the **My Project** folder. Select **Painter.xaml** from the **Startup URI:** ComboBox (Fig. 26.29). Close the projects properties tab.

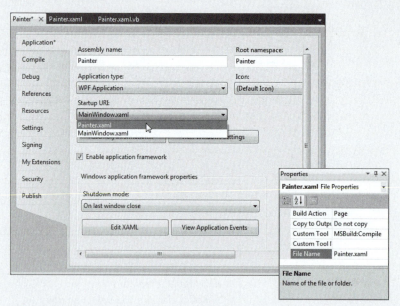

Figure 26.29 Renaming the project files.

2. ***Changing the Window's `Class` attribute and opening the Visual Basic code file.*** Change the `Window`'s `Class` attribute in the XAML to `PainterWindow` (Fig. 26.30). Select **View > Code** to open `Painter.xaml.vb`. Change the class name to `PainterWindow` to match the value set for the `Window`'s `Class` attribute (Fig. 26.31).

(cont.)

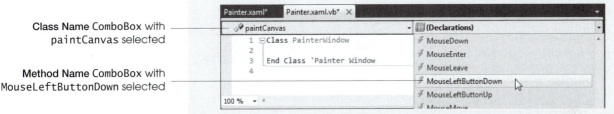

Figure 26.30 Setting the `Window`'s `Class` attribute.

3. **Generating the MouseLeftButtonDown event handler.** To generate the MouseLeftButtonDown event handler, select `paintCanvas` from the **Class Name** ComboBox (Fig. 26.31) in **Code** view. Then select MouseLeftButtonDown from the **Method Name** ComboBox.

Class Name ComboBox with `paintCanvas` selected

Method Name ComboBox with MouseLeftButtonDown selected

Figure 26.31 Creating a `MouseLeftButtonDown` event handler.

This generates the event handler `paintCanvas_MouseLeftButtonDown` (Fig. 26.32). As always, you should add a comment and format your code to improve readability (lines 3–8). The app invokes `paintCanvas_MouseLeftButtonDown` when the user generates the `Canvas`'s `MouseLeftButtonDown` event by pressing the left mouse button when the mouse pointer is over `paintCanvas`.

```
1  Class PainterWindow
2
3     ' handles paintCanvas's MouseLeftButtonDown event
4     Private Sub paintCanvas_MouseLeftButtonDown(sender As Object,
5        e As System.Windows.Input.MouseButtonEventArgs) _
6        Handles paintCanvas.MouseLeftButtonDown
7
8     End Sub ' paintCanvas_MouseLeftButtonDown
9  End Class 'Painter Window
```

MouseButtonEventArgs argument

Figure 26.32 `MouseLeftButtonDown` event handler generated for `paint-Canvas`.

The second argument passed to event handler `paintCanvas_MouseLeftButtonDown` is a variable of type **MouseButtonEventArgs** (line 5). This `MouseButtonEventArgs` object (referenced by `e`) contains information about the `MouseLeftButtonDown` event, including the coordinates of the mouse pointer when the left mouse button is pressed on the `Canvas`.

Note that the *x*- and *y*-coordinates of the `MouseButtonEventArgs` object are relative to the top-left corner of the `Window` or control that raises the event. Point *(0,0)* represents the upper-left corner of the `Window` or control. If you wish to access the *x*- and *y*-coordinates of the mouse, use method **Get-Position** of class `MouseButtonEventArgs` to obtain a **Point** object representing the position of the mouse pointer over the `Canvas`. Use property **X** of the `Point` to access the *x*-coordinate. Use property **Y** of the `Point` to access the *y*-coordinate of the mouse.

(cont.)   4. **Drawing a circle on the Canvas.** Add lines 2–23 of Fig. 26.33 above the event handler MouseLeftButtonDown. Line 3 declares the constant instance variable DIAMETER which is used to set the size of the circle drawn on the Canvas.

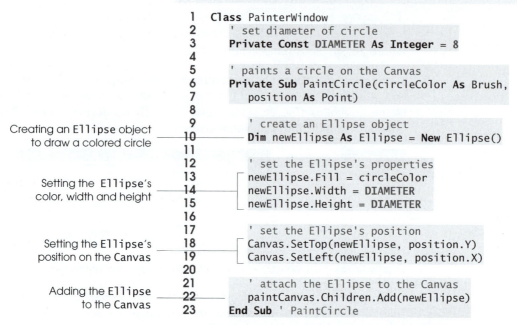

```
1   Class PainterWindow
2       ' set diameter of circle
3       Private Const DIAMETER As Integer = 8
4
5       ' paints a circle on the Canvas
6       Private Sub PaintCircle(circleColor As Brush,
7           position As Point)
8
9           ' create an Ellipse object
10          Dim newEllipse As Ellipse = New Ellipse()
11
12          ' set the Ellipse's properties
13          newEllipse.Fill = circleColor
14          newEllipse.Width = DIAMETER
15          newEllipse.Height = DIAMETER
16
17          ' set the Ellipse's position
18          Canvas.SetTop(newEllipse, position.Y)
19          Canvas.SetLeft(newEllipse, position.X)
20
21          ' attach the Ellipse to the Canvas
22          paintCanvas.Children.Add(newEllipse)
23      End Sub ' PaintCircle
```

Creating an Ellipse object to draw a colored circle (line 10)

Setting the Ellipse's color, width and height (lines 13–15)

Setting the Ellipse's position on the Canvas (lines 18–19)

Adding the Ellipse to the Canvas (line 22)

Figure 26.33 Drawing a circle on the Canvas.

Lines 6–23 define method PaintCircle, which paints a circle on the Canvas in the color represented by its first argument at the location passed as the second argument. A **Brush** is used to fill shapes with color. To see a list of available Brush colors, type the word Brushes followed by a dot, and the *IntelliSense* feature will provide a drop-down list of predefined Brush colors. Line 10 creates an object of class **Ellipse**—the WPF class used to draw an ellipse (a circle is an ellipse with equal width and height). Figure 26.34 shows a diagram of a general ellipse. The dotted rectangle—known as the ellipse's **bounding box**—specifies an ellipse's width, height and location on the Canvas. WPF provides several classes for drawing shapes other than ellipses.

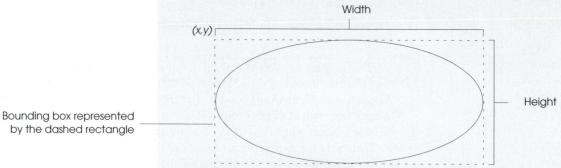

Bounding box represented by the dashed rectangle

Figure 26.34 General ellipse.

The **Fill** property of class Ellipse (line 13 of Fig. 26.33) sets the color of the Ellipse. The Width and Height properties (lines 14–15) set the width and height of the Ellipse, respectively. An Ellipse with equal width and height is a circle. Lines 18–19 set the Ellipse's position on the Canvas. The **SetTop** and **SetLeft** methods of class Canvas set the top and left coordinates, respectively, of an element (the first argument) on the Canvas to a Double value (the second argument).

(cont.)   Line 22 uses the Add method of the paintCanvas's Children property to add the Ellipse to the Canvas. The **Children** property is a collection of all the child elements nested in the Canvas.

5. ***Modifying the MouseLeftButtonDown event handler.*** Add lines 30–32 to the paintCanvas_MouseLeftButtonDown event handler (Fig. 26.35). Line 31 retrieves the position of the mouse cursor relative to the control passed to the GetPosition method—the paintCanvas. Line 32 calls the PaintCircle procedure, passing a black Brush and the mouse cursor's position as the arguments.

```
25      ' handles paintCanvas's MouseLeftButtonDown event
26      Private Sub paintCanvas_MouseLeftButtonDown(sender As Object,
27         e As System.Windows.Input.MouseButtonEventArgs) _
28         Handles paintCanvas.MouseLeftButtonDown
29
30         ' draw a circle on the Canvas at the mouse pointer's position
31         Dim mousePosition As Point = e.GetPosition(paintCanvas)
32         PaintCircle(Brushes.Black, mousePosition)
33      End Sub ' paintCanvas_MouseLeftButtonDown
```

Figure 26.35   Adding code to the MouseLeftButtonDown event handler.

6. ***Running the app.*** Select **Debug > Start Debugging** to run your app. Notice that a small black circle is drawn when the left mouse button is pressed while the mouse pointer is over the Canvas (Fig. 26.36).

7. ***Closing the app.*** Close your running app by clicking its close box.

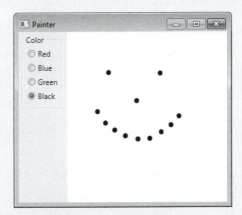

Figure 26.36   Running the app.

SELF-REVIEW   1. To set the color of a shape, set the _____ property of the shape to a Brush of the desired color.

      a) Pencil   b) Color

      c) PaintBrush   d) Fill

2. Black is a member of the _____ class.

      a) SolidColor   b) FillColor

      c) Brushes   d) SystemColor

Answers: 1) d. 2) c.

26.7 Handling the MouseLeftButtonUp Event

The app lets the user click anywhere on the Canvas and place a black circle. To enhance the app further, you'll have it place a green circle on the Canvas when the user releases the left mouse button. A Canvas's **MouseLeftButtonUp** event occurs when the user releases the left mouse button while the mouse pointer is over the Canvas. You'll add this functionality in the following box.

Handling the ***MouseLeftButtonUp*** *Event*	1. *Adding the* ***MouseLeftButtonUp*** *event handler.* Select paintCanvas from the **Class Name** ComboBox, as you did in Fig. 26.31. Then select MouseLeft-ButtonUp from the **Method Name** ComboBox. This creates an empty event handler called paintCanvas_MouseLeftButtonUp (Fig. 26.37).

Reformat the event handler as shown and add the comments in lines 35 and 40 to your app. This header is similar to the header for the MouseLeft-ButtonDown event handler. The MouseLeftButtonUp event handler executes only when the left mouse button is released.

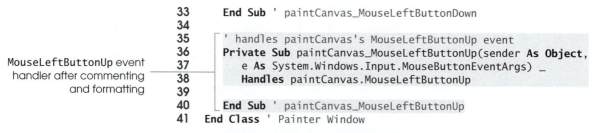

```
33      End Sub ' paintCanvas_MouseLeftButtonDown
34
35      ' handles paintCanvas's MouseLeftButtonUp event
36      Private Sub paintCanvas_MouseLeftButtonUp(sender As Object,
37         e As System.Windows.Input.MouseButtonEventArgs) _
38         Handles paintCanvas.MouseLeftButtonUp
39
40      End Sub ' paintCanvas_MouseLeftButtonUp
41   End Class ' Painter Window
```

MouseLeftButtonUp event handler after commenting and formatting

Figure 26.37 MouseLeftButtonUp empty event handler.

2. *Drawing a circle when the user releases a mouse button.* Add lines 40–42 of Fig. 26.38 to the MouseLeftButtonUp event handler to draw a green circle at the position of the mouse pointer on the Canvas whenever the user releases the left mouse button. The diameter of each "mouse up" circle is the same as the diameter of the Black circles drawn by the MouseLeftButtonDown event handler that's called when left mouse button is pressed.

```
38         Handles paintCanvas.MouseLeftButtonUp
39
40         ' draw a circle on the Canvas at the mouse pointer's position
41         Dim mousePosition As Point = e.GetPosition(paintCanvas)
42         PaintCircle(Brushes.Green, mousePosition)
43      End Sub ' paintCanvas_MouseLeftButtonUp
```

Drawing a green circle

Figure 26.38 MouseLeftButtonUp event handler code.

3. *Running the app.* Select **Debug > Start Debugging** to run your app (Fig. 26.39). Press and hold the left mouse button, move the mouse pointer to a new location and release the button. Note that a Black circle is drawn when you press the left mouse button and that a Green circle is drawn when you release the left mouse button.

4. *Closing the app.* Close your running app by clicking its close box.

(cont.)

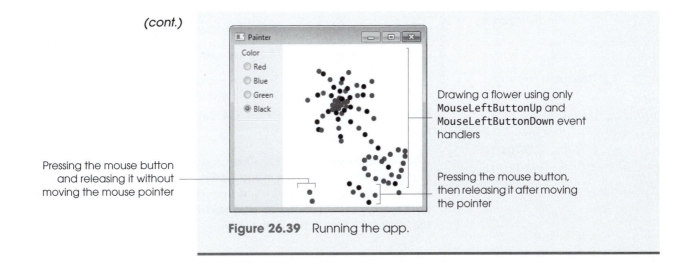

Drawing a flower using only `MouseLeftButtonUp` and `MouseLeftButtonDown` event handlers

Pressing the mouse button and releasing it without moving the mouse pointer

Pressing the mouse button, then releasing it after moving the pointer

Figure 26.39   Running the app.

---

1. Releasing the left mouse button generates a _____ event.

     a) `MouseLeftButtonRelease`   b) `MouseLeftButtonUp`

     c) `MouseOff`   d) `MouseClick`

2. The _____ and _____ methods set the `Ellipse`'s position on the `Canvas`.

     a) `Top`, `Left`   b) `Upper`, `Left`

     c) `SetUpper`, `SetLeft`   d) `SetTop`, `SetLeft`

Answers: 1) b. 2) d.

26.8 Handling the MouseMove Event

Currently, the app allows you to draw only isolated circles when the left mouse button is pressed or released. It does not yet allow you to draw while the mouse is moving. Next, you'll enhance your app to provide more drawing capabilities. The app will be able to continuously draw `Black` circles as long as the mouse is being moved across the `Canvas` with the left mouse button down. If the left mouse button is not pressed, moving the mouse across the `Canvas` does not draw anything. To add this functionality, you'll begin by modifying your two event handlers.

Modifying the Painter App

1. ***Adding a `Boolean` variable to specify whether a mouse button is pressed.*** Add lines 5–6 of Fig. 26.40 to your app. Line 6 declares and initializes the `Boolean` instance variable `shouldPaint`. The app must be able to determine whether the left mouse button is pressed, because the app should draw on the `Canvas` only when the left mouse button is held down.

     You'll alter the `MouseLeftButtonDown` and `MouseLeftButtonUp` event handlers so that `shouldPaint` is `True` when the left mouse button is held down and `False` when the left mouse button is released. When the app is first loaded, it should not "paint" anything, so this instance variable is initialized to `False`.

(cont.)

Declaring and setting
an instance variable
to control painting

```
1   Class PainterWindow
2       ' set diameter of circle
3       Private Const DIAMETER As Integer = 8
4
5       ' specify whether moving the mouse should draw
6       Private shouldPaint As Boolean = False
```

Figure 26.40   Boolean instance variable shouldPaint is declared and set to False.

2. ***Altering the MouseLeftButtonDown event handler.*** Remove the code inside the MouseLeftButtonDown event handler, leaving just the procedure header and the End Sub statement. Add line 33 of Fig. 26.41 to the MouseLeft-ButtonDown event handler to set shouldPaint to True. This indicates that the left mouse button has been pressed.

Allow drawing when left
mouse button is pressed

```
28      ' handles paintCanvas's MouseLeftButtonDown event
29      Private Sub paintCanvas_MouseLeftButtonDown(sender As Object,
30          e As System.Windows.Input.MouseButtonEventArgs) _
31          Handles paintCanvas.MouseLeftButtonDown
32
33          shouldPaint = True ' OK to draw on the Canvas
34      End Sub ' paintCanvas_MouseLeftButtonDown
```

Figure 26.41   Setting shouldPaint to True.

3. ***Altering the MouseLeftButtonUp event handler.*** Remove the code inside the MouseLeftButtonUp event handler, leaving just the procedure header and the End Sub statement. Add line 41 of Fig. 26.42 to set shouldPaint to False. This indicates that the left mouse button has been released, so painting should not continue.

Disable drawing when left
mouse button is released

```
36      ' handles paintCanvas's MouseLeftButtonUp event
37      Private Sub paintCanvas_MouseLeftButtonUp(sender As Object,
38          e As System.Windows.Input.MouseButtonEventArgs) _
39          Handles paintCanvas.MouseLeftButtonUp
40
41          shouldPaint = False ' do not draw on the Canvas
42      End Sub ' paintCanvas_MouseLeftButtonUp
```

Figure 26.42   Setting shouldPaint to False.

4. ***Saving the project.*** Select **File > Save All** to save your modified code.

You've altered the event handlers to set the value of the shouldPaint variable to indicate whether a mouse button is pressed. Next, you'll handle the MouseMove event, which is raised whenever you move the mouse over the **Painter** app's Canvas. You'll define the MouseMove event handler in the following box.

Adding the MouseMove Event Handler

1. ***Adding the MouseMove event handler.*** Select paintCanvas from the **Class Name** ComboBox as in Fig. 26.31. Then select MouseMove from the **Method Name** ComboBox to generate the empty MouseMove event handler paint-Canvas_MouseMove (Fig. 26.43). Reformat the event handler as shown and add comments to lines 44 and 49. Notice that the MouseMove event handler receives a MouseEventArgs parameter (line 46) rather than a MouseBut-tonEventArgs parameter.

(cont.)

MouseMove event handler after commenting and formatting

```
44      ' handles paintCanvas's MouseMove event
45      Private Sub paintCanvas_MouseMove(sender As Object,
46        e As System.Windows.Input.MouseEventArgs) _
47        Handles paintCanvas.MouseMove
48
49      End Sub ' paintCanvas_MouseMove
```

Figure 26.43 MouseMove empty event handler.

2. *Adding code to the MouseMove event handler.* Add lines 49–54 of Fig. 26.44 to the MouseMove event handler, which executes each time the user moves the mouse while it's over the Canvas. The If...Then statement tests the value of shouldPaint. If it's True (the left mouse button is pressed), the PaintCircle method draws a black circle on the Canvas. If it's False (left mouse button is not pressed), then nothing is drawn.

Drawing a circle when the mouse moves and the left mouse button is pressed

```
47        Handles paintCanvas.MouseMove
48
49        ' paint a circle on the Canvas if left mouse button is down
50        If shouldPaint = True Then
51          ' draw a black circle
52          Dim mousePosition As Point = e.GetPosition(paintCanvas)
53          PaintCircle(Brushes.Black, mousePosition)
54        End If
55      End Sub ' paintCanvas_MouseMove
```

Figure 26.44 MouseMove event handler draws a circle on the Canvas if left mouse button is held down.

3. *Running the app.* Select **Debug > Start Debugging** to run your app. Try drawing various shapes and designs on the Canvas.

4. *Closing the app.* Close your running app by clicking its close box.

5. *Saving the project.* Select **File > Save All** to save your modified code.

26.9 Handling Right Mouse Button Events

Now that your app allows the user to draw using the mouse, you're going to add the code that allows the user to "erase" by moving the mouse over the drawing with the right mouse button pressed. You'll learn how to do this in the following box.

Erasing the Canvas

1. *Adding a Boolean variable to specify whether the app should erase while the mouse pointer is moving.* Add lines 5–6 of Fig. 26.45 to your app (above the initialization of shouldPaint). Instance variable shouldErase specifies whether moving the mouse pointer should act like an eraser.

Declaring and setting an instance variable to control erasing

```
1    Class PainterWindow
2      ' set diameter of circle
3      Private Const DIAMETER As Integer = 8
4
5      ' specify whether moving the mouse should erase
6      Private shouldErase As Boolean = False
7
8      ' specify whether moving the mouse should draw
9      Private shouldPaint As Boolean = False
```

Figure 26.45 Boolean instance variable shouldErase is declared and set to False.

(cont.)

2. **Handling the MouseRightButtonDown and MouseRightButtonUp events.** Select paintCanvas from the **Class Name** ComboBox, then add event handlers for the MouseRightButtonDown and MouseRightButtonUp events (Fig. 26.46). Reformat the event handlers and add comments as shown. Add line 65 to the MouseRightButtonDown event handler to set shouldErase to True. Add line 73 to the MouseRightButtonUp event handler to set shouldErase to False.

```
58    End Sub ' paintCanvas_MouseMove
59
60    ' handles paintCanvas's MouseRightButtonDown event
61    Private Sub paintCanvas_MouseRightButtonDown(sender As Object,
62       e As System.Windows.Input.MouseButtonEventArgs) _
63       Handles paintCanvas.MouseRightButtonDown
64
65       shouldErase = True ' OK to erase the Canvas
66    End Sub ' paintCanvas_MouseRightButtonDown
67
68    ' handles paintCanvas's MouseRightButtonUp event
69    Private Sub paintCanvas_MouseRightButtonUp(sender As Object,
70       e As System.Windows.Input.MouseButtonEventArgs) _
71       Handles paintCanvas.MouseRightButtonUp
72
73       shouldErase = False ' do not erase the Canvas
74    End Sub ' paintCanvas_MouseRightButtonUp
75 End Class ' Painter Window
```

Enable erasing — line 65

Disable erasing — line 73

Figure 26.46 Enabling and disabling erasing.

3. **Drawing when the left mouse button is pressed.** Replace the code in event handler paintCanvas_MouseMove with lines 52–61 of Fig. 26.47. If should-Paint is True (line 53), lines 55–56 draw a black circle—the left mouse button is pressed.

```
47    ' handles paintCanvas's MouseMove event
48    Private Sub paintCanvas_MouseMove(sender As Object,
49       e As System.Windows.Input.MouseEventArgs) _
50       Handles paintCanvas.MouseMove
51
52       ' paint a circle on the Canvas if left mouse button is down
53       If shouldPaint = True Then
54          ' draw a black circle
55          Dim mousePosition As Point = e.GetPosition(paintCanvas)
56          PaintCircle(Brushes.Black, mousePosition)
57       ElseIf shouldErase = True Then
58          ' erase by drawing circles of Canvas's background color
59          Dim mousePosition As Point = e.GetPosition(paintCanvas)
60          PaintCircle(paintCanvas.Background, mousePosition)
61       End If
62    End Sub ' paintCanvas_MouseMove
```

Drawing circles if left mouse button is pressed while the mouse moves — lines 53–56

Erasing by drawing circles with the Canvas's background color — lines 57–59

Figure 26.47 Changing the MouseMove event handler to allow erasing.

4. **Erasing when the right mouse button is pressed.** The MouseMove event handler does not actually erase anything. Instead, when shouldErase is True (line 57 of Fig. 26.47), the PaintCircle method (lines 59–60) draws a circle that's the same size as the black circle and has the same color as the Canvas's background. This allows the mouse pointer to act like an eraser. Note that the first argument to PaintCircle is paintCanvas.Background. The **Background** property returns the Canvas's background color as a Brush.

(cont.)

5. ***Running the app.*** Select **Debug > Start Debugging** to run your app. Try drawing various shapes and designs on the Canvas, then try to erase them.

6. ***Closing the app.*** Close your running app by clicking its close box.

7. ***Saving the project.*** Select **File > Save All** to save your modified code.

26.10 Selecting Colors with RadioButtons

Your **Painter** app now allows the user to draw on the Canvas using the left mouse button and to erase parts of the Canvas using the right mouse button. In the next box you'll enhance the **Painter** app by allowing users to choose from several color options using RadioButtons.

Choosing Colors with RadioButtons

1. ***Adding a Brush variable to specify the selected color.*** Add lines 5–6 of Fig. 26.48 to your app (above the initialization of shouldErase). Instance variable brushColor specifies the color in which to draw circles.

Declaring and setting an instance variable to control color

```
1   Class PainterWindow
2       ' set diameter of circle
3       Private Const DIAMETER As Integer = 8
4
5       ' specify the color to draw in
6       Private brushColor As Brush = Brushes.Black
7
8       ' specify whether moving the mouse should erase
9       Private shouldErase As Boolean = False
```
Figure 26.48   Brush instance variable brushColor.

2. ***Handling the RadioButton Checked events.*** Double click the **Red** Radio-Button in **Design** view to generate its Checked event handler. The Checked event is raised when the RadioButton is selected. Note that this is different than a Windows Forms RadioButton, which raises a CheckedChanged event both when it's selected and deselected. Reformat the event handler and add the comments as shown (Fig. 26.49). Add line 88 to the **Red** RadioButton's Checked event handler. This line sets brushColor to Red. Add Checked event handlers for the remaining RadioButtons. Each RadioButton's event handler should set brushColor to the color specified in its Content.

Set brushColor to Red

```
83      ' handles Red RadioButton's Checked event
84      Private Sub redRadioButton_Checked(sender As System.Object,
85          e As System.Windows.RoutedEventArgs) _
86          Handles redRadioButton.Checked
87
88          brushColor = Brushes.Red
89      End Sub ' redRadioButton_Checked
```
Figure 26.49   Changing the paint color.

3. ***Modifying the MouseMove event.*** Replace line 59 of the MouseMove event handler with line 59 of Fig. 26.50. The app now uses brushColor to determine what color to paint in.

(cont.)

```
50    ' handles paintCanvas's MouseMove event
51    Private Sub paintCanvas_MouseMove(sender As Object,
52       e As System.Windows.Input.MouseEventArgs) _
53       Handles paintCanvas.MouseMove
54
55       ' paint a circle on the Canvas if left mouse button is down
56       If shouldPaint = True Then
57          ' draw a black circle
58          Dim mousePosition As Point = e.GetPosition(paintCanvas)
59          PaintCircle(brushColor, mousePosition)
60       ElseIf shouldErase = True Then
61          ' erase by drawing circles of Canvas's background color
62          Dim mousePosition As Point = e.GetPosition(paintCanvas)
63          PaintCircle(paintCanvas.Background, mousePosition)
64       End If
65    End Sub ' paintCanvas_MouseMove
```

Paint in the color specified by brushColor — (line 59)

Figure 26.50   Painting with the selected color.

4. **Running the app.** Select **Debug > Start Debugging** to run your app. Try drawing various shapes and designs of different colors on the Canvas.

5. **Closing the app.** Close your running app by clicking its close box.

6. **Closing the IDE.** Close the Visual Basic IDE by clicking its close box.

Figure 26.51 presents the XAML code and Fig. 26.52 presents the source code for the **Painter** app.

Root element of the XAML document — (line 1)

Window element's attributes correspond to properties — (line 4)

A two-column Grid — (lines 6–9)

Canvas on which to paint — (lines 10–12)

StackPanel that vertically aligns RadioButtons in a GroupBox — (line 16)

Blue RadioButton — (lines 20–21)

```
1    <Window x:Class="PainterWindow"
2       xmlns="http://schemas.microsoft.com/winfx/2006/xaml/presentation"
3       xmlns:x="http://schemas.microsoft.com/winfx/2006/xaml"
4       Title="Painter" Height="350" Width="525" Background="Beige">
5       <Grid>
6          <Grid.ColumnDefinitions>
7             <ColumnDefinition Width="Auto" />
8             <ColumnDefinition />
9          </Grid.ColumnDefinitions>
10         <Canvas Grid.Column="1" Height="Auto"
11            HorizontalAlignment="Stretch" Margin="0" Name="paintCanvas"
12            VerticalAlignment="Stretch" Width="Auto" Background="White"/>
13         <GroupBox Grid.ColumnSpan="1" Header="Color" Height="Auto"
14            HorizontalAlignment="Left" Margin="3" Name="colorGroupBox"
15            VerticalAlignment="Top" Width="Auto">
16            <StackPanel Name="colorStackPanel" Margin="3"
17               HorizontalAlignment="Left" VerticalAlignment="Top">
18               <RadioButton Content="Red" Name="redRadioButton"
19                  Margin="3" />
20               <RadioButton Content="Blue" Name="blueRadioButton"
21                  Margin="3" />
22               <RadioButton Content="Green" Name="greenRadioButton"
23                  Margin="3" />
24               <RadioButton Content="Black" Name="blackRadioButton"
25                  Margin="3" IsChecked="True" />
26            </StackPanel>
27         </GroupBox>
28      </Grid>
29   </Window>
```

Figure 26.51   **Painter** app's XAML markup.

```
 1   Class PainterWindow
 2      ' set diameter of circle
 3      Private Const DIAMETER As Integer = 8
 4
 5      ' specify the color to draw in
 6      Private brushColor As Brush = Brushes.Black
 7
 8      ' specify whether moving the mouse should erase
 9      Private shouldErase As Boolean = False
10
11      ' specify whether moving the mouse should draw
12      Private shouldPaint As Boolean = False
13
14      ' paints a circle on the Canvas
15      Private Sub PaintCircle(ByVal circleColor As Brush,
16         position As Point)
17
18         ' create an Ellipse object
19         Dim newEllipse As Ellipse = New Ellipse()
20
21         ' set the Ellipse's properties
22         newEllipse.Fill = circleColor
23         newEllipse.Width = DIAMETER
24         newEllipse.Height = DIAMETER
25
26         ' set the Ellipse's position
27         Canvas.SetTop(newEllipse, position.Y)
28         Canvas.SetLeft(newEllipse, position.X)
29
30         ' attach the Ellipse to the Canvas
31         paintCanvas.Children.Add(newEllipse)
32      End Sub ' PaintCircle
33
34      ' handles paintCanvas's MouseLeftButtonDown event
35      Private Sub paintCanvas_MouseLeftButtonDown(sender As Object,
36         e As System.Windows.Input.MouseButtonEventArgs) _
37         Handles paintCanvas.MouseLeftButtonDown
38
39         shouldPaint = True ' OK to draw on the Canvas
40      End Sub ' paintCanvas_MouseLeftButtonDown
41
42      ' handles paintCanvas's MouseLeftButtonUp event
43      Private Sub paintCanvas_MouseLeftButtonUp(sender As Object,
44         e As System.Windows.Input.MouseButtonEventArgs) _
45         Handles paintCanvas.MouseLeftButtonUp
46
47         shouldPaint = False ' do not draw on the Canvas
48      End Sub ' paintCanvas_MouseLeftButtonUp
49
50      ' handles paintCanvas's MouseMove event
51      Private Sub paintCanvas_MouseMove(sender As Object,
52         e As System.Windows.Input.MouseEventArgs) _
53         Handles paintCanvas.MouseMove
54
55         ' paint a circle on the Canvas if left mouse button is down
56         If shouldPaint = True Then
57            ' draw a circle in the selected color
58            Dim mousePosition As Point = e.GetPosition(paintCanvas)
59            PaintCircle(brushColor, mousePosition)
60         ElseIf shouldErase = True Then
61            ' erase by drawing circles of the Canvas's background color
62            Dim mousePosition As Point = e.GetPosition(paintCanvas)
63            PaintCircle(paintCanvas.Background, mousePosition)
64         End If
65      End Sub ' paintCanvas_MouseMove
```

Brush used to specify the color used later to paint an **Ellipse**

Create a new **Ellipse** object

Set the color and size of the **Ellipse**

Setting the **Ellipse's** position on the **Canvas**

Adding the **Ellipse** to the **Canvas**

Handling the **Canvas's** **MouseLeftButtonDown** event

Retrieving the mouse pointer's position relative to the **Canvas** at the time of the **MouseMove** event

Figure 26.52 **Painter** app's code. (Part 1 of 2.)

```
66
67        ' handles paintCanvas's MouseRightButtonDown event
68        Private Sub paintCanvas_MouseRightButtonDown(sender As Object,
69           e As System.Windows.Input.MouseButtonEventArgs) _
70           Handles paintCanvas.MouseRightButtonDown
71
72           shouldErase = True ' OK to erase the Canvas
73        End Sub ' paintCanvas_MouseRightButtonDown
74
75        ' handles paintCanvas's MouseRightButtonUp event
76        Private Sub paintCanvas_MouseRightButtonUp(sender As Object,
77           e As System.Windows.Input.MouseButtonEventArgs) _
78           Handles paintCanvas.MouseRightButtonUp
79
80           shouldErase = False ' do not erase the Canvas
81        End Sub ' paintCanvas_MouseRightButtonUp
82
83        ' handles Red RadioButton's Checked event
84        Private Sub redRadioButton_Checked(sender As System.Object,
85           e As System.Windows.RoutedEventArgs) _
86           Handles redRadioButton.Checked
87
88           brushColor = Brushes.Red
89        End Sub ' redRadioButton_Checked
90
91        ' handles Blue RadioButton's Checked event
92        Private Sub blueRadioButton_Checked(sender As System.Object,
93           e As System.Windows.RoutedEventArgs) _
94           Handles blueRadioButton.Checked
95
96           brushColor = Brushes.Blue
97        End Sub ' blueRadioButton_Checked
98
99        ' handles Green RadioButton's Checked event
100       Private Sub greenRadioButton_Checked(sender As System.Object,
101          e As System.Windows.RoutedEventArgs) _
102          Handles greenRadioButton.Checked
103
104          brushColor = Brushes.Green
105       End Sub ' greenRadioButton_Checked
106
107       ' handles Black RadioButton's Checked event
108       Private Sub blackRadioButton_Checked(sender As System.Object,
109          e As System.Windows.RoutedEventArgs) _
110          Handles blackRadioButton.Checked
111
112          brushColor = Brushes.Black
113       End Sub ' blackRadioButton_Checked
114   End Class ' PainterWindow
```

Changing the brushColor to Red when the **Red** RadioButton is selected — (line 88)

Figure 26.52 Painter app's code. (Part 2 of 2.)

SELF-REVIEW

1. Moving the mouse pointer generates a _____ event.

   a) MouseMove   b) MousePositionChanged

   c) MouseOver   d) MouseChanged

2. The _____ event is raised when a RadioButton is selected.

   a) CheckedChanged   b) IsChecked

   c) Checked   d) CheckedEvent

Answers: 1) a. 2) c.

26.11 Wrap-Up

In this chapter, you learned the basics of Windows Presentation Foundation. You learned how to create a GUI using WPF layout containers and content controls. You saw the advantages to WPF's layout strategy vs. that used by Windows Forms. You created a basic GUI using the `Window`, `Grid`, `Canvas`, `StackPanel`, `GroupBox` and `RadioButton` controls.

Next, you learned the essentials of mouse event handling. You handled common mouse events—MouseMove, MouseLeftButtonUp, MouseLeftButtonDown, Mouse-RightButtonUp and MouseRightButtonDown—and how to create mouse event handlers associated with a `Canvas`. You generated these event handlers by selecting the appropriate mouse event from the **Method Name** ComboBox after selecting paint-Canvas from the **Class Name** ComboBox. The skills you learned in this chapter are similar to the skills needed to handle mouse events in Windows Forms app.

You used WPF class `Ellipse` to draw circles in the **Painter** app. You learned how to use a `Brush` object to draw a shape in a solid color specified by one of the predefined `Brush` objects in the `Brushes` class.

The **Painter** app uses mouse events to determine what the user wants to do. The user moves the mouse with the left mouse button held down to draw on the `Canvas`. Moving the mouse across the `Canvas` without pressing a button does not draw anything on the `Canvas`. You provided the **Painter** app with an eraser. When users move the mouse with the right mouse button pressed, the **Painter** app draws circles with the Canvas's background color.

To build the **Painter** app, you used `MouseButtonEventArgs` and `Mouse-EventArgs` objects, which are passed to mouse event handlers and provide information about mouse events. Method `GetPosition` of the `MouseButtonEventArgs` and `MouseEventArgs` objects returned a `Point` object specifying the *x*- and *y*-coordinates where the mouse event occurred.

In the next chapter, we begin our discussion of databases, which organize data so that it can be retained for long periods, yet selected and updated quickly. We'll introduce LINQ to SQL, which allows you to write LINQ queries that extract data from databases. You can then interact with the objects in the query results to insert data in, update data in and delete data from databases.

SKILLS SUMMARY

Creating a GUI with WPF

- Create a new project using the **WPF Application** template.
- Use a `Grid` layout container to divide your GUI into sections. Though we used only columns in this chapter, you can also create rows.
- Use a `Canvas` layout container to position elements using coordinates.
- Use a `StackPanel` layout container to arrange elements either horizontally or vertically (the default).
- Use a `GroupBox` content control to group related elements visually.
- Use `RadioButtons` to enable users to select only one of several options.

Raising Events with a Mouse

- Pressing a mouse's buttons and moving the mouse raise events.

Handling Mouse Events

- The `MouseButtonEventArgs` and `MouseEventArgs` classes contain information about mouse events, such as the `Point` where the mouse event occurred. Each mouse event handler that involves a button receives an object of class `MouseButtonEventArgs` as an argument. The `MouseMove` event handler receives an object of class `MouseEventArgs` as an argument.
- Moving the mouse raises event `MouseMove`.
- Pressing the left mouse button raises event `MouseLeftButtonDown`.
- Pressing the right mouse button raises event `MouseRightButtonDown`.

■ Releasing the left mouse button raises event MouseLeftButtonUp.

■ Releasing the right mouse button raises event MouseRightButtonUp.

Creating an Event Handler for a Mouse Event Associated with a Canvas

■ Select *CanvasName* from the **Class Name** ComboBox, where *CanvasName* is the name of the app's Canvas. Then select the appropriate event from the **Method Name** Combo-Box.

Drawing on a Canvas

■ Shape classes are used to draw shapes on a Canvas or other control.

■ Create an instance of a shape class (by invoking the class's constructor) to access methods for drawing the shape.

■ Display the shape using the Add method of the Canvas's Children property.

Drawing a Solid Ellipse

■ Use the shape class Ellipse to draw an ellipse.

■ Pass a Brush object to the Fill property to specify the shape's color.

■ Specify the color, the coordinates of the bounding box's upper-left corner and the width and height of the bounding box. When the width and height of the bounding box are equal, a circle is drawn.

KEY TERMS

attribute in XAML—Can be used to set an object's property values. Represented in XAML by placing a property name, an equal sign (=) and a value in double quotes inside the opening tag of the object's XAML element.

Background property of class Canvas—Gets or sets the Brush value used as the background color of the Canvas.

bounding box of an ellipse—Specifies an ellipse's location, width and height.

Brush class—Used to fill shapes and controls with colors.

Canvas layout container—A WPF control that enables absolute positioning of its child elements.

child element—A XAML element that's nested inside another element.

Children property of Canvas—Returns a collection of all the child elements nested in a Canvas.

ColumnDefinition element of a Grid—Specifies the attributes of a column in a Grid.

ColumnDefinitions property of a Grid—Provides access to the collection of ColumnDefinitions for a Grid.

content control—A WPF control that can hold one piece of content of any type.

element in XML—Markup that describes a piece of data. Delimited by start and end tags.

Ellipse class—The shape class that draws an ellipse. This class contains properties including Fill, Width and Height. If the width and height are the same, a circle is drawn.

empty element in XML—Shorthand notation for an element with no content between its start and end tags.

end tag—Delimits the end of an XML element.

Extensible Application Markup Language (XAML)—See XAML.

Extensible Markup Language (XML)—See XML.

Fill property of an Ellipse—Specifies the Brush that's used to color the Ellipse.

GetPosition method of classes MouseButtonEventArgs and MouseEventArgs—Returns a Point object representing the position of the mouse pointer over a control.

Grid layout container—A WPF control that organizes its children in rows and columns.

GroupBox content control—A control that places a titled border around its content.

Header property of a GroupBox—Sets the text displayed in a GroupBox's border.

layout container—A control that positions its child controls based on their size and the amount of available space in the container.

mouse event—Generated when a user interacts with an app using the computer's mouse.

MouseButtonEventArgs class—Specifies information about a mouse event involving a button press or release.

MouseLeftButtonDown event—Generated when the left mouse button is pressed.

MouseRightButtonDown event—Generated when the right mouse button is pressed.

MouseEventArgs class—Specifies information about a MouseMove.

MouseMove event—Generated when a mouse pointer is moved.

MouseLeftButtonUp event—Generated when the left mouse button is released.

MouseRightButtonUp event—Generated when the right mouse button is released.

Point class—Contains an X and a Y property representing the coordinates of a point.

SetLeft method of Canvas—Sets the left coordinate of an element (the first argument) on the Canvas to a Double value (the second argument).

SetTop method of Canvas—Sets the top coordinate of an element (the first argument) on the Canvas to a Double value (the second argument).

StackPanel layout container—A WPF control that organizes its children horizontally or vertically (the default).

start tag—Delimits the beginning of an XML element.

Title property of a Window—Specifies the text that appears in the Window's title bar.

Window control—The root control in a WPF app. Analogous to a Form in a Windows Forms app.

Windows Presentation Foundation (WPF)—Microsoft's new graphics framework that allows you to create powerful and flexible GUIs and to create media-rich experiences with animations, audio, video and graphics.

X property of class Point—The property of class Point that specifies the *x*-coordinate.

XAML (Extensible Application Markup Language)—An XML vocabulary for describing WPF user interfaces.

XML (Extensible Markup Language)—Language for creating markup for describing data in a manner that both humans and computers can understand.

XML vocabulary—XML-based markup language that provides a means for describing a particular type of data in a standardized, structured manner. For example, XAML is an XML vocabulary that describes WPF user interface information.

Y property of class Point—The property of class Point that specifies the *y*-coordinate.

CONTROLS, EVENTS, PROPERTIES & METHODS

Canvas   🔲 Canvas   This control allows the user to place elements using coordinates.

■ *In action*

■ *Events*

MouseLeftButtonDown—Raised when the user presses the left mouse button over the Canvas.

MouseLeftButtonUp—Raised when the user releases the left mouse button over the Canvas.

MouseRightButtonDown—Raised when the user presses the right mouse button over the Canvas.

MouseRightButtonUp—Raised when the user releases the right mouse button over the Canvas.

■ *Properties*

Background—Specifies the background color of the Canvas.

Children—Specifies the elements contained in the Canvas.

Grid.Column—Specifies the Grid column in which the Canvas is contained.

Height—Specifies the height of the Canvas.

HorizontalAlignment—Specifies the horizontal alignment of the Canvas.

Margin—Specifies the amount of space around the Canvas.

Name—Specifies the name used to access the Canvas programmatically.

VerticalAlignment—Specifies the vertical alignment of the Canvas.

Width—Specifies the width of the Canvas.

■ *Methods*

Children.Add—Adds the specified element to the Canvas.

SetLeft—Sets the left position of the specified element relative to the top-left corner of the Canvas.

SetTop—Sets the top position of the specified element relative to the top-left corner of the Canvas.

Ellipse   A class that represents the ellipse to draw.

■ *Properties*

Fill—Specifies the color of the ellipse.

Width—Specifies the width of the ellipse.

Height—Specifies the height of the ellipse.

Grid   ☐ Grid   This control allows the user to place elements into an invisible table which controls their positioning.

■ *Properties*

ColumnDefinition—Specifies the properties of a column in a Grid, including width, height and positioning.

ColumnDefinitions—A collection of the columns in a Grid.

GroupBox   (xy) GroupBox   This control groups related controls visually.

■ *In action*

■ *Properties*

Grid.Column—Specifies the Grid column in which the GroupBox is contained.

Header—Specifies the text displayed at the top of the GroupBox.

Height—Specifies the height of the GroupBox.

HorizontalAlignment—Specifies the horizontal alignment of the GroupBox.

Margin—Specifies the amount of space around the GroupBox.

Name—Specifies the name used to access the GroupBox programmatically. The name should be appended with the GroupBox suffix.

VerticalAlignment—Specifies the vertical alignment of the GroupBox.

Width—Specifies the width of the GroupBox.

MouseButtonEventArgs   The class that contains information about mouse events that involve a button press or release.

■ *Method*

GetPosition—Returns a Point representing the position of the mouse pointer when the event occurred.

MouseEventArgs The class that contains information about mouse events.

■ *Method*

GetPosition—Returns a Point representing the position of the mouse pointer when the event occurred.

Point The class that contains information representing a location in the app.

■ *Properties*

X—Specifies the *x*-coordinate of the location.

Y—Specifies the *y*-coordinate of the location.

RadioButton   ⊙ RadioButton   This control allows enables users to select only one of several options.

■ *In action*

◉ Black

■ *Event*

Checked—Raised when the user selects the RadioButton.

■ *Properties*

Content—Specifies the text displayed to the right of the RadioButton.

Height—Specifies the height of the RadioButton.

HorizontalAlignment—Specifies the horizontal alignment of the RadioButton.

IsChecked—Specifies whether the RadioButton is selected.

Margin—Specifies amount of space around the RadioButton.

Name—Specifies the name used to access the RadioButton programmatically. The name should be appended with the RadioButton suffix.

VerticalAlignment—Specifies the vertical alignment of the RadioButton.

Width—Specifies the width of the RadioButton.

StackPanel   ▣ StackPanel   This control arranges its elements horizontally or vertically.

■ *Properties*

Height—Specifies the height of the StackPanel.

HorizontalAlignment—Specifies the horizontal alignment of the StackPanel.

Margin—Specifies amount of blank space around the StackPanel.

Name—Specifies the name used to access the StackPanel programmatically.

VerticalAlignment—Specifies the vertical alignment of the StackPanel.

Width—Specifies the width of the StackPanel.

Window The class that represents an app's GUI.

■ *Properties*

Class—Specifies the Visual Basic class associated with the Window.

Title—Specifies the text displayed in the Window's titlebar.

MULTIPLE-CHOICE QUESTIONS

26.1 The *x*- and *y*-coordinates of the Point object returned by the GetPosition method of class MouseEventArgs are relative to _____.

a) the screen

b) the app

c) the layout container that contains the control that raised the event

d) the control passed as an argument to GetPosition

26.2 The _____ property of the `Ellipse` class specifies the color of the ellipse.

a) `FillEllipse`

b) `Color`

c) `Brush`

d) `Fill`

26.3 The _____ object passed to a mouse event handler contains information about the mouse event that was raised.

a) `MouseArgs`

b) `MouseButtonEventArgs`

c) `MouseEventArgs`

d) Both b and c

26.4 The _____ event is raised when the right mouse button is pressed.

a) `MouseRightButtonDown`

b) `MouseRightClick`

c) `MouseRightDown`

d) `MouseRightPress`

26.5 A _____ object is used to fill a shape with color.

a) `Painter`

b) `Brush`

c) `FillColor`

d) `Marker`

26.6 A _____ event is raised every time the mouse interacts with a control.

a) control

b) mouse pointer

c) mouse

d) user

26.7 The _____ layout container arranges its elements either horizontally or vertically.

a) `Stack`

b) `Canvas`

c) `StackPanel`

d) `Grid`

26.8 The _____ is the default layout container in a WPF app.

a) `Canvas`

b) `Grid`

c) `StackPanel`

d) None of the above

26.9 The _____ layout container allows absolute positioning of its child elements.

a) `Grid`

b) `Canvas`

c) `StackPanel`

d) None of the above

26.10 The _____ content control may not be nested in any other control.

a) `GroupBox`

b) `Window`

c) Both of the above

d) Neither of the above

EXERCISES

26.11 *(Circle Painter App)* The **Circle Painter** app draws a blue circle of a randomly chosen size when the user presses the left mouse button anywhere over the Canvas (Fig. 26.53). The app randomly selects a circle diameter in the range from 5 to 199, inclusive. Using the `Stroke` property rather than the `Fill` property of class `Ellipse` draws the outline of an ellipse. Recall that an ellipse is a circle if the height and width arguments are the same (in this case, the randomly selected `diameter`). Use the *x*- and *y*-coordinates of the `MouseLeftButtonDown` event as the *x*- and *y*-coordinates of the circle's bounding box.

a) *Creating a new WPF app.* Create a new WPF app and name it `CirclePainter`. Rename the `MainWindow.xaml` file to `CirclePainter.xaml`. Change the project's startup URI to `CirclePainter.xaml`. Change the Window's Title to Circle Painter and its Class attribute to `CirclePainterWindow`. Change the class name in the Visual Basic code file to `CirclePainterWindow`.

b) *Adding a Canvas to the app.* Add a Canvas to the app and name it `circleCanvas`. Set its `Width` and `Height` properties to `Auto`, the `Margin` property to 0 and the `HorizontalAlignment` and `VerticalAlignment` properties to `Stretch` so it fills the entire `Grid` cell in which it's contained. Set its `Background` property to `White`.

c) *Creating the PaintCircle method.* Create a Sub procedure called `PaintCircle` which takes as arguments a `Brush` and a `Point` object. The procedure paints a circle on the Canvas in the specified color at the specified location. Generate a random number to use as the circle's diameter, using a `Random` object, and store it in a variable. Create a new `Ellipse` object and set its `Width` and `Height` properties to the randomly generated diameter. Set its `Stroke` property to blue. Set its position using the coordinates of the `Point` passed as an argument.

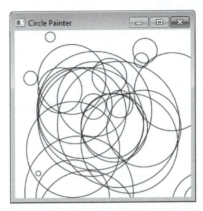

Figure 26.53   Circle Painter app's GUI.

d) ***Adding a MouseLeftButtonDown event handler.*** Create a `MouseLeftButtonDown` event handler. In the event handler, retrieve the *x*- and *y*-coordinates of the location of the mouse pointer when the left mouse button was pressed. Call method `PaintCircle` to paint a blue circle at the mouse pointer's position.

e) ***Running the app.*** Select **Debug > Start Debugging** to run your app. Draw several blue circles and make sure that they're of different sizes.

f) ***Closing the app.*** Close your running app by clicking its close box.

g) ***Closing the IDE.*** Close the Visual Basic IDE by clicking its close box.

26.12 *(Advanced Circle Painter App)* In this exercise, you enhance the app you created in Exercise 26.11. The **Advanced Circle Painter** app draws blue circles with randomly generated diameters when the user presses the left mouse button. When the user presses the right mouse button, the app draws a red circle with a randomly generated diameter (Fig. 26.54).

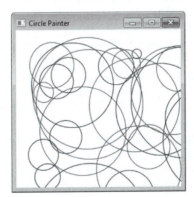

Figure 26.54   Advanced Circle Painter app's GUI.

a) ***Copying the template to your working directory.*** Make a copy of the Circle-Painter directory from Exercise 26.11 in your `C:\SimplyVB2010` directory. Rename the copied directory `AdvancedCirclePainter`. If you have not completed Exercise 26.11, follow the steps in Exercise 26.11 to complete the app.

b) ***Opening the app's template file.*** Double click the `CirclePainter.sln` file in the `AdvancedCirclePainter` directory to open the app.

c) ***Drawing the appropriate circle.*** Create a `MouseRightButtonDown` event handler that draws a red circle at the mouse pointer's position when the right mouse button is pressed.

d) ***Running the app.*** Select **Debug > Start Debugging** to run your app. Draw several blue circles of different sizes using the left mouse button, then draw several red circles of different sizes using the right mouse button.

e) *Closing the app.* Close your running app by clicking its close box.

f) *Closing the IDE.* Close the Visual Basic IDE by clicking its close box.

26.13 *(Line Length App)* The **Line Length** app will draw a straight black line on a Canvas and calculate the length of the line (Fig. 26.55). The line begins at the coordinates where the left mouse button is pressed and stops at the point where the left mouse button is released. The app displays the line's length (that is, the distance between the two endpoints) in the Label **Length =**. Use the following formula to calculate the line's length, where (x_1, y_1) is the first endpoint (the coordinates where the mouse button is pressed) and (x_2, y_2) is the second endpoint (the coordinates where the mouse button is released). To calculate the distance (or length) between the two points, use the equation:

$$d = \sqrt{(x_1 - x_2)^2 + (y_1 - y_2)^2}$$

To draw a straight line, you need to use the **Line** class. When drawing lines, use the **Stroke** property to specify the line's color rather than the Fill property. Use the Line's X1, Y1, X2 and Y2 properties to specify its start point and end point. Then add it as a child of the Canvas.

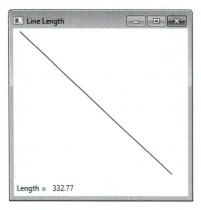

Figure 26.55 Line Length app's GUI.

a) *Creating a new WPF app.* Create a new WPF app and name it LineLength. Change the Window's Title to Line Length.

b) *Adding the layout containers.* Add a Canvas to the WPF app's Grid. Name the Canvas lineCanvas. Add a StackPanel to the Grid and name it outputStackPanel— check the XAML to be sure the StackPanel is nested in the Grid element, *not* in the Canvas.

c) *Adding the output Labels.* Add two Labels to the StackPanel. Name the first Label lengthLabel and set its Content property to Length =. Name the second Label lengthOutputLabel and delete the text in its Content property. Set the Width and Height properties of both Labels to Auto.

d) *Setting properties of the layout containers.* Set the StackPanel's Orientation property to Horizontal to arrange its elements horizontally. Set the Width and Height properties to Auto. Set the HorizontalAlignment and VerticalAlignment properties to Left and Bottom, respectively. Set the Margin property to 0. Set the Canvas's Width and Height properties to Auto, the Margin property to 0 and the HorizontalAlignment and VerticalAlignment properties to Stretch. Set the Canvas's Background property to White.

e) *Renaming the project files.* Rename the MainWindow.xaml project file to LineLength.xaml. Change the startup URI to LineLength.xaml. Change the Window's Class attribute to LineLengthWindow. Change the class name in the Visual Basic code file to LineLengthWindow.

f) *Declaring instance variables.* Select **View > Code** to open the Visual Basic code file. Declare and initialize two Point variables in which you store the start points and end points of the Line.

g) *Creating the Length method.* Define a Function procedure named Length that uses the formula given in the exercise description to return the distance between two endpoints as a Double. The Function procedure should use the following statement to perform the line-length calculation, where xDistance is the difference between the two points' *x*-coordinates and yDistance is the difference between their *y*-coordinates:

```
Math.Sqrt((xDistance ^ 2) + (yDistance ^ 2))
```

h) *Adding a MouseLeftButtonDown event handler.* Create a MouseLeftButtonDown event handler for the Canvas. Add code to store the coordinates of the first endpoint of the line. Clear the lengthOutputLabel by setting its Content property to the empty String.

i) *Adding a MouseLeftButtonUp event handler.* Create a MouseLeftButtonUp event handler. First store the coordinates of the line's second endpoint. Then call the Length method to obtain the distance between the two endpoints (the line's length). Finally, display the line on the Canvas and the line's length in the **Length =** Label, as in Fig. 26.55.

j) *Running the app.* Select **Debug > Start Debugging** to run your app. Draw several lines and view their lengths. Verify that the length values are accurate.

k) *Closing the app.* Close your running app by clicking its close box.

l) *Closing the IDE.* Close the Visual Basic IDE by clicking its close box.

What does this code do? ▶ **26.14** Consider the MouseMove event handler below. What happens when the user moves the mouse? Assume that displayLabel has been placed in the GUI.

```
1    Private Sub paintCanvas_MouseMove(sender As Object,
2       e As System.Windows.Input.MouseEventArgs)
3       Handles paintCanvas.MouseMove
4
5       Dim position As Point = e.GetPosition(paintCanvas)
6
7       displayLabel.Content = "I'm at " & _
8          position.X & ", " & position.Y & "."
9    End Sub ' paintCanvas_MouseMove
```

What's wrong with this code? ▶ **26.15** The following code should draw a solid Blue circle of diameter 5 that corresponds to the movement of the mouse. Find the error(s) in the code:

```
1    Private Sub paintCanvas_MouseMove(sender As Object,
2       e As System.Windows.Input.MouseEventArgs) _
3       Handles paintCanvas.MouseMove
4
5       Dim position As Point = e.GetPosition(paintCanvas)
6
7       If shouldPaint = True Then
8          ' create an Ellipse object
9          Dim newEllipse As Ellipse = New Ellipse()
10
11         ' set the Ellipse's properties
12         newEllipse.Stroke = Brushes.Blue
13         newEllipse.Width = 5
14         newEllipse.Height = 10
15
16         ' set the Ellipse's position
17         Canvas.SetTop(newEllipse, position.X)
18         Canvas.SetLeft(newEllipse, position.Y)
19
20         ' attach the Ellipse to the Canvas
21         paintCanvas.Children.Add(newEllipse)
22      End If
23   End Sub ' PaintCanvas_MouseMove
```

Programming Challenge ▶ **26.16 (*Advanced Painter App*)** Extend the Painter app to enable a user to change the size of the circles drawn and to undo or clear the painting (Fig. 26.56).

Figure 26.56 Advanced Painter app's GUI.

a) ***Copying the template to your working directory.*** Copy the directory C:\Examples\ch27\Exercises\AdvancedPainter to your C:\SimplyVB2010 directory.

b) ***Opening the app's template file.*** Double click AdvancedPainter.sln in the AdvancedPainter directory to open the app.

c) ***Adding the Size options.*** Add a GroupBox to the StackPanel in column 0 of the Grid. Change its Header property to **Size**, its Margin to 3 and its Width property to Auto. Add a StackPanel to the **Size** GroupBox and change its Width to Auto and its Margin to 3, then set the GroupBox's Height to Auto. Add three RadioButtons to the StackPanel, then set the StackPanel's Height property to Auto. Set the Width and Height of each RadioButton to Auto and the Margin to 3. Set the Content properties of the RadioButtons to Small, Medium and Large as in Fig. 26.56 and name each one accordingly. Set the IsChecked property of the **Medium** RadioButton to True.

d) ***Adding the Undo and Clear options.*** Add two Buttons to the StackPanel in column 0. Name the first Button undoButton and change its Content property to Undo. Set its Margin property to 3, 10, 3, 3 to add extra space between the **Undo** Button and the GroupBox above it. Name the second Button clearButton and change its Content property to Clear. Set its Margin to 3.

e) ***Declaring an enumeration to store the circle diameter sizes.*** Declare an enumeration Sizes to store the possible values of diameter. Set constant SMALL to 4, MEDIUM to 8 and LARGE to 10.

f) ***Adding event handlers for the Size RadioButtons.*** The **Size** RadioButton's event handlers should set instance variable diameter to Sizes.SMALL (for the **Small** RadioButton), Sizes.MEDIUM (for the **Medium** RadioButton) or Sizes.LARGE (for the **Large** RadioButton).

g) ***Coding the mouse event handlers.*** The MouseLeftButtonDown, MouseRightButtonDown, MouseLeftButtonUp and MouseRightButtonUp event handlers behave exactly as they do in the **Painter** app.

h) ***Coding the MouseMove event handler.*** The MouseMove event handler behaves the same way as the one in the **Painter** app. The color of the brush that draws the circle when shouldPaint is True is specified by brushColor. The eraser color is specified by the Canvas's Background property, and its size is specified by diameter.

i) ***Coding the Undo Button's event handler.*** The **Undo** Button's event handler removes the last circle added to the Canvas. Double click the **Undo** Button in **Design** view to generate its Click event handler. Use an If...Then statement to determine if there are any circles left on the Canvas. [*Hint:* The Canvas's Children property is a collection, so you can use the Count property to retrieve the number of items in Children.] Use the RemoveAt method of the Canvas's Children property to remove the last circle added.

j) ***Coding the Clear Button's event handler.*** The **Clear** Button's event handler should remove all the circles from the Canvas. Use the `Clear` method of the Canvas's `Children` property to remove all the circles from the Canvas.

k) ***Running the app.*** Select **Debug > Start Debugging** to run your app. Start drawing on the Canvas using different brush sizes and colors. Use the right mouse button to erase part of your drawing.

l) ***Closing the app.*** Close your running app by clicking its close box.

m) ***Closing the IDE.*** Close the Visual Basic IDE by clicking its close box.

27

Address Book App

Databases and LINQ

A **database** is an organized collection of data. A **database management system (DBMS)** provides mechanisms for storing, organizing, retrieving and modifying data. Today's most popular DBMSs manage relational databases, which organize data simply as tables with *rows* and *columns*.

Some popular proprietary DBMSs are Microsoft SQL Server, Oracle, Sybase and IBM DB2. PostgreSQL and MySQL are popular *open-source* DBMSs that can be downloaded and used *freely* by anyone. In this chapter, we use Microsoft's free **SQL Server Express**, which is installed with Visual Basic Express and Visual Studio. It can also be downloaded separately from Microsoft (www.microsoft.com/express/sql).

SQL Server Express provides most of the features of Microsoft's full (fee-based) SQL Server product, but has some limitations, such as a maximum database size of four gigabytes and allowing only one application at a time to interact with a database. A SQL Server Express database can be easily migrated to a full version of SQL Server—we did this with our deitel.com website once our database became too large for SQL Server Express.

Chapter 20 introduced LINQ to Objects and used it to to manipulate data stored in arrays. **LINQ to SQL** allows you to manipulate data stored in a *SQL Server or SQL Server Express* relational database. The SQL in LINQ to SQL stands for *SQL Server, not SQL*. As with LINQ to Objects, the IDE provides *IntelliSense* for your LINQ to SQL queries.

This chapter introduces general concepts of relational databases, then explores LINQ to SQL and the IDE's tools for working with databases. In later chapters, you'll see other practical database and LINQ to SQL applications, such as a web-based bookstore and a web based airline reservation service. Databases are at the heart of almost all "industrial strength" applications.

27.1 Relational Databases

A **relational database** organizes data simply in **tables**. Figure 27.1 illustrates a sample `Employees` table that might be used in a personnel system. The table stores the attributes of employees. Tables are composed of **rows** (also called **records**) and **columns** (also called **fields**) in which values are stored. This table consists of six rows (one per employee) and five columns (one per attribute). The attributes are the employee's ID, name, department, salary and location. The ID column of each row is the table's **primary key**—a column (or group of columns) requiring a *unique* value that cannot be duplicated in other rows. This guarantees that each primary key value can be used to identify *one* row. A primary key composed of two or more columns is known as a **composite key**. Good examples of primary-key columns in other applications are a book's ISBN number in a book information system or a part number in an inventory system—values in each of these columns must be unique. LINQ to SQL *requires every table to have a primary key* to support updating the data in tables. The rows in Fig. 27.1 are displayed in ascending order by primary key. But they could be listed in decreasing (descending) order or in no particular order at all.

Table Employees

	ID	Name	Department	Salary	Location
	23603	Jones	413	1100	Trenton
	24568	Kerwin	413	2000	Trenton
Row	34589	Larson	642	1800	Los Angeles
	35761	Myers	611	1400	Orlando
	47132	Neumann	413	9000	Trenton
	78321	Stephens	611	8500	Orlando
	Primary key		Column		

Figure 27.1 Employees table sample data.

Each *column* represents a different data *attribute*. Some column values may be duplicated between rows. For example, three different rows in the Employees table's Department column contain the number 413, indicating that these employees work in the same department.

You can use LINQ to SQL to define queries that select subsets of the data from a table. For example, a program might select data from the Employees table to create a query result that shows where each department is located, in increasing order by Department number (Fig. 27.2).

Department	Location
413	Trenton
611	Orlando
642	Los Angeles

Figure 27.2 Distinct Department and Location data from the Employees table.

SELF-REVIEW

1. A relational database organizes data simply in _____ .

   a) groups b) tables

   c) sources d) objects

2. A column (or group of columns) of each row is the table's _____ key, requiring a unique value that cannot be duplicated in other rows.

   a) foreign b) source

   c) primary d) composite

Answers: 1) b. 2) c.

27.2 A Books Database

We now consider a simple Books database that stores information about some Deitel publications. First, we overview the database's tables. A database's tables, their fields and the relationships among them are collectively known as a **database schema**. LINQ to SQL uses a database's schema to define classes that enable you to interact with the database. Next, we show how to use LINQ to SQL to retrieve information from the Books database. The database file—Books.mdf—is provided with this chapter's examples. SQL Server database files have the .mdf ("master data file") file-name extension.

Authors Table of the Books Database

The database consists of three tables: Authors, Titles and AuthorISBN. The Authors table (described in Fig. 27.3) consists of three columns that maintain each author's unique ID number, first name and last name, respectively. Figure 27.4 contains the data from the Authors table.

Column	Description
AuthorID	Author's ID number in the database. In the Books database, this integer column is defined as an **identity** column, also known as an **autoincremented** column—for each row inserted in the table, the AuthorID value is increased by 1 automatically to ensure that each row has a unique AuthorID. This is the *primary key*.
FirstName	Author's first name (a string).
LastName	Author's last name (a string).

Figure 27.3   Authors table of the Books database.

AuthorID	FirstName	LastName
1	Harvey	Deitel
2	Paul	Deitel
3	Greg	Ayer
4	Dan	Quirk

Figure 27.4   Data from the Authors table of the Books database.

Titles Table of the Books Database

The Titles table (described in Fig. 27.5) consists of four columns that maintain information about each book in the database, including its ISBN, title, edition number and copyright year. Figure 27.6 contains the data from the Titles table.

Column	Description
ISBN	ISBN of the book (a string). The table's primary key. ISBN is an abbreviation for "International Standard Book Number"—a numbering scheme that publishers worldwide use to give every book a *unique* identification number.
Title	Title of the book (a string).
EditionNumber	Edition number of the book (an integer).
Copyright	Copyright year of the book (a string).

Figure 27.5   Titles table of the Books database.

ISBN	Title	Edition-Number	Copyright
0131752421	Internet & World Wide Web How to Program	4	2008
0132222205	Java How to Program	7	2007
0132404168	C How to Program	5	2007
0136053033	Simply Visual Basic 2008	3	2009
013605305X	Visual Basic 2008 How to Program	4	2009
013605322X	Visual C# 2008 How to Program	3	2009
0136151574	Visual C++ 2008 How to Program	2	2008
0136152503	C++ How to Program	6	2008

Figure 27.6   Data from the `Titles` table of the `Books` database.

AuthorISBN Table of the Books Database

The `AuthorISBN` table (described in Fig. 27.7) consists of two columns that maintain ISBNs for each book and their corresponding authors' ID numbers. This table associates authors with their books. The `AuthorID` column is a **foreign key**—a column in this table that matches the primary-key column in another table (that is, `AuthorID` in the `Authors` table). The `ISBN` column is also a foreign key—it matches the primary-key column (that is, `ISBN`) in the `Titles` table. Together the `AuthorID` and `ISBN` columns in this table form a *composite primary key*. Every row in this table uniquely matches one author to one book's ISBN. Figure 27.8 contains the data from the `AuthorISBN` table of the `Books` database.

Column	Description
AuthorID	The author's ID number, a foreign key to the `Authors` table.
ISBN	The ISBN for a book, a foreign key to the `Titles` table.

Figure 27.7   `AuthorISBN` table of the `Books` database.

AuthorID	ISBN	AuthorID	ISBN
1	0131752421	2	0132222205
1	0132222205	2	0132404168
1	0132404168	2	0136053033
1	0136053033	2	013605305X
1	013605305X	2	013605322X
1	013605322X	2	0136151574
1	0136151574	2	0136152503
1	0136152503	3	0136053033
2	0131752421	4	0136151574

Figure 27.8   Data from the `AuthorISBN` table of the `Books` database.

Foreign Keys

A database might consist of many tables. A goal when designing a database is to minimize the amount of duplicated data among the database's tables. Foreign keys, which are specified when a database table is created, link the data in multiple tables.

Every foreign-key value must appear as another table's primary-key value so the DBMS can ensure that the foreign key value is valid. For example, the DBMS ensures that the `AuthorID` value for a particular row of the `AuthorISBN` table

(Fig. 27.8) is valid by checking that there is a row in the Authors table with that AuthorID as the primary key.

Foreign keys also allow related data in multiple tables to be selected from those tables—this is known as **joining** the data. There is a **one-to-many relationship** between a primary key and a corresponding foreign key (for example, one author can write many books and one book can be written by many authors). This means that a foreign key can appear *many* times in its own table but only *once* (as the primary key) in another table. For example, the ISBN 0131450913 can appear in several rows of AuthorISBN (because this book has several authors) but only once in Titles, where ISBN is the primary key.

Entity-Relationship Diagram for the Books Database

Figure 27.9 is an **entity-relationship (ER) diagram** for the Books database. This diagram shows the tables in the database and the relationships among them. The first compartment in each box contains the table's name. The names in italic font are primary keys—*AuthorID* in the Authors table, *AuthorID* and *ISBN* in the AuthorISBN table, and *ISBN* in the Titles table. Every row *must* have a value in the primary-key column, and the value of the key must be *unique* in the table; otherwise, the DBMS will report an error. The names *AuthorID* and *ISBN* in the AuthorISBN table are *both* italic—together these form a *composite primary key* for the AuthorISBN table.

The lines connecting the tables in Fig. 27.9 represent the relationships among the tables. Consider the line between the Authors and AuthorISBN tables. On the Authors end of the line, there's a 1, and on the AuthorISBN end, an infinity symbol (∞). This indicates a one-to-many relationship—for *each* author in the Authors table, there can be an *arbitrary number* of ISBNs for books written by that author in the AuthorISBN table (that is, an author can write any number of books). Note that the relationship line links the AuthorID column in the Authors table (where AuthorID is the primary key) to the AuthorID column in the AuthorISBN table (where AuthorID is a foreign key)—the line between the tables links the primary key to the matching foreign key.

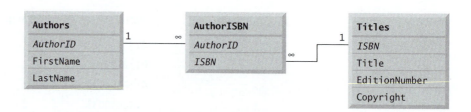

Figure 27.9 Entity-relationship diagram for the **Books** database.

The line between the Titles and AuthorISBN tables illustrates a one-to-many relationship—one book can be written by many authors. Note that the line between the tables links the primary key ISBN in table Titles to the corresponding foreign key in table AuthorISBN. The relationships in Fig. 27.9 illustrate that the sole purpose of the AuthorISBN table is to provide a **many-to-many relationship** between the Authors and Titles tables—an author can write *many* books, and a book can have *many* authors.

SELF-REVIEW

1. A database's tables, their fields and the relationships between them are collectively known as a database _____ .

  a) schema   b) master/detail view

  c) architecture   d) relation

2. Foreign keys also allow related data in multiple tables to be selected from those tables—this is known as _____ the data.

     a) extracting   b) filtering

     c) composing   d) joining

Answers: 1) a. 2) d.

27.3 LINQ to SQL

LINQ to SQL enables you to access data in *SQL Server databases* using the same LINQ syntax introduced in Chapter 20. You interact with the database via classes that are automatically generated from the database schema by the IDE's **LINQ to SQL Designer**. For each table in the database, the IDE creates two classes:

- A class that represents a row of the table: This class contains properties for each column in the table. LINQ to SQL creates objects of this class—called **row objects**—to store the data from individual rows of the table.

- A class that represents the table: LINQ to SQL creates an object of this class to store a collection of row objects that correspond to all of the table's rows.

Relationships between tables are also taken into account in the generated classes:

- In the class for a row object, an additional property is created for each foreign key. This property returns the row object of the corresponding primary key in another table. For example, the LINQ to SQL class that represents the rows of the Books database's AuthorISBN table also contains an Author property and a Title property—from any AuthorISBN row object, you can access the full author and title information.

- In the class for a row object, an additional property is created for the collection of row objects with foreign-keys that reference the row object's primary key. For example, the LINQ to SQL class that represents the rows of the Books database's Authors table contains an AuthorISBNs property that you can use to get all of the ISBNs for books written by that author. The IDE automatically adds the "s" to "AuthorISBN" to indicate that this property represents a collection of AuthorISBN objects. Similarly, the LINQ to SQL class that represents the rows of the Titles table also contains an AuthorISBNs property that you can use to get all of the AuthorIDs for the co-authors of a particular title.

Once generated, the LINQ to SQL classes have full *IntelliSense* support in the IDE. Section 27.6 demonstrates queries that use the relationships among the Books database's tables to join data.

IQueryable *Interface*

LINQ to SQL works through the **IQueryable interface**, which inherits from the IEnumerable interface introduced in Chapter 20. When a LINQ to SQL query on an IQueryable object executes against the database, the results are loaded into objects of the corresponding LINQ to SQL classes for convenient access in your code.

DataContext *Class*

All LINQ to SQL queries occur via a **DataContext class**, which controls the flow of data between the program and the database. A specific DataContext derived class, which inherits from the class System.Data.Linq.DataContext, is created when the LINQ to SQL classes representing each row of the table are generated by the IDE. This derived class has properties for each table in the database, which can be used as data sources in LINQ queries. Any changes made to the DataContext can be saved back to the database using the DataContext's **SubmitChanges method**, so with LINQ to SQL you can modify the database's contents.

SELF-REVIEW 1. Link to _____ enables you to access data in SQL Server databases using LINQ syntax.

    a) Server   b) SQL

    c) Schema   d) Source

2. You interact with LINQ to SQL via classes that are automatically generated by the IDE's LINQ to SQL _____ based on the database schema.

    a) Schema   b) Relation

    c) Entity   d) Designer

Answers: 1) b. 2) d.

27.4 Querying a Database with LINQ

In this section, we demonstrate how to *connect* to a database, *query* it and *display* the results of the query. There is little code in this section—the IDE provides *visual programming* tools and *wizards* that simplify accessing data in applications. These tools establish database connections and create the objects necessary to view and manipulate the data through Windows Forms GUI controls—a technique known as **data binding**.

Our first example performs a simple query on the Books database from Section 27.2. We retrieve the entire Authors table and use data binding to display its data in a DataGridView—a control from namespace System.Windows.Forms that can display data from a data source in tabular format. The basic steps we'll perform are:

- Connect to the Books database.
- Create the LINQ to SQL classes required to use the database.
- Add the Authors table as a data source.
- Drag the Authors table data source onto the **Design** view to create a GUI for displaying the table's data.
- Add a few statements to the program to allow it to interact with the database.

The GUI for the program is shown in Fig. 27.10. All of the controls in this GUI are automatically generated when we drag a data source that represents the Authors table onto the Form in **Design** view. The BindingNavigator at the top of the window is a collection of controls that allow you to navigate through the records in the DataGridView that fills the rest of the window. The BindingNavigator controls also allow you to add records, delete records and save your changes to the database. If you add a new record, note that empty (NULL) values are not allowed in the Books database, so attempting to save a new record without specifying a value for each field will cause an error.

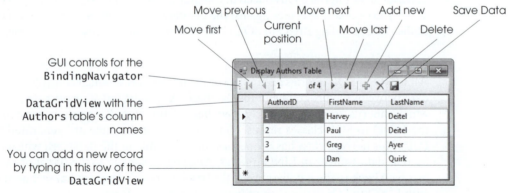

Figure 27.10   GUI for the **Display Authors Table** application.

Creating LINQ to SQL Classes

This section presents the steps required to create LINQ to SQL classes for a database.

Step 1: Creating the Project

Create a new **Windows Forms Application** named `DisplayTable`. Change the name of the source file to `DisplayAuthorsTable.vb`. The IDE updates the Form's class name to match the source file. Set the Form's **Text** property to `Display Authors Table`.

Step 2: Adding a Database to the Project and Connecting to the Database

To interact with a database, you must create a **connection** to the database. This will also give you the option of copying the database file to your project.

1. In Visual Basic 2010 Express, select **View > Other Windows > Database Explorer** to display the Database Explorer **window**. By default, it appears on the left side of the IDE. If you're using a full version of Visual Studio, select **View > Server Explorer** to display the **Server Explorer**. From this point forward, we'll refer to the **Database Explorer**. If you have a full version of Visual Studio, substitute **Server Explorer** for **Database Explorer** in the steps.

2. Click the **Connect to Database** icon () at the top of the **Database Explorer**. If the Choose Data Source **dialog** appears (Fig. 27.11), select **Microsoft SQL Server Database File** from the **Data source:** list. If you check the **Always use this selection** CheckBox, the IDE will use this type of database file by default when you connect to databases in the future. Click **Continue** to display the Add Connection **dialog**.

Figure 27.11   **Choose Data Source** dialog.

![Error-Prevention Tip icon] **Error-Prevention Tip**

SQL Server Express allows only one application at a time to access a database file. Ensure that no other program is using the database file before you attempt to add it to the project.

3. In the **Add Connection** dialog (Fig. 27.12), the **Data source:** TextBox reflects your selection from the **Choose Data Source** dialog. You can click the **Change...** Button to select a different type of database. Next, click **Browse...** to locate and select the `Books.mdf` file in the `Databases` directory included with this chapter's examples. You can click **Test Connection** to verify that the IDE can connect to the database through SQL Server Express. Click **OK** to create the connection.

Figure 27.12 Add Connection dialog.

Step 3: Generating the LINQ to SQL classes

After the database has been added, you must select the database from which the LINQ to SQL classes will be created. LINQ to SQL uses the database's schema to help define the classes.

1. Right click the project name in the **Solution Explorer** and select **Add > New Item...** to display the **Add New Item** dialog. Select the **LINQ to SQL Classes** template, name the new item Books.dbml and click the **Add** button. The **Object Relational Designer window** will appear (Fig. 27.13). You can also double click the Books.dbml file in the **Solution Explorer** to open the **Object Relational Designer**.

Figure 27.13 Object Relational Designer window.

2. Expand the Books.mdf database node in the **Database Explorer**, then expand the **Tables** node. Drag the Authors, Titles and AuthorISBN tables onto the **Object Relational Designer**. The IDE prompts whether you want to copy the database to the project directory. Select **Yes**. The **Object Relational Designer** will display the tables that you dragged from the **Database Explorer** (Fig. 27.14). Notice that the **Object Relational Designer** named the class that represents items from the Authors table as Author, and named the class that represents the Titles table as Title. This is because one object of the Author class represents one author—a single row from the Authors table. Similarly, one object of the Title class represents one book—a single row from the Titles table.

3. Save the Books.dbml file.

Figure 27.14   **Object Relational Designer** window showing the selected tables from the Books database and their relationships.

When you save Books.dbml, the IDE generates the LINQ to SQL classes that you can use to interact with the database. These include a class for each table you selected from the database and a derived class of DataContext named BooksData-Context that enables you to programmatically interact with the database.

Data Bindings Between Controls and the LINQ to SQL Classes

The IDE's automatic data binding capabilities simplify creating applications that can view and modify the data in a database. You must write a small amount of code to enable the autogenerated data-binding classes to interact with the autogenerated LINQ to SQL classes. You'll now perform the steps to display the contents of the Authors table in a GUI.

Step 1: Adding the Author LINQ to SQL Class as a Data Source

To use the LINQ to SQL classes for data binding, you must first add them as a data source.

1. Select **Data > Add New Data Source...** to display the **Data Source Configuration Wizard**.

2. The LINQ to SQL classes are used to create objects representing the tables in the database, so we'll use an **Object data source**. In the dialog, select **Object** and click **Next >**. Expand the tree view as shown in Fig. 27.15 and ensure that **Author** is checked. An object of this class will be used as the data source.

3. Click **Finish**.

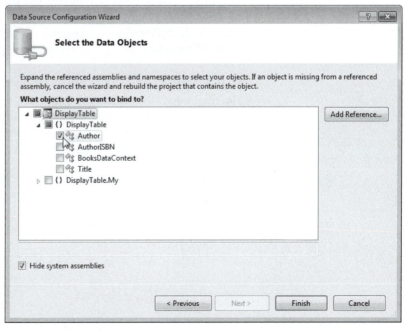

Figure 27.15   Selecting the Author LINQ to SQL class as the data source.

The `Authors` table in the database is now a data source that can be used by the bindings. Open the **Data Sources window** (Fig. 27.16) by selecting **Data > Show Data Sources**. You can see the `Author` class that you added in the previous step. The columns of the database's `Authors` table should appear below it, as well as an `AuthorISBNs` entry representing the relationship between the database's `Authors` and `AuthorISBN` tables.

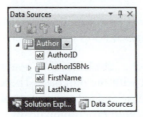

Figure 27.16 **Data Sources** window showing the `Author` class as a data source.

Step 2: Creating GUI Elements

Next, you'll use the **Design** view to create a GUI control that can display the `Authors` table's data.

1. Switch to **Design** view for the `DisplayAuthorsTable` class.

2. Click the **Author** node in the **Data Sources** window—it should change to a drop-down list. Open the drop-down by clicking the down arrow and ensure that the `DataGridView` option is selected—this is the GUI control that will be used to display and interact with the data.

3. Drag the **Author** node from the **Data Sources** window onto the Form in **Design** view.

The IDE creates a `DataGridView` (Fig. 27.17) with the correct column names and a **`BindingNavigator`** (`AuthorBindingNavigator`) that contains `Buttons` for moving between entries, adding entries, deleting entries and saving changes to the database. The IDE also generates a **`BindingSource`** (`AuthorBindingSource`), which handles the transfer of data between the data source and the data-bound controls on the Form. Nonvisual components such as the `BindingSource` and the non-visual aspects of the `BindingNavigator` appear in the component tray—the gray region below the Form in **Design** view. We use the default names for automatically generated components throughout this chapter to show exactly what the IDE creates. To make the **DataGridView** occupy the entire window, select the `DataGridView`, then use the **Properties** window to set the Dock property to `Fill`.

Step 3: Connecting the `BooksDataContext` to the `AuthorBindingSource`

The final step is to connect the `BooksDataContext` (created with the LINQ to SQL classes in Section 27.3) to the `AuthorBindingSource`, so that the application can interact with the database. Figure 27.18 shows the small amount of code needed to obtain data from the database and to save any changes that the user makes to the data back into the database.

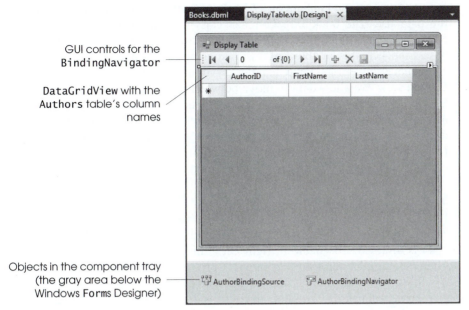

GUI controls for the
`BindingNavigator`

`DataGridView` with the
`Authors` table's column
names

Objects in the component tray
(the gray area below the
Windows `Forms` Designer)

Figure 27.17   Component tray holds nonvisual components in **Design** view.

```
 1    ' Fig. 27.18: DisplayTable.vb
 2    ' Displaying data from a database table in a DataGridView.
 3    Public Class DisplayTable
 4       Private database As New BooksDataContext() ' data context
 5
 6       ' load data from database into DataGridView
 7       Private Sub DisplayTable_Load(ByVal sender As System.Object,
 8          ByVal e As System.EventArgs) Handles MyBase.Load
 9
10          ' use LINQ to order the data for display
11          AuthorBindingSource.DataSource =
12             From author In database.Authors
13             Order By author.AuthorID
14             Select author
15       End Sub ' DisplayTable_Load
16
17       ' save the changes into the database
18       Private Sub AuthorBindingNavigatorSaveItem_Click(
19          ByVal sender As System.Object, ByVal e As System.EventArgs) _
20          Handles AuthorBindingNavigatorSaveItem.Click
21
22          Validate() ' validate input fields
23          AuthorBindingSource.EndEdit() ' indicate edits are complete
24          database.SubmitChanges() ' write changes to database file
25       End Sub ' AuthorBindingNavigatorSaveItem_Click
26    End Class ' DisplayTable
```

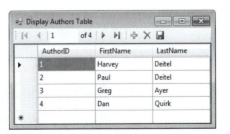

Figure 27.18   Displaying data from a database table in a `DataGridView`.

As mentioned in Section 27.3, a DataContext object is used to interact with the database. The BooksDataContext class was automatically generated by the IDE when you created the LINQ to SQL classes to allow access to the Books database. Line 4 creates an object of this class named database.

Create the Form's Load handler by double clicking the Form's title bar in **Design** view. We allow data to move between the DataContext and the Binding-Source by creating a LINQ query that extracts data from the BooksDataContext's Authors property (lines 12–14), which corresponds to the Authors table in the database. The AuthorBindingSource's **DataSource property** (line 11) is set to the results of this query. The AuthorBindingSource uses the DataSource to extract data from the database and to populate the DataGridView.

Step 4: Saving Modifications Back to the Database

If the user modifies the data in the DataGridView, we'd also like to save the modifications in the database. By default, the BindingNavigator's **Save Data** Button (🖫) is disabled. To enable it, right click this Button's icon and select **Enabled**. Then, double click the icon to create its Click event handler.

Saving the data entered into the DataGridView back to the database is a three-step process (lines 22–24). First, all controls on the form are validated (line 22)—if any of the controls have event handlers for the Validating event, those execute. You typically handle this event to determine whether a control's contents are valid. Second, line 23 calls **EndEdit** on the AuthorBindingSource, which forces it to save any pending changes in the BooksDataContext. Finally, line 24 calls **Submit-Changes** on the BooksDataContext to store the changes in the database. For efficiency, LINQ to SQL saves only data that has changed.

Step 5: Configuring the Database File to Persist Changes

By default, when you run the program in debug mode, the database file is overwritten with the original database file each time you execute the program. This allows you to test your program with the original content until it works correctly. When you run the program in release mode (*Ctrl* + *F5*), any changes you make to the database persist automatically. You can persist changes between program executions in debug mode by selecting the database in the **Solution Explorer** and setting the **Copy to Output Directory** property in the **Properties** window to **Copy if newer**.

SELF-REVIEW

1. The IDE provides visual programming tools and wizards that simplify accessing data in your projects. These tools establish database connections and create the objects necessary to view and manipulate the data through the GUI—a technique known as _____ .

   a) data binding
   c) joining
   b) smart tagging
   d) master/detailing

2. A(n) _____ is a collection of controls that allow you to navigate through the records displayed in a GUI. These controls also allow you to add records, delete records and save your changes to the database.

   a) DatabaseSchema
   c) BindingNavigator
   b) EntityRelationship
   d) BindingSource

Answers: 1) a. 2) c.

27.5 Dynamically Binding Query Results

Now that you've seen how to display an entire database table in a DataGridView, we show how to perform several different queries and display the results in a DataGridView. The **Display Query Results** application (Fig. 27.19) allows the user to select a query from the ComboBox at the bottom of the window, then displays the results of the query.

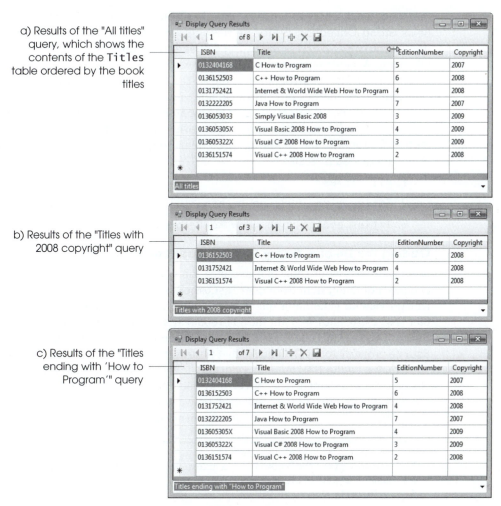

a) Results of the "All titles" query, which shows the contents of the `Titles` table ordered by the book titles

b) Results of the "Titles with 2008 copyright" query

c) Results of the "Titles ending with 'How to Program'" query

Figure 27.19   Sample execution of the **Display Query Results** application.

Creating the Display Query Results GUI

Perform the following steps to build the **Display Query Results** application's GUI.

Step 1: Creating the Project

First, create a new **Windows Forms Application** named `DisplayQueryResult`. Rename the source file to `TitleQueries.vb`. Set the Form's **Text** property to `Display Query Results`.

Step 2: Creating the LINQ to SQL Classes

Follow the steps in Section 27.4 to add the Books database to the project and generate the LINQ to SQL classes.

Step 3: Creating a `DataGridView` to Display the `Titles` Table

Follow *Steps 1* and *2* in Section 27.4 to create the data source and the `DataGridView`. In this example, select the `Title` class (rather than the `Author` class) as the data source, and drag the **Title** node from the **Data Sources** window onto the form.

Step 4: Adding a `ComboBox` to the `Form`

In **Design** view, add a `ComboBox` named `queriesComboBox` below the `DataGridView` on the `Form`. Users will select which query to execute from this control. Set the `ComboBox`'s **Dock** property to `Bottom` and the `DataGridView`'s **Dock** property to `Fill`.

Next, you'll add the names of the queries to the ComboBox. Open the Combo-Box's **String Collection Editor** by right clicking the ComboBox and selecting **Edit Items**. You can also access the **String Collection Editor** from the ComboBox's smart tag menu. A **smart tag menu** provides you with quick access to common properties you might set for a control (such as the Multiline property of a TextBox), so you can set these properties directly in **Design** view, rather than in the **Properties** window. You can open a control's smart tag menu by clicking the small arrowhead (▶) that appears in the control's upper-right corner in **Design** view. In the **String Collection Editor**, add the following three items to queriesComboBox—one for each of the queries we'll create:

1. All titles
2. Titles with 2008 copyright
3. Titles ending with "How to Program"

Coding the Display Query Results Application

Next you must write code that executes the appropriate query each time the user chooses a different item from queriesComboBox. Double click queriesComboBox in **Design** view to generate a queriesComboBox_SelectedIndexChanged event handler (Fig. 27.20, lines 7–37) in the TitleQueries.vb file. In the event handler, add a Select Case statement (lines 12–34) to change the TitleBindingSource's Data-Source property to a LINQ query that returns the correct set of data. The data bindings created by the IDE *automatically* update the TitleDataGridView *each time* we change its DataSource. The **MoveFirst method** of the BindingSource (line 36) moves to the first row of the result each time a query executes. The results of the queries in lines 16–18, 22–25 and 30–33 are shown in Fig. 27.19(a), (b) and (c), respectively.

```
 1   ' Fig. 27.20: TitleQueries.vb
 2   ' Displaying the result of a user-selected query in a DataGridView.
 3   Public Class TitleQueries
 4      Private database As New BooksDataContext() ' data context
 5
 6      ' loads data into TitleBindingSource based on user-selected query
 7      Private Sub queriesComboBox_SelectedIndexChanged(
 8         ByVal sender As System.Object, ByVal e As System.EventArgs) _
 9         Handles queriesComboBox.SelectedIndexChanged
10
11         ' set the data displayed according to what is selected
12         Select Case queriesComboBox.SelectedIndex
13            Case 0 ' all titles
14               ' use LINQ to order the books by title
15               TitleBindingSource.DataSource =
16                  From book In database.Titles
17                  Order By book.Title
18                  Select book
19            Case 1 ' titles with 2008 copyright
20               ' use LINQ to get and sort titles with 2008 copyright
21               TitleBindingSource.DataSource =
22                  From book In database.Titles
23                  Where book.Copyright = "2008"
24                  Order By book.Title
25                  Select book
26            Case 2 ' titles ending with "How to Program"
27               ' use LINQ to get titles ending with
28               ' "How to Program" and sort them
29               TitleBindingSource.DataSource =
30                  From book In database.Titles
31                  Where book.Title.EndsWith("How to Program")
```

Figure 27.20 Displaying the result of a user-selected query in a DataGridView. (Part 1 of 2.)

```
32                    Order By book.Title
33                    Select book
34          End Select
35
36          TitleBindingSource.MoveFirst() ' move to first entry
37      End Sub ' queriesComboBox_SelectedIndexChanged
38
39      ' display results of all titles query when Form loads
40      Private Sub TitleQueries_Load(ByVal sender As System.Object, _
41          ByVal e As System.EventArgs) Handles MyBase.Load
42
43          ' set the ComboBox to show the default query that
44          ' selects all books from the Titles table and executes the
45          ' queriesComboBox's SelectedIndexChanged event handler
46          queriesComboBox.SelectedIndex = 0
47      End Sub ' TitleQueries_Load
48
49      ' save changes from the BooksDataContext into the database
50      Private Sub TitleBindingNavigatorSaveItem_Click(
51          ByVal sender As System.Object, ByVal e As System.EventArgs) _
52          Handles TitleBindingNavigatorSaveItem.Click
53
54          Validate() ' validate input fields
55          TitleBindingSource.EndEdit() ' indicate edits are complete
56          database.SubmitChanges() ' write changes to database file
57
58          ' after saving, display the results of the "all titles" query
59          queriesComboBox.SelectedIndex = 0
60      End Sub ' TitleBindingNavigatorSaveItem_Click
61  End Class ' TitleQueries
```

Figure 27.20 Displaying the result of a user-selected query in a `DataGridView`. (Part 2 of 2.)

Customizing the Form's Load Event Handler

Create the `TitleQueries_Load` event handler (lines 40–47) by double clicking the title bar in **Design** view. When the Form loads, it should display the complete list of books from the `Titles` table, sorted by title. Rather than defining the same LINQ query as in lines 15–18, we can programmatically cause the `queriesCombo-Box_SelectedIndexChanged` event handler to execute simply by setting the `queriesComboBox`'s `SelectedIndex` to 0 (line 46).

Saving Changes

Follow the instructions in the previous example to add a handler for the `Binding-Navigator`'s **Save Data** Button (lines 50–60). Note that, except for changes to the names, the three lines are identical. The last statement (line 59) displays the results of the `All titles` query in the `DataGridView`. Recall that the changes to the database persist between executions if you execute the program in release mode (*Ctrl + F5*).

SELF-REVIEW
1. The IDE displays _____ for many GUI controls to provide you with quick access to common properties you might set for a control, so you can set these properties directly in **Design** view.

   a) binding navigators   b) composite keys

   c) query operators   d) smart tag menus

2. The _____ method of the `BindingSource` moves to the first row of the result.

   a) `InitEntry`   b) `MoveFirst`

   c) `StartRow`   d) `FirstRecord`

Answers: 1) d. 2) b.

27.6 Retrieving Data from Multiple Tables with LINQ

In this section, we concentrate on LINQ to SQL features that simplify querying and combining data from multiple tables. The **Joining Tables with LINQ** application (Fig. 27.21) uses LINQ to SQL to combine and organize data from multiple tables, and shows the results of queries that perform the following tasks:

■ Get a list of all the authors and the ISBNs of the books they've authored, sorted by last name then first name (Fig. 27.21(a)).

■ Get a list of all the authors and the titles of the books they've authored, sorted by last name then first; for each author sort the titles alphabetically (Fig. 27.21(b)).

■ Get a list of all the book titles grouped by author, sorted by last name then first; for a given author sort the titles alphabetically (Fig. 27.21(c)).

a) List of authors and the ISBNs of the books they've authored; sort the authors by last name then first name

b) List of authors and the titles of the book's they've authored; sort the authors by last name then first name; for a given author, sort the titles alphabetically

c) List of titles grouped by author; sort the authors by last name then first name; for a given author, sort the titles alphabetically

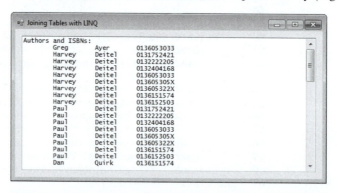

Figure 27.21   Outputs from the **Joining Tables with LINQ** application.

GUI for the Joining Tables with LINQ Application

For this example (Fig. 27.22–Fig. 27.25), create a Windows Forms application named JoinQueries and rename the Form.vb file as JoiningTableData.vb. We set the following properties for the outputTextBox:

■ Font property: Set to Lucida Console to display the output in a fixed-width font.

■ Anchor property: Set to Top, Bottom, Left, Right so that you can resize the window and the outputTextBox will resize accordingly.

■ Scrollbars property: Set to Vertical, so that you can scroll through the output.

Follow the steps from previous sections to set up the connection to the database and the LINQ to SQL classes.

Creating the BooksDataContext

The code combines data from the three tables in the Books database and displays the relationships between the book titles and authors in three different ways. It uses LINQ to SQL classes that have been created using the same steps as the first two examples. As in previous examples, the BooksDataContext object (Fig. 27.22, line 7) allows the program to interact with the database.

```
1    ' Fig. 27.22: JoiningTableData.vb
2    ' Using LINQ to perform aggregate data from several tables.
3    Public Class JoiningTableData
4        Private Sub JoiningTableData_Load(ByVal sender As System.Object,
5            ByVal e As System.EventArgs) Handles MyBase.Load
6
7            Dim database As New BooksDataContext() ' data context
8
```

Figure 27.22   Creating the BooksDataContext for querything the Books database.

Combining Author Names with the ISBNs of the Books They've Written

The first query (Fig. 27.23, lines 11–14) joins data from two tables and returns a list of author names and the ISBNs representing the books they've written, sorted by Last-Name then FirstName. The query takes advantage of the properties that LINQ to SQL creates based on foreign-key relationships between the database's tables. These properties enable you to easily combine data from related rows in multiple tables.

```
9             ' get authors and ISBNs of each book they co-authored
10            Dim authorsAndISBNs =
11                From author In database.Authors
12                From book In author.AuthorISBNs
13                Order By author.LastName, author.FirstName
14                Select author.FirstName, author.LastName, book.ISBN
15
16            outputTextBox.AppendText("Authors and ISBNs:")
17
18            ' display authors and ISBNs in tabular format
19            For Each element In authorsAndISBNs
20                outputTextBox.AppendText(
21                    String.Format("{0}{1}{2,-10} {3,-10} {4,-10}", vbCrLf,
22                    vbTab, element.FirstName, element.LastName, element.ISBN))
23            Next
24
```

Figure 27.23   Getting a list of authors and the ISBNs of the books they've authored.

The first From clause (line 11) gets one author from the Authors table. The second From clause (line 12) uses the generated AuthorISBNs property of the Author class to get only the rows in the AuthorISBN table that link to the current author—that is, the ones that have the same AuthorID as the current author. The combined result of the two From clauses is a collection of all the authors and the ISBNs of the books they've authored. The two From clauses introduce two range variables into the scope of this query—other clauses can access both range variables to combine data from multiple tables. Line 14 combines the FirstName and Last-Name of an author from the Authors table with a corresponding ISBN from the AuthorISBNs table.

Combining Author Names with the Titles of the Books They've Written
The second query (Fig. 27.24, lines 27–31) gives similar output, but uses the foreign-key relationships to go one step further and get the actual title of each book that an author wrote. The first From clause (line 27) gets one title from the Titles table. The second From clause (line 28) uses the generated AuthorISBNs property of the Title class to get only the rows in the AuthorISBN table that link to the current title—that is, the ones that have the same ISBN as the current title. Each of those book objects contains an Author property that represents the foreign-key relationship between the AuthorISBNs table and the Authors table. This Author property gives us access to the names of the authors for the current book.

```
25        ' get authors and titles of each book they co-authored
26        Dim authorsAndTitles =
27            From title In database.Titles
28            From book In title.AuthorISBNs
29            Let author = book.Author
30            Order By author.LastName, author.FirstName, title.Title
31            Select author.FirstName, author.LastName, title.Title
32
33        outputTextBox.AppendText(vbCrLf & vbCrLf & "Authors and titles:")
34
35        ' display authors and titles in tabular format
36        For Each element In authorsAndTitles
37            outputTextBox.AppendText(
38                String.Format("{0}{1}{2,-10} {3,-10} {4}", vbCrLf, vbTab,
39                element.FirstName, element.LastName, element.Title))
40        Next
41
```

Figure 27.24 Getting a list of authors and the titles of the books they've authored.

Line 29 introduces the **Let query operator**, which allows you to declare a new variable in a LINQ query—usually to create a shorter name for an expression. The variable can be accessed in later statements just like a range variable. The author variable created in the Let clause refers to book.Author. The Select clause (line 31) uses the author and title variables introduced earlier in the query to get the FirstName and LastName of each author from the Authors table and the Title of each book from the Titles table.

Organizing Book Titles by Author
Most queries return results with data arranged in a relational-style table of rows and columns. The last query (Fig. 27.25, lines 45–51) returns hierarchical results. Each element in the results contains the name of an Author and a list of Titles that the author wrote. The LINQ query does this by using a nested query in the Select clause. The outer query iterates over the authors in the database. The inner query takes a specific author and retrieves all titles that the author worked on. The Select clause (lines 47–51) creates an anonymous type with two properties:

- The property Name (line 47) combines each author's name, separating the first and last names by a space.
- The property Titles (line 48) receives the result of the nested query, which returns the Title of each book written by the current author.

The nested For Each...Next statements (lines 57–67) use the properties of the anonymous type created by the query to output the hierarchical results. The outer loop displays the author's name and the inner loop displays the titles of all the books written by that author.

```
42          ' get authors and titles of each book
43          ' they co-authored; group by author
44          Dim titlesByAuthor =
45            From author In database.Authors
46            Order By author.LastName, author.FirstName
47            Select Name = author.FirstName & " " & author.LastName,
48              Titles =
49                From book In author.AuthorISBNs
50                Order By book.Title.Title
51                Select book.Title.Title
52
53          outputTextBox.AppendText(
54            vbCrLf & vbCrLf & "Titles grouped by author:")
55
56          ' display titles written by each author, grouped by author
57          For Each author In titlesByAuthor
58            ' display authors
59            outputTextBox.AppendText(
60              String.Format("{0}{1}{2}:", vbCrLf, vbTab, author.Name))
61
62            ' display titles written by that author
63            For Each title In author.Titles
64              outputTextBox.AppendText(
65                String.Format("{0}{1}{1}{2}", vbCrLf, vbTab, title))
66            Next title
67          Next author
68        End Sub ' JoningTableData_Load
69   End Class ' JoningTableData
```

Figure 27.25 Getting a list of titles grouped by authors.

Notice the duplicate Title identifier in the expression book.Title.Title used in the inner Order By and Select clauses (lines 50–51). This is due to the database having a Title column in the Titles table, and is another example of following foreign-key relationships. The range variable book iterates over the rows of AuthorISBN for the current author's books. Each book's Title property contains the corresponding row from the Titles table for that book. The second Title in the expression returns the Title column from that row of the Titles.

SELF-REVIEW

1. The _____ query operator allows you to declare a new variable in a query—usually to create a shorter name for an expression. The variable can be accessed in later clauses just like a range variable.
   a) Let   b) Declare
   c) Set   d) Define

2. To join data from multiple tables you use the properties that LINQ to SQL creates based on _____ relationships between the database's tables. These properties enable you to easily access related rows in other tables.
   a) primary-key   b) schema-key
   c) foreign-key   d) composite-key

Answers: 1) a. 2) c.

27.7 Creating a Master/Detail View Application

Figure 27.26 demonstrates a so-called **master/detail view**—one part of the GUI (the master) allows you to select an entry, and another part (the details) displays detailed information about that entry. In this example, if you select an author from the **Author:** ComboBox, the application displays the details of the books written by that author (Fig. 27.26(b)). If you select a book title from the **Title:** ComboBox, the application displays the co-authors of that book (Fig. 27.26(c)).

a) **Master/Detail** application when it begins execution before an author or title is selected; no results are displayed in the `DataGridView` until the user makes a selection from one of the `ComboBoxes`

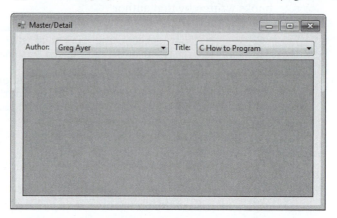

b) Select **Harvey Deitel** from the **Author:** drop-down list to view books he's co-authored

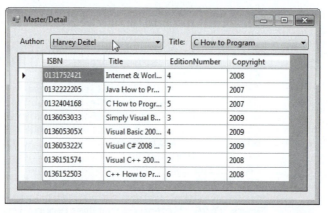

c) Select **C++ How to Program** from the **Title:** drop-down to view the authors who wrote that book

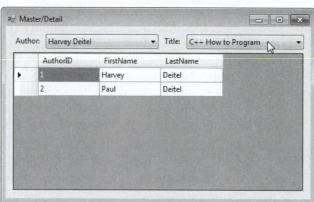

Figure 27.26 Master/Detail application.

Creating the Master/Detail GUI

You've seen that the IDE can automatically generate the BindingSource, BindingNavigator and GUI elements when you drag a data source onto the Form. While this works for simple applications, those with more complex operations involve writing more substantial amounts of code. Before explaining the code, we list the steps required to create the GUI.

Step 1: Creating the Project

Create a new **Windows Forms Application** called `MasterDetail`. Name the source file `Details.vb` and set the Form's `Text` property to **Master/Detail**.

Step 2: Creating LINQ to SQL Classes

Follow the instructions in Section 27.4 to add the `Books` database and create the LINQ to SQL classes to interact with the database.

Step 3: Creating GUI Elements

Add two `Labels` and two `ComboBoxes` to the top of the `Form`. Position them as shown in Fig. 27.27. The `Label` and `ComboBox` on the left should be named `authorLabel` and `authorComboBox`, respectively. The `Label` and `ComboBox` on the right should be named `titleLabel` and `titleComboBox`. Set the `Text` properties of the `Labels` to `Author:` and `Title:`, respectively. Also change the `DropDownStyle` properties of the `ComboBoxes` from `DropDown` to `DropDownList`—this prevents the user from being able to type in the control.

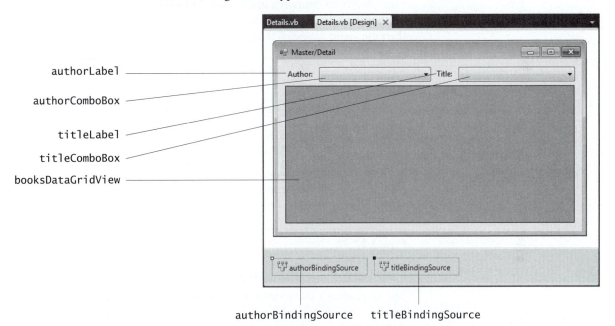

Figure 27.27 Finished design of **Master/Detail** application.

Next, create a `DataGridView` called `booksDataGridView` to hold the details that are displayed. Unlike previous examples, do not automatically create it by dragging a data source from the **Data Sources** window—this example sets the data source programmatically. Instead, drag the `DataGridView` from the **Toolbox**. Resize the `DataGridView` so that it fills the remainder of the `Form`. Because this control is only for *viewing* data, set its `ReadOnly` property to `True` using the **Properties** window.

Finally, we need to add two `BindingSources` from the **Data** section of the **Toolbox**, one for information from the `Titles` table and one for information from the `Authors` table. Name these `titleBindingSource` and `authorBindingSource`, respectively. As in the previous examples, these appear in the component tray. These `BindingSources` are used as data sources for the `DataGridView`—the data source switches between them, depending on whether we want to view a list of `Titles` or a list of `Authors`. With the GUI creation complete, we can now write the code to provide the master/detail functionality.

Coding the Master/Detail Application

Nested Class AuthorBinding

As you saw in Fig. 27.26, the **Author:** ComboBox displays each author's full name. This example uses data binding to display the names in the ComboBox. When you bind a collection of objects to a ComboBox's DataSource property, the ComboBox normally displays the result of calling ToString on each object in the collection. If the String representation is not appropriate, you can specify *one* property of each object in the collection that should be displayed. In this example, we want to display each author's first and last name.

Recall that the author's name is stored as *two* database fields, so the auto-generated Author class does not have single property that returns the full name. For this reason, we use a class called AuthorBinding (Fig. 27.28, lines 8–11) to help display the author's full name. Class AuthorBinding's Name property stores an author's full name, and the Author property stores the Author object that contains the author's information from the database. Class AuthorBinding is intended for use only in this example, so we defined it inside class Details—it's a so-called **nested class**. Class definitions may be nested inside other classes when they're intended to be used only by their enclosing classes—that is, they're not meant for use by other programs.

```vb
1   ' Fig. 27.28: Details.vb
2   ' Using a DataGridView to display details based on a selection.
3   Public Class Details
4      Private database As New BooksDataContext() ' data context
5
6      ' this class helps us display each author's first
7      ' and last name in the authors drop-down list
8      Private Class AuthorBinding
9         Public Property Author As Author ' contained Author object
10        Public Property Name As String ' author's full name
11     End Class ' AuthorBinding
12
```

Figure 27.28 Nested class AuthorBinding in class Details.

Configuring the Data Sources

The ComboBox's **DisplayMember property** is set to the String "Name" (Fig. 27.29, line 17), which tells the ComboBox to use the Name property of the objects in its DataSource to determine what text to display for each item. The DataSource in this case is the result of the LINQ query in lines 21–27, which creates an AuthorBinding object for each author. The authorComboBox will contain the Name of each author in the query result. Recall from Chapter 23 that object initializers (like lines 23–27) can initialize an object without explicitly calling a constructor.

```vb
13        ' initialize data sources when the Form is loaded
14        Private Sub Details_Load(ByVal sender As System.Object,
15           ByVal e As System.EventArgs) Handles MyBase.Load
16
17           authorComboBox.DisplayMember = "Name" ' AuthorBinding.Name
18
19           ' set the authorComboBox's DataSource to the list of authors
20           authorComboBox.DataSource =
21              From author In database.Authors
22              Order By author.LastName, author.FirstName
23              Select New AuthorBinding With
24              {
25                 .Author = author,
```

Figure 27.29 Configuring the ComboBoxes' and DataGridView's data sources. (Part 1 of 2.)

```
26              .Name = author.FirstName & " " & author.LastName
27          }
28
29      titleComboBox.DisplayMember = "Title" ' display Title.Title
30
31      ' set the titleComboBox's DataSource to the list of titles
32      titleComboBox.DataSource =
33          From title In database.Titles
34          Order By title.Title
35          Select title
36
37      booksDataGridView.DataSource = Nothing ' no data source yet
38   End Sub ' Details_Load
39
```

Figure 27.29 Configuring the ComboBoxes' and DataGridView's data sources.
(Part 2 of 2.)

For the titleComboBox, we specify that each book's Title should be displayed (line 29). The LINQ query in lines 33–35 returns a sorted list of Title
objects and assigns it to the titleComboBox's DataSource.

Initially, we don't want to display any data in the DataGridView. However,
when you set a ComboBox's DataSource, the control's SelectedIndexChanged
event handler is called. To prevent this when the program first loads, we explicitly
set the DataGridView's DataSource property to Nothing (line 37).

The BindingSource of a DataGridView

Simple GUI elements like ComboBoxes can work directly from a data source, such
as the result of a LINQ to SQL query. However, a DataGridView requires a BindingSource as its DataSource. While building the GUI, you created two Binding-
Source objects—one for displaying a list of Authors and one for displaying a list of
Titles. You can change the columns and data displayed in the DataGridView
merely by changing its DataSource between the two BindingSource objects. The
DataGridView automatically determines the column names it needs to display
from its BindingSource and refreshes itself when the BindingSource changes.

Method authorComboBox_SelectedIndexChanged

The authorComboBox_SelectedIndexChanged event handler (Fig. 27.30, 41–57)
performs three distinct operations. First, it retrieves the selected Author (lines 46–
47) from the authorComboBox. The ComboBox's SelectedItem property returns an
Object, so we convert the SelectedItem property's value to the type AuthorB-
inding—recall that the ComboBox's DataSource was set to a collection of
AuthorBinding objects. Then, the event handler accesses the AuthorBinding's
Author property to retrieve the wrapped Author object.

```
40      ' display titles that were co-authored by the selected author
41      Private Sub authorComboBox_SelectedIndexChanged(
42          ByVal sender As System.Object, ByVal e As System.EventArgs) _
43          Handles authorComboBox.SelectedIndexChanged
44
45          ' get the selected Author object from the ComboBox
46          Dim currentAuthor =
47              CType(authorComboBox.SelectedItem, AuthorBinding).Author
48
49          ' set the titleBindingSource's DataSource to the
50          ' list of titles written by the selected author
51          titleBindingSource.DataSource =
52              From book In currentAuthor.AuthorISBNs
53              Select book.Title
```

Figure 27.30 Displaying the books for the selected author.

```
54
55        ' display the titles in the DataGridView
56        booksDataGridView.DataSource = titleBindingSource
57     End Sub ' authorComboBox_SelectedIndexChanged
58
```

Figure 27.30 Displaying the books for the selected author.

Next, the event handler uses LINQ to retrieve the `Title` objects representing books that the `currentAuthor` worked on (lines 52–53). The results of the LINQ query are assigned to the `DataSource` property of `titleBindingSource` (line 51). The event handler sets the `titleBindingSource` because we want to display `Title` objects associated with the `currentAuthor`. Finally, the `DataGridView`'s `DataSource` is assigned `titleBindingSource` to display the books this author wrote (line 56).

Method *titleComboBox_SelectedIndexChanged*

The `titleComboBox_SelectedIndexChanged` event handler (60–75) is nearly identical to `authorComboBox_SelectedIndexChanged`. Line 65 gets the selected `Title` from the `ComboBox`. Lines 69–71 set the `authorsBindingSource`'s DataSource to the list of `Authors` for the current book. Finally, the `DataGridView`'s `DataSource` is assigned `authorBindingSource` to display the authors who wrote this book (line 74).

```
59        ' display the authors of the selected title
60        Private Sub titleComboBox_SelectedIndexChanged(
61           ByVal sender As System.Object, ByVal e As System.EventArgs) _
62           Handles titleComboBox.SelectedIndexChanged
63
64           ' get the selected Title object from the ComboBox
65           Dim currentTitle = CType(titleComboBox.SelectedItem, Title)
66
67           ' set the authorBindingSource's DataSource to the
68           ' list of authors for the selected title
69           authorBindingSource.DataSource =
70              From book In currentTitle.AuthorISBNs
71              Select book.Author
72
73           ' display the authors in the DataGridView
74           booksDataGridView.DataSource = authorBindingSource
75        End Sub ' titleComboBox_SelectedIndexChanged
76     End Class ' Details
```

Figure 27.31 Displaying the authors of the selected book.

SELF-REVIEW

1. In a(n) _____ view, one part of the GUI allows you to select an entry, and another part displays detailed information about that entry.

   a) boss/worker b) master/detail
   c) data binding d) entity-relationship

2. A `ComboBox`'s _____ property indicates which property to display in the `ComboBox` from each object in its `DataSource`.

   a) `DisplayMember` b) `QuerySource`
   c) `SelectProperty` d) `DataContext`

Answers: 1) b. 2) a.

27.8 Address Book Case Study

Our next example (Fig. 27.32) implements a simple AddressBook application that enables users to perform the following tasks on the database AddressBook.mdf (which is included in the directory with this chapter's examples):

■ Insert new contacts

■ Find contacts whose last names begin with the specified letters

■ Update existing contacts

■ Delete contacts

We populated the database with six fictional contacts.

a) Use the BindingNavigator's controls at the top of the window to navigate through the contacts in the database; initially there are six contacts in the database

b) Type a search String in the **Last Name:** TextBox then press **Find** to locate contacts whose last names begin with that String; only two names start with "Br" so the BindingNavigator indicates two matching records

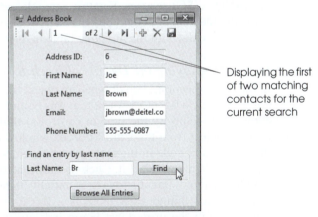

Displaying the first of two matching contacts for the current search

c) Click the **Browse All Entries** Button to clear the search String and to allow browsing of all contacts in the database.

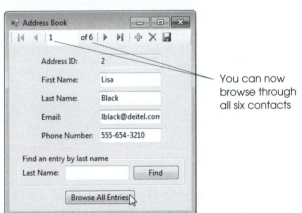

You can now browse through all six contacts

Figure 27.32   Manipulating an address book.

Rather than displaying a database table in a DataGridView, this application presents the details of one contact at a time in several TextBoxes. The Binding-Navigator at the top of the window allows you to control which *row* of the table is displayed at any given time. The BindingNavigator also allows you to add a contact, delete a contact and save changes to a contact. When you run the application, experiment with the BindingNavigator's controls. The CD- or DVD-like buttons of the BindingNavigator allow you to change the currently displayed row. Adding a row clears the TextBoxes and sets the TextBox to the right of **Address ID** to zero. When you save a new entry, the **Address ID** field is automatically changed from zero to a unique number by the database.

Recall from Section 27.4 that to allow changes to the database to *persist* between executions of the application, you can run the program in release mode (*Ctrl + F5*).

Creating the Address Book Application's GUI

We discuss the application's code momentarily. First we show the steps to create this application.

Step 1: Creating the Project

Create a new **Windows Forms Application** named AddressBook. Rename the Form AddressBook and its source file Contacts.vb, then set the Form's **Text** property to Address Book.

Step 2: Creating LINQ to SQL Classes and Data Source

Follow the instructions in Section 27.4 to add a database to the project and generate the LINQ to SQL classes. For this example, add the AddressBook database and name the file AddressBook.dbml. You must also add the Addresses table as a data source, as we did with the Authors table in *Step 1* of Section 27.4.

Step 3: Displaying the Details of Each Row

In the earlier sections, you dragged an object from the **Data Sources** window to the Form to create a DataGridView that was bound to the data in that object. The IDE allows you to specify the type of control(s) that it will create when you drag and drop an object from the **Data Sources** window onto a Form. In **Design** view, click the Addresses node in the **Data Sources** window. Note that this becomes a drop-down list when you select it. Click the down arrow to view the items in the list. The item to the left of DataGridView is initially highlighted in blue, because the default control that's bound to a table is a DataGridView. Select the **Details** option (Fig. 27.33) in the drop-down list to indicate that the IDE should create a set of Label/TextBox pairs for each column-name/column-value pair when you drag and drop Address onto the Form.

Figure 27.33 Specifying that an Address should be displayed as a set of Labels and TextBoxes.

Step 4: Dragging the Address Data-Source Node to the Form

Drag the Address node from the **Data Sources** window to the Form. This automatically creates a BindingNavigator and the Labels and TextBoxes corresponding to the columns of the database table. The fields may be placed out of order, with the

Email at the top. Reorder the components, using **Design** view, so they're in the proper order shown in Fig. 27.32.

Step 5: Making the `AddressID` TextBox ReadOnly
The `AddressID` column of the `Addresses` table is an autoincremented identity column, so users should not be allowed to edit the values in this column. Select the `TextBox` for the `AddressID` and set its `ReadOnly` property to `True` using the **Properties** window.

Step 6: Adding Controls to Allow Users to Specify a Last Name to Locate
While the `BindingNavigator` allows you to browse the address book, it would be more convenient to be able to find a specific entry by last name. To add this functionality to the application, we must create controls to allow the user to enter a last name and provide event handlers to perform the search.

Add a `Label` named `findLabel`, a `TextBox` named `findTextBox`, and a `Button` named `findButton`. Place these controls in a `GroupBox` named `findGroupBox`, then set its `Text` property to **Find an entry by last name**. Set the `Text` property of the `Label` to **Last Name:** and set the `Text` property of the `Button` to **Find**.

Step 7: Allowing the User to Return to Browsing All Rows of the Database
To allow users to return to browsing all the contacts after searching for contacts with a specific last name, add a `Button` named `browseAllButton` below the `findGroupBox`. Set the `Text` property of `browseAllButton` to **Browse All Entries**.

Coding the Address Book Application

Method `RefreshContacts`
As we showed in previous examples, we must connect the `AddressBindingSource` that controls the GUI with the `AddressBookDataContext` that interacts with the database. In this example, we do this in the `RefreshContacts` method (Fig. 27.34, lines 8–17), which is called from several other methods in the application. Method `RefreshContacts` sets the `AddressBindingSource`'s `DataSource` property to the result of a LINQ query on the `Addresses` table. We created a `Private` method in this example, because there are three locations in the program where we need to update the `AddressBindingSource`'s `DataSource` property.

```vb
1   ' Fig. 27.34: Contacts.vb
2   ' Manipulating an address book.
3   Public Class Contacts
4       ' LINQ to SQL data context
5       Private database As New AddressBookDataContext()
6
7       ' fill the AddressBindingSource with all rows, ordered by name
8       Private Sub RefreshContacts()
9           ' use LINQ to create a data source from the database
10          AddressBindingSource.DataSource =
11              From address In database.Addresses
12              Order By address.LastName, address.FirstName
13              Select address
14
15          AddressBindingSource.MoveFirst() ' go to the first result
16          findTextBox.Clear() ' clear the Find TextBox
17      End Sub ' RefreshContacts
18
```

Figure 27.34 Creating the `BooksDataContext` and defining the method RefreshContacts for use in other methods.

Method Contacts_Load

Method Contacts_Load (Fig. 27.35) calls RefreshContacts (line 23) so that the first record is displayed when the application starts. As before, you create the Load event handler by double clicking the Form's title bar.

```
19    ' when the form loads, fill it with data from the database
20    Private Sub Contacts_Load(ByVal sender As System.Object,
21       ByVal e As System.EventArgs) Handles MyBase.Load
22
23       RefreshContacts() ' fill binding with data from database
24    End Sub ' Contacts_Load
25
```

Figure 27.35 Calling RefreshContacts to fill the DataGridView when the application loads.

Method AddressBindingNavigatorSaveItem_Click

Method AddressBindingNavigatorSaveItem_Click (Fig. 27.36) saves the changes to the database when the BindingNavigator's save Button is clicked. We call RefreshContacts after saving to re-sort the data and move back to the first element.

```
1     ' save the changes made to the data
2     Private Sub AddressBindingNavigatorSaveItem_Click(
3        ByVal sender As System.Object, ByVal e As System.EventArgs) _
4        Handles AddressBindingNavigatorSaveItem.Click
5
6        Validate() ' validate input fields
7        AddressBindingSource.EndEdit() ' indicate edits are complete
8        database.SubmitChanges() ' write changes to database file
9
10       RefreshContacts() ' change back to initial unfiltered data on save
11    End Sub ' AddressBindingNavigatorSaveItem_Click
12
```

Figure 27.36 Saving changes to the database when the user clicks the **Save Data** Button.

The AddressBook database is configured to require values for the first name, last name, phone number or e-mail. We have not checked for errors to simplify the code—if any of the fields are empty when you attempt to save, a SqlException exception (namespace System.Data.SqlClient) will be thrown.

Method findButton_Click

Method findButton_Click (Fig. 27.37) uses LINQ to select only people whose last names start with the characters entered in the findTextBox. The query sorts the results by last name then first name (lines 45–48). When you enter a last name and click Find, the BindingNavigator allows the user to browse only the rows containing the matching last names. This is because the data source bound to the Form's controls (the result of the LINQ query) has changed and now contains only a limited number of rows.

```
38       ' load data for the rows with the specified
39       ' last name into the AddressBindingSource
40      Private Sub findButton_Click(ByVal sender As System.Object,
41         ByVal e As System.EventArgs) Handles findButton.Click
42
43         ' use LINQ to find people with the specified last name
44         AddressBindingSource.DataSource =
45            From address In database.Addresses
46            Where address.LastName.StartsWith(findTextBox.Text)
47            Order By address.LastName, address.FirstName
48            Select address
49
50         AddressBindingSource.MoveFirst() ' go to first result
51      End Sub ' findButton_Click
```

Figure 27.37   Finding the contacts whose last names begin with a specified `String`.

Method `browseAllButton_Click`

Method `browseAllButton_Click` (Fig. 27.38) allows users to return to browsing all the rows after searching for specific rows. Double click `browseAllButton` to create a `Click` event handler. Have the event handler call `RefreshContacts` (line 57) to restore the data source to the full list of people and clear the `findTextBox`.

```
53       ' reload AddressBindingSource with all rows
54      Private Sub browseAllButton_Click(ByVal sender As System.Object,
55         ByVal e As System.EventArgs) Handles browseAllButton.Click
56
57         RefreshContacts() ' change back to initial unfiltered data
58      End Sub ' browseAllButton_Click
59   End Class ' Contacts
```

Figure 27.38   Allowing the user to browse all contacts.

SELF-REVIEW   1. The IDE allows you to specify the type of control(s) that it creates when you drag and drop a(n) _____ member onto a `Form`.

    a) foreign-key   b) auto-incremented

    c) data-context   d) data-source

2. The _____ option indicates that the IDE should create a set of `Label`/`TextBox` pairs for each column-name/column-value pair in the data source.

    a) `KeyValue`   b) `NameValue`

    c) `Details`   d) `MasterDetail`

Answers: 1) d.   2) c.

27.9 Tools and Web Resources

Our extensive LINQ Resource Center at `www.deitel.com/LINQ` contains many links to additional information, including blogs by Microsoft LINQ team members, sample chapters, tutorials, videos, downloads, FAQs, forums, webcasts and other resource sites.

A useful tool for learning LINQ is LINQPad (`www.linqpad.net`), which allows you to execute and view the results of any Visual Basic or C# expression, including LINQ queries. It also supports connecting to a SQL Server database and querying it using SQL and LINQ to SQL.

27.10 Wrap-Up

This chapter introduced the relational database model, LINQ to SQL and the IDE's visual programming tools for working with databases. You examined the contents of a simple Books database and learned about the relationships among the tables in the database. You used LINQ and the LINQ to SQL classes generated by the IDE to retrieve data from, add new data to, delete data from and update data in a SQL Server Express database.

We discussed the LINQ to SQL classes automatically generated by the IDE, such as the DataContext class that controls interactions with the database. You learned how to use the IDE's tools to connect to databases and to generate LINQ to SQL classes based on a database's schema. You then used the IDE's drag-and-drop capabilities to automatically generate GUIs for displaying and manipulating database data.

In the next chapter, we demonstrate how to build web applications using Microsoft's ASP.NET technology. We introduce the concept of a three-tier application, which is divided into three pieces that can reside on the same computer or be distributed among separate computers across a network such as the Internet. One of these tiers—the information tier—typically stores data in a database.

SUMMARY

Introduction

- A database is an organized collection of data.

- A database management system (DBMS) provides mechanisms for storing, organizing, retrieving and modifying data.

- SQL Server Express provides most of the features of Microsoft's full (fee-based) SQL Server product, but has some limitations, such as a maximum database size of 4 gigabytes and allowing only one application at a time to interact with a database.

- A SQL Server Express database can be easily migrated to a full version of SQL Server.

- LINQ to SQL allows you to manipulate relational data stored in a SQL Server or SQL Server Express database.

Section 27.1 Relational Databases

- A relational database organizes data simply in tables.

- Tables are composed of rows and columns (also called fields) in which values are stored.

- A column (or group of columns) of each row is the table's primary key—a column (or group of columns) requiring a unique value that cannot be duplicated in other rows. This guarantees that a primary key value can be used to uniquely identify a row.

- A primary key composed of two or more columns is known as a composite key.

- Each column represents a different data attribute.

- Rows are unique (by primary key) within a table, but some column values may be duplicated between rows.

Section 27.2 A Books Database

- A database's tables, their fields and the relationships between them are collectively known as a database schema.

- LINQ to SQL uses a database's schema to define classes that enable you to interact with the database.

- A foreign key is a column in one table that matches the primary-key column in another table.

- Foreign keys, which are specified when a database table is created, link the data in multiple tables.

- Every foreign-key value must appear as another table's primary-key value so the DBMS can ensure that the foreign-key value is valid.

- Foreign keys also allow related data in multiple tables to be selected from those tables—this is known as joining the data.

- There's a one-to-many relationship between a primary key and a corresponding foreign key—a foreign key can appear many times in its own table but only once (as the primary key) in another table.

- An entity-relationship (ER) diagram shows the tables in a database and their relationships.

- Every row must have a value in the primary-key column, and the value of the key must be unique in the table.

Section 27.3 LINQ to SQL

- LINQ to SQL enables you to access data in SQL Server databases using LINQ syntax.

- You interact with LINQ to SQL via classes that are automatically generated by the IDE's LINQ to SQL Designer based on the database schema.

- LINQ to SQL requires every table to have a primary key to support modifying the data in the tables.

- The IDE creates a class for each table. Objects of these classes represent the collections of rows in the corresponding tables.

- The IDE also creates a class for a row of each table with a property for each column in the table. Objects of these classes (row objects) hold the data from individual rows in the database's tables.

- In the class for a row object, an additional property is created for each foreign key. This property returns the row object of the corresponding primary key in another table.

- In the class for a row object, an additional property is created for the collection of row objects with foreign-keys that reference the row object's primary key.

- Once generated, the LINQ to SQL classes have full *IntelliSense* support in the IDE.

Section 27.4 Querying a Database with LINQ

- The IDE provides visual programming tools and wizards that simplify accessing data in your projects. These tools establish database connections and create the objects necessary to view and manipulate the data through the GUI—a technique known as data binding.

- A DataGridView (namespace System.Windows.Forms) displays data from a data source in tabular format.

- A BindingNavigator is a collection of controls that allow you to navigate through the records displayed in a GUI. The BindingNavigator controls also allow you to add records, delete records and save your changes to the database.

Creating LINQ to SQL Classes

- To interact with a database, you must create a connection to the database.

- In Visual Basic 2010 Express, use the **Database Explorer** window to connect to the database. In full versions of Visual Studio 2010, use the **Server Explorer** window.

- After connecting to the database, you can generate the LINQ to SQL classes by adding a new **LINQ to SQL Classes** item to your project, then dragging the tables you wish to use from the **Database Explorer** onto the **Object Relational Designer**. When you save the .dbml file, the IDE generates the LINQ to SQL classes.

Data Bindings Between Controls and the LINQ to SQL Classes

- To use the LINQ to SQL classes for data binding, you must first add them as a data source.

- Select **Data > Add New Data Source...** to display the **Data Source Configuration Wizard**. Use an **Object** data source. Select the LINQ to SQL object that you wish to use as a data source. You can now drag that data source from the **Data Sources** window onto the Form to create a GUI control that can display the table's data.

- By default, the IDE creates a DataGridView with the correct column names and a BindingNavigator that contains Buttons for moving between entries, adding entries, deleting entries and saving changes to the database.

- The IDE also generates a BindingSource, which handles the transfer of data between the data source and the data-bound controls on the Form.

- The result of a LINQ query on the `DataContext` can be assigned to the `BindingSource`'s `DataSource` property. The `BindingSource` uses the `DataSource` to extract data from the database and to populate the `DataGridView`.

- To save the user's changes to the data in the `DataGridView`, enable the `BindingNavigator`'s **Save Data Button** (🖫). Then, double click the icon to create its `Click` event handler. In the event handler, you must validate the data, call `EndEdit` on the `BindingSource` to save pending changes in the `DataContext`, and call `SubmitChanges` on the `DataContext` to store the changes in the database. For efficiency, LINQ to SQL saves only data that has changed.

Section 27.5 Dynamically Binding Query Results

- The IDE displays smart tag menus for many GUI controls to provide you with quick access to common properties you might set for a control, so you can set these properties directly in **Design** view. You can open a control's smart tag menu by clicking the small arrowhead (▶) that appears in the control's upper-right corner in **Design** view.

- The `MoveFirst` method of the `BindingSource` moves to the first row of the result.

Section 27.6 Retrieving data with Multiple Tables with LINQ

- To join data from multiple tables you use the properties that LINQ to SQL creates based on foreign-key relationships between the database's tables. These properties enable you to easily access related rows in other tables.

- The `Let` query operator allows you to declare a new variable in a query—usually to create a shorter name for an expression. The variable can be accessed in later clauses just like a range variable.

- Most queries return result with data arranged in relational-style rows and columns. With LINQ to SQL you can create queries that return hierarchical results in which each item in the result contains a collection of other items.

Section 27.7 Creating a Master/Detail View Application

- In a master/detail view, one part of the GUI (the master) allows you to select an entry, and another part (the details) displays detailed information about that entry.

- Class definitions may be nested inside other classes.

- A `ComboBox`'s `DisplayMember` property indicates which property to display in the `ComboBox` from each object in its `DataSource`.

- You can change the columns and data displayed in a `DataGridView` by changing its `DataSource`. The `DataGridView` automatically determines the column names it needs to display from the `BindingSource`.

Section 27.8 Address Book Case Study

- The IDE allows you to specify the type of control(s) that it creates when you drag and drop a data-source member onto a `Form`. The **Details** option indicates that the IDE should create a set of `Label`/`TextBox` pairs for each column-name/column-value pair in the data source.

TERMINOLOGY

autoincremented database column—An identity column.

BindingNavigator class—Contains `Button`s for moving between entries, adding entries, deleting entries and saving changes to the database.

BindingSource class—Handles the transfer of data between the data source and the data-bound controls on the `Form`.

column of a database table—Fields in which values are stored.

composite key—A primary key composed of two or more columns.

data binding—Techniques for establishing database connections and creating the objects necessary to view and manipulate the data through Windows Forms GUI controls.

database—An organized collection of data.

database management system (DBMS)—Provides mechanisms for storing, organizing, retrieving and modifying data.

database schema—A database's tables, their fields and the relationships among them.

DataContext class—controls the flow of data between the program and the database.

DataGridView class—A control from namespace System.Windows.Forms that can display data from a data source in tabular format.

DataSource property of class BindingSource—Extract data from the database and to populate the DataGridView.

DisplayMember property of the ComboBox control—Tells the ComboBox to use the Name property of the objects in its DataSource to determine what text to display for each item.

EndEdit method of class BindingSource—Forces it to save any pending changes in the BooksDataContext.

entity-relationship (ER) diagram—Shows the tables in the database and the relationships among them.

field in a database table—Columns in which values are stored.

foreign key—A column in this table that matches the primary-key column in another table

identity column in a database table—Also known as an autoincremented column.

IQueryable interface—Inherits from the IEnumerable interface.

joining database tables—Foreign keys allow related data in multiple tables to be selected from those tables.

Let query operator (LINQ)—Allows you to declare a new variable in a LINQ query—usually to create a shorter name for an expression.

LINQ to SQL—Allows you to manipulate data stored in a SQL Server or SQL Server Express relational database.

LINQ to SQL Designer—Used to interact with the database via classes that are automatically generated from the database schema.

many-to-many relationship—A relationship between database tables where one record in a given table can be associated with many records in another table and vice versa.

master/detail view—One part of the GUI (the master) allows you to select an entry, and another part (the details) displays detailed information about that entry.

MoveFirst method of class BindingSource—Moves to the first row of the result each time a query executes.

nested class—Class definitions may be nested inside other classes when they're intended to be used only by their enclosing classes—that is, they're not meant for use by other programs.

primary key—A column (or group of columns) in a database table requiring a unique value that cannot be duplicated in other rows the table.

relational database—Organizes data simply in tables.

row object—Stores the data from individual rows of the table.

smart tag menu—Provides you with quick access to common properties you might set for a control, so you can set these properties directly in **Design** view, rather than in the **Properties** window.

SubmitChanges method of a DataContext—Stores the changes in the database.

table in a database—Composed of rows (also called records) and columns (also called fields) in which values are stored.

MULTIPLE-CHOICE QUESTIONS

27.1 A _____ is a primary key composed of two or more columns..

    a) multicolumn   b) many-to-many key

    c) DataGridView   d) composite key

27.2 The _____ method of a DataContext stores the changes in the database.

    a) CommitChanges   b) StoreChanges

    c) SubmitChanges   d) JoinChanges

27.3 A database _____ describes the database's tables, their fields and the relationships among them.

    a) binding navigator   b) schema

    c) master/detail view   d) entity/detail view

27.4 The _____ method of class `BindingSource` forces any pending changes to be saved in the `DataContext`.

a) `SaveChanges`   b) `BindChanges`

c) `CommitChanges`   d) `EndEdit`

27.5 A row of a database table is also called a _____ .

a) record   b) field

c) collection   d) relation

27.6 An identity column in a database table is also known as a(n) _____ column.

a) identification   b) autoincremented

c) field   d) integrity

27.7 A table in a database is composed of rows (also called records) and columns (also called _____) in which values are stored.

a) stacks   b) groups

c) fields   d) primary key

27.8 The _____ class controls the flow of data between the program and the database.

a) `BindingNavigator`   b) `DataContext`

c) `DataGripView`   d) `BindingSource`

27.9 Class definitions may be _____ inside other classes when they're intended to be used only by their enclosing classes—that is, they're not meant for use by other programs. _____ .

a) restricted   b) locked

c) contained   d) nested

27.10 The _____ is a control from namespace `System.Windows.Forms` that can display data from a data source in tabular format.

a) `DataGridView` class   b) `DataSource`

c) `DataContext`   d) `DataDisplay`

SELF-REVIEW EXERCISES

27.11 Fill in the blanks in each of the following statements:

a) A table in a relational database consists of _____ and _____ in which values are stored.

b) The _____ uniquely identifies each row in a relational database table.

c) A relational database can be manipulated in LINQ to SQL via a(n) _____ object, which contains properties for accessing each table in the database.

d) The _____ control (presented in this chapter) displays data in rows and columns that correspond to the rows and columns of a data source.

e) Merging data from multiple relational database tables is called _____ the data.

f) A(n) _____ is a column (or group of columns) in a relational database table that matches the primary-key column (or group of columns) in another table.

g) A(n) _____ object serves as an intermediary between a data source and its corresponding data-bound GUI control.

h) The _____ property of a control specifies where it gets the data it displays.

i) The _____ clause declares a new temporary variable within a LINQ query.

27.12 State whether each of the following is *true* or *false*. If *false*, explain why.

a) Providing the same value for a foreign key in multiple rows causes the DBMS to report an error.

b) Providing a foreign-key value that does not appear as a primary-key value in another table is an error.

c) The result of a query can be sorted in ascending or descending order.

d) A `BindingNavigator` object can extract data from a database.

e) LINQ to SQL automatically saves changes made back to the database.

ANSWERS TO SELF-REVIEW EXERCISES

27.1 a) rows, columns. b) primary key. c) `DataContext`. d) `DataGridView`. e) joining. f) foreign key. g) `BindingSource`. h) `DataSource`. i) `Let`.

27.2 a) False. Multiple rows can have the same value for a foreign key. Providing the same value for the primary key in multiple rows causes the DBMS to report an error, because duplicate primary keys would prevent each row from being identified uniquely. b) True. c) True. d) False. A `BindingNavigator` allows users to browse and manipulate data displayed by another GUI control. A `DataContext` can extract data from a database. e) False. You must call the `SubmitChanges` method of the `DataContext` to save the changes made back to the database.

EXERCISES

27.3 *(Display Authors Table Application Modification)* Modify the **DisplayTable** application in Section 27.4 to contain a `TextBox` and a `Button` that allow the user to search for specific authors by last name. Include a `Label` to identify the `TextBox`. Using the techniques presented in Section 27.4, create a LINQ query that changes the `DataSource` property of `AuthorBindingSource` to contain only the specified authors.

27.4 *(Display Query Results Application Modification)* Modify the **Display Query Results** application in Section 27.5 to contain a `TextBox` and a `Button` that allow the user to perform a search of the book titles in the `Titles` table of the `Books` database. Use a `Label` to identify the `TextBox`. When the user clicks the `Button`, the application should execute and display the result of a query that selects all the rows in which the search term entered by the user in the `TextBox` appears anywhere in the `Title` column. For example, if the user enters the search term "Visual," the `DataGridView` should display the rows for *Simply Visual Basic 2008*, *Visual Basic 2008 How to Program*, *Visual C# 2008 How to Program* and *Visual C++ 2008 How to Program*. If the user enters "Simply," the `DataGridView` should display only the row for *Simply Visual Basic 2008*. [*Hint:* Use the `Contains` method of the `String` class.]

27.5 *(Baseball Database Application)* Build an application that executes a query against the `Players` table of the `Baseball` database included in the `Databases` folder with this chapter's examples. Display the table in a `DataGridView`, and add a `TextBox` and `Button` to allow the user to search for a specific player by last name. Use a `Label` to identify the Text-Box. Clicking the `Button` should execute the appropriate query.

27.6 *(Baseball Database Application Modification)* Modify Exercise 27.5 to allow the user to locate players with batting averages in a specific range. Add a `minimumTextBox` for the minimum batting average (`0.000` by default) and a `maximumTextBox` for the maximum batting average (`1.000` by default). Use a `Label` to identify each `TextBox`. Add a `Button` for executing a query that selects rows from the `Players` table in which the `BattingAverage` column is greater than or equal to the specified minimum value and less than or equal to the specified maximum value.

27.7 *(Project: AdventureWorks Sample Database)* In this exercise, use Microsoft's sample `AdventureWorks` database. There are several versions available, depending on what version of SQL Server you're using and your operating system. We used the `AdventureWorks LT` version of the database—a smaller version with fewer tables and less data than the full version. The files for SQL Server 2008 can be downloaded from

```
msftdbprodsamples.codeplex.com/Release/ProjectReleases.aspx?
   ReleaseId=24854
```

The installer allows you to select which version of the database to install.

Use the `AdventureWorks` database in an application that runs multiple queries on the database and displays the results. First, it should list customers and their addresses. As this is a large list, limit the number of results to ten. [*Hint:* Use LINQ's `Take` clause at the end of the query to return a limited number of results. The `Take` clause consists of the `Take` operator, then an `Integer` specifying how many rows to take.] Second, if a category has subcategories, the output should show the category with its subcategories indented below it. The queries described here require the `AdventureWorks` tables `Address`, `Customer`, `CustomerAddress` and `ProductCategory`.

27.8 *(Project: AdventureWorks Master/Detail view)* Use the Microsoft `AdventureWorks` database from Exercise 27.7 to create a master/detail view. One master list should be customers, and the other should be products—these should show the details of products the customers purchased, and customers who purchased those products, respectively. Note that there are many customers in the database who did not order any products, and many products that no one ordered. Restrict the drop-down lists so that only customers that have submitted at least one order and products that have been included in at least one order are displayed. The queries in this exercise require the `Customer`, `Product`, `SalesOrderHeader` and `SalesOrderDetail` tables.

Guestbook App

Web App Development with ASP.NET

In this chapter, we introduce **web-app development** with Microsoft's **ASP.NET** technology. Web-based apps create web content for web-browser clients.

We present several examples that demonstrate web-app development using **Web Forms, web controls** (also called **ASP.NET server controls**) and Visual Basic programming. Web Form files have the file-name extension **.aspx** and contain the web page's GUI. You customize Web Forms by adding web controls including labels, textboxes, images, buttons and other GUI components. The Web Form file represents the web page that's sent to the client browser. We often refer to Web Form files as **ASPX files**.

An ASPX file created in Visual Studio has a corresponding class written in a .NET language—we use Visual Basic in this book. This class contains event handlers, initialization code, utility methods and other supporting code. The file that contains this class is called the **code-behind file** and provides the ASPX file's programmatic implementation.

To develop the code and GUIs in this chapter, we used Microsoft's **Visual Web Developer 2010 Express**—a free IDE designed for developing ASP.NET web apps. The full version of Visual Studio 2010 includes the functionality of Visual Web Developer, so the instructions we present for Visual Web Developer also apply to Visual Studio 2010. The database example (Section 28.7) also requires SQL Server 2008 Express. See the *Before You Begin* section of the book for additional information on this software.

In the next chapter, we present several additional web-app development topics, including:

- Master pages to maintain a uniform look-and-feel across the Web Forms in a web app

- Creating password-protected websites with registration and login capabilities

- Using the **Web Site Administration Tool** to specify which parts of a website are password protected

- Using ASP.NET AJAX to quickly and easily improve the user experience for your web apps, giving them responsiveness comparable to that of desktop apps.

28.1 Web Basics

In this section, we discuss what occurs when a user requests a web page in a browser. In its simplest form, a *web page* is nothing more than an *HTML (Hyper-Text Markup Language) document* (with the extension `.html` or `.htm`) that describes to a web browser the document's content and how to format it.

HTML documents normally contain *hyperlinks* that link to different pages or to other parts of the same page. When the user clicks a hyperlink, a **web server** locates the requested web page and sends it to the user's web browser. Similarly, the user can type the *address of a web page* into the browser's *address field* and press *Enter* to view the specified page.

Web development tools like Visual Web Developer typically use a "stricter" version of HTML called *XHTML (Extensible HyperText Markup Language)*. ASP.NET produces web pages as XHTML documents.

URIs and URLs

URIs (Uniform Resource Identifiers) identify resources on the Internet. URIs that start with `http://` are called *URLs (Uniform Resource Locators)*. Common URLs refer to files, directories or server-side code that performs tasks such as database lookups, Internet searches and business app processing. If you know the URL of a publicly available resource anywhere on the web, you can enter that URL into a web browser's address field and the browser can access that resource.

Parts of a URL

A URL contains information that directs a browser to the resource that the user wishes to access. Web servers make such resources available to web clients. Popular web servers include Microsoft's Internet Information Services (IIS) and Apache's HTTP Server.

Let's examine the components of the URL

```
http://www.deitel.com/books/downloads.html
```

The `http://` indicates that the HyperText Transfer Protocol (HTTP) should be used to obtain the resource. HTTP is the web protocol that enables clients and servers to communicate. Next in the URL is the server's fully qualified **hostname** (`www.deitel.com`)—the name of the web server computer on which the resource resides. This computer is referred to as the **host**, because it houses and maintains resources. The hostname `www.deitel.com` is translated into an **IP (Internet Protocol) address**—a numerical value that uniquely identifies the server on the Internet. A **Domain Name System (DNS) server** maintains a database of hostnames and their corresponding IP addresses, and performs the translations automatically.

The remainder of the URL (`/books/downloads.html`) specifies the resource's location (`/books`) and name (`downloads.html`) on the web server. The location could represent an actual directory on the web server's file system. For *security* reasons, however, the location is typically a *virtual directory*. The web server translates the virtual directory into a real location on the server, thus hiding the resource's true location.

Making a Request and Receiving a Response

When given a URL, a web browser uses HTTP to retrieve and display the web page found at that address. Figure 28.1 shows a web browser sending a request to a web server. Figure 28.2 shows the web server responding to that request.

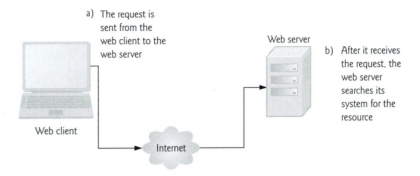

Figure 28.1   Client requesting a resource from a web server.

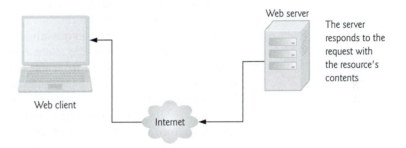

Figure 28.2   Client receiving a response from the web server.

1. _____ identify documents on the Internet. The identifiers that start with http:// are called URLs.

    a) IP addresses   b) hostnames

    c) headers   d) URIs

2. A hostname is translated into a unique IP address that identifies the server. This translation is performed by a _____.

    a) host   b) HTTP server

    c) DNS server   d) validator

Answers: 1) d. 2) c.

28.2 Multitier App Architecture

Web-based apps are **multitier apps** (sometimes referred to as *n*-**tier apps**). Multitier apps divide functionality into separate **tiers** (that is, logical groupings of functionality). Although tiers can be located on the *same* computer, the tiers of web-based apps commonly reside on *separate* computers for security and scalability. Figure 28.3 presents the basic architecture of a three-tier web-based app.

Information Tier

The **information tier** (also called the **bottom tier**) maintains the app's data. This tier typically stores data in a relational database management system. For example, a retail store might have a database for storing product information, such as descriptions, prices and quantities in stock. The same database also might contain customer information, such as user names, billing addresses and credit card numbers. This tier can contain multiple databases, which together comprise the data needed for an app.

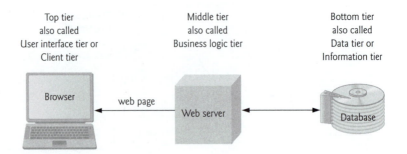

Top tier	Middle tier	Bottom tier
also called	also called	also called
User interface tier or	Business logic tier	Data tier or
Client tier		Information tier

Figure 28.3 Three-tier architecture.

Business Logic

The **middle tier** implements **business logic**, **controller logic** and **presentation logic** to control interactions between the app's clients and its data. The middle tier acts as an intermediary between data in the information tier and the app's clients. The middle-tier controller logic processes client requests (such as requests to view a product catalog) and retrieves data from the database. The middle-tier presentation logic then processes data from the information tier and presents the content to the client. Web apps typically present data to clients as web pages.

Business logic in the middle tier enforces *business rules* and ensures that data is reliable before the server app updates the database or presents the data to users. Business rules dictate how clients can and cannot access app data, and how apps process data. For example, a business rule in the middle tier of a retail store's web-based app might ensure that all product quantities remain positive. A client request to set a negative quantity in the bottom tier's product information database would be rejected by the middle tier's business logic.

Client Tier

The **client tier**, or **top tier**, is the app's user interface, which gathers input and displays output. Users interact directly with the app through the user interface (typically viewed in a web browser), keyboard and mouse. In response to user actions (for example, clicking a hyperlink), the client tier interacts with the middle tier to make requests and to retrieve data from the information tier. The client tier then displays to the user the data retrieved from the middle tier. The client tier never directly interacts with the information tier.

SELF-REVIEW

1. The client tier, or _____ tier, is the app's user interface, which gathers input and displays output.

    a) top   b) bottom

    c) session   d) middle

2. Business logic in the _____ tier enforces business rules and ensures that data is reliable before the server app updates the database or presents the data to users.

    a) top   b) bottom

    c) session   d) middle

Answers: 1) a. 2) d.

28.3 Your First Web App

Our first example displays the web server's time of day in a browser window (Fig. 28.4). When this app executes—that is, a web browser requests the app's web page—the web server executes the app's code, which gets the current time and displays it in a Label. The web server then returns the result to the web browser that made the request, and the web browser renders the web page containing the time. We executed this app in both the Internet Explorer and Firefox web browsers to show you that the web page renders identically in each.

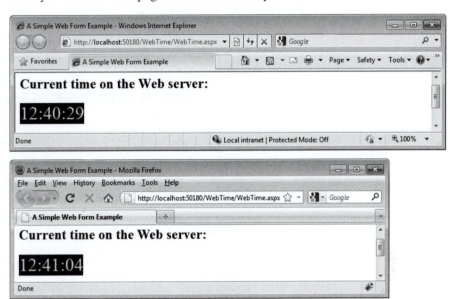

Figure 28.4   WebTime web app running in both Internet Explorer and Firefox.

Testing the App in Your Default Web Browser

To test this app in your default web browser, perform the following steps:

1. Open Visual Web Developer.

2. Select **Open Web Site...** from the **File** menu.

3. In the **Open Web Site** dialog (Fig. 28.5), ensure that **File System** is selected, then navigate to this chapter's examples, select the WebTime folder and click the **Open** Button.

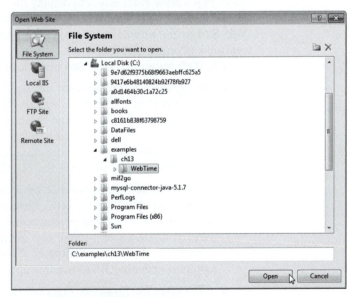

Figure 28.5   **Open Web Site** dialog.

4. Select WebTime.aspx in the **Solution Explorer**, then type *Ctrl + F5* to execute the web app.

Testing the App in a Selected Web Browser

If you wish to execute the app in another web browser, you can copy the web page's address from your default browser's address field and paste it into another browser's address field, or you can perform the following steps:

1. In the **Solution Explorer**, right click `WebTime.aspx` and select **Browse With...** to display the **Browse With** dialog (Fig. 28.6).

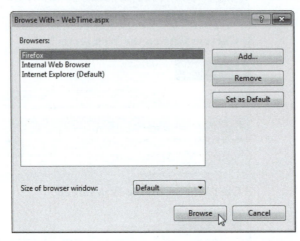

Figure 28.6 Selecting another web browser to execute the web app.

2. From the **Browsers** list, select the browser in which you'd like to test the web app and click the **Browse** `Button`.

If the browser you wish to use is not listed, you can use the **Browse With** dialog to add items to or remove items from the list of web browsers.

Building the `WebTime` App

Now that you've tested the app, let's create it in Visual Web Developer.

Step 1: Creating the Web Site Project

Select **File > New Web Site...** to display the **New Web Site** dialog (Fig. 28.7). In the left column of this dialog, ensure that **Visual Basic** is selected, then select **Empty Web Site** in the middle column. At the bottom of the dialog you can specify the location and name of the web app.

The **Web location:** ComboBox provides the following options:

- **File System:** Creates a new website for testing on your local computer. Such websites execute in Visual Web Developer's built-in ASP.NET Development Server and can be accessed only by web browsers running on the same computer. You can later "publish" your website to a production web server for access via a local network or the Internet. Each example in this chapter uses the **File System** option, so select it now.

- **HTTP:** Creates a new website on an IIS web server and uses HTTP to allow you to put your website's files on the server. IIS is Microsoft's software that's used to run production websites. If you own a website and have your own web server, you might use this to build a new website directly on that server computer. You must be an Administrator on the computer running IIS to use this option.

- **FTP:** Uses File Transfer Protocol (FTP) to allow you to put your website's files on the server. The server administrator must first create the website on the server for you. FTP is commonly used by so-called "hosting providers" to allow website owners to share a server computer that runs many websites.

Figure 28.7   Creating an **ASP.NET Web Site** in Visual Web Developer.

Change the name of the web app from WebSite1 to WebTime, then click the **OK Button** to create the website.

Step 2: Adding a Web Form to the Website and Examining the Solution Explorer

A **Web Form** represents one page in a web app—we'll often use the terms "page" and "Web Form" interchangeably. A Web Form contains a web app's GUI. To create the WebTime.aspx Web Form:

1. Right click the project name in the **Solution Explorer** and select **Add New Item...** to display the **Add New Item** dialog (Fig. 28.8).

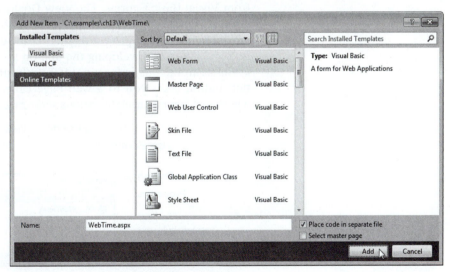

Figure 28.8   Adding a new **Web Form** to the website with the **Add New Item** dialog.

2. In the left column, ensure that **Visual Basic** is selected, then select **Web Form** in the middle column.

3. In the **Name:** TextBox, change the file name to WebTime.aspx, then click the **Add** Button.

After you add the Web Form, the IDE opens it in **Source** view by default (Fig. 28.9). This view displays the markup for the Web Form. As you become more familiar with ASP.NET and building websites in general, you might use **Source** view to perform high precision adjustments to your design or to program in the JavaScript language that executes in web browsers. For the purposes of this chapter, we'll keep things simple by working exclusively in **Design** mode. To switch to **Design** mode, you can click the **Design** Button at the bottom of the code editor window.

Source mode shows only the Web Form's markup

Split mode allows you to view the Web Form's markup and design at the same time

Design mode allows you to build a Web Form using similar techniques to building a Windows Form

```
WebTime.aspx ×
Client Objects & Events          (No Events)
1    <%@ Page Language="VB" AutoEventWireup="false"
2
3    <!DOCTYPE html PUBLIC "-//W3C//DTD XHTML 1.0
4
5    <html xmlns="http://www.w3.org/1999/xhtml">
6    <head runat="server">
7        <title></title>
8    </head>
9    <body>
10       <form id="form1" runat="server">
11       <div>
12
13       </div>
14       </form>
15   </body>
16   </html>
100 %
Design  |  Split  |  Source     <form#form1>  <div>
```

Figure 28.9 Web Form in **Source** view.

The Solution Explorer

The **Solution Explorer** (Fig. 28.10) shows the contents of the website. We expanded the node for WebTime.aspx to show you its code-behind file WebTime.aspx.vb. Visual Web Developer's **Solution Explorer** contains several buttons that differ from Visual Basic Express. The **View Designer** button allows you to open the Web Form in **Design** mode. The **Copy Web Site** button opens a dialog that allows you to move the files in this project to another location, such as a remote web server. This is useful if you're developing the app on your local computer but want to make it available to the public from a different location. Finally, the **ASP.NET Configuration** button takes you to a web page called the **Web Site Administration Tool**, where you can manipulate various settings and security options for your app.

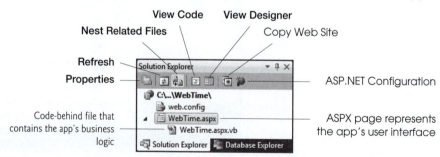

View Code · View Designer
Nest Related Files · Copy Web Site
Refresh · Properties · ASP.NET Configuration
Code-behind file that contains the app's business logic · ASPX page represents the app's user interface

```
Solution Explorer
C:\...\WebTime\
    web.config
    WebTime.aspx
        WebTime.aspx.vb
Solution Explorer    Database Explorer
```

Figure 28.10 **Solution Explorer** window for an **Empty Web Site** project.

If the ASPX file is not open in the IDE, you can open it in **Design** mode three ways:

■ Double click it in the **Solution Explorer**

- Select it in the **Solution Explorer** and click the **View Designer** (⊞) `Button`
- Right click it in the **Solution Explorer** and select **View Designer**
- To open the code-behind file in the code editor, you can
- Double click it in the **Solution Explorer**
- Select the ASPX file in the **Solution Explorer**, then click the **View Code** (⊟) `Button`
- Right click the code-behind file in the **Solution Explorer** and select **Open**

The Toolbox

Figure 28.11 shows the **Toolbox** displayed in the IDE when the project loads. Part (a) displays the beginning of the **Standard** list of web controls, and part (b) displays the remaining web controls and the list of other control groups. We discuss specific controls listed in Fig. 28.11 as they're used throughout the chapter. Many of the controls have similar or identical names to Windows `Forms` controls presented earlier in the book.

a)   b)

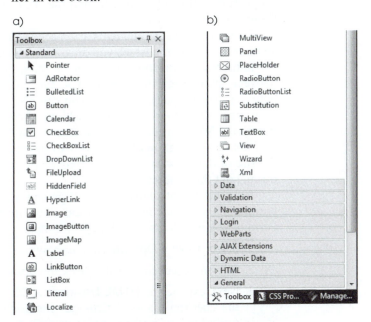

Figure 28.11   **Toolbox** in Visual Web Developer.

The Web Forms Designer

Figure 28.12 shows the initial Web Form in **Design** mode. You can drag and drop controls from the **Toolbox** onto the Web Form. You can also type at the current cursor location to add so-called static text to the web page. In response to such actions, the IDE generates the appropriate markup in the ASPX file.

Cursor appears here by default ——

Cursor's current location in the document

Figure 28.12   **Design** mode of the Web Forms Designer.

Step 3: Changing the Title of the Page

Before designing the Web Form's content, you'll change its title to A Simple Web Form Example. This title will be displayed in the web browser's title bar (see Fig. 28.4). It's typically also used by search engines like Google and Bing when they index real websites for searching. Every page should have a title. To change the title:

1. Ensure that the ASPX file is open in **Design** view.

2. View the Web Form's properties by selecting DOCUMENT, which represents the Web Form, from the drop-down list in the **Properties** window.

3. Modify the Title property in the **Properties** window by setting it to A Simple Web Form Example.

Designing a Page

Designing a Web Form is similar to designing a Windows Form. To add controls to the page, drag-and-drop them from the **Toolbox** onto the Web Form in **Design** view. The Web Form and each control are objects that have properties, methods and events. You can set these properties visually using the **Properties** window or programmatically in the code-behind file. You can also type text directly on a Web Form at the cursor location.

Controls and other elements are placed sequentially on a Web Form one after another in the order in which you drag-and-drop them onto the Web Form. The cursor indicates the insertion point in the page. If you want to position a control between existing text or controls, you can drop the control at a specific position between existing page elements. You can also rearrange controls with drag-and-drop actions in Design view. The positions of controls and other elements are relative to the Web Form's upper-left corner. This type of layout is known as *relative positioning* and it allows the browser to move elements and resize them based on the size of the browser window. Relative positioning is the default, and we'll use it throughout this chapter.

For precise control over the location and size of elements, you can use *absolute positioning* in which controls are located *exactly* where you drop them on the Web Form. If you wish to use absolute positioning:

1. Select **Tools > Options...**, to display the **Options** dialog.

2. If it isn't checked already, check the **Show all settings** checkbox.

3. Next, expand the **HTML Designer > CSS Styling** node and ensure that the checkbox labeled **Change positioning to absolute for controls added using Toolbox, paste or drag and drop** is selected.

Step 4: Adding Text and a Label

You'll now add some text and a Label to the Web Form. Perform the following steps to add the text:

1. Ensure that the Web Form is open in **Design** mode.

2. Type the following text at the current cursor location:

```
Current time on the Web server:
```

3. Select the text you just typed, then select **Heading 2** from the **Block Format** ComboBox (Fig. 28.13) to format this text as a heading that will appear in a larger bold font. In more complex pages, headings help you specify the relative importance of parts of that content—like sections in a book chapter.

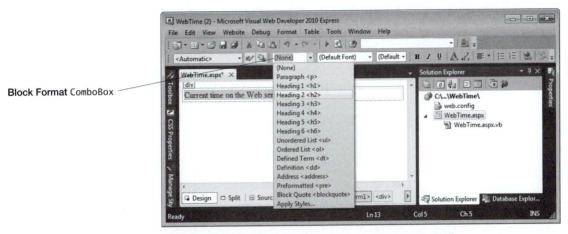

Block Format ComboBox

Figure 28.13 Changing the text to **Heading 2** heading.

4. Click to the right of the text you just typed and press the *Enter* key to start a new paragraph in the page. The Web Form should now appear as in Fig. 28.14.

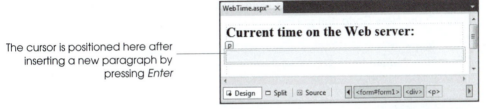

The cursor is positioned here after inserting a new paragraph by pressing *Enter*

Figure 28.14 WebTime.aspx after inserting text and a new paragraph.

5. Next, drag a Label control from the **Toolbox** into the new paragraph or double click the Label control in the **Toolbox** to insert the Label at the current cursor position.

6. Using the **Properties** window, set the Label's (ID) property to timeLabel. This specifies the variable name that will be used to programmatically change the Label's Text.

7. Because, the Label's Text will be set programmatically, delete the current value of the Label's Text property. When a Label does *not* contain text, its name is displayed in square brackets in **Design** view (Fig. 28.15) as a placeholder for design and layout purposes. This text is not displayed at execution time.

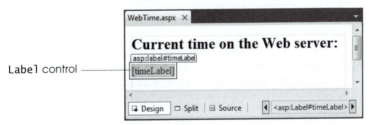

Label control

Figure 28.15 WebTime.aspx after adding a Label.

Step 5: Formatting the Label

Formatting in a web page is performed with CSS (Cascading Style Sheets). The details of CSS are beyond the scope of this book. However, it's easy to use CSS to format text and elements in a Web Form via the tools built into Visual Web Developer. In this example, we'd like to change the Label's background color to black, its foreground color yellow and make its text size larger. To format the Label, perform the following steps:

1. Click the Label in **Design** view to ensure that it's selected.

2. Select **View > Other Windows > CSS Properties** to display the **CSS Properties** window at the left side of the IDE (Fig. 28.16).

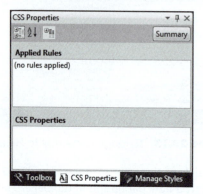

Figure 28.16   **CSS Properties** window.

3. Right click in the **Applied Rules** box and select **New Style...** to display the **New Style** dialog (Fig. 28.17).

New style's name ─────

Font category allows you to style an element's font

Background category allows you to specify an element's background color or background image

Preview of what the style will look like ─────

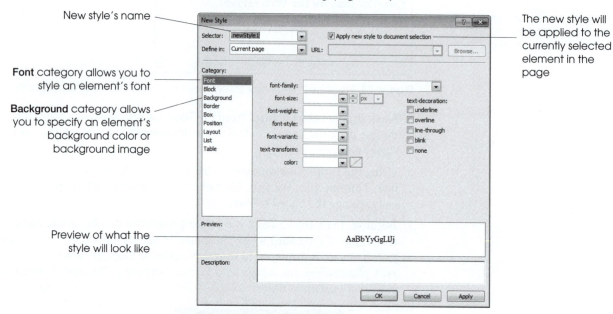

The new style will be applied to the currently selected element in the page

Figure 28.17   **New Style** dialog.

4. Type the new style's name—.timeStyle—in the **Selector:** ComboBox. Styles that apply to specific elements must be named with a dot (.) preceding the name. Such a style is called a CSS class.

5. Each item you can set in the **New Style** dialog is known as a CSS attribute. To change timeLabel's foreground color, select the **Font** category from the **Category** list, then select the yellow color swatch for the **color** attribute.

6. Next, change the **font-size** attribute to xx-large.

7. To change timeLabel's background color, select the **Background** category, then select the black color swatch for the **background-color** attribute.

The **New Style** dialog should now appear as shown in Fig. 28.18. Click the **OK** Button to apply the style to the `timeLabel` so that it appears as shown in Fig. 28.19. Also, notice that the `Label`'s `CssClass` property is now set to `timeStyle` in the **Properties** window.

Bold category names indicate the categories in which CSS attribute values have been changed

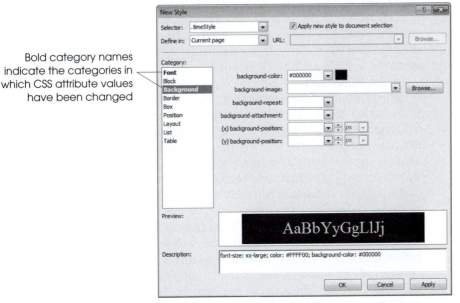

Figure 28.18   **New Style** dialog after changing the Label's font size, foreground color and background color.

Figure 28.19   **Design** view after changing the Label's style.

Step 6: Adding Page Logic

Now that you've designed the GUI, you'll write code in the code-behind file to obtain the server's time and display it on the Label. First, open `WebTime.aspx.vb` by double clicking its node in the **Solution Explorer**. In this example, you'll add an event handler to the code-behind file to handle the Web Form's **Init event**, which occurs when the page is first requested by a web browser. The event handler for this event—named **Page_Init**—initialize the page. The only initialization required for this example is to set the `timeLabel`'s `Text` property to the time on the web server computer. To create the `Page_Init` event handler:

1. Select **(Page Events)** from the left ComboBox at the top of the code editor window.

2. Select **Init** from the right ComboBox at the top of the code editor window.

3. Complete the event handler by inserting the following code in the `Page_Init` event handler:

```
' display the server's current time in timeLabel
timeLabel.Text = DateTime.Now.ToString("hh:mm:ss")
```

Step 7: Setting the Start Page and Running the Program

To ensure that WebTime.aspx loads when you execute this app, right click it in the **Solution Explorer** and select **Set As Start Page**. You can now run the program in one of several ways. At the beginning of Section 28.3, you learned how to view the Web Form by typing *Ctrl + F5* to run the app. You can also right click an ASPX file in the **Solution Explorer** and select **View in Browser**. Both of these techniques execute the ASP.NET Development Server, open your default web browser and load the page into the browser, thus running the web app. The development server stops when you exit Visual Web Developer.

If problems occur when running your app, you can run it in debug mode by selecting **Debug > Start Debugging**, by clicking the **Start Debugging** Button (▶) or by typing *F5* to view the web page in a web browser with debugging enabled. You cannot debug a web app unless debugging is *explicitly* enabled in the app's **Web.config** file—a file that's generated when you create an ASP.NET web app. This file stores the app's configuration settings. You'll rarely need to manually modify Web.config. The first time you select **Debug > Start Debugging** in a project, a dialog appears and asks whether you want the IDE to modify the Web.config file to enable debugging. After you click **OK**, the IDE executes the app. You can stop debugging by selecting **Debug > Stop Debugging**.

Regardless of how you execute the web app, the IDE will compile the project before it executes. In fact, ASP.NET compiles your web page whenever it changes between HTTP requests. For example, suppose you browse the page, then modify the ASPX file or add code to the code-behind file. When you reload the page, ASP.NET recompiles the page on the server before returning the response to the browser. This important behavior ensures that clients always see the *latest* version of the page. You can manually compile an entire website by selecting **Build Web Site** from the **Debug** menu in Visual Web Developer.

Examining WebTime.aspx's Code-Behind File

Figure 28.20 presents the code-behind file WebTime.aspx.vb. Line 3 begins the declaration of class WebTime. In Visual Basic, a class declaration can span multiple source-code files—the separate portions of the class declaration in each file are known as **partial classes**. The **Partial modifier** indicates that the code-behind file is part of a larger class. Like Windows Forms apps, the rest of the class's code is generated for you based on your visual interactions to create the app's GUI in **Design** mode. That code is stored in other source code files as partial classes with the same name. The compiler assembles all the partial classes that have the same into a single class declaration.

```
1   ' Fig. 28.20: WebTime.aspx.vb
2   ' Code-behind file for a page that displays the current time.
3   Partial Class WebTime
4      Inherits System.Web.UI.Page
5
6      ' initializes the contents of the page
7      Protected Sub Page_Init(sender As Object,
8         e As System.EventArgs) Handles Me.Init
9
10        ' display the server's current time in timeLabel
11        timeLabel.Text = DateTime.Now.ToString("hh:mm:ss")
12     End Sub ' Page_Init
13  End Class ' WebTime
```

Figure 28.20 Code-behind file for a page that displays the current time.

Line 4 indicates that WebTime inherits from class **Page** in namespace **System.Web.UI**. This namespace contains classes and controls for building web-based apps. Class Page represents the default capabilities of each page in a web app—all pages inherit directly or indirectly from this class.

Lines 7–12 define the Page_Init event handler, which initializes the page in response to the page's Init event. The only initialization required for this page is to set the timeLabel's Text property to the time on the web server computer. The statement in line 11 retrieves the current time (DateTime.Now) and formats it as *hh:mm:ss*. For example, 9 AM is formatted as 09:00:00, and 2:30 PM is formatted as 02:30:00. As you'll see, variable timeLabel represents an ASP.NET Label control. The ASP.NET controls are defined in namespace System.Web.UI.WebControls.

SELF-REVIEW
1. With _____ positioning, controls and other elements are placed sequentially on a Web Form one after another in the order in which you drag-and-drop them onto the Web Form; the cursor indicates the insertion point in the page.

    a) sequential   b) relative

    c) tiered   d) absolute

2. A Web Form's _____ event occurs when the page is first requested by a web browser.

    a) Load   b) Request

    c) Init   d) Session_Start

Answers: 1) b. 2) c.

28.4 Standard Web Controls: Designing a Form

This section introduces some of the web controls located in the **Standard** section of the **Toolbox** (Fig. 28.11). Figure 28.21 summarizes the controls used in the next example.

Web control	Description
TextBox	Gathers user input and displays text.
Button	Triggers an event when clicked.
HyperLink	Displays a hyperlink.
DropDownList	Displays a drop-down list of choices from which a user can select an item.
RadioButtonList	Groups radio buttons.
Image	Displays images (for example, PNG, GIF and JPG).

Figure 28.21   Commonly used web controls.

A Form Gathering User Input

Figure 28.22 depicts a form for gathering user input. This example does not perform any tasks—that is, no action occurs when the user clicks **Register**. As an exercise, we ask you to provide the functionality. Here we focus on the steps for adding these controls to a Web Form and for setting their properties. Subsequent examples demonstrate how to handle the events of many of these controls. To execute this app:

1. Select **Open Web Site...** from the **File** menu.

2. In the **Open Web Site** dialog, ensure that **File System** is selected, then navigate to this chapter's examples, select the WebControls folder and click the **Open** Button.

3. Select WebControls.aspx in the **Solution Explorer**, then type *Ctrl + F5* to execute the web app in your default web browser.

Heading 3 paragraph
Paragraph of plain text
Image control
A table containing four Images and four TextBoxes
TextBox control
DropDownList control
HyperLink control
RadioButtonList control
Button control

Figure 28.22   Web Form that demonstrates web controls.

Creating the Web Site

To begin, follow the steps in the section Building the WebTime App (page 692) to create an **Empty Web Site** named WebControls, then add a Web Form named WebControls.aspx to the project. Set the document's Title property to "Web Controls Demonstration". To ensure that WebControls.aspx loads when you execute this app, right click it in the **Solution Explorer** and select **Set As Start Page**.

Adding the Images to the Project

The images used in this example are located in the images folder with this chapter's examples. Before you can display images in the Web Form, they must be added to your project. To add the images folder to your project:

1. Open Windows Explorer.

2. Locate and open this chapter's examples folder (ch28).

3. Drag the images folder from Windows Explorer into Visual Web Developer's **Solution Explorer** window and drop the folder on the name of your project.

The IDE will automatically copy the folder and its contents into your project.

Adding Text and an Image to the Form

Next, you'll begin creating the page. Perform the following steps:

1. First create the page's heading. At the current cursor position on the page, type the text "Registration Form", then use the **Block Format ComboBox** in the IDE's toolbar to change the text to **Heading 3** format.

2. Press *Enter* to start a new paragraph, then type the text "Please fill in all fields and click the Register button".

3. Press *Enter* to start a new paragraph, then double click the **Image** control in the **Toolbox**. This control inserts an image into a web page, at the current cursor position. Set the Image's (ID) property to userInformationImage. The **ImageUrl** property specifies the location of the image to display. In the **Properties** window, click the ellipsis for the ImageUrl property to display the **Select Image** dialog. Select the images folder under **Project folders:** to display the list of images. Then select the image user.png.

4. Click **OK** to display the image in **Design** view, then click to the right of the Image and press *Enter* to start a new paragraph.

Adding a Table to the Form

Form elements are often placed in tables for layout purposes—like the elements that represent the first name, last name, e-mail and phone information in Fig. 28.23. Next, you'll create a table with two rows and two columns in **Design** mode.

1. Select **Table > Insert Table** to display the **Insert Table** dialog (Fig. 28.23). This dialog allows you to configure the table's options.

2. Under **Size**, ensure that the values of **Rows** and **Columns** are both 2—these are the default values.

3. Click **OK** to close the **Insert Table** dialog and create the table.

By default, the contents of a table cell are aligned vertically in the middle of the cell. We changed the vertical alignment of all cells in the table by setting the valign property to top in the **Properties** window. This causes the content in each table cell to align with the top of the cell. You can set the valign property for each table cell individually or by selecting all the cells in the table at once, then changing the valign property's value.

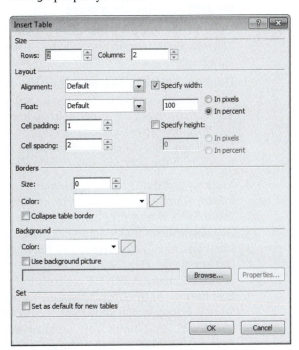

Figure 28.23   **Insert Table** dialog.

After creating the table, controls and text can be added to particular cells to create a neatly organized layout. Next, add `Image` and `TextBox` controls to each the four table cells as follows:

1. Click the table cell in the first row and first column of the table, then double click the `Image` control in the **Toolbox**. Set its (ID) property to `firstNameImage` and set its `ImageUrl` property to the image `fname.png`.

2. Next, double click the `TextBox` control in the **Toolbox**. Set its (ID) property to `firstNameTextBox`. As in Windows Forms, a **TextBox** control allows you to obtain text from the user and display text to the user.

3. Repeat this process in the first row and second column, but set the Image's (ID) property to `lastNameImage` and its `ImageUrl` property to the image `lname.png`, and set the TextBox's (ID) property to `lastNameTextBox`.

4. Repeat *Steps 1* and *2* in the second row and first column, but set the Image's (ID) property to `emailImage` and its `ImageUrl` property to the image `email.png`, and set the TextBox's (ID) property to `emailTextBox`.

5. Repeat *Steps 1* and *2* in the second row and second column, but set the Image's (ID) property to `phoneImage` and its `ImageUrl` property to the image `phone.png`, and set the TextBox's (ID) property to `phoneTextBox`.

Creating the Publications Section of the Page

This section contains an `Image`, some text, a `DropDownList` control and a `Hyper-Link` control. Perform the following steps to create this section:

1. Click below the table, then use the techniques you've already learned in this section to add an `Image` named `publicationsImage` that displays the `publications.png` image.

2. Click to the right of the `Image`, then press *Enter* and type the text `"Which book would you like information about?"` in the new paragraph.

3. Hold the *Shift* key and press *Enter* to create a new line in the current paragraph, then double click the **DropDownList** control in the **Toolbox**. Set its (ID) property to `booksDropDownList`. This control is similar to the Windows Forms ComboBox control, but doesn't allow users to type text. When a user clicks the drop-down list, it expands and displays a list from which the user can make a selection.

4. You can add items to the `DropDownList` using the **ListItem Collection Editor**, which you can access by clicking the ellipsis next to the DropDownList's Items property in the **Properties** window, or by using the **DropDownList Tasks** smart-tag menu. To open this menu, click the small arrowhead that appears in the upper-right corner of the control in **Design** mode (Fig. 28.24). Visual Web Developer displays smart-tag menus for many ASP.NET controls to facilitate common tasks. Clicking **Edit Items...** in the **DropDownList Tasks** menu opens the **ListItem Collection Editor**, which allows you to add `ListItem` elements to the Drop-DownList. Add items for `"Visual Basic 2010 How to Program"`, `"Visual C# 2010 How to Program"`, `"Java How to Program"` and `"C++ How to Program"` by clicking the **Add** Button four times. For each item, select it, then set its Text property to one of the four book titles.

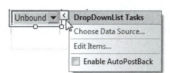

Figure 28.24 DropDownList Tasks smart-tag menu.

5. Click to the right of the DropDownList and press *Enter* to start a new paragraph, then double click the **HyperLink** control in the **Toolbox** to add a hyperlink to the web page. Set its (ID) property to booksHyperLink and its Text property to "Click here to view more information about our books". Set the **NavigateUrl** property to http://www.deitel.com. This specifies the resource or web page that will be requested when the user clicks the HyperLink. Setting the **Target** property to _blank specifies that the requested web page should open in a new browser window. By default, HyperLink controls cause pages to open in the same browser window.

Completing the Page

Next you'll create the **Operating System** section of the page and the **Register** Button. This section contains a **RadioButtonList** control, which provides a series of radio buttons from which the user can select only one. The **RadioButtonList Tasks** smart-tag menu provides an **Edit Items...** link to open the **ListItem Collection Editor** so that you can create the items in the list. Perform the following steps:

1. Click to the right of the HyperLink control and press *Enter* to create a new paragraph, then add an Image named osImage that displays the os.png image.

2. Click to the right of the Image and press *Enter* to create a new paragraph, then add a RadioButtonList. Set its (ID) property to osRadioButtonList. Use the **ListItem Collection Editor** to add the items shown in Fig. 28.24.

3. Finally, click to the right of the RadioButtonList and press *Enter* to create a new paragraph, then add a **Button**. A Button web control represents a button that triggers an action when clicked. Set its (ID) property to registerButton and its Text property to Register. As stated earlier, clicking the **Register** button in this example does not do anything.

You can now execute the app (*Ctrl* + *F5*) to see the Web Form in your browser.

SELF-REVIEW   1. An Image control's _____ property specifies the location of the image to display. _____.

   a) ImageUrl   b) VisibleURL
   c) TargetURL   d) DisplayURL

2. A _____ control is similar to the Windows Forms ComboBox control, but doesn't allow users to type text.
   a) RadioButtonList   b) LinqDataSource
   c) HyperLink   d) DropDownList

Answers: 1) a. 2) d.

28.5 Validation Controls

This section introduces a different type of web control, called a **validation control** or **validator**, which determines whether the data in another web control is in the proper format. For example, validators can determine whether a user has provided information in a required field or whether a zip-code field contains exactly five digits. Validators provide a mechanism for validating user input on the client. When the page is sent to the client, the validator is converted into JavaScript that performs the validation in the client web browser. JavaScript is a scripting language that enhances the functionality of web pages and is typically executed on the client. Unfortunately, some client browsers might not support scripting or the user might disable it. For this reason, you should *always* perform validation on the server. ASP.NET validation controls can function on the client, on the server or both.

Validating Input in a Web Form

The Web Form in Fig. 28.25 prompts the user to enter a name, e-mail address and phone number. A website could use a form like this to collect contact information from visitors. After the user enters any data, but before the data is sent to the web server, validators ensure that the user *entered a value in each field* and that the e-mail address and phone-number values are in an acceptable format. In this example, (555) 123-4567, 555-123-4567 and 123-4567 are all considered valid phone numbers. Once the data is submitted, the web server responds by displaying a message that repeats the submitted information. A real business app would typically store the submitted data in a database or in a file on the server. We simply send the data back to the client to demonstrate that the server received the data. To execute this app:

1. Select **Open Web Site...** from the **File** menu.

2. In the **Open Web Site** dialog, ensure that **File System** is selected, then navigate to this chapter's examples, select the Validation folder and click the **Open** Button.

3. Select Validation.aspx in the **Solution Explorer**, then type *Ctrl + F5* to execute the web app in your default web browser.

In the sample output:

- Fig. 28.25 shows the initial Web Form
- Fig. 28.26 shows the result of submitting the form before typing any data in the TextBoxes
- Fig. 28.27 shows the results after entering data in each TextBox, but specifying an invalid e-mail address and invalid phone number
- Fig. 28.28 shows the results after entering valid values for all three Text-Boxes and submitting the form.

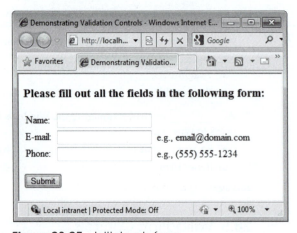

Figure 28.25   Initial web form.

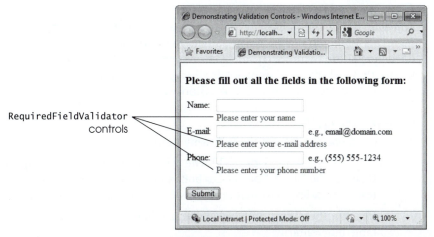

Figure 28.26 Web Form after the user presses the **Submit Button** without having entered any data in the **TextBox**es; each **TextBox** is followed by an error message that was displayed by a validation control.

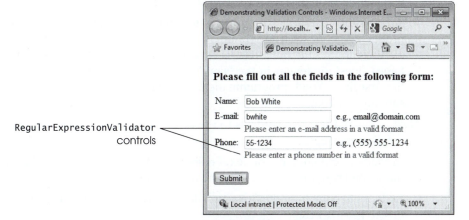

Figure 28.27 Web Form after the user enters a name, an invalid e-mail address and an invalid phone number in the **TextBox**es, then presses the **Submit Button**; the validation controls display error messages in response to the invalid e-mail and phone number values.

Figure 28.28 Web Form after the user enters valid values for all three **Text-Box**es and presses the **Submit Button**.

Creating the Web Site

To begin, follow the steps in Section 28.3 to create an **Empty Web Site** named Validation, then add a Web Form named Validation.aspx to the project. Set the document's Title property to "Demonstrating Validation Controls". To ensure that Validation.aspx loads when you execute this app, right click it in the **Solution Explorer** and select **Set As Start Page**.

Creating the GUI

To create the page, perform the following steps:

1. Type "Please fill out all the fields in the following form:", then use the **Block Format** ComboBox in the IDE's toolbar to change the text to **Heading 3** format and press *Enter* to create a new paragraph.

2. Insert a three row and two column table. You'll add elements to the table momentarily.

3. Click below the table and add a Button. Set its (ID) property to submitButton and its Text property to Submit. Press *Enter* to create a new paragraph. By default, a Button control in a Web Form sends the contents of the form back to the server for processing.

4. Add a Label. Set its (ID) property to outputLabel and clear its Text property—you'll set it programmatically when the user clicks the submitButton. Set the outputLabel's Visible property to False, so the Label does *not* appear in the client's browser when the page loads for the first time. You'll programmatically display this Label after the user submits valid data.

Next you'll add text and controls to the table you created in *Step 2* above. Perform the following steps:

1. In the left column, type the text "Name:" in the first row, "E-mail:" in the second row and "Phone:" in the row column.

2. In the right column of the first row, add a TextBox and set its (ID) property to nameTextBox.

3. In the right column of the second row, add a TextBox and set its (ID) property to emailTextBox. Then type the text "e.g., email@domain.com" to the right of the TextBox.

4. In the right column of the third row, add a TextBox and set its (ID) property to phoneTextBox. Then type the text "e.g., (555) 555-1234" to the right of the TextBox.

Using RequiredFieldValidator Controls

We use three **RequiredFieldValidator** controls (found in the **Validation** section of the **Toolbox**) to ensure that the name, e-mail address and phone number TextBoxes are not empty when the form is submitted. A RequiredFieldValidator makes an input control a required field. If such a field is empty, validation fails. Add a RequiredFieldValidator as follows:

1. Click to the right of the nameTextBox in the table and press *Enter* to move to the next line.

2. Add a RequiredFieldValidator, set its (ID) to nameRequiredFieldValidator and set the ForeColor property to Red.

3. Set the validator's **ControlToValidate** property to nameTextBox to indicate that this validator verifies the nameTextBox's contents.

4. Set the validator's **ErrorMessage** property to "Please enter your name". This is displayed on the Web Form only if the validation fails.

5. Set the validator's `Display` property to Dynamic, so the validator occupies space on the Web Form only when validation fails. When this occurs, space is allocated dynamically, causing the controls below the validator to shift downward to accommodate the `ErrorMessage`, as seen in Fig. 28.28(a)–(c).

Repeat these steps to add two more `RequiredFieldValidators` in the second and third rows of the table. Set their (ID) properties to `emailRequiredFieldValidator` and `phoneRequiredFieldValidator`, respectively, and set their `ErrorMessage` properties to "Please enter your email address" and "Please enter your phone number", respectively.

Using `RegularExpressionValidator` Controls

This example also uses two `RegularExpressionValidator` controls to ensure that the e-mail address and phone number entered by the user are in a valid format. Regular expressions are beyond the scope of this book; however, Visual Web Developer provides several *predefined* regular expressions that you can simply select to take advantage of this powerful validation control. Add a `RegularExpressionValidator` as follows:

1. Click to the right of the `emailRequiredFieldValidator` in the second row of the table and add a `RegularExpressionValidator`, then set its (ID) to `emailRegularExpressionValidator` and its `ForeColor` property to Red.

2. Set the `ControlToValidate` property to `emailTextBox` to indicate that this validator verifies the `emailTextBox`'s contents.

3. Set the validator's `ErrorMessage` property to "Please enter an e-mail address in a valid format".

4. Set the validator's `Display` property to Dynamic, so the validator occupies space on the Web Form only when validation fails.

Repeat the preceding steps to add another `RegularExpressionValidator` in the third row of the table. Set its (ID) property to `phoneRequiredFieldValidator` and its `ErrorMessage` property to "Please enter a phone number in a valid format", respectively.

A `RegularExpressionValidator`'s `ValidationExpression` property specifies the regular expression that validates the `ControlToValidate`'s contents. Clicking the ellipsis next to property `ValidationExpression` in the **Properties** window displays the **Regular Expression Editor** dialog, which contains a list of **Standard expressions** for phone numbers, zip codes and other formatted information. For the `emailRegularExpressionValidator`, we selected the standard expression **Internet e-mail address**. If the user enters text in the `emailTextBox` that does not have the correct format and either clicks in a different text box or attempts to submit the form, the `ErrorMessage` text is displayed in red.

For the `phoneRegularExpressionValidator`, we selected **U.S. phone number** to ensure that a phone number contains an optional three-digit area code either in parentheses and followed by an optional space or without parentheses and followed by a required hyphen. After an optional area code, a phone number must contain three digits, a hyphen and another four digits. For example, (555) 123-4567, 555-123-4567 and 123-4567 are all valid phone numbers.

Submitting the Web Form's Contents to the Server

If all five validators are successful (that is, each `TextBox` is filled in, and the e-mail address and phone number provided are valid), clicking the **Submit** button sends the form's data to the server. As shown in Fig. 28.28(d), the server then responds by displaying the submitted data in the `outputLabel`.

Examining the Code-Behind File for a Web Form That Receives User Input

Figure 28.29 shows the code-behind file for this app. Notice that this code-behind file does not contain any implementation related to the validators. We say more about this soon. In this example, we respond to the page's **Load** event to process the data submitted by the user. This event occurs each time the page loads into a web browser—as opposed to the Init event, which executes only the first time the page is requested by the user. The event handler for this event is **Page_Load** (lines 7–30). To create the event handler, open Validation.aspx.vb in the code editor and perform the following steps:

1. Select **(Page Events)** from the left ComboBox at the top of the code editor window.

2. Select **Load** from the right ComboBox at the top of the code editor window.

3. Complete the event handler by inserting the code from Fig. 28.29.

```
1   ' Fig. 28.29: Validation.aspx.vb
2   ' Code-behind file for the form demonstrating validation controls.
3   Partial Class Validation
4      Inherits System.Web.UI.Page
5
6      ' Page_Load event handler executes when the page is loaded
7      Protected Sub Page_Load(sender As Object,
8         e As System.EventArgs) Handles Me.Load
9
10        ' if this is not the first time the page is loading
11        ' (i.e., the user has already submitted form data)
12        If IsPostBack Then
13           Validate() ' validate the form
14
15           If IsValid Then
16              ' retrieve the values submitted by the user
17              Dim name As String = nameTextBox.Text
18              Dim email As String = emailTextBox.Text
19              Dim phone As String = phoneTextBox.Text
20
21              ' create a table indicating the submitted values
22              outputLabel.Text = "Thank you for your submission<br/>" &
23                 "We received the following information:<br/>"
24              outputLabel.Text &=
25                 String.Format("Name: {0}{1}E-mail:{2}{1}Phone:{3}",
26                    name, "<br/>", email, phone)
27              outputLabel.Visible = True ' display the output message
28           End If
29        End If
30     End Sub ' Page_Load
31  End Class ' Validation
```

Figure 28.29 Code-behind file for a Web Form that obtains a user's contact information.

Differentiating Between the First Request to a Page and a Postback

Web programmers using ASP.NET often design their web pages so that the current page reloads when the user submits the form; this enables the program to receive input, process it as necessary and display the results in the same page when it's loaded the second time. These pages usually contain a form that, when submitted, sends the values of all the controls to the server and causes the current page to be requested again. This event is known as a **postback**. Line 12 uses the **IsPostBack** property of class Page to determine whether the page is being loaded due to a postback. The first time that the web page is requested, IsPostBack is False, and the page displays only the form for user input. When the postback occurs (from the user clicking **Submit**), IsPostBack is True.

Server-Side Web Form Validation

Server-side Web Form validation *must* be implemented *programmatically*. Line 13 calls the current Page's **Validate** method to validate the information in the request. This validates the information as specified by the validation controls in the Web Form. Line 15 uses the **IsValid** property of class Page to check whether the validation succeeded. If this property is set to True (that is, validation succeeded and the Web Form is valid), then we display the Web Form's information. Otherwise, the web page loads without any changes, except any validator that *failed* now displays its ErrorMessage.

Processing the Data Entered by the User

Lines 17–19 retrieve the values of nameTextBox, emailTextBox and phoneTextBox. When data is posted to the web server, the data that the user entered is accessible to the web app through the web controls' properties. Next, lines 22–27 set outputLabel's Text to display a message that includes the name, e-mail and phone information that was submitted to the server. In lines 22, 23 and 26, notice the use of <br/> rather than vbCrLf to start new lines in the outputLabel—
 is the markup for a line break in a web page. Line 27 sets the outputLabel's Visible property to True, so the user can see the thank-you message and submitted data when the page reloads in the client web browser.

SELF-REVIEW

1. A _____ control ensures that its ControlToValidate is not empty when the form is submitted.

   a) RegularExpressionValidator   b) RequiredFieldValidator

   c) ProgrammaticValidator   d) NonEmptyValidator

2. A(n) _____ control determines whether the data in another web control is in the proper format..

   a) edit   b) format

   c) validation   d) configuration

Answers: 1) b. 2) c.

28.6 Session Tracking

Originally, critics accused the Internet and business of failing to provide the customized service typically experienced in "brick-and-mortar" stores. To address this problem, businesses established mechanisms by which they could *personalize* users' browsing experiences, tailoring content to individual users. Businesses achieve this level of service by tracking each customer's movement through the Internet and combining the collected data with information provided by the consumer, including billing information, personal preferences, interests and hobbies.

Personalization

Personalization makes it possible for businesses to communicate effectively with their customers and also improves users' ability to locate desired products and services. Companies that provide content of particular interest to users can establish relationships with customers and build on those relationships over time. Furthermore, by targeting consumers with personal offers, recommendations, advertisements, promotions and services, businesses create customer loyalty. Websites can use sophisticated technology to allow visitors to customize home pages to suit their individual needs and preferences. Similarly, online shopping sites often store personal information for customers, tailoring notifications and special offers to their interests. Such services encourage customers to visit sites more frequently and make purchases more regularly.

Privacy

A trade-off exists between personalized business service and protection of privacy. Some consumers embrace tailored content, but others fear the possible adverse consequences if the info they provide to businesses is released or collected by tracking technologies. Consumers and privacy advocates ask: What if the business to which we give personal data sells or gives that information to another organization without our knowledge? What if we do not want our actions on the Internet—a supposedly anonymous medium—to be tracked and recorded by unknown parties? What if unauthorized parties gain access to sensitive private data, such as credit-card numbers or medical history? These are questions that must be addressed by programmers, consumers, businesses and lawmakers alike.

Recognizing Clients

To provide personalized services to consumers, businesses must be able to recognize clients when they request information from a site. As we have discussed, the request/response system on which the web operates is facilitated by HTTP. Unfortunately, HTTP is a *stateless protocol*—it *does not* provide information that would enable web servers to maintain state information regarding particular clients. This means that web servers cannot determine whether a request comes from a particular client or whether the same or different clients generate a series of requests.

To circumvent this problem, sites can provide mechanisms by which they identify individual clients. A session represents a unique client on a website. If the client leaves a site and then returns later, the client will still be recognized as the same user. When the user closes the browser, the session ends. To help the server distinguish among clients, each client must identify itself to the server. Tracking individual clients is known as **session tracking**. One popular session-tracking technique uses cookies (discussed in the next section); another uses ASP.NET's `HttpSessionState` object (used in the section Session Tracking with `HTTPSessionState` on page 713). Additional session-tracking techniques are beyond this book's scope.

Cookies

Cookies provide you with a tool for personalizing web pages. A cookie is a piece of data stored by web browsers in a small text file on the user's computer. A cookie maintains information about the client during and between browser sessions. The first time a user visits the website, the user's computer might receive a cookie from the server; this cookie is then reactivated each time the user revisits that site. The collected information is intended to be an anonymous record containing data that's used to personalize the user's future visits to the site. For example, cookies in a shopping app might store unique identifiers for users. When a user adds items to an online shopping cart or performs another task resulting in a request to the web server, the server receives a cookie containing the user's unique identifier. The server then uses the unique identifier to locate the shopping cart and perform any necessary processing.

In addition to identifying users, cookies also can indicate users' shopping preferences. When a Web Form receives a request from a client, the Web Form can examine the cookie(s) it sent to the client during previous communications, identify the user's preferences and immediately display products of interest to the client.

Every HTTP-based interaction between a client and a server includes a header containing information either about the request (when the communication is from the client to the server) or about the response (when the communication is from the server to the client). When a Web Form receives a request, the header includes information such as the request type and any cookies that have been sent previ-

Portability Tip

Users may disable cookies in their web browsers to help ensure their privacy. Such users will experience difficulty using web apps that depend on cookies to maintain state information.

ously from the server to be stored on the client machine. When the server formulates its response, the header information contains any cookies the server wants to store on the client computer and other information, such as the MIME type of the response.

The **expiration date** of a cookie determines how long the cookie remains on the client's computer. If you do not set an expiration date for a cookie, the web browser maintains the cookie for the duration of the browsing session. Otherwise, the web browser maintains the cookie until the expiration date occurs. Cookies are deleted when they **expire**.

Session Tracking with `HttpSessionState`

The next web app (Figs. 28.30–28.34) demonstrates session tracking using the .NET class `HttpSessionState`. When you execute this app, the `Options.aspx` page (Fig. 28.30), which is the app's **Start Page**, allows the user to select a programming language from a group of radio buttons. When the user clicks **Submit**, the selection is sent to the web server for processing. The web server uses an `HttpSessionState` object to store the chosen language and the ISBN number for one of our books on that topic. Each user that visits the site has a unique `HttpSessionState` object, so the selections made by one user are maintained separately from all other users. After storing the selection, the server returns the page to the browser (Fig. 28.31) and displays the user's selection and some information about the user's unique session (which we show just for demonstration purposes). The page also includes links that allow the user to choose between selecting another programming language or viewing the `Recommendations.aspx` page (Fig. 28.34), which lists recommended books pertaining to the programming language(s) that the user selected previously. If the user clicks the link for book recommendations, the information stored in the user's unique `HttpSessionState` object is read and used to form the list of recommendations. To test this app:

1. Select **Open Web Site...** from the **File** menu.

2. In the **Open Web Site** dialog, ensure that **File System** is selected, then navigate to this chapter's examples, select the `Sessions` folder and click the **Open** Button.

3. Select `Options.aspx` in the **Solution Explorer**, then type *Ctrl + F5* to execute the web app in your default web browser.

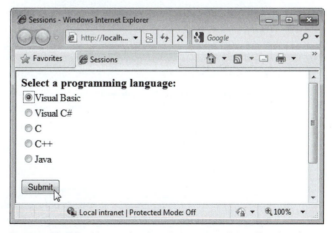

Figure 28.30   User selects a language from the `Options.aspx` page, then presses **Submit** to send the selection to the server.

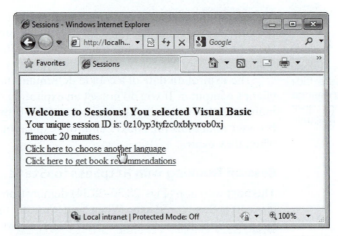

Figure 28.31 `Options.aspx` page is updated to hide the controls for selecting a language and to display the user's selection; the user clicks the hyperlink to return to the list of languages and make another selection.

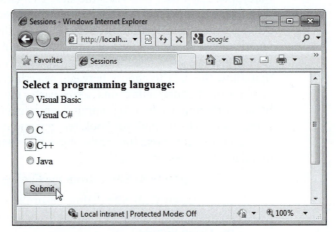

Figure 28.32 User selects another language from the `Options.aspx` page, then presses **Submit** to send the selection to the server.

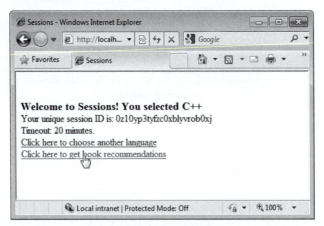

Figure 28.33 `Options.aspx` page is updated to hide the controls for selecting a language and to display the user's selection; the user clicks the hyperlink to get a list of book recommendations.

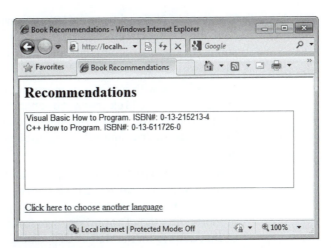

Figure 28.34 `Recommendations.aspx` displays the list of recommended books based on the user's selections

Creating the Web Site

To begin, follow the steps in Section 28.3 to create an **Empty Web Site** named `Sessions`, then add two Web Forms named `Options.aspx` and `Recommendations.aspx` to the project. Set the `Options.aspx` document's `Title` property to `"Sessions"` and the `Recommendations.aspx` document's `Title` property to `"Book Recommendations"`. To ensure that `Options.aspx` is the first page to load for this app, right click it in the **Solution Explorer** and select **Set As Start Page**.

`Options.aspx`: Selecting a Programming Language

`Options.aspx` (Fig. 28.30) contains the following controls arranged vertically:

1. A `Label` with its (ID) property set to `promptLabel` and its `Text` property set to `"Select a programming language:"`. We used the techniques shown in *Step 5* of Section 28.3 to create a CSS style for this label named `.labelStyle`, and set the style's `font-size` attribute to `large` and the `font-weight` attribute to `bold`.

2. The user selects a programming language by clicking one of the radio buttons in a `RadioButtonList`. Each radio button has a `Text` property and a `Value` property. The `Text` property is displayed next to the radio button and the `Value` property represents a value that's sent to the server when the user selects that radio button and submits the form. In this example, we'll use the `Value` property to represent the ISBN for the recommended book.

   Create a `RadioButtonList` with its (ID) property set to `languageList`. Use the **ListItem Collection Editor** to add five radio buttons with their `Text` properties set to `Visual Basic`, `Visual C#`, `C`, `C++` and `Java`, and their `Value` properties set to `0-13-215213-4`, `0-13-215142-1`, `0-13-299044-X`, `0-13-266236-1` and `0-13-257566-3`, respectively

3. A `Button` with its (ID) property set to `submitButton` and its `Text` property set to `Submit`. In this example, we'll handle this `Button`'s `Click` event. You can create its event handler by double clicking the `Button` in **Design** view.

4. A `Label` with its (ID) property set to `responseLabel` and its `Text` property set to `"Welcome to Sessions!"`. This `Label` should be placed immediately to the right of the `Button` so that the `Label` appears at the top of the page when we hide the preceding controls on the page. Reuse the CSS style you created in *Step 1* by setting this `Label`'s `CssClass` property to `labelStyle`.

5. Two more Labels with their (ID) properties set to idLabel and time-outLabel, respectively. Clear the text in each Label's Text property—you'll set these programmatically with information about the current user's session.

6. A HyperLink with its (ID) property set to languageLink and its Text property set to "Click here to choose another language". Set its NavigateUrl property by clicking the ellipsis next to the property in the **Properties** window and selecting Options.aspx from the **Select URL** dialog.

7. A HyperLink with its (ID) property set to recommendationsLink and its Text property set to "Click here to get book recommendations". Set its NavigateUrl property by clicking the ellipsis next to the property in the **Properties** window and selecting Recommendations.aspx from the **Select URL** dialog.

8. Initially, the controls in *Steps 4–7* will not be displayed, so set each control's Visible property to False.

Session Property of a Page

Every Web Form includes a user-specific HttpSessionState object, which is accessible through property **Session** of class Page. Throughout this section, we use this property to manipulate the current user's HttpSessionState object. When a page is first requested, a unique HttpSessionState object is created by ASP.NET and assigned to the Page's Session property.

Code-Behind File for Options.aspx

Fig. 28.35 presents the code-behind file for the Options.aspx page. When this page is requested, the Page_Load event handler (lines 9–40) executes before the response is sent to the client. Since the first request to a page is not a postback, the code in lines 12–39 *does not* execute the first time the page loads.

```
 1    ' Fig. 28.35: Options.aspx.vb
 2    ' Process user's selection of a programming language by displaying
 3    ' links and writing information in an HttpSessionState object.
 4    Partial Class Options
 5       Inherits System.Web.UI.Page
 6
 7       ' if postback, hide form and display links to make additional
 8       ' selections or view recommendations
 9       Protected Sub Page_Load(sender As Object,
10          e As System.EventArgs) Handles Me.Load
11
12          If IsPostBack Then
13             ' user has submitted information, so display message
14             ' and appropriate hyperlinks
15             responseLabel.Visible = True
16             idLabel.Visible = True
17             timeoutLabel.Visible = True
18             languageLink.Visible = True
19             recommendationsLink.Visible = True
20
21             ' hide other controls used to make language selection
22             promptLabel.Visible = False
23             languageList.Visible = False
24             submitButton.Visible = False
25
```

Figure 28.35 Process user's selection of a programming language by displaying links and writing information in an HttpSessionState object. (Part 1 of 2.)

```
26            ' if the user made a selection, display it in responseLabel
27            If languageList.SelectedItem IsNot Nothing Then
28               responseLabel.Text &= " You selected " &
29                  languageList.SelectedItem.Text
30            Else
31               responseLabel.Text &= "You did not select a language."
32            End If
33
34            ' display session ID
35            idLabel.Text =
36               "Your unique session ID is: " & Session.SessionID
37
38            ' display the timeout
39            timeoutLabel.Text =
40               "Timeout: " & Session.Timeout & " minutes."
41         End If
42      End Sub ' Page_Load
43
44      ' record the user's selection in the Session
45      Protected Sub submitButton_Click(sender As Object,
46         e As System.EventArgs) Handles submitButton.Click
47
48         ' if the user made a selection
49         If languageList.SelectedItem IsNot Nothing Then
50            ' add name/value pair to Session
51            Session.Add(languageList.SelectedItem.Text,
52               languageList.SelectedItem.Value)
53         End If
54      End Sub ' submitButton_Click
55   End Class ' Options
```

Figure 28.35 Process user's selection of a programming language by displaying links and writing information in an `HttpSessionState` object. (Part 2 of 2.)

Postback Processing

When the user presses **Submit**, a postback occurs. The form is submitted to the server and the `Page_Load` event handler executes. Lines 15–19 display the controls shown in Fig. 28.31 and lines 22–24 hide the controls shown in Fig. 28.30. Next, lines 27–32 ensure that the user selected a language and, if so, display a message in the `responseLabel` indicating the selection. Otherwise, the message "You did not select a language" is displayed.

The app contains information about the `HttpSessionState` object (`Session`) for the current client. Property **SessionID** (displayed in lines 35–36) contains the **unique session ID**—a sequence of random letters and numbers. The first time a client connects to the web server, a unique session ID is created for that client and a temporary cookie is written to the client so the server can identify the client on subsequent requests. When the client makes additional requests, the client's session ID from that temporary cookie is compared with the session IDs stored in the web server's memory to retrieve the client's `HttpSessionState` object. `HttpSessionState` property **Timeout** (displayed in lines 39–40) specifies the maximum amount of time that an `HttpSessionState` object can be inactive before it's discarded. By default, if the user does not interact with this web app for 20 minutes, the `HttpSessionState` object is discarded by the server and a new one will be created if the user interacts with the app again. Figure 28.36 lists some common `HttpSessionState` properties.

Property	Description
Count	Specifies the number of key/value pairs in the Session object.
IsNewSession	Indicates whether this is a new session (that is, whether the session was created during loading of this page).

Figure 28.36 `HttpSessionState` properties. (Part 1 of 2.)

Properties	Description
Keys	Returns a collection containing the Session object's keys.
SessionID	Returns the session's unique ID.
Timeout	Specifies the maximum number of minutes during which a session can be inactive (that is, no requests are made) before the session expires. By default, this property is set to 20 minutes.

Figure 28.36 HttpSessionState properties. (Part 2 of 2.)

Software Design Tip

A Web Form should not use instance variables to maintain client state information, because each new request or postback is handled by a new instance of the page. Maintain client state information in HttpSessionState objects, because such objects are specific to each client.

Software Design Tip

A benefit of using HttpSessionState objects (rather than cookies) is that HttpSessionState objects can store any type of object (not just Strings) as attribute values. This provides you with increased flexibility in determining the type of state information to maintain for clients.

Method submitButton_Click

In this example, we wish to store the user's selection in an HttpSessionState object when the user clicks the **Submit** Button. The submitButton_Click event handler (lines 45–54) adds a key/value pair to the HttpSessionState object for the current user, specifying the language chosen and the ISBN number for a book on that language. The HttpSessionState object is a dictionary—a data structure that stores **key/value pairs**. A program uses the key to store and retrieve the associated value in the dictionary.

The key/value pairs in an HttpSessionState object are often referred to as **session items**. They're placed in an HttpSessionState object by calling its **Add** method. If the user made a selection (line 49), lines 51–52 get the selection and its corresponding value from the languageList by accessing its SelectedItem's Text and Value properties, respectively, then call HttpSessionState method Add to add this name/value pair as a session item in the HttpSessionState object (Session).

If the app adds a session item that has the same name as an item previously stored in the HttpSessionState object, the session item is replaced—the names in session items *must* be unique. Another common syntax for placing a session item in the HttpSessionState object is Session(*Name*) = *Value*. For example, we could have replaced lines 51–52 with

```
Session(languageList.SelectedItem.Text) =
    languageList.SelectedItem
```

Recommendations.aspx: Displaying Recommendations Based on Session Values

After the postback of Options.aspx, the user may request book recommendations. The book-recommendations hyperlink forwards the user to the page Recommendations.aspx (Fig. 28.34) to display the recommendations based on the user's language selections. The page contains the following controls arranged vertically:

1. A Label with its (ID) property set to recommendationsLabel and its Text property set to "Recommendations:". We created a CSS style for this label named .labelStyle, and set the font-size attribute to x-large and the font-weight attribute to bold. (See *Step 5* in Section 28.3 for information on creating a CSS style.)

2. A ListBox with its (ID) property set to booksListBox. We created a CSS style for this label named .listBoxStyle. In the **Position** category, we set the width attribute to 450px and the height attribute to 125px. The px indicates that the measurement is in pixels.

3. A HyperLink with its (ID) property set to languageLink and its Text property set to "Click here to choose another language". Set its NavigateUrl property by clicking the ellipsis next to the property in the **Properties** window and selecting Options.aspx from the **Select URL** dialog. When the user clicks this link, the Options.aspx page will be

reloaded. Requesting the page in this manner *is not* considered a post-back, so the original form in Fig. 28.30 will be displayed.

Code-Behind File for Recommendations.aspx

Figure 28.37 presents the code-behind file for Recommendations.aspx. Event handler Page_Init (lines 7–27) retrieves the session information. If a user has not selected a language in the Options.aspx page, the HttpSessionState object's Count property will be 0 (line 11). This property provides the number of session items contained in a HttpSessionState object. If the Count is 0, then we display the text **No Recommendations** (line 20), clear the ListBox and hide it (lines 21–22), and update the Text of the HyperLink back to Options.aspx (line 25).

```
1  ' Fig. 28.37: Recommendations.aspx.vb
2  ' Creates book recommendations based on a Session object.
3  Partial Class Recommendations
4     Inherits System.Web.UI.Page
5
6     ' read Session items and populate ListBox with recommendations
7     Protected Sub Page_Init(sender As Object,
8        e As System.EventArgs) Handles Me.Init
9
10       ' determine whether Session contains any information
11       If Session.Count <> 0 Then
12          For Each keyName In Session.Keys
13             ' display one of Session's name/value pairs
14             booksListBox.Items.Add(keyName &
15                " How to Program. ISBN#: " & Session(keyName))
16          Next
17       Else
18          ' if there are no session items, no language was chosen, so
19          ' display message and clear and hide booksListBox
20          recommendationsLabel.Text = "No Recommendations"
21          booksListBox.Items.Clear()
22          booksListBox.Visible = False
23
24          ' modify languageLink because no language was selected
25          languageLink.Text = "Click here to choose a language"
26       End If
27    End Sub ' Page_Init
28 End Class ' Recommendations
```

Figure 28.37　Session data used to provide book recommendations to the user.

If the user chose at least one language, the loop in lines 12–16 iterates through the HttpSessionState object's keys (line 12) by accessing the HttpSessionState's **Keys** property, which returns a collection containing all the keys in the session. Lines 14–15 concatenate the keyName, the String " How to Program. ISBN#: " and the key's corresponding value, which is returned by Session(keyName). This String is the recommendation that's added to the ListBox.

SELF-REVIEW　1. A _____ is a piece of data stored in a small text file on the user's computer; it maintains information about the client during and between browser sessions.

　　a) Session_Tracker　　　　　　b) postback
　　c) DOCUMENT　　　　　　　　d) cookie

2. The HttpSessionState object is a _____—a data structure that stores key/value pairs.

　　a) table　　　　　　　　　　b) list
　　c) dictionary　　　　　　　d) GridView

Answers: 1) d. 2) c.

28.7 Case Study: Database-Driven ASP.NET Guestbook

Many websites allow users to provide feedback about the website in a guestbook. Typically, users click a link on the website's home page to request the guestbook page. This page usually consists of a form that contains fields for the user's name, e-mail address, message/feedback and so on. Data submitted on the guestbook form is then stored in a database located on the server.

In this section, we create a guestbook Web Form app. The GUI (Fig. 28.38) contains a `GridView` data control, which displays all the entries in the guestbook in tabular format. This control is located in the **Toolbox**'s **Data** section. We explain how to create and configure this data control shortly. The `GridView` displays **abc** in **Design** mode to indicate data that will be retrieved from a data source at runtime. You'll learn how to create and configure the `GridView` shortly.

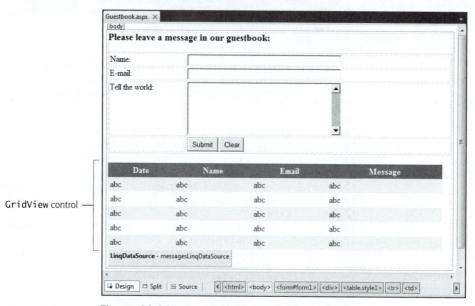

Figure 28.38 Guestbook app GUI in **Design** mode.

The Guestbook Database

The app stores the guestbook information in a SQL Server database called `Guestbook.mdf` located on the web server. (We provide this database in the `databases` folder with this chapter's examples.) The database contains a single table named `Messages`.

Testing the App

To test this app:

1. Select **Open Web Site...** from the **File** menu.

2. In the **Open Web Site** dialog, ensure that **File System** is selected, then navigate to this chapter's examples, select the `Guestbook` folder and click the **Open** Button.

3. Select `Guestbook.aspx` in the **Solution Explorer**, then type *Ctrl + F5* to execute the web app in your default web browser.

Figure 28.39(a) shows the user submitting a new entry. Figure 28.39(b) shows the new entry as the last row in the `GridView`.

a) User enters data for the
name, e-mail and message,
then presses **Submit** to send
the data to the server

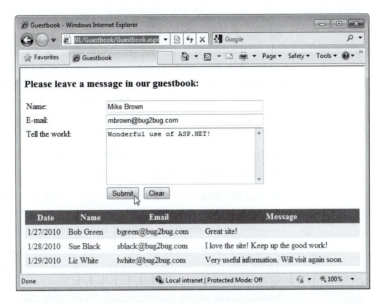

b) Server stores the data in
the database, then refreshes
the `GridView` with the
updated data

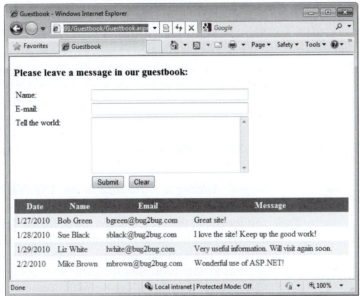

Figure 28.39 Sample execution of the **Guestbook** app.

Building a Web Form that Displays Data from a Database

We now explain how to build this GUI and set up the data binding between the `GridView` control and the database. Many of these steps are similar to those performed in Chapter 27 to access and interact with a database in a Windows app. We discuss the code-behind file in the section "Modifying the Code-Behind File for the **Guestbook** App on page 725. To build the **Guestbook** app, perform the following steps:

Step 1: Creating the Web Site

To begin, follow the steps in the Building the `WebTime` App section on page 692 to create an **Empty Web Site** named `Guestbook` then add a Web Form named `Guestbook.aspx` to the project. Set the document's `Title` property to `"Guestbook"`. To ensure that `Guestobook.aspx` loads when you execute this app, right click it in the **Solution Explorer** and select **Set As Start Page**.

Step 2: Creating the Form for User Input

In **Design** mode, add the text Please leave a message in our guestbook:, then use the **Block Format** ComboBox in the IDE's toolbar to change the text to **Heading 3** format. Insert a table with four rows and two columns, configured so that the text in each cell aligns with the top of the cell. Place the appropriate text (see Fig. 28.38) in the top three cells in the table's left column. Then place Text-Boxes named nameTextBox, emailTextBox and messageTextBox in the top three table cells in the right column. Configure the TextBoxes as follows:

- Set the nameTextBox's width to 300px.

- Set the emailTextBox's width to 300px.

- Set the messageTextBox's width to 300px and height to 100px. Also set this control's TextMode property to MultiLine so the user can type a message containing multiple lines of text.

Finally, add Buttons named submitButton and clearButton to the bottom-right table cell. Set the buttons' Text properties to Submit and Clear, respectively. We discuss the buttons' event handlers when we present the code-behind file. You can create these event handlers now by double clicking each Button in **Design** view.

Step 3: Adding a GridView Control to the Web Form

Add a GridView named messagesGridView that will display the guestbook entries. This control appears in the **Data** section of the **Toolbox**. The colors for the GridView are specified through the **Auto Format...** link in the **GridView Tasks** smart-tag menu that opens when you place the GridView on the page. Clicking this link displays an **AutoFormat** dialog with several choices. In this example, we chose **Professional**. We show how to set the GridView's data source (that is, where it gets the data to display in its rows and columns) shortly.

Step 4: Adding a Database to an ASP.NET Web App

To use a SQL Server Express database file in an ASP.NET web app, you must first add the file to the project's App_Data folder. For security reasons, this folder can be accessed only by the web app on the server—clients cannot access this folder over a network. The web app interacts with the database on behalf of the client.

The **Empty Web Site** template does not create the App_Data folder. To create it, right click the project's name in the **Solution Explorer**, then select **Add ASP.NET Folder > App_Data**. Next, add the Guestbook.mdf file to the App_Data folder. You can do this in one of two ways:

- Drag the file from Windows Explorer and drop it on the App_Data folder.

- Right click the App_Data folder in the **Solution Explorer** and select **Add Existing Item...** to display the **Add Existing Item** dialog, then navigate to the databases folder with this chapter's examples, select the Guestbook.mdf file and click **Add**. [*Note:* Ensure that **Data Files** is selected in the ComboBox above or next to the **Add** Button in the dialog; otherwise, the database file will not be displayed in the list of files.]

Step 5: Creating the LINQ to SQL Classes

As in Chapter 27, you'll use LINQ to interact with the database. To create the LINQ to SQL classes for the Guestbook database:

1. Right click the project in the **Solution Explorer** and select **Add New Item...** to display the **Add New Item** dialog.

2. In the dialog, select **LINQ to SQL Classes**, enter Guestbook.dbml as the **Name**, and click **Add**. A dialog appears asking if you would like to

put your new LINQ to SQL classes in the App_Code folder; click **Yes**. The IDE will create an App_Code folder and place the LINQ to SQL classes information in that folder.

3. In the **Database Explorer** window, drag the Guestbook database's Messages table from the **Database Explorer** onto the **Object Relational Designer**. Finally, save your project by selecting **File > Save All**.

Step 6: Binding the GridView to the Messages Table of the Guestbook Database

You can now configure the GridView to display the database's data.

1. Open the **GridView Tasks** smart-tag menu, then select **<New data source...>** from the **Choose Data Source** ComboBox to display the **Data Source Configuration Wizard** dialog.

2. In this example, we use a **LinqDataSource** control that allows the app to interact with the Guestbook.mdf database through LINQ. Select LINQ, then set the ID of the data source to messagesLinqDataSource and click **OK** to begin the **Configure Data Source** wizard.

3. In the **Choose a Context Object** screen, ensure that GuestbookData-Context is selected in the ComboBox, then click **Next >**.

4. The **Configure Data Selection** screen (Fig. 28.40) allows you to specify which data the LinqDataSource should retrieve from the data context. Your choices on this page design a Select LINQ query. The **Table** drop-down list identifies a table in the data context. The Guestbook data context contains one table named Messages, which is selected by default. *If you haven't saved your project* since creating your LINQ to SQL classes (*Step 5*), the list of tables *will not appear*. In the **Select** pane, ensure that the checkbox marked with an asterisk (*) is selected to indicate that you want to retrieve all the columns in the Messages table.

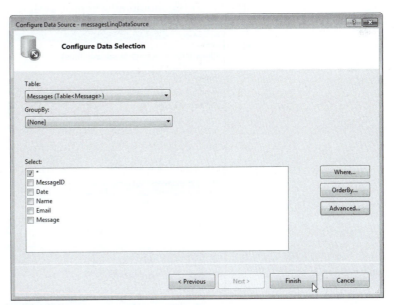

Figure 28.40   Configuring the query used by the LinqDataSource to retrieve data.

5. Click the **Advanced...** button, then select the **Enable the LinqData-Source to perform automatic inserts** CheckBox and click **OK**. This configures the LinqDataSource control to automatically insert new

data into the database when new data is inserted in the data context. We discuss inserting new guestbook entries based on users' form submissions shortly.

6. Click **Finish** to complete the wizard.

A control named `messagesLinqDataSource` now appears on the Web Form directly below the `GridView` (Fig. 28.41). This control is represented in **Design** mode as a gray box containing its type and name. It will *not* appear on the web page—the gray box simply provides a way to manipulate the control visually through **Design** mode—similar to how the objects in the component tray are used in **Design** mode for a Windows Forms app.

The `GridView` now has column headers that correspond to the columns in the `Messages` table. The rows each contain either a number (which signifies an autoincremented column) or **abc** (which indicates string data). The actual data from the `Guestbook.mdf` database file will appear in these rows when you view the ASPX file in a web browser.

Step 7: Modifying the Columns of the Data Source Displayed in the `GridView`

It's not necessary for site visitors to see the `MessageID` column when viewing past guestbook entries—this column is merely a unique primary key required by the `Messages` table within the database. So, let's modify the `GridView` to prevent this column from displaying on the Web Form.

1. In the **GridView Tasks** smart tag menu, click **Edit Columns** to display the **Fields** dialog (Fig. 28.42).

2. Select **MessageID** in the **Selected fields** pane, then click the ⊠ Button. This removes the `MessageID` column from the `GridView`.

3. Click **OK** to return to the main IDE window, then set the `Width` property of the `GridView` to 650px.

The `GridView` should now appear as shown in Fig. 28.38.

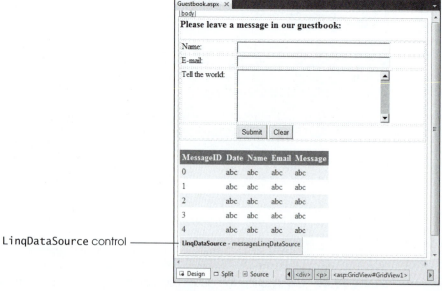

LinqDataSource control ⎯⎯⎯⎯⎯⎯⎯⎯⎯⎯

Figure 28.41   **Design** mode displaying `LinqDataSource` control for a `Grid-View`.

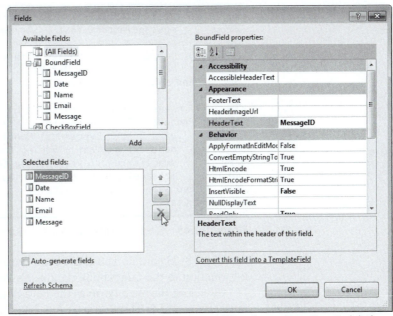

Figure 28.42   Removing the `MessageID` column from the `GridView`.

Modifying the Code-Behind File for the Guestbook App

After building the Web Form and configuring the data controls used in this example, double click the **Submit** and **Clear** buttons in **Design** view to create their corresponding `Click` event handlers in the code-behind file (Fig. 28.43). The IDE generates empty event handlers, so we must add the appropriate code to make these buttons work properly. The event handler for `clearButton` (lines 36–41) clears each `TextBox` by setting its `Text` property to an empty string. This resets the form for a new guestbook submission .

```
1    ' Fig. 28.43: Guestbook.aspx.vb
2    ' Code-behind file that defines event handlers for the guestbook.
3    Partial Class Guestbook
4       Inherits System.Web.UI.Page
5
6       ' Submit Button adds a new guestbook entry to the database,
7       ' clears the form and displays the updated guestbook entries
8       Protected Sub submitButton_Click(sender As Object,
9          e As System.EventArgs) Handles submitButton.Click
10
11         ' create dictionary of parameters for inserting
12         Dim insertParameters As New ListDictionary()
13
14         ' add current date and the user's name, e-mail address and
15         ' message to dictionary of insert parameters
16         insertParameters.Add("Date", Date.Now.ToShortDateString())
17         insertParameters.Add("Name", nameTextBox.Text)
18         insertParameters.Add("Email", emailTextBox.Text)
19         insertParameters.Add("Message", messageTextBox.Text)
20
21         ' execute an INSERT LINQ statement to add a new entry to the
22         ' Messages table in the Guestbook data context that contains
23         ' current date and user's name, e-mail address and message
24         messagesLinqDataSource.Insert(insertParameters)
25
26         ' clear the TextBoxes
27         nameTextBox.Text = String.Empty
```

Figure 28.43   Code-behind file for the guestbook app. (Part 1 of 2.)

```
28          emailTextBox.Text = String.Empty
29          messageTextBox.Text = String.Empty
30
31          ' update the GridView with the new database table contents
32          messagesGridView.DataBind()
33      End Sub ' submitButton_Click
34
35      ' Clear Button clears the Web Form's TextBoxes
36      Protected Sub clearButton_Click(sender As Object,
37          e As System.EventArgs) Handles clearButton.Click
38          nameTextBox.Text = String.Empty
39          emailTextBox.Text = String.Empty
40          messageTextBox.Text = String.Empty
41      End Sub ' clearButton_Click
42  End Class ' Guestbook
```

Figure 28.43 Code-behind file for the guestbook app. (Part 2 of 2.)

Lines 8–33 contain submitButton's event-handling code, which adds the user's information to the Guestbook database's Messages table. To use the values of the TextBoxes on the Web Form as the parameter values inserted into the database, we must create a **ListDictionary** of insert parameters that are key/value pairs.

Line 12 creates a ListDictionary object. Lines 16–19 used the ListDictionary's Add method to store key/value pairs that represent each of the four insert parameters—the current date and the user's name, e-mail address, and message. Invoking the LinqDataSource method Insert (line 24) inserts the data in the data context, adding a row to the Messages table and automatically updating the database. We pass the ListDictionary object as an argument to the Insert method to specify the insert parameters. After the data is inserted into the database, lines 27–29 clear the TextBoxes, and line 32 invokes messagesGridView's **DataBind method** to refresh the data that the GridView displays. This causes messagesLinq-DataSource (the GridView's source) to execute its Select command to obtain the Messages table's newly updated data.

SELF-REVIEW

1. A _____ control allows a web app to interact with a database through LINQ.

   a) RadioButtonList   b) ASP_Server

   c) RequiredFieldValidator   d) LinqDataSource

2. A GridView's _____ method refreshes the data that the GridView displays.

   a) DataBind   b) Synchronize

   c) Update   d) Refresh

Answers: 1) d. 2) c.

28.8 Wrap-Up

In this chapter, we introduced web-app development using ASP.NET and Visual Web Developer 2010 Express. We began by discussing the simple HTTP transactions that take place when you request and receive a web page through a web browser. You then learned about the three tiers (that is, the client or top tier, the business logic or middle tier and the information or bottom tier) that comprise most web apps.

Next, we explained the role of ASPX files (that is, Web Form files) and code-behind files, and the relationship between them. We discussed how ASP.NET compiles and executes web apps so that they can be displayed in a web browser. You also learned how to build an ASP.NET web app using Visual Web Developer.

The chapter demonstrated several common ASP.NET web controls used for displaying text and images on a Web Form. We also discussed validation controls, which allow you to ensure that user input on a web page satisfies certain requirements.

We discussed the benefits of maintaining a user's state information across multiple pages of a website. We then demonstrated how you can include such functionality in a web app by using session tracking with `HttpSessionState` objects.

Finally, we built a **Guestbook** app that allows users to submit comments about a website. You learned how to save the user input in a SQL Server database and how to display past submissions on the web page.

In the next chapter, you'll learn the difference between a traditional web app and an **Ajax (Asynchronous JavaScript and XML) web app**. You also learn how to use **ASP.NET AJAX** to quickly and easily improve the user experience for your web apps, giving them responsiveness comparable to that of desktop apps. To demonstrate ASP.NET AJAX capabilities, you enhance the validation example by displaying the submitted form information without reloading the entire page. The only modifications to this web app appear in `Validation.aspx` file. You use Ajax-enabled controls to add this feature.

SUMMARY

- ASP.NET technology is Microsoft's technology for web-app development.
- Web Form files have the file-name extension `.aspx` and contain the web page's GUI. A Web Form file represents the web page that's sent to the client browser.
- The file that contains the programming logic of a Web Form is called the code-behind file.

Section 28.1 Web Basics

- URIs (Uniform Resource Identifiers) identify documents on the Internet. URIs that start with `http://` are called URLs (Uniform Resource Locators).
- A URL contains information that directs a browser to the resource that the user wishes to access. Computers that run web server software make such resources available.
- In a URL, the hostname is the name of the server on which the resource resides. This computer usually is referred to as the host, because it houses and maintains resources.
- A hostname is translated into a unique IP address that identifies the server. This translation is performed by a domain-name system (DNS) server.
- The remainder of a URL specifies the location and name of a requested resource. For security reasons, the location is normally a virtual directory. The server translates the virtual directory into a real location on the server.
- When given a URL, a web browser performs uses HTTP to retrieve and display the web page found at that address.

Secion 28.2 Multitier App Architecture

- Multitier apps divide functionality into separate tiers—logical groupings of functionality—that commonly reside on separate computers for security and scalability.
- The information tier (also called the bottom tier) maintains data pertaining to the app. This tier typically stores data in a relational database management system.
- The middle tier implements business logic, controller logic and presentation logic to control interactions between the app's clients and the app's data. The middle tier acts as an intermediary between data in the information tier and the app's clients.
- Business logic in the middle tier enforces business rules and ensures that data is reliable before the server app updates the database or presents the data to users.
- The client tier, or top tier, is the app's user interface, which gathers input and displays output. Users interact directly with the app through the user interface (typically viewed in a web browser), keyboard and mouse. In response to user actions, the client tier interacts with the middle tier to make requests and to retrieve data from the information tier. The client tier then displays to the user the data retrieved from the middle tier.

Section 28.3 Your First Web App

Building the WebTime App

- **File System** websites are created and tested on your local computer. Such websites execute in Visual Web Developer's built-in ASP.NET Development Server and can be accessed only by web browsers running on the same computer. You can later "publish" your website to a production web server for access via a local network or the Internet.

- **HTTP** websites are created and tested on an IIS web server and use HTTP to allow you to put your website's files on the server. If you own a website and have your own web server computer, you might use this to build a new website directly on that server computer.

- **FTP** websites use File Transfer Protocol (FTP) to allow you to put your website's files on the server. The server administrator must first create the website on the server for you. FTP is commonly used by so called "hosting providers" to allow website owners to share a server computer that runs many websites.

- A Web Form represents one page in a web app and contains a web app's GUI.

- You can view the Web Form's properties by selecting DOCUMENT in the **Properties** window. The Title property specifies the title that will be displayed in the web browser's title bar when the page is loaded.

- Controls and other elements are placed sequentially on a Web Form one after another in the order in which you drag-and-drop them onto the Web Form. The cursor indicates the insertion point in the page. This type of layout is known as relative positioning. You can also use absolute positioning in which controls are located exactly where you drop them on the Web Form.

- When a Label does not contain text, its name is displayed in square brackets in Design view as a placeholder for design and layout purposes. This text is not displayed at execution time.

- Formatting in a web page is performed with Cascading Style Sheets (CSS).

- A Web Form's Init event occurs when the page is first requested by a web browser. The event handler for this event—named Page_Init—initializes the page.

Examining WebTime.aspx's Code-Behind File

- A class declaration can span multiple source-code files—the separate portions of the class declaration in each file are known as partial classes. The Partial modifier indicates that the class in a particular file is part of a larger class.

- Every Web Form class inherits from class Page in namespace System.Web.UI. Class Page represents the default capabilities of each page in a web app.

- The ASP.NET controls are defined in namespace System.Web.UI.WebControls.

Section 28.4 Standard Web Controls: Designing a Form

- An Image control's ImageUrl property specifies the location of the image to display.

- By default, the contents of a table cell are aligned vertically in the middle of the cell. You can change this with the cell's valign property.

- A TextBox control allows you to obtain text from the user and display text to the user.

- A DropDownList control is similar to the Windows Forms ComboBox control, but doesn't allow users to type text. You can add items to the **DropDownList** using the **ListItem Collection Editor**, which you can access by clicking the ellipsis next to the DropDownList's Items property in the **Properties** window, or by using the **DropDownList Tasks** menu.

- A HyperLink control adds a hyperlink to a Web Form. The NavigateUrl property specifies the resource or web page that will be requested when the user clicks the HyperLink.

- A RadioButtonList control provides a series of radio buttons from which the user can select only one. The **RadioButtonList Tasks** smart-tag menu provides an **Edit Items...** link to open the **ListItem Collection Editor** so that you can create the items in the list.

- A Button control triggers an action when clicked.

Section 28.5 Validation Controls

- A validation control determines whether the data in another web control is in the proper format.

- When the page is sent to the client, the validator is converted into JavaScript that performs the validation in the client web browser.

- Some client browsers might not support scripting or the user might disable it. For this reason, you should always perform validation on the server.

- A `RequiredFieldValidator` control ensures that its `ControlToValidate` is not empty when the form is submitted. The validator's `ErrorMessage` property specifies what to display on the Web Form if the validation fails. When the validator's `Display` property is set to `Dynamic`, the validator occupies space on the Web Form only when validation fails.

- A `RegularExpressionValidator` uses a regular expression to ensure data entered by the user is in a valid format. Visual Web Developer provides several predefined regular expressions that you can simply select to validate e-mail addresses, phone numbers and more. A `RegularExpressionValidator`'s `ValidationExpression` property specifies the regular expression to use for validation.

- A Web Form's `Load` event occurs each time the page loads into a web browser. The event handler for this event is `Page_Load`.

- ASP.NET pages are often designed so that the current page reloads when the user submits the form; this enables the program to receive input, process it as necessary and display the results in the same page when it's loaded the second time.

- Submitting a web form is known as a postback. Class `Page`'s `IsPostBack` property returns `True` if the page is being loaded due to a postback.

- Server-side Web Form validation must be implemented programmatically. Class `Page`'s `Validate` method validates the information in the request as specified by the Web Form's validation controls. Class `Page`'s `IsValid` property returns `True` if validation succeeded.

Section 28.6 Session Tracking

- Personalization makes it possible for e-businesses to communicate effectively with their customers and also improves users' ability to locate desired products and services.

- To provide personalized services to consumers, e-businesses must be able to recognize clients when they request information from a site.

- HTTP is a stateless protocol—it does not provide information regarding particular clients.

- Tracking individual clients is known as session tracking.

Cookies

- A cookie is a piece of data stored in a small text file on the user's computer. A cookie maintains information about the client during and between browser sessions.

- The expiration date of a cookie determines how long the cookie remains on the client's computer. If you do not set an expiration date for a cookie, the web browser maintains the cookie for the duration of the browsing session.

Session Tracking with `HttpSessionState`

- Session tracking is implemented with class `HttpSessionState`.

`Options.aspx`: Selecting a Programming Language

- Each radio button in a `RadioButtonList` has a `Text` property and a `Value` property. The `Text` property is displayed next to the radio button and the `Value` property represents a value that's sent to the server when the user selects that radio button and submits the form.

- Every Web Form includes a user-specific `HttpSessionState` object, which is accessible through property `Session` of class `Page`.

- `HttpSessionState` property `SessionID` contains a client's unique session ID. The first time a client connects to the web server, a unique session ID is created for that client and a temporary cookie is written to the client so the server can identify the client on subsequent requests. When the client makes additional requests, the client's session ID from that temporary cookie is compared with the session IDs stored in the web server's memory to retrieve the client's `HttpSessionState` object.

- `HttpSessionState` property `Timeout` specifies the maximum amount of time that an `HttpSessionState` object can be inactive before it's discarded. Twenty minutes is the default.

- The `HttpSessionState` object is a dictionary—a data structure that stores key/value pairs. A program uses the key to store and retrieve the associated value in the dictionary.

- The key/value pairs in an `HttpSessionState` object are often referred to as session items. They're placed in an `HttpSessionState` object by calling its `Add` method. Another common syntax for placing a session item in the `HttpSessionState` object is `Session(Name) = Value`.

■ If an app adds a session item that has the same name as an item previously stored in the `HttpSessionState` object, the session item is replaced—session items names *must* be unique.

Recommendations.aspx: Displaying Recommendations Based on Session Values

■ The `Count` property returns the number of session items stored in an `HttpSessionState` object.

■ `HttpSessionState`'s `Keys` property returns a collection containing all the keys in the session.

Section 28.7 Case Study: Database-Driven ASP.NET Guestbook

■ A `GridView` data control displays data in tabular format. This control is located in the **Toolbox**'s **Data** section.

Building a Web Form that Displays Data from a Database

■ To use a SQL Server Express database file in an ASP.NET web app, you must first add the file to the project's `App_Data` folder. For security reasons, this folder can be accessed only by the web app on the server—clients cannot access this folder over a network. The web app interacts with the database on behalf of the client.

■ A `LinqDataSource` control allows a web app to interact with a database through LINQ.

Modifying the Code-Behind File for the Guestbook App

■ To insert data into a database using a `LinqDataSource`, you must create a `ListDictionary` of insert parameters that are formatted as key/value pairs.

■ A `ListDictionary`'s Add method stores key/value pairs that represent each insert parameter.

■ A `GridView`'s DataBind method refreshes the data that the `GridView` displays.

KEY TERMS
Add method of class `HttpSessionState`—Method called to place key/value pairs (session items) in an `HttpSessionState` object.

AJAX (Asynchronous JavaScript and XML)—Web-app-development technology that enables you to quickly and easily improve the user experience for your web apps, giving them responsiveness comparable to that of desktop apps.

ASP.NET—Microsoft technology used to develop web apps which create web content for web-browser clients.

ASP.NET AJAX—Quickly and easily improves the user experience for your web apps, giving them responsiveness comparable to that of desktop apps.

ASP.NET server control—Web controls including labels, textboxes, images, buttons and other GUI components.

ASPX file—Web Form files.

.aspx filename extension—The file-name extension for Web Form files.

bottom tier—Maintains the app's data (also called the information tier).

business logic—Enforces business rules and ensures that data is reliable before the server app updates the database or presents the data to users. Business rules dictate how clients can and cannot access app data, and how apps process data.

Button control—Represents a button that triggers an action when clicked.

client tier—The app's user interface (also called the top tier), which gathers input and displays output.

code-behind file—An ASPX file created in Visual Studio that has a corresponding class written in Visual Basic. This class contains event handlers, initialization code, utility methods and other supporting code. The file that contains this class is called the code-behind file and provides the ASPX file's programmatic implementation.

controller logic—Processes client requests (such as requests to view a product catalog) and retrieves data from the database.

ControlToValidate property of a validation control—Set the validator's ControlToValidate property to nameTextBox to indicate that this validator verifies the nameTextBox's contents.

cookies—Provide you with a tool for personalizing web pages. A cookie is a piece of data stored by web browsers in a small text file on the user's computer. A cookie maintains information about the client during and between browser sessions.

Count property of class HttpSessionState—Provides the number of session items contained in a HttpSessionState object.

DataBind method of a GridView—Refreshes the data that the GridView displays.

Display property of a validation control—Set this property to Dynamic, so the validator occupies space on the Web Form only when validation fails.

DNS (domain name system) server—Maintains a database of hostnames and their corresponding IP addresses, and performs the translations automatically.

DOCUMENT property of a Web Form—Represents the Web Form, from the drop-down list in the **Properties** window.

DropDownList control—Similar to the Windows Forms ComboBox control, but doesn't allow users to type text. When a user clicks the drop-down list, it expands and displays a list from which the user can make a selection.

ErrorMessage property of a validation control—Message displayed on the Web Form only if the validation fails.

expiration date of a cookie—Determines how long the cookie remains on the client's computer.

GridView control—Displays data in a grid format.

host—Houses and maintains resources.

hostname—The name of the web server computer on which the resource resides.

HttpSessionState class—The .NET class for session tracking.

HyperLink control—Adds a hyperlink to the web page.

Image control—Inserts an image into a web page, at the current cursor position.

ImageUrl property of an Image web control—Specifies the location of the image to display.

information tier—Maintains the app's data (also called the bottom tier). This tier typically stores data in a relational database management system.

Init event of a Web Form—Occurs when the page is first requested by a web browser.

IP (Internet Protocol) address—A numerical value that uniquely identifies the server on the Internet.

IsPostBack property of Page class—Determine whether the page is being loaded due to a postback.

IsValid property of Page class—Checks whether the validation succeeded.

key/value pair—Used by programs to store and retrieve a key's associated value in the dictionary.

Keys property of HttpSessionState class—Returns a collection containing all the keys in the session.

LinqDataSource control—Allows the app to interact with the database through LINQ.

ListDictionary class—Insert parameters that are key/value pairs that enable you to use the values of the TextBoxes on a Web Form as the parameter values inserted into a database.

Load event of Web Form—Occurs each time the page loads into a web browser.

middle tier—Implements business logic, controller logic and presentation logic to control interactions between the app's clients and its data. The middle tier acts as an intermediary between data in the information tier and the app's clients.

multitier apps—Divide functionality into separate tiers (that is, logical groupings of functionality). Also called *n*-tier apps.

***n*-tier apps**—See multitier apps.

Page class—Represents the default capabilities of each page in a web app—all pages inherit directly or indirectly from this class.

Page_Init event handler—An event handler that initializes the page.

Page_Load event handler—Responds to the page's Load event to process the data submitted by the user.

partial class—The separate portions of the class declaration in each source-code file.

Partial modifier—Indicates that the code-behind file is part of a larger class.

personalization—Makes it possible for businesses to communicate effectively with their customers and also improves users' ability to locate desired products and services.

postback—Sends the values of all the controls to the server when a form is submitted and causes the current page to be requested again.

presentation logic—Processes data from the information tier and presents the content to the client.

RadioButtonList control—Provides a series of radio buttons from which the user can select only one.

RegularExpressionValidator validation control—Ensures that the data entered by the user is in a valid format.

RequiredFieldValidator control—Ensures that the name, e-mail address and phone number TextBoxes are not empty when the form is submitted.

session item—Key/value pairs in an HttpSessionState object.

Session property of Page class—Manipulates the current user's HttpSessionState object

session tracking—Tracking individual clients.

SessionID property of HttpSessionState class—Contains the unique session ID—a sequence of random letters and numbers.

System.Web.UI namespace—Contains classes and controls for building web-based apps.

Target property of a HyperLink control—Setting the Target property to _blank specifies that the requested web page should open in a new browser window.

TextBox control—Allows you to obtain text from the user and display text to the user.

tier in a multitier app—Logical groupings of functionality. Although tiers can be located on the same computer, the tiers of web-based apps commonly reside on separate computers for security and scalability.

Timeout property of HttpSessionState class—Specifies the maximum amount of time that an HttpSessionState object can be inactive before it's discarded.

top tier—The app's user interface, which gathers input and displays output.

unique session ID of an ASP.NET client—A sequence of random letters and numbers. The first time a client connects to the web server, a unique session ID is created for that client and a temporary cookie is written to the client so the server can identify the client on subsequent requests.

Validate property of Page class—Validates the information in a request. This validates the information as specified by the validation controls in the Web Form.

validation control—Determines whether the data in another web control is in the proper format. Also called a validator.

validator—Determines whether the data in another web control is in the proper format.

Visible property of an ASP.NET control—Allows you to either display or hide an element in the client's browser when the page loads for the first time.

Visual Web Developer 2010 Express—A free IDE designed for developing ASP.NET web apps.

web app development—Create web content for web-browser clients.

web control—Also called ASP.NET server controls, include labels, textboxes, images, buttons and other GUI components.

Web Form—Has the file-name extension .aspx and contains the web page's GUI.

web server—Locates the requested web page and sends it to the user's web browser.

Web.config ASP.NET configuration file—A file that's generated when you create an ASP.NET web app.

28.1 _____ is a web-app-development technology that enables you to improve the user experience for your web apps, giving them responsiveness comparable to that of desktop apps.

a) session tracking   b) object-oriented programming

c) multitier   d) ASP.NET Ajax

28.2 An ASPX file created in Visual Studio that has a corresponding class written in Visual Basic. This class contains event handlers, initialization code, utility methods and other supporting code. The file that contains this class is called the _____ file and provides the ASPX file's programmatic implementation.

a) web-app   b) controller

c) code-behind   d) code-source

28.3 Setting the _____ property of a validation control to `Dynamic` causes the validator to occupy space on the Web Form only when validation fails.

a) `Transparent`   b) `Display`

c) `Invalid`   d) `ValidationFailed`

28.4 _____ is the .NET class for session tracking.

a) `HttpSessionState`   b) `HttpSessionTrack`

c) `Session`   d) `Page`

28.5 Although tiers in a multitier app can be located on the same computer, the tiers of web-based apps commonly reside on separate computers for _____ .

a) performance   b) scalability

c) security   d) both b) and c)

28.6 The _____ property of an ASP.NET control allows you to either display or hide an element in the client's browser when the page loads for the first time.

a) `OnLoad`   b) `DisplayOption`

c) `Visible`   d) None of the above.

28.7 A Web Form has the file-name extension _____ and contains the web page's GUI.

a) `.aspx`   b) `.wf`

c) `.wbf`   d) `.asp`

28.8 A _____ locates the requested web page and sends it to the user's web browser.

a) web client   b) domain name server

c) web server   d) `Page_Locate` event handler

28.9 A(n) _____ control inserts an image into a web page at the current cursor location.

a) `ImageInsert`   b) `Image`

c) `ImageEmbed`   d) `Embed`

28.10 To insert data in a database using a `LinqDataSource`, you must create a _____ of insert parameters that are formatted as key/value pairs.

a) `List`   b) `PairsList`

c) `ListDictionary`   d) `KeyValueList`

28.11 State whether each of the following is _true_ or _false_. If _false_, explain why.

a) Web Form file names end in `.aspx`.

b) `App.config` is a file that stores configuration settings for an ASP.NET web app.

c) A maximum of one validation control can be placed on a Web Form.

d) A `LinqDataSource` control allows a web app to interact with a database.

28.12 Fill in the blanks in each of the following statements:

a) Web apps contain three basic tiers: _____, _____, and _____.

b) The _____ web control is similar to the `ComboBox` Windows control.

    c) A control which ensures that the data in another control is in the correct format is called a(n) _____.

    d) A(n) _____ occurs when a page requests itself.

    e) Every ASP.NET page inherits from class _____.

    f) The _____ file contains the functionality for an ASP.NET page.

ANSWERS TO SELF-REVIEW EXERCISES

28.1 a) True. b) False. `Web.config` is the file that stores configuration settings for an ASP.NET web app. c) False. An unlimited number of validation controls can be placed on a Web Form. d) True.

28.2 a) bottom (information), middle (business logic), top (client). b) `DropDownList`. c) validator. d) postback. e) `Page`. f) code-behind.

EXERCISES

28.3 *(WebTime Modification)* Modify the `WebTime` example to contain drop-down lists that allow the user to modify such `Label` properties as `BackColor`, `ForeColor` and `Font-Size`. Configure these drop-down lists so that a postback occurs whenever the user makes a selection. When the page reloads, it should reflect the specified changes to the properties of the `Label` displaying the time.

28.4 *(Page Hit Counter)* Create an ASP.NET page that uses session tracking to keep track of how many times the client computer has visited the page. Set the `HttpSession` object's `Timeout` property to `DateTime.Now.AddDays(1)` to keep the session in effect for one day into the future. Display the number of page hits every time the page loads.

28.5 *(Guestbook App Modification)* Add validation to the **Guestbook** app in Section 28.7. Use validation controls to ensure that the user provides a name, a valid e-mail address and a message.

28.6 *(WebControls Modification)* Modify the example of Section 28.4 to add functionality to the **Register** `Button`. When the user clicks the `Button`, validate all of the input fields to ensure that the user has filled out the form completely, and entered a valid email address and phone number. If any of the fields are not valid, appropriate messages should be displayed by validation controls. If the fields are all valid, direct the user to another page that displays a message indicating that the registration was successful followed by the registration information that was submitted from the form.

28.7 *(Project: Web-Based Address Book)* Using the techniques you learned in Section 28.7, create a web-based address book with similar functionality to the **Address Book** app that you created in Section 27.8. Display the address book's contents in a `GridView`. Allow the user to search for entries with a particular last name.

29

Books Database App

Web App Development with ASP.NET: A Deeper Look

In the last chapter, we introduced ASP.NET and web app development. In this chapter, we introduce several additional ASP.NET web-app development topics, including:

- Master pages to maintain a uniform look-and-feel across the Web Forms in a web app
- Creating a password-protected website with registration and login capabilities
- Using the **Web Site Administration Tool** to specify which parts of a website are password protected
- Using ASP.NET Ajax to quickly and easily improve the user experience for your web apps, giving them responsiveness comparable to that of desktop apps.

29.1 Case Study: Password-Protected Books Database App

This case study presents a web app in which a user logs into a password-protected website to view a list of publications by a selected author. The app consists of several ASPX files. For this app, we'll use the **ASP.NET Web Site** template, which is a starter kit for a small multi-page website. The template uses Microsoft's recommended practices for organizing a website and separating the website's style (look-and-feel) from its content. The default site has two primary pages (**Home** and **About**) and is pre-configured with login and registration capabilities. The template also specifies a common look-and-feel for all the pages in the website—a concept known as a master page.

We begin by examining the features of the default website that is created with the **ASP.NET Web Site** template. Next, we test-drive the completed app to demonstrate the changes we made to the default website. Then, we provide step-by-step instructions to guide you through building the app.

Examining the ASP.NET Web Site Template

To test the default website, begin by creating the website that you'll customize in this case study. Perform the following steps to create the site:

1. Select **File > New Web Site...** to display the **New Web Site** dialog.

2. In the left column of the **New Web Site** dialog, ensure that **Visual Basic** is selected, then select **ASP.NET Web Site** in the middle column.

3. Choose a location for your website, name it Bug2Bug and click **OK**.

Fig. 29.1 shows the website's contents in the **Solution Explorer**.

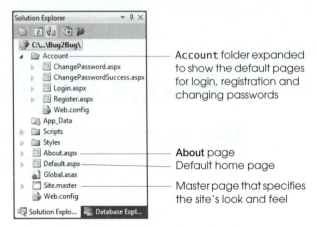

Figure 29.1   The default **ASP.NET Web Site** in the **Solution Explorer**.

Executing the Website

You can now execute the website. Select the Default.aspx page in the **Solution Explorer**, then type *Ctrl + F5* to display the default page shown in Fig. 29.2.

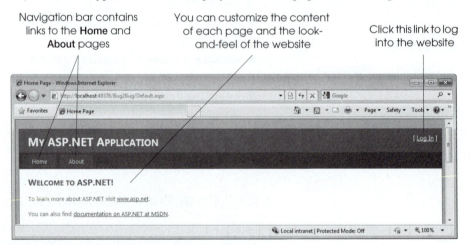

Figure 29.2   Default **Home** page of a website created with the **ASP.NET Web Site** template.

Navigation and Pages

The default **ASP.NET Web Site** contains a home page and an about page—so-called **content pages**—that you'll customize in subsequent sections. The navigation bar near the top of the page allows you to switch between these pages by clicking the link for the appropriate page. In the Configuring the Website section, you'll add another link to the navigation bar to allow users to browse book information.

As you navigate between the pages, notice that each page has the same look-and-feel. This is typical of professional websites. The site uses a **master page** and cascading style sheets (CSS) to achieve this. A master page defines common GUI elements that are inherited by each page in a set of content pages. Just as Visual Basic classes can inherit instance variables and methods from existing classes, content pages can inherit elements from master pages—this is a form of visual inheritance.

Login and Registration Support

Websites commonly provide "membership capabilities" that allow users to register at a website and log in. Often this gives users access to website customization capabilities or premium content. The default **ASP.NET Web Site** is pre-configured to support registration and login capabilities.

In the upper-right corner of each page is a **Log In** link. Click it to display the **Login** page (Fig. 29.3). If you're already registered with the site, you can log in with your username and password. Otherwise, you can click the **Register** link to display the **Register** page (Fig. 29.4). For the purpose of this case study, we created an account with the username `testuser1` and the password `testuser1`. You do not need to be registered or logged in to the default website to view the home and about pages.

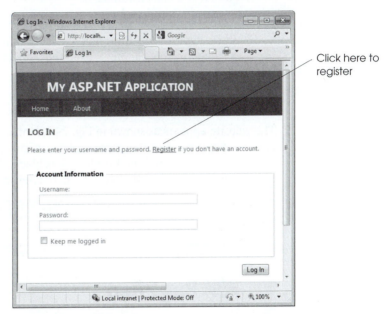

Click here to register

Figure 29.3 **Login** page.

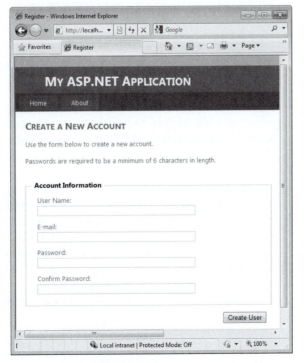

Figure 29.4 **Register** page.

Test-Driving the Completed App

This example uses a technique known as **forms authentication** to protect a page so that only registered users who are logged in to the website can access the page. Such users are known as the site's members. Authentication is a crucial tool for sites that allow only members to enter the site or a portion of the site. In this app, website visitors must log in before they're allowed to view the publications in the Books database.

Let's open the completed Bug2Bug website and execute it so that you can see the authentication functionality in action. Perform the following steps:

1. Close the app you created in Fig. 29.2—you'll reopen this website later so that you can customize it.

2. Select **Open Web Site...** from the **File** menu.

3. In the **Open Web Site** dialog, ensure that **File System** is selected, then navigate to this chapter's examples, select the Bug2Bug folder and click the **Open** Button.

4. Select the Default.aspx page then type *Ctrl + F5* to execute the website.

The website appears as shown in Fig. 29.5. Notice that we modified the site's master page so that the top of the page displays an image, the background color of the top of the page is white and the **Log In** link is black. Also, the navigation bar contains a link for the **Books** page that you'll create later in this case study.

Figure 29.5 **Home** page for the completed **Bug2Bug** website.

Try to visit the **Books** page by clicking the **Books** link in the navigation bar. Because this page is password protected in the Bug2Bug website, the website automatically redirects you to the **Login** page instead—you cannot view the **Books** page without logging in first. If you've not yet registered at the completed Bug2Bug website, click the **Register** link to create a new account. If you have registered, log in now.

If you are logging in, when you click the **Log In** Button on the **Log In** page, the website attempts to validate your username and password by comparing them with the usernames and passwords that are stored in a database on the server—this database is created for you with the **ASP.NET Web Site** template. If there is a match, you are **authenticated** (that is, your identity is confirmed) and you're redirected to the **Books** page (Fig. 29.6). If you're registering for the first time, the server ensures that you've filled out the registration form properly and that your password is valid (at least 6 characters), then logs you in and redirects you to the **Books** page.

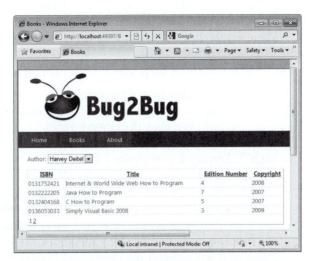

Figure 29.6   Books.aspx displaying books by Harvey Deitel (by default).

The **Books** page provides a drop-down list of authors and a table containing the ISBNs, titles, edition numbers and copyright years of books in the database. By default, the page displays all the books by Harvey Deitel. Links appear at the bottom of the table that allow you to access additional pages of data—we configured the table to display only four rows of data at a time. When the user chooses an author, a postback occurs, and the page is updated to display information about books written by the selected author (Fig. 29.7).

Figure 29.7   Books.aspx displaying books by Greg Ayer.

Logging Out of the Website
When you're logged in, the **Log In** link is replaced in the upper-right corner of each page (not shown in Figs. 29.6–29.7) with the message "Welcome *username*," where *username* is replaced with your log in name, and a **Log Out** link. When you click **Log Out**, the website redirects you to the home page (Fig. 29.5).

Configuring the Website
Now that you're familiar with how this app behaves, you'll modify the default website you created in the Examining the ASP.NET Web Site Template section. Thanks to the rich functionality of the default website, you'll have to write almost no Visual Basic code to create this app. The **ASP.NET Web Site** template hides the details of authenticating users against a database of user names and passwords, displaying appropriate success or error messages and redirecting the user to the correct page based on the authentication results. We now discuss the steps you must perform to create the password-protected books database app.

Step 1: Opening the Website

Open the default website that you created in the Examining the ASP.NET Web Site Template section.

1. Select **Open Web Site...** from the **File** menu.

2. In the **Open Web Site** dialog, ensure that **File System** is selected, then navigate to the location where you created your version of the Bug2Bug website and click the **Open** Button.

Step 2: Setting Up Website Folders

For this website, you'll create two new folders—one that will contain the image that is used on all the pages and one that will contain the password-protected page. Password-protected parts of your website are typically placed in a separate folder. As you'll see shortly, you can control access to specific folders in a website.

You can choose any name you like for these folders—we chose Images for the folder that will contain the image and ProtectedContent for the folder that will contain the password-protected **Books** page. To create the folders, perform the following steps:

1. Create an Images folder by right clicking the location of the website in the **Solution Explorer**, selecting **New Folder** and typing the name Images.

2. Create a ProtectedContent folder by right clicking the location of the website in the **Solution Explorer**, selecting **New Folder** and typing the name ProtectedContent.

Step 3: Importing the Website Header Image and the Database File

Next, you'll add an image to the Images folder and the database file to the App_Data folder.

1. In Windows Explorer, locate the folder containing this chapter's examples.

2. Drag the image bug2bug.png from the images folder in Windows Explorer into the Images folder in the **Solution Explorer** to copy the image into the website.

3. Drag the Books.mdf database file from the databases folder in Windows Explorer to the project's App_Data folder. We show how to retrieve data from this database later in the section.

Step 4: Opening the Web Site Administration Tool

In this app, we want to ensure that only authenticated users are allowed to access Books.aspx (created in the Creating a Content Page That Only Authenticated Users Can Access section) to view the information in the database. Previously, we created all of our ASPX pages in the web app's root directory. By default, any website visitor (regardless of whether the visitor is authenticated) can view pages in the root directory. ASP.NET allows you to restrict access to particular folders of a website. We do not want to restrict access to the root of the website, however, because users won't be able to view any pages of the website. To restrict access to the **Books** page, it must reside in a directory other than the root directory.

You'll now configure the website to allow only authenticated users (that is, users who have logged in) to view the pages in the ProtectedContent folder. Perform the following steps:

1. Select **Website > ASP.NET Configuration** to open the **Web Site Administration Tool** in a web browser (Fig. 29.8). This tool allows you to configure various options that determine how your app behaves.

2. Click either the **Security** link or the **Security** tab to open a web page in which you can set security options (Fig. 29.9), such as the type of authentication the app should use. By default, website users are authenticated by entering username and password information in a web form.

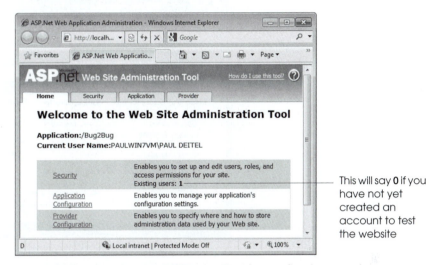

Figure 29.8   **Web Site Administration Tool** for configuring a web app.

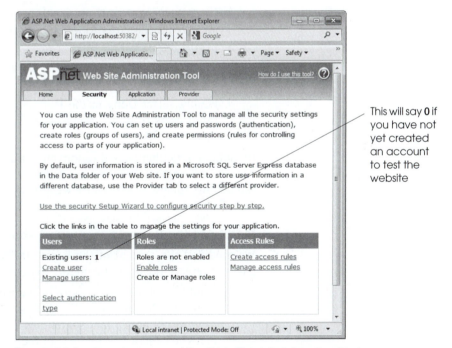

Figure 29.9   **Security** page of the **Web Site Administration Tool**.

Step 5: Configuring the Website's Security Settings

Next, you'll configure the ProtectedContent folder to grant access only to authenticated users—anyone who attempts to access pages in this folder without first logging in will be redirected to the **Login** page. Perform the following steps:

1. Click the **Create access rules** link in the **Access Rules** column of the **Web Site Administration Tool** (Fig. 29.9) to view the **Add New Access Rule** page (Fig. 29.10). This page is used to create an **access rule**—a rule that grants or denies access to a particular directory for a specific user or group of users.

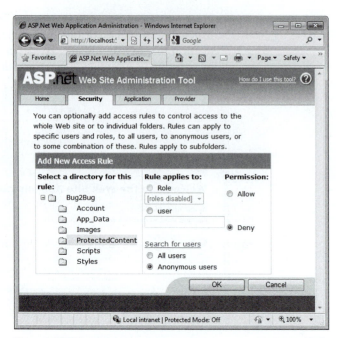

Figure 29.10 **Add New Access Rule** page used to configure directory access.

2. Click the ProtectedContent directory in the left column of the page to identify the directory to which our access rule applies.

3. In the middle column, select the radio button marked **Anonymous users** to specify that the rule applies to users who have not been authenticated.

4. Finally, select **Deny** in the **Permission** column to prevent unauthenticated users from accessing pages in the ProtectedContent directory, then click **OK**.

By default, unauthenticated (anonymous) users who attempt to load a page in the ProtectedContent directory are redirected to the Login.aspx page so that they can identify themselves. Because we did not set up any access rules for the Bug2Bug root directory, anonymous users may still access pages there.

Modifying the Default.aspx and About.aspx Pages

We modified the content of the home (Default.aspx) and about (About.aspx) pages to replace the default content. To do so, perform the following steps:

1. Double click Default.aspx in the **Solution Explorer** to open it, then switch to **Design** view (Fig. 29.11). As you move the cursor over the page, you'll notice that sometimes the cursor displays as ⊘ to indicate that you cannot edit the part of the page behind the cursor. Any part of a content page that is defined in a master page can be edited only in the master page.

2. Change the text "Welcome to ASP.NET!" to "Welcome to Our Password-Protected Book Information Site". Note that the text in this heading is actually formatted as small caps text when the page is displayed in a web browser—all of the letters are displayed in uppercase, but the letters that would normally be lowercase are smaller than the first letter in each word.

This cursor indicates a part of a content page that cannot
be edited because it's inherited from a master page

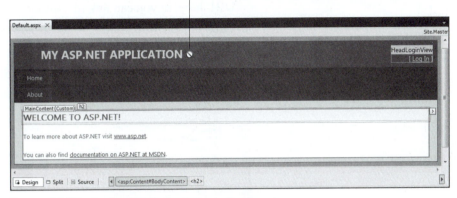

Figure 29.11 `Default.aspx` page in **Design** view.

3. Select the text of the two paragraphs that remain in the page and replace them with "To learn more about our books, click here or click the Books tab in the navigation bar above. You must be logged in to view the Books page." In a later step, you'll link the words "click here" to the **Books** page.

4. Save and close the `Default.aspx` page.

5. Next, open `About.aspx` and switch to **Design** view.

6. Change the text "Put content here." to "This is the Bug2Bug password-protected book information database example."

7. Save and close the `About.aspx` page.

Creating a Content Page That Only Authenticated Users Can Access

We now create the `Books.aspx` file in the `ProtectedContent` folder—the folder for which we set an access rule denying access to anonymous users. If an unauthenticated user requests this file, the user will be redirected to `Login.aspx`. From there, the user can either log in or create a new account, both of which will authenticate the user, then redirect back to `Books.aspx`. To create the page, perform the following steps:

1. Right click the `ProtectedContent` folder in the **Solution Explorer** and select **Add New Item....** In the resulting dialog, select **Web Form** and specify the file name `Books.aspx`. Ensure that the CheckBox **Select master page** is checked to indicate that this Web Form should be created as a content page that references a master page, then click **Add**.

2. In the **Select a Master Page** dialog, select `Site.master` and click **OK**. The IDE creates the file and opens it.

3. Switch to **Design** view, click in the page to select it, then select **DOCUMENT** from the ComboBox in the **Properties** window.

4. Change the `Title` property of the page to Books, then save and close the page

You'll customize this page and create its functionality shortly.

Linking from the `Default.aspx` Page to the `Books.aspx` Page

Next, you'll add a hyperlink from the text "click here" in the `Default.aspx` page to the `Books.aspx` page. To do so, perform the following steps:

1. Open the `Default.aspx` page and switch to **Design** view.

2. Select the text "click here".

3. Click the **Convert to Hyperlink** ( ) Button on the toolbar at the top of Visual Web Developer to display the **Hyperlink** dialog. You can enter a URL here, or you can link to another page within the website.

4. Click the **Browse...** Button to display the **Select Project Item** dialog (Section 29.12), which allows you to select another page in the website.

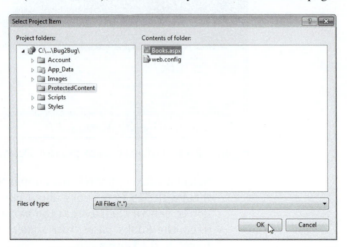

Figure 29.12   Selecting the `Books.aspx` page from the **Select Project** Item dialog.

5. In the left column, select the `ProtectedContent` directory.

6. In the right column, select `Books.aspx`, then click **OK** to dismiss the **Select Project Item** dialog and click **OK** again to dismiss the **Hyperlink** dialog.

Users can now click the click here link in the `Default.aspx` page to browse to the `Books.aspx` page. If a user is not logged in, clicking this link will redirect the user to the **Login** page.

Modifying the Master Page (`Site.master`)

Next, you'll modify the website's master page, which defines the common elements we want to appear on each page. A master page is like a base class in a visual inheritance hierarchy, and content pages are like derived classes. The master page contains placeholders for custom content created in each content page. The content pages visually inherit the master page's content, then add content in the areas designated by the master page's placeholders.

For example, it's common to include a **navigation bar** (that is, a series of buttons or menus for navigating a website) on every page of a site. If a site encompasses a large number of pages, adding markup to create the navigation bar for each page can be time consuming. Moreover, if you subsequently modify the navigation bar, every page on the site that uses it must be updated. By creating a master page, you can specify the navigation-bar in one file and have it appear on all the content pages. If the navigation bar changes, only the master page changes—any content pages that use it are updated the next time the page is requested.

In the final version of this website, we modified the master page to include the Bug2Bug logo in the header at the top of every page. We also changed the colors of some elements in the header to make them work better with the logo. In particular, we changed the background color from a dark blue to white, and we changed the color of the text for the **Log In** and **Log Out** links to black. The color changes require you to modify the CSS styles for some of the master page's elements. These styles are defined in the file `Site.css`, which is located in the website's `Styles` folder. You will not modify the CSS file directly. Instead, you'll use the tools built into Visual Web Developer to perform these modifications.

Inserting an `Image` in the Header

To display the logo, we'll place an `Image` control in the header of the master page. Each content page based on this master page will include the logo. Perform the following steps to add the `Image`:

1. Open `Site.master` and switch to **Design** view.

2. Delete the text `MY ASP.NET APPLICATION` at the top of the page.

3. In the **Toolbox**, double click **Image** to add an `Image` control where the text used to be.

4. Edit the `Image` control's `ImageUrl` property to point to the `bug2bug.png` image in the `Images` folder.

Customizing the CSS Styles for the Master Page

Our logo image was designed to be displayed against a white background. To change the background color in the header at the top of the page, perform the following steps:

1. Just below the **Design** view is a list of `Button`s that show you where the cursor is currently located in the master page (Fig. 29.13). These `Buttons` also allow you to select specific elements in the page. Click the **<div.header>** `Button` to select the header portion of the page.

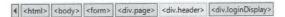

Figure 29.13   `Buttons` for selecting parts of a page in **Design** view.

2. Select **View > Other Windows > CSS Properties** to display the CSS properties (at the left of the IDE) for the currently selected element (the header of the page).

3. At the top of the **CSS Properties** window, click the **Summary** `Button` to show only the CSS properties that are currently set for the selected element.

4. Change the `background` property from `#4b6c9e` (the hexadecimal value for the current dark blue background) to `white` and press *Enter*.

5. The **Log In** and **Log Out** links use white text in the default website. Now that the background of the header is white, we need to change the color of these links so they'll be visible. In the upper-right corner of the master page click the **HeadLoginView** control, which is where the **Log In** and **Log Out** links get displayed.

6. Below the **Design** view, click the **<div.loginDisplay>** `Button` to display the styles for the **HeadLoginView** in the **CSS Properties** window.

7. Change the `color` property from `white` to `black` and press *Enter*.

8. Click inside the box below **HeadLoginView**. Then, below the **Design** view, click the **<a#HeadingLoginStatus>** `Button` to display the styles for the **Log In/Log Out** link in the **CSS Properties** window

9. Change the `color` property from `white` to `black` and press *Enter*.

10. Some style changes must be made directly in the `Site.css` file because the styles are applied only at runtime. On many websites, when you move the mouse over a hyperlink, the color of the link changes. Similarly, once you click a hyperlink, the hyperlink is often displayed in a different color the next time you visit the page to indicate that you've already clicked that link during a previous visit. The predefined styles in this website set the color of the **Log In** link to white for both of these

cases. To change these to black, open the `Site.css` file from the `Styles` folder in the **Solution Explorer**, then search for the following two styles:

```
.loginDisplay a:visited
.loginDisplay a:hover
```

and change each style's `color` property from `white` to `black`.

11. Save the `Site.master` and `Site.css` files.

Adding a Books Link to the Navigation Bar

Currently the navigation bar has only **Home** and **About** links. Next, you'll add a link to the **Books** page. Perform the following steps:

1. In the master page, position the mouse over the navigation bar links, then open the smart-tag menu and click **Edit Menu Items**.

2. In the **Menu Item Editor** dialog, click the **Add a root item** ( ) Button.

3. Set the new item's `Text` property to `Books` and use the up arrow Button to move the new item up so that the order of the navigation bar items is Home, Books and About.

4. Set the new item's `NavigateUrl` property to the `Books.aspx` page in the `ProtectedContent` folder.

5. Click **OK**, then save the `Site.master` file to complete the changes to the master page.

Customizing the Password-Protected Books.aspx **Page**

You are now ready to customize the `Books.aspx` page to display the book information for a particular author.

Generating LINQ to SQL Classes Based on the Books.mdf Database

The `Books.aspx` page will provide a `DropDownList` containing authors' names and a `GridView` displaying information about books written by the author selected in the `DropDownList`. A user will select an author from the `DropDownList` to cause the `GridView` to display information about only the books written by the selected author.

To work with the Books database through LINQ, we use the same approach as in the **Guestbook** case study (Section 28.7). First you need to generate the LINQ to SQL classes based on the Books database, which is provided in the `databases` directory of this chapter's examples folder. Name the file `Books.dbml`. When you drag the tables of the Books database from the **Database Explorer** onto the **Object Relation Designer** of `Books.dbml`, you'll find that associations (represented by arrows) between the two tables are automatically generated (Fig. 29.14).

Figure 29.14   **Object Relation Designer** for the Books database.

To obtain data from this data context, you'll use two `LinqDataSource` controls. In both cases, the `LinqDataSource` control's built-in data selection functionality won't be versatile enough, so the implementation will be slightly different than in Section 28.7. So, we'll use a custom `Select` LINQ statement as the query of a `LinqDataSource`.

Adding a `DropDownList` to Display the Authors' First and Last Names
Now that we have created a `BooksDataContext` class (one of the generated LINQ to SQL classes), we add controls to `Books.aspx` that will display the data on the web page. We first add the `DropDownList` from which users can select an author.

1. Open `Books.aspx` in **Design** mode, then add the text `Author:` and a `DropDownList` control named `authorsDropDownList` in the page's editable content area (which has a white background). The `DropDown-List` initially displays the text `Unbound`.

2. Next, we'll bind the list to a data source, so the list displays the author information in the `Authors` table of the `Books` database. Because the **Configure Data Source** wizard allows us to create `LinqDataSources` with only simple `Select` LINQ statements, we cannot use the wizard here. Instead, add a `LinqDataSource` object below the `DropDownList` named `authorsLinqDataSource`.

3. Open the smart-tag menu for the `DropDownList` and click **Choose Data Source...** to start the **Data Source Configuration Wizard** (Fig. 29.15). Select `authorsLinqDataSource` from the **Select a data source** drop-down list in the first screen of the wizard. Then, type `Name` as the data field to display in the `DropDownList` and `AuthorID` as the data field that will be submitted to the server when the user makes a selection. [*Note:* You must manually type these values in because `authorsLinqData-Source` does not yet have a defined `Select` query.] When `authors-DropDownList` is rendered in a web browser, the list items will display the names of the authors, but the underlying values associated with each item will be the `AuthorID`s of the authors. Click **OK** to bind the Drop-DownList to the specified data.

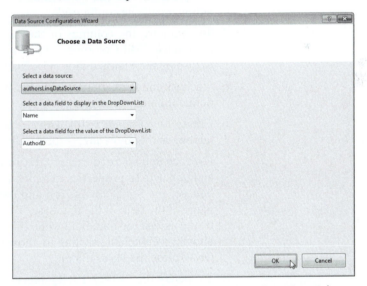

Figure 29.15   Choosing a data source for a `DropDownList`.

4. In the Visual Basic code-behind file (`Books.aspx.vb`), create an instance of `BooksDataContext` named `database` as an instance variable.

5. In the **Design** view of `Books.aspx`, double click `authorsLinqData-Source` to create an event handler for its **Selecting** event. This event occurs every time the `LinqDataSource` selects data from its data context, and can be used to implement custom `Select` queries against the data context. To do so, assign the custom LINQ query to the **Result** property of the event handler's `LinqDataSourceSelectEventArgs` argument. The query results become the data source's data. In this case, we

must create a custom anonymous type in the Select clause with properties Name and AuthorID that contain the author's full name and ID. The LINQ query is

```
From author In database.Authors
Select Name = author.FirstName & " " & author.LastName,
    author.AuthorID
```

The limitations of the **Configure Data Source** wizard prevent us from using a custom field such as Name (a combination of first name and last name, separated by a space) that isn't one of the database table's existing columns.

6. The last step in configuring the DropDownList on Books.aspx is to set the control's **AutoPostBack** property to True. This property indicates that a postback occurs each time the user selects an item in the Drop-DownList. As you'll see shortly, this causes the page's GridView (created in the next step) to display new data.

Creating a GridView to Display the Selected Author's Books

We now add a GridView to Books.aspx for displaying the book information by the author selected in the authorsDropDownList.

1. Add a GridView named titlesGridView below the other controls in the page's content area.

2. To bind the GridView to data from the Books database, create a Linq-DataSource named titlesLinqDataSource beneath the GridView.

3. Select titlesLinqDataSource from the **Choose Data Source** drop-down list in the **GridView Tasks** smart-tag menu. Because titles-LinqDataSource has no defined Select query, the GridView will not automatically be configured.

4. To configure the columns of the GridView to display the appropriate data, select **Edit Columns...** from the **GridView Tasks** smart-tag menu to display the **Fields** dialog (Fig. 29.16).

5. Uncheck the **Auto-generate fields** box to indicate that you'll manually define the fields to display.

6. Create four BoundFields with the HeaderText ISBN, Title, Edition Number and Copyright, respectively.

7. For each BoundField except Edition Number, set the SortExpression and DataField properties to match the HeaderText. For Edition Number, set the SortExpression and DataField to EditionNumber—the name of the field in the database. The SortExpression specifies to sort by the associated data field when the user chooses to sort by the column. Shortly, we'll enable sorting to allow users to sort this GridView. Clock **OK** to close the **Fields** dialog.

8. To specify the Select LINQ query for obtaining the data, double click titlesLinqDataSource to create its Selecting event handler. Assign the custom LINQ query to the LinqDataSourceSelectEventArgs argument's Result property. Use the following LINQ query:

```
From book In database.AuthorISBNs
Where book.AuthorID = authorsDropDownList.SelectedValue
Select book.Title
```

9. The GridView needs to update every time the user makes a new author selection. To implement this, double click the DropDownList to create an event handler for its SelectedIndexChanged event. You can make the GridView update by invoking its DataBind method.

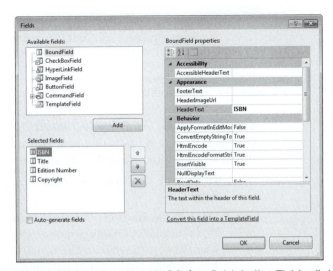

Figure 29.16 Creating `GridView` fields in the **Fields** dialog.

Code-Behind File for the Books Page

Figure 29.17 shows the code for the completed code-behind file. Line 7 defines the data context object that is used in the LINQ queries. Lines 10–18 and 21–29 define the two `LinqDataSource`'s `Selecting` events. Lines 32–37 define the authors-`DropDownList`'s `SelectedIndexChanged` event handler, which updates the `Grid-View`.

```vb
1   ' Fig. 29.17: ProtectedContent_Books.aspx.vb
2   ' Code-behind file for the password-protected Books page.
3   Partial Class ProtectedContent_Books
4      Inherits System.Web.UI.Page
5
6      ' data context queried by data sources
7      Private database As New BooksDataContext()
8
9      ' specify Select query that creates a combined first and last name
10     Protected Sub authorsLinqDataSource_Selecting(ByVal sender As Object,
11        ByVal e As System.Web.UI.WebControls.LinqDataSourceSelectEventArgs) _
12        Handles authorsLinqDataSource.Selecting
13
14        e.Result =
15           From author In database.Authors
16           Select Name = author.FirstName & " " & author.LastName,
17              author.AuthorID
18     End Sub ' authorsLinqDataSource_Selecting
19
20     ' specify the Select query that gets the specified author's books
21     Protected Sub titlesLinqDataSource_Selecting(ByVal sender As Object,
22        ByVal e As System.Web.UI.WebControls.LinqDataSourceSelectEventArgs) _
23        Handles titlesLinqDataSource.Selecting
24
25        e.Result =
26           From book In database.AuthorISBNs
27           Where book.AuthorID = authorsDropDownList.SelectedValue
28           Select book.Title
29     End Sub ' titlesLinqDataSource_Selecting
30
31     ' refresh the GridView when a different author is selected
32     Protected Sub authorsDropDownList_SelectedIndexChanged(
33        ByVal sender As Object, ByVal e As System.EventArgs) _
34        Handles authorsDropDownList.SelectedIndexChanged
```

Figure 29.17 Code-behind file for the password-protected **Books** page. (Part 1 of 2.)

```
35
36            titlesGridView.DataBind() ' update the GridView
37       End Sub ' authorsDropDownList_SelectedIndexChanged
38    End Class ' ProtectedContent_Books
```

Figure 29.17   Code-behind file for the password-protected **Books** page. (Part 2 of 2.)

Configuring the GridView to Enable Sorting and Paging

Now that the GridView is tied to a data source, we modify several of the control's properties to adjust its appearance and behavior.

1. In **Design** view, use the GridView's sizing handles to set the width to 580px.

2. Next, in the **GridView Tasks** smart-tag menu, check **Enable Sorting** so that the column headings in the GridView become hyperlinks that allow users to sort the data in the GridView using the sort expressions specified by each column. For example, clicking the Titles heading in the web browser will cause the displayed data to appear sorted in alphabetical order. Clicking this heading a second time will cause the data to be sorted in reverse alphabetical order. ASP.NET hides the details required to achieve this functionality.

3. Finally, in the **GridView Tasks** smart-tag menu, check **Enable Paging**. This causes the GridView to split across multiple pages. The user can click the numbered links at the bottom of the GridView control to display a different page of data. GridView's **PageSize** property determines the number of entries per page. Set the PageSize property to 4 using the **Properties** window so that the GridView displays only four books per page. This technique for displaying data makes the site more readable and enables pages to load more quickly (because less data is displayed at one time). As with sorting data in a GridView, you do not need to add any code to achieve paging functionality. Figure 29.18 displays the completed Books.aspx file in **Design** mode.

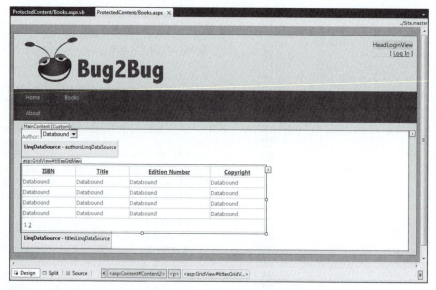

Figure 29.18   Completed Books.aspx page in **Design** mode.

29.2 ASP.NET Ajax

In this section, you learn the difference between a traditional web aplication and an **Ajax (Asynchronous JavaScript and XML) web app.** You also learn how to use **ASP.NET Ajax** to quickly and easily improve the user experience for your web apps. To demonstrate ASP.NET Ajax capabilities, you enhance the validation example by displaying the submitted form information without reloading the entire page. The only modifications to this web app appear in the `Validation.aspx` file. You use Ajax-enabled controls to add this feature.

Traditional Web Apps

Figure 29.19 presents the typical interactions between the client and the server in a traditional web app, such as one that uses a user registration form. The user first fills in the form's fields, then submits the form (Fig. 29.19, *Step 1*). The browser generates a request to the server, which receives the request and processes it (*Step 2*). The server generates and sends a response containing the exact page that the browser renders (*Step 3*), which causes the browser to load the new page (*Step 4*) and temporarily makes the browser window blank. The client *waits* for the server to respond and *reloads the entire page* with the data from the response (*Step 4*). While such a **synchronous request** is being processed on the server, the user cannot interact with the web page. Frequent long periods of waiting, due perhaps to Internet congestion, have led some users to refer to the World Wide Web as the "World Wide Wait." If the user interacts with and submits another form, the process begins again (*Steps 5–8*).

This model was designed for a web of hypertext documents—what some people call the "brochure web." As the web evolved into a full-scale apps platform, the model shown in Fig. 29.19 yielded "choppy" user experiences. Every full-page refresh required users to reload the full page. Users began to demand a more responsive model.

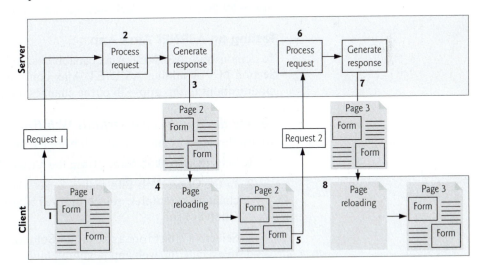

Figure 29.19   Traditional web app reloading the page for every user interaction.

Ajax Web Apps

Ajax web apps add a layer between the client and the server to manage communication between the two (Fig. 29.20). When the user interacts with the page, the client requests information from the server (*Step 1*). The request is intercepted by the ASP.NET Ajax controls and sent to the server as an **asynchronous request** (*Step 2*)—the user can continue interacting with the app in the client browser while the server processes the request. Other user interactions could result in additional requests to the server (*Steps 3* and *4*). Once the server responds to the original request (*Step 5*), the ASP.NET Ajax control that issued the request calls a client-side function to process the data returned by the server. This function—known as a **callback function**—uses **partial-page updates** (*Step 6*) to display the data in the existing web page *without reloading the entire page*. At the same time, the server may be responding to the second request (*Step 7*) and the client browser may be starting another partial-page update (*Step 8*). The callback function updates only a designated part of the page. Such partial-page updates help make web apps more responsive, making them feel more like desktop apps. The web app does not load a new page while the user interacts with it. In the following section, you use ASP.NET Ajax controls to enhance the `Validation.aspx` page.

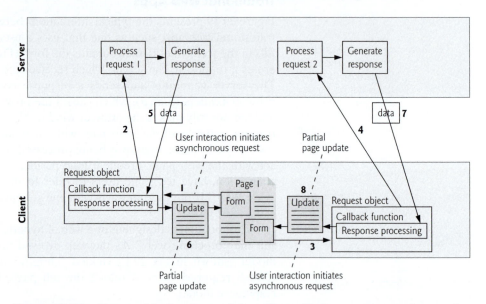

Figure 29.20   Ajax-enabled web app interacting with the server asynchronously.

Testing an ASP.NET Ajax App

To demonstrate ASP.NET Ajax capabilities we'll enhance the **Validation** app from Section 28.5 by adding ASP.NET Ajax controls. There are no Visual Basic code modifications to this app—all of the changes occur in the `.aspx` file.

Testing the App in Your Default Web Browser

To test this app in your default web browser, perform the following steps:

1. Select **Open Web Site...** from the Visual Web Developer **File** menu.

2. In the **Open Web Site** dialog, select **File System**, then navigate to this chapter's examples, select the `ValidationAjax` folder and click the **Open** Button.

3. Select `Validation.aspx` in the **Solution Explorer**, then type *Ctrl + F5* to execute the web app in your default web browser.

Figure 29.21 shows a sample execution of the enhanced app. In Fig. 29.21(a), we show the contact form split into two tabs via the `TabContainer` Ajax control. You can switch between the tabs by clicking the title of each tab. Fig. 29.21(b) shows a `ValidatorCalloutExtender` control, which displays a validation error message in a callout that points to the control in which the validation error occurred, rather than as text in the page. Fig. 29.21(c) shows the updated page with the data the user submitted to the server.

a) Entering a name on the
Name tab then clicking the
Contact tab

b) Entering an e-mail address
in an incorrect format and
pressing the *Tab* key to move
to the next input field causes
a callout to appear informing
the user to enter an e-mail
address in a valid format

c) After filling out the form
properly and clicking the
Submit button, the submitted
data is displayed at the
bottom of the page with a
partial page update

Figure 29.21   Validation app enhanced by ASP.NET Ajax.

The ASP.NET Ajax Control Toolkit

You'll notice that there is a tab of basic **AJAX Extensions** controls in the **Toolbox**. Microsoft also provides the **ASP.NET Ajax Control Toolkit** as part of the ASP.NET Ajax Library

    ajax.codeplex.com

The toolkit contains many more Ajax-enabled, rich GUI controls. Click the **Download Button** to begin the download. The toolkit does not come with an installer, so you must extract the contents of the toolkit's ZIP file to your hard drive. Note the location where you extracted the files as you'll need this information to add the ASP.NET Ajax Controls to your **Toolbox**.

Adding the ASP.NET Ajax Controls to the Toolbox

You should add controls from the Ajax Control Toolkit to the **Toolbox** in Visual Web Developer (or in Visual Studio), so you can drag and drop controls onto your Web Forms. To do so, perform the following steps:

1. Open an existing website project or create a new website project.

2. Open an ASPX page from your project in **Design** mode.

3. Right click the **Toolbox** and choose **Add Tab**, then type ASP.NET Ajax Library in the new tab.

4. Right click under the new **ASP.NET Ajax Library** tab and select **Choose Items...** to open the **Choose Toolbox Items** dialog.

5. Click the **Browse** Button then locate the folder where you extracted the ASP.NET Ajax Control Toolkit. In the WebForms\Release folder, select the file AjaxControlToolkit.dll then click **Open**.

6. Click **OK** to close the dialog. The controls from the Ajax Control Toolkit now appear in the **Toolbox**'s **ASP.NET Ajax Library** tab.

7. Initially the control names are not in alphabetical order. To sort them alphabetically, right click in the list of Ajax Control Toolkit controls and select **Sort Items Alphabetically**.

Using Controls from the Ajax Control Toolkit

In this section, you'll enhance the app you created in Section 28.5 by adding ASP.NET Ajax controls. The key control in every ASP.NET Ajax-enabled app is the **ScriptManager** (in the **Toolbox**'s **AJAX Extensions** tab), which manages the JavaScript client-side code (called scripts) that enable asynchronous Ajax functionality. A benefit of using ASP.NET Ajax is that you do not need to know JavaScript to be able to use these scripts. The **ScriptManager** is meant for use with the controls in the **Toolbox**'s **AJAX Extensions** tab. There can be only one ScriptManager per page.

Common Programming Error

Putting more than one ScriptManager and/or ToolkitScriptManager control on a Web Form causes the app to throw an InvalidOperationException when the page is initialized.

ToolkitScriptManager

The Ajax Control Toolkit comes with an enhanced ScriptManager called the **ToolkitScriptManager**, which manages the scripts for the ASP.NET Ajax Toolkit controls. This one should be used in any page with controls from the ASP.NET Ajax Toolkit.

Open the Validation website you created in Section 28.5. Then drag a ToolkitScriptManager from the **ASP.NET Ajax Library** tab in the **Toolbox** to the top of the page—a script manager must appear before any controls that use the scripts it manages.

Grouping Information in Tabs Using the TabContainer Control

The **TabContainer control** enables you to group information into tabs that are displayed only if they're selected. The information in an unselected tab won't be displayed until the user selects that tab. To demonstrate a TabContainer control, let's split the form into two tabs—one in which the user can enter the name and one in which the user can enter the e-mail address and phone number. Perform the following steps:

1. Click to the right of the text **Please fill out all the fields in the following form:** and press *Enter* to create a new paragraph.

2. Drag a TabContainer control from the **ASP.NET Ajax Library** tab in the **Toolbox** into the new paragraph. This creates a container for hosting tabs. Set the TabContainer's Width property to 450px.

3. To add a tab, open the **TabContainer Tasks** smart-tag menu and select **Add Tab Panel**. This adds a **TabPanel object**—representing a tab—to the TabContainer. Do this again to add a second tab.

4. You must change each TabPanel's HeaderText property by editing the ASPX page's markup. To do so, click the TabContainer to ensure that it's selected, then switch to **Split** view in the design window. In the high-lighted markup that corresponds to the TabContainer, locate Header-Text="TabPanel1" and change "TabPanel1" to "Name", then locate HeaderText="TabPanel2" and change "TabPanel2" to "Contact". Switch back to **Design** view. In **Design** view, you can navigate between tabs by clicking the tab headers. You can drag-and-drop elements into the tab as you would anywhere else.

5. Click in the **Name** tab's body, then insert a one row and two column table. Take the text and controls that are currently in the **Name:** row of the original table and move them to the table in the **Name** tab.

6. Switch to the **Contact** tab, click in its body, then insert a two row and two column table. Take the text and controls that are currently in the **E-mail:** and **Phone:** rows of the original table and move them to the table in the Contact tab.

7. Delete the original table that is currently below the TabContainer.

Partial-Page Updates Using the UpdatePanel Control

The **UpdatePanel control** eliminates full-page refreshes by isolating a section of a page for a partial-page update. In this example, we'll use a partial-page update to display the user's information that is submitted to the server.

To implement a partial-page update, perform the following steps:

1. Click to the left of the **Submit** Button and press *Enter* to create a new paragraph above it. Then click in the new paragraph and drag an UpdatePanel control from the **AJAX Extensions** tab in the **Toolbox** to your form.

2. Then, drag into the UpdatePanel the control(s) to update and the control that triggers the update. For this example, drag the outputLabel and the submitButton into the UpdatePanel.

3. To specify when an UpdatePanel should update, you need to define an **UpdatePanel trigger**. Select the UpdatePanel, then click the ellipsis button next to the control's Triggers property in the **Properties** window. In the **UpdatePanelTrigger Collection** dialog that appears (Fig. 29.22), click Add to add an **AsyncPostBackTrigger**. Set the Con-trolID property to submitButton and the EventName property to Click. Now, when the user clicks the **Submit** button, the UpdatePanel intercepts the request and makes an asynchronous request to the server instead. Then the response is inserted in the outputLabel element, and the UpdatePanel reloads the label to display the new text without refreshing the entire page.

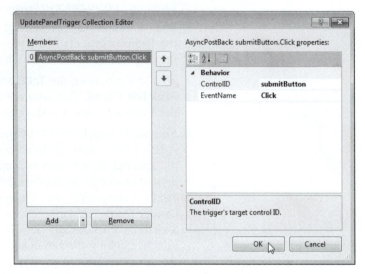

Figure 29.22   Creating a trigger for an `UpdatePanel`.

Adding Ajax Functionality to ASP.NET Validation Controls Using Ajax Extenders

Several controls in the Ajax Control Toolkit are **extenders**—components that enhance the functionality of regular ASP.NET controls. In this example, we use `ValidatorCalloutExtender` **controls** that enhance the ASP.NET validation controls by displaying error messages in small yellow callouts next to the input fields, rather than as text in the page.

You can create a `ValidatorCalloutExtender` by opening any validator control's smart-tag menu and clicking **Add Extender...** to display the **Extender Wizard** dialog (Fig. 29.23). Next, choose `ValidatorCalloutExtender` from the list of available extenders. The extender's ID is chosen based on the ID of the validation control you're extending, but you can rename it if you like. Click **OK** to create the extender. Do this for each of the validation controls in this example.

Changing the Display Property of the Validation Controls

The `ValidatorCalloutExtender`s display error messages with a nicer look-and-feel, so we no longer need the validator controls to display these messages on their own. For this reason, set each validation control's `Display` property to `None`.

Running the App

When you run this app, the `TabContainer` will display whichever tab was last displayed in the ASPX page's **Design** view. Ensure that the **Name** tab is displayed, then select `Validation.aspx` in the **Solution Explorer** and type *Ctrl + F5* to execute the app.

Additional ASP.NET Information

The Ajax Control Toolkit contains many other extenders and independent controls. You can check them out at `www.asp.net/ajax/ajaxcontroltoolkit/samples/`. For more information on ASP.NET Ajax, check out our ASP.NET Ajax Resource Center at

`www.deitel.com/aspdotnetajax`

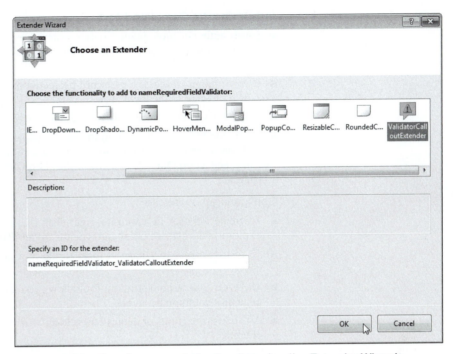

Figure 29.23   Creating a control extender using the **Extender Wizard**.

29.3 Wrap-Up

In this chapter, we presented a case study in which we built a password-protected web app that requires users to log in before accessing information from the Books database. You used the **Web Site Administration Tool** to configure the app to prevent anonymous users from accessing the book information. We used the **ASP.NET Web Site** template, which provides login and registration capabilities for a website. You also learned to create a uniform look-and-feel for a website with a master page.

Finally, you learned the difference between a traditional web app and an Ajax web app. We introduced ASP.NET AJAX and Microsoft's Ajax Control Toolkit. You learned how to build an Ajax-enabled web app by using a `ScriptManager` and the Ajax-enabled controls of the Ajax Extensions package and the Ajax Control Toolkit.

Summary

Section 29.1 Case Study: Password-Protected Books Database Application

- The **ASP.NET Web Site** template is a starter kit for a small multi-page website. The template uses Microsoft's recommended practices for organizing a website and separating the website's style (look-and-feel) from its content.

Examining the ASP.NET Web Site Template

- The default **ASP.NET Web Site** contains a home page and an about page—so-called content pages. The navigation bar near the top of the page allows you to switch between these pages by clicking the link for the appropriate page.

- A master page defines common elements that are inherited by each page in a set of content pages.

- Content pages can inherit elements from master pages—this is a form of visual inheritance.

- Websites commonly provide "membership capabilities" that allow users to register at a website and log in. The default **ASP.NET Web Site** is pre-configured to support registration and login capabilities.

Test-Driving the Completed App

- Forms authentication enables only registered users who are logged in to the website to access a password-protected page or set of pages. Such users are known as the site's members.
- If you attempt to access a password-protected page without logging in, you're automatically redirected to the login page.
- When you successfully log into the website you're considered to be authenticated.
- When you're logged in, the **Log In** link is replaced in the upper-right corner of each page with the message "Welcome *username*," where *username* is replaced with your log in name, and a **Log Out** link. When you click **Log Out**, the website redirects you to the home page.

Configuring the Website

- To create a folder in a website, right click the location of the website in the **Solution Explorer**, select **New Folder** and type the folder name.
- To restrict access to a page, it must reside in a directory other than the website's root directory.
- The **Web Site Administration Tool** allows you to configure various options that determine how your app behaves.
- An access rule grants or denies access to a particular directory for a specific user or group of users.

Modifying the Default.aspx and About.aspx Pages

- As you move the cursor over a content page, you'll notice that sometimes the cursor displays as ⊘ to indicate that you cannot edit the part of the page behind the cursor. Any part of a content page that is defined in a master page can be edited only in the master page.

Creating a Content Page That Only Authenticated Users Can Access

- When you create a new **Web Form** that should inherit from a specific master page, ensure that the CheckBox **Select master page** is checked. Then, in the **Select a Master Page** dialog, select the appropriate master page and click **OK**.

Linking from the Default.aspx Page to the Books.aspx Page

- To convert text to a hyperlink, select the text then click the **Convert to Hyperlink** (🖼) Button on the toolbar at the top of Visual Web Developer to display the **Hyperlink** dialog. You can enter a URL here, or you can link to another page within the website.

Modifying the Master Page (Site.master)

- A master page is like a base class in a visual inheritance hierarchy, and content pages are like derived classes. The master page contains placeholders for custom content created in each content page. The content pages visually inherit the master page's content, then add content in the areas designated by the master page's placeholders.
- The website's styles are defined in the file Site.css, which is located in the site's Styles folder.
- Select **View > Other Windows > CSS Properties** to display the CSS properties (at the left of the IDE) for the currently selected element. At the top of the **CSS Properties** window, click the **Summary** Button to show only the CSS properties that are currently set for the selected element.
- Some style changes must be made directly in the Site.css file because the styles are applied only at runtime.
- To add a link to the navigation bar in the master page, position the mouse over the navigation bar links then open the smart-tag menu and click **Edit Menu Items**. In the **Menu Item Editor** dialog, click the **Add a root item** (🖼) Button. Set the new item's Text property and use the arrow Buttons to move the new item where it should appear in the navigation bar. Set the new item's NavigateUrl property to the appropriate page.

Customizing the Password-Protected Books.aspx Page

- The **Configure Data Source** wizard allows you to create LinqDataSources with only simple Select LINQ statements, so sometimes it is necessary to add a LinqDataSource object with a custom query.

- A LinqDataSource's Selecting event occurs every time the LinqDataSource selects data from its data context, and can be used to implement custom Select queries against the data context. To do so, assign the custom LINQ query to the Result property of the event handler's LinqDataSourceSelectEventArgs argument. The query results become the data source's data.

- Setting a DropDownList's AutoPostBack property to True indicates that a postback occurs each time the user selects an item in the DropDownList.

- You can configure the columns of a GridView manually by selecting **Edit Columns...** from the **GridView Tasks** smart-tag menu.

- Checking **Enable Sorting** in the **GridView Tasks** smart-tag menu changes the column headings in the GridView to hyperlinks that allow users to sort the data in the GridView using the sort expressions specified by each column.

- Checking **Enable Paging** in the **GridView Tasks** smart-tag menu causes the GridView to split across multiple pages. The user can click the numbered links at the bottom of the GridView control to display a different page of data. GridView's PageSize property determines the number of entries per page. This technique for displaying data makes the site more readable and enables pages to load more quickly (because less data is displayed at one time).

Section 29.2 ASP.NET Ajax

- A traditional web app must make synchronous requests and must wait for a response, whereas AJAX (Asynchronous JavaScript and XML) web apps can make asynchronous requests and do not need to wait for a response.

- The ASP.NET Ajax Control Toolkit contains many more Ajax-enabled, rich GUI controls. Click the **Download** Button to begin the download.

- The key control in every ASP.NET Ajax-enabled app is the ScriptManager (in the **Toolbox**'s **AJAX Extensions** tab), which manages the JavaScript client-side code (called scripts) that enable asynchronous Ajax functionality. A benefit of using ASP.NET Ajax is that you do not need to know JavaScript to be able to use these scripts.

- The ScriptManager is meant for use with the controls in the **Toolbox**'s **AJAX Extensions** tab. There can be only one ScriptManager per page.

- The Ajax Control Toolkit comes with an enhanced version of the ScriptManager called the ToolkitScriptManager, which manages all the scripts for the ASP. NET Ajax Toolkit controls. This one should be used in any ASPX page that contains controls from the ASP. NET Ajax Toolkit.

- The TabContainer control enables you to group information into tabs that are displayed only if they're selected. To add a tab, open the **TabContainer Tasks** smart-tag menu and select **Add Tab Panel**. This adds a TabPanel object—representing a tab—to the TabContainer.

- The UpdatePanel control eliminates full-page refreshes by isolating a section of a page for a partial-page update.

- To specify when an UpdatePanel should update, you need to define an UpdatePanel trigger. Select the UpdatePanel, then click the ellipsis button next to the control's Triggers property in the **Properties** window. In the **UpdatePanelTrigger Collection** dialog that appears, click **Add** to add an AsyncPostBackTrigger. Set the ControlID property to the control that triggers the update and the EventName property to the event that is generated when the user interacts with the control.

- Several controls in the Ajax Control Toolkit are extenders—components that enhance the functionality of regular ASP.NET controls.

- ValidatorCalloutExtender controls enhance the ASP.NET validation controls by displaying error messages in small yellow callouts next to the input fields, rather than as text in the page.

■ You can create a `ValidatorCalloutExtender` by opening any validator control's smart-tag menu and clicking **Add Extender...** to display the **Extender Wizard** dialog. Next, choose `ValidatorCalloutExtender` from the list of available extenders.

KEY TERMS

access rule in ASP.NET—A rule that grants or denies access to a particular directory for a specific user or group of users.

Ajax (Asynchronous Javascript and XML)—Web apps add a layer between the client and the server to manage communication between the two.

ASP.NET Ajax Control Toolkit—Contains many more Ajax-enabled, rich GUI controls.

asynchronous request—A request that occurs in the background while the user continues to interact with the app.

authenticating a user—Confirming the user's identity.

AutoPostBack property of a DropDownList ASP.NET control—

callback function—Uses partial-page updates to display the data in the existing web page without reloading the entire page.

content page in ASP.NET—A home page and an about page contained in the default ASP.NET Web Site.

Enable Paging setting for an ASP.NET GridView—Causes the GridView to split across multiple pages.

Enable Sorting setting for an ASP.NET GridView—Causes the column headings in the GridView to become hyperlinks that allow users to sort the data in the GridView using the sort expressions specified by each column.

extender—Components that enhance the functionality of regular ASP.NET controls.

forms authentication—A technique used to protect a page so that only registered users who are logged in to the website can access the page.

master page in ASP.NET—A master page defines common GUI elements that are inherited by each page in a set of content pages.

navigation bar on a website—Allows you to switch between these pages by clicking the link for the appropriate page.

PageSize property of a GridView ASP.NET control—Determines the number of entries per page.

partial page update—Modifies a portion of a webpage (without reloading the webpage) in response to an Ajax request's response

ScriptManager control—Manages the JavaScript client-side code (called scripts) that enable asynchronous Ajax functionality.

synchronous request—The client waits for the server to respond and reloads the entire page with the data from the response. While a synchronous request is being processed on the server, the user cannot interact with the web page.

TabContainer Ajax Control Toolkit control—Enables you to group information into tabs that are displayed only if they're selected.

TabPanel class—Represents a tab to the TabContainer.

ToolkitScriptManager control—Manages the scripts for the ASP. NET Ajax Toolkit controls.

UpdatePanel ASP.NET Ajax Extensions control—Control that provides partial page update capabilities in ASP.NET Ajax.

ValidatorCalloutExtender control—Enhances the ASP.NET validation controls by displaying error messages in small yellow callouts next to the input fields, rather than as text in the page.

Web Site Administration Tool—Specifies which parts of a website are password protected

MULTIPLE-CHOICE QUESTIONS

29.1 With a(n) _____ request the user can continue interacting with the app in the client browser while the server processes the request.

a) trigger
b) asynchronous
c) synchronous
d) callback

29.2 _____ is a technique used to protect a page so that only registered users who are logged in to the website can access the page.

a) User login
b) Postback
c) Forms authentication
d) Access rule

29.3 The default **ASP.NET Web Site** contains a home page and a(n) _____ page.

a) login
b) document
c) description
d) about

29.4 The UpdatePanel control eliminates _____-page refreshes by isolating a section of a page for a _____-page update.

a) full, partial
b) full, full
c) partial, partial
d) partial full

29.5 Setting a DropDownList's _____ property to True indicates that a postback occurs each time the user selects an item in the DropDownList.

a) DropDownPost
b) PostBack
c) AutoPostBack
d) SelectPostBack

29.6 Several controls in the Ajax Control Toolkit are _____—components that enhance the functionality of regular ASP.NET controls.

a) enhancers
b) extenders
c) augmenters
d) amplifiers

29.7 A _____ defines common GUI elements that are inherited by each page in a set of content pages.

a) root page
b) content page
c) login page
d) master page

29.8 The key control in every ASP.NET Ajax-enabled app is the _____ (in the **Toolbox**'s **AJAX Extensions** tab), which manages the JavaScript client-side code (called scripts) that enable asynchronous Ajax functionality.

a) ScriptManager
b) JavaScriptManager
c) TabContainer
d) ClientScriptManager

29.9 A traditional web app must make synchronous requests and must wait for a response, whereas an AJAX (Asynchronous JavaScript and XML) web apps can make requests and do not need to wait for a response.

a) direct
b) enabling
c) asynchronous
d) postback

29.10 If you attempt to access a password-protected page without logging in, you're automatically redirected to the _____.

a) home page
b) login page
c) master page
d) content page

SELF-REVIEW EXERCISES

29.11 State whether each of the following is *true* or *false*. If *false*, explain why.
  a) An access rule grants or denies access to a particular directory for a specific user or group of users.
  b) When using controls from the Ajax Control Toolkit, you must include the ScriptManager control at the top of the ASPX page.
  c) A master page is like a base class in a visual inheritance hierarchy, and content pages are like derived classes.

d) A `GridView` automatically enables sorting and paging of its contents.

e) AJAX web apps make synchronous requests and wait for responses.

29.12 Fill in the blanks in each of the following statements:

a) A(n) _____ defines common GUI elements that are inherited by each page in a set of _____.

b) The main difference between a traditional web app and an Ajax web app is that the latter supports _____ requests.

c) The _____ template is a starter kit for a small multi-page website that uses Microsoft's recommended practices for organizing a website and separating the website's style (look-and-feel) from its content.

d) The _____ allows you to configure various options that determine how your app behaves.

e) A `LinqDataSource`'s _____ event occurs every time the `LinqDataSource` selects data from its data context, and can be used to implement custom `Select` queries against the data context.

f) Setting a `DropDownList`'s _____ property to `True` indicates that a postback occurs each time the user selects an item in the `DropDownList`.

g) Several controls in the Ajax Control Toolkit are _____—components that enhance the functionality of regular ASP.NET controls.

ANSWERS TO SELF-REVIEW EXERCISES

29.1 a) True. b) False. The `ToolkitScriptManager` control must be used for controls from the Ajax Control Toolkit. The `ScriptManager` control can be used only for the controls in the **Toolbox**'s **AJAX Extensions** tab. c) True. d) False. Checking **Enable Sorting** in the **Grid-View Tasks** smart-tag menu changes the column headings in the `GridView` to hyperlinks that allow users to sort the data in the `GridView`. Checking **Enable Paging** in the **GridView Tasks** smart-tag menu causes the `GridView` to split across multiple pages. e) False. That is what traditional web apps do. AJAX web apps can make asynchronous requests and do not need to wait for responses.

29.2 a) master page, content pages. b) asynchronous. c) **ASP.NET Web Site**. d) **Web Site Administration Tool**. e) `Selecting`. f) `AutoPostBack`. g) extenders.

EXERCISES

29.3 *(Guestbook App Modification)* Add Ajax functionality to the `Guestbook` app in Exercise 28.5. Use control extenders to display error callouts when one of the user input fields is invalid.

29.4 *(Guestbook App Modification)* Modify the `Guestbook` app in Exercise 29.3 to use a `UpdatePanel` so only the `GridView` updates when the user submits the form. Because only the `UpdatePanel` will be updated, you cannot clear the user input fields in the **Submit** button's `Click` event, so you can remove this functionality.

29.5 *(Session Tracking Modification)* Use the **ASP.NET Web Site** template that you learned about in this chapter to reimplement the session tracking example in Section 28.6.

Operator Precedence Chart

Operators are shown in decreasing order of precedence from top to bottom, with levels of precedence separated by horizontal lines. Visual Basic operators associate from left to right.

Operator	Type
TypeOf	type comparison
^	exponentiation
+	unary plus
–	unary minus
*	multiplication
/	division
\	integer division
Mod	modulus
+	addition
–	subtraction
&	concatenation
<<	bitwise left shift
>>	bitwise right shift
=	relational is equal to
<>	relational is not equal to
<	relational less than
<=	relational less than or equal to
>	relational greater than
>=	relational greater than or equal to
Like	pattern matching
Is	reference comparison
IsNot	reference comparison
Not	logical negation
And	logical AND without short-circuit evaluation
AndAlso	logical AND with short-circuit evaluation
Or	logical inclusive OR without short-circuit evaluation
OrElse	logical inclusive OR with short-circuit evaluation
Xor	logical exclusive OR

Figure A.1   Operator list (in order of operator precedence).

B

A P P E N D I X

ASCII Character Set

T he digits in the left column of Fig. B.1 are the left digits of the decimal equivalent (0–127) of the character code, and the digits in the top row of Fig. B.1 are the right digits of the character code. For example, the character code for "F" is 70, and the character code for "&" is 38.

Most users of this book are interested in the ASCII character set used to represent English characters on many computers. The ASCII character set is a subset of the Unicode character set used by Visual Basic .NET to represent characters from most of the world's languages.

	0	1	2	3	4	5	6	7	8	9
0	nul	soh	stx	etx	eot	enq	ack	bel	bs	ht
1	nl	vt	ff	cr	so	si	dle	dc1	dc2	dc3
2	dc4	nak	syn	etb	can	em	sub	esc	fs	gs
3	rs	us	sp	!	"	#	$	%	&	'
4	(	)	*	+	,	-	.	/	0	1
5	2	3	4	5	6	7	8	9	:	;
6	<	=	>	?	@	A	B	C	D	E
7	F	G	H	I	J	K	L	M	N	O
8	P	Q	R	S	T	U	V	W	X	Y
9	Z	[	\	]	^	_	'	a	b	c
10	d	e	f	g	h	i	j	k	l	m
11	n	o	p	q	r	s	t	u	v	w
12	x	y	z	{			}	~	del		

Figure B.1   ASCII character set.

GUI Design Guidelines

This appendix contains a complete list of the GUI design guidelines presented at the end of each chapter. The guidelines are organized by chapter; within each chapter section, they're organized by control.

Chapter 3: Welcome App (Introduction to Visual App Development)

Overall Design

■ Use colors in your apps, but not to the point of distracting the user.

Form

■ Choose short, descriptive Form titles. Capitalize words that are not articles, prepositions or conjunctions. Do not use punctuation.

■ Use 9pt Segoe UI font to improve readability for controls that display text.

Label

■ Use Labels to display text that users cannot change.

■ Ensure that all Label controls are large enough to display their text. You can do this by setting AutoSize to True, or by setting AutoSize to False then resizing the Label.

PictureBox

■ Use PictureBoxes to enhance GUIs with graphics that users cannot change.

■ Images should fit inside their PictureBoxes. This can be achieved by setting Picture-Box property SizeMode to StretchImage.

Chapter 4: Designing the Inventory App (Introducing TextBoxes and Buttons)

Overall Design

■ Leave space between the edges of the Form and its controls.

■ Although you can drag a Label control to a location on the Form, the Location property can be used to specify a precise position.

■ Place an app's output below and/or to the right of the Form's input controls.

■ As you drag controls, the IDE displays blue and purple lines called snaplines. The blue lines help you position controls relative to one another. The purple lines help you position controls relative to the control text.

Button

■ Buttons are labeled using their Text property. These labels should use book-title capitalization and be brief while still being meaningful to the user.

■ Buttons should be stacked downward from the top right of a Form or arranged on the same line starting from the bottom right of a Form.

Form

■ Changing the Form's title allows users to identify the Form's purpose.

■ Form titles should use book-title capitalization.

■ Change the Form font to 9pt Segoe UI to be consistent with Microsoft's recommended font for Windows.

Label

■ A Label used to describe the purpose of a control should use sentence-style capitalization and end with a colon. These types of Labels are called descriptive Labels.

■ The TextAlign property of a descriptive Label should be set to MiddleLeft. This ensures that text within groups of Labels aligns.

■ Place each descriptive Label above or to the left of the control (for instance, a TextBox) that it identifies.

■ Align the left or right sides of a group of descriptive Labels if the Labels are arranged vertically.

■ Use a descriptive Label to identify an output Label.

■ Output Labels should be distinguishable from descriptive Labels. This can be done by setting the BorderStyle property of an output Label to Fixed3D.

■ If several output Labels are arranged vertically to display numbers used in a mathematical calculation (such as in an invoice), use the MiddleRight value for the TextAlign property.

■ A descriptive Label and the control it identifies should be aligned on the left if they're arranged vertically.

■ The text in a descriptive Label and the text in the control it identifies should be aligned if they're arranged horizontally.

TextBox

■ Use TextBoxes to input data from the keyboard.

■ Each TextBox should have a descriptive Label indicating the input expected from the user.

■ Make TextBoxes wide enough for their expected inputs.

Chapter 7: Wage Calculator App (Introducing Algorithms, Pseudocode and Program Control)

Overall Design

■ Format all monetary amounts using the C (currency) format specifier.

TextBox

■ When using multiple TextBoxes vertically, align the TextBoxes on their right sides, and where possible make the TextBoxes the same size. Left-align the descriptive Labels for such TextBoxes.

Chapter 8: Dental Payment App (Introducing CheckBoxes and Message Dialogs)

CheckBox

■ A CheckBox's label should be descriptive and brief. When a CheckBox label contains more than one word, use book-title capitalization.

■ Align groups of CheckBoxes either horizontally or vertically.

Message Dialog

■ Text displayed in a dialog should be descriptive and brief.

Chapter 9: Car Payment Calculator App (Introducing the Do While...Loop and Do Until...Loop Repetition Statements)

ListBox

■ A ListBox should be large enough to display all of its content or large enough that scrollbars may be used easily.

■ Use headers in a ListBox when you're displaying tabular data. Adding headers improves readability by describing the information that's displayed in the ListBox.

Chapter 10: Class Average App (Introducing the Do...Loop While and Do...Loop Until Repetition Statements)

Overall Design

■ Transfer the focus to the control that should be used next.

Button

■ Disable a Button when its function should not be available to users.

■ Enable a disabled Button when its function once again should be available to users.

Chapter 11: Interest Calculator App (Introducing the For...Next Repetition Statement and NumericUpDown Control)

NumericUpDown

■ A NumericUpDown control should follow the same GUI Design Guidelines as a TextBox.

■ Use a NumericUpDown control to limit the range of numeric user input.

TextBox

■ If a TextBox will display multiple lines of output, set the Multiline property to True and left align the output by setting the TextAlign property to Left.

■ If a TextBox is used to display output, set the ReadOnly property to True to ensure that the user cannot change the output.

■ If a multiline TextBox will display many lines of output, limit the TextBox height and use a vertical scrollbar to allow users to view additional lines of output.

Chapter 12: Security Panel App (Introducing the Select Case Multiple Selection Statement)

Overall Design

■ If your GUI is modeling a real-world object, its design should mimic the physical appearance of the object.

TextBox

■ Mask passwords or other sensitive pieces of information in TextBoxes.

Chapter 14: Shipping Time App (Using Dates and Timers)

DateTimePicker

■ Use a DateTimePicker to retrieve date and time information from the user.

■ Each DateTimePicker should have a corresponding descriptive Label.

■ If the user is to specify a time of day or a date and time, set the DateTimePicker's ShowUpDown property to True. If the user is to specify only a date, set the DateTimePicker's ShowUpDown property to False to allow the user to select a day from the month calendar.

GroupBox

- GroupBox titles should be concise and should use book-title capitalization.
- Use GroupBoxes to group related controls in a box with a title.

Chapter 17: Flag Quiz App (Introducing One-Dimensional Arrays and ComboBoxes)

ComboBox

- Each ComboBox should have a descriptive Label that describes the ComboBox's contents.
- If a ComboBox's content should not be editable, set its DropDownStyle property to Drop-DownList.

Chapter 18: Sales Data App (Introducing Two-Dimensional Arrays and RadioButtons)

RadioButton

- Use RadioButtons when the user must choose only one option from a group.
- Always place each group of RadioButtons in a separate container (such as a GroupBox).
- Align groups of RadioButtons either horizontally or vertically.

Chapter 19: Microwave Oven App (Building Your Own Classes and Objects)

Panel

- Use Panels to organize groups of related controls where the purpose of the controls is obvious. If the purpose of the controls is not obvious, use a GroupBox rather than a Panel, because GroupBoxes can contain captions.
- Although it's possible to have a Panel without a border (by setting the BorderStyle property to None), use borders on your Panels to improve user interface readability and organization.
- A Panel can display scrollbars when it's not large enough to display all of its controls. To increase usability, we suggest avoiding the use of scrollbars on Panels. If a Panel is not large enough to display all of its contents, increase the size of the Panel.

Chapter 20: Shipping Hub App (Introducing Collections, the For Each...Next Statement and Access Keys)

Overall Design

- Set a control's TabStop property to True only if the control is used to receive user input.
- Use the TabIndex property to define the logical order in which the user should enter data. Usually the order transfers the focus of the app from top to bottom and left to right.
- Use access keys to allow users to "click" a control using the keyboard.

Chapter 21: Typing App (Introducing Keyboard Events, Menus, Dialogs and the Dictionary Collection)

MenuStrip

- Use book-title capitalization in menu-item text.
- Use separator bars in a menu to group related menu items.
- If clicking a menu item opens a dialog, an ellipsis (...) should follow the menu item's text.

Keyword Chart

T he table of Fig. D.1 contains a complete listing of Visual Basic keywords. Many of these keywords are discussed throughout the text.

Visual Basic Keywords			
AddHandler	AddressOf	Alias	And
AndAlso	As	Boolean	ByRef
Byte	ByVal	Call	Case
Catch	CBool	CByte	CChar
CDate	CDbl	CDec	Char
CInt	Class	CLng	CObj
Const	Continue	CSByte	CShort
CSng	CStr	CType	CUInt
CULng	CUShort	Date	Decimal
Declare	Default	Delegate	Dim
DirectCast	Do	Double	Each
Else	ElseIf	End	EndIf
Enum	Erase	Error	Event
Exit	False	Finally	For
Friend	Function	Get	GetType
GetXmlNamespace	Global	GoSub	GoTo
Handles	If	Implements	Imports
In	Inherits	Integer	Interface
Is	IsNot	Let	Lib
Like	Long	Loop	Me
Mod	Module	MustInherit	MustOverride
MyBase	MyClass	Namespace	Narrowing

Figure D.1   Visual Basic keywords. (Part 1 of 2.)

769

Visual Basic Keywords

New	Next	Not	Nothing
NotInheritable	NotOverridable	Object	Of
On	Operator	Option	Optional
Or	OrElse	Overloads	Overridable
Overrides	ParamArray	Partial	Private
Property	Protected	Public	RaiseEvent
ReadOnly	ReDim	REM	RemoveHandler
Resume	Return	SByte	Select
Set	Shadows	Shared	Short
Single	Static	Step	Stop
String	Structure	Sub	SyncLock
Then	Throw	To	True
Try	TryCast	TypeOf	UInteger
ULong	UShort	Using	Varint
Went	When	While	Widening
With	WithEvents	WriteOnly	Xor

The following are reserved, although they're not used in Visual Basic:

EndIf	GoSub	Let	Variant	Wend

Figure D.1   Visual Basic keywords. (Part 2 of 2.)

Primitive Data Types

The table of Fig. E.1 contains the Visual Basic primitive data types, the number of bytes that a value of each type occupies in memory and the range of values that each type supports.

Type	Size in bytes	Value range
SByte	1	–128 to 127, inclusive
Byte	1	0 to 255, inclusive
Boolean	2	True or False
Char	2	0 to 65,535, inclusive (representing the Unicode character set)
Short	2	–32,768 to 32,767, inclusive
UShort	2	0 to 65,535, inclusive
Integer	4	–2,147,483,648 to 2,147,483,647, inclusive
UInteger	4	0 to 4,294,967,295, inclusive
Single	4	negative range: –3.4028235E+38 to –1.401298E–45 positive range: 1.401298E–45 to 3.4028235E+38
Long	8	–9,223,372,036,854,775,808 to 9,223,372,036,854,775,807, inclusive
ULong	8	0 to 18,446,744,073,709,551,615, inclusive
Double	8	negative range: –1.79769313486231570E+308 to –4.94065645841246544E–324 positive range: 4.94065645841246544E–324 to 1.79769313486231570E+308
Date	8	0:00:00 on 1 January 0001 to 23:59:59 on 31 December 9999

Figure E.1 Visual Basic primitive types. (Part 1 of 2.)

771

Type	Size in bytes	Value range
Decimal	16	Range with no decimal point: ±79,228,162,514,264,337,593,543,950,335 Range with 28 places to the right of the decimal point: ±7.9228162514264337593543950335 The smallest nonzero number is ±0.0000000000000000000000000001 (±1E–28)
String	Depends on platform	Up to approximately 2 billion Unicode characters

Figure E.1 Visual Basic primitive types. (Part 2 of 2.)

Additional Primitive Type Information

This appendix is based on information from Section 7.3 of The Microsoft Visual Basic Language Specification (available at msdn2.microsoft.com/en-us/library/ms234437.aspx).

GLOSSARY

A

access key—Keyboard shortcut that allows the user to perform an action on a control using the keyboard.

access modifier—Keywords used to specify what members of a class a client may access. Includes keywords `Public` and `Private`.

access rule in ASP.NET—A rule that grants or denies access to a particular directory for a specific user or group of users.

accessors—Methodlike code units that handle the details of modifying and returning data.

action expression (in the UML)—Used in an action state within a UML activity diagram to specify a particular action to perform.

action state—An action to perform in a UML activity diagram that's represented by an action-state symbol.

action-state symbol—A rectangle with its left and right sides replaced with arcs curving outward that represents an action to perform in a UML activity diagram.

action/decision model of programming—Representing control statements as UML activity diagrams with rounded rectangles indicating *actions* to be performed and diamond symbols indicating *decisions* to be made.

active tab—The tab of the document displayed in the IDE.

active window—The window that's currently being used—sometimes referred to as the window that has the focus.

activity diagram—A UML diagram that models the activity (also called the workflow) of a portion of a software system.

Ada—A programming language, named after Lady Ada Lovelace, that was developed under the sponsorship of the U.S. Department of Defense (DOD) in the 1970s and early 1980s.

Add method of class `Dictionary`—Adds a key/value pair to a `Dictionary` collection.

Add method of class `HttpSessionState`—Method called to place key/value pairs (session items) in an `HttpSession-State` object.

Add method of class `List`—Adds a specified object to the end of a `List`.

Add method of `Items`—Adds an item to a `ListBox` control.

AddHandler statement—Adds an event handler for a specific event.

AddressOf operator—Specifies the location of a method, which can be associated with an event.

ADO.NET—Part of the .NET Framework that's used to interact with databases.

Ajax (Asynchronous Javascript and XML)—Web apps add a layer between the client and the server to manage communication between the two.

algorithm—A procedure for solving a problem, specifying the actions to be executed and the order in which they're to be executed.

Alphabetical icon—The icon in the **Properties** window that, when clicked, sorts properties alphabetically.

And operator—A logical operator used to ensure that two conditions are *both* true before choosing a certain path of execution. Does not perform short-circuit evaluation.

AndAlso operator—A logical operator used to ensure that two conditions are *both* true before choosing a certain path of execution. Performs short-circuit evaluation.

API (app programming interface)—The interface used by a program to access the operating system and various services on the computer.

App_Code folder—The project folder where the app-code files (other than the `aspx.vb` code-behind files) are stored. This is a protected folder that's accessible only to the server.

App_Data folder—The project folder where external sources of data (i.e., the `Bookstore.mdf` database file) are stored. This is a protected folder that's accessible only to the server.

argument—Inputs to a procedure call that provide information needed to perform the procedure's task.

arithmetic and logic unit (ALU)—The "manufacturing" section of the computer. The ALU performs calculations and makes decisions.

arithmetic operators—The operators +, -, *, /, \, ^ and `Mod`.

ARPAnet—The grandfather of today's Internet.

array—A data structure containing data items of the same type.

array bounds—Integers that determine what indices can be used to access an element in an array. The lower bound is 0; the upper bound is the length of the array minus one.

Array.Sort method—Sorts the values of an array into ascending order.

As keyword—Used in variable declarations. Indicates that the following word (such as `Integer`) is the variable type.

ASP.NET—.NET software that helps you create web apps.

ASP.NET Ajax Control Toolkit—Contains many Ajax-enabled, rich GUI controls.

ASP.NET technology—Can be combined with Visual Basic to create web apps.

ASP.NET Ajax—ASP.NET web controls that enable Ajax functionality.

ASP.NET Development Server—A web server that you can use to test your ASP.NET web apps. It's specifically designed for learning and testing purposes to execute web apps on the local computer and to respond to browser requests from the local computer.

ASP.NET server control—Another name for a web control.

ASP.NET Website project—The type of project you create with Visual Web Developer to build an ASP.NET app.

.aspx extension—The file-name extension for ASP.NET Web Forms pages.

ASPX page—File that specifies the GUI of a web page using web controls. Also called Web Forms or Web Form Pages.

assembler—A translator program that converts assembly-language programs to machine language at computer speeds.

assembly—The mechanism used to package compiled .NET code for reuse.

assembly language—A type of programming language that uses English-like abbreviations to represent the fundamental operations on the computer.

assignment operator—The "=" symbol used to assign values in an assignment statement.

assignment statement—A statement that copies one value to another. An assignment statement contains an "equals" sign (=) operator that causes the value of its right operand to be copied to its left operand.

asterisk (*)—Multiplication operator. The operator's left and right operands are multiplied together.

asynchronous request—A request that's performed in the background. The user can continue interacting with the web app while the server processes the request.

authenticating a user—Confirming the user's identity.

attribute—Another name for a property of an object.

attribute in XAML—Can be used to set an object's property values. Represented in XAML by placing a property name, an equal sign (=) and a value in double quotes inside the opening tag of the object's XAML element.

auto-hide—A space-saving IDE feature used for windows such as **Toolbox**, **Properties** and **Solution Explorer** that hides a window until the mouse pointer is placed on the hidden window's tab.

AutoGenerateColumns attribute of a DataGrid—When set to True, indicates that a DataGrid should determine its columns from the source of its data.

AutoSize property of a Label—Determines whether a Label is automatically sized based on its content.

B

BackColor property—Specifies the background color of the Form or a control.

Background property of class Canvas—Gets or sets the Brush value used as the background color of the Canvas.

backslash (\)—Integer division operator. The operator divides its left operand by its right and returns an Integer result.

bandwidth—The information-carrying capacity of communications lines.

BASIC (Beginner's All-purpose Symbolic Instruction Code)—A programming language for writing simple programs. Developed in the mid-1960s by Professors John Kemeny and Thomas Kurtz of Dartmouth College. Its primary purpose was to familiarize novices with programming techniques.

Beep—Causes your computer to make a beep sound.

binary digit—A digit that can assume one of two values.

binary operators—An operator that takes two operands.

Binding markup extension—Binds a property of an object to an attribute of a control.

BindingNavigator—A set of controls that allow you to manipulate and navigate through data in a data source.

BindingSource—A component that manages the data used by a BindingNavigator.

bit—Short for "binary digit"—a digit that can assume one of two values.

block—A group of code statements.

block scope—Variables declared inside control statements, such as an If...Then statement, have block scope. Block scope begins at the identifier's declaration and ends at the block's final statement (for example, Else or End If).

body of a control statement—The set of statements that are enclosed in a control statement.

book-title capitalization—A style that capitalizes the first letter of the each word in the text (for example, **Calculate Total**).

Boolean data type—A data type whose variable can have the value True or False.

Border element—Used to place a border around a WPF control.

BorderStyle property—Specifies the appearance of a Label's border, which allows you to distinguish one control from another visually. The BorderStyle property can be set to None (no border), FixedSingle (a single dark line as a border), or Fixed3D (giving the Label a "sunken" appearance).

BorderStyle property of an Image—Defines the border (such as outset) around an image.

BorderWidth property of an Image—Defines the width of an Image's border.

bottom tier—The tier (also known as the information tier, or the data tier) containing the app data of a multitier app—typically implemented as a database

bounding box of an ellipse—Specifies an ellipse's location, width and height.

break mode—The IDE mode when app execution is suspended. This mode is entered through the debugger.

breakpoint—A location where execution is to suspend, indicated by a solid maroon circle.

Brush class—Used to fill shapes and controls with colors.

Brush object—An object used to specify drawing parameters when drawing solid shapes.

Brushes class—Provides easy access to Brush objects representing the standard colors.

bug—A flaw in a program that prevents it from executing correctly.

built-in data type—A data type already defined in Visual Basic, such as an Integer.

business logic tier—The tier that controls interaction between the client and information tiers. Also called the middle tier.

Button control—When clicked, commands the app to perform an action.

Button element—Displays a button in a WPF GUI.

Button web control—Allows users to perform an action.

ByRef keyword—Used to pass an argument by reference.

byte—Eight bits.

ByVal keyword—The keyword specifying that the calling procedure should pass a copy of its argument's value to the called procedure.

C

C#—A programming language that was designed specifically for the .NET platform. It has roots in C, C++ and Java, adapting the best features of each. Like Visual Basic, C# is object oriented and has access to .NET's powerful library of prebuilt components, enabling you to develop apps quickly.

callback function—Client-side function that processes the response to an asynchronous web request.

callee—The procedure being called.

caller—The procedure that calls another procedure. Also known as the calling procedure.

Cancel value of DialogResult enumeration—Used to determine whether the user clicked the **Cancel** Button of a dialog.

Canvas layout container—A WPF control that enables absolute positioning of its child elements.

caret (^)—Exponentiation operator. This operator raises its left operand to a power specified by the right operand.

Cascading Style Sheets (CSS)—Used to define the look-and-feel of web page elements.

Case Else statement—Optional statement whose body executes if the Select Case's test expression does not match an expression of any Case.

case sensitive—The instance where two words that are spelled identically are treated differently if the capitalization of the two words differs.

Case statement—Statement whose body executes if the Select Case's test expression matches the Case's expression.

Catch block—Also called an exception handler, this block executes when the corresponding Try block in the app detects an exceptional situation and throws an exception of the type the Catch block declares.

Categorized icon—The icon in the **Properties** window that, when clicked, sorts properties categorically.

Central Processing Unit (CPU)—The part of the computer's hardware that's responsible for supervising the operation of the other sections of the computer.

Char data type—Primitive type that represents a character.

Char structure—Stores characters (such as letters and symbols).

character literal—A single character represented as a value of type Char. Create a character literal by placing a single character in double quotes followed by the letter c (e.g., "0"c).

character set—The set of all characters used to write apps and represent data items on a particular computer. Visual Basic uses the Unicode character set.

Chars property of class String—Returns the character located at a specific index in a String.

CheckBox control—A small square GUI element that either is empty or contains a check mark.

CheckBox label—The text that appears next to a CheckBox.

Checked property of the RadioButton control—Displays a small dot in the control when True. When False, the control displays an empty white circle.

Checked property of the CheckBox control—Specifies whether the CheckBox is checked (True) or unchecked (False).

CheckedChanged event—Raised when a RadioButton's state changes.

CheckFileExists property of class OpenFileDialog—Enables the user to display a warning if a specified file does not exist.

child element—XAML element that's nested inside another element.

Children property of Canvas—Returns a collection of all the child elements nested in a Canvas.

class—The type of a group of related objects. A class specifies the general format of its objects; the properties and actions available to an object depend on its class. An object is to its class much as a house is to the blueprint from which a house is constructed.

class definition—The code that belongs to a class, beginning with keywords Public Class and ending with keywords End Class.

Class Keyword—Reserved word required to begin a class definition.

class name—The identifier used to identify the name of a class in code.

Clear method of Items—Deletes all the values in a ListBox control.

Click event—An event raised when a user clicks a control.

Click event of a Button—Raised when the user presses the Button.

client—When an app creates and uses an object of a class, the app is known as a client of the class.

client tier—The user interface of a multitier app (also called the top tier).

Close method of class StreamWriter or StreamReader—Used to close the stream.

COBOL (COmmon Business Oriented Language)—Programming language that was developed in the late 1950s by a group of computer manufacturers in conjunction with government and industrial computer users. This language is used primarily for business apps that manipulate large amounts of data.

code editor—A window where a user can create, view or edit an app's code.

Code view—A mode of the Visual Basic IDE where the app's code is displayed in an editor window.

code-behind file—Visual Basic file that contains a class which provides an ASPX page's functionality.

collection—A class used to store groups of related objects.

Color structure—Represents a color and provides methods for creating custom colors. Also contains several predefined colors as properties.

ColorDialog class—Used to display a dialog from which the user can select colors.

column—The second dimension of a two-dimensional array.

ColumnDefinition element of a Grid—Specifies the attributes of a column in a Grid.

ColumnDefinitions property of a Grid—Provides access to the collection of ColumnDefinitions for a Grid.

ComboBox control—Combines a TextBox with a ListBox.

comment—Text that follows a single-quote character (') and is inserted to improve an app's readability.

compilation error—An error that occurs when program statements violate the grammatical rules of a programming language or when statements are simply incorrect in the current context.

compiler—A translator program that converts high-level-language programs into machine language.

component object box—The ComboBox at the top of the **Properties** window that allows you to select the Form or control object whose properties you want set.

component tray—The area below the Windows Form Designer that contains controls, such as Timers, that are not part of the graphical user interface.

componentization—*See* divide-and-conquer technique.

computer—A device capable that can perform computations and make logical decisions millions, billions and even trillions of times faster than human beings can carry out the same tasks.

computer program—A set of instructions that guides a computer through an orderly series of actions.

computer programmer—A person who writes computer programs.

condition—An expression with a True or False value that's used to make a decision.

conditional If expression—A shorthand representation of an If...Then...Else statement.

consistent state—A way to maintain the values of an object's instance variables such that the values are always valid.

Const keyword—Used to declare a named constant.

constant—An identifier whose value cannot be changed after its initial declaration.

constructor—A special class method that initializes a class's variables when an object of that class is created.

container—An object, such as a GroupBox or Form, that contains other controls.

ContainsKey method of class Dictionary—Determines whether the Dictionary contains the key specified as an argument.

Content attribute of a Button—Specifies the text on the Button.

content page in ASP.NET—A home page and an about page contained in the default ASP.NET Web Site.

content control—A WPF control that can hold one piece of content of any type.

Contents command—The command that displays a categorized table of contents in which help articles are organized by topic.

ContentTemplate element of the UpdatePanel control—Contains the control that initiates an asynchronous request and the controls updated when the UpdatePanel performs a partial page update.

context-sensitive help—A help option (launched by pressing *F1*) that provides links to articles that apply to the current content (that is, the item selected with the mouse pointer).

control—A reusable GUI component, such as a GroupBox, RadioButton, Button or Label.

Control class—A type that can be used to declare variables for referencing controls on the Form. Defines the common properties and methods of Windows Forms controls.

control structure (control statement)—An app component that specifies the order in which statements execute (also known as the flow of control).

control structure (statement) nesting—Placing one control statement in the body of another control statement.

control structure (statement) stacking—A set of control statements in sequence. The exit point of one control statement is connected to the entry point of the next control statement in sequence.

ControlChars.Tab constant—Represents a tab character.

controlling expression—Value compared sequentially with each Case until either a match occurs or the End Select statement is reached. Also known as a test expression.

ControlToValidate property—Specifies the control that's validated by the RequiredFieldValidator.

Convert class—Provides methods for converting data types.

coordinate system—A scheme for identifying every possible point on the computer screen.

CornerRadius attribute of a Border—Specifies the rounding of the corners of a Border.

Count property of Items—Returns the number of ListBox items.

Count property of List—Returns the number of objects in the List.

counter—A variable used to determine the number of times the body of a repetition statement executes.

counter-controlled repetition—A technique that uses a counter variable to determine the number of times that the body of a repetition statement executes. Also called definite repetition.

CType function—Function that converts its first argument to the type specified in its second argument.

CType operator—Converts the object passed as the first argument to the type passed as the second argument.

currency format—Used to display values as monetary amounts.

CustomFormat property of a DateTimePicker control—The DateTimePicker property that contains your format string with which to display the date and/or time when DateTimePicker Format property is set to Custom.

D

data hierarchy—Collection of data items processed by computers that become larger and more complex in structure as you progress from bits, to characters, to fields and up to larger data structures.

Data menu—The menu of the IDE that contains commands for interacting with databases.

Data Source Configuration Wizard—Wizard used to add a data source to the app.

Data Sources window—Window used to connect an app to a data source and create data-bound controls.

data structure—Groups and organizes related data.

data tier—The tier (also known as the information tier, or the bottom tier) containing the app data of a multitier app, typically implemented as a database.

data-bound control—A control that displays information contained in a data source. When the information in the data source changes, the control updates to display the new information.

database—An organized collection of data used to store information for access by apps.

Database Explorer window—Window used to view and manipulate database information in the Visual Basic 2010 Express IDE.

database management system (DBMS)—Provides mechanisms for storing and organizing data.

DataContext class—LINQ to SQL classes representation of a database in the app. Manages interactions between the app and the database.

DataGrid control—Displays data in rows and columns. Can bind a collection of objects to this control via its `ItemSource` property.

DataSource property of class BindingSource—Specifies the data managed by the `BindingSource`.

DataSource property of class ComboBox—Specifies the source of items listed in a `ComboBox`.

Date type—A type whose properties can be used to store and display date and time information.

Date variable—A variable of type `Date`, capable of storing date and time data.

DateChanged event of MonthCalendar control—Raised when a new date (or a range of dates) is selected.

DateTime primitive type—The .NET Framework Class Library type that corresponds to the `Date` keyword.

DateTimePicker control—Retrieves date and time information from the user.

Debug menu—The menu of the IDE that contains commands for debugging and running an app.

debugger—A tool that allows you to analyze the behavior of your app to determine whether it's executing correctly.

debugging—The process of fixing errors in an app.

Decimal data type—Used to store monetary amounts.

decimal digits—The digits 0, 1, 2, 3, 4, 5, 6, 7, 8 and 9.

decision symbol—The diamond-shaped symbol in a UML activity diagram that indicates that a decision is to be made.

declaration—The reporting of a new variable to the compiler. The variable can then be used in the Visual Basic code.

declare a variable—Report the name and type of a variable to the compiler.

DefaultBackColor property—Contains the default background color for a control.

deferred execution—A LINQ query is not executed until you begin to iterate over its results.

definite repetition—*See* counter-controlled repetition.

delimiter—Marks the boundaries between fields in a record of a text file.

descriptive Label—A `Label` used to describe another control on the `Form`. This helps users understand a control's purpose.

design mode—IDE mode that allows you to create apps using Visual Studio 2010's windows, toolbars and menu bar.

Design mode—Displays the ASPX page's GUI at design time.

design units—Any specified units of measurement for the font.

Design view—The IDE view that contains the Windows Forms designer to allow you to layout controls in a Windows Forms app.

Designer.vb file—The file containing the declarations and statements that build an app's GUI.

DetailsView control—A control in the **Data** group of the **Toolbox** that displays property names and values for its data source in a tabular format.

dialog—A window that can display and gather information.

DialogResult enumeration—An enumeration that contains values corresponding to standard dialog `Button` names.

diamond symbol—A symbol (also known as the decision symbol) in a UML activity diagram; this symbol indicates that a decision is to be made.

Dictionary collection—A collection of key/value pairs.

Dim keyword—Indicates the declaration of a variable.

dismiss a dialog—Synonym for closing a dialog.

dithering—Using small dots of existing colors to form a pattern that simulates a desired color.

divide-and-conquer technique—Constructing large apps from small, manageable pieces to make development and maintenance of large apps easier.

Do Until...Loop repetition statement—A control statement that executes a set of body statements *until* its loop-termination condition becomes `True`.

Do While...Loop repetition statement—A control statement that executes a set of body statements *while* its loop-continuation condition is `True`.

Do...Loop Until repetition statement—A control statement that executes a set of statements at least once until the loop-termination condition becomes `True` after the loop executes.

Do...Loop While repetition statement—A control statement that executes a set of statements at least once while the loop-continuation condition is `True` after the loop executes.

Document property of class PrintPreviewDialog—Allows you to specify the document that's displayed in the dialog.

dot operator—*See* member-access operator.

dotted line—A UML activity diagram symbol that connects each UML-style note with the element that the note describes.

Double data type—Stores both whole and fractional numbers. Normally, `Double`s store floating-point numbers.

double-selection statement—A control statement that selects between two different actions or sequences of actions (e.g., an If...Then...Else statement).

double-subscripted array—*See* two-dimensional array.

DrawLine method of class Graphics—Draws a line of a specified color between two specified points.

DrawRectangle method of class Graphics—Draws the outline of a rectangle of a specified size and color at a specified location.

DrawString method of class Graphics—Draws the specified String at the specified location.

DropDownList ASP.NET control—Similar to the Windows Forms ComboBox control, but doesn't allow users to type text. When a user clicks the drop-down list, it expands and displays a list from which the user can make a selection.

DropDownList value of DropDownStyle property—Specifies that a ComboBox is not editable.

DropDownStyle property of class ComboBox—Property of the ComboBox control that specifies the appearance of the ComboBox.

dynamic resizing—A capability that allows certain objects (such as Lists) to increase or decrease in size based on the addition or removal of elements from that object. Enables the List object to increase its size to accommodate new elements and to decrease its size when elements are removed.

E

element—An item in an array.

element in XML—Markup that describes a piece of data. Delimited by start and end tags.

element of a For Each...Next statement—Used to store a reference to the current value of the collection being iterated.

Ellipse class—The shape class that draws an ellipse. This class contains properties including Fill, Width and Height. If the width and height are the same, a circle is drawn.

Else keyword—Indicates the statements to be executed if the condition of the If...Then...Else statement is false.

ElseIf keyword—Keyword used for the nested conditions in nested If...Then...Else statements.

embedded parentheses—Another term for nested parentheses.

empty element in XML—Shorthand notation for an element with no content between its start and end tags.

empty string—A string that does not contain any characters.

Enable Paging setting for an ASP.NET GridView—Causes the GridView to split across multiple pages.

Enable Sorting setting for an ASP.NET GridView—Causes the column headings in the GridView to become hyperlinks that allow users to sort the data in the GridView using the sort expressions specified by each column.

Enabled property—Specifies whether a control such as a Button appears enabled (True) or disabled (False).

Enabled property of a TextBox—When False, specifies that the TextBox does not respond to user input.

Enabled property of class ComboBox—Specifies whether a user can select an item from a ComboBox.

Enabled property of GroupBox control—When False, disables all controls contained in the GroupBox.

End Class keywords—Keywords that indicate the end of a class definition.

End Enum keywords—Ends an enumeration.

End Function keywords—Indicates the end of a Function procedure.

End Select keywords—Terminates the Select Case statement.

End Sub keywords—Indicates the end of a Sub procedure.

end tag—Delimits the end of an XML element.

End Try keywords—Indicates the end of a sequence of blocks containing a Try block, followed by zero or more Catch blocks and an optional Finally block. At least one Catch or Finally block must precede the End Try keywords

EndEdit method of class BindingSource—Saves all edits made to the BindingSource's data.

EndOfStream property of class StreamReader—Returns a Boolean value indicating whether the end of the file has been reached.

EndsWith method of class String—Determines whether a String ends with a particular substring.

Enum keyword—Begins an enumeration.

enumeration—A group of related, named constants.

equality operators—Operators = (is equal to) and <> (is not equal to) that compare two values.

Error List window—A window which displays compilation errors in your code.

Error property—DownloadStringCompletedEventArgs property that specifies the error that occurred, if any, during a web-service invocation.

ErrorMessage property of a RequiredFieldValidator—Specifies the error message that appears when the user does not enter data in a required field of a web form.

event—A user action that can trigger an event handler.

event handler—A section of code that's executed (called) when a certain event is raised (occurs).

event-driven program—A program that responds to user-initiated events, such as mouse clicks and keystrokes.

exception—An indication of a problem that occurs during an app's execution.

Exception Assistant—A window that appears in the IDE indicating where an exception has occurred, the type of exception, and information on handling the exception.

exception handler—A block that executes when the app detects an exceptional situation and throws an exception.

exception handling—Processing problems that occur during app execution.

executable statements—Actions that are performed when the corresponding Visual Basic app is run.

explicit conversion—An operation that converts a value of one type to another type using code to (explicitly) tell the app to do the conversion. An example of an explicit conversion is to convert a value of type Double to type Decimal using a Convert method.

exponentiation operator (^)—This operator raises its left operand to a power specified by the right operand.

expression list—Multiple expressions separated by commas. Used for Cases in Select Case statements, when certain statements should execute based on more than one condition.

extender—Components that enhance the functionality of regular ASP.NET controls.

eXtensible App Markup Language (XAML)—*See* XAML.

extensible language—A language that can be "extended" with new data types. Visual Basic is an extensible language.

eXtensible Markup Language (XML)—*See* XML.

F

field—Group of characters that conveys some meaning. For example, a field consisting of uppercase and lowercase letters can represent a person's name.

file—Collection of data that's assigned a name. Used for long-term persistence of large amounts of data, even after the app that created the data terminates.

File class—Provides methods for file manipulations including creating, copying and deleting files.

File Name property—Specifies the name of a source code file.

FileName property of class OpenFileDialog—Specifies the file name selected in the dialog.

Fill attribute of Rectangle element—Specifies a Rectangle's fill color.

Fill property of an Ellipse—Specifies the Brush that's used to color the Ellipse.

final state—Represented by a solid circle surrounded by a hollow circle in a UML activity diagram; the end of the workflow after an app performs its activities.

Finally block—An optional block of code that follows the last Catch block in a sequence of Catch blocks or the Try block if there are no Catches. The Finally block provides code that always executes, whether or not an exception occurs.

FixedSingle value of a Label's BorderStyle property—Specifies that the Label will display a thin, black border.

Flat value of the FlatStyle property of a Button—Specifies that a Button will appear flat.

FlatStyle property of a Button—Determines whether the Button will appear flat or three-dimensional.

floating-point division—Divides two numbers (whole or fractional) and returns a floating-point number.

focus—Designates the window currently in use.

Focus method—Transfers the focus of the app to the control on which the method is called.

Font class—Contains properties that define unique fonts.

Font property—Specifies the font name, style and size of any displayed text in the Form or one of its controls.

FontDialog class—Used to display a dialog from which the user can choose a font and its style.

FontFamily class—Represents the FontFamily of the Font (a grouping structure to organize fonts with similar properties).

FontStyle enumeration—Provides constants for specifying a font's style, including FontStyle.Bold, FontStyle.Italic, FontStyle.Regular, FontStyle.Strikeout and FontStyle.Underline.

For Each...Next repetition statement—Repetition statment that iterates over each element in an array or collection.

For keyword—Begins the For...Next statement.

For...Next header—The first line of a For...Next repetition statement. The For...Next header specifies all four essential elements for counter-controlled repetition.

For...Next repetition statement—Repetition statement that handles the details of counter-controlled repetition. The For...Next statement uses all four elements essential to counter-controlled repetition in one line of code (the name of a control variable, the initial value, the increment or decrement value and the final value).

Form—The object that represents the Windows app's graphical user interface (GUI).

format control string—A string that specifies how data should be formatted.

Format property of a DateTimePicker control—The property of the DateTimePicker control that allows you to specify a predefined or custom format with which to display the date and/or time.

format specifier—Code that specifies the type of format that should be applied to a string for output.

FormatException class—An exception of this type is thrown when a method cannot convert its argument to a desired numeric type, such as Integer or Double.

formatting text—Modifying the appearance of text for display purposes.

forms authentication—A technique used to protect a page so that only registered users who are logged in to the website can access the page.

Fortran (Formula Translator)—A programming language developed by IBM Corporation in the mid-1950s (and still widely used) to create scientific and engineering apps that require complex mathematical computations.

Framework Class Library—.NET's collection of "prepackaged" classes and methods for performing mathematical calculations, string manipulations, character manipulations, input/output operations, error checking and many other useful operations.

From clause (of a LINQ query)—Specifies a range variable and the data source to query.

FromArgb method of Color structure—A method that creates a new Color object from RGB values and an alpha value.

FullOpen property of class ColorDialog—Property that, when True, enables the ColorDialog to provide a full range of color options when displayed.

Function keyword—Begins the definition of a Function procedure.

Function procedure—A procedure similar to a Sub procedure, with one important difference: Function procedures return a value to the caller, whereas Sub procedures do not.

functionality—The actions an app can execute.

G

GDI+ (Graphics Device Interface)—An app programming interface (API) that provides classes for creating two-dimensional vector graphics.

Get accessor—Used to retrieve a value of a property.

Get/End Get keywords—Reserved words that define a property's Get accessor.

GetName method of class FontFamily—Returns the name of the FontFamily object.

GetPosition method of classes MouseButtonEventArgs and MouseEventArgs—Returns a Point object representing the position of the mouse pointer over a control.

GetUpperBound method of class Array—Returns an array's highest index.

graphical user interface (GUI)—The visual part of an app with which users interact.

Grid layout container—A WPF control that organizes its children in rows and columns.

Grid.Row attribute of a WPF control—Specifies the row in which a control should be placed in the enclosing Grid layout container.

Grid.RowDefinitions element—A nested element of a Grid layout container. Contains a set of RowDefinition elements that define the rows of the Grid and their characteristics.

group (of a For Each...Next statement)—Specifies the array or collection through which you wish to iterate.

GroupBox content control—A control that places a titled border around its content.

GroupBox control—Groups related controls visually.

guard condition—An expression contained in square brackets above or next to the arrows leading from a decision symbol in a UML activity diagram that determines whether workflow continues along a path.

H

Handles clause—Specifies the event handled by an event handler and the object to which the event corresponds.

hardware—The various devices that make up a computer, including the keyboard, screen, mouse, hard drive, memory, CD-ROM, DVD, printer and processing units.

header—A line of text at the top of a ListBox that clarifies the information being displayed.

Header property of a GroupBox—Sets the text displayed in a GroupBox's border.

Height property—This property, a member of property Size, indicates the height of the Form or one of its controls in pixels.

high-level language—A type of programming language in which a single program statement accomplishes a substantial task. High-level languages use instructions that look almost like everyday English and contain common mathematical notations.

Horizontal value of ScrollBars property—Used to display a horizontal scrollbar on the bottom of a TextBox.

host name—Name of a computer where resources reside.

HTML (HyperText Markup Language)—A technology used to describe how a browser should display a web page.

HttpSessionState class—The .NET class for session tracking.

HyperText Transfer Protocol (HTTP)—The protocol used to transmit HTML files over the web.

I

icon—The graphical representation of commands in the Visual Studio 2010 IDE.

ID property of a web control—Specifies the name of a web control for use in code.

identifier—A series of characters consisting of letters, digits and underscores used to name program units such as classes, controls and variables.

IEnumerable interface—Provides methods to iterate through a set of objects, such as an array or a collection.

If...Then statement—Selection statement that performs an action (or sequence of actions) based on a condition. This is also called the single-selection statement.

If...Then...Else statement—Selection statement that performs an action (or sequence of actions) if a condition is true and performs a different action (or sequence of actions) if the condition is false. This is also called the double-selection statement.

Image control—Displays an image in a WPF GUI.

Image property—Indicates the file name of the image displayed in a PictureBox.

Image web control—Displays an image in an ASPX page.

Image.FromFile—A method of class Image that returns an Image object containing the image located at the path you specify.

immutable—Describes an object that cannot be changed after it's created. In Visual Basic, Strings are immutable.

implicit conversion—An operation that converts a value of one type to another type without writing code to (explicitly) tell the app to do the conversion.

Increment property of a NumericUpDown control—Specifies by how much the current number in the NumericUpDown control changes when the user clicks the control's up (for incrementing) or down (for decrementing) arrow.

index—An array element's position number, also called a subscript. An index must be zero, a positive integer or an integer expression that yields a non-negative result. If an app uses an expression as an index, the expression is evaluated first, to determine the index.

index of a List—The value with which you can refer to a specific element in an List, based on the element's location in the List.

indexed array name—The array name followed by an index enclosed in parentheses. The indexed array name can be used on the left side of an assignment statement to place a new value into an array element. The indexed array name can be used in the right side of an assignment to retrieve the value of that array element.

IndexOf method of class String—Returns the index of the first occurrence of a substring in a String. Returns -1 if the substring is not found.

infinite loop—An error in which a repetition statement never terminates.

information tier—Tier containing the app data; typically implemented as a database. Also called the bottom tier or data tier.

initial state—Represented by a solid circle in a UML activity diagram; the beginning of the workflow before the app performs the modeled activities.

initializer list—The required braces ({ and }) surrounding the initial values of the elements in an array. When the initializer list is empty, the elements in the array are initialized to the default value for the array's data type.

input—Data that the user enters into an app.

input device—Devices that are used to interact with a computer, such as keyboards, mice, microphones, scanners and digital cameras.

input unit—The "receiving" section of the computer that obtains information (data and computer programs) from various input devices, such as keyboards, mice, microphones, scanners and digital cameras.

Insert method of a ListBox's Items property—Inserts an item in a ListBox at the location specified by its first argument.

Insert method of class List—Inserts a specified object into the specified location of a List.

Insert method of class String—Returns a new String object with the specified substring inserted at the given index of the original String.

instance variable—Declared inside a class but outside any procedure of that class. Instance variables have module scope.

instant-access app—App that immediately locates a particular record of information.

instantiate an object—Create an object (or instance) of a class.

Int32.MaxValue constant—The largest possible 32-bit Integer (2,147,483,647).

integer—A whole number, such as 919, –11, 0 and 138624.

Integer data type—Stores integer values.

integer division—Integer division takes two Integer operands and yields an Integer result. The fractional portion of the result is discarded.

Integrated Development Environment (IDE)—A software tool that enables you to write, run, test and debug programs quickly and conveniently.

IntelliSense—Visual Basic IDE feature that aids you during development by providing windows that list program items that are available in the current context.

interface—Specifies a set of methods that can be called on an object which implements the interface to perform certain tasks.

internal web browser—The web browser (Internet Explorer) included in Visual Basic 2010 Express, with which you can browse the web.

Internet—A worldwide computer network. Most people today access the Internet through the web.

Internet Information Services (IIS)—A Microsoft web server.

Interval property of a Timer control—The Timer property that specifies the number of milliseconds between Tick events.

invoking a procedure—Causing a procedure to perform its designated task.

IP address—Unique address used to locate a computer on the Internet.

Is keyword—A keyword that, when followed by a comparison operator, can be used to compare the controlling expression of a Select Case statement and a value.

IsControl method of structure Char—Determines whether the Char passed as an argument represents a control key.

IsNot operator—Determines whether two reference variables contain references to different objects or whether a single reference variable refers to an object.

Items property of ComboBox—Collection containing the values displayed in a ComboBox.

Items property of the ListBox control—Returns an object containing all the values in the ListBox.

ItemsPanel of a ListBox—See ListBox.ItemsPanel element.

ItemsPanelTemplate element—Used to redefine the ItemsPanel of a ListBox to change how ListBox items are arranged.

ItemTemplate of a ListBox—See ListBox.ItemTemplate element.

J

Java—A popular programming language that's used to create web pages with dynamic content, to build large-scale enterprise apps, to enhance the functionality of web servers, to provide apps for consumer devices and for many other purposes.

Join method of class String—Concatenates the elements in a String array, separated by the first argument. A new String containing the concatenated elements is returned.

K

key/value pair—Associates a value with a corresponding key, which is used to identify the value. The Session object stores key/value pairs.

keyboard event—Raised when a key on the keyboard is pressed or released.

KeyChar property of class KeyPressEventArgs—Contains data about the key that raised the KeyPress event.

KeyCode property of class KeyEventArgs—Contains data about the key that raised the KeyDown event.

KeyDown event—Generated when a key is initially pressed. Used to handle the event raised when a key that's not a letter or number key is pressed.

KeyEventArgs class—Stores information about special modifier keys.

KeyPress event—Generated when a key is pressed. Used to handle the event raised when a letter or number key is pressed.

KeyPressEventArgs class—Stores information about character keys.

Keys enumeration—Contains values representing keyboard keys.

KeyUp event—Generated when a key is released.

keyword—A word in code reserved by the compiler for a specific purpose. By default, these words appear in blue in the IDE and cannot be used as identifiers.

L

Label—Control that displays text the user can't modify.

Label web control—Displays text on an ASPX page.

Language-Integrated Query (LINQ)—Provides support for writing queries in Visual Basic.

LastIndexOf method of class String—Returns the index of the last occurrence of a substring in a String. Returns -1 if the substring is not found.

layout container—A control that positions its child controls based on their size and the amount of available space in the container.

left operand—The expression on the left side of a binary operator.

length of an array—The number of elements in an array.

Length property of class Array—Contains the length of (or number of elements in) an array.

Length property of class String—Returns the number of characters in a String.

line-continuation character—An underscore character (_) preceded by one or more space characters, used to continue a statement to the next line of code.

LINQ to SQL classes—Creates a model of a database in an app. These classes are used to manipulate the database's contents.

LINQ to XML—LINQ capabilities that enable manipulation of XML data.

LinqDataSource—A data source that uses LINQ to retrieve information from a DataContext object.

List(Of T) class—Has the same capabilities as an array, as well as dynamic resizing.

ListBox control—Allows the user to view items in a list. Items can be added to or removed from the list programmatically.

ListBox web control—Displays a list of items.

ListBox.ItemsPanel element—Defines how the items in a ListBox are arranged in the GUI (e.g., vertically, horizontally, etc.).

ListBox.ItemTemplate element—Defines the look-and-feel of each ListBox item. The default ItemTemplate displays the String representation of each item.

literal String object—A String constant written as a sequence of characters in double quotation marks (also called a string literal).

Load event of a Form—Raised when an app initially executes.

local type inference—Visual Basic 2010 compiler feature that enables it to infer a local variable's type based on the context in which the variable is initialized.

local variable—Declared inside a procedure or block, such as the body of an If...Then statement. Local variables have either procedure scope or block scope.

localhost—Host name that identifies the local computer.

Locals window—Allows you to view the state of the variables and properties in the current scope during debugging.

location bar—The ComboBox in Visual Basic's internal web browser where you can enter the name of a web site to visit.

Location property—Specifies the location (x- and y-coordinates) of the upper-left corner of a control. This property is used to place a control on the Form precisely.

Locked property—Prevents a control from being moved or resized.

logic error—An error that does not prevent the app from compiling successfully, but does cause the app to produce erroneous results.

logical exclusive OR (Xor) operator—A logical operator that's True if and only if one of its operands is True and the other is False.

logical operators—The operators (for example, AndAlso, OrElse, Xor and Not) that can be used to form complex conditions by combining simple ones.

loop—Another name for a repetition statement.

loop-continuation condition—The condition used in a repetition statement (such as a Do While...Loop) that enables repetition to continue while the condition is True and that causes repetition to terminate when the condition becomes False.

loop-termination condition—The condition used in a repetition statement (such as a Do Until...Loop) that enables repetition to continue while the condition is False and that causes repetition to terminate when the condition becomes True.

M

m-by-n array—A two-dimensional array with m rows and n columns.

machine language—A computer's natural language, generally consisting of streams of numbers that instruct the computer how to perform its most elementary operations.

Margin attribute of a WPF control—Specifies the amount of space around the edges of a control.

margin indicator bar—A margin in the IDE where breakpoints are displayed.

MarginBounds.Left property—PrintPageEventArgs property that specifies the left margin of a printed page.

MarginBounds.Top property—PrintPageEventArgs property that specifies the top margin of a printed page.

masking—Hiding text such as passwords or other sensitive pieces of information that should not be observed by other people as they're typed. Masking is achieved by using the PasswordChar property of the TextBox for which you would like to hide data. The actual data entered is retained in the TextBox's Text property.

masking character—Used to replace each character displayed in a TextBox when the TextBox's data is masked for privacy.

master page in ASP.NET—Defines common GUI elements that are inherited by each page in a set of content pages.

Max method of class Math—A method of class Math which returns the greater of its two arguments.

MaxDate property of a DateTimePicker control—The DateTimePicker property that specifies the latest value that the DateTimePicker allows the user to enter.

MaxDropDownItems property of class ComboBox—Property of the ComboBox control that specifies how many items can be displayed in the drop-down list. If the ComboBox has more elements than this, it provides a scrollbar to access all of them.

Maximum property of a NumericUpDown control—Determines the maximum input value in a particular NumericUpDown control.

MaxLength property of TextBox—Specifies the maximum number of characters that can be input into a TextBox.

.mdf file—A SQL Server Express database file.

Me keyword—References the current object.

member-access operator—Also known as the dot operator (.). Allows you to access a control's properties using code.

members of a class—Methods, variables and properties declared within the body of a class.

memory—Another name for the memory unit.

memory unit—The rapid-access, relatively low-capacity "warehouse" section of the computer, which stores data temporarily while an app is running.

menu—Design element that groups related commands for Windows apps. Although these commands depend on the app, some—such as **Open** and **Save**—are common to many apps. Menus are an integral part of GUIs, because they organize commands without cluttering the GUI.

menu bar—Contains the menus for a window.

Menu Designer mode in the Visual Basic IDE—Design mode in the IDE that allows you to create and edit menus and menu items.

menu item (or command)—A command located in a menu that, when selected, causes an app to perform a specific action.

MenuStrip control—Allows you to add menus to your app.

merge symbol (in the UML)—A diamond symbol in the UML that joins two flows of activity into one flow of activity.

message dialog—A window that displays messages to users or gathers input from users.

Message property of an exception object—Provides access to the error message in an exception object.

MessageBox class—Provides a method for displaying message dialogs.

MessageBox.Show method—Displays a message dialog.

MessageBoxButtons constants—The identifiers that specify the Buttons that can be displayed in a MessageBox dialog.

MessageBoxIcon constants—Identifiers that specify the icons that can be displayed in a MessageBox dialog.

method—A portion of a class that performs a task and possibly returns information when it completes the task.

method overloading—Allows you to create multiple methods with the same name but different signatures.

microprocessor—The chip that makes a computer work (that is, the "brain" of the computer).

Microsoft Developer Network (MSDN)—An online library that contains articles, downloads and tutorials on technologies of interest to Visual Basic developers.

middle tier—Tier that controls interaction between the client and information tiers (also called the business logic tier).

Min method of class Math—A method of class Math which returns the lesser of its two arguments.

MinDate property of a DateTimePicker control—Specifies the earliest value that the control allows the user to enter.

Minimum property of a NumericUpDown control—Determines the minimum input value in a particular NumericUpDown control.

minus box—An icon that, when clicked, collapses a node.

Mod (modulus operator)—The modulus operator yields the remainder after division.

modifier key—Key such as *Shift*, *Alt* or *Control* that modifies the way that an app responds to a keyboard event.

module scope—Variable declared inside a class definition but outside any of the classes procedures have module scope. Module scope begins at the identifier after keyword Class and terminates at the End Class statement, enables all procedures in the same class to access all instance variables defined in that class.

MonthCalendar control—Displays a calendar from which a user can select a range of dates.

More Colors dialog—Displays the set of web-safe colors and enables you to create custom colors.

mouse event—Generated when a user interacts with an app using the computer's mouse.

MouseButtonEventArgs class—Specifies information about a mouse event involving a button press or release.

MouseEventArgs class—Specifies information about a MouseMove.

MouseLeftButtonDown event—Generated when the left mouse button is pressed.

MouseLeftButtonUp event—Generated when the left mouse button is released.

MouseMove event—Generated when a mouse pointer is moved.

MouseRightButtonDown event—Generated when the right mouse button is pressed.

MouseRightButtonUp event—Generated when the right mouse button is released.

MoveFirst method of class BindingSource—Moves to the first item in the BindingSource.

Multiline property of a TextBox control—Specifies whether the TextBox is capable of displaying multiple lines of text. If the property value is True, the TextBox may contain multiple lines of text; if the value of the property is False, the TextBox can contain only one line of text.

multiple-selection statement—Performs one of many actions (or sequences of actions) depending on the value of the controlling expression.

multiplication operator—The asterisk (*) used to multiply two operands, producing their product as a result.

multitier app—App (sometimes referred to as an *n*-tier app) whose functionality is divided into separate tiers, which can be on the same machine or can be distributed to separate machines across a network.

mutually exclusive options—A set of options of which only one can be selected at a time.

N

n-tier app—Another name for a multitier app.

name of a variable—The identifier used in an app to access or modify a variable's value.

Name property—Assigns a unique and meaningful name to a control for easy identification.

namespace—Classes in the .NET Framework Class Library are organized by functionality into these directory-like entities.

narrowing conversion—A conversion where the value of a "larger" type is being assigned to a variable of a "smaller" type, where the larger type can store more data than the smaller type. Narrowing conversions can result in loss of data, which can cause subtle logic errors.

navigation bar on a website—Allows you to switch between pages by clicking the link for the appropriate page.

nested For...Next statements—A For...Next statement defined in the body of another For...Next statement. Commonly used to iterate over the elements of a two-dimensional array.

nested parentheses—These occur when an expression in parentheses is found within another expression surrounded by parentheses. With nested parentheses, the operators contained in the innermost pair of parentheses are applied first.

nested statement—A statement that's placed inside another control statement.

NET Framework—Microsoft-provided software that executes apps, provides the Framework Class Library and supplies many other programming capabilities.

.NET Framework Class Library—.NET's collection of "prepackaged" classes and methods for performing mathematical calculations, string manipulations, character manipulations, input/output operations, error checking and many other useful operations.

.NET Initiative—Microsoft's vision for using the Internet and the web in the development, engineering, distribution and use of software.

.NET Platform—The set of software components that enables .NET programs to run—allows apps to be distributed to a variety of devices as well as to desktop computers. Offers a programming model that allows software components created in different programming languages (such as Visual Basic and C#) to communicate with one another.

New keyword—Used to call a constructor when creating an object.

New Project dialog—A dialog that allows you to choose what type of app you wish to create.

New Style dialog—Enables you to specify styles, such as position, for your web controls.

Next method of class Random—A method of class Random that, when called with no arguments, generates a positive Integer value between zero and the constant Int32.MaxValue. When called with arguments, the method generates an Integer value in a range constrained by those arguments.

NextDouble method of class Random—A method of class Random that generates a positive Double value that's greater than or equal to 0.0 and less than 1.0.

nondestructive memory operation—A process that does not overwrite a value in memory.

None value of ScrollBars property—Used to display no scrollbars on a TextBox.

Not (logical negation) operator—A logical operator that enables you to reverse the meaning of a condition: A True condition, when logically negated, becomes False, and a False condition, when logically negated, becomes True.

note—An explanatory remark (represented by a rectangle with a folded upper-right corner) describing the purpose of a symbol in a UML activity diagram.

Nothing keyword—Used to clear a reference's value.

Now property of Date type—Returns the current system time and date.

Now property of type Date—The Date property that retrieves your computer's current time.

NumericUpDown control—Allows you to specify maximum and minimum numeric input values. Also allows you to specify an increment (or decrement) when the user clicks the up (or down) arrow.

O

object initializer—Uses keyword With to assign property values to a newly created object.

Object Relational Designer—Allows you to specify which tables in a database are accessible through an app's LINQ to SQL classes.

object technology—A packaging scheme for creating meaningful software units. The units are large and are focused on particular app areas. There are date objects, time objects, paycheck objects, file objects and the like.

object-oriented programming (OOP)—Models real-world objects with software counterparts.

objects—Software components that model items in the real world.

off-by-one error—The kind of logic error that occurs, for example, when a loop executes for one more or one less iteration than is intended.

one-dimensional array—An array that uses only one index.

opacity—Amount of transparency of the color.

Opacity attribute of Rectangle element—Specifies a Rectangle's transparency—a number from 0 to 1, where 0 is completely transparent and 1 is completely opaque.

OpenFileDialog component—Enables an app to use the **Open** dialog, which allows users to specify a file to be opened

operand—An expression on which an operator performs its task.

Option Strict—When set to On, disallows implicit narrowing conversions (for example, conversion from Double to Decimal). If you attempt an implicit narrowing conversion, the compiler issues a compilation error.

Optional parameter—A parameter that's specified with a default value. If the corresponding argument is omitted in the procedure call, the default value is supplied by the compiler.

Or operator—A logical operator used to ensure that either *or* both of two conditions are true in an app before a certain path of execution is chosen.

Order By clause of a LINQ query—Orders the result of a LINQ query by the specified property.

OrElse operator—A logical operator used to ensure that either *or* both of two conditions are true in an app before a certain path of execution is chosen. Performs short-circuit evaluation.

Orientation attribute of a StackPanel layout container—Determines whether a StackPanel arranges its child elements vertically (the default) or horizontally.

output—The result of running an app.

output device—A device to which information that's processed by the computer can be sent.

output Label—A Label used to display results.

output unit—The section of the computer that takes information the computer has processed and places it on various output devices, making the information available for use outside the computer.

Output window—A window which displays the result of the compilation.

P

PadLeft method of class String—Adds characters to the beginning of a string until the length of the string equals the specified length.

PadRight method of class String—Adds characters to the end of a string until the length of the string equals the specified length.

Page class—Defines the basic functionality for an ASPX page.

Page_Load event handler—Executes when an ASPX page is loaded.

PageSize property of a GridView ASP.NET control—Determines the number of entries per page.

palette—A set of colors.

Panel control—Used to group controls. Unlike GroupBoxes, Panels do not have captions.

parameter—A variable declared in a procedure's parameter list that can be used in the body of the procedure.

Parameter Info **feature of the IDE**—Provides information about procedures and their arguments.

parameter list—A comma-separated list in which the procedure declares each parameter's name and type.

partial page update—Modifies a portion of a webpage (without reloading the webpage) in response to an Ajax request's response

Pascal—A programming language designed for teaching structured programming, named after the 17th-century mathematician and philosopher Blaise Pascal.

pass-by-reference—When an argument is passed by reference, the called procedure can access and modify the caller's argument value directly. Keyword ByRef indicates pass-by-reference (also called call-by-reference).

pass-by-value—When an argument is passed by value, the app makes a copy of the argument's value and passes the copy to the called procedure. With pass-by-value, changes to the called procedure's copy do not affect the caller's argument value. Keyword ByVal indicates pass-by-value (also called call-by-value).

PasswordChar property of a TextBox—Specifies the masking character for a TextBox.

Pen object—Specifies drawing parameters when drawing shape outlines.

persistent data—Data maintained in files which exists after the app that created the data terminates.

personalization—Makes it possible for businesses to communicate effectively with their customers and also improves users' ability to locate desired products and services.

PictureBox—Control that displays an image.

pin (or pushpin) icon—An icon that enables or disables the auto-hide feature.

pixel—A tiny point on your computer screen that displays a color.

plus box—An icon that, when clicked, expands a node.

Pmt function—A built-in Visual Basic function that, given an interest rate, the total number of payments and a monetary loan amount, returns a Double value specifying the amount per payment.

Point class—Contains an X and a Y property representing the coordinates of a point.

position number—A value that indicates a specific location within an array. Position numbers begin at 0 (zero).

postback—Sends the values of all the controls in an ASP.NET page to the server when a form is submitted and causes the current page to be requested again.

precision—Specifies the number of digits to the right of the decimal point in a formatted floating-point value.

presentation logic—Processes data from the information tier and presents the content to the client.

primary key—Field (or combination of fields) in a database table that contains unique values used to distinguish records from one another.

primary memory—Another name for the memory unit.

primitive data type—A data type already defined in Visual Basic, such as Integer.

Print method of class PrintDocument—Prints a document.

PrintDocument class—Allows the user to describe how to print a document.

PrinterSettings.InstalledPrinters.Count property—Determines how many printers are installed on the user's computer.

PrintPage event—Occurs when the data required to print the current page is needed.

PrintPageEventArgs class—Contains data passed to a PrintPage event.

PrintPreviewDialog control—Previews a document in a dialog box before it prints.

Private keyword—Member-access modifier that makes members accessible only to the class that defines the members.

procedural programming language—A programming language (such as Fortran, Pascal, BASIC and C) that focuses on actions (verbs) rather than things or objects (nouns).

procedure—A set of instructions for performing a particular task.

procedure body—The declarations and statements that appear after the procedure header but before the keywords End Sub or End Function. The procedure body contains Visual Basic code that performs actions, generally by manipulating or interacting with the parameters from the parameter list.

procedure call—Invokes a procedure, specifies the procedure name and provides arguments that the callee (the procedure being called) requires to perform its task.

procedure definition—The procedure header, body and ending statement.

procedure header—The first line of a procedure (including the keyword Sub or Function, the procedure name, the parameter list and the Function procedure return type).

procedure name—Follows the keyword Sub or Function and distinguishes one procedure from another. A procedure name can be any valid identifier.

procedure scope—Variables declared inside a procedure but outside a control statement have procedure scope. Variables with procedure scope cannot be referenced outside the procedure in which they're declared.

program control—The task of ordering an app's statements in the correct order.

programmer-defined class (programmer-defined type)—A class defined by a programmer, as opposed to classes predefined in the Framework Class Library.

programmer-defined procedure—A procedure created by a programmer to meet the unique needs of a particular app.

project—A group of related files that compose an app.

properties—Object attributes, such as size, color and weight.

Properties window—The window that displays the properties for a Form or control object.

property—Specifies a control or Form object's attributes, such as size, color and position.

property definition—Defines the accessors for a property.

Property/End Property keywords—Reserved words indicating the definition of a class property.

pseudocode—An informal language that helps you develop algorithms.

pseudorandom numbers—A sequence of values produced by a complex mathematical calculation that simulates random-number generation.

Public keyword—Member-access modifier that makes instance variables or methods accessible wherever the app has a reference to that object.

Q

query—Request information that satisfies given criteria.

query (LINQ)—Retrieves specific information from a data source, such as a collection.

Quick Info box—Displays the value of a variable during debugging.

R

RadioButton control—Appears as a small circle that's either blank (unchecked) or contains a smaller dot (checked). Usu-

ally these controls appear in groups of two or more. Exactly one RadioButton in a group is selected at one time.

RadioButtonList ASP.NET control—Provides a series of radio buttons from which the user can select only one.

Random class—Contains methods to generate pseudorandom numbers.

random-access memory (RAM)—An example of primary memory.

range variable (LINQ)—The control variable for a LINQ query.

ReadAllLines method of class File—Returns an array of Strings containing each line of the file.

ReadLine method of class StreamReader—Reads a line from a file and returns it as a String.

ReadOnly property of a TextBox control—Determines whether the user can change the value of a TextBox.

real-time error checking—Feature of the Visual Basic IDE that provides immediate notification of possible errors in your code. For example, unrecognized identifier errors are indicated by blue, jagged underlines in code.

record—A collection of related fields. Usually a Class in Visual Basic composed of several fields (called member variables in Visual Basic).

record key—Identifies a record and distinguishes it from all other records.

rectangular array—A type of two-dimensional array that can represent tables of values consisting of information arranged in rows and columns. Each row contains the same number of columns.

Redirect method of class Response—Redirects the client browser to another web page.

redundant parentheses—Unnecessary parentheses used in an expression to make it easier to read.

reference—Keyword New creates a new object in memory and returns a reference to that object. You typically store an object's reference in a reference-type variable so you can interact with the object.

reference type—A type that stores the location of an object. Any type that's not a value type is a reference type. Primitive type String is a reference type.

RegularExpressionValidator validation control—Uses a regular expression to ensure that the data entered by the user is in a valid format.

relational operators—Operators < (less than), > (greater than), <= (less than or equal to) and >= (greater than or equal to) that compare two values (also known as comparison operators).

RemoveAt method of class List—Removes the object located at a specified location of a List.

repetition statement—Allows you to specify that an action or actions should be repeated, depending on the value of a condition.

repetition structure (or repetition statement)—Allows the programmer to specify that an action or sequence of actions should be repeated, depending on the value of a condition.

Replace method of class String—Returns a copy of the String for which it's called. Replaces all occurrences of the characters in its first `String` argument with the characters in its second `String` argument.

RequiredFieldValidator control—A validation control which ensures that a web control contains data before the user can submit a web form to a web server.

reserved words (keywords)—Words that are reserved by the Visual Basic compiler.

Response class—Provides methods for responding to a client request.

rethrow an exception—The `Catch` block can defer the exception handling (or perhaps a portion of it) to another `Catch` block by using the `Throw` statement.

Return keyword—Signifies the return statement that sends a value back to the procedure's caller.

Return statement—Used to return a value from a procedure.

return type—Data type of the result returned from a `Function` procedure.

reusing code—The practice of using existing code to build new code. Reusing code saves time, effort and money.

RGB value—The amount of red, green and blue needed to create a color.

Rich Internet Apps (RIAs)—Web apps that offer the responsiveness and rich GUI features of desktop apps.

right operand—The expression on the right side of a binary operator.

row—The first dimension of a two-dimensional array.

RowDefinition element—Nested in a `Grid.RowDefinitions` element to specify the characteristics of a row in a `Grid` layout container.

rules of operator precedence—Rules that determine the precise order in which operators are applied in an expression.

run mode—IDE mode indicating that the app is executing.

runtime error—An error that has its effect at execution time.

S

scope—The portion of an app in which an identifier (such as a variable name) can be referenced. Some identifiers can be referenced throughout an app—others can be referenced only from limited portions of an app (such as within a single procedure or block).

screen scraping—The process of extracting desired information from the HTML that composes a web page.

ScriptManager control—Manages the client-side scripts that enable asynchronous Ajax functionality.

scroll arrows—Arrows at the ends of a scrollbar that enable you to scroll through items.

ScrollBars property of a TextBox control—Specifies whether a `TextBox` has a scrollbar and, if so, of what type. By default, property `ScrollBars` is set to `None`.

secondary storage media—Devices such as magnetic disks, optical disks and magnetic tapes on which computers store files.

secondary storage unit—The long-term, high-capacity "warehouse" section of the computer.

Segoe UI font—The Microsoft-recommended font for use in Windows Vista apps.

Select Case statement—The multiple-selection statement used to make a decision by comparing an expression to a series of conditions. The algorithm then takes different actions based on those values.

Select clause (of a LINQ query)—Specifies the value(s) placed in the results of the query.

Select Resource dialog—Used to import files, such as images, to any app.

SelectedIndex property of class ComboBox—Specifies the index of the selected item. Returns −1 if no item is selected.

SelectedIndexChanged event of ComboBox—Raised when a new value is selected in a `ComboBox`.

SelectedValue property of class ListBox—Returns the value of the selected item.

selection structure (or selection statement)—Selects among alternative courses of action.

SelectionStart property of MonthCalendar control—Returns the first (or only) date selected.

sender event argument—Event argument that contains a reference to the object that raised the event (also called the source of the event).

sentence-style capitalization—A style that capitalizes the first letter of the first word in the text. Every other letter in the text is lowercase, unless it's the first letter of a proper noun (for example, Cartons per shipment).

separator bar—Bar placed in a menu to separate related menu items.

sequence structure (or sequence statement)—Built into Visual Basic—unless directed to act otherwise, the computer executes Visual Basic statements sequentially.

sequential execution—Statements in an app are executed one after another in the order in which they're written.

sequential-access file—File containing data that's read in the order in which it was written to the file.

session item—Key/value pair in an `HttpSessionState` object.

Session object—Object that's maintained across several web pages containing a collection of key/value pairs that are specific to a given user.

session state—ASP.NET's built-in support for tracking data throughout a browser session.

Set accessor—Provides data-validation capabilities to ensure that the value is set properly.

Set/End Set keywords—Reserved words that define a property's `Set` accessor.

SetLeft method of Canvas—Sets the left coordinate of an element (the first argument) on the `Canvas` to a `Double` value (the second argument).

SetTop method of Canvas—Sets the top coordinate of an element (the first argument) on the `Canvas` to a `Double` value (the second argument).

short-circuit evaluation—The evaluation of the right operand in `AndAlso` and `OrElse` expressions occurs only if the first condition meets the criteria for the condition.

ShowDialog method of class FontDialog or ColorDialog—The method that displays the dialog on which it's called.

ShowDialog method of class OpenFileDialog—Displays the Open dialog and returns the result of the user interaction with the dialog.

ShowGridLines attribute of Grid layout container—Displays grid lines so you can see the grid layout as you design and build your GUI.

ShowUpDown property of a DateTimePicker control—The DateTimePicker property that, when True, allows the user to specify the time using up and down arrows, and, when False, allows the user to specify the date using a calendar.

signature—Specifies a procedure's parameters and their types.

simple condition—Contains one expression that evaluates to True or False.

Single data type—Stores floating-point values. Single is similar to Double, but is less precise and requires less memory.

Single method of a LINQ query—Returns a single object from a LINQ query rather than a a collection.

single-entry/single-exit control structure (or statement)—A control statement that has one entry point and one exit point. All Visual Basic control statements are single-entry/single-exit control statements.

single-quote character(')—Indicates the beginning of a code comment.

single-selection statement—The If...Then statement, which selects or ignores a single action or sequence of actions.

size of a variable—The number of bytes required to store a value of the variable's type.

Size property—Property that specifies the height and width, in pixels, of the Form or one of its controls.

SizeMode property—Property that specifies how an image is displayed in a PictureBox.

sizing handle—Square that, when enabled, can be used to resize the Form or one of its controls.

small circles (in the UML)—The solid circle in an activity diagram represents the activity's initial state, and the solid circle surrounded by a hollow circle represents the activity's final state.

software—The set of apps that run on computers.

software reuse—The reuse of existing pieces of software, an approach that enables you to avoid "reinventing the wheel," helping you to develop apps faster.

solid circle (in the UML)—A UML activity diagram symbol that represents the activity's initial state.

solution—Contains one or more projects.

Solution Explorer—A window that provides access to all the projects and their files in a solution.

Sorted property of class ComboBox—When set to True, sorts the items in a ComboBox alphabetically.

Source attribute of an Image—Specifies the URL from which to obtain the image for display in the control.

Source mode—Displays the ASPX page's markup at design time.

special characters—Characters that are neither digits nor letters.

special symbols—$, @, %, &, *, (,), -, +, ", :, ?, / and the like.

Split method of class String—Splits the words in a String whenever a space is reached.

Split mode—Displays the ASPX page's **Source** and **Design** views at the same time.

SQL Server Express—A database management system built by Microsoft.

Sqrt method of class Math—A method of class Math which returns the square root of its argument.

StackPanel layout container—A WPF control that organizes its children horizontally or vertically (the default).

Start Page—The initial page displayed when Visual Studio 2010 is opened.

start tag—Delimits the beginning of an XML element.

StartsWith method of class String—Determines whether a String starts with a particular substring.

state button—A button that can be in the on/off (true/false) state.

statement—A unit of code that, when compiled and executed, performs an action.

Step keyword—Optional component of the For...Next header that specifies the increment or decrement (that is, the amount added to or subtracted from the control variable each time the loop is executed).

straight-line form—The manner in which arithmetic expressions must be written to be represented in Visual Basic code.

stream—A sequence of characters.

StreamReader class—Provides methods for reading information from a file.

StreamWriter class—Provides methods for writing information to a file.

StretchImage—Value of PictureBox property SizeMode that scales an image to fill the PictureBox.

string constant—A String constant written as a sequence of characters in double quotation marks (also called a string literal).

String data type—Stores a series of characters.

string literal—A String constant written as a sequence of characters in double quotation marks (also called a literal String object).

string-concatenation operator (&)—This operator combines its two operands into one string value.

String.Format method—Formats a string.

structured programming—A technique for organizing program control using sequence, selection and repetition structures to help you develop apps that are easy to understand, debug and modify.

Structured Query Language (SQL)—Language often used by relational databases to perform queries and manipulate data in relational databases.

style element—An element that's placed in the head element of a page. Contains CSS style definitions (such as those created with the **New Style** window).

Sub keyword—Begins the definition of a Sub procedure.

Sub procedure—A procedure similar to a Function procedure, with one important difference: Sub procedures do not return a value to the caller, whereas Function procedures do.

submenu—Menu within another menu.

SubmitChanges method of class DataContext—Updates the database on disk with any changes made in the app.

subscript—*See* index.

substring—A sequence of characters in a String.

Substring method of class String—Returns characters from a string, corresponding to the arguments passed by the user, that indicate the start position within a String and the number of characters to return.

Substring method of class String—Creates a new String object by copying part of an existing String object.

synchronous request—The client waits for the server to respond and reloads the entire page with the data from the response. While a synchronous request is being processed on the server, the user cannot interact with the web page.

syntax—Specifies how a statement must be formed to compile without syntax errors.

syntax error—An error that occurs when program statements violate the grammatical rules of a programming language. Syntax errors are a subset of compilation errors.

System.Collections.Generic namespace—Contains collection classes such as List.

System.Drawing.Printing namespace—Allows your apps to access all services related to printing.

System.Web.UI namespace—Contains classes and controls for building web-based apps.

T

TabContainer Ajax Control Toolkit control—Enables you to group information into tabs that are displayed only if they're selected.

TabIndex property—A control property that specifies the order in which focus is transferred to controls on the Form when the *Tab* key is pressed.

table—A two-dimensional array used to contain information arranged in rows and columns.

table in a database—Used to store related information in rows and columns. (Represented in the app by the LINQ to SQL classes.)

TabPanel class—Represents a tab to the TabContainer.

TabStop property—A control property that specifies whether a control can receive the focus when the *Tab* key is pressed.

templates—Starting points for the projects you create in Visual Basic.

temporary variable—Used to store data when swapping values.

Text attribute of a TextBlock—Specifies the text in a TextBlock.

text file—A file containing human-readable characters.

Text property—Sets the text displayed on a control.

Text property of class ComboBox—Returns the currently selected String in the ComboBox.

TextAlign property—Specifies how text is aligned within a Label.

TextBox control—Retrieves user input from the keyboard.

TextChanged event—Occurs when the text in a TextBox changes.

Throw statement—The statement used to throw an exception.

throws an exception—A method throws an exception if a problem occurs while the method is executing.

Tick event of a Timer control—Raised after the number of milliseconds specified in the Timer control's Interval property has elapsed (if Enabled is True).

Timer control—Generates Tick events to run code at specified intervals.

title bar—The top of a window in which the title of the window is displayed.

Title property of a Window—Specifies the text that appears in the Window's title bar.

Title property of an ASPX page—Specifies the page's title that displays in the title bar of the browser.

To keyword—Used to specify a range of values. Commonly used in For...Next headers to specify the initial and final values of the statement's control variable.

Today property of type Date—Returns the current date with the time set to midnight.

ToList method of interface IEnumerable—Returns a List of the items contained in an IEnumerable object.

ToLongDateString method of type Date—Returns a String containing the date in the format "Wednesday, October 30, 2002."

toolbar—A bar that contains buttons that, when clicked, execute commands.

toolbar icon—A picture on a toolbar button.

Toolbox—A window that contains controls used to build and customize Forms.

ToolkitScriptManager control—Manages the scripts for the ASP. NET Ajax Toolkit controls.

Tools menu—A menu of the IDE that contains commands for accessing additional IDE tools and options that enable customization of the IDE.

ToolStripMenuItem class—Class which represents an individual menu item in a MenuStrip.

tooltip—The description of an icon that appears when the mouse pointer is held over that icon for a few seconds.

top tier—Tier containing the app's user interface. Also called the client tier.

ToShortTimeString method of type Date—Returns a String containing the time in the format "4:00 PM."

ToString method—Returns a String representation of the object or data type on which the method is called.

ToUpper method of class String—Returns the uppercase representation of a String. Similarly, ToLower returns the lowercase representation of a String.

transfer of control—Occurs when an executed statement does not directly follow the previously executed statement in a running app.

transferring the focus—Selecting a control in an app.

transition—A change from one action state to another that's represented by transition arrows in a UML activity diagram.

translator program—Converts assembly-language programs to machine languag.

Transmission Control Protocol/Internet Protocol (TCP/IP)—The combined set of communications protocols for the Internet.

Trim method of class String—Removes all whitespace characters from the beginning and end of a String.

truth table—A table that displays the Boolean result of a logical operator for all possible combinations of True and False values for its operands.

Try block—A block of statements that might cause exceptions and statements that should not execute if an exception occurs.

two-dimensional array—An array that contains multiple rows of values.

type of a variable—Specifies the kind of data that can be stored in a variable and the range of values that can be stored.

TypeOf...Is expression—Returns True if the object referenced by the variable is of the specified type.

U

UML (Unified Modeling Language)—An industry standard for modeling software systems graphically.

unary operator—An operator that takes only one operand.

uncaught (unhandled) exception—An exception that does not have an exception handler. Uncaught exceptions might terminate app execution.

Unicode—A character set containing characters that are composed of two bytes. Characters are represented in Visual Basic using the Unicode character set.

uniform resource locator (URL)—Address that can be used to direct a browser to a resource on the web.

unique session ID of an ASP.NET client—A sequence of random letters and numbers. The first time a client connects to the web server, a unique session ID is created for that client and a temporary cookie is written to the client so the server can identify the client on subsequent requests.

UpdatePanel control—ASP.NET Ajax control that performs a partial page update of the controls contained in its ContentTemplate.

UseAntiAlias property of class PrintPreviewDialog—Makes the text in the PrintPreviewDialog appear smoother on the screen.

V

Val function—Filters a number from its argument if possible. This avoids errors introduced by entering nonnumeric data when only numbers are expected. However, the result of the Val function is not always what you intended.

validator—Determines whether the data in another ASP.NET web control is in the proper format.

ValidatorCalloutExtender control—Enhances the ASP.NET validation controls by displaying error messages in small yellow callouts next to the input fields, rather than as text in the page.

value of a variable—The piece of data that's stored in a variable's location in memory.

Value property of a DateTimePicker control—Stores the value (such as a time) in a DateTimePicker control.

value type—A type that's defined as a Structure in Visual Basic. A variable of a value type contains a value of that type. The primitive types (other than String) are value types.

ValueChanged event of a DateTimePicker control—Raised when a user selects a new day or time in the DateTimePicker control.

variable—A location in the computer's memory where a value can be stored.

vector graphics—Graphics created by a set of mathematical properties called vectors, which include the graphics' dimensions, attributes and positions.

Vertical value of ScrollBars property—Used to display a vertical scrollbar on the right side of a TextBox.

Visible property of an ASP.NET control—Allows you to either display or hide an element in the client's browser when the page loads for the first time.

Visual Basic—Programming language introduced by Microsoft in 1991 to make programming Windows apps easier.

visual programming—Technique in which the Visual Basic IDE processes your actions (such as clicking, dragging and dropping controls) and writes code for you.

visual programming with Visual Basic—You use Visual Studio's graphical user interface to conveniently drag and drop predefined controls into place on the screen, and to label and resize them. Visual Studio writes much of the Visual Basic code, saving you considerable effort.

Visual Studio—Microsoft's integrated development environment (IDE), which allows developers to create apps in a variety of .NET programming languages.

Visual Web Developer 2010 Express—A Microsoft tool for building ASP.NET web apps.

volatile memory—Memory that's erased when the machine is powered off.

W

Watch window—A Visual Basic IDE window that allows you to view and modify variable values while an app is being debugged.

web apps—Apps that create web content.

Web.config ASP.NET configuration file—A file that's generated when you create an ASP.NET web app.

web controls—Controls, such as TextBoxes and Buttons, that are used to customize ASPX pages.

Web Form—Another name for an ASPX page.

Web Form Designer—The design area in Visual Web Developer that enables you to visually build your ASPX pages.

Web Form page—Another name for an ASPX page.

web server—Specialized software that responds to client requests by providing resources.

web-safe colors—Colors that display the same on different computers.

Web Site Administration Tool—Specifies which parts of a website are password protected

Where clause (of a LINQ query)—Specifies the conditions that must be met for an item to be included in the results.

whitespace character—A space, tab or newline character.

widening conversion—A conversion in which the value of a "smaller" type is assigned to a variable of a "larger" type—that is, a type that can store more data than the smaller type.

Width property—This setting, a member of property Size, indicates the width of the Form or one of its controls, in pixels.

Window control—The root control in a WPF app. Analogous to a Form in a Windows Forms app.

Windows Form Designer—Used to design the GUI of a Windows Forms app.

Windows Forms app—An app that executes on a Windows operating system (e.g., Windows XP or Vista) and has a graphical user interface (GUI)—the visual part of the app with which the user interacts.

Windows Presentation Foundation (WPF)—Microsoft's new graphics framework that allows you to create powerful and flexible GUIs and to create media-rich experiences with animations, audio, video and graphics.

With keyword—Specifies that the subsequent property assignment statements contained between curly braces refer to the newly created object in an object initializer.

WithEvents keyword—Used in the declaration of an object that can generate events. Enables you to create event handlers for such an object.

workflow—The activity of a portion of a software system.

World Wide Web (WWW)—A communications system that allows computer users to locate and view multimedia documents (such as documents with text, graphics, animations, audios and videos).

World Wide Web Consortium (W3C)—A forum through which qualified individuals and companies cooperate to develop and standardize technologies for the web.

Write method of class StreamWriter—Writes a String to a file.

WriteLine method of class StreamWriter—Writes a String and a line terminator to a file.

X

X property of class Point—The property of class Point that specifies the *x*-coordinate.

***x*-axis**—Describes every horizontal coordinate.

***x*-coordinate**—Horizontal distance (increasing to the right) from the left of the drawing area.

XAML (eXtensible App Markup Language)—An XML vocabulary for describing WPF user interfaces.

XDocument class—Class that enables you to process XML data programmatically.

XDocument.Parse method—Method that parses XML into a form that can be accessed programmatically.

XML (eXtensible Markup Language)—Language for creating markup for describing data in a manner that both humans and computers can understand.

XML descendants property—New Visual Basic 2010 syntax that enables you to specify the elements to select from an XML document for processing in a LINQ to XML expression.

XML axis properties—New Visual Basic 2010 syntax for accessing XML elements directly from Visual Basic code.

XML vocabulary—XML-based markup language that provides a means for describing a particular type of data in a standardized, structured manner. For example, XAML is an XML vocabulary that describes WPF user interface information.

Xor (logical exclusive OR) operator—A logical operator that's True if and only if one of its operands is True and the other is False.

Y

Y property of class Point—The property of class Point that specifies the *y*-coordinate.

***y*-axis**—Describes every vertical coordinate.

***y*-coordinate**—Vertical distance (increasing downward) from the top of the drawing area.

INDEX